GALE ENCYCLOPEDIA OF
MULTICULTURAL AMERICA

THIRD EDITION

EDITED BY THOMAS RIGGS

GALE ENCYCLOPEDIA OF

MULTICULTURAL AMERICA

VOLUME
4

ROMANI AMERICANS–ZUNI

EDITED BY THOMAS RIGGS

GALE
CENGAGE Learning·

Detroit • New York • San Francisco • New Haven, Conn • Waterville, Maine • London

© 2014 Gale, Cengage Learning

WCN: 01-100-101

Gale Encyclopedia of Multicultural America

Thomas Riggs, Editor

Project Editor: Marie Toft

Editorial: Jeff Hunter, Carol Schwartz

Technical Assistance: Luann Brennan, Grant Eldridge, Jeffrey Muhr, Rebecca Parks

Rights Acquisition and Management: Sheila Spencer

Composition: Evi Abou-El-Seoud

Manufacturing: Wendy Blurton

Imaging: John Watkins

Product Design: Kristine Julien

Index: Shana Milkie

For product information and technology assistance, contact us at
Gale Customer Support, 1-800-877-4253.
For permission to use material from this text or product,
submit all requests online at **www.cengage.com/permissions.**
Further permissions questions can be emailed to
permissionrequest@cengage.com.

Cover photographs and art reproduced with the following permission:
For Asian business man, © aslysun/Shutterstock.com; for Indian businessman, © Kenneth Man/Shutterstock.com; for young Sephardic Jewish man, © Howard Sandler/Shutterstock.com; for African American female, © Flashon Studio/Shutterstock.com; for Rastafarian male, © Alan Bailey/Shutterstock.com; for Muslim woman (side view), © szefei/Shutterstock.com; for young woman in white t-shirt and jeans, © Vlasov Volodymyr/Shutterstock.com; for Hispanic woman in white blouse, © Warren Goldswaini/Shutterstock.com; for puzzle vector illustration, © VikaSuh/Shutterstock.com.

While every effort has been made to ensure the reliability of the information presented in this publication, Gale, a part of Cengage Learning, does not guarantee the accuracy of the data contained herein. Gale accepts no payment for listing; and inclusion in the publication of any organization, agency, institution, publication, service, or individual does not imply endorsement of the editors or publisher. Errors brought to the attention of the publisher and verified to the satisfaction of the publisher will be corrected in future editions.

Library of Congress Cataloging-in-Publication Data

Gale Encyclopedia of Multicultural America / Thomas Riggs, editor. — 3rd edition.
   pages cm
   Includes bibliographical references and index.
   ISBN 978-0-7876-7550-9 (set : hardcover) — ISBN 978-0-7876-7551-6 (vol. 1 : hardcover) — ISBN 978-0-7876-7552-3 (vol. 2 : hardcover) — ISBN 978-0-7876-7553-0 (vol. 3 : hardcover) — ISBN 978-1-4144-3279-3 (vol. 4 : hardcover)
   1. Cultural pluralism—United States—Encyclopedias. 2. Ethnology—United States—Encyclopedias. 3. Minorities—United States—Encyclopedias. 4. United States—Ethnic relations—Encyclopedias. 5. United States—Race relations—Encyclopedias. I. Riggs, Thomas.
   E184.A1G14 2014
   305.800973—dc23
                                                            2013049273

Gale
27500 Drake Rd.
Farmington Hills, MI, 48331-3535

ISBN-13: 978-0-7876-7550-9 (set)
ISBN-13: 978-0-7876-7551-6 (vol. 1)
ISBN-13: 978-0-7876-7552-3 (vol. 2)
ISBN-13: 978-0-7876-7553-0 (vol. 3)
ISBN-13: 978-1-4144-3279-3 (vol. 4)

This title is also available as an e-book.
ISBN-13: 978-1-4144-3806-1
Contact your Gale, a part of Cengage Learning sales representative for ordering information.

Printed in the United States of America
1 2 3 4 5 6 7 18 17 16 15 14

TABLE OF CONTENTS

Contents of All Volumes

EDITOR'S NOTE

The third edition of the *Gale Encyclopedia of Multicultural America*—a major revision to the previous editions published in 1995 and 2000—includes 175 entries, each focusing on an immigrant or indigenous group in the United States. Some entries provide historical and cultural overviews of commonly recognized groups, such as Mexican Americans and Japanese Americans, while others discuss much smaller groups—for example, Cape Verdean Americans, Jordanian Americans, and the Ojibwe. The third edition has 23 new entries; the 152 entries from the second edition were thoroughly revised and reorganized, creating up-to-date coverage and a more consistent approach throughout the book. The writing or revision of each entry was reviewed by a scholar with extensive research background in the group.

The structure and content of the *Gale Encyclopedia of Multicultural America* was planned with the help of the project's advisory board. Joe Feagin—professor of sociology at Texas A&M University and a member of the advisory board—revised and updated the encyclopedia's introduction, originally written by Rudolph Vecoli. The introduction provides a broad historical overview of race and ethnicity in the United States, explaining how cultural and legal influences, especially racism, helped shape the experience of indigenous and immigrant groups.

ORGANIZATION

The 175 entries are arranged alphabetically across three volumes. The length of the entries varies from about 4,000 to 20,000 words. All entries share a common structure, providing consistent coverage of the groups and a simple way of comparing basic elements of one entry with another. Birth and death dates are provided for people mentioned in the entries except when dates could not be found or verified. The encyclopedia has more than 400 color images.

Each entry has 14 sections:

Overview: Basic information about the group's origins, homeland, immigration to or migration within the United States, and population and principal areas of settlement.

History of the People: Significant historical events of the group in its original region or country.

Settlement in the United States: For immigrant groups, waves of immigration and notable settlement patterns; for indigenous groups, original area of settlement, as well as migration within North America after the group's contact with Europeans.

Language: Native languages and their influence on the present-day group. Some entries have a section on greetings and popular expressions.

Religion: Religions and religious practices of the group, both in the original country or region and in the United States.

Culture and Assimilation: Traditional beliefs and customs, as well as the status of these traditions in the present-day group; topics include cuisine, dress, dances and songs, holidays, and health care issues and practices. Some entries have a sidebar on proverbs.

Family and Community Life: Topics include family structure and traditions; gender roles; education; dating practices, marriage, and divorce; and relations with other Americans.

Employment and Economic Conditions: Types of jobs commonly done by early immigrants or by indigenous people as they came into contact with European settlers, as well as notable employment trends among later generations of the group.

Politics and Government: Topics include the group's involvement in American politics and government (including voting patterns, significant events, and legislation) and contemporary interest in the parent country.

Notable Individuals: Examples of accomplished members of the group in various fields, with brief summaries.

Media: List of television and radio stations, as well as newspapers and periodicals, that are directed toward the group or provide significant coverage of it.

Organizations and Associations: List of organizations and associations related to the group.

Museums and Research Centers: List of museums and research centers related to the group.

Sources for Additional Study: A bibliography of books and articles about the group, including recent sources.

ACKNOWLEDGMENTS

Many people contributed time, effort, and ideas to the third edition of the *Gale Encyclopedia of Multicultural America*. Marie Toft, senior content project editor at Cengage Gale, served as in-house manager for the project. The quality of the book owes much to her ideas and feedback, as well as to her oversight of the book's production.

We would like to express our appreciation to the advisors, who, in addition to creating the list of new entry topics, helped evaluate the second edition and proposed ideas for producing an improved third edition. We would also like to thank the contributors for their carefully prepared essays and for their efforts to summarize the cultural life of ethnic groups without stereotyping. We are grateful to the many scholars who reviewed entries for accuracy and coverage.

The long process of reorganizing and revising the second-edition entries, as well as preparing the new ones, was overseen by Joseph Campana, project editor, who also helped identify and correspond with the advisors. Anne Healey, senior editor, managed the editing process and was helped by Mary Beth Curran, David Hayes, and Lee Esbenshade, all associate editors. Hannah Soukup, assistant editor, identified and corresponded with the academic reviewers. Other important assistance came from Mariko Fujinaka, managing editor, and Jake Schmitt and Theodore McDermott, assistant editors. The line editors were Robert Anderson, Cheryl Collins, Tony Craine, Gerilee Hunt, Amy Mortensen, Jill Oldham, Kathy Peacock, Donna Polydoros, Natalie Ruppert, and Will Wagner.

Thomas Riggs

# ADVISORY BOARD

CHAIR

David R. M. Beck
Professor, Department of Native American Studies, University of Montana, Missoula.

ADVISORS

Joe Feagin
Ella C. McFadden Professor, Department of Sociology, Texas A&M University.

Patricia Fernandez-Kelly
Professor, Department of Sociology, Office of Population Research, Princeton University.

David Gerber
University at Buffalo Distinguished Professor Emeritus, Department of History, University at Buffalo, The State University of New York.

Rebecca Stuhr
Coordinator for Humanities Collections, Librarian for Classical Studies and History, University of Pennsylvania Libraries, Member, Ethnic & Multicultural Information Exchange Round Table, American Library Association.

Vladimir F. Wertsman
Retired Chair, Publishing and Multicultural Materials Committee, Ethnic and Multicultural Information Exchange Round Table, American Library Association.

LIST OF ACADEMIC REVIEWERS

HOLLY ACKERMAN

Ph. D. Librarian for Latin American, Iberian, & Latino Studies, Duke University, Durham, North Carolina

DEIRDRE ALMEIDA

Director of the American Indian Studies Program, Eastern Washington University, Cheney

BARBARA WATSON ANDAYA

Professor of Asian Studies, University of Hawai'i, Manoa

BARBARA A. ANDERSON

Ronald Freedman Collegiate Professor of Sociology and Population Studies, University of Michigan, Ann Arbor

JOSEPH ARBENA

Professor Emeritus of History, Clemson University, South Carolina

LAURIE ARNOLD

Director of Native American Studies, Gonzaga University, Spokane, Washington

CHRISTOPHER P. ATWOOD

Associate Professor of Central Eurasian Studies, Indiana University, Bloomington

ANNY BAKALIAN

Associate Director of the Graduate Center, City University of New York

CARINA BANDHAUER

Professor of Sociology, Western Connecticut State University, Danbury, Connecticut

CARL L. BANKSTON III

Professor of Sociology, Tulane University, New Orleans, Louisiana

LAURA BARBAS-RHODEN

Associate Professor of Foreign Languages, Wofford College, Spartanburg, South Carolina

DAVID BECK

Department Chair of the Native American Studies Department and Professor of Native American Studies, University of Montana, Missoula

JOHN BIETER

Associate Professor of History, Boise State University, Idaho

ADRIAN VILIAMI BELL

Visiting Assistant Professor of Anthropology, University of Utah, Salt Lake City

BRIAN BELTON

Ph.D., as well as Senior Lecturer, YMCA George Williams College, London, United Kingdom

SAMIR BITAR

Lecturer of Arabic Language and Cultures, Department of Anthropology, and Assistant Director of Outreach-Central and Southwest Asian Studies Center, University of Montana, Missoula

LASZLO BORHI

Senior Research Fellow, Institute of History Hungarian Academy of Sciences, Budapest, Hungary

GREGORY CAMPBELL

Professor of Anthropology, University of Montana, Missoula

MAURICE CARNEY

Independent scholar, Friends of the Congo, Washington D.C

JUAN MANUEL CASAL

Professor and Chair, Department of History, Universidad de Montevideo, Uruguay

ELIZABETH CHACKO

Associate Professor of Geography and International Affairs and Chair of the Department of Geography, George Washington University, Washington, D.C.

ALLAN CHRISTELOW

Professor of History, Idaho State University, Pocatello

STEPHEN CRISWELL

Associate Professor of English and Native American Studies, University of South Carolina, Lancaster

JAMSHEED CHOKSY

Professor of Iranian and Islamic Studies, Indiana University, Bloomington

RICHMOND CLOW

Professor of Native American Studies, University of Montana, Missoula

STEPHANIE COX

Visiting Assistant Professor of French, Carleton College, Northfield, Minnesota

SHAHYAR DANESHGAR

Senior Lecturer of Central Eurasian Studies, Indiana University, Bloomington

JEAN DENNISON

Assistant Professor of Anthropology, University of North Carolina, Chapel Hill

JOSE R. DEUSTUA

Associate Professor of History, Eastern Illinois University, Charleston, Illinois

MUNROE EAGLES

*Program Director of Canadian Studies
and Professor of Political Science, State
University of New York, Buffalo*

SARAH ENGLAND

*Associate Professor of Anthropology and Director
of Social and Behavioral Sciences, Soka
University of America, Alisa Viejo, California*

PHYLLIS FAST

*Professor of Anthropology, University of
Alaska, Anchorage*

SUJATHA FERNANDES

*Associate Professor of Sociology, Queens
College and the Graduate Center of the
City University of New York*

ANN FIENUP-RIORDAN

*Independent scholar, Calista Elders Council,
Bethel, Alaska*

SEAN FOLEY

*Associate Professor of History, Middle
Tennessee State University, Murfreesboro*

JAMES GIGANTINO

*Assistant Professor of History, University of
Arkansas, Fayetteville*

EDWARD GOBETZ

*Professor Emeritus of Sociology, Kent State
University, Ohio*

STEVEN J. GOLD

*Professor of Sociology and Associate Chair in
the Department of Sociology, Michigan
State University, East Lansing*

ANGELA A. GONZALES

*Associate Professor of Development Sociology
and American Indian Studies, Cornell
University, Ithaca, New York*

JONATHAN GOSNELL

*Associate Professor of French Studies, Smith
College, Northampton, Massachusetts*

ISHTAR GOVIA

*Lecturer of Psychology, University of the West
Indies, Mona, Jamaica*

YVONNE HADDAD

*Professor of the History of Islam and
Christian-Muslim Relations, Georgetown
University, Washington, D.C.*

JEFFREY HADLER

*Associate Professor of South and Southeast Asian
Studies, University of California, Berkeley*

MARILYN HALTER

*Professor of History, Institute on Culture,
Religion, and World Affairs, Boston
University, Brookline, Massachusetts*

ANNE PEREZ HATTORI

*Professor of History and Chamorro Studies,
University of Guam, Mangilao*

MICHAEL HITTMAN

*Professor of Anthropology, Long Island
University, Brooklyn, New York*

INEZ HOLLANDER

*Lecturer of Dutch Studies, University of
California, Berkeley*

JON D. HOLTZMAN

*Associate Professor of Anthropology, Western
Michigan University, Kalamazoo*

KATHLEEN HOOD

*Publications Director and Events Coordinator,
The UCLA Herb Alpert School of Music,
Department of Ethnomusicology, University
of California, Los Angeles*

MAREN HOPKINS

*Director of Research, Anthropological
Research, LLC, Tucson, Arizona*

GUITA HOURANI

*Director of the Lebanese Emigration Research
Center, Notre Dame University, Kesrwan,
Lebanon*

SALLY HOWELL

*Assistant Professor of History, University of
Michigan, Dearborn*

TARA INNISS

*Lecturer in History, University of the West
Indies, Cave Hill Campus, Barbados*

ALPHINE JEFFERSON

*Professor of History, Randolph-Macon
College, Ashland, Virginia*

PETER KIVISTO

*Richard A. Swanson Professor of Social Thought,
Augustana College, Rock Island, Illinois*

MICHAEL KOPANIC, JR.

*Adjunct Full Professor of History, University of
Maryland University College, Adelphi, and
Adjunct Associate Professor of History, St.
Francis University, Loretto, Pennsylvania*

DONALD B. KRAYBILL

*Distinguished College Professor and Senior
Fellow, Young Center for Anabaptist and*

*Pietist Studies, Elizabethtown College,
Pennsylvania*

GARY KUNKELMAN

*Senior Lecturer, Professional Writing, Penn
State Berks, Wyomissing, Pennsylvania*

AL KUSLIKIS

*Senior Program Associate for Strategic
Initiatives, American Indian Higher
Education Consortium, Alexandria,
Virginia*

WILLIAM LAATSCH

*Emeritus Professor of Urban and Regional
Studies, University of Wisconsin,
Green Bay*

BRUCE LA BRACK

*Professor Emeritus of Anthropology,
University of the Pacific, Stockton,
California*

SARAH LAMB

*Professor of Anthropology, Brandeis
University, Waltham, Massachusetts*

LAURIE RHONDA LAMBERT

*Doctoral candidate in English and American
Literature, New York University*

JOHN LIE

*C. K. Cho Professor, University of California,
Berkeley*

HUPING LING

*Changjiang Scholar Chair Professor and
Professor of History, Truman State
University, Kirksville, Missouri*

JOSEPH LUBIG

*Associate Dean for Education, Leadership
and Public Service, Northern Michigan
University, Marquette*

ALEXANDER LUSHNYCKY

*President of the Shevchenko Scientific
Society Study Center, Elkins Park,
Pennsylvania*

NEDA MAGHBOULEH

*Assistant Professor, Department of Sociology,
University of Toronto, Ontario*

WILLIAM MEADOWS

*Professor of Anthropology, Missouri State
University, Springfield*

MARIANNE MILLIGAN

*Visiting Assistant Professor of Linguistics,
Macalester College, Saint Paul, Minnesota*

NAEEM MOHAIEMEN

Doctoral student in Anthropology at Columbia University, New York

ALEXANDER MURZAKU

Professor and Chair of World Cultures and Languages, College of Saint Elizabeth, Morristown, New Jersey

GEORGE MUSAMBIRA

Associate Professor of Communication, University of Central Florida, Orlando

GHIRMAI NEGASH

Professor of English & African Literature, Ohio University, Athens

JENNY NELSON

Associate Professor of Media Studies, Ohio University, Athens

RAFAEL NÚÑEZ-CEDEÑO

Coeditor of Probus: International Journal of Latin and Romance Linguistics and Professor Emeritus of Hispanic Studies, University of Illinois, Chicago

GREG O'BRIEN

Associate Professor of History, University of North Carolina, Greensboro

GRANT OLSON

Coordinator of Foreign Language Multimedia Learning Center, Northern Illinois University, DeKalb

THOMAS OWUSU

Professor and Chair of Geography, William Paterson University, Wayne, New Jersey

JODY PAVILACK

Associate Professor of History, University of Montana, Missoula

BARBARA POSADAS

College of Liberal Arts and Sciences Distinguished Professor of History, Northern Illinois University, DeKalb

JASON PRIBILSKY

Associate Professor of Anthropology, Whitman College, Walla Walla, Washington

LAVERN J. RIPPLEY

Professor of German, St. Olaf College, Northfield, Minnesota

MIKA ROINILA

Ph.D., as well as International Baccalaureate Program Coordinator and Fulbright

Specialist, John Adams High School, South Bend, Indiana

WILL ROSCOE

Ph.D., Independent scholar, San Francisco, California

LEONID RUDNYTZKY

Professor and Director of Central and Eastern European Studies Program, La Salle University, Philadelphia

NICHOLAS RUDNYTZKY

Independent scholar and Board member of the St. Sophia Religious Association of Ukrainian Catholics, Elkins Park, Pennsylvania

YONA SABAR

Professor of Hebrew, University of California, Los Angeles

LOUKIA K. SARROUB

Associate Professor of Education, University of Nebraska, Lincoln

RICHARD SATTLER

Adjunct Assistant Professor, University of Montana, Missoula

RICHARD SCAGLION

UCIS Research Professor, University of Pittsburgh, Pennsylvania

HELGA SCHRECKENBERGER

Chair of the Department of German and Russian and Professor of German, University of Vermont, Burlington

BRENDAN SHANAHAN

Doctoral student in North American history, University of California, Berkeley

KEMAL SILAY

Professor of Central Eurasian Studies and Director of the Turkish Studies Program, Indiana University, Bloomington

JEANNE SIMONELLI

Professor of Cultural and Applied Anthropology, Wake Forest University, Winston-Salem, North Carolina

GUNTIS ŠMIDCHENS

Kazickas Family Endowed Professor in Baltic Studies, Associate Professor of Baltic Studies, and Head of Baltic Studies Program, University of Washington, Seattle

MATTHEW SMITH

Senior Lecturer in History, University of the West Indies, Mona, Jamaica

MARY S. SPRUNGER

Professor of History, Eastern Mennonite University, Harrisonburg, Virginia

THOMAS THORNTON

Director for the MSc in Environmental Change and Management, University of Oxford, United Kingdom

ELAISA VAHNIE

Executive Director at the Burmese American Community Institute, Indianapolis, Indiana

DOUGLAS VELTRE

Professor Emeritus of Anthropology, University of Alaska, Anchorage

MILTON VICKERMAN

Associate Professor of Sociology, University of Virginia, Charlottesville

KRINKA VIDAKOVIC-PETROV

Principal Research Fellow, Institute for Literature and Arts, Belgrade, Serbia

BETH VIRTANEN

President, Finnish North American Literature Association

MARTIN VOTRUBA

Director of the Slovak Studies Program, University of Pittsburgh, Pennsylvania

MARY WATERS

M. E. Zukerman Professor of Sociology, Harvard University, Cambridge, Massachusetts

MARVIN WEINBAUM

Professor Emeritus of Political Science, University of Illinois, Urbana-Champaign

BRENT WEISMAN

Professor of Anthropology, University of South Florida, Tampa

THOMAS L. WHIGHAM

Professor of History, University of Georgia, Athens

BRADLEY WOODWORTH

Assistant Professor of History, University of New Haven, West Haven, Connecticut

KRISTIN ELIZABETH YARRIS

Assistant Professor of International Studies and Women's & Gender Studies, University of Oregon, Eugene

XIAOJIAN ZHAO

Professor of Asian American Studies, University of California, Santa Barbara

List of Contributors

NABEEL ABRAHAM

Abraham holds a PhD in anthropology and is a university professor.

JUNE GRANATIR ALEXANDER

Alexander holds a PhD and has been a university professor.

DONALD ALTSCHILLER

Altschiller holds a PhD in library science and works as a university librarian.

DIANE ANDREASSI

Andreassi is a journalist and freelance writer

GREG BACH

Bach holds an MA in classics and is a freelance writer.

CARL L. BANKSTON III

Bankston holds a PhD in sociology and is a university professor.

CRAIG BEEBE

Beebe holds an MA in geography and works in nonprofit communications.

DIANE E. BENSON ("LXEIS")

Benson holds an MFA in creative writing and is a playwright, actor, and director.

BARBARA C. BIGELOW

Bigelow is an author of young adult books and a freelance writer and editor.

D. L. BIRCHFIELD

Birchfield was a university professor and novelist.

BENJAMIN BLOCH

Bloch holds an MFA in creative writing and an MFA in painting.

ELIZABETH BOEHEIM

Boeheim holds an MA in English literature and has been a university instructor.

CAROL BRENNAN

Brennan is a freelance writer with a background in history.

HERBERT J. BRINKS

Brinks was an author and editor and served as a curator at a university library.

K. MARIANNE WARGELIN BROWN

Wargelin Brown holds a PhD in history and is an independent scholar.

SEAN T. BUFFINGTON

Buffington holds an MA and is the president of The University of the Arts.

PHYLLIS J. BURSON

Burson holds a PhD in psychology and works as an independent consultant.

HELEN BUSH CAVER

Caver held a PhD and worked as a university librarian.

CIDA S. CHASE

Chase holds a PhD and is a university professor.

CLARK COLAHAN

Colahan holds a PhD and is a university professor.

ROBERT J. CONLEY

Conley holds an MA in English, is an award-winning novelist, and has served as a university professor.

JANE STEWART COOK

Cook is a freelance writer.

CHRISTINA COOKE

Cooke holds an MFA in creative nonfiction and works as a university instructor and freelance writer.

AMY COOPER

Cooper holds a PhD in anthropology and is a university professor.

PAUL ALAN COX

Cox holds a PhD in biology and is the director of the Institute of Ethnomedicine.

GIANO CROMLEY

Cromley holds an MFA in creative writing and is a university instructor.

KEN CUTHBERTSON

Cuthbertson is a writer, editor, and freelance broadcaster.

ROSETTA SHARP DEAN

Dean is a former school counselor and president of the Sharp-Dean School of Continuing Studies, Inc.

CHAD DUNDAS

Dundas holds an MFA in creative writing and has been a university instructor and freelance writer.

STANLEY E. EASTON

Easton holds a PhD and is a university professor.

TIM EIGO

Eigo holds a law degree and is writer and editor.

LUCIEN ELLINGTON

Ellington holds an EdD and is a university professor.

JESSIE L. EMBRY

Embry holds a PhD in history and is a research professor.

ALLAN ENGLEKIRK

Englekirk holds a PhD in Spanish and is a university professor.

RICHARD ESBENSHADE

Esbenshade holds a PhD in history and has been a university professor and freelance writer.

MARIANNE P. FEDUNKIW

Fedunkiw holds a PhD in strategic communications and is a university instructor and consultant.

DENNIS FEHR

Fehr holds a PhD in art education and is a university professor.

DAISY GARD

Gard is a freelance writer with a background in English literature.

CLINT GARNER

Garner holds an MFA in creative writing and is a freelance writer.

CHRISTOPHER GILES

Giles holds an MA in classics and an MA in history and is a college instructor and administrator.

MARY GILLIS

Gillis holds an MA has worked as a freelance writer and is a painter and sculptor.

EDWARD GOBETZ

Gobetz holds a PhD in sociology and is a retired university professor and former executive director of the Slovenian Research Center of America.

MARK A. GRANQUIST

Granquist holds a PhD and is a university professor.

DEREK GREEN

Green is a freelance writer and editor.

PAULA HAJAR

Hajar holds an EdD and has worked as a university professor and high school teacher.

LORETTA HALL

Hall is a freelance writer and the author of five works of nonfiction.

FRANCESCA HAMPTON

Hampton is a freelance writer and university instructor.

RICHARD C. HANES

Hanes holds a PhD and has served as the Division Chief of Cultural, Paleontological Resources, and Tribal Consultation for the Bureau of Land Management.

SHELDON HANFT

Hanft holds a PhD in history and is a university professor.

RODNEY HARRIS

Harris is a PhD candidate in history.

JOSH HARTEIS

Harteis holds an MA in English literature and is a freelance writer.

KARL HEIL

Heil is a freelance writer.

EVAN HEIMLICH

Heimlich is a freelance writer and university instructor.

ANGELA WASHBURN HEISEY

Heisey is a freelance writer.

MARY A. HESS

Hess is a freelance writer.

LAURIE COLLIER HILLSTROM

Hillstrom is a freelance writer and editor. She has published more than twenty works of history and biography.

MARIA HONG

Hong is a freelance writer and poet and was a Bunting Fellow at Harvard University in 2010-2011.

RON HORTON

Horton holds an MFA in creative writing and has been a high school English instructor and freelance writer.

EDWARD IFKOVIĆ

Ifković is a professor of creative writing and the author of four novels.

ALPHINE W. JEFFERSON

Jefferson holds a PhD in history and is a university professor.

CHARLIE JONES

Jones is a high school librarian.

J. SYDNEY JONES

Jones has worked as a freelance writer and correspondent and has published twelve works of fiction and nonfiction.

JANE JURGENS

Jurgens has been a university instructor.

JIM KAMP

Kamp is a freelance writer and editor.

OSCAR KAWAGLEY

Kawagley held a PhD in social and educational studies and was a university professor.

CLARE KINBERG

Kinberg holds a masters in library and information science and has been a literary journal editor.

KRISTIN KING-RIES

King-Ries holds an MFA in creative writing and has been a university instructor.

VITAUT KIPEL

Kipel held a PhD in mineralogy and an MLS and worked in the Slavic and Baltic Division of the New York Public Library.

JUDSON KNIGHT

Knight holds BIS in international studies, works as a freelance writer, and is co-owner of The Knight Agency, a literary sales and marketing firm.

PAUL S. KOBEL

Kobel is a freelance writer.

DONALD B. KRAYBILL

Kraybill holds a PhD in sociology and is a university professor.

LISA KROGER

Kroger holds a PhD in English literature and has been a university instructor.

KEN KURSON

Kurson is the editor-in-chief of the New York Observer.

ODD S. LOVOLL

Lovoll holds a PhD in U.S. history and is a university professor.

LORNA MABUNDA

Mabunda is a freelance writer.

PAUL ROBERT MAGOCSI

Magocsi holds a PhD in history and is the chair of Ukrainian Studies at the University of Toronto.

MARGUERITE MARÍN

Marín holds a PhD in sociology and is a university professor.

WILLIAM MAXWELL

Maxwell is a freelance writer who has worked as an editor at A Gathering of the Tribes magazine.

THEODORE MCDERMOTT

McDermott holds an MFA in creative writing and has been a university instructor and freelance writer.

JAQUELINE A. MCLEOD

McLeod holds a JD and PhD and is a university professor.

H. BRETT MELENDY

Melendy held a PhD in history and served as university professor and administrator.

MONA MIKHAIL

Mikhail holds a PhD in comparative literature and is a writer, translator, and university professor.

OLIVIA MILLER

Miller is a freelance writer, consultant, and university instructor.

CHRISTINE MOLINARI

Molinari is a freelance writer and editor and an independent researcher.

AARON MOULTON

Moulton holds an MA in Latin American studies. He is a PhD candidate in history and a university instructor.

LLOYD E. MULRAINE

Mulraine holds a DA in English and is a university professor.

JEREMY MUMFORD

Mumford holds a PhD in history and has worked as a university professor.

N. SAMUEL MURRELL

Murrell holds a PhD in biblical and theological studies and is a university professor.

AMY NASH

Nash is a published poet and has worked as a freelance writer and communications manager for Meyer, Scherer, & Rockcastle, Ltd., an architecture firm.

JOHN MARK NIELSEN

Nielsen is the executive director at the Danish Immigrant Museum.

ERNEST E. NORDEN

Norden holds a PhD and is a retired university professor.

SONYA SCHRYER NORRIS

Norris has worked as a freelance writer and website developer.

LOLLY OCKERSTROM

Ockerstrom holds a PhD in English and is a university professor.

KATRINA OKO-ODOI

Oko-Odoi is a PhD candidate in Spanish language literature and a university instructor.

JOHN PACKEL

Packel has worked as a freelance writer and is an associate director at American Express.

TINAZ PAVRI

Pavri holds a PhD in political science and is a university professor.

RICHARD E. PERRIN

Perrin was a university reference librarian.

PETER L. PETERSEN

Petersen holds a PhD in history and is a university professor.

MATTHEW T. PIFER

Pifer holds a PhD in composition and is a university professor.

GEORGE POZETTA

Pozetta held a PhD in history and was a university professor.

NORMAN PRADY

Prady is a freelance writer.

ELIZABETH RHOLETTER PURDY

Purdy is an independent scholar and has published numerous articles on political science and women's issues.

BRENDAN A. RAPPLE

Rapple holds an MBA and PhD and is a university librarian.

MEGAN RATNER

Ratner is a film critic and an associate editor at Bright Lights Film Journal.

WYLENE RHOLETTER

Rholetter holds a PhD in English literature and is a university professor.

LaVERN J. RIPPLEY

Rippley holds a PhD in German studies and is a university professor.

JULIO RODRIGUEZ

Rodriguez is a freelance writer.

PAM ROHLAND

Rohland is a freelance writer.

LORIENE ROY

Roy holds a PhD and MLS and is a university professor.

LAURA C. RUDOLPH

Rudolph is a freelance writer.

ANTHONY RUZICKA

Ruzicka is pursuing an MFA in poetry and has worked as a university instructor.

KWASI SARKODIE-MENSAH

Sarkodie-Mensah holds a PhD, is an author of research guides, and works as a university librarian.

LEO SCHELBERT

Schelbert holds a PhD in history and is a retired university professor.

JACOB SCHMITT

Schmitt holds an MA in English literature and has been a freelance writer.

MARY C. SENGSTOCK

Sengstock holds a PhD in sociology and is a university professor.

ELIZABETH SHOSTAK

Shostak is a freelance writer and editor.

STEFAN SMAGULA

Smagula has written for The Austin Chronicle and Zymurgy magazine and has designed software for Google, Bloomberg L.P., and The Economist. He works as software product designer in Austin, Texas.

HANNAH SOUKUP

Soukup holds an MFA in creative writing.

JANE E. SPEAR

Spear holds an MD and is a freelance writer and copyeditor.

TOVA STABIN

Stabin holds a Masters of Library and Information Science and works as a writer, editor, researcher, and diversity trainer.

BOSILJKA STEVANOVIĆ

Stevanović holds an MS in Library Science and is an independent translator.

SARAH STOECKL

Stoeckl holds a PhD in English literature and is a university instructor and freelance writer.

ANDRIS STRAUMANIS

Straumanis is a freelance writer and editor, as well as a university instructor.

PAMELA STURNER

Sturner is the executive director of the Leopold Leadership Program.

LIZ SWAIN

Swain has worked as a freelance writer and crime reporter and is a staff writer for the San Diego Reader.

MARK SWARTZ

Swartz holds an MA in art history, has served as writer for numerous nonprofits (including the American Hospital Association), and has published two novels.

THOMAS SZENDREY

Szendrey is a freelance writer.

HAROLD TAKOOSHIAN

Takooshian holds a PhD in psychology and is a university professor.

BAATAR TSEND

Tsend is an independent scholar and writer.

FELIX UME UNAEZE

Unaeze is a university librarian.

STEVEN BÉLA VÁRDY

Várdy holds a PhD in history and is a university professor.

GRACE WAITMAN

Waitman is pursuing a PhD in educational psychology. She holds an MA in English literature and has been a university instructor.

DREW WALKER

Walker is a freelance writer.

LING-CHI WANG

Wang holds a PhD and is a social activist and retired university professor.

KEN R. WELLS

Wells is a freelance writer and editor and has published works of young adult science fiction and nonfiction.

VLADIMIR F. WERTSMAN

Wertsman is a member of the American Library Association and the retired chair of the Publishing and Multicultural Materials Committee.

MARY T. WILLIAMS

Williams has worked as a university professor.

ELAINE WINTERS

Winters is a freelance writer, editor, and program facilitator. She has provided professional training for a number of Fortune 500 companies, including Apple, Nokia, and Nortel.

EVELINE YANG

Yang holds an MA in international and public affairs and is a PhD candidate in the Department of Central Eurasian Studies at Indiana University.

ELEANOR YU

Yu is the Supervising Producer at Monumental Mysteries at Optomen Productions.

Introduction

The term multiculturalism is used to describe a society characterized by a diversity of cultures. Religion, language, customs, traditions, and values are some components of culture, and culture also includes the perspectives through which people perceive and interpret society. A shared culture and common historical experience form the basis for a sense of peoplehood.

Over the course of U.S. history two divergent paths have led to this sense of peoplehood. All groups except indigenous Americans (Native Americans), have entered North America as voluntary or involuntary immigrants. Some of these immigrant groups and their descendants have been oppressed by the dominant group—white Americans that have been for centuries primarily of northern European descent—and were defined as inferior racial groups. A *racial group* is a societal group that people inside or outside that group distinguish as racially inferior or superior, usually on the basis of arbitrarily selected physical characteristics (for example, skin color). Historically whites have rationalized the subordination of other racial groups, viewing them as biologically and culturally inferior, uncivilized, foreign, and less than virtuous. To the present day Asian, African, Native, and Mexican Americans have been regularly "racialized" by the dominant white group. Even some non-British European immigrant groups (for example, Italian Americans) were for a short period of time defined as inferior racial groups, but within a generation or two they were defined as white.

Another term often used for certain distinctive social groups is *ethnic group*. While some social scientists have used it broadly to include racial groups, the more accurate use of the term is a group that is distinguished or set apart, by others or its own members, primarily on the basis of national-origin characteristics and cultural characteristics that are subjectively selected. "Ethnic" is an English word derived from the Greek word *ethnos* (for "nation") and was originally used for European immigrants entering in the early twentieth century. Examples are Polish Americans and Italian Americans, groups with a distinctive national origin and cultural heritage. Both racial groups and ethnic groups are socially constructed under particular historical circumstances and typically have a distinctive sense of peoplehood and cultural history. However, the lengthy historical and contemporary experiences of racial discrimination and subordination differentiate certain groups, such as African Americans and Native Americans, from the experiences and societal status of the ethnic groups of European origin that are now part of the white umbrella racial group.

"Multicultural America," the subject of this encyclopedia, is the product of the interaction of many different indigenous and immigrant peoples over the course of four centuries in what is now the United States. Cultural diversity was characteristic of the continent prior to the coming of European colonists and the Africans they enslaved. The indigenous inhabitants of North America numbered at least 7 million, and perhaps as many as 18 million, in the sixteenth century and were divided into hundreds of indigenous societies with distinctive cultures. Although the numbers of "Indians," as they were named by European colonizers, declined precipitously over the centuries as a result of European genocidal killings and diseases, their population has rebounded over the last century. As members of particular indigenous groups (such as Navajo, Ojibwa, and Choctaw) and as Native Americans, they are very much a part of today's cultural pluralism.

Most North Americans, in contrast, are the descendants of immigrants from other continents. Since the sixteenth century, from the early Spanish settlement at St. Augustine, Florida, the process of repopulating the continent has gone on apace. Several hundred thousand Europeans and Africans were recruited or enslaved and transported across the Atlantic Ocean during the colonial period to what eventually became the United States. The first census of 1790 revealed the racial and national origin diversity that marked the U.S. population. Almost a fifth of Americans were of African ancestry. (The census did not include Native Americans.) A surname analysis of the white population revealed that about 14 percent were Scottish and Scotch-Irish Americans and about 9 percent were German Americans—with smaller percentages of French, Irish, Dutch, Swedish, and Welsh Americans. English Americans comprised about 60 percent of the white population. At the time of its birth in 1776, the United States was already a complex racial and ethnic mosaic, with a wide variety of communities differentiated by the extent of racial oppression and by their national ancestry, culture, language, and religion.

The present United States includes not only the original 13 colonies but lands that were subsequently purchased or conquered by an often imperialistic U.S. government. Through this territorial expansion, other peoples and their lands were brought within the boundaries of the country. These included, in addition to many Native American societies, French, Hawaiian, Inuit, Mexican, and Puerto Rican groups, among others. Since 1790 great population growth, other than by natural increase, has come primarily through three eras of large-scale immigration. Arriving in the first major era of immigration (1841–1890) were almost 15 million newcomers: more than 4 million Germans, 3 million each of Irish and British (English, Scottish, and Welsh), and 1 million Scandinavians. A second major era of immigration (1891–1920) brought an additional 18 million immigrants: almost 4 million from Italy, 3.6 million from Austria-Hungary, and 3 million from Russia. In addition, more than 2 million Canadians immigrated prior to 1920. The following decades, from 1920 to 1945, marked a hiatus in immigration because of restrictive and discriminatory immigration policies, economic depression, and World War II. A modest postwar influx of European refugees was followed by a new era of major immigration resulting from the U.S. government abandoning in 1965 its openly discriminatory immigration policy favoring northern European immigrants. Totaling more than 40 million immigrants from 1965 to 2013—and still in progress—this third major era of immigration has encompassed about 20 million newcomers from Mexico and other parts of Central and South America and the Caribbean, as well as roughly 10 million newcomers from Asia. The rest have come from Canada, Europe, the Middle East, and Africa. While almost all the immigrants in the first two eras originated in Europe, a substantial majority since 1965 have come from Latin America, the Caribbean, Asia, Africa, and the Middle East.

Immigration has introduced a great diversity of racial-ethnic groups and cultures into the United States. The 2000 U.S. Census, the latest national census to report on ancestry, provides an interesting portrait of the complex origins of the people of the United States. Responses to the question "What is your ancestry or ethnic origin?" were tabulated for many groups. The largest ancestry groups reported were, in order of magnitude, German, Irish, African American, and English, all with more than 24 million individuals. Other groups reporting more than 4 million were Mexican, Italian, Polish, French, Native American, Scottish, Dutch, Norwegian, Scotch-Irish, and Swedish, with many other groups reporting more than 1 million each. There is also an array of smaller groups: Hmong, Maltese, Honduran, and Nigerian, among scores of others. Only 7 percent identified themselves simply as "American"—and less than one percent only as "white."

Immigration has contributed to the transformation of the religious character of the United States. The dominant Anglo-Protestantism (itself divided among numerous denominations and sects) of early English colonists was over time reinforced by the arrival of millions of Lutherans, Methodists, and Presbyterians and diluted by the heavy influx of Roman Catholics—first by the Irish and Germans, then by eastern Europeans and Italians, and more recently by Latin Americans. These immigrants have made Roman Catholicism the largest U.S. denomination. Meanwhile, Slavic Christian and Jewish immigrants from central and eastern Europe established Orthodox Christianity and Judaism as major religious bodies. As a consequence of Middle Eastern immigration—and the conversion of many African Americans to Islam—there are currently several million Muslims in the United States. Smaller numbers of Buddhists, Hindus, and followers of other religions have also arrived. In many U.S. cities houses of worship now include mosques and temples, as well as churches and synagogues. Religious pluralism is an important source of U.S. multiculturalism.

The immigration and naturalization policies pursued by a country's central government are revealing about the dominant group's public conception of the country. By determining who to admit to residence and citizenship, the dominant group defines the future racial and ethnic composition of the population. Each of the three great eras of immigration inspired much soul-searching and intense debate, especially in the dominant European American group, over the consequences of immigration for the U.S. future. If the capacity of this society to absorb tens of millions of immigrants over the course of more than 17 decades is impressive, it is also true that U.S. history has been punctuated by major episodes of vicious and violent nativism and xenophobia. With the exception of the British, it is difficult to find an immigrant group that has not been subject to significant racial or ethnic prejudice and discrimination. From early violent conflicts with Native Americans to the enslavement of Africans, Americans of northern European ancestry sought to establish "whiteness" as an essential marker of racial difference and superiority. They crafted a racial framing of society in order to legitimate and rationalize their subordination of numerous racial and ethnic groups. For example, the Naturalization Act (1790), one of the first passed in the new U.S. Congress, specified that citizenship in the United States was available only to an immigrant who was "a free white person." By this dramatic provision not only were African Americans ineligible for naturalization but also future immigrants who were deemed not to be "white." From that time to the present, the greater the likeness of immigrants to the northern European Protestants, the more readily they were welcomed by the dominant group.

There were, however, opposing, liberty-and-justice views held by racially and ethnically oppressed groups, as well as a version of this outlook supported by a minority of the dominant European American group. For example, in the nineteenth century, citing democratic ideals and universal brotherhood, many African Americans and some white Americans advocated the abolition of slavery and the human rights of those freed from slavery.

Since at least the 1880s debates over immigration policy have periodically brought contrasting views of the United States into collision. The ideal of the United States as a shelter and asylum for the oppressed of the world has exerted a powerful influence for a liberal reception of diverse newcomers. Early support for this liberal framing of immigration came from the descendants of early immigrants who were racially or ethnically different from the then dominant British American group. Poet Emma Lazarus's sonnet, which began "Give me your tired, your poor, your huddled masses yearning to breathe free, the wretched refuse of your teeming shore," struck a responsive chord among many Americans and was placed on the Statue of Liberty, a gift to the United States by the people of France. Emma Lazarus (1849-87) herself was the daughter of early Sephardic (Portuguese) Jewish immigrants to the colonies.

Over the centuries many U.S. businesses have depended upon the immigrant workers of Europe, Latin America, and Asia to develop the country's factories, mines, and railroads. Periodically, nonetheless, many white Americans have framed this immigration in negative terms—as posing a threat to societal stability, to their jobs, or U.S. cultural and biological integrity. Historically the strength of organized anti-immigrant movements has waxed and waned with the volume of immigration, as well as with fluctuations in the condition of the U.S. economy. Although the immigrant targets of nativistic attacks have changed over time, a constant theme in the framing of them by the dominant group has been the "danger" posed by "foreigners" to the core U.S. values and institutions.

For example, coming in large numbers from the 1830s to the 1850s, Irish Catholics were viewed as the dependent minions of the Catholic pope and thus as enemies of the Protestant character of the United States. A Protestant crusade against these immigrants culminated in the formation of the "Know-Nothing" Party in the 1850s, whose political battle cry was "America for the Americans!" This anti-Catholicism continued to be a powerful strain of nativism well into the middle of the twentieth century, including during the election and presidency of John F. Kennedy, an Irish Catholic American, in the early 1960s.

Despite frequent episodes of xenophobia, during its first decades of existence, the U.S. government generally welcomed newcomers with minimal regulation. In the 1880s, however, two important laws passed by a Congress controlled by (northern) European American politicians initiated a significant tightening of restrictions on some immigration. The first law established certain health and "moral" standards by excluding criminals, prostitutes, lunatics, idiots, and paupers. The second, the openly racist Chinese Exclusion Act, was the culmination of an anti-Chinese movement among European Americans centered on the West Coast. It denied admission to new Chinese laborers and barred Chinese workers already here from acquiring citizenship. Following the law's enactment, agitation for exclusion of Asian immigrants continued as the new Japanese and other Asian immigrant workers arrived. This European American nativism soon resulted in the blatantly racist provisions of the 1924 Immigration Law, which denied entry to "aliens ineligible for citizenship" (that is, those who were not "white"). It was not until 1950s and 1960s that a combination of international politics and civil rights movements, with their democratic ideals, resulted in the elimination of the more overtly racial restrictions from U.S. immigration and naturalization policies.

In the mid- to late-nineteenth century "scientific racism," which reiterated the superiority of whites of northern European origin, was embraced by many scientists and political leaders as justification for immigration restrictions and growing U.S. imperialism on the continent and overseas. By the late-nineteenth century the second immigration era was quite evident, as large numbers of immigrants from southern and eastern Europe entered the country. Nativists of northern European ancestry campaigned for a literacy test and other measures to restrict the entry of what they termed "inferior" European nationalities (sometimes termed "inferior races"). World War I created a xenophobic climate that prepared the way for the immigration acts of 1921 and 1924. Inspired by nativistic ideas, these laws established a national quota system designed to greatly reduce the number of southern and eastern Europeans entering the United States and to bar Asians. The statutes intentionally sought to maintain the northern European racial-ethnic identity of the country by protecting it from "contamination" from abroad.

Until 1965 the U.S. government pursued a very restrictive immigration policy that kept the country from becoming more diverse racially, ethnically, and religiously. The 1965 Immigration Act finally did away with the discriminatory national origins quotas and opened the country to immigration from throughout the world, establishing preferences for family members of citizens, skilled workers, entrepreneurs, and refugees. One consequence was the third wave of immigration. Since then, the annual volume of authorized immigration has increased steadily to about 1 million arrivals each year, and the majority of these new residents have come from Asia and Latin America.

The cumulative impact of the immigration of tens of millions of non-European immigrants since 1965 has aroused intense concerns, mostly in the dominant white group, regarding the demographic, cultural, and racial future of the United States. The skin color, as well as the languages and cultures, of most of the newcomers and their descendants have again been viewed negatively by many whites. Nativistic white advocates of tighter immigration restriction have warned that if current rates of immigration continue, white Americans will likely be a minority of the U.S. population by 2050.

One particular cause of white anxiety is the number of undocumented immigrants from Mexico (down to about 140,000 per year by 2013). Contrary to popular belief, the majority of undocumented immigrants do not cross the border from Mexico but enter the country with student or tourist visas and stay. Indeed, many are Europeans and Asians. The 1986 Immigration Reform and Control Act (IRCA) sought to solve the problem by extending amnesty for undocumented immigrants under certain conditions, imposing penalties on employers who hired them, and making provision for temporary agricultural migrant workers. Although more than 3 million people qualified for consideration for amnesty, employer sanctions failed for lack of enforcement, and for a time the number of undocumented immigrants did not decrease. Congress subsequently enacted the Immigration Act of 1990, which established a cap on immigrants per year, maintained preferences based on family reunification, and expanded the number of skilled workers admitted. The Illegal Immigration Reform and Immigrant Responsibility Act (IIRIRA), passed in 1996, established yet more regulations restricting legal and undocumented immigration and increased border control agents.

In 2006 Congress passed yet more restrictive legislation, the Secure Fence Act. It mandated the building of a billion-dollar border fence and other expensive surveillance technology and increased border enforcement personnel. Over recent decades the extensive border surveillance procedures have played a role in many of the estimated 5,100 lives lost as undocumented men, women, and children have tried to cross an ever more difficult U.S.-Mexico border—with its intensively policed and often extremely hot and waterless conditions--to improve their dire economic situations. Latin American immigration has continued to be a hotly debated U.S. political issue. Responding to the nativist mood of the country, politicians have advocated yet more restrictive measures to reduce immigration, as well as limiting access to government programs by legal and undocumented immigrants.

Forebodings about an "unprecedented immigrant invasion," however, have been greatly exaggerated. In the early 1900s the rate of immigration (the number of immigrants measured against the total population) was higher than in recent decades. While the number of foreign-born individuals in the United States reached nearly 40 million in 2010, an all-time high, they accounted for only 12.9 percent of the population, compared with 14.7 percent in 1910, giving the United States a smaller percentage of foreign-born individuals than some other contemporary nations. Moreover, in the early twenty-first century, Mexican immigration to the United States has been decreasing significantly, to the point that in 2005-10 there was a net zero migration to United States—that is, as many Mexicans were leaving the United States as were coming in. A persuasive argument has also been made that immigrants contribute much more than they take from the U.S. economy and pay more in taxes than they receive in social services. As in the past, new immigrants are often made the scapegoats for the country's broader economic and political problems.

Difficult questions face analysts of U.S. history. How have these millions of immigrants with such differing backgrounds and cultures been incorporated into the society? What changes have they wrought in the character of United States? The problematical concept of "assimilation" has traditionally been used to try to understand the process through which immigrants have adapted to U.S. society. Assimilation theorists view cultural assimilation (acculturation) as the one-way process whereby newcomers assume U.S. cultural attributes, such as the English language and political values, and social-group assimilation as the process of immigrant incorporation into important social networks (work, residence, and families) of the dominant group. In many cases such adaptation has not come easily. Many immigrants of color have culturally adapted to a significant degree but have experienced only limited incorporation into many mainstream networks and institutions because of persisting white racial bias and discrimination.

Indeed, since they have always wielded great social and political power, white Americans as a group have been able to decide who to include and exclude in the country. "Race" (especially skin color) has been the major barrier to full acceptance into historically white-controlled institutions. Asian and Latino Americans, as well as African Americans and Native Americans, have long been excluded from full integration into major white-dominated institutions. Race, language, religion, and national origin have been impediments to access. Social class has also strongly affected interactions among U.S. racial and ethnic groups. Historically, U.S. society has been highly strati-fied, with a close congruence between social class and racial or ethnic group. Thus, a high degree of employment and residential segregation has been central to maintaining the United States as a racially segregated society, with white Americans very disproportionately in the powerful upper and upper-middle classes.

The status of women within American society, as well as within particular racial and ethnic groups, has affected the ability of female immigrants to adapt to their new country. Historically, to a greater or lesser extent depending on their group, women have been restricted to traditional gender roles or have had limited freedom to pursue opportunities in the larger society. The density and location of immigrant settlements have also influenced the incorporation of immigrants into the dominant culture and institutions. Concentrated urban settlements and isolated rural settle-ments, by limiting contacts between immigrants and native-born Americans, tend to inhibit the processes of assimilation.

Historically one important variable is the determination of immigrants themselves whether or not to shed important aspects of their cultures. Through chain migrations, relatives and friends have often regrouped in cities, towns, and the countryside for mutual assistance and to maintain their customary ways in a sometimes hostile and difficult U.S. society. Establishing churches, news-papers, and other institutions, they have built communities and have developed an enlarged sense of peoplehood. Thus, national origin and home cultures have been important in many immigrants' attempts to cope with life in the United States. Theirs is often a selective adaptation, in which they have taken from the dominant U.S. culture what they needed and have kept significant aspects of their home culture that they value. The children and grandchildren of immigrants usually retain less of their ancestral cultures (languages are first to go) and have assumed more attributes of the dominant culture. Still, many have retained, to a greater or lesser degree, a sense of identity with a particular nationality or racial group. These patterns of societal adaptation vary greatly for differ-ent groups, historically and in the present. Immigrant groups of color and their descendants have been racialized by the dominant white group and have thus had quite different experiences from immigrants who are part of distinctive national origin groups within a white America. Racialized immigrant groups often use their home culture and its values and perspectives for resources in fight-ing against the racism and discrimination they face in their everyday lives.

For centuries the core culture of the colonies and early United States was essentially British American in most important aspects, and the immigrants (almost all European until the 1850s) and their offspring had to adapt to that dominant culture. Over time a few aspects of that core culture—such as music, food, and literature—have experienced some significant changes. These aspects of the core culture are today products of syncretism—the melding of different, sometimes discordant elements of the cultures of European and non-European immigrants and their descend-ants. Multiculturalism today is not a museum of immigrant cultures but rather a complex of the living, multitudinous cultures of the contemporary United States interacting with each other. Nonetheless, most of the central social, political, and economic realities of the U.S. core culture are still very much European American (especially British American) in their institutional structures, normative operation, and folkways. These include the major economic, legal, political, and educa-tional institutions.

The country's ideological heritage includes the ideals of freedom and equality from the American Revolution. Such ideals have often been just abstract principles, especially for the dominant white group, that have been handed down from the eighteenth century to the present. However, subordi-nated racial and ethnic groups, taking these ideals very seriously, have employed them as weapons to combat economic exploitation and racial and ethnic discrimination. If the United States has been the "promised land" for many immigrants, that promise has been realized, if only in part, after prolonged and collective societal struggles. Through civil rights and labor movements, they have contributed greatly to keeping alive and enlarging the ideals of freedom, equality, and justice. If the

United States has transformed the numerous immigrant and indigenous groups in significant ways, these groups have on occasion significantly transformed the United States.

How has the dominant white American group historically conceived of this polyglot, kaleidoscopic society? Over the centuries two major models of a society comprised of various racial and ethnic groups have competed with each other. The dominant white model long envisioned a society based on racial "caste"— a society constitutionally and legally divided into those who were free and those who were not. Such a societal order existed for about 85 percent of this country's history (until the late 1960s). While the Civil War destroyed slavery, the Jim Crow system of segregation maintained extreme white oppression of black Americans for another hundred years. This model of intensive racial-ethnic oppression was not limited to black-white relationships. The industrial economy created a caste-like structure in much of the North. For a century prior to the progressive "New Deal" era of the 1930s, U.S. power, wealth, and status in the North were concentrated in the hands of a British-American elite, while U.S. workers there, made up largely of European immigrants and their children, were the low-paid serfs of factories, railroads, and farms. In subsequent decades this pattern has shifted as immigrants of color and their children have often filled many of these jobs on farms and in factories in the North and the South. By the 1960s official Jim Crow segregation ended in Southern and border states, and African Americans continued their movement out of the South to the North, which had begun in earnest in the 1930s and 1940s.

Over the centuries, since at least the 1700s, immigrants to this country have been expected by the dominant group to adapt and conform to the British-American ("Anglo-Saxon") core culture. Convinced of their cultural and biological superiority, Americans of British and other northern European descent have pressured Native Americans, African Americans, Latinos, and Asian Americans to modify or abandon their distinctive linguistic and cultural patterns and conform in a more or less one-way adaptive pattern to the dominant culture and folkways. However, even as they have demanded this conformity, European Americans have erected racial barriers that have severely limited egalitarian social intercourse and integration with those they have framed as racially inferior. Indeed, a prime objective of the U.S. public school system has been the one-way "assimilation" of "alien" children to the dominant cultural values and behaviors. The intensity of this pressure can be seen in the successful attacks, mostly white-led, on various programs of bilingual education, especially those involving the Spanish language of many Latin American immigrants and their descendants.

Nonetheless, over the course of U.S. history, and especially since the early 1900s, this intense one-way adaptation model has been countered by variations on a melting pot perspective. The "melting pot" symbolizes the process in which diverse immigrant groups are assimilated into a new "American blend." There have been many variants of this ideology of the melting pot, including the prevailing one in which the European American is still the cook stirring and determining the immigrant ingredients. In all versions the United States is viewed as becoming a distinctive amalgam of varied cultures and peoples emerging from the racial-ethnic crucible. Expressing confidence in the capacity of the country to incorporate diverse newcomers, the melting pot ideology has also provided the rationale for a more liberal approach to immigrants and immigration policy. Even so, this liberal melting pot ideology has periodically come under increasing attacks from anti-immigrant and other nativist groups, even after the progressive changes in U.S. immigration laws in the 1960s.

A third model of immigrant adaptation emerged during World War I in opposition to intensive pressures on immigrants for one-way "Americanization," a model often termed "cultural pluralism." In this model, while sharing a common U.S. citizenship and loyalty, racial and ethnic groups should be able to maintain and foster their particular languages and distinctive cultures. The metaphors employed for the cultural pluralism model have included a symphony orchestra, a flower garden, and a mosaic. All suggest a reconciliation of group diversity with an encompassing harmony and coherence of racial and ethnic groups. During the 1930s, when cultural democracy was more in vogue, pluralist ideas were more popular. Again during the social movements of the

1960s and the 1970s, cultural pluralism attracted a considerable following. By the early twenty-first century, heightened fears, especially among white Americans, that U.S. society is fragmenting and moving away from the dominance of the English language and Euro-American culture have caused many people to reject any type of significant cultural pluralism.

Questions about racial and ethnic matters loom large as the United States moves ever more deeply into the twenty-first century. Its future as a racially and ethnically plural society and socially just society is vigorously debated. Is the United States more diverse today than in the past? Can discriminatory racial and ethnic barriers be finally removed? Can this multiracial society really be made more just and democratic? The old model of one-way conformity to the white-controlled core culture has lost its ideological and symbolic value for a great many Americans who believe we need to implement a more egalitarian societal model. These Americans see the United States as a respectfully multicultural and truly democratic people in the context of a multicultural world.

Suggested Reading On issues of systemic racism and the creation of U.S. racial groups, see Joe R. Feagin, *Systemic Racism: A Theory of Oppression* (2006) and *The White Racial Frame* (2nd edition, 2013). On conventional assimilation theory, see Milton Gordon's *Assimilation in American Life: The Role of Race, Religion, and National Origins* (1964). On recent assimilation theory and applicable data, see Richard Alba, *Blurring the Color Line: The New Chance for a More Integrated America* (2009). For discussion of racial and ethnic group definitions, see Joe R. Feagin and Clairece B. Feagin, *Racial and Ethnic Relations (2011). Harvard Encyclopedia of American Ethnic Groups* (1980), edited by Stephan Thernstrom, is a standard reference work with articles on racial-ethnic themes and specific groups. Roger Daniels's *Coming to America: A History of Immigration and Ethnicity in American Life* (1991) is a comprehensive history. For a comparative history of racial-ethnic groups, see Ronald Takaki's *A Different Mirror: A History of Multicultural America* (1993). A classic work on nativism is John Higham's *Strangers in the Land: Patterns of American Nativism: 1860-1925* (1963). On the British American elite's history, see E. Digby Baltzell's *The Protestant Establishment: Aristocracy and Caste in America* (1964). On contemporary ancestry groups, see Angela Brittingham and G. Patricia de la Cruz, *Ancestry: 2000* (2004).

Rudolph Vecoli
Updated and revised by Joe Feagin

ROMANI AMERICANS

Evan Heimlich

OVERVIEW

Romani Americans are Americans with Gypsy, or Romani, ancestry. The term *Gypsy* derives from the word *Egyptian*, reflecting a mistaken assumption of the origins of the people who refer to themselves as Roma. According to one hypothesis, Roma trace their roots to a diverse group who were assembled in northern India as a military force to resist the eastward movement of Islam. Romani groups lived in what is the modern Indian state of Rajasthan in northwest India, before migrating west in what DNA and linguistic analysis suggests was about 1000 CE. Over the centuries, they moved into Europe and adapted their language and culture in their migrations, forming a diverse range of Romani subgroups, each with their own unique cultural histories and practices. More recent theorists, such as Wim Willems and Brian Belton, argue that the Romani identity is not in fact hereditary, but instead based on a set of cultural and lifestyle practices that have for centuries been adopted or abandoned by groups from all over the world in response to changing social and economic conditions that placed them at odds with the dominant social structures. Romani Americans represent family groups from England (Romnichals), eastern Europe (Roma, subdivided into Kalderash, Lovari, Machvaya, and others), Romania (Ludar), Spain (Gitanos), Germany, and many other European regions. While Romani people are widely spread throughout Europe, the areas with the most highly concentrated populations are eastern Europe and Spain.

Because Roma are so widely dispersed, and because the number of people who self-identify as Roma is fluid, there is no accurate population count. In the twenty-first century, various scholars and organizations have estimated their numbers to be between 9 and 14 million worldwide. The 2011 World Bank data for Romania, the country with the highest estimates of Roma, puts the country's entire population at over 21 million, 619,000 of which are Roma, though unofficial estimates suggest the true number may be upwards of 2 million. The majority of Romani settlements in Romania and throughout Europe are in impoverished urban areas. Some Roma tend not to assimilate into the societies and cultures of the regions in which they settle—either by choice or due to discrimination; they are often service workers in the regional economies, earning money as performers, fortune-tellers, peddlers, metal salvagers, and used car dealers. There is a high rate of poverty among Roma around the world today, with unemployment over 50 percent in many regions of Europe.

Although small groups of Roma arrived in North America as slaves in the seventeenth century, it was the abolition of Romani slavery in 1864 in southern Romania that led those predominantly living in eastern Europe to migrate throughout the rest of Europe and eventually to the United States. Many from this first wave of Romani immigration to the United States joined groups of Roma living in the South—particularly Louisiana—who had been shipped overseas from France and Spain as slave laborers during the colonial period. Although some Roma moved to rural areas for job opportunities, the Great Depression in the 1930s led many to settle in larger cities such as Chicago and New York City in pursuit of a variety of trades, such as animal husbandry, fortune-telling, and car repair and metallurgy. More recent waves of Romani immigration to the United States have occurred during periods of unrest in eastern Europe, such as the conflicts in Bosnia and Kosovo in the late twentieth century. Roma are still somewhat concealed in U.S. society, mainly by choice to avoid persecution or stereotyping, and have come to be referred to by some scholars as the "invisible minority" or "hidden Americans."

An accurate estimate of the Roma population in the United States is difficult to achieve. If counted in a census at all, it is typically by their country of origin. Estimates of the total population of Roma in the United States range from fewer than 100,000 to one million. The Romani population is spread throughout the rural and urban United States, and the various groups of Roma typically remain within separate insular groups due to their disparate range of cultural practices and dialects. States with large numbers of Romani Americans include New York, Virginia, Illinois, Texas, Massachusetts, California, Washington, and Oregon.

HISTORY OF THE PEOPLE

Early History The linguist W. R. Rishi traces the etymology of the word *Rom* to the Sanskrit word *Rama*, with meanings that include "one who roams about."

The number of Persian, Armenian, and Greek terms in the various Romani dialects reflects their migrations, just as those related to Sanskrit and Hindi point to their common origin. Although a Persian story has been cited as proof they came from a single caste of entertainers, more recent evidence, including blood-type research, points to a gathering of diverse peoples in the Punjab region of India to form an army and its support groups to counter Muslim invaders. In the eleventh century some of this group moved north through Kashmir and west into Persia. After some generations they pushed on to Armenia, then fled Turkish invaders by entering the Byzantine Empire. By the thirteenth century they had reached the Balkan Peninsula; Serbian and Romanian terms came into their language. Thereafter they split into smaller groups that dispersed throughout Europe, absorbed cultural and linguistic influences from their host countries, and developed differences that persist among Romani subgroups today.

In the late fifteenth century Roma reached western Europe from regions dominated by the Ottoman Empire. Their language and appearance set them apart from the resident populations; they repeatedly suffered harassment or worse at the hands of the local majority, and they were often denied the right to own land. Such treatment likely encouraged their traditionally nomadic way of life; however, some groups were not nomadic. Eventually Europeans used "Gypsies" or related words to name not only a particular ethnic group of people, but also other groups of people, unrelated by blood, who maintained a nomadic way of life. For the most part, Roma kept to themselves as a people; however, as Matt Salo suggests in his introduction to *Urban Gypsies*, "The existence of a number of Gypsy-like peripatetic groups, some of which (such as British Travellers) have intermarried with Gypsies … complicate our attempts at classification" of who should count as Romani. Although purists tend to define the group narrowly, the definition of Roma most widely accepted among experts is any people who identify themselves as Romani.

Modern Era Almost all Roma in the United States originated from some part of Europe. Within the category of Roma, the most numerous subgroups are Kalderash and Machwaya. There are other large groups of Roma as well: Baschalde (from Slovakia, Hungary, and the Carpathians), who may number close to 100,000; and Romungre (from Hungary and Transylvania), who may number as many as 60,000. There are some Horahanae, who are Muslims from the South Balkans, and a small population of Sinti Gypsies, who came from northern Europe—Germany, Netherlands, France, Austria, and Hungary—where they, like other Roma, were targets of the Nazis. There are also Bosnian and Polish Roma in the United States. One of the most recent immigrations of a Roma group is that of the Lovara, who arrived in the 1990s. There

are also a few small groups of Rumanian Ludar. Some "black Dutch," from Germany, the Netherlands, and Pennsylvania, intermarried with Romnichals and are counted as Anglo-Americans.

The two groups of Romani Americans about whom scholars know the most are Roma and Romnichals. Many Roma came to the New World from Russia or eastern or central Europe; the Romnichals came from Great Britain. Although these two groups have much in common, they also are divided by cultural differences between Great Britain and eastern Europe. The Romnichals came to the United States several decades earlier than Roma, in the mid-nineteenth century, and ran successful horse-trading operations in New England. Roma arrived in the United States during the late nineteenth century. There are several reasons attributed to the uncertainty surrounding how many Roma are in the United States: many entered the country as undocumented immigrants, and those who were documented were recorded by their country of origin and not as Roma.

The Romani-sponsored Patrin website (www.patrin.org.uk) explains, "Many Roma themselves do not admit to their true ethnic origins for economic and social reasons," a reference to the long tradition of exclusion and persecution that they suffered for centuries in Europe. Most disturbingly, the Nazis rounded up and killed an estimated 200,000 to 1,500,000 Roma during World War II in what is known in Romani as the *Porrajmos*, or "the Devouring." Many Roma who were sent to the Auschwitz concentration camp during the war, particularly Romani children, also became subjects of grotesque medical experiments by the infamous Nazi doctor Josef Mengele. Roman Mirga, a Polish Roma who escaped from Auschwitz, recorded his experience there in a manuscript that was later adapted by Alexander Ramati as a novel titled *And the Violins Stopped Playing* (1986) and as a motion picture of the same title in 1988. Nevertheless, acknowledgement of the atrocities committed against Roma has been slow in coming: the first official recognition by a German leader of the Nazis' Roma executions based on ethnic grounds occurred in 1982. Roma activists continue to draw attention to the current plight of eastern European Roma. Although the collapse of Communist regimes—especially that of Romanian leader Nicolae Ceausescu, which conducted forced sterilizations and other genocidal persecutions of Roma—has alleviated some of the worst oppression, "ethnic cleansing" in eastern Europe is a continuing cause for concern. The Czechoslavakian government also performed forced sterilization on Romani women until 1990, and there have been many criminal complaints of sterilization in eastern Europe since then. Roma continue to face expulsion from both eastern and western member countries of the European Union, most notably France, Germany, and Italy.

Upon the collapse of Communism in Europe in the late 1980s and early 1990s, European Roma sought greater opportunity to organize and establish political representation. In Romania, for example, the *Partida Romilor*, or "Party of the Roma," was founded in 1990 following the overthrow of the Communist government during the 1989 Romanian Revolution. Throughout the 1990s, countries including Hungary, the Czech Republic, and Slovakia implemented policies aimed at providing Roma with a sense of inclusion and the chance to participate in public political discourse. The 1996 formation of the European Roma Rights Center (ERRC) in Budapest, Hungary, marks the introduction of Roma activism on the world stage. Because of continued discrimination against Roma in Europe, including segregation, evictions, and basic social and economic neglect, Roma activism is integral in achieving any sort of equality.

With the advent of Romani activism, more media and cultural attention has been paid to the plight of Roma. Filmmaker Jasmine Dellal created the 2000 PBS documentary *American Gypsy: A Stranger in Everybody's Land*, shedding light on Romani experience by highlighting a Romani family living in Spokane, Washington. George Eli's *Searching for the 4th Nail* (2009) is perhaps the first documentary by a Romani American filmmaker. Recently Romani citizens have appeared in multiple reality television series, such as TLC's *My Big Fat American Gypsy Wedding* and the National Geographic Channel's *American Gypsies*. Both shows have been criticized for perpetuating stereotypes of the Roma. Roma have also made significant appearances in mainstream publications such as *Al Jazeera*, *Time Magazine*, and *Miller-McCune*, spotlighting Romani activism and daily life. Oksana Marafioti's 2012 memoir *American Gypsy* has been praised for its exploration of the Romani American immigrant experience.

SETTLEMENT IN THE UNITED STATES

Roma have come to the United States for reasons similar to those of other immigrants; however, since European powers have tended to discriminate against Romani people, this hostility has hastened Romani emigrations. In the late sixteenth century England deported some Roma to Barbados and Australia, and by the end of the seventeenth century, every European country with New World holdings followed the practice of deporting Roma to the Americas. Suspicion between Roma and established institutions also spurred Romani emigration. Christian churches of Europe attacked Romani fortune-tellers, prompting deportations. Near the end of the nineteenth century, eastern European Roma migrated westward; within this mass movement came the biggest immigrant waves of Roma to the United States.

Although all Europeans have historically treated Roma poorly, Roma tended to fare better in western Europe and the United States than in eastern Europe, where they suffered extremes of racial prejudice, including enslavement in southern Romania. Roma hoped to escape social oppression by immigrating to the New World. Some Roma deported to South America migrated to North America. Some Roma were annexed into America with territory itself: for example, Napoleon transported hundreds of Romani men to Louisiana during the two-year period before selling the Louisiana Territory to the United States in 1803. More recently, toward the end of the twentieth century, the collapse of Communism in eastern Europe has enabled Roma to emigrate more freely, at times with renewed harassment as incentive, bringing new waves of eastern European Roma to the United States.

The traditional stereotype of the Gypsy is the nomad, and some modern Romani Americans continue to travel seasonally in pursuit of their livelihoods. Rather than wander, they move purposefully from one destination to another for work purposes. Historically, some families have reportedly traveled in regular circuits. Awareness of the best cities, small towns, or rural areas as markets for their services has guided all travel. A group might camp for weeks, sometimes months, at especially productive urban areas, returning to these spots year after year.

Nomadic Romani Americans might maintain a sequence of home bases; they often live in mobile homes, settling indefinitely in a trailer park. They may tear down walls and enlarge the doorways of their homes to combine rooms or make them larger to create a wide open space suitable for the large social gatherings that occur in Rom homes. In *Urban Gypsies*, Carol Silverman notes that Kalderash frequently pass along the houses, apartments, or trailers that they modify to a succession of Romani families. While some Romani Americans travel to make their living, others pursue settled careers in a variety of occupations according to their education and opportunities.

While largely hidden from view, Roma who announce their heritage face discrimination on many levels, especially economic. In order to escape worse oppression, early Roma sold themselves into slavery for the price of admission to the United States. Early trades for Roma included woodworking, metalworking, and horse training. Roma who immigrated to the United States after the turn of the twentieth century often sought occupations that enabled them to work independently and primarily on the move. These jobs were often connected to a particular group; Kalderash have a large number of fortune-tellers while Ludar primarily worked as showmen and animal trainers. More recently, many Roma make their living in car repair and reworking and selling scrap metal.

The Romani population has participated in American migrations from countryside into cities, yet estimates suggest that the Romani American population is evenly divided between urban and rural areas. Generally, as noted by Silverman, the urbanization of the Rom in the United States began as early as the

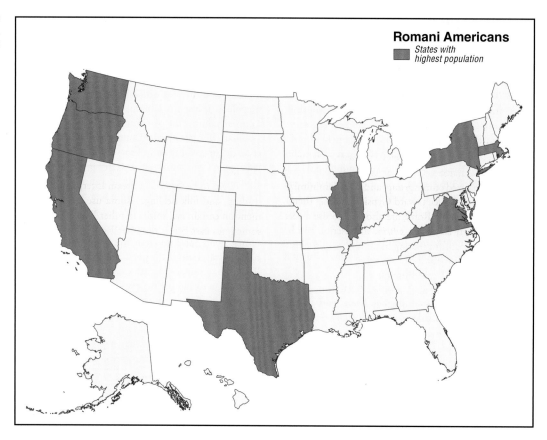

Romani Americans
*States with
highest population*

end of the eighteenth century, when various groups began to spend the winter months camping in vacant lots on the outskirts of cities, and intensified when "a large number of *Rom* flocked to the cities during the 1920s and 1930s to take advantage of various relief programs, and remained there because of gas rationing and because of increasing business opportunities within the city."

Many Americans have either romanticized Roma as exotic foreigners or criminalized them as thieves. Some Americans draw on the supposedly romantic appeal of Romani traditions of dancing, music-making, and living on the road. Americans have maintained or adopted European prejudices against Roma and treat Romani immigrants poorly. Just as Europeans have often attributed the fortune-telling skills of Roma to "black magic," Romani traders have been accused of stealing and fencing stolen goods ever since their earliest migrations into Europe. As a result, English speakers may say that to defraud, swindle, or cheat someone is to "gyp" them. This sensational image of Roma as criminals is not supported by statistical analysis of court records, since conviction rates of Roma Americans for theft is no higher than the rate for other Americans. Nevertheless, laws attempting to deter, prevent, and punish fortune-tellers and thieves in the United States have singled out Romani Americans. In the early twentieth century, Virginia legally barred Roma from telling fortunes. In New

Jersey in the mid-1980s, special regulations and licensing requirements applied to Roma who told fortunes. As recently as 2011, a Fort Lauderdale, Florida–based Romani American named Rose Marks and her family were accused of fraud by the United States government after it was revealed that they had earned some 25 million dollars telling fortunes. Romani households have long been labeled as "dens of thieves" so that charges brought against one resident may apply to any and all. As recently as the 1970s, New Hampshire expelled some Roma on the grounds merely that they were Gypsies.

Because Romani Americans tend to follow economic opportunities, they often reside in the most populous cities, such as Los Angeles, San Francisco, New York, Chicago, Boston, Dallas, Houston, Seattle, and Portland. These urban centers have the largest concentrations of Romani American inhabitants. There are approximately 20,000 Roma living in Texas, with a concentration of Roma in Fort Worth. The Roma also joined the American movement westward, and as a result, many live in California. Virginia is another state with significant numbers of Romani Americans.

LANGUAGE

Most Roma are at least bilingual, speaking the language of the country in which they live as well as some branch of the Romani language, *Romani* or *Romanes*. There are a number of different dialects of Romani, each influenced by the languages of the countries where Roma historically resided. For example, Romani exhibits many characteristics of Greek origin, due to Roma migration throughout the Byzantine Empire prior to the tenth century. Furthermore, linguist Yaron Matras notes that British and American Roma often speak "Angloromani," incorporating Romani words or phrases into English speech.

Silverman explains that when non-Roma ask Kalderash to identify their foreign language, they "usually answer Romanian, Greek, or Yugoslavian," to pass as a less stigmatized ethnic group, and thus to minimize curiosity and prejudice toward Gypsies. Among themselves, some nomadic Roma are also said to use a sort of in-group sign language, *patrin*, to describe conditions of camps for future campers, as well as to provide information useful for fortune-telling. Furthermore, Roma usually use their Romani name only among other Roma and adopt an Americanized name for general and official uses. Particularly because many Roma pick common names, they are hard to trace.

Among younger generations of Romani Americans, especially those who have become more integrated into American society, there has been some decline in the use of Romani. Still, Roma have an expression—*amari čhib si amari zor* ("our language is our strength")—that compels many Romani Americans to preserve the language. The most common varieties of Romani spoken in the United States (by Kalderash and Machwaya) are derived from the Vlach dialects of eastern Europe. Because Romani is primarily spoken and not written, there is no standardized spelling for most words.

Greetings and Popular Expressions Romani greetings and expressions include the following examples (with pronunciation): *P'aves Baxtalo/Baxtali*! ("pah-vis bach-tah-low/bach-tah-lee")—May you be lucky; *Sar san?*—How are you?; *Lačho deves* ("La-cho day-vase")—Good day; and *Xa*! ("kha!")—Eat!

RELIGION

Romani spirituality, part of the core of Romani culture, may derive from Hindu and Zoroastrian concepts of *kintala*—balance and harmony, as between good and evil. When that balance is upset, ancestors send signals to keep people on track. The mysticism of fortune-tellers and tarot readers—though such services to non-Roma are not the same as Roma's own spirituality—has bases in Romani spirituality. Many Roma are Christians with denominational allegiances that reflect their countries of origin.

Most Romani Americans, especially Vlax Roma, are nominally Eastern Orthodox. They celebrate the *pomona* feast for the dead, at which the revelers invite the dead to eat in heaven. Also, preparation for their *slava* (patron saint's day) feast requires thorough cleaning of the interior of the host's house, its furniture, and its inhabitants, as the host transforms a section of the house into a sacred space. The feast ceremony begins with coffee for the guests, prayer, and a candle for the saints.

Roma have tended to syncretize or blend their Romani folk religion with institutional religions such as Christianity. Romani religious beliefs are mostly unrelated to the business of fortune-telling. Silverman points out that, while some Roma "often joke about how gullible non-Gypsies are," others are believers; fortune-tellers generally treat their reading room as sacred and may "consult elder Gypsy women who are known to be experts in dream interpretation, card reading, and folk healing." Roma use code-names to mention certain evil spirits to other Roma, and Roma sometimes cast curses on other Roma (or ward them off). Also, states Silverman, Roma fortune-tellers use diverse religious iconography because "good luck and power can come from the symbols of any religion."

Recently, Christian fundamentalist revival movements have been sweeping through Romani, Romnichal, and other groups of Roma. Since the mid-1980s, through Assemblies of God, various American groups have formed Roma churches. In Fort Worth, Texas, and many other American cities, churches integrate traditional Romani faith with Christian Pentecostal ritual.

CULTURE AND ASSIMILATION

Roma are intensely proud of their heritage and traditions, collectively referred to as *Romaniya*, and have repeatedly shown the ability to adapt without surrendering the essence of their culture. Traditional Romani Americans continue to resist the inroads of acculturation, assimilation, and absorption in the United States. Even groups such as the Gitanos from Spain or Romnichals from England, despite having lost most of their original language, still maintain a strong sense of ethnic identity and exclusiveness. A major issue facing Romani Americans since the 1980s is a worldwide Christian fundamentalist revival that has swept up Roma around the world. As masses of Roma practice versions of Pentecostal Christianity, currents of Romani culture may be undergoing a sea-change.

Roma maintain a powerful group identity. Those who travel see this as setting them apart from other cultures. Those who do not travel point to their language, rituals, and kinship relations as core cultural elements. Another area of difference from mainstream America is their historic attitude toward formal, public schools. Until recently, some Roma sent their children to schools only until puberty to keep them from being exposed to alien practices and teachings. However, in the last two decades, an educated group of Roma has emerged in the United States as well as Europe.

Prejudice against Roma has strengthened their lack of assimilation. One might suppose that economic interactions would dispel the insularity of Roma, while insular social practices pull Roma together. These opposing tensions give Roma a flexible identity. Roma negotiate the split between their business life, which focuses outwardly on non-Roma, and their social life, which focuses inwardly on other Roma.

Contemporary urban Romani Americans usually live interspersed among the non-Roma population, establishing *ofisi* (fortune-telling parlors, one means of livelihood) in working areas or in their homes. Their businesses may make many Roma seem quite assimilated, and at other times the same Roma may seem very traditional. Roma have tended to maintain two distinct standards of public behavior, one among themselves, another among outsiders. "A Gypsy's very survival among non-Gypsies often depends on his [or her] ability to conceal as well as exaggerate his Gypsiness at appropriate times," observes Silverman. For example, an appropriate time for Roma to play to stereotype is while performing as a musician or fortune-teller for audiences who are known to value Romani exoticism. On the other hand, Silverman adds that "a large part of behaving appropriately as a Gypsy involves knowing when to conceal one's Gypsiness." By passing as someone from a less stigmatized group, a Rom can circumvent anti-Romani prejudice. Some Romani Americans may present themselves as Puerto Ricans, Mexicans, Armenians, Greeks, Indians, Native Americans, Arabs, and as other local ethnics in order to obtain jobs, housing, and welfare. For many, notes Silverman, "the process of boundary crossing [is] a performance strategically enacted for survival."

Traditions and Customs Romani patterns of kinship structures, traveling, and economics characterize them as a historic people who have adapted well to modern society. Much scholarship on Roma in the United States treats only the Kalderash and Machwaya. Although other groups differ, Silverman states that the folk belief or folk religion of all ethnic Roma consists mainly of "the taboo system, together with the set of beliefs related to the dead and the supernatural." In general, then, Roma customs are largely intertwined with their religious and spiritual beliefs. Taboos and practices stemming from their belief in the binary system of ritual purity/impurity play a major role in shaping Romani customs. The Romani words *wuzho* (clean, pure) and *marimé* (unclean, contaminated) are used to classify both people and objects.

Among the Kalderash and Machwaya, taboos separate Roma from non-Roma and also separate the contamination of the lower half of the adult Roma's body (especially the genitals and feet) from the purity of its upper half (especially the head and mouth). The waist divides an adult's body; in fact, the Romani word for waist, *maskar*, also means the spatial middle of anything. Because a Romani person who becomes *marimé* can be expelled from the community, to avoid pollution, Roma try to avoid unpurified things that have touched a body's lower half. Accordingly, a Romani person who touches his or her lower body should then wash his or her hands to purify them. Similarly, objects that feet have touched, such as shoes and floors, are impure and, by extension, things that touch the floor when someone drops them are impure as well. Roma mark the bottom end of bedcovers with a button or ribbon in order to avoid accidentally putting the feet-end on their face.

To some Roma, the failure to adhere to such standards of cleanliness by non-Roma makes interaction with non-Roma or Roma who are considered unclean undesirable. Taboos attempt to bar anybody sickly, unlucky, or otherwise impure from joining a meal, and Roma may destroy or discard any cups or utensils used by someone considered *marimé*. According to Silverman, when Roma move into a home, "they often replace the entire kitchen area, especially countertops and sinks, to avoid ritual contamination from previous non-Gypsy occupants."

Taboos apply most fully to adult Roma, who achieve that status when they marry. Childbearing potential fully activates taboos for men and especially for women. At birth, the infant is regarded as entirely contaminated or polluted, because he or she came from the lower center of the body. The mother, because of her intensive contact with the infant, is also considered impure. As in other traditional cultures, mother and child are isolated for a period of time and other female members will assume the household duties of washing and cooking. Between infancy and marriage, taboos apply less strictly to children. For adults, taboos, especially those that separate males and females, relax as they become respected elders.

Cuisine Hancock says in "Romani Foodways: The Indian Roots of Romani Culinary Culture" that for mobile Roma, methods of preparing food have been "contingent on circumstance." Such items as stew, unleavened bread, and fried foods are common, whereas leavened breads and broiled foods are not. Cleanliness is paramount, though, and, "like Hindus and Muslims, Roma, in Europe more than in America, avoid using the left hand during meals, either to eat with or to pass things."

Traditionally, Roma eat two meals a day—one upon rising and the other late in the afternoon. Roma take time to have a meal with other Roma and enjoy *khethanipé*—being together. Roma tend to cook and eat foods of the cultures among which they historically lived; therefore, for many Romani Americans traditional foods are eastern European foods. Those who have adopted Eastern Orthodox Catholicism celebrate holidays closely related to the *slava* feast of southeastern Europe and eat *sarma* (cabbage rolls), *gushvada* (cheese strudel), and a ritually sacrificed animal (often a lamb). Roma consider these and other strong-tasting foods *baxtaló xabé*, or lucky.

For Roma, eating is important. Roma commonly greet an intimate by asking whether or not he or she ate that day, and what. Any weight loss is usually considered unhealthy. If food is lacking, it is associated with bad living, bad luck, poverty, or disease. Conversely, for men especially, weight gain traditionally means good health. The measure of a male's strength, power, or wealth is in his physical stature. Thus, a *Rom baro* is a big man, both physically and politically.

Eating makes Romani social occasions festive and indicates that those who eat together trust one another. It is more than impolite for one Roma to refuse an offer of food from another. Such refusal would suggest that the offerer is *marimé*. Although some Roma will eat in certain restaurants, traditionally Roma cook for themselves. Often more food is served than can be consumed by those present, in order to reserve a portion of the meal for unexpected visitors. While the eastern European roots of many Romani Americans are apparent in their food choices, they have also incorporated aspects of regional American cuisine into their diet. Spicy or strong-flavored ingredients such as black pepper, red pepper, garlic, onion, and vinegar are common to many Romani American recipes, as they are thought to bring good luck.

Traditional Dress Roma have brightly colored traditional costumes that differ according to subgroup. Kalderash women wear dresses with full skirts, and men wear baggy pants and loose-fitting shirts. A scarf often adorns a woman's hair or is used as a cummerbund. Women wear much jewelry, and the men wear boots and large belts. A married Romani woman customarily must cover her hair with a *diklo*, a scarf. However, many Romani women may go bareheaded except when attending traditional communal gatherings.

While Romani Americans sometimes wear traditional, colorful clothing at festivals and celebrations, it is more common for them to wear typical American clothing in public. However, because Romani culture favors open displays of wealth as a signifier of social status, Romani men will often wear business attire—collared shirts, vests, and jackets (though the wearing of ties is not as common)—and Romani women will frequently wear handmade gold jewelry as a sign of their social standing, a practice not uncommon among Americans of all ethnic background.

Holidays and Festivals Roma historically celebrate the holidays (religious or otherwise) of the region in which they settle. The Vlax Roma, one of the largest groups of Roma in the United States, celebrate Christian holidays such as Christmas and Easter with an elaborate feast, often gathering members from the whole community. At Easter a large bowl is passed around with dyed Easter eggs, and each person chooses one. One eastern European ritual that is said to bring *baxt*, or good luck, is called *chognimos*: the visitor brings an egg, and the head of household holds his own egg, and the two slap their hands together to break the eggs. Roma from the Czech Republic refer to Christmas as *Karachonya* and take the holiday as a time to remember the deceased and find reconciliation

among the living. Roma primarily from the Balkans celebrate Ederlezi (also spelled Herdeljezi), the Feast of St. George. This holiday is celebrated by both Muslims and Christians, marking the beginning of spring. "Ederlezi" is also the name of a very famous Romani song named for the holiday.

In addition to religious holidays and weddings, Romani funerals are one of the biggest community celebrations. Groups of Roma travel and gather to mark the passing of one of their own. Romani Americans tend to follow the Vlach tradition of embarking on a three-day period of mourning in which no one is allowed to bathe, shave, or prepare food while they remain in the presence of the deceased. Often, immediately after a Romani American passes away his or her relatives will open a window and light a candle in order to offer the soul a passage to heaven. After the three-day period of mourning an emotional funeral service is held, featuring music, dance, and gift-giving, in which items thought to be needed by the dead in the afterlife, including coins, clothing, good-luck charms, and alcohol, are placed in the grave along with the casket. Romani Americans tend to be buried alongside other members of their family or alongside other Roma if no family members have been buried in the area.

International Romani Day began on April 8, 1971, with the inaugural opening day of the World Romani Congress. The goal of Romani Day is to promote harmony among Roma and to celebrate Roma culture. This is also a day to recognize the hardships and persecution faced by Roma throughout history and today. Since 2000 a nonprofit Romani advocacy group, Voice of Roma, has hosted a May Herdeljezi festival in the San Francisco area aimed at preserving Roma heritage and educating the public about the plight of European Roma. International Roma Day has recently received increased attention from American groups and organizations outside of the Roma community. In 2013 Harvard University celebrated the holiday by hosting a conference on discrimination against Roma in Europe, and Secretary of State Hillary Clinton proclaimed that "From music and art to science and literature, Romani people have contributed in ways large and small to the fabric of countless societies," while decrying that "too often and in too many places, they are forced to live on the margins."

Dances and Songs Music is an essential part of Romani culture and life and has provided Roma with a lasting legacy. Like religious practices, Romani music is heavily influenced by the folk music of the culture where Roma reside. Reflexively, Romani music has influenced many other cultures as well as classical composers such as Franz Liszt and Johannes Brahms. Instruments used in traditional Romani music include the *girnata* (clarinet), the *cimbalom* (hammered dulcimer), the accordion, the violin, and the *darbuka* (hand drum). Roma-style guitar was made famous by the legendary Roma musician Django Reinhardt (1910–1953).

MY BIG FAT AMERICAN GYPSY WEDDING: INSIGHT OR INSULT?

Although Romani Americans are often considered an "invisible" segment of American society, there has been a significant rise in interest in Romani culture in the twenty-first century. Elements of Romani music can be found in numerous genres popular with Americans, including jazz, folk, and punk music. Several books and documentary films on Romani history and culture are now widely available. In what may be the best evidence of their mainstream appeal, Romani Americans became the subject of a reality-television show, the Learning Channel's *My Big Fat American Gypsy Wedding*, which premiered in 2012.

An offshoot of a British show called simply *Big Fat Gypsy Weddings* that premiered in 2010, *My Big Fat American Gypsy Wedding* follows non-Romani dressmaker Sondra Chelli as she prepares outfits to be worn by her Romanichal clients at celebrations including birthdays, baptisms, and weddings. For some, the show offers a revealing glimpse into the lives and traditions of Romani Americans. Many Roma, however, have objected to their portrayal; beyond the fact that show's title uses the pejorative term "Gypsy," the dresses prepared by Chelli are almost universally gaudy and revealing, even those made for adolescent girls. Roma-rights groups have complained that such images play into the stereotype of the exotic, materialistic, and highly sexualized "Gypsy," an image that contrasts sharply with their culture's conservatism, respect for the elderly, and sexual restraint. While *My Big Fat American Gypsy Wedding* has served to counter the notion of Romani Americans as shadowy con artists who reject American society outright, critics argue that it does more harm than good by trading one damaging stereotype for another.

Romani dance is also heavily influenced by the region from which Roma hail, and vice versa. Roma from Bulgaria participate in belly dancing, while the Gitanos in Spain flamenco dance. Sometimes referred to as "the Queen of the Gypsies," Carmen Amaya (1917–1963) was the most famous Gitana flamenco dancer of the twentieth century. She moved to the United States in 1936 to escape the Spanish Civil War. She appeared in a number of Hollywood films and performed at prestigious venues such as Carnegie Hall and the White House, where she was the invited guest of both presidents Franklin Roosevelt and Harry Truman.

Romani music has long been performed throughout the United States. In the 1920s the automobile magnate Henry Ford became fascinated with the Hungarian Romani musical style of *cimbalom*, which features the instrument of the same name. His efforts at reviving old-fashioned dance music—a response to the jazz craze of the era—led him to feature cimbalom music at concerts throughout the United States, and a cimbalom is now housed at the Henry Ford Museum in Dearborn, Michigan. Romani American cimbalom virtuoso Alex Udvary, who has performed with symphonies all over the United States and is considered one of the ten best cimbalom players in the world, has lectured at the Henry Ford Museum about the history of cimbalom music.

According to Carol Silverman, other traditional Romani American musical styles include eastern European modal ballads, usually performed by a solo vocalist of Kalderash descent during family gatherings and community events (the recordings of Sammy "Singing Sam" Stevens are the most famous examples of this style); Muslim Romani Americans from Macedonia perform music in the Turkish-influenced *čoček* style, which typically features traditional instruments such as the clarinet and saxophone alongside more modern instruments such as keyboards and electric guitar and bass and emphasizes improvisation; Banat Roma from Vojvodina, Serbia, are known for their skill with the *tamburica*, a plucked lute with a long, guitar-like neck.

In recent decades, the "gypsy Jazz" of Django Reinhardt and other Roma jazz musicians of the 1930s has been incorporated into American folk, rock, and punk music. American "gypsy punk" and indie-rock bands such as Gogol Bordello, Beirut, Kultur Shock, and DeVotchKa incorporate traditional Romani violins and percussion, along with fast-paced guitar strumming inspired by Reinhardt's frenetic style, into their songs. Since 2005 the New York Gypsy Festival has capitalized on the growing appreciation for gypsy punk and folk music, featuring Romani-style music from bands all over the world. Other music festivals, such as the Midwest Gypsy Swing Fest and DjangoFest, as well as Voice of Roma's "Romani Routes" program, also provide opportunities for Roma and non-Roma alike to celebrate one of the most significant Romani contributions to world culture.

Health Care Issues and Practices Ideas about health and illness among Roma are closely related to a world view (*romania*) that includes notions of good and bad luck, purity and impurity, inclusion and exclusion. Anne Sutherland, in a 1992 essay titled "Health and Illness Among the Rom of California," observes that "these basic concepts affect everyday life in many ways including cultural rules about washing, food, clothes, the house, fasting, conducting rituals such as baptism and the slava, and diagnosing illness and prescribing home remedies." In Romani custom, ritual purification is the road to health. Much attention goes to avoiding diseases and curing them.

The most powerful Romani cure is a substance called *coxai*, or ghost vomit. According to Romani legends, *Mamorio* or "little grandmother," is a dirty, sickness-bringing ghost who eats people, then vomits on garbage piles or in wooded areas. Roma find and gather *coxai* (what scientists call slime mold), on damp forest floors and bake it with flour into rocks. Roma also use *asafoetida*, a pungent spice native to India that is also referred to as "devil's dung," which has a long association with healing and spiritualism in India; according to Sutherland, it has also been used in Western medicine as an antispasmodic, expectorant, and laxative.

An early portrait of a Romani American family that had emigrated from Serbia. FREDERICK C. HOWE / NATIONAL GEOGRAPHIC SOCIETY / CORBIS

Sutherland also recounts several Roma cures for common ailments. A salve of pork fat may be used to relieve itching. The juice of chopped onions sprinkled with sugar is used to treat a cold or the flu; brown sugar heated in a pan is also good for a child's cold; boiling the combined juice of oranges, lemons, water, and sugar, or mashing a clove of garlic in whiskey and drinking it, will also relieve a cold. For a mild headache, one might wrap slices of cold cooked potato or tea leaves around the head with a scarf; or for a migraine, put vinegar, garlic, and the juice of an unblemished new potato onto the scarf. A treatment for stomach trouble is to drink a tea of the common nettle or of spearmint. For arthritis pain, wear copper necklaces or bracelets. For anxiety, sew a piece of fern into your clothes. Sutherland notes that elder Roma tend to "fear, understandably, that their grandchildren, who are turning more and more to American medicine, will lose the knowledge they have of herbs and plants, illnesses, and cures."

When a member of the community falls sick, though, some Romani families turn to doctors, either in private practices or at clinics. As Sutherland notes in her essay in *Gypsies, Tinkers and Other Travellers*, "The Rom will often prefer to pay for private medical care with a collection rather than be cared for by a welfare doctor if they feel this care may be better." In general, Romani cuisine seems to facilitate obesity, and thus heart trouble.

FAMILY AND COMMUNITY LIFE

Traditionally Roma maintain large extended families. Clans of people numbering in the scores, hundreds, or even thousands gather for weddings, funerals, other feasts, or when an elder falls sick. Although Romani communities do not have kings as such, traditionally Kalderash, Machwaya, and Lovara will represent a man as king to outsiders when it needs one to serve as a figurehead or representative. Often, too, a man and his family will tell hospital staffers that he is "King of the Gypsies" so that he will receive better treatment— the title can help provide an excuse for the hospital to allow the large family to make prolonged visits.

Vlax Romani families often cluster to travel and make money, forming *kumpanias*—multifamily businesses. During recent decades in the United States, on the other hand, Romani have been acculturating more closely to the American model by forming nuclear families. After the birth of their first child, some Romani couples may move from the husband's parents' home

A Roma child plays accordian with her father on the New York City Subway. DAVID GROSSMAN / ALAMY

may provide the main income for their families. Men of their families will usually aid the fortune-telling business by helping in some support capacities, as long as they are not part of the "women's work" of talking to customers.

Romani Americans tend to adhere to traditional gender roles, with men working outside the home and occupying positions of authority in the community while women are in charge of most household decisions and finances. In the early and mid-1900s several Romani subgroups in the United States, particularly the Machvaya of New York and California, required Romani women to travel in groups or with male escorts. Today there is a greater sense of autonomy among Vlax Romani women, as many have their own cars and even pursue careers outside of the home. However, some are disenfranchised within the patriarchal Romani culture and may be victims of domestic violence. Those who speak out against such marginalization may be shamed for abandoning the Roma way of life. Nevertheless, in the twenty-first century a number of Romani American women, including Alexandra Oprea, Ethel Brooks, and Petra Gelbart, who come from various subgroups, have given speeches and organized events focused on Romani women.

Education Because of the existence of Romani cultural practices of purity as it pertains to Gadjo (non-Roma) pollution, the history of enslavement and harassment of Romani people by those in power, and the representation of "gypsies" in the rest of society, the relationship between Roma and established educational systems in North America and Europe have been complicated. Romani children are frequently homeschooled for these reasons. In addition to Roma being resistant to public education, many countries have denied Roma access to schooling.

The Decade of Roma Inclusion (2005–2015) is a political commitment put together by European countries (Albania, Bosnia, Bulgaria, Croatia, the Czech Republic, Hungary, Macedonia, Montenegro, Romania, Serbia, Slovakia, and Spain), as "The Decade" website asserts, in order to improve "priority areas of education, employment, health, and housing, and commits governments to take into account the other core issues of poverty, discrimination, and gender mainstreaming." As a result, the Roma Education Fund (REF) was established to desegregate the Roma from the rest of European society and improve the outcome of education in central and southeastern Europe.

There have been no initiatives on that scale within the United States. Ian F. Hancock, Romani scholar and activist and former ambassador to the United Nations, was born in London and experienced a great deal of persecution for his Romani heritage. Hancock began the Romani Studies Department at the University of Texas–Austin, which holds the library of the International Romani Union and the Romani Archives and Documentation Center (RADOC) and regularly offers classes in Romani studies. A report prepared by

into their own. This change has given more independence to newly wedded women as daughters-in-law.

Gender Roles Romani families and communities divide along gender lines. Vlax Romani men wield public authority over members of their community through the *kris*—the Romani form of court. In its most extreme punishment, a kris expels and bars a person from the community. For most official, public duties with non-Roma, too, the men take control. Publicly, traditional Romani men treat women as subordinates.

The role of Romani women, or *Romnya* (plural feminine), in this tradition is not limited to childbearing. She can influence and communicate with the supernatural world; she can pollute a Romani man so that a kris will expel him from the community; and in some cases she makes and manages most of a family's money. Romani women are also thought to have healing powers and are often charged with tending to the sick. Successful fortune-tellers, all of whom are female,

Hancock for RADOC in 2007, "The Schooling of Romani Americans: An Overview," reports that in the 1960s, several programs aimed at encouraging Romani Americans to attend public school began to appear in the United States, particularly on the West Coast. In 1972 a parochial school for Romani Americans was founded in Richmond, California, and other specialized schools were soon founded in Portland, Oregon (1978), and Seattle, Washington (1981), but these programs were short-lived due to a lack of funding and low attendance rates. Hancock explains that there is "no homogeneous Romani population but a number of sharply disparate groups differing from each other in numbers, in degree of acculturation, and in aspects of their language and priorities. All of these factors have a bearing on Romani education." He goes on to suggest that "There is a thirst for education among young Romanies, but satisfying it means making it available in an accessible and attractive way."

EMPLOYMENT AND ECONOMIC CONDITIONS

Mobility and adaptation characterize Romani trades. From their beginnings, their traditional occupations have catered to other groups and at the same time maintained Roma's separation. In their essay in *Urban Gypsies*, Matt and Sheila Salo explain that "the main features of all occupations were that they were independent pursuits, required little overhead, had a ubiquitous clientele, and could be pursued while traveling" in urban and rural areas. Moreover, Roma have adapted to different locales and periods. Silverman discusses a change in occupations in twentieth-century America that parallels the urbanization of the Vlax Roma. After their arrival in the 1880s, Roma followed nomadic European trades such as coppersmithing, refining, and dealing in horses for the men, and fortune-telling for the women. There have also been a great number of Romani animal trainers. Roma would camp in the country and interact mostly with the rural population, venturing into the cities only to sell their services and purchase necessities. As the automobile supplanted horse travel, the Rom became used-car dealers and repairmen, occupations that they still pursue. When metalworking skills became less important, Roma learned new trades, including the selling of items such as watches and jewelry.

As Sutherland points out in *Gypsies, Tinkers and Other Travellers*, "In the *kumpania* men and women cooperate with each other in exploiting the economic resources of their area." Although jobs may be exploited by an individual, the Rom prefer to work in groups called *wortacha*, or partners. These groups are always made up of members of the same sex (although women often take along children of either sex). Wortacha may also include young unmarried Roma who learn the skills of the adults. Adults work as equals, dividing expenses and profits equally. As a token of respect for an elder, an extra amount may be given, but unmarried trainees receive only what others will give them.

Roma do not earn wages from another Roma. As a rule, Roma profit from non-Roma only. In the United States and other countries (including England and Wales), Romani Americans divide geographic territories to minimize competition among Romani businesses.

Roma became dealers of vehicles in the middle of the twentieth century. One Roma subgroup in particular, the Romnichals, took an early American role as horse traders, achieving particular success in Boston. According to Matt and Sheila Salo, "During World War I, Romani Americans brought teams of their horses to the Great Plains to help harvest crops. For a while at least, the label 'horse trader' or 'horse dealer' seemed almost synonymous with 'Gypsy.' The colorful wagons used by Romnichals to advertise their presence to any community they entered further reinforced this identification by the professionally painted side panels depicting idealized horses and the horse trading life." The pride of Romnichals in their ability to trade horses is reflected in the carved figures of horses on the tombstones of horse dealers. Many Roma who arrived in the United States after the horse trade's heyday became involved in selling cars. Other mobile service contributions of Roma have included driveway blacktopping, house painting, and tinsmithing. Roma tinkers, who were mostly Romanian-speaking Roma, were essential to various industries, such as confectioneries, because they re-tinned large mixing bowls and other machinery on-site. They also worked in bakeries, laundries, and anywhere steam jackets operated.

Roma do not earn wages from another Roma. As a rule, Roma profit from non-Roma only. In the United States and other countries (including England and Wales), Romani Americans divide geographic territories to minimize competition among Romani businesses.

Since the 1930s the Vlax group of Romani Americans has virtually controlled the business of fortune-telling. A fortune-teller, or reader, will try to establish a steady relationship with the customer, whether in person, by telephone, or by mail. Readers will also try to use the customer's language, usually English or Spanish. Moreover, readers often adopt and advertise names for themselves that help them claim the ethnicity of their clientele; or they choose an ethnicity renowned for mystical perception, such as Asian, African, or Native American. Their advertisements and shop windows have their undeniable place on American boardwalks, roads, and streets. Romani mysticism has had a notable impact on American culture, represented in fortune-teller costumes and props such as the crystal ball and tarot deck as well as imitations such as commercially produced Ouija boards. New York City supports a great many fortune-tellers, while Los Angeles (where more Roma sell real estate and cars) has relatively few because of strict laws governing fortune-telling. Daughters of successful fortune-tellers often traditionally become fortune-tellers. Their family business is part of their household.

Since the late twentieth century, Romani Americans have become increasingly comfortable in accepting employment among non-Roma, and they no longer rely exclusively on traditional Roma occupations. Romani American men and women now find employment in a wide range of industries, including real estate, teaching, law, construction, health care, and management.

POLITICS AND GOVERNMENT

Special attention from U.S. government authorities has seldom benefited Roma Americans. Some states and districts maintain policies and statutes that prohibit fortune-tellers, require fortune-tellers to pay hundreds of dollars for annual licenses, or otherwise control activities in which Roma engage. Some rules apply specifically to Roma by name, despite the unconstitutionality of such measures, and police departments in areas with large Roma populations often have specialists in "Gypsy crime." For example, Romani American activist Morgan Ahern, founder of the anti-racism organization Lolo Diklo, was one of many children taken from their parents when New York government authorities raided her home in 1955 and found her parents unfit due to their lifestyle and refusal to send her to public school. One excuse for this discrimination is the conflation of nomadic Roma with vagrants. After a long history of avoidance of local authorities, Roma in the United States and elsewhere are becoming more politically active in defense of their civil and human rights; the International Romani Union was recognized by the United Nations in 1978, and in 1997 President Bill Clinton appointed Ian Hancock, a Romani American representative to the United Nations, to the U.S. Holocaust Memorial Council. In the twenty-first century, representatives of the U.S. government, including Ambassador Ian Kelly and Secretaries of State Hillary Clinton and John Kerry, have made pleas to the international community to provide greater opportunity for Roma to integrate into society. Romani Americans have also begun to challenge laws that they feel unfairly target Romani businesses and practices; in 2009, for instance, Maryland-based Romani American Nick Nefedro enlisted the help of the American Civil Liberties Union to challenge a ban on fortune-telling, and the law was overturned by the Maryland Supreme Court in 2010.

NOTABLE INDIVIDUALS

Academia Ian Hancock (1942–) is a scholar of Roma studies and former Romani representative to the UN. Since 1972 he has been a professor at the University of Texas at Austin.

Literature Oksana Marafioti (1967–) is a Romani American writer who published the memoir *American Gypsy* in 2012.

Music Notable Romani American musicians include Eugene Hütz (1972–), lead singer of the Romani American punk rock band Gogol Bordello; Yuri Yunakov, saxophone master from Bulgaria and NEA (National Endowment for the Arts) National Heritage Fellowship winner; and Ismail Lumanovski (1984–), clarinet virtuoso and leader of the New York Gypsy All-Stars.

Scholar and musician Petra Gelbart is a Czech-born Roma musicologist who was a founding member of the band Via Romen and is head of the Initiative for Romani Music at New York University.

Stage and Screen Freddie Prinze (born Freddie Preutzel; 1954–1977), a comedian and actor who starred on the TV show *Chico and the Man* in the 1970s, was Hungarian Roma. His son, Freddie Prinze Jr. (1976–), is an actor who has appeared in movies such as *I Know What You Did Last Summer* (1997) and *Scooby-Doo* (2002).

ORGANIZATIONS AND ASSOCIATIONS

Gypsy Lore Society

This organization consists of scholars, educators, and others interested in the study of the Roma and analogous itinerant or nomadic groups. It works to disseminate information aimed at increasing understanding of Romani culture in its diverse forms. Publishes *Romani Studies*.

Elena Marushiakova, President
5607 Greenleaf Road
Cheverly, Maryland 20785
Phone: (301) 341-1261
Email: studiiromani@geobiz.net;
gls.gypsyloresociety@gmail.com
URL: www.gypsyloresociety.org

Voice of Roma

A nonprofit Roma advocacy group, whose website is considered the premiere source of information on North American Roma on the Internet.

P.O. Box 514
Sebastopol, California 95473
Phone: (707) 823-5858
Email: voiceofroma@gmail.com
URL: www.voiceofroma.com

MUSEUMS AND RESEARCH CENTERS

The Romani Archives and Documentation Center (RADOC)

RADOC is the largest library archives of Roma worldwide.

Calhoun Hall
The University of Texas B5100
Austin, Texas 78712
Phone: (512)-232-7684
Fax: (512)-295-7733
Email: radoc@radoc.net
URL: www.radoc.net

Victor Weybright Archives of Gypsy Studies

These are the archives of the Maryland-based Gypsy Lore Society.

Carmen Hendershott, Archivist
Phone: (212) 229-5308
Fax: (301) 341-1261
Email: ssalo@Capaccess.org
URL: www.gypsyloresociety.org/additional-resources/weybright-archives

SOURCES FOR ADDITIONAL STUDY

Gropper, Rena C., and Carol Miller. "Exploring New Worlds in American Romani Studies: Social and Cultural Attitudes among the American Macvaia." *Romani Studies* 11, no. 2 (2001): 81–110.

Hancock, Ian. "American Roma: The Hidden Gypsy World." *Aperture* 144 (1996): 14–26.

———, and Dileep Karanth. *Danger! Educated Gypsy: Selected Essays*. Hatfield, UK: University of Hertfordshire Press, 2010.

Marafioti, Oksana. *American Gypsy*. New York: Farrar, Straus and Giroux, 2012.

Mayall, David. *Gypsy Identities 1500–2000: From Egypcyans and Moon-Men to the Ethnic Romany*. New York: Routledge, 2004.

Miller, Carol. "American Rom and the Ideology of Defilement." In *Gypsies, Tinkers and Other Travellers*, edited by Farnham Rehfisch, 41–54. New York: Harcourt Brace Jovanovich, 1975.

Rishi, W. R. *Roma: The Panjabi Emigrants in Europe, Central and Middle Asia, the USSR, and the Americas*. Chandigarh, India: Roma Publishers, 1976 and 1996.

Silverman, Carol. *Romani Routes: Cultural Politics and Balkan Music in Diaspora*. New York: Oxford University Press, 2011.

Sutherland, Anne. "The American Rom: A Case of Economic Adaptation." In *Gypsies, Tinkers and Other Travellers*, edited by Farnham Rehfisch, 1–40. New York: Harcourt Brace Jovanovich, 1975.

———. *Gypsies: The Hidden Americans*. London: Tavistock Publications, 1975.

Sway, Marlene. *Familiar Strangers: Gypsy Life in America*. Chicago: University of Illinois Press, 1988.

ROMANIAN AMERICANS

Vladimir F. Wertsman

OVERVIEW

Romanian Americans are immigrants or descendants of people from Romania, an Eastern European country on the Black Sea. Romania is bordered by Ukraine to the north; Moldova to the northeast; Bulgaria to the south; and Hungary, Serbia, and Montenegro to the west. The Carpathian Mountains dominate the Romanian landscape, and the Danube River flows through southern Romania before entering the Black Sea. Slightly smaller than the state of Oregon, Romania measures 91,699 square miles (237,500 square kilometers).

In 2011, according to the National Statistics Institute of Romania, Romania had a population of slightly over 19 million. This is a decrease of more than 2 million since 2002. The decline is a result of hundreds of thousands of Romanians leaving the country to find jobs and settling in various European countries, including Spain, Italy, France, Germany, and Austria, as well as in Israel and the United States. The overwhelming majority of Romanian citizens—88.8 percent—are members of the Romanian Orthodox Church. Approximately 10 percent are Catholics of the Byzantine rite, and there are also small groups of Protestants, Muslims, and Jews. Like many other former members of the Soviet bloc, the Romanian economy is in the midst of transition from communism to capitalism, which has led to uneven growth and has left the country with a lower-middle-income economy. However, the country is rich in natural resources and has a large agricultural sector.

Romanians began to arrive in the United States in significant numbers in the late nineteenth and early twentieth centuries, settling mainly in urban areas and working in factories. During World War II, the threat of German occupation of Romania led to a wave of immigration from Romania to the United States. Whereas prior Romanian immigrants had largely been unskilled laborers, many of these newer immigrants were professionals, a trend that continued after the war. Since the fall of Soviet Communism in 1989 and the elimination of Communist travel restrictions, the tide of Romanian immigration to the United States has increased.

According to the U.S. Census Bureau's American Community Survey estimates for 2009–2011, the population of Romanian Americans was 471,472. States with a significant number of Romanian Americans include California, New York, Florida, Michigan, Illinois, Ohio, and New Jersey.

HISTORY OF THE PEOPLE

Early History The name "Romania," officially in use since 1861, is a derivative of the Latin word *romanus*, meaning "citizen of Rome." The name was given to the country's territory by Roman colonists after Emperor Trajan (circa 53–117 CE) and his legions crossed the Danube River and conquered Dacia, an ancient province located in present-day Transylvania and the Carpathian Mountain region, in 106 CE. Although Roman occupation of Dacia ended in 271 CE, the relationship between the Romans and Dacians flourished. Mixed marriages and the adoption of Latin culture and language gradually molded the Romans and Dacians into a distinct ethnic entity. These ancestors of the modern Romanian people managed to preserve their Latin heritage despite subsequent Gothic, Slavic, Greek, Hungarian, and Turkish conquests, and the Romanian language has survived as a member of the Romance languages group.

Romania has been subjected to numerous occupations by foreign powers since the Middle Ages. In the thirteenth century, the Romanian principalities Moldavia and Wallachia became vassal states of the Ottoman Empire. During the 1700s, Bukovina, Transylvania, and Banat were incorporated into the Austro-Hungarian Empire. Czarist Russia occupied Bessarabia in 1812. In 1859 Moldavia and Wallachia became unified through the auspices of the Paris Peace Conference, and Romania became a national state. At the Congress of Berlin in 1878, Romania obtained full independence from the Ottoman Empire but lost Bessarabia to Russia. In 1881 Romania was proclaimed a kingdom and Carol I (1839–1914) was installed as its first monarch.

Modern Era Following the death of Carol I, his nephew Ferdinand (1865–1927) became king and led the country into World War I against the Central Powers. After the war and the signing of the Treaty of Versailles, Romania regained Transylvania, Banat, Bukovina, and other territories from the fallen Austro-Hungarian Empire. In 1940 controversy over Ferdinand's successor, Carol II (1893–1953), prompted

Romanian military leader Ion Antonescu (1882–1946) to stage a coup d'état, forcing the monarch to renounce his throne in favor of his son, Michael I (1921–). Under Antonescu's influence, Romania became an ally of Nazi Germany during World War II and fought against the Soviet Union. In the last year of the war, Romania switched its alliance to the Soviets, and after the war ended, Antonescu was executed. In national elections held in 1947, members of the Communist party assumed many high-level positions in the new government, and King Michael I was forced to abdicate his throne. Gheorghe Gheorghiu-Dej (1901–1965) of the Romanian Communist party served as premier (1952–1955) and later as chief of state (1961–1965). Two years after Gheorghiu-Dej's death, Nicholae Ceauşescu (1918–1989), a high-ranking Communist official, assumed the presidency of Romania.

On December 22, 1989, the Communist regime was overthrown and Ceauşescu was executed on Christmas Day. In the postcommunist years, various changes occurred, including the institution of a free press, free elections, and a multiparty electorate, bringing to power a democratic government. The country's first president after the fall of Communism was Ion Iliescu (1930–), who served two terms (1990–1995, 2001–2004). Emil Constantinescu (1939–) served as president from 1996 to 2000. Traian Băsescu (1951–) was elected in 2004 and again in 2009, though he was suspended twice for short periods in 2007 and 2012. Since the end of the Communist era, the pace of transforming Romania's economy into a market economy has accelerated, and the country's relations with the United States, Canada, and other Western countries have improved. Today Romania is a member of NATO, the European Union, the World Bank, the World Trade Organization, the Council of Europe, and other important international bodies.

SETTLEMENT IN THE UNITED STATES

Romanians have a recorded presence of almost 250 years on American soil. In the late eighteenth century, a Transylvanian priest named Samuel Damian immigrated to America for scientific reasons. He conducted various experiments with electricity and even caught the attention of Benjamin Franklin (they met and had a conversation in Latin). After living in South Carolina for a few years, Damian left for Jamaica and disappeared from historical record. In 1849 a group of Romanians came to California during the Gold Rush; unsuccessful, they migrated to Mexico. Romanians continued to immigrate to the United States during the mid-nineteenth century, and some distinguished themselves in the Union Army during the Civil War. George Pomutz (1818–1882) joined the Fifteenth Volunteer Regiment of Iowa and fought at such battlefields as Shiloh, Corinth, and Vicksburg. He was later promoted to the rank of brigadier general. Nicholas Dunca (1825–1862), a captain serving in the Ninth Volunteer Regiment of New York, died in the battle of Cross Keyes, Virginia. Another Romanian-born soldier, Eugen Teodoresco, died in the Spanish-American War in 1898.

During the first major wave of Romanian immigration to the United States, between 1895 and 1920, 145,000 Romanians entered the country. They came from various regions, including Wallachia and Moldavia. The majority—particularly those from Transylvania and Banat—were unskilled laborers who left their native regions because of economic depression and forced assimilation, a policy practiced by Hungarian rulers. They were attracted to the economic stability of the United States, which promised better wages and improved working conditions. Many did not plan to establish permanent residency, intending instead to save enough money to return to Romania and purchase land. Consequently, tens of thousands of Romanian immigrants who achieved this goal left the United States within a few years. By 1920 the Romanian American population was approximately 85,000.

Between 1921 and 1939, the number of Romanians entering the United States declined for several reasons. Following World War I, Transylvania, Bukovina, Bessarabia, and other regions under foreign rule officially became part of Romania, thus arresting emigration for a time. In addition, the U.S. Immigration Act of 1924 established a quota system that allowed only 603 new immigrants from Romania per year. The Great Depression added to the decline of new Romanian immigrants to the United States, and by the beginning of World War II, Romanian immigration had reached new lows. Romanians who entered the United States during this period included students, professionals, and others who later made notable contributions to American society.

During World War II, a new surge of immigrants to the United States was generated by the threat of Nazi occupation of Romania. When Communists assumed control of the country in 1947, they imposed many political, economic, and social restrictions on the Romanian people. Through the auspices of the Displaced Persons Act of 1947 and other legislation passed to help absorb the flood of refugees and other immigrants from postwar Europe, the United States admitted refugees who had left Romania due to persecutions, arrests, or fear of being mistreated, and exiles who were already abroad and had chosen not to return to their homeland. Because of the abrupt and dramatic nature of their departure, these refugees and exiles (estimated at about 30,000) received special moral and financial support from various Romanian organizations—religious and secular—in the United States. These immigrants infused an important contingent of professionals, including doctors, lawyers, writers, and engineers, into the Romanian American community and reinvigorated political activity in the community. They established new organizations and churches, and fought against Communist rule in their homeland.

After the Revolution of December 1989, which brought an end to Communist rule in Romania, thousands of new immigrants of all ages came to the United States. The elimination of Communist travel restrictions, the desire of thousands of people to be reunited with their American relatives and friends, and the precarious economic conditions in the new Romania were powerful incentives to immigrate to the United States. Among the newcomers were professionals, former political prisoners, and others who were disenchanted with the new leadership in Romania. In addition many Romanian tourists decided to remain in the United States. Many of these immigrants spoke English and adjusted relatively well, even if they took lower-paying jobs than those for which they were qualified. Others had difficulty finding employment and returned to Romania. Still others left the United States to try their luck in Canada or South America. Those who chose to return to Europe settled in Germany, France, or Italy.

According to the 1990 U.S. Census, there were approximately 365,544 people of Romanian ancestry living in the United States. Twenty years later, according to the American Community Survey (ACS) estimates for 2009–2011, the population of Romanian Americans had increased to 471,472. The ACS estimated that the largest populations of Romanian Americans were residing in California (68,838), New York (56,890), Illinois (33,667), Florida (33,185), Ohio (33,809), Michigan (33,808), and New Jersey (20,963). Other organizations put the number even higher. The Romanian American Network, based in Chicago, claims there are over 1.2 million Romanian Americans, with the largest populations in California (293,633), New York (240,784), Florida (127,123), Michigan (119,624), Illinois (114,529), Ohio (106,017), Pennsylvania (84,958), Georgia (55,228), Texas (47,689), and North Carolina (39,566).

Because early Romanian immigrants were either peasants or laborers, they settled in major industrial centers of the east and midwest and took unskilled jobs in factories. Living near the factories where they worked, first-generation Romanian Americans established communities that often consisted of extended families or those who had migrated from the same region in Romania. Second- and third-generation Romanian Americans, having achieved financial security and social status, gradually moved out of the old neighborhoods, settling in suburban areas or larger cities, or relocating to another state. Consequently, few Romanian American communities are left that preserve the social fabric of the first-generation neighborhoods. However, in larger cities such as Chicago, Romanians have established small enclaves with Romanian restaurants, churches, stores, newspapers, and travel agencies.

Although most Romanian Americans emigrated from Romania, a significant number arrived from countries adjacent to or bordering Romania. The Republic of Moldova, known as Bessarabia before World War II, is essentially a second Romanian country. Sandwiched between Romania and the Ukraine, it occupies an area of 13,010 square miles (33,700 square kilometers). Its

capital is Chişinău (pronounced Keesheenau) and the president is Petru Lucinschi. The population of 4.5 million consists of 65 percent Romanians, 14 percent Ukrainians, 13 percent Russians, 4 percent Gagauz (Turks of Christian faith), and 2 percent Bulgarians. There are also smaller groups of Poles, Belarusians, Germans, and Gypsies. While 98 percent of Moldavians are Eastern Orthodox believers, some are Protestant and Jewish. The official language of Moldova is Romanian (with a Moldavian dialect), and the second language is Russian. The country's flag is the same as Romania's: red, yellow, and blue vertical stripes.

During the Middle Ages, Bessarabia was an integral part of the Romanian principality of Moldavia, but it later became a tributary to the Ottoman Empire. In 1812, following the Russian–Turkish War (1806–1812), Bessarabia was annexed by Tsarist Russia until the 1917 October Revolution. In 1918 Romanians voted to reunite Bessarabia with Romania, but in 1940 the Soviet Union, in a pact with Nazi Germany, gained control of the land. During 1941 to 1944, Romania recaptured the territory but lost it again at the conclusion of World War II, when the Soviet Union incorporated Bessarabia under the name of the Moldovan Soviet Socialist Republic. After the fall of Communism, the country became independent and in 1991 took the name of the Republic of Moldova. It underwent various changes, instituting free elections, a multiparty system of government, and economic reforms, before reaching an understanding in 1996 with separatist movements in two regions, Dnestr and Gagauzia. Although there was a movement for reunification with Romania, the majority of the population opted for independence.

Immigrants from Moldova who came to the United States before World War II, and those who arrived later (about ten thousand immigrated to the United States in the 1990s and early 2000s), consider themselves members of the Romanian American community, using the same language, worshiping in the same Eastern Orthodox churches, and preserving the same heritage. They are also fully integrated in Romanian American organizations and support the reunification of their land of origin with Romania.

Macedo-Romanians, also called Aromanians or Vlachs, live mostly in Albania, although they also live in Greece and Macedonia. In addition they have lived in Yugoslavia and Bulgaria for over two thousand years. Their history goes back to the first and second centuries CE, when the Roman Empire included the territories of today's Romania and neighboring Balkan countries. It is estimated that there are about 600,000 to 700,000 Macedo-Romanians in the Balkans and Romania. Although they know the Romanian language, they also use their own dialect consisting of many archaisms, characteristic regional expressions, and foreign influences. Macedo-Romanians consider themselves Romanian and belong to the same Eastern Orthodox Church. In the United States, there are about five thousand Macedo-Romanians, settled mostly in

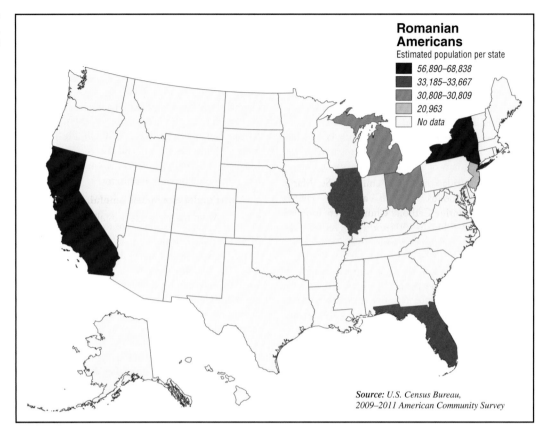

Romanian Americans
Estimated population per state

- 56,890–68,838
- 33,185–33,667
- 30,808–30,809
- 20,963
- No data

*Source: U.S. Census Bureau,
2009–2011 American Community Survey*

the states of Connecticut, New York, Rhode Island, New Jersey, and Missouri. The first wave of immigration took place at the beginning of the twentieth century, while a second wave was recorded after World War II. Family reunifications continue to this day.

Macedo-Romanians are characterized by their hard work, the high esteem in which they keep their families, and the value they place on education. They adjusted well to American life and preserved their cultural heritage via their own organizations. Although the younger generation of Macedo-Romanians are proud of their heritage, they display strong trends of assimilation and tend to use English more than the language of their ancestors.

LANGUAGE

The Romanian language is a Romance language derived from Latin that has survived despite foreign influences (Slavic, Turkish, Greek, and others). In fact, it has many Latin words that are not found in other Romance languages and is more grammatically complex than other Romance languages. Although Romanian uses the Latin alphabet, the letters *k*, *q*, *w*, and *y* appear only in foreign words. In addition Romanian has specific diacritical marks (ă, â, í, ţ, ş). Romanians consider their language sweet and harmonious and are proud of its Latin origin.

For first-generation Romanian immigrants—regardless of the period when they arrived—Romanian was their primary language. In a very short time,

however, such American words as *supermarket*, *basement*, *streetcar*, *laundry*, *high school*, and *subway* became infused in daily speech. As Romanian has become Americanized, subsequent generations have spoken Romanian less often, eventually switching to English as their principal language. Because Romanian is a Latin language, many Romanian American immigrants have an easier time learning English than other immigrants. According to the American Community Survey estimates for 2009–2011, among Romanian Americans ages five and over, 60 percent spoke only English at home. Of those who spoke another language at home, most (86 percent) reported being fluent in English.

Romanian church services and Sunday school are still conducted in Romanian. In several cities, radio programs are broadcast in Romanian, and there are numerous Romanian-language newspapers and periodicals in circulation. The language is also used during official meetings of Romanian organizations and during special cultural programs, as well as in the daily life of some Romanian American families.

Greetings and Popular Expressions Common Romanian greetings and other expressions include *bună seara* (bóona seàra)—good evening; *bună ziua* (bóona zéeoóa)—good day; *salut* (salóot)—greetings, hello; *la revedere* (la rayvaydáyray)—good-bye; *noroc bun* (norók bóon)—good luck; *mulţumesc* (mooltsóomesk)—thank you; *felicitări* (feleecheetáry)—congratulations;

La multzi ani (la múltzi ánee)—Happy New Year; and *Sărbători fericite* (sarbatóry fayreechéetay)—Happy holidays (this greeting is used at Christmas time, for there is no expression like Merry Christmas in Romanian). A greeting used at Easter is *Hristos a inviat* (khristós a ynveeát)—Christ has risen; the reply is *Adevărat a inviat* (adevarát a ynveeát)—In truth He has risen. When raising a toast, Romanians often say, *Sănătate* (sanatátay)—To your health.

RELIGION

The first Romanian American churches, St. Mary's Romanian Orthodox Church and St. Helena Romanian Byzantine Catholic Church, were founded in in Cleveland, Ohio, in 1904 and 1905, respectively. These churches served as community centers where immigrants spent a good part of their social life. In the twenty-first century, the number of Romanian churches proliferated to include 107 churches in the Romanian Orthodox Episcopate of America, 63 in the Romanian Orthodox Archdiocese of America and Canada, 14 in the Romanian Catholic Diocese of Canton, 60 in the Convention of Romanian Pentecostal Churches in USA & Canada, 58 in the Association of Romanian Baptist Churches in the USA & Canada, and 139 in the Alliance of the Romanian Evangelical Churches in USA & Canada.

The vast majority of Romanian American churchgoers (about 60,000) are Eastern Orthodox. Of the 60 Romanian Orthodox parishes in North America, 45 are subordinated to the Romanian Orthodox Episcopate of America, and 15—most of which are located in Canada—are under the Romanian Orthodox Missionary Episcopate of America. The Romanian Church United with Rome, Greek-Catholic, has 15 parishes, serving approximately 4,000 Romanian members.

The Romanian Orthodox Church and the Romanian Catholic Church, are essentially sister churches with a common history, liturgy, customs, and traditions. Both follow the teachings of the apostles but differ in their interpretation of the Pope's infallibility. Members of the Romanian Catholic Church believe in the infallibility of the Pope when he speaks ex cathedra on faith and morality, while Romanian Orthodox followers contend that no person or council in the church is infallible. In 1697 those who embraced the dogma of papal infallibility switched allegiance from the Eastern Orthodox church to the Vatican but preserved all other features and disciplines of the Eastern church. Both churches adhere to the Nicene Creed, and the Liturgy is based on the text of Saint John Chrysostom (circa 347–407 CE), modified by Saint Basil the Great (circa 329–379 CE). There are seven Sacraments: Eucharist, baptism, confirmation, penance, matrimony, holy orders, and anointing of the sick. In the Romanian Orthodox Church, the anointing of the sick is administered by three priests and may be given to the healthy to prevent illness.

ROMANIAN PROVERBS

Lauda de sine nu miroase a bine.

To praise one's self is in vain, it never brings any gain.

Prietenul la nevoie se cunosta.

A friend in need is a friend indeed.

Cainele care latra nu musca.

A barking dog never bites.

Vorba multa este saracia omului.

When there is excessive talk, the deeds are poor.

Modestia e podoaba cea mai de pret.

Modesty is the most precious jewel of a man's soul.

A omului lenea este cel mai mare vrajmas al norocului.

Laziness is the biggest enemy of good luck.

O carte buna poate lua locul unui prieten, dar un prieten nu poate inlocui o carte buna.

A good book can take place of a friend, but a friend cannot replace a good book.

Fie casa mica sau mare, un copil e o binecuvantare.

Whether homes are big or small, a child is a blessing to all.

Un sfat este mai ieftin decat un exemplu bun.

The cheapest article is advice, the most valuable is a good example.

Nu lasa un prieten bun si vechi numai pentru a place unui nou.

Do not leave an old good friend of yours just to please a new one.

Casatoria e un fel de vis, cateodata e infern, alta data paradis.

One thing for sure, each couple can tell, one's home is both paradise and hell.

Lenevia este vrajmasa cea mai mare a norocului.

Idleness is the biggest enemy of good luck.

Cunostinta e putere mare, te sprijina spre avansare.

Knowledge is like a tower in which you test and build your power.

Modestia e podoaba cea mai de pret a sufletului uman.

Modesty is the dearest jewel of a man's soul.

Poti gusta si bea vin, dar nu te lasa invins de el.

Enjoy drinking the wine, but do not become drunk by it.

Services in both churches are conducted in Romanian and are accentuated by song and chants. The cathedrals are richly decorated with icons and images of the saints, although carved images are forbidden. The altar is located in the center of the sanctuary, and a screen or partition called an iconostasis separates the sanctuary from the rest of the church. Only priests and deacons can enter the sanctuary; other parishioners are not permitted to cross beyond the iconostasis. Romanian Orthodox and Romanian Catholic priests usually wear black cassocks, but gray and brown are also permitted. During the Liturgy, vestments are colorful and ornate. The priest's headdress is a cylindrical black hat, whereas bishops wear a mitre, a crown made of stiff material adorned on top with a cross and various small pictures or icons. At the top of the pastoral scepter are two intertwined serpents surmounted by a cross or an image of a saint. Former liturgical colors (black, red, white) are not observed in modern times. Orthodox priests are permitted to marry before ordination, but only unmarried priests can become bishops. Deacons, subdeacons, and readers assist the priests during services. Clergy and laity take part in the administration of the church. In Romanian Orthodox churches, the clergy and laity participate in the election of the clergy, while Romanian Catholic priests are appointed by their bishops.

Of the 2,500 Romanian American Protestants, most are Baptists. The first Romanian Baptist church was founded in Cincinnati, Ohio, in 1910. There are several Romanian Baptist churches in the United States. There are also smaller groups of Romanian Seventh-Day Adventists and Pentecostals under various jurisdictions. Romanian Protestant churches conduct their services in the same manner as their American coreligionists, employing Romanian pastors who are subordinated to various local American jurisdictions. Early Romanian pastors were trained by American missionaries in Romania during the nineteenth century.

CULTURE AND ASSIMILATION

In 1929 Romanian American Christine Avghi Galitzi observed, "Romanians in the United States constitute a picturesque, sturdy group of newly made Americans of whom altogether too little is known" (*A Study of Assimilation among the Roumanians in the United States* [New York: Columbia University Press, 1929]; reprinted in 1969). In the past, insufficient knowledge of Romanian ethnic characteristics generated misconceptions among Americans. Some authors, such as Wayne Charles Miller in his *A Comprehensive Bibliography for the Study of American Minorities* (1976), erroneously categorized Romanians as Slavs because Romania borders several Slavic countries. Other immigration studies, including Carl Wittke's *We Who Built America: The Saga of the Immigrant* (1939; revised 1967) and Joseph Huthmacher's *A Nation of Newcomers* (1967) completely overlooked

Romanians when discussing immigrants from Eastern Europe. In *American Fever: The Story of American Immigration* (1967), Barbara Kaye Greenleaf stereotyped Romanians as wearing sheepskin coats "during all seasons," even though such coats are worn by farmers and shepherds only in the winter.

Romanians who had come from Transylvania with ethnic Hungarians (Transylvania was under Hungarian rule before World War I) were also greatly misunderstood. For some Americans, the mere mention of Transylvania and Romania evoked images of vampires and werewolves as depicted in Bram Stoker's novel *Dracula* (1897) and subsequent film adaptations. Such misconceptions did not deter Romanian ethnic pride, however, which reached its peak during World War II. Today Romanian Americans continue to reaffirm their cultural past. There is a substantial number of Romanian American cultural organizations in the United States.

Traditions and Customs Romanians have a variety of traditions and lore dating back to antiquity. For example, on certain days some farmers would not cut anything with shears, believing it would prevent wolves from injuring their sheep. Tuesdays were considered unlucky days to start a journey or to initiate important business. It was believed that plague could be averted by burning a shirt that was spun, woven, and sewn in less than twenty-four hours, and that a woman who did not want children would be tortured in hell. Girls would not fill their pitchers with water from a well without first breathing upon the well and then pouring some of the water on the ground (a libation to the nymph of the well). Before serving wine, drops would be poured on the floor to honor the souls of the dead. A black cat crossing in front of a pedestrian was a sign of bad luck, as was an owl on the roof of a house, in a courtyard, or in a tree (it also portended a death in the family). Such superstitions were gradually forgotten as Romanian immigrants became acculturated into American society.

Cuisine Romanian cuisine is savory, flavorful, and stimulating to the appetite. Herbs and vegetables are used in abundance, and one-dish meals occupy an important place in the repertoire of recipes. These dishes are very nourishing, inexpensive, and easy to prepare. Romanian Americans enjoy cooking, often modifying old country recipes or creating new dishes. *Mămăligă*, considered a national dish, is a corn mush eaten with butter, cheese, meats, and even marmalade or fruit jelly (as a dessert). *Ciorbă* is a popular sour soup seasoned with sauerkraut or pickled cucumber juice. It contains onions, parsnip, parsley root, rice, and ground beef mixed with pork, and is served after the boiled vegetables are removed.

Gratar is a steak (usually pork) accompanied by pickled cucumbers and tomatoes and combined with other grilled meats. Garlic is a major ingredient used in preparing the steak. *Mititei*, which is similar to hamburgers, consists of ground beef rolled into cylindrical forms and seasoned with garlic. It is often served with *gratar*. *Sarmale* is a stuffed cabbage dish prepared with pork shoulder, rice, black pepper, and chopped onion. *Ghiveci* is a vegetable stew containing carrots, potatoes, tomatoes, green pepper, onions, celery root, eggplant, squash, string beans, fresh peas, cabbage, and cauliflower.

Cozonac and *torte* are various forms of cakes served as desserts. *Ţuică* is a brandy made from plums or wheat. *Vin* is wine and *bere* is beer. Romanian hosts and hostesses usually serve salads in a variety of shapes and compositions as entrées. Christmas dinner often consists of ham, sausages, pastry, fruits, *bere*, *vin*, and a special bread called *colac*. At Easter, lamb, ham, sausages, breads, and painted eggs are prepared, and *vin* and *bere* accompany the feast.

Traditional Dress Romanian traditional, or peasant, costumes are made from handwoven linen. Women traditionally wear embroidered white blouses, skirts that cover the knees (the color varies according to region), and headscarves of various colors according to age and regional tradition (older women usually wear black). The traditional costume for men consists of tight-fitting white pants, a white embroidered shirt that almost reaches the knees, and a wide leather or cotton belt. Men wear several types of hats according to season: black or grey elongated lambskin hats are customary during the winter and straw hats are usually worn during the summer. On festive occasions, men wear black or grey felt hats adorned with a flower or feather. Moccasins are traditional footwear for both men and women; men also wear boots with various adornments according to regional traditions. Romanian Americans wear their national costumes only on special occasions, such as national holidays celebrated in churches, at social gatherings, or while performing at local ethnic festivals.

Dances and Songs On special occasions, dancers perform the *hora*, a national dance in which men and women hold hands in a circle; the *sîrba*, a quick, spirited dance; and the *invârtite*, a pair dance. The *hora* is usually danced by large groups during important events such as the National Day of Romania (December 1). The *sîrba* and *invârtite* are performed during family parties or as part of an artistic program. The dances are accompanied by rhythmic shouts (sometimes with humorous connotations) spoken by the leader of the dance, who also invites members of the audience to join the dancers.

A traditional Romanian orchestra consists of fiddles, clarinets, trumpets, flutes, bagpipes and panpipes, drums, and the *cobza*, an instrument resembling a guitar and a mandolin. Popular songs are traditionally performed during social reunions both in America and Romania. The *doina*, for example, are multiverse tunes evoking nostalgic emotions, from a shepherd's loneliness in the mountains to patriotic sentiments. The *romanţă* is a romantic melody expressing deep feelings of affection.

CIORBA DE PERISOARE (SOUR MEATBALL SOUP)

Ingredients

½ pound ground beef

½ pound ground pork

1 pound beef bones with meat on them

2 small onions

2 slices of sturdy bread

2 tablespoons rice

salt

ground black pepper

1 parsley root, thinly sliced

3–4 carrots, thinly sliced

1 parsnip root

3–4 tablespoons tomato paste

1 bunch of parsley, chopped

2–3 tablespoons vinegar

Preparation

Bring water to boil in a pot. Finely slice 1 onion and put in pot. Add the parsley, parsnip, and carrots. Add the beef (or veal) meat.

In the meantime soak the bread in water then squeeze it. Mash the bread with a fork.

Finely chop the other onion and mix the ground meat, the mashed bread, and the rice. Season with salt and ground black pepper. For a more tender meat composition add 2–3 tablespoons of water. Using wet hands, roll mixture into small meatballs (1 inch).

When the vegetables become tender put the meatballs in the boiling water. Reduce heat and simmer for 30–40 minutes. The meatballs will rise to the surface when the soup is almost done. Add the tomato paste and stir. Add the parsley, and then season with salt and vinegar.

Serve with a dollop of sour cream and optional cayenne pepper.

Serves 8

Holidays In addition to Christmas Day, New Year's Day, and Easter Day, Romanian Americans celebrate the birthday of the Romanian national state on January 24 and Transylvania's reunification with Romania on December 1. Romanian Americans with promonarchist views also celebrate May 10, which marks the ascension of Carol I to the Romanian throne. During these festivities, celebrants sing the Romanian national anthem, "Awake Thee, Romanian," written by Andrei Mureşanu (1816–1863), a noted poet and patriot. Monarchists sing the Romanian royal anthem, which begins with the words "Long live the king in peace and honor." A semiofficial holiday similar to

Regina Kohn, Romanian American, was allowed to enter Ellis Island because she could play violin. New York, 1923. UPI / CORBIS-BETTMANN. REPRODUCED BY PERMISSION.

Valentine's Day is celebrated by lovers and friends on March l, when a white or red silk flower (often handmade) is presented as an expression of love.

Health Care Issues and Practices There are no documented health problems or medical conditions specific to Romanian Americans. Many families have health insurance coverage underwritten by the Union and League of Romanian Societies in America or by other ethnic organizations. Like most Americans, Romanian American business owners and professionals in private practice are insured at their own expense, while employees benefit from their employers' health plans when available.

FAMILY AND COMMUNITY LIFE

During the first three decades of the twentieth century, the Romanian American family underwent profound changes. The first immigrants were typically single males or married men who had temporarily left their families in order to save enough money to send for them later. These immigrants lived in crowded boarding houses and often slept on the floor. On Sundays and holidays, they congregated in saloons or restaurants and at church. Later, Romanian immigrants gathered at the headquarters of mutual aid societies and fraternal organizations where they discussed news from the homeland, read or wrote letters, and sang religious or popular songs. The boarding houses evolved into cooperatives such that boarders provided their own beds and shared all operating expenses (rent, utilities, food, and laundry services).

As Romanian immigrants became better accustomed to the American way of life, they adopted higher standards of living, prepared more nutritious meals, and engaged in such recreational activities as sports and movie going. Since most Romanian American women worked outside the home, economic conditions gradually improved and many Romanian Americans were able to purchase a home, cars, and modern appliances, or rent larger apartments in more prosperous neighborhoods. The typical Romanian household features Romanian embroidery or rugs, the Romanian flag, and other cultural icons, which are displayed in a common area.

Romanians have always held the family in high esteem and are generally opposed to divorce. Although the first wave of immigrants consisted of large families, subsequent generations have chosen to have fewer children, a trend that could be attributed to economic factors. Early immigrants cared very much for their children, did not permit child labor, and instilled in their children the importance of education. While approximately 33 percent of the Romanian immigrants who came to the United States before World War I were illiterate, many managed to learn English or improve their education to obtain or hold onto a job. Encouraged by their parents, second-generation Romanian Americans placed more emphasis on vocational training and college education. By 2011, according to the American Community Survey estimates for 2009–2011, 47.5 percent of Romanian Americans had a bachelor's degree or higher (compared with 28.2 percent of the general U.S. population).

Weddings Romanian American wedding customs have evolved somewhat from the traditions of the old country. For example, the bridal shower, a social custom that was never practiced in Romania, is a gala affair attended by both sexes. Before the wedding ceremony, banns are announced for three consecutive Sundays so that impediments to the marriage—if any—can be brought to the attention of the priest. After that, the couple selects the best man and maid (or matron) of honor, both of whom are called *nașii*, usually a husband and wife or a sister and brother. In most cases, the *nașii* later serve as godparents to the couple's children.

On the day of the wedding, the bridal party meets in the bride's home and leaves for the church, where the groom is waiting along with the best man. In the church there is no instrumental music, and the bridal procession is made in silence. The bride is brought to the altar by her father or another male member of the family, who then relinquishes her to the groom. The priest initiates the ceremony, assisted by a cantor or church choir that sings the responses. After receiving affirmative answers from the couple about their intention to marry and their mutual commitment, the priest blesses the wedding rings and places them in the hands of the bride and groom. Then, metal or floral crowns are placed on the heads of the couple so that they can rule the family in peace, harmony, and purity of heart. The bride and groom then take three bites of a honey wafer or drink wine from a common cup, which symbolizes their bountiful life together. Finally, the hands of the couple are bound together with a ribbon to symbolize how they will share all their joys and sorrows, and the couple walks three times around the tetrapod (a small stand displaying an icon), symbolizing the eternity of their union and obedience to the Holy Trinity. The crowns are removed with a blessing from the priest, who then concludes the ceremony with a few words of advice for the couple. The reception is held either at a private home, hotel, or restaurant. Instead of gifts, guests give money at the reception, which is collected by the *nașii*, who publicly announce the amounts received. The reception is accompanied by music and dancing, including popular Romanian songs and folk dances.

Baptisms When a child is ready for baptism, the *nașii*, or godparents, bring the child to the church, where the priest confers the grace of God by putting his hand on the child. Then the priest exorcises the child by breathing on the child's forehead, mouth, and breast. The godmother, or *nașa*, renounces the service of Satan in the child's name and promises to believe in Jesus Christ and serve only Him. In front of the altar, the priest anoints the child with the "oil of joy" (blessed olive oil) on the forehead, breast, shoulders, ears, hands, and feet. The baptism is completed by dipping the child three times in a font or by sprinkling with holy water. The confirmation immediately follows the baptism and consists of a new anointment of the child with *mir*, a mixture of thirty-three spices blessed by the bishop, on the forehead, eyes, nose, mouth, breast, ears, hands, and feet. It is customary to hold a dinner after the baptism, where guests usually bring gifts in the form of money.

Funerals A death in the family is announced by the ringing of church bells three times a day (morning, noon, and evening) until the day of the funeral. Prayers for the dead are recited by the priest and the Gospel is read during the wake, called *saracusta*. At the church, the funeral service consists entirely of singing; with the assistance of the cantor and choir, the priest sings hymns and prayers for the dead. The priest bids farewell to the family in the name of the deceased and asks for forgiveness of sins against family members or friends. At the cemetery, prayers are recited and the Gospel is read. Before the coffin is lowered into the grave, the priest sprinkles soil on top of it and recites the following: "The earth is the Lord's, and the fullness thereof." Later, the deceased's family offers a *pomana*, which is either a complete meal or sandwiches and beverages. The purpose of the funeral is to remember the dead and to seek forgiveness for the sins of the deceased. At least six weeks following the burial, a memorial service called *parastas* is offered. During the *parastas*, the priest recites a few prayers for the deceased, and a large cake-like bread is then cut into small pieces and served with wine in the church's

vestibule. The mourners state, "May his (or her) soul rest in peace," and reminisce about the deceased.

> *The elimination of Communist travel restrictions, the desire of thousands of people to be reunited with their American relatives and friends, and the precarious economic conditions in the new Romania were powerful incentives to immigrate to the United States. Among the newcomers were professionals, former political prisoners, and others who were disenchanted with the new leadership in Romania.*

Relations with Other Americans As Romanian Americans moved into better residential areas and suburbs, they began to interact with other ethnic groups. Romanian Orthodox worshippers established relationships with Orthodox Serbians, Greeks, Russians, and Ukrainians by attending their churches. Similarly, Romanian Catholics were drawn to Hungarian or Polish Catholics, while Romanian Baptists established friendly relations with Serbian, Croatian, and Bulgarian Baptists. Romanian workers mingled with other ethnic groups in the workplace. All of these factors—including the proliferation of mixed marriages—contributed to the integration of Romanians into mainstream American society.

EMPLOYMENT AND ECONOMIC CONDITIONS

Because early Romanian immigrants settled in the eastern and midwestern regions of the United States, they found work in such industries as iron, rubber, steel, coal, meat packing, and automotive. They were assigned the heaviest and dirtiest jobs, as was the custom with all newly arrived immigrants. After accumulating work experience and perfecting their English language skills, some Romanians advanced to higher positions. Immigrants who settled in California were employed as gardeners and fruit gatherers and packers, and as freight transporters. Macedo-Romanians often held jobs as waiters in the hotel and restaurant industries.

About 9 percent of Romanian immigrants settled in Colorado, North Dakota, South Dakota, Idaho, and Wyoming; they became involved in agriculture and ranching either as farm owners or managers. Romanians were also employed as tailors, bakers, carpenters, and barbers, establishing small businesses in Romanian American neighborhoods. Romanian women found employment in light industry, such as cigar and tobacco manufacturing, or as seamstresses. Younger women became clerks or office secretaries, while others worked as manicurists or hairdressers in beauty salons. Many Macedo-Romanian women took jobs in the textile industry, and some Romanians with entrepreneurial skills opened travel agencies, small banks, saloons, boarding houses, and restaurants.

While maintaining their place in the industries where their parents worked, second-generation Romanian Americans gradually switched from unskilled to skilled occupations. Others became white-collar workers, and many embraced professional careers. Subsequent generations went even further in their educational and professional pursuits. Romanian Americans made such progress that for several decades, few of the adult members of this group had less than a high school education. The professional ranks of Romanians (those educated at American universities) were substantially enlarged by the thousands of professionals who immigrated to the United States after World War II and in the years following the Revolution of 1989. The children of these professionals have typically followed the path of their parents. In addition, many Romanian students sent to the United States to complete their studies have remained after graduation and have found employment. Other Romanian Americans have found work as taxi drivers, clerical workers, and salon attendants, among many other occupations. By 2011, according to the American Community Survey estimates for 2009–2011, 49 percent of employed Romanian Americans worked in management, business, science, and art occupations, 21 percent worked in sales and office jobs, and 15 percent worked in service occupations.

POLITICS AND GOVERNMENT

The formation of the Union and League of Romanian Societies of America (ULRSA) in 1906 marked the beginning of Romanian political activity in the United States on a national scale. Founded in Cleveland, ULRSA brought together dozens of mutual aid and cultural societies, clubs, fraternities, and other groups committed to preserving Romanian ethnicity. It provided insurance benefits, assisted thousands of Romanians in completing their education, and taught newly arrived immigrants how to handle their affairs in a democratic way. As ULRSA gained more power and prestige, its leaders were often courted by local and national politicians to enlist political support from the Romanian American community.

I never really knew how much my ethnic background meant to me until the Romanian Revolution a few years ago. I was never ashamed of my background, I just never boldly stated it. I guess because I live in America I thought that I was just an American, period.

Veronica Buza, "My Ethnic Experience," in *Romanian American Heritage Center Information Bulletin*, September–October 1993.

The leadership of ULRSA (with few exceptions) has held a neutral and unbiased position in American politics. Despite this neutrality, however, many Romanians—especially those who immigrated to America before World War II—have pro-Democratic sentiments, while the majority of postwar immigrants and refugees with strong anticommunist sentiments tilt more toward the Republican party. A small group of Romanian American socialists—primarily workers from Cleveland, Chicago, Detroit, and New York—founded the Federation of the Romanian Socialist Workers of the United States in 1914 and later merged with the pro-communist International Workers Order. Many Romanian Americans also joined local labor unions for the practical reason that they could not obtain work otherwise. Later, as employment opportunities improved, they participated in union activities according to their specific interests, benefits needs, and preferences.

Military Service During World War I, several hundred Romanian volunteers from Ohio and other states enrolled in the American Expeditionary Force in Europe on the French front. Many of these soldiers received commendations for bravery. Over five thousand Romanian Americans served in the American Armed Forces during World War II and over three hundred died in combat. Romanian Americans were also represented in significant numbers during the Korean and Vietnam Wars, and many were promoted to officer ranks. In 1977 Nicholas Daramus became the first Romanian American to be promoted to the rank of full commander in the U.S. Navy.

Relations with Romania Romanian Americans have always been proud of their homeland and have maintained ties beyond typical relations with family or friends. Before and during World War I, Romanian Americans exposed Hungarian persecution of Transylvanians in their newspapers, and many organizations called for the unification of Transylvania and Romania. These organizations also gave generous donations of money, food, and clothing for Romania's orphans, widows, and refugees. In 1919 Romanian Americans submitted to the Paris Peace Conference a four-point motion calling for the reestablishment of Romania's territorial borders (including the restoration of Transylvania and other regions formerly held by foreign powers), equal rights for ethnic minorities, and the establishment of a democracy based on principles adopted in the United States.

In the 1920s and 1930s many Romanian Americans actively supported the National Peasant party founded in Transylvania against antidemocratic political forces. Prominent Romanians such as Queen Marie (1875–1938) visited Romanian American communities, and the Romanian government sent a group of students to complete their studies at various American universities. After World War II, Romanian Americans sent food, medicine, and clothing to refugees and other types of aid to help Romania's devastated economy.

During the years of Communist dictatorship, Romanian American groups sent a formal memorandum to U.S. president Harry Truman protesting the mass deportations of Romanians by Soviet troops in 1952. In 1964 they called upon president Lyndon B. Johnson to exert pressure on the Communists to release Romanian political prisoners and provide exit visas for individuals desiring to join relatives in the United States. Many Romanian Americans who held promonarchist views sought the restoration of Michael I, who was forced by the Communists to abdicate the throne in December 1947. Romanian American Catholics vehemently opposed the suppression of their church in Romania beginning in 1948, when bishops and priests were arrested and murdered, church property was confiscated, and many Romanian Catholics were deported.

Romanian Americans continue to aid their native country during difficult times through the auspices of the ULRSA, the International Red Cross and Red Crescent Movement, and other philanthropic organizations. Presently, some Romanian Americans are involved in developing business ventures in Romania in spite of the precarious conditions of the country's economy and the country's relative unfamiliarity with the capitalist system. There is also a steady flow of scholarly exchanges between Romania and United States, facilitated by grants and scholarships. Many Romanian Americans take an active role in the American Romanian Academy of Arts and Sciences and other academic organizations.

NOTABLE INDIVIDUALS

Although Romanian Americans represent only one-eighth of one percent of America's total population, they have made significant contributions to American popular culture and to the arts and sciences. The following sections list Romanian Americans and their achievements.

Academia Mircea Eliade (1907–1986) was a renowned authority on religious studies, mythology, and folklore. His many publications include *The History of Religions: Essays in Methodology* (1959) and *Zalmoxis, the Vanishing God: Comparative Studies in the Religions and Folklore of Dacia and Eastern Europe* (1972). Many of his works have been translated into several languages. Nicholas Georgescu-Roegen (1906–1994) pioneered mathematical economics and influenced many American economists through his *Analytical Economics: Issues and Problems* (1966). He was considered by his peers, as Paul Samuelson wrote in his foreword to the book, "a scholar's scholar and an economist's economist." Romanian American mathematician Constantin Corduneanu (1928–) edited the journal *Libertas Mathematica*, and Romance philologist Maria Manoliu-Manea (1934–) served as president of the American Romanian Academy of Arts and Sciences.

Mirela Roznoveanu (born Roznovschi) is a well-known writer, poet, literary critic, and journalist who was born in Romania in 1947 and immigrated to the United States in 1991. She became a faculty member at the New York University School of Law and is one of the country's most influential researchers on foreign, comparative, and international law. She has written both in Romanian and English and has published fifteen books, including *The Civilization of the Novel: A History of Fiction Writing from Marayana to Don Quijote* (two volumes; 1983, 1991); *Towards a Cyberlegal Culture* (2001); *Life on the Run* (1997); and *The Life Manager and Other Stories* (2004).

Journalism Theodore Andrica (1900–1990) edited and published two successful periodicals, the *New Pioneer* during the 1940s and the *American Romanian Review* during the 1970s and 1980s. Both publications featured articles on Romanian American life, traditions, customs, and cooking, and documented the achievements of Romanian Americans. Andrica also served as editor of the *Cleveland Press* for twenty years. Vasile Hategan (1915–2003) a Romanian Orthodox pastor wrote several articles on Romanians residing in New York City. John Florea (1916–2000) of *Life* magazine was a photographer during the 1940s and 1950s and a TV director. For several decades, broadcaster Liviu Floda (1913–1997) of Radio Free Europe hosted programs discussing human rights violations by the Communist regime in Romania. He interviewed hundreds of personalities, helped reunite refugee families with American relatives, and wrote dozens of articles on various subjects for Romanian Americans and foreign-language journals.

Literature Peter Neagoe (1881–1960) was the first major Romanian American author. In such novels as *Easter Sun* (1934) and *There Is My Heart* (1936), he depicted the lives of Transylvanian peasants in realistic detail. Illustrator Mircea Vasiliu (1920–2008) wrote *Which Way to the Melting Pot?* (1955) and *The Pleasure Is Mine* (1963), in which he humorously recounts his experiences as an immigrant. In 1947 Anişoara Stan (1902–1954) published *They Crossed Mountains and Oceans*, which focuses on immigrant life in the United States. Stan also wrote *The Romanian Cook Book* (1951), which remains a fundamental source on Romanian cookery and cuisine.

Elie Wiesel (1928–), a writer, journalist, political activist, and professor, was born into a Hasidic family in Romania and survived internment in a concentration camp during the Holocaust. He immigrated to the United States from France in 1955 and published more than fifty books on various subjects. Perhaps his most widely acclaimed book is *Night* (1960), a memoir based on his experiences as a prisoner in the Auschwitz, Birkenau, and Buchenwald concentration camps. He became a Nobel Laureate for Humanism in 1996. Andrei Codrescu (1946–), a poet, novelist, and journalist, added new dimensions to contemporary Romanian American literature through such books as *The Life and Times of an Involuntary Genius* (1975), *In America's Shoes* (1983), and several others that delineate anticommunist sentiments in Romania and the immigrant experience in the United States. Silvia Cinca (1934–), author and president of Moonfall Press, published *Comrade Dracula* (1988), *Homo Spiritus: Journey of Our Magic* (1988), and several other books in Romanian and English.

Music George Enescu (1881–1955) was a composer, violinist, and conductor who lived in the United States before and after World War II. He conducted several symphony orchestras, taught at the Manhattan School of Music in New York City, and earned fame for his "Romanian Rhapsodies," which many American and foreign symphony orchestras have since performed. Ionel Perlea (1900–1970) taught at the Manhattan School of Music and served as musical conductor of the New York Metropolitan Opera for over twenty years despite the fact that his right hand was paralyzed. Stella Roman (1905–1992), an operatic soprano, performed at the Metropolitan Opera in New York during the 1940s and 1950s, specializing in Italian opera spinto roles. Other gifted performers include Christina Carroll (1920–) of the New York Metropolitan Opera; Yolanda Márculescu (died 1992), soprano and music teacher at the University of Wisconsin at Milwaukee; and Lisette Verea (1914–2003), operetta singer and comedienne based in New York City.

Science and Medicine George Emil Palade (1912–2008) of the Yale University School of Medicine shared the 1974 Nobel Prize in Physiology or Medicine for his contributions to research on the structure and function of the internal components of cells. Traian Leucutia (1892–1977), who began his medical career in Detroit in the 1920s, was one of the first scientists to detect the radiation hazards of X-rays. He also served as editor of the *American Journal of Roentgenology, Radium Therapy, and Nuclear Medicine* for several years. Valer Barbu (1892–1986) taught psychiatry and psychoanalysis at Cornell University, the New School of Social Research in New York City, and the American Institute of Psychoanalysis before and after World War II. A disciple of psychoanalyst Karen Horney, Barbu was critical of Freudian analysis.

Constantin Barbulescu (1929–2011), an aeronautical engineer, devised methods of protecting aircraft flying in severe weather. He published his findings in *Electrical Engineering* and other technical journals during the 1940s. Alexandru Papană (1905–1946) tested gliders and other aircraft for Northrop Aircraft in California. Many of Papana's experiences as a test pilot were documented in *Flying* magazine.

Sports World-renowned gymnast Nadia Comăneci (1961–) was the winner of three Olympic gold medals at the 1976 Summer Olympic Games in Montreal. The first female gymnast to be awarded a perfect ten in an Olympic gymnastics event, she defected from Communist Romania in 1989 and became an American naturalized citizen in 2001. After her gymnastics career ended, she became active in many charitable and international organizations and received the Olympic Order (the highest decoration given by the International Olympic Committee) in 1984 and 2004. Dominique Moceanu (1981–) is an American-born gymnast of Romanian descent who earned her first U.S. national team place at the age of ten. She represented the United States in various major international tournaments at the junior level, was the all-around silver medalist at the 1992 Junior Pan American Games, became junior U.S. national champion in 1994, and at age thirteen became the youngest gymnast to win the senior all-around title at the U.S. National Championships. In 1996 she was an Olympic gold medalist.

Charley Stanceu (1916–1969) was the first Romanian American to play baseball in the major leagues. A native of Canton, Ohio, he pitched for the New York Yankees and the Philadelphia Phillies during the 1940s. At 7 feet, 7 inches tall, Gheorghe Mureșan (1971–) became a famous basketball star, playing for the Washington Bullets, and appeared in the film *My Giant* (1998) with Billy Crystal.

Stage and Screen Jean Negulesco (1900–1993) directed *Singapore Woman* (1941), *Johnny Belinda* (1948), *Titanic* (1953), and *Three Coins in a Fountain* (1954), and was known as a portrait artist. Television actor Adrian Zmed (1954–) costarred with William Shatner in the police drama *T. J. Hooker* (1982–1986). In theater, Andrei Șerban (1943–) adapted and directed classical plays at LaMama Theater in New York City, while Liviu Ciulei (1923–2011) is best known for directing classical works.

Visual Arts Constantin Brâncuși (1876–1957) is considered by some art critics to be the father of modern sculpture. He first exhibited his works in the United States in 1913 at the International Exhibition of Modern Art. Many of his pieces (*Miss Pogany, The Kiss, Bird in Space, White Negress*) were acquired by the Museum of Modern Art in New York City, the Philadelphia Museum of Art, and the Art Institute of Chicago. Sculptor George Zolnay (1863–1949) created the Sequoya Statue in the U.S. Capitol, the Edgar Allan Poe monument at the University of Virginia at Charlottesville, and the War Memorial sculpture of the Parthenon in Nashville, Tennessee. Zolnay also served as art commissioner at the 1892 World Columbian Exhibition in Chicago. Elie Cristo-Loveanu (1893–1964) distinguished himself as a portrait artist and professor of painting at New York University during the 1940s and 1950s. His portrait of President Dwight Eisenhower is on display at Columbia University. Mircea Vasiliu (1920–2008), a former diplomat, was a well-known illustrator of children's books.

MEDIA

PRINT

America

An organ of ULRSA, this monthly publication focuses on the activities and achievements of local ULRSA branches and features cultural news and book reviews written in English and Romanian. It is supplemented by an almanac listing important events in the Romanian American community.

Daniela Istrate, Managing Editor
P.O. Box 1037
Andover, Ohio 44003
Phone: (818) 219-9922
Email: d.strate@att.net
URL: http://www.romaniansocieties.com/rom_societies/news.php

Clipa

This weekly magazine, in Romanian, features news from Romania and America.

Dwight Luchian Patton, Director
P.O. Box 4391
Anaheim, California 92803-4391
Phone: (714) 758-8801
Fax: (714) 758-9632
Email: clipa_magazine@yahoo.com
URL: http://www.clipa.com

Crestinul in Actiune (*The Christian in Action*)

This bimonthly Protestant publication, in Romanian, has an interdenominational spirit.

Petru Amarei
3707 West Montrose Avenue
Chicago, Illinois 60618
Phone: (773) 267-0007
Fax: (773) 267-0008
Email: pa@romaniantv.org
URL: www.romaniantv.org/pub_revista.php

Gandacul De Colorado (*The Beetle of Colorado*)

This weekly publication, in Romanian, features achievements of Romanians in the United States and other countries.

Lucian Oprea, Editor
P.O. Box 2521
Estes Park, Colorado 80517
Phone: (970) 222-4751
Email: lucianoprea@gandaculdecolorado.com
URL: www.gandaculdecolorado.com

Meridianul Românesc (*Romanian Meridian*)

This weekly newspaper, in Romanian, contains articles concerning Romania and the Romanian American community, politics, culture, sports, tourism, and other subjects with an independent orientation.

26873 Sierra Highway #505
Santa Clarita, California 91321
Phone: (714) 881-5116
Fax: (714) 780-1325
Email: meridianul@gmail.com
URL: www.meridianul.com

New York Magazin

This weekly publication, in Romanian, features politics in Romania, international events, and sports.

Grigore Culian, Editor
102-02 65th Road
Forest Hills, New York 11375
Phone: (718) 896-8383
Fax: (718) 896-8170
Email: nymagazin@aol.com
URL: www.nymagazin.com

Romanian Journal

This weekly publication, in Romanian, features news about Romanian Americans, Romania, politics, and international events.

Vasile Badaluta, Editor
45-51 39th Place
Sunnyside, New York 11104
Phone: (718) 993-8555
Fax: (718) 993-8334
Email: bigtime@usa.net

Romanian Tribune

This bimonthly publication, in Romanian, contains achievements of Romanian Americans and news from Romania.

7777 North Caldwell Avenue
Suite 103
Niles, Illinois 60714
Phone: (847) 477-3498
Fax: (847) 983-8463
Email: romaniantribune@gmail.com
URL: www.romaniantribune.net/

Solia (*The Herald*)

Published monthly in a bilingual format by the Romanian Orthodox Episcopate of America, this newsletter focuses on parish news and projects, features book reviews, and produces an annual supplement listing important events and a religious calendar.

David Oancea, Editor
2535 Grey Tower Road
Jackson, Michigan 49201-9120
Phone: (517) 522-3656
Fax: (517) 522-5907
Email: solia@roea.org
URL: www.roea.org/soliatheherald.html

RADIO

Viata Romaneasca (*Romanian Life*)

This weekly one-hour radio program is broadcast in Romanian.

Lavinia Simonis
Valentin Fedorovici

P.O. Box 2038
Fair Oaks, California 95628
Phone: (916) 965-7988
Fax: (916) 965-7988
Email: vocearomaneasca@yahoo.com

TELEVISION

Romanian Television Network

Since 1994 this network has broadcasted Romanian-language programming.

Petru Amarei, President
3707 West Montrose Avenue
Chicago, Illinois 60618
Phone: (773) 267-0007
Fax: (773) 267-0008
Email: pa@romaniantv.com
URL: www.rtnchicago.com

Romanian Voice TV

This New York City network transmits news from Romania and the Romanian American community.

Vasile Badaluta
45-51 39th Place
Sunnyside, New York 11104
Phone: (718) 482-9588
Fax: (718) 472-9119
Email: bigtime@usa.net
URL: www.youtube.com/user/RVTVNY

ORGANIZATIONS AND ASSOCIATIONS

American Romanian Academy of Arts and Sciences (ARA)

Founded in 1975, the ARA consists of Romanian scholars and focuses on research and publishing activities regarding Romanian art, culture, language, history, linguistics, sciences, and economics.

Ion Paraschivoiu, President
École Polytechnique de Montréal
P.O. Box 6079
Station Centre-Ville Montréal, Quebec H3C 3A7
Canada
Phone: (514) 340-4711 ext. 4583
Fax: (514) 340-5917
Email: iopara@meca.polymtl.ca
URL: www.meca.polymtl.ca/ion/ARA-AS/

American Romanian Orthodox Youth (AROY)

Founded in 1950, AROY functions as an auxiliary of the Romanian Orthodox Episcopate of America and cultivates religious education and Romanian culture through summer courses, retreats, sports, competitions, scholarships, and other activities.

2535 Grey Tower Road
Jackson, Michigan 49201-9120
Phone: (517) 522-3656
Fax: (517) 522-5907
Email: chancery@roea.org
URL: www.roea.org/aroy.html

Association of Jewish Romanian Americans (AJRA)

AJRA focuses on Jewish community concerns and liaisons with Romanian government representatives.

David Kahan, President
1570 57th Street
Brooklyn, New York 11219
Phone: (718) 972-5074
Fax: (718) 437-4806
Email: davidkahan@juno.com

Association of Romanian Catholics of America (ARCA)

Founded in 1948, the ARCA promotes religious education in the tradition of the Romanian Catholic Church of the Byzantine Rite and cultural preservation, and sponsors special programs designed for youths. The association is also involved in publishing activities.

John E. Stroie, President
1700 Dale Drive
Merrillville, Indiana 46410
Phone: (219) 980-0726
Email: istroia@austin.rr.com

Congress of Romanian Americans (CORA)

CORA promotes the interests of Romanian Americans and cooperation between the Romanian and U.S. governments.

Armand Scala, President and secretary
1000 Gelston Circle
McLean, Virginia 22102
Phone: (703) 356-2280
Fax: (703) 356-1568
Email: web@romanianamericans.org
URL: www.romanianamericans.org/

Iuliu Manu Romanian Relief Foundation

This foundation offers assistance to needy Romanian students and widows of deceased Romanian freedom fighters.

Justin Liuba, President
P.O. Box 230664
Astor Station
Boston, Massachusetts 02123
Phone: (617) 536-6552
Email: jliuba@yahoo.com
URL: www.iuliumaniufoundation.org

North American Romanian Press Association (NARPA)

NARPA works for the improvement of the Romanian press, including the professional ethics of journalists, in the United States and Canada.

Marian Petruta, President
3707 West Montrose Avenue
Chicago, Illinois 60618
Phone: (312) 618-2000
Email: contact@narpa.info
URL: www.narpa.info

Romanian American Chamber of Commerce

This organization promotes the development of successful business relations between Romania and the United States.

URL: www.racc.ro

Romanian American Network

This organization encourages better Romanian American ties to mass media sources and has a library of over twenty thousand books on Romanians and Romania.

Steven Bonica, President
7847 North Caldwell Avenue
Niles, Illinois 60714-3320
Phone: (847) 663-0950
Fax: (847) 663-0960
Email: office@CMMCweb.net
URL: www.ro-am.net

Society for Romanian Studies

Founded in 1985, this organization promotes Romanian language and culture studies in American universities and colleges, and cultural exchange programs between the United States and Romania.

Irina Livezeanu
3502 Posvar Hall
University of Pittsburgh
Pittsburgh, Pennsylvania 15260
Phone: (412) 648-7466
Email: irina@pitt.edu
URL: www.society4romanianstudies.org

Union and League of Romanian Societies of America (ULRSA)

Founded in 1906, ULRSA is the oldest and largest Romanian American organization. It has played an important role in organizing Romanian immigrants and preserving Romanian culture.

Daniela Istrate, President
1801 North Van Ness Avenue
Los Angeles, California 90028
Phone: (818) 219-9922
Fax: (818) 956-1430
Email: d.strate@att.net
URL: www.romaniansocieties.com

MUSEUMS AND RESEARCH CENTERS

Iuliu Maniu American Romanian Relief Foundation (IMF)

This foundation has a sizable collection of Romanian peasant costumes, paintings, and folk art items. It also manages a library of Romanian books that can be borrowed by mail.

Justin Liuba, President
P.O. Box 1151
Gracie Square Station
New York, New York 10128
Phone: (212) 535-8169

Romanian Ethnic Art Museum

This museum has preserved a large collection of Romanian national costumes, wood carvings, rugs, icons, furniture, paintings, and over two thousand Romanian books, as well as English books related to Romania.

R. Grama
3256 Warren Road
Cleveland, Ohio 44111
Phone: (216) 941-5550
Fax: (216) 941-3068

Romanian American Heritage Center

This center collects and preserves historical records relating to Romanian immigrants and their achievements. The collection consists of religious items, brochures, minutes, flyers, and reports donated by various Romanian American organizations, family and individual photographs, and other materials of interest to researchers.

Alexandru Nemoianu
2540 Grey Tower Road
Jackson, Michigan 49201
Phone: (517) 522-8260
Fax: (517) 522-8236

Romanian Cultural Center

A Romanian government agency similar to the U.S. Information Agency, this center has a sizable collection of Romanian books published in Romania and a collection of folk art items. The center organizes cultural programs and assists in providing contacts in Romania.

Doina Uricariu
200 East 38th Street
New York, New York 10016
Phone: (212) 687-0180
Fax: (212) 687-0181
Email: icrny@icrny.org
URL: www.icrny.org

Romanian Museum

This museum features national costumes, rugs, furniture, pottery, and Transylvanian interior decorations, and promotes Romanian artisan exhibits.

Rodica Perciali
1606 Spruce Street
Philadelphia, Pennsylvania 19103
Phone: (215) 732-6780

SOURCES FOR ADDITIONAL STUDY

Diamond, Arthur. *Romanian Americans.* New York: Chelsea House, 1988.

Dima, Nicholas. *From Moldavia to Moldova: The Soviet Romanian Territorial Dispute.* Boulder, Colorado: East European Monographs, 1991.

Galitzi, Christine Avghi. *A Study of Assimilation among the Romanians in the United States.* New York: Columbia University Press, 1929; reprinted, 1969.

Hategan, Vasile. *Romanian Culture in America*. Cleveland, Ohio: Cleveland Cultural Center, 1985.

Wertsman, Vladimir. *The Romanians in America, 1748–1974: A Chronology and Factbook*. Dobbs Ferry, New York: Oceana Publications, 1975.

———. *The Romanians in America and Canada: A Guide to Information Sources*. Detroit: Gale Research Company, 1980.

———. *Romanians in the United States and Canada: A Guide to Ancestry and Heritage Research*. North Salt Lake, Utah: Heritage Quest, 2002.

———. *Salute to the Romanian Jews in America and Canada, 1850–2010: History, Achievements, and Biographies*. Bloomington, Indiana: XLibris, 2010.

Winnifrith, T. J. *The Vlachs: The History of a Balkan People*. London: Duckworth, 1987.

RUSSIAN AMERICANS

Paul Robert Magocsi

OVERVIEW

Russian Americans are immigrants or descendants of immigrants from Russia. The largest country in total land area in the world, Russia occupies one-eighth of the earth's surface and spans ten time zones. It stretches from the plains of Eastern Europe across Siberia as far as the shores of the Pacific Ocean and from north of the Arctic Circle south to the Middle East. The Ural Mountains, which are located mainly in Russia, form the boundary between the two continents it straddles, Europe and Asia. One-third of the country borders fourteen other countries: Norway, Finland, Estonia, Latvia, Lithuania, Poland, Belarus, Ukraine, Georgia, Azerbaijan, Kazakhstan, Mongolia, the People's Republic of China, and North Korea; the other two-thirds are bounded by water. Composed of more than 6.6 million square miles (17 million square kilometers) of territory, Russia is almost twice the size of the United States.

The 2010 Russian census measured the country's population at 142.9 million. Around 80 percent of the people are ethnic Russians, 3.8 percent are Tatars, 2 percent are Ukrainian, and the balance consists of more than ninety smaller ethnic groups. According to a 2011 survey by the Levada Center, a Russian non-governmental polling and sociological research organization, approximately 70 percent self-identify with the (Christian) Russian Orthodox Church, although a 2012 survey by the Independent Research Service (SREDA) produced a figure of 41 percent, and the portion of Russians who actually practice the religion is estimated at between 10 and 20 percent. Along with Slavic ethnicity, Russian Orthodoxy has historically formed a pillar of Russian national identity, and it is currently favored by the government as the national religion. More than 6 percent of the people—Russia's second largest religious population—are Muslim, concentrated in the various Caucasian and Turkic ethnic groups; these are primarily Sunni, with a very small fraction being Shiite. After a period of chaos and extreme hardship following the breakup of the Soviet Union in 1991, the Russian economy stabilized in the late 1990s. It has since grown to be the ninth largest in the world, based largely on exploitation of the country's vast natural resources, especially oil and gas. While a growing and thriving middle class has made its mark both at home and abroad, economic life is still dominated by a small number of extremely wealthy and politically connected "oligarchs," and conditions for many Russians, especially outside the major cities, remain difficult.

In a sense, there are two Russian homelands. One is the present-day state of Russia, which coincides with territory largely inhabited by ethnic Russians. The other includes territories that are beyond Russia proper but were once part of the pre–World War I Russian Empire and later the Soviet Union. Americans who identify their heritage as Russian include first-generation immigrants and their descendants, who came from Russia within its present-day border; people from the Baltic countries, Belarus, and Ukraine who identify as Russians; East Slavs from the former Austro-Hungarian Empire who identified themselves as Russians once in the United States; and Jews from the western regions of the former Russian Empire and the Soviet Union who, aside from their religious background, identify as Russians. These different groups have produced different and distinct patterns of immigration, ranging from settlers crossing from Siberia to Alaska and the West Coast of the United States in the late eighteenth and early nineteenth centuries; to large-scale immigration, mostly by Jews and other minorities, from the Russian Empire during its last decades; to several waves of refugees from the Soviet Union after the 1917 revolution and continuing through the twentieth century. While earlier immigrants largely became farmers or industrial workers, those who came from Soviet and post-Soviet Russia tended to be educated professionals and entered corresponding fields upon arrival. The first decade of the twenty-first century was characterized by "new Russians," or "global Russians," who had benefited from the economic transition of the 1990s and were much more likely to keep one foot in their home country.

In 2011 nearly 3 million people of Russian ancestry lived in the United States, according to the U.S. Census Bureau's American Community Survey estimates—just less than one percent of the entire American population, a number slightly larger than the population of Chicago. (Other sources put the number higher, at around 3.15 million.) The bulk of Russian immigrants have settled in the big cities of the Northeast—New York, Boston, Philadelphia, Washington, D.C.—and in California, though notable

Russian American settlements can also be found in smaller and rural communities in Massachusetts, Pennsylvania, New Jersey, Illinois, and Florida.

HISTORY OF THE PEOPLE

Early History Much of European Russia—the region west of the Urals—was part of a medieval state known as *Kievan Rus'*, which existed from the late ninth century to the thirteenth century. During the Kievan period, Orthodox Christianity reached the area, and the religion remained intimately connected with every state or culture that developed on Russian territory until the twentieth century. A more specifically Russian state was born in the late thirteenth century, in a northern part of *Kievan Rus'*, the Duchy of Muscovy. The state-building process began when the Duchy began to consolidate its power and expand its territory with phenomenal results. By the seventeenth and eighteenth centuries, the growing state included lands along the Baltic Sea and in Belarus, Ukraine, Moldova, and large parts of Poland. The country's borders also moved beyond the Ural Mountains into Siberia, a vast land whose annexation, together with that of Central Asia and the Caucasus region, was completed in the nineteenth century.

As the country grew, its name was amended to the Tsardom of Muscovy, and in 1721 it became the Russian Empire. Throughout the centuries Muscovy/Russia functioned as a centralized state ruled by autocratic leaders whose titles changed as their power and influence expanded. The grand dukes became the tsars of Muscovy, who in turn became emperors. Although the rulers of the Russian Empire were formally called emperors (*imperator*), they were still popularly referred to as tsars and tsarinas.

The tsars wielded absolute power over a vast country populated by a relatively small number of privileged nobles exploiting a destitute peasant majority. The serfs were subject to feudal authority long after it had been abolished in western Europe. Still, certain tsars sought to lift Russia out of its backwardness and played significant roles on the European stage. Peter the Great (reigned 1682–1725) traveled to Holland and England to see the latest advances in science, technology, and organization firsthand and returned to build a new capital, Saint Petersburg, as a symbol of his efforts to drag Russia forward. Catherine the Great (reigned 1762–1796) continued to reform the country's administration and education systems. She corresponded with Voltaire and other leading figures of the French Enlightenment, though without changing the essential dictatorial character of the Russian ruler. The contradiction between the country's scope and potential on the one hand and its isolation from trends towards greater democracy and development experienced in travels to the West produced a deep sense of frustration and an inferiority complex that has continued to dog educated Russians to this day.

By the end of the nineteenth century, the land area of the Russian Empire encompassed more than 8.5 million square miles (22 million square kilometers). The pre-1914 empire was an economically underdeveloped country comprised primarily of poor peasants and a small but growing percentage of poorly paid or unemployed industrial workers. European Russia also encompassed the so-called Pale of Settlement (present-day Lithuania, Belarus, Moldova, large parts of Poland, and Ukraine), the only place where Jews were allowed to reside. The vast majority of these Jews lived in small towns and villages in their own communities known as the *shtetl*, which were made famous in the United States through the setting of the 1964 Broadway musical *Fiddler on the Roof*. The narrative was based on the Yiddish-language stories of Russian Jewish writer Sholem Aleichem (1859–1916), himself an immigrant to New York City late in his life.

The nineteenth century, known as the "Golden Age" of Russian literature, witnessed the appearance of world-renowned figures such as the poet Alexander Pushkin (1799–1837) and the novelists Fyodor Dostoevsky (1821–1881) and Leo Tolstoy (1828–1910), as well as such Romantic composers as Pyotr Tchaikovsky (1840–1893), bringing the nation's culture and political and intellectual thought into international exchange. This flowering by and large remained limited to the aristocratic classes, however, and the chains of serfdom continued to bind and immiserate the peasant masses. In 1861, in response to growing public sentiment against the institution of serfdom and aiming to head off the threat of revolution, Tsar Alexander II emancipated the serfs, after which they continued to struggle with poverty and debt. The drastically unequal social conditions and the country's increasingly outmoded political structure gave rise to a succession of radical movements seeking to transform the tsarist order, making its last decades a time of turbulence and upheaval though also of creativity and change.

Modern Era On the heels of the country's shocking loss in the 1904 to 1905 Russo-Japanese War, widespread strikes and unrest coalesced into what became known as the Revolution of 1905. Tsar Nicholas II responded by instituting several reforms to liberalize the authoritarian political system, most notably the election of a State Duma, or parliament; the appointment of a prime minister; and the formation of a constitutional monarchy, though the balance of power still lay with the tsar and his advisors. At the beginning of World War I, the Russian Empire fought on the side of the Allies (France and the United Kingdom), but internal demonstrations erupted in a series of struggles known as the Russian Revolution, and in March 1917 the tsarist empire collapsed. A weak provisional government left room for a new struggle to erupt in November, fomented by the Bolsheviks (a faction of the Marxist Russian Social-Democratic Workers' Party) and their revolutionary leader, Vladimir Lenin. Russia withdrew from the war, ceding vast areas of land to the Germans. The Bolshevik Revolution was opposed by a significant portion of the population, and the result was a civil war that began in 1918 and lasted until early 1921. The Bolsheviks were ultimately victorious, and in late 1922 they created a new state, the Union of Soviet Socialist Republics, or the Soviet Union. The Soviet Union consisted of fifteen constituent national republics, the largest of which was Russia. Beyond the Russian Republic many inhabitants, especially in the western regions of the Soviet Union, continued to identify themselves as Russians.

The new Soviet state proclaimed as its goal the establishment of Communism worldwide, to be achieved through promoting Bolshevik-style revolutions abroad. Since many countries feared such revolutions, they refused to recognize Bolshevik rule. Thus, the Soviet Union was isolated from the rest of the world community for nearly twenty years. That isolation came to an end during World War II, when the Soviet Union, ruled by Lenin's successor Joseph Stalin from the mid-1920s until his death in 1950, joined the Allied Powers in the struggle against Nazi Germany and Japan. This alliance led to a wholesale change in the U.S. image of Russia, exemplified by Hollywood feature films praising the Russian spirit, Soviet achievements, and even Stalin himself, such as *Mission to Moscow* (1943), and documentaries including *The Battle of Russia* (1943), part of director Frank Capra's series *Why We Fight*.

Following the Allied victory in 1945, the Soviets emerged alongside the United States as one of the two most powerful countries in the world. By 1948, however, the short-lived cooperation quickly turned to conflict, as competing ideologies and aspirations to influence and control inaugurated the Cold War. For nearly the next half-century, the world was divided into two camps: the free or capitalist West, led by the United States; and the revolutionary or communist East, led by the Soviet Union.

By the 1980s the centralized economic and political system of the Soviet Union could no longer function effectively, and in 1985 a new communist leader, Mikhail Gorbachev, tried desperately to reform the system but failed. He did set in motion a new revolution, however, bringing such enormous changes that in late 1991 the Soviet Union collapsed. In its place, each of the former Soviet republics became an independent country, among them Russia. After a period of wrenching economic change under President Boris Yeltsin, highlighted by the privatization of the vast state resources and their concentration in the hands of a relative few oligarchs, Vladimir Putin was elected President in 2000 and reelected in 2004 and 2012. He spent the intervening four years, when he could

not be president because of constitutional limitations, as prime minister. The "Putin era" has seen economic stabilization and the establishment of a significant and thriving middle class but also persistent corruption, organized crime, and charges of a new authoritarianism that harkens back to the history of rule by the Communist Party and the tsars.

SETTLEMENT IN THE UNITED STATES

The first Russians on U.S. territory were part of Russia's internal migration. During the eighteenth century Russian traders and missionaries crossing Siberia reached Alaska, which became a colony of the Russian Empire. By 1784 the first permanent Russian settlement was founded on Kodiak Island, a large island off the Alaskan coast. Soon there were Russian colonies on the Alaskan mainland (Yakutat and Sitka), and by 1812 the Russians had pushed as far south as Fort Ross in California, 100 miles north of San Francisco. In 1867 the Russian government sold Alaska to the United States, and most Russians in Alaska (whose numbers never exceeded five hundred) returned home. Russian influence persisted in Alaska, however, in the form of the Orthodox Church, which succeeded in converting as many as twelve thousand native Inuit and Aleut people.

Large-scale emigration from Russia to the United States only began in the late nineteenth century. Since that time four distinct periods of immigration can be identified: the 1880s to 1914; 1920 to 1939; 1945 to 1955; and 1970s to the present. The reasons for emigration included economic hardship, political repression, religious discrimination, or a combination of those factors.

Between 1881 and 1914 more than 3.2 million immigrants arrived from the Russian Empire. Nearly half were Jews; only 65,000 were ethnically Russian, while the remaining immigrants were Belarusans and Ukrainians. Regardless of their ethnoreligious background, their primary motive was to improve their economic status. Many of the 1.6 million Jews who left, though, primarily did so because they feared *pogroms*—attacks on Jewish property and persons that occurred sporadically in the Russian Empire from the 1880s through the first decade of the twentieth century.

While many Jews from the Russian Empire did not identify themselves as Russians, another group of immigrants adopted a Russian identity in the United States. These were the Carpatho-Rusyns, or Ruthenians, from northeastern Hungary and Galicia in the Austro-Hungarian Empire (today, these lands lie in far western Ukraine, eastern Slovakia, and southeastern Poland). Of the estimated 225,000 Carpatho-Rusyns who immigrated to the United States before World War I, perhaps 100,000 eventually joined the Orthodox Church, where they and their descendants still identify themselves as Americans of Russian background.

The second wave of immigration was less diverse in origin. It was directly related to the political upheaval in the former Russian Empire that was brought about by the Bolshevik Revolution and Russian Civil War that followed. More than two million people fled Russia between 1920 and 1922, among them demobilized soldiers from anti-Bolshevik armies, aristocrats, Orthodox clergy, professionals, businesspersons, artists, intellectuals, and peasants, Jews and non-Jews (the majority). All these refugees had one thing in common—a deep hatred for the new Bolshevik/communist regime in their homeland. Because they were opposed to the communist Reds, these refugees came to be known as the Whites.

Many White Russians fled from the southern Ukraine and the Crimea (the last stronghold of the anti-Bolshevik White Armies), traveling to Istanbul in Turkey before moving on to one of several countries in the Balkans, especially Yugoslavia and Bulgaria; to other countries in east-central Europe; to Germany; or to France, especially Paris and the French Riviera (Nice and its environs). Others moved directly westward and settled in the newly independent Baltic States (today's Estonia, Latvia, Lithuania, and Finland), Poland, Czechoslovakia, or farther on to western Europe. A third outlet was in the Russian far east, from where the White émigrés crossed into China, settling in the Manchurian city of Kharbin. As many as 30,000 left the Old World altogether and settled in the United States. This wave of Russian immigration occurred during the early 1920s, although in the late 1930s several thousand more came, fleeing the advance of Nazi Germany and Japan's invasion of Manchuria. During this period approximately 14,000 immigrants originally from Russia arrived in the United States.

The third wave of Russian immigration to the United States (1945–1955) was a direct outcome of World War II. Large portions of the former Soviet Union had been occupied by Germany during the war, and hundreds of thousands of Russians had been captured or deported to work in Germany or were simply caught behind the lines of the retreating Nazi army, which precipitated them moving further west. After the war many were forced to return home. Others lived in displaced persons camps in Germany and Austria until they were able to emigrate to the United States. During this period approximately 20,000 of Russian displaced persons (DPs), arrived.

Both the tsarist Russian and Soviet governments placed restrictions on emigration. In 1885 the imperial Russian government passed a decree that prohibited all emigration except that of Poles and Jews, which explains the small numbers of non-Jewish Russians in the United States before World War I. By the early 1920s the Bolshevik/communist-led Soviet government implemented further controls that effectively banned all emigration. The second-wave White Russian refugees who fled after the revolution were stripped of their citizenship in absentia in a series of legal measures between 1921 and 1924 and could not lawfully return home; these measures were mitigated by later amnesties and were no longer in force after World War II. The situation was effectively similar for the post–World War II DPs, who were viewed as Nazi collaborators and traitors by the Soviet authorities.

In contrast, the fourth wave of Russian immigration that began in late 1969 was legal. It was formally limited to Jews, who were allowed to leave the Soviet Union for Israel as part of the agreements reached between the United States and the Soviet Union during the era of détente (1971–1980), near the midway point in the Cold War. In return for allowing Jews to leave, the United States and other Western powers expanded the economic, cultural, and intellectual ties with their communist rival. Although Jews leaving the Soviet Union were only granted permission to go to Israel, many had the United States as their true goal, and by 1985 nearly 300,000 had reached the United States. Effectively, the opportunity to emigrate was also extended to Germans and Armenians, with the rationale of family reunification.

After 1985 the more liberal policy of the Soviet government under Mikhail Gorbachev allowed anyone to leave the Soviet Union, and thousands more Jewish and non-Jewish Russians immigrated to the United States. Because Russia has been, since 1991, an independent country with a democratically elected government, immigrants could no longer justify their need to leave home on the grounds of political or religious persecution. This factor resulted in a slowing of Russian immigration during the last decade of the twentieth century and the first decade of the twenty-first.

Of the estimated 2.99 million Americans identified as wholly or partially of Russian ancestry by the U.S. Census Bureau's American Community Survey in 2011, more than 36 percent resided in the Northeast. Among the first wave of immigrants from Russia, the Jews, in particular, went to New York City, Philadelphia, Boston, and other large cities. The non-Jewish Russians from the Russian Empire and the Carpatho-Rusyns settled in these cities as well as in Chicago, Cleveland, Pittsburgh, and the coal-mining towns of eastern Pennsylvania. Nearly 5,000 members of a Russian Christian religious sect known as the Molokans settled in California during the first decade of the twentieth century. They formed the nucleus of what has become a 20,000-member Russian Molokan community that is concentrated today in San Francisco and Los Angeles.

Most White Russian soldiers, aristocrats, professionals, and intellectuals of the second wave of immigrants settled in New York City, Philadelphia, and Chicago, but some moved into farming areas; for example, a group of Don and Kuban Cossacks (descendants of historical warrior communities in southern Russia, who formed the core of the White Russian Army) established what are still vibrant rural centers in southern New Jersey. Those who emigrated from the Russian far east and Chinese Manchuria settled in California, especially in San Francisco and Los Angeles. The fourth wave settled almost exclusively in cities where previous Russian immigrants had gone, especially New York City. Certain sections of the city, such as Brighton Beach in Brooklyn, were transformed into dynamic Russian communities by the 1980s.

While the basic settlement pattern established by the first two waves of immigrants were maintained, the past few have also witnessed migration toward Sun Belt states such as Florida, as well as to California where the original Russian communities have been supplemented by newcomers from the Northeast.

According to the American Community Survey estimates for 2009–2011, the states with the highest populations of Russian Americans included California (437,366), New York (471,517), Florida (235,298), New Jersey (190,965), and Pennsylvania (200,511). Other states with smaller but still significant numbers are Illinois (131,390) and Massachusetts (124,112).

LANGUAGE

Russian is the most widespread of the Slavic languages and is spoken today by more than 250 million people. Most first-generation immigrants used Russian to communicate with family and friends until they had attained a knowledge of English. For others the Russian language took on a symbolic function and was maintained to preserve a sense of Russian identity. For these reasons the Russian language has never died out in the United States and, in fact, the number of native speakers and publications expanded dramatically during the late twentieth and early twenty-first centuries. According to 2010 U.S. Census data, 19.4 percent of Russian Americans speak a language "other than English"—presumably Russian in almost all cases—at home; this rate is significantly higher in certain states, such as New York (27.9 percent) and Alaska (35.5 percent).

Throughout much of the twentieth century, the appearance of Russian-language newspapers, journals, and books in the United States and other countries where Russians lived helped keep traditional Russian culture alive. Following the onset of Bolshevik rule in late 1917, the Soviet state gradually banned all forms of cultural and intellectual activity that did not conform to Stalin's version of Communism. Even the Russian language was transformed: several letters were deleted from the Cyrillic alphabet and new words were introduced that reflected the changes brought about by the Soviet system. Many of these new words were really abbreviations, such as *gensek* ("general secretary"), *gosplan* ("state plan"), *kolkhoz* ("collective farm"), *Komsomol* ("Communist Youth League"), *natsmen* ("national minority"), *vuzy* ("colleges and universities"), and *zarplata* ("salary"). At the same time many words were eliminated, such as

In Brighton Beach, otherwise known as "Little Odessa," Russian immigrants enjoy the winter sun. Brooklyn, NYC. PHILIP SCALIA / ALAMY

gorodovoi ("police officer"), which was replaced with (*militsioner*); *gospodin* ("gentleman," "Mr.") and *gospozha* ("lady," "Mrs."), both of which were replaced by *tovarishch* ("comrade"); and *gubernator* ("governor"), a position which was abolished.

Many Russians who emigrated after the Bolshevik Revolution felt they had a moral duty to preserve the old alphabet as the medium for the "true" Russian language. As a result, until the fall of the Soviet Union in late 1991, there existed two Russian literatures: Soviet Russian literature and Russian literature abroad. Schools were also created in an attempt to preserve the Russian language for the descendants of immigrants. Since the late nineteenth century, many Orthodox Church parishes have had their own Russian-language schools. This tradition is still practiced in some parishes and in summer camps conducted by the Russian Scout movement. At a higher level various Orthodox churches operated Russian-language seminaries, and there were even Russian classes at university-level institutions such as the Russian Collegiate Institute in New York City (1918) and the Russian People's University in Chicago (1918–1920). These efforts proved to be short-lived, although Russian language, literature, history, and culture courses are taught at some high schools and numerous universities throughout the United States. With the arrival of increasingly self-confident and economically stable immigrants after the late 1990s, the number of Russian-language newspapers and radio and television stations has blossomed, especially in large and growing Russian American communities such as Brooklyn. One example is the Russian-language daily newspaper Репортер (*Reporter*), founded in New York in 2011.

Greetings and Popular Expressions Some common Russian expressions (with pronunciation) are: Добрый день (DOBriy den)—"Good day"; Как поживаешь? (kak pazhiVAYESH)—"How are you?"; Спасибо, прекрасно! (SpaSEEba preeKRASna)—"Fine, thanks!"; До свидания! (Da sveeDAneeya)—"Good-bye";

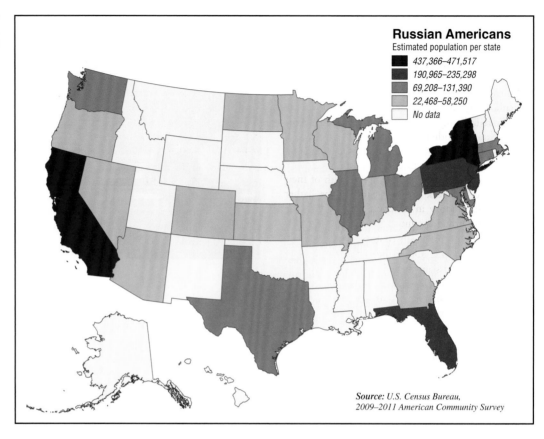

Russian Americans
Estimated population per state

- 437,366–471,517
- 190,965–235,298
- 69,208–131,390
- 22,468–58,250
- No data

Source: U.S. Census Bureau,
2009–2011 American Community Survey

and Выговорите По -английски? (Vi gavaREEtye pa anGLEESkee)—"Do you speak English?"

RELIGION

Based on religious criteria, Russian Americans are classified in three categories: Orthodox Christians, Jews, and nominal Jews. The concept of being a Russian in the United States is often associated with the Orthodox Christian faith. The Russian Orthodox Church traces its roots to the Eastern Christian world. After the Christian church split in 1054 between the western or Latin sphere (centered in Rome) and the eastern or Byzantine-Greek sphere (centered in Constantinople—present-day Istanbul), the Orthodox Church in Russia maintained its spiritual allegiance to the Byzantine East. The second half of the fifteenth century saw the foundation of a jurisdictionally independent Russian Orthodox Church, with its main seat in Moscow. At first the church was headed by a patriarch, but after 1721 it was led by a council of bishops known as the Synod.

Russian Orthodoxy (and Eastern Christianity in general), differs from the Western Catholic Church in several major ways: the Divine Liturgy (not Mass) was conducted in Church Slavonic instead of Latin, priests could marry, and the old Julian calendar was retained. This meant that by the twentieth century, feasts with fixed dates were two weeks behind the commonly used Gregorian calendar. Russian Orthodox Christmas, for instance, is on January 7.

Russian Orthodox Church architecture, both in the homeland and in the United States, also has distinctive features. Church structures are based on a square floor plan (called the Greek cross) covered by a high central dome and surrounded by four or more smaller domes. The domes are usually finished in gold and topped by three-bar crosses. Inside, the dominant element is the *iconostasis*, a screen covered by icons that separates the altar from the congregation. Some traditional churches have no pews, and there is never an organ, because Orthodox belief states that only the human voice is permitted in the worship of God. Russian Orthodox priests are often clad in colorful vestments laden with gold trim. Some priests also wear long beards, which, according to tradition, should not be cut.

Throughout its history in the United States, the Russian Orthodox church has not only ministered to immigrants from Russia but has also functioned as a missionary church, attracting new adherents. Before Alaska was purchased by the United States in 1867, the church had converted more than 12,000 Aleutians and some Eskimos to Orthodoxy. Aside from his spiritual work, the Orthodox Russian Bishop Innokentii Veniaminov (1797–1879) was also the first person to codify a written Aleut language, in which he published a dictionary, grammar guide, Bible, and prayer books.

During the 1890s and the first decade of the twentieth century, Russian Orthodoxy won nearly 50,000 converts in the United States. These were Carpatho-Rusyn immigrants of the Greek or Byzantine Catholic faith living in Pennsylvania, New York, New Jersey, Ohio, and other northeastern industrial states. One of their own priests, the Ruthenian Father Alexis Toth (1853–1909), convinced many Greek Catholic parishioners to return to the Orthodox faith of their ancestors. For his work Toth was hailed as the "father of Eastern Orthodoxy in America," and in 1994 he was made an Orthodox saint.

Among early twentieth century Russian immigrants, Molokans and Old Believers reflect internal divisions in the Russian Orthodox Church that have roots in the Russian Empire. The Molokans evolved from "Spiritual Christian" peasants who rebelled against dietary restrictions of the Orthodox Church before the eleventh century. The Old Believers movement dates from protests against church reforms in the seventeenth century. These immigrants have been most fervent in retaining a sense of Russian identity through an active use of the Russian language in their religious services and in their daily lives.

More significant to most Russian American Christians are the splits that occurred in the Russian Orthodox Church after its establishment in the United States. The divisions were the result of developments in the homeland; they resulted in particular from the reaction of Russians abroad to the Bolshevik Revolution and the existence of the officially atheist Soviet Union. During the 1920s and 1930s, three factions developed within Russian Orthodoxy in the United States. One consisted of the original Russian Orthodox Church that had arrived in Alaska before moving to California and New York. It continued to formally recognize the patriarch, whose office as head of the mother church in Russia was restored by the All-Russian Church Council in 1917. Because Russia was ruled by an uncompromising Soviet government, however, the American branch of the church governed itself as a distinct jurisdiction known as the *Metropolia*. The second Orthodox faction consisted of the post–World War I White Russian émigrés, including some clergy and laypeople of the church who rejected the idea of a patriarch, favoring a church governed by the Synod. These immigrants came to be known as the Russian Orthodox Church Abroad, or the Synod. A third group consisted of individual parishes that remained directly under the jurisdiction of the patriarch in Moscow, even though he was living in a "godless Soviet communist state" and was subject to governmental pressure.

Each of the three factions of the Russian Orthodox Church in the United States had its own bishops, clergy, cathedrals, churches, seminaries, publications, and supporting lay organizations. Each also often denounced the others, so that much of Russian community life in the United States from the 1920s through the 1960s was characterized by fierce rivalry between competing Russian Orthodox Churches.

In 1970 the *Metropolia* reached an agreement with the patriarch in Moscow, was released from its formal subordination to Moscow, and became an independent body: the Orthodox Church of America, which conducts all its services in English. This church is the largest of the three Russian Orthodox churches in the United States. It has absorbed most of the patriarchal parishes. The Synod Abroad remains staunchly Russian in terms of religious tradition and language use and was an enemy of the Soviet Union until that state's demise in 1991.

The large pre–World War I influx of Jews from the Russian Empire consisted mainly of individuals whose lives had been governed by Jewish law and tradition in the thousands of *shtetls* throughout European Russia. Whether these Jews were of the conservative Orthodox or Hasidic tradition, their lives were characterized by attendance at the synagogue, observance of the Sabbath (from sunset on Friday to sunset on Saturday), and deference to the rabbi as community leader. While the authority of the rabbi over most aspects of daily Jewish life could not be fully maintained in the New World, the pre–World War I Russian Jewish immigrants maintained their religious traditions within the confines of the home and synagogue. It was their Jewishness and not any association with Russia that made them indistinguishable from the larger Jewish American society.

For the most part Russian immigrants and their descendants have succeeded in assimilating into mainstream American life. A few groups have avoided acculturation and maintained the traditional lifestyle they brought from their homeland. Such traditionalists include the Orthodox Christian Old Believers and the non-Orthodox Molokan Christian sect.

The arrival of Russian Jews since the early 1970s stands in stark contrast to their pre–World War I predecessors. For nearly seventy years, the Soviet system frowned on all forms of religion, including Judaism. Therefore, by the time of their departure, the vast majority of Soviet Jews had no knowledge of Yiddish or Hebrew and had never been to a synagogue. Living in an officially atheist Soviet Union, many found it politically and socially expedient to forget or even deny their Jewish heritage. Jews were considered members of an ethnic group rather than adherents of a religion, and there was substantial legal discrimination against Jews in the Soviet Union through 1991. When it became possible for Jews to emigrate legally from the Soviet Union, many quickly reclaimed their ancestral religious identity, at least administratively (rather than religiously, or even culturally), which helped them get permission to emigrate. These Russian-speaking nominal Jews found it difficult to relate to English-speaking religious Jews when they arrived in the United States. Although a small percentage of the newcomers learned and accepted the Jewish faith in their new home, most follow no particular religion and have remained simply Russian Americans who are Jews in name only.

CULTURE AND ASSIMILATION

For the most part Russian immigrants and their descendants have succeeded in assimilating into mainstream American life. A few groups have avoided acculturation and maintained the traditional lifestyle they brought from their homeland. Such traditionalists include the Orthodox Christian Old Believers and the non-Orthodox Molokan Christian sect. Whether they live in cities such as San Francisco, Los Angeles, or Erie, Pennsylvania; in rural towns such as Woodburn, Oregon; or in the backwoods of Alaska, these traditionalists have continued to use the Russian language at home and have sometimes succeeded in having it taught in local public schools. The distinct dress and religious-based lifestyle of these groups keep them at a social distance from other Americans and distinguish them from the rest of the community. Another immigrant group, the White Russians—especially those of aristocratic background from the immediate post–World War I era—found it difficult to adapt to an American society that lacked respect for the deference that Russian nobles, princes, princesses, and intellectuals otherwise had come to expect.

The Old Believers, Molokans, and White Russian aristocrats are only a small minority of the Russian American community today. Even among the vast majority who sought to assimilate, however, the goal was not always easy to accomplish. During the seventy-five years of the Soviet Union's existence, many American social institutions and individuals held a negative opinion of that state and often transferred their biases to Russian Americans, who they frequently suspected of being potential communist spies or socialists and anarchists intent on infiltrating and disrupting the American labor movement.

After the breakup of the Soviet Union in the early 1990s, Russians in the United States were linked (some legitimately, some not) to organized crime. A number of Russian speculators tried to take advantage of the radical change in their country's economy. Many of these new Russian businessmen had contacts in or were themselves residents of such Russian American communities as Brighton Beach, where they carried out illegal transactions. It was common to find references in mainstream American media to the dangers of the Russian mafia and, by implication, of all Russians. This trend was also reflected in American cultural products—for example, popular TV series such as *24* (which ran from 2001 to 2010) cast shadowy and ruthless Russian characters as villains.

The wave of so-called "new Russians" who left the more economically stable Russia of the Putin era—arriving prosperous, well educated, fashionable, and attuned to Western values—have mitigated these stereotypes. The image of Russians even "normalized" sufficiently to allow a reality TV series on a glamorized version of life in Brighton Beach, *Russian Dolls* (2011), which mimicked the wildly successful *Jersey Shore*, about Italian Americans. *Russian Dolls* aired on the Lifetime Network until its abrupt cancellation after the first season as a result of controversy and low ratings. The billionaire oligarch Mikhail Prokhorov, who, though remaining a resident of Russia, bought the NBA's New Jersey Nets and moved them to a new home—the $1 billion Barclays Center in Brooklyn—and was involved in a number of Russian American cultural projects in the New York area, is emblematic of what some have called a shift to "global Russians": those who have one foot in Russia but are active in the United States (and elsewhere). According to Russian American journalist Michael Idov in his article "Klub Prokhorov" (*New York* magazine, 30 May 2010), "The term indicates a combination of Russian culture and language with Western education, a well-stamped passport, and liberal Western views."

Cuisine Russian Americans enjoy many traditional dishes, including a variety of rich and tasty soups, which are almost always served with a dollop of sour cream, or *smetana*. Most famous is *borshch*, or borscht, made from beets, cabbage, and meat. In the summer borscht is served cold. *Shchi*, also made with cabbage, includes turnip, carrot, onion or leek, and beef. Popular fish soups, such as *solianka*, contain onion, tomato, cucumber, lemon, butter, and sometimes beef. Many soups also include potatoes or dumplings. Traditional dark Russian bread is made from rye, though wheat is used increasingly. Russian meals are accompanied by vodka.

Holidays The Russian holiday calendar was transformed after the fall of the Communist system in 1991: "ideological" holidays, such as the anniversary of the 1917 Revolution on November 7, were abandoned, and others, such as International Workers' Day on May 1, were modified to reflect the new political climate. While Russian Americans by and large ignored the Soviet holidays, except insofar as they coincided with traditional occasions, their holiday practices (those that diverge from other Americans) now reflect those in Russia.

Since the Russian Orthodox Church still operates on the Julian calendar, Christmas begins on January 7 and continues for twelve days. With Orthodox New Year (also called Old New Year) celebrated on January 13, the intervening week is a time of eating, drinking, singing, and gift-giving, watched over by Father Frost and his granddaughter, Snegurochka. International Women's Day on March 8 was a focal point for the salute of the supposed liberation of women in the Soviet system, but as time went on, it became a more personal occasion for flowers and kisses for female friends, coworkers, and relatives. Russians and Russian Americans continue to mark it as a celebration of more traditional attributes, such as femininity, beauty, and caregiving. Easter is the most festive of Russian Orthodox holidays. Churches are packed with worshippers at midnight services, which include candlelight processions and are followed by the early-morning blessing of Easter baskets filled with edible delicacies and hand-painted eggs.

May 1 has been refashioned into the Spring and Labor Day holiday, with a nod to workers' efforts without the necessity of a struggle for their rights. May 9, the anniversary of the defeat of Nazi forces by the Soviet Red Army in World War II, formerly celebrated as Victory Day, is perhaps the holiday least changed from the Soviet era. It is a day to honor Russian and Russian American veterans of World War II, who wear their uniforms and medals. If they are deceased, they are honored at their grave sites. Russia Day, June 12, is the most important of the completely new holidays created in post-Soviet Russia, marking the 1990 Declaration of Sovereignty of the Russian Federation—Russian Independence Day. Russian Americans also commemorate the day to mark the realization of the dream of Russian exiles since 1917: the end of Soviet Communist rule.

FAMILY AND COMMUNITY LIFE

The Russian extended family, a close-knit unit embracing uncles, aunts, cousins, godparents, and so forth, that prevailed in villages and *shtetls* was difficult, if not impossible, to recreate in the United States. Russian American families became more insular and isolated than they had been in Russia.

Other changes included a decrease in the number of children per family. Among post–World War I White Russian émigrés, there were twice as many men as women. This imbalance led to a high percentage of unmarried men with no children and marriages with women of other ethnic backgrounds. Poverty and unstable economic conditions among émigrés also weighed against having children. Initially, Russian immigrants exhorted their children to choose marriage partners from among their own group. Russian Jews felt that the religious factor was of primary importance. Hence, descendants of pre–World War I Jewish immigrants from Russia largely intermarried with Jews, regardless of their national origins. Non-Jewish Russians were more concerned with maintaining a Russian identity within their family, but marriages with non-Russians soon became the norm.

RUSSIAN PROVERBS

Russian is a language rich in history and meanings; Russian proverbs are especially cherished and abundant. Some Russian proverbs express the sense of pessimism and ingrained injustice honed over centuries of oppressive social orders, such as "The thief who stole an *altyn* (3 kopecks) is hung, and the one who stole a *poltinnik* (50 kopecks) is praised" and "Masters are fighting, servants' forelocks are creaking." Others transpose sayings familiar to English speakers into traditional Russian conditions: "Nobody goes to Tula with one's own samovar." (Tula is famous as city where the best Russian samovars are made) and "If you're afraid of wolves, don't go to the woods."

Gender Roles In traditional Russian society, women were legally dependent on their husbands. The Bolshevik Revolution radically changed the status of women. Under communist rule Russian women were offered equal economic and social responsibilities, which resulted in a high percentage of females entering the labor force. The majority of physicians and health-care workers in general are women. In the family, however, a woman is still expected to perform domestic tasks such as cooking, cleaning, and shopping. Russian American women have played a determining role in maintaining the cultural identity in the family, passing on knowledge of Russian language and culture to younger people and participating in philanthropic works that affect the entire community. Among the oldest of such organizations was the Russian Children's Welfare Society Outside Russia, founded in New York City in 1926 to help orphans and poor children. Today the best-known is the Tolstoy Foundation, set up in 1939 by Alexandra Tolstoy (1884–1979), daughter of the famous nineteenth-century Russian novelist Leo Tolstoy. With branches throughout the world, the Tolstoy Foundation still operates a Russian senior citizen's home and a cultural center in Nyack, New York, that has helped tens of thousands Russians and other refugees to settle more comfortably in the United States.

In more recent years there have been tensions between the "state feminism" promoted by the Soviet Union and a backlash among Russians and Russian Americans that emphasizes more traditional roles for women as a long-repressed aspect of Russian identity. This conflict, while less dramatic and more tempered in the United States by the slow but steady spread of

A boardwalk in Brighton Beach, a Russian enclave in Brooklyn, New York City. JEFF GREENBERG / PETER ARNOLD / GETTY IMAGES

Survey estimates for 2010 determined that 57.4 percent of Russian Americans had at least a bachelor's degree, more than twice the proportion for the U.S. population as a whole.

EMPLOYMENT AND ECONOMIC CONDITIONS

The majority of Russians who arrived in the United States between the 1880s and 1914 entered the industrial labor force in the northeastern United States. This was not a particularly difficult adjustment for the Jews from European Russia, since the large majority of them had been in manufacturing, commerce, and the equivalent of a white-collar service trade at home.

Women immigrants of Russian Jewish background dominated the American garment industry as seamstresses in the small clothing factories and sweatshops of New York City and other urban areas in the northeast. Other Russians (mostly men), including Belarusans and Carpatho-Rusyns, worked in factories in the large northeastern cities as well as in the coal mines of eastern Pennsylvania, the iron and steel factories in the Pittsburgh area, and the slaughtering and meatpacking plants of Chicago. The Russian presence was so pronounced in certain trades that they established their own unions or branches of unions, such as the Russian branch of the Union of Men's and Women's Garment Workers, the Russian-Polish department of the Union of Cloakmakers, the Society of Russian Bootmakers, and the Society of Russian Mechanics.

Although many of the more highly educated White Russians who immigrated after World War I took on menial jobs at first (there are countless legends of Russian aristocrats employed as waiters, taxi drivers, and doormen at night clubs), they eventually found employment that took advantage of their skills. The same was the case among the post–World War II DPs, many of whom found their way into university teaching jobs, federal government employment, publishing, and other occupations that reflected the American interest in studying and sharing information on the Cold War.

The educational and skill level was higher among the Russian, mostly Jewish fourth-wave (Cold War) immigrants. Almost half had a university education, and more than half had been employed in the Soviet Union as engineers, economists, skilled workers, or technicians. In the United States most were able to find similar jobs and improve their economic status. Among the best-known, and highest-paid, of immigrants were several hockey players of non-Jewish Russian background from the former Soviet Olympic team who became a dominant part of teams in the National Hockey League after the 1980s.

The descendants of the large pre–World War I immigration have done very well economically. In the 1930s and 1940s, the American-born offspring of the older immigrants remained in the same industries as their parents (clothing, steel, meat-packing, and

American women's equality work, has also made itself felt in Russian American communities. The generally high level of education of female immigrants over the last few decades, both before and after the fall of the Soviet Union, has mitigated the traditionalist push somewhat.

Another interesting gender angle is presented in a 2004 study by Vera Kishinevsky (1953–) that highlights the conflict between immigrant girls' and women's consumption of traditional Russian food—a source of comfort and bonding in the new environment but also generally very rich—and the often unforgiving set of prescribed body images presented and enforced by American society and media. This tension has led to a prevalence of eating disorders among female Russian Americans.

Education While their families may have been smaller than those of other Americans on average, Russian immigrants tended to place greater emphasis on education. This was certainly the case among Jews, who brought a strong tradition of learning that had characterized Jewish life for centuries. Non-Jewish White Russians were also intent on providing their offspring with the highest possible education (in the Russian language, if possible) so that they could take an appropriate place in Russian society after the anticipated collapse of the Communist regime, when they would return home. Even when it became clear that the Soviet Union would survive, and thus returning to a noncommunist Russia was impossible, higher education was still considered useful for adaptation to American society. It is not surprising, then, that by 1971, among Americans of nine different European backgrounds (Russian, English, Scottish, Welsh, German, Italian, Irish, French, and Polish), Russians between the ages of twenty-five and thirty-four had completed an average of 16 years of education, while all others averaged at most 12.8 years. Four decades later the American Community

so forth), although some moved into managerial or white-collar positions. The third generation entered professions such as medicine, law, engineering, and business in larger numbers. As of 2011, according to the American Community Survey, this advantage had increased further: Russian Americans reported a per capita income of $47,223, more than 75 percent higher than the national average of $26,708. This data indicates that the higher-than-average rate of Russian American employment in management, education, and other professional fields buffered the community from the effects of the recession that began in 2008.

POLITICS AND GOVERNMENT

Aside from their active participation in the labor movement during the early decades of the twentieth century, Russians have not generally become involved in American political life. In a sense, their labor union activity acted as a deterrent to further political work, since many were accused of being socialists or communists and were eschewed by the general public. Russian Americans have never formed a strong voting bloc that would encourage American politicians to solicit their support. Only in the later twentieth century, in such places as the Brighton Beach area of New York City, did local politicians—including Jewish Russian American Stephen Solarz, who moved from the state assembly to the U.S. Congress, serving there from 1975 to 1993—begin to achieve success through courting the Russian vote.

While Russians may have avoided American politics, they maintained a deep interest in their homeland. This was particularly the case among the White Russian immigrants, whose moniker was a political statement in itself. As refugees and political émigrés, most tried to live a Russian life in exile until the hoped-for fall of the Soviet Union would allow them to return home. This almost idyllic belief united them (as it did the post–World War II DPs), even though they represented a wide variety of political persuasions. At an extreme some believed in the return of the monarchy, and one woman living in the New York City area claimed she was Grand Duchess Anastasia (1901–1918), youngest daughter of the last tsar, Nicholas II Romanov, and that she had miraculously survived the assassination of the royal family. The legitimacy of her claims were only conclusively disproved in 2009.

Others rejected the idea of monarchy and awaited the creation of a parliamentary liberal democratic state. The leader of this group was Alexander Kerensky (1881–1970), the last prime minister of Russia before the Bolshevik Revolution. Kerensky had immigrated to New York City on the eve of World War II to escape the Nazi occupation of Paris, where he had been living in exile. Several other factions included regional groups, such as the Don and Kuban Cossacks, who argued for autonomy in a future Russia; socialist and anarchist groups on the

THE RED SCARES

Even before the Soviet Union existed, Russian immigrant workers in the United States, particularly Jews, played a leading role in such organizations as the American branch of the Second International Workingman's Organization (usually called the Second International). For a time before the March 1917 revolution, Leon Trotsky and Nikolai Bukharin, two of Lenin's closest associates, lived in New York City, where they edited a Russian-language socialist newspaper. After the revolution, in a show of anti-Communist fervor, authorities in such places as New York led raids against the headquarters of the Union of Russian Workers and the Russian-dominated American Communist Party. Ironically, this occurred just before the American branch of the Red Cross was about to help find refuge for thousands of Russians fleeing the Communist Soviet Union. As a result of the raids, several thousand Russian Americans were deported, nearly 90 percent of whom were returned to what by then had become Bolshevik-controlled Russia. As late as the 1970s some of these returnees and their descendants maintained an identity as Americans even after living in the Soviet Union for nearly half a century.

After World War II the United States was once again struck by a Red Scare, this time even more widely publicized as a result of the congressional investigations led during the 1950s by the demagogic Senator Joseph McCarthy. The universal association of Russians with Communism forced Russian Americans to maintain a low profile, and some felt obligated to renounce their heritage.

political left; and, on the far right, a Russian fascist organization based in Connecticut during the late 1930s. Among the post–World War II DPs there were also those who believed in Lenin's brand of socialism, which they felt had been undermined by his successor, Stalin. Each of these politically oriented groups had at least one organization and publication that was closely linked to a similar émigré community based in Western Europe.

Despite their various social, propagandistic, and fund-raising activities, none of these Russian American organizations managed to achieve the abolition of Soviet rule in their homeland. Some Russian Americans turned their efforts to their U.S. community and its relationship to American society as a whole. Concerned with the way they and their culture were perceived and depicted in American media and public life, some started lobbying groups, such as the Congress of Russian Americans, in the 1970s.

During the Putin era, though Russian Americans were divided in their opinions of his rule, many without a preexisting political affiliation or ideology became active in supporting the liberal, largely middle-class movement in Russia that sought more democracy and transparency. This stance was exemplified by hundreds who protested on the streets of New

York and Washington, D.C., in December 2011, with signs in both Russian and English, against what they saw as the manipulation of parliamentary elections and suppression of independent voices.

NOTABLE INDIVIDUALS

Academia Americans' present-day understanding of Russia and the Soviet Union is in large part a result of the work of Russian immigrants, including historian of ancient history Michael Rostovtsev (1870–1952); church historians Georges Florovsky (1893–1979), Alexander Schmemann (1921–1983), and John Meyendorff (1926–1992); linguist Roman Jakobson (1896–1982); literary critic Gleb Struve (1898–1985); and historians Michael Florinsky (1894–1981), Michael Karpovich (1888–1959), Alexander Vasiliev (1867–1953), George Vernadsky (1887–1973), Marc Raeff (1923–2008), Nicholas Riasanovsky (1923–2011), and Yuri Slezkine (1956–). Literary theorist Svetlana Boym (1966–), who is also an artist, playwright, and novelist, has figured prominently in academic discourse since the late 1990s.

Art Influential Russian American artists include Gleb Derujinski (1878–1975), a noted sculptor; Israel Tsvaygenbaum (1961–), a painter who lives in Albany, New York; and conceptual artist Ilya Kabakov (1933–). Vitaly Komar (1943–) and Alexander Melamid (1945–), an artistic team who immigrated to New York City in 1978, spawned much discussion and controversy throughout the art and political worlds with their provocative conceptual productions in the 1980s and 1990s.

Literature A number of Russian American authors have flourished. These include the novelist Vladimir Nabokov (1899–1977), who moved from writing in Russian to writing in English in the late 1940s and produced many great fictional works, including the very popular *Lolita* (1958); the novelist and philosopher Ayn Rand (1905–1982; born Alisa Zinovievna Rosenbaum), whose ideas on what she called Objectivism have been embraced by prominent conservative politicians; the short story writer Nina Berberova (1901–1993); and Isaac Asimov (1920–1992), who, while working as a scientist, produced hundreds of volumes of science fiction, popular science, history, and books in numerous other fields. While continuing to write in Russian, the poet and essayist Josef Brodsky (1940–1996; expelled from the Soviet Union in 1972) and the historical novelist and social critic Aleksander Solzhenitsyn (1918–2008; expelled in 1974 and repatriated in 1994) flourished for a time in the United States. Solzhenitsyn was probably the best-known opponent of the Soviet regime. Both of these authors were awarded the Nobel Prize in Literature. At the beginning of the twenty-first century, a new generation of Russian American writers began to explore the frequently fractured nature of the post-Soviet immigrant experience, often with a Jewish admixture. Most prominent among these is the satirical novelist Gary (born Igor) Shteyngart (1972–); others include the novelist and short story writer Lara Vapnyar (1971–), the short story writer Ellen Litman (1973–), and the novelist Irina Reyn (1974–).

Military John Basil Turchin (1821–1901; born Ivan Vasilyevich Turchaninov) served in the Union Army during the Civil War and was promoted to the rank of brigadier general—the first Russian American to be elevated to such a high position.

Music and Dance Classical music, opera, and ballet in the United States have been enriched for more than a century by resident Russian composers and performers, from Sergei Prokofiev (1891–1953), who lived briefly in the United States, to Serge Koussevitzky (1874–1951), conductor of the Boston Symphony Orchestra from 1924 to 1949; classic composers Sergei Rachmaninoff (1873–1943) and Alexander Gretchaninov (1864–1956); popular composers George Gershwin (1898–1937; born Jacob Gershvin) and Irving Berlin (1888–1989; born Israel Beilin), creator of countless standards in the American canon of popular song, including "God Bless America"; cello virtuoso, conductor, and musical director from 1977 to 1994 of the U.S. National Symphony Orchestra Mstislav Rostropovich (1927–2007); George Balanchine (1904–1983), choreographer, founder of the School of American Ballet, and, from 1948 to his death, director of the New York City Ballet; and ballet dancers Natalia Makarova (1940–) and Mikhail Baryshnikov (1948–). The most famous of all was Igor Stravinsky (1882–1971), who in 1939 settled permanently in New York City, from where he continued to enrich and influence profoundly the course of twentieth-century classical music. Dimitri Tiomkin (1894–1979) was a noted composer, musical director, and author of many musical scores for Hollywood films. Pop musician Regina Spektor (1980–) is a classically trained pianist who immigrated to the United States from Moscow when she was nine years old. Spektor's music has been called "anti-folk" and draws on a wide range of genres including punk, hip-hop, jazz, and classical.

Science and Technology Outstanding work has been done by Russian Americans in the scientific fields. Vladimir Ipatieff (1867–1952) was a prominent research chemist; George Gamow (1904–1968), a nuclear physicist, popularized the big bang theory of the origin of the universe; Wassily Leontieff (1906–1999), a Nobel Prize-winning economist, formulated the influential input-output system of economic analysis; Alexander Petrunkevitch (1875–1964) wrote numerous works in the field of zoology; Igor Sikorsky (1889–1972) was an aviation industrialist and inventor of the helicopter; Pitirim Sorokin (1888–1968), a controversial sociologist, argued that Western civilization would be doomed unless it could attain "creative altruism"; Vladimir Zworykin (1889–1982), a physicist and electronics engineer, is known as the father of television; and Sergey Brin (1973–), computer scientist and Internet entrepreneur, cofounded Google.

Stage and Screen Natalie Wood (1938–1981), who was born in San Francisco as Natalia Zacharenko, acted in numerous American films, as did Yul Brynner (1920–1985; born Yuliy Briner) and Kirk Douglas (1916–; born Issur Danielovitch), father of actor Michael Douglas (1944–). Director Sam Raimi (1959–) achieved renown for the *Spider-Man* trilogy but is perhaps best loved for his work on *The Evil Dead* series, a set of four horror films released between 1981 and 2013.

MEDIA

PRINT

Gorizont

This weekly tabloid-style newspaper focuses on business and culture and serves the Russian community of the greater Denver, Colorado, area.

Leonid Reznikov, Executive Editor
P.O. Box 4551
Englewood, Colorado 80155
Phone: (720) 495-0073
Fax: (866) 559-2973
Email: info@gorizont.com
URL: www.gorizont.com

Novyi Zhurnal/New Review

A scholarly publication covering Russian interests.

Marina Adamovich, Editor-in-Chief
611 Broadway
Suite 902
New York, New York 10012-2608
Phone: (212) 353-1478
Fax: (212) 353-1478
Email: newreview@msn.com
URL: http://newreviewinc.com

Репортер (*Reporter*)

This Russian-language daily based in New York City was founded in 2011 to supplant *Novoye Russkova Slovo* (New Russian Word), the oldest Russian daily newspaper in North America and the world until it folded in 2010 after a century of publishing.

Felix Gorodetsky, Founder and Editor-in-Chief
2508 Coney Island Avenue #6
Brooklyn, New York 11235
Phone: (718) 303-8800
Email: reporterruonline@gmail.com
URL: http://reporterru.com

Russian Bazaar

A Russian language weekly for the Tri-State area (New York, New Jersey, and Connecticut), covering local and foreign news, society, and culture.

Natalia Shapiro-Nakhankova, Editor-in-Chief
8518 17th Avenue
Brooklyn, New York 11214
Phone: (718) 266-4444
Fax: (718) 266-5429
Email: rusbazaar@yahoo.com
URL: http://russian-bazaar.com

RADIO

New Life Russian Radio, WKTA-AM (1330)

The largest and longest-running Russian-language broadcasting company in North America, providing music, features, entertainment, and talk to the Chicago Russian community.

Natasha Altman, Program Director
615 Academy Drive
Northbrook, Illinois 60062
Phone: (847) 498-3400
Email: natalia@newliferadio.com
URL: www.newliferadio.com

TELEVISION

RTN

The Russian Television Network offers news and entertainment programs from Russia as well as its own newscasts and programming.

Vlada Khelmnitskaya, Director of Programming
One Bridge Plaza
Suite 145
Fort Lee, New Jersey 07024
Phone: (800) 222-2786
Fax: (201) 461-7462
Email: info@russianmediagroup.com
URL: www.kmnb.com

ORGANIZATIONS AND ASSOCIATIONS

Congress of Russian Americans

A political action umbrella group with branches throughout the country, the congress seeks to promote Russian cultural heritage and to protect the legal, economic, and social interests of Russian Americans.

Alexander Sinkevitch, Treasurer
2460 Sutter Street
San Francisco, California 94115
Phone: (415) 928-5841
Fax: (415) 928-5831
Email: crahq@russian-americans.org
URL: www.russian-americans.org

Orthodox Church in America

The largest church with members of Russian background, it has twelve dioceses throughout North America.

The Very Reverend John A. Jillions, Chancellor
P.O. Box 675
Syosset, New York 11791
Phone: (516) 922-0550
Fax: (516) 922-0954
Email: info@oca.org
URL: http://oca.org

Russian American Community Coalition

This nonprofit community organization serves the Russian-speaking residents of the greater New York City region.

Zina Konovalova, Chair
3101 Ocean Pkwy
Suite 7C
Brooklyn, New York 11235
Phone: (718) 714-6717
Email: info@raccny.com
URL: www.raccny.com

Russian American Cultural Heritage Center

A charitable and educational organization dedicated to collecting and disseminating the history, culture, and heritage of Russian Americans.

Olga Sergeevna Zatsepina, President/CEO
34 Hillside Avenue
Suite 4C
New York, New York 10040
Phone: (212) 567-5834
Email: info@rach-c.org
URL: http://rach-c.org

Russian American Foundation

The foundation promotes development and acceptance of the Russian-speaking community of the greater New York City area and the United States and organizes programs to preserve its heritage.

Marina Kovalyov, President
70 West 36th Street
Suite 701
New York, New York 10018
Phone: (212) 687-6118
Fax: (212) 687-5558
Email: info@russianamericanfoundation.org
URL: www.russianamericanfoundation.org

United Russian American Association

An umbrella organization of the Russian and Russian-speaking community in the greater Houston area.

Elena Suvorova Phillips, President
12122 Moorcreek Drive
Houston, Texas 77070
Phone: (281) 389-7914
Email: president.uraa@gmail.com
URL: www.uraa.us

MUSEUMS AND RESEARCH CENTERS

Immigration History Research Center

The center promotes interdisciplinary research on international migration and houses archives on U.S. immigrant and refugee life.

Erika Lee, Director
311 Elmer L. Andersen Library
222 21st Avenue South
Minneapolis, Minnesota 55455
Phone: (612) 625-4800
Fax: (612) 626-0018
Email: ihrc@umn.edu
URL: www.ihrc.umn.edu

Museum of Russian Art

Dedicated to the preservation and presentation of all forms of Russian art and artifacts, the Museum of

Russian Art is the only North American museum of its kind.

Chris DiCarlo, President and Director
5500 Stevens Ave South
Minneapolis, Minnesota 55419
Phone: (612) 821-9045
Fax: (612) 821-9075
Email: cdicarlo@tmora.org
URL: http://tmora.org

Museum of Russian Culture

The museum houses archival and published materials as well as artifacts pertaining to Russian American life, especially in California.

2450 Sutter Street
San Francisco, California 94115
Phone: (415) 921-4082
Email: contact@mrcsf.org
URL: www.mrcsf.org

New York Public Library, Slavic and Baltic Division

Aside from a rich collection of printed materials on the Russian and Soviet homeland, there is much material on Russians in the United States from the 1890s to the present.

Sumie Ota, Chief Librarian
Stephen A. Schwarzman Building
Fifth Avenue at 42nd Street
New York, New York 10018-2788
Phone: (917) 930-0716
URL: www.nypl.org/locations/tid/36/node/138855

Orthodox Church in America Archives

Includes archival and published materials on Russian Orthodox Church life in North America from the late nineteenth century to the present.

Alexis Liberovsky, OCA Archivist
P.O. Box 675
Syosset, New York 11791
Phone: (516) 922-0550, extension 121
Fax: (516) 922-0954
Email: alex@oca.org
URL: http://oca.org/history-archives/about-archives

SOURCES FOR ADDITIONAL STUDY

Chevigny, Hector. *Russian America: The Great Alaskan Adventure, 1741–1867*. Portland, OR: Binford and Mort, 1979.

Eubank, Nancy. *The Russians in America*. Minneapolis, MN: Lerner Publications, 1979.

Hardwick, Susan Wiley. *Russian Refuge: Religion, Migration, and Settlement on the North American Pacific Rim*. Chicago: University of Chicago Press, 1993.

Idov, Michael. "Klub Prokhorov." *New York*, 30 May 2010.

Jacobs, Dan N., and Ellen Frankel Paul, eds. *Studies of the Third Wave: Recent Migration of Soviet Jews to the United States*. Boulder, CO: Westview Press, 1981.

Kishinevsky, Vera. *Russian Immigrants in the United States: Adapting to American Culture.* New York: LFB Scholarly Publishing, 2004.

Magocsi, Paul Robert. *The Russian Americans.* New York: Chelsea House, 1989.

Morris, Richard A. *Old Russian Ways: Cultural Variations among Three Russian Groups in Oregon.* New York: AMS Press, 1991.

Norton, W. P. "Rediscovering Russian America." *Institute of Modern Russia,* October 19, 2011. http://imrussia.org/en/society/133-rediscovering-russian-america.

Ripp, Victor. *Moscow to Main Street: Among the Russian Emigres.* Boston: Little, Brown, and Co., 1984.

Wertsman, Vladimir. *The Russians in America, 1727–1976.* Dobbs Ferry, NY: Oceana Publications, 1977.

SALVADORAN AMERICANS

Jeremy Mumford

OVERVIEW

Salvadoran Americans are immigrants or descendants of immigrants from the Republic of El Salvador, a nation situated near the northern end of the Central American isthmus. El Salvador is bordered by Guatemala to the northwest, Honduras to the northeast, and the Pacific Ocean to the south. A Spanish-speaking country, El Salvador was given its name—which means "the Savior," referring to Jesus Christ—by the Spanish. Two volcanic mountain ranges dominate El Salvador's landscape; they run parallel to each other, east to west, along the length of the country. Just to the north of the southern range lies a broad central plain, the most fertile and populous region of El Salvador, which includes the nation's capital city, San Salvador, and a handful of smaller cities. Its flag consists of horizontal stripes, two blue and one white, with the national coat of arms in the center. This coat of arms contains branches, flags, green mountains, and the words "Republica de El Salvador en la America Central" and "Dios Union Libertad." Also pictured in the center of the flag are a small red liberty cap and the date of El Salvador's independence from Spain: September 15, 1821. The smallest of the Central American states, the Republic of El Salvador measures 21,041 square kilometers, which makes it about the size of the state of Massachusetts.

The estimated population of El Salvador in 2012 was just over six million, according to the *CIA World Factbook*. Ninety percent of the population is mestizo, meaning of both Spanish and Indian ancestry. Fifty-seven percent of the citizens are Roman Catholic, 21.2 percent are Protestant, and very small numbers are Jehovah's Witness, Mormon, or other religions. The urban population of El Salvador has steadily grown; in 2012, 64 percent of the citizenry lived in cities. Still, a considerable portion of the population remains in the countryside to work the coffee and sugar plantations and other farms. El Salvador has the third-largest economy in Central America, exporting assembled factory products, coffee, sugar, shrimp, textiles, and chemicals. Exports made in *maquilas* (factories contracted by corporations to perform the final assembly and packaging of products) accounted for 45 percent of El Salvador's exports in 2007. Remittances accounted for 17 percent of gross domestic product in 2011 and were received by about a third of all households.

Before 1960 fewer than 10,000 Salvadorans lived in the United States. This number rose dramatically during El Salvador's civil war (1979–1992), when between 500,000 and a million Salvadoran refugees came secretly and without documentation to the United States. The refugees settled mostly in Spanish-speaking communities in San Francisco; Chicago; Houston, Texas; Washington, D.C.; and the New York suburb of Hempstead, Long Island. After the Salvadoran civil war, the country was struck by several natural disasters, including earthquakes, hurricanes, and a volcanic eruption, that further spurred immigration to the United States. About 500,000 Salvadorans have come to the United States each decade since 1980.

By 2010 the Pew Research Center estimated there were 1.7 million people of Salvadoran descent living in the United States, making them the third-largest Latino group in the country. Other estimates were higher, and the EFE World News Service refers to 2.5 million Salvadorans living in the United States in 2010. Pew estimates that only 28 percent of these are American citizens. Thirty-five percent of Salvadorans in the United States reside in California, while another 15 percent live in Texas. Yet smaller communities in New York and Maryland have the highest percentages of Salvadorans among their residents. Increasingly, as Salvadorans decide they are here to stay, they are looking for ways to attain permanent residency and citizenship.

HISTORY OF THE PEOPLE

Early History Before fifteenth-century explorer Christopher Columbus discovered the New World, the land now called El Salvador belonged to the Pipil, nomads of the Nahua language group who were related to the Aztecs of central Mexico. From the eleventh century CE, the Pipil developed their country of Cuzcatlán ("Land of the Jewel") into an organized state and a sophisticated society, with a capital city located near what now is San Salvador. During the 1520s, however, Spanish conquistadors, fresh from the conquest of Mexico, invaded the land of the Pipil. Led by a general named Atlacatl, the Pipil resisted the invasion with initial success but ultimately succumbed to the Spanish forces.

As in Mexico and the rest of Central America, the conquistadors created a divided society in the province they named El Salvador. A small ruling class comprised of people of Spanish birth or descent grew rich from the labor of the Indian population. Intermarriage gradually softened the racial division; today the majority of Salvadorans are mestizos, with both Spanish and Indian ancestors. However, an extreme disparity remains in El Salvador between the powerful and the powerless, between the wealthy landowners—according to legend, the "Fourteen Families"—and the multitudinous poor.

El Salvador became independent from Spain in 1821, after which it joined with Guatemala, Honduras, Nicaragua, and Costa Rica to form the United Provinces of Central America. However, this regional federation dissolved after twenty years. Then, threatened by Mexican and Guatemalan aggression, the Salvadoran government sought to make the country part of the United States. The request was turned down. El Salvador remained independent but gradually came under the influence of American banks, corporations, and government policies. The nineteenth and twentieth centuries brought considerable political turmoil to El Salvador, with the army and the plantation owners trading places in a series of unstable regimes.

One constant in Salvadoran history had been its economy of single-crop export agriculture. In the sixteenth century El Salvador produced cacao, from which chocolate is made; in the eighteenth century it grew the indigo plant, which yields a blue dye used in clothing. Since the late nineteenth century, El Salvador's greatest cash crop has been coffee, although in recent decades the country has also grown cotton and sugar. El Salvador organized its economy with ruthless efficiency, consolidating land into huge plantations worked by landless peasants. As markets changed, cycles of boom and bust hit these people hard.

This unstable social order often became explosive. El Salvador has seen repeated rebellions, each one followed by massive, deadly retaliation against the poor. In 1833 an Indian named Anastasio Aquino led an unsuccessful peasant revolt. Nearly a century later, Agustín Farabundo Martí, a founder of the Salvadoran Communist Party, led another. This was followed by the systematic government murder of rural Indians, leaving an estimated 30,000 dead—an event known as *la matanza*, or "the slaughter."

Modern Era Between 1979 and 1992, Salvadoran guerrillas waged a civil war against the government, fueled in part by the same inequities that motivated Aquino and Martí. The nation's army fought back with U.S. money, weapons, and training from American military advisors. An estimated 75,000 people died during the conflict, most of them civilians killed by the army or by clandestine death squads linked to the government. The guerrilla war and the "dirty war" that accompanied it were a

national catastrophe. In 1992, however, after more than a dozen years of fighting, the army signed a peace accord with the guerrillas' Farabundo Martí National Liberation Front (FMLN). Peace has returned to El Salvador, which is now governed by a reasonably democratic constitution.

SETTLEMENT IN THE UNITED STATES

Salvadoran immigration to the United States is a fairly recent phenomenon, but it has had a profound significance on both countries. The flight of Salvadorans from their own country was the most dramatic result of El Salvador's civil war, draining the nation of between 20 and 30 percent of its population. Half or more of the refugees—between 500,000 and one million—immigrated to the United States, which was home to fewer than 10,000 Salvadorans before 1960, according to Faren Bachelis, in *The Central Americans* (1990). El Salvador's exiled population, as well as its dollars, continued to affect life in the home country.

Salvadoran immigration has changed the face of foreign affairs in the United States. The flood of refugees from a U.S.-supported government forced a national rethinking of foreign policy priorities. This, in turn, transformed the nature of American support for the Salvadoran government and may have helped to end the war in El Salvador. Salvadoran Americans are at the center of an ongoing national debate about U.S. responsibility toward the world's refugees and the future of immigration in general.

Significant Immigration Waves The exodus of Salvadorans from their homeland was prompted by both economic and political factors. Historically El Salvador is a very poor and crowded country. These circumstances have led to patterns of intra-Central American immigration. During the 1960s many Salvadorans moved illegally to Honduras, which is less densely populated. Tension over these immigrants led to war between the nations in 1969, forcing the Salvadorans to return home. El Salvador's civil war from 1979 to 1992 created high unemployment and a crisis of survival for the poor. As in the 1960s, many Salvadorans responded by leaving their native land.

The fear of political persecution has also led Salvadorans to seek refuge in other countries. During the 1980s, death squads—secretly connected with government security forces—murdered many suspected leftists. Operating mostly at night, these groups killed tens of thousands of people during the civil war, according to Bachelis. At the height of the death squad movement, 800 bodies were found each month. As the frenetic pace of assassination continued, the squads resorted to increasingly vague "profiles" by which to identify members of so-called "left-wing" groups—all women wearing blue jeans, for instance, as Mark Danner states in his 1993 *New Yorker* article "The Truth of El Mozote." The bodies of some victims were never recovered; these people form the ranks of the *desaparicinos* (disappeared).

This climate of pervasive terror prompted many Salvadorans to flee their homeland. Some left after seeing friends or family members murdered or after receiving death threats themselves; others fled violence by the guerrillas or the prospect of forced recruitment into the army. About half of the immigrants ended up in refugee camps in Honduras or in Salvadoran enclaves in Costa Rica, Nicaragua, or Mexico. The other half headed for *el norte*—the United States.

Because they left quickly and quietly, without property or established connections in the United States, Salvadoran refugees could seldom obtain U.S. visas. They crossed borders illegally, first into Mexico and then into the United States. Refugees trekked through the desert, swam or rowed the Rio Grande, huddled in secret spaces in cars or trucks, or crawled through abandoned sewer tunnels in order to enter the United States. Many sought aid from professional alien smugglers, known as "coyotes," and were sometimes robbed, abandoned in the desert, or kept in virtual slavery until they could buy their freedom.

Once in the United States, Salvadorans remained a secret population. U.S. law provides that aliens (including illegal ones) who can show they have a tenable fear of persecution can receive political asylum and become eligible for a green card. But according to U.S. Immigration and Naturalization Service (INS) figures, political asylum was granted to very few Salvadorans; in the 1980s only 2.1 percent of applications were approved. Those who were turned down faced possible deportation. Therefore, few Salvadorans made their presence known unless they were caught by the INS.

Salvadoran refugees did not at first see themselves as immigrants or Americans. Most hoped to go home as soon as they could do so safely. In the meantime, they clustered together to maintain the language and culture of their homeland. Dense Salvadoran enclaves sprang up in Latino neighborhoods in San Francisco, Chicago, Houston, Washington, D.C., and the New York suburb of Hempstead, Long Island. The places where a few Salvadorans established themselves became a magnet for friends and relatives. About three-quarters of the Salvadoran town of Intipuca, for instance, moved to Washington, D.C., according to Segundo Montes and Juan Jose García Vásquez in *Salvadoran Migration to the United States* (1988). On Long Island, outreach workers reported that the population of Salvadorans ballooned from 5,000 before the civil war to over 100,000 in 1999. However, the greatest number of refugees settled in Los Angeles, where Salvadorans soon became the second-largest immigrant community. The Pico-Union and Westlake districts of Los Angeles became a virtual Salvadoran city—by some counts second only to San Salvador in population.

Salvadoran refugees during the 1980s were only one current in a broad stream of Central American

Salvadoran refugees hold a meeting. NIK WHEELER / CORBIS / GLOW IMAGES

refugees pouring into the United States. Guatemala and Nicaragua, like El Salvador, endured civil wars during this period. Many people from those countries joined the Salvadorans seeking refuge in the United States.

The Central American influx was secret and illegal, and much of mainstream America was at first ignorant of its magnitude. The INS, however, kept a close eye on the situation. Many Salvadorans who were denied asylum in the States exercised their right to appeal their cases, sometimes all the way up to the Supreme Court. (Until a final decision is reached, the applicant is entitled to temporary working papers.) INS agents suddenly found a huge new bureaucratic workload dropped in their laps, for which they had little experience or funding. According to Ann Crittenden in *Sanctuary: A Story of American Conscience and the Law in Collision* (1988), many agents tried to move immigration cases along by any means necessary, such as intimidating Salvadorans into signing papers in English that put them on the next plane to El Salvador or refusing asylum applications after ten-minute interviews and deporting the applicants before they had a chance to appeal.

The deportation of Salvadoran refugees led many liberal American activists to take an interest in the Central American influx. Disheartened by conservative trends in the United States in the 1980s, these activists found a rallying point in the plight of the refugees. Some saw the Central American refugee crisis as the great moral test of their generation, and U.S. activists established a loose network to aid the refugees. Operating in clear violation of federal laws, they took refugees into their houses, aided their travel across the border, hid them from the authorities, helped them find work, and even gave them legal help. Reviving the ancient custom that a fugitive might find sanctuary inside a church and be safe from capture, the activists often housed refugees in church basements and rectories, giving birth to what later became known as "the sanctuary movement."

Throughout the 1980s the U.S. government extended very little sympathy to Salvadoran refugees. Ironically, the government only began to acknowledge the reality of Salvadoran oppression when persecution and war began to taper off in El Salvador. In 1990 a federal lawsuit brought against the INS by the American Baptist Churches forced the agency to apply a more lenient standard to Central American asylum applications. The settlement prompted the INS to reopen many Salvadoran applications it had already denied and to approve new ones in greater numbers. By this time, however, many Salvadoran Americans had benefited from an amnesty passed in 1986, which "legalized" illegal immigrants who had entered the States before 1982.

In 1991, after years of debate on the issue, Congress awarded Temporary Protected Status (TPS) to Salvadorans who had been in the United States since 1990. This status, known as the Deferred Enforced Departure, allowed qualifying Salvadorans to live and work in the States for fixed periods of time. Although the war in El Salvador ended in 1992, many Salvadoran Americans remained afraid to return to their homeland. Alianza Republicana Nacionalista, the political party most closely associated with the death squads, was in power from after the civil war until 2009, and many of the conditions that brought about the war remained the same. Furthermore, Salvadoran Americans had established roots and new livelihoods in the United States. As reported by the *Los Angeles Times* on December 27, 1992, a 1990 poll found that 70 percent of Salvadorans surveyed did not intend to return to El Salvador, even if they knew they were safe. However, Salvadoran Americans maintain close ties to friends and relatives at home. Within a year after the end of the civil war, about 350,000 Salvadoran Americans visited El Salvador, the *Los Angeles Times* reported on May 19, 1993.

Due to poor INS records and the low profile of undocumented immigrants, statistics regarding Salvadoran immigration are notoriously unreliable. By 1995 the total number of Salvadorans in the United States was somewhere between 500,000 and one million. Approximately one-third of the immigrants were green card holders, who could apply for U.S. citizenship after five years. Between one-fifth and one-third had some form of temporary legal status, and the remaining third were undocumented and, therefore, illegal.

In May 2001, after two major earthquakes followed by hundreds of serious aftershocks, U.S. President George Bush reauthorized the expired TPS for Salvadorans living in the United States since February 13, 2001, the date of the second major earthquake. This allowed them an avenue to live and work legally, if they were willing and able (it could cost several hundred dollars) to register for TPS. The earthquakes had left one in four people in El Salvador homeless, and remittances from the United States were major sources of income. After eighteen months, TPS was renewed for 265,000 Salvadorans living in the United States. When TPS was renewed again in 2003, 2005, 2006, and 2007, Salvadorans, were relieved each time. However, many began seeking routes for permanent residency, and there was growing political debate about the lack of a long-term policy. For example, Steven Camarota of the Center for Immigration Studies said in the Bergen County (New Jersey) *Record*, in 2003 that the government was creating a problem by providing one extension after another to immigrants who had arrived illegally: "The longer we don't enforce the law, the more difficult it becomes to do so, because people put down roots, they become part of a community, they have children born in the U.S."

Over the next few years, the social and political effects of Salvadoran Americans' long-term unstable legal status came to the fore. In 2007, along with renewal of the TPS, the United States increased deportation of undocumented Salvadorans and those with criminal records. Fifteen thousand were deported in 2007, followed by 20,000 the next year. Salvadoran gangs operating in California and New York made headlines such as "Gangland in Suburbia" (*New York Times*, 2009) and "Refocusing Immigration Efforts on Gangs" (*New York Times*, 2010). In 2008, with estimates ranging from 1.1 to 1.5 million Salvadorians in the United States, there were 340,000 Lawful Permanent Residents, nearly 230,000 with TPS, and no clear path to either citizenship or return to El Salvador. The United States was no longer an asylum for refugees; nearly all of the 19,659 Salvadorans admitted to the country for permanent residence in 2008 entered as family-sponsored immigrants and as the immediate relatives of U.S. citizens. Meanwhile, back at home in El Salvador, the leftist Farabundo Martí National Liberation Front (FMLN) Party won the presidency for the first time since the end of the civil war in 1992. For Salvadorans in the United States, according to a *New York Times* report in 2009, this election generated both excitement and debate, and brought out the "one foot here, one foot in the homeland" feeling that had plagued Salvadoran Americans for decades.

According to a 2010 study by the Migration Policy Institute, by 2008 nearly 40 percent of employed Salvadoran American men were working in construction, extraction, and transportation, while nearly half of Salvadoran American women were laboring in the services sector of the economy. The concentration of Salvadoran Americans in low-wage jobs was caused by several issues, including low high school graduation rates and the language barrier.

LANGUAGE

Spanish is the first language of almost all Salvadorans. Salvadoran Spanish is very close to the Spanish spoken in Mexico, Honduras and other Central American

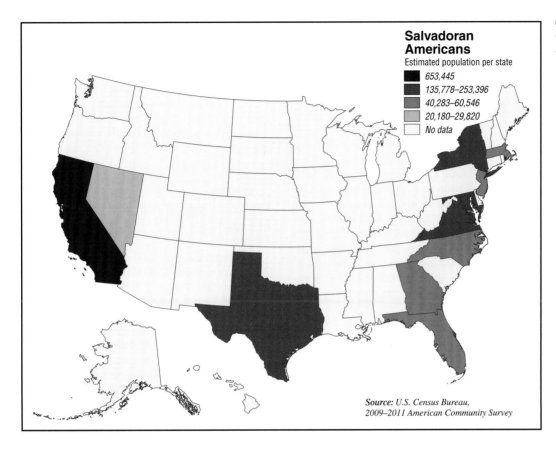

Salvadoran Americans
Estimated population per state
- 653,445
- 135,778–253,396
- 40,283–60,546
- 20,180–29,820
- No data

*Source: U.S. Census Bureau,
2009–2011 American Community Survey*

countries, though it does have distinguishing characteristics. The most commonly noted is the use of the familiar pronoun *vos* with its corresponding verb forms. The familiar and formal in El Salvador are affected by class and urban/rural distinctions and have been retained in the United States in heavily Salvadoran areas such as in Houston. In his authoritative work *Varieties of Spanish in the United States* (2008), John Lipski points out that young Salvadorans born in the United States rarely use the *voseo* verb forms or other particularly Salvadoran Spanish characteristics, though they "may tag *vos* to questions and affirmations as an explicit affirmation of Salvadoran identity." An example is *George tiene mi dinero, vos* ("George has my money").

El Salvador stands apart from neighboring countries in that its indigenous languages are virtually dead. Only a handful of words from the indigenous languages of the Pipil (Nahuat) and K'ekchi Indians have survived in Salvadoran Spanish. One possible explanation for this loss lies in El Salvador's history of widespread violence against the poor. In the aftermath of the 1833 rebellion and during the *matanza* of 1932, government forces singled out Indians to be killed; out of self-protection, many Salvadoran Indians adopted Spanish language and dress. However, Salvadoran *caliche*, or street language, is a Nahuat-inflected Spanish used in the everyday slang by all classes of people, especially the poor and working classes. *Caliche* in the United States is a marker of Salvadoran identity.

Because of their initial determination to return to El Salvador, many immigrants to America at first resisted learning English. However, bilingual education programs, particularly in Los Angeles and Washington, D.C., have been extremely helpful to Salvadoran children. According to the 2010 U.S. Census, 90 percent of Salvadoran Americans spoke Spanish at home and under 50 percent rated their English as "very good."

RELIGION

Most Salvadorans are members of the Roman Catholic Church, although various evangelical Protestant denominations—including Baptists, Seventh-day Adventists, Assemblies of God, and Mormons—also have Salvadoran adherents. In addition, a small number of Salvadorans are Jewish or Muslim, stemming from late-nineteenth-century immigration from the Middle East.

Salvadoran Catholicism bears the strong influence of liberation theology, a Catholic school of thought that evolved in Latin America during the 1960s and 1970s. Liberation theology teaches that Christianity is a religion of the poor. The movement encouraged impoverished Salvadorans to form Christian communities, or "base communities," to improve their lives.

Dedicated both to Bible study and to mutual aid in the secular world, these communities organized credit unions, cooperative stores, labor and peasant unions, and political activist groups.

Liberation theology received an important boost from the approval of the 1968 Latin American Bishops' Conference in Medellín, Colombia. In the late 1970s Salvadoran Archbishop Oscar Romero, though originally selected for his conservative views, became an important patron of the new theology. Young priests carried the message to the Salvadoran countryside with an evangelical fervor, but a shortage of priests in the nation necessitated an increase in the involvement of the Catholic laity. Base communities sprang up both in the cities and rural areas.

Liberation theology's success in organizing the poor had a profound impact on Salvadoran politics. The movement brought new political ideas to the countryside, as the universities did to the cities. Many of the peasants who made up the rural left during the civil war—guerrillas, farmworker federation members, activists who demonstrated in San Salvador—traced the origins of their political consciousness to participation in a base community.

The Salvadoran army was well aware of the effects of the new theology. Starting in the 1970s, it targeted Catholic organizers for harassment and death. In March 1980 Archbishop Romero was assassinated while saying mass; the murder was attributed to a right-wing death squad. Nine months later, four U.S. churchwomen who were working in El Salvador were killed, causing outrage in the States. And in November 1989, six Jesuit priests and two women were killed on the San Salvador campus of the Jesuit-run Central American University.

Several evangelical Protestant denominations have Salvadoran churches. These communities were founded throughout the Salvadoran countryside during the twentieth century by missionaries from the United States. In the 1970s and 1980s the evangelical

Assimilation for Salvadorans in the United States has been deeply affected by the legal, psychological, and economic problems of refugees from war and natural disasters. At least two-thirds of Salvadorans in the United States are undocumented and experience the specific problems related to that status, such as fear of deportation, exploitation in the labor market, and lack of personal safety.

sects increased their missionary efforts, in particular through the influence of American military advisers on soldiers in the Salvadoran army. Both in El Salvador and in the States, Salvadoran evangelicals tend to be more socially and politically conservative than Catholics.

CULTURE AND ASSIMILATION

Assimilation for Salvadorans in the United States has been deeply affected by the legal, psychological, and economic problems of refugees from war and natural disasters. At least two-thirds of Salvadorans in the United States are undocumented and experience the specific problems related to that status, such as fear of deportation, exploitation in the labor market, and lack of personal safety.

Until well into the 1990s, Salvadoran Americans formed an insular community—possessing their own social clubs, doctors, and even banks—and often had little contact with outsiders. Many older immigrants have spent years in the United States without ever learning any English.

Whether they immigrated largely out of fear or a desire for a new life, Salvadorans in the United States, especially the younger generations, are gradually becoming Americanized. Although conditions have improved in El Salvador, few refugees have returned home. To reflect the evolving needs of the Salvadoran American community, the Central American Refugee Center in Los Angeles, one of the largest support organizations for refugees, changed its name to the Central American Resource Center in the 1990s. Although factors such as the insecurity associated with undocumented status, limited job opportunities, and separation from families in El Salvador led to gang problems in the 1990s, the Salvadoran American community began to bounce back in the twenty-first century, with increased pride in its heritage and a feeling of being better acclimated to American culture. According to a 2012 article in *Newsday* about that year's Long Island Salvador Fest, the crowd chanted, "*Cinco, cero, tres,*" the international phone code for El Salvador. The article quotes a twenty-five-year-old Salvadoran American man at the festival who had grown up in the United States: "We came to adapt to other cultures, but somehow we forgot our own cultures. Our roots and our culture are something really important about our community."

Traditions and Customs El Salvador has a rich heritage of folk beliefs and customs, which evolved in a landscape of villages, fields, forests, and mountains. Salvadoran Americans seek to preserve their traditional rural culture, though it is a difficult proposition since most settle in large cities.

Salvadoran folklore is rooted in supernatural beliefs. Tales of ghosts and spirits have been passed orally from generation to generation. One such spirit is the Siguanaba, a beautiful woman who seduces men she finds alone in the forest at night and drives them mad. Slightly less dangerous are the Cadejos, two huge dogs; the black one brings bad luck, while the white one delivers good luck. Another spirit, the Cipitío, is a dwarf with a big hat who eats ashes from fireplaces and strews flower petals in the paths of pretty girls. Such country legends have little meaning in a

Los Angeles barrio. Thus, they are rapidly dying out among Salvadoran American children, a generation thoroughly immersed in the world of American cartoons and comic book characters.

Cuisine Salvadoran food is similar to Mexican food, except it is sweeter and milder. The foundation of the diet is cornmeal tortillas (thicker than the Mexican variety), rice, salt, and beans. The most popular national snack is the *pupusa*, a cornmeal griddle-cake stuffed with various combinations of cheese, spices, beans, and pork. *Pupusas* are served with *curtido*, a cabbage and carrot salad made with vinegar. A more substantial meal is *salpicón*, minced beef cooked with onions and chilies and served with rice and beans. For dessert, many dishes include fried or stewed bananas. *Chicha*, a sweet drink made from pineapple juice, is a popular beverage. The best Salvadoran food is found in private homes, but many Salvadoran restaurants and food stands have opened in Los Angeles and other cities where Salvadoran Americans live.

Both in El Salvador and in Salvadoran American neighborhoods, people love to buy food from street vendors. Popular street foods include *pupusas* and mango slices that are spiced with salt, lime juice, red pepper, and crushed pumpkin and sesame seeds.

Traditional Dress Salvadorans dress in the same Western-style clothing worn by most Latin Americans who are not culturally Indian. Salvadorans in the highlands, where nights can be very cold, occasionally wear brightly colored blankets of traditional Mayan design, but they call these Guatemalan blankets, underscoring their foreign origin. Around their necks, many Salvadorans wear small crosses that are tightly wrapped with colored yarn.

Dances and Songs The most popular musical form in El Salvador is the *cumbia*, a style that originated in Colombia. A typical *cumbia* is performed with a male singer (usually a high baritone or tenor) backed by a male chorus, drums (primarily kettledrum and bass drum), electric guitar and bass, and either a brass section or an accordion. The 2/4 beat is slower than most Latin music; the baseline is heavy and up-front. A very danceable musical form, it is also popular with non-Latin audiences.

Ranchera music, which originated in Mexico, is also well liked by the country people in El Salvador. In the cities, many people listen to rock and rap music from the United States. Mexican American musical styles such as *salsa, merengue,* and *tejano* have become increasingly popular among Salvadorans in the United States. These and other styles from North America are also gaining more listeners in El Salvador.

Traditional Salvadoran music carries influences from the Mayans, Africans, Spanish, and indigenous people from the region. The *güiro*—a hollowed-out gourd used to keep the rhythm—is one of the driving instruments.

SALVADORAN PROVERBS

Salvadoran Spanish is rich in proverbs. Two notable examples are:

Lo que en el corazón se tiene, por la boca sale.

What's in your heart can't stay hidden for long.

Querer pollo por cinco.

To desire finer things but not want to pay their price.

Holidays Many Salvadoran Americans celebrate Independence Day for all of Central America on September 15 of each year. The first week in August is the most important national religious festival, honoring Christ, El Salvador's patron and namesake, as the holy savior of the world. Known simply as the National Celebration, this week is marked in both El Salvador and Salvadoran American neighborhoods with processions, carnival rides, fireworks, and soccer matches. In 2006, the New York State legislature designated August 6 as Salvadoran-American Day, or *El Día del Salvadoreño*.

Health Issues and Practices The single greatest health problem in El Salvador is malnutrition, which especially affects children. This problem is largely absent among Salvadoran Americans. Still, undocumented Salvadoran Americans are often hesitant to visit American doctors or hospitals, for fear of being reported to the immigration authorities. And many communities—including California through 1994's Proposition 187—have sought to deny public health services to undocumented immigrants.

Partly for these reasons, some Salvadoran Americans continue to rely on traditional healers. Such practitioners, known as *curanderos*, use herb teas and poultices, traditional exercises, incantations, and magical touching to heal. Other Salvadoran immigrants are patients of Salvadoran doctors who may have received training at home but have no license to practice in the United States.

Some Salvadoran Americans carry deep emotional scars from the torture they suffered or witnessed in their native country. Many are tormented by rage, continuing fear, and guilt at escaping the violence that claimed the lives of so many of their loved ones. As a result, some members of the immigrant community suffer from depression, alcoholism, and erratic or violent behavior. Few Salvadoran Americans can afford to receive the psychological help they need to work

CHILE LIME MANGO

Ingredients

1 mango, peeled, cored, thickly sliced

2 teaspoons olive oil

1 teaspoon chile flakes

1 tablespoon clear honey

1 lime, juice only

2 lime wedges, to garnish

powdered sugar, for dusting

Preparation

Preheat the oven to broil. Place the mango on an oiled baking tray. Drizzle the mango with the olive oil and sprinkle with chile flakes, honey and lime juice. Place under the broiler for 3–4 minutes, or until golden brown. Dust with powdered sugar.

Serve with lime wedges.

through their traumatic experiences, according to Marcelo Suarez-Orozco in *Central American Refugees and U.S. High Schools.*

FAMILY AND COMMUNITY LIFE

The traditional family in El Salvador, as in Latin America generally, is large and close-knit. The father exercises final authority in all things, and together the parents maintain firm control over their children, above all their daughters. Among Salvadoran Americans, though, this pattern has begun to change. The immigration process and the vastly different conditions of life in the United States have altered Salvadoran family dynamics in dramatic and at times destructive ways.

Because of the nature of their flight to the United States, many Salvadoran refugees made the journey alone: husbands left their wives, parents their children, teenagers their families. Entire families were separated and often stayed that way. Many refugees married non-Salvadorans, sometimes for immigration benefits, and Salvadoran Americans were barred from returning home for any reason without forfeiting a request for asylum.

Some Salvadoran parents who were separated from their children for long periods of time during the immigration process found that when they were finally reunited as a family, they had lost some of their traditional authority and control over the youngsters. Likewise, teenagers who settled in the United States alone grew into adulthood under influences very different from those they would have encountered at home. Even when families moved to the United States together, the dynamics inevitably changed under new cultural influences. Children learned English faster and adapted more readily to their new surroundings than

their parents. They often had to translate or explain things to their parents and argue for their parents with English-speaking storekeepers. In general, they became more knowledgeable and confident than their parents, a role-reversal that proved awkward for both generations.

Salvadoran American parents generally fear that their children may stray too far in America's permissive society. Indeed, many young Salvadoran Americans have formed gangs, especially in Los Angeles, where the culture of Latino youth gangs has deep roots. These gangs distribute drugs, extort money from local merchants (especially street vendors), and battle for turf with Mexican gang members.

Rituals of Family Life Salvadoran Catholicism emphasizes all the sacraments that are practiced in other Catholic countries: baptism, confirmation, marriage in the church, communion at Mass, and last rites. Other occasions are also celebrated in church, such as graduation from school and a girl's *quinceañera,* or fifteenth birthday. Still, when compared with other Central Americans, a surprising number of Salvadorans do not observe church rituals. Church weddings, for instance, are considered prohibitively expensive for the poor, and common-law marriage is frequently practiced.

One ritual of family life that is common even among the poor is *compadrazgo,* or the naming of godparents. Latin Americans of all nationalities practice this custom. They place special importance in the relationship between a child and his or her *padrino* and *madrina* and between the parents and their *compadres,* the friends they honor by choosing them for this role.

Some rituals of the old country have been abandoned by members of the immigrant community. For instance, the traditional Salvadoran practice of interring bodies in family crypts has recently given way to a more Americanized approach to burying the dead. In the early 1980s, most Salvadoran Americans who could afford it arranged to have their bodies sent to El Salvador for burial after death, a process that could cost thousands of dollars. By the mid-1990s, Salvadoran Americans were beginning to reach the painful conclusion that their families would never return to El Salvador; as a result, more and more immigrants are opting for burials in the United States.

Public Assistance Few Salvadoran American families depend entirely on public assistance; a large portion of the immigrant population is undocumented and therefore does not qualify for government benefits. However, the high rate of poverty in the community forces many to seek whatever help they can find—either through assistance for U.S.-born children or through fraudulently obtained benefits. The extent of reliance on public assistance is difficult to estimate due to its underground nature.

Education Salvadorans place a high value on education, partially because of the difficulty of attaining one. Since the National University in San Salvador included a number of Marxist professors and students, the government closed down the campus in 1980. Some professors and students kept classes going in a variety of small buildings and private homes, but this proved challenging.

In the United States access to education has been equally difficult for Salvadorans. Many schools excluded or reported undocumented students until the U.S. Supreme Court decision in *Plyer v. Doe* (1982) established that all children, even illegal immigrants, have a constitutional right to attend public school. This issue remains controversial: California's Proposition 187, approved by voters in 1994, sought again to exclude undocumented students from public schools. The law was challenged and found to be unconstitutional by a federal court, and it was killed in 1999. Though similar laws have been attempted in several other states, the growing Latino electorate has turned the political tide in the twenty-first century. In 2001, for example, California passed the California Immigrant Higher Education Act, known as AB540, allowing eligible undocumented students to attend public community and four-year colleges in California. However, tuition was still out of reach for many Salvadoran immigrant families, which prompted the Salvador American Leadership and Education Fund (SALEF) to step in and award scholarships to AB540-eligible students. By 2010 SALEF had awarded 750 such scholarships. Furthermore, in 2011 California passed the California Development, Relief, and Education for Alien Minors Act, otherwise known as the DREAM Act, which enabled students meeting the AB540 criteria to receive financial aid.

EMPLOYMENT AND ECONOMIC CONDITIONS

Salvadorans have often been referred to as "the Germans of Central America" because of their strong work ethic, according to Walter LaFeber in *Inevitable Revolutions* (1993). Salvadoran Americans are among the hardest-working immigrants, working enough hours at low-paying jobs to send home billions of dollars each year.

Although many Salvadoran refugees worked in agriculture before immigrating to the United States, few of them settled in America's rural areas. In this respect, Salvadorans differ from newly arrived Mexican Americans, many of whom engage in migrant farm labor. Salvadoran immigrants are instead concentrated in unskilled and skilled urban jobs that do not require English. Many Salvadoran American men work in hotel and restaurant kitchens, especially in Los Angeles; others work as day laborers in the building trades. Many Salvadoran American women work as nannies and maids. Both men and women perform cleaning and janitorial services in hotels, commercial buildings, and homes. Some Salvadorans also labor as unlicensed street vendors of food and goods, a line of work that is illegal in Los Angeles and other cities but is nevertheless tolerated and, in fact, contributes to the life and economy of these urban centers.

Although many Salvadoran Americans still toil in the lowest-paying sectors of the American economy, some are starting to become more prosperous. They work long hours, save a great deal, and are gradually moving from the inner cities to the suburbs. With their savings, they have opened restaurants and other service companies, employing other Salvadoran Americans. Additionally, through increased access to education, particularly in California, Salvadoran Americans are more inclined to enter the professional ranks.

Nevertheless, tens of thousands of Salvadoran Americans remain in both urban and suburban ghettoes, alienated from the communities around them. Many live in overcrowded shared or partitioned housing and struggle to get ahead while they support families back in El Salvador. The more prosperous, however, are becoming active members of the communities in which they live. For example, a 2012 article in the *Los Angeles Times* reported that "Salvadorans are opening more businesses, naming schools and roads after community heroes, and even reaching for political power. At least four Salvadoran Americans are running for City Council this year, and for the first time, there is a Salvadoran candidate for mayor."

The incomes of Salvadoran Americans are of vital importance to El Salvador. Salvadoran Americans, even those who are poor, have an incentive to send money to family and friends in El Salvador: a U.S. dollar buys much more there than in the States. According to the Banco Central de Reserva de El Salvador, Salvadorans living in the United States sent home $800 million in 1999; in 2008 this number rose to almost $3.8 billion. These payments, known as remittances, are the largest source of income for El Salvador—larger than either coffee exports or U.S. government aid. For this reason, El Salvador is sometimes said to have a "remittance economy," according to Montes and Vásquez in *Salvadoran Migration to the United States: An Exploratory Study*. It is in part because of this contribution to the economy at home that Salvadoran politicians lobby Washington, D.C., for permanent status for Salvadoran Americans.

In addition to gifts and remittances, Salvadoran Americans have extensive investments in their home country. They may not plan to return permanently, but many are keeping the option open. According to a report in the *San Francisco Chronicle* in 1993, two-thirds of the new housing built in San Salvador during that period was bought by Salvadoran Americans. However, the global economic downturn in the late 2000s had strong ramifications on investment in El Salvador. By 2011 El Salvador was the beneficiary of the least foreign investment in Latin America, as Salvadoran Americans were investing more in the United States.

POLITICS AND GOVERNMENT

Initially, political activity among Salvadoran Americans was primarily limited to the important role they played in legislation regarding their immigration status. In the debate leading to the passage of TPS for Salvadoran refugees and the extensions of that status, Salvadoran organizations lobbied politicians and brought their cases of persecution to the press. At first, refugee organizations were run by Americans, and Salvadorans often appeared in public only with bandannas over their faces. Gradually, Salvadorans and other Central Americans began to take charge of the refugee organizations and assume a higher public profile.

For many years, the Salvadoran American community was not a significant political factor in the United States or at home. The immigrants' organizations had focused not on politics but on relief and jobs in immigrant communities throughout the United States. The relative indifference among most Salvadoran Americans to politics in their native country was attributed to their interest in putting the hatred of the past behind them.

The most ideologically committed of the Salvadoran refugees settled in Mexico, Nicaragua, or Costa Rica, while those who came the United States focused on survival and building a community. Refugees who fled the government and refugees who fled the guerrillas had a lot in common: many would not even discuss their political beliefs, lest they disrupt the fragile solidarity of the refugee community. Furthermore, many Salvadorans on the left who had been active in politics because of the desperate poverty and the class war in El Salvador saw this commitment melt away upon arriving in the United States, where, for the first time, it seemed possible to escape poverty through hard work.

However, when Mauricio Funes, a journalist with CNN en Espanol, ran for president of El Salvador in 2009 as the FMLN candidate, his campaign awakened long-dormant enthusiasm among Salvadoran Americans. Luis Reyes, a co-owner of the upscale Washington, D.C., restaurant Lauriol Plaza, heavily invested time, money, and energy in organizing other successful Salvadoran American business owners to help get Funes elected. Reyes traced this commitment to a decision he had made as a young immigrant in the 1980s not to become involved in El Salvador's civil war. "I'd wanted to participate in a direct way," he said in a 2012 interview with Alexandra Starr in the online journal *Inc.* "Those men [in the 1980s] were fighting for a just cause." Younger Salvadoran Americans, who did not remember the war directly, also became involved. Almost three decades after the civil war, about thirty members of the Salvadoran Union of University Students, an organization on California college campuses, flew to El Salvador to learn about the election firsthand.

At the same time, Salvadoran Americans also became more politically involved in the United States.

"When we first came to the United States, it was just about survival, so that's what our organizations focused on," Salvadoran-born Ana Sol Gutierrez, a Maryland state delegate, said in 2009 at a Salvadoran leadership summit, according to a 2009 article in the *Washington Post*. "Now we have a community that has evolved. … We have to either create new political institutions, or we have to expand those current organizations so they also play a political role." Another Salvadoran American in Maryland's legislature, state senator Victor Ramirez, was cofounder of Latinos for Obama in Maryland in 2008.

NOTABLE INDIVIDUALS

Literature Claribel Alegría (1924–), the most famous living Salvadoran writer, was born in Nicaragua but moved with her family to El Salvador at an early age. She studied at George Washington University in Washington, D.C., and subsequently visited the United States on a regular basis. With her U.S.-born husband, Darwin Flakoll, she lived in various parts of the world—notably Spain and Nicaragua—but always considered herself a Salvadoran. Her autobiographical poetry and fiction (some written in collaboration with her husband) is very popular among both Salvadorans and Salvadoran Americans and provides a rich portrait of bourgeois life in a provincial Salvadoran city.

Many Salvadorans involved in their country's political strife have recorded their feelings in poetry; one such writer, Miguel Huezo Mixco (1954–), was a guerrilla soldier who composed and published verses during campaigns against the army.

After she received the William Carlos Williams Prize from the Academy of American Poets in 1996, the writing of Leticia Hernandez-Linares appeared in newspapers, anthologies, and literary journals, including *Latino Literature Today*, *This Bridge We Call Home*, and *Street Art San Francisco*. Hernandez-Linares, a performer, organizer, and educator as well as a writer, was born in Los Angeles. In 2001 she began organizing and hosting Pinta tu Propio Mundo, an annual women's poetry, performance, and art event; under a new name, Amate: Women Painting Stories; this series became part of the Intersection for the Arts Incubator Program in San Francisco. In 2002 Calaca Press published her poetry chapbook, *Razor Edges of My Tongue*.

Fashion Christy Turlington (1969–) is an internationally known supermodel. The daughter of a Salvadoran woman, she began modeling at the age of fourteen. She appeared on the runways of Paris, Milan, and New York, in the pages of every major fashion magazine, and procured contracts with Maybelline, Calvin Klein, and Vidal Sassoon. Turlington is also a noted animal rights activist and humanitarian who has raised money for Salvadoran causes.

Education Jorge Kattán Zablah (1939–), a Salvadoran who received his Ph from the University of California, Santa Barbara, was chairman of the

Spanish department at the Defense Language Institute in Monterey, California.

Politics and Government Ana Sol Gutierrez (1942–) has served in the Maryland legislature since 2003. She was born in Santa Ana, El Salvador, and came to the United States with her family in 1947 at age five. She was the co-organizer of the First Salvadoran American Leadership Council in 2009.

Victor R. Ramirez (1974–) represents Prince George County in Maryland's legislature. He was born in San Salvador, El Salvador, and moved to the United States with his family in 1974.

Stage and Screen In 2003 Jose Rene "J. R." Martinez (1983–) sustained severe burns to over 34 percent of his body while serving as in the Army infantry in Iraq. Out of that tragedy came an improbable journey of inspiration: he has starred in several television shows and movies and wrote a book, *Full of Heart: My Story of Survival, Strength, and Spirit* (2012).

Sports Born in Los Angeles, Carlos "Famoso" Hernandez (1971–) is the first world champion boxer of Salvadoran descent. He became the International Boxing Federation super featherweight champion in 2003. He retired in 2006 with a record of 39–8, including twenty-three knockouts.

MEDIA

Most Salvadoran Americans rely on the general Spanish-language media offerings in the United States, which are primarily produced by Mexicans, Puerto Ricans, and Cubans. The largest Spanish-language television network is Univision, whose Internet news arm provides updates from each Latin American country, including El Salvador. Some of the largest Spanish-language newspapers in areas where Salvadoran Americans live include *La Opinión* in Los Angeles, *La Voz de Houston* in Houston, *El Tecolote* in San Francisco, *Al Dia* in Dallas/Fort Worth, Texas, *El Nuevo Herald* in Miami, Florida, *El Diario la Prensa* in New York City, and *Mundo Hispanico* in Atlanta, Georgia.

ORGANIZATIONS AND ASSOCIATIONS

Central American Resource Center (CARECEN), Los Angeles

This organization was founded by a group of Salvadoran refugees whose mission was to secure legal status for the thousands of Central Americans fleeing civil war. Over the past twenty-five years, CARECEN has transformed itself from a small grassroots group to the largest Central American organization in the country. Its clients have similarly changed from refugees fleeing war to families who have put down roots in the United States and are building vibrant lives for themselves and their children.

Martha Arevalo, Executive Director
2845 West 7th Street
Los Angeles, California 90005
Phone: (213) 385-7800
URL: www.carecen-la.org

Central American Resource Center (CARECEN), San Francisco

Lariza Dugan-Cuadra, Executive Director
3101 Mission Street
San Francisco, California 94110
Phone: (415) 642-4400
Email: info@carecensf.org
URL: http://carecensf.org/en

Central American Resource Center (CARECEN), Washington, D.C.

1460 Columbia Road NW
Suite C-1
Washington, D.C. 20009
Phone: (202) 328-9799
Fax: (202) 328-7894
Email: info@carecendc.org
URL: www.carecendc.org

Centro Presente

This is a community center for Central Americans in the Boston area.

17 Inner Belt Road
Somerville, Massachusetts 02143
Phone: (617) 629-4731
Fax: (617) 629-2436
URL: www.cpresente.org

El Rescate

Established in 1981, El Rescate empowers immigrants, in particular Latinos, to improve their political and economic status.

Salvador Sanabria, Director
1501 West 8th Street
Suite 100
Los Angeles, California 90017
Phone: (213) 387-3284
Fax: (213) 387-9189
URL: www.elrescate.org/index.html

Salvadoran American Leadership and Education Fund (SALEF)

SALEF exists to foster the civic participation and representation of the Salvadoran and other Latino communities in the United States and to promote economic, educational, and political advancement and democracy in El Salvador.

Carlos Antonio H. Vaquerano, Executive Director
1625 West Olympic Boulevard
Suite 718
Los Angeles, California 90015
Phone: (213) 480-1052
Fax: (213) 487-2530

MUSEUMS AND RESEARCH CENTERS

Migration Policy Institute

The Migration Policy Institute is an independent, nonpartisan, nonprofit think tank in Washington, D.C., dedicated to analysis of the movement of people worldwide.

1400 16th Street NW
Suite 300
Washington, D.C. 20036
Phone: (202) 266-1940
Fax: (202) 266-1900

Pew Hispanic Center

Founded in 2001, the Pew Hispanic Center is a nonpartisan research organization that seeks to improve understanding of the U.S. Hispanic population and to chronicle Latinos' growing impact on the nation. The Center does not take positions on policy issues. It is a project of the Pew Research Center, a nonpartisan "fact tank" in Washington, D.C., that provides information on the issues, attitudes, and trends shaping the United States and the world.

1615 L Street NW
Suite 700
Washington, D.C. 20036
Phone: (202) 419-3600
Fax: (202) 419-3608
Email: info@pewhispanic.org
URL: www.pewhispanic.org

SOURCES FOR ADDITIONAL STUDY

Aizenman, N. C. "Salvadorans Seek a Voice To Match Their Numbers; Summit Aims to Raise Political Visibility." *Washington Post*, 24 Sept. 2009: A10.

Coutin, Bibler, Susan. "Remembering the Nation: Gaps and Reckoning within Biographical Accounts of Salvadoran Émigrés." *Anthropological Quarterly* 4 (2011): 809.

Bachelis, Faren. *The Central Americans*. New York: Chelsea House, 1990.

Bermudez, Esmeralda. "Fully Embracing Their Heritage; Immigrants and offspring Follow Salvadoran Events with Passion." *Los Angeles Times*, 15 March 2009: A33.

Cordova, Carlos B. *The Salvadoran Americans*. Westport, CT: Greenwood Press, 2005.

Crittenden, Ann. *Sanctuary: A Story of American Conscience and the Law in Collision*. New York: Weidenfeld & Nicholson, 1988.

Kowalski, Kathiann M. *Salvadorans in America*. Minneapolis, MN: Lerner Publications, 2006.

Mahler, Sarah J. *Salvadorans in Suburbia: Symbiosis and Conflict*. Boston: Allyn and Bacon, 1995.

Montes, Segundo, Juan Jose, and García Vásquez. *Salvadoran Migration to the United States: An Exploratory Study*. Washington, D.C.: Center for Immigration Policy and Refugee Assistance, Georgetown University, 1988.

Starr, Alexandra. "Luis Reyes: Entrepreneur as Revolutionary." *Inc.* 30 Oct. 2012.

Suarez-Orozco, Marcelo. *Central American Refugees and U.S. High Schools*. Palo Alto, CA: Stanford University Press, 1989.

Watanabe, Teresa. "New Lives, but Old Traditions; Two Local Salvadoran Festivals Celebrate the Customs of the Central American Nation and the Struggles of Those Who Fled War and Created Lives Here." *Los Angeles Times*, 5 Aug. 2007: B1.

SAMOAN AMERICANS

Paul Alan Cox

OVERVIEW

Samoan Americans are immigrants or descendants of immigrants from the Samoan Islands in the South Pacific. The Samoan archipelago consists of fifteen inhabited islands that are located approximately 14 degrees south latitude and between 171 and 173 degrees west longitude. The archipelago is politically divided. The group of islands east of 171 degrees longitude is known as the Territory of American Samoa, or American Samoa, a U.S. territory. The total land area of American Samoa is 199 square miles, about three times the size of the District of Columbia, and includes seven major islands: Tutuila (which includes the territorial capital of Pago Pago), Aunu'u, Ta'u, Ofu, Olosega, Swains Island, and Rose Atoll. The islands west of 171 degrees longitude make up the Independent State of Samoa (Malo Sa'oloto Tuto'atasi o Samoa), known as Samoa. These islands, formerly known as Western Samoa, have a total land area of 2,831 square miles, slightly larger than Delaware. Samoa includes four inhabited islands: Upolu (with Apia, the nation's capital), Manono, Apolima, and Savai'i, which is the largest but also the most underdeveloped of these islands. The major Samoan Islands are volcanic in origin, many with high mountains, pristine rain forests, and surrounding coral reefs. Samoan weather is usually hot and wet, with a mean temperature of 79.5 degrees Fahrenheit and heavy annual rainfall. In the city of Apia, annual rainfall measures about eighty inches.

American Samoa has a population of 55,000, while the Independent State of Samoa has a total population of 194,000. The vast majority of Samoans are Christian, with the major denominations on the islands being Anglican (LMS), Methodist, Catholic, and Mormon. Throughout the islands, many Samoans live as subsistence agriculturalists and fishermen. For those who are employed on a cash basis, American Samoa has a higher mean per capita income at about $8,000 per year, while the Independent State of Samoa has a mean per capita income for laborers of $6,000 per year. While the Independent State of Samoa is one of the poorer countries of the world, the well-being and happiness of the people is very high because of homegrown produce and protein from the sea, the ability to produce houses, mats, canoes, and other aspects of the material culture from locally grown or indigenous plants, and a rich network of family and village relationships.

Samoans began to arrive in the United States in the mid-twentieth century to pursue educational opportunities and religious training. This reflected a broader Samoan diaspora to New Zealand, Australia, and the United States. Since the initial wave of the Samoan diaspora, numerous second- and third-generation Samoans have been born not on the islands but in their new countries.

In the 2010 U.S. Census, over 184,440 Americans reported themselves to be of Samoan descent. Approximately 33 percent of these respondents resided in the state of California, with another 20 percent in Hawaii, 10 percent in Washington, and 37 percent in other states. Thus, the population of Samoan Americans in the fifty United States exceeds the population of American Samoa threefold. Samoan Americans are the single largest non-native Hawaiian Pacific Islander group in the United States, and they continue to grow in numbers. Between the 2000 and the 2010 U.S. Census, their population grew by 38 percent. Most older expatriate Samoans are immigrants, although many of their offspring are natural-born citizens of their host countries. Regardless of birthplace, however, peoples of Samoan descent are linked by a distinctive cultural heritage that continues to flourish on those South Pacific islands.

HISTORY OF THE PEOPLE

Early History The Samoan Islands were colonized between 500 and 800 BCE by an oceanic people distinguished by their production of Lapita pottery—a unique pottery form named after one of the original sites of pottery shard discovery in Melanesia. Based on archaeological, botanical, and linguistic evidence, it seems almost certain that the ancestors of the Samoans originated in Indo-Malaysia, spent several centuries living along coastal areas of New Guinea, and then colonized Samoa and Tonga, another group of islands in the Pacific Ocean. Over time the descendants of these original immigrants colonized other regions, including Tahiti and other areas of eastern Polynesia, the Marquesas, Hawaii, and New Zealand. Once in Samoa, the Lapita potters developed a material culture characterized by a few large stone fortifications, early attempts at irrigation, and the production of highly finished boat timbers.

The quality of the ship timbers produced by the Samoans did not escape notice. Indeed, the first European accounts of Samoa speak admiringly of the handiwork of the islands' indigenous shipwrights. The quality of Samoan boats suggested to Jacob Roggeveen, the first European to discover Samoa, that the Samoans must possess iron tools; he could not believe that such exquisite woodwork could be accomplished with shells and stone adzes. Roggeveen happened upon the islands in 1722 during his ill-fated voyage from the Netherlands to New Ireland. He recorded that the Samoan seamen were a sturdy, healthy group, although he mistook their tattoos for paint. Concerned about the lateness of the season and the poor anchoring terrain, Roggeveen decided not to attempt a landing.

In 1768 Louis Antoine de Bougainville was the second European explorer to visit Samoa. He named the archipelago the Navigator Islands in honor of the superb sailing vessels manned by the natives. Unfortunately, a subsequent expedition to Samoa in 1787, led by Jean-François de Galaup, comte de Lapérouse, met with tragedy when eleven members of the crew were later killed by Samoans. The French claimed the attack was unprovoked, although they admitted the attack came after they had fired muskets over the heads of a few Samoans to persuade them to release a grapnel rope to a longboat. Regardless of the cause of the altercation, Lapérouse fostered a myth of barbarity about the Samoans in the expedition's wake, bitterly remarking in his memoirs that he would leave the documentation of Samoan history to others.

The massacre of the French sailors from the *Astrolabe* in 1787 gave the Samoans a reputation for savagery that deterred future European exploration of the islands, except for a few brief contacts such as the visit of that H.M.S. *Pandora* in 1791. Only a few whalers and warships called at Samoan ports over the next several decades.

In 1828, Tongan Wesleyan missionaries arrived in Samoa, but they had little success in their proselytizing endeavors. In 1830, however, John Williams of the London Missionary Society (LMS) sailed the *Messenger of Peace* to Savai'i under the guidance of a Samoan convert from Rarotonga. He first traveled to Sapapali'i village, home of Malietoa, the highest-ranking chief in Samoa. Williams obtained permission from Malietoa to land Tahitian and Rarotongan missionaries in Samoa. In addition, he secured a commitment from Malietoa to avail himself of the missionaries' teachings. Other religious groups soon followed. The mass conversion of Samoans to Christianity, led by Malietoa and other paramount chiefs, occurred within a year of the missionaries' arrival.

The impact of the European missions on Samoan culture was rapid and profound. Samoans abandoned their former religious beliefs and made dramatic changes to central cultural practices. Warfare as an instrument of political change was discarded, as were polygamy, abortion, "indecent" dances, and certain common articles of clothing (such as the *titi*, a skirt made from *Cordyline terminalis* leaves). The missionaries introduced new agricultural plants and practices, the use of imported cotton cloth for ordinary wear as a wraparound (*lavalava*), and new forms of housing construction. In only a few years, a fundamental restructuring of traditional Samoan society had taken place. *Faifeau* or ministers played a new and pivotal role in this culture, a respected status that continues to this day.

Later, other *papalagi* (foreigners) with less evangelical interests visited Samoa. The U.S. Exploring Expedition visited and mapped Samoa in 1839. Commander Charles Wilkes appointed the son of John Williams as American Vice-Consul. In 1845 George Pritchard joined the diplomatic corps in Apia as British Consul. Both Williams and Pritchard avoided native intrigues and concentrated on assisting in the naval affairs of their respective countries.

The geopolitical importance of Samoa grew over time due to its proximity to southern whaling grounds and the unparalleled harbor of Pago Pago. In 1857 the German firm of Godeffroy greatly expanded trade in copra, establishing a regional center in Samoa. This led to the establishment of a German consulate in 1861. The increased interest in Samoa created significant tensions between the three colonial powers in the islands. Samoa was finally partitioned between the east (Eastern Samoa) and the west (German Samoa) during the 1880s.

Modern Era American Samoa was eventually ceded by the chiefs of Tutuila and Manu'a to the United States and administered by the Department of the Navy as a U.S. territory. The island of Tutuila was ceded on April 17, 1900, by twenty paramount chiefs. The islands of Manu'a were ceded to the United States by the King Tui Manu'a Elisala and the paramount chiefs of Manu'a on July 16, 1904. Both agreements were formally accepted by the U.S. Congress in the Ratification Act of 1929. These agreements created an extraordinary and special relationship between the United States and the American Samoans.

The cession documents make it clear that they were freely signed, without duress, threat, or history of military conflict, by two equally sovereign powers, the United States of America and the Chiefs and Orators of Eastern Samoa. While in English these agreements are often referred to as "Treaties," the Samoan text calls the agreement a "*Feagaiga*," the Samoan term for covenant. In this covenant, the United States pledges to advance the social harmony and well-being ("*faatupuina le fealofani ma le nofolelei*") of the Samoans and to respect the rights of the Samoans to their lands and possessions ("*faamamalu ma tausi le pule taitoatasi o tagata uma oloo nofo nei i Tutuila i o latou fanua poo isi mea*"). The Samoan-language version of the Manu'a agreements adds that American Samoans are to have the same rights as American citizens in Samoa and are never to be consider inferior to Americans ("*ua tusa tagata papalagi mai Amerika ua mau i Samoa, ua le sili le papalagi i Samoa*") and that the chiefs were to retain their traditional authority over their villages. In essence these documents pledged that in return for the chiefs ceding military and political authority to the United States, the United States would respect Samoan customs regarding lands and titles, and that the United States would take care of the Samoans forever.

Although the U.S. military used American Samoa as a coaling station, as a military base for operations in World War II, and later as a refueling station for Strategic Air Command planes as well as a signaling station for U.S. submarines, American efforts to advance the social harmony and well-being of the islands were spotty until the 1960s, when President John F. Kennedy told Governor John Hayden to "get Samoa moving." During the 1960s and 1970s, construction on American Samoa increased dramatically. A hospital, television transmission facilities, an aerial tramway, and modern schools were built. Steps were taken to institute a popular election to determine the Territorial Governor, a position previously filled by appointment from Washington, D.C.

Western Samoa's development during the twentieth century was a little more dramatic. Western Samoa changed hands from German ownership to New Zealand administration during World War I after a bloodless invasion. After the war, Western Samoa was declared a League of Nations Trust Territory under New Zealand administration. A nascent independence movement, called the "Mau," was brutally crushed by New Zealand colonial administrators in 1929. New Zealand subsequently assumed a more benign role in Western Samoa, assisting the country as it prepared for independence in 1962. Today, the Independent State of Samoa is led by a unicameral parliament and prime minister, with His Highness Tuiatua Tupua Tamasese Efi acting as the ceremonial head of state. Prime Minister Tuila'epa Lupesoliai Sailele Malielegaoi, elected in 1998, moved Samoa into closer alignment with its principal Commonwealth trading partners, New Zealand and Australia, by changing all driving to the left side of the road and by administratively moving the dateline so that the Independent State of Samoa, unlike American Samoa, is now on the same side of the dateline as New Zealand and Australia. In addition, perhaps because of the large number of its citizens who are of part-Chinese descent, Samoa has established increasingly cordial relationships with the People's Republic of China. Friendly relationships have also been established in recent years with both Germany and Sweden, the homes of the ancestors of many high-ranking Samoans occupying high levels in Samoan government and commerce.

SETTLEMENT IN THE UNITED STATES

Because of their cultural history as extraordinary voyagers and navigators, their athletic prowess, their innate hospitality, and their remarkable charisma and resiliency, Samoans were well suited to travel and to colonize areas far beyond their home islands. Immigration of Samoans to New Zealand, Australia, and the United States accelerated during the 1950s. Now the number of Samoans living outside of Samoa easily exceeds the combined population of both American Samoa and the Independent State of Samoa. Large populations of expatriate Samoans can be found in Auckland, New Zealand; Honolulu, Hawaii; Los Angeles, California; San Francisco, California; and Salt Lake City, Utah. Smaller groups have settled in Wellington, New Zealand; Sydney, Australia; Laie, Hawaii; Oakland, California; and Independence, Missouri.

Since family remittances constitute the majority of the foreign currency earnings in the Independent State of Samoa, extended families in the islands have a considerable financial stake in encouraging younger Samoans to emigrate. Often Samoan laborers are sent with full airfare support from island families to Auckland, Wellington, Sydney, or Melbourne, or, if visas can be arranged, to Honolulu, Los Angeles, or Utah to assume factory positions or other entry-level positions arranged by overseas members of the families. The wages for factory work or even minimum wage labor in New Zealand, Australia, or the United States greatly exceed the salaries of well-paying jobs in Apia. It is understood by all parties that a significant portion of these wages will be returned to Samoa. On some occasions, village chiefs will call in select village youth and instruct them to prepare to journey overseas.

Financial support for such international voyages are based on Samoan cultural norms, where chiefs are able to request, with little warning, significant financial contributions from uncles, cousins, nieces, distant relatives, etc., to support *fa'alavelave*, the umbrella term for funerals, marriages, and overseas voyages. Thus, the price of international airfares can quickly be raised even by chiefs residing in otherwise poor villages. This complex web of prestige, gift-giving, and culturally unrefusable requests for *fa'alavelave* within extended families characterizes Samoan culture. Resented by some Westernized Samoans, this system of reciprocal gift-giving facilitated by the chiefs functions as what Oxford economic historian Mary Cox terms "an informal insurance system." It has greatly facilitated mass emigration of Samoans to foreign countries. Before enclaves of expatriate Samoans developed in overseas countries, however, the initial wave of Samoan emigration was supported by the New Zealand and American governments.

The Independent State of Samoa, with its historically close ties to New Zealand, sent a number of scholarship students to pursue college degrees in New Zealand, some who subsequently settled in Hawaii or

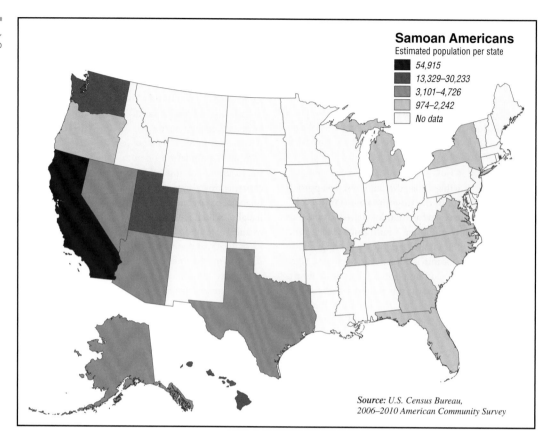

Samoan Americans
Estimated population per state

- 54,915
- 13,329–30,233
- 3,101–4,726
- 974–2,242
- No data

*Source: U.S. Census Bureau,
2006–2010 American Community Survey*

the U.S. mainland. American Samoa saw many of its citizens enroll in U.S. military services, which allowed them to travel to and serve at bases in the U.S. mainland as well as abroad. Samoans who chose to pursue ecclesiastical endeavors were often educated by Anglicans in London. Others entered Catholic seminaries in the South Pacific and studied in Rome, while those who became local lay leaders in the Church of Jesus Christ of Latter-day Saints (Mormon) traveled to Utah. Given the importance of religion in Samoan culture and the status of ministers, expatriate Samoan communities on the U.S. mainland are characterized by the Samoan churches and ministers, which often serve as a focal point for the Samoan American community. The overseas experience encouraged growing numbers of people to emigrate from Samoa.

LANGUAGE

While original immigrants from Samoa were of course fully fluent in the Samoan language, their children and grandchildren often struggle to understand spoken Samoan, particularly the more nuanced rhetorical forms of the language. As has been common for many other immigrant groups to the United States, parents who are not comfortable speaking English typically demand that their children speak perfect English so they can advance in American society. Thus, first-generation offspring of Samoan parents in the United States are usually able to understand simple Samoan

commands, instructions for serving and cooking food, and Samoan terms for discipline and family structure, but may themselves be unable to vocalize Samoan expressions beyond simple greetings or affirmations to spoken requests. These children of first-generation immigrants, learning perfect English at the playground and in the classroom, are therefore often pressed into service as translators for their parents, who seek to navigate the complexities of American social and medical services. The key issue facing newer generations of Samoan Americans is therefore not learning spoken English, but instead finding ways to learn the Samoan language.

In a way that is difficult for native English speakers to comprehend, Samoan culture is deeply interwoven with spoken Samoan. While extraordinary patience is shown to foreigners who attempt to learn the Samoan language, such indulgence is often not shown in villages outside of the capital cities of Pago Pago and Apia to individuals who physically appear to be Samoan but are linguistically isolated from their ancestral population. There is thus an increasing demand for Samoan language courses in the United States, New Zealand, and Australia by second-generation Samoans who wish to reconnect with their own cultural heritage.

The Samoan language is an ancient form of Polynesian dialect. It consists of three basic types of language. Common Samoan is the Samoan language of commerce and normal family interactions, while

Respect Samoan includes honorific terms used for others of equal or greater rank. The third language type employed by Samoans, Rhetorical Samoan, is a set of proverbial, genealogical, and poetic allusions with unique grammars used principally by chiefs in kava ceremonies.

Samoan vowels are pronounced very simply; the French approach to their vowel pronunciation is similar. Consonants are nearly identical to English consonants with two exceptions: the glottal stop indicated by an apostrophe is an unaspirated consonant produced in the bottom of the throat that can best be approximated as the break in the English expression "oh oh." Thus the Samoan word for "thank you,"—*fa'afetai*—is pronounced "fah-ah-fay-tie." The Samoan "g" sound is also difficult for some foreigners to master. It is pronounced similarly to the "ng" in "singalong"; the Samoan word for "gun"—*faga*—is thus pronounced as "fah-ngah." The "n" sound is pronounced as "ng" by Samoans as well. Finally, in colloquial Samoan, the "k" sound is pronounced instead of the "t"; hence *fa'afetai* becomes "fa'afekai." Samoans, however, do not like foreigners to use colloquial pronunciation. In Samoan words all syllables are given equal timing with a slight accent placed on the penultimate syllable.

There are few dialectical differences in spoken Samoan, although a few words and pronunciations differ slightly between American Samoa and the Independent State of Samoa. However, two general exceptions to the rule should be noted. First, just as Oxford dons can be identified by their diction, so can high-ranking Samoan chiefs be identified by their extraordinarily clear and precise manner of speaking. Second, the village of Fitiuta on the island of Ta'u in the Manu'a group of American Samoa does not allow speech using the "k" for "t" substitution. In other words, residents of Fitiuta speak at all time a beautiful formal form of Samoan that can only be related to the exquisitely clear form of Hawaiian spoken by the residents of Niihau island in Hawaii. Ministers of religion are expected to speak, particularly in church services, formal Samoan.

Greetings and Popular Expressions The following are a few common Samoan greetings and their English translations: *Talofa*—Hello; *Fa'afetai*—Thank you; *Tofa*—Good-bye; *Malo*—Congratulations.

Rhetoric Ceremonial Samoan may be one of the world's most complex rhetorical forms. Eloquent oratory has long been an integral part of the Samoan culture. In the case of a village or district dispute, the victor is often the side represented by the most eloquent orator. Oratorical ability in Samoa is a treasured commodity because it has historically brought its finest practitioners prestige, cultural influence, and material goods.

The importance of rhetoric in Samoa has even been institutionalized in the Samoan system of chiefdoms. In Samoan culture there are two types of chiefs: high chiefs, who function very much as the corporate executive officers of the village; and orators, or "talking chiefs," who speak for the village in its dealings with others. Samoan orators are expected to memorize a vast array of information, including the historical events (*taeao*) of Samoa, an exhaustive list of Samoan proverbial expressions, and the genealogies of most of the major families in Samoa. Orators are also expected to be able to speak with power and eloquence in an extemporaneous fashion.

Samoan oratory at a kava ceremony typically contains sophisticated allusions to ancient events, nuanced proverbial expressions, and powerful political insights, which are combined with extensive references to the Bible and the genealogies of those present to produce an exquisitely cerebral poetic work. Samoan oratory is delivered in a cadence and clarity of voice that is clear and ringing. Frequently speeches are yelled out as a sign of respect to visitors. This oral tradition, the highest of all Samoan arts, is the art form most inaccessible to foreigners. Very little Samoan formal rhetoric has ever been translated into English.

RELIGION

Samoan Americans are characterized by deep religiosity and devotion to church attendance, whether they be Catholic, Protestant, or Mormon. Men attending church services typically wear white shirts, ties, and often formal wraparound skirts called *i'e fai taga*. Often Samoan churches form the nucleus of Samoan American communities.

In Samoa, religion plays a huge role that remarkably has been ignored by many anthropologists studying Samoan culture. The Samoan culture is a pious one. Most families in Samoa conduct a nightly *lotu* or vespers service in which the family gathers together, reads from the Bible, and offers prayers. Prayers are offered at every meal. Church attendance in Samoa is almost universal. Ministers of religion occupy a status in Samoa tantamount to that occupied by high chiefs and are granted extraordinary deference. This respect for clergy continues among Samoan Americans, even when services are conducted in English as well as the Samoan language.

Religion in the Samoan setting, however, has a unique Polynesian twist. Most Samoan Americans prefer to organize and participate in Samoan-speaking congregations, with some accommodation made for their non-Samoan-speaking offspring. Singing in a Samoan congregation is enthusiastic and beautiful. The Samoan Bible, which was translated directly from Greek, is quoted extensively in most Samoan services. By and large, Samoans are far better versed in Bible scripture than their Western counterparts.

CULTURE AND ASSIMILATION

Assimilation of Samoan Americans into the mainstream has been facilitated by their prominence in the military, in professional sports, and in their religious communities. The contributions made by Samoan Americans have been many and diverse. The courage and valor of Samoan soldiers became legendary during the Korean conflict and the Vietnam War, and Samoan soldiers of both sexes have given their lives in the recent wars in Iraq and Afghanistan. Prowess on the athletic field led to significant recognition for Samoan Americans in the sports of college and professional football, New Zealand rugby, and even Japanese sumo wrestling. Samoan American political leaders such as Congressman Faleolemavaega Eni Hunkin and governors Peter Coleman and A. P. Lutali have played an increasingly visible role in formulation of U.S. policy in the Pacific Rim.

Many recent immigrants from Samoa, though, have been forced to pursue low-paying jobs as untrained laborers. Others have been forced to rely on governmental entitlement programs for support. A few members of the Samoan community are undocumented aliens who are legally, linguistically, and culturally isolated from their host countries.

Assimilation of Samoan Americans into the mainstream has been facilitated by their prominence in the military, in professional sports, and in their religious communities. The contributions made by Samoan Americans have been many and diverse.

As a group, Samoans in the United States face all the tensions and difficulties encountered by other immigrant groups as they enter new homelands. Many older Samoans, particularly those from the Independent State of Samoa, speak English haltingly. Given the extraordinarily rich web of extended families and village relationships within expatriate communities, it is possible for an older Samoan who does not speak English to still live within the United States with some ease. Yet in areas of significant Samoan population concentration, even Samoan Americans who are fluent in English have faced considerable prejudice.

Members of the newest generation of Samoan Americans sometimes feel linguistically and culturally isolated from the elders. Although many can understand the Samoan spoken by their grandparents, they themselves can speak little, coming from a culture in which children are expected to listen but not speak. They thus feel isolated from, but subject to, Samoan cultural norms. Other young Samoan Americans suffer from the labeling that characterizes most emergent immigrant groups in the United States. While the churches play a large role in helping younger Samoan Americans feel integrated into their own traditional culture, the written works of prominent Samoan American writers and filmmakers are helping to bridge the gap. In his 2012 novel *Akua*, Daniel Pouesi

portrays the sometimes wide gap between Samoan and American culture. A 2011 film by New Zealand–based Samoan filmmaker Tusi Tamasese, *The Orator* (*O le Tulafale*), won strong reviews at the Sundance Film Festival. It was notable as the first feature film made entirely in the Samoan language with English subtitles.

In New Zealand, Hawaii, California, and Utah, there has been a reawakening and organization of expatriate Samoan communities in an attempt to reach out to younger people of Samoan ancestry and inform them of the traditional ways and cultures. Samoan culture, while based largely on hospitality, is at times mystifying to Westerners as well as to the offspring of expatriate Samoans who know little of the ways and language of their ancestral home. Scholars are also sometimes confused, and as a result Samoan culture has been the topic of much controversy. In *Coming of Age in Samoa* (1928), anthropologist Margaret Mead argued that Samoan adolescents are spared the emotional turbulence of American adolescence. She wrote that, unlike their counterparts in Western cultures, young people in Samoa pass relatively easily through adolescence. Her views have been challenged by anthropologist Derek Freeman, who argued that, contrary to the easygoing Samoan nature portrayed by Mead, Samoan culture is hierarchical, power-conscious, and occasionally violent.

The nature of Samoan society is considerably more complex than either camp may wish to admit. Unlike Mead's assertion that Samoans are a "primitive" people, Samoan culture is elaborate and sophisticated and is exemplified by Samoan rhetorical skills, which are extraordinary. Perhaps the most eloquent speeches in the world are made by Samoan orators, who invoke poetry, folk history, genealogical lore, and references to the sea and rain forests as they declaim the dignity of their people. Samoan villages are equally complex in their structure, with a plethora of different levels of *matai*, or chiefs. Villagers are related in various complex ways from a series of common descent groups, and the importance and identity of these common descent groups continue to play an important role in Samoan American communities in the United States.

Matai Titles Conveyance of a *matai* (chiefly) title is a noteworthy cultural event in Samoa. Typically the family of the chief-to-be will prepare kegs of corned beef, fine mats, money, and other items with which to "pay" the village granting the title. Visitors to the ceremony are also hosted in extravagant fashion. Extended and sophisticated rhetoric is exchanged by orators representing the various families in attendance and includes analysis of the genealogical provenance of the title. In some villages the candidate for the chief position is wrapped in a fine mat tied with a bow; the candidate becomes a chief when the bow is untied. Many times paper currency is placed in an ornamental fashion in the chief's headdress. All chief investiture ceremonies, however, regardless of village, culminate in the kava ceremony wherein the candidate drinks kava for the first time as the new chief. Invitation to attend a chief investiture ceremony is an honor, one rarely granted to foreigners.

Conveyance of a chiefly title is far more than an honorific. All people in the village, other than the immediate family, refer to the new chief by the new title. Furthermore, in traditional Samoan culture all the dependents of the new chief use the chief's title as their new surname. Once established, new chiefs are expected to attend village councils, act with a sense of decorum and dignity, support village activities via manual labor and cash donations, and behave with the interests of their families and villages foremost in their minds. As a member of the village chief council, the new chief will participate in decisions reached in consensus with the other chiefs. Some chieftains in Samoa also have special titles such as *Malietoa*, *Tamasese*, *Tupuola*, or *Salamasina*. These titles have national significance. Individuals bearing such titles are awarded respect similar to that given to royal families.

The conveyance of chiefly titles has become a difficult business for expatriate Samoans since in traditional Samoan culture all chiefs' titles are tied to an identifiable piece of land in Samoa. Expatriate Samoans seeking titles usually must return to Samoa for the ceremonies. In New Zealand some chief investiture ceremonies have been held. However, titles so conferred outside of Samoa are controversial within Samoa. Infrequently, foreign diplomats, aid workers, and other foreign visitors are granted honorific titles that have no validity in terms of Samoan land relationships and are not recognized by the Lands and Title Court. Exceptions to this arrangement are rare but do occur. Although nearly all chiefs are men, several women hold chiefly titles, and in at least one case a village conferred a valid title, registered with and recognized by the Land and Titles Court, on a Samoan-speaking foreigner.

Cuisine Samoan cuisine is fairly bland and nuanced in flavor. Samoans eat two or three meals a day consisting of boiled taro or rice cooked with coconut milk, fresh fish, breadfruit, and usually some form of tinned or fresh meat. Corned beef from New Zealand is particularly popular along with turkey tails and lamb flaps for a special dinner. Although traditionally coconut cream for marinating raw fish or cooking starch crops such as green plantains, taro, or breadfruit is produced by grating and then wringing coconut meat, canned coconut cream imported from Thailand or Samoa is increasingly available in stores. Among Samoan Americans, stores or bakeries in the United States that sell Samoan food often become informal centers of Samoan culture.

Because of its importance in traditional Samoan reciprocal gift-giving, food plays a far greater role than in American culture. Visitors to a Samoan family are invariably presented with the most culturally salient or expensive food items as a sign of respect. Visitors to a Samoan home, as a matter of common courtesy, should always receive offered food with graciousness, and formally express gratitude for the meal at its conclusion.

Fruit, although plentiful in the islands, is seldom eaten during mealtime. Raw Samoan cocoa (which for many visitors is an acquired taste) orange leaf tea, lemongrass tea, or coffee is usually served with meals. Samoans do not usually engage in conversation while eating, since the hosts typically do not eat until the guests have finished their meals. Many Samoans have, in recent years, strayed from the traditional diet of starchy roots and fruits to a more Westernized diet. The medical community believes that this dietary change has translated into a high incidence of diabetes among Samoan people. Although in traditional villages Samoans tend to be very trim in appearance, in some expatriate communities obesity is common, possibly as a result of a more sedentary lifestyle.

Traditional Dress American Samoans typically make strong efforts to be appropriately dressed in the context of their neighborhood or city. Around their own household, Samoan Americans often wear attire that is extremely comfortable and common in the islands, most notably the *lavalava*, a single piece of cloth that is worn as a wraparound skirt by both men and women. Brightly colored floral print shirts or blouses, or, in more informal settings, T-shirts, complete the typical outfit. In remote villages some women go without tops while washing clothes or bathing in village pools, but such practices do not occur in the capital cities or among expatriate Samoan populations. While Samoans prefer colorful floral designs in both their lavalava and tops, darker colors are preferred on formal occasions. In such instances, Samoan men often wear a *i'e fai taga*, a tailored lavalava with pockets made from suit cloth material. When combined with leather sandals, white shirt, tie, and suit coat, the *i'e fai taga* is considered appropriate dress for Samoan chiefs whether attending a funeral or hosting government dignitaries. In such settings women will wear a *pulu tasi*, a sort of *mu'umu'u* designed by the early Christian missionaries. On Sundays, Samoans prefer to wear white clothing to church.

For festive occasions, Samoans make and wear flower leis, usually out of frangipani (*pua*, *Plumeria rubra*) or fragrant ylang-ylang (*moso'oi*, *Cananga odorata*) blossoms. Such leis are a common component of high school and college graduation ceremonies involving Samoan Americans, with some young graduates scarcely able to see over the pile of flower and candy leis placed around their necks by loving family members. High-ranking chiefs will sometimes wear brilliant red leis made from the dried syncarps of pandanus (*pa'ogo* or *fala*, *Pandanus tectorius*) to festive occasions as well as more formal forms of chiefly insignia such as coconut fiber fly whisks or orators' staffs. A Samoan American entering a government or civil gathering with an orator staff or fly whisk should be granted deference and seated near the front, as it is likely that he or she will speak on behalf of a significant portion of the Samoan community.

Although Samoan concepts of personal modesty may differ from Western concepts, they are very important to Samoans. The area between the calf of the leg and the thigh is considered to be especially inappropriate for public exhibition. Many traditional Samoan villages ban beachwear such as bikinis and other swimsuits. Some even ban women from wearing trousers. These prohibitions are not enforced, however, among Samoan Americans. While the appearance and garb of Samoan women are subject to a range of cultural restrictions, full-body tattoos are common on Samoan men. The tattooing process is prolonged and painful. It is believed by Samoans to be a means of helping men appreciate the prolonged labor pains involved with childbirth. Samoan American men are proud of their full-body tattoos and are usually pleased to respond to questions about them.

Dances and Songs Among Samoan Americans, birthday parties, weddings, and graduation ceremonies usually involve highly amplified Samoan music and Samoan dancing. Samoans are extraordinary dancers, and presentation of a dance is considered the equivalent of a tangible gift for any visitors lucky enough to witness it.

As discussed in Paul Alan Cox's 1997 book *Nafanua: Saving the Samoan Rainforest*, traditional Samoan dancing is very different from Western dancing in both philosophy and execution. As in all Samoan cultural events, chiefly rank plays an important role. The most prominent dances are performed by the *taupou*, a Samoan maiden who bears chiefly title and wears an elaborate headdress consisting of shells, mirrors, and human hair. To provide counterpoint to her gracious and fluid motions, typically a Samoan orator or young man will dance behind her in a form called the *'aiuli* (which refers to playing a clown) in which he will cavort and roll about. The ability of the *taupou* to totally ignore his antics demonstrates the grace and beauty that commands such a premium in Samoan culture. Samoans believe that offering a dance to a guest, often by bowing in front of them with outstretched arms before beginning, is a highly significant gift. It demonstrates good manners to join in the dancing at an appropriate time.

Among Samoan Americans, traditional dances, including the transfixing but dangerous fire dance, are often performed mixed with hip-hop dancing. On most occasions, the audience for a dance performance will join in at the conclusion, particularly during the special *taualuga* dance performed by the *taupou*.

Holidays Samoan Americans love parades and patriotic celebrations. In larger Samoan American communities, the Fourth of July is typically celebrated with gusto. Both American Samoa and the Independent State of Samoa celebrate their respective national holidays. Christmas, Easter, and other religious holidays are also of great significance to Samoans. In addition, the second Sunday of October is celebrated by most denominations as "White Sunday." On this day, the service revolves around memorized recitations by children. After the service, Samoan children are waited upon by the adults of their family, served a festive meal, and presented with gifts.

In the Independent State of Samoa, Independence Day is celebrated on June 1 with parades, brass bands, and team canoe races (*fautasi*). In American Samoa, Flag Day is similarly celebrated on April 17. Samoan holidays, including those celebrated by Samoan Americans, often involve prayers by ministers, feasting on indigenous delicacies, flowery speeches, choirs or other forms of music, and traditional dance presentations.

Manners In a Samoan house or at a cultural event, people often remove their shoes and leave them at the door. It is usually considered disrespectful to walk across a mat in a Samoan house with shoes on. When walking in front of anybody, a visitor should bend low and say *Tulou* ("too-low").

The presentation of kava is considered to be the highest symbol of respect that can be granted to a visitor. If presented with a cup of kava, the visitor may drip a few drops on the ground (symbolic of returning goodness to the earth) and say *Ia manuia* ("ee-ah mahn-wee-ah"), which means "let there be blessings." At that point he or she can either drink from the cup or return it to the server.

The acceptance of gifts is important in Samoa. No gift offered by a Samoan should be refused. Such refusal might be considered an indication of displeasure with the person presenting the gift. The most common gifts are those of food or mats. Gift-giving is frequently an indication of the status or prestige of both the giver and the receiver. Gifts are given without expectation of reciprocation. During dances or other fund-raising activities, however, cash donations are usually welcomed. It is also considered good manners to publicly offer a significant cash payment to an orator who has given a speech of welcome or greeting.

Display of negative emotions, particularly irritation, anger, or other hostility, is considered to be in very bad taste in Samoa and a sign of weakness. Samoans treat each other with extraordinary politeness even under difficult circumstances.

Health Care Issues and Practices Samoans have a traditional system of healing that plays a very important role in Samoan culture. Traditional Samoan healers use a variety of massage treatments, counseling techniques, and herbal preparations to treat illness. Recent scientific analysis of Samoan healing practices shows them to have some degree of empirical justification: a large number of plants used by Samoans for medical purposes demonstrate pharmacological activity in the laboratory. The U.S. National Cancer Institute, for instance, in 2001 licensed the new anti-HIV compound prostratin, which was discovered in a Samoan plant used by traditional healers, to the not-for-profit AIDS Research Alliance.

Samoans believe that there are some illnesses that cannot be cured by Western medicine. These include illnesses of the to'ala, the reputed center of being located beneath the navel, and cases of spiritual possession. *Musu*, a psychiatric illness of young women characterized by a nearly autistic withdrawal from communication, has been treated successfully in New Zealand by traditional healers. Samoan healers exist and practice, albeit covertly, in most expatriate Samoan communities.

Samoans believe that the major sources of disease are poor diet, poor hygiene, and interpersonal hostility. Because Samoa is a consensus culture with a heavy emphasis on responsibility and family, many believe that an individual who does not support his or her family, who does not shoulder the responsibilities of village life, and who otherwise does not participate in traditional culture has a high risk of becoming ill. Linguistic isolation complicates some medical interaction with the older Samoans, but in general Samoans are appreciative of Western medicine and responsive to prescribed courses of medical treatment.

Samoan Americans are particularly susceptible to high rates of diabetes and other illnesses associated with an industrialized diet and decreased patterns of physical activity. As a population, though, Samoans show lower cholesterol levels than would be expected given their diet and patterns of obesity. Coconut oil, which is high in saturated fat, plays an important part in the Samoan diet, including *palusami* (young taro leaves with coconut cream). The addition of an industrialized diet to traditional fatty foods including corned beef, suckling pig, and coconut cream, combined with a sedentary lifestyle, is a key contributor to cardiovascular illness.

Death and Burial Rituals Samoan funerals include important demonstrations of high Samoan culture. In American Samoa, at a funeral the extended family of the bereaved prepares money, fine mats, kegs of corned beef, pigs, and case goods to present to guests. Visitors attend with a single palm leaf held aloft in front of them. On arrival at the home of the bereaved, the orator representing the visitors stands outside the hut, addresses the dead person with an honorific string of titles, and then speaks to everyone present. After the speech the visitors are invited to sit and wait as other visitors trickle in. The funeral concludes with an orator who acts as a representative for the bereaved family. The orator speaks before distributing gifts to the visitors. In the mainland United States, Samoan families typically conduct funerals at their church or at a mortuary in accordance with American customs.

At funerals and chief investiture ceremonies, a great deal of cash and a large number of fine mats—which may take up to six months to complete—exchange hands. In some instances, more than 2,000 fine mats and as much as $20,000 may be redistributed.

FAMILY AND COMMUNITY LIFE

Samoans have an expansive view of familial bonds. A Samoan *a'iga* or family includes all individuals who descend from a common ancestor. Samoan familial ties are complex and highly interwoven, but also very important; all Samoans are expected to support and serve their extended families. Each extended family has one or more chiefs who organize and run the family.

Family pride is a central part of Samoan culture as well. Individuals in Samoan villages fear breaking village rules not only because of any individual consequences but because of the shame it might bring to their family. In cases of serious transgression, the entire family may be penalized by the village council. In extreme cases the transgressor's chief may be stripped of his title and the family banished from the village. The fear of shaming one's extended family thus serves as a potent deterrent to ill behavior among Samoans. This philosophy extends not only to transgressors but also to victims. An offense committed against anyone, particularly chiefs, elderly individuals—who are revered in Samoan society—or young women, may be seen as an offense to the victim's entire family. In contrast to Western philosophies that laud individualism, Samoan culture emphasizes the importance of family ties and responsibility.

In Samoan culture, serious offenses may be redeemed by an *ifoga* (a "lowering"). This is a ceremony that reflects deep contrition on the part of the perpetrator. In an *ifoga*, all of a transgressor's extended family and village will gather before dawn in front of the residence of the offended or injured party. There they will sit covered by fine mats as the sun rises. They remain in that position until forgiven and invited into the house. They then present fine mats, pigs, and cash as evidence of their contrition. There is no Western equivalent to an *ifoga*, but performance of an *ifoga* in the Independent State of Samoa, even for a serious crime, will often result in waiver or dramatic reduction of the criminal penalties that would have otherwise been assessed.

The Samoan concept of family has profound economic consequences. All Samoans are expected to provide financial support for their families. Many expatriate Samoans routinely send a large portion of their earnings back to their relatives in Samoa. Such foreign remittances constitute a significant portion of the income of Samoa. Although such remittances are a godsend for the relatively weak Samoan economy,

Two Samoan men holding decorative wooden clubs in Laie, Oahu, Hawaii, 1996. PHOTOGRAPH BY CATHERINE KARNOW. CORBIS. REPRODUCED BY PERMISSION.

there is concern that future generations of expatriate Samoans may become so assimilated into Western cultures that this practice will not survive.

Gender Roles Among Samoan Americans, gender roles approximate those of other Americans, with the exception, of course, of cultural performances and interfamily dynamics. Within extended Samoan American families, chiefs, who are typically but not always men, are often shown great deference. Samoan American women are fully engaged in the workforce and are expected to generate significant amounts of the family income.

Although traditional village roles in Samoa are differentiated by gender, these bounds are not absolute. For example, some of the highest chiefly titles in Samoan mythology, such as *Salamasina* or *Nafanua*, are women's titles, and women sometimes function today as orators or high chiefs. Among Samoan Americans, gender roles tend to follow those of other Americans. Samoan American women play active roles in the workforce and as wage earners, and many Samoan American women seek higher education. However, there are some distinctions. It is extremely rare—indeed almost unheard of—for a man to be a *taulasea* or traditional healer, except in the case of bone setters. It is also rare for a woman to be a paramount chief, but when such exceptions occur, the women almost always occupy extraordinarily high rank. The Independent State of Samoa sometimes appoints high-ranking female chiefs as ambassadors or cultural envoys.

In traditional villages in Samoa, both men and women weave, but for different purposes. Women weave *fala*, pandanus leaf mats that cover the floor. They also weave *i'e toga*, fine mats that are exchanged in important culture events. Men weave coconut leaf baskets, used for carrying breadfruit or taro, and *ola*, which are used with a woven shoulder strap to carry fishing gear and fish. Men also weave *'enu*, a special

type of fish trap woven from the aerial roots of *lau falafala* (*Freycinetia reineckei*) vines, but this latter skill remains viable only among one or two residents of Olosega island in American Samoa.

The role of transgendered individuals, or individuals of indeterminate gender, including those who cross-dress, in Samoan culture is different from Western culture. *Fa'afafine* are biological males who dress and adopt the mannerisms of women. They have a cultural niche and are far better accepted than their counterparts in Western culture. *Fa'afafine* occur among American Samoans and are well accepted.

Education Samoans value education very highly. For a developing country, the Independent State of Samoa has an astonishingly high rate of literacy—approximately 98 percent. In traditional villages education is first received at a minister's school, where children are taught to read. Later they attend elementary and secondary schools. The emphasis in Samoan education is largely on rote memorization.

Differences in educational philosophy can be found from island to island, however. Students in the Independent State of Samoa, for instance, pursue an education that in many ways resembles the system taught in New Zealand, while children in American Samoa receive an education that resembles the curriculum taught on the American mainland. In the Independent State of Samoa the best schools are frequently operated by churches. Some of the Catholic schools are particularly prestigious, while the Ah Mu Academy, an elementary school that opened in 2007, caters to students who seek to live according to Mormon behavioral standards.

Although there is a community college in American Samoa and two university campuses in the Independent State of Samoa, many Samoans pursue higher education either in New Zealand or in the United States. Many Samoan Americans major in education, law, or other social sciences.

Courtship and Weddings While older Samoans enjoy the regard in which they are held, younger members of the culture grapple with the complicated process of courtship. In remote villages dating is frowned upon. The culturally acceptable way for young men and young women to meet each other is for the young man to bring presents and food to the young woman's family and to court his intended in the presence of her entire family. In traditional villages, even slight deviation from this pattern may place the young man at some risk of physical harm from the young woman's brothers.

Romantic affairs are, of course, difficult to transact. Typically an intermediary called a *soa* (go-between) is used to communicate the amorous intentions of a young man to the *soa* of the young woman. If romantic interest is reciprocated, young men and young women will visit surreptitiously at night under the cover of darkness. Such liaisons, however, are fraught with danger should the young woman's brothers discover them. Brothers in traditional Samoan culture consider it their familial duty to aggressively screen out unwarranted suitors or inappropriate attempts to court their sister without parental supervision.

Samoan Americans, particularly first- and second-generation immigrants, tend to follow cultural norms for dating. For more traditional Samoans, physical contact between the sexes, including kissing and hand holding, is considered to be in poor taste in public. Even married couples avoid physical contact in public. These traditional practices, however, have changed as Samoan culture has become more Westernized. In Pago Pago and Apia, boys and girls date, attend dances, take in films, and socialize in most of the ways common to Western countries, as do most Samoan Americans in the United States. However, any insult to a young woman, including swearing in her presence, is still taken as a deep offense by her brothers and may result in violence.

A Samoan wedding typically involves feasting, dancing, and much merriment. Weddings are generally held in accordance with local customs or ecclesiastical protocols, followed by a large reception for the bride and groom.

Although Samoan Americans often marry other Samoans or Pacific Islanders, intermarriage with non-Polynesians is becoming increasingly more frequent. Key aspects of Samoan culture include the "informal insurance system" known as *faalavelave*. Setting an annual budget for *faalavelave* so that small cultural payments of $50–$100 USD can be ungrudgingly dispersed throughout the year to distant relatives when requested can help ensure marital harmony and acceptance by the extended Samoan family.

Birth Rituals In Samoa infant children and their mothers occupy special status. New mothers are usually presented with *vaisalo*, a rich drink made of grated coconut, coconut milk, manihot, and the grated flesh of the *vi* apple, *Spondias dulcis*. On occasion fine mats may also be presented to the mother. While Samoan Americans typically give birth in hospitals, some of these ceremonial forms of respect are still followed.

Marriage and Children Samoan Americans tend to maintain traditional views concerning marriage and children. As a result, divorce is less common among Samoan Americans than among other citizens of the United States. In Samoa, marriage has become more common since the advent of Christianity, but many people live together and even raise children without the benefit of marriage. This custom, called *nofo faʻapouliuli*, sometimes functions as a sort of trial marriage in which a Samoan tests the relationship before settling on a single partner. Divorce in Samoa is accepted and plays a similar role as it does in Western cultures.

Illegitimacy does not have the same negative connotations in Samoan culture that it does in other cultures. Children are warmly welcomed into a family and are frequently raised by grandparents or other relatives as their own offspring. In general, children within the Samoan family have a great deal of mobility. It is not uncommon in Samoa for children to be raised by people other than their biological parents. In many cases children are raised by members of extended family or even friends. All children are, regardless of their genetic relationship to the husband and wife in the family, treated equally and expected to assist with family chores. Given the profound importance of extended family relationships among Samoan Americans, distant biological relatives may be raised in the same manner as a couple's own children.

Because of the fluidity of family relationships, Samoans have a very different view of orphans than Westerners have. Although Pratt's 1862 and Milner's 1966 dictionaries of the Samoan language list translations for the English word "orphan" such as *aumatua* and *matuaoti*, respectively, there are in reality no orphans in Samoa because any child who loses his or her biological parents is immediately taken in by a member of the extended family or another unrelated family in the village. Furthermore, the concept of biological parents giving their child up for adoption, with complete severance of parental rights, is alien to the Samoan worldview.

Unfortunately, this difference in cultural norms concerning adoption in 2009 engendered terrible consequences. Poor families in Samoan villages were given *fesoasoani* or aid consisting of rice, tinned goods, and cash payments in return for surrendering their children to an American adoption agency. American adoptive parents were told that these children were in fact orphans or had been abandoned by their parents. These adoptive parents were stunned to hear, however, as their adopted children learned to speak English, that their biological parents, brothers and sisters, and entire families were still alive and well in Samoa. In Samoa, the children's biological parents had been led to believe that their children were being sent to the United States to be educated and would return when they were eighteen years old. Over eighty Samoan children were sent to thirteen cities in the United States under this scheme. When an infant died in the custody of the American adoption service, questions started being raised in both Samoa and the United States. On January 6, 2009, five owners and managers of the now-defunct Focus on Children agency pled guilty in U.S. federal court to a number of misdemeanor charges while the Focus on Children Corp. pleaded guilty to one felony. Some of the children were returned to Samoa, while others, with their Samoan parents' permission, have remained in the United States.

In Samoa, boys and girls are reared in nearly identical fashion until approximately age seven. But girls from eight to ten years old are expected to play

of the strongest records of courage and valor in the U.S. military of any immigrant group. Furthermore, the hierarchal nature of Samoan culture has fitted Samoans well to jobs that require both leadership and respect for the chain of command, such as law enforcement, border patrol, airport security, etc. As traditional voyagers and navigators, Samoan Americans have been particularly attracted to the aviation industry. Samoan American William "Kiso" Keil has had a distinguished career as a pilot for FedEx, and his niece, Violette Keil, is a pilot with Skywest Airlines. The highest paid Samoans are undoubtedly those who play in professional sports, particularly contact sports such as American football, rugby, and professional wrestling. One talented young Samoan American, Futi Tavana, was All-American in college volleyball and now plays professionally in Europe.

Samoans are also natural entertainers. Proficiency in singing, dancing, and playing musical instruments is common and even expected in Samoan culture. As a result, "Polynesian" dance revues in resort communities in Honolulu, Anaheim, Orlando, Branson, etc., are often principally staffed by Samoans.

The traditional emphasis on education has led some Samoan Americans into educational leadership positions at both the secondary and college levels. Many Samoan Americans of the new generation have bachelor's degrees and an increasing number are obtaining advanced degrees.

POLITICS AND GOVERNMENT

American Samoa is administered by an elected governor and territorial legislature as well as a non-voting delegate to the U.S. House of Representatives. Native-born residents of American Samoa are considered American nationals. Since American Samoa is technically considered an unincorporated territory of the United States, under the U.S. Constitution, American Samoans do not pay U.S. income taxes or vote in U.S. presidential elections (although they may vote in presidential primary elections). Many have served in the U.S. armed services.

A former United Nations protectorate under the administration of New Zealand, the Independent State of Samoa is a member of the British Commonwealth and in recent years has continued to more closely align itself with its Commonwealth partners in the South Pacific, New Zealand and Australia.

Because American Samoans do not vote in national elections and the region has been administered in a fairly bipartisan manner by the Department of the Interior, it is difficult to assess Samoan American political leanings. Hawaii, which has been traditionally a strong bastion for the Democratic party, is home to many Samoans, but many Samoan Americans live in the staunchly Republican areas of Orange County, California, and Utah. Given their relatively small numbers, however, it is unlikely that any unified

A Samoan rugby fan at the 2012 USA Sevens Rugby Tournament in Las Vegas, Nevada. EVERETT COLLECTION INC / ALAMY

major roles in caring for other infant children. It is not uncommon in Samoan villages to see eight- or nine-year-old girls packing a six-month-old baby on their hip. Once boys and girls approach puberty, deep cultural taboos take effect that preclude their continued close association. Past puberty, brothers and sisters are not allowed to be alone in each other's presence.

EMPLOYMENT AND ECONOMIC CONDITIONS

Samoans are hard workers. Because of strenuous agricultural activities in their home islands, including carrying 100-pound bags of taro or breadfruit, sometimes for miles, across their backs, their extraordinary athleticism, and the cultural tolerance for pain and discomfort inherent in their voyaging ancestry, Samoans migrating to the United States were willing to take physically demanding and dangerous jobs that others might have avoided. Samoan Americans have one

voting behavior on their part would have more than local political significance, although this may change as the population of Samoan Americans continues to grow and exercise political clout.

Minimum wage laws are a constant concern to those who live in American Samoa. The islands received a waiver from obeying the minimum wage law due to the havoc that implementation would have created for the tuna canneries in American Samoa. In 1997 the waiver was replaced by a board that will use industry standards and fairness to set the minimum wage in American Samoa. Union involvement appears to be fairly minimal among Samoan workers, and the territory as a duty-free port has certain advantages of manufacturing for the U.S. market that have yet to be fully exploited. Furthermore, tourism, particularly in the National Park areas on the islands of Tutuila, Ofu, Olosega, and Ta'u, has yet to achieve its potential, although ecotourism is on the rise. Some of the rain forest and coral reef areas in the National Park of American Samoa are considered to be the most beautiful in the world. The Samoan culture of hospitality is well positioned for future major investments in tourism infrastructure.

The Independent State of Samoa has a lively political climate, with much jousting and intrigue between the different political parties. The Prime Minister and the Cabinet are well educated in both Western and Samoan practices, and most Cabinet members are bilingual. There continues to be, in some circles, discussion of a possible unification of the two Samoan regions into a single independent country. Few American Samoans appear to be in favor of this idea. Their resistance to Samoan unification is driven not only by the tremendous economic disparity between American Samoa and the Independent State of Samoa, but also because of different cultural trajectories. Thus, while there are significant cultural and linguistic similarities between the Independent State and American Samoa, unification seems unlikely. Instead, many Samoans living in Upolu and Savai'i seek to immigrate to American Samoa. Some have even joined the U.S. armed forces. While the U.S. military maintains a presence in American Samoa, the Independent State of Samoa maintains no armed forces beyond a small police force, relying for national security on treaties with New Zealand.

NOTABLE INDIVIDUALS

Business Frank Falaniko Jr. (1956–) is a landscape construction engineer and president of Green City, Inc.

Government Eni Faauaa Hunkin Faleomavaega Jr. (1943–) is a member of the U.S. House of Representatives who served as staff council for the House Subcommittee on National Parks and Lands and later as the American Samoan delegate to the U.S. Congress. He is considered one of the visionary leaders in Asia-Pacific and serves as ranking member on the U.S. House Subcommittee on Asia, the Pacific, and the Global Environment. Another Samoan American politician is Francis "Mufi" Hannemann (1954–), who served as mayor of Honolulu from 2005 to 2010.

Music Mavis Rivers (ca. 1929–1992) was a jazz vocalist who joined her father's band during World War II and sang with the Red Norvo combo, George Shearing, and Andre Previn.

Sports Many Samoans and Samoan Americans have had successful careers in the National Football League (NFL), including Jack Thompson (1956–), who was known as the "Throwin' Samoan" and was a quarterback for the Cincinnati Bengals and the Tampa Bay Buccaneers. Troy Aumua Polamalu (1981–) is an NFL safety and played for the Pittsburgh Steelers in the Super Bowl twice. Tiaina Baul "Junior" Seau Jr. (1969–2012) was an NFL linebacker who played in the Super Bowl for the San Diego Chargers. He also played for the Miami Dolphins and the New England Patriots. Other prominent NFL players of Samoan descent include Siitupe Marcus "Tupe" Peko (1978–), Manase Jesse Sapolu (1961–), Al Noga (1965–), and Mosiula Mea'alofa "Lofa" Tatupu (1982–).

Mekeli Tiu Wesley (1979–) was the Western Athletic Conference Player of the Year for basketball in 2001 while he played for Brigham Young University. James Patrick Johnson (1987–), who was born in Wyoming but is of Samoan descent, has played for the Sacramento Kings and Chicago Bulls NBA basketball teams as a power forward. Peyton Robert Siva Jr. (1990–), who was born in Washington, is a point guard for the Louisville Cardinals men's basketball team. Wallace Aliifua Rank (1958–) was born in California and played for the San Diego Clippers.

Fanene Leifi Pita Maivia (1937–1982) was a professional wrestler and the grandfather of film star Dwayne "The Rock" Johnson.

Gregory Efthimios "Greg" Louganis (1960–) is an American Olympic diver of Samoan descent who won gold medals in the 1984 and 1988 Olympic Games.

Saleva'a Fuauli Atisano'e (Konishiki Yasokichi) (1963–), born in Hawaii and of Samoan descent, was the first non-Japanese-born Grand Master in sumo wrestling.

Stage and Screen Dwayne Johnson (1972–), whose stage name is "The Rock," is a well-known Hollywood actor and WWF champion. He has appeared in *Be Cool, Walking Tall, Race to Witch Mountain, Planet 51, Tooth Fairy, Doom, The Other Guys, Faster, Fast Five,* and *Fast Six.* His 2000 autobiography, *The Rock Says …,* reached number one on the *New York Times* best-seller list.

MEDIA

RADIO AND TELEVISION

American Samoa maintains a television station that
produces local programming under the direction
of the territorial government. Two channels are
broadcast throughout American Samoa. These carry
American network programming in the evening
and locally produced educational programming in
the daytime. The Independent State of Samoa has
television production facilities as well.

Both American and the Independent State of Samoa
operate several radio stations. In the Independent
State of Samoa 2AP is the national radio station and
the major means of communication with individuals
in remote villages. Every evening messages reporting
deaths, births, conferences, or other family news
are aired on 2AP as a way of informing people
who have no other ready access to information on
developments and events on the islands. Samoan-
language radio programs are also broadcast by radio
stations in Auckland, Honolulu, and Salt Lake City.

Samoa Technologies, Inc.

793 Hwy 1 and Faga'alu Park
P.O. Box 793
Pago Pago, American Samoa 96799
Phone: (684) 633-7000
Fax: (684) 633-5727
URL: ksbsfm92.com

South Seas Broadcasting

P.O. Box 6758
Pago Pago, American Samoa 96799

Phone: (684) 633-7793
Fax: (684) 633-4493
URL: southseasbroadcasting.com

PRINT

Samoa News

The daily newspaper of record for American Samoa.

Box 909
Pago Pago, American Samoa 96799
Phone: (684) 633-5599
Fax: (684) 633-4864
URL: samoanews.com

Samoa Observer

Together with the *Samoa Times*, a daily newspaper of
record for the Independent State of Samoa.

P.O. Box 1572
Apia, Samoa
Phone: (685) 23078 / 26977 / 31958 / 31959
Fax: (685) 23965
URL: samoaobserver.ws

ORGANIZATIONS AND ASSOCIATIONS

Polynesian Cultural Center (PCC)

Presents, preserves, and perpetuates the arts, crafts, culture,
and lore of Fijian, Hawaiian, Maori, Marquesan,
Tahitian, Tongan, Samoan, and other Polynesian
peoples.

55-370 Kamehameha Highway
Laie, Hawaii 96762

Phone: (800) 367-7060
Fax: (888) 722-7339
URL: http://polynesianculturalcenter.com

MUSEUMS AND RESEARCH CENTERS

Major libraries with Samoan collections are the O. F.
Nelson Memorial Library in Apia, the Oliveti Library
in Pago Pago, the Turnbull Library in Wellington,
and the Bernice P. Bishop Library in Honolulu.
Major museum collections of Samoan items can be
found at the Dominion Museum in Auckland, New
Zealand, the Bernice P. Bishop Museum in Honolulu,
the Phoebe A. Hearst Museum of Anthropology
(formerly the Lowie Museum of Anthropology) in
Berkeley, and the Ethnological Museum in Basel,
Switzerland.

Alexander Turnbull Library

The Turnbull Library of the National Library of New
Zealand maintains an extensive archive on Samoa,
particularly early explorations.

National Library of New Zealand Te Puna Mātauranga
o Aotearoa
P.O. Box 1467
Wellington 6140
New Zealand
Phone: +64 4 474 3000
Fax: +64 4 474 3035
URL: http://natlib.govt.nz/collections/a-z/
alexander-turnbull-library-collections

Bishop Museum

Maintains extensive collections on Samoan material
culture based on the work of Maori anthropologist Te
Rangi Hiroa, also known as Sir Peter Buck.

1525 Bernice Street
Honolulu, Hawaii 96817
Phone: (808) 847-3511
URL: www.bishopmuseum.org

SOURCES FOR ADDITIONAL STUDY

Baker, Paul T., Joel M. Hanna, and Thelma S. Baker.
*The Changing Samoans: Behavior and Health
in Transition.* Oxford: Oxford University
Press, 1986.

Balick, Michael J., and Paul Alan Cox. *Plants, People,
and Culture: The Science of Ethnobotany.* New York:
Scientific American Library, 1997.

Cox, Paul Alan. *Nafanua: Saving the Samoan Rainforest.*
New York: W. H. Freeman, 1997.

Cox, Paul Alan, and Sandra Anne Banack. *Islands,
Plants and Polynesians: An Introduction to
Polynesian Ethnobotany.* Portland: Dioscorides
Press, 1991.

Davidson, Janet M. "Samoa and Tonga," in *The Prehistory of
Polynesia.* Cambridge: Harvard University Press, 1979.

Fox, James W., and Kenneth Brailey Cumberland. *Western
Samoa.* Christchurch, New Zealand: Whitcombe and
Tombs, 1962.

Freeman, Derek. *Margaret Mead and Samoa: The Making
and Unmaking of an Anthropological Myth.* Cambridge:
Harvard University Press, 1981.

Kennedy, Paul M. *The Samoan Tangle: A Study in Anglo-
German-American Relations.* Dublin: Irish University
Press, 1974.

Milner, George Bertram. *Samoan Dictionary.* London:
Oxford University Press, 1966.

Pouesi, Daniel. *Akua.* Washington, D.C.: Aberdeen
Bay, 2012.

SAUDI ARABIAN AMERICANS

Sonya Schryer Norris

OVERVIEW

Saudi Arabian Americans (also referred to as Saudi Americans) are immigrants or descendants of people from the Kingdom of Saudi Arabia, a country in the Middle East that occupies most of the Arabian Peninsula. The country is home to Mecca and Medina, two holiest cities of Islam, and is bounded by the Red Sea to the west; Iraq, Jordan, and Kuwait to the north; the Persian Gulf (also called the Arabian Gulf), Qatar, and the United Arab Emirates to the east; Oman to the southeast; and Yemen to the southwest. The country measures 899,766 square miles (2,331,000 square kilometers), which is roughly one-third the size of the United States.

The population of Saudi Arabia is growing, and the *CIA World Factbook* estimated it at 26.5 million in July 2012. Officials report that 100 percent of its population practices Islam. According to the *Factbook*, 90 percent of the country is Arab, with Afro-Asians making up the remaining 10 percent of the population. Almost 6 million foreign workers also live in Saudi Arabia, most of them from India, Pakistan, Egypt, Yemen, Bangladesh, and the Philippines. The country's economy is based on its oil reserves, which contain about one-fifth of the world's total petroleum supply. The nation's unemployment rate is around 10 percent, although that figure is 28.2 percent for youths between the ages of 15 and 24.

The first Saudis in the United States came as ambassadors and staff to the Saudi Arabian Embassy in Washington, D.C., in the mid-1940s. In 1999 the Information Department of the embassy reported having no records of any regular Saudi citizens who had lived in the United States for extended periods before the end of World War II. After the war, young Saudi men began coming to the United States to obtain higher education. Saudi Arabia's oil wealth allowed the government to sponsor these students financially. As of 2013, students were provided with tuition, room and board, clothing, medical care, one round-trip plane ticket to visit Saudi Arabia each year, and other benefits. Bonuses were given to those studying science or technology. These Saudis tend to study all across the United States, although a considerable number live in Washington, D.C.

Reliable statistics are not available on the number of Americans of Saudi descent, because in reporting its data, the U.S. Census Bureau includes Saudi ancestry together with other small Arab ancestry groups (including Yemeni, Kuwaiti, and Omani). In the 2000 Census, 7,419 U.S. residents reported having Saudi ancestry—less than 1 percent of the total number of Arab Americans (1.2 million). By 2011 the number of Arab Americans had risen to 1.68 million. In 2011 the U.S. Census Bureau's American Community Survey estimated that the number of people (immigrants or temporary residents) from Saudi Arabia living in the United States was 48,000, half of whom were studying at universities (this number is slightly larger than the population of Chapel Hill, North Carolina). The largest majority of Saudi Arabian Americans live in California; other states with large numbers of Saudi Arabian Americans include Colorado, Florida, Pennsylvania, Texas, and Virginia.

HISTORY OF THE PEOPLE

Early History Beginning in 4000 BCE, trade routes that linked what are now India, China, Africa, and the Middle East crossed the Arabian Peninsula. The city of Mecca lay on one of the more prominent routes taken by Egyptian caravans. The Arabian people belonged to various clans who traced their lineage to Abraham and his son Ishmael, central figures in the Quran, the Old Testament, and the Torah.

The prophet Muhammad (c. 570 CE–632 CE), himself a merchant in Mecca, founded Islam in 622 CE and unified most of the Arabian Peninsula in his lifetime. The momentum of Islam led to the conquering of central Asia, northern Africa, and Spain within one hundred years of Muhammad's death. In practical terms, the widespread observance of Islam improved business relations among regions because Islamic standards of fair dealing practices were respected, regardless of ethnicity, national origin, or language. While Jews and Christians of conquered lands were tolerated as "People of the Book," they were also taxed more heavily than converts to Islam. During the Middle Ages, Arabia enjoyed a scientific, artistic, intellectual, and cultural preeminence unmatched in Europe until the Renaissance. At the beginning of the sixteenth century, the Ottoman Empire first defeated the Mamlukes, the group that had controlled Egypt, Syria, and the Hijaz since the commencement of the thirteenth century; subsequently, the Ottomans conquered the Hijaz.

In the mid-eighteenth century the territory that is now Saudi Arabia came under the control of Muhammad ibn Saud (d. 1765), who had formed an alliance with the religious reformer Muhammad Ibn Abd al-Wahhab (1703–1792). Wahhab was the founder of the Wahhabi movement, a conservative branch of Sunni Islam that demands its adherents live by an exacting interpretation of the Quran, the holy book of Islam, and of the teachings of the prophet Muhammad. Ibn Saud expanded his control through military conquests, advantageous marriages, and the ideology of the Wahhabi movement. The Wahhab/Saud dynasty shaped the moral and political landscape of Arabia. Its control stretched beyond the geographical boundaries of the Arabian Peninsula, and its influence permanently asserted itself in the Najd, the highland of the central Arabian Peninsula.

Modern Era For most of the nineteenth century Arabia was ruled by ibn Saud's descendants (the Saud family, or the Al Saud). However, in 1891 a rival family (the Al Rashid) exiled the Al Saud to Kuwait. In the early decades of the twentieth century, Abdul Aziz Ibn Saud (1876–1953), more simply known as Ibn Saud, successively recaptured key areas until he founded the Kingdom of Saudi Arabia on September 23, 1932.

King Ibn Saud established his authority by ruling in consult with the *ulama* (religious scholars), an indispensable aspect of public leadership in Wahhabi philosophy. As his ancestors had done, he fused political leadership with religious ideology. In 1933 oil was discovered in Saudi Arabia, and the Saudi monarchy used this wealth to bring Arabia to the forefront of global economics.

The discovery of oil has impacted Saudi Arabia's relations with nations around the world, especially with the United States. Oil production began in 1938 under an Arabian-U.S. oil company controlled by a group of private U.S. corporations called Aramco. Upon the death of Ibn Saud in 1953, his son, Saud (1902–1969), ascended the throne. During Saud's eleven-year reign, Saudi Arabia became a founding member of OPEC (Organization of Petroleum Exporting Countries). However, cultural instability and unrest stemming from perceived financial extravagance by the monarchy resulted in the deposition of King Saud in 1964; his half-brother Faisal (1906–1975) was placed on the throne instead. As a rule, Faisal instigated many economic and social reforms that catalyzed positive change in Saudi Arabia. Under his reign, the country's first public school for female students was established.

King Faisal's reign ended abruptly with his assassination by his nephew in 1975, and his brother Khalid (1913–1982) assumed the throne. During his reign, Saudi Arabia underwent many considerable changes. In 1979 the country severed diplomatic ties with Egypt (as a result of disagreement over Egypt's peace agreements with Israel). Also that year, the Grand Mosque in Mecca was taken over by Islamic extremists. The government regained control of the Mosque after a ten-day period and executed the instigators. In 1980 Saudi Arabia assumed complete control of Aramco.

After King Khalid's death of a heart attack in 1982, his brother Fahd (1921–2005) assumed the Saudi throne and maintained close political ties with the United States. He improved the national infrastructure, developed urban areas, created a national public education system, and encouraged the immigration of thousands of foreign employees to the country. He also reintroduced diplomatic interactions with Egypt. In 1990 Saudi Arabia requested the United States to intervene in Iraq's invasion of Kuwait, and in 1991 it assisted the U.S. military in the offensive against Iraq that was code-named Operation Desert Storm. Also during this time, King Fahd introduced several reforms, including the establishment of the Consultative Council (Majlis al-Shura), a body consisting of a chairman and sixty members selected by the ruler.

The king stripped Al-Qaeda founder Osama bin Laden of his Saudi nationality in 1994 after bin Laden's activities as a terrorist leader surfaced. Following a stroke in 1995, King Fahd stepped down and Crown Prince Abdullah assumed control of the kingdom for a brief period. Abdullah set up foreign policy initiatives to create more political distance between Saudi Arabia and the United States. By early 1996 King Fahd had resumed his reign.

During the early years of the twenty-first century, Saudi Arabian and U.S. relations underwent some transformations. Fifteen of the nineteen hijackers in the terrorist attacks on September 11, 2001, were of Saudi nationality. This temporarily strained relations between the two nations. In addition, dissidents within Saudi Arabia had been criticizing the regime's cooperation with the United States in Desert Storm. In 2003 Saudi Arabia refused to support the U.S. invasion of Iraq, and in return the United States removed all troops from Saudi Arabia. Nevertheless, the two nations expressed their intention to remain allies. King Fahd died in 2005, and Abdullah, who as the crown prince had ruled during Fahd's recovery from his stroke, assumed the throne.

King Abdullah sought to reduce Saudi Arabia's reliance on oil revenue. In November 2005 the World Trade Organization admitted Saudi Arabia as a member. Saudi Arabia's relations with the United States gradually became less strained, and more Saudi students traveled to the country to study. During the tumult of the Arab Spring in 2011, in which neighboring countries overthrew their governments, King Abdullah increased welfare expenditures. In June 2011 a group of Saudi women protested the law prohibiting them from driving cars, and in the ensuing months, the king established greater rights for women, including the right to vote and to hold membership on the

Consultative Council. In addition, in 2012 Saudi Arabia allowed women athletes to compete in the Olympic Games for the first time.

SETTLEMENT IN THE UNITED STATES

Although citizens of Middle Eastern countries have been immigrating to the United States since the late nineteenth century, few Middle Eastern Muslims immigrated prior to World War II. In recent decades, greater numbers of Saudi Arabians have immigrated, mostly because of their desire to obtain a university education, and also because of political dissent and dissatisfaction with the restrictions of living in an orthodox Muslim society. In April 1976 Saudi Arabia presented the University of Southern California with an endowment in the amount of $1 million to establish the King Faisal Chair of Islamic and Arab Studies. At that time, more than 150 Saudi students were enrolled at the University of Southern California.

Due to the close political and economic relationship between Saudi Arabia and the United States, a number of other generous educational grants were set up. Saudi men planning to study in the United States were encouraged marry and take their families with them in order to reduce feelings of isolation and culture shock. One incentive included tuition money for a man's spouse to study as well. Unmarried Saudi women were required to have a chaperone to travel outside of Saudi Arabia. According to Richard Nyrop in his book *Saudi Arabia: A Country Study*, "the vast majority [of Saudi students] remained deeply committed to the Saudi values surrounding religion as well as family and social life. The one area where there were measurable changes of opinion was in the attitudes toward women and women's role in society."

Saudi Arabians' interest in studying in the United States declined somewhat, however, when universities in Saudi Arabia that had begun operating in the 1960s became more established. This phenomenon pleased conservative groups, who were concerned about sending so many young people out of the country, particularly to non-Muslim nations. In 1984 approximately 10,000 Saudis were studying outside of Saudi Arabia. By 1992 this figure had dropped to 5,000, with half of these studying at universities in the United States.

By 1999 the trend had reversed. The Saudi Arabian Embassy in Washington, D.C., estimated that 5,000 Saudis were studying in the United States, and that the majority were male. Around the end of the twentieth century, there were twenty-five Saudi student houses scattered across the United States; these organizations were supported by the embassy and the Saudi Cultural Mission. In October 1997 the Saudi Student House at Indiana State University held a "Saudi National Day," featuring traditional food, dancing, a fashion show, displays, slides and videos. At Michigan State University, a Saudi Student House was established in April 1996 to provide Islamic,

educational, social, and athletic services; in 1999 it had 70 members. Saudi students also congregated at mosques and Islamic centers, many of which received support from the embassy.

There are a variety of reasons why so few Saudi Arabians permanently immigrate to the United States. Among these are the wealth of Saudi Arabia, the difficulty of maintaining an Islamic lifestyle in the United States, and a lack of motivation to leave Saudi Arabia.

In the years following September 11 terrorist attacks, the number of Saudi students studying abroad in the United States decreased considerably; by 2004 only 1,000 remained. In more recent years this has changed again; in the 2011–2012 academic year, approximately 24,000 Saudi students were attending U.S. universities, making them the fastest-growing overseas segment, ahead even of China.

To accommodate the needs of Saudi students, many Arab American organizations (both Muslim and Christian) have been established in the United States. They have developed student groups, scholarship networks, newspapers, magazines, television programming, restaurants, cultural centers, and traveling museum exhibits. Saudi Arabians, as well as the Saudi government, have also made financial contributions to Muslim organizations. Despite this trend, though, a relatively small number of Saudis have chosen to live permanently in the United States. The U.S. Immigration and Nationality Act of 1965, which established preferential treatment for educated immigrants, encouraged a limited number of Saudis to seek U.S. citizenship. Those who did settle permanently in the United States were commonly well-educated and lived near cities where they held professional jobs.

The number of people from Saudi Arabia who obtained legal permanent resident status in the United States was also impacted by 9/11. For example, between 2000 and 2002, around 1,100 Saudis obtained legal residency each year. This rate had dropped dramatically by 2003, when only 735 Saudis acquired legal residency in the United States. This number did not rebound to previous rates until 2005.

Census data on the number of Americans of Saudi descent was not available because the U.S. Census Bureau recorded Saudi ancestry in a collapsed "Other Arab" category together with other small Arab ancestry groups (such as Libyan, Yemeni, and Tunisian). For 2009–2011, the Census Bureau's American Community Survey estimated that 227,000 people were in the "Other Arab" category; only a small percentage of these would be people of Saudi ancestry.

More specific Census data was available on the number of U.S. residents born in Saudi Arabia.

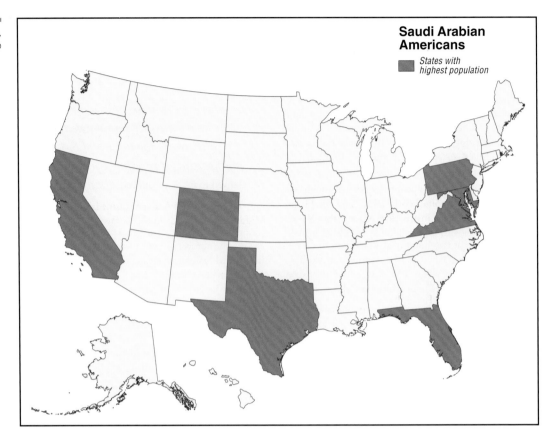

Saudi Arabian Americans

States with
highest population

According to the 2009–2011 estimates compiled by the American Community Survey, 48,621 U.S. residents reported having been born in Saudi Arabia, and these residents were living in 45 of the 50 United States. Apart from California, five additional states reported clusters of over 200 Saudi-born U.S. residents: Colorado, Florida, Pennsylvania, Texas, and Virginia.

There are a variety of reasons why so few Saudi Arabians permanently immigrate to the United States. Among these are the wealth of Saudi Arabia, the difficulty of maintaining an Islamic lifestyle in the United States, and a lack of motivation to leave Saudi Arabia. Saudis are also required to obtain an exit visa from their government in order to leave the country, and they must provide a reason to get it. The limited number of marriages between U.S. and Saudi citizens may also have contributed to the low number of Saudi immigrants.

LANGUAGE

Arabic is the national language of Saudi Arabia, but English is commonly used in business transactions, particularly with foreigners. Of the fourteen main newspapers operating in Saudi Arabia, four are published in English. English is commonly taught in the public schools, and sometimes French is offered in private academies. Because English is a part of the linguistic culture of Saudi Arabia, the language barrier

that other immigrant groups usually encounter does not play as large a role in the immigrant experiences of Saudis in the United States.

Greetings and Popular Expressions The most common greeting in the Arabic language is *"Assalaamu alaikum,"* which means "Peace be upon you." This is often combined with kisses to the right and left cheek. "Hello" in Arabic is *"Marhaba"*; "How are you?" is *"Keef Halek"*; and "Good morning" is *"Sabah Al Kair."* *"Eid Mubarak"* is spoken to wish someone a happy holiday.

RELIGION

Saudi Arabia reportedly has a 100 percent Muslim population. Islam is tightly interwoven into all facets of Saudi life, including government, law, education, social customs, marriage, and family. The Saudi flag, green with white Arabic script, proclaims the first pillar of Islam: "There is no God but Allah and Muhammad is His Messenger." In Saudi Arabia members of religions other than Islam, including foreign workers, are not permitted to exercise their faith publicly, nor may anyone attempt to convert a Muslim.

The vast majority of Saudi Arabians follow Sunni Islam as it is practiced in accordance with the Wahhabi Movement. Sunni Muslims follow the teachings of the Quran and the example of the prophet Muhammad (the *sunna* consists of the personal customs and habits of Muhammad). Sunni Islam is one of two major strains of Islam, the other being Shi'a Islam. The schism between the two groups dates back to factionalism among Muhammad's followers in the years following his death.

Saudi Arabia's "Basic Law of Governance" declares that its constitution is the Quran. The country is therefore governed according to *shari'a*, Islamic law as outlined in the Quran. All facets of life are governed in the Islamic system, which does not dwell on differences of ethnicity, class, or caste, but instead concentrates on bringing people together through an all-encompassing, monotheistic faith. The teachings of Islam include clear instructions on such topics as marriage, family and criminal law, inheritance rights, business, banking, and individual deportment.

Islam stresses submission to God as well as peace. There are five pillars of Islam, all of which must be practiced by Muslims: profession of faith, prayer (five times daily facing in the direction of the holy city of Mecca in Saudi Arabia), almsgiving, fasting during the month of Ramadan, and Hajj, the pilgrimage to Mecca that all Muslims are required to make at least once in their lives. The Hajj is made in the month after Ramadan. Many Saudi Americans make the pilgrimage to Mecca. Although the Saudi Arabian Embassy in the United States limits people to making the pilgrimage only once every five years, approximately 12,000 Saudis living in the United States make this journey annually.

Islam plays a huge role in the lives of Saudi Arabian Americans. In the United States, young Saudi men and women residing with their families frequently experience a greater degree of freedom than do their counterparts in Saudi Arabia. However, they also face expectations, some of which are related to tenets of Islam, that are often more restrictive than those of the average American. For instance, there are constraints concerning the kinds of marriage partners they are permitted: Males can marry non-Muslims, but the woman must be affiliated with the Jewish or Christian faith.

CULTURE AND ASSIMILATION

A majority of Saudi Arabians who migrate to the United States ultimately plan to return to their home country; this is true even of Saudi children who are born on American soil. For this reason, Saudis frequently retain many of the cultural customs from their home country. In addition, because Saudi Arabian Americans frequently marry persons from their country or the same geographic region, they do not become as assimilated into mainstream U.S. cultural practices as they might if they intermarried with those from other cultures or ethnicities.

At the same time, however, it is common for Saudi students studying abroad to assimilate into U.S. culture, even if these practices are temporary. While

Saudis live in the United States, many of them participate in sports leagues, eat fast food, attend concerts by Western music groups, and go to the movies. Because they experience greater freedom while living in the United States, Saudi students often undergo some culture shock concerning frequent and informal interactions with the opposite sex. Many female students reported that they had to become re-acclimated to living under more restrictive conditions upon their return to their home country. For example, female students can drive in the United States, but women are not allowed to drive in Saudi Arabia.

Cuisine Saudi Arabian cuisine is similar to other Middle Eastern foods in that it favors lamb, rice, and a wide variety of vegetables and spices. Both tea and *gahwah*, a coffee of unroasted beans and cardamom, are very popular. Islam forbids both pork and alcohol.

In the United States, Saudi women prepare traditional dishes and learn to work with American foods. There are no specifically Saudi Arabian restaurants in the United States, but many Saudi Americans enjoy the cuisine of other Middle Eastern countries and frequent their restaurants. Sensitive to the desires of Saudi expatriates, Saadeddin Pastry Limited, headquartered in Riyadh, ships Saudi pastries and sweets worldwide for holidays, weddings, and other special occasions.

Many Saudi Arabian Americans partake of popular American food; this might be especially true for students. For example, the *Wall Street Journal* reported that during the influx of Saudi university students to the United States in 2012, Central Washington University administrators were ready to offer *halal* food to Saudi students; this food must be prepared in accordance with Islamic law. However, the Saudi students elected instead to dine at the college town's cafes like other students. Despite the preferences of these students, however, most Saudis and Muslims in general continue to eat only halal foods.

Traditional Dress Traditional Saudi clothing for men consists of a *thobe*, a long-sleeved, loose-fitting garment that covers the body from neck to ankles. Thobes are sewn of cotton or wool and may be plain white or very colorful with fine embroidery. A headpiece called a *ghutrah* is also customary. This is a cotton square of cloth wrapped around the head and secured with an *agal*, a black cord. For special occasions, Saudi men may wear a *bisht*, a gold-edged cloak, over the thobe.

While in the United States, most male Saudi students adopt Western standards of dress, including jeans and T-shirts. The clothing worn by Saudi women in the United States are varied and not confined to traditional Saudi Arabian garb. Jeans and heels are not unheard of. Many women wear the *hijab*, a veil that covers a woman's hair and neck; this type of dress is common among women who are experiencing the freedom available in U.S. culture that is not as acceptable in Saudi Arabia itself. In public, some women wear the *abaya*, a loose black garment that covers them from neck to foot. A variety of veils are worn as well, including the *niqab*, which covers most of the face. A family's religious piety influences how a woman will dress after arriving in the United States. In conservative settings such as the mosque, or for celebrations, both men and women are more likely to wear traditional clothing.

Dances and Songs *Khaleegy* (meaning "gulf"), a popular Saudi women's dance, is characterized as fast and exciting. It is often performed at women's parties in a special dancing costume known as the *thobe al nasha'ar*, and associated songs speak of the beauty of the dancer, often mentioning her hair. In Saudi Arabia in the 1990s and early 2000s, Muhammad Abdou was a popular singer of songs typifying this style. In the United States, the khaleegy came to be included in the repertoires of dancing groups such as the Jawaahir Dance Company of Minneapolis, Minnesota.

The distribution of Saudi music, secular or religious, has been very restricted. Much of it is available only on compact discs and not by digital download. A very limited number of songs are available through Amazon.com and iTunes. Despite these challenges, individual import companies, including Caravelle Fine Middle Eastern Imports, advertise their ability to provide Saudi music in the United States. Increasing interest in Arabic music has led to the publication of several books on the topic, including the translation of Habib Hassan Touma's *The Music of the Arabs* (1996).

Holidays The nation of Saudi Arabia recognizes two religious holidays, both of which are celebrated by Muslims the world over, including by Saudi Arabian Americans. The first is Eid Al-Fitr, which marks the end of the month of Ramadan and lasts for seven days. Fasting during the lunar month of Ramadan is a required practice of all adult Muslims in good health. Few Muslims in the United States are able to take time away from their jobs during Ramadan, which can make religious observance challenging for Muslim Americans. Eid Al-Fitr is celebrated at mosques and Islamic centers with special meals and prayers. Giving *zakat* (alms) at the end of Ramadan is also a religious requirement. Muslims who do not live near mosques often travel to them for holidays. In January 1999, approximately 14,000 Muslims gathered to celebrate Eid Al-Fitr at the Expo Center in Chantilly, Virginia. Because of the huge numbers of Saudi students who have studied abroad in the United States, an increasing number are expanding their celebrations of Ramadan on various college campus across the nation. These students find pleasure in celebrating religious holidays with a community; however, Saudi students can find it difficult to balance this celebration with academic requirements. A majority report that non-Muslim instructors assist them in trying to sustain this balance.

The second important Islamic religious holiday is Eid al-Adha, celebrated at the end of the Hajj; it lasts

for ten days. Due to the lunar nature of the Arabic calendar, known as the *Hijra* calendar, Eid al-Fitr and Eid al-Adha do not fall on the same days each year.

September 23rd, the day Saudi Arabia was declared an independent nation, is often recognized as a time of celebration as well. This day of independence, or Saudi National Day, as it is frequently called, is celebrated at numerous universities around the United States; these functions are frequently sponsored by Saudi student organizations, some of which even receive remunerations from the Saudi government to sponsor their activities. These celebrations allow Saudi students to share their heritage and culture with classmates and faculty, and the celebrations are marked with great joy and festivity. Some students have even compared the celebration to the Western tradition of Halloween, which is not practiced in Saudi Arabia.

Health Issues The United States has had a long-term relationship with Saudi Arabia in the areas of medical research and health care. From the 1960s through the 1980s, Saudi Arabia developed and instituted expansive medical coverage for its citizens, built hospitals, and trained physicians. The United States assisted in this process, and as a result, some Saudi doctors were trained in the United States. In 1999 Saudi Arabia presented George Mason University in northern Virginia with a $1.1 million grant to train twelve Saudi nurses.

Saudi Arabian medical students continue to study at U.S. medical schools to receive a top-quality education, and many of them then return to their home country to practice medicine. Researchers and academics from the United States and Saudi Arabia have also collaborated on studies of certain health issues. The Naval Health Research Center in San Diego, California, completed one such study in 2005 that utilized the efforts of both U.S. and Saudi representatives. The researchers investigated health outcomes among Saudi Arabian National Guard soldiers following the Persian Gulf War. Because the two nations have greatly contrasting social and religious customs, the study explored how these contrastive conditions potentially impacted health outcomes.

One of the maladies that frequently affects various ethnic groups, including Africans, African Americans, and Saudi Arabians, is sickle cell disease. In 1999, with the assistance of the King Faisal Specialist Hospital and Research Center in Riyadh, Saudi Arabia, worldwide collaborative research was conducted to examine additional risk factors pertaining to Saudis with sickle-cell disease. Research conducted in the twenty-first century has identified five areas in Africa and the Saudi Arabia region where mutations that lead to this disease have occurred.

Funerals In Islam the body of a deceased person is bathed three times, the last time with scented oil. Men are washed by men and women by women. Prayers are said during the bathing process and the body is wrapped in a white shroud. If a person dies in the morning, they must be buried that same day. If they die in the afternoon, they must be buried by the following morning. Prayers are recited throughout the burial ceremony. Most frequently, God is praised, forgiveness is asked for the person's sins, and a prayer is recited for all Muslims. No embalming materials are used. The dead are buried five or six feet deep, on their right side, with their head facing Mecca. Coffins are allowed, but more often the person is put to rest only in their shroud. Ornate coffins, tombs, or headstones are prohibited. Muslims in the United States have established cemeteries in their communities to observe these rites and customs.

FAMILY AND COMMUNITY LIFE

A majority of Saudi students in the United States return home after receiving their degrees to begin their professional career. This trend holds true even for children of Saudi Arabians who are born in the United States. However, while young Saudi men and women reside in the United States, they experience a greater degree of freedom than they would while living in their home country. Regardless, adolescents are unlikely to form close relationships with the opposite sex. Girls and boys are kept somewhat apart, as Saudi Arabian Americans tend to preserve the cultural trends of their home country. Historically, women in Saudi Arabia were given less freedom and fewer opportunities than males. This practice has shifted a great deal in the past couple of decades so that women have much greater access to education; however, they still have numerous restrictions placed on their recreational activities and socializing.

Gender Roles Saudi Arabians in the United States sometimes engage in more interactions with persons of the opposite sex than they would in their homeland. This is possible because the restrictions on women in Saudi Arabia, which include a ban on using any form of public transportation, driving, or appearing in public without a male escort, are not always followed in the United States. Female Saudi students who study abroad must do so in the company of a close male relative, but when in the United States, they may engage in activities that they might not otherwise have access to. For example, many Saudi Arabian women might drive a car in the United States. For Saudi Arabian American students, even going to class with members of the opposite sex proves to be an innovative experience. When students return to Saudi Arabia, their views about how men and women can and should interact have often shifted, and sometimes they experience periods of adjustment in acclimating back to stricter cultural practices.

Saudi women retain their last name after marriage, but their activities are regulated by their families and by religious law. Men are legally allowed up to four wives, although technically a woman must agree

SAUDI ARABIAN PROVERBS

Examples of secular Saudi Arabian proverbs include the following: "He who knows not and knows not he knows not is a fool. Shun him"; "He who knows not and knows he knows not is simple. Teach him"; "He who knows and knows not he knows is asleep. Wake him;" "He who knows and knows he knows is wise. Follow him"; "He who loves thinks others are blind; the others think he is crazy"; "Better a thousand enemies outside the house than one inside"; and "He who has health has hope; and he who has hope, has everything."

Proverbs from the prophet Muhammad include: "Riches are not from abundance of worldly goods, but from a contented mind"; "Let go of the things of which you are in doubt for the things in which there is no doubt"; and "God is beautiful and He loves beauty."

Quranic proverbs include: "Whatever good you have is all from God. Whatever evil, all is from yourself"; and "God will not change the condition of men until they change what is in themselves."

to her husband's subsequent marriages. The discord often caused by such arrangements discourages many men from attempting them.

Education Saudi families established the Islamic Saudi Academy for children of primary- and secondary-school age in Alexandria, Virginia, in 1984. The government of Saudi Arabia funded the academy to provide an academic, religious, and Arabic curriculum. As of 2008, it served approximately 1,200 children in kindergarten through the twelfth grade.

The number of Saudi Arabian American students studying in the United States has skyrocketed since the introduction of King Abdullah's scholarship program in 2005, from 1,000 students in 2004 to over 74,000 students in the 2011–2012 academic year. New requirements for changes in Saudi Arabia's infrastructure mean that students are encouraged to study the sciences and engineering. However, students from all majors participate in the scholarship program, which provides students a five-year visa and expenditure coverage. Students pursue both undergraduate and graduate degrees. Saudis who receive sponsorship to study at institutions of higher education in the United States have often agreed to work for the Saudi government for a number of years upon their return.

STUDYING THE SAUDI STUDENT COMMUNITY

The academic areas that have interested Saudi Arabian students have shifted over time. Although they collectively researched a wide variety of topics at the masters and doctoral levels, the majority of students during the late 1970s were studying the social sciences. As more Saudi Arabians received educations in the United States, more dissertations were published about the community of Saudi students. One doctoral dissertation by Abdullah Ahmed Oweidat, titled "A Study of Changes in Value Orientation of Arab Students in the United States" (University of Southern California, 1981), revealed that Saudis and other Arab students who had resided in the United States for at least three years demonstrated values similar to those held by Americans, which were significantly different from those of Arab students who had recently arrived in the United States. Another doctoral dissertation, by Abdallah Mohammed Alfauzan (Mississippi State University, 1992), focused on how Saudi students in the United States viewed women's participation in the workforce in Saudi Arabia. He found that Saudi students in the United States possessed more liberal viewpoints than their counterparts in Saudi Arabia.

Courtship and Weddings During the twentieth century, both Saudi Arabians and Saudi Arabian Americans frequently had their marriages arranged by their parents. More liberal parents would allow their children greater opportunity to select their spouses. In the twenty-first century, Saudi men and women in the United States may exchange phone numbers and interact online.

Islamic marriages are a contract, and while certain aspects are immutable, both parties contribute to the contract according to their needs and desires. For instance, a woman may request the right to travel in her marriage contract. Wedding parties are usually separate for the bride and groom, taking place in different locations and even on different nights. Divorce is permissible as a last resort, but the importance placed on marriage and the family has traditionally kept the divorce rate low. Since the beginning of the twenty-first century, however, Saudi Arabians have been divorcing at an increasing rate. Both men and women are also marrying foreigners in record numbers; this trend is indicative of similar patterns in other societies in the Persian Gulf region.

Saudi men living alone in the United States as students are more likely to return to Saudi Arabia to find a wife than to marry an American woman. In Islam, males are legally permitted to marry any woman "of the Book"—meaning Muslims, Jews, and Christians—but family preferences for other Arabs often hold sway.

The restrictions for Saudi women desiring to marry non-Saudis are severe. Saudi women are prevented from marrying non-Saudis, unless they receive special permission from the authorities. Despite these challenges, however, the number of Saudi women marrying foreigners has increased in the twenty-first century: Over 20,000 marriages were registered between Saudi women and foreign men between 2002 and 2007. One of the most notable Saudi Arabian women who has married a foreigner is Lubna Olayan. Born in Saudi Arabia and educated in the United States, Olayan is married to an American attorney, John Xefos, and serves as CEO of the Riyadh-based Olayan Financing Company (an organization that was started by Olayan's father in 1947).

EMPLOYMENT AND ECONOMIC CONDITIONS

When petroleum mining began in 1938, it was estimated that Saudi Arabia possessed 25 percent of the world's oil supply. King Ibn Saud and subsequent rulers were faced with the challenge of turning an isolated country, almost completely ignored by the Western industrialized nations, into a global economic force. Among other concerns was their desire to obtain the economic benefits of oil production without allowing Western values to corrupt Saudi Arabia.

Ultimately, the United States agreed to train Saudi workers, many of whom had to first be taught to read, and to pay for the oil that resulted from their joint efforts. The enormous influx of money and technical advances lifted Saudi Arabia into the modern twentieth century faster, perhaps, than has happened to any other industrializing society.

In the 2012–2013 academic year, an estimated 130,000 Saudi students were studying in other countries, and typically, around 50 percent of them at U.S. universities. The king's goal for establishing this program was to provide youth with the skills they would need to contribute effectively to the Saudi nation, especially in light of the challenges of a rapidly expanding population and decreasing petroleum reserves.

The execution of this scholarship program has raised some tensions in Saudi Arabia between those who support it and those who received a more religiously based Saudi education and wish to preserve the status quo. Also under debate is the question of how educating women abroad will impact the current conservative practices in place in Saudi Arabia itself when they return home after having experienced Western-style freedoms. Some female students who have studied abroad elect to move to countries like Dubai after they return home. A related trend is that 40 percent of educated female Saudi students cannot find employment in Saudi Arabia because of gender-based cultural and societal restrictions.

POLITICS AND GOVERNMENT

Most Saudis residing in the United States are not citizens and cannot vote or run for political office. Despite this, the Saudi influence on American politics is huge. Saudi Arabia's close political ties with the United States are the result of an economic relationship created by oil. For example, the Saudis accepted over 700,000 troops from thirty-seven nations to fight against Iraq during the Persian Gulf War in 1991. While Saudi Arabia and the United States are linked because of a mutually beneficial relationship over oil, the two countries have not always agreed on issues. Significantly, Saudi Arabia and the United States have differed in foreign policy stances regarding Israel and the Middle East. The relationship has nevertheless remained strong over time, though during the early twenty-first century, an increase in terrorist attacks in Saudi Arabia (thought to be linked to the Saudis' cooperation with the United States during the Persian Gulf War) has strained relations somewhat. In particular, in 2003 Saudi Arabia refused to help with the U.S. invasion of Iraq; that same year, the United States withdrew all of its troops from Saudi soil.

NOTABLE INDIVIDUALS

Academia Tadal Asad (1933–) was born in Saudi Arabia and became an anthropologist at the City University of New York. He developed a genealogical method derived from the philosophy of Friedrich Nietzsche and Michel Foucault.

Art Hend Al-Mansour (1956–), installation artist, was born in Saudi Arabia, where she was trained as a doctor and practiced medicine before immigrating to the United States in 1997. She earned an MFA in 2002 at the Minnesota College of Art and Design, has exhibited throughout the United States, and is a board member of the Arab American Cultural Institute in Minnesota.

Film Summer Bishil (1988–) is an actress who was born in Pasadena, California, to a European-American mother and a Saudi Arabian father. She starred in the 2007 film *Towelhead* and also appeared

Rajaa Al-Sanea is a Saudi Arabian author of the controversial novel *Girls of Riyadh* and currently lives in Chicago, Illinois. KATJA HEINEMANN / AURORA PHOTOS / ALAMY

Yasmin Siraj competes in the Ladies Free Skate during the 2013 Prudential U.S. Figure Skating Championships in Omaha, Nebraska. JONATHAN DANIEL / GETTY IMAGES

in films such as *Crossing Over* (2009) and *The Last Airbender* (2010).

Sports Sarah Attar (1992–) is a track and field athlete who was born in California to an American mother and a Saudi Arabian father. She competed in the London 2012 Olympics for Saudi Arabia, the first time Saudi women were allowed to compete.

Yasmin Siraj (1996–), a U.S. figure skater, earned the silver medal in the 2010 U.S. Figure Skating Championships. Her mother is of Iranian descent and her father is Saudi Arabian.

MEDIA

There are no significant publications specific to Saudis in the United States.

ORGANIZATIONS AND ASSOCIATIONS

American and Saudi Arabian Dialogue (ASAD) Education Center at George Washington University

An organization devoted to finding educational opportunities for Saudi and U.S. students in legal, business, and religious disciplines.

K. Cyrus Homayounpour, Director
805 21st Street NW
Suite 301
Washington, D.C. 20052
Phone: (202) 994-1845
Fax: (202) 994-7718
Email: cyrush@gwu.edu
URL: www.cps.gwu.edu/ASADcenter

Islamic Saudi Academy

A private school that encourages students to achieve high academic goals while maintaining Islamic ideals and proficiency in the Arabic language.

Faridah Turkistani, Director General
8333 Richmond Highway
Alexandria, Virginia 22309
Phone: (703) 780-0606
Email: Faridah.Turkistani@saudiacademy.net
URL: www.saudiacademy.net

Saudi Arabian Cultural Mission to the USA (SACM)

This organization implements the Saudi government's policies regarding education of its citizens in the United States.

8500 Hilltop Road
Fairfax, Virginia 22031
Phone: (703) 573-7226
Fax: (703) 573-2595
URL: www.sacm.org

U.S.–Saudi Arabian Business Council (USSABC)

A membership organization that develops relationships between Saudi and U.S. businesses.

8081 Wolftrap Road
Suite 300
Vienna, Virginia 22182
Phone: (703) 962-9300 or (888) 638-1212
Fax: (703) 204-0332
Email: ussaudi@us-sabc.org
URL: www.us-sabc.org

MUSEUMS AND RESEARCH CENTERS

Arab American National Museum

Exhibits and resources focus on the experience of U.S. immigrants from all Arab countries, including Saudi Arabia.

Kim Silarski, Communications
13624 Michigan Avenue
Dearborn, Michigan 48126
Phone: (313) 582-2266
Fax: (313) 582-1086
Email: ksilarski@accesscommunity.org
URL: www.arabamericanmuseum.org

SOURCES FOR ADDITIONAL STUDY

Al-Farsy, Fouad. *Modernity and Tradition: The Saudi Equation.* New York: Kegan Paul International, 1990.

Barrett, Paul M. *American Islam: The Struggle for the Soul of a Religion.* New York: Farrar, Straus, and Giroux, 2007.

Bronson, Rachel. *Thicker Than Oil: America's Uneasy Partnership with Saudi Arabia.* Oxford, UK: Oxford University Press, 2006.

Chu, Jeff. "Saudi Students: In Their Own Words." *Time*, March 13, 2006.

House, Karen Elliot. *On Saudi Arabia: Its People, Past Religion, Fault Lines, and Future.* New York: Knopf, 2012.

Jones, Toby. *Desert Kingdom: How Oil and Water Forged Modern Saudi Arabia.* Cambridge, MA: Harvard University Press, 2010.

Knickmeyer, Ellen. "Saudi Students Flood in as U.S. Reopens Door." *Wall Street Journal*, Nov. 8, 2012.

Lippman, Thomas. *Saudi Arabia on the Edge: The Uncertain Future of an American Ally.* Dulles, VA: Potomac Books, 2012.

SCOTCH-IRISH AMERICANS

Richard Esbenshade

OVERVIEW

Scotch-Irish Americans are descendants of the Presbyterian "Ulster Scots," who migrated from the Lowland areas of Scotland to northern Ireland (also referred to as Ulster, although present-day Ulster is smaller than the historical Irish province of Ulster) in the seventeenth century as part of a plan to cement Protestant British domination of Ireland. Over the course of the eighteenth century, religious persecution by the official Episcopalian Church of Ireland and economic hardship pushed a significant portion to set off across the sea again, from Ulster to North America. Northern Ireland, barely 12 miles across the Irish Sea from southwestern Scotland at its closest point, consists of the northeasternmost six counties of the Irish island—Antrim, Armagh, Fermanagh, Down, Derry, and Tyrone—which, at the time the Republic of Ireland was established in 1937, remained part of Great Britain. Ulster's landscape consists of fertile lowlands and rugged uplands. Its area is 5,345 square miles (13,843 square kilometers), about the size of Connecticut.

The population of Northern Ireland was just over 1.8 million in 2011, according to the census carried out by the Northern Ireland Statistics and Research Agency. The census listed slightly more than 40 percent of the population as Roman Catholic and a similar proportion as members of various Protestant denominations, led by Presbyterians at 19 percent and Anglicans at just under 14 percent. The majority of the rest either declared themselves nonreligious or declined to state, and there were very small communities of Muslims, Hindus, Sikhs, Buddhists, and Jews (less than 1 percent in total). Over the last century Northern Ireland's history has been characterized by division and bitter strife between cultural groups defined by religion. At the time of the Ulster migration, Scotland was a land of poor farmers; after its incorporation into Great Britain in the early eighteenth century, its economy was industrialized, with heavy involvement in shipbuilding, coal mining, and steelmaking. Northern Ireland's economy has historically been manufacturing based, though it has shifted toward services and the public sector in recent decades. While Northern Ireland has an average standard of living below that of the United Kingdom, as an "advanced" economy and a European Union member, it is a relatively well-off country in a worldwide context—its GDP per capita gives it a ranking between thirtieth and thirty-fifth on a list of the countries of the world.

Ulster Scots began to leave for the American colonies in the early eighteenth century. Most of the early immigrants, lacking the money to pay their passage, came as indentured servants, though they were able to earn their freedom in a few years and generally became independent farmers on the western and southern frontiers. Immigrants in later waves were more likely to be skilled artisans or professionals and to settle in cities and towns along the East Coast. Scotch-Irish immigration tapered off in the twentieth century and had virtually stopped by the time of the Great Depression. In all, an estimated two million had arrived during that time period (in comparison to 200,000 who had made the original trek from Scotland to Northern Ireland in the seventeenth century). By the mid-twentieth century, if not earlier, the Scotch-Irish were completely assimilated into the broader American society, and their occupations and lifestyle were almost indistinguishable from those of other ethnic groups. In recent decades numerous Scotch-Irish Americans have made concerted efforts to reconnect with their ethnic roots and explore their historical and cultural identity, producing a number of books, journals, and organizations dedicated to Scotch-Irish Americana.

According to the U.S. Census Bureau's American Community Survey, an estimated 3.3 million people living in the United States in 2011 self-identified as having Scotch-Irish ancestry; the 2008 figure was 5.8 million. However, both historians and authors of popular books, including Carlton Jackson, Karen F. McCarthy, and James Webb, have estimated that the number of Americans with Scotch-Irish heritage is more than 20 million, more than 6 percent of the U.S. population. Scotch-Irish Americans are most numerous in Pennsylvania, especially in Lancaster County and points further south and west; in the Ohio River Valley, principally in Ohio; and in the South, especially the Shenandoah Valley in Virginia and in the Carolinas, Georgia, and Tennessee. According to the American Community Survey estimates, other states with large numbers of Scotch-Irish Americans included California, Texas, and Florida.

HISTORY OF THE PEOPLE

Early History Because the first inhabitants of Ireland came by way of Scotland around 9,000 years ago, there has been a continuous history of connections between the two lands. Some of these "Scots," as the early Celtic people in Ireland were called, crossed back over to Scotland in the centuries following the retreat of the Romans from the British Isles in the 400s; there they settled the western islands and coast. They brought Christianity and eventually conquered the other tribal groups in Great Britain: the Angles of the southeast, related to the Germanic tribes settling England at the time; the Britons of the southwest, a Celtic people related to the Welsh; and the Picts, also Celtic, who dominated the Highlands. Following the Viking invasions of the 800s and 900s, the four tribes gradually united under Scottish kings. Eventually, the Scots gave their name to the land and all its people, but the kings often ruled in name only, especially in the remote Highlands where local clan leaders retained their independence.

In 1066 Norman invaders from France gained control of England. Powerful new English rulers such as the thirteenth century's Edward I, who was called "the Hammer of the Scots," gained influence over the Scottish kings and helped shape culture in the Lowlands. The Normans also attempted to expand into Ireland. Scots warriors were recruited by their brethren in Ireland to defend the island. The Scots resisted English dominance altogether, often allying with England's enemy, France. Robert the Bruce (1274–1329), the most renowned leader of Scottish defiance, sponsored an invasion of northern Ireland in the fourteenth century, led by his brother Edward, to weaken his English enemies. However, the destruction wrought by Edward on the land alienated the local population to the point where his defeat by the English was cheered, leading to a subsequent steady advance of "Anglo-Irish" power.

The 1503 marriage of Margaret Tudor, daughter of Henry VII, to James IV, the son of Mary, Queen of Scots, united the English and Scottish royal houses. Already king of Scotland, James IV ascended the throne of England as James I on Elizabeth I's death in 1603. His coronation coincided with the defeat of the recalcitrant Gaelic chieftains of northern Ireland, the last bastion of Irish resistance to English domination. Their exile and the confiscation of their lands gave the united Crown the opportunity to further a long-standing "plantation" strategy, fortifying English control by colonizing the region with Protestants. This was accomplished using a system of "undertakers"—wealthy settlers who were granted tracts of land and who undertook to import tenants to cultivate it. Struggling farmers from the Scottish Lowlands proved most suited to the effort of building a new society in a harsh environment, surrounded by hostile Irish natives and eking out a living on often poor lands—qualities that were transferred to the American frontier a century later.

Religion also played a significant role in the migration. The Scottish Reformation, led by John Knox (ca. 1505–1572), had succeeded in toppling the especially corrupt and unpopular Scottish Catholic Church only after a civil war that ended in 1560. The doctrines of the new Church of Scotland were based on Calvinism (or Presbyterianism). James was a Catholic, however, and he turned the Scottish Protestant church into an Episcopalian (Anglican) institution dominated by bishops. The antihierarchical Presbyterians saw in this a "return to papacy." Many ministers fled to Ulster, where the recent conflict had devastated churches and congregations and left an open field for them to fill.

An Irish rebellion centered in the north broke out in 1641 after wealthy Irish Catholics attempted a coup d'état. The 1630 to 1640 Bishops' Wars—a Scottish revolt provoked by Charles I's attempt to impose Anglican conformity on the Scots—had alarmed the Catholics of Ireland, as had the mounting conflict between Charles and Parliament that would became the English Civil War in 1642; the Irish Catholics feared an anti-Catholic invasion of Ireland. There followed eleven years of complicated, multisided war in Ulster, punctuated by a number of massacres that traumatized the Protestant settler community, contributing to a permanent "siege mentality" that historians see as an influential part of the Scotch-Irish cultural mindset. By the time the forces of the English Parliament toppled and executed Charles in 1649 and arrived in Ireland to brutally suppress what had become the Irish Confederate Wars, the Church of Ireland had practically collapsed, and it was replaced by the Irish Presbyterian Church. The English Parliament under Oliver Cromwell confiscated massive tracts of Irish land to punish the rebels, giving the Ulster settlers a firm foothold and spurring a new wave of immigration from Scotland. Scottish Presbyterians became the majority of the population of northern and eastern Ulster. They turned it into the wealthiest part of Ireland while maintaining a separate existence from the Catholic natives around them.

Their ascendance in the region was cemented by the 1690 Battle of the Boyne, in which the Protestant English King William III (also known as William of Orange) defeated Catholic forces led by the recently deposed James II on the east coast of Ireland. Seeking to regain his crown, James had secured most of his army from among the Irish by promising them autonomy, land, and the religious tolerance of England. William's victory finally secured English and Protestant control of Ulster. This occasion is still celebrated in Northern Ireland's Protestant communities with parades and banners featuring William's face every year on July 12. The following seven years were the high point of Scottish immigration to Ireland, with some 50,000 new settlers arriving.

Modern Era After William's death in 1702, the Anglican Queen Anne ascended to the English throne,

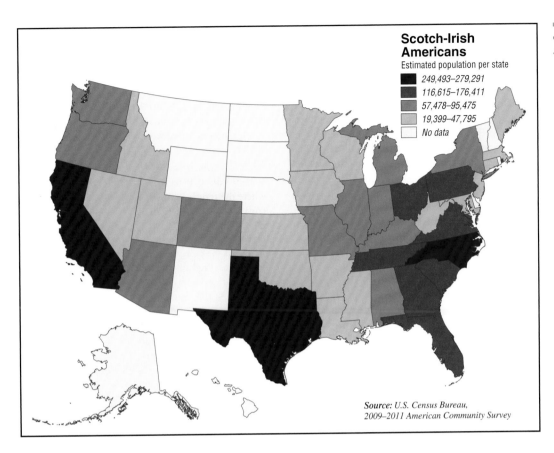

Scotch-Irish Americans

Estimated population per state

- 249,493–279,291
- 116,615–176,411
- 57,478–95,475
- 19,399–47,795
- No data

Source: U.S. Census Bureau, 2009–2011 American Community Survey

causing Irish Protestants to endure once again the experience of being an oppressed religious minority. Nevertheless, the eighteenth century saw a relaxation of sectarian tensions in Ulster coupled with economic advances. Progress was punctuated by stifling trade restrictions imposed by the Crown, intended to preserve English domination. Combined with periodic economic crises and stiff trade competition, the situation caused a substantial portion of the Ulster Scots—as many as 300,000 by the time of the American Revolution in 1775—to set out for new shores yet again, this time to the United States.

In the 1790s, inspired by the French and American Revolutions, liberal Irish Presbyterians joined with Catholics to form the republican United Irishmen, intending to throw off the yoke of British and Anglican rule. At the same time, conflict broke out in County Armagh between Catholics and Anglicans. Spurred by economic competition and, most likely, British provocation, the fighting led to the foundation of the militant Protestant organization the Orange Order. After the suppression of the United Irishmen's attempt at rebellion in 1798, the Order gained the support of Presbyterians as restrictions on them were relaxed.

In the nineteenth century Ulster became the site of the only significant industrialization in Ireland, and Belfast, home to an emerging shipbuilding industry (producing the HMS Titanic, among other giants), grew larger and more prosperous than Dublin. By the beginning of the twentieth century, however, Ireland's significant Catholic majority had initiated a movement across Ireland for Home Rule—some measure of self-government within the British monarchy, though seen by many as a step towards full independence. Most Ulster Protestants opposed the crusade, fearing that abandonment by the Crown would leave them at the mercy of the Catholics. The religious divide mapped onto the political conflict between nationalists and unionists (the Orange Order being the backbone of the latter). The unionists formed the paramilitary Ulster Volunteer Force (UVF) in 1911 to fight the Home Rule threat; nationalists responded in 1913 by establishing the Irish Volunteers, which later evolved into the Irish Republican Army (IRA). The Anglo-Irish War, a guerrilla struggle for Irish independence that reached its peak between 1919 and 1921, was accompanied by street battles in Belfast between Protestants and Catholics. The 1921 Anglo-Irish Treaty partitioned the Irish island into the Irish Free State in the south (succeeded by the Republic of Ireland in 1937) and Northern Ireland. The latter contained the six (of nine) counties of Ulster with the highest proportion of Protestants and remained part of the United Kingdom.

The partition of Ireland was almost universally opposed by Irish nationalists, and IRA actions to destabilize the new Northern Ireland were met with reprisals by the Royal Ulster Constabulary, the newly organized police force for the territory. The cycle of violence intensified periodically over the succeeding decades, often sparked by Orange Order parades. Although formal measures were put in place to ensure Catholics in Northern Ireland representation and political participation, gerrymandering led to permanent domination by hardline Unionists. Growing discrimination led to increasing emigration among Catholics and the sense of being an oppressed minority on the part of those who stayed. In the late 1960s a civil rights movement arose, attracting the support of moderate Protestants, especially students. Security forces and Unionist paramilitary groups responded with intense violence to the movement. Their actions spiraled into thirty years of bloodshed known as "the Troubles," which were characterized by assassinations and bombings carried out by both the IRA and Protestant paramilitary groups (among them the Ulster Defense Association) and widespread arrests by the British Army, mostly of nationalists.

By the time the Belfast Peace Agreement was reached in 1998, more than 3,500 had been killed and over 100,000 physically injured—huge numbers for such a small population. Although the power-sharing agreement between the nationalist and unionist communities has suffered setbacks when one side or the other felt victimized, and recalcitrant offshoots of the main combatants carried out a number of acts of violence in defiance of the agreement, on the whole it has been a model process of reconciliation for divided polities.

SETTLEMENT IN THE UNITED STATES

Ulster Scots first attempted to immigrate to the United States in the seventeenth century in response to a tightening of policies on religious practice by the new Irish Lord Deputy of the Irish Episcopal Church. Presbyterian leader Robert Blair arranged for the ship *Eagle Wing* to sail to Massachusetts in 1836 with 140 passengers, but after two attempts to reach land there, bad weather forced the ship's return and the abandonment of the effort. In the 1680s renewed religious restrictions spawned widespread plans on the part of Ulster Presbyterian congregations to emigrate, but the death of Charles II (whose stated support of religious tolerance was opposed by Parliament and betrayed by his own policies) and subsequent easing of restrictions again delayed the efforts of all but a few, one being Francis Makemie. Colonel William Stevens, an American landowner, invited Makemie to Maryland, where the Ulster Scots clergyman founded the first Presbyterian congregation and became known as the "father of American Presbyterianism."

By 1718 the recurrent religious interference in the Scotch-Irish community was compounded by a six-year drought, causing crop failure and high food prices; a severe smallpox epidemic provided the decisive push. About one thousand Scotch-Irish immigrants sailed to Boston that year in ten different voyages, laying the groundwork for some 250,000 to immigrate by 1775 (by which time they made up 10 percent of the American population). Peaks in immigration occurred from 1725 to 1729, from 1740 to 1741, from 1754 to 1755, and from 1771 to 1775. While Scotch-Irish collective memory has tended to see religious persecution as the strongest cause of emigration, historians favor economic motivations, including periodic famines; ever-rising rents on farmland; the growing practice of "canting," or auctioning of tenancies, which were then bought up by middlemen; and the collapse of the Irish linen trade in 1772 because of English restrictions on manufacturing, a crisis that severely impacted the many Ulster Scots weavers. As the immigration process became regularized, agents fanned out across Ulster to fill ships that were bound for the colonies to bring back heavy bulk goods but were nearly empty for the western crossing; in addition, land promoters who had a financial interest in American settlements (for example, in North Carolina) that needed colonists advertised widely to fill their tracts.

A high proportion of the immigrants—estimated at up to 90 percent at some points—were unable to pay for their passage up front; these people were forced to pledge their labor to an "employer" as an indentured servant for a fixed term after arrival, usually five to seven years; or to become redemptioners, who were typically sold by the ship's captain at an American port. An estimated 100,000 Scotch-Irish arrived in this manner. Later in the century skilled artisans, especially weavers, made their own way to the United States, despite British attempts to ban them from leaving, fearing a precipitous decline in the economic health and control of Ulster. After the failed United Irishmen Rebellion, political motivations propelled more affluent, professional, educated Scotch-Irish to immigrate (though still alongside a larger number of paupers); in contrast to the earlier servants and artisans of modest means, who tended to move south and west towards the frontier, this group was most likely to stay in the cities of the Eastern seaboard, and a good number went to Pittsburgh, an up-and-coming town on the western edge of the new republic. An estimated 100,000 immigrated in the three decades following the American Revolution.

The 1803 British Passenger Act—instituted in part to address often horrible conditions on the ships but also reflecting the Crown's interest in stemming the loss of its citizens—drastically limited the numbers allowed on transatlantic vessels; the Napoleonic Wars of 1803 to 1815 between Great Britain and France also disrupted the flow. The next three decades saw around half a million Ulster immigrants to the United States, however, the majority of them Presbyterians

An 1862 photograph by George Barnard shows a Scotch-Irish family uprooted by the Civil War. It was common for 19th-century Scotch-Irish women to smoke pipes. EVERETT COLLECTION INC / AGE FOTOSTOCK

until 1835. The early 1800s was the period of largest Scotch-Irish immigration, both absolutely and in proportion to the U.S. population. Farmers pressed by overcrowding in northern Ireland and the continued poor production of Irish agriculture, as well as weavers and spinners put out of work by industrialization, made up the bulk of this wave.

Although the mid-nineteenth century exodus caused by the Irish potato famine is one of the most remembered and significant immigrant waves in U.S. history, the proportion coming from Ulster, which suffered the least, declined at that time. The second half of the nineteenth century saw more than a million immigrants from Ulster, most of them Protestant and most of them skilled workers or part of the industrial proletariat, who headed to cities like the professionals had before them. In the twentieth century the Ulster proportion of Irish immigration to the United States steadily declined then practically stopped at the time of the Great Depression. After World War II those Ulster Scots who immigrated to the United States tended to return to Scotland or to England after a time.

While the first Ulster immigrants headed to New England, where they initially saw the English Puritans as refugees from religious persecution like themselves, their strict Calvinism ultimately clashed with what was quickly becoming an oppressive state religion itself. After 1725 their destination shifted to Pennsylvania,

where the legacy of William Penn seemed especially tolerant and welcoming; in addition, the lack of a dominating big-landowner class or a slave plantation economy there was attractive to the modest settlers. Pennsylvania had ample land and also offered more protections for the many who arrived as indentured servants. Discord soon arose, however, because the Scotch-Irish attitude towards the indigenous Native Americans—which was harsh and combative—conflicted with the official Quaker policy of coexistence. From the Scotch-Irish Americans' point of view, the Quaker oligarchy was distant and slow to act, as during the French and Indian War, when those on the frontier (including in western Pennsylvania) were the first target of Indian retaliation.

Although Scotch-Irish constituted a third of the Pennsylvania population by the time of the American Revolution, a critical mass had already begun moving on, through the Cumberland and Shenandoah Valleys to the Carolinas—especially western North Carolina—and Georgia, Tennessee, and Kentucky. Whereas extensive slaveholding was taking hold in the deep South, the middle colonies (especially their interior hill country, where the slave-based plantation economy had less of a foothold) became the places where white labor and self-sufficient settlement were most in demand. The Ulster settlers became the quintessential pioneers, clearing the land, building log cabins, exploiting the soil, and moving on within a few years. Because of this period the Scotch-Irish immigrants became most identified with Appalachia and the South. Bill McGimpsey, president of the Scotch-Irish Society of the United States of America, has also drawn attention to settlements of what he calls "divergent Scotch-Irish" in such places as Montana, New England, and Utah.

According to the U.S. Census Bureau's American Community Survey estimates for 2009 to 2011, there were 3.3 million Americans of Scotch-Irish descent living in the United States. The states with the highest populations included North Carolina (279,291), Texas (278,316), and California (249,493). Other states with large numbers of Scotch-Irish Americans included Florida, Georgia, Ohio, Pennsylvania, South Carolina, Tennessee, and Virginia.

LANGUAGE

The Scots language is a Germanic language descended from Northumbrian Old English and Middle English. It developed in Lowland Scotland and is completely distinct from Scottish Gaelic, a Celtic language spoken in the Highlands and at the early Scottish Court. Scots and English developed separately from the Middle Ages onward. By the time of the English plantation of Ulster, written Scots had largely been superseded by English as a result of the convergence of the Scottish and English kingdoms. The language persisted in its spoken form, however, and was transplanted to Ireland along with the settlers, where it became Ulster Scots. Some linguists dispute the status of Scots as a separate language from English, as opposed to a dialect, saying that it is on the same spectrum as Scottish Standard English. It is spoken by an estimated 30 to 50 percent of Scotland's population, though more than half of the population has said in surveys that they do not in fact consider it a separate language.

Ulster Scots is usually considered to be a dialect of Scots, although some enthusiasts deem it a separate language. It is spoken by, at most, around 2 percent of Northern Ireland's population today. There have been efforts at a linguistic revival since the 1990s, although some write these off as partisan maneuvering to counter the spread of Irish (a Gaelic language), spoken by a higher but still relatively minimal proportion of the population. As a written, literary language, Ulster Scots had become practically extinct by the early twentieth century; however, the recent revival has attempted to reintroduce it as well. Regardless, by the time Scottish nationalists such as poet Robert Burns (1759–1796) were working in Scotland proper to reverse the decline of Scots in its written form, a good portion of the Scotch-Irish who were immigrating to America had already left the realm of Scots culture behind.

The diminution of the Scots and Ulster Scots languages or dialects by the advent of English in the British Isles is almost less extraordinary than the thoroughness of the linguistic assimilation of the Scotch-Irish in the United States, who rather quickly after their arrival gave up most of the distinctive signposts of their culture and language. Thus, knowledge of their ancestral languages is today nonexistent among Scotch-Irish Americans, except for a few words—for example, *craic* ("gossip or loud conversation") and *boggin* ("disgusting"). Linguist Michael Montgomery, however, an expert on Appalachian speech, has identified a substantial Scotch-Irish influence on Appalachian pronunciation, vocabulary, and grammar, in particular on the dialect spoken in eastern Tennessee, that persists to this day. Most Americans would recognize many Scotch-Irish-influenced phrases. Examples are word usages such as "bottom land," "kindling"(as a noun), to "let on" (pretend), and "a far piece" (distance); and grammatical usages such as "used to could," "might could," "done" as a helping verb ("I done told you already"), "y'all," and "who all."

RELIGION

The Scotch-Irish are almost by definition Protestants: their religion is what motivated their resettlement by the Crown from Scotland to Ulster, giving them their particular identity—an identity sharpened by their sense of being surrounded there by a hostile Catholic population. England thereby politicized religion and initiated the discord between the two groups, a discord that still plays itself out in Northern Ireland. The Ulster Scots also suffered constant real and imagined persecution by the official Anglican (Episcopalian) Church, which saw the much less hierarchical structure that formed the essence of Presbyterianism as a threat to ecclesiastical and political authority. This shaped the Scotch-Irish identity still further, as a sect embattled even among Protestants. Once the immigrants reached the United States, conflicts with the dominant Puritan culture in New England and with Quakers—who were alienated by the Scotch-Irish hostility towards the Indians and their reputation for disregarding legality and squatting what they saw as empty lands—in Pennsylvania continued this sense of siege. As resented and disdained Irish Catholics began to make their way to the colonies in larger numbers, the Scotch-Irish used their Protestantism—and anti-Catholicism—to keep from being lumped together with the Catholic "wild Irish."

In their frontier communities their religion was what held the Scotch-Irish together, provided guidance and control over conduct and morality, and determined their outlook on life. Once the resources became available to build a church, worshippers came from miles around to attend an all-day communion, the only regular chance to socialize for families divided onto individual homesteads. A shortage of ministers exacerbated the far-flung nature of the congregations; both the numbers of immigrants and the steady

The pastor and congregants lay their hands on a man during a service at the Church of the Lord Jesus in Jolo, West Virginia, in 2011. Rooted in Appalachian tradition and the New Testament Book of Mark, the "Signs Following" faith encourages adherents to handle deadly snakes, drink poison and speak in tongues. LAUREN POND FOR THE WASHINGTON POST VIA GETTY IMAGES

movement outward made it hard for the Presbyterian Church to keep up. This problem was exacerbated by the Presbyterian requirement that ministers undergo a specific, rigorous university training, including the study of Greek, Latin, and Hebrew, still only available in Scotland. Thus, settlements had to wait years before their plea for a minister—a distant, difficult, and poorly paid posting that was far from attractive to such graduates—could be fulfilled. The American Presbyterian Church established a number of colleges to address this circumstance, including the College of New Jersey in Princeton (today Princeton University) in 1746 and Washington and Jefferson College in western Pennsylvania in 1781. In fact, Presbyterian-founded colleges were the largest group of the 207 prominent colleges in the United States before the Civil War, most of them established by and for Scotch-Irish. Still, the supply of ministers lagged far behind the need. The evangelical "Great Awakening" beginning in the mid-eighteenth century produced a flood of Baptist and Methodist ministers along the

frontier; these ministers converted many Scotch-Irish Presbyterians who were not well served by their church and who were attracted by the passion and excitement of the new approach. This phenomenon caused a temporary schism in the Presbyterian Church between "Old Siders," who resisted change, and "New Siders," who wanted to adapt to the settlers' reality.

Scotch-Irish Americans are thus split today between their traditional Presbyterianism and the more evangelical Protestant churches that dominate the landscape in rural and especially southern parts of the country. Religion still plays a central role in their life and imprints itself on their culture, politics, and sense of identity. Some, in fact, argue that the general religiosity so prominent in American life—the sense that rights are God-given, that political leaders must be pious, and that religious duty saturates everyday life—which stands in stark contrast to the attitudes of other advanced industrial democracies, is in large part a result of the strong influence of the Scotch-Irish and their historical belief in the predestination of the soul.

CULTURE AND ASSIMILATION

The early Scotch-Irish Americans, through their religious evolution, language affinity, and experience with frontier life, became relatively quickly assimilated

Insofar as the dominant European-American orientation was at that time becoming white, Protestant, and plebian, it could almost be said that American mainstream culture assimilated to the Scotch-Irish.

into colonial American culture. In fact, insofar as the dominant European-American orientation was at that time becoming white, Protestant, and plebian, it could almost be said that American mainstream culture assimilated to the Scotch-Irish. In *Born Fighting: How the Scots-Irish Shaped America* (2004), former U.S. senator and secretary of the Navy James Webb characterized their "radical individualism," which has been claimed as the basis for such quintessential American traits as populism, love of country music, military tradition, fanatical attachment to gun rights, and even NASCAR racing—said to have its origins in the adventures of illegal moonshine runners during Prohibition. Thus, by the mid-nineteenth century, the Scotch-Irish had become practically indistinguishable from other Protestant European immigrants. Most histories of the Scotch-Irish end their narrative in this period. The conclusion of Ron Chepesiuk's *The Scotch-Irish: From the North of Ireland to the Making of America* (2000) can stand in for many others: "From this point [around 1830] on, the Scotch-Irish began to make their contribution as Americans and not as Scotch-Irish—that is, not as people of a particular ethnic culture. They intermarried with other ethnic groups, mixing easily and eventually losing their identity as a separate people. By and large, the Scotch-Irish have become absorbed into the mainstream of society."

There have, however, been periodic efforts, at least on the part of elites, to assert and preserve a Scotch-Irish American identity and culture. The Scotch-Irish Society of America was established in 1889, drawing on Presbyterian clergy, newspapermen, and politicians, and held annual congresses; however, after the sixth congress, in Des Moines, Iowa, in 1894, it seems to have disappeared. It was resurrected in the first decade of the twenty-first century as the Scotch-Irish Society of the United States of America and has actively promoted Scotch-Irish heritage and exploration since then. The Ulster American Heritage Symposium has been held biannually, alternating between Northern Ireland and the United States, since 1976; it is organized by the Ulster American Folk Park in Northern Ireland, where the commitment to cultural preservation seems to be stronger. There are also many local efforts; for example, the Clover Scottish

Games and Scotch-Irish Festival has been held annually in Clover, South Carolina, since 1997. A growing number of books on Scotch-Irish history and identity were published in the early twenty-first century, attesting to a renewed interest of individuals in investigating and promoting their heritage.

Dances and Songs Scotch-Irish musical traditions (tempered by the exigencies of early frontier life, especially in the Appalachian region) played a central role in the development of American traditional music styles such as bluegrass. Although fife and drum bands have been cited as the only pure and exclusively Ulster Scots music form, the Scotch-Irish were part of the broader "Anglo-Celtic" tradition of ballad singing, fiddle-based instrumental dance music, and storytelling. Except for the fiddle, traditional folk instruments of Scotland and Ireland, such as the bagpipes and the harp, were too unwieldy to bring on the arduous journey across the sea and into the wilderness; in some cases, including that of the harp, the instruments had already been suppressed by the English Crown back in Ireland. Traditional instruments were therefore replaced by local instruments such as the banjo, guitar, and mandolin. The Scotch-Irish also developed the Appalachian (or mountain) dulcimer, a variation of the *scheitholt*, a zitherlike instrument that German settlers had brought with them.

Musical styles anchored by the fiddle and particular elements such as the Scottish pentatonic (five-note) scale were united with American popular music trends and local elements, including gospel and African American music, to constitute something both distinctly American and deeply connected to the Scotch-Irish homelands. Another influence was early Protestant religious music. Based on the *Scottish Metrical Psalter*, which immigrants carried with them on their journeys, this tradition provided a source for the kinds of vocal harmonies typical to bluegrass and country, as well as to distinctive forms such as shape-note singing. Some musicologists assert that particular ballads were preserved long after their disappearance in the British Isles by Appalachian settlers as a result of their isolation and conservatism. The best-known example is "Bonny Barbara Allan," also known as "Barbary Allan," already popular in North Carolina in the late seventeenth century and still sung today.

The culture of drinking and dancing in the South is also traceable, at least in part, to the Scotch-Irish, with their love of whisky and celebration—another quality that diverged acutely from the dour New England Puritans, with whom the first Scotch-Irish immigrants clashed so sharply. The square dance, especially in its Appalachian form, is traditionally accompanied by jigs and reels from Scotland and Ireland, almost always featuring that most Scotch-Irish of instruments, the fiddle. Today's Texas two-step and "boot-scooting" evolved from ancient ritual dances.

Holidays The most prominent holiday particular to the Scotch-Irish—and even more so to Ulster Scots, or Northern Ireland Protestants—is July 12, the anniversary of William of Orange's victory over the Catholics at the Battle of the Boyne in 1690. This day was commemorated throughout much of the nineteenth century with parades in major American cities that often ended in violence between Protestants and Catholics. The Orange Riot of 1871 was one of the worst incidents of street violence in New York City's history, causing sixty deaths. These provocative demonstrations had practically disappeared in the United States by the end of the nineteenth century, though they continued and intensified in Northern Ireland, where they remain a flashpoint today. Another celebration of Protestant triumph that has led to riots occurs on December 7, the date that the defiant actions of thirteen "apprentice boys of Derry" touched off the 1688 siege of that city by Catholic royal troops. The holiday is celebrated by the brotherhood of the Apprentice Boys of Derry in Northern Ireland and its associated branches in England, Scotland, and the United States. In celebration of ethnic identity, the Scotch-Irish Society of Charleston, South Carolina, organizes the annual "South Carolina Day" on March 18, commemorating the birthday of Scotch-Irish and South Carolinian favorite son John C. Calhoun (1782–1850), vice president, senator, statesman, and political theorist of states' rights.

Health Issues Health concerns among the Scotch-Irish American community are primarily determined by economic factors and, more especially, by location. In Appalachia poverty and ill-health persist despite the initiatives of Lyndon B. Johnson's "War on Poverty" in the 1960s. The dominant industry of the area, coal mining, has left a considerable mark on the health of Scotch-Irish Americans. Black lung, a congestive disease of the lungs caused by the inhalation of coal dust, disables and kills miners at a high rate. This and chronic malnutrition, high infant mortality, and low birth weight remain the scourge of mountain people. West Virginia, Kentucky, and Tennessee still have pockets of poverty as a result of high unemployment and isolation. The pattern of early marriage and large families is still typical, as is a significant problem with domestic violence.

FAMILY AND COMMUNITY LIFE

In contrast to Highland Scots, who immigrated directly to the United States in groups based on their early organization in clans, Scotch-Irish immigrated individually or in small family groups. Homesteading on the frontier was carried out on a family basis, with initially monoethnic Presbyterian congregations constituting the broader community; the Scotch-Irish tended to separate themselves from other frontier dwellers, such as the Germans, whose culture and practices conflicted with their own. Scotch-Irish individualism and lack of the extended clan obligation led to relatively rapid assimilation and intermarriage, exacerbated by the numerous conversions during the Great

GOOD, BAD, AND UGLY PORTRAYALS OF SCOTCH-IRISH AMERICANS

The very term Scotch-Irish is contested (the variant "Scots-Irish" is also used, since in Scotland "Scotch" only applies to whisky). It was a phrase that signified approval when it first arose in the late eighteenth century; Federalists (who advocated good relations with Britain) and other New England elites used the term in opposition to the first Ulster Catholic immigrants and, subsequently, to associate the "ruder" sorts of Irish Protestant immigrants with those "wild Irish." The formulation of a "positive" Scotch-Irish (Protestant) identity, adopted willingly after 1800, has been linked to the defeat of the United Irishmen coalition, as well as to reactionary politics and evangelical religion in the United States and Protestant militancy in Ulster. As the alliance between Protestant and Catholic Irish immigrants unraveled over the course of the nineteenth century, Irish Americans began to criticize the "Scotch-Irish myth," charging that a separate Scotch-Irish identity was just a way to deny any connection to the masses of poorer Irish Catholics who immigrated in the aftermath of the 1845 Irish Potato Famine and, later, to validate the divisive "two nations theory" in Ireland (which asserts that Irish Protestants and Catholics, whether from the north or south, are completely separate peoples, requiring separate political arrangements). Partisans of the term contend that it is justified by their distinct historical experiences, including but not limited to religion. It is notable that during the twentieth century, as the conflict in Northern Ireland escalated, Scotch-Irish involvement in anti-Catholic organizations such as the American Protective Association, strong in the late nineteenth century, practically disappeared.

The "hillbilly" legend, which portrays Appalachian residents as ill-clad, unshod bumpkins fond of brewing "moonshine" (bootleg whiskey) persists. This image became widespread with the "Li'l Abner" comic strip drawn by Al Capp beginning in 1932; the strip reached 60 million readers and became first a Broadway musical and then a film in 1959. In the 1960s the CBS television series *The Beverly Hillbillies* and its spinoffs, *Petticoat Junction* and *Green Acres*, furthered the image of rural people as simpletons. The dignity of most rural Southern life has emerged, however, with the publication of the Foxfire books beginning in the 1970s (which contain oral histories and instructional pieces garnered from southern Appalachian life and culture) and the efforts of folklorists to preserve and document a vanishing way of life. Appalshop, a rural arts and education center in Whitesburg, Kentucky, exemplifies the effort to preserve the Scotch-Irish (and other) heritage of Appalachia on film and also through recorded music.

Awakening and after. Their constant push to resettle also limited community coherence. Wherever they ultimately established themselves, however, frontier families formed tight-knit communities, some more and some less specifically Scotch-Irish in character.

Gender Roles In independent and self-reliant Scotch-Irish frontier families, gender roles were as rigid as in other communities at the time, and women, in charge

Two Scotch-Irish men take a break while tidying up a graveyard. MARIO TAMA/GETTY IMAGES

of the household's domestic economy, were as essential as men to the family's survival. As well as cooking, cleaning, and sewing, mothers were typically charged with educating the children, both in basic literacy and Christian principles; milking the cows, grinding the flour, and baking the bread; gathering available foodstuffs from the forest; and even defending the homestead from Indians and wild animals, often with the husband away from home to trade, scout a new location, or deal with other business. This kind of centrality and independence among women has diminished in modern times as more roles (such as education and security) have been taken on by government institutions; as well, Scotch-Irish cultural conservatism and a certain fundamentalist interpretation of Christianity has spread the notion that a women's place is ideally tied to childbirth, childrearing, and domestic chores. Nevertheless, there is a certain feisty independence among women of Appalachia and other Scotch-Irish heartlands, as exemplified by Scotch-Irish American Dolly Parton (1946–) and her song "9 to 5," with its adoption of the struggles of women in the workplace. "Typically Southern" masculinity, to some extent a product of the Scotch-Irish heritage, emphasizes hypertraditional male tropes of military service, hunting,

auto racing, country music, and all-around hard living. At the same time, a 2013 article by historian James Loewen touted James Buchanan (1791–1868; president from 1857–1861), one of numerous American presidents of Scotch-Irish stock, as our "first gay President."

Relations with Other Americans Scotch-Irish Americans' relations with other groups have often been difficult, especially when their resolve was threatened: their initial contacts with the New England (English) Puritans and then the Pennsylvania Quakers were discordant; rivalry and cultural clashes dogged their encounters with the German settlers who fanned out along the frontier in close parallel with them; and their stance toward the Native Americans, who threatened their further progress westward, was hostile. Probably their most fraught relationship, however, has been with Catholic immigrants, especially Irish Catholics, whose antipathy during their time in Ulster they had hoped to escape.

EMPLOYMENT AND ECONOMIC CONDITIONS

As in their home country, Scotch-Irish in the United States have been drawn to the land as farmers and herders. Others found work in heavy industry, such as the steel mills and coal mines. Hard times during the Great Depression for those isolated in Appalachia or the rural South brought scores of Scotch-Irish to the factories of Detroit and Chicago, where they labored in the auto plants and stockyards. Poverty returned for many of these people as plants shut down and downscaled in the 1960s, creating so-called "hillbilly ghettoes" in major Northern industrial cities. Generations of poverty have created an underclass of displaced Southerners, a social problem that persists today. Author Harriette Arnow (1908–1986) wrote movingly of the plight of these economic migrants in her novel *The Dollmaker* (1954). Having assimilated to a high degree, many Scotch-Irish Americans have benefited from the opportunities that class mobility and a strong work ethic have brought them. Webb asserted in *Born Fighting*, however, that over the course of their history, they have "endur[ed] poverty at a rate that far exceeded the rest of the country."

POLITICS AND GOVERNMENT

Scotch-Irish Americans' political credo is above all "small d" democratic, or populist, fueled by a strong sense of equality, self-reliance, and resentment against elitism and inherited privilege. This stance is exemplified by their most prominent flag bearer, Andrew Jackson (1767–1845; president 1829–1837), the son of immigrants from County Antrim who arrived in the United States two years before his birth and was raised on the Carolina frontier. While he is remembered as a fighter for the common man—and still celebrated by the Democratic Party—Jackson was also a fierce antagonist to Native Americans, responsible for the Trail of Tears and numerous other lesser-known acts of "Indian Removal," and was himself a wealthy slaveholder. Scotch-Irish Americans in general tended not to own slaves and resented the wealthy slaveholders on their lowland plantations. No friends to Abolitionism, the Scotch-Irish in greater numbers fought on the side of the Confederacy during the Civil War than on the side of the Union.

The Scotch-Irish in the Carolinas were a bulwark of the Regulator Movement, an armed resistance against corrupt colonial officials in the 1760s, often seen as a kind of opening act to the American Revolution. But despite a collective memory that valorizes them as a unified bastion of the independence struggle in the revolution itself, in some contexts they joined the Loyalists—not out of any great love for the British but because of their hatred for local patriots they saw as wealthy and controlling. This opposition to the dominance of the affluent establishment in the new republic pushed them to support the Jeffersonians against the Federalists and to increase their involvement in politics, leading up to the Jackson presidency.

Although Scotch-Irish soldiers fought on both sides of the Civil War—including Generals Ulysses S. Grant (1822–1885) for the North and Thomas "Stonewall" Jackson (1824–1863), J. E. B. "Jeb" Stuart (1833–1864), and Nathan Bedford Forrest (1821–1877; Forrest survived the war to become the first Grand Wizard of the Ku Klux Klan) for the South—the bulk of them, residing in Confederate states, fought for the Confederate cause. The Scotch-Irish were closely identified with the Populist movement, strongest in the South and Midwest, which reached its peak in the 1890s and united farmers for a short time against perceived economic injustice. They were also a major force in the twentieth-century union movement, exemplified by their agitation for workers rights in the textile mills of the Southeast and the mines of West Virginia and Kentucky. These efforts were marked by serious outbreaks of violence and strikes—although many have since followed the drift of conservative and Southern politics to become strongly anti-union.

The Scotch-Irish claim that seventeen U.S. presidents have at least some verifiable Scotch-Irish ancestry, including, beyond Jackson, Buchanan, and Grant (served 1869–1877), Grover Cleveland (1837–1908; served 1885–1889 and 1893–1897), William McKinley (1843–1901; served 1897–1901), Woodrow Wilson (1856–1924; served 1913–1921), Richard Nixon (1913–1994; served 1969–1974), and Bill Clinton (1946–; served 1993–2001). As is apparent from this list, it would be very difficult to pin Scotch-Irish Americans down to a particular political party or ideology. To the extent that they are enveloped by the southern white Protestant vote—which is true only partially—they tended to vote Democrat until the ascendance of the Civil Rights Movement in the 1960s, later becoming conservative "Reagan Democrats" and, thereafter, straight Republicans.

NOTABLE INDIVIDUALS

Frontiersmen and Explorers Scotch-Irish Americans' baptism as sojourners to new territories instilled in them a penchant for pushing forward Euro-American expansion. Davy Crockett (1786–1836), the "king of the wild frontier," served in the Tennessee Legislature and the U.S. House of Representatives, where he vehemently opposed the Indian Removal policies of Andrew Jackson, fought the Mexicans in the Texas Revolution, died at the Battle of the Alamo, helped popularize the coonskin cap, and was the subject of countless books, plays, movies, and television portrayals. Sam Houston (1793–1863) was governor of Tennessee, leader of the Texas Revolution, first president of the Republic of Texas, U.S. senator from Texas after its annexation to the United States, governor of Texas, adopted citizen of the Cherokee Nation, and namesake of the fourth-largest American city. Kit Carson (1809–1868) was a mountain man and early explorer of the West (all the way to California), wilderness guide, and Indian fighter; he fought in the Mexican-American War and the Civil War and was, like Crockett, the subject of many portrayals. Neil Armstrong (1930–2012) was the first human to walk on the moon, in 1969, coining the immortal phrase "That's one small step for [a] man, one giant leap for mankind."

Literature Scotch-Irish writers who have enriched American literature include Ellen Glasgow (1873–1945), whose best novel, *Vein of Iron* (1935), concerns the fortunes of Ada Fincastle, the daughter of a hardy Scotch-Irish family of Virginia in the early part of the twentieth century. Larry McMurtry (1936–) is known for his novels set in the American Southwest. His *The Last Picture Show* (1966) and *Lonesome Dove* (1985) enjoyed tremendous success after filmed versions captured fans for the prolific writer's view of his home state of Texas and its rich history. Edgar Allan Poe (1809–1849), master of the macabre, is known primarily for his gothic tales, such as "The Fall of the House of Usher," "The Murders in the Rue Morgue," "The Pit and the Pendulum," and "The Tell-Tale Heart," and for his haunting poems, including "Annabel Lee" and "The Raven." Mark Twain (born Samuel Langhorne Clemens; 1835–1910), author, humorist, abolitionist, and anti-imperialist, wrote the classics *The Adventures of Tom Sawyer* (1876) and *Adventures of Huckleberry Finn* (1884).

Music Scotch-Irish Americans are well represented in country music by such greats as Hank Williams (1923–1953), one of the creators of the modern country sound, and Johnny Cash (1932–2003), the "man in black," country icon and author and performer of such hits as "I Walk the Line," "Folsom Prison Blues," and "Ring of Fire"; his daughter Roseanne Cash (1955–) is also a singer-songwriter, crossing over from country into many other genres, as does Hank Williams Jr. (1953–). Loretta Lynn (1932–), country music singer-songwriter and fifty-year member of the Grand Ole Opry, recalled her childhood growing up in a Kentucky coal-mining community in her song "Coal Miner's Daughter." Bill Monroe (1911–1996) is credited as the "father of bluegrass," the style that took its name from his band the Blue Grass Boys, intended to evoke his home state of Kentucky. Elvis Presley (1935–1977), the "King of Rock and Roll" and towering figure in popular culture, melded African American rhythm and blues with country; he was the best-selling solo artist in the history of popular music.

Science and Medicine Bill Gates (1955–) cofounded Microsoft, which produced the software that made the personal computer revolution possible. He became one of the wealthiest people on earth and with his wife started the Bill and Melinda Gates Foundation, one of the largest foundations in the world, which works globally to reduce poverty and improve health care outcomes. James Irwin (1930–1991) was an astronaut who became the eighth person to walk on the moon on the Apollo 15 mission in 1971. Cyrus McCormick (1809–1884) is credited with the invention of the reaper, although much of

the work was done by an African American slave on the family plantation who was not eligible for a patent because of his status. A particularly enterprising Scotch-Irish woman, Bette Nesmith Graham (1924–1980), born in Dallas, Texas, died with a net worth of more than $47.5 million; a poor typist, she devised a product that would cover mistakes and in so doing created Liquid Paper correction fluid. Andrew Mellon (1855–1937) was a banker, industrialist, U.S. secretary of the treasury, and philanthropist who founded the Mellon Institute of Industrial Research, which later merged with the Carnegie Institute of Technology to form Carnegie-Mellon University, a major research center in Pittsburgh.

Sports William Harrison "Jack" Dempsey (1895–1983), the "Manassa Mauler," was the world heavyweight boxing champion from 1919 to 1926, setting attendance records and becoming a cultural icon. Arnold Palmer (1929–) is one of the most popular professional golfers of all time; "Arnie's Army," as his fans were known, helped launch the sport into the television age. Race car driver Jeffery Martin "Jeff" Gordon (1971–) has racked up the most wins in NASCAR's modern era (since 1972) and was the first NASCAR driver to reach $100 million in career earnings.

Stage and Screen Influential Scotch-Irish Americans in the performing arts include Ava Gardner (1922–1990), the seventh child of poor cotton and tobacco farmers, who became one of Hollywood's leading actresses (*Mogambo*, 1953; and *The Night of the Iguana*, 1964). The careers of the remarkable Huston family span much of the history of the motion picture in the United States. Walter (1884–1950), his son John (1906–1987), and John's daughter Angelica (1951–) have all won Academy Awards. Walter Huston was a memorable character actor, perhaps best remembered for one of his son John's best films as a director, *The Treasure of the Sierra Madre* (1948); granddaughter Angelica was directed by her father in three films, notably *Prizzi's Honor* (1985), for which she won an Oscar for Best Supporting Actress. John Huston's last film, *The Dead*, a 1987 adaptation of James Joyce's short story, also starred Angelica and was scripted by her brother Danny. James Stewart (1908–1997), one of Hollywood's most famous and beloved citizens, is well known for classics such as *Mr. Smith Goes to Washington* (1939), *It's a Wonderful Life* (1947), and *Rear Window* (1954). John Wayne (1907–1979; born Marion Robert Morrison) was the icon of American masculinity, go-to onscreen cowboy and soldier for three decades, and top box office draw of all time. Shirley MacLaine (1934–; born Shirley MacLean Beatty) has had a film career spanning seven decades, during which she won an Academy Award for Best Actress for *Terms of Endearment* (1983). Her brother Warren Beatty (1937–) not only starred in but also produced and directed landmark films, such as *Bonnie and Clyde* (1967) and *Reds* (1981).

MEDIA

PRINT

Celtic Guide

Established in 2012, this monthly online magazine of Celtic history and culture has a substantial Scotch-Irish component. Also available in print.

James A. McQuiston, Editor/Publisher
Email: celticguide@gmail.com
URL: www.thecelticguide.com

Journal of Scotch-Irish Studies

This journal, sponsored by the Center for Scotch-Irish Studies, publishes scholarly studies on the Scotch-Irish people: their history, language, literature, music, material culture, political and legal philosophy, and contributions to the United States in general.

Dr. Joyce Alexander, Editor
Richard K. McMaster, Editor
Center for Scotch-Irish Studies
P.O. Box 71
Glenolden, Pennsylvania 19036-0071
Phone: (610) 532-8061
Email: cntrsis@aol.com
URL: www.scotch-irishsocietyusa.org/journals.html

RADIO AND TELEVISION

TNN (The Nashville Network)

TNN is a twenty-four-hour cable country music channel. Programming includes recorded videos and talk shows, with a strong regional emphasis toward the American South and West. "The Grand Ole Opry," a radio and television simulcast of the weekly performances of leading country music performers from Nashville's Ryman Auditorium, airs each Saturday evening at 8:00 p.m. on TNN and on a syndicated network of radio stations as well. Begun in 1925, it is the nation's oldest radio program.

Emily Cline Bronze
225 East 8th Street
Chattanooga, Tennessee 37402
Phone: (423) 468-5100
Email: tnninfo@watchtnn.com
URL: www.watchtnn.com

The Thistle and Shamrock

This weekly Celtic music and cultural appreciation program features thematically grouped presentations on Scottish, Irish, and Breton music. It is syndicated nationally on National Public Radio.

Fiona Ritchie, Founder, Producer, and Host
P.O. Box 518
Matthews, North Carolina 28106
Email: info@thistleradio.com
URL: www.thistleradio.com

ORGANIZATIONS AND ASSOCIATIONS

ScotchIrish.net

This website focuses on Scotch-Irish/Scots Irish and Ulster Scots and their history and culture. Its tagline is

"brewed in Scotland, bottled in Ulster and uncorked in the USA."

Sophie Sadler
Scotch Irish Online
East 30th Street
New York, New York 10016
Email: sophie@scotchirish.net
URL: www.scotchirish.net

Scotch-Irish Society of the United States of America

A national organization of persons of Scotch-Irish heritage, it was founded to promote and preserve Scotch-Irish history and culture. It sponsors the biennial Scotch-Irish Identity Symposium and publishes a semiannual newsletter.

Bill McGimpsey, President
P.O. Box 53
Media, Pennsylvania 19063
Email: scotchirish@verizon.net
URL: www.scotch-irishsocietyusa.org/index.html

MUSEUMS AND RESEARCH CENTERS

Historical Center of York County, South Carolina

The center holds archives and sponsors programs illuminating the history of the Carolina Piedmont region, with its significant Scotch-Irish settlement.

Stephen Crotts
212 East Jefferson Street
York, South Carolina 29745
Phone: (803) 329-2121, extension 7245
Email: information@chmuseums.org
URL: http://chmuseums.org/history-hc

Scotch-Irish Foundation Collection at the Balch Institute, Historical Society of Pennsylvania

Established in 1949 to preserve books and manuscripts relating to Scotch-Irish history, culture, and heritage, the Scotch-Irish Foundation was dissolved in 2012 and merged into the Historical Society of Pennsylvania. It includes records of the Loyal Orange Institution of the United States of America and related associations from the late nineteenth to the late twentieth centuries.

Lee Arnold, Senior Director of the Library and Collections
1300 Locust Street
Philadelphia, Pennsylvania 19107
Phone: (215) 732-6200
Fax: (215) 732-2680
Email: larnold@hsp.org
URL: http://hsp.org/about-us/the-balch-institute

SOURCES FOR ADDITIONAL STUDY

Chepesiuk, Ron. *The Scotch-Irish: From the North of Ireland to the Making of America*. Jefferson, NC: McFarland and Company, 2000.

Fischer, David Hackett. *Albion's Seed: Four British Folkways in America*. Oxford: Oxford University Press, 1989.

Jackson, Carlton. *A Social History of the Scotch-Irish*. Lanham, MD: Madison Books, 1993.

Lehmann, William C. *Scottish and Scotch-Irish Contributions to Early American Life and Culture*. Port Washington, NY: Kennikat Press, 1978.

Leyburn, James G. *The Scotch-Irish: A Social History*. Chapel Hill: University of North Carolina Press, 1962.

McCarthy, Karen F. *The Other Irish: The Scots-Irish Rascals Who Made America*. New York: Sterling, 2011.

McWhiney, Grady. *Cracker Culture: Celtic Ways in the Old South*. Tuscaloosa: University of Alabama Press, 1988.

Miller, Kerby A. "'Scotch-Irish' Myths and 'Irish' Identities in Eighteenth- and Nineteenth-Century America." *New Perspectives on the Irish Diaspora*, edited by Charles Fanning. Carbondale: Southern Illinois University Press, 2000.

Vann, Barry Aron. *In Search of Ulster-Scots Land: The Birth and Geotheological Imagings of a Transatlantic People, 1603–1703*. Columbia: University of South Carolina Press, 2008.

Webb, James. *Born Fighting: How the Scots-Irish Shaped America*. New York: Broadway Books, 2004.

Scottish Americans

Mary A. Hess

OVERVIEW

Scottish Americans are immigrants or descendants of people from Scotland, a country that occupies roughly the northern one-third of the British Isles. A land of considerable natural beauty, Scotland is surrounded on three sides by water—the Atlantic Ocean to the north and west, and the North Sea to the east. To the south, Scotland shares a border with England. A fault line separates the country into the northern Highlands and the southern Lowlands, the agricultural and industrial center of the country. In addition, there are several island groups offshore, notably the Hebrides, the Shetland Islands, and the Orkney Islands. Deep and narrow inlets known as *firths* penetrate the coastline of Scotland, while inland are distinctive glacial lakes known as lochs, the most famous of which is Loch Ness, the home of the fabled "Nessie," a prehistoric creature said to live in the deepest part of the lake. The country's area is 30,414 square miles (78,772 square kilometers), or about the size of the state of Maine.

According to the 2011 United Kingdom census, Scotland's population is 5,254,800, two-thirds of which live in the Lowlands, most near the country's two largest cites—Edinburgh, the Scottish capital, and Glasgow. The cities of Dundee and Aberdeen reflect Scotland's major industries, particularly fishing and shipbuilding, and its strong ties to maritime commerce. As part of the United Kingdom, Scotland has benefited economically from its use of the British pound. In 2010 Scotland ranked sixth in the world for gross domestic product per capita, with an estimated output of $41,189 per citizen, two spots behind the United States and ten spots ahead of the United Kingdom as a whole. According to the 2009–2010 Scottish Household Survey, 40.9 percent of the population reported having no religion, 33.4 percent belonged to the Church of Scotland, 14.7 percent were Roman Catholic, 7.6 percent belonged to another Christian denomination, and 1.3 percent were Muslim. The majority of Scots identify as white, making up nearly 98 percent of the population; among the Scottish minority ethnic population, Pakistanis are the largest group, followed by Chinese, Indian, and those identifying as mixed heritage.

With the support of the English crown, Scots were among the earliest arrivals to the New World. The first large wave of Scottish immigrants appeared on North American shores in 1652 and was comprised mostly of English prisoners. Throughout the eighteenth and nineteenth centuries Scots arrived on North American soil in vast numbers, with immigration peaking in the first decade of the twentieth century. Over the course of the twentieth century, immigration to the United States remained relatively constant, spiking occasionally during periods of economic trouble in Scotland. In the first decade of the twenty-first century, Scotland's history of net out-migration reversed; for the first time, the country had a net in-migration, welcoming immigrants from around the world.

The U.S. Census Bureau's American Community Survey estimated in 2011 that 5.56 million Americans were descended from Scottish ancestors, making Scottish Americans the tenth most populous ethnic group in the country. According to the American Community Survey estimates, the states with greatest number of Scottish Americans were California, Florida, Texas, Michigan, New York, North Carolina, Pennsylvania, Washington, and Ohio. States reporting the highest concentration of Scottish Americans were Maine, Vermont, Utah, and New Hampshire. However, American Scots have largely been absorbed into the broader population and can be found throughout the nation.

HISTORY OF THE PEOPLE

Early History The earliest recorded history concerning the Scots comes from the Romans, who controlled southern Britain in the first century CE. In 84 CE the Romans defeated the tribal armies of Scotland in battle but were unable to conquer the people. In an attempt to isolate the fierce "barbarians," the Roman emperor Hadrian built a massive stone wall, the remains of which are still visible traversing northern England just south of the Scottish border. By the 600s, four tribal groups had emerged: the Angles of the Southeast, related to the Germanic tribes settling England at the time; the Britons of the southwest, a Celtic people related to the Welsh; the Picts, also Celtic, who dominated the Highlands; and the Scots, a Celtic group that settled the western islands and coast from nearby Ireland. Christianity, brought by missionaries such as St. Ninian and St. Columba, spread slowly among the tribes beginning in about 400.

Following the Viking invasions of the 800s and 900s, the four tribes gradually united under Scottish kings such as Kenneth MacAlpin, who brought the Scots and Picts together in 843 and is often called the first king of Scotland. His descendants succeeded in gaining limited control over rival kings and the feuding clans (groups of families related by blood). Eventually, the Scots gave their name to the land and all its people, but the kings often ruled in name only, especially in the remote Highlands, where local clan leaders retained their independence.

In 1066 Norman invaders from France gained control of England. Powerful new English rulers such as Edward I (1239–1307), who was called "the Hammer of the Scots," gained influence over the Scottish kings and helped shape culture in the Lowlands. Still the Scots resisted English dominance, often allying with England's enemy, France. However, over time the English and Scottish royal houses became closely connected through marriage. On the death of the English queen, Elizabeth I, in 1603, her cousin James VI, already king of Scotland, ascended the throne of England as James I. The Catholic Stuart monarchs faced trouble in both England and Scotland as the religious disputes between Catholics and Protestants wreaked the land. While rebellions continued in Scotland, the union of Scottish and English crowns marked the beginning of an increasing bond between Scotland and her more powerful neighbor. The Treaty of Union (1707) formalized the political connection by incorporating Scotland's government into that of England. This created the United Kingdom and laid the foundation for the British Empire—to which the Scots would contribute greatly in coming centuries.

Political turmoil continued in Scotland during the 1700s with rebellions led by James Stuart (son of James II), who was backed by France and Spain—England's Catholic enemies. The most important of these "Jacobite" (from *Jacobus*, Latin for James) campaigns occurred in 1715 and in 1745, when James' son Charles also surprised Britain by invading from Scotland. These failed attempts engendered a vast body of romantic legend, though, particularly around the figure of Charles, called "Bonnie Prince Charlie" or the "Young Pretender" (claimant to the throne). The Jacobites found more support among the fiercely independent Highlanders, who had remained largely Catholic, than among the stern Protestant Lowlanders. The Scots retained their distinctive character, however, even as they contributed to Britain's prosperity and worldwide power.

Modern Era The modern history of Scotland mirrors the trajectory of many western European nations. In the nineteenth century, the Industrial Revolution arrived in Scotland; first textiles and later steel, mining, shipbuilding, and engineering all propelled Scotland to the forefront of the world economy and made the region one of the most industrialized places in the world. However, such industry was not immune to the Great Depression of the 1920s and 1930s. After World War I, global need for mining and heavy industry declined. Unemployment, combined with housing shortages and widespread health concerns associated with the Industrial Revolution contributed to a mass migration of Scots to destinations around the world. Scotland endured a net population loss throughout that decade, despite rising birth rates. Boom times returned with the beginning of World War II as Allied forces relied on Scotland's industrial production to provide ships, weapons, and engines. Today, Scotland maintains a business-friendly economic environment, but the technological sector has replaced heavy industry as the driving economic force. Rather than shipbuilders at the docks, there are electronic technicians and software designers in "Silicon Glen" (Scotland's version of Silicon Valley).

Nationalism has also come to define modern Scottish history. Since the eighteenth century, Scotland has worked to distinguish itself politically from England. It was not until the second half of the twentieth century, however, that Scottish secession from the United Kingdom was put into motion. The Devolution Referendum of 1979 polled Scottish citizen support for the Scotland Act of 1978, which proposed a Scottish Parliament independent of the United Kingdom Parliament. Despite failing to earn requisite votes, Scotland only had to wait twenty years before the UK Parliament passed the Scotland Act of 1998, paving the way for the formation of the Scottish Parliament in 1999 and establishing an executive power. For Scottish nationalists the next step is independence. Yet the continued devolution of Scotland's government from the UK is not inevitable. Polls in early 2013 showed that 47 percent of Scots opposed independence and 38 percent believed the country would be worse off as an autonomous nation. Arguments against independence include concerns of diminished international influence and economic instability, while pro-independence Scots believe a smaller government would be more manageable and want to see Scottish interests supersede those of the UK. Citizens are scheduled to vote in a referendum set for late 2014.

SETTLEMENT IN THE UNITED STATES
One of the first colonies with a predominantly Scottish population was in Nova Scotia (which translates as "New Scotland") in present-day Canada; it was founded in 1629 by Scotsman William Alexander. Several small British colonies with high concentrations of Scottish immigrants were established in the early seventeenth century in New Jersey and the Carolinas, at East Jersey in 1683 and Stuarts Town in 1684, respectively. These colonies were primarily for Quakers and Presbyterians who were experiencing religious persecution by the Church of Scotland, which at the time was Episcopalian.

Although some Scots were transported to America as prisoners or criminals and were forced into labor as punishment, many voluntarily settled in America as traders or as tobacco workers in Virginia. Many Scots emigrated to escape the political persecution of the Jacobite sympathizers, combined with economic hard times in Scotland. Throughout the late eighteenth century, roughly 40,000 Scots arrived in the United States. Scots emigrated in groups, which reflects their early organization in clans. They became a significant presence in the New World, settling in the original colonies with a particularly strong presence in the Southeast. Toward the turn of the century, increasing numbers of Highland Scots arrived in the South—founding Darien, Georgia, and populating the Upper Cape Fear area of North Carolina—while Lowland Scots settled in the Lower Cape Fear region. This presence remains strong today, as the American South provides a hub of Scottish history and heritage preservation; in fact, North Carolina has one of largest concentrations of people of Scottish descent. Additionally, Scots were strongly represented in the push westward as well, and their participation in military campaigns was significant.

As a booming Scottish population outpaced job availability, substantial numbers of Scots also immigrated to the United States in the nineteenth century to work in industry. Throughout the twentieth century, immigration to the United States would rise when economic conditions in Scotland worsened; this was especially true during the 1920s, when an economic depression hit Scotland particularly hard. Throughout the remainder of the twentieth century, Scots continued to migrate to the United States, but never again with the same volume. Since 1960, immigrants from Europe have accounted for only 12 percent of the total foreign-born U.S. population. By the twenty-first century, the majority of immigrants arriving in the United States were from Asia and Latin America. According to the American Community Survey's estimates for 2011, among the 5.6 million Americans reporting Scottish ancestry, the vast majority (97 percent) were born in the United States. The states with the highest numbers of Scottish Americans included California, Florida, Michigan, New York, North Carolina, Ohio, Pennsylvania, Texas, and Washington.

LANGUAGE

While the majority of Scottish citizens speak English, the language of the land was once the Celtic-derived Scottish Gaelic. In 2001 it was estimated that roughly 60,000 Scottish citizens still spoke the language. These speakers are primarily located in small pockets of the northwestern part of the country, additionally where a variation of this branch of Gaelic persists in some isolated communities in Nova Scotia, Canada.

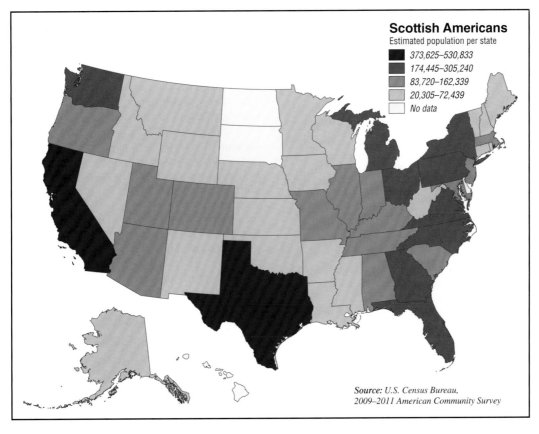

Scottish Americans
Estimated population per state

- 373,625–530,833
- 174,445–305,240
- 83,720–162,339
- 20,305–72,439
- No data

Source: U.S. Census Bureau, 2009–2011 American Community Survey

American Scots or other interested learners can take Scottish Gaelic classes in several U.S. cities such as Seattle or San Francisco. A traditional Scottish Gaelic expression–*Alba gu bràth* (meaning "Scotland until judgment," or "Scotland forever") has become a catch-phrase among contemporary America Scots. A sign of pride in one's heritage, the phrase gained popularity when it was featured as a rallying cry in the 1995 film *Braveheart*, about Scottish folk hero William Wallace.

Excepting recent immigrants, Americans of Scottish ancestry rarely share the characteristic burr (a distinctive trilled "r") that defines Scottish English. However, linguists who have studied Appalachian accents have found continuity in usage and idiom that can be shown to originate in Scottish phrases. Occasionally remnants of the Scottish idiom survive in words such as "dinna," which means "don't," as in "I dinna ken" (I don't know), but this is increasingly rare as even isolated mountain hollows in the South are penetrated by mass media and its homogenizing influence.

RELIGION

Christianity is the predominant religion of Scots and Scottish Americans. The majority of Scottish citizens belong to the national church, the Presbyterian Church of Scotland, affectionately called "the Kirk." Although the Church of Scotland was an austere entity, not given to large churches or displays of wealth in the home nation, it gradually gave way to grand affirmations of material success in the United States. Today most Scottish Americans belong to Protestant denominations, and the Presbyterian Church still plays a significant role in American religious life. The stirring hymn "Onward Christian Soldiers" (1864) exemplifies the Scottish heritage reflected in today's church: "Onward Christian soldiers / Marching as to war / With the Cross of Jesus / Going on before!" Written first as a children's hymn, it became a favorite in Protestant churches.

CULTURE AND ASSIMILATION

Throughout the significant immigration periods of American history, particularly the late nineteenth and early twentieth centuries, cultural norms pressured new arrivals to repress ethnic identity markers in order to appear more "American." Additionally, many Americans detached themselves from strict cultural boundaries by moving away from enclaves and by marrying partners from other backgrounds. As white, Protestant Europeans, this process was particularly easy for Scots. On the whole, the assimilation of Scottish immigrants occurred long ago and has proven to be thorough in American society. Having the benefit of arriving early in U.S. settlement, speaking the local tongue, and appearing in droves, Scottish immigrants played a significant role in shaping American culture. Yet a sense of nostalgic "symbolic ethnicity" eventually led to a resurgence of Scottish Americans' interest in

their ancestry and genealogy in the mid-twentieth century. Such interest in ethnic roots tends to be romanticized, and some Scottish citizens consider American notions of Scottishness to be out of touch or incongruous with real life in contemporary Scotland.

Traditions and Customs There is a cliché about "the wandering Scot" that contains an essential truth—that Scottish people have both a wanderlust and a strong affection for Scotland. This attachment can be seen today in the celebration by Americans of their Scottish roots, which often means both a consciousness of ethnicity as well as taking a journey to discover their ancestral heritage. Many genealogical firms in Great Britain and Ireland specialize in helping these Americans trace their ancestry. Insignia such as a family crest, an article of clothing displaying a traditional plaid pattern (called a tartan), or an interest in traditional customs are all demonstrations of pride in Scottish ethnic identity.

The most significant way in which Scottish Americans connect with their heritage is through participation in regional Scottish clubs and societies. Groups such as the Chicago Scots promote community by fostering contemporary Scottish American culture through lectures, festivals, and institutes like the Scottish American Hall of Fame. These societies also uphold Scottish traditions, support genealogical study, and facilitate travel to Scotland. Present throughout the United States, Scottish societies provide a new iteration of the clan social structure. Rather than close family ties, however, American Scots are bound to one another through a sense of shared history and identity.

Scots enjoy large "gatherings of the clan," which celebrate their heritage and offer opportunities to meet others who share membership in the clan. The Highland Games are one way Scots can celebrate their culture. Originating in Scotland in the early nineteenth century, several countries with substantial Scottish immigrant histories have generated their own Highland Games. In the United States, such events can be found in most states with a large Scottish population (such as New York and Michigan). The games feature sports such as "tossing the caber" (in which men compete to toss a heavy pole farthest) and the hammer throw. Bagpipe music is a very important part of this celebration, as it is at any celebration of clan identity. Dancing, displays of traditional crafts, and other events are also included in the festivities. North Carolina hosts the biggest gathering at Grandfather Mountain each July. Campbells mingle with MacGregors and Andersons, while enjoying Scotch whiskey and traditional cuisine.

Cuisine Main Scottish staples are oatmeal, barley, and potatoes. Oatmeal is made into porridge, a thick, hot breakfast cereal traditionally seasoned with salt. Barley is used primarily in the distillation of Scotch whiskey, now a major source of export revenue. Potatoes ("tatties") are most often eaten mashed. There is also the traditional *haggis* (a pudding made from the heart, liver, and other organs of a sheep, chopped with onions and oatmeal and then stuffed into a sheep's stomach and boiled). This unique meal, served with tatties and "a wee dram" (small portion of whiskey), has taken its place with the tartan and the bagpipes as a national symbol. Scots also enjoy rich vegetable soups, seafood in many forms, beef, oatcakes (a tasty biscuit), and shortbread (a rich, cookie-like confection).

Few of these traditional dishes survived the journey across the Atlantic to become staples in the United States, but some elements of Scottish fare, like potatoes, are indispensable for American grocery shoppers. Shortbread cookies are such a common treat for contemporary Americans that one can easily purchase them pre-made at any grocery store. One of the most recognizable and lasting impacts on the American diet by the Scots is not frequently associated with Scotland: fried chicken. Scots had long been frying chicken in fat, and early settlers in the American Southeast propagated this cooking method, eventually leading to the dish's identification with Southern American traditional food. In general, though, the contemporary Scottish American diet reflects mainstream American food preferences.

Traditional Dress The famous Scottish kilt, a knee-length skirt of a tartan pattern made of wool, was created in the eighteenth century by an Englishman named Thomas Rawlinson. Older kilts were rectangles of cloth, hanging over the legs, gathered at the waist, and wrapped in folds around the upper body. The blanket-like garment served as a bed-roll for a night spent outdoors. Aside from the kilt, fancy "highland" dress includes a *sporan* (leather purse on a belt), stockings, brogues (shoes), dress jacket, and a number of decorative accessories. The plaid is a length of tartan cloth draped over the shoulder and does not properly refer to the pattern, which is the tartan. Women's fancy dress is simpler, though elegant, consisting of a white cotton blouse, perhaps with embroidered patterns, and a silk tartan skirt. Her version of the plaid, a tartan also in silk, is hung over the shoulder and pinned in place with a brooch. This finery, like the tartans, is mostly an invention of the modern age but has become traditional, and it is taken quite seriously. The tartan shows up elsewhere, commonly on ties, caps, and skirts—even on cars and in the costumes of young "punk rockers" in Edinburgh and Glasgow. Today, Scottish Americans most frequently sport kilts and clan tartans on formal occasions, for sporting events, or for national holidays.

Traditional Arts and Crafts Like many early American settlers, Scottish immigrants participated in folk crafts that were first and foremost purposeful and practical for frontier life. Gatherings called "quilting bees," which allowed women to enjoy each other's company while creating a patchwork quilt—were the essence of thrift. Various small pieces of fabric were

SCOTTISH SHORTBREAD

Ingredients

1 cup butter

1 cup sugar

3½ cups flour

Preparation

Preheat oven to 300°F.

Cream butter and sugar. Then add flour, ½ cup at a time. Mix well and knead thoroughly. Add more flour if needed.

Pat the dough into a round, square, or oblong pan. Prick with a fork all the way to the bottom.

Bake in oven for 45–60 minutes. Shortbread should be slightly darker, but not brown. Retain a piece of raw dough for comparison.

sewn together in patterns to create a beautiful and utilitarian bed covering. Today many of these quilts are treasured by the descendants of the women who made them. Quilting is a popular craft that has enjoyed an ever-widening appreciation both as a hobby and folk art; quilts are often displayed in museums, and one of the best collections can be seen in Paducah, Kentucky, home of the American Quilting Society. Another traditional community activity is that of the barn raising and the subsequent dance—a tribute to the pioneer spirit that built America. Neighbors cooperated to erect barns and celebrated their hard work with fiddle music and a square dance late into the night. These gatherings helped shape community in rural areas such as the Midwest and the West.

Dances and Songs There is considerable Scottish influence in the field of country and folk music, directly traceable to the Scots ballad—a traditional form in which a story (usually tragic) is related to the listener in song. The ballad (e.g. "Barbara Allen") originated as an oral tradition and was brought to the southeastern United States by immigrants who preserved the form while adapting melody and lyrics to suit their purpose. Instruments, especially the fiddle and harp, have been transformed into unique-sounding relations such as the hammered dulcimer, pedal steel guitar, and electric mandolins, and they are the staples of today's country music, particularly bluegrass, which emphasizes the heritage of country music in its traditional origins in Scotland and Ireland. Contemporary line dancing also evolved from ancient Scottish ritual dances by way of square dancing. The square dance began with reels and other dances enjoyed by the nobility and transformed to the present popularity of line dancing. Today's "Texas Two-Step" and "Boot-scooting" are lasting relics of these traditions.

SCOTTISH TARTAN

The most distinctive feature of the kilt is its pattern; frequently (and erroneously) referred to as plaid, this pattern—the tartan—is comprised of a combination of crisscrossed, multicolored stripes. Many clans claim their own unique tartan pattern, but the most popular patterns refer to military groups and other institutions. Some Scottish Americans identify with a particular tartan, often choosing their pattern based on allegiance. Yet, plaid patterns have become so commonplace in everyday wear such that many non-Scots may not even realize they could be sporting centuries-old clan insignia.

The musical sound perhaps most closely associated with the Scots is the unmistakable reedy drone of the bagpipe. Historians hypothesize that the bagpipe may have originated in the ancient Middle East or the Iberian Peninsula, but since the mid-sixteenth century the instrument has been associated with the Scottish Highlands. Although several varieties of bagpipe exist across numerous cultures, the Great Highland Bagpipe is most familiar to contemporary Americans. The bagpipe is comprised of four main parts: the blowstick, a wooden rod that forces air into an animal-hide bag; the bag compresses air and passes it into the chanter, a notched tube the piper manipulates to regulate notes or chords; air then emerges from the drones—or protruding sticks—to produce the musical tones. Historically bagpipes have been used in ceremonial contexts which continues today where Americans hear the distinctive instrument in settings like weddings, funerals, military rituals, and in parades.

Holidays Most Scottish holidays are those celebrated throughout Great Britain; however, two holidays are unique to Scotland: Scottish Quarter Day, celebrated forty days after Christmas, and the commemoration of St. Andrew, patron saint of Scotland, on November 30. Scots throughout the world share in the celebration of St. Andrew's Day. A sentimental holiday is the birthday of poet Robert ("Robbie") Burns, celebrated on the poet's birthday, January 25, and called "Burns Night." The event is marked by a traditional "Burns Supper" meal, consisting of haggis and accompanied by recitations of Burns' poetry, memorial speeches highlighting his continued relevance, and performance of Burns' most memorable work, "Auld Lang Syne." Unique to American Scots is the relatively new holiday of National Tartan Day. The first celebration of Tartan Day occurred in New York City in 1982 as a commemoration of the repeal of an act banning tartan wearing. In 2005 a proposal to make April 6 an annual day of celebration of Scottish Heritage was passed by Congress. In the 2010's, this holiday is marked by parades and festivals throughout the United States.

Health Care Issues and Practices Health concerns are primarily determined by economic factors, and especially by location. Having found, for the most part, economic security due to generations of residence and the economic advantage of an early arrival in the United States, many Scots are insured through their employers, are self-employed, or have union benefits. The great exception is in Appalachia, where poverty persists despite the initiatives of John F. Kennedy and Lyndon B. Johnson's "War on Poverty" in the 1960s. The dominant industry of the area, coal mining, has left a considerable mark on the health of Scottish Americans. Black lung, a congestive disease of the lungs caused by the inhalation of coal dust, disables and kills miners at a high rate. This and chronic malnutrition, high infant mortality, and low birth weight remain the scourge of mountain people. West Virginia, Kentucky, and Tennessee still have pockets of poverty as a result of high unemployment and isolation. These concerns are not, however, limited to Americans of Scottish descent.

FAMILY AND COMMUNITY LIFE

Traditional family structure, especially in the Highlands, centered around the clan. There are about ninety original clans. Large clans enrolled smaller ones as allies, and the alliances also became traditional. The clans have loosely defined territories, and prolonged wars, often spanning generations, were once common between clans. The most famous feud was that between the Campbells (who supported the English) and the MacDonalds (Jacobites). Even today there are MacDonalds who will not speak to Campbells and vice-versa.

The adjective "clannish," derived from the Gaelic *clann* (descent from a common ancestor), perfectly describes the sentimental attachment that Scottish Americans feel concerning extended family and heritage. The origin of this term is the tendency of Scots to migrate with their clan and settle in the same location. This tendency was so pronounced that in parts of Kentucky and Tennessee, relatives adopted the use of their middle name as a surname since all their kin shared a common last name. One of the most infamous examples in the United States of the Scottish tendency to clannishness is the Hatfield and McCoy feud of the 1880s in the Tug River Valley along the West Virginia and Kentucky border. The murderous vendetta lasted years and involved disputes over a razorback hog, a romance between a Hatfield son and a McCoy daughter, and various other affronts to family dignity. After nationwide publicity, the feud was finally ended in 1897 after the execution of one of the Hatfields and the jailing of several other participants. However, the phrase, "feuding like the Hatfields and McCoys" is still a part of the American vocabulary.

Gender Roles Scottish identity often aligns itself with displays of overt masculinity. Events like the Highland Games emphasize physical prowess and the use of weapons. In this way, Scottish heritage has come to signify misogyny for some American Scots. The image of a *Braveheart* figure often stands in for all of Scottish heritage, but in reality only reflects a narrow stereotype of Highlander Scots. Contemporary Scottish American culture reflects mainstream American gender roles. According to the American Community Survey estimates for 2011, the percentage of Scottish American women over the age of fifteen who in the labor force was 59 percent, nearly identical to the rate for U.S. women overall. Likewise, as with the general U.S. population, Scottish American women earned less than Scottish American men; the American Community Survey's 2009–2011 estimates showed that among Scottish Americans employed full-time, women's median earnings were 25 percent lower than that of their male counterparts. (For the total U.S. population, women's median earnings were 21 percent lower than men's.)

Education Perhaps due in part to ethnic and social advantages historically accorded to Scottish immigrants, in the early twenty-first century Scottish Americans had higher rates of educational attainment than the general American population. The American Community Survey's estimates for 2009–2011 showed that 95.8 percent of Scottish Americans had attained a high school degree or higher (compared with 85.6 percent of the overall population), and 42.7 percent of Scottish Americans had attained a bachelor's degree or higher (whereas only 28.2 percent of all Americans had achieved the same education levels).

Courtship and Weddings Scottish weddings were historically a time of public celebration in which an entire community would feast and revel together. While this practice may not have been unique to Scots, the tradition of breaking an oatcake over the bride's head is. Commonly in the nineteenth century, the wedding party would crumble a cake over the bride and then distribute it among guests. A symbol of breaking the bride's virgin state, the custom has since fallen by the wayside in favor of less messy rituals.

Less traditional wedding practices also have their origin in Scotland. For example, hand fasting, in which a bride and groom's hands are bound together to symbolize their new unity, has become a common feature in Wiccan and other non-Christian wedding ceremonies today. Accounts report that this ceremony originated as a civil alternative to religious wedding rituals at times when religious officials were unavailable, or as a way to "try out" a bride without having to make a marriage official. In 1939 reformed marriage laws ceased the recognition of hand fasting as official marriage, but today the majority of Scottish marriages are still civil rather than religious.

Philanthropy Philanthropy is a foundational tenet of Scottish culture in the United States. Many immigrants, grateful for the opportunities and successes granted them in the new world, used their

A Scottish Christmas parade. RICHARD T. NOWITZ / CORBIS

advantages to help others find similar opportunities. Industrialist Andrew Carnegie is perhaps the best-known Scottish American philanthropist. Carnegie essentially wrote the book on charitable giving, as his 1889 essay "The Gospel of Wealth" remains a reference for philanthropists into the twenty-first century. His philosophy was based in the belief that money is only valuable inasmuch as it can benefit society, rather than be amassed for individual gain. Carnegie donated hundreds of millions of dollars to build public libraries, endow universities, and fund scholarships. His most famous gift is one of New York's most beautiful public buildings, Carnegie Hall, which has hosted the world's most distinguished performers in the lively arts. Today groups such as the Scots Charitable Society and others carry on Carnegie's vision and work. Charity is a hallmark of Scottish community organizations throughout the United States.

Surnames Typical Scottish surnames carry some historical signification. Many original surnames are patronyms, meaning they were derived from the first name of a person's father; numerous clan names are prefixed by the Gaelic "Mac," meaning "son of" and many of these have proliferated and remain common today. Historically, inhabitants of claimed land often changed their surnames to reflect the clans newly in charge of their land, demonstrating their allegiance and strengthening the clan's power. Other surnames derived from the region of a family's origin or a

SCOTTISH PROVERBS

The following are examples of Scottish proverbs:

Whit's fur ye'll no go past ye.

(Meaning: What's meant to happen will happen.)

Mony a mickle maks a muckle!

(Meaning: Saving a small amount soon builds up to a large amount.)

family's trade. Among the most recognized Scottish surnames are Campbell, Mackenzie, Stewart (Stuart), MacDonald, and Gordon.

EMPLOYMENT AND ECONOMIC CONDITIONS

The Scots people were among the first European settlers, and along with the other colonists from the British Isles they helped create what has been recognized as the dominant culture in America, namely, white and Protestant. By working hard and seizing the opportunities of a rapidly growing country, many Scottish immigrants were able to move up rapidly in American society. Unaffected by barriers of race, language, or religion, they earned a reputation for hard work and thrift that was greatly admired in the young republic.

Historically, American Scots were drawn to the land as farmers and herders just as in their home country. Highland Scots, in particular, were attracted to mountain areas that resembled their homeland, and replicated their lives as herders and small-scale farmers wherever possible. Others were drawn to work in heavy industry, such as the steel mills and coal mines. The nation's railroads provided employment for many, and in the case of Andrew Carnegie, provided a step up in his career as a capitalist. Many sought higher education and entered the professions at all levels, particularly as physicians and lawyers. According to the American Community Survey estimates for 2009–2011, nearly 48 percent of Scottish Americans reported employment in management, business, sciences and arts industries (compared with 36 percent for the total U.S. population).

For others, isolated in Appalachia or the rural South, hard times during the Great Depression brought scores of Scotch-Irish to the factories of Detroit and Chicago, where they labored in the auto plants and stockyards. Poverty returned for many of these people as plants shut down and downscaled in the 1960s, creating so-called "hillbilly ghettoes" in major Northern industrial cities. Generations of poverty have created an underclass of displaced Southerners, which persists as a social problem today. Author Harriette Arnow, born in 1908, wrote movingly of the plight of these economic migrants in her novel *The Dollmaker* (1954).

Scottish Americans have, of course, assimilated to a high degree and have benefited much from the opportunities that class mobility and a strong work ethic have brought them. Despite the economic downturn in the late 2000s, American Scots maintained a lower unemployment rate than the national average.

POLITICS AND GOVERNMENT

Scots were a significant presence in the American Revolution and the Civil War. The divided union was embodied by Generals "Stonewall" Jackson and Jeb Stuart for the Gray and George B. McClellan for the Blue. Many Scots had settled on the frontier and moved westward seeking land and opportunity, and pressed forward to the West, chiefly Texas, Oklahoma, and the Gulf Coast. Texas in particular was a land of opportunity for the land-hungry Scots—Scotch-Irish statesman Sam Houston and his fellows were among the intrepid settlers of that diverse state who fought the Comanche and settled the Plains, effectively expanding the purview of the United States' territory at the cost of Native American cultural and population losses.

Highland Scots and their descendants (who typically settled in the mountains) were active in the anti-slavery movement, while it was more common for the Lowland Scots and the Scotch-Irish to be proslavery. This created a major rift in the mid-South and the lowland areas, which clung to slavery while the highlands in large part chose the Union during the Civil War. Scots figured prominently in all the major political parties in American history, and were perhaps most identified as a group with the Populist movement which reached its peak in the 1890s and united farmers for a short time against perceived economic injustice. The South and Midwest were the stronghold of the populists, led by men like Tom Watson and Ignatius Donnelly. Scots were also a major force in the union movement, exemplified by the agitation for workers' rights in the textile mills of the Southeast and the mines of West Virginia and Kentucky, marked by serious outbreaks of violence and strikes. "Which side are you on?" was a question often heard in these conflicts. Filmmaker Barbara Kopple documented this long and bloody struggle in her prize-winning film *Harlan County, USA* (1977).

Not until the 1970s would Scottish nationalism be a significant force in British politics; nonetheless, in 1979, Scottish voters rejected limited home rule in a referendum. Despite historic, economic, and cultural ties to Britain, Scottish independence is a fervently debated issue. Nationalists believe that Scottish interests have long been placed secondary to England and that independence would enable Scotland to thrive financially, socially, and creatively and effectively allow it to become an equal world power and to exercise full control over its future. The opposition, who constitute the majority of Scots, maintains that Scotland is more stable as a part of the UK, which shares risk and upholds common values. Yet, the issue is not black and white; some opposed to independence support an increase in economic and legislative autonomy while leaving some issues like defense and foreign affairs as the UK's responsibility as a prudent compromise. With no clear decision on the horizon, Scottish citizens anticipate a referendum on independence in late 2014. Although, for many contemporary Scottish Americans, the details of Scotland's politics are less pertinent than the idyllic imagery and clan identities so often referenced in popular media.

Scottish Americans have been involved with U.S. government from the founding of the Republic. As landholders and farmers, they were very much the people Thomas Jefferson had in mind as participants in his agrarian democracy. From legislators to presidents, including President Bill Clinton, the passion of Scottish people for government has been felt in America. Presidents who shared this heritage include Andrew Jackson (1767–1845), Ulysses S. Grant (1822–1885), Woodrow Wilson (1856–1924), and Ronald Reagan (1911–2004), and George W. Bush (1946–).

Since the breakup of the so-called Democratic "Solid South," it is difficult to predict how Scottish Americans vote. In addition, because of assimilation, it is unlikely that there would be a "Scots vote."

NOTABLE INDIVIDUALS

Pioneer and explorer Daniel Boone (1734–1820), was born to parents of Scottish ancestry. After immigrating to the United States, Boone exemplified the aptitude of Scots to adapt to the unrest and harsh climate of the American frontier. Boone was active in building the New Republic, primarily in the American Southeast, where he established settlements and fought to defend the region from the British. His reputation has been celebrated in song and story, as well as movies and television. Daniel Boone was a trailblazer and patriot who continues to capture the imaginations of Americans.

Scottish-born naturalist John Muir (1838–1914), was reared as a strict Calvinist, and reacted to a near loss of his eyesight in an accident by embarking on a spiritual quest for the natural world. He began a walk on foot across the continent, which instilled in him a deep appreciation for the wild land of North America. Through his writings, such as *My First Summer in the Sierra* (1911) and *A Thousand-Mile Walk to the Gulf* (1916), Muir popularized environmental preservation. A fierce advocate for the preservation of the wilderness, Muir influenced President Theodore Roosevelt to become a conservationist. The national parks are a tribute to his foresight and love of America's natural

beauty. Today he is regarded as one of America's great naturalists and the founder of modern nature writing.

Commerce and Industry Industrialist and philanthropist Andrew Carnegie (1835–1919) was born in Dunfermline, Scotland. Arriving in the United States as a child immigrant, Carnegie's meteoric rise to the top echelons of American society has come to epitomize the notion of America as the "Land of Opportunity." Years of hard work and smart investments in the railroad and steel industries earned Carnegie the designation of being among the earliest millionaires in the United States. In addition to his substantial role to the development of American business and infrastructure, perhaps Carnegie's most lasting contribution to American society has been his philosophy of charitable giving. It is estimated that at the time of his death, Andrew Carnegie had donated more than $350 million dollars. Many of these donations went to education and art institutions. Today the world-renowned performance center Carnegie Hall in New York City, Carnegie Mellon University, the Carnegie Trust for the Universities of Scotland, and others bear the great philanthropist's name.

The adjective "clannish," derived from the Gaelic clann *(descent from a common ancestor), perfectly describes the sentimental attachment that Scottish Americans feel concerning extended family and heritage. The origin of this term is the tendency of Scots to migrate with their clan and settle in the same location.*

Fashion Claire McCardell (1905–1958) revolutionized fashion design and dance by popularizing the stretch leotard; a pioneer in women's ready-to-wear clothing, she also created the affordable and practical "popover," a wrap-around denim housedress, and the "Moroccan" tent dress.

Literature Thomas Wolfe (1900–1938), received great acclaim for his novel, *Look Homeward, Angel* (1929). The youngest of eight children, Wolfe grew up in Asheville, North Carolina. After writing plays for several years without success, Wolfe turned to fiction. He drew on his life experiences in the American South to inform his masterpiece, causing some controversy in the small town. He continued to write throughout his life, but by the time he died only half of Wolfe's prolific writings had been published. Today Harvard University and the University of North Carolina–Chapel Hill, the author's alma maters, both maintain collections of his work.

Author Carson McCullers (1917–1967), wrote in a variety of genres, but almost always focused on themes pertaining to the America South. Born Lula Carson

Smith in Georgia, McCullers came from an illustrious legacy in the South, as her grandparents owned plantations and fought for the Confederate army. Among her best known works are *The Heart is a Lonely Hunter* (1940), *Reflections in A Golden Eye* (1941), and *Member of the Wedding* (1946). Two of these titles were adapted to film. Today, she is regarded as one of the South's most important novelists alongside William Faulkner.

Pulitzer Prize–winning author and screenwriter Larry McMurtry (1936–), is known for his Western-themed novels, including *The Last Picture Show* (1966) and *Lonesome Dove* (1985). A native of Texas, McMurtry often draws inspiration from the landscapes and legends of his home state. Not only has McMurtry found success as an author, but several of his works have been adapted to hit films and television series'. The film version of McMurtry's 1975 novel *Terms of Endearment* won five Academy awards, and McMurtry himself won an Oscar in 2005 for his adaptation of E. Annie Proulx's short story *Brokeback Mountain*, about two cowboys in Wyoming.

Music Actor and singer John Raitt (1917–2005) enjoyed Broadway success that transferred to Hollywood musicals. Best known for his portrayal of Curley in *Oklahoma!* (which depicts Scottish customs such as the *shivaree* and the barn dance), Raitt began his career on the stage during a height of Broadway's popularity. Raitt's talent easily translated to the screen, where he appeared frequently to perform his musical hits.

Guitarist, singer, and songwriter Bonnie Raitt (1949–), is the daughter of legendary musician John Raitt. Beginning her career as a folk and roots performer, Raitt has come to be known as a noted interpreter of the blues. Among her best known songs are the pop hit "Something to Talk About" (1991) and the melancholy break-up ballad, "I Can't Make You Love Me" (1991). By the mid-2010s, Raitt had won ten Grammy Awards, solidifying her place in the annals of American music history.

Performance Isadora Duncan (1877–1927) was a major innovator in modern dance, creating a unique expression based on Greek classicism and a belief in liberating the body from the constrictive costumes and especially footwear of classical ballet; her flowing draperies and bare feet made her the sensation of her day; her colorful life story is chronicled in her autobiography, *My Life* (1926).

Science and Medicine Samuel Morse (1791–1872), who revolutionized communications with the telegraph and Morse Code, was also an accomplished portrait painter and a founder of Vassar College in 1861; in 1844 he sent the famous message "What hath God wrought?" from Washington to Baltimore, and between 1857 and 1858 he collaborated with entrepreneur Cyrus Field (1819–1892) in laying the first transatlantic cable.

Visual Arts Craftsman Duncan Phyfe (1768–1854) was born in Scotland, but emigrated as a child, relocating to upstate New York where he became the apprentice of a cabinetmaker. Gaining the patronage of wealthy New York families, Phyfe built a notable reputation for his hard work and popular styles mid-nineteenth century. Phyfe is well-known to generations of Americans who cherish the tables, chairs, and cabinets he created, as well as inspiring imitators of his work—the apex of the Federalist style. Retrospectives of his work continue to be exhibited as recently as 2012.

Stage and Screen Oscar-winning stage and film actor James Stewart (1908–1997) was one of Hollywood's most famous and beloved citizens. Known for classics such as *Mr. Smith Goes to Washington* (1939), *The Philadelphia Story, It's a Wonderful Life* (1947), and *Rear Window* (1954), Stewart's characters defined classic Hollywood heroes. By the late twentieth century, Stewart had largely retired from acting but he remained an active political contributor. Starring in over ninety films, Stewart received numerous Lifetime Achievement awards for his contributions to American film history.

Film and television actor Katharine Hepburn (1907–2003) was known as a strong-willed and talented leading lady. An Oscar-winning actress, Hepburn's numerous films span a career lasting over fifty years. She portrayed the doomed Mary, Queen of Scots in *Mary of Scotland* (1936), and took on the role of Tracy Lord in *The Philadelphia Story* opposite James Stewart, for which she received an Academy Award nomination. Throughout her long and honored career on stage and screen, Hepburn won three Academy Awards and was nominated for eight.

Scottish-born comedian and television personality Craig Ferguson (1962–) immigrated to the United States in the 1990s as an adult. He moved to Los Angeles looking to break into the American movie business after finding moderate success in the United Kingdom. Soon after this move, Ferguson broke onto American television as a character on *The Drew Carey Show* (1996–2003). By the mid-2000s, Ferguson had begun hosting *The Late Late Show*, a late-night talk show, which showcased his sparkling personality and comedic prowess. In 2008 Ferguson became a naturalized American citizen, the process of which he broadcast on his television program.

MEDIA

PRINT

The Highlander Magazine

A bi-monthly magazine of Scottish heritage, largely dealing with Scottish history and traditions.

The Highlander
87 Highland Avenue
Hull, Massachusetts 02045
Phone: (781) 925-0600
Fax: (781) 925-1439
Email: advertising@highlandermagazine.com
URL: www.highlandermagazine.com

Scotia: Interdisciplinary Journal of Scottish Studies

An academic journal presenting research across disciplines, which focus on topics pertaining to Scottish history and culture; published by the Department of History at Old Dominion University.

Old Dominion University
Department of History
8000 Batten Arts and Letters
Norfolk, Virginia 23529
Phone: (757) 683-3949
Fax: (757) 683-5644
URL: http://al.odu.edu/history/

Scottish Banner

Touted as the largest international Scottish newspaper, the *Banner* covers news and events for Scots in North America and Australia. Intended for Scottish expatriates and descendants.

13799 Park Boulevard #271
Seminole, Florida 33776
Phone: (866) 544-5157
Fax: (727) 648-4096
Email: scotbanner@aol.com
URL: www.scottishbanner.com

Scots Heritage Magazine

A quarterly publication with a readership of more than 32,000 worldwide. Available in print and online.

Richard Bath, Editor
P.O. Box 32510
Fridley, Minnesota 55432
Phone: 01631 568000
Fax: (763) 571-8292
Email: editor@scotsheritagemagazine.com
URL: www.scotsheritagemagazine.com

RADIO AND TELEVISION

The Thistle & Shamrock

The Thistle & Shamrock is a weekly Celtic music and cultural appreciation program, featuring thematically grouped presentations on Scottish, Irish, and Breton music. Broadcast on more than 350 National Public Radio stations.

Fiona Ritchie, Producer and Host
P.O. Box 518
Matthews, North Carolina 28106
URL: http://thistleradio.com/

Simply Scottish Radio

Originally a syndicated radio show, *Simply Scottish Radio* aired weekly throughout North America on NPR affiliates. Since 2011 it has been broadcast as a weekly Internet podcast. The show features music, history, news, interviews, and other aspects of Scottish culture. The show was created in 1999 by Andrew McDiarmid Sr. and his son Andrew McDiarmid Jr., who continue to host the show into the 2010s.

Andrew McDiarmid, Jr., Radio Host
Email: radio@simplyscottish.com
URL: www.simplyscottish.com

ORGANIZATIONS AND ASSOCIATIONS

American Scottish Foundation

An organization that promotes Scottish heritage through Scotland House, a cultural center in New York City, and a newsletter, *Calling All Scots*.

Heather L. Bain, Chairman
545 Madison Avenue
New York, New York 10022
Phone: (212) 605-0338
Fax: (212) 605-0222
Email: asfevents@wwbcny.com
URL: www.americascottishfoundation.com

Association of Scottish Games and Festivals

Provides information for its members on Highland Games held in the United States; compiles statistics and maintains a computer database.

Kevin Anderson, Immediate Past-President
RR3–Box 223
Bridgeport, West Virginia 26330
Phone: (304) 534-3737
Fax: (215) 825-8745
Email: daa223@juno.com
URL: www.asgf.org

Council of Scottish Clans and Associations (COSCA)

Provides information on clan organizations for interested individuals or groups and maintains files of clan newsletters and books. The council meets each July at Grandfather Mountain in North Carolina.

Susan L. McIntosh, Board of Trustees President
P.O. Box 427
Pinehurst, North Carolina 28370
Phone: (980) 333-4686
Fax: (280) 229-4699
Email: coscainfo@gmail.com
URL: www.cosca.net

MUSEUMS AND RESEARCH CENTERS

Ellen Payne Odom Genealogical Library

Built in 1989 by an endowment from the estate of Ellen Payne Odom, the library offers individuals resources for genealogical research. Numerous Scottish clans have declared the library an official repository for records.

Lauren Howell, Board of Trustees Chairman
Moultrie-Colquitt County Library
204 5th Street, Southeast
Moultrie, Georgia 31768
Phone: (229) 985-6540
Email: mccls@mccls.org
URL: www.mccls.org/odom_gen.htm

Scottish American History Club and Museum

Run by the Illinois Saint Andrew Society, the largest Scottish Society in the United States, the museum presents information and exhibits pertaining to Scottish contributions to American culture. Aiming to cultivate Scottish identity through education and celebration, the museum is just one of many ways the Chicago Scots promote their heritage.

Kristen Guthrie
Illinois St. Andrew Society
2800 Des Plaines Avenue
North Riverside, Illinois 60546
Phone: (708) 447-5092
Fax: (708) 447-4697
Email: kristenguthrie@chicagoscot.org
URL: www.chicagoscots.org/museum/

Scottish Tartans Museum

Dedicated to the "history and traditions of Scottish Highland Dress," the museum showcases a gallery of kilts and tartans that date to the eighteenth century. In addition to the 500 tartans on display, the museum also provides access to thousands more. The museum, founded by the Scottish Tartan Society has dedicated itself to providing reliable information and encouraging research of traditional Highland garb.

Ronan B. MacGregor, Operating Manager
86 East Main Street
Franklin, North Carolina 28734
Phone: (828) 524-7472
Email: tartans@scottishtartans.org
URL: www.scottishtartans.org

St. Andrews Scottish Heritage Center

Housing a collection of books on history, genealogy, and culture, as well as artifacts and Celtic music, the Scottish Heritage Center aims to educate Americans of Scottish decent and researchers alike. Sponsored by North Carolina's St. Andrews University, the heritage center also hosts educational programming.

Bill Caudill, Director
1700 Dogwood Mile
Laurinburg, North Carolina 28352
Phone: (910) 277-5555

Fax: (910) 277-5020
Email: bill@sapc.edu
URL: www.sapc.edu/shc/index.php

SOURCES FOR ADDITIONAL STUDY

Dobson, David. *Scottish Emigration to Colonial America, 1607–1785*. Athens: University of Georgia Press, 1994.

Duncan, Sim. *American Scots: The Scottish Diaspora and the USA*. Edinburgh: Dinedin Press, 2011.

Fry, Michael. *How the Scots Made America*. New York: St. Martin's Press, 2003.

Lehmann, William C. *Scottish and Scotch-Irish Contributions to Early American Life and Culture*. Port Washington, NY: Kennikat Press, 1978.

McWhiney, Grady. *Cracker Culture: Celtic Customs in the Old South*. Tuscaloosa: University of Alabama Press, 1988.

Parker, Anthony W. *Scottish Highlanders in Colonial Georgia: The Recruitment, Emigration, and Settlement at Darien, 1735–1748*. Athens: University of Georgia Press, 1997.

Ray, Celeste. *Highland Heritage: Scottish Americans in the American South*. Chapel Hill: University of North Carolina, 2001.

———, ed. *Transatlantic Scots*. Tuscaloosa: University of Alabama Press, 2005.

Rethford, Wayne, and June Skinner Sawyers. *The Scots of Chicago: Quiet Immigrants and Their New Society*. Dubuque, IA: Kendall/Hunt Pub. Co., 1997.

Szasz, Margaret Connell. *Scottish Highlanders and Native Americans: Indigenous Education in the Eighteenth-Century Atlantic World*. Norman, University of Oklahoma Press, 2007.

SEMINOLES

Lisa Kroger

OVERVIEW

The Seminole people are a group of Native Americans who banded together in the eighteenth century to occupy the land that is now Florida. The tribe's territory took up most of the Florida peninsula, which is bordered by the Atlantic Ocean on the east and the Gulf Mexico on the west. Much of the region consists of the vast wetlands now known as the Everglades. The group's name is thought to come either from the Creek word *semaló ni* (which means "wild" or "runaway") or from the Spanish word *cimarrón* (which means "untamed" or "wild").

The Seminole are a unique group of Native Americans that were originally from several different tribes, mostly Creeks from Georgia, Alabama, and elsewhere in the southeastern United States. In the late eighteenth century, a group of these Creeks, numbering around 5,000, settled in what was then Spanish land in Florida, establishing at least six villages. Like the Creeks, the Seminoles lived in well-established towns. Their economy was primarily based on agriculture and trade with the Europeans who occupied the area. The Seminoles also took in runaway African slaves, who became known as the Black Seminoles.

Today there are two distinct Seminole political entities recognized by the U.S. government: the Seminole Nation of Oklahoma and the Seminole Tribe of Florida. A third culturally and historically related group, the Miccosukee Tribe of Indians of Florida, is also recognized by the federal government. After the Second Seminole War (1835–1842), during which the Seminoles fought the United States for control of their Florida homeland, the tribe was forced to relocate to what is now Oklahoma. A small faction remained in Florida, escaping the removal by surviving in the Florida Everglades. They now maintain several reservations on Florida land. The Seminole have fought to maintain their distinct heritage among increasing temptation to assimilate to American culture.

In the first decade of the twenty-first century, there were approximately 20,000 enrolled Seminole tribal members (17,000 in the Seminole Nation of Oklahoma, 2,800 in the Seminole Tribe of Florida, and 600 in the Miccosukee Tribe). In the 2010 U.S. Census, a larger number of Americans self-identified as having Seminole ancestry: 31,971. According to the Census, Florida and Oklahoma boast the largest population of Seminoles, and other states with small but significant numbers of Seminoles include California, Texas, New York, and Pennsylvania.

HISTORY OF THE PEOPLE

Early History The Seminoles are originally descended from the Creek Indians from Georgia and Alabama. In the eighteenth century a small faction of the group moved to Florida, seeking not only new places to plant crops but also peace from increasingly hostile relations with British colonists in Georgia and from other Creek tribes who were constantly at war with each other. Around the 1770s, this group took the name of Seminole. During this time, the Seminole tribe also took in remnants of other Native Americans and runaway slaves from nearby plantations.

In the early nineteenth century, the United States invaded Florida, which was then a Spanish territory. The conflict, known as the First Seminole War (ca. 1814 to 1819), pushed the Seminoles further south in the Florida peninsula and ultimately resulted in the United States taking control of Florida in 1821. The new government immediately caused problems for the Seminole tribes, who were unsure of their ownership of their lands. A temporary solution was reached in 1823 when the Treaty of Moultrie Creek gave the Seminoles reservation land in the middle of the Florida peninsula.

More change was imminent for the tribe, however. In 1830 the Indian Removal Act attempted to force the Seminoles to relocate to Oklahoma, then known as Indian Territory, an action that led to the Second Seminole War. Most Seminoles refused to relocate. Led by their chief, Osceola (1804–1838), the remaining Seminoles were determined to fight for the home. The war began on December 28, 1835, when Major Francis Dade and his troops were attacked by 300 Seminoles; later the same day Osceola killed Wiley Thompson, the Indian Agent stationed at Fort King in present-day Ocala. Using their knowledge of the difficult-to-navigate marshes and swamps of the Everglades, the Seminoles were able to survive and attack any U.S. troops nearby using guerrilla-style war tactics. The war would continue for seven years, even after Osceola's death in 1838.

The first of the Seminole removals occurred in 1836 and lasted through 1842. By 1842 the Seminole numbers were diminishing; over 4,000 were forced to Oklahoma. A few hundred remained in the Everglades. The Second Seminole War would become known as the most expensive of the Indian Wars. A final conflict, called the Third Seminole War, took place in 1858, when the remaining Seminoles once again fought to keep their lands in Florida. Although more Seminoles were once again moved to Oklahoma, a small group remained behind.

As the Seminole tribe faced integration into the United States, the people used their culture to appeal to tourists, especially those who flocked to southern Florida. In the early twentieth century, the Seminoles opened tourist villages, selling admission to see ceremonies such as the Green Corn Festival and weddings. These were usually staged performances rather than a real look into the Seminole way of life.

Modern Era Though impoverished and still in hiding, the remnants of the Seminoles lived in the Florida Everglades in relative peace until the twentieth century. Their lands were once again threatened, this time not by military troops but by developers moving deeper into the Florida peninsula, bringing business, plantations, and tourism into southern Florida. The Seminoles faced extinction as they were forced to assimilate to survive. Help came in 1938 when the U.S. Congress set aside more than 80,000 acres of land around the towns of Big Cypress, Hollywood, and Brighton to be Seminole land. The Seminoles, however, did not move immediately because they were still distrustful of the government's motives.

The Indian Reorganization Act of 1934 gave Native Americans the right to their own government under their own constitution. On July 21, 1957, the Seminole tribe established a Seminole Constitution, allowing the nation to be recognized by the United States as the Seminole Tribe of Florida. Around this time, in 1962, a separate group of Seminoles sought their own government, which was given to them under the name the Miccosukee Tribe of Indians of Florida. A small number of "independent" Seminoles also exist (called the Independent Traditional Seminole Nation), refusing enrollment in any tribe.

In 1970 the Seminole nation (both in Oklahoma and Florida) was awarded $12,347,500 by the United States government in reparation for the lands that had been taken from them. In the 1990s and 2000s, the Miccosukee and Seminole tribes of Florida set up governmental programs and social services on their reservation lands, working to increase their tribal roll and improve their members' quality of life. By the turn of the twenty-first century, the Seminoles and the state of Florida had become involved in a series of legal battles over gambling businesses. The tribe was eventually successful, bringing in nearly 95 percent of its income from its casinos in 2001. Other revenue for the tribe comes from tourism and sugarcane and citrus businesses.

SETTLEMENT IN THE UNITED STATES

The Seminole nation was formed on the Florida peninsula in the eighteenth century when the Spanish still occupied the area. Following the Second Seminole War (1835–1842), the majority of the Seminoles were forcibly removed by the U.S. government to what was called Indian Territory (now Oklahoma). A small number remained in Florida; these became the Seminole Tribe of Florida. The Florida Seminole now control several reservations, including Big Cypress, Brighton, Hollywood, Immokalee, Ft. Pierce, and Tampa Reservations. Also in Florida is the Miccosukee Tribe, which controls the Miccosukee Indian Reservation.

The Seminoles who moved to Oklahoma eventually formed the Seminole Nation of Oklahoma, located in Seminole County, Oklahoma. The tribes of Oklahoma and Florida, while all related by their common Seminole heritage, consider themselves separate entities with their own unique cultural identities. According to the U.S. Census Bureau's American Community Survey estimates in 2010, the states besides Oklahoma and Florida with significant numbers of Seminole included Pennsylvania, New York, California, and Texas.

LANGUAGE

The Seminoles have two languages still in use today: Muskogee, also called Florida Creek or Seminole Creek, and Mikasuki. Although the two dialects share linguistic similarities (both are part of the Muskogean language family), they are two separate and distinct languages. Muskogee has dialectal forms in both Florida and Oklahoma, and Mikasuki is primarily found in Florida only. Traditionally, both Muskogee and Mikasuki are spoken languages and are not written (though some have tried to write it phonetically).

Although both languages are still spoken today, Seminole elders are concerned that the languages are endangered. The younger generations have not been learning the languages, which are traditionally passed down orally. Many parents of Seminole children now speak English at home, and many children attend English-speaking public schools. Some parents are choosing to teach their children at home, while those children who attend school on the reservations are often given Mikasuki or Muskogee language lessons. In addition, there have been initiatives to begin teaching the Seminole languages in the public schools.

In Florida many geographical locations, such as cities and rivers, carry names taken from the two Seminole dialects. For example, the Chattahoochee

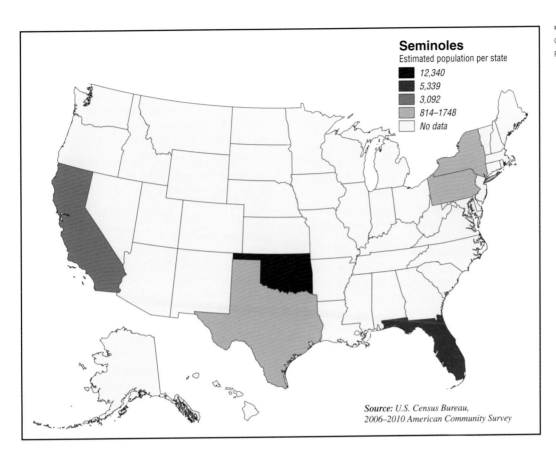

Seminoles
Estimated population per state

- 12,340
- 5,339
- 3,092
- 814–1748
- No data

Source: U.S. Census Bureau,
2006–2010 American Community Survey

River's name comes from the Mikasuki word meaning "marked stones," and the city of Miami's name comes from the Mikasuki word meaning "that place."

Greetings and Popular Expressions Because both Mikasuki and Muskogee are oral languages, it is difficult to find dictionaries with English translations (though a few do exist). Spellings of words are often phonetic and vary from place to place. Muskogee in particular also has different dialects depending on the area of the country, so multiple pronunciations for words do exist.

In Mikasuki, *cheehuntamo* (chee-hun-tah-moh) means "hello"; and *Shonabish* (shoh-nah-bish) means "thank you."

In Muskogee, *istonko* (iss-tone-koh) or *hesci* (hes-sai) means "hello"; and *Mvto* (muh-toh) means "thank you."

RELIGION

Traditional Seminole religion consisted of shamanism, in which a medicine man (called *aiysicks meforsee* in Mikasuki, meaning "takes care of") carries a medicine bundle (or at times multiple bundles) used to protect members of the tribe. The bundle consists of a myriad of things, usually horn, feathers, stones, and other items, all wrapped in deerskin. The medicine man's medicine bundle was carefully guarded, as it had the power to do both good and harm; tradition told

that the medicine contained within the bundle was so strong it could knock down a woman who came too close to it.

In the mid-nineteenth century, Christian missionaries began preaching on Seminole lands in Oklahoma. Southern Baptist missionaries converted Seminoles in Oklahoma as early as 1846. Christian missionaries did not have as much success in Florida, where the Seminoles were wary of outsiders. In 1907, Creek Indian missionaries from Baptist churches in Oklahoma went to Florida to preach among the Seminoles there. In 1936 the First Seminole Indian Baptist Church was established on the Dania Reservation (now the Hollywood Reservation).

As the Seminoles began to convert to Christianity, participation in traditional customs such as the Green Corn Festival decreased. Some Seminoles viewed Christianity as a threat to their heritage and customs, creating tension between some tribal members. By the 1980s, however, many Seminole tribes began to revitalize their culture, including traditions like the Green Corn Festival, and Christianity no longer seemed to be as big of a threat as it once had. Today, most Seminoles are considered Christian, predominately Protestant (particularly Southern Baptist), though they also choose to participate in their ancient rituals as well.

SEMINOLES AND THE MASCOT CONTROVERSY

In the late twentieth century, controversy arose regarding the use of ethnic stereotypes as mascots and names for schools and sports teams. The National College Athletic Association (NCAA) began prohibiting such mascots in college athletics. In response, all colleges with the team name "Indians" replaced their names (Arkansas State University, for example, changed from the Indians to the Red Wolves).

In the interest of keeping their heritage alive, however, the Seminoles have endorsed the use of their name as sport mascots, most notably at Florida State University, where the tribe also helped to create the costume for the school's Chief Osceola mascot. In 2005 the Seminole Tribe of Florida and the Seminole Nation of Oklahoma made their approval public, and the NCAA granted Florida State a waiver of the ban on using mascots deemed culturally insensitive. The Florida Seminole Tribal Council's written resolution stated that the "Seminole Tribe of Florida has an established relationship with Florida State University which includes its permission to use the name 'Seminole' as well as various Seminole symbols and images such as Chief Osceola." Likewise, the Seminoles of Oklahoma voted to defeat a motion that would denounce the use of Native American images in sports.

CULTURE AND ASSIMILATION

The moniker "the unconquered people" applies not only to the Seminoles' ability to resist forced removal by the U.S. government but also to the tribe's fierce attitude about preserving its own culture and heritage in the face of assimilation. Even as their language and customs faced extinction, the Seminoles as a people have fought to keep their heritage alive by teaching the younger generation, as well as the outside world, through festivals (such as the Green Corn Festival) and cultural classes involving traditional arts and crafts.

Traditions and Customs The Seminoles traditionally shared their tribal history through storytelling, an art form that continues to be a great source of pride for the Seminoles; it is usually a featured attraction at festivals. Elders who are expert storytellers pass Seminole traditions to the younger generation. The stories change as the tribe changes, and the storyteller creates his or her own version of the story, but some elements remain consistent, such as the tribe's creation story.

Cuisine Seminoles today eat the same types of foods as other Americans. However, they often cook traditional foods on special occasions and holidays. The traditional Seminole diet used the wild coontie (also called Zamia) plant root to make flour for cooking. Other staples included sweet potatoes, squash, and any meat that was hunted or fished. Most Seminoles

did not have a strict schedule of three meals a day; a pot of *sofkee* (also called *sofk*), a soup or drink made from roasted corn, was kept on the fire for people to enjoy throughout the day as hunger dictated. Sofkee, along with fry bread, is still common in Seminole households today. Another popular traditional dish is *taal-holelke*, or swamp cabbage, in which the heart of the cabbage is boiled with cane syrup and salt.

Traditional Dress The traditional clothing of the Seminoles tends to be of colorful and intricate design. Women would wore long skirts and short blouses that covered their chests, leaving midriffs exposed. A well-dressed woman would also wear many glass-bead necklaces. She would wear her hair in a knot or a bun (in later years, decorative hair pins also became popular) with fringe bangs framing her face. The men's wardrobe consisted of a simple, long shirt, usually belted, and a head turban made from plaid wool shawls. Beneath the turban, the men would shave the sides of their heads, leaving a fringe around the face and a lock of hair on the top of the scalp, which would often be braided. In cold weather, he would often add a colorful cotton coat over his clothing.

By the early twentieth century, with the introduction of the sewing machine to Seminole homes, the Seminoles' dress began to change. The clothes were sewn in a decorative patchwork design with alternating colors. Today this patchwork clothing is frequently worn as ceremonial attire or sold in tourist shops as "Seminole patchwork."

Traditional Arts and Crafts The tradition of arts and crafts in the Seminole community has always been a changing one. The tribe has adapted to the changing world around them as needed; for instance, they might use modern equipment to create their customary crafts. Even as they were resisting assimilation to the culture of the European settlers in the 1700s and 1800s, Seminole craftsmen were using iron tools from the Europeans to build their canoes. In the twenty-first century, Seminole artists often use chainsaws and other modern implements alongside their own traditional tools.

Beadwork is one of the oldest craft traditions in the Seminole community. Traditionally made and worn by women, the beaded necklaces were both a fashion statement and status symbol. The beads were made of glass and often came in bright colors, with blue and red being the favorite. Women would don as many necklaces as they could, sometimes wearing up to 12 pounds of beads around their neck. The older women of the community often wore fewer necklaces; scholars have suggested this was probably due to the discomfort of wearing so many beads at one time. In the twentieth century the beaded necklaces became a tourist attraction, and Seminole women started making the beadwork to sell in Indian villages and at roadside stands.

As tourist interest in the Seminole villages increased at around the start of twentieth century, the Seminoles made more arts and crafts to sell to the onlookers and passersby, and they continue to do so. The Florida Seminoles make woven baskets out of palmetto fiber from the nearby Everglades, sewn together with colorful threads. Another popular craft is dolls, which are woven from the same palmetto fiber as the baskets. These husk dolls are usually dressed in the traditional colorful clothing of the Seminoles and often depict customary hairstyles.

Dances and Songs The Seminole Stomp Dance is traditionally part of the Green Corn Festival, though these dances are occasionally performed at festivals throughout the year. The term "stomp dance" is taken from the style of the dance, which involves stomping and weaving; it is called *opvnkv haco* (meaning drunken or crazy dance) in Muskogee. The dance involves a call-and-response type song in which a leader, usually a medicine man, leads the chant and is answered by the men in chant. The women will shuffle behind with shell shakers adorning their legs. The dance continues for at least four songs, many with over twenty verses. It is meant as a social dance, encouraging men, women, and children to participate. One of the purposes of the dance is to teach the younger generations the songs and traditions of the Seminole tribe.

Holidays One of the primary Seminole holidays, particularly in the Muscogee tradition, is the Green Corn Festival (also known as the Green Corn Dance or Green Corn Ceremony), called *Posketv* in Muscogee. Usually held in June or July, the festival is celebrated as the Seminole New Year. It involves four days of ceremonial dancing, called a stomp dance, around an erected square platform with a ceremonial fire at its center. The men fast and a number of ceremonies occur, including a naming rite for the young men of the tribe and a purification rite during which all offenses and crimes from the past year are forgiven.

A traditional form of recreation for Seminoles is stickball, which is played by many Native Americans in the southeastern United States as part of the Green Corn Dance festivities. The game consists of a small deer-hide ball that is caught and thrown with racquets, which are usually made by local Seminole craftsman. The game is still popular among Seminole boys and girls.

Health Care Issues and Practices Traditional medicine, including the use of medicine men and women, is still alive in many Seminole communities, though these practices do not replace the role of modern medicine and medical doctors. Seminoles still use natural ingredients, such as herbs, roots, and sometimes animal parts, in conjunction with traditional chants, to heal a variety of illnesses, both physical and mental. These customs are generally passed down by the older generation to the younger ones. Many of the practices are still shrouded in mystery because most Seminoles do not discuss their traditional medicine with people from outside the tribe.

While the medicine men and women are still widely respected, most Seminole reservations have

some type of formal health department to offer modern health care to its members.

FAMILY AND COMMUNITY LIFE

Family is an important part of Seminole life and culture. Like many Native American tribes, Seminole society is matriarchal; someone is considered a member of the Seminole tribe if born to a Seminole mother. The society is divided into matrilineal clans; each tribal member becomes a member of his or her mother's clan at birth. The clans originate from a Seminole myth, which tells of animals leaving a mountain through a hole. The Panther tried to exit first but found the hole too small. The Wind opened the hole wider, making the Wind clan first in the clan hierarchy. The Panther was then able to exit, making it the second in clan hierarchy. The animals that followed are, in this order, Wildcat, Bear, Wolf, Deer, and Bird. Other clans were added over time,

Three Florida Seminole women wear traditional clothing. M. TIMOTHY O'KEEFE / ALAMY

A Seminole man in the Florida Everglades. FRILET PATRICK / ALAMY

with as many as forty-seven clans existing at one point. Each clan has a totem, which determines the characteristics of its members. For instance, Wind is thought to be quiet, while Bird is prone to arguments and laughter.

As of 2008, eight Seminole clans existed, most named after animals or other elements of nature: Panther, Bear, Deer, Wind, Big Town, Bird, Snake, and Otter. At one time there were more clans, like the Alligator clan, but those are now extinct. The Panther clan is the largest of the Florida Seminole clans.

Today a person must be at least one-quarter Seminole to register as a member of the tribe; that person would then become a member of his or her mother's (or mother's family's) clan. Tradition discourages people from marrying within their own clan. As a result of the intermarriage between Seminoles and non-Seminoles, not every Seminole belongs to a clan, which is still an important part of twenty-first century tribal life, as it structures ceremonies, voting patterns, and even political leadership.

Gender Roles Seminole gender roles primarily came from the Creek tradition. Men were the hunters and fishermen; they also built the houses and canoes and participated in battles when necessary. The women were expected to prepare the food and raise the children; they also made the clothing and pottery. Early Seminole life was not easy for women. They were restricted from social life during their monthly menstrual cycles and after childbirth. While the boys were educated, girls generally received little or no formal education.

Modern Seminole women have found that gender roles are changing. As early as the 1960s, women were elected as tribal chiefs, something that would have been strictly forbidden according to earlier tradition, which dictated that women were not allowed to hold leadership positions or even speak in public forums. In the twenty-first century, girls are afforded the same educational opportunities as boys, and many Seminole women are pursuing college educations.

Education Although in the past boys may have been formally educated while girls were expected to stay at home, the Seminole tribe of the twenty-first century places a high priority on education for all Seminoles, boys and girls, young and old. While some Seminole children attend public schools, most of the reservations also have schools on-site, where classes are taught to emphasize both the current U.S. academic standards as well as the Seminole culture, including classes on language and heritage. The tribe uses much of the profits it makes from its gaming businesses to improve its education facilities and programs, which extend beyond the traditional K-12 curriculum. The Seminole Tribe of Florida, for example, offers adult vocational courses and college preparatory classes and helps students attend college fairs and university tours. The Seminole Nation of Oklahoma offers similar programs that encourage education among its members. For example, its Head Start Program seeks to prepare its young children (under five years old) for kindergarten. The Seminole Nation also offers job-training programs for adult members seeking full-time employment. College education is highly valued in the Seminole community, and the tribe does what it can to encourage its members to pursue a higher-education degree.

EMPLOYMENT AND ECONOMIC CONDITIONS

As the Seminole tribe faced integration into the United States, the people used their culture to appeal to tourists, especially those who flocked to southern Florida. In the early twentieth century, the Seminoles opened tourist villages, selling admission to see ceremonies such as the Green Corn Festival and weddings. These were usually staged performances rather than a real look into the Seminole way of life. For example, the weddings were staged, the same couples marrying over and over, for the sake of the audiences. Seminole men and women would also sell their arts and crafts, such as beaded necklaces and patchwork fabrics, to tourists who came to their villages.

As the twentieth century progressed, the Seminoles developed new ways to provide revenue and jobs for their members. The Oklahoma and Florida tribes both became involved in gaming, opening numerous gambling resorts and casinos. In 2006 the Seminole Tribe of Florida purchased the popular Hard Rock Cafe chain of hotels and restaurants. The financial gain has allowed the Seminole Tribe of Florida to improve the lives of their members, including spending over $1 million each year on education alone, which has enabled the tribe to offer aid money to college students and improve its own reservation schools.

POLITICS AND GOVERNMENT

The governments of the Florida and Oklahoma Seminoles are two separate entities. The modern Florida Seminole government emerged from the Council Oak. In the first half of the twentieth century, the last descendants of the original Seminoles who hid in the Everglades to avoid relocation would gather around a large oak tree (which still stands today on the Hollywood reservation) to discuss tribal matters. It was at the Council Oak that the beginnings of their constitution began to shape. When the tribe was federally recognized in 1957, it created a constitution establishing a government consisting of a Tribal Council and a Board of Directors. The council is head by an elected chairman, who works with a vice-chairman and council representatives from each reservation. Together, they oversee projects that affect the security of the tribe, such as the gaming industry, police and health care departments, and human-resources programs.

The Oklahoma Seminoles have a similar form of government. Their elected officials, such as the chief and vice-chief, work with their General Council (consisting of twenty-eight elected representatives), which oversee the laws and projects that affect the Seminole Nation of Oklahoma.

Seminoles, as a group, tend to be active in their own government and politics. They will also involve themselves in state and national politics as it affects and protects their own tribal members. They have a history, both in Oklahoma and Florida, of fighting for control of tribal lands (with the Florida land claim settled in 1990

following a long battle). In the twenty-first century, most lobbying of the federal government by Seminoles has involved natural-resource management (especially as it pertains to tribal lands) and gaming rights.

NOTABLE INDIVIDUALS

Art Fred Beaver (1911–1980) was a Muscogee Creek-Seminole artist from Oklahoma. While he had no formal training, his paintings and murals helped to define Oklahoma Native American art.

Noah Billie (1948–2000) was one of the most acclaimed Seminole artists. His mother taught him traditional crafts such as beadwork, but Billie is best known for his paintings, which depict Seminole life and heritage in vivid color. His work can be seen in the Ah-Tah-Thi-Ki Museum on the Big Cypress Seminole Indian Reservation.

Enoch Kelly Haney (1940–) is an artist and politician from Seminole County, Oklahoma. He gained international renown for his sculpture, which includes a 22-foot bronze sculpture that tops the Oklahoma State Capitol Dome. He also made a name for himself in Oklahoma politics. His election to the Oklahoma House of Representatives in 1980 made Haney the first full-blooded American Indian in the Oklahoma Legislature. From 1986 to 2002 he served in the Oklahoma Senate, after which he served a term as the chief of the Seminole Nation of Oklahoma.

Government James Edward "Jim" Billie (1944–) served as chairman of the Seminole Tribe of Florida for over twenty years. He was instrumental in winning legal battles that enabled Florida's Seminole people to operate casinos, which in turn brought revenue to the tribe. Billie also won recognition as a notable musician; his song "Big Alligator" was nominated for a Grammy Award in 1999.

Stage and Screen Randolph Mantooth (1945–) is a character actor, best known for his role as a paramedic on the 1970s TV show *Emergency!* He also appeared in soap operas in the 1980s and alongside comedian John Hensen on *Talk Soup*. Although his father was a full-blooded Seminole, Mantooth has shied away from playing Native American roles.

MEDIA

PRINT

The Seminole Tribune

The official newspaper of Florida's Seminole tribe since 1956, this paper is published monthly and distributed across the United States.

Brett Daly, Senior Editor
3560 North State Road 7
Hollywood, Florida 33021
Phone: (954) 985-5701
Fax: (954) 965-2937
Email: BrettDaly@semtribe.com
URL: www.seminoletribune.org

ORGANIZATIONS AND ASSOCIATIONS

Miccosukee Tribe of Indians of Florida

The federally recognized tribe is a separate entity from the Seminole Tribe of Florida, though they are descendants of the Native Americans who lived in the Everglades. The tribe operates a resort and an Indian Village.

Colley Billie, Chairman
Miccosukee Resort and Gaming
500 S.W. 177th Avenue
Miami, Florida 33194
Phone: (877) 242-6464
URL: www.miccosukee.com

Seminole Nation of Oklahoma

The Seminole Nation of Oklahoma oversees government issues for the Seminole people in the state of Oklahoma, including gaming and legal issues and the promotion of Seminole culture. The organization also runs a newsletter called *Cokv Tvlvme*.

Chief Leonard M. Harjo
Executive Office
P.O. Box 1498
Wewoka, Oklahoma 74884
Phone: (405) 2157-7200
Fax: (405) 257-7209
Email: website@sno-nsn.gov
URL: www.sno-nsn.gov

Seminole Tribe of Florida

The Seminole Tribe of Florida handles government issues for the Seminole people in Florida, as well as working to promote the tribe's culture and heritage.

James E. Billie, Chairman
6300 Stirling Road
Hollywood, Florida 33024
Phone: (800) 683-7800
URL: www.semtribe.com

MUSEUMS AND RESEARCH CENTERS

Ah-Tah-Thi-Ki Museum

Located in the Florida Everglades on the Big Cypress Seminole Indian Reservation, Ah-Tah-Thi-Ki has an indoor gallery with historical artifacts and an outdoor simulated Seminole village.

Paul Backhouse, Museum Director
Big Cypress Seminole Indian Reservation
34725 West Boundary Road
Clewiston, Florida 33440

Phone: (877) 902-1113
Fax: (863) 902-8879
Email: paulbackhouse@semtribe.com
URL: www.ahtahthiki.com

P. K. Yonge Library of Florida History

The University of Florida's P. K. Yonge Library has a collection of microfilm and manuscript archives relating to Seminole and Miccosukee history, including diaries and letters from the Second Seminole War (1835–1842).

James Cusick, Curator for Florida History
University of Florida George A. Smathers Libraries
Department of Special Collections
P.O. Box 117007
Gainesville, Florida 32611-7007
Phone: (352) 273-2755
Fax: (352) 846-2746
Email: jamcusi@uflib.ufl.edu
URL: http://web.uflib.ufl.edu/spec/pkyonge/sem.html

Seminole Nation Museum

The museum was established in 1974 and contains historical artifacts and images, as well as exhibits, to document the stories of the Seminole Nation.

Richard Ellwanger, Director
524 South Wewoka Avenue
P.O. Box 1532
Wewoka, Oklahoma 74884-1532
Phone: (405) 257-5580
Fax: (405) 257-5580
Email: director@theseminolenationmuseum.org
URL: www.theseminolenationmuseum.org

SOURCES FOR ADDITIONAL STUDY

Cattelino, Jessica R. *High Stakes: Florida Seminole Gaming and Sovereignty.* Durham, NC: Duke University Press, 2008.

George, Charles, and Linda George. *The Seminole.* Charleston, SC: Arcadia, 2012.

Pleasants, Julian M., and Harry A. Kersey. *Seminole Voices: Reflections on Their Changing Society, 1970–2000.* Lincoln: University of Nebraska Press, 2010.

Weisman, Brent Richards. *Like Beads on a String: A Culture History of the Seminole Indians in Northern Peninsular Florida.* Tuscaloosa: University of Alabama Press, 1989.

———. *Unconquered People: Florida's Seminole and Miccosukee Indians.* Gainesville: University Press of Florida, 1999.

SENEGALESE AMERICANS

Tova Stabin

OVERVIEW

Senegalese Americans are immigrants or descendants of people from the country of Senegal, the westernmost country of Africa. Senegal is bordered on the west by the Atlantic Ocean, on the east by Mali, on the north by Mauritania, and on the south by Guinea and Guinea-Bissau. Senegal has mostly low-lying plains and a hot, tropical climate. The Cape Verde Peninsula on its coastline is the westernmost point of Africa. Senegal's total land area is 75,955 square miles (196,722 square kilometers), making it slightly smaller than South Dakota.

According to the *CIA World Factbook*, the population of Senegal as of 2012 was 12,969,606. The overwhelming majority of Senegalese, 94 percent, are Muslim. Christians, mostly Roman Catholics, compose 5 percent of the population, and 1 percent reported that they follow traditional African beliefs. The most dominant ethnic group is the Wolof, who make up 43.3 percent of the population; other ethnic groups include the Pular (23.8 percent), Serer (14.7 percent), Jola (3.7 percent), Mandinka (3 percent), Soninke (1.1 percent), European and Lebanese (1 percent), and "other" (9.4 percent). Senegal is a poor country—its per capita GDP (Gross Domestic Product) ranked 194th (out of 228 countries) in the world in 2012. Its unemployment rate in 2007 was 48 percent. Senegal's economy is dependent on foreign aid, donor assistance, and imports of food and many basic necessities.

The first Senegalese to arrive in what would become the United States came as slaves beginning in the seventeenth century. However, not all the slaves who arrived from Senegal were originally Senegalese; many came from other parts of Africa but had left on slave ships from ports in Senegal. Many slaves maintained traditions of their culture and blended them with other African and European cultures to form distinct African American cultures. The first significant voluntary immigration from Senegal began in the late 1970s and early 1980s; these immigrants settled mainly in New York and California, where many found work as street merchants, hair braiders, and restaurant owners. In the late 1990s and the early twenty-first century, Senegalese immigrants to the United States have been primarily young and middle-class.

According to the U.S. Census Bureau's American Community Survey, in 2010 there were an estimated 11,369 people of Senegalese descent in the United States. New York City has the largest community of Senegalese Americans; other communities with significant numbers of Senegalese Americans can be found in Los Angeles, Washington, D.C., Atlanta, Detroit, Portland (Oregon), Minneapolis, Chicago, Houston, and Philadelphia.

HISTORY OF THE PEOPLE

Early History Archeological evidence indicates that, over the course of the first millennium CE, present-day Senegal was populated by migrating groups of Wolof, Fulani, and Serer people and that several empires also expanded into the region. The Ghana Empire, which was the first organized state to expand into Senegal, was established toward the end of the third century and eventually spread north and west but likely did not reach the southern portion of contemporary Senegal until sometime around 800 CE. Offering ports to Europeans trading in gold, ivory, and slaves, the empire prospered and continued ruling until about the tenth century. At some point in the ninth century, likely due to a wave of Fulani people migrating to the area, the Tekrur Empire was established in the northeastern region of Senegal. The Tekrur economy was based on trade with Arab merchants, who brought Islam to the region. In the eleventh century, Tekrur ruler War Jabi converted to Islam and joined forces with the Almoravids, a Berber dynasty from the north that had also converted to Islam, to drive the Ghana Empire out of the region.

The Mali Empire expanded into Senegal from the east in the thirteenth century. It was a wealthy and massive empire that stretched all the way from central Africa to the Atlantic coast. The Mali emperor ruled his domain through a network of alliances with vassals who were permitted to establish kingdoms in various regions of the empire. In the westernmost region of Senegal, a loose confederation of states evolved into the Wolof Empire in the mid-fourteenth century and thrived, with the consent of Mali Empire, whose power was steadily waning. At the same time, the Islamic Songhai Empire declared its independence from the Mali Empire and by the mid-fifteenth century had completely displaced it, taking control of roughly the same tract of land the Mali emperor had ruled.

In 1444, Portuguese sailors arrived at Cape Verde, an archipelago in the Atlantic Ocean approximately 350 miles off the coast of Africa. They later established trading posts on the Senegal River, mainly for ivory and gold and a limited number of slaves after 1500. Other European powers, including the Dutch and English, vied for these profitable trade rights in Senegal. The Dutch West India Company bought the Island of Gorée in 1627. In 1677 France took control of the Island of Gorée, which became a slave trade auction house and departure point. The slave trade intensified in the seventeenth century and reached its peak in the eighteenth century. The arrival of European powers disrupted the centralized Wolof and Songhai societies in the region, creating factions that competed among themselves for trading rights with the Europeans and for power in the region.

Slavery already existed in Senegal (and elsewhere in Africa) when the trans-Atlantic slave trade was established. Slaves were often captives of war who were sold to Muslim traders, who then traded them across the Sahara to the Middle East. Africans provided slaves with work-free days and gave them a plot of land where they could grow a garden for their family or to sell at market. Slaves could marry into the owner's family, and the children of some slaves were considered free. At first the Portuguese treated slaves in a similar way. However, when massive amounts of labor in grueling conditions was needed in the New World (mainly in the Caribbean and Brazil), European and African traders bartered for millions of Africans and exploited them. Between 1500 and 1850, Europeans purchased more than twelve million Africans and took them as slaves to the New World. Slaves were held in deplorable conditions until slave ships could take them, and they continued to be treated inhumanly as slaves. Slave ships departed from what was then called the Island of Goree (now Dakar). A memorial called "The House of Slaves" remains to remind people of the horrors of slavery.

In the 1800s Senegal became part of French West Africa. France abolished slavery in 1848 and granted French citizenship to people in the communities of Dakar, Goree, Rufisque, and Saint-Louis (an area known as the Four Communes), though residents outside of the Four Communes did not receive citizenship. The Senegalese were forced to assimilate to French culture, because the political, judicial, and educational systems were all French. Young Senegalese were offered money to go to France to study and then return to Senegal. For decades, Muslim leaders resisted French rule and the French attempts at forced assimilation. Al-Hajj Umar Tal, considered a freedom fighter, launched a holy war (jihad) against French rule and had some success until 1852, when Major Louis Faidherbe became the governor of the colony and quelled the resistance.

In the 1880s the European "scramble for Africa," as it became known, started. European powers, including Britain, France, Germany, Belgium, and several others, raced to colonize African territories and partition them to avoid going to war. The French, who already had a trading port at the Senegal River, were able to conquer eastward from the Sahel along the Sahara into more of the African interior and take control of (modern day) Senegal, Mali, Niger and Chad. Their aim was to establish a link between the Niger and Nile rivers to control trade. The French extended their territory so vastly that they had the largest colonial region in Africa, with Saint-Louis as its administrative center.

Modern Era In 1914 the Senegal-born political leader Blaise Diagne became the first black African deputy elected to the French Parliament; from then on the deputies from the Four Communes were African. Senegalese soldiers fought with the French during World War II. After the war, France created the French Union, planning to give its colonies more political representation.

In 1959 Senegal and French Sudan (later Mali) merged into the Mali Federation and became fully independent. After only four months Senegal seceded from the union, however, and in 1960 it became a sovereign nation. Léopold Senghor became Senegal's first president, and Mamadou Dia its first prime minister, co-governing with a parliamentary government. Senghor and Dia were, however, political rivals. Dia led an unsuccessful coup in 1962, after which he was imprisoned. Subsequently a new constitution was created providing greater presidential power. The office of prime minister was not re-established until 1970, when Senghor appointed the socialist Abdou Diouf to the position. In 1976 the constitution was amended to allow three political parties: democratic socialist, liberal democratic, and Marxist-Leninists. In 1981 Senghor stepped down from the presidency and Diouf became president, running for the Senegalese Socialist Party, which also dominated the parliamentary elections. Diouf amended the constitution to allow all political parties and eliminated the position of prime minister.

In 1982 Senegal and Gambia nominally joined to form the confederation of Senegambia and attempted to share economic, cultural, and social policies. However, the confederation plan failed when Gambia chose not to seek greater union with Senegal and the agreement was dissolved in 1989.

From the 1980s and continuing into the twenty-first century, the Movement of Democratic Forces in the Casamance (MFDC) have led a separatist rebellion from the southern Diola-majority areas. They have claimed discrimination by the northern Wolofs who dominate the government and who have also tried to impose their language and religion on the south. Nearly every year there have been riots and armed conflicts as well as regular attempts to reach peace agreements. There was a ceasefire agreement in 1997, but

Senegalese Americans

☐ *States with highest population*

the conflict continued. Father Diamacoune Senghor, a leader of the MFDC, signed a peace agreement in 2001, but it did not give full autonomy to Casamance, which created conflict with the different factions of the MFDC. A new peace deal was signed in 2004, but conflicts persisted.

Abdoulaye Wade, from the Senegalese Democratic Party, replaced President Diouf in 2000; the Senegalese Democratic Party also gained control of the National Assembly. It was the first time in decades that a socialist party did not rule Senegal. A new constitution was adopted in 2000. Wade was re-elected in 2007, although some opposition parties boycotted the elections because of complaints of fraud. During Wade's terms he amended the constitution many times and increased presidential power. He also worked on economic policies; in particular, he helped form the New Partnership for Africa's Development (NEPAD), privatized markets, and improved infrastructure. Despite this work, the Senegalese economy still suffered greatly with extremely high unemployment and rampant poverty. A 2008 Gallup survey found that 56 percent of Senegalese who were polled said they would leave Senegal permanently if they could; young people in particular wanted to emigrate. Wade ran again for president in 2012 and lost the election to Macky Sall.

SETTLEMENT IN THE UNITED STATES

It is difficult to say how many Americans may be of Senegalese descent because, according to the World History Center, approximately 430,000 slaves were brought to the United States primarily from western and west central Africa—Senegal to Angola. Many African Americans who are descendants of slaves do not know their exact heritage.

Significant voluntary immigration of Senegalese Americans did not happen until the very late 1970s and early 1980s. Some Senegalese came with assistance from relief agencies due to factors such as riots and armed conflict in Senegal between the Movement of Democratic Forces in the Casamance (MFDC) and the government, drought, and a staggeringly poor economy. Some Senegalese escaping violence were classified as refugees by the Immigration and Naturalization Service (INS). Other Senegalese during these early years came as undocumented immigrants. Many early immigrants were poorly educated. They often worked as street peddlers in New York or in beauty shops.

In 1986 the Immigration Reform and Control Act made it easier for students and professionals to remain in the United States, and the 1990 Diversity Visa Lottery allowed for 55,000 immigrants a year from countries that had traditionally low rates of immigration to the United States. Immigration from Senegal increased, especially immigration by youth. The majority of Senegalese immigrants came to improve their economic situation, often sending money back to their family in Senegal.

According to the Migration Policy Institute (MPI) report "Characteristics of the African Born in the United States," between 1990 and 2000 the number of foreign-born Americans from western Africa increased by 214,941 (192.7 percent). Western African countries and territories included Senegal as well as Benin, Burkina Faso, Cape Verde, Gambia, Ghana, Guinea, Guinea-Bissau, Ivory Coast, Liberia, Mali, Mauritania, Niger, Nigeria, Sierra Leone, St. Helena, and Togo. Individual statistics were not provided for Senegal. According to another MPI report, "African Immigrants in the United States" (2011), among all African-born immigrants living in the United States in 2009, the highest number were from western Africa: 542,032 individuals (or 36.3 percent of all African immigrants). Naturalization rates for Senegalese immigrants specifically, however, were low at 26.2 percent when compared to African immigrants overall (43.7 percent). Also noted was a high gender imbalance for immigrants born in Senegal, with 63.7 percent of Senegalese immigrants being men.

The largest Senegalese American community is in New York City. The southwestern part of Harlem is often known as "Little Senegal" or "Le Petit Sénégal." The neighborhood is home to mosques and the headquarters of the Senegalese American Association. Many Senegalese Americans own and work at beauty shops, electronic stores, and restaurants in the area. There is also a smaller community of Senegalese Americans in Brooklyn. According to the New York Department of City Planning, there were about 2,000 immigrants from Senegal in 2002. Other cities with Senegalese American communities include Los Angeles, Washington, D.C., Atlanta, Philadelphia, Portland (Oregon), Minneapolis, Chicago, Detroit, and Houston.

LANGUAGE

The official language of Senegal is French, which is used for business and in schools. However, it is viewed as the language of the colonizers and is not used in ordinary everyday conversations. Most Senegalese also speak the language of their ethnic group. These languages include Wolof, Fula, Serer, Diola, and Mandinka. The most common language spoken is Wolof. The Wolof people are the majority of the population in Senegal and also dominate it politically and culturally. Approximately 80 percent of people speak Wolof, although it is barely spoken in Casamance and the western part of Senegal, where few Wolof people are found and there is resistance to Wolof domination. Wolof is sometimes spoken by other ethnic groups in addition to their own ethnic language.

Wolof was originally the language of the Lebou (Lebu) people. It is not a tonal language, as is common amongst African languages. Wolof is traditionally written with an Arabic script called *Ajami* or *Wolofal*, although it has also been adapted for Roman script. There are a number of Wolof dialects found in different geographic urban and rural areas, but generally people can understand each other even if they speak different dialects. Young people in urban areas have infused contemporary Wolof with French, English, and Arabic (called Dakar-Wolof). The popular internationally known Senegalese music, *mbalax*, uses Wolof.

Senegalese Americans generally speak English, French, and Wolof; some who are observant Muslims also speak Arabic. According to the 2011 Migration Policy Institute Report "African Immigrants in the United States," Senegalese Americans have one of the highest rates among African immigrants of Limited English Proficiency (LEP), 52.4 percent, and one of the highest rates of speaking a language other than English at home, 93.3 percent.

GREETINGS AND POPULAR EXPRESSIONS

Common Senegalese greetings and expressions include: *Salaam aleekum*—Hello; *Mangi dem*—Goodbye; *Bu la neexee*—Please; *Jërejëf*—Thank you; *Amul sólo*—You're welcome; *Jàmm nga fanaane?*—How was your night? (instead of "Good morning"); *Jàmm nga yendoo?*—How was your day? (meaning "Good afternoon/evening"); and *Na nga def?*—How are you?

RELIGION

The vast majority of Senegalese are Muslims, and mosques are found in areas where there are Senegalese American communities. In some of these mosques, all attendees may be from Senegal or West Africa and speak French, even while belonging to different Muslim denominations. In Harlem in New York City, daily prayers are announced on a loudspeaker near mosques.

Many Senegalese Americans are followers of Cheikh Ahamadou Bamba, who founded the Muridiyya, a Sufi Muslim brotherhood in Senegal. Bamba was a mystic leader and scholar who opposed French colonialism. He was exiled by the French for being a radical Islamist jihadist from 1895 to 1912, which raised his status among his followers. Often in Senegalese American restaurants or music shops, there are paintings and stickers of Bamba. Followers of Muridiyya are called Mourides, which means "one who desires." Mourides are very influential in Senegal politically and socially, and they have a very strong work ethic: they teach of the "twin virtues" of hard work and prayer. They believe in strong adherence to a religious leader called a *shaikh*. The shaikh is to be revered and has mystical powers, using, for instance, amulets, magical spells and Islamic *jinn* (supernatural invisible spirits). Senegalese indigenous beliefs have been integrated into this Islamic sect. The *Da'ira* is a religious association that teaches about spiritual conventions of Muridiyya as well as about social issues. Mouride women have their own separate Da'ira. The first Da'ira in New York was established in 1986 by Senegalese American immigrants.

Mourides in New York City have an annual parade in Harlem at the end of July; New York declared the day Amadou Bamba Day. Additionally, in the late 1990s Mouride immigrants contributed funding to build the House of Islam in New York, a Mouride mosque and community center. There are many stereotypes about Mourides being only street vendors and cabdrivers, and the parade and celebration is an opportunity to educate the general public about Mouride and Senegalese religion and life.

Many Senegalese and Senegalese Americans follow Tidjanya Islam, which considers itself to be a moderate form of Islam.

CULTURE AND ASSIMILATION

Senegalese Americans have various approaches to assimilating into American culture while still maintaining their own culture. Some families have their children live with family in Dakar, and the children only come to New York when they are off from school in Senegal, while other families have their children with them in the United States all year round but send them to Senegal in the summers. Senegalese students have at times been surprised by the extent of racism that they experience in the United States. Often they have been told in Senegal that racism no longer exists in the United States; additionally, they are not used to Africans being a minority. Groups such as the Association of Senegalese in America help immigrants adjust to life in the United States by providing support through, for instance, English classes, as well as organizing community and cultural events. Some Senegalese Americans live in small somewhat insular communities where the majority of the population is Senegalese, such as in Little Senegal in Harlem, where the residents live almost exactly as they had in Senegal, speaking the same language and eating the same foods.

Younger-generation Senegalese Americans, those born in the United States, and those living in more integrated neighborhoods are more assimilated to U.S. culture than older generations and those living in more insulated communities.

Traditions and Customs Senegalese Americans maintain many Senegalese traditions and customs. Some communities, such as in Philadelphia, have Senegalese-style parties called *tan-bers* or *soiree dansantes*, with traditional music and dance. These parties start after midnight, as they would in Senegal. Larger communities have radio programming of Senegalese music, news, food, and updated immigrant information, which is sometimes broadcast in Wolof, Pulaar, Serer, and French, as well as English. Senegalese American educational programs teach youth, especially those born in the United States, about traditional dress, dance, and music, particularly drumming and *griot*—telling stories through songs.

Cuisine In Senegal different ethnic groups have their own traditional foods. French food is also served.

A LANGUAGE BARRIER BETWEEN MOTHER AND SON

A New York University student assignment found changes in language across generations of immigrants. A Senegalese mother said that her son speaks "a type of Wolof" that she cannot understand because of his accent. She explained, "what can I expect, he was born in America and lives in the American environment." She also said that her son used to speak French but no longer does.

Portuguese, West African, and Middle Eastern cuisine have additionally influenced Senegalese food. Most Senegalese are Muslim, so many follow rules of halal, including not eating pork. Because of the coast line of Senegal, fish is often eaten. In Senegalese American restaurants, tilapia is a common fish served. Other ingredients used in Senegalese cuisine include peanuts, millet, couscous (pasta-like balls of semolina flour), rice, plantain, lentils, black-eyed peas, dried baobab (a kind of tropical fruit), okra, cabbage, and yams. Tamarind is a commonly used spice and is also used for drinks. Habanero peppers provide hot spiciness to foods. Many dishes are stewed or marinated in herbs and spices, and then served over rice, millet, or couscous.

One of the most popular dishes is *Ceebu jeen* (rice and fish). It is served in many Senegalese American restaurants, as well as being a common dish served in Senegalese American homes. There are many variations of ceebu jeen, but generally the fish is marinated and then stuffed with vegetables and spices, such as habanero peppers and tamarind, then cooked with a tomato-paste sauce and served over jasmine red broken rice (the red is from the sauce). It is sometimes called the national dish of Senegal. *Ceebu Yapp* (beef and rice, or sometimes lamb and rice) and *Ceebu Guinaar* (chicken and rice) are also popular. In these dishes the meat is fried with spices, onions, and garlic and then is tenderized in a water/mustard/spice mixture and served with rice. Common salads include tamarind coleslaw and *salatu niebe*, with black-eyed peas, tomatoes, cucumbers, and parsley. *Jollof* rice is made with ground spices, such as cinnamon, cumin, coriander, and chilies. *Yassa* is a Casamance dish made with chicken or fish that is marinated in lemon juice, pepper, and onions and then baked and served with rice. Fruit and yogurt dishes are common for dessert, such as banana fritters, batter-fried bananas with sugar on top, and *thiakri*, sweet millet couscous with yogurt. Drinks include *bissap*, made with hibiscus flowers; ginger drinks; tamarind juice; and lemongrass or mint tea. Café Touba is a strong, sweet coffee that many Senegalese Americans drink daily.

CEEBU JENN (RICE AND FISH)

Ingredients

⅔ to 1 cup oil

3 cups short-grain rice

3–6 tablespoons tomato paste

4 wedges of cabbage, about 2 inches at thickest point

4 carrots

2 potatoes, sweet potatoes or other tubers, peeled and chopped

1–2 small eggplants (opt)

3–4 cloves garlic, crushed

½ bunch fresh parsley

salt

pepper

dried red pepper flakes

very hot hot sauce

fresh lemon wedges

4 Tilapia filets

Preparation

Heat oil in large saucepan. Fry fish filets until golden. Add onions, garlic, parsley, dried pepper flakes, and a pinch of salt and pepper. Cook for 5 minutes. Dilute tomato paste with ½ cup water and add to pot. Add 6 cups water and vegetables. Let simmer over medium heat until the vegetables are tender. Remove vegetables, fish and ½ cup liquid.

Use the remaining broth to cook the rice. Add rice and cover. Reduce heat and cook until all liquid is absorbed and you begin to smell the rice on the bottom of the pan toasting.

Once cooked, spread the rice out on a large platter. Arrange the fish and vegetables in the center, then sprinkle the remaining broth over top. Sprinkle with lemon juice.

Serves 4

Senegalese restaurants, such as Le Grand Dakar in Brooklyn, New York, are common in areas with Senegalese American communities, as are grocery stores that carry Senegalese foods. Many restaurant owners and workers speak both Wolof and English, and menus are often also written in English and Wolof. Eating together as a family is very important. In Senegal there is a tradition of all family members sitting around a large bowl of food and eating together. Senegalese Americans often continue this tradition.

Traditional Dress A boubou (*mbubb* in Wolof) or kaftan is the common traditional dress of Senegalese, worn also by Senegalese American immigrants. It is a long, loose-fitting cotton robe, usually worn over drawstring pants (*tubay*). Women's boubous are worn over long skirts called *pagne* that are wrapped around their body. Women usually have matching head wraps that are twisted tower-like and emphasize the head. Bright colors and designs are common, often using wax-resistant print cloths, as is common in western Africa. Blues and greens are common for men; peach and purple are common for women. Traditionally in Senegalese culture, dyeing and weaving are important and respected skills that are often passed down through the generations from mothers to daughters. Patterns can tell family stories or be indications of marital, social, or economic status—generally the more elaborate the pattern and decoration, the higher the social or economic status of the wearer. Religiously oriented Muslim women may wear a *mussor* (head covering). Formal boubous may be used for special occasions— for instance, a man may have a special formal boubou made for his wedding. Tailoring is a very common profession in Senegal; there were an estimated 20,000 tailors in Dakar in 2003. Being a tailor is also a common profession in Senegalese American communities.

Jewelry, embroidery, decorative beads, and hair braiding are important elements of traditional Senegalese attire. Generally, from the time a girl is very young, she will start to have her hair braided with beads and other small objects. Hair braiding is one of the leading professions of Senegalese American immigrants, with women doing the hair braiding and male immigrants often being managers of hair salons. There are also many Senegalese American jewelry establishments, and many street vendors sell beads and other hair accessories as well as jewelry. Influenced by Senegalese culture, hair braiding and weaving in beads and other small objects has become popular in other African American communities.

Dances and Songs Music and dance are integral to Senegalese and Senegalese American culture. Songs are viewed as a way to help tell stories of history and culture and connect with ancestors, as well as to help youth embrace Senegalese culture. Traditional music includes much percussion, mainly drumming, and stringed instruments; it often accompanies dancing. Songs and dances are performed at celebrations, such as weddings, and at social gatherings and fundraisers. Senegalese American music and dance groups also do public performances. Traditional music and dance are taught within the Senegalese American community and in dance and music studios outside the community.

The most widely known percussion instrument is a drum called the *sabar*, which is larger at the top than the middle and then tapers off. It is usually made of a mahogany or a mango wood. A sabar is played with a stick in the right hand for a high accent beat with a lower (tenor or bass) beat played with the left hand. There are sabar groups where there is a lead drummer and the other drummers follow the rhythm of the lead; sometimes there is call and response from the audience. Sabar is also a type of dancing that accompanies sabar drumming and is the most common folkloric dancing. It is high-energy and sensual and includes jumping and much movement of the hips and the arms. It has influenced hip-hop and breakdancing. Sabar has gained some popularity in mainstream culture and is taught in places such as the Alvin Ailey American Dance Theater Extension. The renowned African American singer Stevie Wonder hired a Senegalese dancer to consult on music videos. There is some controversy surrounding sabar dancing; the more religious and fundamentalist segments of the population find it inappropriate and not modest enough. In Senegal different governments have banned some sabar dance steps, and more fundamentalist Muslim leaders have denounced or banned sabar dancing.

There are a number of other common percussion instruments. The *tamal* is shaped like an hourglass and held under your arm; one applies different amounts of pressure to create different sounds. The *balafon* is similar to a xylophone, but is made from a gourd. Various types of bells and rattles are also used. String instruments include the *kora*, which has twenty-four strings and is played like a harp, and the *zalam*, which is like a lute made from a gourd and leather.

An important tradition is the *griot* or *jali*, who tells stories of the past through songs. The griot tradition is sometimes passed down generationally through families. This tradition is evidenced in the Senegalese American community by, for instance, Djimo Koyate of Washington, D.C. Koyate claims to be the 140th *jali* in his family and performs at Senegalese American weddings, family ceremonies, and holiday celebrations. He was part of the African Immigrant Folklife Study Project of the Smithsonian Institute.

Senegalese music is not just known to Senegalese Americans; it is an important part of the World Music scene. *M'balax* is a Senegalese style of Afropop that includes sabar drums (though not necessarily using traditional drumming patterns). M'balax was largely popularized by the renowned Senegalese singer Youssou N'Dour from the group Étoile de Dakar. M'balax music was featured on Paul Simon's *Graceland* album.

Holidays Because the majority of Senegalese Americans are Muslim, Muslim holidays are celebrated within the family, in the community, and often with other West African Muslims. Ramadan is a month when Muslims fast daily from sunrise to sundown. Special food is eaten (in the early morning and late evening), prayers are said, and people grant forgiveness for wrongdoings between family and friends (*baalou akh*). Eid al-Fitr, or Korité, is celebrated to mark the end of Ramadan with feasts and celebration. Eid al-Adha, or Tabaski, honors the willingness of the biblical Abraham (Ibrahim) to sacrifice his son Isaac to God. It takes place at the end of the *Hajj* (the time when

SENEGALESE PROVERBS

Utpi unji upel najaar. (Mankaañ)

A hat is never too big for a farmer.

Ajug kataam di kayik. (Manjaku)

The one who has a spoon does not burn his hands.

Wuuqanaam, o wuuqan xoox of raxun. (Sérère)

It is better to cry alone than ask for people to cry for you.

Cooh kaana sÍs caa kÍduk. (Noon)

It is when the elephant dies, we get to see his teeth.

Yalla Yalla béy sa tool. (Wolof)

Support yourself and heaven will help you.

Gaynaako paaɓi anndi keen laɣooru. (Pulaar)

It is the specialist who knows the ins and outs.

Nna baa be baakoo a maŋ baakuu bo i la. (Mandinka)

My goat is on the other side of the river. It cannot meet my craving for goat.

An faaba da doroke kutu an ŋa, an yimme na jiiba ro a yi. (Soninké)

Your dad bought a boubou, make an effort to add a pocket.

Sahha kënz lhayaat. (Hassaniya)

Health is a treasure.

Ndanke Ndanke Muy Diap Golo Chi Nai. (Wolof)

Slowly, slowly the monkey is coaxed from the underbrush. (anything worthwhile, you need to have patience for)

Ku munn, muun.

One who endures hardships, will smile.

Fen way defar moo gena degg wuy yaq.

Lies that build are better than truths that destroy.

Xuro amul, nakk waxtaana am.

Incomprehension does not exist, just miscommunication.

Muslims are to make a pilgrimage to Mecca in Saudi Arabia). Tamkharit is the Islamic New Year and when Allah decides on people's destinies. Maouloud is the birthday of the prophet Muhammad.

In various Senegalese American communities, there are Senegalese Independence Day celebrations in April with, for instance, music, dancing, food and children's activities; Senegalese Independence Day is April 4. There are special events such as the annual Mourid parade or a gathering when the Senegalese president visits the United States. Senegalese Americans also celebrate American holidays, such as Thanksgiving Day and July 4, and major Christian holidays such as Christmas (although the vast majority are not Christian).

Health Care Issues and Practices Senegalese American approaches to health care are greatly influenced by the norms about health care in their home country. In Senegal the high rate of poverty translates into very little ability to focus on disease prevention. There is also a reticence to talk about disease and health, and the country has a relatively high rate of HIV infection (53rd in the world). To try to combat these norms, organizations such as the Senegalese Association have health fairs to encourage Senegalese Americans to focus on prevention. When health fairs indicate, for instance, certain health issues like high cholesterol rates, community health workers have responded with public media efforts that included Senegalese radio programming discussing ways to decrease cholesterol. Specific health programs target particular issues, such as HIV, by involving the community and its leaders. The Popular Opinion Leader program in New York educates community leaders about HIV prevention and treatment and encourages them to in turn educate their peers. Health clinics try to reach out to immigrants by letting them know that staff at local clinics are also African immigrants who understand the devastation HIV has caused in Africa.

The Senegalese American Association offers family counseling services, believing that the community is best served by other Senegalese or those involved with the community and, thus, know the particular cultural (and linguistic) needs of Senegalese

Sometimes tensions exist between Senegalese Americans and their family members in Senegal, because the Senegalese family members may think that all people in the United States are rich and that relatives who live there should thus be able to provide for most of their financial needs, even while the Senegalese American relatives may in fact be struggling economically.

Americans. The association offers marriage counseling and information about what is legal and illegal in the United States, and information about family law, including child support and domestic violence. Due to its successful program, the counseling services have been supported with government funds.

FAMILY AND COMMUNITY LIFE

Family ties, including to extended family, are strong in Senegalese culture. In Senegal, especially in rural areas, extended families live together, and polygamous relationships are fairly common. While polygamy still happens among Senegalese Americans in the United States, the majority of Senegalese American families live in nuclear family units with a strong commitment to extended family and community. Commitment to the extended family also entails a financial commitment to the rest of one's family that is still in Senegal. Sometimes tensions exist between Senegalese Americans and their family members in Senegal, because the Senegalese family members may think that all people in the United States are rich and that relatives who live there should thus be able to provide for most of their financial needs, even while the Senegalese American relatives may in fact be struggling economically.

Many Senegalese Americans live in tight-knit communities with other Senegalese immigrants, such as Little Senegal in New York and in specific neighborhoods in cities like Chicago and Atlanta. In these communities, many of the customs, traditions, language, dress, food, educational values, and religion of Senegal are maintained. One value that is significantly changing for Senegalese American immigrants is that in Senegal status has more to do with social and marital relations, as well as caste, but in the United States, status is based more on money and material possessions.

Gender Roles Traditionally, in Senegal there were strict gender roles, with women having fewer opportunities, for instance, in education and many areas of employment. While women more often were found in the role of taking care of the household and children, they still had less power than men in most family decisions. Gender roles were stricter, generally, in conservative Muslim households. Since Senegalese independence, gender roles have been changing, with women having greater access to education and the labor market. Senegalese women have also been able to be more active in government policies, including working as government officials.

In the United States there has been progress in the loosening of gender roles within the Senegalese American community. This is largely a result of a changing economic situation. Many Senegalese American women have been earning their own incomes and have been instrumental to their family's economic survival. Hair braiding in particular has been influential in achieving greater gender equality in the Senegalese American community. In Senegal only women (and generally women of a lower caste) are hair braiders, but in the United States, Senegalese American men are often managers of hair salons, not infrequently working under the direction of their wives or other women, although men do not directly braid hair or work with the customers. Additionally, sometimes women are the main economic providers for the family, while men who might be underemployed or unemployed assist with their family's child care or do other household work.

This change in economic status and sometimes household roles has translated into Senegalese American women having stronger voices in family decision making, especially as concerns financial decisions. All these changes are also impacting traditional ideas of masculinity and femininity; men are no longer exclusively in the "outside" world and women in the home. Some men feel threatened by these changes. In an article published in *Africa Today*, Cheikh Anta Babou discusses how Senegalese men who feel threatened by women's new roles sometimes react by being involved in more polygamous relationships. Women, on the other hand, have become stronger in asserting their voices when it comes to making family and household decisions or even filing for divorce if they feel their voices are not being respected. Changes in gender roles in the Senegalese American community are also impacting gender roles in Senegal, as the connections between those in the United States and those in Senegal remain very strong.

While gradually in the twenty-first century more women are immigrating to the United States, in 2009 there were still a higher percentage of Senegalese American men than women immigrants. A high percentage of women immigrate to the United States to join their husbands, while men generally come for economic or educational reasons. Some women also bring their sisters to the United States once they themselves are established.

Education Many Senegalese Americans do not have a college degree, particularly the earlier immigrants. Immigrants who started to arrive in the late 1980s more often had some higher education or came to the United States through school exchange programs for higher education. Cheikh A. Diop University in Senegal, for instance, has partnerships with colleges and universities in the United States. Many Senegalese go to university in Senegal to try to get teaching jobs to help support their families. Sometimes visiting professors to Senegal would see a Senegalese student who they felt had potential and the professor helped the student apply to study and stay in the United States. Other times these students stayed with host families who then would pay for them to continue their education in the United States; many students remained after finishing their studies. Sometimes students worked as French teachers in the United States in exchange for being able to study here.

Senegalese Americans with higher levels of education sometimes live in different communities than less-educated Senegalese Americans. For instance, residents of Little Senegal in New York tend not have a college degree (though a majority have finished high school)

and work in less professional jobs. However, younger generations in these neighborhoods have started to be more interested in and have more opportunities for higher education in the twenty-first century.

In larger Senegalese American communities, K-12 schools may accommodate Senegalese Americans who speak French or Wolof by putting them in English language classes or international classes where English is not the first language of all the students. The Senegalese Association also provides night education courses for adults, including English classes and computer literacy classes.

Courtship and Weddings In Senegal polygamy is fairly common, with men having more than one wife, though most have a limit of four wives. Senegal has the highest rate of polygamy in West Africa; in 2005 half of all marriages were polygamous; the internationally known Senegalese musician Youssou N'Dour married his second wife in 2006. Because polygamy is illegal in the United States, it is somewhat difficult to know how many polygamous marriages there may be. A common practice is for one marriage to be a civil (legal) marriage and the rest to be through religious ceremonies only. Sometimes there is one marriage in the United States and the other marriages take place abroad. Sometimes these polygamous marriages create legal problems for immigrants because the "legal" first wife can be sponsored by her husband, but subsequent wives are not recognized for immigration purposes.

Marriages in Senegal can be arranged by the man's parents, or the couple can simply ask for approval from the family. Arranged marriages are uncommon in the United States, though marrying within one's culture or religion is common. Weddings may combine American, Senegalese, and Muslim customs with, for instance, an American-style wedding cake, a griot singing songs with sabar drumming and dancing, and the ceremony taking place late in the day, after the 5 P.M. Muslim prayer time.

Relations with Other Americans Senegalese Americans experience racism and discrimination in similar manners that other African Americans and people of color do, as well as discrimination for being immigrants, for speaking languages other than English, and for being Muslims. Particular stereotypes that are often reported amongst Senegalese Americans is that "they are all" street vendors and cab drivers, out to get your money. Organizations such as the Senegalese American Association try to educate those outside the culture to understand the lives and culture of Senegalese Americans and the diversity amongst them.

Senegalese American students have reported what they describe as "subtle" forms of discrimination, such as teachers and administrators assuming they are not able to excel academically. One student reported being kept back for some time in a mathematics class, although he excelled in math, because of struggles with English. Others report being kept in ESL (English as a Second Language) or lower-level classes unnecessarily long because there was not room in regular classrooms.

Depending on the size of the community, Senegalese Americans can have different relationships with other Americans. The community of Little Senegal, for instance, is fairly insular, and much of Senegalese traditions and customs are easily found and many people work right inside the community. One resident, for instance, said he heard Wolof spoken in the streets, on the trains, downtown, and at the supermarkets. Relationships outside the community are generally with other African immigrants who are in the neighborhood or at schools, or with other Muslims through religious connections. In smaller communities, such as the one in Bedford-Stuyvesant in Brooklyn, there may be more of an effort and need to reach out beyond the community.

EMPLOYMENT AND ECONOMIC CONDITIONS

Many early Senegalese American immigrants, especially in major cities like New York and Chicago, became street peddlers selling clothes, sunglasses, hair-braiding accessories, umbrellas, purses, African crafts, and incense. It is not uncommon for many of these goods to be counterfeit designer items. Senegalese Americans who work as street merchants or traders often work long hours in all types of weather and risk harassment or worse from police and shop owners, depending on, for instance, their legal status and whether they have permits to be selling. Other common occupations held by Senegalese Americans include restaurant and shop owners (very often beauty salons and hair-braiding shops), cab drivers, jewelers, tailors, hotel workers, and business owners. In places like the south side of Chicago, some Senegalese Americans operate underground businesses out of their home, such as catering and trade in African crafts. Among those who are entrepreneurs, the number of women is slowly increasing. According to a 2009 *New York Times* survey, the top two occupations for Senegalese American immigrants in the United States are sales-related occupations and hairdressers and other grooming services.

In larger Senegalese American communities, such as Little Senegal, many businesses, such as restaurants, grocery stores, and clothing stores, specifically serve the Senegalese American community. Hair-braiding shops that served primarily the Senegalese American community expanded their circle of customers as hair braiding and other African hair styles became popular in African American communities and then in other communities. Those who are professionals tend to be engineers and accountants.

After the terrorist attacks of September 11, 2001, immigration laws became stricter. Senegalese Americans without proper papers and who worked as street merchants or in underground businesses had to be extremely cautious or stop work completely so as not to risk being reported to immigration officials. The global recession that began in 2007 strongly affected the Senegalese American community, and small businesses and street merchants were hit especially hard. According to a 2006 report by the Migration Policy Institute, Senegalese-born immigrants were among the most likely of African-born groups in the United States to be unemployed.

Businesses in places like Little Senegal and elsewhere began to suffer in the twenty-first century, as urban gentrification increased (which made housing costs rise) and the economic downturn continued. In 2007 in Harlem, a business association was formed in the hopes that collective action would be beneficial to businesses that were suffering in hard economic times. One main strategy was to work on diversifying clientele and meeting the needs of a broader market instead of serving only Senegalese and other West Africans. This meant changing stock, for instance, in grocery stores so there were not only foods of interest to the Senegalese and other West Africans, but to a broader group. Additionally, some of the business practices of shop owners were modeled after those of the Sandaga marketplace in Senegal, and such practices were not always effective in the mainstream American culture. For instance, stores often carried a miscellaneous range of unrelated items, with shoe stores selling cooking oil; items were stacked high all over the store or sprawled across the floor so there are not really aisles for browsing and walking; and workers and their friends sometimes sat in stores watching television and were not as attentive to customers as is found in more mainstream U.S. stores. Successful Senegalese American businesspeople and Senegalese Americans with accounting and other professional degrees have also provided assistance to smaller Senegalese American businesses, such as helping them organize their accounts, set up credit, and incorporate other useful Western business practices.

POLITICS AND GOVERNMENT

A majority of Senegalese Americans remain involved in Senegalese politics. In the 2000 elections, Senegalese presidential candidates considered it highly important to win the immigrant vote in the United States; all the main candidates, except Abdoulaye Bathily, went to New York to win the votes of Senegalese Americans. In speeches and meetings in the United States, candidates would address issues of both Senegal and the immigrant community in the United States. According to the *New York Daily News*, 8,600 Senegalese nationals living in the United States were registered to vote in Senegal's 2012 presidential election and about 5,000 of these voted. Over 82 percent of the vote went to Macky Sall, who won the election from Abdoulaye Wade.

Generally, African Americans and immigrants tend to be Democrats and liberal politically; statistics specifically for Senegalese Americans were not aggregated in the early twenty-first century.

NOTABLE INDIVIDUALS

Academia Johnnetta Betsch Cole (1936–) was the first African American female president of Spelman College (1987–1997), a historically black university. From 2002 to 2007 she was president of Bennett College, where she founded the Johnnetta B. Cole Global Diversity and Inclusion Institute. Cole was the first African American to be the board chairperson of United Way of America as well as the first woman to serve on the board of Coca-Cola Enterprises.

Activism Thione Niang is an activist, consultant, and businessperson. One of twenty-eight children in his family, Niang was born in Senegal and moved to the United States as a young man in 2000. Among many other ventures, he founded the Give One Project, which works to empower young men and women to work toward greater social, economic and political participation in their communities in the United States, France, and Senegal.

Music Aliaune Damala Badara Akon Thiam (1973–), known simply as Akon, is an R&B and hip-hop recording artist, songwriter, and producer. He has been nominated and won numerous awards, including an American Music Award for Favorite Soul/R&B Male Artist (2007), five Grammy Award nominations, and the top artists of the year chart by Billboard Legacy (2009, 2011).

Issa (birthdate unknown) is an R&B/pop/reggae singer, songwriter and producer who was named BET's (Black Entertainment Television) Break Out Artist in August 2008 for his single "Used to Be the One," from his album *The Rules of Attraction*. He was also the winner in 2009 of LL Cool J's First Annual Boomdizzle All-Star Competition to discover the next great artist. He was born in Senegal and immigrated to the United States in 2003.

George Lewis (George Louis Francois Zenon, 1900–1968) was a renowned jazz clarinetist called "The Father of Revivalism" and "The King of Traditional Jazz." He played with groups such as the Black Eagle Band, Buddy Petit, the Eureka Brass Band, Chris Kelly, Kid Ory, and the Olympia Orchestra.

Stage and Screen Gabourey Sidibe (1983–) is an actress born in New York to a father who had immigrated from Senegal. She was nominated for an Academy Award for Best Actress for her portrayal of the title character in the 2009 film *Precious* (2009). She also appeared in the film *Yelling to the Sky* (2011) which won a Black Reel Award for best independent film and a Berlin International Film Festival Award, and the film *Tower Heist* (2011).

MEDIA

Radio Tam-Tam on WNWR

Features news and music of the Francophone African community and is broadcast for an hour daily in French and English. The host is Senegalese businessman "Moody" Modibo Diagne. It is live streamed at http://radioradio7.com/radio/WNWR-New-World-Radio-1540-AM-Philadelphia-PA.html.

428 Mt. Airy Avenue
Philadelphia, Pennsylvania 19119
Phone: (610) 664-6780

African Time—WPAT 930-AM Multicultural Radio Broadcasting

News and political discussion in Wolof that is broadcast for an hour weekly. Airs in New York and surrounding areas, and Senegal. The host is Senegalese American Dame Babou. It is live streamed on the Senegalese Association of America's website at http://www.asa-website.org/index.php?option=com_content&view=frontpage&Itemid=68.

449 Broadway
2nd Floor
New York, New York 10013
Phone: (212) 966-1059
Fax: (212) 966-9580
URL: www.wpat930am.com

ORGANIZATIONS AND ASSOCIATIONS

Senegalese Association of America

The Senegalese Association of America's self-stated mission is to "contribute to the economic, political and socio-cultural Senegalese community residing in the United States of America." It organizes classes, seminars, and events such as Senegal Independence Day and International Women's Day celebrations, as well as summer trips to Senegal. Its headquarters are in New York, but there are regional associations across the United States where there are communities of Senegalese Americans, such as in Philadelphia, Houston, and Detroit.

121 St. Nicholas Avenue
New York, New York 10026
Phone: (212) 932-0900
Fax: (212) 932-0880
Email: general@awaweb.org
URL: www.asa-website.org

Senegal-America Project

Organized around collaborative music, poetry and dance of Senegal and the United States, a performance troupe tours to bring common understandings and a network of partnerships works to help address issues of health, education, equity and access. Projects have included funding schools and free health care screenings in Senegal, collaborative recordings with Senegalese and U.S. musicians performing in both countries, and exchange programs for Senegalese and American students.

Phone: (413) 665-1067
Email: tonyvacca@comcast.net
URL: www.tonyvacca.com/senegalamerica/

MUSEUMS AND RESEARCH CENTERS

West African Research Association (WARA)

WARA's mission is to promote research and academic exchange between scholars in West Africa and the United States, and to distribute information on West Africans in Africa and in the diaspora. They are located at Boston University, and their overseas research center is in Dakar.

Boston University
African Studies Center
232 Bay State Road
Boston, Massachusetts 02215
Phone: (617) 353-8902
Fax: (617) 353-4975
Email: wara@bu.edu

SOURCES FOR ADDITIONAL STUDY

Babou, Cheikh Anta. "Migration and Cultural Change: Money, 'Caste,' Gender, and Social Status among Senegalese Female Hair Braiders in the United States." *Africa Today* 55, no. 2 (2008): 3–22.

Badiane, Cheikh Toure. *A Study of Three Senegalese in American Higher Education in Light of Ogbu's Theories.* New York: State University of New York at Binghamton, 2007.

Ebin, Victoria. "'Little Senegal' vs. the New Harlem Renaissance: Senegalese Immigrants and the Gentrification of Harlem." Revision of French essay in *Revue Asylon,* no. 3 (2008). http://www.africanart. org/uploads/resources/docs/vicky_ebin_116th_ st_012110.pdf.

Kane, Ousmane. *The Homeland Is the Arena: Religion, Transnationalism, and the Integration of Senegalese Immigrants in America.* New York: Oxford University Press, 2011.

Kumarathas, Purnima, Halimatou Nimaga, and Hollis Wear. *Harlem's Little Senegal: A Shelter or a Home? A Conversation with Senegalese Immigrants in New York City.* http://www.humanityinaction. org/knowledgebase/133-harlem-s-little-senegal-a- shelter-or-a-home-a-conversation-with-senegalese- immigrants-in-new-york-city.

Louden, Mark L. "African-Americans and Minority Language Maintenance in the United States." *Journal of Negro History* 85, no. 4 (2000): 223–240.

M'Baye, Babacar, and Simon J. Bronner. "Senegalese Communities." In *Encyclopedia of American Folklife,* edited by Simon J. Bronner. New York: ME Sharpe, 2006.

New York University. *Voices of New York: Senegalese Communities in New York City.* http://www.nyuvoicesofnewyork.com/ Communities/2001/senegal.html.

Salzbrunn, Monika. "The Occupation of Public Space through Religious and Political Events: How Senegalese Migrants Became a Part of Harlem, New York." *Journal of Religion in Africa* 34, no. 4 (2004): 468–92.

SERBIAN AMERICANS

Bosiljka Stevanović

OVERVIEW

Serbian Americans are immigrants or descendants of people from Serbia, a country located in the central area of the Balkan Peninsula in southeastern Europe. Over history the borders of Serbia have changed several times. In 2012 Serbia was bordered by Hungary to the north, Romania and Bulgaria to the east, Macedonia to the south, Bosnia-Herzegovina to the west, and Croatia to the northwest. The Republic of Kosovo, located to the southwest between Serbia and Albania, declared independence in 2008, but as of 2012 the Serbian government still considered Kosovo, which is 95 percent ethnic Albanian, to be a region of Serbia. The northernmost region of Serbia is the autonomous Province of Vojvodina. A landlocked country with a varied terrain, Serbia has rich fertile plains in the north and mountains in the south. The country's flag consists of three equal horizontal stripes: blue, white, and red (from top to bottom). Without Kosovo, Serbia is 29,913 square miles (77,474 square kilometers), about the size of South Carolina.

Serbia's population of 7,276,604, based on a July 2012 estimate by the *CIA World Factbook*, consists of 82.9 percent Serbs, 4 percent Hungarians, 1.4 percent Roma, and about 4 percent Bosniaks, Germans, Romanians, Slovenians, and Turks. A 2004 study by the United Nations listed the Roma, officially 108,000 people but unofficially five times that many, as the poorest and most socially vulnerable population in Serbia. About 85 percent of the population belongs to the Serbian Orthodox church, 5.5 percent is Roman Catholic, 3.2 percent Muslim, and 1.1 percent is Protestant. Before World War II there were about 16,000 Jews in Serbia, which was part of Yugoslavia; all but 1,500 of them were murdered by the Nazi and Fascist occupying forces (German, Hungarian, Bulgarian, and Croatian) during the war. The official language is Serbian. Belgrade, located at the confluence of the Sava and Danube rivers, is Serbia's capital and largest city with a metropolitan population of 1.7 million. Belgrade is a cultural, intellectual, and economic hub for all of southeastern Europe.

The first wave of Serbian immigration to the United States occurred in the early 1800s when the regions inhabited by Serbs were still ruled by the Turkish Ottoman Empire and the Austrian Empire.

Early emigrants came from the coastal area of Montenegro and Dalmatia. More significant immigration of ethnic Serbs took place between 1880 and 1914 (from Austria-Hungary and Montenegro); Serbia, already independent, was not a land of emigration. Most of the immigrants were escaping poverty and persecution but planned to return home after making money working in the United States. They first settled in the San Francisco Bay area and New Orleans and later moved into mining and industrial areas of the east and northern Midwest, with communities developing in Illinois, Pennsylvania, Michigan, Montana, California, Louisiana, and Alaska. After World War II, the majority of Serbian immigrants were politically minded refugees who tended to be urban and educated. Another wave of immigrants came when Yugoslavia broke up in the early 1990s; the region was subsequently embroiled in turmoil for the next two decades. Although ethnic Serbs emigrated from several surrounding countries due to conflict and changing borders, connection to Serbia as the central homeland has remained strong among all Serbian Americans.

The American Factfinder estimates that in 2010 there were 187,739 Americans of Serbian descent. More than two-thirds were born in the United States, and between 15,000 and 30,000 entered the United States after the year 2000. Serbian Americans are very integrated into the general population, and because immigrants are recorded by their country of emigration, ethnic Serbs may be recorded as Yugoslavian, Croatian, Slovenian, or Macedonian, for example. There is a large Serbian community in the Chicago, Illinois, metropolitan area, making it the state with the largest population of Serbian Americans. Other states with large numbers of people of Serbian descent include Indiana, California, Ohio, and Pennsylvania. Other notable communities are in the San Francisco Bay Area and San Diego; Cleveland, Ohio; Milwaukee, Wisconsin; and Pittsburgh.

HISTORY OF THE PEOPLE

Early History The Serbs settled in the Balkans in the seventh century during the reign of the Byzantine Emperor Heraclius (610–41 CE). The Serbs are Slavs, whose prehistoric home had been in the general area of today's Byelorussia and Ukraine. In the sixth century CE the Slavs began to leave their land, dispersing themselves to the north, east, west, and south. The Serbs went south, forming part of the South Slavic group (including Croats, Slovenes, Bulgarians, and others).

During the Middle Ages there were several Serbian principalities or states. The first significant principality was ruled by Mutimir (829–917), during whose reign the Serbs accepted Christianity. Zeta, also known as Dioclea, rose to power in the tenth century under the reign of Prince Vladimir. His grandson Bodin (1082–1101) expanded the territory of Zeta to parts of Raška, Bosnia, and Herzegovina.

After Bodin's reign, Zeta weakened, and Raška achieved great political and military power. The ascension to the throne of Raška by the Grand Zhupan Stefan Nemanja (1114–1200) marks one of the most important events in Serbian history. Founding the Nemanjić Dynasty, which was to rule for the next 200 years, he ushered in the Golden Age of Serbian medieval history. An able politician and statesman, Stefan Nemanja ruled from 1168 to 1196, consolidating his political power within the state, undertaking Serbia's territorial expansion, and achieving independence from Byzantium. Religiously, however, Serbia became irreversibly tied to the Eastern rites and traditions of Byzantium. In 1196 Nemanja called an assembly of nobles and announced his abdication in favor of his son Stefan. Stefan married Anna Dondolo, the granddaughter of the Venetian Doge Enrico Dondolo, thus securing his power. In 1217 Pope Honorius III sent his legate with a royal crown for Stefan, who became Stefan Prvovencani, or the First Crowned. The crowning confirmed the independence of Serbia and also brought about the recognition of the Serbian state as a European state.

King Stefan then turned his attention to the creation of an independent and national church. His brother Sava undertook numerous diplomatic missions before he was able to attain this goal, and in 1219 he was consecrated as the first archbishop of the Serbian Autocephalus (autonomous) Church. This event marks another cornerstone in Serbian history and Serbian Orthodoxy, for in 1221 Archbishop Sava was able to crown his brother King Stefan again, this time according to the religious rites and customs of the Eastern Orthodox Church.

Saint Sava is one of the most sacred and venerated historical figures in the minds and hearts of Serbs. Aside from contributing enormously to education and literacy in general, Saint Sava, together with King Stefan, wrote the first Serbian literary work, a biography of their father.

As the Serbian medieval state centered in Raška and Kosovo matured politically, it also developed a solid and prosperous economy. The state's Golden Age reached its apogee during the reign of Czar Dušan Silni, Emperor Dušan the Mighty (1308–1355). An extremely capable ruler, he secured and expanded the Serbian state while richly endowing the Serbian Orthodox Church, which was the center of learning and artistic creativity, predating even the beginnings of the Italian Renaissance. He elevated the head of the church to the patriarchy and consolidated the internal affairs through the emperor's *Zakonik*, the written Code of Laws, unique at that time in Europe. Emperor Dušan's accomplishments were such that Serbs today continue to draw inspiration and solace from the national pride and glory achieved during his time. Near the end of Dušan's reign the Byzantine Turks repelled what they viewed as Serbian expansion, and when Dušan died in 1355, the state was weakened, and rival nobles broke it into several principalities. The most important were the principality ruled by Prince Lazar Hrebeljanović and the one centered in Bosnia, which reached its peak in the fourteenth century during the reign of King Tvrtko.

Tvrtko's army participated in the Battle of Kosovo Polje ("The Field of Blackbirds") on June 28, 1389, which was fought between the Ottoman Turks, led by Sultan Murad I (1319–1389), and the Serbs, led by Prince Lazar (1329–1389). This battle changed the course of Serbian history for centuries to come, for the Serbian defeat was followed by the incorporation of almost all Serbian lands into the Ottoman Empire, where they would remain for the next 500 years. Over the centuries Serbia remained totally isolated from the rest of Europe and could not participate in the enormous political changes or cultural and industrial progress unfolding in other European states.

The land and all other natural resources became the domain of the Ottoman Empire. The Turks became landowners called *spahis*, whereas the Serbs were reduced to the status of *raya*, the populace who worked the land they previously had owned; their labor was called *kulluk*, a term that to this day denotes the work of slaves. Every four years the countryside was raided; small Serbian male children were forcibly taken from their families and brought to Istanbul, where they were raised and trained to become Janissaries, the Ottoman's elite military unit. Another particularly distasteful practice was the use of economic pressures to convert people to Islam.

The enforced serfdom, conscription, and forced conversions caused two massive Serb migrations from Kosovo, one in 1690 and the other in the first half of the eighteenth century. They resettled in a strip of Austrian territory bordering with Ottoman-ruled lands. It was organized as a Military Frontier (*Vojna krajina*) in which Serb settlers, engaged in the protection of Austria against frequent Ottoman raids, were given certain privileges and freedom of religion. The *krajina* comprised the regions of Bania, Lika, Kordun, and Slavonia (in abandoned Croatian territory) and Vojvodina (in south Hungary).

Although the Serbs in Austria were fairly safe, rebellions against Ottoman rule in Serbia continued, causing severe reprisals. Karadjordje (Black

George, or Karadjordjević) Petrović (1752–1817), a merchant, led the First Serbian Uprising against the Turks (1804–1813). Severe Turkish reprisals caused many Serbian leaders to escape north to Vojvodina, where the monasteries at Fruska Gora became Serbian cultural strongholds. Miloš Obrenović (Milosh Obrenovich, 1780–1860), a local administrator, emerged as the leader of the Second Serbian Uprising against the Turks in 1815. In 1830 Serbia was granted autonomy by the Turkish sultan under a hereditary prince. A lengthy feud between the Karadjordjević and Obrenović dynasties ensued.

Serbia received recognition of its independence at the Congress of Berlin in 1878, at the same time as Montenegro; Austria-Hungary was given mandate over Bosnia and Herzegovina (which it subsequently annexed in 1908). Serbia's struggle to establish itself as an independent nation in the nineteenth century was marked by many changes of rulers and forms of government, until a monarchy was established in 1882, followed by a constitutional monarchy in 1903. Serbia also emerged as the strongest Balkan state at the conclusion of the First Balkan War against the Ottoman Empire in 1912, when Serbia, Montenegro, Greece, and Bulgaria formed an alliance (the Balkan League) and defeated the Turks.

Modern Era Fearing Serbia and its leading role in the determination to rid the Balkans of all foreign domination, the Austro-Hungarian government systematically pressured Serbs living in its territory and in independent Serbia both politically and economically, until the tensions between the two nations led to the events that ignited World War I. When Archduke Franz Ferdinand and his wife, Sophie, chose to review the troops in Sarajevo on St. Vitus Day, June 28, 1914—the most sacred date of the Serbian calendar, commemorating the Battle of Kosovo—a small secret association called "Young Bosnia" had Gavrilo Princip, one of its members, carry out the assassination of the archduke and his wife. Austria, accusing Serbia of complicity, responded with an immediate ultimatum, compliance with which would have presented a serious threat to the sovereignty of Serbia. Having just fought two Balkan Wars, and not wanting to get involved in another conflict, Serbia offered a compromise. Austria rejected these terms and declared war on Serbia on July 28, 1914, precipitating World War I.

Although heavily outnumbered and drained of resources from the just concluded Balkan Wars, the Serbian army initially fought successfully against Austria-Hungary, but the addition of the German army to the Austrian side tipped the balance against Serbia. Eventually, the ravaged Serbian army had to retreat through Albania toward the southern Adriatic Sea, where the remnants were picked up by French war ships. After being reconstituted and reequipped, this newly strengthened Serbian army broke through the Salonika Front in late 1916, and over the next year and a half successfully fought its way north, culminating in the recapture of Belgrade in October 1918. This victory significantly contributed to the final collapse of the dual Austro-Hungarian monarchy.

The physical destruction of Serbia had been staggering, but the growing significance of the Pan Slavic movement and Serbia's effort to liberate Serbs and other South Slavs led to the establishment of the Kingdom of the Serbs, Croats, and Slovenes in 1918, including Bosnian Muslims and Macedonians. This postwar state was proclaimed the Kingdom of Yugoslavia ("the land of the South Slavs") in 1929 and consisted of Serbia and lands populated by South Slavs (Serbs, Croats, and Slovenes) formerly under the rule of Austria-Hungary. It was a monarchy ruled by King Alexander Karadjordjević (1888–1934).

Despite the 1934 assassination of King Alexander in Marseille, the country prospered as a result of increased trade and growing industrialization. This period was brought to a sudden halt by the bombing of Belgrade on April 6, 1941, which preceded the invading armies of Nazi Germany and its allies: Italy, Hungary, and Bulgaria. The Yugoslav defenses collapsed within two weeks, and the country was dismembered. Less than a week after the beginning of hostilities, an Independent State of Croatia, headed by Ante Pavelić, the leader of the Croat *Ustaši* (Ustashi) Party, was established as a satellite to the Axis Powers. In addition to Croatia, the Independent State of Croatia included Bosnia, Herzegovina, and a part of Serbia. Serbia was divided into occupation zones controlled by Germany (Central and South Serbia, also Banat in Vojvodina), Hungary (part of Vojvodina), Bulgaria (South Serbia and Macedonia), and Italy (Kosovo and Metohia).

King Peter II and the government of Yugoslavia fled to London. Some Serbian troops, under the leadership of Colonel Draža Mihailović, withdrew to the mountains and organized themselves as guerrillas. They became known as the Yugoslav Army in the Homeland or, more popularly, *Četnik* (Chetnik), from the word *četa*, meaning a small fighting group. Promoted to general and named minister of war by the Yugoslav government in exile, Mihailović's legacy is controversial. Although some believe Mihailović and the Chetniks are national heros, many historians believe they collaborated with occupying forces, particularly in the Italian-held areas.

After Germany attacked the Soviet Union in June 1941, the Yugoslav Communists, under the leadership of Josip Broz Tito, formed another guerrilla movement, which they called the National Liberation Movement, or Partisans. The Partisans and the Chetniks both fought on the side of the antifascist Allies but had disputes with each other. The Chetniks saw their fight as against both the Germans and the other occupying forces (the Croatian Ustashi, the Italians, the Hungarians, and the Bulgarians), and

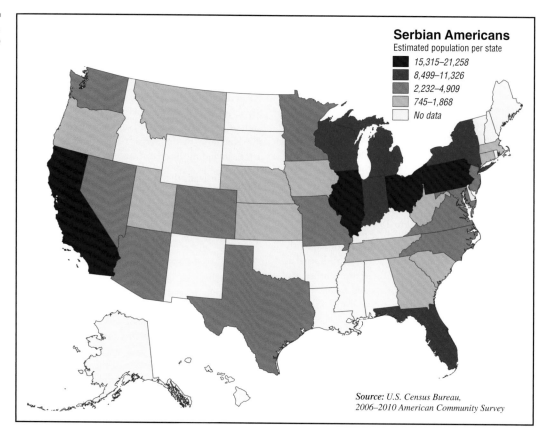

Serbian Americans
Estimated population per state

- 15,315–21,258
- 8,499–11,326
- 2,232–4,909
- 745–1,868
- No data

*Source: U.S. Census Bureau,
2006–2010 American Community Survey*

Tito's Communist Partisans. The Ustashi instituted a reign of terror that led to the massacre of 500,000 to 700,000 Serbs, as well as 50,000 Jews and 20,000 Roma. To counter Tito's and Mihailović's guerrilla attacks and sabotages, the Germans used reprisals against the civilian population: fifty hostages were executed for each wounded German soldier, and one hundred for each one killed. Thus, in one instance alone, the German Nazis executed several thousand Serbs in a single day (October 21, 1941) in the city of Kragujevac, including schoolchildren driven out of their classrooms that morning.

Tito's Partisans gained the support of the antifascist Allies, who withdrew their endorsement of Mihailović's Chetniks, a decision taken at the Tehran Conference in November 1943. Operating mainly in Ustashi territory, namely Croatia and the mountain ranges of Bosnia-Herzegovina, the Partisans were joined by many Serbs who were attempting to escape Ustashi terror. However, the Communists had only partial support of the Serbian population at large.

Emerging victorious at the end of the war, Tito set out to further secure the power of the Communist Party and his own. Purging the country of its enemies, the new government tried and executed General Mihailović. After the redrawing of the internal borders, Tito's Yugoslavia became a federation of six republics: Serbia, Croatia, Slovenia, Bosnia-Herzegovina, Montenegro, Makedonija, and two autonomous

provinces: Kosovo and Vojvodina, which were carved out of the larger Serbia.

From 1974 until Tito's death in 1980, Yugoslavia was ruled by a collective presidency made up of representatives of the six republics in the Yugoslavian Federation and the two autonomous provinces within Serbia, with Tito as chair and president for life. After Tito's death in 1980, the chair rotated; the central authority weakened, and nationalism within each of the republics rose, as did ethnic tensions. The fall of the Berlin Wall in 1989 fostered radical changes in Eastern Europe, including Yugoslavia, where the rising tide of national autonomy led to the country's breakup. Slovenia was the first to declare independence and secede, followed by Croatia (both in June 1991), Macedonia (September 1991), and Bosnia-Herzegovina (March 1992). Serbia and Montenegro became the Federal Republic of Yugoslavia (FRY) in 1992. The war in Croatia (1991–1995) ended with the expulsion of more than 250,000 Serbs. The war in Bosnia-Herzegovina, which ended in 1995 with the Dayton Agreement, was tragic, resulting in significant loss of life, destruction, and a large number of refugees. In 1998 Albanians in Kosovo began armed rebellion against Serbian authorities. In 1999 the war in Kosovo prompted a seventy-eight-day bombing of the Federal Republic of Yugoslavia by NATO (without a UN decision) in support of Kosovo independence (which was finally declared in 2008). The International War

Crimes Tribunal for Yugoslavia in the Hague indicted a number of political and military officials for participating in these wars, most of them Serbs from Croatia and Bosnia, some of whom were accused of genocide. The most prominent was Slobodan Milošević, former president of Serbia, who died of a heart attack in 2006 during the trial. The loose union between Serbia and Montenegro lasted until June 2006, when, after a referendum, Montenegro seceded and declared its independence.

SETTLEMENT IN THE UNITED STATES

Although the earliest Serbian immigrants came to the United States after 1815, the largest wave of immigration took place from 1880 to 1914. There were arrivals between the two world wars followed by refugees and displaced persons after World War II. Arrivals since 1965 have included the influx resulting from the breakup of Yugoslavia and the ongoing violent conflict in the Balkans.

Generally speaking, it is difficult to determine the exact number of Serbs who came to the United States in the early waves of immigration because immigration records often did not distinguish between various Slavic and, especially, South Slavic groups. The term "Slavonic" was most often used in recording immigrants from the various parts of the Eastern Europe. Church records are more helpful in distinguishing the Serbs, for these documents clearly state religious orientation of the parishioners. In addition, census statistics compiled before World War I had further confused the issue by listing immigrants by their country of origin. The Serbs were often included with the Croats and Slovenians as Austro-Hungarians or were registered as Turks. Consequently, of the 257,995 who reported Yugoslavian origin in 1990, it was impossible to tell how many actually had Serbian ancestry.

Many of the earliest Serbian immigrants did not come from Serbia proper; the emergence of Serbia as an independent nation during the nineteenth century offered hope for more political stability and economic development, which led to low emigration. Rather, the Serbs who came to the United States at that time were mostly from areas under the domination of either the Austro-Hungarian or Ottoman empires, or from inland Montenegro.

Poverty and ethnic and religious persecutions were behind the decisions to leave one's village, family, and way of life for the United States, which appealed to able-bodied young men as the land of opportunity. In 1869 the Austrian emperor dissolved the age-old agreement with the Granicaris, the Serbians who protected the frontier from the Ottomans. The Serbs felt betrayed by the emperor, and in the words of Michael Pupin, who came from Vojvodina, they felt "delivered to the Hungarians," who then subjected them to a severe campaign of Magyarization, insisting on official use of the Hungarian language in schools and courts, as well as seeking to convert them to Roman Catholicism.

The greatest number of Serbs arrived during the peak period of immigration to the United States between 1880 and 1914 from lands dominated by the Austro-Hungarian empire (Vojvodina, Lika, Bania, Kordun, Bosnia, Herzegovina, and the coast of Montenegro) as well as from inland Montenegro. Although the overwhelming majority of Serbian immigrants were uneducated, unskilled men in their prime working years—mostly peasants from the countryside—they did not come to the United States particularly to be farmers, and they did not intend to stay. Instead, they wanted to remain long enough to earn money, enabling them to return home and improve the lives of their families, in keeping with a practice called *pečalba* (pechalba). They settled in the mining areas of Pennsylvania, Ohio, West Virginia, northern Minnesota, Montana, Nevada, Arizona, and Colorado, as well as in the big industrial cities of Pittsburgh, Cleveland, and Chicago, working in steel mills and related industries. Others found work with the major meat-packing companies in Chicago, Milwaukee, Kansas City, Omaha, and St. Paul, and in the lumber industries in the Pacific northwest. The Serbian motto *čovek mora da radi*, "a man has to work" served them very well in this country.

The immigrants who arrived after 1945 were refugees from World War II. Among their numbers were former army officers and soldiers who had either been prisoners of war or attached to the Allied Forces, people deported to Nazi Germany as slave laborers, and supporters of General Mihailović during the Civil War who fled following the Communist takeover. Many Serbs, therefore, found a new home in the United States under the Displaced Persons Act of 1948 and the Refugee Relief Act of 1953.

The differences between this wave of Serbian immigration and the previous ones are substantial. The new immigrants came mainly from the urban areas in Serbia proper rather than the rural areas outside Serbia. They came for political reasons rather than economic reasons and tended to see themselves as émigrés (exiles) rather than immigrants. On the whole, these Serbians were educated members of the middle and upper classes—many among them had considerable social status—and they came to join already well-established Serbian communities. Politically minded, these immigrants also saw this country as a safe house in which to develop strategic operations in opposition to the Yugoslav Communist state, rather than as a new homeland.

In the later decades of the twentieth century, immigration was motivated by the economy once again and was the result of economic and political failures of the Communist system. These immigrants did not experience the sense of cohesiveness of earlier groups. Until the dissolution of Yugoslavia, which began in 1991, the newest immigrants had come and gone freely between the United States and Yugoslavia/Serbia. Some worked for American companies, some for Yugoslav companies in the United States, and many, after staying abroad for a number of years, went back to Yugoslavia with hard currency and marketable skills.

Between 1981 and 2009 more than 90,000 persons from Serbia and Montenegro received Permanent Resident Status in the United States; of these, about 30,000 were classified as refugees and asylees. The Kosovo War (1998–1999), including NATO bombing with the goal of getting the Serbs out of Kosovo, led to mass dislocations of Serbs, Albanians, and others in the region. In September 1999 the United States began admitting the first of 5,000 Serbian refugees, most of whom were married to Americans or were considered at risk politically. They were identified by the U.N. refugee agency from among half a million Serbs who took refuge in Serbia from Croatia and Bosnia during the war. Over the next several years, there were several dozen high-profiles cases of Bosnian Serb war criminals who had falsified papers in order to enter the United States. States with the largest population of Serbian Americans include Illinois, Pennsylvania, Ohio, California, and Indiana.

LANGUAGE

The Serbian language is part of the Slavic language group that also includes Russian, Ukrainian, Belarusian, Polish, Czech, Slovak, Croatian, Bulgarian, and Macedonian. In the seventh century two Greek missionaries, Cyril and Methodius, created the Slavic alphabet, called Cyrillic, which is still used by the Russians, Serbs, Ukrainians, Belarusians, Bulgarians, and Macedonians. The Old Slavonic, or Staroslovenski, was the original literary language of all the Slavs. It evolved into the Church Slavonic, or Crkvenoslovenski, which in turn engendered the Serb Church Slavonic, the Serb literary language up until the nineteenth century.

In the early nineteenth century Vuk Stefanović Karadžić (1787–1864), known as the father of the "modern" Serbian language, reconstructed the Cyrillic alphabet to correspond to the sounds in spoken Serbian, adding some letters and discarding others that were not used in spoken Serbian. He also promoted the use of spoken language as the literary language, resulting in a reawakening of Serbian culture in general. He published the first Serbian dictionary in 1818 and collected and published volumes of epic and lyrical poetry that had survived in the oral tradition. His voluminous correspondence is an important political and literary document.

Immigrants were confronted with the modification of their language as it came into contact with English, and they began to incorporate many English words into everyday use, especially those that were needed to communicate in a more complex society and that did not exist in their rural vocabulary. Another American influence can be seen in the fact that many immigrants changed their names for simplification. Often the changing of names was done by either the

immigration officers at the time of entry into the United States or by the employers at the factories or mines who were not accustomed to dealing with complicated Slavic names. At other times, the immigrants themselves opted for simple American names, either for business reasons or to escape being a target for ridicule. Also, some changes were the result of the immigrants' desire to show loyalty to their adopted country; thus, the names were either simply translated—Ivan into John, Ivanović into Johnson—or the diacritical marks over the letters "ć" and "š" were dropped and replaced by English-sounding equivalents such as "Sasha" for "Saša" and "Simich" for "Simić." By 2010 more than 62 percent of Serbian Americans spoke only English, whereas 37 percent spoke more than one language, and 12 percent rated their English as less than very good.

Greetings and Popular Expressions Some basic greetings and sayings in Serbian include: *dobro jutro* ("dobro yutro")—good morning; *dobar dan* (pronounced as written)—good day; *dobro veče* ("dobro vetche")—good evening; *zdravo* (pronounced as written)—greetings; *hvala* ("khvala")—thank you; *dobro došli* ("dobro doshli")—welcome.

RELIGION

The Serbs accepted Christianity in the ninth century due to the work of two Greek brothers, Cyril and Methodius, who were missionaries from Salonika; they were also called "Apostles of the Slavs." Since that time, and especially since King Stefan Prvovenčani established the Serbian Orthodox Autonomous church in 1219, the Serbs have strongly associated their religion with their ethnic heritage. *Srpstvo*, or being Serbian, expresses this concept of the Serbian identity as encompassing the nation, its historic heritage, church, language, and other cultural traditions. Serbian communal life in the United States mainly evolved and, to a large degree, still revolves around the church parish.

Orthodoxy, which means "correct worship," partly differs from Roman Catholicism in dogmatic issues, such as teachings about the immaculate conception of the Virgin Mary, purgatory, and the procession of the Holy Spirit, and clerical practices, such as not allowing priests to marry. Some Orthodox Christians, including Serbs, use the Julian calendar, which is thirteen days behind the Gregorian calendar. Thus, for example, the Serbs celebrate Christmas on January 7 instead of December 25.

Serbian churches, both in the United States and in the homeland, feature the altar, a carved iconostasis, and richly painted icons. A ceremonial pedestal or chair called a *Nalonj*, placed at a respectable distance from the altar, is used to exhibit the icon of the saint the particular church is named after. Upon entering the church everyone stops there to make the sign of the cross and kiss the icon.

The first Serbian churches in the United States were established in Jackson, California, in 1894, followed by McKeesport, Pennsylvania (1900), Douglas, Alaska (1902), and Steelton, Pennsylvania (1903). At that time most Serbian churches were under the jurisdiction of the Russian Orthodox Church in the United States, though served by Serbian priests. The first American-born Serbian Orthodox priest, the Reverend Sebastian Dabovich (1863–1940), the son of a Serbian pioneer in California, was appointed head of the Serbian mission in the United States by the patriarch in Moscow in 1905.

In 1921 a separate Serbian Orthodox Diocese in North America and Canada was created under the leadership of the Reverend Mardary Uskokovich, who later became the first bishop of the new diocese, establishing his seat in Libertyville, Illinois, in 1927. From 1940 to 1963 the diocese was headed by Bishop Dionisije Milivojević. After World War II the diocese was instrumental in arranging for the immigration of refugees, as well as placing refugee priests. Diocese publications included *Pravoslavni glasnik* (*Orthodox Herald*), established in 1937–1938; *Glasnik* (*Herald*), launched in 1963; and *Staza pravoslvlja* (*Path of Orthodoxy*), which dates to 1968.

In 1963 the Serbian Diocese of North America suffered a painful schism and split into two groups: one wanted an independent Serbian Orthodox church in the United States, and the other insisted on maintaining canonical unity with the patriarchy in Belgrade. The immigrant community became bitterly divided. The old settlers felt that the primary role of the church was to uphold Orthodoxy and to maintain the spiritual life in the communities; the newer immigrants saw the need to defend themselves against the communist threat.

The official reconciliation took place in 1991 and was followed by work on a new church constitution. The Holy Liturgy was jointly celebrated on February 15, 1992, by the Patriarch Pavle of Belgrade and the Metropolitan Irinej, the head of the Free Diocese in America, whose seat is in New Gracancia (Third Lake, Illinois).

CULTURE AND ASSIMILATION

It can be argued that assimilation into American life and society's acceptance of the new immigrants was uneven at best. On the one hand, some Serbs were impressed by the freedom and openness of the Americans, as well as by the opportunities available to all. On the other hand, late nineteenth-century Americans, feeling threatened by the large numbers of new immigrants from southern and eastern Europe, increasingly expressed anti-immigrant sentiment. The Immigration Restriction League founded in Boston in 1894 attempted to curb this type of immigrant tide by advocating the literacy test, which required immigrants over sixteen years of age to be literate. Since the eastern and southern Europeans were less literate than their counterparts from northern and western Europe, it was clear where the actions of the League were going to lead. The immigration laws from 1921 and 1924 established a national origins system and set annual quotas for each nationality based on the percentage

U.S. Secretary of State Hillary Clinton tours the Gracanica Serbian Monastery with Bishop Teodosije (L) and U.S. Ambassador to Kosovo Christopher Dell (R) in 2010. MANDEL NGAN / AFP / GETTY IMAGES

of the total of that nationality already living in the United States. This was based on the 1890 and 1910 censuses, which respectively assigned 2 percent and 3 percent annual quotas, or 671, and later 942, per year for all immigrants from Yugoslavia.

The majority of the earlier Serbian immigrants endured the hardships and found that the degree of freedom and the opportunities available to them in the United States were worth staying for. However, the Great Depression of the 1930s adversely affected the old Serbian immigrant communities. Discouraged, many returned to their homeland.

Cuisine Serbian cuisine over the centuries has adopted the tastes and flavors of Balkan, Middle Eastern (Turkish), and Central European (Hungarian, Austrian) foods. Roast suckling pig and lamb are still served on festive occasions. Serbs are also fond of casserole dishes with or without meat; pies (consisting of meat, cheese, or fruit); all kinds of fried foods, and an assortment of cakes, cookies, and condiments that rival the displays in Vienna and Budapest.

A few representative dishes include *šarma*, stuffed cabbage made from leaves of sour cabbage or from wine leaves, and ground beef or veal, often in combination with chopped pork, onions, and smoked meat for added flavor. Serbs especially appreciate *gibanica*, or *pita*, a cheese pie made with Feta or cottage cheese (an American substitute for the cheese used in the homeland), or the combination of both; butter; filo pastry leaves; eggs; and milk. *Ćevapčići*, the summertime favorite for cookouts, are small barbecued sausagelike pieces prepared from a combination of freshly ground pork, lamb, veal, and beef, and served with raw onions.

At Saint Sava Serbian Orthodox Church in Jackson, California, the firing of shotguns into the air on Christmas morning has been a tradition for more than one hundred years and represents a merging of Old West and Serbian traditions.

Serbs like to drink wine, beer, and especially the plum brandy called *šljivovica*, which is the national drink, made from *šljiva*, or plums, the Serbian national fruit. Another word for šljivovica is *rakija*, which is once-distilled plum brandy; twice-distilled šljivovica is called *prepečenica*. Serbs drink at all kinds of celebrations: weddings, baptisms, and *krsna slavas* (a family's patron saint day), and every raised glass is accompanied with the exclamation: *Živeli*, or "Live long." It is not surprising that many Serbs found California to be the perfect place for continuing the family tradition of growing grapes to produce wine or plums for šljivovica.

Traditional Dress Serbian traditional clothing consists of richly embroidered, colorful garments, which are worn today only by the dancers in folkloric dance ensembles or perhaps at other events inspired by folk motives, such as picnics, harvests, or church festivals. Each region has its own particular motives and ways of wearing these costumes, making it easy to discern one from another. The typical costume for women from Serbia proper consists of a fine linen blouse richly embroidered with floral or folk motifs; a vest called a *jelek*, cut low under the breast, which is made of velvet, embroidered with silver and gold thread, and worn tightly around the waist; an ample colorful skirt accompanied by an embroidered apron and a white linen petticoat worn longer than the skirt to show off the hand-crocheted lace; knitted and embroidered stockings; and a pair of handmade leather slipperlike footwear called *opanci*. The hair is long and braided; the braids are sometimes worn down the back or twisted in a bun around the head.

The costume for men consists of a head cap called a *šajkača*, a white linen shirt, a wool jacket, and pants. The jacket is short with sober decorations, and the pants are worn tight around the knees. A richly decorated sash is tied around the waist. Knitted and embroidered socks and *opanci* (leather shoes) are worn on the feet. The fabrics used were always homegrown, spun, or woven, and the costumes were made at home. The early immigrants stood out in an American crowd by the way their clothes looked, which provided an easy target for ridicule. Today, these costumes have given way to standard dress, and if still in existence, are brought out only at folk festivals.

Dances and Songs Music plays a very important role in the Serbian American community. The early Serbian immigrants from the Military Frontier areas brought with them their native mandolin-like string instrument called a tamburica (tamburitza), which varies in five different sizes and ranges. George Kachar, one of the first teachers of tamburitza in the United States, brought the love for his music from his homeland to a small mining town in Colorado, where he taught during the 1920s. His most remarkable students were four Popovich brothers who later became famous as the Popovich Brothers of South Chicago. Having started by traveling from community to community, they gained prominence by delighting Serbian American audiences for sixty years with their art, while also achieving national recognition for appearances at the White House and by participating in the "Salute to Immigrant Cultures" during the Statue of Liberty celebrations held in 1986.

During the annual Tamburitza Extravaganza Festival, as many as twenty bands from around the country perform for three days, with performers vying for the Tamburitza Hall of Fame. The new students and performers are actively recruited and trained by the Duquesne University Tamburitzans, which maintains a folklore institute, grants scholarships for promising students, and makes good use of the enthusiasm generously shared by the junior team called "Tammies." A few active tamburitza manufacturers in the United States continue to assure an adequate supply of this favorite instrument.

The immigrants who came to the United States after World War II brought in a different style of music performed on accordions. Drums, keyboards, and the amplified modern instruments came into use in the last few decades. These musical groups mostly play the newly composed folk music, which combines traditional instruments, melodies, and styles with modern instruments, lyrics, and production techniques. Generally speaking, be they older or newer immigrants, the Serbs sing of love and death, of parting and hope, of the tragedy that accompanied them throughout their history, and of the heroic deeds that helped them triumph over adversity. One of the most beloved and nostalgic songs is "Tamo deleko" ("There Far Away"), referring to the distance of the homeland.

The *gusle*, another symbol of Serbianism, is a string instrument similar to a violin. Gusle musicians have used it since the earliest days of the Serbian kingdom in accompanying the chanting of epic poetry. Although this instrument is capable of rendering only a few melancholy notes, the *guslar*, or bard, manages to evoke myriad emotions. During the Ottoman period of Serbian history the *guslari* traveled from village to village bringing news and keeping alive ancient Serbian heroic epics and ballads, which played a role of utmost importance in the development and preservation of the Serbian national conscience and character.

The *kolo*, meaning the circle, is the Serbian national dance, and by extention the Serbian American dance. Danced in a circle as well as in a single line, the dancers hold each other's hands or belts, and no one, from teenagers to grandparents, can resist the lively tunes and sprightly motions. A good number of folk dancing ensembles throughout the United States have kept alive the rich repertoire of folk dancing, and it is difficult to imagine any kind of Serbian celebrations without a performance of one such ensemble.

Holidays The two most important religious holidays of the year for Serbian Americans are *Božić* (Christmas) and *Uskrs* (Easter). Both are celebrated for three days. *Božić* starts with *Tucindan* (two days before Christmas) when a young pig is prepared to be barbecued for Christmas dinner, or *Božićna večera*. On the day before Christmas—called *Badnji Dan*—the *badnjak*, or Yule log, is placed outside the house, and the *pečenica*, or roasted pig, is prepared. In the evening, straw is placed under the table to represent the manger, the Yule log is cut and brought in for burning, and the family gathers for a Lenten Christmas Eve dinner. *Božićni Post*, the Christmas Lenten, is observed for six weeks prior to Christmas, during which a diet without milk, dairy products, meat, or eggs is maintained. This

SERBIAN AMERICAN CHOIRS

Serbian American choirs, performing mainly at social functions, were formed early on. These included the Gorski Vijenac (Mountain Wreath) Choir in Pittsburgh in 1901, and the Branko Radičević Choir in Chicago in 1906. They were founded both by laity and the clergy, often priests together with singers. Vladimir Lugonja (1898–1977) founded the Serbian Singing Federation of the USA and Canada (SSF) in 1931. Many choirs joined in, connected with the church parishes, and totaled thirty by World War II. Their membership in the federation was contingent on their singing in church. Since 1935 the federation has been sponsoring annual concerts and competitions where both secular and liturgical music are performed. A number of Serbian priests have come from the ranks of the SSF; many are well-known directors and conductors such as Adam Popovich, director of South Chicago's Sloboda. A respected veteran of the Serbian American choir movement, Popovich and his choir performed at the White House for Dwight D. Eisenhower's presidential inauguration.

The SSF continues to be active today, not only sponsoring annual festivals, workshops, and conventions but also awarding annual college scholarships to members. Information on the federation can be found on the organization's website at www.serbiansingingfederation.org.

strict observance is practiced by fewer people today, as most are willing to fast only for a week prior to Christmas.

On Christmas Day *česnica*, a round bread, is baked from wheat flour. A coin placed inside the bread brings good luck throughout the year to the person who finds it. The family goes to church early on Christmas Day, and upon return home the most festive meal of the year is served. The father lights a candle and incense, and says a prayer. The family turns the česnica from left to right and sings the Christmas hymn "Rozdestvo Tvoje," which glorifies the birth of Christ. The česnica is broken, and each member of the family receives a piece, leaving one portion for an unexpected guest. Each person kisses the person next to him three times with the greeting *Hristos se rodi* ("Christ is born") and receives in reply *Vaistinu se rodi* ("Indeed He is born").

In the United States the burning of the *badnjak* is done at church after Christmas Eve mass. An elaborate Lenten Christmas Eve dinner is served in the parish hall for those who wish to participate.

Traditionally three Sundays before Christmas are dedicated to the family: *Detinjci*, Children's Day; *Materice*, Mother's Day; and *Očevi*, Father's Day. On each of these days the celebrants are tied to an object, and their release is obtained with a gift.

These traditions continued into the twenty-first century in Serbian Orthodox churches across the

United States. At Saint Sava Serbian Orthodox Church in Jackson, California, the firing of shotguns into the air on Christmas morning has been a tradition for more than one hundred years and represents a merging of Old West and Serbian traditions, explained Saint Sava's pastor, Milletta Simonovich: "In the old country (Yugoslavia) it is a tradition to stand in front of one's home and shoot at the sky at midnight Christmas Eve to announce the birth of the Christ child." From Holy Trinity Serbian Orthodox Christian Church in Butte, Montana, to the large community in Chicago, Illinois, the traditions are kept alive. Some in the United States continue a Serbian tradition of planting a small garden of wheat, called a *pšenica* (pshe-ni-tza), on December 19, St. Nicholas Day, which allows the wheat to sprout by January 7, Christmas Day, releasing the shoots of new life—a biblical metaphor for Jesus' birth.

Uskrs (Easter) is considered the holiest of holidays. A seven-week Lenten period, Great Lent, is observed, also without meat, eggs, milk, or dairy products. *Vrbica*, or Palm Sunday, is observed on the last Sunday before Easter when the willow branches are blessed and distributed to all present. This service is rendered especially beautiful and significant by the presence of children, dressed in fine new clothes worn for the first time, with little bells hanging from their necks on Serbian tricolor ribbons—red, blue, and white—waiting for the whole congregation to start an outside procession encircling the church three times while singing hymns.

Easter celebrations cannot be conceived without roasted lamb and colored eggs. The eggs symbolize spring and the renewal of the life cycle as well as *Vaskrsenje*, the Easter Resurrection. The Serbian tradition is to color at least the first ten eggs a deep red, representing happiness, rebirth, and Christ's blood on the cross, with designs drawn on with wax before coloring. The eggs may be dyed by boiling with an onion that makes a caramel-red color. Families sometimes bring their baskets of eggs to church for blessing, and they may exchange them with other families saying, *Hristos voskrese* ("Christ is risen"). The response is *Voistinu voskrese* ("Indeed He is risen").

The Easter Mass is the most splendid one. The doors of the iconostasis, which remained closed until the symbolic moment of *Hristovo Voskresenje*, or "Christ's Resurrection," open wide; the church bells ring, and the priest dressed in his gold vestments steps forward. The congregation sings a hymn of rejoicing, and a procession led by the banner of Resurrection encircles the church three times while the worshippers carry lit candles. The greetings *Hristos voskrese*, "Christ is risen," and *Voistinu voskrese*, "Indeed He is risen," are exchanged three times. The influx of immigrants from Serbia in the 1990s to the Seattle area revitalized the celebration of Easter at St. Sava's Serbian Orthodox church in Issaquah, Washington. In 2012 Gerogiana Gavrilovich, one of the original founders of St. Sava's

Church, said that more than half of the church's current members were refugees, providing a youthful energy to what had been an aging congregation.

The most important Serbian tradition is the yearly observance of *Krsna Slava*, the Patron Saint Day. This uniquely Serbian religious holiday is celebrated once a year in commemoration of the family's conversion to Christianity, when each family chose its patron saint, which derived from the custom of worshipping protective spirits. Passing from father to son, this joyous holiday is observed with friends and family enjoying sumptuous foods, often with music and dancing as well. The central elements, which enhance the solemnity of Krsna Slava are *slavska sveca*, a long candle that must burn all day; the votive light lit in front of the icon representing the picture of the family's patron saint; and incense burning. Two foods are specially prepared: *koljivo*, or sometimes called *žito*, made with boiled wheat, sugar, and ground nuts; and *krsni kolač*, which is a ritual round bread baked solely for this occasion. It is decorated with dough replicas of birds, wheat, grapes, barrels of wine, or whatever else an inspired mother of the family can think of, aside from the obligatory religious seal representing the cross. The priest visits the homes and conducts a ceremony in which the *kolač* is raised three times, symbolizing the Holy Trinity. He and the head of the family cut a cross on the bottom of the kolač into which a little wine is poured to symbolize the blood of Christ. This family-based holiday continues to be celebrated in the United States, albeit with a few updates. For instance, according to a 2006 report in the *Kansas City Star*, one family moved their Slava from the more traditional December to May to make it easier for far-flung relatives to attend. One year they started earlier than usual to accommodate the priest's schedule.

Every year on June 28 the Serbs commemorate *Vidovdan*, or Saint Vitus Day. One of the most sacred national and spiritual holidays, it commemorates a defeat on June 28, 1389, when the Serbs led by Prince Lazar lost their kingdom to the Turks in the Battle of Kosovo. The heroism and death of Prince Lazar and his martyrs who died that day for *krst casni i zlatnu slobodu*, or the "venerable cross and golden freedom," are commemorated in epic songs and celebrated each year by churches and communities across the United States. The Serbs might be the only people who celebrate a disastrous defeat as a national holiday, but what they are really celebrating is the ability to withstand adversity. For the last 600 years the Serbs have maintained the tradition of respecting their ancestors for living out the old proverb *bolje grob nego rob*, or "better a grave than a slave." To Serbs in the United States and in the homeland Kosovo Polje ("The Field of Blackbirds," where the Battle of Kosovo took place) is a sacred national site.

The commemoration of Vidovdan took on additional meanings after February 2008 when Kosovo declared independence from Serbia. In a February 23,

2008, *San Diego Union-Tribune* article titled "Violent Demonstrations Persist over Kosovo Independence," Secretary of State Condoleezza Rice is quoted as saying: "We believe that the resolution of Kosovo's status will really, finally, let the Balkans begin to put its terrible history behind it. I mean, after all, we're talking about something from 1389–1389! It's time to move forward." Yet in a speech on Vidovdan 2008 at the Serbian Orthodox Church of the Assumption of the Virgin Mary, Fair Oaks, California, Serbian American M. J. Pejakovich said, "Ms. Rice, I was born in the USA, as was my mother. I have never set foot in Kosovo or Serbia, yet I can without hesitation say, 'Kosovo is mine. Kosovo is ours. Kosovo is Serbia. Kosovo defined what it means to be a Serb … While I have never set foot on Kosovo Polje, the lessons of that day, the love of freedom and the recognition of the sacrifices necessary to be a Christian will never die in the Serb heart—and will never die in the Christian heart." Other Serbian churches used the commemoration of Vidovdan to raise charity for the Serbian minority in Kosovo. At the St. Sava Serbian Orthodox Church in San Gabriel, California, Father Petar Jovanovic wrote on June 28, 2008, "By organizing The Kosovo Charity Banquet we want to show our support and solidarity with our brothers and sisters, in the once again occupied Kosovo. Our moral and financial support for our churches, monasteries and refugees, as well as for the Serbian people that still live in Kosovo, show that we are deeply conscious of the cradle of our heritage."

Death and Burial Rituals Serbian Orthodox funerals in the United States are organized and conducted by the priest. There are no funerals on Sunday or days of celebration, but typically funerals are conducted just a few days after someone passes away. These ceremonies follow the customs of the Serbian Orthodox Church. The church arranges for an all-night vigil over the body before burial, and prayers are said. The eulogy and sermon are often in Serbian. Catherine Rankovic describes her father's funeral in a suburb of Milwaukee, Wisconsin: "Presiding at my father's funeral was a newcomer, less than ten years in the States: a bony, severe Very Reverend priest with a dry, gray beard. He spoke abruptly and never in English. It was said that he'd spent ten or twenty years in Tito's prisons. Who knew what he thought?" Prayers are also sung at the cemetery. Rankovic writes, "The priest, in his black cassock, intoned into the sharp September wind, and the two respondents sang the antiphons, mostly 'Gospodi po-mi-luy,' meaning 'Lord, have mercy.'"

Serbian Orthodox visit the cemetery quite often in the first year after a death, bringing a candle, flowers, and flags, and sometimes eating near the grave. In 2006 a father near Chicago recounted how he honored his Serbian customs by visiting the cemetery each weekend in the first year after his son was killed. A report describes how he "opens the trunk of their car and pulls out plastic bags of supplies: a bouquet of flowers, a single rose and candles, as well as Slim Jims, ginger ale, and sausages." The food and drink are intended for the soul of the lost loved one.

FAMILY AND COMMUNITY LIFE

In their homeland Serbians were primarily farmers; all the family members lived together in a *zadruga*, a large family cooperative where everyone worked on the family land, maintaining strong family ties, as well as observing a strict hierarchical order from the head of the *zadruga*, called *starešina*, down to the youngest child. In the United States, however, each family member's occupation could be different, leading to less interdependence among the family members without destroying the closeness of family ties. To a great extent Serbian and Serbian American households still include grandparents or other elderly relatives needing care and help. It is also a common practice to have grandparents care for young children while their parents are working, as well as take charge of housekeeping in general. Elderly parents (or close relatives) live out their lives at home surrounded by their children and grandchildren. The structure of a typical Serbian American family also retains close relationships with the extended family—aunts, uncles, and cousins—going back a few generations, thus placing emphasis on strong emotional ties as well as offering a good family support system.

Kumstvo, or godparenthood, is a tradition deeply embedded in the Serbian culture. The parents of an unborn child choose a *kum* or a *kuma* (a man or a woman to be a godparent), who names the baby at the baptismal ceremony. The godparents also have the responsibility of ensuring the moral and material well-being of the child if need be and are considered very close family.

Although Serbian immigrants tended to live in closely knit, homogeneous colonies, they were never so totally isolated as to prevent any penetration of American influence, and that interaction inevitably led to changes in many aspects of their lives. Their children and grandchildren only rarely adhere to the old ways, and as a result the immigrant heritage became a strange mixture of old-country and American cultural elements.

Gender Roles Traditionally Serbian culture is male-dominated, and men are considered the head of the household. However, in post–World War II Yugoslavia, women had more access to education and legal equality. Under Tito, for instance, women gained equal rights in marriage, and divorce became easier and more common. Still, Serbian culture tolerates a lower status for women. It was reported in 2011 that 30 percent of homicides in the Republic of Serbia were victims of domestic violence.

Women's organizations among Serbian Americans are various groups of sisterhoods known as Kolo Srpskih Sestara, or Serbian Sisters Circles. They were organized in the beginning of the twentieth century

in Pittsburgh, Cincinnati, and Chicago. They are active in fundraising activities and support children's camps and charities. Being closely associated with the Serbian church, they, unfortunately, were affected by the schism in the church.

Education In the United States the Serbian churches maintain parish Sunday schools where children learn the language, customs, and traditions of their ancestors. The Serbian Orthodox Diocese at the St. Sava Monastery in Libertyville, Illinois, runs a summer camp as well as the parish school. The children of immigrants have mostly attended public schools, and in the early days it was often the case that these children were the only source of information about American culture and history for Serbian adults.

Courtship and Weddings It is said that nothing is like a Serbian wedding. Though the ceremony may be similar to Russian or Greek Orthodox weddings, there are many Serbian traditions that have been kept alive in the United States. The festivities may begin the night before the wedding with the making of rosemary wreathes or corsages to be worn the next day during the wedding. Some report that in the United States, red roses have replaced the traditional rosemary. The day of the wedding begins with the pre-wedding Skup (gathering), often at the home of the bride, with friends, relatives, food, music (perhaps with a traditional tamburitza), dancing, and bartering for the bride. The bartering, conducted by a representative of the groom called a "dever," is playful and entertaining, as in this description of a Skup in Pittsburgh: "the dever's first offer of a Pittsburgh Steeler Terrible Towel coupled with a case of famous Pittsburgh Iron City beer was promptly rejected. A velvet bag full of USA Gold dollars was offered next, but promptly refused as not being 100 percent gold. A wad of money unrolled at last.…" From the Skup the wedding party heads to the church for the ceremony. The two witnesses, one

known as the *stari svat* (godfather or "old man of the wedding") and the other the *kum* (the best man), wear special sashes called *peškir*. The *peškir* may be white, embroidered, or feature the Serbian flag (Trobojka).

The traditional Orthodox wedding ceremony is divided into two parts, the Betrothal and the Crowning. The Betrothal begins with the blessing and exchange of rings. The bride and groom are handed candles, which they hold throughout the service. The right hands of the bride and groom are tied together, and they are "crowned." They then drink wine from a common cup and take a "walk," their first steps together as a couple. On their way out of the church, young children may throw coins at the newlyweds as a way to wish them good fortune.

Organizations In the early stages of Serbian immigration, fraternal mutual aid societies and insurance companies preceded the church as the centers of Serbian American community life. These were formed for economic reasons, as the new arrivals needed to find ways to protect themselves against the hazards of dangerous and life-threatening work in mines, foundries, or factories. In the early years the Serbs readily joined other Slavic groups, such as the Slavonic Benevolent Organization founded in San Francisco in 1857, which served all South Slavs.

In time Serbian immigrants formed their own organizations, starting as local groups, lodges, assemblies, and societies whose goals were the preservation of culture, social welfare, and fraternal sentiment. The first such organization was the Srpsko crnogorsko literarno i dobrotvorno društvo (Serbian-Montenegrin Literary and Benevolent Society) founded in San Francisco in 1880, then Srpsko jedinstvo (Serbian Unity) in Chicago in 1894. Other societies followed and began to form federations, such as the Srpsko crnogorski savez (Serbian-Montenegrin Federation), whose headquarters were in Butte, Montana, and which ceased to exist because most of its members left to fight in the Balkan Wars (1912–1913) and in World War I.

EMPLOYMENT AND ECONOMIC CONDITIONS

Although historically Serbs have placed high value on education, early immigrants were largely illiterate or had very little education due to their circumstances living in rural areas of Austria-Hungary, in poor Montenegrin villages, or under Turkish occupation. In the United States they worked, as already stated, in predominantly heavy industrial areas. In time they began to attend evening English-language classes offered by the adult-education programs in public schools, which proved to be enormously valuable to them and especially to their children.

The younger generations took an increased interest in education and slowly began to break away from the factory jobs and move to white-collar occupations. According to the 2010 U.S. Census, higher than average numbers of Serbian Americans graduate high school and college: 93 percent of Serbian Americans graduate high school, and 40 percent have at least a bachelor's degree. Although Serbian American professionals can be found in nearly every American industry, a great many tend to opt for engineering, medicine, law, or other professions. Lately, however, more and more young people are attracted by financial service industries, such as banking, insurance, and stock brokerage. Boys and girls are educated alike, and everyone is free to set career goals to his or her own liking. There are a number of Serbian American women working in professions that were once thought to be the province of men, especially medicine and engineering.

POLITICS AND GOVERNMENT

Although their participation in American political life has evolved slowly, Serbs have demonstrated a great deal of fervor for politics. Generally speaking, most Serbian Americans are more likely to be concerned with the government's policies and attitude toward the countries in the Balkan region than with local politics.

World War I was the turning point in political activities and unity with other Slavic groups, and such activities had more to do with the politics in the homeland than in the United States. Exiled Serbians, Croatians, and Slovenians in the United States and England began to call for the union of the South Slavs into an independent state. As a result, the Yugoslav Committee was formed, its purpose being to inform and influence the American people, as well as to recruit for war and raise money. Thousands of South Slavs joined either the Serbian army or the U.S. army, and thousands of Serbian emigrants returned from the United States to fight for Serbia.

Among the immigrants who arrived in the United States after 1945, many were very politically engaged and considered the United States as a base for pursuing political goals related to Yugoslavia and, after 1989, Serbia. A number of political organizations were formed to reflect the differing views carried over from the mother country concerning the new regime and the affiliations with particular groups during World War II. After 1945 most of the large numbers of newcomers who joined the Serbian American community in the United States were Chetniks. Forming political organizations, they continued their fight against Tito's Communist dictatorship as best they could. Another faction, albeit much smaller in number, was an ultra-right-wing group called Ljotićevci, which was founded by Dimitrije Ljotić (1891–1945). These two groups polarized the attention of the Serbian American immigrants and heightened political awareness among Serbian American communities.

Many men and women of Serbian descent who have joined the mainstream of American politics today as mayors, governors, and senators have testified to the fact that a degree of "American" political maturity has been reached by this ethnic group in spite of its still intense identification with the motherland, as exemplified by the career of Rose Ann Vuich (1927–2001), who was the first woman to serve in the California State Senate. Vuich was born in California to a Serbian immigrant citrus farmer.

Serbian Americans continued to debate the political issues of the former Yugoslavia over the course of the two decades following the 1991–1992 breakup of Yugoslavia. They felt the policy of the U.S. government—through the presidencies of George H. Bush, Bill Clinton, George W. Bush, and Barack Obama—was incomprehensibly against the interests of their homeland. Serbian Americans were alarmed by what they considered to be the premature recognition of the independence of Slovenia, Croatia, and Bosnia-Herzegovina, first by most of the member states of the European community and then by the United States on April 7, 1992. Although the Serbian American community was at great odds with the Yugoslav President Slobodan Milošević, they perceived the U.S. government as siding against the Serbian minorities in Bosnia, Croatia, and Kosovo. Serbian Americans demonstrated against U.S. policy during the 1999 bombing of Yugoslavia and again on February 17, 2008, when Kosovo declared independence from Serbia and President George W. Bush extended formal recognition shortly thereafter. For many Serbian Americans, Kosovo is their Holy Land, "the cradle of Serbdom, and their inalienable, historical, national, and cultural heritage," according to Milana ("Mim") Karlo Bizic, curator of the 2001 Serb National Federation's Centennial Historic Photo Exhibit, which was held in Pittsburgh.

Military The degree of participation of Serbian Americans in the armed forces, as well as in the intelligence community, is high. During World War I thousands of American Serbs went to Serbia, an ally, to fight, whereas others established a number of humanitarian organizations to send help abroad. The response was overwhelming during World War II as well. A large number distinguished themselves in battle, and some were awarded the Congressional Medal of Honor.

Many Serbian Americans had distinguished careers in the military. Examples include Colonel Nicholas Stepanovich, U.S. Army, who had a brilliant career as a lawyer and military leader and was appointed by President Dwight D. Eisenhower to the U.S. ambassadorial staff to the United Nations; and Colonel Tyrus Cobb, U.S. Army, who served in Vietnam both in war and in peace missions. The recipient of the Defense Superior Service Medal, Colonel Cobb was appointed to the National Security Council and was selected by President Ronald Reagan to accompany him on summits to Geneva, Moscow, and Iceland. Many other Serbian Americans served in the Office of Strategic Services (later known as the Central Intelligence Agency [CIA]), including Nick

Lalich, George Vujnovic, and Joe Veselinovich. The Vietnam War and the Persian Gulf War have also claimed Serbian American decorated heroes as well, such as Lance Sijan, for whom a building is named at the U.S. Air Force Academy in Colorado Springs, Colorado.

Labor Unions The labor movement and the labor unions in the United States found some of their staunchest supporters among the Serbs. Having worked very hard to earn their living and having given strength and youth to their new homeland, they felt, as many other Americans did, that strong unions presented opportunities to rectify many poor work situations. They were active with the United Mine Workers of America, the American Federation of Labor, the Congress of Industrial Organizations, and the Textile Workers Union of America, among others. The contributions of the Serbs to the labor movement are numerous, as exemplified by Eli Zivkovich, who organized the story of the unionization of textile workers in North Carolina, as depicted in the film *Norma Rae* (1979).

Serbian Americans also made significant contributions in the field of labor law as exemplified by the tireless efforts of Robert Lagather, an attorney. The son of a mine worker and a miner himself as a young man, Lagather had a deep commitment to improving the working conditions in the mines, and the role he played in the Federal Mine and Safety and Health Act of 1977 testifies to his determination and dedication.

NOTABLE INDIVIDUALS

Academia Political science professor Alex N. Dragnich (1912–2009) served in the Office of Strategic Services during World War II and as the cultural attaché and public affairs officer in the American Embassy in Yugoslavia. Dragnich wrote extensively on Serbian subjects and was the author of eleven books, including *Serbs and Croats: The Struggle in Yugoslavia* (1992).

Radmila Milentijevic was a history professor at the City College of the City University of New York. Born in Belgrade in 1931, she moved to the United States in the 1950s to attend the University of Chicago. In 1997 she moved back to Serbia to become the Serbian government's information minister in the administration of Slobodan Milošević. In 2012 she published a book about Albert Einstein and his first wife, who was Serbian.

Mateja Matejic, born in 1924 and emigrated from Serbia in 1945, was a professor of Slavic languages at Ohio State University and an Serbian Orthodox priest. He was an authority on medieval Serbian literature and translated many works.

Michael Boro Petrovich (1922–1989) was a professor of history at the University of Wisconsin at Madison specializing in Russian, Soviet, East European, and Balkan history.

Art John David Brčin (1899–1983) was a sculptor who immigrated to the United States in 1914. Drawing his inspiration from American subjects, Brčin sculpted busts of President Abraham Lincoln, Mark Twain, and many others. He also created large reliefs depicting scenes from American history.

Journalism Walt Bogdanich (1950–) became the investigations editor for the business and finance desk of the *New York Times* in January 2001. In 2008 he won the Pulitzer Prize for Investigative Reporting for the series "A Toxic Pipeline," which tracked how dangerous and poisonous pharmaceutical ingredients from China have flowed into the global market. Mr. Bogdanich also won the Pulitzer Prize in 1988 for Specialized Reporting for his articles in *The Wall Street Journal* on substandard medical laboratories and in 2005 for National Reporting for his series "Death on the Tracks," which examined the safety record of the U.S. railroad industry.

Alex Machaskee was the publisher, president, and chief executive of the *Plain Dealer*, Cleveland's largest newspaper, from 1990 to 2006. He was born in Warren, Ohio, in the late 1930s.

Literature Novelist and publishing executive William (Iliya) Jovanovich (1920–2001) wrote many works, including *Now, Barabbas* (1964), *Madmen Must* (1978), and *A Slow Suicide* (1991). Jovanovich was the president of Harcourt, Brace and Jovanovich for thirty-six years, from 1954 to 1990.

Natasha Radojčić-Kane (1966–) was the author of two novels as well as short stories and nonfiction published in *The New York Times*, among many other publications. She was born in Belgrade, and her mother was a Bosnian feminist who told her that "it was essential for a woman to have her own money and to know how to drive." She was a cofounder of the literary journal *H.O.W. Journal*.

Poet and translator Charles Simic (1938–) was awarded the 1990 Pulitzer Prize for Poetry for his collection *The World Doesn't End*. He won the Wallace Stevens Award in 2007 and was a coeditor of the *Paris Review*. Also in 2007 Simic was appointed the fifteenth Poet Laureate Consultant in Poetry to the Library of Congress. He published more than twenty collections of poetry, six books of essays, a memoir, and numerous translations.

Tea Obreht's (1985–) 2011 debut novel, *The Tiger's Wife*, won the 2011 Orange Prize for Fiction. Obreht was born Tea Bajraktarević in Belgrade, Yugoslavia.

Politics Djordje Šagić (1795–1873), later known as George Fisher, was born in a Serbian settlement in western Hungary and came to the United States in 1815, having agreed to become a bond servant upon his arrival. He jumped ship at the mouth of the Delaware River in order to escape his pledge and was named Fisher by the bystanders who watched him swim ashore. Wandering from Pennsylvania to Mississippi to Mexico and eventually to Texas, he joined in the battle for independence from Mexico, helped to organize the first supreme court of the republic, and held a number of positions in the Texas state government. Fisher also published a liberal Spanish-language newspaper. In 1851 he went to Panama and from there to San Francisco. While in California he served as secretary of the land commission, justice of the peace, and county judge. He finished his wandering and wondrous life as the council for Greece in 1873.

Awarded the GOP Woman of the Year in 1972, Helen Delich Bentely (1923–) was a member of the U.S. House of Representatives from Maryland from 1985 to 1995. Rose Ann Vuich (c.1927–2001) served in the California State Senate from 1976 to 1992 and received the Democrat of the Year Award in 1975. Vuich was the first woman to serve in the California State Senate.

Rod Blagojevich (1956–) served as the governor of Illinois from 2003 to 2009. His father, Radislav, was an immigrant steel plant laborer from a village near Kragujevac, Serbia. His mother, Mila Govedarica, was a Serb originally from Gacko, Bosnia, and Herzegovina. In 2008 Blagojevich was charged with corruption for trying to sell the Senate seat vacated by President Obama. He was impeached and removed from office by the Illinois Senate and was convicted of federal extortion charges in 2010.

George V. Voinovich, born in 1936 in Cleveland, Ohio, began his political career as a Republican member of Ohio's House of Representatives in 1967. He served as the mayor of Cleveland from 1979 to 1989 and as the governor of Ohio from 1991 to 1998. He was first elected to the Senate in 1999 and served until his retirement in 2011. During his time in Washington, he was considered the Senate's leading expert on the Balkans.

Milan Panić (1929–), born in Belgrade, was the California-based multimillionaire founder of ICN Pharmaceuticals. He served as prime minister of the Federal Republic of Yugoslavia from 1992 to 1993. The legality of retaining U.S. citizenship while holding this office was questioned based on a constitutional prohibition against a U.S. citizen accepting office on behalf of a foreign nation. He ran for president of Serbia in 1992 but lost to Slobodan Milošević.

Born in Belgrade, Serbia (former Yugoslavia), Danielle Sremac grew up in Cleveland, Ohio. Throughout the 1990s, she served as a visible spokesperson for Serbian Americans, working for Republika Srpska, one of the main political entities in Bosnia-Herzegovina, and director of the Institute for Balkan Affairs. She also appeared on hundreds of national and international television and radio programs. She has authored two books, *The War of Words: Washington Tackles the Yugoslav Conflict* (1999) and *Heart of Serbia: A Cultural Journey* (2012).

Etching of Nikola Tesla (1856–1943), naturalized American physicist and electrical engineer, who was born in Croatia to Serbian parents. Tesla was the inventor of polyphase electrical power systems and the AC induction motor. SSPL / GETTY IMAGES

Science Nikola Tesla (1856–1943), "the electrical wizard," astonished the world with his demonstration of the wonders of alternating current at the World Columbian Exposition in Chicago in 1893; in the first half of the twentieth century, this became the standard method of generating electrical power. Tesla also designed the first hydroelectric power plant in Niagara Falls, New York. Having introduced the fundamentals of robotry, fluorescent light, the laser beam, wireless communication and transmission of electrical energy, the turbine and vertical take-off aircraft, computers, and missile science, Tesla was possibly the greatest inventor the world has ever known. His work spawned technology such as satellites, beam weapons, and nuclear fusion.

Michael Idvorsky Pupin's (1858–1935) scientific contributions in the field of radiology include rapid X-ray photography (1896), which cut the usual hour-long exposure time to seconds; the discovery of the secondary X-ray radiation; and the development of the first X-ray picture used in surgery. His other interests covered the field of telecommunications. The "Pupin coil," which uses alternate current, made long-distance telephone lines and cables possible. He also invented the means to eliminate static from radio receivers as well as the tuning devices for radios. Pupin successfully experimented with sonar U-boat detectors and underwater radars, as well as the passage of electricity through gases. In addition to his scientific contributions, Pupin was a prominent Serbian patriot. He tirelessly campaigned on behalf of Serbia during World War I. In his Pulitzer Prize-winning autobiography *From Immigrant to Inventor*

(1925) Pupin stated: "[I] brought to America something … which I valued very highly, and that was: a knowledge of and a profound respect and admiration for the best traditions of my race … no other lesson had ever made a deeper impression upon me." The Pupin Institute at Columbia University was founded in his memory.

Miodrag Radulovacki (1933–) was named the University of Illinois at Chicago's Inventor of the Year, along with his colleague David Carly, for their work on sleep apnea. Raised north of Belgrade in Sremski Karlovci, a small town on the Danube, he came to the United States to pursue his dream of being a scientist. He earned his MD and PhD in neurophysiology from the University of Belgrade School of Medicine, where he specialized in sleep research. Dr. Radulovacki was a foreign member of the Serbian Academy of Sciences and Arts beginning in 2003.

Sports Professional basketball player Pete Maravich (1947–1988) was perhaps best known as "Pistol Pete" Maravich. He is considered one of the fifty greatest basketball players of all time.

Stage and Screen Peter Bogdanovich is a film director and historian, writer, actor, producer, and critic. Some of his best-known films are *What's Up, Doc?* (1972) and *Paper Moon* (1973). He was born in 1939 in Kingston, New York, to an Eastern Orthodox Serbian father and an Austrian-Jewish mother. A prolific writer, he was the author of more than a dozen books, and he also appeared in as many films and TV shows as he directed.

Actor Karl Malden (1912–2009) born Mladen Sekulovich, received an Academy Award for his performance in *A Streetcar Named Desire* in 1951 and was nominated for a second Oscar in 1954 for his work in *On the Waterfront*. Malden is best known for his starring role in the television series "The Streets of San Francisco" and for his series of television commercials for American Express.

Steve Tesich (born Stoyan Tesich [1942-July 1, 1996]) was a well-known screenwriter, playwright, and novelist who received an Academy Award for Best Screenplay in 1979 for *Breaking Away*. His other screenplays include The World According to Garp (1982) and *Eleni* (1985). Tesich's plays include *Passing Game* (1977).

MEDIA

PRINT

Amerikanski Srbobran (The American Serb Defender)

Published by the Serb National Federation since 1906, this is the oldest and largest circulating Serbian bilingual biweekly newspaper in the United States, covering cultural, political, and sporting events of interest to Serbian Americans.

Cissy M. Rebich
938 Penn Avenue
Fourth Floor
Pittsburgh, Pennsylvania 15222
Phone: (412) 642-7372
Fax: (412) 642-1372
Email: snf@snflife.org
URL: www.snflife.org

Serb World U.S.A.

A continuation of *Serb World* (1979–1983), this bimonthly, illustrated magazine was established in 1984. It features articles about Serbian American immigrants' cultural heritage and history, as well as other topics relating to Serbian Americans.

Mary Nicklanovic-Hart
P.O. Box 50742
Tucson, Arizona 85703
Phone: (602) 624-4887
URL: www.serbworldusa.com

Serbian Studies

Founded in 1980, this scholarly journal is published biannually by the North American Society for Serbian Studies. It offers broad coverage of history, political science, art, and the humanities.

Ljubica Dragana Popovich, Editor
Phone: (773) 702-0035
Email: lfr@gwu.edu
URL: www.serbianstudies.org

Liberty: The Official Publication of the Serb National Defense Council of America

Founded in 1952 by the Serb National Defense Council of America, this publication is an illustrated biweekly featuring articles on Serbian history and culture.

5782 N. Elston Avenue
Chicago, Illinois 60646
Phone: (773) 775-7772
Fax: (773) 775-7779
Email: info@snd-us.com
URL: http://liberty.snd-us.com/index.php

Serbian Sounds of Music

The American Serbian Club of Pittsburgh sponsors this radio show every Sunday from 4:00 p.m. to 5:00 p.m. on WEDO 810 AM.

Valery Tassari
Phone: (412) 242-0570
Email: valtassari@yahoo.com

ORGANIZATIONS AND ASSOCIATIONS

Serb National Federation (SNF)

Founded in 1906, the SNF has lodges throughout the United States and Canada. Its activities transcend business interests to include sponsoring and promoting many programs from sports to scholarship within the Serbian American community.

George Martich
938 Penn Avenue
4th Floor
Pittsburgh, Pennsylvania 15222
Phone: (412) 642-7372
Fax: (412) 642-1372
Email: snf@snflife.org
URL: www.snflife.org

Serbian American Museum St. Sava (SAMS)

Founded in 1951, this organization is one of the oldest Serbian cultural institutions in Chicago. The museum offers exhibits highlighting Serbian culture and also sponsors community events.

448 Barry Avenue
Chicago, Illinois 60657
Phone: (773) 549-9690
Fax: (773) 549-9690
Email: info@serbianamericanmuseum.org
URL: http://serbianamericanmuseum.org/

Serbian National Defense Council of America (Sprska Narodna Odbrana)

Established in 1941 with chapters throughout the United States and abroad. Activities focus on political and cultural Serbian interests.

Slavko Panović, President
5782 North Elston Avenue
Chicago, Illinois 60646
Phone: (773) 775-7772
Fax: (773) 775-7779

Serbian Singing Federation (SSF)

Founded in 1931, the Serbian Singing Federation organizes annual festivals and promotes the cultural, liturgical, and ethnic music of Serbia. The SSF sponsors an annual choral festival.

P.O. Box 71007
Madison Heights, Michigan 48071
Phone: (248) 542-4004
Email: request@serbiansingingfederation.org
URL: www.serbiansingingfederation.org

MUSEUMS AND RESEARCH CENTERS

North American Society for Serbian Studies

The NASSS is an organizational member of the Association for Slavic, East European, and Eurasian Studies (ASEEES). Its mission is to research and promote Serbian literature, history, and culture. The organization attracts Serbian scholars from the United States, Canada, and Mexico, who meet at annual conferences of the ASEEES.

Phone: (773) 702-0035
Email: petkovic@uchicago.edu
URL: www.serbianstudies.org

The Njegoš Endowment for Serbian Language & Culture at Columbia University

The endowment was founded in 1997 with the goal of supporting instruction in Serbian language, literature, and culture at Columbia University.

East Central European Center
Columbia University MC3336
New York, New York 10027
URL: www.columbia.edu/cu/ece/academics/regional/serbia.html

SOURCES FOR ADDITIONAL STUDY

Kisslinger, J. *The Serbian Americans*. New York: Chelsea House, 1990.

Pavlovich, Paul. *The Serbians: The Story of a People*. Toronto: Serbian Heritage Books, 1988.

Petrov, Krinka Vidakovic. "An Outline of the Cultural History of the Serbian community in Chicago." *Serbian Studies* 20, no. 1 (2006): 33+.

Radovich, Milan. "The Serbian Press." In *The Ethnic Press in the United States: A Historical Analysis and Handbook*, edited by Sally M. Miller, 337–51. Westport, CT: Greenwood Press, 1987.

Ramirez, Anthony. "Upheaval over Kosovo's Independence Echoes in a New York Enclave." *New York Times*, February 24, 2008.

Rankovich, Catherine. "Reflections of a Serbian-American." *Progressive*, June 1999: 24.

Simic, Andrei. "Understanding Hyphenated Ethnicity: the Serbian-American Case." *Serbian Studies* 21, no. 1 (Winter-Spring 2009): 37.

Singleton, Frederick Bernard. *A Short History of the Yugoslav Peoples*. New York: Cambridge University Press, 1993.

Tomashevich, George V. *Portraits of Serbian Achievers*. Toronto: Serbian Literary Company, 2000.

Webster, Andy. "Balkan Tale: Blood Ties, and Ties to Home." *New York Times*, July 3, 2008.

SICILIAN AMERICANS

Laura C. Rudolph

OVERVIEW

Sicilian Americans are immigrants or the descendants of immigrants from the island of Sicily in the Mediterranean Sea. Located off the tip of the Italian Peninsula, Sicily is the largest Mediterranean island and is part of the Italian Republic. Inside the Republic of Italy is the *Regione Siciliana*, a special autonomous region in which Sicilians enjoy extensive powers of self-government. As a result of its close proximity to both Italy (separated by the Strait of Messina by less than two miles) and North Africa (separated by less than 100 miles), Sicily has traditionally been regarded as a bridge between Africa and Europe. The terrain is largely mountainous, with Europe's largest volcano, Mount Etna, representing the highest peak at 3,260 meters. The capital is Palermo, which has a population of 500,000 and is the largest city in Sicily. At 9,920 square miles (25,700 square kilometers), Sicily is a little larger than the state of Vermont.

According to the Italian National Institute of Statistics, Sicily was home to 5,004,598 people in 2011. Its ethnically diverse population reflects centuries of foreign rule. The major ethnic groups include native Sicilians, Arabs, Greeks, Spanish, and northern Italians. Although the vast majority of Sicilians are Roman Catholics, there are smaller numbers of Greek Orthodox Christians. Sicily, like other parts of southern Italy, has a higher unemployment rate than those in the northern half of the peninsula; the 2011 unemployment rate in Sicily was 19.5 percent, twice that of Italy's in general. About 100,000 of Sicily's five million citizens are employed by either the state or related agencies. Due to its fertile land, Sicily is known for its agriculture, with products such as wheat, olives, tomatoes, and artichokes.

The first significant wave of Sicilian immigrants to the United States began in the late 1880s, and over the next four decades, more than one million of them sailed for America. The heaviest concentrations of Sicilian immigrants were in New York, Chicago, Boston, New Orleans, Louisiana, and San Francisco, where jobs for unskilled workers were readily available. The U.S. Immigration Act of 1924 sharply reduced the number of people allowed to immigrate to the United States; among Italians, the number was 3,845 per year. In the decades since then, Sicilian Americans have largely assimilated into the U.S. landscape, though they have retained a distinct identity as an immigrant community, separate even from other Italian American populations.

Sicilian Americans are included in general population counts for Italian Americans, which the U.S. Census Bureau estimated at 17.8 million in 2010, a number roughly equivalent to the population of Florida. Out of the 4.5 million Italians who immigrated to the United States between 1880 and 1930, one out of every four was a Sicilian. The immigrants represented virtually every area in Sicily, and they settled primarily in major industrial centers in New York, New Jersey, Massachusetts, California, Illinois, and some parts of the South, including Louisiana and Texas. Subsequent generations of Sicilian Americans gradually moved away from the old neighborhoods, as economic prosperity enabled them to fulfill the immigrant dreams of their grandparents by owning their own houses in the suburbs. Nevertheless, large numbers of Sicilian Americans continue to live in urban areas.

HISTORY OF THE PEOPLE

Early History Sicily's strategic location in the Mediterranean has prompted centuries of invasion and occupation by foreign powers, closely paralleling the rise and fall of virtually every empire since the eighth century BCE. The name "Sicily" is thought to have originated with the Sicels, one of three peoples who occupied Sicily during the Neolithic Age. Thereafter, during the seventh and eighth centuries BCE. the Greeks established colonies, including Messina, Syracuse, and Gela, under which Sicily flourished culturally. Although the Carthaginians arrived at roughly the same time as the Greeks, they were confined to the northwest of the island and exerted a lesser influence. However, by the third century BCE, the Greek Empire declined and the Romans established control, which lasted until the fifth century CE. Sicily was subsequently occupied by the Ostrogoths, the Byzantines, and the Arabs.

Sicily flourished once again under Norman rule, which began around 1000 CE. Frederick II's reign (1211–1250) produced an outpouring of literary, scientific, and architectural works, representing a cultural peak. After his death, however, Sicily passed into the hands of France, an oppressive occupation that ended with the bloody "Sicilian Vespers" revolt in 1282. Thereafter, for the better part of the next six centuries, the Spanish ruled Sicily, with periodic occupation from other countries. In the first half of the nineteenth century, after uniting with the Kingdom of Naples, Sicily became known as the Kingdom of the Two Sicilies. Sicily's foreign kings, the Spanish-French-Austrian admixture of one line in the House of Bourbon, were ousted when the Kingdom of Sardinia annexed the Two Sicilies in 1860 as part of a wave of political unrest. Weary from years of invasion, the Sicilians rallied under Giuseppe Garibaldi, who won control of the island in 1860. There was great hope that unification into a larger Italy would help Sicilians leap forward into the progress and promise of nineteenth-century life. They enthusiastically supported the unification of Italy, which was completed during the *Risorgimento* of 1860–1870. The unification with Italy did not, however, prove particularly beneficial to Sicily. Quickly deemed part of "the Southern problem"—a cultural divide that separated the more progressive, worldly northern Italians from their peasant brethren in the south—Sicilians were forced to endure military conscription and a heavy tax burden. The *Mafioso* (or Mafia), an underground element often linked with criminal activity, quickly became a stronghold of power in Sicily. Efforts on the part of Sicilians to revolt against the new laws were quickly suppressed, often brutally.

Modern Era Tensions remained between northern and southern Italy into the early part of the twentieth century. In the 1920s Benito Mussolini came into power in Italy and established a right-wing fascist dictatorship. Mussolini waged unofficial war on the Sicilian *Mafioso* and official war against the Allies during World War II. Sicily proved to be a crucial battleground in the Allied effort and was successfully conquered in a July–August 1943 campaign. The Allied victory forced Mussolini's fall from power, and following the war, a large separatist movement began in Sicily, which agitated for its own rule. Although the Sicilians were not able to achieve this goal, they were not wholly unsuccessful. Sicily remained a region of the newly created Republic of Italy, but it was granted regional autonomy in 1946, giving it control over the tax revenues it collected. However, social, political, and economic problems continued to plague the region. High illiteracy and unemployment rates, coupled with natural disasters, served to reinforce rather than lessen the poverty of the Sicilians. Moreover, freed from the restrictive measures of Mussolini's regime, the *Mafioso* quickly regained a large portion of power in Sicily. Since the last part of the twentieth century, there have been serious efforts to lessen the influence and control of the Mafia and to rejuvenate the economy. In 2007 law enforcement made one of its most high-profile arrests, seizing Salvatore Lo Piccolo, who was

in hiding near Palermo. Lo Piccolo had been eluding justice since a murder conviction was handed down by a court in 1983, and he had been reportedly leading *La Cosa Nostra* (the Sicilian Mafia) since the arrest of another infamous ringleader, Bernardo Provenzano, in 2006. Both arrests were part of a nearly two-year initiative to take down key figures in the Sicilian Mafia and effectively leave it leaderless. A grassroots movement, loosely known as *Addiopizzo*! ("Goodbye, protection money!"), has emerged on the island to encourage tourism and investment in a new, less corrupt Sicily.

SETTLEMENT IN THE UNITED STATES

Sicilians have a recorded presence of more than 300 years on American soil, but their immigration remained relatively slow until the latter part of the nineteenth century. However, several Sicilian immigrants distinguished themselves in the decades leading up to that time. During the Civil War, for example, Enrico Fardella was commissioned a colonel in the Union Army and was rapidly promoted to brigadier general for distinguished services. And Father Luigi Venuta, a former professor from the University of Palermo, built the Church of St. Joseph in Newark and several school buildings in New Jersey shortly after the Civil War.

Sicilians began leaving their homeland for a new life in the United States in large numbers in the 1880s and 1890s. Before 1880 fewer than 1,000 Sicilians immigrated to America per year, but by 1906, there were up to 100,000 a year, following a general pattern of immigration that included large numbers from the rest of southern Italy. Sicilians represented about one out of every four of the 4.5 million Italians who came to the United States between 1880 and 1930.

The surge of Italian immigrants to the United States happened for several reasons. After the unification of Italy was completed in 1870, Sicilians were confident their lot would improve after centuries of *la miseria* (poverty). They were quickly disillusioned. Sicily suffered a series of agricultural crises, which precipitated a sharp drop in the grain and citrus markets. The discovery of sulfur in America greatly reduced the role of volcano-rich Sicily in that foreign market. In addition, there was widespread economic exploitation of Sicilians, who were heavily taxed under the new government. Eventually Sicilians banded together against the intolerable conditions, largely in the form of peasants' and workers' organizations termed *mutuo soccorso* (mutual aid societies). These societies contributed in part to the formation of the *Fasci*, a Socialist-directed movement. By the 1890s, the Fasci movement had become a powerful force, with revolts that were increasingly threatening to those in power. Between 1892 and 1894, the Fasci was forcibly suppressed by the government and ordered to disband. Many of the former leaders of the movement fled to the United States, while other Sicilians responded to the deteriorating economic conditions by leaving, too.

The main areas of Sicilian settlement in the United States were the major industrial centers of the late-nineteenth and early-twentieth centuries, such as New York City, New Jersey, Chicago, Boston, parts of Massachusetts and Rhode Island, and the San Francisco Bay Area. Gulf Coast states such as Louisiana and Texas also became destinations for Sicilian immigrants. As with other Sicilian immigrants who had chosen coastal communities, those in the southern United States were proficient commercial fishermen, a trade that had been honed on their island homeland.

Sicilian immigrants tended to cluster according to the regions from which they had emigrated. For example, East 69th Street in New York City was dominated by Sicilians from the village of Cinisi. Farther south in Manhattan, in Little Italy, tenement buildings on Elizabeth Street were home to Sicilians from Sciacca and Palermo, among other places. The North End in Boston accommodated Sicilians from several fishing villages, as did San Francisco's North Beach community. Furthermore, part of New Orleans' French Quarter came to be dubbed "Little Palermo."

Sicilian immigration to the United States dropped sharply after the passage of the U.S. Immigration Act of 1924. The act reduced the number of Italians who were allowed to immigrate to the United States annually to a paltry 3,845. Southern Europeans were viewed as less likely to assimilate—or "Americanize," in the parlance of the era—and, thus, were deemed less desirable, while immigrants from northern European countries were favored in the annual quotas issued by the U.S. government. Media stories about organized-crime rings operating in Italian-immigrant enclaves in the United States magnified ongoing prejudice against Italians, especially southern Italians. Even inside Italy itself, Sicilians faced enormous discrimination: because the island is located so close to northern Africa and has been home to mariners over the centuries, its ethnic composition is different than that of mainland Italy. Other Italians derided Sicilians as "Africans." There was another minor immigration surge after World War II, partly the result of Sicilian Americans' phenomenal aid in the Allied invasion of Sicily, which led to a campaign to take the Italian Peninsula in 1943 from Mussolini and his fascist German allies.

In general, employment patterns for Sicilian Americans have mirrored those of the larger Italian American population. They were initially laborers, fishermen, and food-service industry workers who went on to become small-business owners. They entered the grocery business or opened restaurants, and many sacrificed to send their children to American colleges. Today's Sicilian Americans, like Italian Americans in general, can be found in the sciences, the medical and legal professions, and politics.

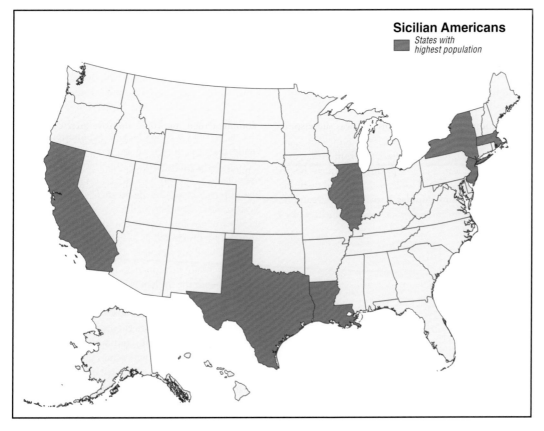

Sicilian Americans

States with highest population

LANGUAGE

Although the official language of Sicily is Italian, Sicilians have a fully developed a language of their own, complete with regional dialects (*parrati*). The Sicilian language derives from Latin and reflects the influence of centuries of occupation. Many of their words have Greek, Arab, French, or Spanish origins. The spelling is fundamentally phonetic, and the stress falls on the next-to-last syllable unless indicted by an accent mark. The vowels are pronounced as follows: the Sicilian *a* is pronounced like the English "a" in "father;" *e* like "e" in "west"; *i* like "ea" in "feast"; a short *i* like "i" in "fit"; *o* like "aw" in "saw"; and *u* like "o" in "do." Most of the consonants are pronounced the same as in English, with a few exceptions: *e* before *e* or *i* is pronounced like the "ch" in "church"; *c* before *a, o,* or *u* is pronounced like the "k" in "kite"; the *h* is always silent; and both letters in double consonants must be distinctly pronounced. There is no future tense.

Like many immigrants in general, some earlier Sicilian immigrants never learned to speak English. Many, however, adapted their Sicilian to the English language to form a hybrid dialect comprised of both Sicilian and English words. The children of the immigrants usually spoke both English and Sicilian. Most Sicilian Americans converted to the English language by the end of the twentieth century, causing a sense of alarm that the cultural heritage of their language would be lost. Various organizations were subsequently formed to promote the study of the language, including Arba Sicula, based in the New York City area.

> To this day, some Sicilians who also believe in the Evil Eye try not to forget to put their first stocking on the left leg, in order to ensure a day of good luck. And if, while praying at midnight, they should hear the baying of a dog, they will expect *male notizia* (bad news).
>
> "Southern Italian Folklore in New York City." *New York Folklore Quarterly* 11, 1965.

Greetings and Popular Expressions Common Sicilian greetings and other expressions include the following:

Milli grazii
    Many thanks

Cuntenti di canuscirivi
    Glad to meet you

Addiu
    Goodbye

Una bona idea
    A good idea

Sì, daveru
    Yes, indeed

Scusatimi
    Excuse me

Pir favuri
    Please

Saluti
    Health

Santa
    Saint

Cu piaciri
    With pleasure

Benissimu
    Fine

Bon
    Good

Cuntenti
    Content

Oggi
    Today

Dumani
    Tomorrow

Amicu
    Friend

Gentillissimu
    Very kind

RELIGION

Sicilians have a long history of religious activity in the Americas. As early as the seventeenth century, Catholic missionaries sailed to the West Coast in an effort to convert Native Americans to Christianity, including Palermo's Father Francesco Mario Piccolo, who joined Father Eusebio Kino in Spanish-controlled *Nueva Espana* in 1689. Father Piccolo served on Kino's historic exploration of Baja California and proved to be a skilled mapmaker. Piccolo was promoted to a supervisory role in the missions in 1705 and had spent a total of forty years in California before his death there in 1729. Father Saverio Saeta, another Sicilian, was also instrumental in early missionary efforts and was posthumously honored by his church as a religious martyr after his death in the Pima Revolt in 1751.

The Jesuit missionaries, however, had little in common with the Sicilian immigrants who arrived en masse between 1880 and 1920. While the vast majority of Sicilian immigrants were Roman Catholics, many of their religious beliefs were based on a mixture of Catholicism, paganism, and superstition. Tied to an agricultural world, their semi-religious traditions and customs had been celebrated for centuries, virtually untouched and unchallenged from the unrest provoked in other countries during the Protestant Reformation. Their faith was an important extension of their local identity, and the *feste* honoring the patron saints of their villages were sacred rituals. For Sicilians who often felt helpless and vulnerable against the elements in their impoverished rural lives, the superstitions, saints, and customs of their folk religion provided solace.

Early Sicilian immigrants to the United States brought their folk religion with them. Their sheltered enclaves, which were based on village ties from their native land, allowed them to continue practicing their religion as they had done in Sicily. The communities continued the practice of the *feste*, and many held fast to their belief in witchcraft such as the "evil eye" (the ability to bring misfortune or even physical harm to someone through a mere glance). The more assimilated communities of American Roman Catholics were appalled at the Sicilians' treatment of the Catholic faith, as were the Protestants. In their eyes, the Sicilians' festival processions and worship of saints smacked of paganism and idolatry, and to the Protestants, the practices represented the worst of Catholic excess. Furthermore, Sicilians were unaccustomed to regular attendance at church or confessions and harbored a general distrust toward members of the clergy.

Tensions ran especially high between Sicilian Catholics and Irish Catholics. Irish American priests and archbishops were predominant in the American Catholic hierarchy in the early decades of the twentieth century, and they resented the Sicilians' potential encroachment. Eventually Sicilians founded their own parishes, where they could practice their faith as they preferred. Immigrants from the area of Palermo founded the Brooklyn, New York, church of St. Rosalia, while those from Patti province communed around their own patron saint, the Black Madonna of Tindari, a statue of which became the centerpiece of a longtime parade in New York City's Little Italy. Sicilians from other villages quickly followed suit in forming their own parish communities. Second and third generation Sicilians, however, gradually phased out most of the more superstitious and supernatural elements from the homeland, preferring to practice religion in more conventional ways. The younger generations found the folk elements to be an old-fashioned and embarrassing reminder of their parents' and grandparents' immigrant status. In general, the *feste* honoring the various patron saints still take place, but they are seen as cultural rather than religious celebrations.

CULTURE AND ASSIMILATION

Many of the earliest Sicilian immigrants were young males or heads of households who intended to work for a short time in the United States before returning to Italy. However, over half eventually sent for their families and permanently established themselves in various cities across the United States. In a "chain migration," other families from a Sicilian village would then immigrate to the same area. There was, as a result, little assimilation at first, even among Sicilians who had emigrated from different regions.

Early Sicilian immigrants held fast to the various dialects and celebrations of their native villages. Many never learned to speak English, and there was little intermarriage with other immigrant groups. Sheltered from the larger culture, the "Little Sicilies" that the immigrants created mimicked the world they had left behind. Mutual aid societies such as the Caltanissetta (Sicily) Society in Baltimore, Maryland, and the Trinacria Fratellanza Siciliana in Chicago aided the immigrants with housing, employment, and general acclimation. Sicilian cuisine and entertainment could be found in virtually every Sicilian settlement area. Sicilian dances and songs were performed at the local music halls, as were puppet shows, a traditional Sicilian entertainment. Agrippino Manteo's widely popular "Papa Manteo's Life-Size Marionettes" attracted large Sicilian audiences throughout the early part of the twentieth century. And weekly newspapers such as the *Corriere Siciliano* (*The Sicilian Courier*) brought immigrants news from Sicily.

The Sicilians' seemingly stubborn resistance to assimilation was fueled in part by the hatred they aroused in their new country. Sicilians were often judged by Americans, other immigrants, and even fellow Italians to be an "inferior race," one that was destined to remain in ignorance and poverty. This prejudice generated a vicious cycle of limited economic and educational opportunities. Arrivals from northern Italy were foremost among those who spurned the Sicilians, continuing an animosity that had existed in their native country. Northern Italians, who had a greater number of skilled laborers among them, were therefore more likely to land higher-paying jobs than Sicilians, the majority of whom were peasants. Furthermore, northern Italian immigrants were more established in North America and had begun to achieve a relative degree of prosperity. They were reluctant to be lumped with the newly arrived Sicilians. Nevertheless, they struggled to disassociate themselves from the Sicilian immigrants. In many instances, northern Italians would move out of neighborhoods when the Sicilians began to populate them. A 1975 article by F. Ianni and E. Reuss in *Psychology Today* quotes a northern Italian immigrant: "Trust family first, relatives second, Sicilians third, and after that, forget it."

If the northern Italians were suspicious and dismissive of the Sicilians, then the rest of America was openly hostile. Sicilians were labeled "dirty," "diseased," and "political anarchists" and were accused of introducing a criminal element into the United States, namely the Mafia. The notorious underworld activities of Sicilian Americans such as Charles "Lucky" Luciano were duly reported in newspapers across the United States. The image of the Sicilian "mobster" had devastating consequences for the entire immigrant group. Numerous innocent Sicilians were charged and convicted of heinous crimes, usually with flimsy circumstantial evidence to support their cases. When the jury system failed to convict, citizens sometimes took matters into their own hands. For example, in 1891 in New Orleans, eleven Sicilians were lynched by a mob of "good citizens" who were outraged at the not-guilty verdict returned in a trial. Similar incidents on a smaller scale occurred in other towns throughout Louisiana well into the next century.

Given the amount of hatred these first Sicilian immigrants encountered in the United States, it is not surprising that they preferred to remain in sheltered enclaves surrounded with familiar village dialects and customs. Even as other immigrants began to consider themselves "Americans," Sicilians continued to identify themselves by their particular villages. Nor were they entirely sure of their place in the emerging Italian American culture as a whole. Although the United States grouped Sicilians under the category of "Italians," Sicilians were reluctant to do so. The unification of Italy and Sicily was fewer than 100 years old, and the bitterness it had wrought ran deep among Sicilians. However, second and third generation Sicilian Americans were less concerned with such distinctions and were more apt to label themselves "Italian Americans."

*In Sicily the family was a strong defense against the desperate and unrelieved poverty that characterized life. Each family member contributed to the all-encompassing and often heartbreaking effort to survive. First loyalties were reserved for the closest kin (*casa*). This was an economic necessity, as each family competed with other families for survival.*

Ultimately, Sicilian immigrants followed an assimilation pattern similar to northern Italians, albeit at a noticeably slower rate. As educational opportunities increased, so too did chances for economic advancement. As with Italian Americans overall, Sicilians proved they were "American" in the fullest sense of the word during World War II. Sicilian Americans were able to provide crucial military aid, particularly during the Sicilian campaign of 1943. World War II marked something of a turning point as second and third generation Sicilians achieved financial security and social acceptance. Although images of Mafia lords continue to dog the Sicilians, they are far from being the victims of hatred and discrimination they once were.

Moreover, descendants of early Sicilian immigrants have become interested in exploring their Sicilian roots and learning about the culture of their ancestors. Toward the end of the twentieth century,

this renewed interest helped to fuel a celebration of the distinctiveness of the Sicilian heritage. The City University of New York (CUNY), for example, has a foreign exchange program for students wishing to study in Sicily. In addition, the Italian Cultural Center in Stone Park, Illinois, is home to the Sicilian Heritage Museum, established in 2004. The Regional Association of Sicilians in America and the Sicilian American Cultural Association work to promote and endow the collection.

Traditions and Customs Sicilians have a variety of traditions, many of which are derived from quasi-religious beliefs. For example, according to an old folk belief, bread made during the first three days of May will result in mold and roaches throughout the house. This belief can be traced to a legend about a woman making bread who denied a crumb to a beggar and was generous to devils masquerading as knights. The mistake resulted in the dangers inherent in making bread during the first three days of May. This custom has been largely abandoned by Sicilian Americans.

Other traditions and customs came from the agricultural lifestyle of Sicilians, who would ritually taste every new product that came from the earth while reciting the words, "Whatever I eat today, may I eat it next year." Dried figs were left in a basket and were not touched until the feast day of St. Francis of Assisi, in the belief that moths would ruin them unless they were protected by the saint. Many of these agricultural traditions and customs were difficult to transfer to the urbanized, industrial cities of North America, and so they disappeared with immigration.

Cuisine Sicilian cuisine is savory and flavorful, and it reflects the influence of a diverse cultural inheritance, particularly from Arabs. The food is hot and spicy, and eggplants, olives, pine nuts, and capers are plentiful, along with the ubiquitous pasta and tomatoes.

Some of the main dishes include *pasta con le sarde* (sardines, raisins, pine nuts, and capers); *frittedda* (peas, fava beans, and artichokes); *pasta con pescespada* (pasta with swordfish); *pasta con le melanzane* (pasta and eggplant); and *cuscus* (Sicilian couscous). Special dishes include the *ragu Siciliano delle feste* (Sicilian feast day ragout). Sicilians are also known for their desserts, including *gelato Siciliano* (Sicilian ice cream) and *cannoli* (a fried pastry stuffed with ricotta cheese and candied fruit). *Cassata* is also made with ricotta and candied fruit, in addition to almond paste and sponge cake, and *martorana* is a form of marzipan for which Sicilians are well known.

The poverty that characterized Sicily in the early decades of the twentieth century forced Sicilians to exist at a mere sustenance level. It is ironic that numerous Sicilian peasants were unable to enjoy many of the foods unique to their region until they immigrated to the United States and could afford to do so. Food became a central part of the immigrants' lives and found a prominent place in many of the religious and cultural celebrations. Toward the end of the twentieth century in the United States, there was a renewed interest in Sicilian cooking. Among New York City eateries known for their authentic Sicilian dishes are three in the borough of Brooklyn: Joe's on Avenue U, Ferdinando's on Union Street, and Gino's in the Bensonhurst neighborhood. Sicilians' most enduring contribution to American cuisine may be the *sfinciuni* (*sfincione* in Italian). This is a deep-dish square pizza pie whose basic toppings are onion, tomato sauce, bread crumbs, and sometimes anchovies.

Traditional Dress The traditional costumes of Sicilian women consist of dimity bodices, red and dark-blue (or white and dark-blue) striped skirts of home-woven cloth, striped aprons, calfskin slippers with pointed toes, dark-blue stockings, and kerchiefs of cotton wrapped around the neck and bosom. Men wear white cotton hose, home-woven cloth shirts with wide collars, heavy shoes, and a wide-brimmed hat made out of palm leaves. The festival dress of women consists of a dark-blue velvet bodice, a silk skirt, dark-blue stockings, a white twill mantlet, striped leather shoes with ties of black ribbon in the front, a silver hair clasp, filigree drop earrings, numerous finger rings, and necklaces of coral and amber. The men wear a dark-blue velvet suit, a white cotton cap, a red cotton sash, and two handkerchiefs of red, yellow, or green. Sicilian Americans do not dress traditionally anymore except at special events such as heritage parades.

Dances and Songs Sicilians have many unique songs, the majority of which celebrate agricultural and religious themes. For instance, during the olive harvest or grape gathering, certain songs would be sung for each stage of the harvesting process. Many of the folk songs are mournful, haunting melodies, but others are quite ribald. Traditional instruments include bagpipes, reed flutes, drums, and wind instruments. Several songs combine dancing and singing, such as the "Aria of the Fasola," in which a man and woman sing to each other. Some of the traditional dances include the *nail, polyp, tarascon, capona,* and *fasola.* Sicilian dances and songs were a vibrant part of the entertainment found in the communities of the first Sicilian immigrants, but they were gradually replaced with more Americanized forms of entertainment, such as movies. However, traditional Sicilian songs and dances can still be heard and seen at celebrations and special occasions, especially wedding receptions.

Holidays Along with traditional Catholic and American holidays such as Christmas, New Year's, and Easter, Sicilian Americans have traditionally celebrated several feast days. Sicilian immigrants brought with them their *feste,* which honor the patron saints of the various villages they had left. The *feste* were

Sicilian American Lady Gaga has rocketed to unprecedented popularity around the world. ZUMA PRESS, INC / ALAMY

not only celebratory, but they also reinforced the ties the immigrants still had to their native villages. Immigrants from Palermo honored Saint Rosalia, those from Catania honored Saint Agatha, and still others honored Saint Gandolfo, Saint Joseph, and Saint Anthony. Lavish processions complete with parades, fireworks, and traditional Sicilian songs and dances characterized the *feste.* The festivals were not, however, limited to honoring of the patron saints of Sicilian villages. Immigrants from Palermo continued the practice of honoring Madonna del Lume (Holy Mother of Light) in San Francisco; a procession would lead down to the Fisherman's Wharf for the ancient Blessing of the Fishing Fleet, after which celebrations with music and dancing would take place. The *feste* celebrations of the Sicilian Americans continue to take place and are equally lavish, if not more so. Many celebrations, such as the annual *feste* honoring St. Joseph in New Orleans, are attended by Sicilians and non-Sicilians alike.

Health Care Issues and Practices Sicilians have not been prone to any particular health problems,

SICILIAN PROVERBS

A cani tintu catina curta.

> To bad dogs, a short chain is given.

Cu gaddu e senza gaddu, diu fa journa.

> With a rooster or without a rooster, God will still make the dawn.

Non essiri duci sinno tu mancianu, non essiri amaru sinno ti futanu.

> Do not be too sweet lest you be eaten, do not be too sour lest you be shunned.

I palori nimici fannu ridiri chiddi di l'amici fanni chianciri.

> The words of your enemies can make you laugh, but those of a friend can make you cry.

Nenti mi ratta a manu comu i me unga.

> Nothing scratches my hand like my own nails.

Nun si po' aviri la carni senz' ossu.

> You can't have meat without the bone.

Cu mancia fa muddichi.

> A person eating must make crumbs.

U pesci fet d'a testa.

> A fish starts smelling bad from the head.

though illnesses did occur during early immigration. Accustomed to the mild climate and open spaces of Sicily, immigrants fared badly among the crowded conditions of city tenements. The closeness of their living spaces and lack of fresh air was both mentally and physically harmful. Many Sicilians suffered from depression or were victims of the various diseases that swept through entire city blocks of tenements. Sicilians were especially vulnerable to tuberculosis, and many returned to Sicily gravely ill. During the mass migration, so many immigrants returned to Sicily to die that several villages set up sanitariums to receive them. As they began to move out of the tenements, later generations of Sicilian Americans were no longer exposed to the conditions that bred disease.

Death and Burial Rituals After a death in a Sicilian American family, there is an outpouring of food, flowers, and money from friends and relatives. Even distant kin are expected to pay respects. During the wake, which can last up to four days, the casket is left open, and the mourners can kneel and

say a prayer. At the funeral, relatives are arranged in order of how close they were to the deceased, and afterward a procession goes to the cemetery. Sicilian American funerals have come to incorporate American traditions such as shortening the duration of the wake. In general, however, they tend to be more openly emotional and elaborate than other American funerals.

FAMILY AND COMMUNITY LIFE

In Sicily the family was a strong defense against the desperate and unrelieved poverty that characterized life. Each family member contributed to the all-encompassing and often heartbreaking effort to survive. First loyalties were reserved for the closest kin (*casa*). This was an economic necessity, as each family competed with other families for survival.

A new emphasis was placed on extended relatives during the immigration process. Although the economic competition in Sicily fostered less of a sense of cooperation beyond the *casa*, a distinction was generally made for a second tier of kin (*parenti*), which played a peripheral role. During the immigration process, however, the *parenti* increased in importance, in many cases becoming the first link in a migration chain. The *parenti* provided much-needed emotional and financial support, eventually commanding almost as much loyalty as the *casa*.

Gender Roles Resolutely patriarchal, the traditional Sicilian family deferred to the father on every decision. However, the mother's role was also important; while she did not possess an equal share of authority, she was responsible for running the household. Children were expected to share in household duties from an early age.

Sicilian immigrants carried with them fixed rules concerning women's roles. Fathers perceived a fierce obligation to guard the chastity of their daughters, and when the daughters were old enough to marry, they were then protected and dominated by their husbands. Wives and daughters stayed strictly within the boundaries of running the household and did not work outside of the home. Such a system could not be maintained in the United States. When it was possible, wives continued to work in the house, and their daughters helped them cook, clean, and care for the younger children, but many women, even those who were unmarried, were forced by sheer economic necessity to seek jobs. They worked in factories and in the garment industry, and in the south, they labored in the fields alongside the men.

The old patriarchal system was obviously at odds with the new expectations of and roles for women. Fathers were unable to supervise the activities of their daughters in the manner to which they had been accustomed. At school, daughters learned "American ways" that were considered, by Sicilian standards, unsuitable and compromising to their chastity. In increasing numbers Sicilian daughters desired an education beyond the household arts. The men were not in the habit of considering formal education to be important for females, and they resisted. Gradually, however, the role of the Sicilian American woman underwent a revision. Like many women in America, Sicilian females now demand educational and career opportunities. Among today's Sicilian Americans, traditional family values have receded into history. Nevertheless, *la famiglia* continues to play an important role in the lives of Sicilian Americans.

Education In agriculture-based Sicily, basic survival was of primary importance, and children were expected to start contributing from an early age. If a child was studying in school rather than working in the fields, a family's well-being would be jeopardized, so a formal education was not highly valued. In addition, schools were not easily accessible to the majority of Sicilians; only the wealthy were able to take advantage of the limited opportunities. Consequently, there was a high illiteracy rate among agricultural workers in Sicily, which remained true as late as the twenty-first century.

Because the first Sicilian immigrants were primarily agricultural workers, formal education continued to be a low priority. Sicilian immigrants were also wary of the values being taught to their children in the schools. Children frequently had part-time jobs in addition to their schoolwork, which lessened their chances of success in an educational setting. Their limited education translated into limited economic opportunities, creating a web of poverty.

After World War II, however, the children and grandchildren of these immigrants became largely cognizant of the need for education. Second and third generation Sicilian Americans were acclimated to the extent that they no longer felt threatened or intimidated by American schools, and they utilized the G.I. Bill to pursue their educations. Like many other Americans today, Sicilian Americans strive to provide their children with college educations.

Weddings The importance of weddings has not diminished among latter generations of Sicilian Americans. As an extension of Sicilian Americans' religious faith, weddings are observed in the manner of Roman Catholicism. They also tend to be lavish and expensive. The majority of the expenses fall on the daughter's family, but in view of the rising costs of weddings, the financial burden is, in some instances, now distributed more evenly. Nevertheless, because of the importance placed on weddings, it is not considered inappropriate for a family to go into debt to pay for one. The celebration begins early, as the bride is given several pre-wedding showers, at which she receives gifts and money. Male friends and relatives of the groom throw him stag parties. The wedding itself is generally an all-day celebration, culminating with a large reception. Some of today's Sicilian Americans, however, have pared down the guest lists.

Baptisms Like weddings, baptisms are extremely special to Sicilian Americans. The godparents are chosen carefully, for that role represents a substantial investment of time and money. The baptism is performed as soon after the birth as possible; traditionally, an unbaptized baby was thought to be susceptible to the devil. The godparents furnish the clothing the baby wears during the ceremony. In the more traditional ceremonies, a religious medal is sometimes included to ward off the "evil eye." After the ceremony, a party takes place that generally lasts until evening.

EMPLOYMENT AND ECONOMIC CONDITIONS

Because the first Sicilian immigrants generally were unskilled laborers, the jobs they found in the United States were of the lowest sort. They worked in factories and on the railroads, operated pushcarts, dug tunnels, labored at construction sites, unloaded ships' cargo on the docks, and cleaned streets. Sicilians in New Orleans worked in the sugarcane fields, while those in San Francisco and Boston gravitated toward the waterfront, where they were in the fishing trade. Sicilian women worked mainly in the garment industry, in factories, or alongside their husbands in the fields. Only a fortunate few men had been artisans in Sicily, and they fared much better. Skilled laborers were able to find jobs as carpenters, masons, bakers, and plumbers.

In many ways, early Sicilian immigrants were exploited, sometimes even before they left their native land. A type of labor recruitment system evolved in which a *padrone* (a fellow Sicilian who operated as a middle man between immigrants and American bosses) lured Sicilian men to the United States with the promise of paid passage and a guaranteed job. *Padrones* were paid handsomely for providing American companies with large numbers of employees, but the Sicilians they recruited were charged high interest for the "loan" of their passage money and were treated as slaves by their new employers.

The road to financial security was long and difficult. Since many families hovered near the poverty level, their children had to leave school early in order to supplement their parents' income. As there was no chance of learning a trade, children, like their parents, were unable to rise above the status of unskilled laborer. There were exceptions, however, such as Vincenzo La Rosa, who founded the La Rosa Macaroni Company in Brooklyn in 1914. Likewise, Salvador Oteri built a successful wholesale fruit business based in New Orleans, and Giuseppe Cacioppo founded New York's Grandview Dairy, Inc. in 1901. All three men amassed millions of dollars. Nevertheless, the majority of the Sicilians found it difficult to break out of the cycle of poverty, a problem that was exacerbated by the Great

Depression. Like other Americans, however, Sicilians benefited from the economic prosperity following World War II. Third and fourth generation Sicilian Americans are represented in virtually every professional field, including medicine, law, higher education, and business.

POLITICS AND GOVERNMENT

Many of the first Sicilian immigrants expected to return to Sicily after they had earned an appropriate amount of money. While the naturalization rate was low for Italians in general, it was even lower for Sicilians, who cared little about American politics or governmental policies and were more inclined to stay abreast of developments in their native country. Many of these immigrants had been active members of the Fasci movement and were well acquainted with political activity.

Ultimately, it was the type of work Sicilians found in the United States that brought them to the political forefront with their push toward organized labor. They grew heavily involved in the struggle for labor unions, and some became associated with anarchists and other extreme-left movements. However, unsafe working conditions, low pay, and long hours had begun to take a toll on American workers long before the Sicilian mass immigration began. The rapidly expanding capitalist economy in the early twentieth century further widened the gap between American "bosses" and workers. America was ripe for union activity, but the efforts thus far had proved ineffectual. As the initial success of the *Fasci Siciliano* had proved, Sicilians were adept at organizing workers. Sicilian immigrants brought this knowledge with them to America at precisely the time when organized labor was ready to utilize their experience.

Two disruptive strikes by dress and coat makers in New York City in 1909 and 1910 were led by Salvatore Ninfo, a Sicilian immigrant and a key figure in the International Ladies Garment Workers' Union. Ninfo was one among several labor activists of Sicilian heritage who was triumphant on this front. Other Sicilians agitated for safer working conditions and shorter hours for their work digging subway tunnels in New York City. Giovanni Vaccaro led a series of successful cigar-factory strikes in Tampa, Florida, between 1910 and 1920. The Clothing Workers of America Union organized similar strikes, including a big one in 1919 that was led in great part by Antonio "Nino" Capraro. Sicilian American women also contributed to the push for organized labor, namely Capraro's wife, Maria Bambache Capraro, who played a vital role in the needle workers' strike in 1919.

As naturalization rates increased, Sicilian Americans began to switch from radical union activity to formal politics. During the 1920s and 1930s, Sicilians voted primarily Democratic. In addition, they began to send Sicilian Americans into office, including the first Italian representative to Congress,

Vincent Palmisano (1882–1953), a Democrat from Maryland. Sicilians have since then been elected to most offices on the local, state, and national levels. In 1986 President Ronald Reagan appointed Antonin Scalia, the son of a Sicilian-immigrant father, to the U.S. Supreme Court, a powerful symbol of the acceptance of Sicilian Americans into the political mainstream. Sonny Bono (1935–1998), whose father was born in Sicily, first gained fame on the CBS television variety show *Sonny & Cher* and was elected mayor of Palm Springs, California, in 1988. Six years later he was elected to the U.S. House of Representatives from California's 44th Congressional district. Bono died in a skiing accident during his second term in Congress.

NOTABLE INDIVIDUALS

Academia Pietro Bachi (1787–1853) was Sicilian-born and the first Italian language instructor at Harvard University, with his tenure commencing in 1825. Bachi also wrote several books on the Italian, Spanish, and Portuguese languages, including *A Grammar of the Italian Language* (1829).

Like Bachi, Luigi Monti (1830–1914) taught Italian at Harvard and contributed to the academic world with written works, such as *A Grammar of the Italian Language* (1855). He later became the American consul at Palermo, where he wrote about his experiences in his book *Adventures of a Consul Abroad* (1878).

Josephine Gattuso Hendin (1944–) became a professor of American literature at New York University. Her books *The World Around Flannery O'Connor* (1970) and *Vulnerable People: A View of American Fiction Since 1945* (1978) were highly lauded. She later published *The Right Thing to Do* (1988), which draws heavily on her experiences of growing up in a Sicilian household.

Stage and Screen Director Frank Capra (1897–1991) is best known for nostalgic, optimistic movies such as *It Happened One Night* (1934), *Mr. Deeds Goes to Town* (1936), *You Can't Take It With You* (1938), *Mr. Smith Goes to Washington* (1939), *Arsenic and Old Lace* (1944), and *It's a Wonderful Life* (1947). Capra won three Oscars for Best Director, as well as one for Best Documentary for his propaganda series *Why We Fight* (1942).

Martin Scorsese (1942–), another director, was born to a Sicilian American father and an Italian American mother. He reached iconic status after making gritty dramas such as *Taxi Driver* (1976), *Raging Bull* (1980), and *Goodfellas* (1990). His 2006 film *The Departed* earned him the Oscar for Best Director.

Cartoonist Joseph Barbera (1911–2006) cofounded one of television's most successful animation studios with William Hanna. Hanna-Barbera produced *The Flintstones* and *Scooby-Doo* franchises and later became part of the Cartoon Network.

Actor Al Pacino (1940–) has earned much critical acclaim, notably for his performances in *The Godfather*

(1972) and *The Godfather Part II* (1974), films about a Sicilian American Mafia family for which he received Oscar nominations. He was also nominated for his roles in *Justice for All* (1979), *Dick Tracy* (1990), and *Glengarry Glen Ross* (1992). He won the Oscar for Best Actor for his work in *Scent of a Woman* (1992).

Actor-screenwriter Sylvester Stallone (1946–) first gained fame with *Rocky* (1976), the story of an underdog prizefighter that became the basis for several successful sequels.

Sibling actors Aida Turturro (1962–) and John Turturro (1957–) are known, respectively, for their roles in the hit HBO series *The Sopranos* (1999–2007) and films by Spike Lee and the Coen Brothers.

Character actor Vincent Schiavelli (1948–2005) appeared in scores of notable films, including *One Flew Over the Cuckoo's Nest* (1975) and *Ghost* (1990). He wrote two books about his Sicilian heritage, *Bruculinu, America: Remembrances of Sicilian-American Brooklyn* (1998) and *Many Beautiful Things: Stories and Recipes from Polizzi Generosa* (2002).

Ben Gazzara (1930–2012) was an actor who appeared in films such as *The Strange One* (1957), *Anatomy of a Murder* (1949), and *Husbands* (1970), as well as the television series *Arrest and Trial* (1963–1964) and *Run for Your Life* (1965–1968).

Music Frank Sinatra (1915–1998) is among the most famous entertainment figures in American history. He recorded more than 800 songs, including "I'm Walking Behind You" (1953), "I've Got the World on a String" (1953), "From Here to Eternity" (1953), "Learnin' the Blues" (1955), "Chicago" (1957), "Witchcraft" (1957), and "Nice 'N' Easy" (1960). In the 1940s, he also began to appear in motion pictures and was soon commanding starring roles. His film credits include *Anchors Aweigh* (1945), *On the Town* (1949), and *From Here to Eternity* (1953), for which he won the Oscar for Best Supporting Actor. Sinatra was the recipient of numerous honors, notably a lifetime achievement designation by the Kennedy Center Honors in 1983 and the Presidential Medal of Freedom in 1985.

Nick LaRocca (1889–1961) contributed to the emergence of jazz. He was an inspired cornet player and founded the original Dixieland Jazz Band. "Livery Stable Blues" (1917) and "Tiger Rag" (1917) are two of his better-known songs.

Natalie Merchant (1963–) achieved international success as the lead singer in the band 10,000 Maniacs. In 1995 Merchant launched a successful solo career with her album *Tigerlily*. She continued to release solo albums into the twenty-first century.

Singer-songwriter Lady Gaga (1986–) was born Stefani Germanotta and attended Roman Catholic schools in New York City before becoming a superstar, starting with her album *The Fame* (2008).

Sports Boxer Tony Canzonerie (1908–1959) held the featherweight (1928), lightweight (1930–1933, 1935–1936), and junior welterweight (1931–1932, 1933) world championships and is considered one of the most fearless, aggressive fighters of all time. He was elected to the International Boxing Hall of Fame in 1956.

Joe DiMaggio (1914–1999), who played for the New York Yankees from 1936 to 1951 and was known as the "Yankee Clipper," is one of the most beloved baseball players in the history of the sport. Among his many achievements, he set a record in 1941 with a 56-game hitting streak, won three American League Most Valuable Player awards, and was voted into the National Baseball Hall of Fame in 1955.

MEDIA

Numerous Sicilian-oriented newspapers and radio broadcasts existed during the years of the Sicilian mass immigration. However, as the assimilation of Sicilians into American culture became more complete, these sources gradually disappeared. While there are currently no newspapers or radio shows specifically targeted to Sicilian American audiences, the internet has allowed a growing number of interested Sicilian Americans to access the Sicilian newspapers and live-stream Sicilian radio. The Palermo daily newspaper *Giornale di Sicilia* (www.gds.it) and PrimaRadio Sicilia (www.primaradio.net) are examples of each.

ORGANIZATIONS AND ASSOCIATIONS

Arba Sicula (AS)

Founded in 1979, AS focuses on the promotion and preservation of the Sicilian language and Sicilian literature, and culture. It publishes a biannual journal of Sicilian arts and history, *Arba Sicula* (translated as "Sicilian Dawn") and the biannual newsletter *Sicilia Parra*. Arba Sicula also sponsors Sicilian language festivals, organizes cultural events in the New York City area, and conducts an annual tour of Sicily.

Dr. Gaetano Cipolla, President
Languages and Literatures Department
St. John's University
Jamaica, New York 11439
Phone: (718) 990-5203
Email: cipollag@stjohns.edu
URL: http://arbasicula.org

National Sicilian American Foundation

This organization was founded in 1997 to promote Sicilian heritage and culture in America, and forge ties with Sicily.

Joe Lucchesi, President
P.O. Box 503
Santa Clara, California 95052
URL: http://nsaf.net

La Confederazione Siciliani Nord America/Sicilian Confederation of North America

Founded in 2007, it strengthens ties among Sicilian-heritage groups in the United States and Canada through an annual convention.

Gerry Puccio, President
777 Lonesome Dove Trail
Hurst, Texas 76054
URL: http://csna2012.org

Order Sons of Italy (OSIA)

The Order Sons of Italy, established in 1905, focuses on the preservation of the cultural heritage of Italian Americans, including those of Sicilian ancestry. It maintains cultural ties to Italy, offers scholarships, publishes the *Italian America* magazine, and operates an antidefamation arm called the Commission for Social Justice.

Joseph J. DiTrapani, National President
219 East Street NE
Washington, D.C. 20002
Phone: (202) 547-2900
Fax: (202) 546-8168
URL: www.osia.org

National Italian American Foundation (NIAF)

An organization dedicated to protecting and preserving the Italian American heritage and culture, and to strengthening the ties between the United States and Italy.

Joseph V. Del Raso, President
1860 19th Street NW
Washington, D.C. 20009
Phone: (202) 387-0600
Fax: (202) 387-0800
Email: information@niaf.org
URL: www.niaf.org

MUSEUMS AND RESEARCH CENTERS

Balch Institute for Ethnic Studies at the Historical Society of Pennsylvania

The center houses a formidable library containing valuable information and resources on multicultural groups in the United States, including Sicilian Americans.

Lee Arnold, Senior Director
1300 Locust Street
Philadelphia, Pennsylvania 19107
Phone: (215) 732-6200
Fax: (215) 732-2680
URL: http://hsp.org/about-us/the-balch-institute

The Center for Migration Studies (CMS)

A New York City-based educational institute originally founded in 1964 by members of a Roman Catholic religious order, the Congregation of the Missionaries of St. Charles-Scalabrinians, whose focus was on helping Italian Americans remain faithful to the religion. The Scalabrinian Fathers and Brothers eventually directed their energies toward serving immigrant communities. The CMS works to track migration data, promote tolerance, and safeguard social-justice rights. It publishes the scholarly journal *International Migration Review*.

Donald M. Kerwin, Jr., Executive Director
27 Carmine Street
New York, New York 10014
Phone: (212) 337-3080
Fax: (646) 998-4625
Email: cms@cmsny.org
URL: http://cmsny.org/

Immigration History Research Center (IHRC)

Located at the University of Minnesota, the IHRC is a valuable archival source for Sicilian Americans. The collection includes newspapers, books, and manuscripts.

Erika Lee, Director
311 Elmer L. Andersen Library
222 21st Avenue South
Minneapolis, Minnesota 55455
Phone: (612) 625-4800
Fax: (612) 626-0018
Email: ihrc@umn.edu
URL: www.ihrc.umn.edu

SOURCES FOR ADDITIONAL STUDY

Gabaccia, Donna. *From Sicily to Elizabeth Street*. Albany: State University of New York Press, 1984.

———. *Militants and Migrants: Rural Sicilians Become American Workers*. New Brunswick, NJ: Rutgers University Press, 1988.

Johnson, Colleen Leahy. *Growing Up and Growing Old in Italian-American Families*. Rutgers University Press, 1985.

Mangione, Jerre, and Ben Morriale. *La Storia: Five Centuries of the Italian American Experience*. New York: HarperCollins, 1992.

Mazzucchelli, Chiara. *"Heart of My Race": Questions of Identity in Sicilian/American Writings*. Boca Raton: Florida Atlantic University, 2007.

Salomone-Marino, Salvatore. *Customs and Habits of the Sicilian Peasants*, Translated by Rosalie Norris. London: Associated University Presses, 1981.

Raab, Selwyn. *Five Families: The Rise, Decline, and Resurgence of America's Most Powerful Mafia Empires*. New York: Thomas Dunne/St. Martin's Press, 2005.

Sammartino, Peter, and William Roberts. *Sicily: An Informal History*. New York: Cornwall, 1992.

Schiavelli, Vincent. *Bruculinu, America: Remembrances of Sicilian-American Brooklyn*. New York: Houghton Mifflin, 1998.

SIERRA LEONEAN AMERICANS

Francesca Hampton

OVERVIEW

Sierra Leonean Americans are immigrants or descendants of people from the West African country of Sierra Leone. Located on what was once called the "Rice Coast" of West Africa, Sierra Leone is bordered by the Atlantic Ocean to the west, Guinea to the north and east, and Liberia to the south. Its inland areas include heavy rain forest, swamp, plains of open savanna, and hill country, rising to 6,390 feet at Loma Mansa (Bintimani) in the Loma Mountains. The country is sometimes called "Salone" by Sierra Leonean immigrants. At 27,699 square miles (71,740 square kilometers), it is slightly smaller than the state of Maine.

The *CIA World Factbook* estimated the population of Sierra Leone to be 5,485,998 in 2012. About 60 percent were Muslim, 10 percent were Christian, and 30 percent held indigenous beliefs, though other sources list higher numbers of Christians. Sierra Leoneans often practice more than one religion or combine religions. The country includes the homelands of twenty African peoples, including the Mende, Lokko, Temne, Limba, Susu, Yalunka, Sherbro, Bullom, Krim, Koranko, Kono, Vai, Kisi, Gola, and Fula. The Temne (35 percent) and Mende (31 percent) make up the majority of the country's population. Sierra Leone's capital, Freetown, was founded as a refuge for former slaves, known as Krio (also spelled Kriole or Creole), repatriated by the British in the eighteenth century. These Krio make up about 2 percent of the Sierra Leonean population. The country also has small numbers of Europeans, Syrians, Lebanese, Pakistanis, and Indians. Sierra Leone is a very poor country with large income inequality, yet it is rich in natural resources, including large diamond reserves. Its progress into the twenty-first century was severely hampered by a civil war (1989–2002).

The first Sierra Leoneans in the United States arrived between 1750 and 1800 on slave ships traveling from Bance (or Bunce) Island in the Sierra Leone River to Charleston, South Carolina. They were then enslaved by rice plantation owners in the Carolinas and Georgia. Immigration from Sierra Leone was not again recorded until 1961. In the 1970s and 1980s Sierra Leoneans moved to the United States largely to access higher education. Over the following decades most immigrants from Sierra Leone were educated

and immigrated to escape the danger of civil war and its devastating effects on the country's economy.

According to the U.S. Census, 16,343 people of Sierra Leonean descent lived in the United States in 2010. Of these, about 4,800 were born in the United States and some two-thirds were American citizens. About 5,700 entered the United States after 2000. According to the 2010 American Community Survey, the majority of Sierra Leoneans who immigrated to the United States in the first decade of the twenty-first century settled in New York, Pennsylvania, Maryland, and Virginia. Unofficial estimates from the Sierra Leonean newspaper *Cocorioko* and the United Brothers and Sisters of Sierra Leone report that other states with significant Sierra Leonean Americans include Massachusetts, California, New Jersey, and Ohio. In 2006 Congress designated an area along the southeastern coast of the United States—from the northern border of Pender County, North Carolina, to the southern border of St. Johns County, Florida, and 30 miles inland, including seventy-nine barrier islands—as the Gullah Geechee Cultural Heritage Corridor. An estimated 250,000 Gullah, or (in Georgia) Geechee, people lived in the corridor and trace at least part of their heritage to West Africa's Rice Coast.

HISTORY OF THE PEOPLE

Early History Scholars and archaeologists believe there have been people living in the region that is today Sierra Leone for at least 2,500 years. The Bullom (or Sherbro), Limba, and Kisi are among the oldest nonmigratory groups found in Sierra Leone. However, Sierra Leone was on the fringes of the great West African empires of the Mandingo (or Malinka) and Songhai to the north and east and Benin to the south. Historians believe that early migrations and invasions gave the country a diverse ethnic population. The breakup of the Malinka Empire in the later fourteenth century pushed largely Muslim groups into Sierra Leone from the north and east. The Mende, Kono, and Vai tribes of today are believed to be descended from invaders who pushed up from the south.

The name *Sierra Leone* derives from the term *Sierra Lyoa*, or "Lion Mountain," given to the land in 1462 by Portuguese explorer Pedro Da Cinta when he observed its wild and forbidding hills. Within Sierra

Leone the Portuguese constructed the first fortified trading stations on the African coast. Like the French, Dutch, and Brandenburgers, they began to trade manufactured goods, rum, tobacco, arms, and ammunition for ivory, gold, and slaves.

In the early part of the sixteenth century, the area was invaded repeatedly by the Temne. Like the Kisi, the Temne are a Bantu people who speak a language related to Swahili. They moved south from Guinea after the breakup of the Songhai Empire. Led by Bai Farama, the Temne attacked the Susus Limba, and Mende, as well as the Portuguese, and created a strong state along the trade route from Port Loko to the Sudan and Niger. They sold many of these conquered peoples to the Europeans as slaves. In the late sixteenth century the Susus, who were converting to Islam, revolted against the Christian Temne and set up their own state on the Scarcies River. From there they dominated the Temne, converting many of them to Islam. Another Islamic theocratic state in the northwest was established by the Fula, who often attacked and enslaved nonbelievers among the Yalunka.

Taking advantage of the warfare, British slavers arrived on the Sierra Leone River during the late sixteenth century and built factories and forts on Sherbro, Bunce, and Tasso islands. These islands were often the last view that Sierra Leoneans had of their native land before being sent into slavery in the Americas. European slave agents hired African and mulatto mercenaries to help them capture villagers or purchase them as debtors or prisoners of war from local chiefs. Relations between these groups were not always friendly. In 1562 Temne warriors reneged on a deal with a European slave trader and drove him away with a fleet of war canoes.

As controversy over the ethics of the slave trade arose in Britain, the English abolitionist Granville Sharp convinced the British government to repatriate a group of freed slaves onto land purchased from Temne chiefs on the Sierra Leone peninsula. In May 1787 these first settlers arrived in what would become the capital of Sierra Leone, Freetown. In 1792 they were joined by 1200 freed American slaves who had fought with the British army in the American Revolutionary War. Unhappy with the land they had been offered in Nova Scotia at the war's conclusion, these black loyalists sent ex-slave Thomas Peters on a protest mission to Britain. The Sierra Leone Company, now in charge of the new colony, helped them return to Africa.

The arrival of these ex-slaves marked the beginning of a culture uniquely influential in West Africa called Creole, or Krio. Along with a steady influx of native Sierra Leoneans from the interior tribes, more than eighty thousand other Africans displaced by the slave trade joined those in Freetown during the next century. In 1807 the British Parliament voted to end the slave trade, and Freetown soon became a crown colony and an enforcement port. British naval vessels based there upheld the ban on slave trading and captured numerous outbound slavers. The Africans released from the holds of slave ships were settled in Freetown and in nearby villages. Within a few decades this new Krio society, who were English- and Creole-speaking, educated, and predominantly Christian, with a subgroup of Yoruba Muslims, began to influence the whole coast and even the interior of West Africa as they became teachers, missionaries, traders, administrators, and artisans. By the middle of the nineteenth century, according to the *Encyclopedia of Africa South of the Sahara* (1999), they had formed "the nucleus of the bourgeoisie of late nineteenth-century coastal British West Africa."

Sierra Leone gradually gained its independence from Britain. Beginning in 1863, native Sierra Leoneans were given representation in the government of Freetown. Limited free elections were held in the city in 1895. Sixty years later the right to vote was extended to the interior, where many tribes had long traditions of participatory decision making. Full independence was granted to Sierra Leone in 1961. As a new tradition of elective democratic government became firmly established throughout the country, interior tribes such as the Mende, Temne, and Limba gradually regained a dominant position in politics.

Modern Era Sierra Leone's first years as an independent democracy were very successful, thanks to the benevolent leadership of the first prime minister, Sir Milton Magai, a member of the Evangelical United Brethren Church who was born in southern Sierra Leone to Mende parents. He encouraged a free press and honest debate in Parliament and welcomed nationwide participation in the political process. When Magai died in 1964 he was succeeded by his half-brother, Albert Magai, head of the Sierra Leone People's Party (SLPP). Attempting to establish a one-party state and accused of corruption, the SLPP lost the next election in 1967 to an opposition party, the All People's Congress (APC), led by Siaka Stevens. Stevens was unseated briefly by a military coup but returned to power in 1968, this time with the title of president. Although popular in his first years in power, Stevens lost much influence in the latter years of his regime through his government's reputation for corruption and the use of intimidation to stay in power. Stevens was succeeded in 1986 by his handpicked successor, Major General Joseph Saidu Momoh, who worked to liberalize the political system, restore the faltering economy, and return Sierra Leone to a multiparty democracy. Unfortunately, events on the border with Liberia in 1991 crushed Momoh's efforts and ushered in more than a decade of brutal civil war.

Allied with the Liberian forces of Charles Taylor's Patriotic Front, a small group of Sierra Leonean rebels calling themselves the Revolutionary United Front (RUF) crossed the Liberian border into Sierra Leone in 1991. Distracted by this rebellion, Momoh's

APC party was overthrown in a military coup led by Valentine Strasser, leader of the National Provisional Ruling Council (NPRC). Under Strasser's rule some members of the Sierra Leonean army began to loot villages. Large numbers of villagers died of starvation because the economy was disrupted. As the army's organization weakened, the RUF advanced. By 1995 it was on the outskirts of Freetown. In a frantic attempt to hold onto power, the NPRC hired a South African mercenary firm, Executive Outcomes, to reinforce the army. The RUF suffered significant losses and were forced to retreat to their base camp.

Strasser was eventually overthrown by his deputy, Julius Bio, who held long-promised democratic elections. In 1996 the people of Sierra Leone chose their first freely elected leader in three decades, President Ahmad Tejan Kabbah. Kabbah was able to negotiate a peace agreement with the RUF rebels, but the results were short-lived. Another coup rocked the country, and Kabbah was overthrown by a faction of the army calling itself the Armed Forces Revolutionary Council (AFRC). The AFRC suspended the constitution and arrested, killed, or tortured those who resisted. Diplomats throughout Sierra Leone fled the country. Many Sierra Leonean citizens launched a campaign of passive resistance to the AFRC. The brutal stalemate was broken when troops from Nigeria, Guinea, Ghana, and Mali, part of the Economic Council of West African States Monitoring Group (ECOMOG), routed the AFRC and restored Kabbah to power in 1998.

Although the AFRC was defeated, the RUF remained a destructive force. It embarked on a campaign of renewed terror called "No Living Thing." According to testimony reprinted on the *ReliefWeb* website on June 11, 1998 ("Humanitarian Crisis Looming over Sierra Leone: U.S. Amb. Carson Details U.S. Assistance and Policy"), Ambassador Johnnie Carson told the U.S. House of Representatives Subcommittee on Africa, "The RUF threw [a five-year-old boy who survived] and sixty other villagers into a human bonfire. Hundreds of civilians have escaped to Freetown with arms, feet, hands, and ears amputated by the rebels." The ambassador also reported that the RUF forced children to participate in the torture and killing of their parents before being drafted as soldier trainees. After several failed peace agreements, the war officially ended on July 28, 2002.

The role of Sierra Leone's abundant diamond mines in the civil war is both documented and disputed. While many have argued that control of the mines was a cause of the civil war, historians agree that diamond sales fueled the war, as diamonds were traded for weapons. Recovery from the war was slow but determined. Between one and two million Sierra Leoneans were internally displaced, and almost 300,000 sought refuge in Guinea, Liberia, or other countries, including the United States. The traditional, rice-farming villagers of the interior became more alienated from the better-educated, wealthier elite of Freetown. Ethnic hostilities between elements of the majority Mende, the Temne, and other groups, continued for another decade, and more than 17,000 foreign troops were used to disarm the many rebel groups.

The Sierra Leone Truth and Reconciliation Commission (SLTRC) gathered testimony throughout the country from 2002 to 2004, held hearings, issued recommendations, and continued to follow up with hope that it will "not only expose perpetrators and identify victims but also [serve] as a mirror through which all Sierra Leoneans can examine their own roles in the conflict." The United Nations and the Sierra Leone government also established, in 2002, the Special Court for Sierra Leone in which to try any persons who committed war crimes and crimes against humanity. On April 26, 2012, former Liberian President Charles Taylor was convicted by the court of crimes against humanity and sentenced to fifty years in prison.

By 2010 Sierra Leone was showing strong signs of stability, if not growth. The UN Security Council lifted the remaining sanctions against Sierra Leone, saying the government had fully reestablished control over its territory, and former rebel fighters had been disarmed and demobilized under the auspices of a professional national army. In 2012 Ernest Bai Koroma, an ethnic Temne, devout Christian, and insurance salesman, was elected to a second five-year term as president of Sierra Leone.

SETTLEMENT IN THE UNITED STATES

In the film *Family Across the Sea* (1991), anthropologist Joe Opala presented several proofs connecting Sierra Leone to a unique group of African Americans whose way of life centers on the coasts and Sea Islands of the Carolinas and Georgia. These are the Gullah, or Geechee, speakers, descendants of slaves imported from Barbados or directly from Africa to work rice plantations along the southeast coast of the United States beginning in the eighteenth century. Between 1701 and 1810 approximately 300,000 African slaves arrived on the shores of South Carolina. It is estimated that approximately 24 percent of slaves brought into the area came from Sierra Leone; they were prized by buyers in Charleston specifically for their skills as rice farmers. Opala has found letters establishing the facts of this regular commerce between South Carolina plantation owner Henry Lawrence and Richard Oswald, his English slave agent resident on Bunce Island in the Sierra Leone River.

Between 1787 and 1804 it was illegal to bring new slaves into the United States. However, a second infusion of 23,773 Africans arrived in South Carolina between 1804 and 1807 as new cotton plantations on the Sea Islands began to expand their need for labor and landowners petitioned the South Carolina legislature to reopen the trade. The importation of Africans was made permanently illegal in the United States in 1808, but Sierra Leoneans and other West Africans continued to be kidnapped or purchased by renegade slavers long after the ruling. The coastlines of South Carolina and Georgia, with their numerous rivers, islands, and swamps, provided secret landing sites for the underground sale of slaves. The fact that Sierra Leoneans were among these slaves is documented by the famous court case of the *Amistad*. In 1841 illegally captured members of the Mende, Temne, and other tribes managed to take control of their slave ship, the *Amistad*. When the *Amistad* eventually reached American waters, those on board were able to secure their freedom after the U.S. Supreme Court ruled in their favor.

Large numbers of Gullah-speaking American citizens, many of whom are of Sierra Leonean descent, continue to live in the Sea Islands and the coastal areas of South Carolina and Georgia. Some islands with significant populations are Hilton Head, St. Helena, and Wadmalaw. In the decades before the American Civil War, many Gullah-speaking slaves attempted to escape from their South Carolina and Georgian plantations. Of these, many went south, taking refuge with the Creek Indians in Florida. Along with the Creek and other embattled tribes, they created the society of the Seminoles and retreated deeper into the Florida swamps. Following the Second Seminole War, which lasted from 1835 to 1842, many Sierra Leoneans joined their Native American allies on the Trail of Tears, a forced march to Wewoka in Oklahoma territory. Others followed Wild Cat, the son of Seminole chief King Phillip, across the Rio Grande from Texas to a Seminole colony in Mexico. Still others remained in Florida and assimilated into Seminole culture.

There was no further Sierra Leonean immigration to the United States until the country gained independence in 1961. Beginning in about 1965, when U.S. immigration law changed from a country-by-country quota to an overall annual quota of 170,000, Sierra Leoneans began immigrating to the United States for education, with most returning home at the end of their studies to help build their new nation. In the 1970s and 1980s an increasing number of Sierra Leoneans entered the United States to escape the economic and political hardships in their homeland. While many continued to pursue their education, they also worked to help support family members at home. Although many of these students, also returned to Sierra Leone when they completed their schooling, others sought resident status so that they could continue to work in the United States.

By 1990, 4,627 American citizens and residents reported their first ancestry as Sierra Leonean. When civil war swept through Sierra Leone in the 1990s, a new wave of immigrants came to the United States. Many of these immigrants gained access through visitor or student visas. This trend continued between 1990 and 1996, as 7,159 more Sierra Leoneans legally entered the United States. After 1996 some refugees from Sierra Leone were able to enter the United States with immediate legal residence status as beneficiaries of immigration lotteries. Others received the newly established Priority 3 designation for refugees with close family links in the United States.

During the first decade of the twenty-first century, overall immigration from Africa dramatically increased. Of the 1.1 million black African immigrants from that decade, 3 percent, or 34,000, were from Sierra Leone. Another 75,000 came from Liberia and Guinea, the countries closest to Sierra Leone in West Africa. Between 2000 and 2010 a yearly average of 2,240 Sierra Leoneans were granted legal permanent resident status in the United States, with the highest in one year being 3,572 in 2006. About one-third of all of these immigrants already had immediate relatives living here. One-fourth or fewer were admitted each year between 2003 and 2012 as part of the Diversity Immigrant Visa (DV) program, which makes available 50,000 permanent resident visas annually to persons from countries with low rates of immigration to the United States. To be eligible for the DV lottery, prospective immigrants must have at least twelve years of formal schooling or two years' work experience in a field considered desirable in the United States. In 2010 about 2,000 Sierra Leoneans were granted permanent resident status; more than half had immediate relatives in the United States or were family sponsored, 415 won the DV Lottery, and 484 were granted refugee or asylee status.

Sierra Leonean academics and professionals are scattered all over the United States, but the vast majority live in areas where other Sierra Leonean immigrants have settled. According to the 2010 U.S. Census American Community Survey estimates of 2006–2010, there are over 16,343 Sierra Leoneans living in the United States. More than half (8,739) lived in Maryland and Virginia. The largest concentration of Sierra Leonean immigrants lives in the Baltimore–Washington, D.C. metropolitan area. Other sizable enclaves exist in the suburbs of Alexandria, Fairfax, Arlington, Falls Church, and Woodbridge in Virginia and in Landover, Lanham, Cheverly, Silver Spring, and Bethesda in Maryland. About 5,000 live in the Northeast in the states of New York and Pennsylvania. According to unofficial estimates from the Sierra Leonean newspaper *Cocorioko* and the United Brothers and Sisters of Sierra Leone, there are also significant Sierra Leonean American communities in the Boston and Los Angeles metropolitan areas, as well as in New Jersey and Ohio. There is also the Gullah/Geechee population in Georgia, North Carolina, South Carolina, and Florida.

LANGUAGE

Because of its long colonial association with Britain, English is one of the four official languages of Sierra Leone. Most Sierra Leonean Americans speak it as a

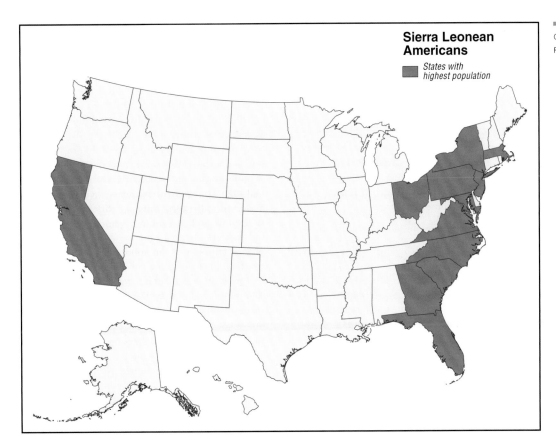

Sierra Leonean Americans

■ States with highest population

first or second language. The two main indigenous languages are Mende and Temne, each with many dialects. The Mende language group, which resembles Mandinka in structure, includes Mende, Susu, Yalunka, Koranko, Kono, and Vai. Mende is spoken by about 1.5 million people in the southern part of Sierra Leone, and about 600,000 more speak Mende as a second language. Most Mende speakers can also speak Krio but prefer Mende in informal situations. The Semi-Bantu language group includes Temne, Limba, Bullom (or Sherbro), and Krim. Temne has many dialects and is spoken by about 30 percent of Sierra Leoneans, mostly in the northern areas. The melodic Krio language is also widely spoken by Sierra Leonean Americans. Krio was created in Freetown from a blend of various European and African languages. With the exception of the passive voice, Krio utilizes a full complement of verb tenses. The grammar and pronunciation of Krio is similar to that of many African languages.

The language spoken by the Gullah/Geechee people of coastal South Carolina and Georgia is very similar to Krio. The Gullah language retains a great deal of West African syntax and combines English vocabulary with words from African languages such as Ewe, Mandinka, Igbo, Twi, Yoruba, and Mende. Much of the grammar and pronunciation

of the Gullah languages has been modified to fit African language patterns.

Greetings and Popular Expressions Gullah phrases, terms, and expressions include the following: *beat on ayun*—mechanic (literally, "beat on iron"); *troot ma-wt*—a truthful person (literally, "truth mouth"); *sho ded*—cemetery (literally, "sure dead"); *tebl tappa*—preacher (literally, "table tapper"); *ty ooonuh ma-wt*—hush, stop talking (literally, "tie your mouth"); *krak teet*—to speak (literally, "crack teeth"); and *I han shaht pay-shun*—he steals (literally, "his hand is short of patience").

Popular Krio expressions and terms include the following: *Ah tell god tanki*—I give thanks to God (literally, "I tell God thank you"); *pikin*—an infant (from picaninny, anglicized from the Spanish); *pequeno nino*—little child; *plabba* or *palaver*—trouble or the discussion of trouble (from the French word *palabre*); and *long rod no kil nobodi*—a long road kills no one.

RELIGION

The religious practices of both the Gullah/Geechee people and twentieth- and twenty-first century-immigrants from Sierra Leone were influenced by Christianity, Islam, and traditional West African practices. Evangelical Christianity, primarily Methodist

SIERRA LEONEAN PROVERBS

A rich variety of proverbs exist in the Sierra Leonean languages, and witty exchanges of proverbs are a conversational tradition. Krio, the most common language spoken by Sierra Leoneans, contains some of the most colorful proverbs:

Inch no in masta, kabasloht no in misis

> An implication knows its master (just as) a dress knows its mistress. (This proverb is used to warn people that you are aware they are speaking about you.)

Ogiri de laf kenda foh smehl

> Ogiri laughs at kenda on account of its smell. (Kenda and ogiri, when uncooked, are both rank-smelling seasonings.)

Mohnki tahk, mohnki yehri

> Monkey talks, monkey listens. (People who think alike will understand one another.)

We yu bohs mi yai, a chuk yu wes (Kono)

> An eye for an eye, a tooth for a tooth.

Bush noh de foh trwoe bad pikin

> Bad children may not be thrown into the bush. (No matter how bad a child may act, he can't be disowned by his family.)

> The Temne have their own witty proverbs, one example of which is "The snake that bites a Mende man gets turned into soup for the Mende man."

and Baptist beliefs, was very appealing to the enslaved Africans, particularly the ideal of millenarianism, which pointed out the corruption of current rulers and the evil of slavery and looked forward to dramatic change when the low would be brought high. The Old Testament drama of deliverance from slavery spoke directly to them. Calvinist and some Baptist preachers openly opposed slavery and promoted equality between the races and literacy and education for all people in order to attain a better understanding of God. In addition, Methodists and Baptists encouraged emotional expression of faith. Enslaved Africans worshiped together in one-room meeting places called praise houses. These small buildings became the center of the Gullah community. A West African practice that was translated into Christian practice is the Ring Shout (or Shouting), in which men and women form a circle and sing, clap their hands, and shuffle or stomp their feet in a fast-paced, rhythmic beat, reminiscent of ceremonial dances that were a part of African religious traditions.

In the twenty-first century, most Gullah/Geechee people are devout Christians whose spirituality is part of every aspect of their lives. Their Christian practices are still a fusion of West African traditions and their experience of slavery. One specifically African belief is the tripartite human being consisting of a body, a soul, and a spirit. When the body dies, the soul may go on to heaven while the spirit remains to influence the living. The Gullah traditionally believe the spirits of their ancestors participate in their daily affairs, protecting and guiding them and sometimes interceding for them. An essential element in all Sierra Leonean spiritual traditions is the respect and homage paid to ancestors. In the ongoing conflict between good and evil forces, ancestors can intervene to advise and help or to punish enemies. Evil human beings or deceased persons who were not correctly helped to "cross over" may return as harmful spirits. Sierra Leonean American immigrants retain these beliefs to varying degrees.

Among the slaves brought to Charleston from the Rice Coast were many Muslims, and the remnants of Islam can be found in the Gullah community in names and oral histories. From the colonial era through the antebellum era, the Sea Islands of Sapelo, St. Simons, and St. Helena hosted the largest community of African Muslims in North America. Despite some knowledge of their Muslim heritage, the Gullah/Geechee had lost most of their Islamic practices by the twentieth century.

Although 2012 population surveys provided no statistical information on the religion of Sierra Leonean Americans, religious institutions, mosques, Islamic centers, and churches were extremely important to the immigrant communities as both social and spiritual homes. In 1989 Sierra Leonean Muslims in the Washington, D.C., area opened the Fullah Progressive Union (FPU) Islamic and Cultural Center (also known as the Fullah Islamic School), and by 2012 the FPU Washington, D.C., chapter had purchased its own building. Prior to the Fullah Islamic School opening, Sierra Leonean Muslims had attended mosques where Saudi and Pakistani Islamic traditions were taught, but, according to research in anthropologist JoAnn D'Alisera's *An Imagined Geography: Sierra Leonean Muslims in America* (2004), some families felt that their specific Sierra Leonean traditions were getting lost. D'Alisera found that Sierra Leonean American Muslims struggled with what they perceived as "authentic" or traditional Islam as practiced in the more international mosques versus the more familiar practices of Sierra Leonean Muslims. For instance, in Sierra Leone, Muslim women do not cover their faces. In areas outside of Washington, D.C., where there are fewer Muslims, which mosque one prays at may be less of an issue. In the Somerset, New Jersey, area, there are three "jamaat" (gathering places for prayer) but only one small mosque.

The percentage of Sierra Leonean Americans who practice Christianity seems to have grown in the early years of the twenty-first century, according to Hamjat Jallomy Bah, a young Sierra Leonean American living in New Jersey. He explained that authentic Muslim practice places more demands that are less compatible with life in the United States, including regular daily prayer and modest dress code, and says, "Once we get out of the watching eyes of our parents and community back in Africa we tend to be more casual with the Muslim religion, and some of us are switching over to Christianity." Bah's comment illustrates what seems to be a generational divide noted by other Sierra Leonean immigrants. The older generation wants to stay very connected to Africa, while the younger generation wants to leave the customs of Africa behind, yet still stay in community with other Sierra Leoneans. Among Sierra Leonean Muslims in Washington, D.C., where the largest concentration lived in the 1990s, cab drivers and food vendors would arrange their spaces and schedules to allow for prayer and to be recognized as Muslims. Audiotapes and stickers with verses from the Quran adorned the spaces, and prayer mats were nearby. However, maintaining these practices was challenging for several reasons. In post-2001 America, Muslims became associated with terrorists and were avoided by some paying customers. In addition, there are differences between Islam as practiced in Sierra Leone and as practiced in the large mosques in the United States.

CULTURE AND ASSIMILATION

The Gullah/Geechee people were able to preserve some of their original language, culture, and identity for a number of reasons. First, unlike most other enslaved African peoples, they managed to remain together in large concentrations. This was initially a result of their expertise as rice farmers at a time when few white laborers had these skills. Buyers sought out Sierra Leonean captives in the slave markets specifically for this ability. According to Opala, "It was African technology which created the intricate dikes and waterways which transformed the low country marshes of the southeast coast into thousands of acres of rice farms." A second reason for the preservation of Gullah culture in the United States was that the slaves had a greater resistance to malaria and other tropical diseases than whites. Lastly, there were large numbers of Sierra Leoneans living in the south. In St. Helena Parish, for example, the population of slaves in the first ten years of the nineteenth century grew by 86 percent. The ratio of blacks to whites in Beaufort, South Carolina, was almost five to one. This ratio was higher in some areas, and black overseers managed whole plantations while the owners resided elsewhere.

When the American Civil War ended in 1865, opportunities for the Gullah to buy land in the isolated Sea Islands were far greater than for African Americans on the mainland. Although the parcels rarely exceeded ten acres, they allowed their owners to avoid the type of sharecropping and tenant farming that characterized the lives of most African Americans during the Jim Crow years. "The 1870 Census shows that 98 percent of St. Helena's population of 6,200 was black and that 70 percent owned their own farms," wrote Patricia Jones-Jackson in *When Roots Die.*

Beginning in the 1950s, however, Gullahs residing on the Sea Islands were adversely affected by an influx of resort developers and the construction of bridges to the mainland. On many islands where the Gullah once represented an overwhelming majority of the population, they began facing minority status. However, there was also a resurgence of interest in Gullah heritage and identity, and in 2006 the area was designated the Gullah Geechee Cultural Heritage Corridor by an act of Congress, and several approaches to preserving their culture were pursued.

The Gullah/Geechee people were able to preserve some of their original language, culture, and identity for a number of reasons. First, unlike most other enslaved African peoples, they managed to remain together in large concentrations. This was initially a result of their expertise as rice farmers at a time when few white laborers had these skills.

Immigrants from Sierra Leone, although scattered over a variety of states, tended to congregate in communities for mutual support. Many socialized or celebrated customs that brought them together regularly. The reemergence in some cases of family and tribal support networks made the transition to a new country easier than it might have been. Although it was not uncommon for newer arrivals to work two or three jobs to support themselves and their families who remained in Sierra Leone, others were able to attain respect and professional status in a variety of well-paid careers.

Cuisine Rice is still a staple both in Sierra Leone and among Sierra Leonean Americans. Another common staple is cassava prepared with palm oil in stews and sauces. This is often combined with rice, chicken, and/or okra and may be eaten at breakfast, lunch, or dinner. Rice also forms the basis of all three meals for the Gullah of the Sea Islands. It is combined with different meats, gumbos, greens, and sauces, many of which are still prepared and eaten according to the old traditions, although, unlike in Sierra Leone, pork or bacon is a frequent addition. A popular Gullah recipe is Frogmore Stew, which contains smoked beef sausage, corn, crab, shrimp, and seasonings. Sierra Leoneans also enjoy

Marquetta Goodwine is Queen Quet, chieftess of the Gullah/Geechee Nation. AP IMAGES / THE POST AND COURIER, STEPHANIE HARVIN

culture, for example, the *booba* is tucked in. Among the Temne, it is worn more loosely. Mandingo women may sport a double ruffle around a lowered neckline and sometimes wear their blouses off-shoulder.

Dances and Songs With its colorful mixture of African and Western cultures, Sierra Leonean music is extremely creative and varied and forms an essential part of daily life both in Freetown and the interior. The instruments are dominated by a great variety of drums. Drumming groups may also include a lively mix of castanets, beaten bells, and even wind instruments. Sierra Leoneans from northern parts of the country, the Korankos, add a type of xylophone, the *balangi*. Another popular instrument is the *seigureh*, which consists of stones in a rope-bound calabash. The seigureh is used to provide background rhythm. Longer musical pieces are guided by a master drummer and contain embedded signals within the overall rhythm that indicate major changes in tempo. Some pieces may add the continuous blowing of a whistle as a counterpoint. In Freetown, traditional tribal music has given way to various calypso styles that incorporate Western instruments such as the saxophone. In the United States, many Sierra Leonean music and dance traditions are kept alive by the Ko-Thi Dance Company of Madison, Wisconsin. Groups like the Beaufort, South Carolina, Hallelujah Singers perform and record traditional Gullah music.

One hallmark of Sierra Leonean culture is the incorporation of dance into all parts of life. A bride may dance on her way to the home of her new husband. A family may dance at the grave of one who has been dead three days. According to Roy Lewis in *Sierra Leone: A Modern Portrait*, "The dance is … the principal medium of folk art; it is the one which European influences are least likely to affect. There are dances for every occasion, for every age and both sexes." Because rice serves as one of the foundations of Sierra Leone's economy, many dances incorporate the movements used to farm and harvest this crop. Other dances celebrate the actions of warriors and may involve dancing with swords and catching them out of the air. *Buyan* is the "dance of happiness," a delicate interchange between two teenage girls dressed entirely in white and wearing red kerchiefs. The *fetenke* is danced by two young boys, moving heel to toe and waving black scarves. At times, whole communities may come together to dance in celebration of the Muslim festival of Eid al-Fitr or the culmination of Poro or Sande secret society initiations. These dances are usually led by master drummers and dancers. For Sierra Leonean Americans, dancing continues to be a defining part of many gatherings and a joyful part of daily life.

Health Care Issues and Practices Sierra Leone, like many tropical countries, is home to a variety of diseases. Because of the civil war, in which many health care facilities were destroyed, health conditions

prawn palava, a dish that contains onions, tomatoes, peanuts, thyme, chili peppers, spinach, and prawns. It is usually served with boiled yams and rice.

Traditional Dress Sierra Leonean Americans are likely to wear both Western clothing and traditional African dress. For men, the traditional clothing consists of either pull-on pants with matching embroidered tunic, or longer gown and hat or cap. Headgear consisting of wrapped cloth in a Muslim style, Western-style hats, or ornate circular caps are common. Among women, *cabbaslot* dresses, which are long and have puffed sleeves, are sometimes popular. Tribal women generally favor wrapped headgear and a two-piece costume that consists of a skirt, or *lappa*, and a blouse, or *booba*. The way in which these garments are worn varies according to tribe. In the Mende

plummeted at the end of the twentieth century. The Koroma government (2007) invested 13 percent of the gross domestic product in health care, ranking it sixth in the world in health care investment, according to the *CIA World Factbook*. Yet in 2012, Sierra Leone still ranked very poorly in life expectancy, maternal death rates, and other health measures. During the 1990s until the end of the civil war, Sierra Leonean refugees admitted to the United States were likely to have been subjected to multiple traumas, including separation from and loss of family, malnutrition, and serious wounds.

Although most Sierra Leonean American births now occur in hospitals, the delivery of a child traditionally took place far from men, and the mother would be assisted by the women of the Sande society. After the birth, soothsayers were consulted to speak about the child's future, and offerings were made to the ancestors.

Another health issue affecting the Sierra Leonean American population has been the controversy surrounding the practice of female circumcision. Seventy-five percent of Sierra Leonean women are said to uphold the practice, which involves removing the clitoris as well the labia majora and minora of pre-pubescent girls, often in unhygienic conditions and usually without anesthesia. Organizations such as the National Council of Muslim Women and the secret Bondo Society defend the practice. A leading spokesperson for female circumcision, Haja Isha Sasso, argues that "the rite of female circumcision is sacred, feared and respected. It is a religion to us." Josephine Macauley, a staunch opponent of female circumcision, remarked in the *Electronic Mail & Guardian* that the practice is "cruel, unprogressive and a total abuse of the children's rights." Many prominent Americans have criticized the practice, calling it genital mutilation, not circumcision, and some Sierra Leonean women have sought refuge against it.

Funerals According to Krio custom, the burial of a person's body does not represent the end of the funeral service. The person's spirit is believed to reside in a vulture's body and cannot cross over without additional ceremonies being held three days, seven days, and forty days after death. Hymns and wailing begin at sunrise on those days, and cold, pure water and crushed *agiri* are left at the gravesite. Memorial services are held for a departed ancestor on the fifth and tenth anniversaries of the death. The Gullah believe that it is very important to be buried close to family and friends, usually in dense woods. Some families still practice the old tradition of placing articles on the grave that the dead person might need in the afterlife, such as spoons and dishes.

Traditional Arts and Crafts The Gullah/Geechee tradition of making *fanner*, which are flat, tightly woven, circular sweetgrass baskets, is one of the most visible links between that culture and West African culture. These baskets have been sold in city

FROGMORE STEW

Ingredients

2 tablespoons crab boil seasoning per gallon water (or more to taste)

several lemons, halved

12 redskin potatoes

1 pound spicy smoked sausage, cut into 1-inch slices

6 ears fresh corn, broken into halves or thirds

2 pounds shrimp

butter, melted

cocktail sauce

sour cream

ketchup

Preparation

Fill a large steamer pot halfway with water. Add crab-boil seasoning and several halved lemons.

When the seasoned water comes to a boil, add redskin potatoes and boil for 20 minutes; then add slices of spicy smoked sausage and boil for 5–10 minutes. Add the corn and cook another 5 minutes. Then add the shrimp. Cook for 3 minutes, drain, and pile on a table.

Serve with lots of paper towels and icy beverages, plus melted butter for the corn, cocktail sauce for the shrimp, and sour cream or ketchup for the potatoes.

markets and on the streets of Charleston since the 1600s. In Sierra Leone these baskets are still used to winnow rice.

FAMILY AND COMMUNITY LIFE

Family and clan relationships are extremely important to Sierra Leonean Americans. According to Lewis, "What belongs to one, belongs to all, and a man has no right to refuse to take in a relative or share his meal or his money with a relative. This is the African social tradition." In traditional villages, the basic social unit was the *mawei*, or (in Mende) *mavei*. The mawei included a man, his wife or wives, and their children. For wealthier men, it might also include junior brothers and their wives and unmarried sisters. Wives were lodged, whenever possible, in several houses, or *pe wa*. If wives lived together in a house, the senior wife supervised the junior wives. Because polygamy is illegal in the United States, these marriage customs have created a serious problem in some immigrant households. In a few cases, the polygamous relationships have been continued secretly or on an informal basis.

Generally, a Sierra Leonean man has a special relationship with his mother's brother, or *kenya*.

The kenya is expected to help him, especially in making his marriage payment. In many cases the man marries the kenya's daughter. The father's brothers are respected as "little fathers." His daughters are regarded as a man's sisters. Sisters of both parents are considered "little mothers," and it is not uncommon for a child to be raised by nearby relatives rather than by his own parents. To varying degrees, Sierra Leoneans in the United States have maintained connections to clans, and several support groups based on ethnic or chieftaincy affiliations have formed, such as the Fullah Progressive Union and the Krio Heritage Society.

Within the Gullah/Geechee community, spouses brought into the community from the outside world are often not trusted or accepted for many years. Disputes within the community are largely resolved in the churches and praise houses. Deacons and ministers often intervene and try to resolve the conflict without punishing either party. Taking cases to courts outside the community is frowned upon. After marriage, a couple generally builds a house in or nearby the "yard" of the husband's parents. A yard is a large area that may grow into a true clan site if several sons bring spouses, and even grandchildren may grow up and return to the group. When the dwellings consist of mobile homes, they are often placed in kinship clusters.

Gender Roles Women generally occupy lower positions than men in Sierra Leonean society, although there are instances of women being selected as chief of the Mende culture. When a woman is chosen to be chief, she is not allowed to marry. However, she is permitted to take consorts. Women can also attain a high position in the Bundu, a woman's society that guards the rites of circumcision, or the Humoi Society, which guards kinship rules. Unless she is a senior wife, a woman has relatively little say in a polygamous household. In traditional culture, women in their early teens are generally wedded to men in their thirties. Divorce is permitted, but children are often required to live with the father. It was the custom in the Mende culture that a widow, although she might follow Christian burial rites, could also make a mudpack with the water used to wash the husband's corpse and smear herself with it. When the mud was washed off, all of her husband's proprietary rights were removed as well, and she could marry again. Any woman who does not marry is looked on with disapproval. In the United States, the status of Sierra Leonean women is improving as some attain college degrees and professional status.

Education Education is highly valued within the Sierra Leonean immigrant community. Many immigrants enter the United States with student visas or after earning degrees from British universities or from Fourah Bay College in Freetown. Recent immigrants attend school as soon as economic stability of the family is achieved. Many Sierra Leonean American children also receive education in their cultural traditions through initiation into the cross-tribal Poro (for boys) and Sande (for girls) secret societies.

Some members of the Gullah/Geechee community have earned college degrees at mainland universities. As the Sea Islands have become increasingly developed, mainstream white culture has had a tremendous impact on the Gullah educational system. However, Gullah language and traditions are still energetically

A Koumankele African dance and drum ensemble perform at the 5th annual fundraiser for Shine On Sierra Leone at a private residence in Venice, California. JOHN M. HELLER / GETTY IMAGES ENTERTAINMENT / GETTY IMAGES

preserved and promoted by organizations such as the Gullah/Geechee Sea Island Coalition and by the Penn Center at Penn School on St. Helena Island.

Courtship and Weddings Sierra Leonean marriages traditionally have been arranged by the parents with the permission of the Humoi Society, which enforced the rules against incest in the villages. In Sierra Leone such an engagement could even be made for an infant or small child, called a *nyahanga*, or "mushroom wife." A suitor made a marriage payment called a *mboya*. Once betrothed, he took immediate responsibility for the girl's education, including the payment of fees for her Sande initiation training. A girl might refuse to marry this man when she came of age. If she did so, however, the man must be repaid for all expenses incurred. Among poorer men and immigrants to the United States, courtship frequently begins with friendship. Cohabitation is permitted, but any children who are born into this relationship belong to the woman's family if a mboya has not been paid. When a husband is ready to take possession of his wife and the bride price has been paid, it was the Mende custom for the girl's mother to spit on her daughter's head and bless her. The bride was then taken, dancing, to her husband's door.

Relationships outside of marriage are not uncommon in polygamous situations. For men, this can mean the risk of being fined for "woman damage" if he is caught with a married woman. When a couple who is in an extramarital relationship appears in public, the man refers to the woman as his *mbeta*, which means sister-in-law. In private, he may call her *sewa ka mi* (loved one), and she may call him *han ka mi* (sigh of mine).

In the United States, weddings combine traditions in creative and celebratory ways. A 2012 article in the Sierra Leonean newspaper the *Patriotic Vanguard* described the wedding of Peter Tarpeh and Aminata Bangura. The marriage ceremony took place at the Dawatul Islamia mosque, or *masjid*, in Somerset, New Jersey, a place chosen by the couple even though they don't live there, because of the large Sierra Leonean community. Somerset is also located between the largest concentrations of Sierra Leoneans in Washington, D.C., New York, and Boston. The large reception had an emcee and featured many toasts to the bride and groom, and dancing where the bride "demonstrated that she can actually dance to the latest tunes from Sierra Leone. She danced with joyous abandon and she was showered with money by friends, relatives and well-wishers."

Relations with Other Americans Sierra Leonean Americans commonly marry and make friends outside of their own clan, and friendships are formed with other African immigrants. Sociologists have noted many times that white Americans tend to categorize African immigrants apart from African American descendants of slaves. Paul Stoller, an anthropologist

BABY-NAMING CEREMONIES

Sierra Leonean Americans use religious or ethnic ceremonies or rituals in an effort to hold onto a sense of homeland. For instance, naming ceremonies in which children are given their African name create important ties for the child, family, and community. Regardless of family religion, the infant is presented to the community one week after birth in a ceremony called *pull-na-door* (put out the door). Family members gather to name the child and celebrate his or her arrival into the world. In preparation, beans, water, chicken, and plantain are put on stools and on the floor overnight as offerings to the ancestors. In her book *An Imagined Geography: Sierra Leonean Muslims in America* (2004), anthropologist JoAnn D'Alisera describes a Sierra Leonean Muslim baby-naming that she attended in a Washington, D.C., home in 1991: "The table in the living room was set up with the usual West African-style fare, for such events: *plasause* (a leaf and palm oil based stew) and rice, roasted *halal* meat on skewers, samosas, salad, fruit and ginger beer." The mother and child were draped in an African print cloth, and an imam led the ceremony with verses from the Quran and a sermon. The imam whispered the baby's name into her ears and spoke the name several times out loud for all to hear and acknowledge.

at West Chester University in Pennsylvania who has spent years studying West African street vendors in New York City, including Sierra Leoneans, noted that suppliers offer more generous credit to African immigrants than to other African Americans. Other social scientists have made similar discoveries. D'Alisera recalled that, time and again, whites would assume her Sierra Leonean subjects were better educated and more hardworking than other African Americans.

Among the Gullah people, there has been a long association with various Native American peoples. Over time, the Gullah intermarried with descendants of the Yamasee, the Apalachicola, the Yuchi, and the Creeks.

EMPLOYMENT AND ECONOMIC CONDITIONS

Since the Civil War, Gullah/Geechee communities in the southern United States have traditionally relied on their own farming and fishing activities in order to earn a living. They sell produce in Charleston and Savannah, and some take seasonal jobs on the mainland as commercial fishermen, loggers, or dock workers. During the 1990s, life on the Sea Islands began to change as developers started to build tourist resorts. A dramatic rise in land values on some islands, while increasing the worth of Gullah holdings, led to increased taxes, and many Gullah were forced to sell their land. Increasingly, Gullah students have become a minority in local schools and discover that, upon graduation, the only jobs available to them are as service workers at the resorts. "Developers just come in and roll over them and change their culture, change their way of life, destroy the environment and therefore the culture has to be changed," remarked Emory Campbell, former director of the Penn Center on St. Helena Island. The establishment of the Gullah Geechee Cultural Heritage Corridor in 2006 was expected to turn this trend around by increasing heritage tourism to the area.

In large metropolitan areas where the majority of immigrants from Sierra Leone have settled, many Sierra Leoneans have earned college degrees and entered a variety of professions. New immigrants often come to the United States with a strong desire to succeed. Sierra Leoneans commonly take entry-level jobs as taxi drivers, cooks, nursing assistants, and other service workers. Many go on to higher education or start their own businesses, although the responsibility to support family members who remained in Sierra Leone can slow their progress toward these goals.

In his book *African Diaspora Identities*, John A. Arthur found that a majority of women from African countries, including Sierra Leone, who attain college degrees in their home countries emigrate within five years of graduation, the majority of them to the United States. These degrees are in medicine, pharmacy, business, law, and nursing. Some 80 percent enter the United States on their own (without a family), and a majority are seeking to advance their degrees and improve their employment opportunities.

POLITICS AND GOVERNMENT

In 2001 Sidique Wai, a Sierra Leonean Muslim, was reportedly the first continental African to seek political office in the United States when he ran unsuccessfully for the 35th district seat in Brooklyn, New York. Sierra Leonean immigrants remain very involved in the political activities of their homeland. Before the outbreak of the civil war, Sierra Leonean Americans returned often to their homeland and were welcomed as long-lost relatives. During Sierra Leone's steep economic decline under the rule of All People's Congress President Siaka Stevens (1968–1985), Sierra Leonean students and other immigrants formed several multiethnic organizations in opposition to the ALP's one-party rule. From the 1970s onward, several ethnically based "descendants" organizations sprang up in the United States, including the Kono Descendants, the Gbonkolenken Descendants, and the Tegloma (Mende) Federation. By the twenty-first century most of these organizations were reaching out to all Sierra Leoneans and working to deemphasize ethnic divisions. For instance, Tegloma, which had more than twenty chapters in the United States, with the majority of its members from the southern and eastern regions of Sierra Leone, had an a open door

policy to anybody originating from, or interested in, Sierra Leone. The organizations also organized joint events such as a 2011 celebration in Dallas at which Tegloma joined Ebilleh, Kono Descendants Union, Fullah Progressive Union and many other regional Sierra Leone organizations to promote the culture and unity of Sierra Leone in the diaspora. These organizations focus much of their energy on fundraising for educational, health, and social welfare projects in the homeland. Since a 1989 visit to the Sea Islands by then-President Momoh, there has been a marked increase in interest among the Gullah in their Sierra Leonean roots.

NOTABLE INDIVIDUALS

Academia Cecil Blake, former cabinet minister in the Sierra Leonean government (2000–2001), was on the faculty of the Department of Africana Studies at the University of Pittsburgh. He is the author of many books and articles on African governmental issues.

Marquetta Goodwine, born on St. Helena Island, is an author and Gullah historian. In 1996 she founded the Gullah/Geechee Sea Island Coalition and was elected by her people as the first Queen Mother of the Gullah/Geechee Nation.

Abioseh Porter, born and raised in Sierra Leone, is the head of the Department of English and Philosophy at Drexel University in Philadelphia and serve as the editor of the *Journal of the African Literature Association (JALA)*.

Activism Joseph Cinqué (born Sengbe Pieh, 1814–1879) was well known in the United States for his leadership in the takeover of the slave ship *Amistad* in 1839. In the U.S. Supreme Court, with the help of ex-president John Quincy Adams, he successfully maintained the rights of Sierra Leoneans and other Africans to defend themselves against illegal capture by slave smugglers.

Government Omotunde Johnson, an economics researcher and consultant, was the division head of the International Monetary Fund until 2000.

J. Sorie Conteh, born in Sierra Leone, received a BA from the University of Rochester in New York and a PhD in anthropology and African studies from Indiana University. He was a political affairs officer at the Permanent Observer Mission of the African Union to the United Nations in New York. Conteh was later the political affairs officer at the United Nations Mission in Iraq and Kuwait, and also at the United Nations Mission in Eritrea and Ethiopia. He is the author of four novels: *The Diamonds*, *In Search of Sons*, *Family Affairs*, and *Journey to Dreamland*. He has published several short stories and articles on the effects of diamond mining in Sierra Leone, female circumcision, secret societies, African culture, and democracy in Africa.

Journalism Kwame "Cumale" Fitzjohn was a founder of Global African Media. A native of Sierra Leone, he attended both Fourah Bay College and the University of Maryland. In the 1990s he served as Washington correspondent for the BBC World Service for Africa and contributor to *West Africa Magazine*. Beginning in the early 2000s, Kwame served as an anchor on American public television and was a producer and on-air personality for the television program *The African World*.

Literature Ishmael Beah (1980–) is the author of the memoir *A Long Way Gone: Memoirs of a Boy Soldier* (2004). A native Sierra Leonean who was forced to become a child soldier for the government in the civil war, Beah escaped and immigrated as a refugee to the United States in 1998. As a spokesperson for Human Rights Watch Children's Rights Division Advisory Committee, Beah has spoken before the United Nations, the Council on Foreign Relations, the Center for Emerging Threats and Opportunities (CETO) at the Marine Corps Warfighting Laboratory, and many other panels on children affected by the war.

Journalist, novelist, and folklorist Joel Chandler Harris (1845–1908) wrote a number of books, including *The Complete Tales of Uncle Remus, Free Joe, and Other Georgian Sketches*, and *On the Plantation: A Story of a Georgia Boy's Adventures during the War*.

Yulisa Amadu Maddy (1936–) wrote *African Images in Juvenile Literature: Commentaries on Neocolonialist Fiction* and *No Past, No Present, No Future*.

Pede Hollist, a native of Sierra Leone, is an associate professor of English at the University of Tampa, Florida. His first novel was *So the Path Does Not Die* (2012). His published short stories include "Foreign Aid," "Resettlement," "Going to America," and "BackHomeAbroad."

An author and professor of English and African studies at Georgia State College and University, Eustace Palmer is one of the pioneer critics of African literature. He has also published numerous books and articles on English and African literature. He was the associate editor of *African Literature Today* for several years and served as president of the African Literature Association from 2006 to 2007. His third novel, *A Tale of Three Women*, was published in 2011.

Ronald Daise is the chairman of the Gullah Geechee Cultural Heritage Corridor Commission and vice president for creative education at Brookgreen Gardens in Murrells Inlet, South Carolina. A native of St. Helena Island, South Carolina, he starred as "Mr. Ron" in Nick Jr. TV's award-winning *Gullah Gullah Island* children's series of the 1990s. His 2007 book *Gullah Branches, West African Roots* chronicles cultural connections of language, spirituality, dietary practices, and beliefs between the Gullah and Ghana and Sierra Leone.

Music Ferne Caulker founded the Ko-Thi Dance Company in Madison, Wisconsin. David Pleasant is a Gullah music griot and African American master drummer. Heyden Adama Bangura (1989–) is a Sierra Leone music star and model based in Seattle, Washington.

Politics Robert Scott Smalls (1839–1915) was born into slavery in Beaufort County, South Carolina. He served in both the South Carolina Senate and the U.S. Congress and was a delegate to the South Carolina Constitutional Convention.

MEDIA

PRINT

Cocorioko Newspaper

Sierra Leone's biggest and most widely read newspaper, published in the United States and Freetown.

Rev. Leeroy Wilfred Kabs-Kanu, Publisher
Email: kabbskanu@aol.com
URL: www.cocorioko.net

Gullah Sentinel

Established by Jabari Moteski in 1997, the *Sentinel* is printed biweekly and distributed throughout Beaufort County, South Carolina, and may be read for free online.

B. Ballentine, Operations Manager
909 Bladen Street
Beaufort, South Carolina 29902
Phone: (843) 982-0500
Fax: (843) 982-0631
Email: gullah@thegullahnews.net
URL: www.thegullahnews.net

ORGANIZATIONS AND ASSOCIATIONS

Friends of Sierra Leone (FOSL)

Formed in 1991 by a small group of former Peace Corps volunteers, FOSL is a nonpolitical organization that strives to educate Americans and others about Sierra Leone's people, cultures, and history and to support small-scale development and relief projects in Sierra Leone.

Peggy Murrah, President
P.O. Box 15875
Washington, D.C. 20003-0875
Email: president@fosalone.org
URL: www.fosalone.org

Gbonkolenken Descendants Foundation

Based in the Netherlands, the foundation aims to promote solidarity among expatriate Sierra Leoneans and to help develop the Gbonkolenken Chiefdom in the Tonkolili South Constituency in the northern province of Sierra Leone through education, health projects, and food relief for its residents.

Email: info@gbonkolenken.eu
URL: www.gbonkolenken.eu

National Organization of Sierra Leoneans in North America (NOSLINA)

Based in Washington, D.C., NOSLINA is an organization whose goal is to campaign for an end to the brutal civil war in Sierra Leone, to restore democracy, to promote sustainable development, and to initiate community health projects.

Suna Nallo, Executive Director
Phone: (410) 412 4311
Email: noslina2011@aol.com
URL: www.noslina.org

MUSEUMS AND RESEARCH CENTERS

Gullah Museum of Hilton Head Island

The mission of the Gullah Museum of Hilton Head Island is to revive, restore, and preserve the Hilton Head Island Gullah history.

Louise Miller Cohen, Founder and Director
187 Gumtree Road
Hilton Head Island, South Carolina 29926
Phone: (843) 681-3254
Fax: (843) 681-3354
URL: www.gullahmuseumhhi.org

The Penn Center

Located on St. Helena Island, South Carolina, this institution was established in 1862 as a school for freed slaves. It now promotes the preservation of Gullah culture and sponsors the annual Gullah festival.

16 Penn Center Circle West
St. Helena Island, South Carolina 29920
Phone: (843) 838-2432
Fax: (843) 838-8545
Email: info@penncenter.com
URL: www.penncenter.com

SOURCES FOR ADDITIONAL STUDY

Bailey, Cornelia Walker. *God, Dr. Buzzard, and the Bolito Man: A Saltwater Geechee Talks about Life on Sapelo Island.* New York: Doubleday, 2000.

Copeland, Larry. "Coastal Residents Aim to Preserve Rich African Culture." *USATODAY.com*, April 24, 2011. http://usatoday30.usatoday.com/news/nation/2011-04-22-gullah-geechee-south-carolina.htm.

D'Alisera, JoAnn. "Images of a Wounded Homeland: Sierra Leonean-American Children and the New Heart of Darkness." In *Family Ties: Immigrant Families in America*, edited by Nancy Foner, 114–34. New York: New York University Press, 2009.

———. *An Imagined Geography: Sierra Leonean Muslims in America.* Philadelphia: University of Pennsylvania Press, 2004.

———. "Public Spaces/Muslim Places: Locating Sierra Leonean Muslim Identity in Washington, D.C." *African Diaspora* 3, no. 1 (2010): 93–109.

Davis, Paul. "US-Sierra Leone Slavery History with Interview of Joe Opala." SierraLeoneResources.org, February 13–15, 2005. http://www.richard.jewell.net/SierraLeone/Articles/artcl-SLslavehist.html.

Jalloh, Alusine. "Sierra Leoneans in America and Homeland Politics." In *The United States and West Africa*, edited by Alusine Jalloh and Toyin Falola. Rochester, NY: University of Rochester Press, 2008.

Jones-Jackson, Patricia. *When Roots Die: Endangered Traditions on the Sea Islands.* Athens: University of Georgia Press, 1987.

Lowther, Kevin. *The African American Odyssey of John Kizell: A South Carolina Slave Returns to Fight the Slave Trade in His African Homeland.* Columbia: University of South Carolina Press, 2012.

Morgan, Philip, ed. *African American Life in the Georgia Lowcountry: The Atlantic World and the Gullah Geechee.* Athens: University of Georgia Press, 2010.

SIKH AMERICANS
Tova Stabin

OVERVIEW

Sikh Americans are part of a religious and cultural group that traces its origins to the Punjab, a cross-national region on the Indian subcontinent that includes northern India and eastern Pakistan. In India the Punjab is one of twenty-eight states, and in Pakistan it is one of four provinces. The entire Punjab region is bordered on the north by the Himalayan Mountains, on the south by the Rajputana Desert, on the west by the Indus River, and on the east by the Yamuna River. The name *Punjab* comes from the Persian words *panj* (five) and *aab* (water) because of the five rivers in the region's central plain: the Jhelum, the Chenab, the Ravi, the Sutlej, and the Beas. The lower plains of the Punjab are exceptionally fertile, due to their proximity to the Himalayas, which is a bountiful source of water and minerals. The entire Punjab area is 98,729 square miles (253,706 square kilometers), roughly the size of Oregon.

According to the Census of India, the 2013 population of Punjab, India, was 36 million, with more than 60 percent of the population identifying as Sikh. The other major religions in the area are Hinduism (37 percent) and Islam (1.5 percent). The 2007 population of Punjab, Pakistan, was 86.4 million, and the estimated 2013 population was 95.4 million, according to the World Gazetteer, a source of population data and other statistics. While Pakistan remains a place of importance to Sikhs, only about 20,000 remain there; the majority of the population there follows Islam. According to the *World Religion Database*, as of 2010 there were about 25 million Sikhs in the world, making up about .035 percent of the world population. The Punjab is among the wealthiest, most self-sufficient regions in both India and Pakistan. The province of Punjab is especially important to Pakistan, producing almost 70 percent of the country's food.

Sikhs began to immigrate to the United States in the late 1800s and early 1900s. According to the book *Buddhists, Hindus and Sikhs in America* (2008), by 1915 there were approximately 6,000 Sikhs in the United States, primarily on the West Coast. Most came from the Punjab region and were male peasant farmers, though some also came from Hong Kong and Shanghai, China, where they were serving in the British armed services (India at the time was part of the British Empire). Because many came from agricultural communities, often these immigrants became agriculture workers in California; some worked in Oregon and Washington lumber mills and on railroad construction. After World War II, Sikh immigrants were also educated people looking for employment or further educational opportunities in the United States. Most Sikh university students stayed in the United States when they graduated. Another wave of immigrants came to the United States in the mid-1980s to the 1990s, mainly due to political unrest in India, particularly conflicts between the government and Sikhs who wanted to create a separate independent state.

It is difficult to determine the number of Sikhs in the United States because the U.S. Census Bureau does not ask about religious affiliation, and surveys have yielded results that vary by a wide margin. For example, the American Religious Identification Survey from 2008 estimated that there were about 78,000 adult Sikhs living in the United States at the time. Meanwhile, the World Religion Database at Boston University estimates there are about 280,000 Sikhs in the United States, based on estimates of the number of Punjabi immigrants from India and Pakistan and an assumption about the proportion of them who are Sikh. The Sikh Coalition, an advocacy group, maintains that there are more than 500,000 Sikh Americans but does not cite a source for that figure. It is also difficult to determine the states where the highest numbers of Sikh Americans reside. The Association of Religion Data Archives, which estimates that there are around 314,000 Sikh Americans living in the United States, reports that the states with the largest number of Sikh American congregations include California, New York, Texas, Florida, Ohio, Arizona, Virginia, Michigan, Maryland, and Pennsylvania.

HISTORY OF THE PEOPLE

Early History Sikhism was founded sometime around 1499 or shortly thereafter by Guru Nanak, who was born in 1469 in what is now Pakistan, near the present-day city of Lahore. From the start of his schooling at age five, Nanak was a prodigy who excelled at reading symbols and conversing on theological matters with adults. At age thirty he had a vision on the bank of a local river that indicated he should preach the path to enlightenment and God. Without telling anyone where he was going, he disappeared for three days and returned with a message containing the some of the basic tenets that would serve as the foundation of Sikh thought. He renounced polytheism and forsook idol worship and the caste system. Nanak proclaimed belief in a single, incomprehensible God and encouraged followers to live a simple, honest life, helping others in need and praying regularly. Over the remainder of his life, Nanak embarked on five grand journeys, one in each direction and the last in all four directions, accustoming himself to the joy and suffering of the material world, spreading his message, and recruiting followers. He took the name "Guru," which means teacher or enlightened one.

From the time of Guru Nanak's death in 1538 until 1708, there were nine other Sikh guru spiritual leaders. The fifth Sikh guru, Guru Arjan Dev, built the Harmandir Sahib, the "Golden Temple" (also called the Darbar Sahib), in 1574 in Amritsar, Punjab, India. It is considered the most holy temple for the Sikhs. In 1604 Guru Arjan compiled the *Guru Granth Sahib*, the holy book of scripture that contains the poems and songs of Guru Arjan and former gurus as well as works from a few Muslim and Hindu holy people, particularly the mystical poet and religious reformer Kabir (1440–1518). During Guru Arjan's leadership, the ruling emperor saw Sikhism as a threat to the government, and in 1606 Guru Arjan was tortured and executed for his religious beliefs.

Guru Hargobind, the sixth Guru and only son of Guru Arjan, had assumed leadership days before his father was martyred. During his initiation ceremony he refused to wear the woolen cord that was worn around the head and instead asked for a sword. When it was placed on the wrong side of his body, he asked for another sword for the other side and continued to wear two swords during his life, explaining that one sword was for spiritual power and the other was for power in the secular world. Subsequent gurus also wore two swords symbolizing these dual powers. Guru Hargobind militarized the Sikhs and encouraged followers to learn how to use weapons and horses and to be physically active.

The Sikhs lived in relative peace with political leaders until the reign of the Mughal emperor Aurangzeb, who ruled India from 1658 until 1707 and actively sought to convert the entire country to Islam. In 1675 Aurangzeb executed Guru Tegh Bahadur, the ninth guru; subsequently Bahadur's son, Guru Gobind Singh, became the leader of the Sikhs when he was just nine years old. In 1699, before a large crowd, Guru Singh formally initiated the first five Sikhs into the *Khalsa*, meaning "pure ones." These initiates were to be the temporal leaders of the Sikhs, to uphold the ideals of cleanliness, virtue, and self-defense. They were to maintain a standard to which others would aspire. When he was dying in 1708, Guru Singh proclaimed that there would be no other human gurus after him and informed his followers that Sikh scripture, the

Guru Granth Sahib, would be their Guru. In other words, the Sikhs were instructed to view their holy scripture as a living guide rather than investing an individual with authority over the group.

After the death of Guru Singh, Banda Singh Bahadur (1670–1716) led the Sikhs in battle against the Mughals, successfully raiding their capital in Sirhind (in present-day Indian Punjab) before he was captured and executed in 1716. Regarded as a martyr for the Sikh cause, Bahadur inspired many others to follow his example, and by the mid-nineteenth century the Sikhs had significantly increased their territory. In 1799 Ranjit Singh captured the city of Lahore, and in 1801 established an independent Sikh state in the Punjab with himself as leader. Under his rule the Sikhs, who were a minority in the area, lived peacefully with the Hindus and Muslims. Ranjit Singh died in 1839, and just ten years later, in 1849, the British, who had been steadily wresting control of India from the Mughals for decades, annexed the Sikh kingdom.

Despite nearly a decade of enmity between the two groups, in 1857, the British asked the *Khalsa* army to help fight a group of northern Indian soldiers who had rebelled against British rule. With the help of the Sikhs, the British were able to quell the rebellion and thus started an era of cooperation between the British and Sikhs. Sikh leaders became honorary magistrates, Sikhs could join the British Army and maintain their traditions (such as wearing turbans/*dastaars*), and the British gave economic support to the Punjab.

Modern Era The Sikhs fought alongside the British during World War I, but soon afterward their relationship became hostile again, the tension culminating with the April 19, 1919, Massacre of Amritsar, the holy city for the Sikhs. A few days prior to the massacre, Amritsar was put under martial law with Brigadier General Reginald Dyer in charge. On April 13 many thousands of Sikhs had begun arriving in Amritsar from surrounding areas to celebrate a Sikh festival, and most were unaware that public gatherings had been forbidden. On April 19 they gathered at the park Jallianwala Bagh, where a pro-Indian nationalist peaceful demonstration had been scheduled. General Dyer surrounded the park and without warning had his soldiers shoot into the crowd, killing an estimated 379 and wounding 1,200.

During World War II an estimated 300,000 Sikhs fought as British Indian soldiers, despite their troubled history with the British and the continued calls for independence throughout India. More Sikhs volunteered for the army than any other Indian group. Some Indians did not want to fight for the British without first securing a promise of independence after the war. However, many Sikhs felt that talk of independence should wait until after fascism was defeated.

In 1947 the British finally succumbed to Indians' demand for independence and agreed to leave the region. According to the terms negotiated with leaders of the independence movement, the British partitioned the territory along religious lines into two independent states, with India becoming a primarily a Hindu nation and Pakistan becoming a Muslim nation. The terms of the partition called for the Punjab region to be divided, and most of the Sikhs from what became Pakistan took up residence in India because they were not welcome among the Muslims of Pakistan. Much violence occurred among Muslims, Hindus, and Sikhs during the massive cross-border migrations in the aftermath of the partition.

From the start, the Sikhs have had a tumultuous relationship with the Indian government. In 1950, when the Indian constitution was adopted, the Sikhs refused to endorse it because the new government did not grant the Sikhs their own state, as had been promised. After years of protest from the Sikhs, in 1966 the Indian government divided Punjab (India) into three parts—the states of Punjab and Haryana and their shared capital, Chandigarh—with Punjab containing a majority of Sikhs. Despite this concession, the Sikhs remained unsatisfied, and a separatist movement arose with many Sikhs demanding their own country.

Tension escalated throughout the reign of Indira Gandhi (no relation to Mahatma Gandhi), who ruled India from 1966 to 1977 and from 1980 to 1984, when she was assassinated by Sikh bodyguards. For many years Gandhi attempted to win Hindu support by oppressing Sikhs, and when she was found guilty of election fraud in 1975 there was a large nonviolent protest by the Sikh community. At this time Gandhi suspended the constitution, declared a state of emergency, and issued a five-year economic plan to reduce poverty and boost production. Approximately 50,000 Sikhs were jailed, among many others.

During the early 1980s, over 250,000 Sikhs were arrested for demanding water rights and more autonomy in Punjab. In April 1984 Gandhi declared martial law in Punjab and on June 3 she launched Operation Blue Star, a military attacking the Golden Temple, where separatists led by militant Sikh leader Jarnail Singh Bhindranwale were taking refuge and were believed to be storing weapons. The army also attacked numerous other temples in Punjab in an attempt to root out suspected militants, with reports varying between 20 and 125 raids. These attacks commenced on the anniversary of the fifth guru's martyrdom, which meant that the temples were densely populated and the Sikh population was especially vulnerable. Three days of fighting ensued at the Golden Temple, and somewhere between 5,000 and 10,000 Sikhs were killed. The temple was also severely damaged, as was as a rare collection of documents from its library.

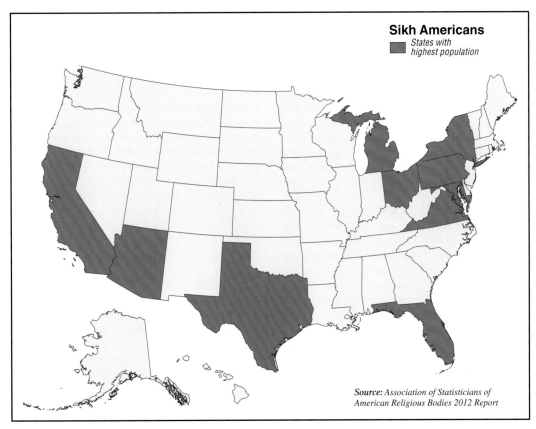

Sikh Americans

States with highest population

Source: Association of Statisticians of American Religious Bodies 2012 Report

Four months later, on October 31, 1984, Gandhi was assassinated at her residence by two Sikh bodyguards. After the assassination, violent organized mob attacks, including state-sponsored pogroms, targeted Sikhs. Many were injured, killed, or lost their homes and other property in cities across India. While the government claimed there were only 2,700 Sikh deaths, estimates by the media and human rights groups claimed there were anywhere between 10,000 and 17,000. After the 1984 attack, the movement for a separate state called Khālistān that would include the Indian state of Punjab and the surrounding areas where people spoke Punjabi, gathered more strength. Human rights violations against Sikhs continued for over a decade.

Through the latter part of the 1990s and into the twenty-first century, tension had waned to such at point that in 2004, Manmohan Singh, a well-respected economist, became the first Sikh prime minister of India. He was re-elected in 2009. Some Sikhs, however, continued the movement for a separate state. For example, Dalijit Singh Bittu, a leader of the Sikh Student Federation, formed the Shiromani Khalsa Dal (SKD) in 2004 with the objective of "creating a free, sovereign, and a separate Sikh state in Punjab." After a large rally in remembrance of those who died in Operation Blue Star, prominent members of the SKD were arrested for sedition. In the early part of the twenty-first century, Sikhs have continued to seek justice and compensation for human rights abuses.

SETTLEMENT IN THE UNITED STATES

Among the first Indians to come to the United States, the Sikhs began immigrating to central California from the Punjab in 1899. In the beginning of the twentieth century, some Sikhs immigrated to the western coast of Canada (which, like India, was part of the British Empire) and then moved to the United States. Others came directly to California, Oregon, and Washington. Most of the Sikhs of this first migration, over 7,000 total, were single men, mostly soldiers, farmers, and peasants from the Punjab. They came to make money or raise the status of their families back home by sending money or by returning to the Punjab and purchasing land. The California valleys were similar to the land in the Punjab and, thus, they were able to be successful as farmers and agricultural workers. Other Sikhs worked in Oregon or Washington lumber mills or on railroad construction. Sikhs began coming together as communities soon after immigration. By 1912 the first Sikh association, the Pacific Coast Khalsa Diwan Society, was founded. In 1915 the first *gurdwara*, or temple, Gurdwara Sahib Stockton, opened in Stockton, California.

During this early immigration Sikhs, like many others from Asia, experienced considerable discrimination. For example, in 1907 riots broke out in Bellingham, Washington, when about 400 to 500 men, mostly from the Asiatic Exclusion League, attacked the homes of Indian immigrants. There was

also governmental discrimination. In 1913 California passed a law stipulating that Asians were not allowed to own land, and other states followed suit. The Immigration Act of 1917 prevented immigration from South Asia and other parts of the world. After that, some Sikhs came to the United States illegally through Mexico. In the 1920s some Sikhs returned to India to participate in the struggle for India's independence. The U.S. Sikh population continued to decline through the 1930s, and by the early 1940s there were about 1,500 Sikhs in the United States.

A second wave of immigration came as a result of changes in immigration laws starting in the late 1940s. For example, the Luce-Celler Bill of 1946 lifted restrictions on immigrants coming from South Asia. The 1965 Immigration Act allowed immediate family members of those living in the United States to immigrate and permitted up to 20,000 professionals to immigrate from each Asian country if they could find work in the United States. Sikhs who were professionals immigrated to major cities where jobs in fields such as medicine, business, or engineering were available. Many went to Chicago and New York, in particular to the borough of Queens, where there were diverse immigrant communities. About 5,000 Sikhs came to the United States between 1948 and 1965.

A third wave of Sikh immigrants came to the United States starting the mid-1980s, primarily because of increased tension in India in the aftermath of Operation Blue Star. Many Sikhs also came at this time seeking jobs in the technology sector. Educated youth who were part of the student movement in India and who were sometimes particularly targeted in India, sought refuge in the United States. Some of these newer immigrants were more religious than the more established and assimilated Sikh Americans, who, for instance, might no longer wear traditional dress and would cut their hair, which the religion forbids.

Despite significant influx into urban areas in the east and Midwest, the greatest concentration of Sikh Americans remains in California, with many still working rural jobs. There are also significant populations of Sikh Americans living in New York, Texas, Florida, Ohio, Arizona, Virginia, Michigan, Maryland, and Pennsylvania. In addition, there are Americans who have converted to Sikhism, the greatest numbers being in California and New Mexico. American Sikhs are sometimes called "Western Sikhs."

LANGUAGE

Punjabi is the Sikh language. It is an Indo-Aryan language derived from the Shauraseni language of medieval India that became a unique language in the eleventh century. Punjabi is written from left to right and has thirty-five letters. Indian Punjabi is written with the Gurmukhi syllabic alphabet, standardized by Guru Angad Dev Ji, the second Sikh guru (the word means "from the mouth of the Guru"). Muslims in Pakistan use Shahmukhi script. There are many

Punjabi dialects, such as Malwi (spoken in the eastern part of Punjab, India), Doabi (spoken in Punjab, India, between the rivers of Beas and Sutlej), and Jhangochi or Rachnavi (the oldest dialect of Punjabi, spoken in a variety of areas throughout the Punjab region).

Understanding sacred texts, such as the Guru Granth Sahib, and Sikh literature in Punjabi are an important part of Sikh identity and pride. This identity was not difficult to retain in the state of Punjab in India, where Punjabi is the everyday language, but it is more challenging in the United States, where Punjabi is used for worship and for some other *gurdwara* (temple) activities. Most gurdwaras have a Sunday school where children are taught Punjabi and the Gurmukhi script. There are also Sikh summer camps where Punjabi is taught. However, few Sikh children are fluent enough to have an in-depth of understanding of religious tracts. Some Sikh communities are beginning to accept transliteration of the Guru Granth Sahib into Roman script, and some are even translating it into English to be alongside the original or replacing the original, in the hopes of maintaining understanding of the sacred text. Sikh American immigrants also sometimes speak Hindi (the "unofficial" national language of India) and are often multilingual, as is common in India.

Greetings and Popular Expressions

Sat sri akaal.

Hello (used for Good morning, good evening, and good night; literally means "immortal God is the truth").

Tussi kiwen ho? / ki gal hai?

How are you?

Main theek haan.

I am fine.

Tu-adey nal mil kar bahut khusi hoi.

Pleased to meet you.

Zukriā.

Thank you.

Tuhada naan ki hai?

What is your name?

Mera naan haga …

My name is …

Tusi kithe dey ho?

Where are you from?

Theek hai.

Okay.

Maaf karna.

Excuse me.

Maaf karo.

Sorry.

RELIGION

Sikhism is a monotheistic religion with many names for God, the most common being Waheguru. For Sikhs, God is neither male nor female, is not born, and never dies. Sikhs believe meditation, *Simran*, brings one closer to God and also helps one live a more peaceful life.

> *Sikhs put a high degree of importance on equality, respect for all, being charitable, doing good deeds, and participating in religious rituals. Men and women have equal status in religious customs. Sikh doctrine provides a model for a simple, virtuous life that sustains both the individual and the community as a whole.*

Sikhs put a high degree of importance on equality, respect for all, being charitable, doing good deeds, and participating in religious rituals. Men and women have equal status in religious customs. Sikh doctrine provides a model for a simple, virtuous life that sustains both the individual and the community as a whole. *Kirat Karo*, one of the central tenets in the religion, is defined as honest, hard work, and is closely related to another important Sikh concept, *dharmasal*, or the practice of righteousness. Sikhs should not be greedy, should only take what they need to live simply, and should help those less fortunate. Another related concept is *Seva*, which calls for service, to both other people and God. Seva can include, for instance, making financial donations, community service, or having positive loving relationships. In Sikhism, drinking, smoking, drugs, and adultery are prohibited.

Temples are called *gurdwaras*, and every gurdwara has a Guru Granth Sahib, the Sikh holy book. If a room in a home has the holy book in it, it can be considered a gurdwara. The Harmandir Sahib, Golden Temple, in the Punjab, is the most renowned and revered temple. The Guru Granth Sahib is treated with reverence: each morning it is taken from a small room, put on a cushioned platform, and covered with the *ramalla*, an embroidered cloth. When people enter the gurdwara, they bow to the Guru Granth Sahib out of respect. Specific verses are read for special occasions such as weddings. All acts of worship or special ceremonies, such as weddings, begin and end with *ardas*, standardized Sikh prayers. During services there is usually a prayer leader (but no formal clergy) who reads from the Guru Granth Sahib and who is called a *granthi*. There are also musicians who sing hymns and play traditional instruments called *ragis*. People sit on the floor to show all are equal, although men and women traditionally sit on opposite sides of the room. After the service, a *karah prasad* (a sweet food that has been blessed; it is made from semolina, sugar, and ghee) is eaten, offerings are made, and a meal is shared. Gurdwaras have prayer halls and a *langer* hall or community kitchen. Most gurdwaras also have libraries and a classroom.

POST-9/11 VIOLENCE AGAINST AMERICAN SIKHS

In the wake of the terrorist attacks in the United States on September 11, 2001, many Americans began to view Muslim and Arab Americans with suspicion, with some even committing random acts of violence against innocent Muslims as a form of retaliation. Although Sikhs and Muslims have very little in common in terms of spiritual beliefs or geographical origins, they are sometimes confused with Muslims because Sikh men frequently grow long beards and wear turbans. This confusion often makes Sikhs the target of discrimination or violence, as was the case with the tragic shooting of ten Wisconsin Sikhs by a white supremacist in 2012.

On August 5, 2012, Wade Michael Page, a forty-year-old former soldier and white supremacist, opened fire at the Sikh Temple of Wisconsin in Oak Creek, Wisconsin, killing six and injuring four others before committing suicide as police closed in. While Page did not leave any clues as to why he targeted the Sikh temple, many observers have attributed the act to anti-Muslim extremism. In the aftermath of the shooting, Sikh leaders made efforts to point out the differences between Islam and Sikhism but also emphasized the fact that, had the victims been Muslims, the attack would have been equally heinous in their eyes. As Satpal Singh, chairperson of the World Sikh Association, said in response to the attack, "whether somebody is Muslim or Sikh, we should do as much as we can to reduce hate crimes."

When they are old enough to understand the vows they taking, Sikhs may participate in in an initiation ceremony called the *Amrit Sanskar* to formally join the Khalsa, or community of Sikhs, as prescribed by Guru Gobind Singh, the tenth and final human guru, in 1699. When a Sikh is initiated he or she takes on the name *Singh* (lion) if male and *Kaur* (princess) if female, just as the Guru Gobind did for the first Sikhs to symbolize equality. Sikhs use this name as a middle name or sometimes a last name.

People who join the Khalsa are expected to maintain or abide by the five Ks, which remind adherents of their obligations as Sikhs. The first of these five Ks is *Kesha*, which requires Sikhs to keep uncut hair, including beards. Men tie their hair up and cover it with a turban called a *dastaar* or a *pagri* (more general term for male turban). Women generally wear a scarf called a *chuni* draped over their hair but are allowed to wear turbans. *Kangha*, the second of the Ks, is a small wooden comb worn all the time and used twice a day to keep uncut hair neat and tangle-free. It shows the importance of cleanliness and order and symbolizes "combing away" impure thoughts. *Kara* is a steel or iron bracelet worn on the right arm. It symbolizes moral strength, the "unbroken circle of oneness," integrity, resilience, and the Sikh commitment to God and doing right actions. *Kaccha* are loose shorts worn

underneath the clothes that represent devotion, purity, self-control, and the prohibition of adultery, and the *Kirpan* is a ceremonial sword usually worn on a *gatra* (cloth belt) that symbolizes God's supreme power, self-defense (defending your faith), and fighting injustice and defending the weak.

Much of Sikh American community life revolves around the gurdwara. In addition to being a house of prayer and *langer* (dining hall), in the United States and elsewhere outside India, the gurdwara has also often served as a meeting place, school, social hub, employment information center, and a place for political activity and Punjabi culture and language. It is the place for Sikh Americans to be comfortably and fully Sikhs. For Sikh Americans, questions frequently arise regarding which traditions are strict core religious beliefs and which are cultural traditions that can be altered and changed in the United States. For example, whether the Guru Granth Sahib has to be in Punjabi or can be translated into English has become an issue in the Sikh American community. There is also debate about the meals served after services. Traditionally, these meals are Punjabi food, but some gurdwaras are beginning to serve more American foods, which are more familiar to many and easier to purchase and prepare. Some Sikhs see the actual food as a cultural tradition that can change, while other Sikhs view the preparing, serving, and sharing of the food as religious edict.

CULTURE AND ASSIMILATION

In the Sikh American community, religious issues are intricately enmeshed with cultural, social, and political issues and thus factor into attempts by Sikhs either to withdraw from American culture or assimilate into it. From the first wave of immigrants to the most recent, Sikhs in the United States have been discriminated against by individuals and institutions and in the media, albeit in a variety of forms and intensities in different eras and locations. For instance, early immigrants (pre-1967) were often not allowed to own land, marry white people in some states, travel abroad (and thus, were unable to return to visit family and their home culture in the Punjab), or participate in the political process. Some of the earlier immigrants in particular gave up the outward signs of their religion, such as wearing a *daastar* (turban) or carrying a *kirpin*, in order to succeed in employment or other mainstream activities, or to avoid discrimination and harassment. Some of these Sikh Americans later returned to donning more traditional dress and activities when more and newer immigrants arrived who adhered more to these symbols because they were more religious and were less assimilated into Western culture. However, newer immigrants tended to be more middle-class or upper-middle-class, well-educated, and urban-based and thus could often more easily integrate into Western life.

Traditions and Customs Sikh Americans typically take great pride in retaining Sikh traditions and customs. For example, many attend services in the

On August 5, 2012, six Sikhs were killed during a religious service at a temple near Milwaukee, Wisconsin by a white supremacist. In Plymouth, Michigan, hundreds of Detroit-area Sikhs held a memorial service and candlelight vigil at the Hidden Falls Gurdwara temple for victims of the shooting. JIM WEST / ALAMY

gurdwara and sing traditional hymns (*shabad kirtan*) while temple musicians (*ragis*) play music and help prepare the langer meal. In daily life, many Sikhs adhere to at least some of the five Ks, such as wearing turbans or not cutting their hair.

Cuisine Most Sikh Americans prefer native Punjabi cooking to American food. The main ingredients used in Punjabi cuisine include wheat, corn, dairy products like *malai* (cream) and *paneer* (a mild type of curdled cheese, like cottage cheese), and spices such as coriander, cloves, cinnamon, ginger, chili, and cumin. Some foods are made in a *tandoor* oven, which is a clay oven kept at very high temperatures. However, most Sikh Americans use an electric or gas oven. Common foods include *roti* (flat bread), *dhal*, *kulcha* (a baked bread), *sarson ka saag* (a curry type of gravy made from mustard leaves and spices, sometimes served on spinach and with roti), *rajma* (spiced kidney beans in gravy), *chole* (a spicy chickpea curry), and *kadhi* (curd curry). Although meat is banned for those who have gone through the Amrit Sanskar initiation ceremony, many Sikh Americans eat do not abide by this prohibition. Some Sikhs refrain from beef but eat fish and poultry.

All food served in the gurdwara, however, is vegetarian. A *lassi* is a common drink made with yogurt and water. Lassis can be prepared as sweet drinks (when mixed with fruit such as a mango), salty drinks, or savory drinks (mixed with, for example, roasted cumin).

Traditional Dress In order for one to be a Khalsa, a Sikh must wear the specific "spiritual" clothing, which is referred to as *bana* (literally meaning vocation or calling). In addition to the five Ks (e.g., uncut hair, comb, bracelet, ceremonial underwear or cotton shorts, and ceremonial sword), a turban must be worn. All attire must be modest. Often, a *salwar kameez* outfit is worn, which consists of loose-fitting drawstring cotton pants, a long shirt with open seams, or an overdress for women. Women also may wear a *dupatta*, a head scarf or shawl. The salwar kameez is worn by many people, not just Sikhs, in much of south and central Asia and Afghanistan. Sikh Americans may wear all or part of these traditional clothes. Devout Sikh Americans may adhere to all of these traditions on a daily basis, while other Sikh Americans may wear some of these, such as the turban, in daily life while reserving items such as a salwar for attending services

SIKH PROVERBS

The following are proverbs from the Guru Granth Sahib:

- Love me when I least deserve it, because that's when I really need it.

- The giver of peace is eternally blissful.

- Pride in social status is empty; pride in personal glory is useless.

- Some are stuck in falsehood, and false are the rewards they receive.

- Through selfless service, eternal peace is obtained.

at the gurdwara or for special occasions or holidays. Sikh Americans, especially youth, often dress in typical American clothing such as jeans and t-shirts. Many in the Sikh American communities have banned this type of dress in the gurdwara, however, to maintain a sense of propriety. Sometimes shawls and scarves are kept in the gurdwara and people are asked to cover themselves if they are considered to be inappropriately dressed.

The color of dress and turbans has various interpretations. For instance, some Sikhs believe that the color saffron represents devotion to Sikhism, that blue represents ancient Sikh warriors, and that white represents renouncing worldly matters. Other Sikhs feel that the colors of their turbans symbolize part of the Golden Temple, with white symbolizing the marble walls and saffron the golden dome. Black turbans tend to be more common among younger Sikhs. How turbans are tied also can vary. The traditional style worn in India is with a blunt rounded apex at the front, while Orthodox Sikhs use a more rounded style, and some younger Sikh Americans put a pointed apex at the front, a style begun by Sikhs in Kenya and Uganda.

Dances and Songs Many Sikhs view music as a way to attain spiritual happiness and transcendence. Services begin with the singing of *shabad kirtan*, or hymns from scripture. Specific hymns are used for different occasions and holidays. *Ragas* are scales of five to seven tones used for the *kirtans* and can be used in different combinations for different prayers. Traditional instruments accompany singing and can be categorized as either note instruments or rhythm instruments. *Svaravad* instruments are the note instruments and can include a *baja* or *vaja* (a harmonium, which is a type of hand-operated pump organ), *rabab* (a member of the lute family), *taus* (a large stringed instrument), *dilruba* (an eighteen-stringed instrument), and *sitar* (a seven-stringed instrument). *Tal*

vad instruments keep the rhythm of the music and can include the *jorri* or *tabla* (two small drums played mostly with the palm and fingers), *mridangam* (similar to a tabla, but longer and only a single drum) and different types of cymbals, such as *kartal* (handheld cymbals). Sacred instruments are often handmade.

The Sikh religion does not permit nonreligious dancing and dancing with partners of the opposite sex. However, religious and cultural dances are permitted, including dances such as *bhangra*, *tiranjan*, and *giddha*. These are performed for celebrations, community building, and special occasions. Bhangra, a Punjabi folk dance, originated as part of the April harvest celebration of Baisakhi and was done in circles accompanied by *dhols*, or large drums. There are Sikh American bhangra dance troupes that perform publicly, such as at the 2010 Smithsonian Folklife Festival. Bhangra has become a popular form of dance, often mixed with hip-hop or Bollywood-type dancing. Depending on the religious orthodoxy of Sikh Americans, this "fusion" bhangra dancing may or may not be acceptable.

Holidays Sikh Americans celebrate a range of holidays, including anniversaries of the ten gurus' births and deaths, certain Indian and Punjabi holidays, and American holidays such as Thanksgiving and the Fourth of July. Generally, during Sikh religious holidays, Sikh Americans spend time at the gurdwara with particular prayers, music, the communal dinner and other religious rituals, as well as having family time and eating special foods. Days on which gurus are remembered are called *gurpurb*, from the words *gur* (short for guru) and *purb* (which means a sacred or important day). Gurpurb celebrations usually include reading the entire scripture from start to finish (1,430 pages), which two days of round-the-clock reading (forty-eight hours) and is called *akhand-path*. Food is continuously served during akhand-path. Sikhs may come and go during any of the time of the reading. In some Sikh American communities there are processions during gurpurbs just as there are in India.

Baisakhi, or Vaisakhi, which commemorates the day Guru Gobin Singh established the Khalsa community, is considered by many to be the most important Sikh holiday. The holiday happens on the first day of the month of *Baisakh* in the Punjabi calendar, generally around mid-April. There is often a parade led by five Sikhs in saffron-colored traditional robes and turbans carrying swords; they symbolize the original five Sikhs that Guru Gobin Singh initiated into Sikhism. According to holiday tradition, the saffron cloth wrapped around the flagpole outside the temple is taken down, unwrapped, and washed with yogurt as a symbol of renewal and washing away one's sins from the past year; a new cloth is then wrapped around the flagpole before it is again placed in front of the gurdwara. In some cities, such as New Orleans, Washington, D.C., and New York, Sikh Americans celebrate Baisakhi with a parade. In New York City the parade often draws more than 20,000 spectators and includes a langer meal for all participants and spectators. In addition to being a joyous celebration, Baisakhi also commemorates the April 1919 massacre at the hands of the British in Jallianwala Bagh Park in Amritsar.

Holla Mohalla is another important holiday. Like Baisakhi, this holiday was initiated by Guru Govind Singh, who believed that Sikhs should be physically fit. On this holiday Sikhs once conducted mock battles and tests of physical prowess. In contemporary times, there are often martial-arts demonstrations and other physical competitions or games. Readings and poetry of Guru Govind Singh are recited. Generally Holla Mohalla happens around March (the first day of the lunar month *Chet*) and is also a celebration of the coming of spring. Holla Mohalla celebrations can last for about a week, although generally in the United States the celebrations are held on weekends to be more accommodating to Western work and school schedules.

Sikhs celebrate the birthday of Guru Nanak in the winter, and beginning in 2010 the founder's birthday was observed in the White House. In 2012, 160 Sikhs from around the United States were invited to the celebration with many senior officials from President Barack Obama's administration. Sikh Americans also observe the martyrdom of the fifth Sikh, Guru Arjan, who built the Golden Temple and was assassinated in 1606. In India Sikhs honor Guru Arjan by handing out cold drinks to people on the street, in subways, and in other places, and some Sikh American communities continue this tradition, handing out lassis or other drinks.

Sikh Americans also celebrate *melas*, which are festivals that have both religious and cultural significance. Diwali, for instance, is the winter Indian festival of lights and is considered the New Year's Day in the Indian calendar. Sikhs and Sikh Americans also celebrate this day as the day in 1619 when Guru Hargobind was released from prison. In the United States many Sikhs light candles and display colorful lights in temples. Sometimes there are fireworks displays.

Sikh Americans participate in the fair following the 15th Annual Sikh Independence Day Parade on April 20, 2002. RICHARD B. LEVINE / NEWSCOM

Sikh Americans also come together to celebrate with others specifically from the Punjab, whether they are Sikh or not. Starting in the early 1990s, for instance, there has been an annual Punjabi American Festival in Yuba City, California, with bhangra and giddha dancing, arts and crafts, Punjabi cuisine, henna tattoos, talent contests, and other displays of Punjabi culture. The festival draws up to 80,000 people.

FAMILY AND COMMUNITY LIFE

Unlike in India, where Sikhs live mostly in extended families, Sikhs in the United States generally live in nuclear families. Nevertheless, Sikh Americans still have strong ties not only within nuclear families but also with extended family and community members. Community life centers around the gurdwara, which is the place of worship but in the United States very often plays the role of a community center as well and is a place for Sikhs to affirm their traditions, customs, language, and culture. Hospitality is an important concept in Sikh family and community life, as exhibited, for instance, by the strong tradition of anyone visiting a gurdwara being offered food.

Gender Roles Sikhism promotes gender equality in religious rituals and life. The scriptures specifically say that men and women have equal souls and are allowed to participate equally in religious rituals and services, including reading from the scripture and singing hymns. However, gender equality is not necessarily a reality in the religious community and family life of Sikh Americans. Men are generally leaders and organizers of the gurdwaras, for instance, and the most widely known and important religious historical leaders were men. There are few historical religious female role models. Some of the gurus' mothers and sisters are well-known figures, such as Mata Tripta, who was the mother of the first guru, but these women are only known by their relationship to men. Additionally, gender roles persist in many instances of family and public life. For instance, even when women have jobs or professions outside the home, they are still expected to assume traditional roles as mothers and housekeepers.

Education A Sikh is supposed to be a disciple, a student of the gurus, who themselves were supposed to be teachers as well as students. Guru Nanak, for instance, believed in the concept of *goshati* (discussion), where teachers and students put questions to each other and learn from each other by engaging in a balanced conversation. Guru Nanak also considered careful observance of the physical world and sustained contact with other people, especially strangers, to be essential to learning. He used his five great journeys as a way of engaging in these practices.

Sikh American communities often have Sunday schools and summer camps where Sikh children learn to speak Punjabi and read its written script, Gurmukhi. Sikh American Sunday schools and camps also teach prayer, rituals, customs, culture, and arts. In addition, they focus on leadership skills and have parent seminars so parents can communicate with their children about the basic ideals of Sikhism.

While the first Sikh American immigrants were primarily farmers, later immigrants were often well-educated and came to the United States for further education or were highly educated professionals seeking jobs. There are numerous Sikh American organizations that provide scholarship opportunities to help Sikhs in the United States attend college or gain professional training. These include scholarships from the Association of Sikh Professionals and the Sikh Human Development Foundation (SHDF). There are a number of colleges and universities that have Sikh Studies or endowed chairs for Sikh Studies (often funded by successful Sikh American entrepreneurs), such as the University of Michigan, the University of California at Santa Barbara, Hofstra University, and the University of Birmingham.

Courtship and Weddings Traditional Sikh marriage ceremonies are called *Anand Karaj*, meaning blissful ceremony. Generally, weddings take place in the gurdwara, where a prayer is recited to bless and begin the ceremony and a hymn, randomly selected, is read. Four marriage hymns, called *lavan*, are read, and the bride and groom circle the Guru Granth Sahib (scriptures) four times, once for each hymn. Traditionally, the bride walks slightly behind the groom, but in more ceremonies, especially in the United States, the man and woman walk side by side in a show of equality. Each lavan represents an aspect of the couple's obligations. The first lavan is about the couple fulfilling family and community obligations; the second is about the couple bonding to each other with love and respect; the third is about detaching from worldly matters and maintaining faith in challenging times; and the fourth is about translating one's love into service to God and about having a balanced life. Circling the Guru Granth Sahib is a symbol of the never-ending movement of life and the couple's love, which has no beginning and no end. The congregation joins in a concluding hymn called an *ardaas*. After the ceremony, there is often a wedding reception (not necessarily in the gurdwara, but in a rented hall or community center) that includes usually a large meal, music, dancing, and gifts.

Traditionally, Sikh marriages are arranged, but that is no longer common in the Sikh American community, and it is also becoming less common in the Punjab. However, despite more Western-style dating patterns and a greater frequency of love marriages, family involvement and input is still of great import, especially as a relationship becomes more serious and moves toward engagement. Interfaith marriages are not expressly forbidden, but there is a strong value on marriage between Sikhs in order to maintain one's faith and to raise children in the faith. Younger-generation Sikh Americans are intermarrying more, however. While dating, Sikhs commonly go out in large groups, often with other family members present. Many Sikh Americans recoil from these traditional practices and long to date as American couples do, but they often encounter considerable resistance from parents who are not willing to accept this aspect of American culture.

EMPLOYMENT AND ECONOMIC CONDITIONS

In the late 1970s and early 1980s, when certain professional jobs, such as that of a physician, were becoming more difficult to find in the American Northeast, some Sikh Americans moved to the South, to places such as Raleigh-Durham, North Carolina, and Augusta and Atlanta, Georgia, where they established small Sikh American communities, built gurdwaras, and established organizations such as the Sikh Religious Society of South Carolina.

By the 1980s the Silicon Valley technology industry had started to flourish, and some South Asian immigrants, including Sikhs, were brought to the United States to work at discounted wages. While these discounted wages were more than Indian wages and were generally equivalent to middle-class U.S. wages, because of the very high standard of living in the Silicon Valley, these Sikhs still sometimes struggled economically. The situation began to change during the 1990s and early 2000s, when India became a high-level training place for computer engineers and the software business.

Other Sikh Americans continued to struggle economically. In New York City, for instance, during the 1990s and 2000s, male South Asian immigrants, including many Sikhs, made up a majority of taxi drivers, with estimates varying from 70 to 90 percent of all drivers. Some of these immigrants had come to the United States without higher education or professional experience, but South Asian immigrant taxi drivers generally had a high level of educational attainment (compared to other cab drivers) and had worked in professional jobs. In many cases their educational credentials were not accepted in the United States.

POLITICS AND GOVERNMENT

While there are no specific studies on Sikh American voting patterns, a 2012 Pew Research Report on Asian Americans reported that 65 percent of Indian Americans (whose highest percentage are Sikhs) are Democrats or lean Democrat. Whatever the case, Sikhs were a highly visible part of the political landscape at both the Republican and Democratic national conventions in the run-up to the 2012 presidential election. Sikh Americans had an important presence at the Democratic National Convention in 2012; twenty-six Sikh Americans were part of the California delegation. Sikh American leader Ishwar Singh provided an invocation during the Republican National Convention in Tampa in 2012.

Sikh Americans have been involved in politics to help promote their civil rights, deal with hate crimes, and educate the public about Sikhs. In 2003 Sikh leaders met with the director of the White House Office of Public Liaison, Tim Goeglein, and discussed hate-crime issues and how to promote understanding of Sikh life. In 2005 the White House hosted a Sikh American Heritage Dinner honoring Sikhs and their involvement in civic life. About 225 people attended, and speakers included then-senators Hillary Rodham Clinton and Rick Santorum and Congresspersons Tom David and Jim McDermott. In 2012 the first-ever briefing on Sikh American civil rights was held at the White House.

Sikhs in the United States have also been involved in many causes for social justice and fairness in the media. For instance, Sikh American cab drivers in New York City were instrumental in organizing the largest ever New York taxi drivers' strike, held by the New York Taxi Workers Alliance in 1998. It involved 12,200 cab drivers protesting new and restrictive rules imposed by the mayor. In 2012, when late-night television host Jay Leno showed a photo of the Harmandir Sahib (Golden Temple) and joked that it was presidential candidate Mitt Romney's summer home (to poke fun at Romney's wealth), many Sikh Americans protested with petitions and letters. Sikh American Randeep Dhillon filed a law suit against NBC for libel on behalf of himself and the Punjabi All Regions Community Organization.

NOTABLE INDIVIDUALS

Business Gurbaksh Singh Chahal (1982–) was born in Punjab, India, and moved with his family to California in 1985. Chahal is an Internet entrepreneur whose start-ups include ClickAgents, an online ad network, and BlueLithium, which helped online advertisers target customer behavior and was named one of the top 100 private companies by AlwaysOn for three years consecutive years. Chahal was named Innovator of the Year in 2007 and earned the Leaders in Management Award in 2010. His memoir *The Dream* (2008) was well received.

Ishar Bindra (1921–) was born in the Punjab, fought with the Indian army, and immigrated to the United States after he retired in India in 1979. Bindra is a businessman and philanthropist who founded the Jeetish Group of Companies, which includes apparel, commodities, and real estate companies. He was awarded the Life Time Achievement Award by the World Punjabi Society (2005) and the Life Time Achievement Award (2006) by the Sikh Council of Religious Education.

Government Dalip Singh Saund (1899–1973) was born in the Punjab and was the first Asian American to be elected to Congress (in 1956 from California's 29th district). He won three terms and was gaining notoriety in American politics when he had a debilitating stroke during his campaign for a fourth term.

Ricky Kashmir Gill (1987–), the son of Indian immigrants, was the mayor of Yuba City, California, from 2009 to 2010, a member of its city council from 2006 to 2009, and a member of the California State Board of Education in 2004. In 2012 he unsuccessfully ran for Congress as a Republican.

Nimrata Kaur Randhawa Haley (1972–), better known as Nikki Haley, was born in South Carolina to Indian immigrants and received an accounting degree from Clemson University. Haley was elected governor of South Carolina in 2012. A Republican, she was the first Sikh governor in the United States and the first female governor of South Carolina. She had previously served in the South Carolina House of Representatives from 2005 to 2010.

Preetinder Singh "Preet" Bharara (1968–) was born in Punjab, India, to a Sikh father and Hindu mother and immigrated to New Jersey. He attended Harvard University and Columbia Law School. A lawyer, Bharara was nominated by President Barack Obama to be the U.S. attorney for the Southern District of New York and was unanimously confirmed by the U.S. Senate in 2009. In 2012 *Time* magazine named him one of the 100 most influential people in the world.

Journalism Valarie Kaur is a writer, award-winning filmmaker, civil rights advocate, and interfaith leader. She has been a regular contributor to TV shows such as *Melissa Harris-Perry* (MSNBC) and magazines and newspapers such as *CNN*, the *Washington Post*, the *New York Times*, and *Salon*. Kaur and her film partner Sharat Raju produced the documentaries *Divided We Fall* (2008), *Alienation* (2011), *Stigma* (2011), *The Worst of the Worst: Portrait of a Supermax* (2012), and *Oak Creek: In Memoriam* (2013), about the mass shooting at the Wisconsin gurdwara in 2012.

Music Snatam Kaur Khalsa (1972–) is an American Sikh singer and songwriter who performs devotional music (kirtan) and lectures on peace throughout the world. She was born in Trinidad and moved to California when she was two years old. Her albums include *Prem* (2002), *Shanti* (2003), *Grace* (2004), *Anand* (2006), *The Essential Snatam Kaur: Sacred Chants For Healing* (2010), *Raas* (2011), and *Heart of the Universe* (2012).

Religion Harbhajan Singh Khalsa Yogi (1929–2004) introduced kundalini yoga to the United States in 1968. He gained a worldwide following and in 1969 founded the nonprofit 3HO (Healthy, Happy, Holy Organization) Foundation, which spread to thirty-five countries. In 1971 he was named chief religious and administrative authority for the Western Hemisphere by the Akal Takhat, the Sikh seat of religious authority in Amritsar. He became a U.S. citizen in 1976.

Science and Medicine Narinder Singh Kapany (1926–) is a physicist who is often called "the father of fiber optics." He has also worked on biomedical instruments, solar energy, and pollution monitoring. He founded companies such as Optics Technology, Kaptron, and K2 Optronics and holds over one hundred patents.

Sports Alexi Singh Grewa (1960–) won a gold medal in the 1984 Olympics in cycling. As of 2013, he was still the only Sikh American ever win a gold medal. He grew up in Colorado, the son of a Sikh father and a German mother. His father had immigrated to the United States in 1956.

Stage and Screen Waris Ahluwalia (1975–) is an actor, writer, producer, and jewelry designer. His best-known films are *The Life Aquatic with Steve Zissou* (2004), *Inside Man* (2006), *Hotel Chevalier* (2007), and *The Darjeeling Limited* (2007). He was born in Punjab, India, and immigrated with his family to New York when he was five.

Tanveer Kaur Atwal (1994–) is an actress who acted in the movie *The Matrix Revolutions* (2003). She also appeared in the television series *The Office* (2006). She was born in California to Sikh parents.

MEDIA

PRINT

Punjab Mail USA

Punjab Mail USA is a Punjabi-language newspaper, published weekly and distributed all over the West Coast.

Gurjatinder Singh Randhawa, Chief Editor
10481 Grant Line Road #175
Elk Grove, California 95624
Phone: (916) 320-9444
Fax: (916) 209-8726
Email: punjabmailusa@yahoo.com
URL: http://web.punjabmailusa.com/

Sher-E-Panjab

This nationally distributed weekly Punjabi newspaper has been published from New York since 1999.

Phone: (516) 783-1001
Fax: (516) 783-1004
Email: editor@sher-e-panjab.com
URL: www.sher-e-panjab.com

Sikhchic

Sikhchic is an online Sikh magazine (in English) covering arts, religion, sports, news, food, humor, fashion, and travel.

Email: editor@sikhchic.com
URL: www.sikhchic.com

RADIO

Punjabi Radio USA

Established in 2010, Punjabi Radio broadcasts 24/7 from Bakersfield, California, to Reno, Nevada, and Washington State, as well as to other areas in the

West. It includes a number of music shows, talk shows, arts and cultural shows, business shows, and news from India, the United States, and other places around the world where Punjabis live.

3750 Mckee Road
Suite A
San Jose, California 95127
Phone: (408) 272-5200
Fax: (408) 493-4552
Email: info@punjabiradiousa.com
URL: www.punjabiradiousa.com

ORGANIZATIONS AND ASSOCIATIONS

Sikh American Chamber of Commerce (SACC)

The SACC was founded in 2011 to promote successful entrepreneurship in the Sikh American community.

120 Wood Ave South
Suite 608
Iselin, New Jersey 08830
Phone: (732) 379-6180
Fax: (646) 349-2572
Email: info@sikhamericanchamber.org
URL: www.sikhamericanchamber.org

Sikh American Legal Defense and Education Fund (SALDEF)

A civil rights and educational organization, SALDEF was founded in 1996 to empower Sikh Americans through advocacy, education, and media relations.

Jasjit Singh, Executive Director
1012 14th Street NW
Suite 450
Washington, D.C. 20005
Phone: (202) 393-2700
Fax: (202) 318-4433
URL: www.saldef.org

The Sikh Coalition

The Sikh Coalition is a civil and human rights community organization founded in response to the 9/11 attacks and the heightened incidence of racism that ensued. Provides legal services for those whose civil or human rights have been violated and promotes civic discourse and education.

Sapreet Kaur, Executive Director
50 Broad Street
Suite 1537
New York, New York 10004
Phone: (212) 655-3095
URL: www.sikhcoalition.org

The Sikh Foundation

Founded in 1967, the foundation promotes the heritage and future of Sikhism to Sikhs in the West, particularly youth. Its projects include working on academic courses in Sikh studies, art exhibits, and renovation and conservation of historical Sikh monuments.

Sonia Dhami, Director of Cultural Affairs
580 College Avenue
Palo Alto, California 94306

Phone: (650) 494-7454
Fax: (650) 494-3316
Email: info@sikhfoundation.org
URL: www.sikhfoundation.org

World Sikh Council—America Region (WSC-AR)

This umbrella organization was established to promote Sikh interests at the national and international level, focusing on education and advocacy.

P.O. Box 3635
Columbus, Ohio 43210
Phone: (888) 340-1702
Fax: (888) 398-1875
Email: contact@worldsikhcouncil.org
URL: www.worldsikhcouncil.org

MUSEUMS AND RESEARCH CENTERS

Center for Sikh and Punjab Studies

The center was opened in 2004 as a venue for research and scholarly exchange at the University of California, Santa Barbara. It promotes undergraduate and graduate teaching, disseminates knowledge through publications and outreach activities, and assists other universities.

Gurinder Singh Mann
3051 Humanities & Social Sciences Building
University of California
Santa Barbara, California 93106
Phone: (805)-893-5115
Email: mann@religion.ucsb.edu
URL: www.global.ucsb.edu/punjab

Sikh History Museum and Library

This library, located at the Stockton Gurdwara in California, was founded in 2012 as the first Sikh museum and library in the United States. Its main artifact is the hand-cranked printing press used by the revolutionary Gadar Party leaders to print the *Gadar*, the first Punjabi-language newspaper in the United States, which was published from 1913 to 1948.

Stockton Gurdwara Sahib
1930 South Grant Street, Stockton
California 95206
Email: stocktonsikhtemple@gmail.comhttp://sikhcentury.us/sikh-history-museum-library/

Sikh Research Institute

The Sikh Research Institute provides educational resources, including podcasts and videos for students, and organizes events, programs, and training sessions.

Ravinder Singh, Acting Executive Director
P.O. Box 690504
San Antonio, Texas 78269
Phone: (210) 757-4555
Fax: (469) 324-2954
Email: info@sikhri.org
URL: www.sikhri.org

SOURCES FOR ADDITIONAL STUDY

Angelo, Michael. *The Sikh Diaspora: Tradition and Change in an Immigrant Community*. New York: Routledge, 1997.

Hawley, John Stratton, and Gurinder Singh Mann. *Studying the Sikhs: Issues for North America*. Albany: State University of New York Press, 1993.

Mahmood, Cynthia Keppley, and Stacy Brady. *The Guru's Gift: An Ethnography Exploring Gender Equality with North American Sikh Women*. Mountain View, CA: Mayfield Publishers, 2000.

Mann, Gurinder Singh. *Sikhism*. Upper Saddle River, NJ: Prentice Hall, 2004.

———, Paul Numrich, and Raymond Williams. *Buddhists, Hindus, and Sikhs in America*. New York: Oxford University Press, 2008.

Sidhu, Dawinder S., and Neha Singh Gohil. *Civil Rights in Wartime: The Post-9/11 Sikh Experience*. Burlington, VT: Ashgate, 2009.

Singh, Patwants. *The Sikhs*. New York: Random House, 1999.

Verma, Rita. *Backlash: South Asian Immigrant Voices on the Margins*. Rotterdam, The Netherlands: Sense Publishers, 2008.

SIOUX

D. L. Birchfield

OVERVIEW

The Sioux are a cluster of Native American tribes who originated in the areas of present-day Wisconsin, Minnesota, Illinois, and Iowa. Since the early nineteenth century, the Great Sioux Nation has consisted of three subgroups: the Eastern Dakota (made up of the Santee and Sisseton), the Western Dakota (the Yankton and Yanktonai), and the Lakota (the Teton or Teton Sioux). These Sioux tribes of today were once part of one of the largest American indigenous groups north of Mexico, second in numbers only to the Algonquian people. In the pre-Columbian era (the time in the Americas from prehistory until significant European influence occurred), the Siouan peoples occupied an immense geographical area of the North American continent, from the Rocky Mountains to the Mississippi River and from the Great Lakes to the Gulf of Mexico. Scholars have been able to connect this disparate and widespread grouping of peoples through language. Long before contact with non-Indians, those who spoke the original Siouan language separated into numerous distinct tribes. Some of these many tribes include the Osage and Crow of the Great Plains, the Winnebago in Wisconsin, the Biloxi on the Gulf Coast, and the Catawba in the Southeast. The name *Sioux* originates from the Ottawa word *na-towe-ssi* (which in term was derived from a word from an earlier language meaning "foreigner"); the French wrote it as *Nadouessioux*. The Sioux subgroup names *Lakota* and *Dakota* are Siouan words meaning "friend" or "ally."

The earliest records—those of French trappers in present-day Wisconsin and Minnesota in around 1660—logged approximately 28,000 Sioux in the years just prior to the European exploration and settlement of the later seventeenth century. By the early eighteenth century, the Sioux had moved west, following buffalo herds and trading opportunities and also fleeing conflict with other tribes, particularly the Cree, Ottawa, and Chippewa. Historical and anthropological research asserts that in their original location, the Sioux were semisedentary woodland people with an economy based on fishing, hunting, gathering, and some corn cultivation. They manufactured items for trade, such as beaded garments, and groups sometimes held trading fairs, partly as a means of staying in contact with their neighbors. Several Siouan groups endured years of conflict with neighboring tribes, however.

Tribal groups belonging to today's Great Sioux Nation have sixteen reservations and communities across five western U.S. states—Minnesota, Nebraska, South Dakota, North Dakota, and Montana—as well as several Canadian reserves. Numerous treaties between Sioux groups and the U.S. government over the course of two centuries gradually restricted Sioux territory. By the late nineteenth century, the tribes had been pushed westward and northward so that they chiefly resided in the northern Great Plains and Canada. The lands of the Sioux have been a focal point for some of the most dramatic events of Native American activism in modern times, including the 1973 siege of Wounded Knee. Alongside political action, the Sioux have experienced great interest in and revitalization of their traditional practices; Sioux writers, poets, and political leaders are among the most influential leaders in the North American Native American community today, and the traditions of the Sioux religion have had an influence far beyond the Sioux people.

The 2010 U.S. Census stated that 170,110 individuals identified as Sioux at that time, either solely or in combination with another race. Roughly half of these people live on reservations. The most populous Sioux reservation is the Oglala Lakota reservation of Pine Ridge in the southwest corner of South Dakota, which in 2010 was home to 18,824 people (16,906 of whom identified as Native American). Many Sioux have migrated to metropolitan areas, and some have found flourishing urban Native American communities, particularly in Chicago and Minneapolis. Family ties remain strong, however, and many urban Sioux travel frequently to their home reservation. According to the 2010 U.S. Census American Community Survey estimates for 2006 to 2010, states with large populations of Sioux tribes include California, Colorado, Montana, and South Dakota. Smaller but still significant numbers reside in Minnesota, Nebraska, North Dakota, Oklahoma, Texas, and Washington.

HISTORY OF THE PEOPLE

Early History According to scholars' reconstruction of linguistic patterns, all of the Siouan-language peoples originated in the wooded and riparian areas of present-day Wisconsin, Minnesota, Illinois, and Iowa. French trappers first encountered Dakota Sioux in the region surrounding Lake Superior around 1660. By this time, however, the Sioux had begun to disperse northward and westward because of conflicts with Ojibwe and Chippewa Indians. The Eastern Dakota migrated toward Lake Michigan, the Lakota moved into the Black Hills region of South Dakota, and the Yankton-Yanktonai settled along the Missouri River. Eventually, all of the groups pushed farther west and north, settling in Montana, North Dakota, and Canada. As they moved onto the expansive northern Great Plains in the eighteenth and nineteenth centuries, the Sioux tribes adopted tipi structures and became more reliant on buffalo as a primary source of food and materials.

After the first recorded European contact with Sioux tribes in the late seventeenth century, Sioux experience was shaped by an ever-growing European presence on the North American continent. Routes west, whether for trapping, hunting, gold mining, or homesteading, played a pivotal role in redefining Sioux national independence. By the mid-eighteenth century, streams of men from the East first passed through western hunting territories on their way to the gold fields of Montana, Idaho, and California. They drained traditional hunting grounds, depleted resources, and presented the threat of warfare. Moreover, these newcomers brought with them smallpox, measles, and other contagious diseases to which the Sioux had no immunity and which ravaged their population, reducing their numbers by an estimated one-half, despite U.S. efforts to inoculate some American Indians. This tide continued unabated well into the next century.

Beginning in earnest in the mid-nineteenth century, missionary influence on Sioux culture had a long-standing impact. Early missionary interaction with Sioux groups primarily took place in Minnesota, where two Congregational missionaries, Samuel W. and Gideon H. Pond, transcribed and generated an orthography of the Sioux language they encountered. Their work facilitated a broader reach for mission work within Sioux tribes in other areas. Their orthography initiated a strong educational component to missionary work, as efforts to increase literacy among the Sioux offered another way to introduce Christianity to the Sioux.

The nineteenth century also inaugurated an era of treaty-making and treaty-breaking between the U.S. government and Indian tribes. It was not uncommon for either party to violate treaty agreements, leading to a breakdown in negotiations, at times resulting in dire consequences. This was the case with the Dakota War of 1862, also known as the Sioux Uprising of 1862 or the Minnesota Massacre. Led by Chief Little Crow, the Minnesota Mdewakanton Dakota Sioux launched sweeping attacks on European settlements throughout the Minnesota River Valley and in northern Minnesota in efforts to expel the white newcomers. Opposed by the Minnesota Militia and later by the U.S. Army, Dakota combatants surrendered after about six weeks of fighting, having suffered hundreds of casualties. During subsequent military trials 300 Sioux were sentenced to death; the number was reduced to thirty-eight through an intervention by President Abraham Lincoln. On December 26, 1862, the thirty-eight Sioux warriors were hanged for their role in the conflict in what remains the largest mass execution in U.S. history. The event drove some Santee Sioux bands into Canadian territories, where they remain today in independent settlements.

Meanwhile, armed conflict between Sioux groups and the U.S. government persisted in other regions. In Red Cloud's War (1866–1868), Oglala Lakota chief Red Cloud led Lakota, Northern Cheyenne, and Northern Arapaho fighters in a rebellion against the U.S. Army's presence in, and European settlers' intrusion into, the fertile Powder River Valley of Wyoming. The conflict consisted of small raids and attacks on three garrisons. The Lakota victory resulted in the signing of the Treaty of Fort Laramie (1868), which established the Great Sioux Reservation on the western half of the South Dakota Territory and secured the Powder River Valley as "unceded Indian territory" for those who chose not to relocate to the reservation. Representing a watershed moment in Native American history, the treaty banned whites from settling in these areas or even passing through without permission. Significantly, the treaty also guaranteed Lakota control over the Black Hills area of present-day South Dakota (*Paha Sapa*, meaning "the heart of everything that is"), a sacred site for the Lakota Sioux peoples. The agreement achieved temporary peace in the Sioux lands of the Great Plains.

In the 1870s, however, the discovery of gold in the Black Hills, confirmed by Lieutenant Colonel George Armstrong Custer in 1874, brought hordes of miners to the area in blatant violation of the treaty and of Sioux sovereignty. The Great Sioux War of 1876 to 1877, which pitted the Lakota Sioux and Northern Cheyenne against the U.S. Army, lasted one year and resulted in significant casualties on both sides of the conflict. Notably, nearly three hundred U.S. soldiers died at the Battle of the Little Bighorn in June 1876, including the much-lauded Custer. Despite the tribes' victory at Little Bighorn, they were weakened and lacking in resources, and the majority finally surrendered. Renowned Lakota Sioux leader Sitting Bull and a party of fighters fled to Canada, where they remained, refusing to surrender or negotiate. In 1880 they returned and conceded defeat. Significantly, the war resulted in the breaking up of the Great Sioux Reservation into smaller reservations more widely dispersed across the northern Great Plains. While many

Lakota Sioux remained in the region of the former Great Sioux Reservation, referred to today as the Pine Ridge Reservation, other groups established their own settlements, such as the Cheyenne River Community in northwest central South Dakota.

As white settlers decimated the bison herds and the U.S. government violated its treaties as well as its promises to protect and subsidize reservation life, Sioux reservation lands dwindled further. The last decade of the nineteenth century saw a crescendo of violence in what is widely considered the final battle of the American-Indian Wars, the Battle of Wounded Knee (1890). On the Pine Ridge Reservation, unrest and a growing interest in the Ghost Dance, a pan-Indian, anti-white spiritual movement led by Paiute prophet Wovoka, frightened whites into attempting to interfere in traditional practices. U.S. officials endeavored to arrest Sitting Bull and inadvertently killed him instead. Soon afterwards, U.S. soldiers asked Lakota Ghost Dancers to surrender their weapons, and the confrontation escalated into a full-scale battle. The loss of life among the Sioux far outweighed the fallen U.S. soldiers; nearly half the Sioux casualties were women and children, leading many to call the incident the Wounded Knee Massacre. It was the last armed conflict between the Plains Indians and the U.S. government; the site was later declared a National Historic Landmark.

Modern Era At the end of the nineteenth century and into the twentieth, Sioux resources were further depleted, and U.S. policies increasingly alienated the tribes from long-standing spiritual and cultural customs. Within a generation many Sioux found themselves paupers in their native land, with no alternative but to accept reservation life. Catholic and Protestant churches continued to establish missions on the reservations to acculturate the Sioux, setting up boarding schools where Indian children were instructed in Western mores. In the mid-twentieth century, the U.S. government put into effect an official policy of "termination" of Indian nations that was supported by Congress, some states, and some tribes; the aim was to dissolve the unique political relationship between the U.S. government and tribal groups and to bring tribal members under state jurisdiction. Some tribal members saw it as a chance to be free of paternalism, but the policy resulted in further limiting Indian land rights, weakening Native Americans' autonomy, and revoking programs supporting tribal economies, health care, and culture. While the 1975 Indian Self-Determination and Education Assistance Act effectively put an end to the termination policy, only within recent decades have attempts been made by the U.S. government to redress past wrongs.

Such gains have not come without bloodshed and strife, however. During the civil rights era of the 1960s, Native Americans of many tribes organized political activist groups, the best-known being

Sioux girl, c. 1900. THE LIBRARY OF CONGRESS

the American Indian Movement (AIM), founded in 1968 in Minneapolis to address the predicaments of urban Indians. The originators were mainly Ojibwe, but Russell Means, an Oglala Lakota from the Pine Ridge Reservation, joined in the first year and became a primary organizer of protest events. After attracting members nationwide, the organization led a march to Washington, D.C., in 1971 and took over the national office of the Bureau of Indian Affairs (BIA), issuing a list of twenty demands. Takeovers of Alcatraz Island in the San Francisco Bay and Mount Rushmore also demonstrated AIM's efforts to reclaim traditional Native American lands. These protests often had high Sioux participation. Perhaps no other event typifies the problems encountered by traditional Indians in seeking the redress of long-standing grievances with the United States more than the Siege of Wounded Knee in 1973, a standoff between Lakota Sioux and the U.S. government in which activists demanded justice for treaty violations.

In the latter half of the twentieth century, Sioux tribes gained increased measures of self-determination while the BIA's legal and economic power diminished. Once dependent on the BIA to provide funding, the Sioux benefitted from the establishment of the Office of Economic Opportunity in 1974, which provided an alternate means of accessing funds and gave tribal leaders power to distribute the funds as they saw fit. Another significant expansion in Sioux tribes' sovereignty came with the passage of the Indian Self-Determination and Education Assistance Act in 1975. The act gave tribes the ability to contract and administer programs formerly run by the BIA, allowing them much more control over day-to-day reservation management. For the Sioux, one marked effect of these changes was to spur economic growth and development of tribal enterprises, which has had lasting impacts, albeit with varying degrees of success.

In the early 1990s several Sioux tribes participated in a national trend by entering into the gaming industry; the Shakopee Mdewakanton Sioux, Prairie Island Sioux, and Lower Brule Sioux all established casinos on their reservations. These enterprises have brought economic development to reservation communities through increased cash flow and employment opportunities. The era of self-determination has not yielded the same rewards for all Sioux tribes, however. The Standing Rock Sioux attempted to establish almost twenty businesses on their North Dakota reservation between 1970 and 1995, without success. For less economically successful reservations, the turn of the twenty-first century has witnessed the breakdown of traditional customs, rampant alcoholism, and pervasive health issues. Some of these challenges are occasioned by the rural settings in which the majority of reservations are located. The first decades of the twenty-first century also brought extensive efforts across Sioux country to reassert tribal identity through cultural programs and language education, as well as efforts to address reservation troubles through a variety of initiatives, ranging from job training and career counseling to preventative health measures and youth drug and alcohol education. In one success story the U.S. Department of Housing and Urban Development awarded a nearly one-million-dollar Sustainable Communities Planning Grant to a community development corporation on the Pine Ridge Reservation in 2010 that was intended to establish around a dozen initiatives for sustainable development in a variety of sectors.

SETTLEMENT IN THE UNITED STATES

By the early nineteenth century, the Eastern and Western Dakota and the Lakota had separated enough that marked differences in language, politics, and culture existed among them. The Western Dakota, also called the Yankton and Yanktonai settled between the Minnesota River Valley and the Missouri River. The Santee, or Eastern Dakota, took up residence in Minnesota, extending their range into northern Iowa and the eastern part of the Dakota Territory. The Lakota, sometimes referred to as the Teton, moved farthest west into the western parts of North and South Dakota, eventually reaching Montana, thanks to the adoption of horses for mobility.

During the reservation years (beginning in the 1850s), Sioux groups were established in disparate reservations, the first permanent ones being the Crow Creek Reservation in central South Dakota, established in 1862, and the Santee Sioux Reservation in Niobrara, Nebraska, established in 1863. Today, the westernmost is the Fort Peck Assiniboine and Sioux Reservation in northeastern Montana, and the southernmost is the Nebraska Santee Reservation. At the northern end of the group of reservations, the Spirit Lake Reservation is in the east central part of North Dakota. Minnesota has the four easternmost Sioux reservations. The location of the greatest Sioux population and the most Sioux-owned square miles is South Dakota, with nine reservations.

Some of these communities are home to a single Sioux tribe, such as South Dakota's Rosebud Reservation, the home of the Sicangu Oyate (a Lakota tribe); and the Yankton Sioux Reservation of the Yankton Sioux, also in South Dakota. Many contemporary reservations, however, are inhabited by people descended from a variety of Sioux bands, including Standing Rock, which straddles the North Dakota–South Dakota border and is home to Dakota, Lakota, and Yankton-Yanktonai, including many separate bands of each. The largest Sioux reservations in square acreage are Pine Ridge, Cheyenne River, and Standing Rock.

States without Sioux reservations that also have a significant number of Sioux residents include California, Colorado, Oklahoma, Texas, and Washington. In recent decades an increased number of individuals identify as mixed heritage; among the 170,110 Sioux counted in the 2010 U.S. Census, 53,633 identified as Sioux in combination with one or more other race.

LANGUAGE

Members of the Siouan language family can be found almost everywhere east of the Rocky Mountains except on the southern Plains and in the Northeast. The northern Plains are home to the Crow, Hidatsa, and Dakota (Sioux) speakers. The Omaha, Osage, Ponca, Kansa, and Quapaw languages are spoken on the central Plains; Winnebago is spoken in Wisconsin; on the Gulf Coast are speakers of the Tutelo, Ofo, and Biloxi languages; and in the Southeast are Catawba speakers. Moreover, Siouan languages are not restricted to the United States but extend far into the prairie provinces of Canada. The immense geographical spread of the languages within this family is testimony to the importance of Siouan-speaking peoples in the history of the continent.

Tribes speaking languages belonging to the Macro-Siouan language group are numerous, but those American Indian tribes ethnically identifying as Sioux speak three main, geographically varied but mutually intelligible dialects from within the subcategory of Dakota languages. These are Lakota, Western Dakota (Yankton-Yanktonai), and Eastern Dakota (Santee-Sisseton), all of which have further splintered into several subdialects. The largest difference among the main Dakota dialects is the pronunciation of key sounds; one example is that where Lakota speakers employ an "l" sound, Santee-Sisseton Dakota speakers use a "d" sound and the Yankton-Yanktonai use an "n." Europeans utilized these variations to differentiate among the tribes: they concluded that since the Lakota

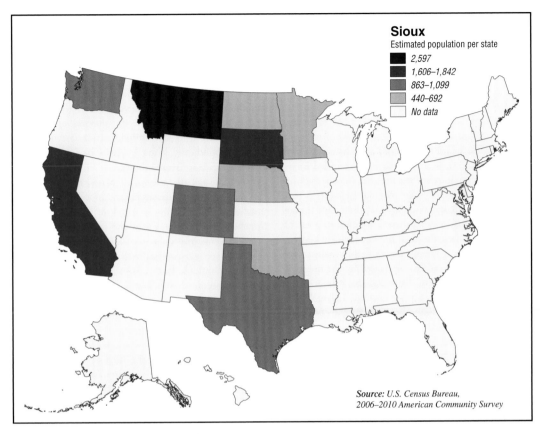

Sioux
Estimated population per state

- 2,597
- 1,606–1,842
- 863–1,099
- 440–692
- No data

*Source: U.S. Census Bureau,
2006–2010 American Community Survey*

and Dakota tribes' languages reflect their names, then the Yankton-Yanktonai's use of "n" implied their name to be Nakota, when in fact this title referred to a distinct tribe that had broken away from the Sioux. Like English, the Dakota languages use a subject-object-verb phrase structure and is an agglutinative language, meaning that it incorporates prefixes, infixes, and suffixes with specific rules. For example, English uses the suffix "s" or "es" to denote plural objects, and in Dakota the suffix "pi" denotes multiples. The three languages are assumed to be mutually intelligible, but Lakota and Yankton-Yanktonai speakers have difficulty understanding Santee-Sisseton speakers because their vocabulary has diverged further.

The 2010 U.S. Census counted 18,616 people who self-reported as Dakota speakers. In 2010 fewer than 6,000 individuals were estimated to speak Lakota, most of whom were over sixty-five years of age. Few people under thirty years old were considered fluent.

In the late twentieth century, community leaders began to make significant efforts to revive Siouan languages. In the early twenty-first century, education programs for every age group and ability level were available in both Dakota and Lakota languages. The Pine Ridge Reservation initiated an immersion child-care program in 2012 to begin Lakota language education for children under the age of two. Established in 2002, the nonprofit organization Lakota Language

Consortium, headquartered in Bloomington, Indiana, has dedicated itself to regenerating a vibrant linguistic culture through the production of Lakota-language learning tools, teacher training, and community events. Summer camps such as those run on the Cheyenne River Reservation in South Dakota and by the Gibbs House in Minnesota also encourage young people to use the Siouan language of their forebears. Students from North Dakota, South Dakota, and Manitoba competed in a Dakota-language Scrabble tournament in 2006. Education programs are offered at the university level as well, including at the University of North Dakota, the University of Minnesota, and the University of Colorado at Boulder, where students can continue their academic study of Siouan languages and cultures.

The Sioux were also masters of sign language, a long-standing vehicle of communication among native peoples of the North American continent. The Lakota Sioux language can be heard in the video documentary *Wiping the Tears of Seven Generations* (1992), directed by Gary Rhine and Fidel Moreno, which includes recorded interviews with a number of Sioux members of the Wounded Knee Survivors' Association relating their grandparents accounts of the 1890 massacre at Wounded Knee.

Greetings and Popular Expressions A common greeting in both Dakota and Lakota is *hau*, or *haw* (how)—"hello," with variations for gender. In

Lakota, *Waste*! (wash-tay) means "Good!" In Dakota, *Tokiya da he*? (doh-key-ah-DAH-hey) means "Where are you going?" "Thank you" is *pilamaya* (pee-la-ma-ya) in Lakota and *pidamayaye* (pee-da-ma-ya-yay) in Dakota.

RELIGION

No Native American religion has been more closely studied or more widely known than the Sioux religion, partly because of John Niehardt's popular book *Black Elk Speaks* (1932), in which Niehardt recorded interviews with the Sioux spiritual leader. Another reason for the prominence of Sioux religious practices is that AIM adopted many of them into their Pan-Indian Movement, thus carrying these principles to areas of the continent where they had not been widely known. The so-called New Age movement within mainstream American culture was also captivated by the religious practices of the northern Plains Indians, primarily the Cheyenne and the Sioux (practices that are largely foreign to Indians in many other areas of the continent but that are perceived by many Americans as representative of Native Americans in general). Yet, until the American Indians Religious Freedom Act of 1978, many Indian religious practices were discouraged in the United States.

The basic unit of traditional Sioux family and community life was the tiyospaye, a small group of related families. In the era of the buffalo, the tiyospaye was a highly mobile unit capable of daily movement when necessary.

Many of the Plains tribes share similar belief systems. The Siouan peoples' faith is characterized by its integration into daily life and its emphasis on community and relationships. "All my relatives" is a common phrase among Dakota and Lakota people. The sanctity of land and reverence for specific holy sites are additional aspects of many Native American religions that are shared by Siouan peoples. For the Sioux *Paha Sapa*, known in American culture as the Black Hills, is among the most sacred locations.

Teachings of the Lakota religion focus on respect, bravery, and generosity. The Lakota developed a complex mythology that encompassed many deities whose works and tricks were passed down orally. Among the most significant Lakota gods are Inyan, the first god, who created earth from a part of himself; Maka, the earth; Škan, the sky; and Waken Tanka, the "Great Spirit," a supreme being that is a part of all things animate and inanimate. White Buffalo Calf Woman, a mystical woman of legend, is also highly revered for bestowing the Sioux with their seven sacred ceremonies, which form the practical basis for all the Sioux religions. These ceremonies include Canupa, the sacred pipe ceremony; Inipi, the

sweat lodge ceremony, intended to heal and purify; Nagi Unhapi, the soul-keeping ritual, performed to mourn the deceased and help their souls transition to the afterlife; Hanblecha, a vision quest to achieve insight or knowledge; Wiwangwacipi, the Sun Dance, which several American Indian groups practice variations of—this ritual involves the offering of flesh by participants; Hunkapi, the making of relatives, whereby two unrelated individuals choose to form a familial bond; and Ishna Ta Awi Cha Lowan, which prepares girls for womanhood.

The long prohibition of Native American religious freedom interrupted the continuity of ceremonial customs, resulting in a lack of knowledge of the practices and a decrease in the importance of these rites in Sioux life. Since the 1970s the revival of traditional practices, specifically the Sun Dance and sweat lodge ceremonies, has continued unabated; participation has become representative of political and cultural commitment. In 1997 more than forty Sun Dance ceremonies were held on the Pine Ridge Reservation. The most commonly practiced among the seven sacred ceremonies are the Canupa, Inipi, Hanblecha, and Wiwangwacipi. At the turn of the twenty-first century, the practice of these ceremonies varied widely and depended on the individual community.

Discussion of contemporary Native American religious practice is incomplete without mention of the influence of Christianity. As a result of missionary work among the Sioux begun in the mid-nineteenth century, by the mid-twentieth century an overwhelming majority claimed affiliation with some Christian denomination. Today Christian services are predominantly utilized for rites such as funerals, although these customs are often performed in conjunction with traditional practices.

CULTURE AND ASSIMILATION

Beginning in the late nineteenth century, the U.S. government attempted to force American Indians, including the Sioux, to assimilate into American culture. This assimilation is defined by the primary weapon of cultural genocide practiced by the United States: missionary-run boarding schools, where little regard for traditional culture, language, or beliefs was observed. With some exceptions, many of these schools were reviled for their practices. Forcibly removed from their homes and isolated from their families, Sioux children were often grouped with children from other tribes and nations who did not share their language or practices; in some schools students were punished if they were caught speaking their native tongue or observing traditional customs. Their hair was cropped, they were directed to adopt Christianity, and school and dormitory life were conducted on a military model. Oftentimes these schools offered poor living conditions, practiced severe punishment, and perpetuated prejudices that demeaned the Native American children for their race and

religion. Many Sioux children attended the school located at Flandreau, South Dakota, while some were removed to schools in the East, to Hampton Institute in Virginia or to the Indian school at Carlisle, Pennsylvania, and others attended the Santa Fe Indian School and the Haskell Institute in Lawrence, Kansas. This era was marked by the lowest population statistics for Native Americans and the near-extinction of many traditional ways. It was with determination and resilience that the Sioux were able to retain their language and religion, while learning English and adjusting to the demands of American culture. Today, Siouan peoples have reached an uneasy position in which they are members of and participants in mainstream U.S. culture but still regard themselves and are treated by others as outsiders.

Traditions and Customs The Sioux are skilled artisans at beadwork, quillwork, carving, pipe making, drum making, flute making, and leatherwork of all kinds—from competition powwow regalia to saddles and tack. These crafts have been handed down from generation to generation. Intertribal powwow competitions, festivals, and tribal fairs bring forth impressive displays of Sioux traditional crafts. In the twenty-first century, concerted efforts have been made to maintain these aspects of Siouan culture through museum exhibitions,

educational materials, workshops, and classes, as well as by documenting traditional methods and practices.

Contemporary art and craft techniques are also an important part of Sioux culture and represent a profitable economic venture for many Sioux artists. The annual Northern Plains Art Market, hosted by Sinte Gleska University in Sioux Falls, South Dakota, is a juried art show that showcases works of contemporary fine art, in a variety of media, by enrolled Northern Plains Indians. Founded in 1988 as an economic development project, the market also provides a venue for Northern Plains Indian artists to sell their works.

Cuisine Holding a particular reverence for food as a source of life, the Sioux had a special relationship with their dietary staple, the buffalo. As they become more integrated into mainstream U.S. culture, so too did their eating habits. Several traditional buffalo meat dishes are still prepared today, often with time-saving changes or updated ingredients easily found in modern grocery stores. One Lakota bison dish is *wohanpi* soup, which consists of bison meat, turnips, and wild potatoes; today, beef often replaces buffalo in the recipe. *Wasna* (pemmican), is dried, pounded bison meat combined with dried chokecherry and tallow. It was considered a sacred food because of its high protein content and healing properties. Meat could last for three to four years in this form. The process is recreated today and used in some ceremonies; the month-long preparation can be expedited with modern appliances for more frequent consumption.

Chokecherries, a wild berry found across the Northern Great Plains, also featured heavily in the Sioux diet. The berries could be dried and mixed with corn kernels and tallow then fried to make *Wahuwapa Wasna*, or corn balls, a Dakota recipe. *Wojapi*, a berry pudding, was a Northern Plains dessert recipe once made with fresh wild chokecherries and served with fry bread. Contemporary cooks have adapted the recipe using fresh, frozen, dried, or canned berries.

Traditional Dress Northern Plains tribes such as the Assiniboine Sioux used buffalo, elk, deer, and sheep hides to make clothing. While men were in charge of hunting, women prepared hides and fashioned garments. Traditional Sioux dressmakers decorated clothing with paint made from natural materials and with animal quills, teeth, bones, or shells, integrating beads after being introduced to them by Europeans. Design elements were unique to the artisan's tribe and symbolized important aspects of their group's culture.

Among various aspects of traditional Sioux life, clothing production is one of the best-preserved and most commonly practiced today. Women continue to prepare, craft, and decorate garments using precontact methods, passing down these practices to younger generations. Today, beaded dresses, shirts, moccasins, and other hand-worked attire are reserved for special occasions such as weddings, powwows, and naming celebrations. Some individuals also choose to incorporate this element of their heritage into non-Indian occasions—for instance, wearing traditional regalia to high school graduation. Integrating traditional dress into mainstream Western ceremonies such as commencement occasionally presented controversy in the twenty-first century; in 2010 Lakota high school student Aloysius Dreaming Bear sued his school district for denying his request to wear tribal regalia to receive his diploma. Although he lost the suit, the court case raised questions of free speech and cultural sensitivity. Throughout the United States, high schools maintain various policies for the ceremony.

Dances and Songs Siouan singing and dancing is most publically on display at secular, intertribal powwows that take place throughout North America, often in the summer months. The drums that typify powwow gatherings are an important element in Sioux culture and are treated with reverence, as they are believed to have their own spirits. Powwows featuring dance competitions are the ones at which visitors are most welcome. The competitions are broken into categories by type of dance, age of participants, and gender. Many powwow dances have evolved from war dances, and dancers wear elaborate pan-tribal attire, adding an element of showmanship to the events.

The Sun Dance, one of the seven sacred ceremonies of the Sioux, has gained wide notoriety for the tribe. Also known as the Offerings Lodge ceremonial, it is practiced by several Plains groups with tribal variations. Within each tribe the songs and dances performed during this ceremony have been passed down from generation to generation. Traditional drumming is typical, as is fasting, making offerings, and the use of a ceremonial pipe. Most notable to outsiders, however, is the ritual piercing that accompanies some variations of the Sun Dance. While only men participate in the ceremony, preparations for a successful event necessitate input from the entire community. Other community members often watch the ritual. The most famous Sun Dance occurs in early August on the Pine Ridge Reservation. Another Sun Dance takes place in early July on the Rosebud Reservation. Tourist attendance at these religious events is discouraged in order to preserve the sanctity of the occasion.

Holidays On many Sioux reservations federal holidays are observed in the same manner as they are off the reservation, with business and bureaucratic closures. Many Sioux also celebrate Christian religious holidays such as Christmas. Naming ceremonies remain an important traditional event in Sioux communities, with young people receiving a Native American name and, often, gifts. Tribal fairs are held during the summer at Devil's Lake and Fort Totten, North Dakota; and at Lower Brule, Rosebud and Eagle Butte, South Dakota. A day of remembrance for many Sioux is December 26, the date in 1862 of the hanging of thirty-eight Sioux men at Wounded Knee. Communities across Sioux country commemorate this day, and annually a small group of Sioux have memorialized the tragedy with a multiday, multistate journey on horseback called the Big Foot Ride.

Health Care Issues and Practices All of the health problems associated with poverty in the United States can be found among the contemporary Sioux. Diabetes, heart disease, substance abuse, and mental illness occur in Sioux communities at rates consistently higher than those experienced by white Americans. Alcoholism has proven to be especially debilitating. Statistics from the Pine Ridge prove staggering: one in four children born on the reservation are diagnosed with fetal alcohol-related ailments, and the adult life expectancy is roughly twenty-five years shorter than the average American's.

Initiatives on many Sioux reservations seek to address these issues by promoting an active lifestyle and healthy food choices. First Lady Michele Obama's nationwide initiative to encourage children to become more active, "Let's Move!," was launched as "Let's Move! In Indian Country" in 2011 with the help of Assiniboine/Sioux actor Chaske Spencer (best known for his role in the *Twilight* movies). One third of U.S. reservations, including Pine Ridge and Lower Brule, combat alcohol-fueled illness and crime by banning alcohol. The Cheyenne River Sioux voted to ban drugs and alcohol in 2000 and proposed arresting pregnant women found drinking; these resolutions went into effect in 2001 amid concerns over tribal sovereignty and individual rights.

While many Sioux rely on modern medicine for treatment, traditional healing practices still exist; the Oglala Lakota and others continue to employ herbal remedies, and the role of healers in Sioux communities in general persists, although they often serve in ceremonial or leadership capacities rather than treating illnesses.

FAMILY AND COMMUNITY LIFE

The basic unit of traditional Sioux family and community life was the *tiyospaye*, a small group of related families. In the era of the buffalo, the tiyospaye was a highly mobile unit capable of daily migration when necessary. A tiyospaye might include thirty or more households. From these related households a headman achieved the position of leadership by demonstrating characteristics valued by the group, such as generosity, wisdom, fortitude, and spiritual power gained through dreams and visions.

Fraternal and women-specific societies were significant to the functioning of the group. During migrations fraternal societies helped young men develop leadership skills by assigning them roles in maintaining orderly camp movements. Membership was by invitation only and restricted to the most promising young males. Another kind of fraternity, the *akicita*, was a military group that policed Sioux camps while tribal members were on the move or hunting bison. The *nacas* societies were comprised of older men with proven abilities. The most important of the nacas, the *Naca Omincia*, functioned as something of a tribal council. Operating by consensus, it had the power to declare war and negotiate peace. A few members of the Naca Omincia were appointed *wicasa itancans*, who were responsible for implementing decisions of the larger body.

Acculturation, assimilation, and intermarriage have made inroads into Sioux traditional family and community relationships. Many vestiges of traditional Lakota community organizational structure have been replaced, at least on the surface—originally as a result of the 1934 Indian Reorganization Act. The act ostensibly returned to Native American tribes aspects of self-regulation and self-determination previously denied them but also demanded a certain amount of conformity to U.S. government structures. The more isolated and rural portions of the population tend to be more traditional. One important leader in Sioux society was the *yuwipi* man, a healer respected for his wisdom and curative powers. The wicasa itancans consulted the yuwipi man on important tribal decisions; the Lakota still ask the advice of the healer on important matters today.

Gender Roles Historically a patriarchal society, the Sioux assigned men and women different tasks; their roles were perceived as complementary and were

SIOUX PROVERBS

- Speak truth in humility to all people. Only then can you be a true man.

- With all things and in all things, we are relatives.

- A people without a history is like the wind over buffalo grass.

- The tongue is very sacred, so do not hurt anyone's heart by talking.

- To us, gentleness and kindness are some of the most important things.

- If we understand our history, we can learn from it.

equally valued within the community. The precedent of White Buffalo Calf Woman, an important legend within Lakota mythology, strengthened the value of women in Lakota communities. Women were primarily responsible for raising children and other home-centered duties. Hunting, on the other hand, was a communal activity; after scouting parties found a buffalo herd, entire families would mobilize to drive the herd toward the hunters, who were most often men.

In the early twenty-first century, many Sioux women were still the primary caretakers of the children, often acting as the head of single-parent households. Although they had also moved toward equality in terms of educational achievements and had become a larger presence in the workforce, Sicangu Lakota women of the Rosebud Reservation complained to researcher Christina G. Mello ("Gender and Empowerment: Contemporary Lakota Women of Rosebud," 2004), "Women are taught to work, raise children, sew, cook, and take care of their homes, but nothing is expected of the men."

In addition to male and female, the Sioux recognize a third gender of "two-spirit" people, called *berdaches* or *Badés*. A berdache is a biological man who either chooses or is spiritually guided to assume a woman's role in the community by dressing as a woman and performing women's work. In some Sioux tribes the berdaches were not ostracized but rather were valued for their insight and seen as sacred people, whereas in other Sioux groups, the berdaches were discouraged from divergent practices. As Christianity and other Western mores took hold in Sioux communities, the tradition of the berdache diminished, but in the 2010s, as gay, lesbian, and queer identities became increasingly acceptable in mainstream culture, this

two-spirit traditions has revived. Among the Lakota, berdache individuals are also called *winkte*, which translates as "to become woman."

Courtship and Weddings Traditional courtship among the Sioux was spearheaded by young lovers' parents. Some marriages were arranged by parents, occasionally to create strong political alliances or increase a family's social position. Other matches were not prearranged. Offerings of gifts such as food, blankets, or clothing by a groom's parents signified a formal request for courtship rights. Young women were considered ready to marry after their first menstruation, and young men were expected to have participated in at least one war party before marriage. The wedding ceremony was accompanied by a feast and dance performance. Accounts of polygamy and intrafamilial marriages in the past among some Sioux groups have been recorded. Today, many of the traditional protocols have fallen to the wayside. In the age of Internet dating, Native American and Lakota-specific websites allow single people to meet others with a similar background and to connect regardless of geography. Divorce rates among American Indians are on par with rates for the general U.S. population.

Education Historically, white Americans used education as a tool for assimilating and acculturating Native Americans, resulting in some negative attitudes toward education. On the Pine Ridge Reservation, only 27.2 percent of the population had attained a high school diploma in 2000, though the 2010 U.S. Census recorded almost 80 percent of American Indians nationwide with a high school (or equivalency) education level. The majority of Sioux students are enrolled in public schools, but some communities have private schools, such as the Red Cloud Indian School on the Pine Ridge Reservation, which has 600 students, and St. Joseph's Indian School in South Dakota. Many of these private schools maintain religious affiliations but also emphasize Native culture, language, and religion.

One manifestation of the Native American impetus toward self-determination and autonomy was the tribal college movement. American Indian tribes founded institutes of higher education as a way to provide more opportunity to their communities and foster the academic study of indigenous cultures. Sinte Gleska on the Rosebud Reservation was among the first of these universities. Other institutes affiliated with Siouan tribes including Fort Peck Community College, Oglala Lakota College, and Sisseton Wahpeton Community College. These institutions typically serve both Sioux and nonnative populations. Primary aims include enhancing life for Sioux people through educational opportunities, occupational training, and increased awareness of Native issues and perspectives. College and university programs focused on American Indian issues and cultures had spread across the United States and Canada by the early twenty-first century.

EMPLOYMENT AND ECONOMIC CONDITIONS

The economic reality for Sioux peoples varies widely between rural and urban areas and from one reservation to another. Some reservations that are more isolated from urban industrial centers have attracted very little industry and experience some of the highest levels of unemployment and poverty of any communities within the United States. According to the 2010 U.S. Census report, Shannon County on the Pine Ridge Reservation had the lowest per capita income in the country, and unemployment was estimated at 70 percent; in Ziebach County on the Cheyenne River Indian Reservation, more than 60 percent of the residents lived below the poverty line in 2010. On many Sioux reservations, various U.S. government agencies and programs are the largest employers. Extractive industries also provide some employment, but the economic benefits go largely to non-Indians, and many traditional Sioux refuse to participate in economic activities that scar and pollute their land. The discovery of uranium upstream from the Pine Ridge Reservation, which generated commercial proposals for extraction, has been a divisive issue within Sioux communities. Despite possibly bringing an economic boom to the area, the proposed mine could cause disastrous environmental impacts and health complications for nearby residents. In 2013 the Oglala Sioux Tribe demanded drastic changes be made to the permit process for licensing the proposed mine; citing violations of EPA standards, the tribe requested a more detailed environmental impact statement.

In the late nineteenth and early twentieth centuries, the U.S. government tried to force the Sioux to become farmers. While large-scale agriculture proved unappealing for Sioux, some western Sioux communities overcame the limitations of small land allotments to make cattle ranching economically viable. In the West, Sioux have also distinguished themselves on the professional rodeo and all-Indian rodeo circuits.

In addition to ranching, casinos have proven to be a source of economic development, as evidenced by the Dakota Nation Gaming Enterprise, run by the Sisseton-Wahpeton Oyate Tribe and comprising three casino-resort complexes across North and South Dakota; and the Mystic Lake Casino and Hotel operated by the Shakopee Mdewakanton Sioux Community in Minnesota. In general, these casinos attract non-Native customers who contribute to the local tribal economy. With casinos, hotels, shopping centers, and restaurants near Fargo, North Dakota, and Sisseton, South Dakota, the Dakota Nation Gaming Enterprise employs more than four hundred individuals and earns $30 million in annual revenue. The Shakopee Mdewakanton Sioux Community, located in Prior Lake, Minnesota, outside of the Twin Cities metropolitan area, opened its Mystic Lake Casino and hotel in 1992. The casino and several other local business ventures have made this Sioux community the largest employer in the county, with 4,200 employees; the tribe has made more than $258 million in donations to other tribes, organizations, and schools since 1996. Western Lakota reservations are more rural, and their casinos are not as profitable.

POLITICS AND GOVERNMENT

Each of the sixteen federally recognized reservations with Sioux affiliations has its own tribal government; the majority of these were formed under the Indian Reorganization Act of 1934. Intended to increase Native American self-government and autonomy, the act impelled numerous tribes and communities to create or adopt written constitutions following guidelines established by the U.S. government. The contemporary governmental structure of the Lakota Sioux tribal division is similar to that of other Sioux governments. The Lakota Nation's National Sioux Council is comprised of delegates from the Lakota reservations at Cheyenne River, Standing Rock, Lower Brule, Crow Creek, Pine Ridge, Rosebud, Santee, and Fort Peck. The council meets annually to discuss matters affecting the entire Lakota population. The body honors the traditional model of Lakota government, in which the heads of individual bands gather to represent the tribe, which sends representatives to the Greater Sioux Council. Essentially a federal structure, the council is required to function by voting rather than consensus, which was a quintessential American Indian method of decision making.

Each contemporary Lakota reservation is governed by its own elected tribal council that adheres to a constitution and is led by a president or chairperson. The Cheyenne River Reservation tribal council, for example, is a supreme governing body for the Cheyenne River Sioux. It is empowered to enter into negotiations with foreign governments, such as the government of the United States; to pass laws and establish courts; to appoint tribal officials; and to administer the tribal budget. Certain kinds of actions taken by the tribal council, however, are subject to the authority of the U.S. secretary of the interior, a reminder that the Sioux do not have complete sovereignty over their land. The Cheyenne River tribal council consists of eighteen members, fifteen of whom are locally elected from six voting districts (the districts being apportioned according to population) and three who are elected at large—the chairperson, the secretary, and the treasurer. The council elects a vice-chairperson from among its members. Other Sioux Nation reservations are similarly run.

Only enrolled tribal members who meet residency requirements may vote or hold office at Cheyenne River. Tribal members must be one-quarter or more Cheyenne River Sioux, and their parents must also have been residents of the reservation (a controversial policy in recent years). A two-thirds vote of the tribal council, however, may enroll a person of Cheyenne River Indian blood who does not meet either the blood quantum or the parental residency requirements. Voters must meet a thirty-day residency requirement; to hold office the residency requirement is one year.

Like many American Indian groups, the Sioux Nation has faced challenges in dealing with the U.S. government, particularly over Native rights and land issues. One major dispute centered on the Black Hills, a sacred site for the Sioux. After alternately offering to protect the lands and then withdrawing support, the U.S. government took control of the area in the late nineteenth century when it established the reservation system. Beginning in the 1920s the Sioux Nation waged a legal battle against the federal government to reclaim the Black Hills land. In 1980 the case reached the U.S Supreme Court, which ruled in favor of the Sioux Nation and awarded the tribes $106 million dollars. The Sioux refused to accept monetary payment, continuing to demand land rights to the Black Hills.

NOTABLE INDIVIDUALS

Academia Yankton Sioux author and anthropologist Ella Deloria (1889–1971) produced landmark ethnographic and anthropological work on both traditional and contemporary Sioux culture and language. Her books include *The Sun Dance of the Oglala Sioux* (1929), *Dakota Texts* (1932), *Dakota Grammar* (1941), and *Speaking of Indians* (1944). Deloria also wrote a number of fictional works, including the much-lauded posthumously published novel *Waterlily* (1988), which deals with matters of kinship and community in a traditional Dakota camp, told from the perspective of a Dakota woman. Throughout her life, Deloria worked as a lecturer and consultant and was regarded as an expert on the Dakota people. Her alma mater, Columbia University, annually awards the Ella C. Deloria Undergraduate Research Fellowship in honor of Deloria's spirit and commitment.

Sioux author, professor, and attorney Vine Deloria Jr. (1933–2005), Ella Deloria's nephew, was one of the most articulate speakers for the recognition of Indian political and religious rights. Born at Standing Rock on the Pine Ridge Reservation, he held degrees in divinity from the Lutheran School of Theology and in law from the University of Colorado, where he also served as a professor. A prolific writer, Deloria published more than twenty books in his lifetime. His writings include the influential text *Custer Died for Your Sins: An Indian Manifesto* (1969) and *We Talk, You Listen: New Tribes, New Turf* (1970). Deloria's legacy is inextricably tied to the rise of American Indians as a political force in the 1970s. A leader in the Red Power Movement, he skillfully articulated an Indian perspective, bringing Native issues and rights to the national stage.

Activism Helen Peterson (1915–2000), an Oglala Sioux woman born on the Pine Ridge Reservation, was an activist for American Indian rights. From the 1950s through the 1970s, Peterson worked tirelessly for Native American rights reforms. As the executive director of the National Congress of the American Indian (1954–1962), she organized tribal leaders, lobbied congress, and coordinated voting drives in an effort to promote the American Indian cause. Peterson also served as an official on the Indian Affairs Commission and founded a Christian church for urban Native Americans, the Church of the Four Winds. She retired from politics in 1985 and lived until her death in Washington state.

Rosebud Sioux politician and author Robert Burnette (?–1984) was an active supporter of Native American rights for more than three decades. He served as the chairman of the Rosebud Sioux Tribal Council from 1954 to 1961 and 1974 to 1975. He also served as the executive chairman of the National Congress of the American Indian and led the United Sioux Tribes. Burnette authored two books, *The Tortured Americans* (1971) and, with John Koster, *The Road to Wounded Knee* (1974).

Oglala Sioux activist and actor Russell Means (1939–2012), rose to prominence as the first national director of AIM in 1970. Born on the Pine Ridge Reservation and raised in California, Means was instrumental in fostering the group's activism and protest tactics. He participated in or led many of the AIM's protest occupations throughout the 1970s, including the Alcatraz Occupation, the takeover of Mount Rushmore, the ill-fated occupation of the Bureau of Indian Affairs, and the occupation of Wounded Knee. After the dissolution of the AIM, Means continued to work for indigenous rights throughout his life. He unsuccessfully ran for political office both on and off the reservation. Means also had a career late in life as an actor, appearing in *The Last of the Mohicans* (1992) and lending his voice to the animated Disney movie *Pocahontas* (1995).

Art Yankton Dakota graphic artist Oscar Howe (1915–1983) is one of the best-known Native American artists in the United States. Known as *Mazuha Koshina* (trader boy), Howe was born at Joe Creek on the Crow Creek Reservation in South Dakota. He earned degrees from Dakota Wesleyan University and the University of Oklahoma and was a professor of fine arts and an artist in residence at the University of South Dakota for fifteen years. His work is characterized by poignant images of Indian culture in transition depicted in a modern style.

Sicangu Sioux and Omaha artist Robert Penn (1946–1999) was a painter and teacher. Born in Omaha, Nebraska, and raised on the Rosebud Reservation, Penn began his artistic career as a young child. During his undergraduate studies at the University of South Dakota, Penn was taken on as a protégé of the Yanktonai Dakota artist Oscar Howe. Throughout his college years, Penn taught art classes and worked as an illustrator. He taught at the Rosebud Reservation Sinte Gleska University, the

Santee Community College, and Mary College before returning to Vermillion, South Dakota, where he lived and painted until the end of his life. Today, Penn's paintings and multimedia works can be seen at the Smithsonian Institution, the Minneapolis Institute of Art, and the Vincent Prince Gallery in Chicago.

Literature Lakota Sioux poet, author, and professor Elizabeth Cook-Lynn (1930–), born on the Crow Creek Reservation, is a granddaughter of Gabriel Renville, a linguist who helped develop Dakota dictionaries. A Dakota speaker herself, Cook-Lynn has gained prominence as a professor, editor, poet, and scholar; she is emeritus professor of American and Indian studies at Eastern Washington State University, and in 1985 she became a founding editor of *Wicazo Sa Review*, a biannual scholarly journal for Native American studies professionals. Her book of Sioux-focused songs, stories, and poetry *Then Badger Said This* (1977) and her short fiction published in journals established her as a leader among American Indian creative voices. Cook-Lynn continued to publish through the end of the twentieth century and into the twenty-first, producing a book of poetry, three collections of short stories, and four works of nonfiction. With *A Separate Country: Postcoloniality and American Indian Nations*, released in 2011, she maintained her position in the forefront of American Indian politics and letters.

Virginia Driving Hawk Sneve (1933–), a Rosebud Sioux, is the author of eight children's books and other works of historical nonfiction for adults. In 1992 she won the Native American Prose Award from the University of Nebraska Press for her book *Completing The Circle*.

Oglala Sioux Robert L. Perea (1944–), born in Wheatland, Wyoming, graduated from the University of New Mexico. Half Chicano, he has published short stories in anthologies such as *Mestizo: An Anthology of Chicano Literature* (1978) and *The Remembered Earth: An Anthology of Contemporary Native American Literature* (1979). In 1992 Perea won the inaugural Louis Littlecoon Oliver Memorial Prose Award from his fellow creative writers and poets in the Native Writers' Circle of the Americas for his short fictional piece "Stacey's Story."

Philip H. Red-Eagle Jr. (1945–), a Wahpeton-Sisseton Sioux, is a founding editor of *The Raven Chronicles*, a multicultural journal of literature and the arts in Seattle. In 1993 Red-Eagle won the Louis Littlecoon Oliver Memorial Prose Award for his manuscript novel *Red Earth: A Vietnam Warrior's Journey* (2007), which draws from his experiences in the Vietnam War.

Fellow Seattle resident and Sioux poet Tiffany Midge, an enrolled member of the Standing Rock Sioux Tribe, earned an MFA from the University of Idaho. She won the 1994 Diane Decorah Memorial Poetry Award from the Native Writers' Circle of the

Americas for her book-length poetry manuscript *Outlaws, Renegades and Saints: Diary of a Mixed-Up Half-Breed* (1996). In 2010 Midge published the chapbook *Guiding the Stars to Their Campfire, Driving the Salmon to their Beds*, as well as numerous individual poems in other publications and anthologies. In 2013 she won the inaugural Kenyon Review Earthworks Prize for Indigenous Poetry.

Susan Power, who is also enrolled at Standing Rock, gained national attention with the 1994 publication of her first novel, *The Grass Dancer*. Power received both a BA and a law degree from Harvard University before deciding to pursue fiction and earning an MFA from the University of Iowa. Following the appearance of her illustrious debut novel, Power's short stories appeared in several well-regarded publications such as the *Paris Review* and *Ploughshares*. In 1998 she published her second novel, *Strong Heart Society*, followed by *Roofwalker* (2002).

Religion Yankton Sioux Vine Deloria Sr. (1901–1990) was the first Native American to be nominated to a national leadership position within the Episcopalian Church. Following in his father's missionary footsteps, Deloria Sr. studied theology, later becoming an Episcopal priest and serving as a missionary on the Standing Rock Reservation as well as for numerous other Indian congregations over a forty-year career. Recognized for his work in Sioux communities, Deloria Sr. was named archdeacon of South Dakota. Along with his son, Vine Deloria Jr., and his sister, Ella, Deloria Sr. was honored by the Indian Council Fire for his leadership and achievement in Indian affairs.

MEDIA

PRINT

Lakota Country Times

The official newspaper for the Pine Ridge and Rosebud Reservations.

Vi Waln, Editor
316 Main Street
Martin, South Dakota 57551
Phone: (605) 685-1868
Fax: (605) 685-1870
Email: editor@lakotacountrytimes.com
URL: www.lakotacountrytimes.com

Sicangu Sun Times

A newspaper for the Great Rosebud Sioux Indian Reservation.

P. R. Gregg-Bear, Chief Editor
BIA Route 1
P.O. Box 750
Rosebud, South Dakota 57570
Phone: (605) 747-2058
Fax: (605) 747-2789
Email: sicangusun@mail.com
URL: www.sicangusuntimes.com

Sota Iya Ye Yapi

The official weekly newspaper of the Sisseton-Wahpeton Oyate of the Lake Traverse Reservation.

C. D. Floro, Managing Editor
P.O. Box 5
Wilmot, South Dakota 57279
Phone: (605) 938-4452
Fax: (605) 938-4678
Email: earthskyweb@cs.com
URL: www.earthskyweb.com/sota.html

Todd County Tribune

News source serving Todd County, South Dakota, including the Rosebud Reservation.

Angel Johnson, Office Manager
P.O. Box 229
Mission, South Dakota 57555
Phone: (605) 856-4469
Email: tribnews@gwtc.net
URL: www.trib-news.com

Wotanin-Wowapi

Newspaper of the Fort Peck Assiniboine and Sioux tribes.

Bonnie Red Elk, Editor
400 Court Avenue
Box 1027
Poplar, Montana 59255
Phone: (406) 768-5387
Fax: (406) 768-5743
Email: wotanin@nemontel.net
URL: http://wotaninwowapi.nativeweb.org

RADIO

KEYA-FM (88.5)

In operation since 1975, KEYA is the second-oldest Indian owned and operated radio station in the United States.

Kimberly Thomas, General Manager
P.O. Box 190
Belcourt, North Dakota 58316
Phone: (701) 477-5686
Fax: (701) 477-3252
Email: keya@utma.com
URL: http://keya.utma.com/885

KGVA-FM (88.1)

Calling itself "the voice of the Nakota and White Clay Nations," this radio station broadcasts from the Fort Belknap College on Fort Belknap Reservation and is Montana's only Native radio station.

Gerald Stiffarm, Station Manager
P.O. Box 159
Harlem, Montana 59526
Phone: (406) 353-4656
Fax: (406) 353-4808
Email: kgvaradiostation@yahoo.com
URL: http://kgvafm.org

KILI-FM (90.1)

"The voice of Lakota Nation" is a public, nonprofit station broadcasting on the Pine Ridge, Rosebud, and Cheyenne reservations.

P.O. Box 150
Porcupine, South Dakota 57772
Phone: (605) 867-5002
Fax: (605) 867-5634
Email: on.air.person@gmail.com
URL: www.kiliradio.org/kiliradio/KILI_home.html

KINI-FM (96.1)

Operated by the St. Francis Mission, KINI broadcasts to
the Rosebud Reservation.

P.O. Box 499
St. Francis, South Dakota 57572
Phone: (605) 747-2291
Fax: (605) 747-5791
Email: kinifm@gwtc.net
URL: www.kinifm.com

KLND-FM (89.5)

"The Lodge of Good Voices" broadcasts from Little
Eagle, South Dakota, to serve the Standing Rock
and Cheyenne River communities. Owned by the
Native American company Seventh Generation Media
Services, Inc., KLND-FM is an affiliate of Native Voice
One, airing Native American news, music, and other
cultural programming.

11420 SD Highway 63
McLaughlin, South Dakota 57642
Phone: (605) 823-4661
Fax: (605) 823-4660
Email: zbolts@hotmail.com
URL: www.nv1.org/index.html

ORGANIZATIONS AND ASSOCIATIONS

Fort Belknap Indian Community

Represents the Assiniboine-Sioux and Gros Ventre.

Tracy King, President
Fort Belknap Agency
158 Tribal Way
Harlem, Montana 59526
Phone: (406) 353-2205
Fax: (406) 353-4541
URL: www.ftbelknap.org

Oglala Lakota Nation

Predominantly represents Oglala Sioux but also serves the
Brule Sioux and Northern Cheyenne.

Bryan Brewer, President
P.O. Box H
Pine Ridge, South Dakota 57770-2070
Phone: (605) 867-5821
Fax: (605) 867-1449
URL: www.oglalalakotanation.org/oln/Home.html

Prairie Island Indian Community

Represents the Mdewakanton division of the Santee Sioux.

Johnny Johnson, President
5636 Sturgeon Lake Road
Welch, Minnesota 55089
Phone: (651) 385-2554
Fax: (651) 385-4180
URL: www.prairieisland.org

Rosebud Sioux Tribe

Represents the Oglala, Oohenonpa, Minneconjou, Upper
Brule, Waglukhe, and Wahzhazhe Sioux.

Cyril Scott, President
P.O. Box 430
11 Legion Avenue
Rosebud, South Dakota 57570-0430
Phone: (605) 747-2381
Fax: (605) 747-2243
URL: www.rosebudsiouxtribe-nsn.gov

Santee Sioux Tribe of Nebraska

Represents the Santee Sioux, including Mdewakanton,
Wahpekute, Sisseton, and Wahpeton.

Roger Trudell, Chairman
425 Frazier Avenue North
Suite 2
Niobrara, Nebraska 68760
Phone: (402) 857-2302
Fax: (402) 857-2307
URL: www.santeedakota.org/santee_sioux_tribe_of_
nebraska.htm

Shakopee Mdewakanton Sioux Community

Represents the Mdewakanton division of the Santee
Sioux.

Charles R. Vig, Chairman
2330 Sioux Trail N.W.
Prior Lake, Minnesota 55372
Phone: (952) 445-8900
Email: info@shakopeedakota.org
URL: www.shakopeedakota.org

Sisseton-Wahpeton Oyate

Represents the Sisseton Sioux.

Robert Shepherd, Chairman
P.O. Box 509
Agency Village, South Dakota 57262-0509
Phone: (605) 698-3911
Fax: (605) 698-3708
Email: webadmin@swo-nsn.gov
URL: www.swo-nsn.gov

Standing Rock Sioux Tribe

Predominantly represents the Teton Sioux, including
Hunkpapa and Sihasapa, but also serves the Lower
and Upper Yanktonai.

Charles W. Murphy, Chairman
P.O. Box D
Fort Yates, North Dakota 58538-0522
Phone: (701) 854-8500
Fax: (701) 854-8595
URL: www.standingrock.org

MUSEUMS AND RESEARCH CENTERS

Akta Lakota Museum and Cultural Center

An education outreach center of the St. Joseph's Indian
School, the museum is dedicated to honoring the
Lakota Sioux people's culture through interactive

displays about the Lakota belief system, the
importance of the buffalo, and daily life. The
museum also contains a gallery exhibiting modern
Lakotan art, sculpture, and crafts.

St. Joseph's Indian School, P.O. Box 89
Chamberlain, South Dakota 57325
Phone: (800) 798-3452
Email: aktalakota@stjo.org
URL: http://aktalakota.org

Oglala Lakota College Historical Center

Located on the Oglala Lakota College campus, the
historical center contains exhibits of historical
artwork, photographs, and artifacts curated to
convey a deeper understanding of the Oglala
Lakota people and the struggle to maintain their
way of life.

Marilyn Pourier
P.O. Box 490
Kyle, South Dakota 57752
Phone: (605) 455-6000
Fax: (605) 455-2787
URL: www.olc.edu

Red Cloud Indian School Heritage Center

Located on the Pine Ridge Indian Reservation, the
heritage center offers access to numerous pieces of
historical Lakota art and artifacts as well as exhibits
of works by contemporary American Indian artists of
any descent.

Peter J. Strong, Director
100 Mission Drive
Pine Ridge Indian Reservation, South Dakota 57770
Phone: (605) 867-5491
Email: heritagecenter@redcloudschool.org
URL: www.redcloudschool.org

Sicangu Heritage Center

Located at Sinte Gleska University on the Rosebud
Reservation, the Sicangu Heritage Center serves
as the official archival repository for the Rosebud
Sioux Tribe, exhibits tribal and regional artifacts,
and hosts lectures. The center houses university and
tribal records, video and audio recordings, maps,
photographs, written documents, and other Lakota
and Rosebud artifacts.

Marcella Cash, Archivist/Director
Sinte Gleska University
Antelope Lake Campus
P.O. Box 675
Mission, South Dakota 57555
Phone: (605) 856-8211
Fax: (605) 856-5027
Email: heritagecenter@sintegleska.edu
URL: www.sintegleska.edu/heritage-center.html

Sioux Indian Museum at the Journey Museum

The museum's extensive permanent exhibit includes
historic garments, weaponry, household items, and
other artifacts of daily life for the northern Plains
Indians. Temporary exhibits often feature work by
contemporary Sioux Indian artists and craftspeople.

222 New York Street
Rapid City, South Dakota 57701
Phone: (605) 394-2381
Fax: (605) 384-6182
Email: SIM@journeymuseum.org
URL: www.journeymuseum.org/index.php?pg=sioux

Wounded Knee Museum

Described as a "narrative" museum, the facility exhibits
interactive displays that lead visitors through the story
of several Sioux families involved in the Wounded
Knee conflict with the U.S. government in 1890. In
addition the museum contains exhibits related to
other areas of American Indian life.

207 10th Avenue
P.O. Box 348
Wall, South Dakota 57790
Phone: (605) 279-2573
Email: info@woundedkneemuseum.org
URL: www.woundedkneemuseum.org/index.htm

SOURCES FOR ADDITIONAL STUDY

Gagnon, Gregory O. *Culture and Customs of the Sioux Indians.* Santa Barbara, CA: Greenwood, 2011.

Gibbon, Guy. *The Sioux: The Dakota and Lakota Nations.* Malden, MA: Blackwell, 2003.

Hyman, Colette A. *Dakota Women's Work: Creativity, Culture, and Exile.* St. Paul: Minnesota Historical Society, 2012.

Lakota: Seeking the Great Spirit. San Francisco: Chronicle Books, 1994.

Neihardt, John. *Black Elk Speaks: Being the Life Story of a Holy Man of the Oglala Sioux.* Lincoln: University of Nebraska Press, 1961.

Paha Sapa: The Struggle for the Black Hills. VHS. Directed by Mel Lawrence. New York: HBO Studio Productions, 1993.

Petrillo, Larissa, Melda Trejo, and Lupe Trejo. *Being Lakota: Identity and Tradition on Pine Ridge Reservation.* Lincoln: University of Nebraska Press, 2007.

Ross, A. C. *Mitakuye Oyasin: "We Are All Related."* Denver: Wicóni Wasté, 1997.

Skins. Directed by Chris Eyre. Century City, CA: First Look Pictures, 2002.

Wiping the Tears of Seven Generations. DVD/VHS. Directed by Gary Rhine and Fidel Moreno. Los Angeles: Kifaru Productions, 1992.

SLOVAK AMERICANS

June Granatir Alexander

OVERVIEW

Slovak Americans are immigrants or descendants of people from Slovakia, a nation in east-central Europe. Slovakia is bordered by Poland to the north, Hungary to the south, the Czech Republic to the west, and Ukraine to the east. Slovakia's topography varies widely, and in addition to dense forests and low fertile plains, the vast Carpathian mountain range stretches along Slovakia's northern border with peaks that reach altitudes as high as 8,711 feet (2,655 meters). Slovakia is a relatively small country, with a land mass of 18,919 square miles (49,000 square kilometers), making it roughly twice the size of the state of New Hampshire.

In July 2012 the *CIA World Factbook* estimated Slovakia's population as 5.48 million. According to the 2001 Slovakian census, the population was overwhelmingly Roman Catholic, with 68.9 percent of the population identifying itself as Catholic. In the same survey, 10.8 percent identified as Protestant, with 4.1 percent claiming Greek Catholic and 13.8 percent claiming no religious affiliation. Despite its small size since its separation from the Czech Republic in 1993, Slovakia has become the world's sixty-fourth largest economy, with relatively cheap and skilled labor, low taxes, and a favorable geographical location, making it very attractive to foreign investment, particularly in the automotive and electronic sectors.

Significant immigration of Slovaks to the United States began in the 1870s, when large numbers of southern and eastern Europeans arrived. Slovaks gravitated to areas where industries were expanding and needed unskilled labor. More than half the Slovak immigrants went to Pennsylvania, primarily to the mill towns and coal mining districts in the state's northeastern and western regions. Other popular destinations included Ohio, New Jersey, New York, and Illinois. Most Slovaks "chain migrated," that is, they went to places where previous Slovak immigrants already lived. Between 1908 and 1910, 98.4 percent of Slovaks entering the country were joining relatives or friends.

According to the U.S. Census Bureau's American Community Survey estimates, in 2011 there were approximately 764,554 persons of Slovak ancestry living in the United States, a number similar in size to the population of Fort Worth, Texas. The number does not account from those who identified themselves as Slavic or Czechoslovakian, which might also include many Slovaks. While much of the Slovak American population has assimilated throughout the United States, the traditional industrial and mining areas of western Pennsylvania and Ohio still contain significant Slovak populations. However, there are also large numbers of Slovak Americans in Illinois, New York, Florida, Michigan, Indiana, Connecticut, California, and New Jersey.

HISTORY OF THE PEOPLE

Early History Throughout most of its history, modern-day Slovakia was not an independent country. Its inhabitants were subject peoples of the multi-national medieval Hungarian Empire, and later, the Austro-Hungarian Empire. When the Austro-Hungarian Empire collapsed in near the end of World War I in 1918, Slovaks joined with the neighboring Czechs to create an independent Czechoslovakia. Except for a short period of independence during World War II (1939–1945), Slovakia remained part of that multi-national state until 1993.

The history of Slovakia reaches back to the fifth and sixth centuries, when Slavic tribes migrated into the region south of the Carpathian Mountains. These ancestors of modern-day Slovaks established villages and developed an agricultural economy in the Middle Danube Basin. In the mid-ninth century Slavs from Bohemia, Moravia, and the Danube region united in a loose union to form the Great Moravian Empire, which comprised most of latter-day Czechoslovakia, southern Poland, and western Hungary. The empire was the first unification of the ancestors of the Czech (Bohemian and Moravian) and Slovak peoples. In the 860s Christianity was introduced into the empire, supported by Saints Cyril and Methodius, the "Apostles of the Slavs." In 907 the Magyars, a seminomadic people from the northeast, invaded the empire and established the Kingdom of Hungary, which incorporated modern-day Slovakia. As a result of the Magyar invasion, the traditional Slovak lands remained part of Hungary until the 1918 dissolution of the Austro-Hungarian Empire. This collapse of the Great Moravian Empire split the Bohemian Czechs, Moravians, and Slovaks, who stayed separate for the next one thousand years.

Despite some interruptions, like the thirteenth-century Mongol invasion and subsequent famine, the years as part of the kingdom of Hungary were fairly positive times for Slovakia and the Slovak people. As an integral part of the Hungarian kingdom, Slovakia both contributed to and benefited from the state's status as a major power in Central Europe and as a European cultural center, with the Slovak capital of Poszony (now called Bratislava) eventually becoming the capital of the kingdom of Hungary after the invasion of Ottoman Turks.

During the 1520s the Hungarian kingdom began to break up as a result of European power-politics. Seeking an ally against the powerful Habsburg Empire of Charles V, the French king Francis I brokered an "impious alliance" with the Muslim Ottoman Empire of Suleiman the Magnificent, hoping the Turks would attack the Habsburg Empire and relieve the pressure on France. Because the Hungarian kingdom lay between the Habsburg and Ottoman lands, the area inevitably became a battleground for the two huge empires.

In 1526, at the battle of Mohacs, the Turks defeated a Hungarian army and destroyed much of the native Hungarian leadership. In the ensuing political instability two separate Hungarian kingdoms were created, one in the north and west ruled by the Holy Roman Empire of the Habsburgs and one in the east ruled by John Zápolya. While the Slovak lands became part of the new Habsburg Kingdom of Hungary, the transfer of hegemony did little to create political stability as another Ottoman invasion in 1541 led to over a century of conflict and the destruction of much of the formerly Hungarian lands.

After their failure to take Vienna in 1683, Ottoman control over the former Hungarian Kingdom began to wane, with the Habsburg Empire leading the effort to eject them from the region completely. Treating those lands taken from the Turks as conquered territories, the Habsburg Empire soon extended its control over much of the old Hungarian lands. The replacement of Ottoman control by Habsburg control soon sparked resistance in Hungary, eventually leading in 1703 to a revolt against Austrian rule. While this uprising, named the Rákóczi Rebellion after its leader, Francis II Rákóczi, a Roman Catholic magnate, was eventually crushed by Habsburg military forces, the ferocity of the uprising did lead the Habsburg authorities to seek a legal and workable basis for Habsburg rule in Hungary.

Their solution, the Pragmatic Sanction of 1713, made the Habsburg emperor the king of Hungary, but under the constraints of the Hungarian constitution. The new arrangement formalized the relationship between Hungary and the Habsburg Empire, but in practice it did little to lessen Austrian control over Hungarian affairs: Austria retained control over Hungarian foreign affairs, defense, and finance.

Modern Era The strained relationship between Hungary and the larger empire of the Habsburgs would remain until the early twentieth century, when World War I opened the way for the dismemberment of the Habsburg Empire and the liberation of its subject peoples. One important result of this was the reunification of the Czech and Slovak lands, sundered by the invasion of the Magyars 1,000 years before. This reunion was formalized on October 28, 1918, with the creation of the modern Czecho-Slovakia.

Many Slovak supporters of an independent Czecho-Slovakia had envisioned the new state as a federation of two independent peoples, with two autonomous regions. Instead, the country's constitution of 1920 changed the name to Czechoslovakia, without a hyphen, and established a centralized government with a single capital city, Prague. Instituting a centralized government, instead of a system that granted Slovaks autonomy, led to tensions between Czechs and Slovaks in the 1920s and 1930s. Economic domination by Prague and the Great Depression accentuated the political and cultural divisions between the two lands.

As result of the Munich Agreement (September 1938) and Hitler's invasion of Czechoslovakia in March 1939, Slovakia's political leaders proclaimed autonomy in a Czecho-Slovak state. Under pressure from Hitler, Slovakia declared independence under German protection in order to avoid an invasion from a Hungary determined to regain to its pre–World War I borders. While Slovakia was able to exert some measure of self-rule under President Jozef Tiso for several years after independence, it was ultimately dependent on Germany for its existence and subservient to the demands of German foreign policy. Deportations of Jews started in March 1942 and were only halted in October after the intervention of Slovak bishops and pressure from the Vatican. By then 58,000 had been deported to death camps in Poland. When some partisan and a dissident group in the army arose and rebelled against the Tiso regime in August 1944, Germany intervened and suppressed what is termed the Slovak National Uprising by October. Thereafter, Slovakia remained under German occupation until the Soviet Red Army liberated the country in the spring of 1945.

In 1945 Slovakia and the Czech lands were reunified. In postwar elections the Communist Party enjoyed significant victories, especially in the Czech lands, but the anticommunist Democratic Party in Slovakia secured a 62 percent majority. In 1948 the Czechoslovak Communist Party leaders engineered a coup and took over the government. For the following four decades, Slovakia remained part of Czechoslovakia and under Communist control. When Slovak Communist leader Alexander Dubček tried to democratize the country in 1968, the Soviet Union, together with several other Warsaw Pact members, intervened to crush the reform movement. In 1969

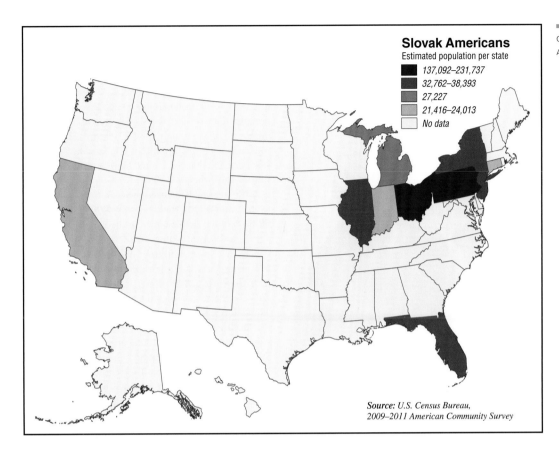

Slovak Americans
Estimated population per state

- 137,092–231,737
- 32,762–38,393
- 27,227
- 21,416–24,013
- No data

*Source: U.S. Census Bureau,
2009–2011 American Community Survey*

the government granted Slovakia slightly more self-rule within the region and designated Bratislava as the capital city.

In the fall of 1989 Slovaks joined Czechs in the Velvet Revolution that toppled the Communist-controlled government in December. In April 1990 Czechoslovakia was renamed the Czech and Slovak Federative Republic. In June the country held its first free elections since 1945. As reforms and measures to privatize the economy were introduced, relations between Czechs and Slovaks deteriorated. After the June 1992 elections, Czech and Slovak government officials decided that the two regions should separate. Because it was achieved without bloodshed or serious animosities, the breakup of the former Czechoslovakia is often called the Velvet Divorce (in Prague) or the Gentle Revolution (in Slovakia). On January 1, 1993, Slovakia became independent. Slovakia's first prime minister was Vladimír Mečiar.

Since becoming independent, the Slovak Republic has achieved a measure of success in integrating into European institutions, entering NATO and the European Union in 2004. Although high unemployment has continued to plague Slovakia and many young Slovaks have sought higher wages working abroad, the state has made considerable success in attracting foreign investment. Regional disparities exist, however, and the eastern regions, which had sent many immigrants to the United States before World War I, continue to have lower wages and problems with job creation. While relics of communism and some corruption have persisted in putting a break on more substantial progress, Slovakia has managed to build a stable democratic form of government and has a relatively free press.

SETTLEMENT IN THE UNITED STATES

A few Slovaks immigrated to the United States before the American Civil War, but their numbers were small. Large-scale Slovak immigration to the United States began in the late 1870s, steadily increased during the following two decades, and peaked in 1905, when 52,368 Slovaks entered. Slovak immigration declined precipitously during World War I and started up again after hostilities ended in 1918. However, the movement came almost to a complete halt in the 1920s when American immigration laws virtually stopped eastern European immigration into the United States. According to immigration records, 480,201 Slovaks entered the country between 1899 and 1918. The 1920 U.S. Census found that there were 274,948 foreign-born Slovaks in the United States. Slovak immigrants and their children totaled 619,866.

Statistics on Slovak immigration, however, are imprecise, and it is difficult to determine the number that actually immigrated to the United States.

Slovak immigrant, New York, 1900s. NGS IMAGE COLLECTION / THE ART ARCHIVE AT ART RESOURCE, NY

until the number of female immigrants rose sharply after 1907. Between 1899 and 1910, 266,262 Slovak males and 111,265 Slovak females had entered the United States.

Over time, many temporary Slovak migrants decided to stay in the United States and sent for their families. The reasons for staying varied. Some were unable to save enough money to buy land and in some regions of their homeland no land was available; some decided that the United States promised a better future; and others married in the United States and decided to stay. Whatever their motives, from 1880 to the mid-1920s, between 450,000 and 500,000 Slovaks moved permanently to the United States.

Slovak immigrants were committed to saving money and fulfilling obligations to families left behind. As a result they routinely sent money to Europe. In 1899 alone, more than $4 million was channeled to the Slovak region of Hungary. The determination to save money, compounded by the fact that so many Slovaks were males who had come alone, influenced living standards. In general, Slovaks tried to live cheaply. Laborers often roomed in boardinghouses, where they could get a bed and daily meals for as little as ten dollars per month. These boardinghouses were typically run by Slovak immigrants, a husband and wife who either owned or rented a large house. For these Slovak families, taking in boarders became an important source of additional income.

Slovak immigration began during a period when anti-foreign sentiment was on the rise in the United States. The response by Americans to Slovak immigrants reflected the common anti-foreign attitude, and reformers strove to Americanize them and other immigrants. Furthermore, the desire by Slovaks to live cheaply, the large number of males, and their concentration in unskilled industrial jobs reinforced beliefs that immigrants were creating social and economic problems for the United States. Slovaks were not usually singled out as presenting special problems. Because Slovaks did not have a separate identifiable homeland and most Americans did not know that there was a Slovak people, they often referred to Slovak immigrants simply as Slavs, Slavic, Slavish, or by the pejorative terms "Hunky" or "Bohunk." Based on their geographic origin, Slovaks fell into the general category of undesirable immigrants. Judging persons from both eastern and southern Europe as biologically and intellectually inferior and a threat to American society, some native-born Americans demanded that these "undesirables" be barred from the country. The immigration laws of the 1920s that curtailed eastern and southern European immigration severely reduced the number of Slovaks who could enter the United States. Between 1929 and 1965, U.S. quotas permitted only 2,874 people from Czechoslovakia to immigrate annually to the United States. In the decades after immigration restriction

Before 1899, U.S. immigration officials listed immigrants by country of birth. Thus, until 1899 Slovaks were recorded as Hungarians, since they came from Hungary. Even after immigrants were enumerated by nationality, the Magyarization policies had been so effective that some Slovaks did not identify themselves as Slovaks but rather identified with their region. Many of them acquired a strong sense of national self-consciousness after coming to the United States.

Perhaps one-third of the Slovaks who came to the United States were not immigrants but instead migrants. Often called "birds of passage," they worked temporarily in the United States and then returned to Europe. They wanted to earn money to buy property in their homeland. It was common for Slovaks to make several trips between the United States and Upper Hungary. At least 19 percent of the Slovaks who entered an American port from 1899 to 1910 had been in the United States one or more times before. Not until 1908 did immigration officials subtract the number of immigrants leaving from the total numbers entering the United States. Still, it is clear that temporary migrants formed an especially large contingent of the early stages of the Slovak immigration and remained a common feature of the movement. Between 1908 and 1910, for example, 80,797 Slovaks entered the United States while 41,726 left. Its temporary nature also affected the composition of the Slovak immigration. Most Slovak immigrants were unskilled laborers, and men typically outnumbered women by more than two to one,

went into effect, Slovaks were lost in popular perceptions and culture, as they were lumped into generalizations about the massive turn-of-the-century immigration.

According to the 2011 U.S. Census Bureau's American Community Survey estimates for 2009–2011, over 760,000 Americans claimed Slovak descent. The majority of Slovak Americans reside in the Northeast and Midwest, and the two states with the highest numbers of Slovak Americans in 2011 were Pennsylvania (an estimated 231,737) and Ohio (an estimated 137,092). Other states with smaller, but significant, populations are New York, New Jersey, Michigan, Indiana, Illinois, Florida, Connecticut, and California.

LANGUAGE

Slovak belongs to the Slavic language group. Although similar to other Slavic languages, especially Czech, Slovak is linguistically distinct, with its own grammar and vocabulary. Slovak has three general dialects (western, central, and eastern) that roughly correspond with geographical areas in Slovakia. Each dialect also has numerous local and regional variations. Slovak, like other Slavic languages, has diacritical marks that govern the pronunciation of both consonants and vowels. The accent is on the first syllable in literary Slovak, but on the second syllable in eastern dialects.

Slovak was the primary language spoken among immigrants, but the language has not persisted among successive generations in the United States, with American Community Survey estimates in 2011 showing that only 5.4 percent speak a language other than English. Several factors have contributed to this decline. First, children gave way to the pressure in American society to abandon foreign languages. Second, immigrants were often barely literate; most only received a grammar school education in Hungary and were also forced to learn only Magyar after fourth grade. Although they taught their children, especially the older sons and daughters, to speak Slovak, they could not teach them to read and write the language. Slovaks established parochial schools where nuns provided some language instruction, but these classes often either proved inadequate or students did not remain in school long enough to become literate in Slovak.

In common with many immigrant groups, measures are being taken to ensure the survival of the native tongue among Slovak Americans. Slovak is taught at a few Sunday schools for children and at universities, including the University of Pittsburgh, and several American libraries have Slovak-language collections. Slovak is, however, a very difficult language, and intermarriage and Americanization pressures have mostly prevailed, so that only a handful of third-generation Slovaks know the language of their ancestors.

The Slovak language was modified slightly in the United States as English, or modern, technical terms were introduced into the vocabulary. The absence of diacritical marks in English meant that either the spelling or the pronunciation of many Slovak names was changed. For example, a person with the name *Karčis* (pronounced "Kar-chis") had the option to change the pronunciation to the English ("Kar-kis") or keep the pronunciation and change the spelling to *Karchish*.

Greetings and Popular Expressions Common Slovak greetings include the following: *Dobréráno* ("dobreraahno")—Good morning; *Dobrydeň* ("dobree den")—Good day; *Dobrývečer* ("dobrevecher")—Good evening; *Dobrúnoc* ("dobroonots")—Good night; *Prosím* ("proseem")—Please, if you please, excuse me; *Ďakujem* ("djakooyem")—Thank you; *Dobrúchuť* ("dobrookoot")—Eat well!, bon appetit!; *Na zdravie* ("nazdravye")—To [your] health!, cheers! (a toast); and *VeseléVianoce* ("veselehvyanotse")—Merry Christmas.

RELIGION

Early Slovak immigrants included Catholics, Lutherans, and Calvinists, but the majority of Slovaks were Roman Catholic. The first Slovak Roman Catholic churches were founded in 1885 in Hazleton, Pennsylvania, and Streator, Illinois. During the next four decades Slovak Catholics established nearly 250 churches in the United States. The universality of the Latin Mass and Catholic theology meant that Slovaks continued to practice their religion as they had done in their homeland, but immigrants also had to observe holy days and laws unique to the American Catholic Church. The requirement that individual congregations pay all church expenses was the most significant difference between Slovak Catholic churches in Europe and the United States. Because parishes had to be self-supporting, lay organizations sponsored numerous fund-raising social events, and ethnic churches became centers of community activities.

A small number of Slovak Byzantine-rite Catholics also migrated to the United States. They organized a few churches, but more often they cooperated with other Byzantine-rite Catholics, especially Carpatho-Rusyns, to establish ethnically mixed parishes. Among Slovak Americans, intermarriage of Byzantine and Roman-rite Catholics was frequent. Byzantine-rite Catholics professed the same creed as followers of the Roman-rite, and both were under papal authority. However, services in the Byzantine rite were conducted in Old Church Slavonic, which used the Cyrillic alphabet. The fact that Byzantine-rite clergymen could marry while Roman-rite priests could not became a significant difference in the United States. Having a married clergy created problems for Byzantine-rite Catholics because some American bishops refused to accept wedded priests in their dioceses. This refusal caused some Byzantine-rite Catholic Slovaks to join the Russian Orthodox Church in America.

Lutherans made up the second-largest body of Slovak immigrants. They organized their first congregation in 1883 in Freeland, Pennsylvania, and during the next half century Lutheran Slovaks established more than seventy congregations and missions. In 1902, Lutheran Slovaks formed their own synod, an executive and judicial body made up of clergy and laypersons. Conflicts developed when the Slovak Synod became affiliated with the Evangelical Lutheran Synodical Conference of America in 1908. Some Slovak Lutheran clergy and laypersons refused to adopt liturgical changes that were subsequently demanded by the conference, which caused serious divisions. Continued disagreements over liturgical and theological principles led to the formation in 1919 of the Slovak Zion Synod, which became affiliated with the United Lutheran Church in America in 1962. Most Lutheran Slovaks belong to congregations associated either with the Lutheran Church of America or the Synodical Conference.

Slovak churches survived for decades as ethnic institutions while experiencing some change. By the 1930s Slovak Protestant churches were introducing English into their services. Catholics continued to use Latin until the 1960s, when the Catholic Church began to use the vernacular. As the immigrant generation died and their descendants moved out of ethnic neighborhoods, some Slovak churches declined or were taken over by new immigrant groups. Vibrant Slovak Lutheran and Catholic churches still exist in cities and small towns—especially in Pennsylvania, Ohio, New York, and New Jersey—but they are gradually declining as fourth and fifth generations intermarry and move increasingly to the suburbs or migrate to other areas of the United States for employment.

CULTURE AND ASSIMILATION

Slovak immigrants exemplified the pattern evident among most ethnic groups in the United States: they adjusted to American society and preserved some traditions and values while altering others. Values and beliefs that Slovaks brought with them were rooted in their rural past and reflected the concerns of agricultural communities. Slovaks placed great value on owning property and a home, and they highly valued the family and the honoring of family obligations.

Traditions, Customs, and Beliefs Slovaks have traditionally been a deeply religious people. Some religious holy days were customarily observed with village processions, while others were less dramatic. On some saints' feast days, Slovak villagers came together as a community to pray for a favor associated by legend with a saint. For example, on the feast of Saint Mark (April 25) they prayed for rain and good weather during the upcoming growing season. Although Slovaks were fervently religious, their beliefs and customs were a blend of folklore and superstitions linked to the Christian calendar. A vast array of superstitions permeated their culture. For example, until the middle of the twentieth century, some Slovaks still performed rituals to protect their villages from demons and witches.

Slovaks also carried out numerous rituals, especially during the Christmas season, which they believed foretold their future. On November 30 they poured lead into boiling water and relied on the shape of the cooled droplets to make predictions about the forthcoming year. Young women had several rituals that they believed might reveal who their husbands would be. On Christmas Eve, Slovaks cracked nuts and used the condition of the meat as an indicator of what the upcoming year might hold for them. On Christmas Eve, the head of the household gave food from the dinner table to the family's animals in the hope of ensuring the livestock's health. No food was ever wasted, not even crumbs.

Traditional Dress In Slovakia the typical folk costume for women consisted of a puffed-sleeve blouse, a vest, a short but full skirt, an apron, a bonnet or headscarf, and calf-high boots. Men's costumes included a hat, a shirt overlaid with a vest, trousers, and boots. Men's trousers, typically form-fitting but occasionally flared, were usually white or off-white linen or wool with colorful embroidery. Both male and female folk costumes made of homespun cloth and sheepskin were multicolored and featured intricate embroidery. Specific styles, colors, and items included in the attire varied from village to village and from region to region. In fact, peasant costumes could be so distinctive that they simultaneously indicated a person's village and religion. A headdress also revealed a woman's marital status. Married Slovak women braided their hair and only showed their full hair to their own families. In the United States, Slovak folk costumes have become nostalgic or quaint artifacts worn only for interethnic or Slovak events.

Cuisine Soup is a staple of the Slovak daily diet. Cabbage, potatoes, and dumplings, all prepared in a variety of ways, are regular fare on Slovak tables. Meat, especially in Slovakia's poorer eastern region, was not a common ingredient in soups or main dishes, though some traditional dishes served throughout Slovakia are meat-based. *Klobasa* (a sausage with garlic) and *holubky* (cabbage leaves stuffed with pork, rice, and onions) are the most popular. Duck and chicken are reserved for special occasions, but for particularly festive celebrations goose is preferred. Although desserts are not part of the daily diet, Slovak culinary specialties include several filled *kolače* (sweet yeast baked goods). The most popular *koláč* contains prune, ground nut, or crushed poppy-seed fillings. Depending on the filling, *pirohy* (small dumplings) are served as main dishes or as desserts.

Slovaks attach great importance to serving traditional foods on Christmas and Easter, the only major holidays observed by Slovaks in both the homeland and the United States. Although in regional variations, several dishes served at Christmas and Easter are considered authentic Slovak cuisine. On Christmas Eve the main dishes consist of *bobalky* (bite-size rolls served either in sauerkraut and butter or in a poppy-seed sauce) and a special mushroom soup. Traditional Easter specialties include Slovak *paska* (a sweet, yeast bread with raisins) and homemade *hrudka,* also known as *syrek* (a bland, custard-style imitation cheese).

Holidays In their Slovak homeland, the celebration of Christmas and Easter were events for both family and village. While Slovak American Christmas celebrations have taken on American features with a greater emphasis on gifts and a midday turkey dinner, many Americans of Slovak descent adhere to the custom of the family coming together for traditional Slovak foods on Christmas Eve (called the Vilija supper). Visiting family during both the Christmas and Easter seasons has also remained an obligatory custom among Slovak Americans.

Health Care Issues and Practices Neither Slovak immigrants nor their American descendants have unique health problems. Data from the 1990 U.S. Census indicated that average rates of disability among both young and elderly Slovaks were the same as for most other ethnic groups in the United States. The same is true for the number of Slovaks institutionalized. Immigrants and subsequent generations suffered from afflictions characteristic of other working-class Americans, especially at the turn of the century. In addition to a high rate of tuberculosis, workers were often killed or permanently maimed in industrial accidents. Some Slovaks who toiled in mines have been stricken with the respiratory problems that afflict miners.

Slovaks had local folk remedies. It has not been documented how extensively immigrants used these folk cures or how long such practices persisted in the United States. Although no systematic study of Slovak health attitudes has been done, there is no evidence that folk cures had any real impact on Slovak health practices in the United States.

FAMILY AND COMMUNITY LIFE

Immigration is a disruptive process, especially for families. Although chain migration meant that Slovaks typically went to where relatives and friends had already settled, families were temporarily torn apart. Men immigrated alone, lived in boardinghouses, and later summoned their families or fiancées to join them. The process also worked in reverse as children immigrated first and then sent for the elderly parents they had left behind in Europe. Although Slovaks typically maintained a close-knit family system, by the mid-twentieth century Slovak Americans were moving from cities to suburbs. During the latter decades, the third and fourth generations were also moving from dying mill towns to metropolitan regions.

Marriage patterns influenced Slovak American family and community dynamics. For the immigrant generation, the norm was marriage between Slovaks.

The second generation followed the same trend into the 1920s and 1930s, but by the post–World War II era, it had become more common for Slovak Americans to marry people from other ethnic groups, especially other Slavic peoples and Hungarians. Dating patterns differed from generation to generation and even within the same generation. Early in the twentieth century, dating in the United States was typically limited to events sponsored by Slovak fraternal benefit societies, churches, or ethnic social groups. Attending religious services and sharing in a family dinner also were common among couples. By the mid-1920s the Slovak American youth had adopted the dating practices common among their American peers. They enjoyed dances, movies, amusement parks, and other entertainment characteristic of the changing contemporary popular culture.

Traditional culture and religious values combined to make divorce uncommon among Slovak immigrants. Reliable data on divorce rates for specific ethnic groups are unavailable but, given general trends in the United States, the empirical evidence suggests that dissolutions involving Slovaks surely rose in the latter part of the twentieth century.

Gender Roles Both socially and economically, Slovakia has been a male-dominated society. Many Slovaks have maintained the traditional Catholic view of gender and gender roles in society. While economic opportunity for women has recently begun to expand in Slovakia, a 2008 European Union report on gender roles noted that the nation has continued to maintain a sharp division between men and women in the workforce, particularly in the areas of pay and advancement.

While Slovak Americans have had over a century to assimilate into American society, U.S. Census figures suggest that they have maintained a somewhat more conservative view of gender roles than the majority of Americans. According to 2010 estimates by the U.S. Census Bureau's American Community Survey, marriage rates among Slovak Americans were higher than the national rates for both sexes (for men, 57 percent compared to a the national rate of 50.1 percent for men; and for women, 51.9 percent compared to the national rate of 46.6 percent). Divorce rates for both sexes were also below the national rates (8.4 percent versus 9.7 percent for men; 10.3 percent versus 12.2 percent for women). Furthermore, the number of female-run households was considerably smaller among Slovak Americans (7.6 percent compared to the national rate of 13.1 percent).

Slovak American women, however, have taken advantage of increased economic opportunity. According to the 2010 American Community Survey estimates, 58.5 percent of Slovak American women over the age of sixteen were in the workforce, particularly in the management, business, science, and arts occupations, which accounted for over 48 percent of those employed. As in Slovakia, these women continue to make less than their male counterparts, with median earning for full-time male workers estimated at $60,505 compared to $44,431 for women.

Education Slovak culture traditionally did not place a high emphasis on education. The Hungarian government's Magyarization policy, together with the agricultural nature of Slovak society, worked against developing a culture that valued formal education. Between 24 percent and 30 percent of the turn-of-the-century Slovak immigrants over the age of fourteen could neither read nor write. Those who had attended school had done so for only a few years. With this background, many immigrant parents, especially during the pre–World War I era, did not hesitate to put their children to work at early ages. In the 1920s more Slovak American children regularly attended school and more completed twelve years of education. Nevertheless, Slovak American parents generally advocated practical learning over an education in the sciences or liberal arts. Rather than stressing social mobility, both first- and second-generation parents typically encouraged children to get a secure job, even if that meant working in a factory. The value system of both first- and second-generation Slovaks placed women in the traditional role of wife, mother, and homemaker; therefore, education was considered even less valuable for daughters than for sons.

Slovak Americans' tendency to downplay formal education had an impact for much of the twentieth century, but by the start of the twenty-first century, their rates of education were higher than those for the overall U.S. population. According to the 2011 American Community Survey estimates, among the Slovak American population age twenty-five years and over, 94.1 percent had at least a high school diploma or equivalency (higher than the U.S. rate of 85 percent), and 37.1 percent had received a bachelor's degree or higher (while the U.S. rate was 27.9 percent).

During the 1930s Slovak American fraternals actively lobbied for social security, unemployment benefits, "minimum wage, maximum hours" legislation, and the legalization of unions. Slovak immigrants and their children helped organize and joined unions, especially in the steel and mining industries where so many of them worked.

Weddings Slovak weddings were lengthy affairs that, depending on the village's size, could involve nearly all the inhabitants. Preparatory rituals for the marriage, the ceremony, and subsequent celebrations could last a week. During the festivities, usually three days after the actual marriage ceremony, a bonnet was placed on the new bride's head, and she was accepted as a married woman. In the United States, Slovak immigrants gradually adopted a mixture of American and Slovak customs, with the polka being the main music played by an ethnic band.

EMPLOYMENT AND ECONOMIC CONDITIONS

The vast majority of early Slovak immigrants to the United States had been common or farm laborers in their homeland. Having few skills, Slovak immigrants found jobs as manual laborers in heavy industries, especially in steel and allied industries that produced durable goods. A large number of Slovaks also toiled in coal mines. In 1910 surveys revealed that 82 percent of Slovak American males labored as miners or in iron and steel mills. Some Slovak women were employed as domestics, but in cities they often worked in food processing, tobacco, and textile plants. Fewer employment opportunities existed for women in small mill towns. Those who were unable to find domestic service jobs typically remained unemployed and helped at home until they married. Widows and married women often ran boardinghouses, where they cooked and did the laundry for residents.

The majority of second-generation Slovak males followed their fathers' paths and became industrial laborers, although some entered the professions or acquired skills. Subsequent generations have deviated from this course. The 1990 U.S. Census found that only 5.7 percent of Slovak Americans were self-employed, while the vast majority remained wage and salary workers; however, in the type of jobs they differed from their parents or grandparents. In 1990 only 26 percent of Slovaks had jobs in manufacturing, mining, and construction. Most Slovaks were employed in white-collar jobs. In the late twentieth and early twenty-first centuries, the closing of plants in the industrial Northeast and Midwest adversely affected second- and third-generation Slovak Americans, especially those beyond middle age.

According to the American Community Survey's 2010 estimates, 63.1 percent of the Slovak American population over the age of sixteen was in the workforce, including 58.5 percent of women. Of those in the workforce in 2010, 46.4 percent worked in management, business, science, and arts occupations; 13.7 percent in service occupations; 6.7 percent in natural resources, construction, and maintenance occupations; and 8.9 percent in production, transportation, and material moving occupations. Women outnumbered men in management occupations (49 percent to 43.8 percent) and in service occupations (31.9 percent to 12.3 percent), while men outnumbered women in natural resources, construction, and maintenance occupations (12.8 percent to 0.5 percent) and production, transportation, and material moving occupations (14.3 percent to 3.5 percent).

According to 2010 estimates, among Slovak Americans per capita income per individual was

$36,190 and for households $61,275. During the same period, 5.6 percent of all Slovak American individuals lived below the poverty line (whereas the U.S. rate was 15 percent). Among single-parent families with no husband present, the poverty rate was 13.2 percent, including 24.9 percent of those with children under eighteen (by comparison, the U.S. rates were 30.3 percent and 39.5 percent).

POLITICS AND GOVERNMENT

Slovak involvement in politics has changed over the decades. At the turn of the century, few immigrant workers regularly participated in political activities. Such involvement was typically limited to leaders of Slovak fraternal societies. Founded to provide insurance, disability benefits, and unemployment compensation, and to stimulate ethnic consciousness among Slovaks, fraternals also encouraged or required members to become American citizens. Fraternal leaders believed that having a membership comprised mainly of American citizens would enhance the societies' political clout. These organizations worked hard to influence legislation that affected immigrants. They also became involved in American domestic issues, especially those that concerned working-class Americans. During the 1930s Slovak American fraternals actively lobbied for social security, unemployment benefits, "minimum wage, maximum hours" legislation, and the legalization of unions. Slovak immigrants and their children helped organize and joined unions, especially in the steel and mining industries where so many of them worked. In his powerful novel *Out of This Furnace* (1941), Thomas Bell, a second-generation Slovak, vividly describes the work experiences and union activities of Slovaks in western Pennsylvania, where he grew up during the Great Depression.

An accurate picture of the political activities of Slovak immigrants and successive generations is difficult to discern. In 1920, when citizenship data was recorded by "country of birth," only 45.8 percent of persons from Czechoslovakia had become American citizens and could vote. During the 1930s the New Deal programs drew working-class Slovaks to the Democratic Party. Through the 1950s Slovaks seemed to remain loyal to the Democratic Party in state and local elections, but the pattern in national elections is less clear. In 1960 President John F. Kennedy's Catholicism and Cold War liberalism attracted Slovak American Catholics. The specific voting patterns and political activities of Slovak Americans during the following three decades have not been studied, but empirical evidence suggests that the same religious, class, regional, and related differences that divide the U.S. population and influence Americans' political behavior in general also fragment Americans of Slovak descent.

In geographic areas where Slovaks have concentrated, they have been elected to local and state offices. One of the first Slovak Americans elected to the United States Congress was Joseph M. Gaydos

THE PITTSBURGH AGREEMENT

Slovak American organizations have worked to stay involved in the politics of their homeland. Specifically to counter the Hungarian government's intensified Magyarization efforts, in 1907 Slovak American journalists and national fraternal leaders organized the Slovak League of America. During World War I, the league and Slovak fraternal societies worked to secure American and international support for the creation of an independent Czecho-Slovakia. Their activities included lobbying American politicians and trying to influence public opinion. The league and its supporters pressured Thomas Masaryk, the future first president of Czechoslovakia, into signing the Pittsburgh Agreement on May 30, 1918. The document ostensibly provided for Slovak autonomy within the newly created state. According to the agreement's provisions Slovakia was to have its own independent administration, parliament, and court system. The Pittsburgh Agreement subsequently became one of the most controversial documents in Czechoslovakia's history. Its provisions were not incorporated into Czechoslovakia's constitution, and a centralized government was established instead. During the 1920s and 1930s several Slovak American organizations tried unsuccessfully to persuade Czechoslovakia's government to implement the Pittsburgh Agreement. During the Cold War, Slovak organizations actively supported American policies and those of other countries that opposed the totalitarian government in Czechoslovakia.

(1926–), who represented Pennsylvania's 20th district from 1968 through 1992. Other Slovak Americans in the U.S. Congress include Representative Daniel A. Mica (1944–), a Democrat who represented Florida's 11th congressional district from 1979 to 1989, as well as his brother, John L. Mica (1943–), who began serving as a Republican U.S. Representative for Florida's 7th congressional district in 1993. Joseph Sestak (1951–), a Democrat, served two terms representing the 7th congressional district of Pennsylvania from 2007 to 2011, and as of 2013 he was the highest ranking military official ever to have served in Congress. Peter John "Pete" Visclosky (1949–) began serving as the U.S. Representative for northwest Indiana's 1st congressional district in 1985.

NOTABLE INDIVIDUALS

Aerospace Eugene Cernan (1935–), the son of a Slovak father and a Czech mother, was a U.S. naval officer and astronaut who participated in the Gemini space flights and the Apollo moon missions. In 1972 Cernan was commander of the last Apollo Moon mission, Apollo 17, and was the last man to walk on the moon.

Art and Entertainment Steve Ditko (1927–), the son of Slovak immigrants from Johnstown, Pennsylvania, was an American comic book artist most notable for his creation of iconic Marvel Comics characters Spider-Man and Doctor Strange. Ditko also created characters

The first comic book to feature Spider Man hit the stands in 1962. The comic series was created by Stan Lee and Slovak American Steve Ditko. SOLENT NEWS / SPLASH NEWS/NEWSCOM

Pennsylvania, was an educator, philosopher, and diplomat who served as U.S. Ambassador to the United Nations Commission on Human Rights in 1981 and 1982 and led the U.S. delegation to the Conference on Security and Cooperation in Europe. In 1994 he was awarded the Templeton Prize for Progress in Religion.

Tom Ridge (1945–), whose maternal grandparents emigrated from Slovakia, served as a member of the U.S. Congress (1983–1995), the governor of Pennsylvania (1995–2001), and the first United States Secretary of Homeland Security (2003–2005).

Military Michael Kocak (1882–c.1918), was born in Gbely in western Slovakia and received the Congressional Medal of Honor for single-handedly eliminating a German machine-gun nest and then leading twenty-five French colonial troops in a successful attack on another machine-gun position.

Michael Strank (d. 1945) was from the Rusyn village of Jarabina in northeastern Slovakia and immigrated to the United States in 1922; his family gave their language as Slovak to immigration officials. He was one of the six men immortalized by the famous photograph of the raising of the American flag atop Mount Suribachi, Iwo Jima, on February 23, 1945.

Religion Andrew G. Grutka (1908–1993), Catholic bishop of Gary, Indiana, from 1956 to 1984, ranked among the most influential clergyman of Slovak descent in the United States. He acquired a national and international reputation for his dedication to ecumenism, civil rights, and racial equality and wrote the Second Vatican Council statement on racial issues. Having both parents from Slovakia, Grutka became the leading figure of Slovak Americans among the clergy and helped found the Slovak Institute of Saints Cyril and Methodius in Rome. He also became a leading spokesman for religious freedom when the Communists ruled Czechoslovakia.

Sports Charles (Chuck) Philip Bednarik (1925–) was a Slovak American football player from Bethlehem, Pennsylvania. Over a twenty-six-year career with the Philadelphia Eagles, Bednarik, a linebacker, was an eight-time Pro Bowl selection, a ten-time All-Pro selection, a two-time NFL Champion, and a member of the National Football League 75th Anniversary All-Time Team. He was inducted into the Pro Football Hall of Fame in 1967.

George Blanda (1927–2010), professional football player, was the son of a Slovak-born coal miner in Pittsburgh. Blanda played twenty-six seasons and at the time of his retirement had scored more points than any player in NFL history. An eleven-time All-Pro, Blanda was a member of the AFL All-Time Team and was a 1981 inductee into the Pro Football Hall of Fame.

William John Hartack Jr. (1932–2007) was a Hall of Fame jockey and the son of a Slovak coal miner from Culver, Pennsylvania. He was one of two jockeys to ever win five Kentucky Derbies, and from 1955 to 1957 he won more races than any other jockey in the

for rival comics publisher DC Comics and later created characters for Charlton Comics that reflected his own interest in Ayn Rand's Objectivist philosophy.

D. (Daniel) Carleton Gajdusek (1923–2008), a Slovak American from Yonkers, New York, shared with Baruch S. Blumberg the Nobel Prize for Physiology or Medicine in 1976. He was recognized for groundbreaking research on causal agents of degenerative neurological disorders.

Literature Thomas Bell (1903–1961), originally Adalbert Thomas Belejcak, was a second-generation Slovak American author of six novels. His best-known novel, *Out of This Furnace* (1941), vividly portrays the life of Slovak immigrants and their children and grandchildren from the turn of the century into the Great Depression of the 1930s.

Politics and Public Service Michael Novak (1933–), the son of immigrants from Johnstown,

United States. Hartack was featured on the cover of *Sports Illustrated* magazine in 1956 and 1964 and on the cover of *Time* magazine in 1958.

Kelly Robert Pavlik (1982–) was a professional boxer from a Slovak neighborhood in Youngstown, Ohio. He was the WBC and WBO Middleweight champion from September 2007 until 2010. He retired in early 2013.

Stage and Screen Steve McQueen, (1930–1980), born Štefan Ihnát but adopted by an Irish family, was an American film actor. Known as "The King of Cool," McQueen was one of the first of Hollywood's anti-heroes and became one of the world's biggest box-office draws during the decades of the 1960s and 1970s. An avid racer of automobiles and motorcycles, McQueen became a film icon through his roles in such films as *Bullitt* and *The Great Escape*.

Paul Newman (1928–2008) was an American film actor, activist, and entrepreneur of mixed Slovak and Jewish descent. An Academy Award, Golden Globe, BAFTA, and Emmy award-winning actor, Newman was best known for films such as *Sweet Bird of Youth, The Hustler, Butch Cassidy and the Sundance Kid, The Sting,* and *The Color of Money.* Newman was also a cofounder (with writer A. E. Hotchner) of Newman's Own, a food company that began in 1982 by selling salad dressing. The company has since expanded its offerings to conclude an array of condiments and soft drinks as well as a line of organic foods. Newman's Own donates its after-tax profits to charity.

MEDIA

PRINT

Fraternally Yours (Ženská Jednota)

A monthly publication of the First Catholic Slovak Ladies Association. Archived issues are available online.

Carolyn Bazik, Editor
P.O. Box 1617
Reading, Pennsylvania 19603
Phone: (610) 373-2743
Fax: (610) 375-8333
Email: zjbazik@comcast.net
URL: www.fcsla.org/fraternally.shtml

Národnénoviny (National News)

A monthly publication of the National Slovak Society.

Lori Crowley, Editor
351 Valley Brook Road
McMurray, Pennsylvania 15317-3337
Phone: (724) 731-0094
Fax: (724) 731-0145
Email: crowleynss@yahoo.com
URL: http://nsslife.org/publications.php

Slovák v Amerike

A monthly publication founded in 1889 that bills itself as "the oldest Slovak newspaper in America." Published in Slovak.

Ján Varga, Editor in Chief
P.O. Box 2060
Linden, New Jersey 07036
Phone: (917) 847-9298
Fax: (908) 486-8020
Email: office@slovakvamerike.com
URL: www.slovakvamerike.com

Zornicka

A monthly publication of the Ladies Pennsylvania Slovak Catholic Union.

Margaret A. Ferri, Public Relations Director
71 South Washington Street
Wilkes-Barre, Pennsylvania 18701
Phone: (717) 823-3513
Fax: (717) 823-4464
Email: lpscu@lpscu.org
URL: www.lpscu.org/zornicka.html

ORGANIZATIONS AND ASSOCIATIONS

Czechoslovak Genealogical Society International (CGSI)

Founded in 1988, the CGSI promotes genealogical research as well as interest in the culture of former Czechoslovakia. It publishes a quarterly newsletter (*Našerodina*; Our Family), which contains well-researched articles about genealogy, history, and culture of the peoples of the former state and immigrant life in America.

Ginger Simek, President
P.O. Box 16225
St. Paul, Minnesota 55116-0225
Phone: (651) 964-2322
Email: info@cgsi.org
URL: www.cgsi.org

First Catholic Slovak Ladies Association (FCSLA)

Founded in 1892, the FCSLA is a religious fraternal organization that provides insurance benefits to more than 105,000 members. It also promotes the preservation of Catholicism and ethnic culture among Slovak American Catholics.

Cynthia M. Maleski, President
24950 Chagrin Boulevard
Beechwood, Ohio 44122
Phone: (800) 464-4642
Fax: (216) 464-9260
Email: info@fcsla.com
URL: www.fcsla.org

Friends of Slovakia

Friends of Slovakia is a nonprofit organization of volunteers founded in 2001 to enhance the relationship between Slovakia and the United States in all its various aspects, including promotion of increased cultural and economic exchanges between the two countries.

Joseph T. Senko, Chairman
704 Blueberry Hill Road
McLean, Virginia 22101
Phone: (703) 671-0926
Email: information@friendsofslovakia.org
URL: www.friendsofslovakia.org/fos/index.htm

National Slovak Society (NSS)

Founded in 1890, the NSS is a secular fraternal organization that provides insurance benefits to more than 13,700 members. It also promotes the preservation of ethnic culture among Slovak Americans.

David G. Blazek, President
351 Valley Brook Road, McMurray
Pennsylvania 15317-3337
Phone: (724) 731-0094
Fax: (724) 731-0145
Email: info@nsslife.org
URL: http://nsslife.org/

Sokol USA

Founded in 1896, Sokol USA (formerly the Slovak Gymnastic Union Sokol) is a secular gymnastic association that promotes physical fitness and Slovak culture in the United States. The Slovak Catholic Sokol split from it in 1905 in order to found a religious-based gymnastic society.

Joseph Bielecki, President
276 Prospect Street
P.O. Box 189, East Orange
New Jersey 07019-0189
Phone: (973) 676-0280
Email: SOKOLUSAHQS@aol.com
URL: www.SokolUSA.org

MUSEUMS AND RESEARCH CENTERS

Balch Institute for Ethnic Studies

Now part of the Historical Society of Pennsylvania, the Balch Institute has Slovak books and periodicals as well as the records and papers of many Slovak fraternal organizations.

Lee Arnold, Senior Director of the Library and Collections
1300 Locust Street, Philadelphia
Pennsylvania 19107
Phone: (215) 732-6200
Fax: (215) 732-2680
Email: larnold@hsp.org
URL: http://hsp.org/about-us/the-balch-institute

Immigration History Research Center

Located at the University of Minnesota, the center is the largest repository in the world of materials on immigrants from eastern and southern Europe. Among its holdings are Slovak newspapers, fraternal and non-fraternal publications, and books. Its manuscript collections include the records of several Slovak organizations, fraternal societies, churches, and prominent persons.

Erika Lee, Director
311 Elmer L. Andersen Library
222 21st Ave South, Minneapolis
Minnesota 55455
Phone: (612) 625-4800
Fax: (612) 626-0018
Email: ihrc@umn.edu
URL: http://ihrc.umn.edu/

Jankola Library and Slovak Museum

The largest Slovak library in the United States, with more than 30,000 volumes. Its goal is to promote and preserve Slovak intellectual and cultural life by providing books and reading material and exhibiting artifacts and memorabilia pertaining to Slovak and Slavic history, language, and culture.

Sister M. Catherine Laboure Bresnock, Director
Villa Sacred Heart, Danville
Pennsylvania 17821
Phone: 570-275-5606
Fax: 570-275-3581
Email: jankolalib@jlink.net
URL: http://jankolalibrary.sscm.org/

Slovak Institute

This institute has extensive holdings of books, newspapers, periodicals, and other documents related to Slovak immigration and life in the United States.

Andrew F. Hudak, Jr., President
10510 Buckeye Road, Cleveland
Ohio 44104
Phone: (216) 721-5300
Fax: (216) 791-8268
Email: slovakinstitute@cbhs.net
URL: www.slovakinstitute.com

Slovak Studies Association

An independent, nonprofit association promoting interdisciplinary scholarly research, publication, and teaching related to the Slovak experience the world over, and to helping scholars interested in Slovak studies

Dr. Kevin Deegan-Krause, President
315 South Bellefield Avenue
203C Bellefield Hall, Pittsburgh
Pennsylvania 15260-6424
Phone: (412) 648-9911
Fax: (412) 648-9815
Email: slovakstudies@gmail.com
URL: www.aseees.org/organizations/ssa.html

SOURCES FOR ADDITIONAL STUDY

Čulen, Konštantín. *History of Slovaks in America*. Edited by Michael J. Kopanic Jr. and Steve G. Potach. St. Paul, MN: Czechoslovak Genealogical Society International, 2007.

Kopanic, Michael J. "The Slovaks." In *Identity, Conflict, and Cooperation: Central Europeans in Cleveland, 1850–1930*, edited by David C. Hammack, John J. Grabowski, and Diane L. Grabowski, 249–306. Cleveland: Western Reserve Historical Society, 2003.

Krajsa, Joseph, et al., comps. *Slovaks in America: A Bicentennial Study*. Middletown, PA: Jednota Press, 1978.

Rechcígl, Miloslav. *Czechs and Slovaks in America*. Boulder, CO: East European Monographs, 2005.

Stasko, Jozef. *Slovaks in the United States of America: Brief Sketches of Their History, National Heritage, and Activities*. Cambridge, Ontario: Good Books Press, 1974.

Stolarik, M. Mark. *Growing Up on the South Side: Three Generations of Slovaks in Bethlehem, Pennsylvania, 1880–1976.* Lewisburg, PA: Bucknell University Press, 1985.

Stolarik, M. M. *Where Is My Home?: Slovak Immigration to North America (1870–2010).* Bern: Peter Lang, 2012.

Urbanic, Allan, and Beth Feinberg. *A Guide to Slavic Collections in the United States and Canada.* New York: Haworth Information Press, 2004.

Zecker, Robert. *Streetcar Parishes: Slovak Immigrants Build Their Nonlocal Communities, 1890–1945.* Selinsgrove, PA: Susquehanna University Press, 2010.

SLOVENIAN AMERICANS

Edward Gobetz

OVERVIEW

Slovenian (or Slovene) Americans are immigrants or descendants of people from Slovenia, a country in South Central Europe. Slovenia is bordered to the west by Italy and the Adriatic Sea, to the north by Austria, to the east by Hungary, and to the south and southeast by Croatia. Three major European geographic regions meet in Slovenia: the Alps, the Pannonian Plain and the Mediterranean. Slovenia's total land area is 7,827 square miles (20,273 square kilometers), slightly smaller than the state of New Jersey.

According to the Statistical Office of the Republic of Slovenia, the country had a population of 2,058,123 in 2012. More than half of the population was Catholic (57.8 percent), and there were small percentages of Muslims (2.4 percent), Orthodox (2.3 percent), and Protestants (0.9 percent). Another 3.5 percent were believers without any religious denomination, 22.8 percent declared no association with religion, and 10.1 percent identified themselves as nonbelievers. In 2012 Slovenia also counted almost 417,000 immigrants, most of them from former southern Yugoslav republics, especially Bosnia, Croatia, and Serbia, meaning that almost every fifth resident of Slovenia was an immigrant.

Slovenian immigrants have a history in the United States that extends to the period before the American Revolution, but the largest group arrived between 1870 and 1924. Most were poor peasant farmers who found work first in the mining communities of Michigan and Minnesota and later in industrialized cities such as Cleveland, Pittsburgh, and Chicago. Slovenians who came to the United States after World War II were mainly political refugees who were better educated and included more professionals than the economic immigrants of the earlier periods whose purpose in migrating to the United States was to seek employment and improve their financial position. Since Slovenia achieved its independence in 1991, immigration has slowed to a trickle. Between 1992 and 2002 average annual immigration to the United States was just seventy people.

According to the U.S. Census Bureau's American Community Survey estimates for 2006–2010, there were an estimated 174,784 Slovenian Americans residing in the United States, an amount close to the population of Salt Lake City. However, because Slovenians have self-identified under a variety of labels—including Slav, Slavic, Slavish, and Slavonian—the number of Americans of Slovenian descent is likely underreported by a considerable margin. About a third of the reported Slovenian American population lives in Ohio. Pennsylvania, Illinois, and Minnesota—all historic settlement areas for Slovenian immigrants—also have substantial Slovenian American populations as do Wisconsin and California.

HISTORY OF THE PEOPLE

Early History Most historians believe that Slovenians settled in present-day Slovenian lands between 568 and 650 CE, but this has been challenged by a group of writers who argue that Slovenians are descendants of an ancient West Slavic people called (Slo) Veneti, Vendi, or Wends—a people that predated the Romans. All scholars agree, however, that Slovenians lived in present-day Slovenia by 650 CE. They enjoyed a brief independence at the dawn of their known history when they developed an early form of democracy, culminating in the famous ritual of the installation of the dukes of Karantania (Slovenian Carinthia). According to Harvard historian Crane Brinton, "the picturesque Slovenian ceremony was well known to political philosophers, and indeed through Bodin known to Thomas Jefferson … [being] a small but significant variable that went into the making of modern Western democratic institutions." (*Catholic Historical Review*, 1969).

After allying themselves with the Bavarians against the warlike Avars and jointly defeating them in 743 CE, the northern Karantanian Slovenians lost independence to their Bavarian allies, who refused to leave, and a year or two later to the Franks, who subdued the Bavarians. Following the mysterious disappearance of Prince Kocelj, the Slovenians of Pannonia, too, came under the rule of Frankish overlords in 874. For more than a millennium the Slovenian people were under the political administration of their more powerful neighbors: the Bavarians, the Franks, the Holy Roman Empire, and the Austrian Empire. According to British author Bernard Newman, "It was manifestly impossible for a small people to gain and hold freedom when surrounded by acquisitive great powers, but the Slovenes determined on cultural rather than political liberty. It was a miracle of survival almost without parallel." (*Unknown Yugoslavia*, London: Herbert Jenkins, 1960, 199)

The Christianization of the Slovenians had been conducted by missionaries from Aquileia (now in northern Italy) and Salzburg (then an ethnically mixed territory). The most famous missionaries were the Irish bishop St. Modestus in the mid-eighth century, who labored in Karantania, and brothers St. Cyril and St. Methodius from Salonika, who spread the Christian faith and literacy in Slovenian Pannonia in the late 860s and 870s and established a seminary to educate Slovenian boys for the priesthood.

In addition to constant Germanization pressures, which began with the Christianization process, the Slovenians suffered almost two centuries of sporadic Turkish raids, especially from 1408 to 1578. An estimated 100,000 Slovenians perished, and an equal number of young boys and girls were taken to Turkey, where the boys were trained as Turkish soldiers (*janissaries*) and the girls were put into harems or domestic service. In 1593, however, Slovenian and Croatian forces united and decisively defeated the Turks in the battle of Sisak in Croatia. Under the leadership of Count Andrej Turjaški (Andreas of Turjak, Slovenia), the threat of subsequent Turkish raids on Slovenian and neighboring lands was considerably diminished. Slovenians were also involved in numerous uprisings against the exploitative foreign nobility, the most famous of which was the joint Slovenian-Croatian revolt of 1573, in which more than a third of the rebels perished in battle and many of the survivors were tortured and executed.

As Newman and other foreign observers noted, the Slovenians concentrated on cultural, rather than political, freedom and opportunities. Scholars have pointed out how Slovenians benefited not only Austria, with which they were for centuries associated, but also the world. Examples include Jurij (George) Slatkonia (1456–1522), from Ljubljana, Slovenia, who in 1498 founded and led the Vienna Court Musical Establishment, including the Vienna Boys Choir, and became the first resident bishop of Vienna in 1513. Joseph Stefan (1835–1983), a physicist and author of Stefan's fourth-power law, was also one of many Slovenian rectors of the University of Vienna. Frederic Pregl from Ljubljana (1869–1930), the father of microanalysis, won the 1923 Nobel Prize in Chemistry. His disciple, P. A. Levene, according to *Asimov's Biographical Encyclopedia of Science and Technology* (1972), "brought Pregl's world-famous methods to the United States." Described by some as a people of servants, the Slovenians also gave Germany, when it was Europe's most powerful state, its second chancellor (1890–1894), Leon von Caprivi (originally Kopriva).

Modern Era Slovenia was part of the Habsburg Empire from the fourteenth century until 1918, with the exception of a four-year period in which it was part of the Illyrian Provinces (comprising Krain, or central Slovenia, central Croatia, and Dalmatia), established by Napoleon in 1809 to fend off Austria. Despite this long occupation, Slovenia maintained its Slovenian language and culture. In 1918, at the end of World War I, Slovenia became a part of the new Kingdom of Serbs, Croats, and Slovenes, which was renamed Yugoslavia in 1929. The uneasy union was terminated by the invasion of the Axis powers in 1941. After a brutal occupation by the Axis forces and a cruel Communist revolution (1941–45), Communist-dominated Yugoslavia was under the totalitarian rule of Josip Broz, known as Marshall Tito. Slovenia was Yugoslavia's most prosperous republic during this period, yet it was dominated by Communists (the only allowed political party) who never represented as much as 7 percent of the Slovenian population yet controlled nearly all politics, finances and economy, education, the judiciary branch, and, of course, the media.

In the years immediately following Tito's death in 1980, Slovenia resisted Belgrade's plans to further concentrate federal political and economic power and developed an openness in cultural, civic, and economic areas that was rare in the Communist world. In September 1989 the General Assembly of the Yugoslav Republic of Slovenia asserted its right to secede from Yugoslavia by adopting an amendment to its constitution. On December 23, 1990, a referendum was held in which 88.5 percent of Slovenians voted for independence. On June 25, 1991, the Republic of Slovenia declared its independence, and after a ten-day war, Yugoslavia ended its attack and gradually withdrew its forces from Slovenia. On January 15, 1992, the European community recognized independent Slovenia, and other countries soon followed suit, including the United States on April 7, 1992.

With historical ties to Central Europe, Slovenia has become an independent modern state. On May 22, 1992, it became a permanent member of the United Nations. In 2004 the country became a member of NATO and the European Union. Three years later Slovenia joined the Eurozone—the seventeen-member union of European countries that have adopted the euro as common currency and sole legal tender. In 2008 Slovenia became the first post-Communist country to hold the presidency of the Council of the European Union. Yet, in contrast to other countries formerly under former Communist domination, Slovenia did not exclude Communist leaders from political and economic power, nor did it manage to substantially diminish their control of banks, the courts, and leading mass media. This has resulted in continued Communist abuses and strong polarization, not only in politics but also in the population at large. Not a single Communist war criminal or mass murderer was sentenced or imprisoned or blocked from power. Unlike the European Union States, Slovenia never officially condemned Communism. Communists were often favored with inflated pensions or "cultural" subsidies, and some have become notorious tycoons. In 2012 and 2013 the old guard used its power to increasingly obstruct democratic government. It encouraged or organized mass protests, often under Communist symbols such as red flags and red stars, to block needed financial and other reforms and to topple Slovenian Spring leaders, especially second-term prime minister Janez Janša—an imprisoned Communist dissenter who became secretary of defense during the 1991 War of Independence and who, as prime minister of Slovenia (2004–2008), was president of the European Council in 2008.

SETTLEMENT IN THE UNITED STATES

The first proven settler of mixed Slovenian-Croatian ancestry was Ivan Ratkaj, a Jesuit priest who reached the New World in 1680. He was followed by Mark Anton Kappus, who came to the New World in 1687 and distinguished himself as a missionary, educator, writer, poet, and explorer. In the 1730s Slovenians and Croatians established small agricultural settlements in Georgia. During the Revolutionary War a small number of Slovenian soldiers fought with George Washington's forces. Between 1831 and 1868 the Slovenian-born scholar, missionary, and bishop Frederic Baraga labored on a vast 80,000-square-mile area of virgin territory that included parts of what is now Michigan, Wisconsin, Minnesota, and Canada, where he and his followers built some of the first churches, schools, and orphanages. Four of his Slovenian fellow missionaries also became American bishops. This was also the time when early Slovenian settlements were established. Andreas Skopec (Skopez) reached Fryburg, Pennsylvania, in 1846 and was joined by several Slovenian compatriots. Slovenian settlements followed in the mining town of Calumet, Michigan, in 1856; the farming community of Brockway, Minnesota, in 1865; and several rural areas in Michigan, Illinois, and Iowa. Historian and biographer John Zaplotnik recorded the beginnings of Slovenian communities in Omaha, Nebraska, in 1868; Joliet, Illinois, in 1873; New York City in 1878; and Cleveland, Ohio, in 1881.

Following the missionaries and other trailblazers, the largest numbers of Slovenian immigrants reached the United States between 1880 and World War I, particularly from 1905 to 1913. The exact numbers are impossible to pinpoint, because Slovenians were often identified either as Austrians or jointly with Croatians, or under a number of other labels. These immigrants were mostly men from poorer areas of Slovenia hoping to find a better life in the United States—the land of opportunity—and arrange for their wives or sweethearts to follow as soon as they had saved enough money. Many of them found work in mines and steel mills, where initially they earned two dollars for a ten-hour day. Some grew discouraged and returned to their homeland, but others married and settled in Slovenian communities. Many single men were anxious to find wives of their own culture; they persuaded young Slovenian women to immigrate to the United States by offering them jobs in their boarding houses, restaurants, and saloons, hoping to marry them. The growing communities attracted new immigrants, who were pleased to find countrymen who shared their culture and spoke their language.

The 1910 U.S. Census reported 183,431 persons of Slovenian mother tongue: 123,631 "foreign-born" and 59,800 born in the United States. By 1920, the Slovenian population in the United States had reached

> The first night in America I spent, with hundreds of other recently arrived immigrants, in an immense hall with tiers of narrow iron-and-canvas bunks, four deep. ... The bunk immediately beneath mine was occupied by a Turk. ... I thought how curious it was that I should be spending a night in such proximity to a Turk, for Turks were traditional enemies of [my people]. ... Now here I was, trying to sleep directly above a Turk, with only a sheet of canvas between us.
>
> Louis Adamic in 1913, cited in *Ellis Island: An Illustrated History of the Immigrant Experience*, edited by Ivan Chermayeff et al. (New York: Macmillan, 1991)

228,000. These numbers were disputed as an underestimate of the actual Slovenian American population, because often descendants of earlier settlers no longer knew Slovenian. Also, many Slovenians coming from Austria tried to escape widespread anti-Slavic prejudice by identifying themselves as Austrian, and many who should have been reported as Slovenian appeared under such headings as Slav, Slavic, Slavish, or Slavonian, a problem recognized by the U.S. Census officials. World War I and subsequent restrictive regulations of 1924 ended mass immigration of Slovenians to the United States. The next significant wave of Slovenian immigration occurred after World War II (1945–1956), with an influx of political rather than economic immigrants. Again, because of different labels given these immigrants, such as Yugoslav, the numbers are difficult to determine. Concerning all Slovenian Americans, some writers placed their number in the 1980s at 250,000 to 300,000. Others, assuming the Slovenian population growth between 1910 and 1980 was the same as that of the American population at large, suggested that Americans with some Slovenian parentage should number over 500,000, yet in many cases only a fraction of increasingly mixed ethnic roots would be Slovenian and such persons could justifiably identify with a more dominant ancestral category or

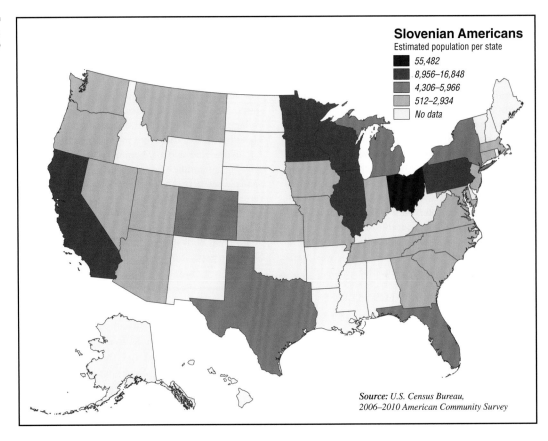

Slovenian Americans
Estimated population per state

- 55,482
- 8,956–16,848
- 4,306–5,966
- 512–2,934
- No data

*Source: U.S. Census Bureau,
2006–2010 American Community Survey*

with none at all. In the twenty-first century, an estimated 90 percent of Slovenian Americans are second generation or beyond.

From the very beginning, Slovenian immigrants have been widely scattered in many states. Despite the underestimates of their numbers, the U.S. Census probably correctly identifies the states with the highest concentration of Slovenian Americans. Ohio, where nearly 50 percent live, is the unrivaled leader, with greater Cleveland being the home of the largest Slovenian community in the United States and also the largest settlement of Slovenians living outside of Slovenia. Pennsylvania (14.5 percent) is next, followed by Illinois (11.7 percent). Minnesota and Wisconsin each have a little over 6 percent of the Slovenian population. California, Colorado, Michigan, Florida, New York, Texas, Indiana, Washington, Kansas, and Maryland all have even smaller numbers. According to the U.S. Census of 2000, there was no single U.S. state in which Slovenians were not represented. The 2000 U.S. Census also indicated that Slovenian Americans were the ancestral group with the smallest percentage living in poverty in the United States. According to the U.S. Census Bureau's American Community Survey estimates for 2006–2010, Ohio was the state with the largest population of Slovenian Americans. Other states with large numbers of Americans of Slovenian descent included Illinois, Pennsylvania, Wisconsin, California, and Minnesota.

LANGUAGE

Slovenian is a Slavic language that uses the Latin alphabet. It is also the language of the oldest preserved written documents of any Slavic people, the so-called *brižinski spomeniki* (the Freising Monuments), dating from 1000 CE. Primož Trubar published the first printed books in Slovenian starting in 1551, less than a century after the invention of the Guttenberg press and at a time when Latin was the prevalent scholarly language. Through a millennium of incorporation into German-speaking lands, the Slovenian language was the pivotal vehicle of Slovenian culture, consciousness, identity, and national survival. Because the Slovenians were few in number, they were eager to preserve their mother tongue while simultaneously learning other languages.

Indeed, Slovenians have long been noted for their exceptional linguistic skills. For example, many Slovenian missionaries in the United States preached in five or more languages. Several colleges and universities have from time to time taught the Slovenian language, including Kent State University (which also established an annual Slovenian Studies Award), Columbia University, the University of Illinois, Indiana University, the University of Kansas, Ohio State University, University of Pittsburgh, and others. There are also several libraries with Slovenian language collections.

Among foreign-born Slovenians over the age of five in the United States in 2000, slightly more than 22 percent spoke only English in the home. Of the approximately 75 percent who spoke Slovenian in the home, almost 45 percent were also proficient in English. About 30 percent of all Slovenians in the United States are bilingual—English and some Slovenian—but the younger generation tends to use English to the exclusion of their ancestors' language.

The Slovenian writing system is phonetically precise in that a letter, with very few exceptions, always has the same sound. Most letters are the same as in English (except that Slovenian lacks the letters *w* and *y*), and many letters also have the same sound as in English. For the rest, the following pronunciation guide may be of help: *a* is pronounced as in *art* (never as in *safe*); *e* as in *get* (never as in *eve*); *i* as in *ill* (never as in *like*); *o* as in *awe*; *u* as in *ruler* (never as in *use*); *c* as in *tsar* (never as in *cat*); *g* as in *go* (never as in *age*); *j* as the *y* in *yes* (never as in *just*); *lj* as the *lli* in *million*; *nj* as the *gn* in *monsignor*; *č* as in *church*; *š* as in *she*; *z* as in *zipper*; and *ž* as the *ge* in *garage*.

Greetings and Popular Expressions *Dobro jutro*—good morning; *dober dan*—good day; *dober večer*—good evening; *dobrodošli*—welcome; *jaz sem (Janez Zupan)*—I am (John Zupan); *to je gospod (gospa, gospodična) Stropnik*—this is Mr. (Mrs., Miss) Stropnik; *kako ste*—how are you; *hvala, dobro*—thank you, well; *na svidenje*—so long; *zbogom*—good-bye; *lahko noč*—good night; *prosim*—please; *hvala*—thank you; *na zdravje*—to your health; *dober tek*—enjoy your meal; *vse najboljše*—the best of everything; *oprostite*—excuse me; *čestitke*—congratulations; *kje je*—where is; *kje je restavracija (hotel)*—where is a restaurant (hotel); *kje je ta naslov*—where is this address; *me veseli*—I am pleased; *žal mi je*—I am sorry; *sem ameriški Slovenec (ameriška Slovenka)*—I am an American Slovenian; *vse je zelo lepo*—everything is very nice; *Slovenija je krasna*—Slovenia is beautiful; *še pridite*—come again; *srečno pot*—have a safe trip.

RELIGION

Coming from a country with strong Catholic traditions and where hills and valleys are dotted with beautiful, centuries-old churches, many Slovenian Americans cling to their religious roots. They have built their own churches and other religious institutions all over the United States. Following the example of the missionaries, priests and seminarians came from Slovenia, and U.S.-born descendants of immigrants gradually joined the clergy. St. Vitus Catholic Church in Cleveland, Ohio is the largest Slovenian church in the United States; many visitors, including Slovenian Cardinal Franc Rode, have compared it to a cathedral. Since 1924 the Slovenian Franciscan Commissariat of the Holy Cross in Lemont, Illinois, has played a pivotal unifying role among Slovenian Catholics in the United States. It established the Mary Help of Christians Shrine (with a replica painting from Brezje,

Slovenia) and represents the most popular Slovenian pilgrimage in North America. It comprises a monastery, a high school, a retreat house, and the Alvernia Manor for the Aged. It used to publish the annual *Koledars* (*Almanacs*) and still publishes the monthly magazine *Ave Maria*. In 1994 the spacious Slovenian Cultural and Pastoral Center was built in Lemont. Meanwhile, in 1971 the Slovenian Chapel of Our Lady of Brezje was dedicated inside the National Shrine of the Immaculate Conception in Washington, D.C., becoming another significant Slovenian religious landmark in the United States. Numerous pilgrims from throughout the United States, Canada, and other countries visit St. Peter's Cathedral in Marquette, Michigan, the resting place of its first bishop, Frederic Baraga.

Slovenian Americans, like other groups, have belonged to at least two ideologically distinct categories the Catholics (conservatives) and the freethinkers (progressives), or "rightists" and "leftists." In the past, each had its own newspapers, magazines, and other institutions. Depending on times and people involved, relations between the two factions have ranged from hostile to tolerant to friendly competition. Some friction also developed between the freethinkers and socialists, who were descendants of earlier Slovenian immigrants, and the Slovenian Catholics, who immigrated to the United States after World War II. The new immigrants resented the freethinkers' support of Communist dictator Josip Broz Tito, whom they viewed as a mass murderer, while progressives looked with suspicion at the newly arrived refugees. In general, the friction has subsided.

A greater threat for religion developed in the late twentieth century. Many Slovenian parishes struggled for survival as the older generation died off, the Slovenian population migrated to the suburbs, the younger generation experienced increased Americanization and secularization, and the parishes found themselves with a lack of Slovenian priests. Some churches closed, and while others—such as St. George's in Chicago—remained active, the predominant ethnicity of the congregation changed from Slovenian to Latino. Some, like St. Joseph's Church in Joliet, Illinois, have continued to be the center of a thriving Slovenian community. In rare instances, ethnic churches that have closed have been replaced by new ones in new neighborhoods, as happened in Milwaukee-West Allis, Wisconsin, and in Bridgeport-Fairfield, Connecticut. In Cleveland two thriving Slovenian parishes remain, St. Vitus and St. Mary of the Assumption, each of which is more than a hundred years old.

Many Slovenians worship in other American Catholic parishes, while an extremely small number have joined other religions. The children of young couples are frequently enrolled in local Catholic schools, which means that their parents also join such non-Slovenian parishes. Many of these people still return to Slovenian parishes at least on special occasions—at Christmas and Easter, for annual festivals, celebrations of holidays, Corpus Christi processions, Palm Sunday festivities with Slovenian *butare* (ornamented bundles of branches), and so on. St. Mary of the Assumption Parish in Cleveland even presents the Passion liturgy in Slovenian, conducted by schoolchildren in biblical attire (ranging from Roman soldiers to Mary and Christ). According to the Slovenian Ethnic Parish Survey of 1976, to which twenty-seven parishes responded, the use of Slovenian languages in what were once predominantly Slovenian parishes is on the decline. Only stronger parishes remain bilingual, often with one Sunday Mass in English and another in Slovenian, which is paralleled by the church choirs. Yet it is not unusual for ethnic identity to persist to some extent even when ethnic languages are no longer used. The shortage of Slovenian priests has become a serious problem, as exemplified for instance in the once-thriving Slovenian St. Joseph parish in Calumet, Michigan, in San Francisco, and elsewhere. These trends have continued in the decades since the parish survey due to a number of factors, including an overall decline in the number of people joining the priesthood and a tendency of Catholic parishes to lose their ethnic character as subsequent generations of an immigrant group become more Americanized.

There is a group of Slovenian Protestants who refer to themselves as Windish. Although numerically small, this community has long used a Slovenian regional dialect in interaction, its services, and its press and has displayed considerable ethnic and religious vitality, especially in St. John's Windish Lutheran Church in Bethlehem, Pennsylvania, and a few other Slovenian Protestant institutions.

The belief that the American and Slovenian cultures at their best are not only compatible but complement and enrich each other seems to appeal to large numbers of Slovenian Americans who have visited the country of their ancestors.

CULTURE AND ASSIMILATION

Until 1918 the bulk of Slovenian immigrants were Slovenian by ethnicity and Austrian by citizenship or statehood. Men usually had a working knowledge of German, which facilitated their adjustment in the American workplace where, at that time, many foremen and workers were from German-speaking countries. Yet, the American population began to differentiate between Germans, genuine German Austrians, and various non-German ethnic groups, including the Slovenians, who were looked down upon as inferior and often given such pejorative labels as "Polacks," "Hunkies," and "Bohunks." Residents of cities with larger settlements

of immigrants became aware of further subdivisions and reserved "Hunkies" for Hungarians, "Bohunks" for Czechs and Slovaks, and "Grainers" or "Grenish" (a corruption of the term "Krainers" from the Slovenian province of Krain, also known as Kranjska or Carniola) for Slovenians. Numerous accounts and studies suggest that for more than half a century after 1880 there was strong anti-Slavic and anti-Slovenian prejudice in the United States. Although Slovenians were not included among the forty "races" or ethnic groups whose hierarchical position in the United States has been studied since 1926 by means of the Bogardus Social Distance Scale, statistical scores and narrative reports in leading textbooks suggest there was an intense and widespread prejudice against all Slavic groups.

Initially most Slovenians coped with the problems of being low-status or despised strangers in a foreign land by establishing their own ethnic communities, including churches, schools, and business establishments. They also organized self-help groups such as fraternal societies, social and political clubs, and national homes as their new community centers. A high degree of self-sufficiency among Slovenians helped them adjust relatively well within their own ethnic community and facilitated adjustment in the American workplace and in society at large. Many applied the leadership skills they had learned in their ethnic neighborhoods to wider American society, often rising from club or lodge officers to become ward leaders, city councilmen, mayors, and other American political, business, and civic leaders. This trend continued through World War II but has declined since then. With few exceptions, this gradual, piecemeal adjustment to the United States seemed to work remarkably well. Slovenians in general proudly avoided being on welfare; in times of crises they helped each other.

Many Slovenian immigrants have acquired English with relative speed and facility. This was especially true of the missionaries and priests who immigrated to the United States in the nineteenth century and of post–World War II refugees. It was less true of working-class immigrants who arrived between 1880 and 1930. Slovenians have been anxious to own homes, often with vegetable and flower gardens. In the mid-1950s, approximately 48 percent of Slovenian refugees had become homeowners after being in the United States only ten years on average. Newspapers such as the *Cleveland Press* and the *Cleveland Plain Dealer* often mentioned clean, family-owned homes, with attached vegetable and flower gardens, as a characteristic of Slovenian ethnic communities. As the emphasis in the United States has shifted from Anglo-conformity to pluralism, large numbers of Slovenian immigrants and their descendants are eager to learn and preserve the best elements of their ethnic culture and blend them into their American heritage.

Traditions and Customs The belief that the American and Slovenian cultures at their best are not only compatible but complement and enrich each other seems to appeal to large numbers of Slovenian Americans, especially those who have visited the country of their ancestors (and are therefore familiar with present-day Slovenia instead of just the old country they had heard about from their parents or grandparents). Although Slovenia is a relatively small country, many customs are regional. Picturesque Slovenian national costumes, worn only on festive occasions, enrich many traditional affairs and often add diversity and color to various American festivals and celebrations.

Slovenian traditions that are still practiced include several cultural festivals. Miklavževanje, the feast of St. Nicholas Sveti Miklavž), takes place on or around December 6. The good old saint, dressed as a bishop and accompanied by angels and *parkelji* (little devils), visits Slovenian parish halls and schools and, after solemnly exhorting the young to be good, distributes gifts. *Maškarade*, or Slovenian-style carnivals, are another opportunity for merrymaking. Attendees disguise themselves with masks and silly attire.

Funerals Slovenian American wakes and funerals are usually attended by large numbers of mourners, including relatives, friends, and members of organizations to which the deceased belonged. Often, groups gather for private or club-scheduled prayers at the funeral homes; on rare occasions there are honor guards in uniforms or national costumes. After the funeral Mass and attendance at the cemetery, guests are invited to a meal as the bereaved family shows its appreciation for their attendance and those attending reinforce their solidarity with relatives of the deceased, helping ease the transition from sadness to normalcy.

In general, Slovenian American funerals tend to be similar to those of the U.S. population at large, with either a religious or secular tone. In addition to, or instead of, flowers, mourners often give money to help out the bereaved family or donate to a specified charity in memory of the deceased. Providing for a decent funeral was one of the first tasks of fraternal organizations' insurance in the years before Social Security and other safety nets.

Cuisine Slovenian and Slovenian American women are known for being excellent cooks and bakers. Many culinary specialties prepared by Slovenian American women (and sometimes men) have long been sold in ethnic communities at social gatherings and fundraisers. Some of the most popular goodies include *potica* (or *poteetsah*), a nut roll that is as Slovenian as apple pie is American. Among the usual varieties of *poticas* are walnut, raisin (or mixed), poppyseed, and tarragon. Apple, cherry, apricot, cheese, and other varieties of *štrudel* are also tempting delicacies, as are *krofi*, the Slovenian variety of doughnuts, and *flancati*, or angel wings, a flaky, deep-fried pastry. Savory dumplings (*cmoki*) and *štruklji*, meat-filled or liver-filled for soups, are also popular, as well as dumplings filled with apricots, plums, finely ground meat, or cheese, which can be served as the main meal, or baked and sweetened as dessert. In addition to all kinds of chicken, pork, and beef

POTICA

Ingredients

For dough:

2 cups white flour

2 tablespoons yeast

2 tablespoons water or milk

5½ tablespoons sugar

3 egg yolks

1 cup milk

½ cup butter

¼ teaspoon rum

½ teaspoon lemon or orange peel

¼ teaspoon vanilla extract

salt

For the filling:

7 tablespoons honey

7 tablespoons milk

2 cups ground walnuts

7 tablespoons sugar

2 eggs

¼ teaspoon vanilla essence

¼ teaspoon ground cinnamon

¼ teaspoon ground cloves

¼ teaspoon lemon peel

¼ teaspoon rum

Preparation

For dough:

Put flour in a bowl; add salt.

In a cup, dissolve the yeast in a tablespoon of water or milk.

In a medium bowl, mix the eggs, sugar, rum, vanilla extract, and lemon or orange peel.

Heat milk with butter until just hot (with butter melted). Add hot butter/milk mixture to the flour; stir to remove lumps and then add that to the egg mixture. Stir again; add dissolved yeast and stir into a medium thick dough. Knead until it is elastic inside and smooth on the outside. Make sure the dough does not stick to the bowl and that it does not get too hard. Cover the dough with a plastic sheet and allow to rise at room temperature until doubled in size.

While dough is rising, make filling:

Melt honey in tepid milk, and then add half of the walnuts, sugar, eggs, aromas, spices and rum.

When dough has risen, preheat oven to 375°F. Knead the dough once, then roll it out. Spread the filling on the rolled-out dough and sprinkle with the other half of walnuts. The temperature of the filling should be equal to that of the dough. Roll tightly, put in a bread pan, prick, and leave to rise until doubled in size. Before baking, coat with a thin layer of milk and egg mixture. Bake for 50 minutes.

dishes, including *paprikash* and *goulash*, Carniolan sausages (*kranjske klobase*) are also favorites. The Slovenian American astronaut Sunita Williams took some of these *klobase* on her space trip in 2006–2007, which received much publicity in the American news outlets.

Zganci (buckwheat crumbles) is a very popular food in Slovenia and is experiencing a revival in the United States as studies show how healthy it is. The same is true of such once-despised peasant meals as beans and sauerkraut, which former Ohio Governor Frank J. Lausche was known to consume right in the kitchen of the Capitol during his time in office (1945–1947 and 1949–1957). Somewhat exotic are rice or blood sausages, mentioned in several books by journalist Jim Klobuchar, the father of Minnesota senator Amy Klobuchar. Imported award-winning Slovenian wines are supplemented by domestic wine from Slovenian American wineries, especially in Ohio and California, while some families, even those who no longer grow their own grapes, continue to make their own wine. Some old-timers also enjoy *slivovitz*, a strong plum brandy, imported or in some areas homemade, which others use only to "strengthen" and flavor their tea, and many would never taste.

Dances and Songs Early immigrants, often single men who worked hard and long hours during the week as miners, lumberjacks, or steel workers, loved to relax on weekends at Slovenian saloons, clubs, national halls, or picnic grounds. There they listened and danced to familiar tunes of joyful Slovenian polka music.

Polka dancing has long been a principal form of entertainment among a large section of Slovenian Americans. Many folk-dancing organizations, such as Eleanor Karlinger's at St. Vitus; SNPJ Circle 2 (the Slovenian Junior Chorus), Kres (Bonefire) Folklore Group, and Folklore Institute Dancers in Cleveland; Slovenian Radio Club Dancers in Chicago; and others in various Slovenian American communities, have been popular attractions for Slovenian and American audiences of all ages.

Singing societies—some singing primarily for enjoyment and socializing, others striving for perfection—have been popular among Slovenian Americans for more than a century. A popular saying is that three Serbians make up an army; three Croatians, a political party; and three Slovenians, a singing society. Although preserving Slovenian songs has usually been the primary goal of these singing societies, an assortment of American patriotic and other songs are frequently included. Cleveland singing groups Zarja and Glasbena Matica, under such prominent professional directors as John Ivanusch and Anton Schubel, were also known for their excellent operas, glowingly reviewed by American music critics. Although the number of singing societies has decreased, an impressive amount are still active and popular.

Starting in Cleveland in the mid-1960s, Rudy Knez directed the large and very popular Slovenian Young Accordionists Orchestra. In addition to individual button box and piano accordionists, gradually and

especially in recent decades a surprisingly large number of polka orchestras have been established throughout the United States. With the national popularity of musicians such as the Grammy Award-winning Frankie Yankovic, this Slovenian music, often with an added American beat, has gained an ever-larger audience. Eddie Simms (Simoncic) played Slovenian tunes in some Holywood movies. In 1987 the American Slovenian Polka Foundation, led by Polka Ambassador and radio personality Tony Petkovsek, established The National Cleveland-Style Polka Hall of Fame.

In 1973 Father Frank Perkovich celebrated the first Polka Mass at the landmark Slovenian Resurrection Church in Eveleth, Minnesota. The Polka Mass, which combined Slovenian polka and waltz melodies with lyrics for liturgy, was soon celebrated all across Minnesota's Mesabi Iron Range and in the Twin Cities. Later Father Perkovich went on tours, celebrating the unique Mass in churches across the United States, including Alaska and Hawaii, and, ultimately, in Pope John Paul II's presence in Rome, which helped silence various critics who objected to this type of music. The Polka Mass became a key event at several Slovenian festivals throughout North America, and Father Perkovich's recording sold more than 100,000 copies.

Holidays Christmas, until 1987 an ordinary working day under the Communist regime in Slovenia, is the most universally celebrated holiday by Slovenians and Slovenian Americans, not only by Catholics but also by other Slovenian groups. Easter is very important to Catholics, and Easter customs that have been passed on through generations among Slovenian Americans include the painting of *pisanke* (the Slovenian version of Easter eggs) and select Easter foods, such as *želodec* (stomach casings filled with meat, symbolizing the tomb) and *hren* (horseradish, symbolizing the nails used in the Crucifixion). *Potica* (walnut roll) is a must on any festive occasion, including Easter. Corpus Christi, occasionally with processions, and Assumption Day (August 15) are observed by churchgoing Slovenian Americans, although much less so than Christmas and Easter. Slovenian national days are celebrated by much smaller numbers of heritage-conscious Slovenian Americans, among them especially Prešeren Day (Slovenian Culture Day) on February 8, in honor of Slovenia's greatest poet, Dr. France Prešeren (1800–1849); Labor Day (May 1 and 2), especially by the so-called Progressive Slovenians; and Slovenian Statehood or Independence Day, commemorating the nation's independence from Yugoslavia on June 25, 1991. While most Slovenian Americans celebrate Mother's Day on the second Sunday of May, many Slovenian American communities, especially those with their own parishes and schools, also celebrate the Slovenian *Materinski dan* at the end of March, both at home and with public programs (songs, recitations, plays, and dances) staged by children in honor of their mothers. People commonly give their mothers a red carnation, the Slovenian national flower.

SLOVENIAN PROVERBS

Otroci so največje bogastvo.

Children are our greatest wealth.

Smeh je pol zdravja.

Laughter is half of health.

Več glav več ve.

More heads know more.

Prijatelja v nesreči spoznaš.

You get to know who is a friend when times are tough.

Laž ima kratke noge.

A lie has short legs.

Lepa beseda lepo mesto najde.

A nice word finds a nice place.

Čas je zlato.

Time is gold.

Kakor si boš postlal, tako boš ležal.

As you make your bed, so will you sleep.

Bolje doseči malenkost v pravici kot mnogo v krivici.

It's better to achieve a little something justly than plenty unjustly.

Mrtvi nas učijo živeti.

The dead teach us how to live.

Health Care Issues and Practices Slovenian culture has long emphasized the value of good health. One of the most frequently quoted sayings is "*Zdravje je največje bogastvo*"—"Health is the greatest wealth." Following the Czech lead, the most influential Slovenian youth organizations, which often included "youngsters" fifty or seventy years old, were the conservative Eagles (*Orli*) and liberal Falcons (*Sokoli*). They adopted an ancient Roman guideline as their own slogan, "*Mens sana in corpore sano*"—(A healthy mind in a healthy body), paying attention to development of both good character and physical fitness. Both Sokols and, to a lesser extent, Orli were also active in a number of Slovenian American communities, but these organizations no longer exist. Active participation in athletics, gymnastics, walking, hiking, mountain climbing, and a variety of sports, especially skiing, where trips and various competitions by age groups are still organized each year, are viewed as contributing to good mental and physical health. Alcohol consumption and smoking, on the other hand, have been among the unhealthy practices in which Slovenians on both sides of the ocean continue to indulge.

In the past, overcrowded boarding houses and life in depressing urban areas with air, water, and noise pollution contributed a new variety of health hazards for early workers. Occupational risks lurked in steel mills and coal mines, where workers experienced accidents and were exposed to increased air pollution, extremes of heat and cold, or coal dust that resulted in black lung disease, which drastically shortened the life of countless miners. In some mining towns, from Pennsylvania to Wyoming, there is an alarming absence of older men; their widows survive with nothing but their modest homes and low benefits to compensate them for their families' share in building a more prosperous United States.

As working and living conditions have generally improved, and some good health habits learned in childhood have persisted, the physical and mental health of Slovenian Americans is now comparable to that of other Americans. It is unclear whether or not home remedies, such as medicinal herbs, used in many Slovenian immigrant households have been among the contributing factors to better health. A conclusion of "slightly better" than "national health" was reached by Sylvia J. O'Kicki, who examined a group of Slovenian Americans in Pennsylvania with comparable cohorts selected from the National Health Interview Survey of 1985. She stated,

> When the group of Slovene Americans without any regard to the level of ethnicity is compared to the national American sample they differ favorably in health status and the practice of health behaviors. … Those who are actively involved in the heritage and traditions of the ethnic group report a more favorable health status and practice of more favorable health behaviors.

FAMILY AND COMMUNITY LIFE

Extended families were common among early Slovenian immigrants, but nuclear families prevail today. Increasingly, children move away from their parental homes once they are permanently employed, as is common in the United States. However, many Slovenian American parents still prefer to have their children live at home until marriage, saving money for their own homes. The oldest child is often expected to be a responsible role model for younger children, and the youngest child is widely believed to be shown the most affection by all. Actual differences by order of birth are probably comparable to those of American families, although group-specific research is not available. Slovenian Americans have frowned upon putting their parents or elderly relatives into homes for the aged, but since employment of women has increased and families have become more mobile, the practice is becoming more common.

Gender Roles A 1993 study revealed that traditional attitudes toward gender roles have persisted in Slovenia after independence. Although the employment of women outside the home has increased,

CELEBRATING SLOVENIAN WINEMAKING

To celebrate the tradition of winemaking, many Slovenian American communities host vintage festivals (*trgatve*, sometimes spelled *trgatev*) in the fall. Merrymakers dance and socialize, often under clusters of tempting grapes hanging from an improvised ceiling. Those who reach for the grapes and are caught by mock police are sent to "jail," where all can see their sad fate. A relative or friend must free the "thief" (or *tat*) by paying a ransom or fine, which is used for a worthy cause. Another traditional celebration is Martinovanje (St. Martin's feast), when the good saint changes lowly grape juice into tasty wine.

Slovenian women still perform most of the household tasks, and too little value is attached to domestic tasks. Slovenian women are more liberal than men in their views of gender roles, and most indicate a preference for working outside the home even when the family's economic needs do not require them to do so. Slovenian men, regardless of age, tend to be more traditional in their attitudes toward gender. A decade-long study that ended in 2000 showed that college-age Slovenian males became more traditional over time, in comparison to female students in Slovenia.

Slovenian immigrants brought their traditional attitudes toward gender roles with them when they came to the United States, but beginning with late-nineteenth-century immigrants, women played an increasingly important economic role in the Slovenian American community. Ironically, that increased economic role was directly related to domestic responsibilities. Women were largely responsible for managing the boarding house operations that housed the single males who immigrated to work in the mines and mills. Often female relatives were brought over from the old country to help with the extra domestic work these boarding houses required. In 1926 the Slovenian Women's Union of America was founded in Chicago with the multiple purposes of preserving Slovenian heritage and encouraging Slovenian women to continue their education and to participate in public life. It is perhaps indicative of changing gender roles that in 2011 the venerable organization changed its name to the Slovenian Union of America, in part to encourage male members to join.

Slovenian American women have played a pivotal role not only as homemakers but also in ethnic churches, language schools, charity projects, and, increasingly, in political campaigns. As the old Slovenian proverb states "*Žena tri vogle podpira*," or "The woman supports three corners [of a four-corner home]."

Courtship and Weddings In general, Slovenian American parents are anxious for their children to marry someone from their own ethnic and religious group, although ethnic homogeny has been decreasing among members of American-born generations. Young people have adopted dating and other American customs, such as bridal showers. Those living in Slovenian communities often still prefer huge ethnic weddings with hundreds of guests in attendance (where the number of guests suggests the couple's importance or popularity), lots of food, open bars, and countless varieties of Slovenian pastries, plus a huge American wedding cake. In addition to Slovenian music and dancing, some couples reenact the traditional Slovenian unveiling ceremony. In this ceremony, which praises the bride's beauty and innocence, the bride's white veil is removed and a red carnation is pinned in her hair, symbolizing her transition from maidenhood into married life. In addition to other wedding gifts, it is customary to contribute envelopes with money to help the newlyweds start a family.

As in Slovenia before World War II, divorce among Slovenian Americans has been less common than among Americans in general, although it has recently increased, especially in ethnically and religiously mixed families. U.S. Census data for 2000 revealed that 8.2 percent of Slovenian Americans were divorced; by 2011 that number had increased to 9.7 percent (only slightly less than that of the overall U.S. population, which was 10.8 percent), according to the American Community Survey estimates for 2009–2011.

Education Beginning with the post–World War II immigrants, Slovenians entering the United States have usually been well educated. According to U.S. Census data, among the foreign-born Slovenians in the United States in 2000, more than 70 percent had a high school diploma (compared to a national average of 72 percent for the same period), nearly 30 percent held at least a bachelor's degree, and 13 percent had graduate or professional degrees. For second-generation immigrants and beyond, education, whether in parochial or public schools, has been an agent of change, helping young Slovenian Americans to navigate between their Slovenian identity that was linked to their homes and family customs and the public American identities they needed to succeed in the United States.

Cultural and educational exchanges have long existed on both sides of the ocean. Countless Slovenian orchestras, many singing groups, and some dancing ensembles have visited Slovenian American communities, as have such internationally prominent pianists as Dubravka Tomsic, the Slovenian Octet, symphony conductors, and famous opera singers such Bernarda Fink. Additionally, many Slovenian American groups, including Glasbena Matica, Korotan, Kres, Zarja, and Jadran, appeared in Slovenia and other European countries. Reciprocal student exchanges, ranging from high schools to universities, have been mutually beneficial. Slovenian university students have also competed at MIT in International Genetically Engineered Machine (iGEM) competitions with teams from some

130 universities, including Harvard, MIT, Stanford, Princeton, and Cambridge, winning the prestigious BioBrick Trophy in 2006, 2008, and 2010.

EMPLOYMENT AND ECONOMIC CONDITIONS

With the exception of missionaries, priests, and some 6,000 to 10,000 ideological political refugees escaping Marshall Tito's Communist reign after World War II, the bulk of Slovenians in the United States were economic immigrants; that is, they tended to come from the poorest areas and the most economically disadvantaged families. Most were craftsmen or of poor peasant stock, joined to a lesser extent by those who wanted to avoid being drafted, a few adventurers, and a very small number of socialists or other political dissenters.

Some of the earliest immigrants took advantage of the open lands and homesteading, establishing such Slovenian pioneer farming communities as St. Stephen's and St. Anthony's in Minnesota, and, later, in Traunik, Michigan. A substantial number also worked as lumberjacks. Although many immigrants initially intended to return to Slovenia after they had earned enough money to establish themselves in their native country, and some did just that, a large majority decided to remain in the United States. In the 1880s, when land became more difficult to obtain and earnings elsewhere had become more attractive, the major wave of Slovenian immigrants settled in industrial cities and mining towns, where their labor was in demand.

It is impossible to pinpoint an exact breakdown of employment because Slovenians were frequently identified as Austrians or Yugoslavs, or they were combined in categories with Croatians or South Slavs. Because Slovenians coming from under Austrian administration were better educated than other South Slav groups, the statistical distribution was probably more favorable for them than when shown in combination with other groups. The available data on the South Slavs in general are nevertheless suggestive. Thus, in 1921, 42 percent of the South Slavs were workers in steel, iron, and zinc mines, smelters, and refineries; 12 percent worked in the coal mines; 6.5 percent in the lumber industry; 6 percent in stockyards; and 5 percent in fruit growing. Chemical works, railroads, and electrical manufacturing employed 4 percent each; professions accounted for 3.5 percent; and farming for only 3 percent.

Considerable numbers of Slovenian immigrants, however, soon became skilled workers. In the early decades of the twentieth century many Slovenian Americans worked in the automobile industry in Detroit, Toledo, Cleveland, and Pittsburgh. Using their skills from the old country, both men and women were also strongly represented in the straw-hat industry in New York. Other skills survived as useful hobbies: home-building and carpentry skills; butchering, sausage making, and meat-processing skills; wine making; and apiculture (bee keeping), which was very popular and helped many Slovenian immigrants provide honey for family and friends. Women were usually good cooks, bakers, dressmakers, and gardeners, and they canned large quantities of fruit and vegetables to provide basic necessities for their families, while some of them also used their skills, especially as dressmakers and cooks, in American industrial and business companies. Habits of hard work, honesty, frugality, and mutual help, particularly in times of hardship, helped Slovenian immigrants survive and succeed in a strange new land.

Today, Slovenian Americans can be found in almost all occupations. Many are professionals; others own businesses, agencies, factories and stores; still others are workers, foremen, or executives with large American companies. Among Slovenian immigrants in 2000, nearly 75 percent over the age of sixteen were employed in salaried positions. Management, professional, and related occupations accounted for 45.1 percent of salaried employees, with sales and office occupations representing an additional 20.7 percent. A large number of Slovenian Americans have achieved positions of leadership and prominence in American society.

POLITICS AND GOVERNMENT

In numerous towns, such as Ely, Eveleth, Chisholm, and Gilbert in Minnesota, Slovenian Americans have long been strongly represented on city councils and as mayors. They were also elected mayors in such larger communities as Euclid and Wickliffe, Ohio; Portland, Oregon; and Indianapolis. In Cleveland, the city with the largest number of Slovenians in the United States, Slovenians have long served as ward leaders, council members, council presidents, and heads of various departments of municipal government.

A young Slovenian American man who has lived and worked in New York for more than twenty years is among many people of Slovenian descent who have recently moved to the region looking for better opportunities in their careers. MANCA JUVAN / IN PICTURES / CORBIS

Frank J. Lausche, Ohio's only five-time governor and a senator from Ohio from 1957 to 1969, first won national attention as a fearless judge who, with the help of Gus Korach, a Slovenian worker, broke up widespread organized crime and corruption in a true-life drama that resulted in local and national publicity. A sizable number of Americans of Slovenian heritage have been elected to U.S. Congress. Tom Harkin, whose mother was an immigrant born in Slovenia, was elected in 1984 to represent Iowa in the Senate (he was previously a U.S. congressman); George Voinovich (Ohio), also Slovenian on his mother's side, was a member of the U.S. Senate from 1999 to 2011; and Amy Klobuchar (Minnesota), descendant of Slovenian immigrants, had been in 2006 the first female elected U.S. senator from Minnesota and was elected to her second term in 2012. Slovenian American U.S. representatives have included John A. Blatnik (served 1947–1975) and James L. Oberstar (served 1975–2011) from Minnesota, Ray P. Kogovsek from Colorado (served 1979–1985), Philip Ruppe from Michigan (served 1967–1979), Joseph Skubitz from Kansas (served 1963–1978), and Paul Gosar from Arizona (elected 2011).

Most Slovenian Americans supported the Democratic party over the years, with the exception of a small socialist subgroup who were attracted to independent candidates such as Eugene Debs just before World War I and Norman Thomas in the 1930s. Republicans gained support during and after the presidency of Ronald Reagan. Since then, Slovenian preferences have reflected those of Americans at large.

Military Slovenian Americans have been well represented in the military. Slovenian immigrant Louis Dobnikar, serving on the destroyer *Kearney*, was the first Clevelander and one of the first eleven Americans killed during World War II. John Hribar, a volunteer marine from Krayn, Pennsylvania (named after Kranj, Slovenia), was one of several Slovenian American heroes of Iwo Jima. At least eleven Slovenian Americans became generals, including U.S. Air Force Lieutenant General Anthony Burshnick (also commandant of Cadets of the U.S. Air Force Academy from 1982 to 1984 and Commander-in-Chief of the U.S. Military Airlift Command for three years prior to his retirement in 1991); Frank Gorenc, born in Slovenia, who had a distinguished career in the U.S. Air Force, culminating in 2013 when he was promoted to four-star general and was named commander of U.S. Air Forces in Europe and Africa; and his brother, Stanley Gorenc, who retired in 2007 as chief of safety, Headquarters U.S. Air Force, holding the rank of major general. The same rank was also achieved by former astronaut and undersecretary of the United States Air Force Ronald Sega, and, earlier, by the first Slovenian four-star general of the U.S. Army, Ferdinand Chesarek. The Archives of the Slovenian Research Center of America also contain materials on six Slovenian American admirals, including Ronald Zlatoper, who received his fourth star in 1994 and served with distinction as commander of the Pacific Fleet, the largest and most powerful navy in the world. Edward H. Rupnik, rear admiral of Medical Corps, U.S. Navy, was the commander of the Naval Medical School, National Medical Naval Center in Bethesda, Maryland. Some Slovenian American women have risen to the ranks of colonel in the Army and captain in the Navy.

Relations with Slovenia Slovenian Americans have not established permanent lobbying organizations in Washington, D.C., but they frequently used existing societies and institutions, ad hoc committees, or temporary councils or unions to advocate or support various causes on behalf of their home country. These include the Slovenian League, Slovenian National Union, and Slovenian Republican Alliance during World War I; various relief committees, the Union of Slovenian Parishes, and Slovenian American National Council during World War II; and the Slovenian American Council, which substantially supported the first free elections that toppled the Communist dictatorship in Slovenia in 1990. A special ad hoc committee, Americans for Free Slovenia, together with scores of other organizations and institutions, especially the *American Home* newspaper, the Slovenian Research Center of America, and thousands of individuals, helped secure the American recognition of independent Slovenia in 1992. For several decades after World War II, the Slovenian language section of Voice of America Information Agency played an important role by bringing objective information to its listeners in Slovenia.

NOTABLE INDIVIDUALS

A large number of Slovenian Americans have achieved positions of leadership and prominence in American society.

Academia James J. Stukel, born in 1937 in Joliet, Illinois, earned his BS in engineering from Purdue University and a PhD in engineering from University of Illinois. There he rose through the ranks from research assistant to professor to chancellor. From 1995 to 2005 he served as the fifteenth president of University of Illinois. Chancellor and President Stukel conceived and developed the Great Cities Institute to improve the quality of life in Chicago through teaching, research, and service. After his retirement in 2005, a James J. Stukel Professorship and the James J. Stukel Twin Towers at the Chicago campus were named in his honor.

Frederick Stare (1910–2002) obtained doctorates in biochemistry and nutrition from the University of Wisconsin in Madison in 1934 and in medicine from University of Chicago in 1941. A year later he established the first Department of Nutrition at Harvard University and served as its chairman until 1976, seeing it grow from 3 to 150 members. A prolific author of about a thousand publications, he was globally recognized as the most influential nutritionist of his time. A professorship of nutrition and epidemiology at Harvard University Public School of Health has been named in his honor.

Arthur Bergles, born in 1935 in New York City, earned a doctorate in mechanical engineering at MIT in 1962 and was chairman of its Engineering Projects Laboratory until 1969. He subsequently served as professor and chairman of the mechanical engineering department at Georgia Tech, as professor and chairman of the mechanical engineering department at Iowa State University, and as the Clark and Crossan Professor of Engineering and Director of the Heat Transfer Laboratory at Rensselaer Polytechnic Institute in New York until 1999, when he became research professor of engineering at University of Maryland. He has authored more than five hundred publications, served on editorial boards of eighteen journals, was president of the 120,000-member American Society of Mechanical Engineers, and won many distinctions and awards, including membership in the Royal Academy of Engineering in the United Kingdom, in the National Academy of Science in Italy, and in the Slovenian Academy of Arts and Sciences.

Walter J. Koroshetz obtained his M in 1979 from the University of Chicago, where he completed his two-year residency. He continued his research, teaching, and administrative activities at Massachusetts General Hospital, which is affiliated with Harvard Medical School. In 1990 he became director of the neurology residency program, then a researcher and a practicing neurologist, and a principal project investigator in stroke and Alzheimer's research. In 1994 he was appointed Director of the Neurointensive Care Service and Acute Stroke Service. In 2007 he was named deputy director at the Center for Neuroscience and Regenerative Medicine at the National Institutes of Health.

Mark Zupan, born in 1959 in Rochester, New York, obtained his B in economics from Harvard University in 1981 and became an award-winning teaching fellow there while working on his Ph, which he received from MIT in 1987. He received the Golden Apple Teaching Award at the University of Southern California in 1989 and the Burlington Resources Foundation Faculty Achievement Award for Outstanding Scholarship in 1992. In 1997 he became dean and professor of economics at the Eller College of Business and Public Administration in Tucson, Arizona, and in 2004 he was appointed dean of William E. Simon School of Business Administration at the University of Rochester.

Aeronautics August Raspet (1913–1960) was a noted inventor and designer of modern lightweight airplanes. Raspet was president of the American Aerophysics Institute from 1947 to 1949, when he left to take a position at Mississippi State College. He served

Téa Obreht is an American novelist of Bosniak/Slovenian descent. Her debut novel, *The Tiger's Wife* (2011), won the 2011 Orange Prize for Fiction. BEOWULF SHEEHAN / ZUMAPRESS / NEWSCOM

as the head of the aerophysics department there from 1953 to 1960. Raspet died in a plane crash in 1960.

Joe Sutter (1921–), the son of a Slovenian immigrant, led the team that designed the Boeing 747, which, according to Neil Armstrong, "forever changed long distance travel." Sutter is known as "The Father of the 747" and has won numerous awards, including the United States Medal of Technology and the Wright Brothers Memorial Trophy, given annually to an individual for contributions to the advancement of air travel.

Ronald Sega (1962–) is a retired major general in the United States Air Force and a former NASA astronaut. From 1995 to 1996 he served as NASA's director of operations in Russia, where he helped to train American astronauts and Russian cosmonauts for missions to the Russian space station Mir. He was flight engineer on the U.S.-Russian space shuttle mission STS-60 in 1994 and payload commander for the STS-76 mission in 1996.

Jerry M. Linenger (1955–), a retired Navy flight surgeon, flew on the STS-64 mission (1994) and launched again on the STS-81 mission on January 12, 1997, joining two Russian cosmonauts on space station Mir. Completing a nearly five-month mission, he logged approximately 50 million miles and more than 2,000 orbits around the Earth. After establishing a number of American records, he returned to Earth on May 24, 1997, having spent more continuous time in space than any male American.

NASA astronaut Sunita Williams (1965–) was launched to the International Space Station on December 9, 2006, and returned to Earth on April 26, 2007. In 2008 she became NASA deputy chief of the Astronaut Office. She returned to space on July 15, 2012, as part of Expedition 32/33. She became the commander of the International Space Station on September 17, 2012, being the second woman to achieve this feat. As of November 2012, she had made seven spacewalks, achieved the record for longest single space flight for a woman, and was also the first astronaut to run the Boston Marathon from a space station (while strapped to a treadmill).

Art Gregory Prusheck (1887–1940) has frequently been described by art critics as "the best of modernistic painters of Chicago." His art, recognized with numerous awards (including the Jenkins Prize and the Carr Prize), underwent gradual transformation from naturalism to abstract symbolism and expressionism. He exhibited widely throughout the United States and Europe, and his work has been preserved in several museums, art galleries, and personal collections. His original Slovenian name was Gregor Perusek.

Paul Kos (1942–) is one of the founders of the Bay Area Conceptual Art Movement, which thrived in the 1960s and 1970s. He was among the first artists to use video and sound in his installations. Kos received fellowships from the Rockefeller Foundation and the National Endowment of the Arts. His most famous installations include "The Sound of Ice Melting," for which Kos arranged ten microphones around a 25-pound block of ice, and "Tower of Babel," a large steel spiral with video monitors depicting people speaking fifty languages.

Bogdan Grom (1918–), who works in New Jersey and in Trieste, Italy, is a prominent sculptor, painter, and illustrator whose art has been displayed in New York's Rockefeller Center and in many museums around the world. Grom began his career working in watercolor and oil but ventured into many new areas, including graphics, sculpture, and multimedia. He has been featured in American and European art monographs and films.

Literature Louis Adamic (1899–1951) is a well-known Slovenian American writer who first won national recognition with *The Native's Return* in 1934. He authored many other highly influential books, including *A Nation of Nations, From Many Lands, Dinner at the White House, Dynamite*, and *What's Your Name?* During World War II he edited *Common Ground*, the first journal of multiethnic American literature.

Frank Mlakar (1913–1967), a "disciple" of Adamic, wrote the novel *He, the Father* (1950), which *Time* magazine described as a "powerful Dostoevskian story" (August 7, 1950). Many other Slovenian American writers and poets are featured in *Anthology of Slovenian American Literature* (1977).

Music Frankie Yankovic (1915–1998) was a Grammy Award-winning Slovenian American polka musician who became known as "America's polka king." He began his career in Cleveland music halls, but his sophisticated blending of elements of classical music and jazz into the traditional polka reached a wider audience. This brand of music came to be known as the Slovenian-style polka, which is marked by its lively rhythm and swing.

Raymond Premru (1934–1998), professor at the Oberlin Conservatory of Music, was an internationally prominent trombonist and composer of numerous works, including Concerto for Orchestra, commissioned in 1976 for the American Bicentennial by the Cleveland Orchestra, and Symphony No. 2, commissioned by the same orchestra in 1988.

Anton Schubel (1899–1965) was an opera singer in Europe and the United States as well as a musical pedagogue and promoter of cultural exchange. He was particularly known as a talent scout for Carnegie Hall who discovered many of the country's most talented singers and musicians.

Mickey Dolenz (1945–) the son of Slovenian-born actor George Dolenz, was the drummer and lead singer of the Monkees, a band that grew out of a television sitcom of the same name and achieved lasting fame due to hits such as "Last Train to Clarksville" and "I'm a Believer." In 2010 Dolenz released "King for a Day," a tribute to Carole King.

Politics Frank J. Lausche (1895–1990), the son of Slovenian immigrants, was a successful Ohio politician. A Democrat, he served as mayor of Cleveland from 1941 to 1944 and as governor of Ohio from 1945 to 1947 and 1949 to 1957. He also served two terms as a U.S. senator, representing Ohio from 1957 to 1969.

Tom Harkin (1939–) is a five-term U.S. senator from Iowa. Elected in 1984 after serving in the U.S. House of Representatives for a decade, Harkin, a Democrat, was named chairman of the Senate Committee on Health, Education, Labor, and Pensions in 2009. Harkin was a jet pilot in the United States Navy from 1962 to 1967.

George Voinovich (1936–), a popular Republican politician from Ohio, who served as a U.S. senator from 1999 to 2011. In the 2004 Senate race, Voinovich won every county in Ohio and earned more votes than any Senate candidate in the state's history. Voinovich also served as mayor of Cleveland (1979–1989) and governor of Ohio (1991–1998).

Amy Klobuchar (1960–), a member of the Minnesota Democratic-Farmer-Labor Party, was the first woman to be elected to the U.S. Senate from Minnesota. She took office on January 3, 2007, and was re-elected in 2012.

Sports Eric Heiden (1958–) won five speed-skating gold medals in the 1980 Winter Olympic Games in Lake Placid, New York. Before retiring from competition, Heiden also achieved success in cycling and cross-country skiing. Heiden attended Stanford University Medical School and worked as an orthopedic surgeon in Sacramento, California, and Salt Lake City. Eric's sister, Beth (1959–), won a bronze medal in speed skating in the 1980 Winter Olympics. After the Olympics, Beth attended the University of Vermont, where she was an All-American cross-country skier.

Gymnast Peter Vidmar (1961–) won two gold medals and a silver medal at the 1984 Summer Olympics in Los Angeles.

Anže Kopitar (1987–) played center for the Los Angeles Kings in the National Hockey League. The first Slovenian to play in the NHL, Kopitar led the Kings to the franchise's first Stanley Cup Championship (2012).

Stage and Screen Laura LaPlante (1904–1996) was a star of silent films. From 1921 to 1930 she was the leading female actor at Universal Studios. Her most famous film is the 1927 horror film *The Cat and the Canary*. LaPlante also starred in many comedies, including *Skinner's Dress Suit* (1926), and was known for bringing a touch of levity to all her roles, no matter the genre of the film.

Audrey Totter (1917–) was a Hollywood actor who starred in hard-boiled classics such as *The Postman Always Rings Twice* (1946) and *Lady in the Lake* (1947). Her last recorded acting role was in a 1987 episode of *Murder, She Wrote* (CBS).

Frank Gorshin (1933–2005), film and television actor, comedian, and impersonator (for example, of Burt Lancaster, James Cagney, and Richard Burton), is perhaps best remembered as playing the Riddler on television's *Batman* series, starring Adam West and Burt Ward, that ran from 1966 to 1968. In his final years he portrayed comedian George Burns on Broadway in the one-man show *Say Goodnight, Gracie*, which was nominated for a 2003 Tony Award for best play.

Journalist Charles Kuralt (1934–1997) appeared on the CBS Evening News with Walter Cronkite for a quarter century, airing segments called "On the Road." He was also the first anchor of CBS News Sunday Morning. Kuralt won numerous awards, including two Emmys and two George Foster Peabody Awards. In 1983 he was named Broadcaster of the Year by the International Radio and Television Society.

MEDIA

PRINT

As older generations die out, knowledge of the Slovenian language has drastically decreased. Two generations ago, Slovenian Americans supported several printed dailies and weeklies, but very few printed media survive.

Ave Maria

Established in 1908, *Ave Maria* is currently the only completely Slovenian American monthly. It is published by Franciscan Fathers of Lemont in Illinois and partly supported by the government of Slovenia.

Dr. Bernardin Susnik, Editor
P.O. Box 608
Lemont, Illinois 60439
Email: bs1935@sbcglobal.net

KSKJ Voice

The official publication of the American Slovenian Catholic Union (KSKJ), the *KSKJ Voice* is published monthly, both online and in print. It is available in print only to KSKJ Life members. Published bilingually, with a very limited Slovenian section, it traces its origin to *Amerikanski Slovenec*, which began publication in 1891.

Frank Janczak, CEO and publisher
2439 Glenwood Avenue
Joliet, Illinois 60435
Email: Janice@skjlife.com
URL: ww.kskjlife.com/index.php/news-you-can-use/voice

Prosveta (Enlightment)

Biweekly, bilingual official publication of the Slovene National Benefit Society (SNPJ), *Prosveta* has been published since 1908. It initially was printed predominantly in Slovenian, but by 1994 the Slovenian language entries had been reduced to a single weekly page or less. It appears both in print and online.

Jay Sedmak, Editor
247 West Allegheny Road
Imperial, Pennsylvania 15126-0774
Phone: (724) 695-1100
Fax: (724) 695-1555
Email: prosveta@snpj.com
URL: www.snpj.org/Publications

Slovenian American Times (SAT, Slovenski ameriški časi)

This independent bilingual monthly newspaper concentrates on Slovenian community news and news from Slovenia, as well as on Slovenian history, culture, and sports. In print since 2008, it began after the cessation of *Ameriška Domovina* (*The American Home*), which had been published under a variety of names since 1899.

Breda Loncar, Editor
33977 Chardon Road
Suite 120
Willoughby Hills, Ohio 44094
Phone: (440) 833-0020
Fax: (440) 833-0021
Email: bloncar@slovenianamericantimes.com
URL: slovenianamericantimes.com

Zarja (The Dawn)

Zarja was published in both Slovenian and English, as a monthly magazine and an official organ of the Slovenian Women's Union, for more than fifty years. With changes intended to attract male members, the renamed Slovenian Union of America continues to publish the magazine in English only.

Debbie Pohar, Editor
431 N. Chicago Street
Joliet, Illinois 60432
Phone: (815) 727-1926
Fax: (312) 268-7744
Email: sua@slovenianunion.org
URL: slovenianunion.org/zarja

RADIO

Slovenian Hour, WCPN (90.3)

Cleveland Public Radio director Tony Ovsenik presents
a weekly program covering local community and
Slovenian news, interviews, and commentaries, plus
a rich variety of Slovenian songs and music.

Tony Ovsenik, Producer
31731 Miller Avenue
Willoughby Hills, Ohio 44029
URL: www.wcpn.org

WCSB-FM (89.3)

Songs and Melodies from Beautiful Slovenia presents a rich
variety of Slovenian songs and music, community news,
and news from Slovenia, all in Slovenian language.

Ed Mejac, Producer
2405 Somrack Drive
Willoughby Hills, Ohio 44094
Email: emejac@sbcglobal.net
URL: wcsbrario.com

WELW-AM (1330)

Tony Petkovsek's *Polka Radio and Slovenian Show*
broadcasts Slovenian and other polka music in
addition to Slovenian and ethnic community news,
mostly in English and partly in Slovenian.

Tony Petkovsek, Producer
665 2nd Street
Unit 8
Fairport Harbor, Ohio 44077
Email: email@247polkaheaven.com

ORGANIZATIONS AND ASSOCIATIONS

American Slovenian Catholic Union (KSKJ)

Established in 1894 as a self-help organization that also
"strived to preserve and promote Catholic and
Slovenian heritage, while helping its members to be
active American citizens," it is the largest Slovenian
Catholic organization in the United States. Like most
other fraternal organizations, it functions through
local lodges scattered throughout the country but is
coordinated by a national board of directors and an
executive committee. Promoting friendship and Catholic
charity, it conducts numerous religious, educational,
cultural, sports, recreational, and social activities, and
it provides its members with payments of death and
sickness benefits, scholarships, and low-interest loans.

Anthony Mravle, CEO
2439 Glenwood Avenue
Joliet, Illinois 60435
Phone: (815) 730-3510
URL: www.kskjlife.com

Slovene National Benefit Society (SNPJ)

Founded in 1904, SNPJ is currently the largest
Slovenian American organization. Once a
stronghold of the labor movement, with some
prominent socialists among its leaders, it is now
administered mostly by American-born, English-
speaking leaders, usually of Slovenian descent.
As a nonprofit fraternal benefit society, it offers
low-cost insurance, tax-deferred savings plans,
scholarships, pageants and debutante balls,
singing and music circles, Slovenefest and other
heritage programs, and a wide variety of other
benefits and activities, including athletic, cultural,
and social projects.

Joseph C. Evanish, National President
247 West Allegheny Road
Imperial, Pennsylvania 15126
Phone: (800) 843-7675
Fax: (412) 695-1555
Email: snpj@snpj.com
URL: www.snpj.com

Slovenian American Union (SAU)

Established in 1926, SAU has been the leading
Slovenian American women's organization of
Catholic orientation. Fraternal activities are
organized on a local (lodge), regional, and
national basis and include scholarship and
educational programs, heritage projects,
numerous charity and athletic projects, tributes
to honorees such as mothers of the year, cooking
classes and contests. Originally named the Slovenian
Women's Union of America, the name of the
organization was changed in 2011 in order to attract
male members.

Bonnie Prokup, National President
431 N. Chicago Street
Joliet, Illinois 60432
Phone: (815) 727-1926
URL: slovenianunion.org

MUSEUMS AND RESEARCH CENTERS

Museum of the Slovenian Women's Union of America

The museum has a collection of Slovenian memorabilia,
books, pictures, slides, records, Slovenian national
costumes, and handicrafts. It also functions as a gift
shop in which various Slovenian items, including
books and souvenirs, can be purchased.

431 N. Chicago Street
Joliet, Illinois 60432
Phone: (815) 723-4514

Slovenian Heritage Center

The center has a museum with three specified categories.
One is dedicated to Slovenia alone, with maps, coats
of arms, books, pictures, and artifacts. The second
covers Slovenian American history and houses a library
of Slovenian and Slovenian American authors. The
third area deals with the Slovene National Benefit
Society (SNPJ) history and also serves as a lecture and
conference room.

Maurice Sinan, Director
270 Martin Road
Enon Valley, Pennsylvania 16120
Phone: (724) 336-5180
Fax: (724) 336-6176
Email: snpj@snpjheritage.com
URL: www.snpjheritage.org/facilities/
SNPJ-Slovenian-Heritage-Center/Home

Slovenian Museum and Archives

Opened in July 2009 with the declared mission to collect, preserve, and share Slovenian culture, history, and immigrant experience and provide an educational, cultural, and literary resource for families, including an archive and museum space filled with cultural treasures. It has organized a number of exhibits, lectures, and conferences. It also houses a Slovenian genealogy office that conducts an oral history project and is developing a research library.

Bob Hopkins, President, Slovenian National Home
6407 St. Clair Avenue
Cleveland, Ohio 44003
Email: staff@smacleveland.org

Slovenian Research Center of America, Inc.

Research center dedicated to research, education, publications, lectures, and exhibits on Slovenian heritage. An American and international network of Slovenian volunteer associates has assisted in more than sixty years of research, particularly on Slovenian contributions to the United States and the world, resulting in the richest contemporary archival collection of its kind. Other areas of research include lifestyles, activities, and integration of Slovenian immigrants and their descendants.

Dr. Edward Gobetz, Director
29227 Eddy Road
Willoughby Hills, Ohio 44092
Phone: (440) 944-7237
Email: gobedslo@aol.com

SOURCES FOR ADDITIONAL STUDY

Adamic, Louis. *The Native's Return: An American Immigrant Visits Yugoslavia and Discovers His Old Country*. New York and London: Harper, 1934.

Arnez, John A. *Slovenia in European Affairs: Reflections on Slovenian Political History*. New York: League of CSA, 1958.

Blake, Jason. *The Essential Guide to Customs & Culture, Culture Smart! Slovenia*. London: Kuperard, 2011.

Gobetz, G. Edward. *Adjustment and Assimilation of Slovenian Refugees*. New York: Arno, 1980.

———, ed. *Slovenian Heritage, Volume I*. Willoughby Hills, Ohio: Slovenian Research Center of America, 1980.

———, and Adele Donchenko, eds. *Anthology of Slovenian American Literature*, Willoughby Hills, Ohio: Slovenian Research Center of America, 1977.

Mrak, Mojmir, Mitja Rojec, and Carlos Silva-Jauregui, eds. *Slovenia: From Yugoslavia to the European Union*. Washington, D.C.: The World Bank, 2004.

Odorizzi, Irene M. Planinsek. *Footsteps through Time*. Arlington, VA: Washington Landmark Tours, 1978.

Plut-Pregelj, Leopoldina, and Carole Rogel. *Historical Dictionary of Slovenia*. Lanham and London: Scarecrow, 1996.

Prisland, Marie. *From Slovenia to America: Recollections and Collections*. Milwaukee: Bruce, 1968.

SOMALI AMERICANS

Kristin King-Ries

OVERVIEW

Somali Americans are immigrants or descendants of people from the Federal Republic of Somalia, a long, narrow, hook-shaped country on the tip of East Africa. Somalia is one of four countries that make up the Horn of Africa, and it has the longest stretch of coastline on the African continent. The Somali border is almost equal parts land and coastline. On the land side, Somalia borders Djibouti in the northwest, Ethiopia in the west, and Kenya in the south. The coastal side fronts the Arabian Sea to the north and the Indian Ocean to the south. Somalia's total land area is 242,216 square miles (637,540 square kilometers), slightly smaller than the state of Texas.

According to a World Bank report from 2011, the population of Somalia was 9,556,873. The population was overwhelmingly young; according to Index Mundi, the average age in 2012 was 17.8 years old. Almost all Somali citizens are Muslim, a vast majority of those Sunni Muslims. A tiny minority practice other religions, including Christianity (0.01 percent). In the south, some groups of ethnic minorities practice animism, the traditional faith of their ancestors. Ethnic Somalis make up 85 percent of the population. The largest minority group is Bantu, followed by Arabs, Pakistanis and Italians, in that order. Somalia's economy is one of the poorest in the world, ranking 174 out of 195 countries in a list compiled by the United Nations in 2011. As of the early 2010s, agriculture (primarily in the form of livestock) accounts for almost 60 percent of the gross domestic product, followed by service (33.5 percent) and industry (7.3 percent). Despite the lack of a stable government since 1991, in the capital city of Mogadishu certain sectors of the economy, particularly livestock, telecommunications, and money-transfer companies, have remained viable through the early part of the twenty-first century.

Somalis began to arrive in the United States in small numbers after Somalia declared its independence from Italian and British colonial rule in 1960. The Somalis arriving in the United States were mostly single male college or graduate students, most of who returned home after completing their educations. When civil war broke out in Somalia in the mid-1980s, the number of its citizens coming to the United

States grew exponentially. Fighting between rebel factions spread across the country, leading to the collapse of the central government in 1991. According to the 1990 U.S. Census, there were 2,070 people of Somali descent living in the United States. By 1992 the U.S. government had given visas to thousands of Somali refugees. This second wave of Somali immigrants were primarily families fleeing the violence. However, not all Somalis arrived in the United States as refugees. A growing number were coming to the United States to pursue educational or professional opportunities. When security in Somalia improved in 2012, small numbers of Somalis in the United States began returning to Somalia help rebuild the county.

According to the U.S. Census Bureau's American Community Survey (ACS) estimates for 2006–2010, there were 100,011 people of Somali ancestry living in the United States. A report written by the Minnesota Historical Society indicated that approximately one of every three Somali Americans lived in Minnesota in 2013, most of them in the Twin Cities. Areas with significant Somali American populations include Columbus, Ohio; Washington, D.C.; Washington state, especially Seattle; Arizona; Virginia; Texas; New York; and California, especially San Diego.

HISTORY OF THE PEOPLE

Early History Cave paintings and stone implements found in northern Somalia are evidence that Somalia has been inhabited since as far back as 9000 BCE. The ancient civilization had a writing system that remains undeciphered in the twenty-first century. Other discoveries from ancient Somalia include cemeteries that date back to the fourth millennium BCE, as well as pyramid-like structures, ruined cities, and stone walls. From approximately 2000 BCE, Somalia (then known as the Kingdom of Punt) traded incense, ebony, and livestock, among other products, with ancient Egypt and Maecenaean Greece. Later, Somali sailors transported cargo on their ships from the city-states to trade with merchants from Phoenicia, Ptolemic Egypt, Greece, Persia, and the Roman Empire.

By the early fourth century CE, Coptic Christianity had made its way from Egypt to an area that included what are now the countries of Somalia and Ethiopia, where it became the official religion.

Muslims began to arrive in Somalia approximately three centuries later, settling in the coastal cities. Early Muslims included Arabs who migrated to Somalia as well as Somali traders whose conversion had resulted from their travels to the Arabian Peninsula. For hundreds of years, Muslims and Christians in Somalia and Ethiopia coexisted peacefully.

Due in part to the stark geographic differences between the two countries, Ethiopia and Somalia developed distinctly different societies. Ethiopia's fertile, mountainous terrain was favorable for farming and produced sufficient resources to sustain a centralized population, making a unified government a viable option. The arid lowlands of Somalia, by contrast, lacked the resources to support a large, centralized populace. Only 10 percent of the land was arable, so the terrain was better suited to a dispersed nomadic population and a less centralized government of clan networks.

The Muslim-Christian truce ended with the Muslim conquest of the Christian stronghold of Shoa (also spelled Shewa), a region of northern Ethiopia that includes present-day city of Addis Ababa. Many wars ensued, and ultimately the Christians defeated the Muslims, in part because the greater degree of social organization afforded by their geography permitted them to sustain battle longer. Christian rule continued in parts of Somalia into the Middle Ages.

By the 1400s the Muslims had made progress against the Ethiopian empire, reclaiming lost territory and enlisting support of their neighbors. Eventually, the two states agreed to a truce and enjoyed several decades of peace. Commerce flourished with merchants from across Europe, Asia, and Arabia. In the fifteenth and sixteenth centuries, Mogadishu was a city of enormous wealth. There were large homes, impressive palaces, and ornate mosques. In around 1527, Muslims in present-day Somalia invaded Ethiopia, and a Portuguese expedition joined the fight to protect Ethiopia on behalf of their fellow Christians. Together, Ethiopian and Portuguese forces won the war. Portugal continued to take control of East Africa, but cooperation between the Ottoman Empire and Somalia was a constant threat to the Portuguese. In the second half of the century, a Somali-Ottoman offensive forced the Portuguese to flee important cities such as Mombasa (in what is now Kenya). However, the Portuguese regrouped and succeeded in retaking most of their former territory.

From the 1700s to the mid-1800s, the sultans of Zanzibar brought Bantu slaves to Somalia from further south on the east coast of Africa, creating an underclass of Bantu Somalis. Bantu slaves worked in oases and in the river valleys of the south. They eventually became concentrated in the Juba Valley, close to the Kenyan border. During the nineteenth century, many Bantu slaves converted to Islam in an attempt to end their enslavement.

In the late 1800s Somalia got caught in the "Scramble for Africa," a race among European powers to colonize the continent and extract wealth from the land. The country was at one point occupied by colonial powers Britain and Italy, with Britain as the dominant power. The independent state of Ethiopia and the British colonial territory of Kenya also claimed regions of Somalia as their possessions. British Somaliland covered much of nomadic northern Somalia, and Italian Somaliland occupied the more agrarian southern part of the country. France occupied a section of the coast around Djibouti. Beginning in 1899 the Somali resistance movement fought for two decades to end British colonial rule. British troops killed roughly one-third of the population of northern Somalia before the colonial government succeeded in crushing the resistance.

Modern Era During World War II, another war broke out in Somalia, this one caused by colonial governments who trained and armed rival clans in order to attack each other by proxy. The British-backed Somali clans from the north joined with militias from Ethiopia and Kenya to battle the Italian-backed Somali clans from the south. After World War II, Somalia received United Nations trusteeship status in 1949 in preparation for its independence. Ten years later, in 1960, the former British and Italian colonies merged, and the country declared independence, becoming a socialist republic called the United Republic of Somalia.

Integrating the northern and southern parts of the country, however, proved difficult due to the legacy of roughly eighty years of colonial rule, during which time various regions had developed dramatic differences in linguistic, institutional, educational, and legal systems. By the end of the 1960s, the new government had lost favor with the majority of its citizens, and concerns about corruption had become common. After Somalia's president was assassinated in a coup in 1969, General Mohamed Siad Barre formed a new government.

Barre served as the head of Somalia's newly created socialist state for the next twenty years. Claiming that socialism united and tribalism divided, Barre's government declared a ban on clan and kinship ties. Although Somalis resisted the policy, one group who benefited was the Bantus, whose lack of clan affiliation had made them vulnerable in the past. Even after they had gained their freedom in the early twentieth century, the Bantus' status in Somalia remained marginal. During the 1930s and 1940s, the fascist Italian colonial government and Somali landlords continued to treat Bantu farmers like slaves. After independence in 1960s, the Bantus again suffered from discrimination, in part due to a lack of clan affiliation, and in part due to the obvious racial and cultural differences from ethnic Somalis. Barre's treatment of the Bantu was also far from ideal. When he ordered the invasion of Ethiopia in 1977, Bantus were subject to forced conscription.

In response to Somalia's invasion of Ethiopia, the Soviet Union withdrew its support from Somalia, and Barre lost a powerful ally. Though popular at first, the general lost many supporters with his autocratic style and his practice, despite the official ban, of placing members of his own clan in high government positions. By the mid-1970s failed economic policies and a severe drought had led to widespread famine and political unrest. An influx of outside resources helped militias of rival clans to flourish. The Majarteen clan in the north received support from the Ethiopian army, and the southern Hawiye clan received support from Italy. The Barre regime's practice of pitting rival clans against one another exacerbated the unstable situation and hastened its downfall.

Fighting between factions started in the mid-1980s, and by 1990 civil war had broken out between the militias of rival clans. Opposition forces under generals such as Mohamed Farrah Aidid and Ali Mahdi Mohamed ousted Barre's government. The longtime leader was exiled in 1991, leaving a power vacuum in Somalia that went unfilled for over twenty years. With the collapse of the government and still without the protection of a clan, the Bantu ethnic group suffered even more severely at the hands of warring factions than their fellow citizens. A human-rights organization called the Minority Rights Group International reported that, after the fall of the Barre government, dominant clans in places such as the Juba Valley regularly seized Bantu farmland, extorted protection money, and raped Bantu women.

The U.S. government sent troops to Somalia in 1992 as part of a UN peacekeeping force, but the effort proved unsuccessful and the army withdrew in 1994. One incident in particular, known as Black Hawk Down, led to the U.S. troop withdrawal. On October 3 and 4, 1993, two U.S. military helicopters were shot down during an attempt to capture high-ranking lieutenants of the Somali National Army. Instead of raiding a safe house as planned, U.S. troops were caught in an all-night street battle that left eighteen U.S. servicemembers dead and eighty wounded. Hundreds if not thousands of Somalis died. After the withdrawal of the UN forces, war and clan violence went unchecked for up to a decade, devastating the country, crippling the economy, and causing over a million Somalis to flee abroad. Since 2001 the U.S. government has periodically conducted military operations in Somalia, most commonly in the form of drone strikes, against suspected al-Qaeda and al-Shabaab (a Somalia-based Islamic militant group) joint forces believed to be plotting terrorist attacks against the United States.

During the war years the Somali diaspora extended from refugee camps in neighboring countries such as Djibouti, Kenya, Ethiopia, and Yemen, to places across the globe, including Australia, Europe, Scandinavia, Canada, and the United States. Somali refugees continued to discriminate against the Bantus by taking the lion's share of camp resources and pushing the Bantu to live in quarters on the periphery of the camps, where they were vulnerable to bandit attacks. In 2004 the U.S. State Department granted asylum to an estimated 15,000 Bantu refugees. President Abdullahi Yusuf Ahmed and his ministers, backed by the Ethiopian and U.S. governments, established a secular government in 2004 called the Transitional Federal Government (TFG), but it failed to unify the country. There were deep divisions within the TFG, and it faced strong opposition from a group of fundamentalist Islamic militias called Islamic Courts.

Despite these continued challenges, by 2011 Somalia was on the road to national reconciliation. The UN supported negotiations between the TFG and international partners such as the African Union, the Kenyan army, and representatives from the United States and the European Union, which resulted in the Kampala Accord, ending the transitional government and establishing a new republic. In 2012 a federal parliament was selected and a provisional constitution adopted. Parliament then elected Hassan Sheikh Mohamud as president, and Mohamud appointed a prime minister and a cabinet. The same year, the new republic joined several international organizations, including the United Nations, the International Monetary Fund, and the World Bank. The United States officially recognized the new government in January 2013.

SETTLEMENT IN THE UNITED STATES

After Somalia declared independence in 1960, a small number of Somali citizens began to seek employment opportunities and education abroad in places such as the United States. For example, Somali engineers moved to Seattle to work for Boeing designing aircrafts. Young men also came to the United States to attended college, university, or in some cases even high school. These men typically returned to Somalia as soon as they finished their education.

In 1991 a second major wave of Somali immigrants began to arrive, this time fleeing violence and unrest in their homeland. They sought to enter countries such as the United States and Canada in far larger numbers than ever before. A 2009 UN report by Hassan Sheikh and Sally Healy stated that the total number of Somalis living outside Somalia was approximately one million. This group consisted primarily of refugees who often came directly from refugee camps in Kenya and Ethiopia. The road to U.S. immigration was a long, multistep process for these immigrants. Somalis living in the camps first had to apply for refugee status in order to get permission to travel to the United States. Once here, they had to apply for Legal Permanent Resident status. Refugees who succeeded in obtaining legal status still faced the possibility of deportation. If found guilty of committing a crime or sending funds to groups engaged in terrorist activity, Somali refugees were sent home. The distinction between terrorist groups and patriotic organizations was not always clear. Some Somali Americans, including women, have been arrested for raising funds for the Islamist group al-Shabaab, which they see as an organization that simply supports people in their homeland, but which the U.S. government has designated as a terrorist organization.

Somalis from the second wave of immigration settled primarily in cities such as Minneapolis–St. Paul, Minnesota; Atlanta; San Diego; Seattle; and Columbus, Ohio. Somali Americans chose to live in places such as Minneapolis in the early 1990s because of the availability of factory work in meat-packing plants, tech jobs, and other types of work where limited knowledge of English was sufficient. In many instances, the Somali refugees had experienced violence directly. Many had also lost family and friends to the violence in their country. As a result, post-traumatic stress disorder (PTSD) played a significant role in the lives of these new immigrants. Somalis who came to the United States to escape the war were also drawn to cities with services geared toward refugees, including help in dealing with trauma. According to a 2012 U.S. Department of State report, an estimated 400,000 Somalis died during the two decades of war, and a 2012 report from the United Nations High Commissioner on Refugees (UNHCR), the UN's Refugee Agency, stated that 1.4 million people had been internally displaced within Somalia as of January 1, 2012, and another 2.5 million had fled the country.

Somali immigrants to the United States faced many hurdles in their adopted home. Differences in language, religion, culture, and clothing made them stand out. The bright, colorful dresses and headscarves worn by Somali women made them even more visibly different from their new peers than Somali men. Often Somali immigrants were the target of discrimination and racism because of their dark skin and religious beliefs. In the United States, where the majority religion is Christianity, Muslim customs and practices are unfamiliar to most people, creating misunderstandings and conflicts. After the terrorist attacks on September 11, 2001, Somali Americans became targets of growing anti-Muslim sentiment. Acts of discrimination against Somali Americans increased. One such incident occurred two months after the bombings, when federal agents raided several Somali businesses in Seattle, seizing their inventories, destroying their reputations, and closing them down, based on unsubstantiated suspicions of funding terrorist organizations. All charges were found to be without merit, and the men were never prosecuted. However, a great deal of damage had been done to the businesses.

Some Somali refugees moved from their place of initial settlement to places with larger concentration of Somalis, such as Minneapolis. According to the American Community Survey's estimates for 2010, Minnesota was the state with the largest population of Somali Americans, with an estimated 32,449. Other states with small, but significant, numbers included California (7,150), Arizona (3,028), Ohio (10,078), Washington (9,543), Virginia (3,460), Texas (3,601), and New York (3,053).

In the second decade of the twenty-first century, drought, famine, and lack of economic opportunity persisted in some areas of Somalia, and a stream of refugees continued to seek asylum elsewhere. Due to the stabilizing political situation, there was reverse migration as well. The UN-brokered Kampala Accord of 2011 ended the eight-year Transitional Federal Government, thus necessitating a new election. In the first few months after President Mohamud's 2012 government was established, 14,353 Somali refugees living in Kenya returned home. Refugees in Saudi Arabia, Ethiopia, Europe, and the United States also started to return, albeit in smaller numbers. The urban population of Somalia grew during the decades between 1991 and 2011, from roughly 20 percent to 40 percent, due in large part to refugees leaving the countryside and flocking to the cities in search of greater employment and educational opportunities. By the 2010s Mogadishu's population exceeded one million people, while other cities, such as Hargeysa, in the hills of the north, had at most 100,000. President Mohamud visited Minnesota in early 2013 to urge Somali Americans to come home and help rebuild Somalia. The UNHCR anticipated that as many as 100,000 households of displaced persons would attempt to return home by December 2013.

LANGUAGE

Somalia's official language is called Somali. It is the first language of ethnic Somalis, who make up 85 percent of the population. A Yemeni dialect of Arabic is also widely spoken in Somalia because of Yemen's geographic proximity and the close ties between the two countries. Other languages spoken in Somalia include Amharic, Oromo, Swahili, Italian, and English. According to the American Community Survey's 2010 estimates, only 9.4 percent of Somali Americans reported speaking exclusively English at home, and 48.9 percent described themselves as speaking English "less than very well."

The Somali language belongs to the Cushitic branch of the Afro-Asiatic family of languages, which includes Oromo (the predominant language spoken in Ethiopia) and Egyptian. Spoken Somali is a tonal language. It is similar to Mandarin Chinese in that is has four different tones, which are not indicated in writing.

Over the past millennium, Somali has been written using four different alphabets: an Arabic-based alphabet known as Wadaad's writing, which is made up of thirty-two characters; Borama, a Somali alphabet with twenty-seven characters; Osmanya, another Somali alphabet, made up of thirty characters; and a Latin-based alphabet made up of thirty-two letters. Wadaad's writing was introduced in Somalia in the thirteenth century as part of an effort by Muslims to teach the Quran. It was used for hundreds of years.

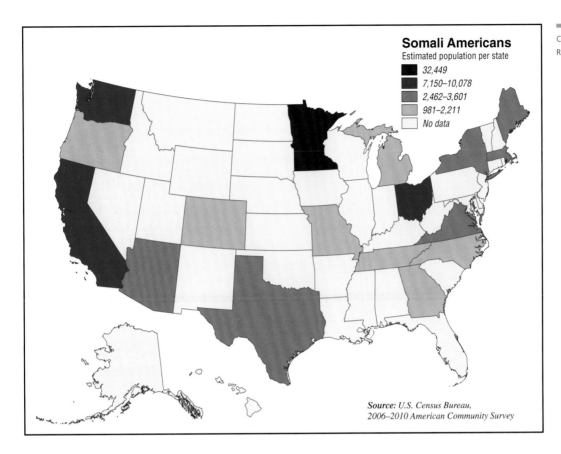

Somali Americans
Estimated population per state

- 32,449
- 7,150–10,078
- 2,462–3,601
- 981–2,211
- No data

Source: U.S. Census Bureau, 2006–2010 American Community Survey

The Osmanya alphabet was created early in the twentieth century and served as the official alphabet for a few decades. Osmanya largely fell out of use when a Latin-based alphabet was adopted as the official Somali alphabet in 1972. Borama was never widely used.

Greetings and Popular Expressions In the Somali language, *Subax wanaagsan* (pronounced "subah wanaksin") means "Good morning"; *Habeen wanaagan* ("habayn wanaksin") means "Good night"; *Iska waran* ("iska warran") means "Hello"; and *Jaaw* ("chow") means "Good-bye."

RELIGION

The vast majority of Somalis and Somali Americans are Sunni Muslims. Religion informs much of their daily life. A person's diet, dress, and behavior are all informed by the Islamic faith. Sunnis pray five times a day and abstain from eating pork and drinking alcohol. During the holy month of Ramadan, they fast: there is no public eating, smoking, or drinking from sunrise to sunset.

CULTURE AND ASSIMILATION

The Somalis who have settled in the United States as refugees maintain strong ties to the country of their birth, continuing to send money home and sponsoring relatives to come to the United States. They tend to settle in concentrated groups, where they recreate Somali culture, maintain Somali customs, speak the Somali language, and eat traditional Somali food rather than adopt the practices of their new country. By contrast, those who arrived from Somalia when they were young children or were born in the United States tend to be more integrated into American culture and less connected with Somalia. They have grown up speaking English. Some have rejected their parents' traditions, wearing American-style clothing and following other mainstream trends. In this group, some have never been to Somalia to visit. They feel less of a sense of duty to support extended family in Somalia and are more resistant to sending money. The most recent arrivals are people who immigrated to the United States for economic reasons. This group tends to maintain strong ties to Somalia through marriage, charitable giving, and financial investment. Because many Somali Americans fled their country for political or economic reasons, they arrived with few resources and little education. As a result, a majority continue to face challenges in terms of finding well-paid work and decent housing. Differences in religion make assimilation difficult for many. For instance, according to Islamic law as interpreted by Sunni Muslims, all must pray five times a day and women must be fully covered in public by wearing a burqa (which covers everything but the eyes).

Traditions and Customs Somalis traditionally shake hands when meeting or saying good-bye.

RESENTMENT AND MISINTERPRETATIONS

In order to escape the high crime rates, overcrowding, hectic pace of life, and underfunded school systems, many Somali Americans left larger U.S. cities in favor of smaller cities and towns. Those who ventured into rural areas often encountered resentment, which was exacerbated by Americans' unfamiliarity with Somali culture and religious differences. A highly publicized example of this dynamic occurred in Lewiston, Maine, between 2001 and 2002. In the course of a year, over 1,000 Somalis moved to Lewiston, a working-class city with a population of 36,000. False rumors were spread that the U.S. government was giving Somalis free cars, air conditioners, and groceries, along with $10,000 in cash. The mayor exacerbated the non-Somali residents' growing sense of resentment when he wrote an open letter to the newcomers, asking them to tell other Somalis to stay away. The Somali American community wrote an outraged response, and Lewiston suddenly found itself at the center of a national debate on immigration. Advocates for both sides of the issue came to town, including at least two white supremacist groups, to hold rallies and circulate petitions. A pro-immigration rally of 4,000 people in 2003 helped to defuse the situation.

The most sensational news concerning Somali American communities often related to support for Islamist groups in Somalia. When a group of twenty Somali American youths from the Minneapolis area disappeared in 2007, there were reports that they had returned to Somalia to fight on the side of al-Shabaab. Young Somali Americans began disappearing from other U.S. cities around the same time. The mainstream U.S. media often portrayed the motive as support for Islamic extremism. Others argued that the young men had joined the fighting to protect their homeland in response to a 2006 Ethiopian incursion into Somalia. International news coverage in 2009 of the surge in Somali piracy on the East African coast did little to improve the image of Somali Americans.

Nevertheless, Somali Americans have achieved success in a number of areas, notably as small business owners; many operate restaurants, markets, and money-transfer businesses. In cities such as Columbus, Ohio, there are Somali shopping centers and car dealerships. The Somali American community has worked hard to educate and reach out to other Americans, with positive results. Many, such as the men in Seattle whose businesses were raided, have received public support from fellow Americans in response to post-9/11 persecution and violations of their civil rights.

The right hand is always used because the left hand is considered unclean. When an important person walks into a room, it is customary for others to stand up in a show of respect. Somali men consider it a sign of friendship to hug and kiss each other on the cheek when saying hello. In Somali society, verbal acumen and agility are highly valued. Reciting poetry is one example of a praiseworthy skill. On the other hand, it is considered impolite to argue or discuss politics. Being impatient and asking direct questions are also frowned upon.

Cuisine Somalia is a Muslim country where Islamic dietary laws are strictly observed. The term *halal* is used to describe food that is sanctioned by the Quran. The dietary laws forbid consumption of pork, alcohol, carnivorous animals, birds of prey, blood, or blood products. In order to qualify as halal, meat must be slaughtered properly and in the name of Allah. Halal grocery stores and restaurants owned and operated by Somalis exist in Somali American communities throughout the United States that cater to this population.

Traditional staples in Somalia included milk, ghee (clarified butter), meat, and rice mixed with onion. Somali food in the twenty-first century reflects the country's social and colonial history. It is a combination of Somali, Ethiopian, Turkish, Middle Eastern, Indian, and Italian dishes. Somali Americans eat a number of traditional dishes, including *ambola*, a dish of red beans, rice, and salt served with sesame oil and sugar; and *malawa*, which resembles an American pancake and is often served with honey. Meat curry, which consists of vegetables, ground beef, spices, and sometimes goat meat, is also popular among Somali Americans, as is *iskudahkaris*, a Tanzanian dish that combines fried onions and vegetables with rice.

Somali Americans also enjoy *roti* and *chapathi*, two kinds of Indian bread. Roti is pan-cooked without oil, and chapathi is pan-fried with oil or butter. While many older Somali Americans continue to observe halal, eat traditional foods, and drink sweet tea in the United States, Somali American youth have adopted aspects of the Western diet. Fast food, fries, soda pop, and high-fat snacks like cheese are becoming popular with the younger generation.

Traditional Dress Traditional dress styles in Somalia have been strongly influenced by the Islamic religion. However, in the late twentieth and early twenty-first centuries, many Somalis have adopted Western dress styles such as jeans and t-shirts, reserving traditional dress for special occasions. Western clothing is especially common among young people and those in urban areas, while traditional dress is more common in the rural areas of the country.

A traditional garment for men is two white cotton sheets, one used as a skirt and the other as a shawl. Another traditional piece of men's clothing is a *macawiis*, similar to a sarong. Men also wear turbans and embroidered caps. Somali businessmen wear Western suits and ties to work.

Traditionally, women were forbidden to wear revealing clothes or clothes with bright colors. Full-length dresses were common. One traditional style is a *guntiino*, a dress that ties at the shoulder and is worn for everyday use. At weddings and religious celebrations, a different kind of long dress is worn, called a *dirac*. Unmarried women typically do not cover their heads but wear their hair braided. Married women wear scarves called *shash* on their heads. The more religious the woman, the more covering she wears. Religious women wear a *jilbab* (garment that leaves only the head and hands uncovered) and very religious women wear a burqa (a garment that covers everything but the eyes). The first generation of Somali refugees and the latest arrivals continue to wear traditional Somali clothing for the most part. Among the second generation of Somali Americans, those born or raised in the United States, some choose to observe tradition while others wear Western clothing like their American peers.

Traditional Arts and Crafts The oldest Somali artworks are the cave paintings in the north and the tomb decorations in the south. Pottery, wood carving, and architecture are some other traditional Somali arts. Traditional Somali art shows Islamic influences. In the 2010s Somali American artists began making their mark on the U.S. art scene. Mohamud Mumin is an example of a contemporary Somali American who has gained recognition for his work. The Minneapolis-based photographer is best known for his portraits of Somali refugees who have achieved success in their adopted country. In 2012 he had a solo show at Minneapolis's Whittier Gallery featuring larger-than-life portraits of Somali American men.

Dances and Songs Somalia's musical tradition has its roots in the country's folklore. Unlike Western music, which is based on a scale of seven pitches per octave, much of Somali music is played with five pitches per octave. Somali music shares similarities with the music of its close neighbors, Ethiopia and Yemen, but it has its own distinct sound. Much Somali music is played on a guitar-like instrument called the *oud* and accompanied with small drums. The earliest form of popular music, called *balwo*, is a combination of poetry and dance music. It emerged in the 1930s.

Recent Somali immigrants attend a class at the Somali Community Development Center of Southwest Kansas in Garden City. The center offers lessons in English and American civics in order to prepare recent immigrants for eventual citizenship. ADAM REYNOLDS / CORBIS

SUQAAR

Ingredients

1½ cups of beef, cubed

¼ cup of oil

½ of a small onion, finely chopped

2 cups of water

½ teaspoon of ground cumin

½ of a chile pepper, finely chopped

½ green pepper, diced

1 potato, diced

1 carrot, diced

½ chicken boullion cube

¼ teaspoon of salt

1 clove garlic, crushed

½ cup fresh cilantro, chopped

Preparation

Simmer beef in water to cover for 30–45 minutes or until it is very tender. Drain water from the meat and add the oil and onions. Cook on medium heat until the onions are soft. Add the water, cumin powder, chile pepper, green pepper, potato, carrot, chicken cube, salt, garlic and cilantro. Stir well. Cover and simmer for 20 minutes or until vegetables are tender. Stir after 10 minutes and add a little water if necessary.

Serves 4

Recipe courtesy of Abdirazzak Mohamed

Balwo was followed in the 1940s by *qaraami*, which remained popular into the twenty-first century. In the 1970s and 1980s, during the reign of General Barre, most music was banned. The prohibition inspired numerous protest songs. A few twenty-first-century Somali bands play traditional music, notably Waaberi and Horseed. Other musicians, such as Ahmed Cali Cigal and Maryam Mursal, have created new styles that blend traditional Somali music with more recent popular forms, including jazz and rock. *Heeso* is another very popular style of contemporary music. In Somalia in the 2010s, popular music can be downloaded from Somali music portals on the Internet.

There are many traditional folk dances in Somalia, including *dhantur* (also known as *dhaantu*), *buraanbur*, *niiko*, and *gaaleeyso*. In dhantur, dancers move to the beat of drumming and singing and sometimes help keep the beat by clapping. The men and women each form a line, and the two groups interweave and dance in circles around each other but do not touch. Buraanbur, performed by women, involves sung poetry. Niiko is a traditional wedding dance involving small pelvic movements. It is performed by one woman or a group of women. Gaaleeyso is a men's dance involving stomping and footwork. In some dances partners are taken. Traditional dancing remains popular with Somalis in Somalia and abroad, including Somali Americans.

Holidays For government and business purposes, Somalis use the Gregorian calendar (the solar calendar used in the United States and the rest of the West), but Islamic holidays are determined by the Islamic lunar calendar, which is based on the phases of the moon. As a result, the dates of holidays shift every year by eleven or twelve days in relation to the Gregorian calendar. Somalis celebrate several major religious holidays, including Eid Milad-un-Nabi (the birth of Muhammad; also called Mawlid), the Ascension of Muhammad, Eid al-Fitr (the end of Ramadan), and Eid al-Adha (the Feast of Sacrifice). Ramadan is an entire month of fasting during the day and feasting at night. Somalis are expected to make the *hajj* (pilgrimage to Mecca in Saudi Arabia) at least once in their lives. The traditional Islamic practice of ritual killing of a lamb or goat for religious holidays continues to be observed by many Somali Americans.

Non-religious holidays celebrated in Somalia are Labour Day (May 1); New Year's (January 1); Independence Day, marking the independence of the State of Somaliland (June 26); and Republic Day, marking the independence of the Trust Territory and the creation of a Somali state (July 1). Like religious holidays, secular holidays are often marked with a feast in which friends, family, and poor people are invited to share.

Health Care Issues and Practices One traditional method of treating illnesses involved the use of herbal medicine. Other rituals, such as prayer and fire burning, were practiced by traditional doctors, or *dhaawayaal*. Today traditional doctors in Somalia are sometimes still called upon to treat physical conditions like contagious diseases or broken bones that people believe have been caused by spirits. However, Western medicine is gaining traction, especially in urban areas.

According to a 2003 EthnoMed report on Somali diet, health issues for Somali Americans are often connected to acculturation and dietary changes, including anemia, poor dental health, allergies, diabetes, and childhood and postpartum obesity. A relatively new concern at the time of the report was eating disorders among Somali teens. In 2008 the *Journal of Consulting and Clinical Psychology* published the results of a mental health study of Somali teens born outside the United States. The study reported that war-related post-traumatic stress disorder was common in this population and that it exacerbated other conditions normally experienced by refugees, such as depression from resettlement and the negative effects of perceived discrimination.

Death and Burial Rituals In Somalia a *wadaad* presides over the funeral ceremony, saying prayers and chanting. At the burial site, the body is lowered into a large grave and placed into a niche carved into the earth. The shroud is removed so that the body touches the dust. The niche is closed with stones or wood, then the grave is filled with sand. All the adult men who are in attendance take turns shoveling or dropping a handful of sand into the ground. Throughout the ceremony all in attendance chant, "Death is Allah's law."

After the grave is filled, women sprinkle water over it. Once that is done, everyone leaves the site immediately. While women may wail and cry, men are discouraged from doing so. At least one feast is held in honor of the deceased. The first such feast is held on the day of the burial and includes the grave diggers and the presiding wadaad. The wadaad reads from the Quran during the meal, and those who knew the deceased recount stories of the person's life. Traditionally, a second feast would happen on the one-year anniversary of the burial. However, this custom is observed less often in the twenty-first century.

Somali Americans have encountered difficulty observing traditional death and burial rituals in the United States. Refugees often do not make enough money to be able to afford to pay for the honors, burial rites, and gravesites. Often American funeral homes and cemeteries do not understand Somali customs and cannot or will not accommodate them. In the early twenty-first century traditional funerals were on the decline among Somali immigrants, both for these reasons and because as a group they were young and not yet concerned with death.

Recreational Activities Women gather with friends at one of their homes, while men often gather in coffee shops to talk, play games such as *shah* (similar to chess), and drink tea. A related activity that has a long tradition is storytelling. Traditional dancing and singing continue to be popular, especially in rural areas of Somalia. Men also enjoy competing against each other in wrestling matches and running and jumping contests.

Football (soccer) is the most popular sport in contemporary Somalia. From organized clubs to informal pick-up games, it is played by boys all over the country. Basketball has gained popularity, even with girls. However, girls traditionally were required to help out at home more than boys and had less time for play. In contemporary Somalia, girls enjoy playing games with friends, playing with dolls, dancing to popular music, and playing basketball.

Somali Americans have numerous clubs and cultural centers in the United States where they go to socialize, play soccer and basketball, sing in choirs, and participate in other activities.

FAMILY AND COMMUNITY LIFE

Somali culture is organized around clans, and clans have family at their core. Traditionally, nuclear families lived together. Polygamy is legal in Somalia, and approximately 20 percent of the population lives in a polygamous household (one husband with multiple wives). Each wife has her own section of the family compound, but they all share the cooking space and areas for socializing. Marriages in Somalia were traditionally arranged by the family. In the early twenty-first century, however, love matches were on the rise. In the United States, the practice of polygamy is illegal and therefore not a part of Somali American culture.

Female genital circumcision is a traditional practice that marked a rite of passage and was traditionally considered necessary for marriage. Although the practice was outlawed by the U.S. federal government in the 1990s for girls under eighteen, a 2005 study conducted by the African Women's Health Center in Boston estimated that over two hundred thousand women in this country had been or were at risk of being circumcised. According to the EthnoMed website, it is not uncommon for Somali Americans to get around the law by sending their girls to Somalia to be circumcised.

In 2008 the Journal of Consulting and Clinical Psychology published the results of a mental health study of Somali teens born outside the United States. The study reported that war-related post-traumatic stress disorder was common in this population and that it exacerbated other conditions normally experienced by refugees, such as depression from resettlement and the negative effects of perceived discrimination.

Gender Roles Before independence men typically worked outside the home. In nomadic areas they took care of the camels and cattle while younger children tended to the less valuable animals, such as sheep and goats. Men were also required to participate in clan politics. The women cared for the children, cooked, and farmed. In the cities, men worked in business or trade. Men were in control of the family, and a woman who helped support her family financially was encouraged to make her husband the head of household. Women in Somalia generally do not socialize with men outside of their homes. Nomadic women in particular are still expected to do what is asked of them by their husbands, fathers, and brothers. However, President Barre's socialist government made efforts toward gender equality, and since then Somali women have had more opportunities, freedoms, and rights than women in many Muslim countries, such as Saudi Arabia (though they still have less freedom than women in certain other Muslim countries, such as Turkey and Indonesia). In addition, decades of war casualties have turned many Somali women into heads of household. Some of those living abroad or in urban areas have adopted a more Western dress code and behavioral norms.

Education Prior to colonization, most of the schools in Somalia were Quranic schools. Girls were prohibited from attending school. In the north, the

A Somali refugee works at a community garden in Boise, Idaho. DAVID R. FRAZIER PHOTOLIBRARY, INC. / ALAMY

schools is better in urban areas. Because of a lack of funding, parents often shoulder the financial burden of operating schools, so children from families with means stand a better chance of attending school.

The more stable areas of the country have made efforts to correct the situation. In 2012 the regional government in northern Somalia began to survey the state of education in order to assess needs and plan for the future. The government in the south hopes to begin a similar project as soon as the political situation improves. Somalis living abroad who have professional experience in education have been encouraged to return home to train teachers and administrators and to share their expertise with the Education Ministry.

According to the 2006–2010 American Community Survey (ACS) estimates, 59.2 percent of Somali Americans over the age of eighteen had a high school degree or higher (whereas the graduation rate for the U.S. population overall was 85 percent). Among Somali Americans, 11 percent of the population had a bachelor's degree or higher (compared to 27.9 percent for the overall U.S. population).

Courtship and Weddings Opportunities for courtship in Somalia differed depending upon where the couple lived. In rural communities, couples were permitted to get acquainted when a young woman led her family camel to the well for a drink. This was seen as a rite of passage for the young woman, who would dress in her best clothes and jewelry. The young man would hang out near the well and offer to fill her water bucket, giving them a chance to talk. Another chance to court was at the marriage dances held for newlyweds. On these occasions, unmarried people were allowed to dance and mingle. Chances to court were more frequent in towns and cities. School, market, and ceremonies, along with marriage dances, provided occasions to members of the opposite sex to meet and talk. Prowess in conversation was considered an important feature in a mate.

A young man traditionally asked the father or a male relative of his intended for permission to marry. Both families had to approve of the match. If they did not, the marriage did not happen or the couple eloped. Elopement was seen by some as romantic and exciting, though foregoing the support of their families meant hardship for the couple.

Traditionally, marriage created three levels of relationships: a relationship between the couple, a relationship between the families, and a relationship between clans. Family and clan featured prominently in a young Somali man or woman's decision on who to marry. Although a young person often selected his or her own partner, once the selection was made, the family became heavily involved in the planning. The parents of the groom had to pay a bride price, more to demonstrate the family's financial stability than to enrich the bride's parents. This was followed with a religious ceremony presided over by a priest or *wadaad*.

British colonial government placed a heavy emphasis on vocational training for young men. In the south, the Italian colonial government's emphasis was on preparing young men for careers in farming, business, and shipping. The official adoption of Somali script in the 1970s expanded opportunities for education. More people learned to read and write due to government-sponsored literacy campaigns, and public primary education paved the way for the children of poor parents to seek an education. However, schooling beyond that level remained an unattainable goal for many. According to a 2012 UNICEF report, only 24 percent of the Somali population was literate as of 2000.

Education in Somalia has suffered due to the turmoil and unrest that has plagued Somalia since 1991. Resources are scarce; with things such as electricity and textbooks in short supply, getting an education has proved challenging, especially for girls. Access to

Prior to the twenty-first century, marrying outsiders was very rare. In the early twenty-first century Somali Americans from the second wave of immigrants began to marry non-Somalis, though it was far from common practice. Donna Gabaccia, director of the Immigration History Research Center at the University of Minnesota, told Minnesota Public Radio in 2011 that Somali women were leading the trend. This reflected a larger trend among immigrants groups in general. As a whole, immigrant women were far more likely than their male counterparts to marry outside of their ethnic group. "Today it's a very strong and pronounced pattern that girls are more likely to marry out than boys," she said. "I don't think that really anyone in the scholarly world completely understands that phenomenon or why that should be." Some members of the older generation of Somali Americans reported feeling uncomfortable with their white sons- and daughters-in-law because of language and culture barriers.

According to a 2012 report from Public Radio International, gay marriage was traditionally a taboo subject among most Somalis, largely because Islam forbids such a union. But with state political campaigns for and against gay marriage on the rise in the twenty-first century, avoiding the subject became difficult for Somali immigrants in their new home. Somali Americans were divided on the issue. While many supported a ban on gay marriage for religious reasons, others opposed the ban for religious reasons—because it defined marriage too narrowly and infringed on the their belief in the right to polygamy. Still others, primarily young people who had been assimilated into American culture, did not object to gay relationships.

EMPLOYMENT AND ECONOMIC CONDITIONS

A 2010 news segment from a public radio station in San Diego, KPBS, quoted Abdi Mohamoud, the director of the Horn of Africa Community Center, on the subject of employment for Somali immigrants. "Many of them are just settling for whatever jobs they could get, part-time, odd jobs, you tend to see some customer service at hotels … maybe some janitorial, housekeeping, security guards." The American Community Survey (ACS) reported in 2010 that an estimated 37.1 percent of Somali Americans in the workforce worked in the production, transport, and material-moving industries. Service and sales jobs accounted for 44.1 percent of the jobs. Another 16.5 percent worked in management, business, science, or the arts. According to the ACS, 20.5 percent of Somali Americans were unemployed.

The ACS also reported that an estimated 28.7 percent of Somali American families earned less than $10,000 a year. In 2010 the median household income for Somali Americans was $19,000, about $33,000 less than the median for the U.S. population overall. A high percentage of Somali American families were living below the poverty line, including 61 percent of families with children under eighteen. (By comparison, the national rate for the families of all foreign-born Americans living below the poverty line was 18 percent, and the rate for the population as a whole was 10 percent.)

POLITICS AND GOVERNMENT

Politics in Somalia traditionally revolved around clans. This remained true in the early twenty-first century. Clans provide members with benefits as well as drawbacks. Internal conflict was common. Historically clans provided protection, access to water, and political clout. Nevertheless, clan affiliation retained a position of great importance in Somali society; when forced to choose between loyalty to one's clan versus loyalty to one's country, clan loyalty often carries the day, to the extent that clan partisanship has presented a threat to national unity.

The earliest Somali immigrants to the United States avoided political participation. Of the small numbers of Somalis who came before the 1990s, few intended to make the United States their home. When Somalis began arriving in larger numbers during the 1990s, most were fleeing refugee camps and therefore lacked the resources, education, and English-language fluency critical to political involvement.

Over the next twenty years, many Somali Americans became successful business leaders in their communities, and by 2010 the group as a whole had become far more civically engaged. According to a 2012 article in the *Minneapolis Star Tribune*, Somalis had gained political clout in Minnesota. This trend had been seen in other areas where there were Somali American communities, such as Atlanta, Georgia. An increasing number of Somali Americans had registered to vote, helped out on political campaigns for Somali and non-Somali candidates, run for office, and formed a political action committee. In 2010 Hussein Samatar was elected to the Minneapolis Board of Education. Samatar was one of the first Somali Americans elected to political office.

NOTABLE INDIVIDUALS

Academia Abdi Kusow, born in Somalia, earned a PhD in 1998 at Wayne State University in Detroit, Michigan before becoming a professor of sociology at Iowa State University. He has published a number of scholarly works on Somalia, including *Putting the Cart Before the Horse: Contested Nationalism and the Crisis of the Nation-state in Somalia* (2004). He has spoken at international policy forums around the world.

Abdi Ismail Samatar (1950–) received his PhD at the University of California, Berkley, in 1985. He is a professor of geography at the University of Minnesota. Samatar has authored numerous works, most notably *An African Miracle: State and Class Leadership and Colonial Legacy in Botswana* (1999).

Mohamed Haji Mukhtar (1947–) is a scholar whose work focuses on Somali history and language. Mukhtar was educated at Al-Azhar University in Cairo. He was a two-time recipient of the Fulbright-Hays Fellowship as well as the recipient of a National Endowment for the Humanities Fellowship. Early in his career he taught at Somali National University in Mogadishu, and later he became a professor of history at Savannah State University in Savannah, Georgia. In addition, Mukhtar has produced and corresponded for the BBC African Service.

Activism Fatima Jibrell (1947–) is a Somali American activist who focuses on environmental and women's issues. She cofounded the Horn of Africa Relief and Development Organization (now called Horn Relief), where she also served as the executive director. Jibrell cofounded Sun Fire Cooking and played an important role in the formation of the Women's Coalition for Peace.

Literature Afdhere Jama (1980–) is a Somali American writer and filmmaker who self-identifies as queer and Muslim. His films include *Angelenos* (2013), *Bits* (2012), and *Ani* (2009).

Visual Arts Mohamud Mumin, a Minneapolis-based Somali American photographer, is best known for his portraits of Somali refugees who have achieved success in their adopted country.

MEDIA

PRINT AND DIGITAL

Somaliland News Network

Based in Atlanta, Georgia, the network's website offers news in English and Somali. In addition, there are links to news articles, TV, audio and video reports covering Somalia.

Email: snn@snnnews.net
URL: www.snnnews.net

Voice of America–Africa News

This Washington, D.C.–based website includes written content and audio broadcast news reports related to Somalia.

330 Independence Avenue SW
Washington, D.C. 20237
Phone: (202) 203-4019
URL: http://www.voanews.com/english/Africa/index.cfm

TELEVISION

Somali TV Minnesota

A TV station based in Minneapolis, Minnesota, covering culture, news, and religion for and about Somali Americans. The station broadcasts Somali sporting events and Somali TV shows. It can be viewed streaming on the Internet and is accessed by Somali Americans across the country.

Phone: (612) 782-7135
URL: www.somalitv.org; www.livestream.com/somalitvofmn

ORGANIZATIONS AND ASSOCIATIONS

Somali American Community Center of Colorado

The mission of the organization is to help Somali Americans by promoting education, providing access to technology, and assisting with integration into American society.

Mohamed Nur, President
1582 S. Parker Road
Suite 201
Denver, Colorado 80231
Phone: (303) 369-5998
Fax: (303) 369-5225
Email: SomaliCommunityCenter@msn.com
URL: www.somaliamerican.org

Somali-Bantu Community Association of Onondaga County

This organization offers language classes and other resources to help refugees and immigrants coming to the United States become acclimated with their new country. The group also supports cultural programs designed for all people of Bantu heritage.

Haji A. Adan, Executive Director
P.O. Box 655
Syracuse, New York 13205
Phone: (315) 214-4480
Fax: (315) 422-8080
Email: info@somalibantucommunity.org
URL: www.somalibantucommunity.org

Somali Family Care Network

The Somali Family Care Network is based in Fairfax, Virginia, and works with community-based organizations that assist refugees. The network focuses on building capacity and providing technical assistance with the aim of helping refugees become self-sufficient members of American society.

Raqiya D. Abdalla, President
2724 Dorr Avenue
Suite 100
Fairfax, Virginia 22031
Phone: (703) 560-0005
Fax: (703) 639-0051
Email: info@somalifamily.org
URL: www.somalifamily.org

Somali Community Services of Seattle

The community center provides Seattle's large Somali American population, especially refugees, with basic services to help with the transition into American society.

3320 Rainier Avenue S.
Seattle, Washington 98144
Phone: (206) 760-1181
Fax: (206) 760-1186
Email: somcss@yahoo.com
URL: http://somcss.org.somcss.org/

SOURCES FOR ADDITIONAL STUDY

Abdullahi, Mohamed Dirive. *Culture and Customs of Somalia*. Westport, CT: Greenwood Press. 2001.

Ajrouch, Kristine J., and Abdi M. Kusow. "Racial and Religious Contexts: Situational Identities among Lebanese and Somali Muslim Immigrants in North America." *Ethnic and Racial Studies* 30, no. 1 (2007): 72–94.

Ellis, B. Heidi, et al. "Mental Health of Somali Adolescent Refugees: The Role of Trauma, Stress, and Perceived Discrimination." *Journal of Consulting and Clinical Psychology* 76, no. 2 (2008): 184–93.

Holtz, Michael. "Proposed Gay Marriage Amendment Forces Somali Immigrants to Confront Taboo." *Public Radio International*, July 20, 2012. http://www.pri.org/stories/politics-society/proposed-gay-marriage-amendment-forces-somalis-in-minnesota-to-confront-long-held-taboo.html.

Kusow, Abdi, ed. *Putting the Cart Before the Horse: Contested Nationalism and the Crisis of the Nation-State in Somalia*. Trenton, NJ: Red Sea Press, 2004.

Robbe, Abdi. *The Somali Diaspora: A Journey Away*. Minneapolis: University of Minnesota Press, 2008.

Sharma, Amita. "Somalis Adjust to U.S. Life, but Integration and Jobs Still Problems." *KPBS*, September 28, 2010. http://www.kpbs.org/news/2010/sep/28/somali-refugees-adjust-life-us-assimilation-and-un/.

Van Hear, Nicholas. "Refugee Diasporas or Refugees in Diaspora." In *Encyclopedia of Diasporas: Immigrant and Refugee Cultures around the World*, edited by Melvin Ember, Carol R. Ember, and Ian Skoggard, 580–89. New York: Springer, 2004.

SOUTH AFRICAN AMERICANS

Judson Knight and Lorna Mabunda

OVERVIEW

South African Americans are immigrants or descendants of people from South Africa, a country located at the southern tip of the African continent. South Africa is bordered by five countries—Namibia to the northwest; Botswana to the north; and Zimbabwe, Mozambique, and Swaziland to the northeast—and completely surrounds a sixth, Lesotho. The Indian Ocean is to the south and east, while the Atlantic Ocean sits to the southwest and west. The two oceans meet at Cape Agulhas, which is the southernmost point in Africa. South Africa's total land area is 471,443 square miles (1,221,037 square kilometers), slightly larger than the combined land of Texas, New Mexico, and Oklahoma.

According to the 2011 national census, South Africa had a population of 51,770,560. Almost 80 percent were Christians, while another 15 percent professed no religious affiliation. The remainder included Muslims (1.5 percent), Hindus (1.2 percent), and very small groups practicing Judaism, traditional African religions, and other faiths. Ethnically, the nation was about 79.5 percent black, 9 percent white, 9 percent "Coloured" (mixed racial heritage), and 2.5 percent Asian. South Africa has Africa's largest economy and is among the half-dozen wealthiest nations on the continent in terms of per capita income. Yet both the United Nations and the U.S. Central Intelligence Agency rank it among the world's top ten nations in terms of income inequality. The country is rich in natural resources, particularly metals, and it is the world's leading producer of platinum.

The first South Africans came to the United States in the wake of the 1848 gold rush in California, where they worked as prospectors. One century later, in 1948, the imposition of a system of formalized racial segregation in South Africa known as apartheid prompted more immigration, as South Africans fled the political oppression in their home country. After apartheid ended in 1994, some white South Africans chose to leave the country, but thanks to President Nelson Mandela's efforts to maintain peace and economic stability, many more chose to remain in the land of their birth.

The American Community Survey estimates that for the period 2009–2011 there were about 56,000 people of South African descent living in the United States (about 2 percent of the total sub-Saharan African immigrant population). The largest concentration of South African Americans—about one-sixth of the total—is in California (particularly San Diego), followed by Florida, New York, Texas (particularly Austin), Georgia (particularly Atlanta), and New Jersey. Other states with small but significant populations of South Africans—that is, at least 1,000 people each—include North Carolina, Illinois, Arizona, Virginia, Massachusetts, Pennsylvania, Ohio, Washington, Colorado, Maryland, and Michigan.

HISTORY OF THE PEOPLE

Early History By the early part of the Common Era, Khoisan peoples—speakers of so-called "click languages"—dominated the region, but they would be displaced by the migration of Bantu peoples to the area beginning in the fourth or fifth century CE. A large linguistic group that originated in West Africa, the Bantu were noted for their ironworking abilities, which gave them a technological edge over the Khoisan hunter-gatherers. Soon the Bantu, whose numbers included speakers of the Zulu and Xhosa languages, became dominant in what is now South Africa.

Portuguese mariner Diogo Cão landed on the shores of present-day Namibia in 1485, but it was not until three years later that Europeans, led by Cão's countryman Bartholomeu Dias, first reached the area today known as South Africa. In May 1488, Dias saw what he called the Cape of Storms, which his monarch, John II, later renamed the much more positive Cape of Good Hope.

Permanent white settlement began in 1652, when Jan van Riebeeck established a supply station for the Dutch East India Company on the site of what would become Cape Town. The Dutch brought with them slaves from various colonies along the Indian Ocean and soon began migrating inland, where they clashed with the Xhosa population. The white settlers, who included migrants not only from Holland but also from other European nations, spoke a Dutch dialect that became Afrikaans, a language in its own right. In time the white settlers of southern Africa would become known as Afrikaners, and those living in what became South Africa would be called by the Afrikaner term *Boer*, meaning "farmer."

Great Britain seized the Cape of Good Hope in 1795, ostensibly to prevent the French First Republic from taking control of it, and established the Cape Colony in 1806. Also vying for dominance were the Zulu, led by their legendary chieftain Shaka, as well as the Matabele subgroup of Zulu, and the Xhosa, all of whom fought against the British invaders. Conflict with these groups, both European and African, led some 12,000 Boers to undertake what became known as the Great Trek, a migration to the north and northeast in the 1830s and 1840s. Ultimately the Boer migrants, who came to be known as *Voortrekkers*, or "pioneers," established a number of independent political entities, including the Orange Free State, Transvaal, and Natalia republics.

The Boers' discovery of precious natural resources—diamonds in 1867 and gold in 1885—not only spawned what came to be known as the Mineral Revolution but also sparked two Anglo-Boer wars (1880–1881, 1899–1902). The latter conflict, sometimes referred to simply as the Boer War, was an extraordinarily brutal conflict that saw the first use of concentration camps, but it established British imperial power in the region as an unshakable reality. In 1909 the Cape and Natal colonies, joined by the Orange Free State and Transvaal in 1910, formed the Union of South Africa, a British dominion.

Modern Era The Union of South Africa began formalizing racial segregation with the passage in 1913 of the Natives Land Act, which restricted indigenous land ownership to only about 7 percent of the country. The following year, the country entered World War I as a member of the British Empire. South African troops, including many thousands of black, Asian, and mixed-race personnel, fought not only in Europe but also closer to home. In addition to seizing the German colony of South-West Africa (which remained under South African control until it received independence as Namibia in 1990), loyalists to Britain—most notably Jan Smuts and Louis Botha—fought two battles against pro-German Boer factions in 1914.

The 1931 Statute of Westminster made South Africa a self-governing dominion within the Empire, which meant that when World War II came eight years later, the nation's leadership theoretically had a choice regarding whether to enter on the British side. This question of loyalties split the United Party, formed in 1934 by the union of the South African and National parties in an effort to unite Afrikaner- and English-speaking whites. Ultimately Smuts, head of the pro-British group, took control. He suppressed pro-Nazi groups at home and emerged as the British Empire's most important non-British general, becoming a member of the Imperial War Cabinet in 1939 and a Field Marshal of the British Empire in 1941. In addition to seizing Madagascar in 1942 and thus preventing German and Japanese forces from establishing an Indian Ocean link, South African forces fought in North Africa, Italy, and, in the war's final months, East Asia.

Despite his popularity, Smuts's pro-British stance made him a target for conservative Afrikaners, whose National Party won control in 1948. That year was notable for the establishment of formalized segregation, or apartheid, which—along with the National Party itself—would remain in place for the next forty-six years. A flurry of new legislation delineated the intricacies of apartheid: for example, the Prohibition of Mixed Marriages Act (1949) forbade marital union across races; the Population Registration Act (1950) required all persons over eighteen years of age to carry racial identification cards; and the Reservation of Separate Amenities Act (1953) provided for segregated public facilities.

A whites-only referendum in 1961 established South Africa as an independent nation and removed it from the British Commonwealth, thus enabling the nation's leadership to chart its own course amidst growing opposition both abroad and at home. The first major antiapartheid riots broke out at Sharpeville, where government troops killed sixty-nine black protesters on March 21, 1960. A series of riots in 1976 led to the deaths of some 600 blacks, and the murder of resistance leader Stephen Biko in 1977 sparked further tensions. Among the most prominent antiapartheid entities within the country's borders was the African National Congress (ANC), formed in 1912 as the South African Native National Congress and renamed in 1923. Its most famous member was Nelson Mandela, whose imprisonment starting in the early 1960s attracted increasing world attention during the quarter-century that followed.

Other nations began responding to apartheid by enacting sanctions against South Africa, which was banned from many international cultural-exchange programs, as well as the Olympic Games and other international athletic competitions. The United Nations imposed an arms embargo and passed resolutions condemning apartheid. Widespread popular reaction in the West, simmering for several decades, exploded in the 1980s, with antiapartheid protests on many college campuses. Under pressure from stockholders, many foreign banks and multinational corporations broke their South African ties, while the U.S. government and American businesses faced increasing pressure for full economic divestiture from South Africa. Meanwhile, the country became embroiled in wars with the communist governments of nearby Angola and Mozambique during much of the 1980s and fought a sustained conflict with the Southwest African People's Organization (SWAPO) in South-West Africa, which it had retained as a colony against international protests.

As pressure mounted, change began sweeping South Africa, whose National Party regime began slowly dismantling the framework of apartheid. The

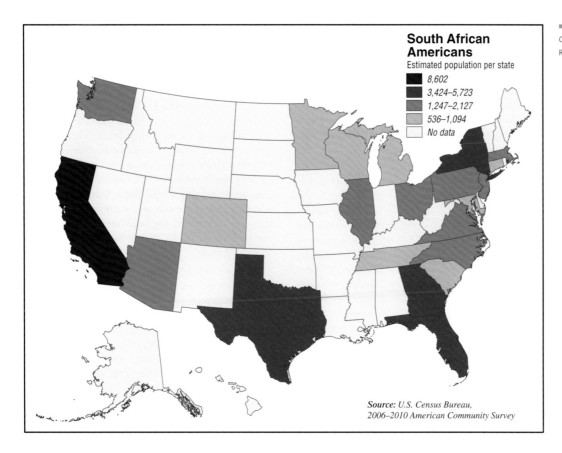

South African Americans

Estimated population per state

- ■ 8,602
- ■ 3,424–5,723
- ▨ 1,247–2,127
- ▨ 536–1,094
- □ No data

Source: U.S. Census Bureau,
2006–2010 American Community Survey

new constitution in 1983 extended the vote to Asians and Coloureds, and two years later, the government repealed laws banning interracial sex and marriage. In 1986 President P. W. Botha ordered an end to pass laws and allowed blacks to take an advisory role in government. However, he also launched attacks against ANC strongholds in neighboring countries, and a massive strike by some two million black workers in 1988 helped lead to his resignation in 1989. Under the subsequent administration of F. W. de Klerk, the government removed its ban on the ANC and released Mandela in 1990. In 1991 de Klerk announced plans to end apartheid, and in 1994 the nation held free elections. The ANC won the majority, making Mandela the first president of the "new" South Africa.

The end of apartheid hardly spelled the end of troubles in South Africa, however. Unemployment soared and poverty was rampant, while the pandemic of HIV/AIDS (human immunodeficiency virus/ acquired immunodeficiency syndrome) continued to ravage much of sub-Saharan Africa, claiming lives at an alarming rate. In November 2003, the government approved an ambitious program, which included drug distribution centers, to combat the pandemic; however, Thabo Mbeki, who replaced Mandela as president in 1999, had become notorious as an AIDS "denialist" by maintaining that HIV is not the sole

cause of AIDS. Mbeki won reelection in 2004, but his government acquired a reputation for corruption that led to the firing of a top official, Jacob Zuma, in June 2005. Ultimately, however, all charges against Zuma would be dropped. In a stunning reversal, Mbeki became the focus of corruption enquiries, while Zuma emerged as president in 2009.

Residents of South African townships launched violent protests against their poor living conditions in July 2009, and civil servants staged a nationwide strike in August 2010. Meanwhile, ANC power began to erode as new opposition forces, including the Democratic Alliance and the Congress of the People (COPE), gained seats in parliament. More allegations of corruption forced Zuma to remove two cabinet ministers in October 2011, and in the following month the ANC suspended youth leader Julius Malema. Also in November 2011, the National Assembly approved a so-called information bill that, according to critics, suppressed free speech. ANC leaders, on the other hand, described the bill as a necessary measure for protecting national security. In the summer of 2012, government forces opened fire on platinum workers in Marikana, killing three dozen people and injuring twice as many more. Unrest among platinum workers continued throughout the remainder of the year, which ended with Zuma's reelection as ANC leader in December of that year.

SETTLEMENT IN THE UNITED STATES

Because the number of South African Americans is minuscule compared to that of, say, Mexican Americans or Filipino Americans, waves of South African immigration have been proportionately small. Nevertheless, it is possible to discern immigration patterns, beginning in the late nineteenth century and continuing to the present, with significant spikes corresponding to the establishment, promulgation, and abolition of apartheid.

White South Africans' experience as gold miners made them natural candidates for employment in the gold fields of California and Alaska, and the first notable instance of South African immigration to the United States occurred in the period following the discovery of gold in California in 1848. South African immigrants continued trickling into California during the latter part of the nineteenth century. By that time, the gold-rush years were long past and adventurous prospectors had been replaced by professionals who settled in for the long, arduous challenge of extracting gold from subterranean deposits. Afrikaners, with their knowledge gained in the gold fields of the Transvaal, proved ideal for the task, and many settled in California, with smaller numbers migrated northward in the period following the discovery of gold in Alaska in 1894.

South Africans' homeland is a heterogeneous agglomeration of ethnicities that, on the surface at least, seems not so different from the vast melting pot of the United States. However, with their country's history of segregation even more severe (and more recent) than that of the American South under the Jim Crow laws, South African immigrants have been viewed in a way that, whether fairly or not, tends to set them apart.

A new group of South African immigrants arrived some fifty years later, following the institutionalization of apartheid. However, there was not a large influx, perhaps because few blacks could afford to leave their homeland. Even so, poor black South Africans enjoyed a higher average standard of living than did many of their counterparts in the rest of the continent, and South Africa itself experienced a large immigration of native Africans from other countries, even at the height of apartheid.

As unrest increased in the late twentieth century, larger populations of South African immigrants began arriving in the United States. These included not only small numbers of white opponents to the regime and relatively well-educated blacks but also a group of South African Jews who formed a community on the north side of Chicago. The end of apartheid, in contrast, spawned waves of "white flight" from the homeland, but this exodus was not as severe or widespread as many had predicted. Mandela sought to retain as many whites as possible, urging multiracial policies in an attempt to counteract a potential backlash of blacks against their former oppressors.

Of the whites who left South Africa in the years leading up to and following the end of apartheid, most did not go to the United States. They were far more likely to settle in Australia or New Zealand, countries whose British cultural heritage more closely parallels South Africa's. Furthermore, the climate in Oceania is similar to that of South Africa, and its location far south of the equator means that the seasonal changes—summer at the beginning of the calendar year and winter in the middle—are similar to those in South Africa.

Those South Africans who did settle in the United States have tended to follow a pattern of movement typical of Americans in general. In other words, the areas of relatively high South African American concentration have not remained static over time. Whereas the Midwest and the northeastern United States were home to the largest South African American populations in the late twentieth century, the population had shifted southward, toward the Sun Belt states, by the second decade of the twenty-first century. California, Florida, Georgia, New York, Texas, and New Jersey became home to largest number of South African Americans. Other states with smaller populations of people of South African descent included Arizona, Colorado, Illinois, Maryland, Michigan, North Carolina, Massachusetts, Virginia, Washington, Pennsylvania, and Ohio.

LANGUAGE

Among South African Americans, English is the overwhelmingly dominant language: about 70 percent of the population over five years of age speaks only English at home. Other South African Americans typically speak one of South Africa's eleven official languages, which are (in addition to English) Afrikaans, Ndebele, Northern Sotho, Southern Sotho, Swati, Tsonga, Tswana, Venda, Xhosa, and Zulu. According to the American Community Survey for 2009–2011, only 2 percent of South African Americans spoke English less than "very well."

Greetings and Popular Expressions South African and South African American expressions reflect the cultural diversity of South Africa, with roots in English, Afrikaans, and various native languages. Many ethnicities, for instance, recognize *tom* as a word for money. *Bundu*, a variant of *boondocks*, is the South African term for what Australians would call the Outback. And whereas Americans go "four-wheeling," South Africans go *bundu-bashing* in a four-wheel drive vehicle, perhaps a *bakkie* (pronounced "bucky"), meaning a small truck.

Some expressions would be familiar to speakers of British English, such as *cheers* for "good-bye", *ta* for "thanks," or *cheeky* for "rude." Other expressions, however, might befuddle a speaker of American English. For example, *tinkle* might be a colloquial euphemism for urination in the United States, but among persons of South African descent, it refers to a telephone call, as in, "Give me a tinkle and we'll plan that *braai* [backyard barbecue]." And whereas a person from the United States would consider *lavatory* to be an appropriate, if a bit formal, term for a sink, among South African Americans, it refers to a toilet bowl. Proper hygiene would involve washing one's hands in what South Africans call a *basin*. Similarly, like British English speakers, South Africans use the verb *flog* not to mean "whip" but rather "to hawk or sell something."

A number of South African and South African American expressions involve a blurring of words, sometimes from different linguistic roots. A common greeting, for instance, is *howzit*, meaning, "How is it going?" while *sawright* serves to indicate that something is "all right." Somewhat more obscure to a person from another culture are expressions such as *thisarvie* for "this afternoon." Meanwhile, *struesbob*, a shortened form of "as true as God," is used to indicate that a person is telling the truth even if it seems to be a stretch. When a South Africans are not certain of the answer to a question, they might say *ag*, which is pronounced "akh," as in "Ag, I don't know where the baby threw his dummy [pacifier]." *Ag* is just one of many interjections, along with *jislaaik* (pronounced "yis-LIKE"), an expression of shock or astonishment. Finally, there is the term *Saffa* by which South African expatriates refer to themselves, in much the same way that their counterparts from Australia or New Zealand call themselves Aussies or Kiwis respectively.

RELIGION

People of South African origin generally adhere to Judeo-Christian faiths, practiced by most whites and some blacks; traditional and tribal faiths, chiefly among blacks; and the various East Asian religions of the Indian, Chinese, and other minorities. There are also Muslim South Africans, adherents of nontraditional "new religions," and people who profess no religious faith at all.

The Reformed Church of Holland, a Protestant denomination that arose during the 1600s, has a strong following among the Afrikaners, who mix Reformed Church beliefs with Calvinism. (In the past, Afrikaners used religion as a justification for apartheid, pointing out that John Calvin himself, a major figure in the Protestant reformation, supported separation of the races and a strong role for the church in government.) English, Coloureds, and black South African Christians typically belong to either the Anglican or Catholic churches. The prominent role of Bishop Desmond Tutu, a black Anglican minister, illustrates the more interracial character of these churches in contrast to the Afrikaner version of the Reformed Church. The 1980s and 1990s saw the rise

MULTILINGUAL LIFE IN SOUTH AFRICA

In South Africa language has long been a source of discord. The June 16, 1976, riots in the Soweto township, for instance, began as a protest against the use of Afrikaans as the medium of instruction in black schools. At the time, Afrikaans was the dominant language in matters of politics and internal administration, while communication with the outside world regarding business and science typically took place in English.

In the new South Africa television broadcasts can be heard in the most prevalent languages: English, Sotho, Xhosa, Zulu, and Afrikaans. Radio broadcasts are even more varied. English, however, remains the principal language, with the other dialects primarily confined to regions where native speakers predominate. Though none of the major languages is spoken by a majority of the populace, 98 percent of South Africans use at least one of them as their home or first language. Most blacks, in fact, are multilingual, speaking their tribal languages along with English and, in some cases, Afrikaans.

of charismatic movements, which placed an emphasis on healing and other powers of the Holy Spirit, primarily among black South Africans. Finally, there is a significant community of Jewish South Africans, many of whom have immigrated to the United States.

Although large numbers of Xhosa, Zulu, and members of other black ethnic groups have accepted Christianity, traditional beliefs have not died out and, in many cases, are mingled with Christian practices. Adherents to the Xhosa traditional religion worship a supreme being called uThixo or uQamata, and the Zulus pray to a deity named uNkulunkulu (The Very Big One). In both cases, the supreme being is primarily a creator, with little role in the personal lives of believers. The Sothos' worship of Modimo is mingled with ancestor worship, and indeed ancestors play a significant part in most traditional black African faiths.

CULTURE AND ASSIMILATION

On the one hand, South African immigrants have tended to assimilate easily within the larger culture of the United States. This is especially true for white South Africans, who, unlike their black compatriots with tribal backgrounds, have fewer traditional practices that might make them stand out among their American neighbors. South Africans' homeland is a heterogeneous agglomeration of ethnicities that, on the surface at least, seems not so different from the vast melting pot of the United States. However, with their country's history of segregation even more severe (and more recent) than that of the American South under the Jim Crow laws, South African immigrants have been viewed in a way that, whether fairly or not, tends to set them apart.

This has been true of both black and white immigrants: Mark Mathabane, a black writer and immigrant who settled in North Carolina, writes in the autobiographical *Kaffir Boy in America* (1989): "I marveled at the reach of apartheid: it could influence the way people thousands of miles away thought, felt, and acted; it could silence them at will; it could defeat them without a shot being fired." In her 1994 essay "An Incomplete Replacing: The White South African Expatriate," Sheila Roberts, a white writer who moved to the United States in part because she opposed apartheid, recalls, "From the beginning I was seen by American friends and colleagues as not only an authority on South Africa but also a representative of the 'opposition.'"

It is ironic, given their complex and multifarious heritage, that South Africans of all groups have been stereotyped and reduced to a mere political identity. The same ethnic diversity that has often made South Africa a focal point of tension has also produced a richly varied culture. Furthermore, this diversity exists not only between the major ethnic groups but also within them. For example, great distinctions exist between the two major sectors of white South African society: Afrikaners consider themselves Africans, not Europeans, whereas South Africans with an English heritage tend—like their counterparts in Australia, New Zealand, and Canada—to identify more closely with Great Britain.

Traditions and Customs Interestingly, Afrikaners and South African blacks share much of the same folklore. Indeed, in a further detail that illustrates the racial complexity of South Africa, many of those shared traditions can be traced to Asian roots. For instance, *goel*, or ghost stories, originated from indentured laborers from India and Malaysia. Adopted by whites and blacks alike, many of these stories revolve around the harsh southeastern wind, known as the "Cape Doctor," that blows over Cape Town in the summertime.

Of course the Zulu, Xhosa, and Sotho peoples each have multifaceted cultural traditions all their own. According to Zulu myth, at one time people did not die but simply continued living; thus, in Zulu culture, old age is seen as a blessing. A Zulu legend recounts how the creator told a chameleon to go and tell the people of the world that they did not have to die. However, the chameleon took so long to do the job that the angered creator sent a lizard in his place to tell them that indeed they would die. It is only for this reason that death exists.

The Xhosa have their own tales of human origins, which revolve around a heroic Adam figure known simply as Xhosa. There is a large body of Xhosa folktales, called *intsomi*, as well as praise poems, or *isibongo*, regarding the adventures of past heroes. The Xhosa have several interesting dietary restrictions: women are typically not supposed to eat eggs, and a man is not supposed to drink milk in a village where he might later take a wife.

The Sotho, known as excellent horsemen, are distinguished by their bright blankets and cone-shaped

South African author Mark Mathabane spent much of his childhood in South Africa before coming to the U.S. to play tennis in college. He subsequently wrote the critically acclaimed novel, *Kaffir Boy*. WILLIAM F. CAMPBELL / TIME LIFE PICTURES / GETTY IMAGES

hats. An example of the latter appears on the flag of Lesotho, whose population is primarily Sotho. The Sotho tradition also includes praise poems and folk tales, one of the most prominent of which is a tale concerning a boy named Santkatana, who saves the world by killing a giant monster.

In Zulu traditional culture, a birth is celebrated by the sacrifice of animals to ancestors. Also important is a young girl's puberty ceremony, signifying the fact that she has come of age and is eligible for marriage. The Xhosa have much more intricate coming-of-age ceremonies for both sexes. Boys are segregated from the rest of the group for several weeks, during which time their heads are shaved and they undergo a number of rituals, such as the smearing of white clay over their entire bodies. This rite of passage culminates with circumcision. Girls are also separated from the group, though for a shorter period, and during this time the community celebrates the coming of womanhood with dances and animal sacrifices. The Sotho have similarly complex rituals surrounding puberty and circumcision, which is performed on girls as well as boys.

English and Coloured South Africans celebrate birthdays in a manner familiar to most Americans brought up in Anglo-Saxon traditions. The same is true of Afrikaners, though birthday parties are perhaps a bigger part of life than they are with other groups. This is the case in particular with regard to one's twenty-first birthday celebration, at which the honoree is presented with a key symbolizing the passage into maturity.

Cuisine As in many other aspects of South African life, the national cuisines are as varied as the ethnic groups. A lot of these foods have remained popular among segments of the South African American population. Afrikaners favor a meat-and-potatoes diet that includes items such as *boerewors*, a spicy pork sausage; *putu pap* (the second word is pronounced "pup"), a porridge-like dish made of boiled corn meal; and *biltong*, a beef, ostrich, or antelope jerky. English South Africans, as one might expect, eat a diet similar to that of the British, though with local variations such as *bredies*, or stew.

Vegetable dishes are often mixtures of items such as spinach, potatoes, and roasted, sweetened pumpkin. Slap chips are similar to American French fries, only larger and less crisp; hence, the first part of the name (pronounced "slup"), which refers to their softness or limpness. They are served salted and doused in vinegar.

The Zulu diet places a heavy emphasis on products of the cow, including beef and milk products such as *amasi*, or curdled milk. *Mealie-meal* (cooked corn meal) and yams are also favorites. Among the Xhosa, goat, mutton, and beef are popular, as are corn and bread. Particularly notable is a spicy hominy dish called *umngqusho*. Dishes popular among South

BOBOTIE

Ingredients

1 thick slice good quality, crustless bread

1½ cups milk

2 tablespoons oil

2 teaspoons butter

2 onions, sliced

2 cloves garlic, crushed

2 tablespoons curry powder

2 teaspoons salt

2 tablespoons chutney

1 tablespoon smooth apricot jam

1 tablespoon Worcestershire sauce

1 teaspoon turmeric

2 tablespoons brown vinegar

2¼ pounds ground beef

7 tablespoons sultanas (do not substitute raisins, they are too sweet)

3 eggs

pinch each salt and turmeric

bay leaves

Preparation

Soak bread in milk. Heat oil and butter in large pan and fry onions and garlic. When onions are soft, add curry powder, salt, chutney, jam, Worcestershire sauce, turmeric, and vinegar. Mix well. Drain and mash bread, reserve milk. Add bread to pan together with ground beef and sultanas. Cook over low heat, stirring. When meat loses its pinkness, remove from stove. Add 1 beaten egg, mix well, then spoon into a greased, 11-by-7 inch baking dish and level the top.

Beat remaining eggs with reserved milk (you should have ½ cup left), the salt, and turmeric. Pour over meat mixture and put a few bay leaves on top. Stand dish in a larger pan of water (this is important to prevent drying out) and bake, uncovered, at 350°F for 1 hour or until set.

Serve with rice, coconut, chutney, nuts and bananas.

Serves 10

Africans of mixed race include *bredies* and an Indian-style meat pastry called *samoesas*. South Africa's Indian minority may also have provided the term for tangerines, *naartjie*—an apparent reference to the Hindi *tamie nartie*, used to refer to citrus fruit.

Other food items that are popular among South Africans in the United States are *Marie* biscuits, a hard, dry cookie baked for dipping in tea; cream crackers, light and puffy sweets; *morogo* or *imifino*, a wild leaf stew; *bobotie*, a minced beef curry; a fried bread called *vetkoek*; and *sosaties*, which are made of marinated lamb and apricots. Meals may be washed down with homemade beer, fine wines, coffee, or the corn meal–based *mechow*. A strong English tea called Red Bush is very popular, as are Chinese and Indian varieties; these are often sweetened with condensed milk.

Among the most notable South African restaurants in the United States is New York City's Braai, a barbecue bar and grill in Hell's Kitchen. The menu includes *sop en slaai*, or soup and salad, such as *die braai slaai*, among whose ingredients are oranges, goat cheese, and roasted garlic, and entrees such as *ribbetjies*, or ribs. Other prominent South African restaurants include Shebeen Pub & Braai in Charlottesville, Virginia; Karoo Café in Provincetown, Massachusetts; and 10 Degrees South in Atlanta, Georgia.

Traditional Dress Most South African Americans dress the same way most people do in the United States, though some—primarily from nonwhite groups—might don traditional costumes on festive occasions. Zulu men sport the *amabheshu*, an apron of goatskin or leather worn at the back. Beads are common among men, women, and children, and popular items for men are frilly goatskin bands worn on both arms and legs. The Xhosa, too, are known for their striking attire, including blankets with detailed patterns that both men and women wear as shawls. The Sotho also wear brightly colored blankets but as coats; in addition, they are typically store-bought since the Sotho have no tradition of hand-making these items. In areas north of Johannesburg, a strong Ndebele influence is reflected in beadwork, as well as geometric designs painted on houses.

Dances and Songs The range of peoples, cultures, and traditions in South Africa is reflected in the diversity of the nation's music. Though emanating from more rural areas, traditional music continues to influence contemporary urban forms. Traditional instruments include homemade horns, drums, and stringed instruments, and among neo-traditional styles are variants on the indigenous music of the Ndebele, Pedi, Shangaan, Sotho, and Zulu peoples. For example, the Tsonga are associated with the *mbila*, a traditional instrument played along with drums and horns. Often Tsongan music is used to accompany the tribe's traditional dance forms. From the countryside have come such forms as *mbube*, a complex choral gospel music.

Singing and dancing is a significant part of black South African traditional life, and praise poems—traditional odes in celebration of a person, place, or event—form a key element in their music. The Xhosa practice group singing and hand-clapping but have also borrowed from Western styles introduced by missionaries. An example of this influence is the hymn-like "*Nkosi Sikele' iAfrika*," or "God Bless Africa," which was written by a Xhosa schoolteacher in 1897 and later became South Africa's national anthem.

SOUTH AFRICAN PROVERBS

- Knowledge is like a lion; it cannot be gently embraced.

- Once you have found your first diamond, you will never give up looking.

- If you are looking for a fly in your food, it means that you are full.

- Roasted locusts eaten at night bring dangerous dreams.

- The heart is like a goat that has to be tied up.

- Behold the iguana puffing itself up to make itself a man.

- The woman who always complains and is never satisfied with anything is like an annoying flea on the foot.

- Two wives, two pots of poison.

- An Elder does not break wind in public, but in a latrine.

- When two elephants meet on a narrow bridge, they get nowhere until one of them backs down or lies down.

- Until the lions have their historians, tales of hunting will always glorify the hunter.

- When you shoot a zebra in the black stripe, the white dies too; shoot it in the white and the black dies too.

- The one chased away with a club comes back, but the one chased away with reason does not.

- The best time to plant a tree is twenty years ago; the next best time is now.

In the 1930s *marabi* became very popular. Like its cousin, American big-band jazz, *marabi* is a characterized by the repetition of short melodic phrases. *Kwela*, with its distinctive blend of homemade guitar, saxophone, and pennywhistle, gained popularity in the 1940s. By the 1960s, whites, too, had become avid fans of township jazz, which had sprouted into *kwela's* instrumental music and *mbaqanga*, a vocal jazz style. Cape Malays developed their own Cape jazz, marked by strains of Eastern sounds that reflect their southeast Asian heritage.

In the 1980s, the townships gave birth to their own brand of pop music. Like the West's synthetic new wave sounds of the era, "township music" is punctuated by synthesizers and drum machines, though it maintains the vocal harmonies for which South Africans are famous. South African music also received a boost on the world scene when American pop singer Paul Simon teamed up with the a cappella group Ladysmith Black Mambazo for the highly acclaimed album *Graceland* in 1986. In the 1990s native vocal artistry and praise poetry combined with American rap and hip-hop to create uniquely South African forms. Another style that developed in the 1990s was *kwaito*, which blends traditional sounds with those of house music, rhythm and blues, and hip-hop.

At least one popular Afrikaner song bears a direct link to U.S. history: "*Daar Kom die* Alabama" ("There Comes the *Alabama*") celebrates the Confederate raider C.S.S. *Alabama*, which pursued the U.S.S. *Sea Bride* all the way to Cape Town in August 1863. All of Cape Town, is it said, came out to greet the ship from far-off America.

Holidays Among the significant public holidays in South Africa are Family Day (April 5); Freedom Day (April 27), which commemorates the first day on which black South Africans were allowed to vote; Worker's Day (May 1); Youth Day (June 16), which honors protestors killed in the 1976 Soweto township riots; National Women's Day (August 9); Heritage Day (September 24); the Day of Reconciliation (December 16), instituted to foster national unity in postapartheid South Africa; and Boxing Day or the Day of Goodwill (December 26). Religious holidays include Good Friday, along with the nonreligious Easter Monday holiday, Ascension Day in April or May, and Christmas. New Year's Day, of course, is also a holiday.

English and/or Afrikaners celebrate Founder's Day (April 6), which commemorates the founding of the Cape Colony in 1652; Republic Day (May 31), the anniversary of the declaration of the Republic of South Africa in 1961; Kruger Day (October 10), the birthday of early Afrikaner leader S. J. P. Kruger (1825–1904); and the Day of the Vow. The latter, which commemorates the Boer defeat of the Zulu at the Battle of Blood River in 1838, is on December 16, which in 1994 officially became the Day of Reconciliation.

Health Care Issues and Practices By and large, South African Americans have participated in the U.S. health care system. According to the U.S. Census Bureau, in the period of 2009 to 2011, approximately 83 percent of the civilian noninstitutionalized South African American population had private health insurance and another 11 percent had public coverage.

South Africans' homeland has a severe HIV/ AIDS problem. The United Nations estimated that some 5.7 million South Africans, or about 12 percent of the national population, had HIV/AIDS, making it the nation with the highest prevalence in the entire

world. (The other top five countries with the highest prevalence of HIV/AIDS are all neighbors of South Africa.) The spread of HIV/AIDS from South Africa to the United States was not a significant concern due to the imposition of an immigration ban in the late 1980s that prevented persons with HIV/AIDS from entering the country. However, in 2010 President Barack Obama lifted the ban.

FAMILY AND COMMUNITY LIFE
The U.S. Census Bureau estimated that for the period of 2009 to 2011, there were more than 20,000 South African American households, resulting in an average household size of 2.55 persons. Just over 69 percent of all South African American households were families, with the average family size being 3.06. Six out of seven South African American family households had two parents, while female householders slightly outnumbered their male counterparts in nonfamily households.

Among a population of more than 44,000 South African Americans fifteen years of age or older, 57 percent were married. (This figure does not include people who were married but separated.) Just under 31 percent had never been married, a figure somewhat smaller than for South Africans living in South Africa. Among some 22,500 South African American males age fifteen or over, nearly 60 percent were married and not separated. The number of South African American females fifteen or older was smaller—about 21,800— as was the percentage of those who were married and not separated, which was about 55 percent. Among both males and females, approximately 30 percent had never been married.

As with many immigrant groups from developed nations, the birth rate was not particularly high among South African Americans: of some 15,700 women ages fifteen to fifty, just 684 had given birth within the previous twelve months, a figure equivalent to about 4 percent of all eligible persons.

Gender Roles In the past, Afrikaners were known for their highly conservative views, not only regarding racial relations but also women's roles. This came in part from a strong fundamentalist religious tradition, namely a strict interpretation of family guidelines provided by the Apostle Paul in the New Testament. Among the perhaps unintended consequences that followed the end of apartheid, however, was a rise in employment opportunities for Afrikaner women. This rise was accompanied by a decline in the practice of gender separation that had typified many social interactions among Afrikaners.

Gender relations in black South African ethnic groups have also been characterized by patriarchy. The Xhosa, for instance, have a tradition of polygamy, and the man is king in the typical Xhosa home, a notion that is also upheld by the Zulu. The latter have their own polygamous tradition, one that today even extends to dating. Thus, it is not uncommon for a young Zulu man to have several girlfriends. English, Coloured, and Asian families tend to be more or less traditional and patriarchal, depending on the family and the degree to which they embrace Western lifestyles.

Education The South African American population is educated to a degree well above the national average for all groups. The American Community Survey for 2009–2011 showed that about 17,000 South African Americans three years of age or older were enrolled in school and that of this group, the largest portion (about 36 percent) was in college or graduate school. Out of some 36,000 South African Americans twenty-five or older, nearly 97 percent had at least a high school diploma, while 31 percent had bachelor's degrees and more than 23 percent had graduate or professional degrees.

Courtship and Weddings Gender relations among Afrikaners in the past were conducted according to highly conservative guidelines. Thus, males and females spent much of their time apart. When a man took an interest in a woman, the courtship was formal and traditional. Should the two wish to marry, it was incumbent on the man to ask the woman's father for her hand in marriage. On three Sunday mornings prior to the wedding, the couple's names would be read in church, and if there were no objections, the marriage would be performed. This practice had declined by the end of the twentieth century, however,

and courtships are now conducted along lines more familiar to American and European youth.

Courtship among Coloureds has also tended to be highly formal, in part because apartheid-era laws banning interracial dating required people of both sexes to be highly circumspect. Arranged marriages have played a significant in the lives of South African groups ranging from Indians to Sotho. The Zulu, on the other hand, have their own traditional courtship practices that deviate somewhat from the patriarchal standard typical of most tribal societies. Thus a Zulu girl is the one who initiates contact by sending a "love letter"—actually, a string of beads whose colors carry specific meanings—to the boy in whom she is interested. The Xhosa have perhaps the most relaxed practices, with boys and girls typically meeting at dances, some of which last all night.

Relations with Other Americans The subjects of family and community, as applied to South Africans in general—and particularly to South Africans in the United States—are closely tied to the complex political and racial history of South Africa. South African Americans have continued to be haunted by the legacy of apartheid. A sense of connectedness to the old country has affected family and community relations, tending to strengthen the bonds of Afrikaner to Afrikaner and black South African to black South African.

For English-speaking South Africans, however, this dynamic has not been as strong, simply because their accents make many of them indistinguishable from Britons or Australians to most Americans. Yet this, too, has created tensions within families. Thus, South African expatriate author and professor Sheila Roberts writes of her son in "An Incomplete Replacing: The White South African Expatriate":

> By the time he was twelve and able to understand the full infamy of South African racism, he grew so ashamed of his South African heritage that he not only began inventing a different past for himself, but he expected me not to tell people I was from South Africa. Rather, I should say I was from Britain: my accent would carry the lie. At times I went along with his request if he was with me, particularly if there was not much opportunity for a following conversation in which I would have to fabricate an intricate and unlikely past. Other times I would resist. I didn't like the lie.

EMPLOYMENT AND ECONOMIC CONDITIONS

South African Americans have meshed rather seamlessly with the U.S. labor force. According to the U.S. Census Bureau, of nearly 44,000 South African Americans age sixteen and older in the period of 2009 to 2011, over 71 percent were in the labor force. This amounted to nearly 29,000 workers, the vast majority

Patrick Soon-Shiong is a South African American surgeon and founder, chairman, and CEO of Abraxis BioScience, a biotechnology company developing cancer treatment. ZUMA PRESS, INC. / ALAMY

of whom commuted an average of 25.1 minutes to work. (The remaining 7 percent worked at home.) Out of this working population, over 59 percent were employed in management, business, science, or the arts; another 20 percent worked in sales and office occupations; just over 12 percent held service jobs; nearly 5 percent were involved in production, transportation, and material moving occupations; and the remainder—just under 4 percent—worked in natural resources, construction, and maintenance. As one might expect, the vast majority of employed persons (about 83 percent) worked as private wage and salary workers, with about 9 percent employed by the government. Self-employed persons accounted for most of the remaining 8 percent.

During the late twentieth century, a number of South African entrepreneurs established successful businesses throughout the United States. Atlanta, Georgia, was a case in point: Goldberg's Deli and Avril's Exclusives (a car detailing shop), both owned and operated by Jewish immigrants from South Africa, were practically across the street from one another on Roswell Road in the city's prosperous north end. Atlanta was also the home of Firearms Training Systems, Inc., a facility for training law enforcement, military, and security personnel in the use of firearms through simulations of real-world situations. Its founder was South African race-car driver Jody Scheckter, who in 1979 won the Formula One championship for Ferrari.

Using inflation-adjusted dollars, the U.S. Census Bureau estimated a median household income of $82,236 per year for South African Americans in 2011—a figure well above the national average. Nearly 91 percent of South African Americans had earnings (as opposed to, or in addition to, other forms of income such as Social Security, retirement benefits, or public assistance), and their mean annual income was $123,576. The per-capita income for South African Americans was $48,002, about 15 percent higher than the U.S. per-capita income of $41,560 in 2011. Only about 5 percent of South African American families were at the poverty rate or below.

POLITICS AND GOVERNMENT

Given the racially and politically charged nature of their homeland, it might be reasonable to expect South African Americans to be highly involved politically. Just as Cuban Americans and other refugees from communist countries are often outspoken proponents of free enterprise and limited government, South African Americans would seem to be keenly motivated by racial issues. However, theirs is a much smaller and less visible group than Cuban Americans, and the South African American population is too segmented and widely dispersed to be regarded as a unitary group. However, it is possible to glean at least some sense of their political views and experiences on the basis of purely anecdotal information.

In his 1989 memoir *Kaffir Boy in America*, Mark Mathabane recalls staying at "the I-House," a dormitory for international students in New York City. While there he experienced tension with fellow black South Africans and others of African origin when, as he writes, he "made it known that I would not isolate myself from other students out of some false sense of black pride or solidarity." He also met two white South Africans active in the United Democratic Front (UDF), an antiapartheid group, from whom he learned "about the shock of finding themselves reviled by Americans as racist simply because they were white South Africans. … But what was even more shocking to [them] was being shunned by most black South Africans at I-House." He listened to them express their frustrations and then told them, "I consider you brothers, too. But remember that to people in whom apartheid has bred paranoia, your very connection with the UDF is reason to be wary of you since all the opposition groups in South Africa, particularly the UDF, are full of government informants."

South African expatriate writer Sheila Roberts also encountered the hostility that often greeted white South Africans in the United States during the years of apartheid, an experience she describes in her 1994 essay "An Incomplete Replacing: The White South African Expatriate." When she was buying tickets to a movie with her son in Lansing, Michigan, in 1986, the theater clerk noticed her accent and asked where she was from. Roberts recalls:

> As soon as I said, "South Africa," my son walked away, ashamed as always at any reference to our country. The young woman looked at me with cold curiosity. As she handed me the tickets, she announced that "we" should nuke "that place." Then she used a catchphrase from the Vietnam War, though she was too young to know where it came from. She said we should turn it into a parking lot.

As illustrated by the experiences of Roberts and Mathabane, Americans seemed to be highly aware of the situation in South Africa during the 1980s. However, many of their responses tended to be based in emotion rather than intellect, with Roberts's theater clerk being an extreme example. And though former South Africans opposed to apartheid naturally applauded their neighbors' growing awareness, this did little to address their own complex feelings about their home country. Roberts experienced a situation typical of many immigrants: her children readily became assimilated to the United States, while her own heart remained tied to her native country. "The idea of returning" to South Africa, she writes, "stayed with me as a consoling, if impossible, escape through the hard years of my children's teens."

NOTABLE INDIVIDUALS

Business Elon Musk (1971–) is an entrepreneur and inventor who cofounded PayPal and the electric carmaker Tesla Motors and created private space transport company SpaceX. Born in Pretoria, South Africa, Musk was the son of a Canadian mother and a South African father. He left his homeland in 1988 at age seventeen rather than serve in the South African military, making his way to North America. After four years in Canada, Musk came to the United States, where he earned a bachelor's degree in physics from the University of Pennsylvania, as well as a business degree from the Wharton School.

Patrick Soon-Shiong (1952–), born to Chinese immigrants in Port Elizabeth, South Africa, is a surgeon, medical researcher, and professor at the University of California at Los Angeles, as well as an entrepreneur and philanthropist. He earned a medical degree at the University of Witwatersrand and a Master of Science degree at the University of British Columbia. In addition to being the chairman and chief executive officer of the Chan Soon-Shiong Institute for Advanced Health, National LambdaRail, the Healthcare Transformation Institute, and NantWorks, LLC, he was a minority owner of the Los Angeles Lakers basketball team.

Fashion Colin Cowie (1962–) is a style guru, party planner, interior designer, television personality, and author of books on entertaining, weddings, and related subjects. He was born in Kitwe, Federation of Rhodesia and Nyasaland (now Zambia) and grew up in South Africa, moving to the United States in 1985. A regular on the CBS *Early Show* for many years, he later hosted Lifetime Television's *Get Married*, a daily wedding-planning show. He was profiled in such publications as *Architectural Digest, In Style, Town & Country*, and *Modern Bride*, and his books include *Extraordinary Weddings* (2007), *Effortless Elegance* (1996), and *Colin Cowie Chic* (2007).

Film Daniel Mindel (1958–) is a cinematographer noted for his work on the films of John Boorman, Ridley Scott, and Tony Scott. Born in Johannesburg, Mindel was educated in Australia and Britain. After working as assistant cameraman on Boorman's *The Emerald Forest* (1985), he moved to the United States, where the two Scotts and other directors employed him on commercials. During the 1990s he worked as camera operator or photographer on a number of films, including *Thelma & Louise* (1992) and *Crimson Tide* (1995), before serving as second-unit director on Ridley Scott's *G.I. Jane* (1997) and director of photography on Tony Scott's *Enemy of the State* (1998). He later worked with J. J. Abrams on *Star Trek* (2009) and its sequel, *Star Trek into Darkness* (2013).

Government Elizabeth Furse (1936–) is the first person born in Africa to win election to the U.S. Congress, where she served as a Democratic representative from Oregon from 1993 to 1999. Born in Nairobi, Kenya, she grew up in South Africa. During the early 1950s—long before opposition to apartheid became a popular cause—the teenage Furse was an activist in her homeland. She moved to England in 1956, and later to California, where she became involved with the United Farm Workers movement under the direction of Cesar Chavez. She relocated to Seattle, Washington, in 1968, became a U.S. citizen in 1972, and settled in Oregon in 1978.

Journalism Jani Allan (1952–) was already a well-known journalist, first in South Africa and later in the United Kingdom, before she relocated to the United States in 2001. She was born in England and was adopted by a couple who moved to Johannesburg when she was a baby. After earning an honors degree in English literature at the University of Witwatersrand, she worked in various jobs, including modeling, before beginning a career in journalism. Her work as columnist for the *Sunday Times* in Johannesburg brought her attention, and it also made her the target of an assassination attempt that forced her to flee to London. Allan returned to South Africa in 1996, but five years later, she immigrated to the United States.

Lara Logan (1971–), born in Durban, South Africa, is a correspondent for *60 Minutes* and chief foreign affairs correspondent for CBS News. She graduated the University of Natal in 1992 with a degree in commerce. After working with several Durban newspapers, she went on to Reuters Television and then worked as a freelancer for various major international news organizations. Her reporting from Afghanistan during the early days of the U.S. war against the Taliban in 2001 brought her to prominence, and a number of important assignments followed. Logan herself became part of the news when, while covering the Egyptian revolution against President Hosni Mubarak in February 2011, she was beaten and sexually assaulted in Cairo's Tahrir Square. During the 2012 U.S. presidential campaign, she sharply criticized President Barack Obama's administration for its claims that Mideast terrorist groups were on the wane, as well as its attempts to downplay the September 11, 2012, murder of four U.S. diplomatic personnel by terrorists in Benghazi, Libya.

Literature Athol Fugard (1932–) is a South African writer known for his antiapartheid plays and his novel *Tsotsi* (1980), which was made into a movie that won an Academy Award for Best Foreign Language Film in 2005. Born in the Eastern Cape, Fugard grew up enjoying the privileges of Afrikaners, but his experience as a government clerk in Johannesburg made him increasingly aware of the injustice inherent in the apartheid system. His play *The Blood Knot* (1961) earned him international recognition but also made him a target of his country's government. Eventually he relocated to the United States and became a citizen, though he also retained his South African citizenship.

Sheila Gordon (1927–), a native of Johannesburg, is a novelist whose works included *Waiting for the Rain* (1987), *The Middle of Somewhere* (1990), and *Unfinished Business* (1975). She moved to the United States as an adult and ultimately settled in Brooklyn, New York.

Mark Mathabane (1960–) is an author and lecturer whose works included *Kaffir Boy: the True Story of a Black Youth's Coming of Age in Apartheid South Africa* (1986) and *Kaffir Boy in America: An Encounter with Apartheid* (1989). Born in a Johannesburg ghetto, Mathabane grew up experiencing the misery of life as a black South African under apartheid. His grandmother worked for a wealthy white family in whose library he first discovered literature in the form of Robert Louis Stevenson's *Treasure Island*. This exposure to the outside world began to build a dream in him of escaping the constraints of his upbringing. Mathabane found a mentor in Wimbledon star Stan Smith, who helped him gain a tennis scholarship to Limestone College in South Carolina in 1978.

Sheila Roberts was a writer and teacher who criticized apartheid both in fiction and nonfiction. Born in Johannesburg in 1937, she came to prominence with works such as the story collection *Outside Life's Feast*, which won the Olive Schreiner Prize in 1975, and *He's My Brother*, a 1977 novel banned by the South African government. She moved to the United States in 1977 and became a professor of creative writing at the University of Wisconsin–Milwaukee. Roberts died in 2009.

Music Dave Matthews (1967–) is the lead vocalist, the songwriter, and a guitarist for the Dave Matthews Band, as well as an actor and political activist. The Johannesburg native relocated to New York State when he was two years old, after his father took a job with IBM. The family returned to South Africa in 1977, but in 1985 Matthews fled the country to avoid conscription in its armed services. He ultimately settled in Charlottesville, Virginia, where in 1991 he formed his band. The Dave Matthews Band had a string of top-selling albums, beginning with *Remember Two Things* (1993). Between 2000 and 2010, it sold the most concert tickets of any act in North America.

Goapele Mohlabane (1977–) known by her first name, is a soul and R&B singer-songwriter. She was the daughter of a black South African father and a Jewish Israeli mother whose work as antiapartheid activists brought them together. They raised her and her brother, who later came to prominence as a rap DJ, in an Oakland, California, community of South African exiles. Influenced by a range of artists, including South Africa's Miriam Makeba and Hugh Masekela, Goapele began her career as a recording artist with *Closer* (2001). *Break of Dawn* (2011) was her fourth album.

Singer-songwriter Goapele's father was an exiled South African political activist. Goapele grew up in a South African exile community in California. FREDERICK M. BROWN / GETTY IMAGES

Trevor Rabin (1954–) is a guitarist, vocalist, and songwriter best known for his work with the British progressive rock band Yes, for which he cowrote the hit "Owner of a Lonely Heart." Born in Johannesburg, Rabin grew up learning piano and guitar, and he performed for the entertainment division of the South African armed forces during his period of compulsory service. He played in a number of bands, including a brief stint with the antiapartheid group Freedom's Children, before establishing himself as a highly sought-after studio musician. This led to an invitation to join Yes in 1982, and in the following year he helped propel the resurgent group to chart-topping success with its album *90125*. Rabin left Yes in 1994 and went on to an award-winning career as composer for such motion pictures as *Armageddon* (1998), *National Treasure* (2004), and *The Sorcerer's Apprentice* (2010).

Religion Robert G. Hamerton-Kelly (1938–), born in Cape Town, South Africa, is a Methodist pastor, theologian, and author. He studied at Cambridge in England before earning his ThD from Union Theological Seminary in New York. Hamerton-Kelly was the dean of the chapel at Stanford University from 1972 to 1986 and went on to work as a senior research scholar at the school's Center for International Security and Arms Control until 1997. Hamerton-Kelly wrote a number of theological works, beginning with *God the Father: Theology and Patriarchy in the Teaching of Jesus* (1979).

Sports David DeCastro (1990–) is a guard for the Pittsburgh Steelers in the National Football League (NFL). Born to South African American parents in Bellevue, Washington, DeCastro played on the Bellevue High School team alongside future San Diego Chargers guard Stephen Schilling. In college he played for Stanford University, earning honors as an All-American. DeCastro was selected in the first round of the 2012 NFL draft.

Eric Clifford "Cliff" Drysdale (1941–) is a former professional tennis player and announcer. He was born in Nelspruit, Transvaal, and first gained attention in the 1960s as a member of the "Handsome Eight," a group of rising tennis stars. Drysdale went on to win five singles and six doubles titles. After retiring as a player in the 1970s, he became a naturalized U.S. citizen and pursued a second career as a tennis commentator for ESPN.

Johan Kriek (1958–) is a professional tennis player and activist. Born in Pongola near the border with Swaziland, he attended the Afrikaans High School for Boys in Pretoria and began his rise to international prominence in the 1970s. In a career that included triumphs over Andre Agassi, Jimmy Connors, John McEnroe, and Bjorn Börg, Kriek won the Australian Open twice, reached the semifinals at the French Open and U.S. Open, and made it to the quarterfinals at Wimbledon. He won fourteen singles and eight doubles titles and, at one point, was ranked number one in the world. Kriek, who settled in Virginia, also founded the Global Water Foundation, a nonprofit group established for the purpose of providing clean water to needy communities worldwide.

Gary Player (1935–), a native of Johannesburg, is regarded as one of the greatest figures in the history of professional golf. The son of a miner who had to take out a loan to buy him his first set of golf clubs, Player turned professional in 1953 and won the U.S. Open in 1965. Over the course of his career, he won 165 tournaments. Player became the only non-American to win the Grand Slam, or all four majors (Masters, U.S. Open, British Open, and PGA Championship). After retirement, he engaged in a number of business ventures and divided his time between residences in Florida and South Africa.

He was inducted into the World Golf Hall of Fame in 1974.

Roy Wegerle (1964–) is professional soccer player and golfer. The Pretoria native signed with the Tampa Bay Rowdies in 1984 and went on to play for a number of U.S. professional teams, as well as the 1994 and 1998 U.S. World Cup teams. After marrying an American in 1991, he became a U.S. citizen. Knee injuries forced Wegerle to leave soccer after 1998, at which point he pursued a career as a golfer.

Stage and Screen Embeth Davidtz (1965–) is a film and television actress. She was born to South African parents in Lafayette, Indiana, and moved with her parents back to their native country when she was nine years old. Davidtz, who had to learn Afrikaans in order to obtain an education, graduated from high school in Pretoria in 1983 and then earned a degree in English literature at Rhodes University in Grahamstown. Her acting credits include the movies *Schindler's List* (1993), *Bridget Jones's Diary* (2001), and *The Amazing Spider-Man* (2012) and a stint on the popular TV series *Mad Men*.

Charlize Theron (1975–) is an actress and fashion model who was born in Benoni, Transvaal, and grew up on a farm speaking Afrikaans. Theron had a turbulent childhood: when she was sixteen, her mother shot and killed her father, an abusive alcoholic. (The killing was ruled self-defense.) The striking and statuesque Theron showed early promise as a model, and at age nineteen, she went to Los Angeles to seek a career in film. While trying to cash a check from her mother at a Hollywood Boulevard bank, she got in a shouting match with a recalcitrant teller, and this attracted the attention of a film agent who was waiting in line. After a few forgettable film roles, Theron began attracting attention in movies such as *The Devil's Advocate* (1997). She rose to prominence with her portrayal of serial killer Aileen Wuornos in *Monster* (2003), a role that earned her an Academy Award for Best Actress. She was the first South African ever to win an Oscar in a major category. Theron became a U.S. citizen in 2007, though she retained her South African citizenship.

Arnold Vosloo (1962–), a native of Pretoria, is a film actor best known for his role as Imhotep in *The Mummy* (1999) and *The Mummy Returns* (2001) and for his portrayal of the eponymous superhero in the *Darkman* movies during the 1990s. Vosloo was raised in an acting family, and he achieved early successes on the stage and screen in his homeland before moving to the United States in the late 1980s. His exotic good looks—Vosloo has often been cited as a virtual double for British actor Billy Zane—helped land him a number of roles playing non-Western characters, such as a Middle Eastern terrorist on the TV series *24*. Vosloo became a naturalized U.S. citizen in 1988.

MEDIA

Juluka

Magazine containing news of interest to South Africans in America.

P.O. Box 34095
Bethesda, Maryland 20827
Phone: (301) 652-5754

ORGANIZATIONS AND ASSOCIATIONS

Braai Connection

A social and networking club founded in 1987. Organizes recreational outings and publishes a quarterly newsletter for southern Africans in North America.

Derek Selbo
2037 S. Orchard Street
Boise, Idaho 83705
Phone: (858) 775-4524
URL: www.braai-connection.org

South African Chamber of Commerce in America (SACCA)

Encourages trade, joint ventures, and investment between South Africa and the United States, assists entrepreneurs on both continents in exploring business opportunities, and works with U.S. and South African authorities to solve problems that inhibit trade and investment.

Claude W. Roxborough, III, President, SACCA U.S.
23 Damon Park
2nd and 3rd Floor
Arlington, Massachusetts 02474
Phone: (617) 615-9379

Fax: (954) 761-7810
Email: info@sacca.biz
URL: www.sacca.biz

South Africans in Austin

Organized for South Africans living in Austin, Texas, the club offers a wide variety of information sources for South African Americans through its website.

John Els
URL: www.sa-austin.com

SOURCES FOR ADDITIONAL STUDY

Davids, Nashira. "We Want out of SA." *Sunday Times* (Johannesburg), February 22, 2012.

Hammer, Ben. "Serving Urban Populations … A Continent Away: Bronx Community College Works to Expand Educational, Employment Opportunities for Black South Africans." *Black Issues in Higher Education* 20, no. 14 (2003): 36.

Mathabane, Mark. *Kaffir Boy in America: An Encounter with Apartheid.* New York: Scribner, 1989.

Offenburger, Andrew, et. al, eds. *A South African & American Comparative Reader: The Best of Safundi and Other Selected Articles.* Scottsdale, AZ: Safundi, 2002.

Roberts, Sheila. "An Incomplete Replacing: The White South African Expatriate." In *Displacements: Cultural Identities in Question,* edited by Angelika Bammer, 172–81. Bloomington: Indiana University Press, 1994.

Vail, LeRoy, and Landeg White. *Power and the Praise Poem: South African Voices in History.* Charlottesville: University of Virginia Press, 1991.

Van Rooyen, Johann. *The New Great Trek: The Story of South Africa's White Exodus.* Pretoria, South Africa: Unisa Press, 2000.

Spanish Americans

Clark Colahan

OVERVIEW

Spanish Americans are immigrants or descendants of people from Spain, a southwestern European nation occupying the greater part of the Iberian Peninsula. The Spanish mainland shares a border with Portugal to the west and France to the north. The Mediterranean Sea borders mainland Spain's southern and eastern shores. Spain also consists of seventeen additional autonomous communities, most of which are islands northwest of Africa, near Morocco. Spain's total land area is 195,365 square miles (505,992 square kilometers). Some of the country's major regions are Castile, which contains the capital city of Madrid; Cataluña, which contains Barcelona; Andalucía, which contains Seville; Extremadura; Galicia; and the Basque Country. Spain is the fifth-largest country in Europe, roughly the size of California.

Data from the National Statistics Institute of Spain indicates that the nation had a population of approximately 47.2 million in 2011. According to an April 2012 study by the Spanish Center of Sociological Research, about 71 percent of Spaniards self-identify as Catholics, 2.7 percent as practicing another faith, and about 24 percent as practicing no religion, among which 9.4 percent are atheists. Spain is a member of the United Nations, the North Atlantic Treaty Organization (NATO), the Organisation for Co-operation and Development (OECD), and the World Trade Organization (WTO).

The first Europeans to settle in what is now the United States, Spanish immigrants arrived on the mainland in 1565, when the first-known Spanish settlement was established in what now is known as St. Augustine, Florida. This was followed by several other colonial-era Spanish settlements, in modern-day New Mexico, California, Arizona, Texas, and Louisiana. Most Spanish immigrants at this time came to the New World seeking new land to explore, claim, and farm. Spain is a developed country with the twelfth-largest economy in the world (by nominal gross domestic product) and—like the United States—very high living standards. As of 2005 Spain had the tenth-highest quality-of-life index rating in the world. However, since 2008 Spain's economy has weakened, and the unemployment rate has risen dramatically, from 8 percent of the population in 2007 to 26 percent in 2012.

According to the U.S. Census Bureau's American Community Survey estimates for 2009–2011, approximately 682,000 U.S. residents identified themselves as Spaniards (that is, having ancestors from Spain). Including people who have come to the United States from countries and territories in the Western Hemisphere once colonized by Spain, such as Mexico, Puerto Rico, and Cuba, the number of Spanish Americans in the United States is approximately 24 million. The majority of Spanish Americans have settled in California, with other large settlements in Texas, New Mexico, Colorado, Florida, and New York. Smaller populations of Spanish Americans also live in Arizona and New Jersey.

HISTORY OF THE PEOPLE

Early History The origins of Spain's Latin name, Hispania, is much debated. Some believe it to have been a name, meaning "land of rabbits," given by Carthaginian settlers who arrived on the peninsula around 800 BCE. Another theory suggests that the name may have derived from the Basque word for "border." Colonized by a series of important civilizations, Spain became heir to the cultures not only of Carthage but also of Greece and Rome. It was the home country of legionaries, several emperors, and philosophers, including Seneca, the founder of Stoicism. Later, with the fall of the Roman Empire in approximately 476 CE, it was settled by Germanic Visigoths, then Arabs and Moors.

In the fifteenth century—under the rule of King Ferdinand and Queen Isabella, the same monarchs under whom Christopher Columbus's famous envoy was launched—Christian forces recaptured Spain from the Moors. Historians view the sixteenth and seventeenth centuries as the golden era of Spain, when the country acquired great power and wealth from its New World possessions and its arts and literature flourished. In the eighteenth and nineteenth centuries, however, Spain's wealth declined, as a vast amount of money was spent by the country's monarchs on a number of European wars and revenues declined from the New World territories. This period culminated with France's Napoleon Bonaparte forcing Spain's King Charles IV and his son Ferdinand VII into exile in 1808. For a brief time, the Spanish Crown was given to Joseph Bonaparte. It was reclaimed, however, by Ferdinand VII in 1814 and then passed to his daughter Isabella, an unpopular queen who ruled until 1868. Her rule was challenged in a series of civil wars known as the Carlist Wars, and she was eventually overthrown by rebel forces made up of both liberals and conservatives led by General Juan Prim. The overthrow became known as the Glorious Revolution, and Isabella was forced into exile. For the following two years, Spain was led by Prince Amadeus of Italy, who had been enlisted to rule by the victorious leaders of the revolution. After Prince Amadeus's rule, Spain existed for two years as a republic before restoring monarchal status to Isabella's son, Alfonso XII, who held the throne from 1874 to 1885.

Spain maintained neutrality in World War I, which allowed the country a degree of economic stability. In the years following the war, however, public unrest led to an increase in worker revolts, strikes, and riots. Eventually the reigning monarch, Alfonso XIV, was forced to leave the country, and Spain's second incarnation as a republic was proclaimed in 1931. A new constitution was drafted at this time, after which Spain experienced a short period of unification under the new coalition. In the mid-1930s, however, the worldwide economic depression that preceded World War II generated much social and political unrest in Spain. The country's political climate fostered a sharp divide between right- and left-wing factions. Tensions reached a head in 1936 with a military revolt in Morocco that marked the beginning of the Spanish Civil War, which lasted until 1939 and pitted the country's conservative fascist party, led by General Francisco Franco, against Republican loyalists on the left. The loyalists, despite receiving some aid from the Soviet Union, were defeated largely because of military support provided from the fascist governments of Germany's Adolf Hitler and Italy's Benito Mussolini.

After the Spanish Civil War, Franco aligned Spain more closely with Germany, though Spain again remained neutral in World War II. In 1955 Spain became a member of the United Nations. Franco, meanwhile, governed Spain as a dictator until his death in 1975.

Modern Era The contemporary history of Spain essentially began with the death of Franco, followed by the accession of King Juan Carlos I to the throne and the reestablishment of a parliamentary monarchy. The Spanish Constitution of 1978, which is still in force, defined the status of Spain's autonomous entities (*autonomías*) and established Spain as a parliamentary monarchy, with a prime minister responsible to the bicameral Cortes (Congress of Deputies and Senate) elected every four years. On February 23, 1981, rebels in the Spanish security forces seized the Cortes and attempted to impose a military-backed government. However, a majority of military forces remained loyal to King Juan Carlos, who used his personal authority to overcome the coup attempt.

In October 1982 the Spanish Socialist Workers Party (PSOE), led by Felipe González, won both the Congress of Deputies and Senate by an absolute majority. Gonzalez and the PSOE ruled for the following thirteen years. During this period, Spain joined both NATO and the European Union.

In March 1996 José María Aznar's People's Party (PP, or *Partido Popular* in Spanish) won a plurality of votes. Aznar lobbied to decentralize powers in the region and stir the economy through privatization of businesses, labor-market reform, and measures designed to increase competition in selected markets, such as telecommunications. During Aznar's initial term, Spain integrated fully into European institutions, including the European Monetary Union. Spain also took part, alongside the United States and other NATO allies, in military operations in the former Yugoslavia. Spanish planes participated in the air war against Serbia in 1999, and Spanish armed forces and police personnel were employed in the international peacekeeping forces in Bosnia and Kosovo. President Aznar and the PP won reelection in March 2000 by a landslide, garnering absolute majorities in both houses of parliament.

A decades-long conflict with Basque separatists had made fighting terrorism a top priority for the Aznar government. The Euskadi Ta Askatasuna (ETA) had relied on terrorist tactics since its 1959 founding, attempting to establish Basque nationalism through violent means. After the terrorist attacks on the United States on September 11, 2001, Aznar became a key ally in the United States' fight against terrorism. Spain backed military action against the Taliban in Afghanistan and took a leading role within the European Union (EU) as it pushed for increased international cooperation on terrorism. The Aznar government also supported U.S. intervention in Iraq.

Spanish parliamentary elections on March 14, 2004, were held only three days after a devastating terrorist attack on Madrid commuter rail lines that killed 191 and wounded more than 1,400. This event was thought to have increased voter turnout, resulting in a victory for the PSOE and its leader, José Luis Rodríguez Zapatero, who took office on April 17, 2004.

As he promised during his campaign, Zapatero removed all Spanish soldiers from Iraq. His government also approved a same-sex marriage law, which was supported by the majority of the Spanish population. However, the Roman Catholic Church and social conservatives, many of whom were associated with the People's Party, strongly opposed the law.

The Spanish general election of 2011 took place on November 20. It was the eleventh general election since the transition to renew seats for both chambers of the Cortes: 350 seats for the Congress of Deputies and 208 of the 266 seats of the Senate. It was a snap election, called by Zapatero four months earlier than expected after his government's perceived failure in attempting to reverse the fortunes of Spain's flagging economy, and it was the first time since 1996 that the country's general election was not run concurrently with an Andalusian regional election. Andalusia held its election separately in March 2012.

After several years of unpopular decisions and austerity cuts, the PSOE, in power since 2004, was defeated in a landslide by the PP. The PP received 44.6 percent of the vote and 186 of the 350 seats in the lower house, an absolute majority of the seats, which ensured that PP leader Mariano Rajoy would become the next prime minister.

SETTLEMENT IN THE UNITED STATES

In the first century of Spain's presence in the New World, many of the explorers and soldiers came from Andalucía (in the south) and Extremadura (in the west), two of the poorest regions of the country. The early and lasting influence of these immigrants explains why the standard dialect spoken today in the Western Hemisphere retains the pronunciation used in the south of Spain instead of the characteristics of the older variant still spoken by those living north of Madrid. In the nineteenth and twentieth centuries, the region that produced the most emigrants was Galicia, together with similar parts of Old Castile that border it on the south. During most of this time, Galicia was an isolated, non-industrialized corner of the peninsula. Its inheritance laws either divided farms among all the siblings in a family, resulting in unworkably small *minifundios*, or denied land entirely to all but the first born. In either case, the competition for land was intense, compelling many Galicians to seek their fortunes elsewhere.

Adjoining Galicia to the east on Spain's north coast is Asturias. Until the nineteenth century, the economic situation in Asturias was similar to that in Galicia, but it later became a national leader in industrial development based on coal mining, metalworking, and shipbuilding. From 1900 to 1924, thousands of Spaniards came to the United States from Asturias. Many of these immigrants labored in heavy industries such as the mining of coal and zinc.

The southern provinces of Spain, which include Almería, Málaga, Granada, and the Canary Islands, have been another major source of Spanish immigration to the United States. A number of factors combined to compel citizens to leave these regions: the hot, dry climate; the absence of industry; and a *latifundio* system of large ranches that placed agriculture under the control of a landed caste.

Basques have also immigrated to the United States in large numbers. Traditionally both hardy mountain farmers as well as seafaring people, Basques stood out in the exploration of the Americas, both as soldiers and members of the crews that sailed for the Spanish. Prominent in the civil service and colonial administration, they were accustomed to overseas travel and

"THE BLACK LEGEND"

Stereotypes of Spanish immigrants derive in part from the *leyenda negra*, or the "black legend," a particular style of propagandalike writing that was aimed specifically at vilifying the *conquistadores* and the Spanish Empire. The "black legend" was created and spread by the English in the sixteenth and seventeenth centuries when England and Spain were rivals for European domination. Revulsion is expressed at the alleged cruelty of the Spanish sport of bullfighting, which is believed by its supporters to exalt individual worth through the demonstration of almost chivalric courage. Other stereotypical images, including exaggerated ideas of wild emotional intensity, create the misperception of Spain as the land of the tambourine and castanets, fiery flamenco dancing, and the reckless sensuality of Georges Bizet's opera heroine Carmen. Most of these stereotypes are connected to a degree with the southern region of Andalucía. As in matters of religion, northern Spaniards often view the character of life in their own regions as profoundly different.

residence. Another reason for their emigration besides the restrictive inheritance laws in the Basque Country, was the devastation from the Napoleonic Wars in the first half of the nineteenth century, which was followed by defeats in the Carlist Wars.

In colonial times there were a number of Spanish-controlled settlements in America. The first settlement was in what would become Florida, followed by others in New Mexico, California, Arizona, Texas, and Louisiana. In 1598, when the first town in New Mexico was established, there were about 1,000 Spaniards north of Mexico; today, their descendants are estimated at 900,000. Since the founding of the United States, an additional 250,000 immigrants have arrived either directly from Spain or following a relatively short sojourn in a Latin American country.

The earliest Spanish settlements north of Mexico (known then as New Spain) were the result of the same forces that later led the English to come to that area. Exploration had been fueled in part by imperial hopes for the discovery of wealthy civilizations. Many of the first settlers to New Mexico, for instance, were sent by the Spanish leadership in Mexico City to stake claim to new land and to build colonies that could serve as shields for the profitable silver mines in northern Mexico against attacks by European powers.

Immigration to the United States from Spain was minimal but steady during the first half of the nineteenth century, with an increase during the 1850s and 1860s. Much larger numbers of Spanish immigrants entered the country in the first quarter of the twentieth century—27,000 in the first decade and 68,000 in the second—due to the same circumstances of rural poverty and urban congestion that led other

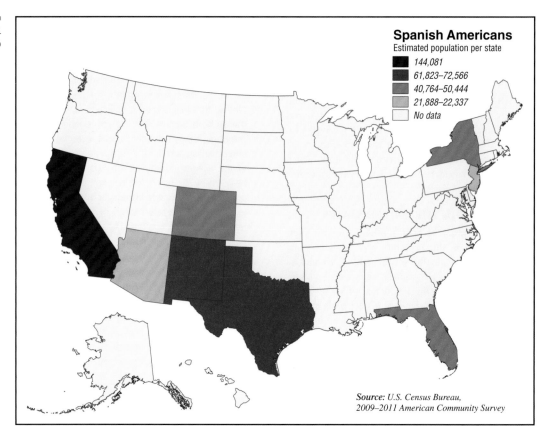

Spanish Americans
Estimated population per state

- 144,081
- 61,823–72,566
- 40,764–50,444
- 21,888–22,337
- No data

Source: U.S. Census Bureau, 2009–2011 American Community Survey

Europeans to emigrate in that period. In 1921, however, the U.S. government enacted a quota system that favored northern and western Europeans, limiting the number of entering Spaniards to 912 per year, a number soon reduced further to 131.

The Spanish presence in the United States continued to diminish, declining sharply between 1930 and 1940 from a total of 110,000 to 85,000. Many immigrants moved back to Spain. Historically, Spaniards have often lived abroad, usually in order to make enough money to return home to an enhanced standard of living and higher social status. In Spanish cities located in regions that experienced heavy emigration at the beginning of the twentieth century, such as the port city of Gijón in Asturias, there are wealthy neighborhoods usually referred to as concentrations of *indianos*, people who became rich in the New World and then returned to their home regions.

Beginning with the fascist revolt against the Spanish Republic in 1936 and the devastating civil war that ensued, General Francisco Franco established a reactionary dictatorship that ruled Spain for forty years. At the time of the fascist takeover, a small but prominent group of liberal intellectuals fled into exile in the United States. The civil war wreaked havoc upon Spain's economy. The country's infrastructure was damaged, many workers were killed in fighting, and businesses were hindered. The poor economic

conditions lasted nearly twenty years under Franco's rule. As a result, when relations between Spain and most other countries were at last normalized in the mid-1960s, 44,000 Spaniards immigrated to the United States in that decade alone. In the 1970s, with prosperity emerging in Spain, the numbers declined to about 3,000 per year. Europe enjoyed an economic boom in the 1980s, and the total number of Spanish immigrants for those ten years dropped to only 15,000. The 1990 U.S. Census recorded 76,000 foreign-born Spaniards in the country, representing only four-tenths of a percent of the total populace. In contrast, the largest Hispanic group—Mexicans born outside the United States—numbered over 2 million, approximately 21 percent.

Five areas of the United States have had significant concentrations of Spaniards: New York City, Florida, California, the mountain regions of the West, and the industrial areas of the Midwest. For nineteenth-century U.S. immigrants, New York City was the most common destination. Until 1890 most Spaniards in the United States lived either in the city itself, with a heavy concentration in Brooklyn, or in communities in New Jersey and Connecticut. By the 1930s, however, these neighborhoods had largely disintegrated, with the second generation moving to the suburbs and assimilating into the mainstream of American life.

At the end of the nineteenth century, Florida attracted the second-largest group of Spaniards in the country through its ties to the Cuban cigar industry. Most of the owners of factories were originally from Asturias, and in the second half of the century, they immigrated in substantial numbers—first to Cuba, later to Key West, and eventually to Tampa, Florida—taking thousands of workers with them. Several thousands of their descendants still live in the vicinity.

California is home to descendants of southern Spanish pineapple and sugar cane workers who had moved to Hawaii at the beginning of the twentieth century. The great majority of those immigrants moved on to the San Francisco area in search of greater opportunities. In southern California's industrial sector, there have been large numbers of skilled workers from northern Spain.

The steel and metalworking centers of the Midwest attracted northern Spaniards. In addition, rubber production and other kinds of heavy industry accounted for large groups of Spaniards in Ohio, Illinois, Michigan, and Pennsylvania. In the U.S. censuses of 1920, 1930, and 1940, West Virginia was among the top seven states in number of Spanish immigrants, due to sizable contingents of Asturian coal miners. However with the decline of the manufacturing sector of the American economy such centers of industry have largely lost their drawing power, accelerating the dispersal and assimilation of these Spanish communities into other sectors of the workforce.

According to the American Community Survey estimates for 2009–2011, California was the state with the largest population of Spanish Americans (144,081). Other states with large numbers of Americans of Spanish descent are Texas, New Mexico, Colorado, Florida, New York, Arizona, and New Jersey.

LANGUAGE

While Spain's centralist regimes of the past favored a standard national language, the its government today encourages the schooling in and general use of regional dialects. For example, Galicians, who occupy the northwest corner of the peninsula, speak Gallego. It is a language that reflects in vocabulary and structure the region's proximity to Portugal to the south and Castile to the east. Residents of Cataluña speak Catalan, a romance language that shares many features with other romance languages, such as Spanish and French, but is nonetheless distinct. In Castile, the country's central region, the residents speak Castellano, which is also the language of most Latin American countries and, outside of Spain, is commonly thought of as the standard Spanish dialect.

As Spanish becomes more and more the second language in the United States, the American-born generations of families that emigrated from Spain have been increasingly likely to retain it in both its spoken and written forms. Current communication with Hispanic countries is highly developed, including such media as newspapers, magazines, films, and Spanish-language television networks. Consequently, immigrants arriving in recent years have found themselves less obliged to learn English than their predecessors. These newcomers integrate easily into the Latin American communities that in several parts of the country function mainly in Spanish.

Strong believers in the value of their culture, Spanish Americans make every effort to keep their native language alive in the home. Many, however, are opposed to bilingual education in the schools, a position grounded in their awareness of the need to assimilate linguistically in order to compete in an English-speaking society.

Common expressions among Spaniards include: *¿Qué hay?* (pronounced "kay I," meaning "What's new?") and *Hasta luego* (pronounced "ahsta lwego," meaning "See you later"). Spaniards can easily be distinguished from other Spanish speakers by their ubiquitous use of *vale* (pronounced "bahlay"), employed identically to the American "okay."

RELIGION

Many Spanish Americans are less active in Catholicism than were past generations. They rarely change their religious affiliation, though, and still participate frequently in family-centered ecclesiastical rituals. In both Spain and the United States, events such as first communions and baptisms are viewed as social obligations and serve to strengthen clan identity.

Strong believers in the value of their culture, Spanish Americans make every effort to keep their native language alive in the home. Many, however, are opposed to bilingual education in the schools, a position grounded in their awareness of the need to assimilate linguistically in order to compete in an English-speaking society.

CULTURE AND ASSIMILATION

The presence of Spanish Americans has seemed less pronounced in recent decades, due to their willingness to blend in with the Hispanic sector and a general decrease in the flow of Spaniards to the United States. Features of a knightly ruling class still indirectly influence Hispanic societies, including those in the United States. These qualities include a firm grounding in family and other personal relations, a thorough *personalismo* that leads to loyalty in business and politics and to friendships in personal life. *Personalismo*, especially among males, is deeper and more common than among Anglos and is thought to provide greater security for one's self and family than the provisions of government.

The Spanish work ethic is compatible with the values of both pre- and post-industrial Europe. Though

Spanish American Isabel Arevalo, 1933. CORBIS-BETTMANN. REPRODUCED BY PERMISSION.

they often work long, intensive hours, Spaniards have generally not felt that a job in itself will guarantee either success or happiness. Instead, leisure has a primary value: it is meant to maintain essential social contacts and is identified with upward social movement. Another element of the Spanish character is an aristocratic concern with a public image that is in harmony with group standards. The opinions of others serve to validate a Spaniard's sense of self, as exemplified by the Spanish phrase *¿Quédirán?* (What will they say?).

Cuisine Spanish food varies from region to region, though the use of olive oil instead of butter is widespread. Seafood is also a common element of Spanish meals; few parts of the peninsula are without daily deliveries of fresh fish and shellfish from the coast, and these items are the featured ingredients in the rice-based casserole of the Mediterranean coast called *paella*. Much of the agriculture in the south of Spain is involved with olive production, and a typical dish of this region is *gazpacho*, a thick, cold tomato and vegetable soup originally concocted to be served during the heat of the day to harvest workers. The southern town Jérez de la Frontera, where a particular type of white grape is grown to make the popular fortified wine known as sherry, contributed the word "sherry" to the English language. In the opposite corner of the country, the Galicians and Asturians drink hard cider and eat a stew called *favada*, made from two kinds of sausage, garlic, saffron, and white beans. Some Spanish foods that are particularly common in the United States are *gazpacho*, *paella*, *tapas* (various types of appetizers), *flan* (a dessert), and *churros* (a Spanish-type doughnut).

Traditional Dress The most commonly pictured Spanish clothing—as in representations of the annual spring fair in Seville, Spain, that served as the

prototype for the California Rose Parade—is the traditional Andalucian ruffled dress for women and the short, tightly fitted jacket for men. This jacket is cut for display both while on horseback and in the atmosphere of stylized energy and romance that characterizes flamenco dancing. Throughout much of Spain, however, holiday attire is based on everyday work clothes, but richly embroidered and appointed. The western region surrounding Salamanca has an economy based on cattle raising, and the extravagantly large hat and embroidered jacket worn by that province's *charros* were passed on to the Mexican cowboys.

Dances and Songs Flamenco is perhaps the most recognized Spanish style of music and dance in the United States. It is mainly associated with the southern region of Andalucía, where Arabic and Romani influences are strong. Flamenco music is characterized by rapid, rhythmic hand clapping and a specialized form of guitar playing. The dancing that accompanies this music is typically done in duet fashion and includes feet stomping and castanet playing. Dancers generally wear the traditional Andalucian costumes described above: ornate, ruffled dresses for women and short, tightly fitting jackets for men. In the United States, flamenco can be found in restaurants in major urban areas that have significant Spanish American populations.

Holidays Most Spanish holidays are also found in American culture through the shared influence of Catholicism. One exception is the Sixth of January, *Día de los Reyes Magos*, "Day of the Three Wise Men." Known in English as Epiphany (formerly Twelfth Night), this holiday has remained vital in Spain as the occasion when Christmas gifts are given. In the United States, Spanish children usually are the beneficiaries of a biculturalism that supplies them with gifts on January 6 as well as on Christmas.

FAMILY AND COMMUNITY LIFE

In keeping with their strong regional identifications in Spain, Spanish Americans have established centers for Galicians, Asturians, Andalucians, and other such groups. Writing in his 1992 book *Arts, Culture and Society in Spanish Emigration to America*, Moisés Llordén Miñambres, a specialist in emigration patterns from Spain, regards this as a given—a natural condition—and refers in passing to how the "ethnic" groupings of recent Spanish immigrants reflect the individual characteristics of the "countries" from which they come. This diversity is reflected in the number of clubs and associations formed by Spanish Americans. A listing by Llordén Miñambres shows twenty-three in New York City, eight in New Jersey, five in Pennsylvania, four in California, and lesser numbers in Indiana, Ohio, Illinois, Massachusetts, Michigan, New York State, Rhode Island, Vermont, and Florida.

Llordén Miñambres divides these organizations into several categories: Beneficent societies, such as the Unión

SPANISH AMERICANS
PROVERBS

En boca cerrada no entra mosca (*"en boca therrada no entra mosca"*).

Don't put your foot in your mouth.

Uvas y queso saben un beso (*"oobas ee keso saben un beso"*).

Grapes and cheese together taste as good as a kiss.

Salud, dinero y amor, y tiempo para disfrutarlos (*"saluth, deenayro, ee ahmor, ee tyempo pahra deesfrutahrlos"*).

Health, wealth, and love, and time to enjoy them.

Benéfica Española of New York, have aimed to provide charitable help for the needy and also information and recommendations to Spanish immigrants. Mutual-aid societies such as the Española de Socorros Mutuos, or "La Nacional", founded in New York in 1868, began as examples of trade-union associations and were important in providing families with medical care and help during economic crises. Members of educational and recreational societies often have been drawn from among the more successful members of the local Spanish community; activities include literary readings, musical performances, banquets, and dances. Also prevalent are athletic associations, such as the Sporting Club of New York; Spanish chambers of commerce; and cultural associations such as the Instituto Cervantes in New York, which offers courses in Spanish language, arranges lectures, and collaborates with museums and other cultural centers.

Gender Roles The structure of the Spanish family has come to resemble the American and European model, as grandparents often live in their own house or a retirement home and women frequently have jobs. The obligation of children to care for elderly parents, however, is somewhat stronger among Spaniards—even those raised in the United States—than among the general American population; a parent often lives part of the year with one child and part with another. The traditional practice of one daughter not marrying in order to live with and care for the parents during their last years has not been maintained in the United States. The notion that Spanish mothers are completely devoted to their children—especially the boys—while fathers spend much of their time socializing outside the home is not as true as it once was. Yet despite the various changes within the family structure that have expanded female roles, the majority of political and community leaders in Spain are still men.

Today, Spanish women often serve "double duty," functioning in their traditional household roles while also holding jobs. In recent years, however, Spain has been recognized for demonstrating a greater commitment to gender equality. In 2004 major legislation was introduced addressing gender-based violence, while the 2007 Law on Guaranteeing Equality between Women and Men sought comprehensive reform for social inequality between the genders. A predominantly female cabinet that was appointed in 2008 under Prime Minister José Zapatero also helped establish new standards for female political participation. These changes echo the developmental U.S. gender roles in the past fifty years, and they have made the assimilation into American culture less problematic for Spaniards.

Education Because careers outside the home are now the norm for Spanish women, differences in the schooling males and females pursue are minimal. In Spain, similar to France, there is a greater emphasis on vocational school, as opposed to a getting a broader liberal arts education. Additionally, in the Spanish system of education, there are no grades; students either pass or fail exams at the end of courses, determining whether or not they advance. Unlike in the United States, Spanish culture does not attach a great stigma to failing results. These differences can make it difficult of Spanish immigrants to adapt to the U.S. educational system. As in the United States, higher education is stressed in Spain. Approximately 89 percent of Spaniards graduate from high school, compared to 86 percent of all Americans. Thirty-one percent of those graduates go on to complete a bachelor's degree (compared to 28.5 percent of all Americans) and 13.2 percent obtain a graduate or professional-level degree (compared to 10.6 percent of all Americans). Consequently, a significant number of Spanish physicians, engineers, and college professors have become successful in the United States.

Courtship and Weddings At one time, young Spanish women were allowed to date only when accompanied by a chaperon, but this custom has been entirely discarded. Family pressure for a "respectable" courtship—a vestige of the strongly emphasized Spanish sense of honor—has largely eroded in both Spain and the United States. Long engagements, however, have persisted, giving the couple and their relatives a chance to get to know each other.

Traditional Spanish weddings are often characterized as being less extravagant than full-blown American weddings. It is not customary for the male to present the female with an engagement ring, and there are no bridesmaids or groomsmen during the ceremony. Often the couple exchange *las arras*, or unity coins, which symbolize the sharing of lives and property. Also in Spanish ceremonies, the mother of the groom walks him down the aisle just as the father walks with the bride. Throughout most of Spain, the wedding band is worn on the middle finger of the

Spanish American artist Richard Serra is depicted with an exhibition at one of the Gagosian Galleries. DAILY MAIL / REX / ALAMY

right hand, except in Catalonia, where it is worn on the left hand. According to the American Community Survey estimates for 2009–2011, among the Spanish-born population living in the United States (over the age of fifteen), 59 percent were married, 22 percent were never married, 11 percent were divorced or separated, and 8 percent were widowed.

EMPLOYMENT AND ECONOMIC CONDITIONS

Spain's history of patriarchal politics fostered a culture that, until recent years, kept women from fully participating in the labor market. According to current data from the Organization for Economic Co-operation and Development (OECD), 53 percent of Spanish women participate in Spain's workforce. According to the American Community Survey's estimates for 2009–2011, 65 percent of the Spanish American population over the age of fifteen was in the labor force, as were 61 percent of Spanish American women. Throughout the history of Spanish immigration to the United States, the percentage of skilled workers has remained uniformly high. In the first quarter of the twentieth century, for example, 85 percent of Spanish

immigrants were literate, and 36 percent were either professionals or skilled craftsmen.

A combination of aptitude, motivation, and high expectations led to successful entry into a variety of fields. Of Spanish American workers 41 percent are in management, business, science, or the arts, 26 percent are in sales or office occupations, and 24 percent are in educational services, health care, or social assistance fields. Seventy-four percent of Spanish Americans are private-wage and salary workers, 19.5 percent are government workers, and 6.4 percent are self-employed. The median household income for Spanish Americans in 2011 was $54,808, while the median family income was $65,712. (Household income statistics reflect one or more individuals living at the same residence—not necessarily married or related—and family income statistics apply to blood-related or married individuals living at the same residence.) Single-female households earned an average of $33,723 per year, while single-male households made $46,421.

POLITICS AND GOVERNMENT

With the outbreak of the Spanish Civil War in 1936, a number of intellectual political refugees found asylum in the United States. Supporters of the overthrown Spanish Republic, which had received aid from the Soviet Union while under attack from fascist forces, were sometimes incorrectly linked to communism, but their arrival in the United States well before the "red scare" of the early 1950s spared them the worst excesses of McCarthyism. Ever since the dictatorial government of Spain under Franco, Spanish Americans have tended to vote Democratic as a lasting response to that politically oppressive era. Until the end of the dictatorship in Spain in 1975 political exiles in the United States actively campaigned against the abuses of the Franco regime. They gained the sympathy of many Americans, some of whom formed the Abraham Lincoln Brigade during the war and fought in Spain against the fascists.

NOTABLE INDIVIDUALS

Art Richard Serra (1939–) is a sculptor whose large steel works have appeared outdoors in the United States, Canada, Germany, and the Netherlands, among other places. Serra's massive, often zigzagging and rusting sculptures have drawn both lavish praise for their arresting visual qualities and harsh criticism for taking up too much space. Serra also made a number of successful short films and documentaries, notably *Television Delivers People* (1973), which criticizes mass media and American corporate life.

Business Thomas García-Borras (1926–), a leading figure in the American heating oil business, was born in Barcelona and arrived in the United States in 1955. In 1983 he published *Manual for Improving Boiler and Furnace Performance*, and he was also president of U.S. Products Corporation in Las Vegas.

Literature Poet Angel González (1925–), an Asturian who experienced the Spanish Civil War as a child, is known as the clearest and most honored lyrical voice to describe the emotional fatigue and near-despair of life under the Franco dictatorship. Living in the United States but traveling frequently throughout the Hispanic world from the 1960s until 1992, he taught during most of that period at the University of New Mexico. He then retired in Spain.

Alfred Rodriguez (1932–), writer, has won literary prizes in both Spain and the United States, including the Spanish government's Golden Letters award for outstanding Spanish-language narrative written in the United States. Born in Brooklyn to immigrants from Andalucía, he sojourned in Spain during the bleakest years that followed the civil war. His work continues the classic Spanish tradition of the *picaresque* tale, a penetrating and grimly humorous exploration of the strategies for survival in decayed or traumatized societies.

Novelist Ramón Sender (1902–1982) settled in the United States after fleeing the Franco regime to Mexico and then Guatemala. A professor of Spanish literature at the University of New Mexico, University of Southern California, and University of California, he published in the United States under the pen name of José Losángeles. He is well known for his depiction of the impact of political events on human lives, as in the short novel *Requiem por un campesino español* (*Requiem for a Spanish Peasant*, 1960). He managed to keep a sense of humor throughout the aftermath of the Spanish Civil War, and humor is paramount in his Nancy novels, in which the protagonist is a typical American undergraduate student.

Music Pablo Casals (1876–1973), an internationally celebrated cellist, was among the political refugees from the Spanish Civil War. In addition to his lyrically beautiful playing, he was known for his adaptations of Spanish folk music, especially from his own region of Cataluña. He was also active in efforts to help other victims of the civil war.

Jerry Garcia (1942–1995) was the wildly popular guitarist and singer for the counter-cultural band the Grateful Dead. Fans of the group, known as Dead Heads, were known to follow the group from stop to stop on its tours. Garcia's father was born in La Coruña, Spain.

Julio Iglesias (1943–) is a singer of international fame, having sold more than 300 million records in fourteen languages worldwide. Born in Madrid, Iglesias released his first full-length album in 1969 and quickly became a star. His son, Enrique Iglesias (1975–), is a singer-songwriter who has sold more than 100 million records internationally.

Politics Henry Cisneros (1947–) served as mayor of San Antonio, Texas, from 1981 to 1989. During President Bill Clinton's administration, Cisneros was secretary of Housing and Urban Development.

William Blaine "Bill" Richardson III (1947–) was governor of New Mexico from 2003 to 2011. Richardson was elected to the U.S. House of Representatives in 1980, and in 2004 he served as chairman of the Democratic National Convention.

Science and Medicine Luis W. Alvarez (1911–1988) was a physicist who worked on the Manhattan Project during World War II and won the Nobel Prize in Physics in 1968. He spent the majority of his professional career on the faculty at the University of California, Berkeley.

Neurologist Luis García-Buñuel (1931–) was born in Madrid and immigrated to the United States in 1956. He headed neurology services in several American hospitals and in 1984 became chief of staff at the Veterans Administration Medical Center in Phoenix, Arizona.

Sports Mary Joe Fernández Godsick (1971–), born María José Fernández, is a tennis player who finished second in the Australian Open in 1990 and 1992 and the French Open in 1993. She also won the gold medal in women's doubles in the 1992 and 1996 Olympics.

Keith Barlow Hernandez (1953–) played Major League Baseball for the St. Louis Cardinals and New York Mets. He won the World Series with the Cardinals in 1982 and again with the Mets in 1986. The winner of eleven consecutive Rawlings Gold Glove Awards, Hernandez is also remembered for his clutch hitting and leadership in the clubhouse.

Anthony "Tony" La Russa Jr. (1944–) was a major league infielder who went on to become one of the most successful managers of all time. When he retired after the 2011 season, La Russa ranked third among major league managers with 2,728 wins. La Russa managed the Oakland Athletics to three consecutive World Series appearances (1988–1990), winning the championship against the San Francisco Giants in 1989. He also won two World Series titles as manager of the St. Louis Cardinals, in 2006 and 2011. La Russa won Major League Baseball's Manager of the Year Award four times.

Louis Victor Piniella (1943–) achieved success in Major League Baseball both as a player and manager. As a player, he won two World Series with the New York Yankees (1977, 1978). As a manager, he won a World Series title with the Cincinnati Reds in 1990 and had several winning seasons with the Seattle Mariners in the late 1990s and early 2000s.

Stage and Screen Cameron Michelle Diaz (1972–) became widely known after starring in the blockbuster romantic comedies *My Best Friend's Wedding* (1997) and *There's Something about Mary* (1998). The recipient of numerous Golden Globe nominations, Diaz has also done voiceovers in animated movies, including the part of Princess Fiona in the *Shrek* franchise, and she has taken roles in dramatic films such as *Any Given Sunday* (1999) and *Gangs of New York* (2002).

Emilio Diogenes Estévez (1962–), the son of Martin Sheen and brother of Charlie Sheen, was an actor, writer, and director. He was part of the "Brat Pack" in the 1980s, a group of famous young actors that included Judd Nelson, Allie Sheedy, Molly Ringwald, Anthony Michael Hall, and Demi Moore. His acting credits include the popular *The Mighty Ducks* film series.

Rita Hayworth (1918–1987), born Margarita Carmen Cansino, was one of Hollywood's biggest movie stars during the 1940s. At the height of her fame, she appeared on the cover of *Life* magazine five times. Her father, Eduardo Cansino Sr., was a dancer and actor born in Seville, Spain.

Maria Rosario Pilar Martinez Molina Baeza (1951–), better known by her stage name Charo, reached a wide American audience with her numerous appearances on the ABC television show *The Love Boat* in the late 1970s and early 1980s. Charo, who became famous for her catchphrase "cuchi-cuchi" and for wearing provocative clothing, was a successful singer and flamenco guitarist in addition to being a popular comedienne.

Charlie Sheen (1965–), born Carlos Irwin Estévez, is an actor known for his roles in such films as *Platoon* (1986), *Wall Street* (1987), and *Major League* (1989). From 2003 to 2011, he starred on the television show *Two and a Half Men*. He was fired from that show due to conflicts with the producers but went on to star in another sitcom, *Anger Management*, starting in 2012.

Martin Sheen (1940–), born Ramón Antonio Gerardo Estévez, is the father of Emilio Estévez and Charlie Sheen. He is perhaps most famous for his role as President Josiah Bartlet in the television series *The West Wing* (1999–2006). Some of his movie credits include *Apocalypse Now* (1979), *Wall Street* (1987), *The Departed* (2006), and *The Amazing Spider-Man* (2012).

Raquel Welch (1940–), born Jo Raquel Tejada, rose to fame in the mid-1960s. She is perhaps best remembered for posing in an animal-skin bikini in the 1966 British film *One Million Years B.C.* Her other movies include *Bedazzled* (1967), *Bandolero!* (1968), *100 Rifles* (1969), and *Myra Breckinridge* (1970). She is of both Spanish and Bolivian descent.

MEDIA

PRINT

El Diario/La Prensa

A major Spanish-language newspaper founded in 1913.

Rosanna Rosado, Publisher
West Coast Headquarters
700 South Flower
Suite 3000
Los Angeles, California 90017
Phone: (213) 622-8332
East Coast Headquarters
1 Metrotech Center
18th Floor
Brooklyn, New York 11201
Phone: (212) 807-4785
Fax: (212) 807-4617
URL: www.eldiariony.com

Nat Geo Mundo (Spanish National Geographic)

A magazine about travel, geography, and the natural sciences.

1211 Avenue of the Americas
31st Floor
New York, New York 10036
Phone: (212) 822-9083
Email: support@foxhispanicmedia.com
URL: www.natgeomundo.com

RADIO

WADO-AM (1280)

A Spanish-language station serving New York City. Owned by Univision, it broadcasts news and talk shows.

85 Madison Avenue
Floor 3
New York, New York 10022
Phone: (212) 310-6000
URL: http://wado1280am.univision.com/

WAMA-AM (1550)

A Spanish-language sports radio station serving the
Tampa, Florida, area.

5203 North Armenia Avenue
Tampa, Florida 33603
Phone: (813) 875-0086

WKDM-AM (1380)

Serves the New York City area with Spanish-language
programming.

449 Broadway
2nd Floor
New York, New York 10013
Phone: (212) 966-1059
Email: geneh@mrbi.net

TELEVISION

Telemundo

An American television network that broadcasts in
Spanish.

Emilio Romano, President
2340 West 8th Avenue
Hialeah, Florida 33010
Phone: (305) 884-8200
URL: www.telemundo.com

Univisión

Spanish-language television network in the United States.

605 Third Avenue
12th Floor
New York, New York 10158
Phone: (305) 487-5464
Email: btejera@us.univision.com
URL: www.univision.com

ORGANIZATIONS AND ASSOCIATIONS

Hispanic Institute

Provides an effective education forum for an informed
and empowered Hispanic America.

Gus K. West, Board Chair and President
906 Pennsylvania Avenue SE
Washington, D.C. 20003
Phone: (202)-544-8284
Fax: (202) 544-8285
Email: thi@thehispanicinstitute.net
URL: www.thehispanicinstitute.org

Repertorio Español

Presents and tours Spanish classic plays, contemporary
Latin American plays, zarzuela (Spanish light opera),
and dance.

Gilberto Zaldívar, Producer
138 East 27th Street
New York, New York 10016
Phone: (212) 225-9999
Fax: (212) 225-9085
URL: www.repertorio.org

Unión Española de California

Organizes cultural events from the traditions of Spain.

Francisco Perez, President
2850 Alemany Boulevard
San Francisco, California 94112
Phone: (415) 587-5504
Email: info@unionespanolasf.org
URL: www.unionespanolasf.org

MUSEUMS AND RESEARCH CENTERS

Hispanic Society of America

A free museum that exhibits paintings, sculpture,
ceramics, textiles, costumes, and decorative arts
representative of the Hispanic culture.

Mitchell A. Codding, Director
613 West 155th Street
New York, New York 10032
Phone: (212) 926-2234
Fax: (212) 690-0743
URL: www.hispanicsociety.org

Southwest Museum (part of the Autry National Center)

Collections include artifacts from the Spanish colonial and
Mexican eras.

234 Museum Drive
Los Angeles, California 90065
Phone: (323) 667-2000
URL: http://theautry.org

SOURCES FOR ADDITIONAL STUDY

Fernández-Shaw, Carlos. *The Hispanic Presence in
North America from 1492 to Today.* Translated by
Alfonso Bertodano Stourton et al. New York: Facts
On File, 1991.

Gómez, R. A. "Spanish Immigration to the United
States." *The Americas* 19, no. 1 (July 1962):
59–78.

King, John, editor. *The Cambridge Companion to
Modern Latin American Culture.* London: Cambridge
University Press, 2004.

McCall, Grant. *Basque Americans.* Saratoga, CA: R & R
Research Associates, 1973.

Michener, James A. *Iberia: Spanish Travels and Reflections.*
Greenwich, CT: Fawcett, 1968.

Pereda, Prudencio de. *Windmills in Brooklyn.* New York:
Atheneum, 1960.

Rosenthal, Debra J. *Race Mixture in Nineteenth-Century
U.S. and Spanish American Fictions: Gender, Culture,
and Nation Building.* Chapel Hill: University of North
Carolina Press, 2003.

SRI LANKAN AMERICANS

Olivia Miller

OVERVIEW

Sri Lankan Americans are immigrants or descendants of people from the Democratic Socialist Republic of Sri Lanka, an island in the Indian Ocean approximately twenty miles off the southeastern tip of India. The country has an equatorial climate, with little seasonal temperature variation. Sri Lanka's distinctive central highlands house three rainforests—the Peak Wilderness Protected Area, the Horton Plains National Park, and the Knuckles Conservation Forest. The central highlands receive the highest amount of rainfall on the island and effectively create arid zones in the northeast and on the southeastern coast. The country occupies an area of 25,332 square miles, which is about the size of West Virginia.

According to the 2012 report by the Sri Lanka Department of Census and Statistics, Sri Lanka has a population of 20,277,597 people. Close to 75 percent of the people identify as native Sinhalese, while the rest of the population belongs to various ethnic minorities, including Sri Lankan Tamils (11.2 percent), Muslims (9 percent), and Indian Tamils (4.2 percent), as well as Burghers, Malays, Parsis, and Vaddhas. Seventy percent of the population is Buddhist, 13 percent is Hindu, 10 percent is Islamic, and 7 percent is Christian. Sri Lanka enjoys a robust economy that continues to grow at a rate greater than found in other South Asian countries. The country's economy relies strongly on exports, such as textiles and clothing, as well as tea, rubber, coconut, precious stones, and spices, such as cinnamon, cardamom, nutmeg, pepper, and cloves. Sri Lanka also has a lucrative tourism industry.

Sri Lankans began arriving in the United States in the late nineteenth century, settling in small communities and seeking employment on tea and coffee plantations; a second wave of immigration occurred in the early 1950s. Immigration records, however, did not provide for Sri Lankan as a classification until 1975. The most substantial immigration followed a long period of civil unrest that began in 1975, leading to a civil that lasted from 1983 to 2009, when the military defeated the insurgent forces. The United States Immigration Service estimates that during the twenty-six years of conflict approximately 20,000 Sri Lankans immigrated to the United States. Conversely, during the same period between 200,000 and 300,000 Sri Lankans, particular Tamils, immigrated to Canada.

The 2010 U.S. Census indicated that 45,381 people of Sri Lankan descent lived in the United States. The largest Sri Lankan community is located in New York City, while other sizable communities are located in Chicago; Miami; Newark, New Jersey; Los Angeles; Washington, D.C.; and Houston. According to the U.S. Census American Community Survey for 2006–2010, the states with the largest number of Sri Lankan Americans include California (10,590), New York (5,430), New Jersey (2,241), and Texas (2,337).

HISTORY OF THE PEOPLE

Early History Serendib, the old Arab name for Sri Lanka, is the source of the word "serendipity," which means "making happy discoveries by chance." Sri Lanka has also been called Ceylon, Teardrop of India, Resplendent Isle, Island of Dharma, and Pearl of the Orient, names that reveal its richness and beauty and the intensity of affection it has evoked. Sri Lanka means the "resplendent land."

Sri Lanka has had a continuous record of settled and civilized life for more than two millennia. The actual origins of the Sinhalese are shrouded in myth. Most historians believe that the Sinhalese came to Sri Lanka from northern India during the sixth century BCE. Buddhism and a sophisticated system of irrigation became the pillars of classical Sinhalese civilization, which flourished in the north-central part of the island from 200 BCE to 1200 CE. The first major literary reference to the island is found in the great Indian epic the *Ramayana*, thought to have been written around 500 BCE.

Portuguese traders, in search of cinnamon and other spices, seized Sri Lanka's coastal areas and spread Catholicism throughout the island. In 1658 the Dutch conquered the Portuguese and took control of Sri Lanka. Although the Dutch were ejected by the British in 1796, Dutch law remains an important part of Sri Lankan jurisprudence. In 1815 the British defeated the king of Kandy, last of the native rulers, and created the Crown Colony of Ceylon. The British established a plantation economy based on tea, rubber, and coconuts. In 1931 the British granted Ceylon limited self rule. On February 4, 1948, Ceylon became an independent nation.

Modern Era Sri Lanka, which celebrated fifty years of independence in 1998, is one of southern Asia's oldest and most stable democracies. Sri Lankan politics since independence have been strongly democratic. Two major parties, the United National Party and the Sri Lanka Freedom Party, have generally alternated rule. In 1972 a new constitution was introduced that changed the country's name from Ceylon to Sri Lanka, declared it a republic, made protection of Buddhism a constitutional principle, and created a weak president appointed by the prime minister. In 1978 the Republic of Sri Lanka became the Democratic Socialist Republic of Sri Lanka. The ruling party introduced a new constitution based on the French model, a key element of which was the creation of a strong presidency.

Sri Lanka has made significant progress in shifting from a socialist, centralized economy to a more open and free market-oriented economy and society. It has relatively high economic growth, high literacy rates, and low fertility and mortality rates. Agriculture remains the primary source of income for Sri Lanka's predominantly rural population. Unsustainable agricultural and logging practices have resulted in substantial land degradation and reduction in the size of forest reserves. Sri Lanka was one of the first countries to develop a national environmental action plan for biodiversity conservation, protection of coastal zones, and land and water management.

Since its independence Sri Lanka has been plagued by hostilities between the majority Sinhalese and the minority Tamils. Beginning in 1983 a civil war waged by Tamil separatists in the country's north and east region claimed close to 100,000 lives and severely damaged the economy. The war was largely confined to Sri Lanka's northeastern province, which is six to eight hours by road from the capital of Colombo. However, terrorist bombings directed against politicians and others have occurred in Colombo and elsewhere in the country. Between 1983 and 2009 the Sri Lankan government fought the Liberation Tigers of Tamil Eelam (LTTE), an insurgent organization fighting for a separate state for the country's Tamil minority. In May 1997 the fighting intensified after the government launched a major offensive aimed at opening a land route to the Jaffna peninsula through LTTE-controlled territory in the north. The offensive resulted in approximately 5,000 casualties on both sides and the displacement of tens of thousands of citizens. The unresolved ethnic conflict in the north and the east were key issues that prevented Sri Lanka from attaining its development potential.

Fighting continued to escalate between 1997 and 2000 as LTTE made considerable gains, capturing the Iyakachchi and Elephant Pass military complexes. Following a sustained effort by the military, the government forced LTTE from the city of Jaffna in 1999. In early 2000 Norway persuaded both sides to enter into peace talks, and in December LTTE agreed to a cease-fire; however, the insurgents launched a series of attacks in April 2001. Three months later LTTE carried out an attack on Bandaranaike Airport, destroying civilian and military planes and crippling Sri Lanka's tourist industry.

In the wake of the terrorist attacks in the United States on September 11, 2001, LTTE was persuaded by the international community to participate in peace talks. The two sides met in Thailand, with subsequent rounds of talks being held in Thailand, Germany, Japan, and Norway. The two sides agreed to pursue a federal solution, in which the central government would share power with regional authorities, and held elections later in 2001. Although the elections were successful, relations between the factions were tenuous, leading to a breakdown in the peace process in April 2003 when LTTE suspended any further talks until it was included in the reconstruction process. In October of that year LTTE produced its own peace proposal, establishing an Interim Self Governing Authority (ISGA) that would be controlled by LTTE in the north and east. The proposal was met with resistance and criticism from the south, which argued that Prime Minister Ranil Wickremashinghe caved to LTTE's demands. The hard-liners in President Chandrika Kumaratunga's party pressured her to take action, leading her to declare a state of emergency and assume control over the ministry of mass media, the interior ministry, and the defense ministry. She allied her governement with the United People's Freedom Alliance in opposition to the ISGA and called for new elections. Elections were held on April 8, 2004, and Mahinda Rajapakse of the UFPA was appointed prime minister.

Amidst further political turmoil Sri Lanka was ravaged by a tsunami that hit the island on December 26, 2004, which resulted in more than 35,000 deaths and left even more people homeless. LTTE and the government attempted to form a post-tsunami operational management structure; however, disagreements between LTTE and the JVP dissolved the structure, increasing tensions between the warring factions. In August 2005 an LTTE member allegedly assassinated Foreign Minister Lakshman Kadirgamar, further marginalizing LTTE from the international community.

In 2005 Sri Lanka's Supreme Court terminated Kumaratunga's second term and issued an order calling for new elections. Prime Minister Mahinda Rajapaksa, the UFPA candidate, narrowly defeated Wickremasinghe, the UNF candiate. Rajapaksa campaigned on a strong policy against LTTE, causing LTTE leader Velupilla Prabhakaran to issue an ultimatum that challenged the government's peace policy. At the end of the year and in early 2006, hostilities again erupted between the two parties, resulting in increased civilian casualties. Norway attempted to lead peace talks, but the ongoing violence prevented any real developments. Government-led offensives against LTTE continued in 2006, and the government

In Los Angeles, 2010, two children from Sri Lanka take part in a U.S. Citizenship and Immigration Services art project for children who will be taking the Oath of Allegiance. Children were asked to create images depicting their interpretation of the theme, "We Are America." KEVORK DJANSEZIAN / GETTY IMAGES

formally abandoned the cease-fire agreement in 2007. The government pursued LTTE in the north and the east, culminating in the decisive Battle of Aanandapuram on April 5, 2009, in which many of LTTE's commanders were killed. On May 16, 2009, government troops captured the last remaining coastline held by LTTE. The next day LTTE commanders admitted defeat. Rajapaksa advocated for a political solution, bringing the first signs of peace to the nation in decades.

Following the civil war Sri Lanka became one of the fastest-growing economies in the region. In spite of the country's economic success, Sri Lanka remained embroiled in ethnic tensions as the majority Sinhalese and minority Tamil attempted to reconcile the grievances that sparked the civil war. Some of the Tamil leaders continued to advocate for a separate state, while other leaders sought a federal-based approach with the Sinhalese government. Some military leaders dismissed the Tamils' claims and continued to view the civil war as the fault of Tamils who advocated violence and terrorism. Some Tamil groups avoid using the term "Sri Lanka."

SETTLEMENT IN THE UNITED STATES

The earliest Sri Lankans to enter the United States were classified as "other Asian." Immigration records show that between 1881 and 1890 1,910 "other Asians" were admitted to the United States. It is unlikely that many of these were from Sri Lanka. In 1975 immigration records classified Sri Lankans as a separate category for the first time. That year 432 Sri Lankans immigrated to the United States. Between the 1950s and 1970s immigration from Sri Lanka was closely related to education and professionalism. Many of them took advantage of scholarship programs that had been organized by the U.S. government and individual universities. Once these students had graduated, they decided to remain in the United States. During the 1960s and 1970s many Sri Lankans, Tamils and Sinhalese, who immigrated to the United States arrived as medical school students. Sri Lanka was one of the South Asian countries where the U.S. government enlisted recruits to U.S. medical colleges, and quite a few Sri Lankan medical students took advantage of this opportunity. Many stayed after graduation.

Although Sri Lankan Tamils make up less than 15 percent of the Sri Lankan population, at least 50 percent of Sri Lankan Americans are of Tamil descent. This is partly due to the violence that erupted between Sinhalese and Tamils. After the outbreak of hostilities between the government and armed Tamil separatists in the early 1980s, several hundred thousand Tamil civilians fled Sri Lanka. By 1996 63,068 were housed in refugee camps in south India, another 30,000 to 40,000 lived outside the Indian camps, and more than 200,000 Tamils had sought political asylum in the West. According to U.S. Immigration and Naturalization records, 1,277 Sri Lankans were naturalized in 1996. Of this group 615 had arrived in 1995 and 254 had arrived in 1994, compared with only 68 arrivals in 1993 and 17 before 1985. Sri Lankan refugees admitted to the United States in 1991 (54) and in 1993 (62) contrasted with typical yearly admissions of 2 in 1989 and 6 in 1992. This increase coincided with an escalation of ethnic violence in Sri Lanka. During the 1980s an average of 400 Sri Lankans immigrated to the United States each year. In 1998 322 Sri Lankans were winners of the DV-99 diversity lottery. The diversity lottery is conducted under the terms of Section 203(c) of the Immigration and Nationality Act and makes available up to 55,000 permanent-resident visas annually to persons from countries with low rates of immigration to the United States.

According to the 2010 U.S. Census, there were 45,381 Americans with Sri Lankan ancestry, indicating an 85 percent increase in the population between 2000 and 2010. In addition to fleeing from the escalation of violence between the Sinhalese and Tamils, Sri Lankans also looked for stable economic and educational opportunities. Sri Lankans continued to settle in established communities in large urban centers, including New York; Los Angeles; Washington, D.C.; San Jose; and Houston. California was the state with the highest population of Americans of Sri Lankan descent in 2010. Other states where large numbers of Sri Lankan Americans reside include New York, New Jersey, and Texas. Compared with other South Asian groups, Sri Lankan Americans earned the highest income per capita, $38,312, and 61 percent owned their home. Approximately 9 percent of Sri Lankan Americans fell below the poverty line. Sri Lankan Americans also had the highest rate of foreign-born members in their community (76 percent) compared with other Asian American groups.

LANGUAGE

Sinhala and Tamil are official languages in Sri Lanka. The Sinhalese are the largest ethnic group in the country, totaling close to 75 percent of the population in 2012. Sinhala is an Indo-Aryan language genetically related to such major south Asian languages as Hindi and Bengali. As a descendant of Sanskrit (the language of the *Mahabharatha* and *Ramayana*), Sinhala is also related to European languages such as Greek and Latin. Two varieties of Sinhala are commonly distinguished—the literary and colloquial. Agreement between the verb and the subject is found only in the literary variety.

It is likely that groups from northern India introduced an early form of Sinhala when they migrated to Sri Lanka around 500 BCE, bringing with them the agricultural economy that has remained dominant during the twentieth century. From ancient times, however, Sinhala has included a large number of words and constructions that were borrowed from Tamil, and modern speech includes many words and expressions

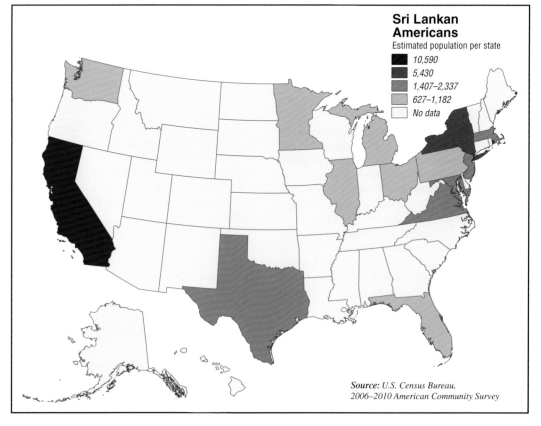

Sri Lankan Americans

Estimated population per state

- 10,590
- 5,430
- 1,407–2,337
- 627–1,182
- No data

Source: U.S. Census Bureau, 2006–2010 American Community Survey

from European languages, especially English and Portuguese. There are twelve Sinhala vowel sounds, and there are also double vowels, which are extended sounds. Double consonants are split to finish the previous syllable and begin the following syllable.

Tamils and most Muslims speak Tamil, part of the South Indian Dravidian linguistic group. Because Sri Lanka was a British colony from 1815 to 1948, many Sri Lankans were only educated in English rather than their indigenous language. As a result, most Sri Lankans who immigrated to the United States prior to 1970 spoke English. Some Sri Lankan American children speak Tamil or Sinhala, but most of them speak only English. Many Sri Lankan adults speak Sinhala or Tamil, especially if they are first-generation Sri Lankan Americans. Socially most Sri Lankan Americans speak English.

Greetings and Popular Expressions The palms clasped together, with a gentle bow of the head and the word "*Ayubowan*," meaning "Wishing you a long life," is the traditional welcome used by Sinhalas. "*Shaaa*" is an exclamation of pleasure and surprise, as one might say upon seeing a beautiful sight. "*Ayi yoo*" and "*appoo*" are exclamations of unpleasant surprise, used for everything from hearing a bit of gossip to witnessing an auto wreck. An expression that originated in village culture and continues to be used by modern Sri Lankans is "*Koheede Yanne*?" meaning "Where are you going?" In village life everyone is interested in where people are heading on the road.

RELIGION

Sri Lanka is a multireligious country of Buddhists, Hindus, Christians, and Muslims. The various religious groups practice their faiths in separate communities that are allowed to express their religious convictions. Sinhalese are predominantly Buddhists, which constitute the majority in Sri Lanka (70 percent). Tamils belong to the Hindu faith and find themselves part of a larger religious group in the United States, as the overwhelming majority of Asian Indian immigrants are also Hindu. Theravada Buddhism (one of two types of Buddhism) was introduced to Sri Lanka in the third century BCE, when a branch of the sacred bo tree under which the Buddha attained enlightenment was brought to the island from India. According to legend, the tree that grew from this branch is near the ruins of the ancient city of Anuradhapura in the north of Sri Lanka. The tree is said to be the oldest living thing in the world and is an object of great veneration. There is no central religious authority in Theravada Buddhism, and the monastic community has divided into a number of orders with different styles of monastic dress and recruitment. The modern orders originated in the eighteenth century.

CULTURE AND ASSIMILATION

While many Sri Lankans arrive in the United States prepared to earn advanced degrees and move into good jobs, some are shocked at how quickly life moves in their new country. For example, for the Venerable Wipulasara, a

Sri Lankan monk who settled in Tampa, meditation had to come between running errands, buying groceries, and taking courses at the local high school to improve his English. Wipulasara created a *vihar*, a small Buddhist temple, in his apartment. Another concession Wipulasara made to American culture was to change the color of his light orange robe because people confused him with highway workers who also wore light orange.

Second-generation Sri Lankans are almost completely Americanized. Nathan Katz, chairman of the religious studies department at Florida International University in Miami, told the *St. Petersburg Times* that "most immigrants come to America and more or less lead the life they want until they have children. Then they want them to learn the old values." Parents often send their children to religion courses. Young people sometimes need to resort to helping each other with the assimilation process. An alliance of students who grew up in the United States but are children of people from India, Sri Lanka, Nepal, and other nations formed the Atlanta-based United Indian Student Alliance, hosting yearly conferences attended by more than a thousand students from thirty universities.

Traditions and Customs Learning is so valued within Sri Lanka that a solemn ritual, the *akuru kiyaweema* ceremony, takes place to commemorate a child's mastery of the first letter when old enough to manipulate the fingers, usually around age three. An astrologer determines every detail of the ceremony: the time of day it should take place, which way the child should sit, and what colors should be worn. The person who teaches the first letter to the child must be an educated, respected person who knows and loves the child. The child and teacher sit together on a mat, and the teacher lights a brass lamp. Milk, rice, and Sri Lankan sweetmeats are set out in precise order, along with the slate on which the child will scrawl the letter. Usually it is "ah," the first letter of the alphabet. However, very few Sri Lankan Americans observe this custom.

Cuisine The traditional Sri Lankan meal is served with all dishes on the table at once: rice, fish and meat curries, soup, vegetables, and accompaniments. Each guest takes a serving of everything with the right hand. The food should not touch the hand above the middle knuckles, and the left hand does not make direct contact with the food but is used to pass and serve dishes.

Sri Lanka boasts a variety of spicy foods and styles of cooking, reflecting the diversity of its ethnic communities. The most noticeable influences have been Portuguese, Dutch, Moor, and Malay. Since ancient times other cultures have traded with Sri Lanka for the spices that grow there. Some of the world's best spices, including cinnamon and cloves, are indigenous to Sri Lanka. Sri Lankan cuisine is distinguished from that of its neighboring countries by its spices, which are fast roasted before they are ground and added to the food. Sri Lankans use two different curry powders. One is referred to as plain curry powder and is

Sri Lankan Americans in Queens Village, New York, pray at an interfaith prayer ceremony at the Buddhist Vihara Temple to aid tsunami victims in Sri Lanka. Over 220,000 people died when the devastating tsunami hit Southeast Asia on December 26, 2004. ANTHONY CORREIA / GETTY IMAGES

similar to the Indian yellow curry powder. The other is referred to as black or roasted curry powder and is used for meats. Along with curry, seasonings include hot red peppers, tamarind, garlic, ginger, cardamom, cinnamon, curry leaves, fenugreek, and tiny black mustard seeds. Red chili peppers were introduced to Sri Lanka by the Portuguese. Modern-day Sri Lankan food has Indian, Portuguese, Dutch, and even a touch of British flavor mixed in. Because foods spoil quickly in Sri Lanka's tropical location, most foods are cooked in liquids to ensure that all ingredients are cooked thoroughly. Rice is eaten at least once a day, usually with very hot curry.

Coconut milk, the liquid obtained from squeezing the meat of the coconut, is central to Sri Lankan cooking. Almost every dish is prepared in coconut milk. *Sambols* are hot, spicy relishes. *Seeni sambol* is a sweet, hot onion dish. Coconut *sambol*, or *pol sambol*, as it is known in Sri Lanka, is probably the country's most popular dish. It is made from onion, coconut, and red chili and is served in every home and restaurant. Another favorite dish is egg hoppers. Traditionally a breakfast food, egg hoppers are made of a rice flour and coconut milk to which an egg is added while being cooked in a pan that looks like a small wok.

Ambul thiyal is a traditional fish preparation that can be kept without refrigeration for several days. This dish is prepared by placing a fish in a clay pot over an open fire, replacing the lid with another clay pot containing firewood or tinder, and cutting the fish into cubes. Chopped green chilies and bay leaf are then added. *Goraka*, a spice made from an orange fruit, is ground and mixed with a little water. Salt and pepper are added to the *goraka*, which is poured onto the fish in an earthenware pot. The dish is cooked over a moderate flame until it is very dry.

Traditional Dress Sri Lankan men did not wear garments on their upper body prior to the sixteenth century. This distinction was reserved for royalty and warriors, who wore protective clothing or armor. The lower garment, the *dhoti*, was worn from the waist to below the knees. Ancient Sinhalese garments, especially those of the upper classes, were divided and neatly arranged in folds horizontally. During very cold weather, a mantle would be worn over the usual dress.

During ancient times Sinhalese women did not cover the upper part of their bodies. Middle-class women wore only a cloth around their hips while at home and used another piece of cloth to cover their shoulders when they went outdoors. Upper-class women were often bare-breasted but typically wore fabric draped over their shoulders and tied above the navel, as well as more elaborate sarongs. Lower-class female attendants wore a breast band.

With the arrival of the Portuguese in the early sixteenth century, Sinhalese dress underwent a dramatic change. Sri Lankan men quickly adopted the types of shirts, trousers, socks, and shoes worn by Portuguese settlers. Prior to this time only upper-class Sinhalese wore shoes. In the Kandyan kingdom women wore a short frock with sleeves that covered the arms. The frock was made of fine white calico wrought with blue and red thread in flowers and branch designs. Kandyan men and women wore jewelry. The men wore gold chains, pendants, girdles, and finger rings. Women wore chains, pendants, girdles, and rings in addition to earrings (*kundalabharana*), anklets (*pa-salamba*), bracelets, and toe rings (*pa-mudu*).

From the sixteenth to nineteenth centuries, respectable women covered their upper bodies, while women of the low castes and the untouchables (*Rodi*) were prohibited from doing so. On their lower bodies women wore a garment that was similar to a *dhoti*. For upper-class women this garment extended to the ankles. Upper-class women also wore more elaborate lower garments in an array of colors. Women in the lower classes were usually naked from the waist up, and their lower garments did not extend below their knees. During the seventeenth century, upper-class men wore doublets of white or blue calico around the middle torso, a white one next to the skin, and a blue one over the white, with a blue or red sash at the waist. A knife with a carved handle inlaid with silver protruded from the garment folds at the chest.

Sri Lankan culture continually evolved as people not only rejected and resisted European and Indian cultural pressures but also adopted and mimicked other cultural aspects of the country's colonizers. Like language and cuisine, clothing represents the cultural changes Sri Lankans underwent during colonization. Western views of decency and propriety altered traditional Sri Lankan dress to be less revealing and more conservative. Disagreements over what counts as authentic dress, or even if such authenticity existed, point to how the various international influences shaped Sri Lankan culture. By the twentieth century Sri Lankan men had begun to wear a shirt and sarong—fabric wrapped around the waist like a kilt. Traditional dress for women is a sari, a long garment made of cotton, crepe, silk, or chiffon, which is draped over the body. Following Sri Lanka's independence in 1948 and its growth as an exporter of textiles, Sri Lankan men and women of all classes adopted what represents a merging of multiple cultures. As noted by scholar Nira Wickramasinghe, the contemporary combinations of traditional sari and jackets are the result of a series of alterations and reflect more the whims of European colonists than the historical dress of the Lankan culture.

The traditional dress, however, is far from universal. A Sinhalese girl may wear a half sari with a jacket, while Tamil girls may wear a half sari that resembles a skirt with a blouse. Sinhalese men wear typically wear a sarong with a shirt called a Baniyama, while Tamil men traditionally wear a patta vetty, a shirt accompanied by a long piece of cloth wrapped around the waist. As Sri Lanka's export market grew, so did its access to Western styles. Contemporary Sri Lankan dress is a mix of Eastern and Western fashions, but younger generations more readily adopt Western trends such as jeans and T-shirts. Western brand-name clothes are more readily available, and people of the working class largely abandoned the traditional sarongs and saris. Most professional Sri Lankans wear Western clothing, and the same is true for Sri Lankan Americans.

Dances and Songs *Bharata natyam* is a classical dance form of India that was adopted by Sri Lankans. During this dance a sari-clad feminine figure, covered with jewels and flowers, strikes a graceful pose. In Sri Lanka announcements of *arangetram*, the traditional first performance by a young artist, are published every month. Since the 1970s Kandyan dances, originally religious dances performed only by males, have become more prevalent in Sri Lankan culture. Dancers wear elaborate chest pieces and headdresses. The dance is now performed by members of any caste.

Sri Lanka is also known for *tovil* dances (described by early Europeans as "devil dances"), dramatic healing rituals performed by masked dancers who represent demons and characters such as *Nag Raksa*, the king of the cobras, and *Gurulu Raksa*, the king of birds. Dancers are trained from around age ten by their elders. The dance lasts throughout one night and is accompanied by the *Yak bera*, the devil drum. The best-known of the *tovil* dances is the *Sanni Yakuma*, when eighteen demons of disease are summoned around a sick person's house. Sri Lankan Americans perform the *Bharata natyam* and the *Sanni Yakuma* for special occasions.

Sri Lankan music was heavily influenced by India. W. D. Amaradeva (1927–), known as Sri Lanka's greatest singer and composer, mixed North Indian (Hindustani) classical music and Sinhala folk music associated with dance, drama, ritual, and social customs. Buddhist chants and narrative styles are also a part of Sri Lanka's musical heritage. *Baila* is a genre of music borrowed from the Portuguese, known for its upbeat style and played with Western instruments. Baila is still the music of choice at middle-class parties.

Holidays The one national holiday celebrated by most Sri Lankans and Sri Lankan Americans is the Sinhala/Tamil new year on April 13 or 14. It is

SRI LANKAN PROVERBS

Sri Lankan culture has several sayings and proverbs drawn from various cultures that once ruled the country, as well as from the dominant religions of Buddhism and Hinduism. The following come from the Buddhist tradition:

- A defrocked monk will be unable to mix with society.

- Whatever you love, you are its master. Whatever you hate, you are its slave.

- If one speaks with a pure mind, happiness will follow him like one's shadow that never leaves.

- O man, correct thine own self first, then turn to guide others.

- A wise man shall not let himself get tarnished.

- May all beings be well and happy, may there be peace on earth and goodwill among men.

- He prayeth best that loveth best, all things both great and small.

- Any coconut leaf will win, meaning that a party can nominate a coconut leaf and the loyal villages will vote for it.

celebrated by cooking and sharing sweets, swinging, pillow fights, and other games. The full moon day of each month, Poya Day, is also considered a holiday. In addition, Sri Lankan Americans celebrate a wide variety of Buddhist, Hindu, Christian, and Muslim festivals and holidays that correspond to their religious preferences.

For Buddhists the day of the full moon in May is the most important full moon holy day of the entire year. On this day Gautama Buddha was born, gained enlightenment, and passed away. Sri Lankan Buddhists celebrate this holiday, known as *Vesak*, by attending religious ceremonies at temples and decorating their homes with lanterns made of colored paper and sticks. *Vesak*, along with all other Buddhist holy days, is still celebrated by Sri Lankan Americans.

Tamils celebrate the harvest festival, *Thai Pongal*, which means "January of milk rice." It is celebrated on the first day of the month of *Thai* on the Tamil calendar. *Pongal* refers to the sweet dish of rice and milk. The festival is a celebration of life and renewal, and participants are encouraged to put aside personal animosities and rivalries. Tamil Americans also celebrate

this holiday. During October and November Hindus in Sri Lanka and the United States celebrate *Deepavali*, or the festival of lights, which symbolizes the destruction of forces of darkness and evil and the re-enthronement of the light of God in the heart.

FAMILY AND COMMUNITY LIFE

The caste system was traditionally used to create social divisions within Sri Lanka. The Goyigama caste of the Sinhalese, traditionally associated with land cultivation, is dominant in the population and in public influence. In the lowlands of Sri Lanka, however, other castes based on commercial activities are influential. The influence of caste in Sinhala society has weakened in recent times, and now a family's wealth can be equally important in determining social status and marriageable partners. The Tamil Vellala caste resembles the Goyigama in its dominance and traditional connection with agriculture, but it is completely separate from the Sinhalese caste. Within their separate caste structures, Sinhalese and Tamil communities are fragmented through customs that separate higher from lower orders. However, differences in wealth arising from the modern economic system have created wide class cleavages that cut across boundaries of caste, religion, and language.

Sri Lankan Americans experience even more pressure to abandon caste restrictions when they acclimate to American lifestyles. Maintaining caste distinctions is not possible for the most part in business and social settings.

Many Sri Lankan Americans live in single family units without relatives, although relatives may migrate to the same community. In Sri Lanka, among all ethnic and caste groups, the most important social unit is the nuclear family of husband, wife, and unmarried children. According to ethnographic studies in *The Sri Lanka Reader*, the youngest child will often remain with the family. Even after marriage the youngest female child continues to assist parents with domestic activities. Although women increasingly work outside the home, they take great pride in providing for their children. Among all sections of the population, however, relatives of the wife and the husband form an important social network that supports the nuclear family and encompasses the majority of its important social relations.

Following Western trends Sri Lanka's social structure has moved away from caste into a class structure based on economics: upper, middle, lower, and poor. In the upper and upper-middle class, economic mobility is the norm. Male and female children are educated well into their twenties, with many women pursuing jobs that were traditionally reserved for men. Lower-class men and women typically abandon their educations to pursue employment to help support the family. Poor families are much more fragmented. Often either the mother or father will be away from the home or country as a migrant worker. Poor families rely heavily upon their extended family to support them and to care for their children. Women are expected to work, and young women typically abandon their education to pursue jobs in textiles.

In the United States local Sri Lankan associations are found across the country. These associations function as important centers for socializing and celebrating Sri Lankan culture. Buddhist and Hindu temples serve as places where Sinhalas and Tamils, respectively, gather and reinforce their community ties.

Gender Roles Since the country's independence in 1948, Sri Lankan women have gained legal rights to education and employment. Prior to 1921 the female literacy rate among Christians in Sri Lanka was 50 percent, among Buddhists 17 percent, among Hindus 10 percent, and among Muslims 6 percent. After independence women entered the educational system in equal numbers with men. A continuing problem in all fields of technical education was extreme gender differentiation in job training; women tended to enroll in home economics and teaching courses rather than in science courses. Sri Lankan American women are encouraged to attend college and pursue a career.

Although the constitution provides for equal employment opportunities in the public sector, women have no legal protection against discrimination in the private sector, where they sometimes are paid less than men for equal work. Women also often experience difficulty in rising to supervisory positions and face sexual harassment. Women constitute approximately one-half of Sri Lanka's workforce and have equal rights under national, civil, and criminal law. However, issues related to family law, including divorce, child custody, and inheritance, are adjudicated by the customary law of each ethnic or religious group. In 1995 the government raised the minimum age of marriage for women from twelve to eighteen. Muslims, however, were allowed to continue their customary marriage practices. During the political turmoil of the civil war, women not only continued to serve as prominent political figures but also led humanitarian efforts that benefited women and children; however, the levels of violence against women during the conflict have yet to be fully tallied, and humanitarian agencies acknowledge that real numbers may never be known.

Education Sri Lankan Americans are highly educated. Most immigrants have completed some college, and many have advanced degrees. Until colonial times the educational system was designed primarily for a small elite. Since independence in 1948 Sri Lanka has also made important gains in education, reaching near universal literacy and primary school enrollment rates. Children from age five to ten attend primary school; from age eleven to fifteen they attend junior secondary school (terminating in the ordinary level examination); and from age sixteen to seventeen they attend senior secondary school (terminating in the advanced level examination). Those who qualify can go on to the university system, which is run by the

SRI LANKAN WOMEN IN POLITICS

Although there are no legal impediments to the participation of women in politics or government, social mores within some communities limited women's activities outside the home for most of the twentieth century. Nevertheless, Sri Lanka elected the world's first female prime minister, Sirimavo Bandaranaike, in 1960. Bandaranaike served as prime minister for three terms (1960–1965, 1970–1977, and 1994–2000). In November 1994 a woman, Chandrika Kumarathunga, was elected president for the first time. Kumarathunga served until 2005. Following the 2010 elections, only ten women held seats in parliament, representing eight of the twenty-two districts.

state. As of 2012 there were fifteen public universities with more than 18,000 students in twenty-eight disciplines, plus 2,000 graduate and certificate students. However, improvements in the educational system created economic difficulties because many graduates were qualified for jobs that did not exist. Women, who made up about 25 percent of the labor force in the 1980s, were particularly affected. Many Sri Lankans who settle in the United States do so in search of better employment opportunities.

Courtship and Weddings In the past most marriages were arranged. Today some marriages between young people are still arranged, but children can decline the mate chosen by their parents. In rural areas marriages have traditionally been arranged between teenagers. The average age at marriage began to increase in the last decades of the twentieth century. This is attributed to the longer periods of time that are needed to obtain a college education and establish a stable career. For Sri Lankan American couples, marriages are very rarely arranged.

In rural areas of Sri Lanka, traditional marriages did not require legal registration or a ceremony. The couple simply started living together, with the consent of their parents, who were usually related. Most Sri Lankan families have limited financial resources and do not spend large sums on wedding parties. However, all families seek to hold as fancy a wedding ceremony as possible to benefit the children and impress their friends and neighbors. Wealthier families, especially in urban areas, have a ceremony. The bride may receive a substantial dowry, determined beforehand during negotiations between her family and her future in-laws. Matchmakers and astrologers pick the time for the marriage.

Contemporary wedding ceremonies have been influenced by British and Western culture. Brides wear white, carry flowers, and are preceded by bridesmaids and flower girls as in the typical wedding in the West. This contrasts with the Kandyan Sinhalese (referring to more traditional upland dwellers named after the Kingdom of Kandy) bride in her traditional costume of the *Osariya* (sari) and the complementing regalia. The Kandyan bride tries to dress lavishly, typically wearing a grand sari with gold and silver thread, pearls, stones, beads, and sequins.

The bridal headgear, the *nalalpata*, is a headband with a gold gem-studded forehead plate and was traditionally worn by a ruler. The *nalalpata* was tied to the forehead of a young prince during a ceremony. A Sinhala wedding is the only time that the *nalalpata* is worn. It is placed on the middle of the forehead with one stem extending down the part of the hair and another two branches extending across the forehead up to the ear. Traditionally the *nalalpata* was a piece of jewelry embedded with red stones.

Learning is so valued within Sri Lanka that a solemn ritual, the akuru kiyaweema *ceremony, takes place to commemorate a child's mastery of the first letter when he or she is old enough to manipulate the fingers, usually around age three.*

The bride wears a mass of chains at the neck. *Padakkam*, or pendants, are the important part of the chains. Starting from the *nalalpata* pendant, each successive chain shows off pendants with Sinhala designs. The *peti malaya* is the last and longest chain encircling the rest. *Peti malaya* means a garland of flowers or petals. The design of the pendants may vary. The *agasthi malaya* is a chain made of agate. Some chains have seeds placed at intervals along the chain. The *seri valatu* is a broad bangle with three smaller bangles joined together. The earrings, known as *dimithi*, have the shape of an overturned cup with tiny pearls dangling from two ear studs. Some brides wear armlets to ward off bad luck. These wedding traditions are still observed by many Sri Lankan Americans.

Interactions with Other Ethnic Groups
According to United Nations statistics, Sri Lanka ranks second in the world in human rights violations. Sri Lankans fight bitterly along ethnic lines. In Sri Lanka the different ethnic communities live in separate villages or sections of villages. In towns and cities they often inhabit different neighborhoods. The fact that primary education is in either Tamil or Sinhala effectively segregates the children of the different communities at an early age. Ethnic segregation is reinforced by fears that ethnic majorities will try to dominate positions of influence and repress the religious, linguistic, or cultural systems of minorities. The Sinhalese are the dominant ethnic group within Sri Lanka. However, they often feel intimidated by the large Tamil population in nearby India. The combined Tamil populations of India and Sri Lanka outnumber the Sinhalese at least four to one.

The ethnic groups of Sri Lanka have been in conflict with each other since the nineteenth century. Ethnic divisions are not based on race or physical appearance, although some Sri Lankans claim to be able to determine the ethnicity of a person by facial characteristics or color. There is nothing in the languages or the religious systems in Sri Lanka that officially promotes the social segregation of ethnic groups. Because historical circumstances have favored one or more of the groups at various times, there has been hostility and competition for political and economic power. However, Sri Lankan Americans peacefully voice their ethnic differences through fund-raising and political lobbying efforts. Others work to erase those differences and promote good relations across ethnic and religious lines.

EMPLOYMENT AND ECONOMIC CONDITIONS

According to U.S. Census statistics, many Sri Lankan immigrants are highly educated professionals who came to the United States seeking employment opportunities. Many start their own companies and become well known in their industries. For example, Sri Lankan American entrepreneurs formed an organization among South Asian businessmen called the Indus Entrepreneurs that aims to provide a support network for entrepreneurs. The 2010 census found that many Sri Lankans were employed as computer specialists, physicians and surgeons, teachers, and engineers.

Sri Lanka has a developing, mixed public and private economy based on agriculture, services, and light industries. Agriculture accounts for approximately one-fourth of the gross domestic product (GDP) and employs two-fifths of the workforce. Services are the largest sector of the GDP and employ one-third of the workforce. Foreign banks were allowed to open "offshore" branches in Sri Lanka in 1979 as part of a government effort to promote the country as an international financial center for South Asia. In 1990 a successful new stock exchange was founded. All exchange controls on current account transactions were eliminated, and more than forty state firms were privatized. The development of a capitalist economy in Sri Lanka led to the development of a new working class. These upwardly mobile, primarily urban professionals formed a new class that transcended divisions of race and caste. This class, particularly its uppermost strata, was educated in Western culture.

POLITICS AND GOVERNMENT

Large numbers of educated Sri Lankans, both Sinhalese and Tamil, lived in the United States, Britain, and western Europe during the 1970s and 1980s. Tamils in the United States played a role in publicizing the plight of their countrymen in the American media and provided the militant movement with financial support. For example, the *Sacramento Bee* reported on the efforts of a Sri Lankan American professor at

Sacramento State University who was a member of the Tamil minority and worked in the United States to help end the bloodshed in Sri Lanka by urging the U.S. government to end military support for the Sri Lankan government. The Tamil Nadu Foundation, Inc., lobbies for Tamil goals and seeks to influence U.S. policies toward Sri Lanka. An increasing number of Western countries have sharply criticized Sri Lanka's human rights record.

NOTABLE INDIVIDUALS

Academia Ananda Kentish Coomaraswamy (1877–1947) was a philosopher born in Ceylon (now Sri Lanka) who moved to the United States in 1917. His writings proved to be integral in providing Westerners with an understanding of Sri Lankan and Indian religions, art, and culture.

Film Chandran Rutnam is a Sri Lankan–born film director and producer. Rutnam worked on production crews for various Hollywood films, including *Indiana Jones and the Temple of Doom* (1984). He directed films such as *The Road from Elephant Pass* (2009) and *A Common Man* (2012) and produced a variety of films.

Government Roy Wijewickrama is a Sri Lankan American who was elected to a four-year term as a North Carolina District Court judge in 2010. He had previously served as North Carolina's assistant district attorney and as a tribal prosecutor for the Eastern Band of Cherokee Indians.

Literature Rosemary Rogers (1932–) is a Sri Lankan–born author of romance novels. Her first book, *Sweet Savage Love* (1974), topped the best-seller list.

Indran Amirthanayagam (1960–) is a first-generation Sri Lankan American poet and essayist who wrote in English, French, and Spanish. Amirthanayagam published two collections of poetry in English—*The Splintered Face* (2008) and *Ceylon R.I.P.* (2001)—and two collections in Spanish—*El Infierno de los Pajaros* (2001) and *El Hombre que Recoge Nidos* (2005), both of which were originally published in Mexico. His French poems were published in Côte d'Ivoire.

V. V. Ganeshananthan is a Sri Lankan American writer whose short fiction has appeared in *Granta*, *Esquire*, and *Himal Southasian*. Her debut novel, *Love Marriage* (2008), which she began as an undergraduate at Harvard, received favorable reviews and was listed by the *Washington Post* as one of the best books of 2008.

Music Dilan Jayasinha, known as DeLon, is a hip-hop artist born in California to parents who immigrated from Sri Lanka. DeLon's success stemmed from the support of the Sri Lankan community, which helped him become the first Sri Lankan with a single on the U.S. *Billboard* charts in 2005.

Stage and Screen Bernard White (1959–) is a Sri Lankan American actor who has appeared in supporting roles in numerous films and television programs, including *Raising Helen*, a comedy starring Kate Hudson; *Land of Plenty*, a drama about post-9/11 life in an urban California Middle Eastern neighborhood; and *Criminal Minds*, a CBS police drama.

MEDIA

E-Lanka News

Online news source based in Sri Lanka. E-Lanka covers a variety of topics, including politics, sports, science, entertainment, business, and technology.

No. 11/1, Pagoda Rd, Nugegoda
10250
Sri Lanka
Email: editor@e-lankanews.com
URL: www.e-lankanews.com

Lankapage

Online publication providing international and local news concerning Sri Lanka.

616 LaGrange Street, West Lafayette
Indiana 47906
URL: www.lankapage.com

Lankatown.com

Online source established in 2001 that provides links to blogs, community events, politics, news items, and dating services relevant to Sri Lankan Americans.

URL: www.lankatown.com

Lankaweb

Online nonprofit, volunteer-run clearinghouse of news articles concerning Sri Lanka and the diaspora.

Email: editor@Lankaweb.com
URL: www.lankaweb.com

ORGANIZATIONS AND ASSOCIATIONS

Sri Lanka Association of Washington, D.C.

Provides resources that focus on social, cultural, educational, and recreational activities and supports nonpolitical endeavors to benefit Sri Lankans living in the United States.

Roy Braine, President
Phone: (240) 654-2067
Email: roybraine@hotmail.com
URL: www.slawdc.com

Sri Lanka Foundation

Promotes Sri Lankan culture in the United States and globally and highlights the cultural and social events of the expatriate Sri Lankan community.

1930 Wilshire Blvd
Suite 1100
Los Angeles, California 90057
Phone: (213) 483-0126
Fax: (213) 413-1233
Email: info@srilankafoundation.org
URL: www.srilankafoundation.org

Sri Lankan Association of New York

Fosters social and fraternal activities among Sri Lankans residing in the United States and promotes Sri Lankan culture for the benefit of future generations. It is a nonpolitical, nonreligious social organization.

Vidura Jayasuriya, President
Phone: (301) 871-5138
URL: www.slanyusa.com

Sri Lankan Youth Organization

Primarily focused on youth in Sri Lanka, the United States, and Canada, this organization provides support networks designed to navigate the tensions between traditional Sri Lankan culture and American cultures.

Aruni Ganewatta, President
Phone: (323) 929-7596
Email: info@slyo.org, slyousa@gmail.com
URL: www.slyo.org

Tamil American Peace Initiative

Works to inform and engage the American people and American policymakers on issues involved in peace-building in Sri Lanka.

Dr. Karunyan Arulanantham, Executive Director
P.O. Box 33936
Washington, D.C. 20033-3936
Phone: (202) 448-5238
Email: info@tamilamerican.org
URL: www.tamilamerican.org

MUSEUMS AND RESEARCH CENTERS

Federation of Tamil Sangams of North America

An umbrella organization of Tamil Sangams functioning within the North American continent.

Dr. Dhandapani Kuppuswamy, President
Email: president@fetna.org
URL: www.fetna.org

Tamil Nadu Foundation, Inc.

Formed in 1974 to assist Tamil people through scholarships and relief projects. It sponsors an annual conference.

S. Deivanayagam, President
12100 Franklin Street
Beltsville, Maryland 20705-1174
Phone: (931) 528-2259
Email: deivy@tntech.edu
URL: www.tnfusa.org

SOURCES FOR ADDITIONAL STUDY

De Silva, Chandra Richard. *Sri Lanka: A History.* New Delhi: Vikas, 1987.

Hennayake, Nalani. *Culture, Politics, and Development in Postcolonial Sri Lanka.* Lanham, MD: Lexington Books, 2006.

Mahinda, Deegalle, ed. *Buddhism, Conflict and Violence in Modern Sri Lanka.* New York: Routledge, 2006.

Nubin, Walter. *Sri Lanka: Current Issues and Historical Background.* New York: NOVA Science Publishers, Inc., 2002.

Ratnapala, Nandasena. *Sinhalese Folklore, Folk Religion, and Folk Life.* Dehiwala, Sri Lanka: Sarvodaya Research, 1980.

Wickramasinghe, Nira. *Sri Lanka in the Modern Age: A History of Contested Identities.* Honolulu: University of Hawaii Press, 2006.

Wright, Gillian. *Sri Lanka.* Lincolnwood, IL: Passport Books, 1994.

SUDANESE AMERICANS

Ron Horton

OVERVIEW

Sudanese Americans are immigrants or descendants of people from the Sudan region of northeast Africa. In 2011 the country of Sudan was divided into two separate countries, Sudan and South Sudan. The two countries share borders with several other African countries; Egypt lies to the north, while to the west are Libya, Chad, and the Central African Republic; to the south are Democratic Republic of the Congo, Uganda, and Kenya; and to the east are Ethiopia, Eritrea, and the Red Sea. The White Nile River flows northward through Sudan and South Sudan and empties into Lake Nubia (called Lake Nasser in Egypt), which is the world's largest man-made lake at 2,030 square miles (5,250 square kilometers). Sudan and South Sudan's location on the Nile River makes it a prime spot for settlements with rich, fertile soil, ample fishing, and productive hunting grounds. According to the *CIA World Factbook*, the area of Sudan (718,723 square miles; 1.86 million square kilometers) and South Sudan (248,777 square miles; 644,329 square kilometers) together are more than 967,500 square miles (2.5 million square kilometers), which is roughly one-fourth the size of the United States.

According to the *CIA World Factbook*, in 2013 the population of Sudan was 316.7 million, and the population of South Sudan was 11.1 million, for a combined total of 327.8 million inhabitants. The majority of Sudan is Sunni Muslim with a sparse minority of Christians, while South Sudan is predominately animist and Christian. There are multiple ethnic groups living in Sudan, including a majority of Arabs as well as Fur, Beja, Nuba, and Fallata. South Sudan has nearly twenty ethnic groups residing in a much smaller area, including Dinka, Kakwa, Bari, Azande, Shilluk, Kuku, Murle, Mandari, Didinga, Ndogo, Bviri, Lndi, Anuak, Bongo, Lango, Dungotona, and Acholi. Both Sudan and South Sudan's economies rely predominately on agriculture, although oil exportation brings significant revenue to the area as well. When South Sudan became a sovereign nation in 2011, an oil profit-sharing agreement that had been in place since 2005 was disbanded, sending both nations' already ravaged economies into further turmoil.

The first Sudanese began immigrating to the United States in the mid-1980s as a result of civil war between the North and South. These immigrants worked predominately blue-collar jobs in agriculture, construction, transportation, and the service industry. In 2001 the United States accepted roughly 4,000 orphaned refugees, predominantly from the South, known as the "Lost Boys of the Sudan." Along with these "Lost Boys," other Sudanese continued to immigrate to the United States in the twenty-first century. While many of these refugees worked in blue-collar positions, others attended universities in the hopes of sending money to their relatives or returning to war-torn Sudan to help rebuild their country.

According to the U.S. Census Bureau's American Community Survey estimates for 2006–2010, there were 38,380 Sudanese Americans living in the United States. This number is roughly the same as the seating capacity at Boston's Fenway Park, home of Major League Baseball's Red Sox. Large populations of Sudanese Americans have settled in predominately urban areas in New York, Iowa, Virginia, Nebraska, California, Texas, and Washington, D.C. Other states with significant numbers include Minnesota, New Jersey, North Carolina, Pennsylvania, and Tennessee. Although the more than forty tribes in Sudan and South Sudan tend to stay in their own insulated communities, the members of these ethnic groups often merge into one greater Sudanese community in the United States.

HISTORY OF THE PEOPLE

Early History The history of the region that is now Sudan and South Sudan dates back to 590 BCE, when the Meroitic people settled in the area. Located between the Atbara and Nile rivers, the Meroitic homeland was invaded by Ethiopians and later divided among three different Nubian kingdoms—Alawa, Makuria, and Nobatia—which eventually converted to Christianity. In 641 CE Islamic Arabs arrived and began to slowly take over the region. Much of Northern Sudan's culture derives from these early Arabic and Nubian roots.

Led by Amara Dunqus, the Funj people, also known as the Blue Sultanate, arrived in Nubia in 1504. This group eradicated the last remnants of the Alawa Christian kingdom and instituted Arabic language and culture. The Funj maintained control of the area until the early 1800s, when Egyptians, motivated by the ivory and slave trade, began invading and taking members of Sudanese tribes as slaves. In 1820, after conquering Egypt, Muhammad Ali Pasha (1769–1849), the Turkish viceroy of the Ottoman sultan in Istanbul, invaded northern Sudan. He imposed heavy taxes on the Sudanese and was seen as an unjust, exploitative ruler, which led to an uprising that Ali brutally suppressed, laying waste to much of the Sudanese countryside, burning the land, and killing its inhabitants.

During the nineteenth century Sudan saw a series of political changes under rulers such as Turko-Egyptian governor general Uthman Bey, who founded the capital city of Khartoum in 1824, and Ali Khurshid Agha Pasha, appointed governor general in 1826. Khurshid promoted agriculture, reduced taxes, expanded the slave trade, and pushed for exploration and expansion on the Nile past the Sudd (a vast swampland that serves as a barrier between North and South Sudan). In 1838 Khurshid was succeeded by Ahmad Pasha Abu Widan, who focused on maintaining a strong internal government rather than expanding the empire. While this helped the area surrounding Khartoum to flourish, it also allowed for an influx of missionaries to enter southern Sudan and spread Christianity among the nomads and native tribes. In 1863 Isma'il Pasha became viceroy of Egypt, and he took a great interest in Sudan bringing it into the modern era. He built government schools, railroads, telegraph wires, and a postal service, and he brought other aspects of Western culture to the country. He also rebuilt the army and continued to push for expansion of the empire to include Darfur and the lands south of the Sudd.

Sudan remained under Turko-Egyptian control until 1881, when the Sudanese leader Muhammad Ahmad took over. He ruled until 1885, when he left control of the government to three of his disciples. Struggles between the Turko-Egyptian government and the Sudanese native followers of Ahmad ensued, and after Egypt became a British colony in 1882, the struggle continued between Great Britain and Sudan until 1898, when the British, under the leadership of Lord Kitchener, defeated the Sudanese at the Battle of Omdurman.

Modern Era In 1899 Egypt and Britain signed an agreement that established their joint rule over both Egypt and Sudan. While the British acted in an advisory fashion for Egypt, they ruled Sudan more formally as a British imperial colony. They divided the country into two sections, with a predominately Arab north and mostly Christian and animist south. In 1916 the British successfully invaded Darfur (the region to the west of Sudan) and made it a province of Sudan. Although Britain withdrew its forces from Egypt in 1936, it continued to rule Sudan until January 1, 1956. In 1955, the year prior to independence, the First Civil War erupted when southern insurgents led by a secessionist group called the Anyanya revolted against the northern area of the country. Thus, while the Sudan was free of British rule, there was a great deal of contention between the North and South, as most of the power and control of resources was given to the North, with less than a half dozen of the 800 governmental positions being held by Southerners.

In 1958 General Ibrahim Abboud took control of the government as dictator, banning political parties and trade unions. Two opposing groups, the United Front and the Professional Front, successfully deposed Abboud in 1964, forcing his resignation and replacing his dictatorship with a parliamentary system, but this new government proved to be disorganized and weak, and lasted only five years. In 1969 Jaafar Nimeiri staged a military coup and seized control of the government. His reign lasted more than fifteen years, during which time he initially recognized Southern Sudan as an autonomous region under the Addis Ababa Peace Agreement of 1972, which marked the end of the civil war.

Under Nimeiri the economy initially thrived due to sustained agricultural projects, increased oil production, and the export of Sudan's natural resources. In 1978 massive oil fields were discovered predominately in Southern Sudan, which could have led to continued growth of the economy but instead caused more problems between the two regions as all of the nation's refineries were in the north and most of the oil reserves were in the south. The tension between the predominately Islamic Arab North and Christian South continued to escalate into the 1980s, and in 1983 Nimeiri instigated the Second Sudanese Civil War when he revoked South Sudan's independence, broke the area into three regions, and imposed sharia (Islamic religious) law. A group of southern soldiers under the leadership of John Garang of the Dinka tribe fled to Ethiopia to form the Sudanese People's Liberation Army (SPLA), which, though it had originated in the South, claimed to be a movement for all displaced Sudanese.

In April 1985 Nimeiri was deposed in a military coup led by Abdul Rahman Suwar ad-Dahhab, who established a temporary civilian cabinet made up of the Democratic Unionist Party, the National Islamic Front, and the Umma Party before elections could be held a year later. The new leader, Prime Minister Sadiq al-Mahdi of the Umma Party, began a series of peace negotiations with Garang's SPLA that repealed sharia law and called for a cease-fire in 1988. This peace did not last long; in June 1989 the Revolutionary Command Council led by General Omar Hassan Ahmed al-Bashir took control, declaring a state of emergency and abolishing newspapers, public gatherings, political parties, and trade unions. This military dictatorship led the United Nations to intervene, passing a resolution in 1992 citing human rights violations in the country. The military conceded governmental control shortly thereafter but appointed Bashir the new president of Sudan before doing so.

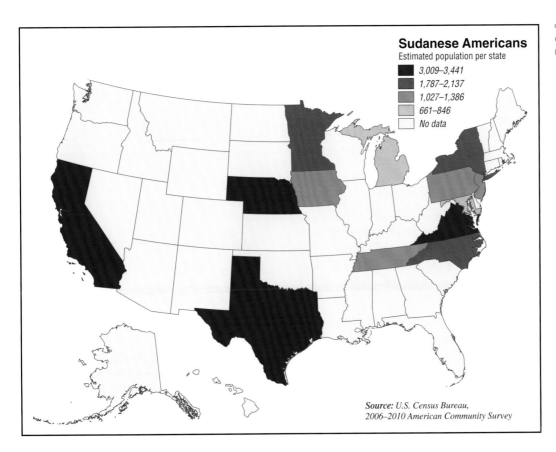

Sudanese Americans
Estimated population per state

- 3,009–3,441
- 1,787–2,137
- 1,027–1,386
- 661–846
- No data

Source: U.S. Census Bureau, 2006–2010 American Community Survey

In 1994 Bashir's government cut all relief programs to the South, which led to a mass exodus of South Sudanese. Southern rebel groups continued to challenge the government, and violence erupted between the areas again. Bashir won the 1996 elections, the first in seven years. Protests from other Islamic fundamentalist groups claiming electoral fraud led to the drafting of a constitution, the establishment of a multiparty system, and the right to religious freedom in 1998, but later that year Bashir revoked all these rights. During this same time, the United States launched a missile attack on a factory in Khartoum suspected of producing chemical weapons to terrorists.

The tensions between North and South continued to escalate over the next half decade, but peace talks progressed at the beginning of the twenty-first century. On January 2, 2005, the government of Sudan and the SPLA signed the Comprehensive Peace Agreement (CPA), which called for the equal division of oil revenues, the demobilization of child soldiers on both sides; and the repeal of sharia law in the South. The CPA also set a six-year timetable for establishing and independent country in South Sudan.

More than two million people died and over four million were displaced as a result of the two civil wars (1955–1972 and 1983–2005) in the Sudan region. In the early and mid-1990s a group of over 20,000 orphaned boys from the Dinka and Nuer ethnic groups in South Sudan, many of whom were away from home tending cattle when their villages were raided, fled the Northern armies and journeyed by foot to refugee camps in Ethiopia and Kenya. The kids came to be known collectively as "The Lost Boys of the Sudan." In the late 1990s and early 2000s, numerous countries, including the United States, established resettlement programs to find new homes for the Lost Boys. The 2005 CPA offered the Lost Boys an opportunity to return home and help rebuild South Sudan.

Exactly six years after the signing of the CPA, in a referendum held in January 2011, almost 99 percent of South Sudanese voted to declare independence. On July 9, 2011, South Sudan became an independent nation. Since that time, the new country has been ravaged by inter-ethnic warfare and continued conflict with Sudan. The most bitter of the tribal clashes is between the Nuer White Army and the Murle Tribe in the Jonglei state on the Ethiopian border. As of 2013, Sudan and South Sudan were fighting over possession of the Heglig oil fields, which lie on the border of the two countries. The European Union, the United States, and the United Nations have sided with Sudan on the issues and have urged South Sudan to keep its military out of the area.

The Darfur region, which is located in the west-central region of Sudan and is roughly the size of France, has been in a state of humanitarian crisis since 2003, when two rebel factions, the Sudanese Liberation Army (SLA) and the Justice and Equality Movement (JEM), broke away from the Sudanese government. Sudan responded by sending out Arab militias known as the Janjaweed to attack these rebel forces. The Janjaweed have been accused of genocide against villagers; the International Criminal Court (ICC) issued arrest warrants for the former Sudanese minister of state Ahmad Harun and the Janjaweed leader Ali Kushayb. Sudanese president Omar al Bashir has been indicted by the ICC for crimes against humanity. More than 400,000 people in the Darfur region have been killed, and 2.5 million have been displaced.

SETTLEMENT IN THE UNITED STATES

The U.S. Census Bureau lists immigrants from Sudan and South Sudan under the category of Sudanese, so it is not possible to determine whether Sudanese immigrants have come from Sudan or South Sudan by consulting Census data. The majority, however, are displaced South Sudanese seeking asylum from their war-torn country, which has only been a sovereign nation since 2011.

According to the American Community Survey's estimates for 2006–2010, there were approximately 38,000 people of Sudanese ancestry living in the United States. Of these, nearly half had arrived in the United States in 2000 or later. The first wave of Sudanese immigrants from the southern portion of Sudan (which is now South Sudan) arrived in the mid-1980s and made American citizens and the U.S. government more aware of the issues facing the displaced populations of southern Sudan.

In the 1990s, after walking some 1,000 miles for nearly three years, thousands of orphaned boys from the Dinka and Nuer ethnic groups, called the Lost Boys, were relocated to refugee camps in Ethiopia and Kenya. They stayed there for nearly a decade before immigrating to the United States in the spring of 2001, when the U.S. government allowed roughly 4,000 Sudanese Lost Boy refugees to resettle in the United States. Girls were not eligible for the program because in order to be admitted one had to be an orphan. As a matter of policy at the refugee camps, boys were housed in one area and girls were adopted by Sudanese families there. The camps established this policy in deference to Sudanese culture, according to which girls could not be abandoned if there were families that could take them in.

Thus, although some women and girls came to the United States during this immigration wave, the majority of them were young men of Dinka and Nuer ethnicity. These young immigrants were spread out over thirty-eight different cities in the United States, and many of them were forced to separate from friends and family members, who were either left behind in African refugee camps or relocated to different cities in the United States. Many suffered from post-traumatic stress disorder (PTSD) and required significant

assistance upon arrival. The Alliance for the Lost Boys of Sudan helps to empower the Lost Boys in the United States and also serves to educate Americans about the issues facing these Sudanese refugees in the United States, the refugee camps, and South Sudan.

The United States imposed economic, financial, and trade sanctions on Sudan in 1997 for its alleged support of international terrorism and its human rights violations. After the terrorist attacks of September 11, 2001, the United States temporarily stopped admitting Sudanese refugees, but the process started again several years later in response to the crisis in Darfur. Relations between the United States and Sudan have been strained in post-9/11 era, as Khartoum has been viewed as a hotbed of terrorist activity. More sanctions were imposed in 2007 in response to the crisis in Darfur, blocking the assets of Sudanese businesses and citizens with ties to violence in the region. According to the American Community Survey's estimates for 2006–2010, California, Nebraska, Texas, New York, and Virginia had large populations of Sudanese Americans. Iowa, Minnesota, New Jersey, North Carolina, Pennsylvania, and Tennessee also had small, but significant, numbers of Sudanese Americans.

LANGUAGE

There are approximately 100 different languages spoken in Sudan, including forms of Arabic, the Nubian language to the far north, the Dinka language in the south, the Beja language in the far east, the Fur language in the far west, and English. Arabic was the official language of Sudan until 2005, when the constitution added English as a second official language. The language predominantly spoken in Sudan is Arabic, the varieties of which include Sudanese Arabic, Najdi Arabic, Hejazi Arabic, and Chadic Arabic. In South Sudan multiple tribal languages, English, and Dinka are spoken.

Most South Sudanese who come to the United States speak English, having learned it in refugee camps before their entry into the United States. Immigrants from Sudan often speak both Arabic and English, using Arabic with their fellow countrymen and English in their everyday life and work environments. According to the 2006–2010 American Community Survey's estimates, 60 percent of Sudanese Americans over the age of five, were fluent in English. However, the vast majority, 85 percent, spoke a language other than English in their homes. Many Sudanese Americans are teaching their children the native languages of their original tribes, not only to encourage them to embrace their culture but also to enable them to communicate with native people if they choose to return to the Sudan region someday.

RELIGION

Almost 97 percent of the population in Sudan practices Islam. The remaining 3 percent of the population is animist or Christian. In South Sudan the population is primarily Christian or animist, with a small Islam minority of immigrants from the north. An independent study by the Pew Research Forum in 2010 estimated that, of the approximately 10 million people living in South Sudan, there were roughly 6 million Christians, 3.25 million followers of various African animist religions, and about 610,000 Muslims. Of the Christian religions, the South Sudanese are Roman Catholic and Episcopalian in the greatest numbers. The Episcopal Church of Sudan, located in South Sudan, claimed to have over 2 million members as of 2005. As in many other African countries, Christianity and animism are often practiced simultaneously.

Sudanese immigrants to the United States generally follow either Christianity or Islam in their new home, depending on which religion they followed in Sudan or South Sudan. Few maintain their animist African tribal religions in the United States, with the exception of celebrating holidays or other cultural celebrations among friends and family. Because most Sudanese immigrants come from South Sudan, they are commonly Roman Catholic or Episcopalian. Most of the Sudanese followers of Islam are of the Sunni Muslim branch, which is often referred to as the orthodox version of the faith.

CULTURE AND ASSIMILATION

While many Sudanese refugees still maintain the traditions and customs of their homeland, most choose to assimilate into the general culture of the United States. Sudanese Americans tend to celebrate Sudanese customs and traditions during holidays or at cultural festivals, while they live their day-to-day life as mainstream Americans. For many, this process of assimilation began in the African refugee camps, where those seeking asylum in the United States intermixed with Sudanese from other regions and prepared to become naturalized U.S. citizens.

Traditions and Customs One ancient custom in some of the Sudanese tribes is ritual facial scarification. Different tribes have their own unique marks that vary in meaning based on tribe, clan, and region. For women, scars can be signs of beauty, marital status, or number of children. For men, the marks can denote bravery or convey wealth or social status. Along with scarring, some tribes use lip tattoos and piercings for the same purposes.

Cuisine Sudanese cuisine is as varied as the many different peoples that live throughout the two countries. Sudan is predominately Arabic and influenced by religious practices of Islam. People who live in the northern part of Sudan are known for simpler foods. One of the most popular dishes among these people is *gourrassa*, a circular wheat cake. They also enjoy *ful*, a dish made of beans cooked in oil. Sweet potatoes are also popular.

South Sudan has more than twenty different ethnic groups living in remote villages, so their dietary habits vary from tribe to tribe. The people who live in the southern part of South Sudan, which has numerous rivers and lakes, rely heavily on fish as a dietary staple. A popular dish in that region is *kajaik*, a dried-fish stew served with porridge.

Sudanese cuisine is most diverse in the central region, which includes parts of Sudan and South

A Sudanese refugee child in California. SANDY HUFFAKER / CORBIS

Sudan and has had the greatest exposure to external influences throughout the history of the area. Red pepper and other spices were introduced to the central region by the Syrian and Arab traders who arrived during Turko-Egyptian rule. People in this region eat a bread called *kissra*, which is made from corn or millet. It is generally eaten with stews that may include meat, onions, dried okra, eggplant, potatoes, spices, yogurt, milk, and peanut butter. Among these stews are *waika*, *bussaara*, *miras*, and *sabaroag*. Stews are served with porridge called *aseeda*, which is made from flour, wheat, or corn. Popular appetizers include *elmaraara* and *umfitit*, which are both made from sheep organs.

Sudanese Americans tend to celebrate Sudanese customs and traditions during holidays or at cultural festivals, while they live their day-to-day life as mainstream Americans. For many, this process of assimilation began in the African refugee camps, where those seeking asylum in the United States intermixed with Sudanese from other regions and prepared to become naturalized U.S. citizens.

People who live in the eastern portion Sudan and South Sudan enjoy a banana-paste-based dish called *moukhbaza*. In the western portion of both countries, the diet is heavily based on milk, cheeses, and meat, as the region is a major cattle-producing area. A popular dish in this region is *sharmout abiyad*, which is served with *aseeda dukhun* (porridge made from millet grain).

The Sudanese usually cook outdoors in courtyards on a charcoal-fueled grill called a *kanoon*. Meals are generally served on a large communal tray that is shared by a large group of people. Food is eaten with the right hand using bread as a utensil. Popular drinks include strong spiced coffee, hibiscus and other herbal teas, and beverages made from regional fruits such as *aradaib*, *guddaim*, and *karkadai*. For the Dinka and Nuer, which are herding societies, milk is a traditional beverage that makes up a large portion of their diet.

Because many Sudanese immigrants to the United States spend extended periods of time in refugee camps, their dietary habits tend to change as they enter the United States. For example, many Sudanese who stayed in Ethiopian camps continue to enjoy Ethiopian foods, such as *njerra* bread with spiced sauces, when they take up residence in the United States. While Sudanese Americans still enjoy eating with friends and family members, their communal meals tend to consist of more American items, including at times fast food and other items purchased at local grocers.

Traditional Dress In adherence to Islam, many northern Sudanese women cover their bodies from head to toe and wear veils. Sudanese Muslim men wear a *jalabiyah* (a long, white robe commonly worn in Egypt) and a turban or small cap on their heads. Rural tribesman of the South wear little to no clothing, in the tribal tradition of their ancestors. Nubians, for instance, wear garments made of cotton, animal skin, or wool with females wearing a *toab* (loincloth), a *rahat* (leather belt), and an upper body covering called a *shaigga*. Men generally wear a single piece of cloth covering the waist to the knees, but some nomadic tribesmen's clothing was influenced by the Arabs with a *araaqi* (knee-length robe), a *sirwaal* (knee-length pantaloons), and a small hat or turban called a *taqiya*. Clothing or lack thereof could sometimes also be used to denote social status. Muslim Sudanese Americans may dress in traditional garb, especially the women, who may wear veils and robes, but many of them dress like average American citizens. Most South Sudanese adopt traditional Western dress in the refugee camps even before they reach the United States.

Dances and Songs Because some Islamic cultures do not embrace dance or song, Sudanese music is more typically associated with the various Sudanese tribes. When Islamic singing is permitted, it is often in the form of recitations of the Quran over music. When sharia law was imposed in 1989, some musicians, poets, and singers were imprisoned and others fled the country. One type of traditional Sudanese tribal music is Hausa, a form of folk music popular in Nigeria, Sudan, and other Central African countries. Hausa music, which originated with the Hausa people of West Africa, uses traditional instruments like a one-stringed fiddle called the *goje*, the *kalanga* talking drum, and the *kakaki* trumpet accompanied by a singer of folk tales or praises. Modern forms of music exist in South Sudan as well, including such genres as reggae, hip-hop, R&B, Afro-Beat, pop, and rap. There is a genre of lyrical music accompanied by drums and stringed instruments in North Sudan. It was popular among the various Sudanese liberation movements as a form of nationalistic music mixed with folk music about the deeds of certain military and political heroes.

Dancing is also popular among the various tribes of Sudan and South Sudan. Sufi Dervishes are folk dancers who enter a state of altered consciousness through dance. While Sufism is a form of Islam, the group is apolitical and resembles early Christian mystic groups in some of its practices. Members of the Sufi order perform these dances in rituals called *Dhikr* ceremonies. These ceremonies are usually held on Thursdays and Sundays. Another traditional form of music and dance is the *Zar*, a female cleansing ritual first introduced to northern Sudanese and Egyptians by southern slaves. The Zar ritual is based in Islam, Christian mysticism, and animism, and it is performed to purge evil spirits from the dancer through the use of a prop associated with the spirits.

In 2009 a group of male and female dancers of Sudanese descent living in the San Francisco Bay Area

SUDANESE PROVERBS

- A fool will not even find water at the Nile.

- He who imagines at the time of harvest that he is really well off and need not trouble to cultivate, finds when the rains come round again that he is a poor man.

- He who does not work when the dawn reddens, will have to work for others when he is blind.

- A locust in the hand is better than a thousand flying things.

- A young crocodile does not cry when he falls in the water.

- The hen with baby chicks doesn't swallow the worm.

- It is a fool who rejoices when his neighbor is in trouble.

formed a group called Shabbal, which is a colloquial Arabic term for a dance move where the female swings her head, letting her hair gently touch her partner's face in an act of appreciation. Shabbal seeks to promote diversity and preserve their cultural heritage through dance and music, which they have performed at events such as the annual Celebrate Sudan Festival in Berkeley, California.

Holidays Secular holidays in South Sudan include Peace Agreement Day (January 9), International Labor Day (May 1), SPLA Day (May 16), Independence Day (July 9), and Martyr's Day (July 30). March 3 is celebrated in both Sudan and South Sudan as National Unity Day, when the Addis Ababa Peace Agreement was signed in 1972.

Other holidays observed in Sudan and South Sudan are Islamic or Christian religious holidays. Christians observe Christmas, Easter, and Lent. Muslims observe Ramadan (fasting), Eid al-Fitr (fast-breaking), and Kurban Bairam (the Big Festival, called Eid al-Adha in many parts of the world). The latter, lasting four to five days, marks the end of the *hajj*, the annual Muslim pilgrimage to Mecca, and is spent visiting family and generally involves slaughtering a ram for feasting. Sham al-Nassim (Spring Holiday), celebrated the first Monday after Easter, is based on an ancient Egyptian festival and involves family gathering and outdoor picnics. Moulid al-Nabi (the Prophet's Birthday), celebrated roughly three months after Kurban Bairam, takes place in public squares and town mosques with feasting, entertainment, and religious celebrations. Animist religions have celebrations and holidays focused on agricultural events; for instance, a rainmaking ceremony is held to ensure a strong growing season and various harvest festivals once the year's agricultural yield is harvested. The Dinka tribe traditionally celebrates the harvest in autumn, when the whole tribe gathers, cattle are sacrificed, and a feast is held.

FAMILY AND COMMUNITY LIFE

Traditionally, the Northern Sudanese have a higher opportunity for economic success and the attainment of education. Some Southern Sudanese Christians were able to attend religious schools in order to elevate their status, but in general members of the various tribes were born into a caste system that was determined at birth. Other tribes, like the Dinka and Nuer, enabled people to progress from their birth class by performing deeds or excelling at agriculture or tending cattle.

Gender Roles Sudan is a male-dominated culture, and women hold lesser status than men. In Sudan and South Sudan, women typically perform domestic duties and take care of the children. Because most of the tribes of South Sudan live a rural lifestyle, working the land or tending cattle, women take an active role in whatever tasks need doing around the house and in the fields as well. In their home country, men and women live relatively separate lives, spending time with members of their own sex, the women socializing at home and the men socializing in clubs or cafes. In the United States, these habits may vary a bit, as immigrants tend to spend time with other Sudanese regardless of gender; thus, there is more socializing between men and women.

Courtship and Weddings Typically in Islamic cultures, women are supposed to remain virgins before marriage, although it is not mandatory for men. Weddings are celebrated in an elaborate manner, often lasting several days and including hundreds of guests. Newlyweds typically live with the bride's parents for the first year of marriage or until they have their first child. Divorce is allowed within the Muslim faith by either the man or the woman, although the woman is often disgraced after a divorce and unable to return to her home or marry again. Sudanese Christian wedding ceremonies are similar to those held in European and American Christian churches, because these rituals originated in those Western countries.

Among the tribes of South Sudan, getting married can involve many steps. For instance, for a traditional Dinka marriage, the groom first declares interest in the bride by asking her family; then he has his best friend declare the groom's intentions to the village elders. A ceremony follows this declaration if the bride's family accepts the offer. The next step involves meeting with the bride's extended family to decide on a dowry price, which is usually paid in cattle by the groom's family. The marriage ceremony is celebrated by a gathering of the families to support the union. Divorce is only granted if the woman is unable to conceive. Dinka tribesman in Sudan often marry multiple wives. Sudanese Americans tend to marry amongst their own culture, and often men return to their home country to bring their significant others back to the United States.

Education Typically, the northern region of Sudan is considered to be more educated, as it is more urban and has public schools and universities. Muslim students attend schools called *khalwa* to study the Quran and learn to be members of the Muslim community. Boys usually receive more education than girls, attending school between the ages of five and nineteen. Girls stop going to school around the age of ten and then undergo training in domestic duties at home. South Sudan has church-run schools for the Christian population, but the majority of tribespeople do not attend school, choosing to work at subsistence living instead of seeking formal education.

Sudanese Americans value education and have made a significant effort to succeed in American schools. According to the 2006–2010 American Community Survey estimates, 81.9 percent of Sudanese Americans age twenty-five or older had earned a high school degree or higher, and 31 percent had earned a bachelor's degree or higher. These rates were equivalent or higher than the rates for the U.S. population in general (of whom 85 percent had graduated from high school and 27.9 percent had a bachelor's degree or higher).

EMPLOYMENT AND ECONOMIC CONDITIONS

Many Sudanese immigrants who come to the United States do so in order to gain an education and return to their homeland to start businesses, work in the medical field, or help in rebuilding the newly independent South Sudan. Others choose to stay in the United States, either working full-time or attending college to earn a degree. According to the 2006–2010 Community Survey estimates, of the Sudanese Americans sixteen years of age and older in the civilian labor force, 21 percent were in management, business, science, and arts occupations; 24 percent were in service occupations; 18 percent were in sales and office occupations; 4 percent were in natural resources, construction, and maintenance occupations; and 32 percent were in production, transportation, and material-moving occupations. Many Sudanese immigrants attend universities or vocational schools at night and work during the day. They often work several jobs in order to send money back to support their families in Sudan or to bring them over to the United States. The first wave of Lost Boy refugees were given three months of assistance by the U.S. government before they had to get a job and repay their plane fare and travel expenses.

POLITICS AND GOVERNMENT

Many Sudanese Americans have worked to establish foundations, organizations, and other humanitarian efforts to help their relatives and countryman still living in Sudan. John Dau (1974–), one of the Lost Boys featured in the movie *God Grew Tired of Us*, came to the United States in 2001, and in 2004 he established the John Dau Foundation (www.johndau-foundation.org), a nonprofit organization dedicated to reforming health care, training health workers, and setting up clinics in South Sudan. Another Sudanese Lost Boy, Valentino Achak Deng, worked with the author Dave Eggers to publish *What Is the What: The Autobiography of Valentino Achak Deng*, a novel based on Deng's life, in 2006. That year Deng and Eggers also set up an educational foundation for Sudanese refugees called the Valentino Achak Deng Foundation (www.valentinoachakdeng.org), to help rebuild war-torn South Sudan and give Sudanese increased access to education both at home and in the United States. All proceeds from sales of *What Is the What* are donated to the foundation.

NOTABLE INDIVIDUALS

Business Zack Dafaallah (1960–) immigrated to California from Sudan in 1987. He is a business entrepreneur educated at the University of Khartoum and California State University–Fullerton. With the help of mentor Michael D. Ames, Dafaallah began mentoring graduate and undergraduate students and started the Titan Entrepreneurs Network. Dafaallah also started the nonprofit organization Sudanese American National Affairs and Development Foundation, which helps Sudanese immigrant children adjust to life in the United States while still embracing their native culture.

Fashion Alek Wek (1977–) is a South Sudanese model of Dinka ethnicity who migrated first to England and later to the United States. She began modeling in 1995, appearing in Tina Turner and Janet Jackson videos, doing advertisements for Clinique and Victoria's Secret, and modeling for famous designers such as Calvin Klein, Chanel, and Donna Karan. She was named MTV's Model of the Year in 1997 and was the first African model to appear on the cover of *Elle* magazine. Aside from her modeling career, Wek also serves on the U.S. Committee for Refugee's Advisory Council in an effort to promote humanitarian relief to South Sudan.

Religion Mohammed Adam El-Sheikh is a Sudanese American religious leader. El-Sheikh completed undergraduate school in Sudan and came to the United States in 1978 to earn a master's degree from Howard University, after which he earned a law degree from George Washington University and a PhD from Temple University. He then served as Imam or mosque leader at Masjid Al-Rahmah in Baltimore, helped found the Muslim American Society, and served as executive director of the Fiqh Council of North America, which is a group of North American Muslim legal scholars and interpreters of Islamic law.

Sports Manute Bol (1962–2010) was by far the most famous Sudanese American athlete, with a professional basketball career lasting from 1985 to 1996. He was born in South Sudan and was of Dinka ethnicity. Bol immigrated to the United States in his late teens, attending Cleveland State University and University of Bridgeport in Connecticut before playing for several professional teams, including the Washington Bullets, Golden State Warriors, Philadelphia 76ers, and Miami Heat. His career highlight was being the only NBA player in history to block more shots than points scored. Bol was an activist for Sudanese aid, starting the Ring True Foundation for Sudanese refugees and devoting much of his time and monetary resources to the Sudanese cause. Manute Bol died in Charlottesville, Virginia, from kidney failure.

Deng Gai (1982–), former professional basketball player, is a South Sudanese American immigrant who attended high school in Connecticut and then Fairfield University, also in Connecticut. In 2005 he was drafted by the Philadelphia 76ers, but he only played in two games. He continued playing basketball for USBL (United States Basketball) and ABA (American Basketball Association) teams. His career achievement was as 2005's NCAA Division 1's basketball season blocks leader.

MEDIA

AllAfrica

AllAfrica accesses and posts daily news about the Sudan and all of Africa from more than 130 African news sources with locations in various African countries as well as Washington, D.C.

Email: info@allafrica.com
URL: http://allafrica.com/sudan/

The New Sudan Vision

This news source, founded in 2006, is dedicated to bridging the information gap among Sudanese and Sudanese Americans based in Africa and North America.

Email: office@newsudanvision.com
URL: www.NewSudanVision.com

South Sudan News Agency

This online news source, founded in 2008 and launched in 2010, features topics of interest to the South Sudan people. It covers news, politics, editorials, current issues, and more. Its headquarters are in Colorado Springs, Colorado.

Email: info@southsudannewsagency.com
URL: www.southsudannewsagency.com

ORGANIZATIONS AND ASSOCIATIONS

Alliance for the Lost Boys of Sudan

This foundation seeks to inform Americans on issues facing Sudanese American immigrants and helps to educate and empower the Lost Boys of Sudan living in the United States.

Joan Hecht, Founder/President
8241 Wallingford Hills Lane
Jacksonville, Florida 32256
Phone: (904) 363-9821
Email: info@allianceforthelostboys.com
URL: www.allianceforthelostboys.com

The John Dau Foundation

This foundation, started by Lost Boy John Dau, strives to help in health care and humanitarian efforts for South Sudan.

P.O. Box 503
Skaneateles, New York 13152
Phone: (800) 759-4443
Email: info@johndaufoundation.org
URL: www.johndaufoundation.org

Sudan Development Foundation

This foundation seeks to aid in the rebuilding of South Sudan by educating immigrants to create sustainable, healthy and self-reliant communities both in the United States and Sudan.

Abraham Awolich, President
139 Elmwood Avenue
Burlington, Vermont 05401
Phone: (802) 264-4887
Email: info@sudef.org
URL: www.sudef.org

Valentino Achak Deng Foundation

Based in the United States, this organization helps to rebuild Southern Sudan through increasing education in the United States and in South Sudan.

849 Valencia Street
San Francisco, California 94110
Phone: (415) 550-8840
Email: info@valentinoachakdeng.org
URL: www.valentinoachakdeng.org

SOURCES FOR ADDITIONAL STUDY

Bixler, Mark. *The Lost Boys of Sudan: An American Story of the Refugee Experience*. Athens: University of Georgia Press, 2006.

Burr, Millard. *Revolutionary Sudan: Hasan Al-Turabi and the Islamist State, 1989–2000*. Boston: Brill Academic Publishers, 2003.

Collins, Robert O. *A History of Modern Sudan*. New York: Cambridge University Press, 2008.

Eggers, Dave. *What Is the What*. New York: Vintage, 2007.

Holt, P. M., and M. W. Daly. *A History of Sudan: From the Coming of Islam to the Present Day*, 5th ed. New York: Longman, 2000.

Holtzman, Jon. *Nuer Journeys, Nuer Lives: Sudanese Refugees in Minnesota*. Boston: Allyn and Bacon, 2007.

Khalid, Mansur. *War and Peace in Sudan: A Tale of Two Countries*. New York: Columbia University Press, 2003.

Shandy, Dianna. *Nuer-American Passages: Globalizing Sudanese Migration*. Gainesville: University Press of Florida, 2007.

SWEDISH AMERICANS

Mark A. Granquist

OVERVIEW

Swedish Americans are immigrants, or the descendants of immigrants, from the Scandinavian nation of Sweden. Making up the eastern half of the Scandinavian Peninsula in northern Europe, Sweden only shares a direct border with Norway and Finland, with its nearest neighbors across the Baltic Sea being Finland, Estonia, Latvia, and Lithuania to the east and Poland, Germany, and Denmark to the south. Sweden measures 173,745 square miles (449,964 square kilometers) in area, roughly the combined size of California and Massachusetts.

A September 2012 estimate published by Statistika Centralbyrån (Statistics Sweden) placed the Swedish population at roughly 9.5 million. Virtually all Swedes officially belong to the Lutheran State Church of Sweden, though there are small groups of Pentecostal, Methodist, Covenant, Baptist, and Roman Catholic worshippers. With a nominal gross domestic product of roughly $540 billion, Sweden's economy was ranked twenty-first in the world in the International Monetary Fund's 2011 estimates. However, the World Economic Forum's 2012–2013 Global Competitiveness Report, which rates nations' creativity, production, and ability to compete in the global market, placed Sweden fourth—topped only by Switzerland, Singapore, and Finland.

The Swedish were among the first to settle in America, establishing the colony of New Sweden in what is now Delaware in 1638. But the majority of today's Swedish American population is descended from the million or more Swedish immigrants who came to the United States after its western expansion in the late nineteenth and early twentieth centuries, settling primarily in Illinois (particularly in and around Chicago), Michigan, Minnesota, and Wisconsin. After World War II, the nature of Swedish immigration to the United States changed significantly, with fewer agricultural and industrial workers arriving and considerably more scientists and engineers. By the late twentieth and early twenty-first centuries, the largest demographic of Swedish immigrants to the United States comprised physicists, chemists, geneticists, and engineers, who either joined research teams and design projects or completed advanced degrees at U.S. institutions offering placement on such teams.

The U.S. Census Bureau's 2006–2010 American Community Survey—compiled for a 2011 report—placed the number of Americans of Swedish descent at roughly 4.3 million, a number roughly equivalent to the population of Kentucky. Largely in keeping with early settlement patterns, the states with the largest number of Swedish Americans are still Minnesota, Illinois, Michigan, and Wisconsin, joined now by California and Washington. While early immigrants tended to form isolated communities, contemporary Swedish Americans are, generally speaking, fully absorbed into the general population.

HISTORY OF THE PEOPLE

Early History Swedes are descended from the Gothic tribes that moved into Sweden following the melting glaciers, probably during the Neolithic period. The various Gothic settlements were centered in eastern Sweden and the island of Gotland in the Baltic Sea. During the Viking period (800–1050 BCE) the Swedes pushed eastward into Russia and were trading as far south as the Black Sea. In Russia, these Swedes (labeled by the local Slavs as the "Rus") ruled many areas, but were found especially in the trading town of Novgorod. By about 1000, most of central and eastern Sweden was united in the kingdom of the Svear, although this was disputed by their powerful neighbors, the Danes and the Norwegians. Christianity was introduced to the Swedes by St. Ansgar in 829, although it was slow to take hold and was not fully established until the late twelfth century, under the rule of King Eric IX. Medieval Sweden was slowly incorporated into the European world and began to form the political and social structures characteristic of its society even to this day. King Magnus VII was able to unite Norway and Sweden under his rule in 1319, but the union was unstable and did not last. In 1397 Norway and Sweden were united with Denmark, under the rule of the Danish queen Margaret in the Union of Kalmar.

Modern Era Sweden felt slighted in the Danish-dominated union, however, and after a Danish massacre of Swedish nobles in 1520, the Swedes rose against the Danes and, led by King Gustav Vasa, freed themselves from Danish rule in 1523. Swedish king Gustavus Adolphus fought for the Protestants in the

Queen Silvia Gustaf of Sweden and Philadelphia Mayor Michael Nutter visit the American Swedish Historical Museum in Philadelphia, Pennsylvania, for the 375th anniversary of the founding of New Sweden. BILL MCCAY / GETTY IMAGES

Thirty Years War (1618–1648) and gained possessions for Sweden in northern Germany; King Charles X gained further territory in Poland and the Baltic States following victories against Denmark, Russia, and Poland. Sweden's age of glory, during which it controlled the production and distribution of nearly all grain, iron, and furs in Europe and settled an area along the colonial American Delaware River called New Sweden, ended with the rise of Russia, which defeated the Swedes in the Northern War (1700–1721).

The late eighteenth century saw Sweden join the Enlightenment culture, most notably characterized by the introduction of the world's first Freedom of the Press Act by Sweden and Finland in 1766. Significant individual contributions were made during this period by botanist, physician, and zoologist Carl Linnaeus (1707–1778), whose work pioneered both the modern taxonomical system and the science of ecology as it is known today. Such progress was made possible in part by the adoption of parliamentary governance. This so-called Age of Freedom came to an end—along with the principles of the Enlightenment—when King Gustav III (1746–1792), who had come to power in 1771, declared Sweden an absolute monarchy in a French-supported coup d'état in 1772.

It has been speculated that Gustav III's despotism significantly weakened Sweden's economy, which remained almost exclusively agricultural while much of Europe industrialized. This left Sweden weakened and vulnerable during the Napoleonic wars, and in 1809 it was forced to cede Finland to Russia after a series

of military defeats but received Norway as compensation in 1814 (a union that lasted until 1905). During the nineteenth century, Sweden underwent economic, social, and political transformations that only partially stemmed a large-scale immigration to North America. These changes are commonly believed to have laid the sociopolitical groundwork for the adoption and growth of democratic principles in Sweden as it finally began to industrialize around 1870.

Parliamentary governance was reinstituted in Sweden in 1917, forming the constitutional monarchy and representative democracy still in place today. Sweden maintained political and military neutrality throughout World Wars I and II, though it did manufacture military equipment for Germany under duress during the latter war. Beginning in 1943, however, Sweden aided the Norwegians in their resistance against Nazi Germany and mounted efforts to rescue numerous Danish Jews slated for internment. As the war drew to a close, Sweden stepped up its efforts, aiding in numerous internment rescue missions and providing various other humanitarian services to its European neighbors.

Political neutrality slowly fell out of favor during global financial crises in both the 1970s and late 1980s. Though it had long declined participation in global organizations, namely the North Atlantic Treaty Organization (NATO), popular and political pressure to correct a devastated economy led Sweden to join the newly formed European Union (EU) in 1995. Since that time, Sweden has also joined NATO, providing logistical and military support for operations in Kosovo and Afghanistan. From July to December of 2009, Sweden chaired the EU, with Swedish prime minister Fredrik Reinfeldt (born in 1965) serving as president of the European Council for that term.

SETTLEMENT IN THE UNITED STATES

In 1638, during Sweden's era as a European power, a Swedish merchant company founded the colony of New Sweden in Delaware. This became an official Swedish colony under the leadership of governor Johan Printz but struggled because of indifference from the Swedish government; the colony never prospered, reaching a total of only about five hundred inhabitants. In 1655 the Dutch took the colony by force; the Dutch were in turn defeated by the English eleven years later. A Swedish-speaking enclave existed in the Delaware River valley until the nineteenth century, however. In fact, Swedes from this area played key roles in early Revolutionary America. John Hanson of Maryland, a descendant of the New Sweden settlers, was the first president of the U.S. Congress, from 1781 to 1782.

The immigration of Swedes to the United States during the nineteenth century was a movement of youth—young Swedes leaving their homeland for improved economic opportunity in the United States. The first waves of immigration were more rural and family oriented, but as the immigration continued this pattern changed. Young, single men (and later women) left Sweden to find employment in American cities. There were those who resented the political, social, and religious confinement of nineteenth-century Sweden, of course, but research has shown that the overwhelming motivation driving the emigrants westward over the Atlantic was economic advancement.

Trade and adventure brought a small number of Swedes to the United States in the early national expansion, but large-scale immigration did not occur until the construction of the railroads, as the rail companies began advertising the sale of their newly acquired lands. From 1851 to 1930, more than 1.2 million Swedes immigrated to the United States, a number that represented perhaps 25 percent of the total population of Sweden at the time.

The first great wave arrived between 1868 and 1873, as famine in Sweden and opportunity for land in the United States drove 100,000 Swedes, mainly farming families, from their homeland. They relocated primarily in the upper Midwest. The largest wave of immigrants, approximately 475,000, arrived between 1880 and 1893, again due to economic struggles in Sweden. This time not only farmworkers emigrated, but also loggers, miners, and factory workers from the cities. The American depression of 1893 slowed Swedish immigration until the first decade of the twentieth century, when 220,000 Swedes came to the United States. World War I halted emigration again, and improved economic conditions in Sweden have kept it to a minimum since 1920.

The geographical dispersal of Swedish immigrant settlement also changed during the course of the nineteenth century, varying with economic conditions and opportunities. The initial wave of immigration in the 1840s and 1850s was directed toward rural areas of Illinois and Iowa, especially in areas surrounding the Mississippi River valley and Chicago. In the 1860s and 1870s immigration shifted toward Minnesota and the upper Midwest, and the Swedish population of Minneapolis grew substantially. In the 1880s rural migration spread to Kansas, Nebraska, and the Dakotas. With the changing complexion of immigration later in the century (more single youth heading toward urban areas) came the growth of immigration to both coasts. Significant Swedish American centers were established in Connecticut, Massachusetts, and Maine in the east and in Washington and California in the west, along with a Swedish colony in Texas.

> Most dear to me are the shoes my mother wore when she first set foot on the soil of America. You must see these shoes to appreciate the courage my parents had and the sacrifices they made giving up family and security to try for a better life, but not knowing what lay ahead. We came to this country as many others did, POOR! My mother's shoes tell a whole story.
>
> Birgitta Hedman Fichter, 1924, cited in *Ellis Island: An Illustrated History of the Immigrant Experience*, edited by Ivan Chermayeff et al. (New York: Macmillan, 1991).

By the turn of the twentieth century, about 60 percent of Swedish Americans were settled in urban areas. In fact, by 1900 Chicago was the second-largest Swedish city in the world (second only to Sweden's capital and largest city, Stockholm). Among American cities with significant Swedish populations were Minneapolis, New York City, Seattle/Tacoma, Omaha, and San Francisco. Smaller cities with a relatively high concentration of Swedes included Worchester, Massachusetts; Jamestown, New York; and Rockford, Illinois. By 1930, Swedish America (a term generally referring only to first- and second-generation Swedish Americans) had peaked at a population of 1.5 million, and secondary, internal migrations had dispersed the Swedes around the country.

The U.S. Census Bureau's 2006–2010 American Community Survey placed the total number of Americans with Swedish ancestry at roughly 4.3 million, with their geographic dispersal changing very little since the early twentieth century. By the Census Bureau's estimations, the states with the largest Swedish populations (by percentage of total state population) were still Minnesota (9.9 percent), North Dakota (5.0%), Nebraska (4.9 percent), Utah (4.3%), and South Dakota (3.9 percent).

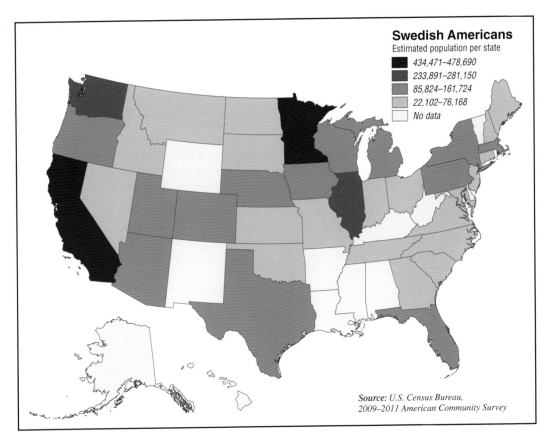

Swedish Americans
Estimated population per state

- 434,471–478,690
- 233,891–281,150
- 85,824–161,724
- 22,102–76,168
- No data

*Source: U.S. Census Bureau,
2009–2011 American Community Survey*

Coming from a Protestant, northern European country, Swedish immigrants have generally been well accepted by mainstream America and have tended to blend in easily with their neighbors, especially in the Midwest. Overall, they are a literate, skilled, and hard-working group and have assimilated into mainstream American culture seamlessly.

LANGUAGE

Swedish is a North Germanic language, related to Norwegian, Danish, and German. Although most Swedes speak Swedish, which is the national language, there are also a number of official minority languages in Sweden: Finnish, Sami, Romani, Yiddish, and Meänkieli, a Finnish dialect. Into the modern period there were some Swedish dialects present in various regions of the country, but by the twentieth century these variations had largely disappeared. Swedish uses the standard Roman alphabet, along with the additional vowels "ä," "ö", and "å." The language is pronounced with a particular "sing-song" lilt, and in areas of heavy Scandinavian settlement in the United States (especially the upper Midwest) this lilt is apparent among English-speaking descendants of the Scandinavian immigrants.

For the immigrants in the United States, Swedish remained the standard language, especially at home and at church, but the settlers soon learned enough English to manage their affairs. Some picked up a fractured combination of English and Swedish, which was derisively called "Swinglish." As the cultural world of Swedish America developed, English words and expressions crept into the community, and a distinctive form of American Swedish developed that maintained older linguistic traditions of the Sweden of the 1860s and 1870s. The immigrant community was divided over the question of language, with some urging the retention of Swedish, and others seeking a rapid transition to English. For many older immigrants, especially of the first generation, English remained a very foreign language with which they were not comfortable. Swedish remained the language of the churches and social organizations, but the transition to English was rapid, especially among the children of the immigrants. By 1920 English was beginning to replace Swedish in the immigrant community. Bilingual approaches were a temporary measure in many immigrant organizations, a measure intended to meet the needs of both younger and older members of the immigrant community. As of 2010, however, the U.S. Census Bureau's American Community Survey estimated that only 96.6 percent of Swedish Americans reported speaking only English at home, and 99.5 percent reported being proficient in English.

Greetings and Popular Expressions

God morgon ("goo mor-on")

Good morning

God dag ("goo dahg")

Good day, or good afternoon

God afton ("goo ahf-ton")

Good evening

God natt ("goo naht")

Good night

Pååterseende ("paw aw-ter-seh-en-deh")

I'll be seeing you

Adjö ("ah-yoe")

Good-bye

Hur står det till? ("hewr stohr deh teel")

How are you?

Tak ("tahk")

Thanks!

Förlåt ("foer-loht")

Excuse me

Var så god ("vahr soh goo")

You're welcome

Lycka till! ("leuk-kah teel")

Good luck

Vi ses i morgon ("vee sehs ee mor-on")

See you tomorrow

RELIGION

The Church of Sweden, the official state church of the country, is a part of the Lutheran family of Protestant Christianity and is by far the largest religious institution in Sweden. Having converted to Christianity rather late in the medieval period, Sweden early on joined the Protestant Reformation of the sixteenth century. Under the direction of King Gustav Vasa the Catholic Church organization in Sweden was transformed to Lutheranism, which became the official religion of the state. In fact, until the mid-nineteenth century it was illegal for Swedes to be anything *but* Lutheran or to engage in private religious devotions or study outside of church sponsorship. The priests of the Church of Sweden were civil servants. Besides their religious duties these priests kept the citizenship and tax records and functioned as the local representatives of governmental power. This state church system was prone to abuse and stagnation, and many Swedes, both clergy and laity, sought to reform and renew it over the years.

In the eighteenth and nineteenth centuries a movement called Pietism made its way from Germany into Scandinavia, seeking to reform the church and the lives of individual believers. Stressing personal conversion and morality, the Pietists were critical of the state church and pressed for reform of both the church and the government. They also sought a change in governmental policy to allow for more freedom of religious expression in Sweden, including religious practices outside the Church of Sweden. Over the course of the century many of the changes proposed by the Pietists were enacted by the church and the government.

It is this religious background that Swedish immigrants brought to the United States. They were officially Lutheran, but many were unhappy with state church Christianity in Sweden and sought different forms of religious expression. A few early immigrants came to the United States to escape religious persecution. For the vast majority, however, the motivation was economic, although they welcomed the chance to worship in their own way. Some found other forms of Protestantism more to their liking, and they formed Swedish Baptist and Swedish Methodist groups, which in turn exported these movements to Sweden.

In the 1840s and 1850s various Swedish Americans began religious activities among their fellow immigrants. Notable names include: Gustav Unonius (Episcopalian); Olof and Jonas Hedstrom (Methodist); Gustaf Palmquist and F. O. Nilsson (Baptist); and L. P. Esbjörn, T. N. Hasselquist, Erland Carlsson, and Eric Norelius (Lutherans). In 1851 the Swedish American Lutherans organized as part of an American Lutheran denomination, but they later broke away to form the independent Augustana Synod, the largest religious group in Swedish America. The Baptists and Methodists also formed their own denominational groups related to their American counterparts. The growth of these groups was fueled by the waves of immigrants after 1865, and the denominations struggled to keep up with the demand for pastors and congregations.

The Augustana Synod practiced a Lutheranism influenced by Pietism. Other immigrants thought that Augustana was still too Lutheran and sought a freer type of Christian organization that relied more heavily on Pietist traditions. Both within and outside Augustana congregations these immigrants formed mission societies that were the core of future congregations. During the 1870s and 1880s, despite the wishes of Augustana leaders, this movement broke away from Augustana and Lutheranism, forming independent congregations. The movement eventually yielded two other Swedish American denominations, the Swedish Mission Covenant Church (1885) and the Swedish Evangelical Free Church (1884). These two groups, along with the Lutherans, Methodists, and Baptists were the largest religious groups in the Swedish American community.

The immigrant religious denominations were easily the largest and most influential organizations within Swedish America. These groups soon began to form congregations, schools, hospitals, nursing homes, orphanages, and seminaries to serve the needs of their

SWEDISH KRINGLE

Ingredients
Dough:

1 cup all-purpose flour

½ cup butter

1 tablespoon water, or as needed

Filling:

1 cup water

½ cup butter

1 cup all-purpose flour

3 eggs

1 teaspoon almond extract

Glaze:

1 cup powdered sugar

1 tablespoon heavy cream

1 tablespoon butter, softened

1 teaspoon almond extract

Preparation

Preheat oven to 350°F.

To make the dough:

Cut butter into flour using a knife or pastry blender. Add water as needed and mix until crumbly, leaving pea sized chunks. On a floured surface, roll the dough out to 3 or 4 inches wide. Place on a rectangular cookie sheet.

To make the filling:

In a small saucepan over high heat, bring 1 cup water and ½ cup butter to a boil. Remove from heat and stir in flour; mix until smooth. Beat in eggs 1 at a time, mixing well after each. Stir in 1 teaspoon almond extract. Spread over dough.

Bake for 55–60 minutes. The pastry will fall a little as it cools.

To make the glaze:

While kringle is baking, combine powdered sugar, cream, 1 tablespoon butter, and 1 teaspoon almond extract. Spread over pastry as soon as it's removed from the oven.

Serves 8

community. Much of the cultural and social life of the immigrant communities was channeled through the churches. Still, these religious groups only formally enrolled about 20 percent of all immigrants with 70 percent in Augustana and the remaining 30 percent in the other denominations. The churches reached out beyond their membership to serve many others in the immigrant community, but some Swedes chose to join American churches or no church at all. It was a tremendous change for these immigrants to leave a mandatory state church system for one they had to intentionally join and in which they had to financially support a specific congregation.

These immigrant churches weathered acculturation and assimilation better than other immigrant institutions. Most churches made the transition to English during the 1920s and 1930s and continued to grow in the twentieth century. Augustana joined with other American Lutherans in 1962; the Methodists merged with American Methodism in 1942, and the Evangelical Free Church began to encompass other Scandinavian free church movements in 1950. The Baptist General Conference and the Evangelical Covenant Church remain independent organizations. Many of the congregations and colleges of these immigrant religious groups retain a strong interest in their ethnic heritage, with Augustana leading the most significant efforts toward Swedish American cultural preservation well into the twenty-first century.

CULTURE AND ASSIMILATION

In general, Swedish immigrants made a fairly quick and smooth transition to life in their new country, and most became quickly Americanized. As a northern European people, the Swedes shared a common religious and social heritage with Americans, as well as a common linguistic base (English being a Germanic language). Swedish immigrants settled over a wide range of areas. Because they were drawn mostly to cities rather than to tight-knit rural settlements, they were immersed immediately in American culture. In addition, there was a growing interest in, and influence from, America in nineteenth-century Sweden. During the first decade of the twentieth century, the Swedish American community was continually replenished by newcomers; however, World War I brought with it xenophobic attitudes, which resulted in a drastic drop in immigration after 1914 and forced the Swedish American community to assimilate rapidly.

The concept of Swedish America furthered the acculturation process. In an essay in *The Immigration of Ideas* (1968), Conrad Bergendoff described the community as "a state of thinking and feeling that bridged the Atlantic." In this enclave, which existed from the Civil War until the Great Depression, first- and second-generation immigrants created their own society, helping one another make the transition to a new culture. After World War I this community was rapidly integrated into the larger American society. The most telling indicator of this was the transition from the use of Swedish to English. By 1935 the majority of Swedish Americans primarily spoke the language of their new home.

With assimilation and acculturation, though, came a renewed interest in Swedish history and culture as children and grandchildren of immigrants sought to preserve some of the traditions of their homeland. Many institutions dedicated to this preservation were established: historical and fraternal societies, museums, and foundations. It was this dynamic that historian Marcus Hansen observed in his own generation, prompting his famous axiom, "What the son wishes to forget, the grandson wishes to remember."

Relations with Other Americans Swedish immigrants have typically interacted most readily with other Nordic American groups, namely Danes, Norwegians, and Finns. American Swedes have long held a particularly close affinity with the Finns, many of whom were Swedish-speaking settlers from western Finland (Sweden had ruled Finland from the Middle Ages until 1809). There was a special, good-natured rivalry between the Swedes and the Norwegians in the United States, which still results in quite a few "Swede" and "Norwegian" jokes. Swedes have also mixed easily with the German Americans, especially those who are Lutheran.

Cuisine Traditional Swedish dishes represent the cooking of the Swedish countryside, which is heavily weighted toward meat, fish, potatoes, and other starches. Pickled herring, a fish commonly found in the Baltic and North Seas, is a traditional Swedish staple. *Gravlax* is raw, cured salmon served on crisp bread, which are flat wafers made of rye. Pea soup and pancakes are traditionally served together, and crawfish are popular in the summertime. One of the most ubiquitous elements of Swedish cuisine is lingonberry jam, which is made from the tart red lingonberry (similar to the cranberry) and is used to flavor everything from meatballs to pancakes. In the area of baked goods, Swedish American cooks produce delicious breads, cookies, and other delights, including *kringla*, a pretzel-like pastry, and *prinsesstårta*, a sponge cake made with cream.

The holiday seasons, especially Christmas, are times for special ethnic dishes such as *lutefisk* (whitefish that has been air-dried and either heavily salted or soaked in lye), baked goods, meatballs, and ham, which are arranged on a buffet-style smorgasbord and washed down with gallons of strong, thick Swedish coffee or *glögg*, a Swedish mulled wine.

Traditional Dress The immigrants did not have a particularly distinctive way of dressing and generally adopted the clothing styles of their new homeland. Some brought with them the colorful, festive clothing representative of their region of Sweden, but such ethnic costumes were not worn often. The distinctive regional festive dress of nineteenth-century Sweden has, however, been revived by some Americans of Swedish descent seeking to get in touch with their roots. This traditional dress, which for women and girls consists of a woolen skirt, cotton bodice, apron, linen blouse, and headdress, is sometimes worn for ethnic celebrations or dance competitions.

Swedish American girls perform at the annual Svenskarnas Dag in Minneapolis, Minnesota. STEVE SKJOLD / ALAMY

Holidays Along with the traditional holidays celebrated by Americans, many Swedish Americans celebrate two additional holidays. Along with other Scandinavians, Swedes celebrate the summer solstice, or Midsummer's Day, June 21. This is a time for feasting and outdoor activities. In many areas of Swedish America this day is celebrated as *Svenskarnas dag* (Swedes' Day), a special festival of Swedish American culture and solidarity, with picnics, parades, and ethnic activities such as dancing around a maypole. December 13 is Saint Lucia Day. Remembering an early Christian saint who brought light in the darkness of the world, a young woman is selected to be the "Lucia bride." Dressed in a white gown with a wreath of candles on her head, she leads a procession through town and serves special breads and sweet rolls. The Luciafest is an important holiday leading into the celebration of Christmas.

Health Care Issues and Practices The United States in the nineteenth century was often a dangerous place for immigrants; many worked hazardous jobs, and health care was frequently lacking. As the Swedish American community began to form, various immigrant groups, especially the churches, established medical and other types of organizations to care for the arriving Swedes. Hospitals, clinics, nursing homes, sanitariums, and orphanages were all a part of the network of care for the immigrants. Swedish American medical institutions remain in operation to this day, especially in the urban centers of the Midwest.

Some Swedish immigrants and their Swedish American descendants sought medical careers, receiving their training mainly in the United States. After completing their education, some returned to Sweden to practice there. The only significant Swedish influence on American medicine was in the field of physical therapy, where techniques from Sweden were introduced into American medical centers.

There are few diseases or conditions that seem to be specific to the Swedish American community. Problems that are prominent in Sweden—such as heart disease, depression, and alcoholism—are also seen within the Swedish American community, as well as in the rest of the United States.

FAMILY AND COMMUNITY LIFE

When the first major wave of Swedish immigrants came to the United States in the 1840s and 1850s, the settlers traveled in large groups comprised of entire families, often led by a pastor or other community leader. These groups established the beginnings of the ethnic communities that are still today identifiably Swedish American. Family and social structures became the bedrock of the larger community, and often these communal settlements maintained the characteristics and customs of the areas in Sweden from which the immigrants had come.

Swedish America was thus founded on a tight communal and familial structure, and these characteristics were present both in rural and urban settlements. But this pattern was soon altered by a number of factors, including the increased immigration of single young people, the geographical dispersion of the Swedish immigrants, and secondary migrations within the United States. Although Swedish Americans rarely intermarried (and if they did, it was usually with other Scandinavian Americans), Swedes assimilated rapidly into American society, and by the second or third generation were indistinguishable from the general Anglo-American population. Their family patterns and social organization also became indistinct from that of the wider population.

Gender Roles Gender dynamics within the Swedish American community are largely indistinguishable from those of the larger American community. Early settlement saw patriarchal family and community structures, with men holding almost all positions of prominence and being responsible for business matters, and women staying at home to raise the children and maintain the household. Boys were afforded more opportunities for education and professional advancement, and girls were prepared for a family life of their own.

Much like the rest of mainstream America, however, these dynamics have shifted with each new wave of social progress. Today, all areas of education and employment are open to and acceptable for pursuit by all members of a family or community, and marriages are generally treated as partnerships, with each partner contributing more equally than before to all aspects of family and community life.

Education Because of widespread literacy in nineteenth-century Sweden, Swedish immigrants were almost universally literate (at least in Swedish), and education was of primary importance to them. They eagerly embraced the American public school system, enrolling their children and organizing their own public schools wherever these might be lacking. Swedish immigrants saw education as the primary means for their children to advance in the United States and are known for their high level of educational attainment. Besides participating in the formation of public institutions of higher education (the University of Minnesota is one good example), Swedish Americans also formed their own private colleges; many remain today, including Augustana College (Rock Island, Illinois), Gustavus Adolphus College (St. Peter, Minnesota), Bethany College (Lindsborg, Kansas), Uppsala College (East Orange, New Jersey), North Park College (Chicago, Illinois), and Bethel College (St. Paul, Minnesota). Other colleges and secondary schools operated for a time in the immigrant community, but many of these have not survived. Swedish American churches founded most of these schools, along with theological seminaries to train their own pastors. According to the 2010 American Community Survey, 95.3 percent had attained a high school degree or higher and 38.5 percent had achieved a bachelor's degree or higher. Literary and publishing activities were strong in the immigrant communities; presses brought forth streams of newspapers, journals, and books representing a broad spectrum of Swedish American opinions.

EMPLOYMENT AND ECONOMIC CONDITIONS

A common stereotype of nineteenth-century Swedish immigrants was that they were either farmers and agricultural laborers in the rural areas, or domestic servants in urban areas. There was a grain of truth in this stereotype, as such occupations were often filled by newly arrived immigrants. For the most part, Swedish immigrants were literate, skilled, and ambitious, quickly moving up the employment ladder into skilled positions or even white-collar jobs. Many Swedes exhibit a streak of stubborn independence and, accordingly, most sought economic activities that would allow them to work with their own talents and skills. For some this meant work within the Swedish American community, serving the needs of the immigrants. For others it meant independent work in the larger American community as skilled trade workers or independent businesspeople in low-capital, high-labor fields such as woodworking and metalworking, printing, and building contracting.

At the turn of the twentieth century, Swedish American men were employed in agriculture (33 percent), industry (35 percent), business and communication (14 percent), and as servants and laborers (16 percent). Among women, common occupations included servants and waitresses (56 percent), and seamstresses or laundresses (13 percent), with smaller groups of laborers and factory workers. As the Swedes adapted to American society, their employment patterns began to emulate that of the society as a whole, and they moved into educated positions in teaching, business, and industry.

Coming from a country that in the nineteenth century was largely rural, many Swedish immigrants were attracted to the United States by the prospect of free or cheap agricultural land, mainly in the upper Midwest or Great Plains states. By 1920 there were over sixty thousand Swedish American farmers in the United State on more than 11 million cultivated acres (4,451,000 hectares), and five out of six of these farmers owned their land. Swedish American farmers were industrious and intelligent and soon picked up American agricultural methods for use on their farms. For the most part, the older agricultural techniques from Sweden were not applicable to American farms, and Swedish Americans made few unique contributions to American agriculture. Later immigrants often headed to the forests and mines of the upper Midwest and increasingly to the Pacific northwest. Here they worked as lumberjacks and miners, two professions that were common in Sweden.

In the urban areas, Swedish Americans were best known for their skilled work in construction trades, and in the woodworking and metalworking industries. Swedish contractors dominated the construction business in the Midwest; at one point it was estimated that 80 percent of the construction in Minneapolis and 35 percent in Chicago was carried out by Swedes. The Swedish contractors also employed many of their fellow immigrants as carpenters, plumbers, masons, and painters, providing vital employment for new arrivals. Over half the Swedish American industrial workers in 1900 were occupied in woodworking and metalworking. In addition, Swedes were represented in the printing and graphics, as well as the design industries.

Swedes were also employed in the engineering and architecture fields, with many designing industrial and military machinery. Two Swedish Americans, Captain John Ericsson and Admiral John Dahlgren, revolutionized American naval power during the Civil War with their invention of the ironclad warship and the modern naval cannon, respectively. Other technical achievements and inventions of Swedish Americans include an improved zipper (Peter Aronsson and Gideon Sundback), the Bendix drive (Vincent Bendix), an improved disc clutch (George William Borg), and xerographic copying (Chester Carlson).

Contemporary Swedish American employment patterns are nearly indistinguishable from those of mainstream America. The U.S. Census Bureau's 2011 American Community Survey report that approximately 25 percent of Swedish Americans are employed in education, health care, and social assistance; 11 percent in science and professional management and administration; 11 percent in retail; and just under 10 percent in manufacturing. All other fields of occupation combine to account for less than 45 percent of Swedish American employment.

POLITICS AND GOVERNMENT

Sweden has a long history of representative government, with the nobles, the clergy, and the peasants all represented in the Swedish Parliament. This tradition was never overcome, even by the most autocratic of Swedish kings. At the beginning of the nineteenth century the voting franchise in Sweden was rather limited, although this changed drastically toward the end of the century.

One of the reasons Swedes came to the United States was to experience greater political freedom and to help shape their local communities. Swedish Americans from the old Delaware colony were active in the politics of colonial America and were elected to the legislatures of Delaware and Pennsylvania. The Swedes were also generally on the American side of the Revolutionary War and remained politically active when it ended. John Morton (1724–1777) of Pennsylvania was a delegate to the Continental Congress and voted for and signed the Declaration of Independence in 1776. John Hanson (1715–1783) of Maryland was one the leading political figures of that state and was elected to the Continental Congress three times. In 1781 Hanson was elected by Congress as the first president of the United States in Congress Assembled, or the chief executive of Congress, before the office of the presidency was established.

Through the early national period Swedish Americans usually favored the Democrats over the Whigs, but later they broke with the Democrats over the issue of slavery. Swedish Americans became enthusiastic supporters of the newly rising Republican Party and of Abraham Lincoln. The Swedes' relationship with the Republican Party became so firm and widespread as to be axiomatic; it was said that the average Swedish American believed in three things: Swedish culture, the Lutheran Church, and the Republican Party. In the late nineteenth century Swedes became a powerful force in local Republican politics in the upper Midwest, especially in Minnesota and Illinois. In 1886 John Lind (1854–1930) of Minnesota became the first Swedish American elected to Congress. Lind uncharacteristically switched to the Democratic Party and was then elected the first Swedish American governor of Minnesota in 1898.

Not all Swedish Americans subscribed to the Republican philosophy, of course. Many immigrants, especially those who arrived in the later waves, were strongly influenced by socialism in Sweden and brought this philosophy with them to the United States. Swedish American socialists founded their own organizations and newspapers and became active within the American socialist community. Most of this socialistic activity was local in nature, but some Swedes became involved on a national level. Joe Hill (born Joel Hägglund) was a celebrated leader in the Industrial Workers of the World but was accused of murder and executed in Utah in 1915.

Although socialism was a minority movement among the Swedish Americans, it did reflect many of their concerns. Swedes tended to be progressives within their parties. They believed strongly in the rights of the individual, were deeply suspicious of big business and foreign entanglements, and pushed progressive social legislation and reforms. One of the early leaders in this movement was Charles Lindbergh Sr. (1859–1924), father of the famed aviator, who was elected as a Republican to Congress from Minnesota in 1906. In Congress he espoused midwestern populist ideals, opposed big business interests, and spoke forcefully against American involvement in World War I. After the war, many Scandinavians in Minnesota left the Republican Party for the new Farmer Labor Party, which adopted many of the populist ideals common among the Swedes. Magnus Johnson was elected as a Farmer Labor senator from Minnesota in 1923, and Floyd Olson served that party as governor of Minnesota from 1931 to 1936. Many Swedes left the Republican Party in 1932 to vote for Franklin D. Roosevelt in the presidential election, and some remained in the Democratic Party. A split occurred within the Swedish American community after Roosevelt's presidency, and that division exists to this day. Urban Swedish Americans are evenly divided between the Democratic and Republican Parties, while rural Swedish Americans remain overwhelmingly Republican.

As with many ethnic immigrant groups, Swedish Americans have been underrepresented in national politics, with about thirteen senators and fifty representatives, mainly from the Midwest. On the state level there have been at least twenty-eight governors (ten in Minnesota) and many state and local officials. Modern Swedish American politicians have included governors Orville Freeman (Minnesota), James Thompson (Illinois), and Kay Orr (Nebraska), Senator Warren Magnusson (Washington), and Representative John B. Anderson (Illinois). Swedish Americans have achieved notable success on the Supreme Court, including the appointment of two chief justices, Earl Warren and William Rehnquist.

As small independent farmers and business owners, Swedish Americans have not been overwhelmingly involved in American labor union activities. Many in skilled professions in the wood and metal industries were involved in the formation of craft unions. In addition, given the Swedish domination of the building trades in the Midwest, there were many who became involved with the construction trade unions, most notably Lawrence Lindelof, president of the International Brotherhood of Painters and Allied Trades from 1929 to 1952. Some Swedish American women were involved in the garment and textile unions; Mary Anderson joined a trade union as a shoe stitcher in Chicago, was hired by the International Boot and Shoe Workers Union, and eventually was appointed director of the U.S. Department of Labor's Women's Bureau.

Swedish Americans have fought for America in all of its wars, from the Revolution to the present day. During the Revolutionary War, Swedes from Maryland and Delaware fought, for the most part, on the colonists' side, some in the army, but many more in the newly formed American navy. About ninety army and navy officers from Sweden came over temporarily to fight on the American side, either directly with American troops or, more typically, with French forces (Sweden was allied with France at the time). One of these officers, Baron von Stedingk, who would later become a field marshal in the Swedish army and Swedish ambassador to Russia.

At the start of the Civil War the Swedish American population numbered about twenty thousand, and their enthusiasm for Lincoln and the northern cause is seen in the fact that at least three thousand Swedes served in the Union army, mainly in the Illinois and Minnesota regiments. A number of others served in the Union navy, and it was here that Swedish Americans were best known. Admiral John Dahlgren was in command of a fleet blockading southern ports and introduced a number of modern advances in the area of naval weaponry. Captain John Ericsson, a naval engineer, developed the North's first practical ironclad ships, which fought with great effectiveness and revolutionized naval warfare. Swedish Americans in the South at the time were concentrated mainly in Texas, although their numbers were small, and some did enlist to fight for the Confederacy.

Leading up to World War I, Swedish American sympathies were typically with Germany, although the strongest sentiments were toward neutrality and isolationism, as espoused by Charles Lindbergh Sr. When the United States did enter the war on the Allied side in 1917, however, many Swedish Americans rushed to show their patriotism by enlisting in the army and by buying war bonds. In the 1920s and 1930s, Swedes generally returned to their isolationist and neutralist ways, and Charles Lindberg Jr. took up the cause where his father had left off. However, another famous Swedish American, author Carl Sandburg, forcefully urged American intervention in Europe against the Nazis, writing many articles and works opposing the German regime. In both world wars many Swedish Americans served with great distinction, including Major Richard Bong, who received the Medal of Honor in 1944 for destroying thirty-six Japanese planes in combat. Given their general engineering and technical expertise, many Swedish Americans rose to positions of importance in command, such as John Dahlquist, deputy chief of staff to General Dwight Eisenhower, and Arleigh Burke and Theodore Lonnquest, who eventually rose to the rank of admiral in the navy. Many other Swedish Americans rose to prominence in the defense industry, especially Philip Johnson, who headed Boeing Aircraft Company during World War II.

Swedish Americans have historically been very interested in the development of Sweden, and a lively correspondence is still maintained between Swedes on both sides of the Atlantic. Modern Sweden is a dramatically different country than the one the immigrants left; while Swedish Americans often have a hazy impression of a backward, rural country, the reality is quite different. The Sweden of the twentieth century has often been characterized as taking the "middle way," positioning itself as a neutral, socialist country between the capitalist West and the Communist East, ruled for most of fifty years by the Social Democratic Party. Some Swedish Americans have applauded the changes that have occurred in modern Sweden, while others have deplored them. During the Vietnam War era of the 1960s and 1970s, relations between Sweden and the United States were somewhat strained, but the rapport between the two nations has improved significantly since then, particularly following Sweden's decision to lend military and logistical support to American and international military operations in Kosovo (1998–1999), Iraq (2003–2011), and Afghanistan (2001–).

NOTABLE INDIVIDUALS

Art The most widely known Swedish American painter is probably Birger Sandzén (1871–1945), who lived and worked in the rolling prairies of central Kansas around Lindsborg; his works are found in many museums in Europe and the United States. A more recent artist, known for his pop art sculptures, is Claes Oldenburg (1929–). Other notable artists have included Henry Mattson (1887–1971), John F. Carlson (1875–1947), and Bror Julius Nordfeldt (1878–1955). Swedish American sculptor Carl Milles (1875–1955) achieved international fame for his work, especially for his outdoor sculpture; Milles studied with August Rodin in Paris, and went on to be artist-in-residence at Cranbrook Academy of Art in Michigan.

Business Many Swedish Americans have made names for themselves in American business. Eric Wickman (1887–1954) founded Greyhound Corporation and built it into a national enterprise. Charles R. Walgreen (1873–1939) started the national chain of drugstores, and Curtis Carlson (1914–1999) parlayed business and service sectors into the Carlson Companies, which operates hotels (Marriot), restaurants, and travel agencies. John W. Nordstrom (1871–1963) of Seattle founded the department store chain that bears his name. Some Swedish Americans rose through the ranks to become leaders in American industry, including Eric Mattson of Midland National Bank; Robert O. Anderson (1917–2007) of Atlantic Richfield; Rudolph Peterson (1904–2003) of Bank of America; Philip G. Johnson (1894–1944) of Boeing; and Rand V. Araskog (1931–) of ITT.

Exploration One of the best known of all Swedish Americans is the aviator Charles Lindbergh Jr. (1902–1974); his father and namesake was a congressman and politician, but the younger Lindbergh is known for making the first solo flight across the Atlantic in 1927; a national hero, Lindberg served as a civilian employee of the U.S. War Department. Another famous explorer of sorts was Edwin (Buzz) Aldrin (1930–), the Apollo 11 astronaut who in 1969 was the second person to step onto the moon.

Stage and Screen The most famous Swedish immigrants in this field were Greta Garbo (1905–1990), who was born in Sweden and came to the United States in 1925, and Ingrid Bergman (1915–1982), who was born in Stockholm and came to the United States in 1939. Both studied at the Royal Academy Theatre School in Stockholm before earning roles and stardom in Hollywood. Other Swedish American actresses of note include Viveca Lindfors (1920–1995), Ann-Margret (Olson) (1941–), Gloria Swanson (1899–1983), and Candice Bergen (1946–)—the daughter of popular ventriloquist Edgar Bergen (1903–1978), well known for his television appearances. Other Swedish American actors have included Werner Oland (1879–1938) and Richard Widmark (1914–2008), and contemporary actors with documented Swedish ancestry include Val Kilmer (1959–), James Franco (1978–), Jake Gyllenhaal (1980–) and his sister Maggie Gyllenhaal (1977–), and Uma Thurman (1970–).

Literature Although Swedish Americans produced a vast quantity of written literature, some of it was written in Swedish and is unknown outside the immigrant community. Second- and third-generation

Swedish American poet Carl Sandburg (1878–1967) with his grandchild at his goat farm in North Carolina, c. 1950s. EVANS / THREE LIONS / GETTY IMAGES

A young girl and boy wear traditional Swedish costumes. PHOTOGRAPH BY RAYMOND GEHMAN. CORBIS. REPRODUCED BY PERMISSION.

Swedish American community. Following Lind to the United States were such singers as Christiana Nilsson (1843–1921), lyric tenor Jussi Björling (1911–1960), and soprano Birgit Nilsson (1918–2005). Still, the most popular Swedish American musicians have been second- and third-generation artists, including Kris Kristofferson (1936–), a legendary country singer and songwriter (and, later, movie actor) perhaps best known for writing Janis Joplin's classic "Me and Bobby McGee," and singer and teen heartthrob Rick Nelson (1940–1985), whose twin sons Gunnar (1967–) and Matthew (1967–) had success in the early nineties as the band Nelson.

Politics Several second- and third-generation Swedish Americans have risen to prominent positions in U.S. politics. Most notable among contemporary officials are Earl Warren (1891–1974), whose mother was a Swedish immigrant, served three terms as governor of California before being appointed chief justice of the United States in 1953. His rulings helped end lawful segregation, and he headed the commission that investigated the assassination of President John F. Kennedy. William Rehnquist (1924–2005), whose paternal grandparents immigrated from Sweden, served as the U.S. assistant attorney general under President Richard Nixon from 1969 to 1971 before being appointed as an associate justice on the U.S. Supreme Court in 1972. He held that post until 1986, when he was named the chief justice of the United States. He served as chief justice until his death on September 3, 2005. Jennifer M. Granholm (1959–), whose paternal grandfather immigrated from Sweden to Canada in the 1930s, has served both as the fifty-first attorney general of the state of Michigan, from 1999 to 2003, and as the forty-seventh governor of Michigan, from 2003 to 2011.

Science Many Swedish Americans have become distinguished in the field of science, especially in chemistry and physics. Carl David Anderson (1905–1991) won the Nobel Prize in Physics for his discovery of positrons. Another Swedish American Nobel laureate is Glenn T. Seaborg (1912–1999), who won the 1951 Nobel Prize for Chemistry for his work with transuranium elements.

MEDIA

PRINT

Nordstjernan (Nordic Reach)

Established in 1872, this weekly is one of the few remaining Swedish American newspapers printed in English and Swedish. It is published in four editions: a U.S. national edition and city-specific editions for New York, Chicago, and San Francisco. It also publishes select special-interest books and the magazine Nordic Reach.

Ulf Mårtensson, Editor and Publisher
P.O. Box 1710

Swedish Americans, however, have included a number of writers in English who have earned national reputations. The most famous of these authors were Carl Sandburg (1878–1967), who produced nationally known poetry and novels but whose most famous work is his four-volume biography of Abraham Lincoln, a work that won Sandburg a Pulitzer Prize; Ray Bradbury (1920–2012), a science fiction, fantasy, and horror writer best remembered for his dystopian classic *Fahrenheit 451*; and Nelson Algren (1909–1981), who has written extensively about the hard realities of urban and working class life but best known for the novels *The Man with the Golden Arm* and *A Walk on the Wild Side*.

Music The most famous Swedish American composer is Howard Hanson (1896–1981) who grew up in the immigrant community of Wahoo, Nebraska. For many years Hanson was director of the Eastman School of Music in Rochester, New York, and he is one of the best-known twentieth-century American composers of classical music. A number of immigrants from Sweden have become important singers of classical music and opera. Jenny Lind (1820–1887), referred to as the "Swedish Nightingale," was already famous in Europe when P. T. Barnum brought her to the United States in 1850 for the first of more than ninety concerts in three years. Lind took America by storm, eventually returning to Europe but not before giving generous support to charities within the

New Canaan, Connecticut 06840
Phone: (203) 299-0381
Fax: (203) 299-0380
Email: info@nordstjernan.com
URL: www.nordstjernan.com

Swedish American Genealogist

This quarterly is published by the Swenson Swedish Immigration Research Center at Augustana College and contains articles on genealogical research, as well as local and family history.

Elisabeth Thorsell, Editor
Email: sag@etgenealogy.se
Hästskovägen 45
se-177 39, Järfälla
Sweden

Swedish American Historical Quarterly

Published by the Swedish American Historical Society, this periodical contains articles on the history and culture of Swedish Americans.

Byron J. Nordstrom, Quarterly Editor
Gustav Adolphus College
Department of History
St. Peter, Minnesota 56082
Phone: (507) 933-7435
Fax: (507) 933-7041

ORGANIZATIONS AND ASSOCIATIONS

American Swedish Institute

Founded in 1929, the American Swedish Institute seeks to preserve the Swedish cultural heritage in the United States. The institute, housed in the mansion of a former Swedish American journalist, offers classes, activities, exhibits, concerts and workshops, along with a library and archives.

Peggy Korsmo-Kennon, Chief Operating Officer
2600 Park Avenue
Minneapolis, Minnesota 55407
Phone: (612) 871-4907
Fax: (612) 871-8682
Email: info@asimn.org
URL: www.asimn.org

Swedish American Historical Society

Founded in 1950, the society is dedicated to the preservation and documentation of the heritage of Swedish Americans. It publishes a quarterly journal, Swedish American Historical Quarterly, and Pioneer Newsletter, as well as books in this area.

Timothy J. Johnson
3225 West Foster Avenue
Box 48
Chicago, Illinois 60625
Phone: (773) 583-5722
Email: info@swedishamericanhist.org
URL: www.swedishamericanhist.org

Swedish Council of America

Formed in 1973, the Swedish Council of America is a cooperative agency that coordinates the efforts of over a hundred different Swedish American historical, cultural, and fraternal organizations. The Swedish Council publishes a monthly magazine called Sweden and America, which is a useful forum for current Swedish American activities.

Gregg White, Executive Director
2600 Park Avenue
Minneapolis, Minnesota 55407
Phone: (612) 871-0593
Email: swedcoun@swedishcouncil.org
URL: www.swedishcouncil.org

The Swedish American Chambers of Commerce USA

SACC-USA is the parent organization for more than twenty regional Swedish American chambers of commerce across the United States, all of which promote both Swedish American economic access and fair, productive trade policy between Sweden and the United States.

Therese Linde, President
House of Sweden
2900 K Street NW
Suite 403
Washington, D.C. 20007
Phone: (202) 536-1520
Email: info@sacc-usa.org
URL: www.sacc-usa.org

Vasa Order of America

Founded in 1896, it is the largest Swedish American fraternal organization in the United States, with more than 31,000 members in 326 lodges nationwide.

William Lundquist, Grand Master
1456 Kennebec Road
Grand Blanc, Michigan 48439
Phone: (810) 695-3248

MUSEUMS AND RESEARCH CENTERS

American Swedish Historical Museum

Collects and displays artifacts and documents of Swedish Americans to preserve the Swedish American culture. The building is modeled after a seventeenth-century Swedish manor house.

Tracey Beck, Executive Director
1900 Pattison Avenue
Philadelphia, Pennsylvania 19145-5901
Phone: (215) 389-1776
Fax: (215) 389-7701
Email: info@americanswedish.org
URL: www.americanswedish.org

American Swedish Institute Museum

Provides exhibits and activities for and about Swedish Americans, including displays of the institute's collections, as well as traveling exhibits.

Curt Pederson, Curator
2600 Park Avenue
Minneapolis, Minnesota 55407
Phone: (612) 871-4907
Fax: (612) 871-8682

Email: info@asimn.org
URL: www.asimn.org

Bishop Hill

Located in northwestern Illinois, this is a folk museum dedicated to preserving the life of the pioneer Swedish immigrants in the United States. Founded in 1846, Bishop Hill was the home of a religious communal settlement organized by Erik Jansson. Although the communal settlement collapsed after Jansson's death, a Swedish American community remained. In the twentieth century the Bishop Hill Heritage Association began restoring the settlement to its original condition.

Todd DeDecker, Administrator
103 North Bishop Hill Street
P.O. Box 92
Bishop Hill, Illinois 61419
Phone: (309) 927-3899
URL: www.bishophill.com

Swedish American Museum Center (of Chicago)

Located in the Andersonville neighborhood of Chicago, an area of historical immigrant settlement, this museum collects and displays artifacts and documents of Swedish immigration, maintains an archives, and sponsors special exhibits and activities.

Karin Moen Abercrombie, Executive Director
5211 North Clark Street
Chicago, Illinois 60640
Phone: (773) 728-8111
Fax: (773) 728-8870
Email: museum@samac.org
URL: www.swedishamericanmuseum.org

Swenson Immigrant Research Center

Situated on the campus of Augustana College, this center has a large collection of historical documents, records, and artifacts on Swedish Americans. The Swenson center is an especially good resource for genealogical and historical study.

Dag Blanck, Director
Augustana College

Box 175639
Thirty-Eighth St.
Rock Island, Illinois 61201-2296
Phone: (309) 794-7204
Fax: (309) 794-7443
Email: sag@augustana.edu
URL: www.augustana.edu/x13856.xml

SOURCES FOR ADDITIONAL STUDY

Barton, H. Arnold. *A Folk Divided: Homeland Swedes and Swedish Americans, 1840–1940*. Carbondale: Southern Illinois University Press, 1994.

Blanck, Dag, and Harald Rundblom, eds. *Swedish Life in American Cities*. Uppsala, Sweden: Centre for Multiethnic Research, 1991.

Carlsson, Sten. *Swedes in North America, 1638–1988: Technical, Cultural, and Political Achievements*. Stockholm: Streiffert, 1988.

Erling, Maria. "What America Wanted and Swedish American Youth." *Currents in Theology and Mission* 39, no. 3 (2012): 229–38.

Hasselmo, Nils. *Swedish America: An Introduction*. Minneapolis: Brings Press, 1976.

Ljungmark, Lars. *Swedish Exodus*. Translated by Kermit Westerberg. Carbondale: Southern Illinois University Press, 1979.

Lundström, Catrin. "Women with Class: Swedish Migrant Women's Class Positions in the USA." *Journal of Intercultural Studies* 31, no. 1 (2010): 49–63.

Olsson, Christopher, and Ruth McLaughlin, eds. *American-Swedish Handbook*, 11th ed. Minneapolis: Swedish Council of America, 1992.

Rundblom, Harald, and Hans Norman, eds. *From Sweden to America: A History of the Migration*. Minneapolis: University of Minnesota Press, 1976.

Schnell, Steven M. "Creating Narratives of Place and Identity in 'Little Sweden, U.S.A.'" *Geographical Review* 93, no. 1 (2003): 1–29.

Scott, Larry E. *The Swedish Texans*. San Antonio: University of Texas Institute of Texan Cultures, 1990.

SWISS AMERICANS

Leo Schelbert

OVERVIEW

Swiss Americans are immigrants or descendants of immigrants from Switzerland, a country in Western Europe. Switzerland is bordered by Germany to the north, France to the west, Italy to the south, and Austria and the Principality of Liechtenstein to the east. The country lies in the central part of the Alps, a 500-mile-long mountain range that stretches westward from France's Riviera into what was northern Yugoslavia. Four main passes (Grimsel, Furka, St. Gotthard, and Oberalp) allow passage from northern Europe across the Alps to Italy, making Switzerland a country of transit. The Swiss nation is a confederation of twenty-six member states called cantons. The country covers 15,941 square miles (25,655 square kilometers), an area slightly larger than the state of Maryland.

In 2012 the population of Switzerland was estimated to be 7.9 million by the *CIA World Factbook*. The country is ethnically diverse, as indicated by its four official languages (German, French, Italian, and Romansh). According to the 2010 Swiss census, 38.6 percent of the population was Catholic, 28 percent was Swiss Reformed, 4.5 percent was Muslim, 5.7 percent belonged to other Christian denominations and other faiths, and 20.1 percent claimed no religion. Switzerland is one of the most economically prosperous nations in the world. Much of this wealth is generated through the country's substantial banking and trade sectors, but Switzerland is also home to numerous manufacturing companies. While the country is most famous for producing watches, Swiss companies also manufacture machinery, precision instruments, and chemicals.

The first substantial wave of immigration from Switzerland to what is now the United States occurred in the early eighteenth century, when Swiss immigrants seeking religious freedom and agricultural opportunity began to settle primarily in the British colonies of Pennsylvania, Virginia, and South Carolina. Although a substantial number of Swiss immigrants arrived in the United States in the latter half of the twentieth century, most of them were businesspeople and other professionals, such as academics, who did not remain in the United States permanently. This trend has continued into the twenty-first century, because many Swiss citizens who move to the United States are employees of American branches of Swiss companies.

According to the U.S. Census Bureau's American Community Survey estimates for 2009–2011, the number of U.S. residents claiming Swiss ancestry was 963,967. Most of these, 96 percent, were born in the United States. The vast majority of Swiss Americans have been assimilated and absorbed into the broader U.S. population and thus no longer live in a distinct immigrant community. That said, areas of significant historical Swiss immigration, such as the rural Midwest and cities such as Chicago and New York, continue to boast significant Swiss American populations.

HISTORY OF THE PEOPLE

Early History The Swiss Confederation emerged in the late thirteenth century from an alliance of three regions: the modern-day cantons Uri, Schwyz, and Unterwalden. The so-called *Bundesbrief* of 1291 documents their alliance. In it the three regions pledge mutual support to keep internal order and to resist aggression. The Confederation grew by wars of conquest and by alliances arranged with important towns located at the access routes of the passes to Italy, such as Luzern, Zürich, and Bern. By 1513, thirteen cantons had united the rural population with the urban elite of artisans and entrepreneurs. Both groups were intent on gaining and preserving independence from the nobility, a unique development in European history. The Confederation's defeat at the battle of Marignano in upper Italy in 1515 ended the nation's expansion. This loss led to the gradual emergence of armed neutrality, a basic feature of Switzerland's political tradition. However, the Reformation split the people into Catholic and Swiss Reformed hostile camps and nearly destroyed the Confederation.

Modern Era During the seventeenth and eighteenth centuries smaller oligarchies came to power in the Swiss cantons but were overthrown in 1798 in the wake of the French Revolution. In 1848, after five decades of foreign intervention and internal uncertainty, a new constitution was adopted. The previous system of autonomous states became one federal state, though the people remain the actual sovereign.

Neutrality in foreign affairs and universal military service of men are considered central to the Swiss political tradition, which may have kept the country out of two devastating world wars. Though the country was virtually surrounded by Hitler's troops during World War II, it managed to avoid hostilities by engaging in some trade and financial agreements with Germany, housing an unknown quantity of gold and treasure looted from victims of Nazi persecution that was later repaid in a $1.25 billion settlement involving the top Swiss banks and a separate Holocaust Fund initiated by the Swiss government. Switzerland is also home to the International Red Cross, which played an important role in providing medical service to civilians and prisoners of war during both World War I and World War II.

After World War II, Switzerland entered into an era of unprecedented peace and prosperity and embraced a number of sweeping social changes. In 1971 women were granted the right to vote on a federal level, and the first female member of the federal government, Elisabeth Kopp, was elected in 1984. In 1999 the Swiss voted to adopt a revised constitution which ratified a number of unwritten laws and eliminated some outdated provisions. In 2002 the country voted to join the United Nations, overcoming longstanding concerns about maintaining its signature neutrality in foreign affairs. The country did, however, resist joining the European Union, leaving it on sound financial footing during the economic collapse and global recession that swept through most of Europe in 2008 and 2009. Despite such resistance to internationalism, Switzerland's economy is fully dependent on the export of quality products and on special expertise in finance as well as the production of machinery, pharmaceuticals, watches, and precision instruments.

> My mother had to try and keep track of us. She finally took us and tied us all together so that we would stay together. And that's the way we came off the boat.
>
> Gertrude Schneider Smith, 1921, cited in *Ellis Island: An Illustrated History of the Immigrant Experience*, edited by Ivan Cwhermayeff et al. (New York: Macmillan, 1991).

SETTLEMENT IN THE UNITED STATES

The first known Swiss in what is now the territory of the United States was Theobald von Erlach (1541–1565). In 1564 he was a leading member of a French attempt to create a permanent foothold in North America. He perished when some 900 French soldiers were shipwrecked by a hurricane in September 1565 and killed by the Spanish. Some "Switzers" also lived at Jamestown during the regime of Captain Smith. In 1657 the French Swiss Jean Gignilliat received a large land grant from the proprietors of South Carolina. In 1710 some 100 Swiss joined Christoph von Graffenried (1661–1743), who founded New Bern in present-day North Carolina.

Between 1710 and 1750, some 25,000 Swiss are estimated to have settled in British North America, especially in Pennsylvania, Virginia, and South Carolina. Many were members of the Reformed church and were actively recruited by entrepreneurs such as Jean Pierre Purry (1675–1736), the founder of Purrysburg, South Carolina. About 4,000 Swiss Mennonites settled in Pennsylvania, many of whom had first gone to the Palatinate from which the next generation emigrated in search of fertile, affordable land and greater toleration of their creed.

In the late 1750s an influential group of French Swiss officers in the British service assumed leadership roles in the fight against indigenous peoples resisting white incursions into the trans-Appalachian West, the French, and the insurgent colonials. In the middle decades of the eighteenth century a group of Swiss Jesuits labored in the Southwest of the present United States to promote the northward expansion of New Spain.

Between 1798 and 1850, about 100,000 Swiss went abroad (the proportions between temporary and permanent migrations cannot be determined) and some 50,000 foreigners located in Switzerland. Between 1850 and 1914 those leaving the Confederation numbered about 410,000, those entering it from abroad about 409,000. Those leaving were attracted by the newly conquered lands taken from indigenous peoples in Australia, New Zealand, and in the Western Hemisphere by expanding neo-European nations such as Argentina, Brazil, or the United States. The emigrants seem to have been rooted in the lure of faraway lands or in the desire to escape parental control, intolerable marriages, or oppressive village traditions.

In the first half of the nineteenth century, large numbers of Swiss settled in the rural Midwest, especially in Ohio, Indiana, Illinois, and Wisconsin, and—after 1848—in California. Some 40 percent of Swiss went to urban areas such as New York, Philadelphia, Cincinnati, Chicago, St. Louis, San Francisco, and Los Angeles. In 1920, for instance, New York counted 9,233 Swiss, Chicago 3,452, San Francisco 2,105, and Philadelphia 1,889. As to states, in 1930 California numbered 20,063 Swiss, New York 16,571, New Jersey 8,765, and Wisconsin, Ohio, and Illinois some 7,000 each.

The socioeconomic status of newcomers from Switzerland spanned the spectrum from the well-to-do to the poor. A sample analysis from 1915 of 5,000 Swiss men in the United States yielded the following distribution: a third belonged to lower-income and lower-status groups; about 44 percent were solidly middle class; and about 22 percent were well situated.

In 1804 a special grant of the U.S. Congress enabled a group of French Swiss winegrowers to settle on the Ohio River and establish the town of Vevay, Indiana. This viticulture, which they had hoped to

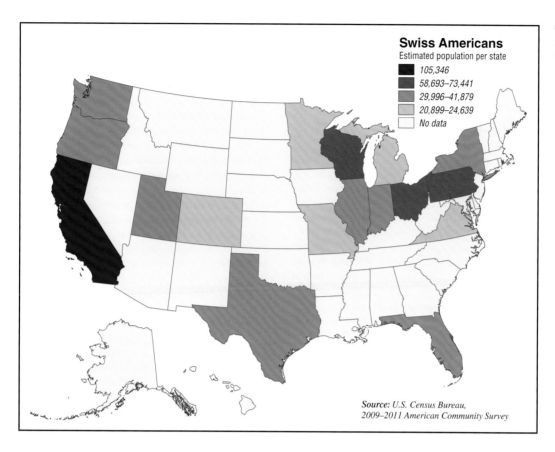

Swiss Americans
Estimated population per state

- 105,346
- 58,693–73,441
- 29,996–41,879
- 20,899–24,639
- No data

Source: U.S. Census Bureau, 2009–2011 American Community Survey

introduce as a permanent feature into the Midwestern economy, became insignificant by midcentury and was replaced by the cultivation of maize and other staples. In 1817 and 1825 Swiss Mennonites founded the agricultural settlements Sonnenberg and Chippewa in Ohio, respectively, and in 1838 they founded Berne, Indiana; the latter remains conscious of its Swiss origin. By the efforts of the Köpfli and Suppiger families, the town of Highland emerged in southern Illinois in 1831 and eventually attracted some 1,500 Swiss settlers. In the same decade John August Sutter (1803–1880), who was of Swiss descent, established New Helvetia in California, then still under Mexican sovereignty. When gold was discovered on his property in 1848, thousands of gold seekers overran his extensive domain, and the city of Sacramento was platted, and became California's capital in 1854.

In 1825 several Swiss, who had joined Lord Selkirk's Red River colony in Canada in 1821, settled at Gratiot's Grove northeast of Galena, Illinois. In 1845 New Glarus was founded in southern Wisconsin's Green County, today the best-known settlement of Swiss origin. Numerous Swiss also settled in the towns of Monroe, Washington, and Mount Pleasant. In 1848 Bernese Swiss established Alma on the Mississippi, which counted some 900 Swiss in 1870. A French Swiss group connected with the

Protestant Plymouth Brethren established a community in Knoxville, Tennessee, in the same year.

In the spring of 1856 a group of Swiss and Germans established a Swiss Colonization Society in Cincinnati, Ohio, to create a culturally homogeneous settlement. After an extensive search Tell City was laid out in 1858 on the Ohio River in Perry County, Indiana. In the post-Civil War era, Helvetia was founded in West Virginia (1867) as a result of active recruitment by that state. In the 1880s Peter Staub (1827–1904) initiated the settlement of Grütli in Grundy County, Tennessee. During the same decade 1,000 Swiss who had converted to Mormonism went to Utah and settled mainly at Midway near Salt Lake City and at St. George on Utah's southwestern border. Between 1870 and 1914 several thousand Italian Swiss went to California, where they established vineyards and dairy farms.

The Great Depression and World War II diminished Swiss immigration. Between 1931 and 1960 about 23,700 Swiss arrived, and between 1961 and 1990, about 29,100. Many of these Swiss did not stay permanently, however, because they were mainly professionals and business people employed in American branches of Swiss firms. The 1980 Census counted 235,355 people of single, and 746,188 of multiple Swiss ancestry. In 1990 there was a total of 607,833 persons of Swiss ancestry, 5.9 percent of whom were Swiss-born. According to the U.S. Census Bureau, in 2011 there were an estimated 963,967 U.S. residents claiming Swiss ancestry (American Community Survey estimate for 2009–2011), 96 percent of whom were born in the United States.

LANGUAGE

Some 73 percent of Swiss speak High German or forms of various Low German dialects called *Schwyzerdütsch* (Swiss-German); 20 percent speak French, and the rest speak any of several regional dialects (5 percent Italian and 1 percent Romansh). Most Swiss learn as their first language a regional form of German, French, or Italian, which remains their principal form of communication, but in school they also learn a different language such as High German, standard French, or standard Italian. The children where Romansh is spoken also learn German or French. For most Swiss immigrants to the United States, therefore, to enter a different linguistic world was not a new experience, and they mastered multiculturalism with relative ease.

Greetings and Popular Expressions Depending on their local origin, Swiss greet each other by a variety of forms. Widespread among German Swiss is *Grüezi* ("groitsee") or *Grüezi wohl*, derived from [*Ich*] *grüsse dich*—I greet you; also the French-derived *Salü* ("saly") and *Tschau* from the Italian *Ciao*, used both when first meeting and when parting. In a common dialect of Romansh, people say *Bien di* ("biandee")—Good day; on parting the French Swiss will use the form *A revere* for the standard French *Au revoir* and the German Swiss *Uf wiederluäge* ("oof weederlooaga")—See you. In German-speaking rural Switzerland the standard form for goodbye is still widespread, *Bhüet di Gott*— May God protect you.

RELIGION

Swiss immigrants belong to various religions. The first Swiss to arrive in North America in large numbers were the Swiss Mennonites, a group that derived from the Anabaptist communities of the Radical Reformation of the 1520s. They rejected infant baptism, thus declaring the whole of ecclesiastical Christendom as heathen. They also repudiated the state as symbolized by the sword and the oath. The Swiss Mennonite settlements that emerged in Pennsylvania and Virginia in the first half of the eighteenth century were expert in farming, and they formed congregations of some 25 to 30 families. Each religious community was semi-autonomous and guided by a bishop and by preachers and deacons who were not specially schooled. The only full members were adults who had proven their faith by a virtuous life, the demands of the community, and accepted baptism as a symbol of submission to God's will. Rules set by the religious leaders ordered the manner of dress, forms of courtship, the schooling of children, and dealings with the outside world. If a member failed to conform, the person would be banned and

avoided even by the next of kin. In the late nineteenth century many Mennonite congregations—influenced by the Dutch Mennonites, American Protestantism, and American secular culture—gave up the older traditions. They moved into towns and took up occupations increasingly removed from farming. Only some conservative Swiss Mennonites and Amish still hold on to the sixteenth-century forms of their creed.

Numerous Swiss immigrants belong to the Swiss Reformed church, as formulated by Huldrych Zwingli (1484–1531). He adapted Christian doctrine to the needs of a rising urban bourgeoisie. Municipal power increased, monastic institutions were secularized, and the rule of the urban elites strengthened. Many members of the Swiss Reformed church settled in colonial Pennsylvania, Virginia, and the Carolinas. Their views and ecclesiastical organization were similar to those of Presbyterians, with whom they easily merged. One of the largest Swiss Reformed Churches in the United States is the Swiss United Church of Christ in New Glarus, Wisconsin, founded by Swiss settlers in 1850.

Some 50,000 Swiss Catholics arrived in the United States after the 1820s, including about 20,000 Italian Swiss who settled in California between 1887 and 1938. Depending on their language, Swiss Catholics joined either German, French, Italian, or ethnically undefined American parishes. They found, however, a very different parish organization in the United States that curtailed the Swiss practice of lay jurisdiction over secular affairs.

Several Swiss religious orders were actively engaged in establishing the Catholic Church in the United States. In 1842 Franz von Sales Brunner (1795–1859) introduced the Order of the Precious Blood into Ohio. In 1852 monks from the ancient Benedictine monastery of Einsiedeln founded St. Meinrad, Indiana, the nucleus of the Swiss Benedictine Congregation of the United States formed in 1881. In 1956 the congregation united some twelve foundations with 645 monks. Benedictine sisters were also deeply involved in promoting Catholic education and charity. Anselma Felber (1843–1883) established a community at Conception, Missouri, which later moved to Clyde. Gertrude Leupi (1825–1904) founded a convent in Maryville, later transferred to Yankton, South Dakota.

CULTURE AND ASSIMILATION

Although Swiss in the United States are often mistaken for German, French, or Italian immigrants, their involvement in American life has been quite extensive. Since the Swiss came from Western Europe's oldest democracy and have forged a national unity out of ethnically diverse constituencies, they find American culture compatible with their own. For instance, when John J. Zubly, a delegate to the Second Continental Congress, published the widely distributed pamphlet *The Law of Liberty* in 1775, he appended "A Short and Concise Account of the Struggles of Swisserland for

Liberty" to it. He paralleled the Swiss with American colonials, the Austrian emperor with the British king, and viewed their struggle as the same quest for liberty.

Traditions and Customs Although Switzerland is a highly industrialized country with a powerful financial and industrial elite involved in global markets, Swiss culture remains identified with an idealized rural tradition. In New Glarus, a major tourist attraction in southern Wisconsin, a William Tell and Heidi festival is held each year. The chalet, a house style of rural origin, remains identified with the Swiss, although it is common only in certain Swiss regions.

Yodeling and the Alphorn, again native only to some rural Swiss regions, continue to serve as emblems of Swiss culture, as do the various *Trachten*—colorful and often beautifully crafted garb for women and men. *Trachten* originate in distinct regions, but tend to become fused into a blended version, sometimes mixed with Tyrolian or Bavarian motifs. The so-called Swiss barn is also widely found in Pennsylvania and some midwestern states. It is built into an incline with a large entrance to the hayloft on an upper level and the entrances to the stables on the opposite lower level. The dominance of rural motifs in Swiss American culture points to a central feature of Swiss self-interpretation: Switzerland's origins are shaped by the traditions of rural communities. Their emblems symbolize Swiss culture however far removed they might be from modern day Swiss and Swiss American reality.

Cuisine Predictably, Swiss cuisine varies according to ethnic influences. Another historic division is equally telling, however: that between country and city. Thus, two dishes eaten today by all Swiss are the simple cheese fondue, eaten for centuries by Swiss in rural regions, and veal with a sauce of white wine and cream, formerly enjoyed by city dwellers. Cheese, however, is popular in almost any form. As for other regional cuisine, German areas favor pork, often accompanied by *rösti*, a dish of diced potatoes mixed with herbs, bacon, or cheese, and fried to a golden brown.

Because Swiss Americans played such an important part in developing rural communities in the nineteenth century, Swiss cuisine became popular in the American Midwest and in other areas with high concentrations of Swiss. Restaurants featuring Swiss foods like fondue, rösti, and *spätzli*, a modified version of the German egg noodle dish *spätzle,* are common in these areas, and importers such as Albert Uster Imports in Maryland offer Swiss immigrants all the comforts of home.

Health Care Issues and Practices Swiss Americans follow general trends in Western medicine and health care. People in rural areas have remained connected with healing traditions based on telepathic methods and herbs and herbal ointments. In mental health the influence of Carl Gustav Jung (1875–1961)

Ida Zahler, with her eleven children, after they arrived from Switzerland, 1926. UPI / CORBIS-BETTMANN. REPRODUCED BY PERMISSION.

has been significant. Jung viewed mental problems as soluble in part by a skillful evocation of symbols shared by all in a postulated collective subconscious that transcends cultural boundaries. Swiss-American psychoanalyst Adolf Meyer (1866–1950), who served as the president of the American Psychiatric Association from 1927 to 1928, brought famed analysts Sigmund Freud and Gustav Jung to the United States for the first time in 1909. Since then, numerous Jung Institutes have appeared in the United States to promote Jungian ideas, which also have influenced American literary scholarship.

FAMILY AND COMMUNITY LIFE

Swiss family life is well regulated and conservative. Few women hold careers outside the family, and young people tend to be cooperative and well behaved. The Swiss American family is indistinguishable from other American families, which have changed from a patriarchal to an egalitarian and child-centered outlook. The Swiss American family is predominantly middle class. According to the 1990 census the median income of Swiss American families was over $42,000 and only 3.8 percent had an income below the poverty line. By 2010 the median income increased to around $79,500, and the poverty level for Swiss American families fell to 3.5 percent. More than one-half all Swiss American families had two wage-earners in 2010, though in families with children under the age of six the number was under 50 percent, suggesting that stay-at-home parenting remains relatively common.

Swiss people tend to get married later in life and to have fewer children than the global average. In 2004 the average number of children per family in Switzerland was 1.42, well below the world average of 2.65, and in 2009 the number of married couples without children surpassed those with children for the first time. These statistics generally hold true for Swiss Americans as well; of the 258,250 households containing married couples in 2010 only 87,170 (or 33 percent) had children under the age of 18, and the average family size was 2.94, below the national average of 3.25.

Swiss Americans re-create organizations they have known at home for mutual support as well as for enjoyment and social contact. They celebrate August 1 as the Swiss national holiday and commemorate important battles of the fifteenth-century Swiss struggle for independence with parades, speeches, and conviviality. At such events there is yodeling, singing, flag throwing (an artful throwing and catching of a Swiss flag on a short handle high into the air), and sometimes a reading of the *Bundesbrief* of 1291. The festivities also include traditional dishes such as rösti and *bratwurst*, in addition to dancing and the playing of folk music on the accordion, clarinet, and fiddle. Popular Swiss American festivals include Swiss Days held annually in Midway, Utah, in late summer, and the annual Wilhelm Tell Festival in New Glarus Wisconsin ("America's Little Switzerland"), celebrating the story of Swiss national hero Wilhelm Tell.

EMPLOYMENT AND ECONOMIC CONDITIONS

In the eighteenth century, Swiss immigrants were mainly farmers and artisans. Like other German-speaking newcomers, their methods of farming differed from those of the English. Mennonite and Amish farmers fenced their properties, built stables for their cattle, sometimes even before their houses, and tilled well-manured fields. By the mid-eighteenth century they also had developed the Conestoga wagon, a large, heavily built structure that was suited for the arduous trek across the Alleghenies.

The occupational profile of Swiss immigrants reflected the general trends of Western economies. A statistical analysis for the years 1887 to 1938 counted 42 percent in the industrial workforce; 25 percent in agriculture; 6.5 percent in commerce; 4.5 percent in the hotel and restaurant business; and 4.3 percent in the professions. A large percentage of Swiss immigrants also worked as domestics.

Viticulture was introduced into the Midwest by French Swiss farmers and was also extensively practiced by Italian Swiss from Canton Tessin who went to California in large numbers after the 1870s. Bernese Swiss used their expertise in dairy farming, especially in Wisconsin. Nicolas Gerber (1836–1908), for instance, opened a Limburger cheese factory in New Glarus in 1868, as did Jacob Karlen (1840–1920) in nearby Monroe in 1878. Gottlieb Beller (1850–1902) developed a system of storage that allowed cheese production to remain responsive to fluctuating market demand. Leon de Montreux Chevalley (1854–1926) founded butter, cheese, and condensed-milk factories in Portland, Oregon. Jacques Huber (1851–1918) introduced silk manufacturing to New Jersey; by 1900 he had established a firm with plants in Union City, Hackensack, and other cities of the mid-Atlantic states. Albert Wittnauer (1856–1908) used his Swiss training in watchmaking to establish a successful business in New York City.

By 1900 world-renowned firms such as Nestlé had established plants in the United States. The Swiss pharmaceutical companies Ciba-Geigy, Hoffmann-La Roche, and Sandoz emerged in the twentieth century as important forces in the United States economy and diversified their productive activities. Aargauische Portlandcement-Fabrik Holderbank Wildegg, a Swiss cement company, incorporated in 1912 and reorganized in 1930 as Holderbank Financière Glaris, introduced superior, cost-efficient cement production into North America. In 2001 the firm changed its name to Holcim, and a subsidiary—Holcim (US) Inc.—dominates today's U.S. cement market.

In the late twentieth and early twenty-first centuries, Swiss Americans were among the more prosperous immigrant groups. In 2010, just 3 percent of Swiss Americans in the labor force were unemployed, as opposed to 5.1 percent nationally. Swiss Americans also had a median household income of $63,682, above the national median of $62,982. The most common industries for Swiss Americans include health care, education, manufacturing, finance, and insurance. Because of strong economic ties between the United States and Switzerland, there are hundreds of Swiss companies operating throughout the Midwest, providing strong opportunities for Swiss Americans with extensive knowledge of Swiss culture and business practices.

POLITICS AND GOVERNMENT

In the eighteenth century, Geneva was an autonomous city-state but allied with the Swiss Confederation. The writings of two of its citizens influenced the founders of the United States engaged in creating a new governmental structure. Jean Jacques Rousseau (1712–1778) expounded the idea that government rested on a social contract. Jean Jacques Burlamaqui (1694–1748) stressed in his *Principles of Natural and Political Law* that a government should guarantee its citizens secure happiness.

The relations between the United States and Switzerland have been generally friendly but not without tensions. At times outsiders view Swiss neutrality and direct democracy as inefficient; yet Switzerland's neutral stand allows it to represent American interests in countries with which the United States has broken off diplomatic ties. The constitutional revisions of 1999 strengthened the rights of Swiss expatriates to vote in national elections, encouraging those who have left the country to maintain their engagement in Swiss politics. In 2006 the Swiss government launched the Swiss Roots program, which supports outreach organizations for people of Swiss heritage and educational programs throughout the United States and the world.

Switzerland and the United States also share strong economic ties: the United States is the number-one foreign investor in Swiss businesses and industries, and Switzerland is the sixth-largest investor in the United States. There are more than 700 Swiss

Swiss American, Captain "Sully" Sullenberger poses in the cockpit of a 1958 DC7 to benefit the Historical Flight Foundation in 2011. Sullenberger is famous for his near-perfect crash landing of a jetliner in the Hudson River in 2009, in which all passengers survived. LARRY MARANO / GETTY IMAGES

companies operating in the United States, primarily in the Midwest.

NOTABLE INDIVIDUALS

The Swiss have had easy access to all aspects of life in the United States. The selection that follows features a few individuals according to their field of endeavor.

Architecture William Lescaze (1896–1969), born and educated in Geneva, Switzerland, moved to the United States in 1921 and rose to prominence as a builder of skyscrapers; he also authored several treatises on modern architecture. In bridge-building Othmar Ammann (1879–1965), born in Feuerthalen, Canton Schaffhausen, achieved world renown; after studies in Zurich he went to New York City in 1904 and in 1925 was appointed chief engineer of the Port Authority of New York; he built the George Washington and other suspension bridges noted for innovative engineering and bold and esthetic design.

Arts Mari Sandoz (1896?–1966), the daughter of Swiss immigrants, published several works of enduring value, among them the biography of her father, titled *Old Jules*, and a biography of Crazy Horse, the noted leader of the Sioux; her works reveal an unusual understanding of not only the world of the white settlers but also the mental universe of indigenous peoples such as the Sioux and Cheyenne. Jeremias Theus (1719–1774) worked in Charleston, South Carolina, as a successful portrait painter. Peter Rindisbacher (1806–1834) produced valuable paintings documenting his family's move to Canada's Red River colony in 1821 and to Wisconsin in 1826; his works featuring Native Americans are also highly valued for their accuracy. The same holds for the numerous works of Karl Bodmer (1809–1893) who served for thirteen months as pictorial chronicler for the Prince zu Neuwied's journey to the Upper Missouri in 1832. Fritz Glarner (1899–1972), like Bodmer a native of Zurich, began working in New York in 1936, creating works in the style of constructivism.

Business and Industry Lorenzo Delmonico (1813–1881) from Marengo, Canton Tessin, went to New York at age nineteen, and in 1843 he opened the Delmonico Hotel, which popularized continental European cuisine in American cooking.

Medicine Adolf Meyer (1866–1950), born in Niederwenigen, Canton Zurich, was influential in American psychiatry; after studies at European universities he worked in various American psychiatric institutions and insisted on the study of symptoms, on bedside note-taking, the counseling of the families of patients, and their further care after discharge; in 1898 he published a classical work on neurology and after 1910 chaired the department of psychiatry at Johns Hopkins Medical School and also directed the Henry Phipps Clinic. Henry E. Sigerist (1891–1957) taught at Johns Hopkins University from 1932 to 1942, directing its Institute of History and Medicine; he had previously been a professor at the University of Leipzig, Germany, and emerged as a leading historian and as an advocate of socialized medicine.

Military In the American Revolution John André (1751–1780), born in Geneva, Switzerland, and an officer in the British army, was captured as a spy in 1780 and hanged by the revolutionaries; the British honored his bravery by a tomb in Westminster Abbey. At the end of the Civil War another Swiss named Henry Wirz (1823–1865) was also hanged for his alleged crimes as commander of the Confederacy's Andersonville Prison where some 12,000 Union soldiers perished; his responsibility for the terrible conditions at Andersonville remains controversial.

Music Rudolf Ganz (1877–1972), who immigrated to the United States in 1900, became an influential pianist, the conductor of the St. Louis Symphony Orchestra from 1921 to 1927, and president of the Chicago Musical College of Roosevelt University from 1933 to 1954. The composer Ernest Bloch (1880–1957) of Geneva, Switzerland, taught and wrote music at various American institutions of the Midwest and the West Coast; among his works the orchestral poems titled *Helvetia*, *America*, and *Israel* intimate his threefold cultural orientation.

In popular music, singer-songwriter Jewel (1974–), pop singer Cyndi Lauper (1953–), and folk artist Elvis Perkins (1976–) are of Swiss extraction.

Politics In the 1770s John Joachim Zubly (1724–1781) of St. Gallen, Switzerland, emerged as a leading critic of the British; he was an ordained Swiss Reformed minister, a member of the Georgia Provincial Congress, and delegate to the Second Continental Congress; yet he rejected independence and viewed the union between the colonies and Great Britain as sacred and perpetual. Albert Gallatin (1761–1849) became successful in the early years of the American republic; he arrived from Geneva in 1780 and eventually moved to western Pennsylvania, where he entered politics. He was elected to the state legislature in 1792 but was disbarred by the Federalists. He then served in the House and emerged as a leader of Jefferson's party; from 1801 to 1813 he served as secretary of the treasury, then as diplomat in France, England, and Russia. After his retirement from politics he became a scholar of Native American languages, cofounded New York University, and was a leading opponent of the War against Mexico in 1847. Another leading Jeffersonian was William Wirt (1772–1834). The son of Swiss

A series of human-shaped stone figures by Swiss-born artist Ugo Rondinone are depicted at the Rockefeller Center Plaza in New York during his "Human Nature" street exhibition in April, 2013. EMMANUEL DUNAND / AFP / GETTY IMAGES

immigrants; he was a noted orator and jurist and served as attorney general of the United States from 1817 to 1829. Emanuel Lorenz Philipp (1861–1925) rose to prominence in Wisconsin politics, which he entered in 1903. He served as governor from 1915 to 1921 and promoted cooperation between farmers, workers, and business.

Religion Michael Schlatter (1716–1790) from St. Gallen, Switzerland, went to Pennsylvania in 1746 and there organized numerous parishes of the Swiss Reformed Church. Johann Martin Henni (1805–1881) became in 1875 the first Catholic archbishop of Milwaukee. He was born in Misanenga, Canton Graubünden, went to the United States in 1828, became vicar general of the diocese of Cincinnati, and served as editor of the *Wahrheitsfreund*, the first Catholic German-language newspaper. Philip Schaff (1819–1893) of Chur, Canton Graubünden, was a major historian of church history at Union Theological Seminary in New York for twenty-five years. He was a strong advocate of Christian ecumenism, author of numerous scholarly works, and stressed the historical approach to questions of theology.

Science Ferdinand Hassler (1770–1843) was born in Aarau, Switzerland, and studied in Jena, Göttingen, and Paris, then accepted an appointment as professor of mathematics and natural philosophy at West Point. His 1807 plan for a coastal survey of the United States was began in 1817 and the precision of Hassler's work makes it still valid today. Louis Rodolphe Agassiz (1807–1873) became internationally known as a scientist and explorer. Born in Motier, Canton Fribourg, he studied the natural sciences at various European universities. He published a major work on fish and proposed the theory of a previous ice age. After he went to Boston in 1846, he undertook scientific expeditions to South America and was appointed to the chair of zoology and geology at Harvard University, where he began work on his influential ten-volume *Contributions to the Natural History of the United States*. His son Alexander Agassiz (1835–1910) also became a noted natural scientist in his own right. Adolphe Bandelier (1840–1914) was a pioneer in the ethnology and archeology of the American southwest. Born in Bern, Switzerland, he went with his family to Highland, Illinois, in 1848, and returned to Switzerland in 1857 to study geology at the University of Bern. On his return he did extended research in Mexico, the American southwest, and Bolivia, and he authored numerous studies on Native American cultures of those regions.

Sports National Football League quarterback Ben Roethlisberger (1982–), legendary pool player Rudolph "Minnesota Fats" Wanderone (1913–1996), Olympic alpine skier Caroline Lalive (1979–), and National Hockey League goaltender Cory Schnieder (1986–) are all Swiss-Americans.

Swiss American actor Renee Zellweger, best known for her roles in *Jerry Maguire, Cold Mountain,* and *Bridget Jones's Diary,* among others. LARRY BUSACCA / GETTY IMAGES

Stage and Screen Actors and actresses of Swiss ancestry include Meryl Streep (1949–), Renée Zellweger (1969–), Yul Brynner (1920–1985), Michelle Pfeiffer (1958–), Liev Schreiber (1976–), and James Caviezel (1968–). In addition, famed director George Lucas and television personality Ryan Seacrest are of Swiss descent.

Technology Machinist John Heinrich Kruesi (1843–1899), born in Heiden, Canton Appenzell, joined Thomas A. Edison in Newark, New Jersey, in the early 1870s and transformed Edison's ideas into workable instruments. In 1887 he became general manager and chief engineer of the Edison Machine Works in Schenectady, New York. The Swiss Louis Joseph Chevrolet (1878–1941) came to the United States in 1900, became a successful racing-car champion, winning the 500-mile Indianapolis race in 1919. In 1911 he cofounded the Chevrolet Motor Car Company in Detroit but soon left the enterprise. In 1929 he built a workable airplane engine and later designed a helicopter.

MEDIA

PRINT

Swiss American Historical Society Review

Published three times a year with a circulation of 400, this journal offers scholarly and popular articles of Swiss American interest relating to history, literature, genealogy, and personal experience.

Leo Schelbert, Editor
2523 Asbury Avenue
Evanston, Illinois 60201
Phone: (708) 328-3514
Email: lschelbe@uic.edu

Swiss Review

Founded in 1973, this quarterly magazine has a circulation of over 300,000. It publishes regional news from Swiss communities for the Swiss abroad, and has editions in German, French, Italian, English, and Spanish.

Wal Baur, U.S. Swiss American Editor
2364 Sunset Curve
Upland, California 91784-1069
Phone: (909) 931-7708
Email: wbaur@roadrunner.com
URL: http://www.revuew.ch

RADIO

World Radio Switzerland

An English-language radio station operating in Switzerland, available for streaming over the Internet.

Philippe Mottaz, Director
Phone: +41 58 236 74 44
Fax: +41 58 236 74 54
Email: isabelle.schoen@worldradio.ch
URL: http://www.worldradio.ch

ORGANIZATIONS AND ASSOCIATIONS

American-Swiss Foundation

Involves American and Swiss corporations and individuals interested in maintaining friendship and cultural exchange with Switzerland. Provides a forum for meetings and discussions. Conducts monthly events featuring Swiss and American speakers in New York.

Patricia Schramm, President
317 Madison Avenue
Suite 2320
New York, New York 10017
Phone: (212) 754-0130
Fax: (212) 754-4512
Email: info@americanswiss.org
URL: http://www.americanswiss.org

North American Swiss Alliance

Fraternal benefit life insurance society for persons of Swiss birth or ancestry.

Victoria Donahue, Manager
26777 Lorain Road

Suite 321
North Olmsted, Ohio 44070
Phone: (440) 734-3131

Swiss-American Business Council

A nonprofit association seeking to foster relationships between American and Swiss businesses.

Sutha Heck, Office Manager
P.O. Box 64975
Chicago, Illinois 60601
Phone: (312) 508-3340
Email: events@sabcnow.com
URL: http://www.sabcnow.com

Swiss American Historical Society (SAHS)

Founded in 1927, it moved from Chicago to Madison, Wisconsin, in 1940. Became dormant in the 1950s but was reactivated in 1963 under the leadership of Heinz K. Meier (1929–1989). Publishes the *SAHS Review* three times a year, holds annual and occasional regional meetings, and supports the SAHS Publication Series with Lang Publishers, New York.

Fred Gillespie, President
55 Twin Pine Way
Glen Mills, Pennsylvania 19342-1606
Email: Fred.Gillespie@state.de.us
URL: http://www.swissamericanhistory.org/forum/portal.php

MUSEUMS AND RESEARCH CENTERS

Archives of the Archabbey St. Meinrad

Houses 13 volumes of transcripts of materials located at the Benedictine Abbey of Einsiedeln, Switzerland, relating to St. Meinrad's founding in 1854. Despite the fire of 1887 that destroyed valuable sources, letters of the founding generation and extensive correspondence with other monasteries and ecclesiastical institutions are preserved and provide insight into the Benedictine dimension of transplanted Swiss Catholicism.

St. Meinrad College and School of Theology
St. Meinrad, Indiana 47577
Phone: (812) 357-6566

Balch Institute for Ethnic Studies

Dedicated to preserving and documenting the multicultural heritage of the United States. Houses a collection on the Swiss, including papers of the Swiss American Historical Society. Merged with the Pennsylvania Historical Society in 2002.

Kim Sajet, President
1300 Locust Street
Philadelphia, Pennsylvania 19107
Phone: (215) 732-6200
Fax: (215) 732-2680
Email: ksajet@hsp.org
URL: http://www.hsp.org

Lovejoy Library

Located at Southern Illinois University in Ewardsville, houses the Highland, Koepfli, and Suppiger

Collections. The materials highlight the founding and evolution of the Highland settlement, which began in 1831, as well as the Swiss in Illinois. They are complemented by materials at the Madison County Historical Museum, also at Edwardsville, and by the Illinois Historical Survey Library at the University of Illinois at Urbana.

Campus Box 1063
30 Hairpin Drive
Edwardsville, Illinois 62026
Phone: (618) 650-4636
URL: http://www.siue.edu/lovejoylibrary/

Mennonite Historical Library

Located at Goshen College, has an extensive collection of works on Swiss Mennonite history and of Swiss Mennonite and Amish family histories and genealogies.

Harvey Hiebert, Librarian
1700 South Main Street
Goshen, Indiana 46526
Phone: (574) 535-7418
Fax: (574) 535-7438
Email: mhl@goshen.edu
URL: http://www.goshen.edu/mhl/

New Glarus Swiss Historical Village and Museum

Presents artifacts from the town's early history in several thematically arranged buildings. An exhibition hall features special exhibits of Swiss American interest.

John Marty, President
612 7th Avenue
New Glarus, Wisconsin 53574
Phone: (608) 527-2317
URL: www.swisshistoricalvillage.org

Swiss Center of North America

Founded in 2003 through grants from both the Wisconsin Department of Commerce and the Swiss government, houses a research library and museum and hosts events celebrating Swiss culture.

507 Durst Road, New Glarus
Wisconsin 53574
Phone: (608) 527-6565
Email: info@theswisscenter.org
URL: http://theswisscenter.org

SOURCES FOR ADDITIONAL STUDY

American Letters: Eighteenth and Nineteenth Century Accounts of Swiss Immigrants, edited by Leo Schelbert. Camden, ME: Picton Press, 1995.

Basler, Konrad. *The Dorlikon Emigrants: Swiss Settlers and Cultural Founders in the United States*, translated by Laura Villiger. New York: Peter Lang, 1996.

Bowen, Ralph. *A Frontier Family in Minnesota: Letters of Theodore and Sophie Bost, 1851–1920*. Minneapolis: University of Minnesota Press, 1981.

Freitag, Duane H. *Sauerkraut, Suspenders, and the Swiss: A Political History of Green County's Swiss Colony, 1845–1945*. Bloomington, IN: iUniverse Inc., 2012.

Gratz, Delbert L. *Bernese Anabaptists and Their American Descendants*. Scottdale, PA: Herald Press, 1953.

Grueningen, John Paul *The Swiss in the United States*. Madison, WI: Swiss American Historical Society, 1940.

Hoelscher, Steven D. *Heritage on Stage: The Invention of Ethnic Place in America's Little Switzerland*. Madison: University of Wisconsin Press, 1998.

Kleber, Albert. *History of St. Meinrad Archabbey 1854–1954*. St. Meinrad, IN: St. Meinrad Archabbey, 1954.

Schelbert, Leo. "On Becoming an Emigrant: A Structural View of Eighteenth and Nineteenth Century Swiss Data." *Perspectives in American History* 7 (1973): 440–95.

The United States and Switzerland: Aspects of an Enmeshment; Yearbook of German American Studies 1990, Volume 25, edited by Leo Schelbert. Lawrence: University of Kansas for the Society for German American Studies, 1991.

Tritt, D. G., ed. *Swiss Festivals in North America: A Resource Guide*. Morgantown, PA: Masthof Press, 1999.

SYRIAN AMERICANS

J. Sydney Jones

OVERVIEW

Syrian Americans are immigrants or descendants of people from Syria, an Arab republic of southwestern Asia. Syria is bordered by Turkey on the north, Iraq on the east and southeast, Jordan on the south, Israel and Lebanon on the southwest, and the Mediterranean Sea on the west. At 71,500 square miles (185,226 square kilometers), the country is slightly larger than the state of Washington.

Officially called the Syrian Arab Republic, the country had an estimated population in 2012 of 22.7 million. The people are primarily Muslim, with some 1.5 million Christians and a few thousand Jews. Ethnically, the country is made up of an Arab majority with a large number of Kurds as the second-largest ethnic group. Other groups include Armenians, Turkmen, and Assyrians, as well as Chechens and Circasians. During the first decade of the twenty-first century, Syria underwent modest economic reform; however, because of political turmoil and upheaval in 2011, the economy has suffered. In addition, international sanctions and a decrease in the nation's capacity to produce and consume goods and services as a result of the civil war have threatened the economic stability of the country and lowered its standard of living.

The earliest Syrians immigrated to the United States after 1880. Between 1899 and 1919, almost 90,000 Syrians (68 percent of them unmarried males) arrived in the United States. Many worked in the world's fairs held in Philadelphia, Chicago, and St. Louis at the end of the nineteenth century and the beginning of the twentieth, and a large number of these workers remained in those cities after the fairs ended. Restrictions on immigration quotas slowed the numbers of Syrians arriving in the United States after 1924, but when these restrictions were abolished with the Immigration Act of 1965, a massive wave of immigrants arrived, with an estimated 40,000 entering between 1961 and 1990. Ten percent of this group immigrated under the Refugee Act of 1980.

According to the American Community Survey of the U.S. Census Bureau, 153,392 Syrian Americans—close to the population of Sioux Falls, South Dakota—resided in the United States in 2011. Syrian Americans live in every state, and they tend to live in urban city centers. There are small communities of Syrian Americans in Toledo, Ohio; New Orleans; and Cedar Rapids, Iowa. Cities with an especially dense population of Syrian Americans include New York, Boston, and Detroit and Dearborn, Michigan. New York City has the largest number of Syrian Americans, many of whom reside in Brooklyn. California, especially Los Angeles, and Houston have also gained popularity among Syrian Americans in recent decades. The states with the most Syrian American residents are California, Pennsylvania, New York, New Jersey, Florida, Michigan, Texas, and Massachusetts.

HISTORY OF THE PEOPLE

Early History Syria has a long and storied history. From ancient times, the area that came to be known as Syria had a succession of rulers, including Mesopotamians, Hittites, Egyptians, Assyrians, Babylonians, Persians, and Greeks. Pompey brought Roman rule to the region in 63 BCE, making Greater Syria a Roman province. The Christian era brought centuries of unrest. The Arab Muslims invaded in 633–634 CE, and Damascus surrendered to Muslim troops in 635. By 640 the conquest was complete. Four districts—Damascus, Hims, Jordan, and Palestine—were created, with Damascus the capital. The region enjoyed relative peace and prosperity, as well as religious toleration, for the next century under the Umayyad reign. The Umayyad lineage was the Umayyad caliphate—the second Islamic caliphate established after the passing of Muhammad. The Arabic language was used predominantly in the region at this time.

The Abbasid dynasty, centered in Iraq, overthrew the Umayyads in 750 CE. This dynasty ruled from a new capital established at Baghdad and erected a symbolic caliph in Cairo. It was in power until around 1250 CE. The dynasty culture flourished in the tenth and eleventh centuries, with Baghdad the most cultured city in the world. During this time the European Crusaders made repeated incursions in an attempt to recapture the Holy Land. Saladin, a noted Muslim sultan and war hero, took Damascus in 1174, effectively expelling the Crusaders from their occupying positions, and established centers of learning as well as trading centers and a new land system that stimulated economic life.

During the thirteenth century Mongol invasions wracked the region. By 1322 Mongol leaders had converted to the Muslim religion and become integrated into the existing culture. At the end of the fourteenth century, Tamerlane—a well-known Asian conquerer—captured Syria, and in 1401 Baghdad was destroyed. The Mamluk Sultanate controlled the region until 1516, when the Turkish Ottomans defeated Egypt and occupied all of ancient Syria. Ottoman control would last for four centuries, during which time the Ottomans created four jurisdictional districts—Damascus, Aleppo, Tripoli, and Sidon—each ruled by its own governor. Early governors encouraged agriculture based on the economic structure they established; subsequently, cereals, cotton, and silk were produced for export. Aleppo became an important center for trade with Europe, and Italian, French, and English merchants began to settle in the region. Christian communities were allowed to flourish, especially during the seventeenth and eighteenth centuries.

By the eighteenth century, however, Ottoman rule was beginning to weaken. Bedouin incursions from the desert increased, and general prosperity and security declined. A brief period of Egyptian domination was again replaced by Ottoman rule in 1840, but tensions were growing between the religious and ethnic groups of the region. With the massacre of Christians by a Muslim mob in Damascus in 1860, Europe began to intervene in the affairs of the moribund Ottoman Empire. A group of Western powers established an autonomous district in Lebanon but left Syria under Ottoman control for a time. Meanwhile, French and British influence gained in the region, and the population steadily became more Westernized. But Arab-Turk relations worsened, especially after the Young Turk revolution of 1908, an event that inaugurated a return to parliamentary Ottoman government. The Young Turk movement allowed for the meeting of many intellectuals and dissidents and resulted in a vision of a democratic, multinational state possibly consisting of Bulgarians, Jewish people, Arabs, Greeks, and Armenians. Arab nationalists were inspired by this movement in Syria.

New arrivals in the United States from Greater Syria ranged from seekers of religious freedom to those who wished to avoid Turkish conscription. But by far the largest motivator was the American dream of personal success.

Modern Era During World War I Syria was transformed into a military base of the Ottoman Empire, which declared a jihad against France, Russia, and Britain before joining forces with the Germans. However, nationalist Arabs under Faysal—an Arab statesman and king of Iraq from 1921 to 1933—stood alongside the British with military leaders T. E. Lawrence and Edmund Allenby, two men who were legendary for their diplomacy and military prowess. After the war the region was ruled for a time by Faysal, but a French mandate from the League of Nations placed the newly partitioned region under French control until independence could be arranged. In fact, the French had no interest in such independence, and British and Free French troops (soldiers who continued to fight against the Axis powers after the collapse of France) occupied the country until 1946, when a Syrian civilian government took over. It was only with World War II that a free Syria was finally established.

There were manifold challenges for such a government, including the reconciliation of a number of religious groups. These included the majority Sunni Muslim sect with the two other dominant Muslim groups, the Alawites—a Shi'ite group—and the Druzes. There were also Christians, divided into a half dozen sects, and Jews. Additionally, ethnic and economic-cultural differences had to be dealt with, from peasant to Westernized urbanite, from Arab to Kurd to Turk. With the failure of a civilian government made up mostly of Sunni landowners, a bloodless coup brought Colonel Husni as-Zaim to power, but he was, in turn, soon toppled. Control over the nation passed swiftly from al-Zaim to Colonel Sami al-Hinnawi and Colonel Adib al-Sheeshakli.

A series of such coups followed, as did an abortive union with Egypt from 1958 to 1961. Increasingly, governing power rested with the Pan Arabist Ba'th Socialists in the military. On March 14, 1971, General Hafiz al-Assad was sworn in as president of the titular democracy after seizing power from Colonel Salah al-Jadid. Assad remained in power until his death in 2000, enjoying a measure of popularity from nationalists, workers, and peasants for his land reform and economic development.

Modern Syrian foreign policy has largely been driven by the Arab-Israeli conflict; Syria has suffered several defeats at the hands of the Israelis. The Syrian Golan Heights are still under Israeli occupation and remain a contentious issue between the two countries. Arab relations were strained by Syria's support of Iran against Iraq in the ten-year Iran-Iraq War. Syrian-Lebanese relations have also proved to be a volatile issue; until the Cedar Revolution of 2005, Syria maintained more than 30,000 troops in Lebanon. During the Cold War Syria was an ally of the Soviet Union, receiving arms aid from that country. With the fall of Communism, however, Syria turned toward the West to form alliances. After the Iraqi invasion of Kuwait in 1990, Syria sent troops to aid in the UN-led liberation of Kuwait.

Upon President Hafiz al-Asad's death in 2000, his son Bashar was elected by popular referendum. During his first term Syrian troops were removed

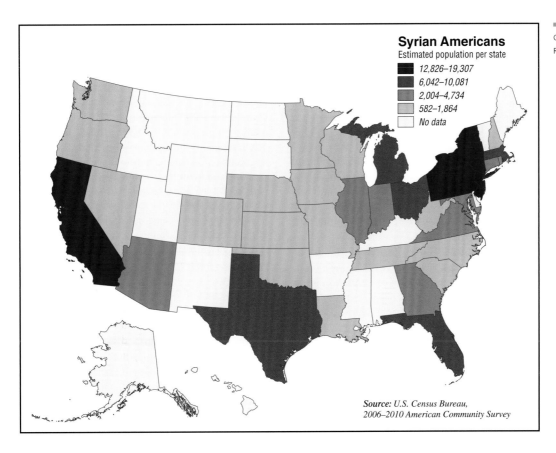

Syrian Americans
Estimated population per state

- 12,826–19,307
- 6,042–10,081
- 2,004–4,734
- 582–1,864
- No data

Source: U.S. Census Bureau,
2006–2010 American Community Survey

from Lebanon. Although Bashar was elected to a second term as president in 2007, many protests erupted against the government beginning in 2010. During its long reign, since 1963, the Ba'th Party has brought order to the country, but largely at the cost of true democratic government; foes of the administration are harshly repressed. Almost the entire country has engaged in protests at one point or another, with the government making some concessions as a result. The king remains in power, however, despite protestors' calls for his resignation. Subsequently, intense conflicts have taken place between the government and rebel groups. Many nations have issued economic sanctions against Syria, including the United States, members of the European Union, Turkey, and the Arab League.

SETTLEMENT IN THE UNITED STATES

Until World War I the majority of Greater Syrian immigrants to the United States came from the Christian villages around Mount Lebanon. Estimates of the number of early immigrants run between 40,000 and 100,000. Philip Hitti, who wrote an authoritative early history titled *The Syrians in America* (1924), even asserted that "it [was] safe to assume that there [were] …] about 200,000 Syrians, foreign-born and born of Syrian parents, in the United States" at that time. It is estimated that between 1900 and 1916, about 1,000 official immigrants a year came from the districts of

Damascus and Aleppo, parts of modern-day Syria, or the Republic of Syria. Most of these early immigrants settled in urban centers in the eastern United States, including New York and Boston, or in Detroit.

Immigration to the United States occurred for several reasons. Emigrants from Greater Syria ranged from seekers of religious freedom to those who wished to avoid Turkish conscription. But by far the largest motivator was the American dream of personal success. Economic improvement was the primary incentive for these early immigrants. Many of the earliest made money in the United States and then returned to their native soil to live. The tales told by these returning men fueled further immigration waves. This, in addition to early settlers in the United States sending for their relatives, created what is known as *chain immigration*. This phenomenon was intensified by Syrian Americans working at the world's fairs in 1876 (Philadelphia), 1893 (Chicago), and 1904 (St. Louis). Some 68 percent of the early immigrants were single males, and at least half were illiterate.

Although the number of arrivals in the United States was not large, the effect in the villages from which these people emigrated was lasting. Restrictions imposed by both the Ottoman government and the United States limited the number of Syrians who moved to the United States, especially after the passage of the U.S. Johnson-Reed Act in 1924; this quota act greatly reduced immigration from the eastern Mediterranean region to the United States, effectively halting further Syrian immigration until the Immigration Act of 1965 opened the doors once again to Arabs. Another wave of immigration thus started in the mid-1960s; in fact, more than 75 percent of all foreign-born Arab Americans identified on the 1990 U.S. Census came to the United States after 1964. Many of these people were Palestinian refugees, Egyptians, or Lebanese, so exact numbers are difficult to determine. This challenge is exacerbated by the fact that many people associated with the Ottoman Syria consider themselves to be Lebanese and still others self-identify as Palestinians or Jordanians, as opposed to Syrians.

During the last decades of the twentieth century and the first decades of the twenty-first, Syrians settled in every state, continuing to concentrate in urban centers. The largest communities of Syrians live in New York City, especially in the borough of Brooklyn. In particular, the area around Atlantic Avenue has become known as "Little Syria," preserving the look and feel of ethnic business and traditions. Boston also harbors a significant Syrian population, as do two city centers in Michigan: Detroit and Dearborn. In addition, many Syrians reside in New England and upstate New York, especially descendants of early peddlers who opened small mercantile operations. New Orleans; Toledo, Ohio; and Cedar Rapids, Iowa, all have small but significant numbers of Syrian Americans. In the past few decades, Syrian Americans have also congregated in California, especially Los Angeles. Large communities of Syrian immigrants have settled in Houston since the last few years of the twentieth century. Finally, other states with significant populations of Syrian Americans include Florida, New Jersey, and Pennsylvania.

LANGUAGE

Language use by Syrian Americans is loosely linked to the languages spoken in the home country, but different trends have impacted the way Syrian Americans have used language during the last few decades of the twentieth century and since the beginning of the twenty-first. Arabic is the primary language in Syria. However, some ethnic groups maintain their own languages, especially outside the urban areas of Aleppo and Damascus, with Kurdish, Armenian, and Turkish being spoken in various areas. In general, Syrians are Arabic speakers who have their own dialect of the formal language, one that separates them as a group from other Arab-speaking peoples. Subdialects of each dialect exist depending on the place of origin; for example, Aleppo and Damascus each have a distinctive subdialect with accent and idiomatic peculiarities unique to the region. For the most part, dialect speakers can be understood by others, especially those closely related to the Syrian dialect, such as Lebanese, Jordanian, and Palestinian.

The availability of print materials published in Arabic in the United States has impacted the way that Syrian Americans use language. More immigrants sustained their use of Arabic when there was a rich profusion of Arab newspapers and magazines in the United States. However, many immigrants wished to assimilate quickly into traditional U.S. culture. This predisposition, combined with a lower number of new immigrants due to quota restrictions, resulted in the decline of Arabic publications and the practice of speaking Arabic in the last few decades of the twentieth century. Parents ceased teaching their children the language around the same time, and thus, their linguistic traditions were lost within a few generations in the United States. Among newer immigrants, however, language traditions are stronger. Arabic classes for young children are once again common. Church services are held in Arabic in many locations, and the appearance of the Arabic language in commercial signs advertising Arab businesses also demonstrates an increased use of Arabic among Syrian Americans.

According to the 2011 American Community Survey, 93 percent of Syrian Americans over the age of five speak English, including in the home. Only 11.1 percent of the Syrian American population rate themselves as speaking English less than "very well." The survey shows that 66.1 percent speak English only and 33.9 percent of the population speaks another language in addition to English.

Greetings and Popular Expressions Syrian greetings often come in triplicate, with response and counterresponse. The most typical greeting is the casual *Marhaba* (Hello), which elicits the response *Ahlen* (Welcome) or *Marhabteen* (Two hellos). Both can earn the counterresponse of *Maraahib* (Several hellos). The morning greeting is *Sabaah al-kehir* (The morning is good), followed by *Sabaah an-noor* (The morning is light). The evening greeting is *Masa al-kheir*, responded to with *Masa n-noor*. Greetings understood throughout the Arabic world are *Asalam 'a laykum* (Peace be with you), followed by *Wa 'a laykum asalaam* (Peace be upon you too).

The formal introduction is *Ahlein* or *Ahlan was Sahlan*, and a popular toast is *Sahteen May* (Your health increase). "How are you?" is *Keif haalak?*; this is often responded to with *Nushkar Allah* (We thank God). Elaborate linguistic differentiations are made for gender and for salutations made to a group as opposed to an individual.

RELIGION

Although Islam is the predominant religion of Syria, most of the early immigrants to the United States from Syria were Christian. Syrian immigrants to the United States after 1965 are more likely to be Muslim. As a collective, the Syrian American community holds membership in a number of religious groups, from Sunni Muslims to Greek Orthodox Christians.

Christian Syrian Americans belong to various branches of Catholicism, mostly of the Eastern rite: Armenian Catholics, Syrian Catholics, and Catholic Chaldeans, as well as Latin-rite Roman Catholics, Melkites, and Maronites. Additionally, there are Greek Orthodox, Syrian Orthodox, Nestorians, and Protestants. The first Syrian churches built in New York between 1890 and 1895 were Melkite, Maronite, and Orthodox.

Muslim Syrian Americans identify with one of several branches and can be strongly impacted by the tendencies and distinct rituals of their particular Muslim branch. In Syria, the Sunni sect is the largest, accounting for 75 percent of the population. Shi'ite is the second-largest, and next is the Druzes, a Muslim branch that was the affiliation of many of the early Syrian immigrant peddlers.

Because the Ottomans developed a so-called "millet system" (a means of dividing citizens into political entities by religion), religious affiliation in Syria was almost tantamount to belonging to a nation. Identification with a particular religious group became, over the centuries, a second dimension of identity for Syrians, along with family ties. Despite these perceived distinctions, all Middle Eastern religions share common values, including charity, hospitality, and respect for authority and age; nevertheless, these individual sects experience some friction in their sentiments toward other branches. The differences between the various Catholic faiths are not major dogmatic ones, however. For example, some churches conduct services in Arabic and Greek, others only in Aramaic.

As noted, the earliest Syrian American immigrants were largely Christian. As of 2013 there were nearly 250 churches and missions in the United States serving the Orthodox Christians of Syria. Melkite, Maronite, and Orthodox churches confirm and baptize the faithful and use wine-soaked bread for the Eucharist. Often, ceremonies are held in English to serve the assimilated membership. Popular saints for the Maronites are St. Maron and St. Charbel; for the Melkites, St. Basil; and for the Orthodox, St. Nicholas and St. George.

Some Muslims and Druzes arrived in the early waves of immigration, but most have come since 1965. As of 2010 there were 2,106 mosques in the United States. Part of Muslim ritual is praying five times a day. When no mosque is available for worship, small groups get together and rent rooms in commercial districts, where they can hold midday prayer.

The political upheaval in Syria in the twenty-first century has created challenges and tragedies that affect both Muslims and Christians. The bloodshed and skirmishes of the civil war are a cause for worry among religious Syrian Americans of both faiths and have prompted them to call for the U.S. government to intervene.

CULTURE AND ASSIMILATION

Several factors combined to promote the rapid assimilation of early Syrian immigrants into traditional U.S. culture. Primary among these was that, instead of congregating in urban ethnic enclaves, many of the first immigrants from Greater Syria took to the road as peddlers, selling their wares up and down the eastern seaboard. Despite their relatively low numbers compared to other immigrant groups, the first arrivals stood out from other recent immigrants, due largely to their traditional clothing and their occupation as peddlers. The circulation of negative stereotypes and the resulting xenophobia prompted Syrian immigrants to integrate into the mainstream culture more quickly than other groups. Intent on building a successful business, these peddlers used their daily dealings with rural Americans to absorb the language, customs, and mannerisms of their new homeland, and they tended to blend in rapidly with the American way of life. Most swiftly Anglicized their names and, as many of them were already Christian, adopted more mainstream American religious denominations.

The assimilation and Americanization of the early Syrian Americans, in fact, has been so successful that it proves challenging to ascertain the ethnic origins of some families. The same is not true, however, for Syrians who arrived in the United States during the last few decades of the twentieth century. This group is generally better educated than some of the earlier Syrian immigrants, and a larger percentage of them are Muslim. In general, they are not overeager to give up their Arab identities and be absorbed into mainstream U.S. culture. This is partly a result of renewed

A peddler with a huge brass pitcher strapped to his back sells cold drinks in the Syrian quarter of New York City. CORBIS. REPRODUCED BY PERMISSION.

SYRIAN SALAD

Ingredients

6 cucumbers, diced

4 roma tomatoes, seeded and diced

5 green onions, sliced

1 red bell pepper, seeded and diced

1 cup garlic, chopped

1 cup fresh parsley, chopped

½ cup fresh mint leaves, minced

½ cup olive oil

2 tablespoons fresh lemon juice

1 tablespoon salt

1 tablespoon ground black pepper

Preparation

Toss the cucumbers, tomatoes, onions, bell pepper, garlic, parsley, and mint together in a bowl. Drizzle the olive oil and lemon juice over the salad and toss to coat. Season with salt and pepper to taste.

Serves 6

vigor of multiculturalism in the United States and due to the different mentality in the minds of the more recent arrivals.

Traditions and Customs Family is the foundation for much of the traditions and belief systems in Syria. A well-known saying sums up the importance of family in society: "Myself and my brother against my cousin; myself and my cousin against the stranger." Such strong family ties breed a communal spirit in which the needs of the group are more determinant than those of the individual. However, for many Syrian Americans, much of this traditional family system has unraveled with life in the United States, especially in families where both parents participate in the workforce. The fabric of the tight-knit family has become loosened in an environment that encourages so much individual achievement and personal freedom.

In Syria, as in all Arab societies, honor and status are important; these characteristics can be acquired through financial achievement and the exertion of power. Even people who do not embody these qualities must conduct themselves honestly and with sincerity. The virtues of magnanimity and social graciousness are integral to Syrian life, as these characteristics are considered important in many Islamic societies.

Cuisine Many standard foods from the Syrian heartland are also common in the United States and are standard fare for Syrian Americans. These items include pita bread and crushed chickpea or eggplant spreads (*hommos* and *baba ganouj*). *Tabouli*, a salad made from bulgur wheat, tomatoes, onions, lemons, and garlic, is also popular. Other typical foods include cheeses, yogurts, and many of the fruits and vegetables common to the eastern Mediterranean region, including pickles, hot peppers, olives, and pistachios. Followers of Islam are forbidden to consume pork, but other meats, such as lamb and chicken, are staples.

Much Syrian food is highly spiced, and dates and figs are employed in ways not usually found in typical American food. Stuffed zucchini, grape leaves, and cabbage leaves are common dishes. A popular sweet is *baqlawa*, which is made of phyllo dough filled with ground walnuts or pistachios and drizzled with sugar syrup.

Traditional Dress Traditional native Syrian dress included *shirwal*, which are baggy black pants, but this type of ensemble is almost completely a thing of the past for both Syrian Americans and native Syrians. Instead, native dress is reserved exclusively for ethnic dance performers. Some Syrian Muslim women wear the traditional *hijab* in public, derived from Muslim teaching that people in general, but women in particular, should be modest. A hijab may consist of a long-sleeved coat as well as a white scarf that covers the hair, but for some the scarf alone is sufficient. The number of female Syrian Americans who wear the hijab has increased along with the larger number of Muslim Syrian American in the United States.

Dances and Songs Arabic or Middle Eastern music is a living tradition that spans some thirteen centuries. Its three main divisions are classical, religious, and folk, the last of which has been expanded in modern times into a newer pop tradition. Central to all music from Syria and Arab countries are monophony and heterophony, vocal flourishes, subtle intonation, rich improvisation, and the Arab scales so different from those of Western tradition. These characteristics give Middle Eastern music its distinctive, exotic sound, at least to Western ears.

Maqam, or melodic modes, are basic to music of the classical genre. There are set intervals, cadences, and even final tones to these modes. Additionally, classical Arabic music uses rhythmic modes similar to medieval Western music, with short units that come from poetic measurements. Islamic music relies heavily on chanting from the Quran and has similarities to Gregorian chant. While classical and religious music have regular characteristics throughout a vast amount of land and culture, Arabic folk music reflects individual cultures such as Druze, Kurdish, and Bedouin.

Musical instruments used in classical music are primarily stringed, with the *ud*, a short-necked instrument similar to the lute, being the most typical. The spike-fiddle, or *rabab*, is an important stringed instrument that is bowed, and the *qanun* resembles a zither. For folk music, the most common instrument is the long-necked lute, or *tanbur*. Drums are also a common accompanying instrument in this vital musical tradition.

Holidays Both Christian and Muslim Syrian Americans celebrate a variety of religious holidays. Adherents of Islam observe three main holidays: *Ramadan*, the thirty-day period of fasting during daytime hours; *'Eid al-Fitr*, the five days marking the end of Ramadan; and *Eid al-Adha*, "The Feast of Sacrifice." Ramadan, held during the ninth month of the Islamic calendar, is a time in which self-discipline and moderation are employed for physical and spiritual cleansing (similar to the Christian Lenten period). The end of Ramadan is marked by 'Eid al-Fitr, something of a cross between Christmas and Thanksgiving, an ebullient festival time for Arabs. The Feast of Sacrifice, on the other hand, commemorates the intervention of the Angel Gabriel in the sacrifice of Ishmael. According to the Quran, the Muslim holy book, Abraham was willing to sacrifice his son Ishmael for God, but Gabriel intervened at the last moment, substituting a lamb for the boy. With the growing numbers of Syrian Americans, these holidays have become more widely observed and celebrated in the United States.

Christian Syrian Americans celebrate saints' days, Christmas, and Easter; however, the Orthodox Easter falls on a different Sunday than the Western Easter. Increasingly, Arab Muslims are also celebrating Christmas, not as a religious holiday but as a time for families to get together and exchange gifts. Syria's independence day, April 17, has traditionally been little celebrated in the United States; however, since the political uprisings in Syria, celebrations have begun to appear more frequently in major metropolitan areas. Groups like the Syrian American Council sponsor and organize these festivities.

Health Care Issues and Practices In general, the Syrian American population has no specific medical issues that are applicable to the population as a whole. The group does demonstrate higher-than-average rates of anemia as well as lactose intolerance. Syrian Americans typically rely on the family as a resource for dealing with psychological issues, as opposed to seeking outside help. Thus, while Arab medical doctors are common, Arab American psychologists and psychiatrists are more difficult to find.

FAMILY AND COMMUNITY LIFE

Syrian American families are generally close-knit, patriarchal units. Nuclear families in the United States have largely replaced the extended family of the Syrian homeland. Formerly, the oldest son held a special position in the family: he would bring his bride to his parents' house, raise his children there, and care for his parents in their old age. Like much else about traditional Syrian lifestyles, this custom has also broken down over time in both the United States and Syria.

Gender Roles For Syrian Americans, the longer they have resided in the United States, the more likely

SYRIAN AMERICAN RAPPER OMAR OFFENDUM

Music served as a medium of protest in response to violence that took place in Syria beginning in 2011. One performer in particular—Syrian American rapper Omar Offendum—has used a mainstream musical genre, rap, to spread messages that describe the collective hope of many Syrian Americans for peace. His music also communicates the hope for more harmonious relations between Syria and the United States. He integrates both Arabic and English into his music. Offendum has been banned from Syria because his work is considered controversial.

it is that traditional gender roles have become dismantled. Increasingly, men and women share a more equal role in Syrian American households, with the wife often out in the workplace and the husband also taking a more active role in childrearing. However, women still maintain responsibility for much of the domestic requirements of the family, including the rearing of children. In some cases, they might also provide assistance to their husbands in the family business. Indeed, many of the more recent Syrian American female immigrants arrived on a preference visa, and they lead active careers outside the home as professional doctors, scientists, and computer engineers. According to the 2011 American Community Survey, 56.7 percent of Syrian American females age sixteen and older were in the workforce.

Education A tradition of higher education was already in place with many early Syrian immigrants due in part to the preponderance of Western religious institutions established in Greater Syria from the late nineteenth century onward. Americans, Russians, French, and British operated these institutions. Emigrants from Damascus and Aleppo in Syria were also accustomed to institutions of higher education, although generally the more rural the immigrant, the less emphasis was placed on his or her education in the early Syrian American community.

Over time the attitude of the Syrian community has paralleled that of the United States as a whole: education is now more important for all children, not just the males. During the last decades of the twentieth century and into the early twenty-first century, women have been pursuing university studies in rising numbers. Today, higher education is highly prized among Syrian Americans. The 2011 American Community Survey reports that almost 90 percent of the Syrian American population (male and female) had earned a high school diploma. According to the same survey, almost half of male Syrian Americans age twenty-five

SYRIAN PROVERBS

- The camel limped because of pain in his hip.

- We taught them how to beg, they raced us to the gates. (To beat someone at his own game.)

- A beggar and he bargains! (Beggars can't be choosers.)

- With the lack of horses, we saddle the dogs! (There's nothing suitable, so they come with a useless alternative.)

- He hit me and cried, and then he raced me to complain! (It's all his fault, yet he pretends to be the victim.)

- Ask one who has experience rather than a physician. (Experience without learning is better than learning without experience.)

- He married the monkey for its money, the money went and the monkey stayed a monkey. (As you make your bed, so you must lie on it.)

- Whoever gets between the onion and its skin will get nothing but its stink. (Never get between a man and his wife.)

and older (48.7 percent) had earned a bachelor's degree, as well as more than a third of female Syrian Americans of the same age (36 percent). For most Syrian American professionals, the sciences are the preferred area of study, with large numbers becoming engineers, pharmacists, and doctors.

Courtship and Weddings Although many Syrian Americans have fully adopted the practices and customs of mainstream U.S. culture, the more conservative Syrian Americans and recent immigrants often practice arranged marriages, including endogamous (within group) marriages between cousins, which are intended to benefit the prestige of both families. Courtship is a chaperoned, heavily supervised affair; casual dating, such as that practiced in mainstream American culture, is disapproved of in these more traditional circles.

Among Syrian Americans who have become more assimilated into mainstream American culture, however, many young people retain control of the decision of who they will marry, though parental guidance and input have a heavy influence. Within these spheres, dating proves to be more relaxed. At the same time, for

many Muslim Syrian Americans, dating is allowed only after a ritual engagement. The enactment of a marriage contract, *kitb al-kitab*, sets up a period of time, usually lasting from several months to a year, during which the couple becomes more familiar with each other. The marriage is consummated only after a formal ceremony. Most Syrian Americans tend to marry within their religious community, if not their ethnic community. Thus, an Arab Muslim woman, for example, would be more likely to marry a non-Arab Muslim, such as an Iranian or Pakistani, than a Christian Arab.

Syrian Americans, like all Middle Easterners in general, consider marriage to be a solemn vow not to be entered into lightly. This belief likely contributes to the low divorce rates among Syrian Americans. According to the 2011 American Community Survey, 53 percent of Syrian Americans reported being married, with only 9.3 percent listing themselves as divorced and 1.6 percent as separated. In general, Syrian Americans do not approve of the practice, often seen in the mainstream United States, of engaging in a multiple divorce-remarriage pattern—and the group discourages divorcing due to reasons of personal unhappiness.

Syrian American couples tend to have children at a younger age than Americans, and they tend to have larger families as well. Boys are often given more freedom concerning behavior than girls.

EMPLOYMENT AND ECONOMIC CONDITIONS

Many of the first Syrian immigrants came to the United States with the goal of gaining wealth. Young men from villages all over Greater Syria immigrated in the late nineteenth century in hopes of getting rich quick in the relatively lucrative endeavor of door-to-door peddling. An estimated 90 to 95 percent of early Syrian American immigrants became peddlers. These individuals comprised the early distribution system of numerous small manufacturers, and they peddled all types of products, from buttons to suspenders to scissors. Such work had obvious advantages for immigrants: it took little or no training and investment; required a limited vocabulary; and provided instant, if meager, remuneration. Eager Syrian emigrants were herded into ships and headed off to "Amrika" or "Nay Yark," and many of them ended up in Brazil or Australia as a result of unscrupulous shipping agents.

At the turn of the twentieth century, peddlers were a common sight. The United States was in a period of transition, and peddlers served as migratory entrepreneurs, carrying backpacks or riding on carriages selling their wares. Although immigrants from many countries engaged in this trade, Syrian Americans were unique in that they stuck primarily to backpack peddling and rural America in their efforts to cover back roads in areas ranging from Vermont to North Dakota. In fact, this work took Syrian Americans to every state in the continental United States, helping distribute the settlement of Syrian Americans widely across the country.

Enterprising peddlers frequently used this experience as a step toward owning their own businesses. Estimates reflect that by 1908 there were already 3,000 Syrian-owned businesses in the United States, ranging from restaurants to stores to other industries. Many U.S.-educated Syrian Americans also soon obtained professional positions, including those of doctor, lawyer, and engineer. By 1910 a small group of Syrian millionaires provided evidence of the idea that the United States was a "land of opportunity." Dry goods were a particular Syrian specialty, especially clothing: this tradition can be seen in the modern clothing empires Farah and Haggar, both are which were founded by early Syrian immigrants. Many early Syrian immigrants joined the auto industry, resulting in large Syrian American communities in Detroit and Dearborn, Michigan.

Immigrants who arrived in the mid-twentieth century tended to be more educated than the first wave of immigrants, and they found employment in fields from computer science to banking to medicine. With cutbacks in the auto sector in the 1970s and 1980s, factory workers of Syrian descent, as well as Lebanese, Yemeni, and Palestinian immigrants, were particularly hard hit. Many were forced to go on public assistance, an extremely difficult decision for families for whom honor is synonymous with self-reliance.

The 2011 American Community Survey shows that 65.5 percent of the Syrian American population older than sixteen years of age was employed in the labor force. Syrian Americans work in a variety of positions, including management (47.3 percent); service occupations (13.6 percent); sales and office positions (27.3 percent); natural resources, construction, and maintenance jobs (4.0 percent); and production and transportation (6.8 percent). The median family income was $38,067. Just over 9 percent of Syrian Americans qualified for and used food stamps from the Supplemental Nutrition Assistance Program (SNAP), and 2.6 percent drew on cash public assistance as a source of income.

POLITICS AND GOVERNMENT

Initially, Syrian Americans were quiet politically. They never collectively belonged to one political party or the other; rather, their political affiliation reflected the larger American population, with business owners among the group often voting Republican, and blue-collar workers opting more frequently to vote Democrat. As a political entity, they traditionally have not had the clout of other ethnic groups. One early issue that roused Syrian Americans, as it did all Arab Americans, was the 1914 decision in *Dow v. United States*, which established that Syrians were Caucasians and thus could not be refused naturalization on the grounds of race. Since that time Syrian Americans have been elected to offices from judgeships to the U.S. Senate.

Syrian Americans protest Syrian president Bashar al-Assad at a demonstration in front of the United Nations in 2012. AP IMAGES / MARK LENNIHAN

Syrian American political action of the mid- to late twentieth century focused on the Arab-Israeli conflict. The partitioning of Palestine in 1948 brought behind-the-scenes protests from Syrian leaders. After the 1967 Arab-Israeli War (also called the Six-Day War) between Israel and the United Arab Republic, Jordan, and Syria, Syrian Americans began to join political forces with other Arab groups to try to affect U.S. foreign policy regarding the Middle East. Included in this group are Palestinian and Lebanese Americans. The Association of Arab University Graduates hoped to educate the American public about its perspective on the Arab-Israeli dispute, and the National Association of Arab Americans was formed in the early 1970s to lobby Congress in this regard. In 1980 the American Arab Anti-Discrimination Committee was founded to counteract negative Arab stereotyping in the media, and the Arab American Institute was founded in 1985 to promote Arab American participation in U.S. politics. As a result, smaller regional action groups have also been organized, supporting Arab American candidates for office as well as candidates sympathetic to the Arab American viewpoint in international and domestic affairs.

With the rise of political unrest in Syria, many Syrian Americans became much more politically active and vociferous. Numerous Syrian American organizations (including the Syrian American Foundation and the American Syrian Arab Cultural Association) were formed and have taken as their mission the goal of unifying the "voice" of Syrian Americans and establishing more harmonious ties between the United States and Syria. Other groups, such as the Syrian American Medical Society, were formed to offer networking possibilities between Syrian American physicians and their colleagues in Syria in order to foment greater collaboration and cooperation across the profession. Still other entities, like the Syrian American Women's Charitable Association, were founded to

Syrian children, New York City, c. 1910. CORBIS. REPRODUCED BY PERMISSION.

provide assistance to those in need in Syria. Although these organizations are not overtly political, their existence and objectives intimate the desire of Syrian Americans to foster more peaceful relations between the country in which they reside and their country of ethnic or actual origin.

In addition to these organizations, more intense political conflicts in Syria itself have catalyzed the growing involvement of Syrian Americans in political matters. In particular, the violence taking place in Syria under the regime of President Bashar al-Assad in 2011 and 2012 caused the country to become the topic of much debate in President Barack Obama's administration. Many Syrian Americans believed that the United States should be conducting greater intervention, especially because of the high tallies of civilian casualties, which number in the tens of thousands.

NOTABLE INDIVIDUALS

There is not always a clear distinction between places of origin when dealing with Syrian immigration history. For individuals as well as for immigration records, the confusion between Greater Syria and modern Syria poses some difficulties. However, the following list of notable Syrian Americans is mostly comprised of individuals who either arrived in the first wave of Greater Syrian immigration or were the offspring of such immigrants. Thus, in the largest possible sense, these notable individuals are Syrian American.

Academia Halim Barakat (1936–) was born in Kafroun in Syria and raised in Beirut. Barakat earned a PhD in social psychology from the University of Michigan. He has held teaching and research positions at the University of Texas-Austin, Harvard, and Georgetown. The author of twenty books on sociology, he has also published novels and short stories. Elaine Hagopian (1941–) is a professor of sociology at Simmons College in Boston. She is a leading activist

against discrimination in the United States. She served as president of the Arab American University Graduates.

Business Steve Jobs (1955–2011), cofounder and former CEO of Apple, was born to a Syrian father and American mother and was adopted by American parents. He left Harvard before finishing his degree to found Apple, one of the most successful and visionary companies in the world.

Government Mitch Daniels (1949–), the former Republican governor of the state of Indiana, became president of Purdue University in 2013. As governor Daniels engaged in extreme budget cuts. Philip Habib (1920–1992) was a career diplomat who helped negotiate an end to the Vietnam War. Queen Noor (born Lisa Najeeb Halaby; 1951–) is the widow of King Hussein of Jordan and has been queen dowager of Jordan since 1999. Her paternal grandfather was a Syrian immigrant to the United States, and she was born in Washington, D.C.

Journalism Born in the United States to Syrian parents from Aleppo, Hala Basha-Gorani (1970–) is an anchor and a news correspondent for CNN. Anthropologist and journalist Barbara Nimri Aziz was the executive director of Radius of Arab-American Writers (RAWI).

Literature Nadra Haddad (1881–1950) was an early Syrian immigrant who had a *diwan* (collection of poetry) published in New York in 1941. He served as part of the Pen League, which included other literary figures who wrote in Arabic. The literature from this group became famous in the authors' countries of origin. William Peter Blatty (1928–) wrote *The Exorcist* (1971) and adapted it into the screenplay for the 1973 movie. Born in Damascus in Syria, poet and author Mohja Kahf (1967–) immigrated to the United States in 1971. Her work concentrates on the experiences of Muslim Americans.

Music Malik Jandali (1972–) was born in Germany and raised in Homs, Syria. He studied music in the United States at the university level. Jandali is a world-renowned classical performer and has received numerous awards for his piano playing. He is also a highly respected composer. Choreographer, dancer, and singer Paula Abdul (1962–) has won Grammys and Emmys and was a judge on the television series *American Idol*. Paul Anka (1941–) was a popular singer and songwriter in the 1950s. Frank Zappa (1940–1993) was a well-known rock musician.

Science and Medicine Michael DeBakey (1908–2008) pioneered bypass surgery and invented the heart pump. Elias J. Corey (1928–) of Harvard University won the 1990 Nobel Prize for Chemistry. M. Safwan Badr was a professor of medicine at Wayne State University and the division chief and program director of the university's Sleep Fellowship program.

Stage and Screen F. Murray Abraham (1939–) was the first Syrian American to win an Academy

Award, for his role in *Amadeus* (1984). Moustapha Akkad (1930–2005) directed *Mohammed, Messenger of God* (1976) and *Lion in the Desert* (1981) as well as the *Halloween* thrillers (1981–2002). Teri Hatcher (1964–) is an actress known for her television roles as Lois Lane on *Lois and Clark* and Susan Mayer on *Desperate Housewives*. Jerry Seinfeld (1954–) is a comedian, actor, and writer best known for his hugely successful sitcom *Seinfeld*.

MEDIA

PRINT

American-Arab Message

Religious and political weekly founded in 1937 and printed in English and Arabic.

Imam M. A. Hussein
4045 West 13 Mile Road
Royal Oak, Michigan 48073
Phone: (313) 868-2266
Fax: (313) 868-2267

The Link

Bimonthly national periodical published by the nonprofit organization Americans for Middle East Understanding (AMEU).

John F. Mahoney, Executive Director
475 Riverside Drive
Room 245
New York, New York 10025-0241
Phone: (212) 870-2053
URL: www.ameu.org

Washington Report on Middle East Affairs

Nonprofit publication since 1928; strives to provide neutral and balanced information about U.S. interactions with states in the Middle East.

P.O. Box 53062
Washington, D.C. 20009
Phone: (800) 368-5788
URL: www.wrmea.org

RADIO

Arab Network of America

Broadcasts one to two hours of Arabic programming weekly in urban areas with large Arab American populations, including Chicago, Detroit, Los Angeles, New York, Pittsburgh, San Francisco, and Washington, D.C.

Eptisam Malloutli, Radio Program Director
150 South Gordon Street
Alexandria, Virginia 22304
Phone: (800) ARAB-NET

WBAI Radio

Radio station financed by listeners; member of the Pacifica chain of radio stations. Offers programming to listeners in New York City and to a global audience via the Internet.

Church Street Station
P.O. Box 7032, New York
New York 10008
URL: www.wbai.org

TELEVISION

Arab Network of America (ANA)

Arab Network of America, created in the early 1990s, was the first television station specifically designed to offer programming to meet the needs and interests of Arab Americans.

Laila Shaikhli, TV Program Director
150 South Gordon Street
Alexandria, Virginia 22304
Phone: (800) ARAB-NET

TAC Arabic Channel

Arabic-language programming for a family audience. Programs include movies, news, and children's shows.

Jamil Tawfiq, Director
P.O. Box 936
New York, New York 10035
Phone: (212) 425-8822
URL: www.allied-media.com/ARABTV/ the_arabic_channel_NY.html

ORGANIZATIONS AND ASSOCIATIONS

American Syrian Arab Cultural Association

Established in 1995 as a nonprofit, nonsectarian, cultural, and educationally focused group. Its objective is to familiarize the American people with Arabic culture and to offer lectures, seminars, and other activities and events to fulfill this purpose. The group strives to provide Syrian American youth, as well as other Arab Americans, with a sense of community and to offer information about Arabic and Syrian culture and heritage.

P.O. Box 1425
Troy, Michigan 48099
Phone: (248) 988-1166
Email: info@asaca-usa.org
URL: www.asaca-usa.org

Syrian American Council (SAC)

This grassroots organization located in Washington, D.C., strives to offer educational, civic, financial, and humanitarian opportunities for Syrian Americans. The group also advocates for harmonious relations between the United States and Syria and for maintaining peace and stability in Syria itself.

20 F Street NW
Washington, D.C. 20001
Phone: (657) 777-3191
Email: info@sacouncil.com
URL: www.sacouncil.com

Syrian American Foundation

The foundation was established in southern Ohio to advocate for freedom and human rights in Syria;

unify and empower Syrian Americans and offer them a sense of community; seek democracy for Syria and ensure the nation's human and civil rights; and provide scientific, educational, and humanitarian assistance to the residents of Syria.

Email: info@syrian-american.org
URL: www.syrian-american.org

Syrian American Medical Society

Syrian American Medical Society provides opportunities for networking between Syrian American physicians and their medical counterparts in Syria. The organization is a nonprofit, nonpolitical, humanitarian group whose members include medical professionals of Syrian descent.

Phone: (866) 809-9039
Fax: (330) 286-0325

or

Fax: (330) 319-8989
Email: SAMS@sams-usa.net
URL: sams-usa.net
P.O. Box 1015, Canfield
Ohio 44406

Syrian American Society

Syrian American Society members are Syrians of all types of religious, geographic, and political backgrounds. The group's goal is for Syrians to have political, economic, and religious rights, both in their home country and in other nations where they reside. They want to create a stronger sense of community between Syrians living in the home country and those living outside of it.

7226 West 90th Place
Bridgeview, Illinois 60455
URL: www.syrianamericansociety.org/bootstrap

Syrian American Women's Charitable Association

Nonprofit, nongovernmental group designed to assist comparable charitable groups in Syria. The mission of the group is to serve the humanitarian needs of impoverished, ill, and elderly people in Syria, regardless of sexual orientation, religion, political leanings, or background characteristics. The group was established in 1993.

2452 Parallel Lange, Silver Spring
Maryland 20904
Email: feedback@sawa.org
URL: www.sawa.org

Syrian Arab American Association

Formed in Southern California in 1992 with the objective of fostering a sense of community in younger generations of Syrian Americans. The nationwide organization also strives to cultivate bridges of mutual acceptance and appreciation between the United States and Syria and is designed to help Syrian Americans connect and network with one another.

Phone: (818) 800-0977
Email: mysaaa.ca@gmail.com
URL: www.mysaaa.org

MUSEUMS AND RESEARCH CENTERS

Arab American National Museum

Features exhibits on various characteristics of Arab civilization. Provides information and displays collections regarding Arabic contributions to science, medicine, mathematics, and astronomy. Also offers information about the history of Arab immigration.

13624 Michigan Avenue
Dearborn, Michigan 48126
Phone: (313) 582-2266
URL: www.arabamericanmuseum.org

Brookings Institute

Privately owned, not-for-profit research organization that operates with the objective of conducting independent research and providing innovative policy solutions.

1775 Massachusetts Avenue NW
Washington, D.C. 20036
Phone: (202) 797-6000
URL: www.brookings.edu/research/topics/syria

Pew Research Center for the People and the Press

Nonpartisan fact tank that informs the public about worldwide issues through public opinion polling, demographic research, media content analysis, and other empirical social science research. It is a subsidiary of the Pew Charitable Trusts.

1615 L Street NW
Suite 700
Washington, D.C. 20036
Phone: (202) 419-4300
Fax: (202) 419-4349
URL: pewresearch.org

SOURCES FOR ADDITIONAL STUDY

Abu-Laban, Baha, and Michael W. Suleiman, eds. *Arab Americans: Continuity and Change.* Normal, IL: Association of Arab American University Graduates, 1989.

Gualtieri, Sarah. *Between Arab and White: Race and Ethnicity in the Early Syrian American Diaspora.* Berkeley: University of California Press, 2009.

Haddad, Yvonne Yazbeck. *Becoming American? The Forging of Arab and Muslim Identity in Pluralist America.* Baylor, TX: Baylor University Press, 2011.

Hitti, P. K. *The Syrians in America.* Piscataway, NJ: Gorgias Press, 2005.

Kayal, Philip, and Joseph Kayla. *The Syrian Lebanese in America: A Study in Religion and Assimilation.* Boston: Twayne Publishers, 1975.

Saliba, Najib E. *Emigration from Syria and the Syrian-Lebanese Community of Worcester, MA.* Ligonier, PA: Antakya Press, 1992.

Sherman, William C. *Prairie Peddlers: The Syrian-Lebanese in North Dakota.* Bismarck, ND: University of Mary Press, 2002.

Younis, Adele L. *The Coming of the Arabic-Speaking People to the United States.* Staten Island, NY: Center for Migration Studies, 1995.

TAIWANESE AMERICANS

J. Sydney Jones

OVERVIEW

Taiwanese Americans are immigrants or descendants of immigrants from Taiwan, also called Nationalist China or the Republic of China, a country located 100 miles from mainland China. The Taiwan Strait, formerly known as the Straits of Formosa, separates Taiwan from the southeastern Chinese province of Fujian. To the north of Taiwan is the East China Sea with the Ryukyu Islands, Okinawa, and Japan; to the south, the Baishi Channel in the South China Sea separates Taiwan from the Philippines; to the east lies the Pacific Ocean. The country is mountainous, especially the eastern two-thirds of the island. It has jurisdiction over twenty-two islands in the Taiwan group and another sixty-four in the Pescadores Archipelago to the west. About twice the size of New Jersey, it measures 13,892 square miles (35,990 square kilometers).

According to a Taiwanese government estimate in October 2012, the country's inhabitants numbered 23.3 million, making it one of the most densely populated places on earth. Of these, only 330,000 are non-Chinese: the aboriginal inhabitants of the island, who are related to Malay people of Indonesia, Malaysia, and the Philippines. Of the remaining majority, 85 percent are descendants of early Chinese migrants to the island; most are from the provinces of Fujian and Guangdong and are of the Fujianese and Hakka ethnic groups. The remaining 14 percent of the population is made up of "mainlanders," Chinese people from a variety of mainland provinces who were either born in China or are descendants of families who fled the Communist Chinese armies during the Chinese Civil War (1945–1949). Daoism and Buddhism are the major religions of Taiwan. A blending of the philosophical tenets of Confucianism with these two major religions has resulted in a hybrid religion, often referred to as Chinese popular religion. Christianity is also represented, and though it is a relatively minor religion, it has had a strong influence in the spheres of education and health care. There are also some Muslims living in the urban areas of the country. Taiwan's trade economy makes it one of the wealthier countries in Asia, with relatively low unemployment. The island's major industries are textiles, electronics, machinery, shipbuilding, and agriculture.

Although immigration to the United States from Taiwan began in the late 1800s, the first large groups of Taiwanese immigrants arrived in the mid-twentieth century, seeking educational opportunities at universities along the East and West Coasts. Passage of the Immigration and Nationality Act of 1965 resulted in increased immigration of skilled workers to the United States from Taiwan. In the 1990s new immigration laws, such as the Immigration Act of 1990, favored educated entrepreneurs, and businessmen and women brought their families to the United States to start new businesses or bridge business relationships between the United States and Taiwan.

The 2010 U.S. Census identified 215,441 Taiwanese Americans living in the United States (about as many people as live in the city of New Orleans, Louisiana), although because Taiwanese people are subsumed into the category "other Asian" on the census form, the actual population may be higher. According to the U.S. Census Bureau's American Community Survey estimates for 2006-2010, the largest population of Taiwanese Americans reside in California (51,094), particularly the Los Angeles and San Francisco areas. Other states with small but significant numbers include New Jersey (6,083), New York (9.896), Texas (9,138), Washington ((4,709), Illinois (3,959), Massachusetts (3,592), Virginia (3,152), and Maryland (3,006).

HISTORY OF THE PEOPLE

Early History The derivation of the Chinese word *Tai-wan* is unknown, though its literal meaning is "terraced bay." Until the sixteenth century it was primarily inhabited by a native Malayo-Polynesian population. In Chinese records from before the Han dynasty (206 BCE–222 CE), Taiwan is referred to as Yangchow and later Yinchow. In 239 CE the Chinese emperor sent an expeditionary force to explore the island, an event that forms one of the bases of Beijing's current claim of sovereignty over the island. The explorers established no permanent settlement on the island. Several centuries later China sent further missions to the island. It was clearly identified in court records of the Ming dynasty as having been charted by the explorer Cheng Ho in 1430 and given its current name. Few Chinese ventured across the treacherous waters of the Straits of Formosa, however, and the island was largely an operational base for Chinese and Japanese pirates.

In the sixteenth century other countries discovered the island's existence. The Portuguese passed it en route to Japan in 1517, dubbing it *Ilha Formosa*, or Beautiful Island. In 1624 the Dutch established a settlement in southwestern Taiwan, and the Spanish settled in the north at present-day Chi-lung. The Dutch seized the Spanish settlements in the north in 1642. In order to increase agricultural production, the Dutch East India Company encouraged Chinese migration, and the numbers of Fujianese and Hakka settlers grew to some 200,000 by 1662, when events in China brought an end to the Dutch presence on the island.

With the fall of the Ming dynasty in 1644, the Manchus of the Qing dynasty had consolidated and enlarged their rule of mainland China, moving south of the Great Wall to bring all of China under their control by 1683. During these turbulent years many Chinese fled to Taiwan to escape the Manchus, just as, centuries later, Nationalist forces would flee there to avoid the Communist offensive. The island thus became a center of Chinese resistance to the Manchus as Ming diehards fought on. One Ming loyalist was the half-Japanese Zheng Cheng-gong, also known as Koxinga, who led an army of 100,000 troops and 3,000 junks against the Manchurian invasion; Koxinga's success in battle led to a long military career. Ultimately, he turned against the Dutch in Taiwan, expelling them and establishing a Ming-style dynasty on the island. This government in exile lasted until 1683, when the Manchus invaded Taiwan, absorbing it into the empire to be administered by Fujian province. Two hundred years later, Taiwan became a separate province of China.

The centuries of relative peace and prosperity under Manchu control led to dramatic increases in population on the mainland. Meanwhile, on the island, the aboriginal people were increasingly relegated to the eastern, more mountainous regions. Rice and sugar became Taiwan's main exports to China. In the nineteenth century European interest in the China trade grew. Two ports were opened in Taiwan in 1858: Tainan in the southwest and Tanshui in the northwest, the latter just downstream of the city of Taipei on the Tanshui River. China began to take more notice of its rebellious province to the west, but its years of misrule there had sown the seeds of distrust in Taiwan. In 1884 the Qing dynasty reorganized rule on the island, sending Liung Ming ch'uan to administer it, which he did capably. In 1886 Taiwan was made an independent province, with Taipei as its capital city.

Modern Era In 1894 China and Japan fought the first Sino-Japanese War over control of Korea. China was quickly defeated and, in the ensuing treaty, lost its province of Taiwan. For the next fifty years, the Japanese occupied the island, carrying out a Japanization policy of Taiwan's people and culture. Japanese was instituted as the language of instruction, bureaucracy, and business. Initially, the island provided mainly rice and sugar to Japan. By the 1930s, relatively cheap hydroelectric power in Taiwan allowed the development of textile, chemical, and machinery-producing industries. Although repressive, the Japanese regime improved the sanitation and educational systems on the island. With the onset of World War II, Taiwan became a Japanese staging area for invasions of Southeast Asia. After the Japanese surrendered to the Allies in September 1945, Taiwan was returned to China with uncertain status. In October China's Nationalist Party leader, Chiang Kai-shek, sent military forces to the island to replace Japanese officials with those of the Republic of China.

Just as oppressive as the Japanese regime, the nationalist government was not popular. It viewed the Taiwanese as traitors for not having opposed the Japanese during the war. Unrest among the population led to a rebellion. Known as *er er ba*, from the Chinese for the date of the onset of the trouble—February 28, 1947—the insurrection was brutally put down by the mainland government, with the loss of Taiwanese lives estimated at 10,000. In the 1990s some amends were made to the families of the victims, and February 28 became Peace Day in Taiwan.

In 1949 communist forces under Mao Tse-tung defeated the nationalists on the mainland, establishing the People's Republic of China. Chiang Kai-shek, his government, and a portion of his army fled to Taiwan to set up a nationalist government in exile. Mao's forces were on the brink of invading the island when the Korean War broke out in 1950. The U.S. Seventh Fleet was sent to the Taiwan Strait to protect Taiwan from attack. For the next two decades, the Republic of China (or Nationalist China) in Taiwan was the representative for United States-China relations. Chiang ran an autocratic regime there and dreamed of eventually returning to the mainland. In the bipolar world of the Cold War, Taiwan maintained a precarious independence. Partly with the help of American aid and partly with a policy of import substitution (producing at home rather than importing), Taiwan grew into a manufacturing power. By the 1960s it was exporting vast quantities of textiles, electronic equipment, and machinery to the West, fueling an 11 percent annual growth rate in the Taiwanese economy between 1960 and 1973.

In 1971 the United States began to normalize relations with communist China, and Taiwan lost its seat at the United Nations. Official diplomatic relations were established between the People's Republic and the United States in 1979. Equally dramatic changes were taking place in Taiwan. After Chiang Kai-shek's death in 1975, his son Chiang Ching-kuo took power and attempted to cultivate a more populist image. He finally lifted martial law in 1987, a year before his death. He was succeeded by Lee Teng-hui, a native Taiwanese. From 1988 to 1996 Lee oversaw liberal changes in the political process, and in 1996 he became the first popularly elected president of Taiwan.

The country continues to perform a delicate balancing act, attempting to normalize relations with the People's Republic while at the same time insuring its own independence.

SETTLEMENT IN THE UNITED STATES

Mainland Chinese immigrants began arriving in the United States in significant numbers about a century before the Taiwanese. These early immigrants, largely from Guangdong province, came to the West Coast during the Gold Rush. A backlash of anti-Chinese sentiment followed. Discriminatory laws, such as the Chinese Exclusion Act of 1882, denied them the right of entry to the United States based on ethnicity and race. When China and the United States became allies during World War II, the ban on Chinese immigration ended, although early quota limits for Chinese and Asians in general were low. In 1965 President Lyndon B. Johnson signed the Hart-Celler (Immigration and Nationality) Act, which allowed for an annual quota of 20,000 Chinese and the entry of family members as nonquota immigrants. Because Taiwanese immigrants were considered Chinese under the quota laws, their immigration patterns were influenced by the same legal restrictions.

Another jump in Taiwan's productivity in the 1980s created a class of transnationals called taikongren or "astronauts." These immigrants shuttle back and forth between the United States, where their families reside, and Taiwan.

The first Taiwanese immigrated to the United States between the end of World War II and 1965. The majority of these were students continuing their education at American universities, mainly on the east and West Coasts and in certain places in the Midwest, such as Chicago. The numbers were low. Some stayed after graduation to find careers in the United States. Early Taiwanese immigrants also included wives of

Novelist Maxine Hong Kingston (1940–) writes about the experiences of Chinese immigrants to the U.S. ANTHONY BARBOZA / GETTY IMAGES

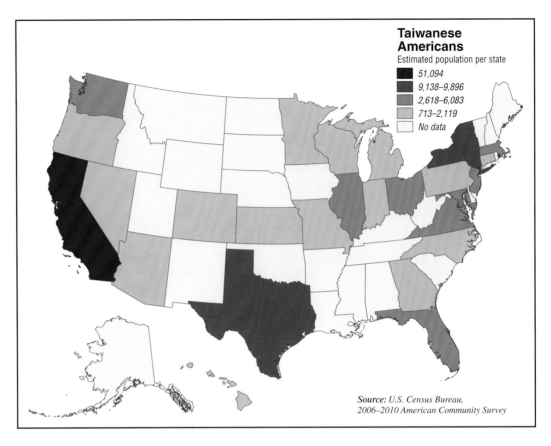

Taiwanese Americans
Estimated population per state

- 51,094
- 9,138–9,896
- 2,618–6,083
- 713–2,119
- No data

*Source: U.S. Census Bureau,
2006–2010 American Community Survey*

U.S. servicemen who had been stationed in Taiwan after the Korean War. A third group of early immigrants sought better economic conditions and opportunities than they could find at home. This contingent often ended up working in Chinese restaurants or in service industries. A large number of Taiwanese immigrants settled in the Chinatowns of large American cities. Although they were classified as Chinese when they arrived, many of the early immigrants felt isolated from the general Chinese American population by cultural traditions and language: the majority of Chinese immigrants of the period spoke Cantonese, while immigrants from Taiwan spoke Taiwanese or Mandarin Chinese.

After the 1965 Immigration Act was passed, more Taiwanese came to the United States. The lack of diplomatic relations between mainland China and the United States meant that for more than a decade, the only Chinese allowed to immigrate were those from Taiwan. Individuals with technical and scientific skills, as well as those in the hotel and restaurant business, found easier admittance. This second wave of immigration lasted until 1979. Once the United States recognized mainland China, relations with Taiwan became more nebulous. Taiwanese immigrants since 1979 have faced increased difficulties because they hold passports from a "nonexistent" nation. In 1982 Taiwan's quota was 20,000, and many of the immigrants were trained professionals for whom there were

insufficient jobs in Taiwan. Student immigrants added to the brain drain from Taiwan; educational opportunities increased in the United States, and many students who were granted temporary visas decided to stay, finding jobs and gaining more permanent residency. Work opportunities were more plentiful in the United States, and young men of draft age could also avoid compulsory military service in Taiwan.

Another jump in Taiwan's productivity in the 1980s created a class of transnationals called *taikongren* or "astronauts." These immigrants shuttle back and forth between the United States, where their families reside, and Taiwan. The Immigration Act of 1990 established preferences for those willing to invest in new U.S. businesses.

The number of Taiwanese immigrants to the United States is difficult to calculate, because, as of 2010, U.S. Census figures group all of the approximately 3.4 million Chinese Americans in one category. This group includes American-born Chinese, as well as immigrants from China, Hong Kong, Singapore, Southeast Asia, and Taiwan. The U.S. Department of Homeland Security estimates that from 2000 to 2009 some 92,000 Taiwanese immigrated to the United States, which yields an average of a little more than 9,000 each year. In 2011, 6,206 Taiwanese arrived, whereas about 83,000 immigrants were admitted from mainland China. In both cases the overwhelming majority of immigrants who listed an occupation were professionals, technicians, or managers. The stereotype of the Taiwanese engineer or computer scientist is not necessarily the norm, however. Large numbers of blue-collar workers in service and garment industries and more women are now immigrating to the United States.

Large communities of Taiwanese Americans are scattered throughout the United States, but the majority are concentrated in California and on the East Coast. In California Taiwanese communities are particularly prevalent in Los Angeles, San Jose, and San Francisco. In the greater Los Angeles area, for example, the town of Monterey Park has been called "Little Taipei." Large Taiwanese populations in suburban southern California also occur throughout the San Gabriel Valley. In the East sizeable communities have been established in the Flushing neighborhood in the New York borough of Queens, while in Texas, Houston draws Taiwanese immigrants. Smaller populations also reside in New Jersey, Washington, Illinois, Massachusetts, Virginia, and Maryland.

The flow of capital from Taiwan follows these immigrants, and as a result they have been able to revitalize some failing communities and to culturally influence others. Instead of the Chinatowns of old, however, Taiwanese immigrants create islands of culture in suburbia, with all-Chinese shopping malls and strip malls offering everything from Chinese food shops to bookshops and pharmacies. Signs mix intricate Chinese characters with English words in a kind of international linguistic mélange. Entering these malls is like being transported to Taiwan. This is especially true in Monterey Park and San Jose, where the Taiwanese community has its own clubs, churches, and newspapers. In larger urban areas, such as Flushing, the Taiwanese are part of a more varied multicultural milieu that includes Chinese, Pakistanis, Indians, Koreans, Thai people, and other Asian Americans.

LANGUAGE

Taiwanese Americans speak a variety of languages, but their first language is generally Mandarin (or standard) Chinese, known as *kuo yu*, or "national dialect." It derives from Beijing Mandarin and is about as similar to that dialect as American English is to British English. In addition, the various ethnic groups comprising the Taiwanese American community have their own dialects. The Fujian and Hakka speak the native Taiwanese dialect, which is based on the Minnan vernacular of southern Fujian province, and some Hakka also speak their own idiom. Chinese characters are still romanized using the Wade-Giles system in Taiwan, though the country is beginning to adopt the pinyin system used on the mainland. Thus Peking (in the Wade-Giles system), the capital of communist China, is now known as Beijing; and Taipei, Taiwan's capital in the Wade-Giles system, has become Taibei in pinyin.

Especially in written language, Taiwanese Americans often combine English with Chinese. In larger urban areas Chinese-language radio and television stations provide listeners and viewers with programming in Mandarin or Cantonese dialects.

Greetings and Popular Expressions Common greetings and other expressions (with pronunciation) include *tsao* (tsow)—"good morning"; *ni hao ma* (knee how ma)—"how are you"; *tsao chien* (tsow chyen)—"goodbye, see you later"; *pai tuo* (pie twa)—"please"; *hsieh hsieh* (shye shye)—"thanks"; *pu ko chi* (pookócheh)—"you're welcome"; *tai hau le* (tie how le)—"great, wonderful."

RELIGION

For newcomers to the United States, religious affiliation can provide an important networking resource. Taiwanese Americans practice a rich diversity of religions. Whereas Christians are a distinct minority in Taiwan (about one million, divided between Roman Catholic and Protestant), a large percentage of Taiwanese Americans identify as Christian, partly because churches provide a social gathering point for immigrants. Protestants outnumber Catholics, and a significant number of Taiwanese Americans belong to evangelical or fundamentalist Baptist churches. Presbyterian churches, which often offer services in Mandarin or Taiwanese dialect, are also popular. Taiwanese American Christian churches offer the full panoply of options, including Bible study for the young and social functions such as dinners and talks.

Other Taiwanese Americans favor the traditional religions of Taiwan and China. These consist of Buddhism (with the largest following), Daoism, Confucianism, and a hybrid popular religion. Taiwanese Buddhists follow the Mahayana school, which is similar to the Buddhism of Japan, Korea, Vietnam, and much of China. Buddhism in the United States has seen particularly rapid expansion in recent years, with new temples established in Los Angeles, San Francisco, Houston, and New York. This growth reflects the increasing popularity Buddhism is enjoying in Taiwan: from 1983 to 1995 adherents multiplied sixfold. Xi Lai Temple, near Monterey Park, is particularly noteworthy as the largest overseas temple of the Fo Guan Shan Zen Buddhist Centre in Taiwan. Completed in 1988, Xi Lai Temple cost $26 million and is a colorful and stunning architectural presence, attracting the faithful and tourists alike. One hall alone has ten thousand golden Buddhas. It speaks for the presence of Buddhism in the United States, as do the Jade Buddha Temple in Houston and the Zhuangyen Monastery in Carmel, New York.

Taiwanese popular religion blends the three traditional faiths with ancestor worship and the belief in certain local gods and goddesses. It is represented in the United States by various temples built for worshipping these deities, among them *Tudigong* (god of the earth), *Guanyin* (goddess of mercy), and *Mazu* (goddess of the sea). The Ma Tsu Temple, dedicated to Mazu, for example, was established in San Francisco in 1986.

Taiwanese faith-based organizations all serve functions beyond religion, incorporating activity halls for lectures as well as instruction in Chinese language. Religious observance is not restricted to formal temples and churches. Many Taiwanese Americans create shrines in their homes and observe lunar festivals, activities that bond the community to folk traditions and religious practices.

CULTURE AND ASSIMILATION

Like many other immigrants from Asia, the Taiwanese tend to settle in areas where large numbers of their fellow countrymen already live. Families create networks of mutual aid just as they might in Taiwan. "They have developed a complex organizational life, as social hierarchy is an important aspect of Taiwanese American life," Hsiang-shui Chen pointed out in *Chinatown No More* (1992), a study of Taiwanese immigrants in Queens. Thus the Taiwanese American community tends to remain cohesive, preserving its values, languages, and cultural traditions amid the bustle of contemporary American life. According to Chen, Taiwanese Americans are no longer segregated into the Chinatowns of old. They often own a business or hold a job in the inner cities of metropolitan areas such as San Jose, Los Angeles, or Houston. Collectively they are differentiating themselves from their Chinese counterparts by "attempting to define their distinctive social and political history," according to Linda Trinh Võ and Rick Bonus in *Contemporary Asian American Communities: Intersections and Divergences* (2002). In this way the new Taiwanese immigrant community is looser than it was, while preserving much of the reciprocal support that characterized the older Chinatown communities.

Traditions and Customs Taiwanese traditions blend those of the groups that have occupied the island state. There are instances of Fujian culture, of traditions from Guangdong, and of customs from Japan, as a result of the fifty-year occupation by that country. These practices have also been heavily influenced by Western trends, because Taiwan itself is a modern economic power. Taiwanese American belief systems have generally followed a middle ground between East and West.

Concepts relating to nature, space, and time unite the Chinese sense of harmonic living in tune with the natural order and the Western scientific, materialistic worldview. Ancient belief systems revolved around the *Dao*, or the Way—the manner in which humans become one with the natural workings of the universe. The traditional belief in *qi*, or life force, leads to a view of a world divided into the polar opposites yin and yang, as represented in such dichotomies as male-female, cold-hot, dry-wet, light-dark. Additionally, the world is seen as comprised of five elements: fire, wood, air, water, and earth. Seasons and relationships are determined by the ebb and flow of opposites and of the five elements. The tradition of *feng shui*, wind and water, is an ancient Chinese science that seeks harmony in interior and exterior design and architecture by balancing yin-yang and allowing for proper flow of qi. This tradition has gained popularity outside of the Taiwanese and Chinese communities, resulting in the use of feng shui principles in much of the Western world as well.

A unique perception of time also informs Taiwanese American life, in which both the lunar calendar and Western Gregorian calendar are used. The latter solar calendar is employed in business, school, and public life, whereas the lunar calendar determines the dates of festivals and religious observances. Based on the phases of the moon, the lunar calendar consists of twelve months with twenty-four solar divisions and is eleven days shorter than the Western calendar year. The lunar calendar and almanacs are also used to determine auspicious and inauspicious days for carrying out various endeavors, from starting a business to getting married. Some Taiwanese believe that certain days are unlucky: the third, seventh, thirteenth, eighteenth, twenty-second, and twenty-seventh days of the lunar month, for example, are held by some to be bad luck days. Such old beliefs, however, are dying out among the younger generation of Taiwanese both in Taiwan and in the United States.

Other widespread beliefs among both Chinese and Taiwanese include a taboo against the number four, which sounds much like the word for death. Buildings often exclude a fourth and even a fourteenth or twenty-fourth floor to avoid possible bad luck, a custom similar to that regarding the number thirteen in Western societies. Many other convictions revolve around the play of homonyms. It is bad luck to share a pear, *li*, because the word sounds like the Chinese word "to separate," pronounced *lei*. After breaking an object, a person will quickly say *Sui sui ping an*, a play on the words for "pieces" and "year after year," turning the bad situation into a wish for eternal happiness. Similarly, at Chinese New Year, the characters for luck and happiness are taped to windows upside down because the word for "down" sounds similar to that for "to come": presented in this configuration, the words mean luck or happiness will come to you.

Cuisine Taiwanese cuisine is largely influenced by Fujian cooking, from which it gains its use of broth and seafood. Popular cooking methods include barbecuing and the use of hot-pots—pots kept simmering at the table—in addition to pan frying, boiling, and stir-frying. Among Taiwanese Americans, traditional Taiwanese dishes remain popular and are also increasingly sought after outside the community, as numerous Taiwanese restaurants catering to a broad clientele have opened around the country, especially in California.

Taiwanese cooking employs a wide assortment of foodstuffs, from meats such as beef and pork to poultry and all types of seafood. Such meats as turkey and pork are often cooked in a variety of spices and are served over bowls of rice. Although rice usually forms the base of meals, noodle dishes and soups are also popular, as are boiled dumplings (*shuijiao*), prepared with crabmeat in addition to the usual pork and leek stuffing. Seafood appears in such delicacies as oysters in black bean sauce, prawns wrapped in seaweed, cucumber crab rolls, and clam and winter melon soup. With its tropical and subtropical climate, Taiwan grows fruits and vegetables in abundance, including papaya, mango, pineapple, melons, citrus, asparagus, eggplant, pea pods, Chinese cabbage and mushrooms, bok choy, and leafy greens of the spinach family. Bean curd in various guises is also a common ingredient. As a result of Western influence in Taiwan, dinner rolls, cakes, and bread are also more prevalent in Taiwanese cuisine than in other Chinese fare. Beverages such as beer and rice wine (sake) are typical, as is Western style soda, and tea continues to be an omnipresent beverage among Taiwanese.

The Taiwanese use chopsticks, a skill most children master by the time they are five. Deep, curved Chinese spoons in plastic or porcelain also make a change from Western cutlery. Knives are usually unnecessary at table as meat is diced or sliced in preparation. It is customary to hold the rice bowl close to the mouth, scooping the rice in with chopsticks. These are rested on the table or the rim of the rice bowl and never pointing down into the bowl, a position that could bring bad luck.

Music Music functions in ceremonial and entertainment settings in Taiwanese society, both in the United States and in Taiwan. It follows the dead to their burial, heralds marriages and birthdays, and provides the framework for Chinese opera and puppet plays. The ancient Chinese musical system uses a scale of seven notes, focusing on five core tones with two changing tones. The five main tones are tied to the Chinese concept of the five basic elements. The Taiwanese musical tradition follows the classical Chinese model and, in addition, has its own folk variations. Popular instruments include the *se*, a zither with twenty-five strings and movable bridges; the *chin*, another stringed instrument; and several types of two-string fiddles. This kind of traditional Taiwanese music, often accompanying a puppet show, is performed at festivals and cultural heritage events around the United States as a way to preserve Taiwan's cultural legacy among immigrant communities.

The Taiwanese employ three different varieties of musical ensemble at festive or ritual occasions, each tracing its development back to imperials times and the musicians that accompanied highly ranked officers. Drums are an integral part of traditional Taiwanese music, and for special occasions, a drum group, or *guting*, performs, comprising several sorts of drums, gongs, and cymbals as well as the double-reeded pipe called the *suona*. *Bayin* ensembles, employing eight tones, are used for weddings and funerals with a *guting* following. A third type of amateur folk ensemble plays *beiguan* music at temples for a god's or goddess's birthday. Folk songs and ballads have become more popular, inspired by both aboriginal music and Japanese musical styles.

Taiwan has produced stars on the Mandarin and Taiwanese pop music scenes, including Teresa Teng, a singer who was known all over East Asia and is beloved by immigrant communities in the United States. Taiwanese Americans also listen to Western music in all its forms.

Traditional Dress Taiwanese Americans wear traditional clothing when participating in events that promote Chinese culture; otherwise, they have assimilated in their dressing habits. In formal settings women traditionally wear the *chi pao*, a long, high-collared dress with a side slit. It is generally made of silk that may be brocaded with designs or plain. A shorter version is used for informal occasions. Formerly worn by men as well as women, the *chan sang*, literally meaning "long clothes," is similar but with a looser waist.

Dances and Songs Taiwanese Americans keep their traditional dances alive as part of their heritage and cultural awareness. These dances are mainly ritualistic, emphasizing formal, stiff body movements with the feet kept close to the ground. Such dances appear in folk celebrations and rituals as well as in opera, where each movement is highly symbolic, telling of emotions or changes in time and space. Traditional drama often includes a chaotic, swirling, acrobatic blend of fight and dance, for instance when armies clash or monks attack devils. This latter form of dance is closely related to Taiwan's martial art, *guoshu*, of which there are many varieties.

Within a strong tradition of folk dancing among Taiwanese, the lion and dragon dances are the most typical. In ancient times the people performed such dances to bring rain or avoid plagues, employing drums, masks, and animated movements. Modern performances of the lion and dragon dances are intended to bring good luck or liven up festive occasions. The dragon mask and costume in particular are works of folk art in themselves, with the entire body of the dancer covered in colorful fabric. Contemporary choreographers have blended this folk tradition with elements of modern dance, creating a uniquely Taiwanese form of ballet.

Holidays In addition to observing all the American holidays—Christmas, New Years, Thanksgiving, Fourth of July, and Easter—Taiwanese Americans celebrate with several festivals that are peculiar to the lunar calendar and have seasonal significance. The most important for all Chinese Americans

TAIWANESE PROVERBS

Taiwanese culture is rich in proverbs, many of them paired counterparts. Thus, "When Heaven feeds men, they're fat as can be, when people feed people, there remains only one bone" (Thiⁿ chhī lâng pûi chut chut, lâng chhⁿ lâng chhun chit ki kut) is a warning to rely on God rather than on fellow humans. Similarly, advice about good leadership is served up in the following dualism: "Top not straight, bottom then crooked" (Siōng put chèng, hā chek oai), which is similar to the English proverb "A fish rots from the head down." These Taiwanese sayings are also popular in China, where proverbs abound.

is the Lunar New Year, which is tied to the coming of spring and is thus also known as *chunjie*, or "spring festival." The advent of the new year is a time for housecleaning, but during the year's first days, housework must stop lest good luck be swept away. The dominant color is red: people hang swaths of red paper with calligraphic wishes for good luck or good health and wear festive red clothing at gatherings. On New Year's Day family comes together to give gifts and visit close friends. Celebrants prepare special foods determined by similarity in sound to words representing good luck or wealth; for example, fish, *yu*, is a popular New Year's dish because it sounds the like the word for "abundance." Parades and dramatic performances take place over many days, before and after Chinese New Year.

The Lantern Festival, *dengjie*, takes place on the fifteenth day of the Lunar New Year and traditionally marks the end of New Year celebrations. In the United States this festival marks the beginning of spring banquets given by many Taiwanese organizations. In summer the Dragon Boat Festival honors the death of a popular poet and minister of the Zhou dynasty of China, Qu Yuan (c. 340–278 BCE), who committed suicide in the Mi Lo River as a protest against government corruption. Legend has it that villagers attempted to recover his body with a flotilla of boats; modern-day boat races in Taiwan honor the day. The same legend tells that the people threw rice dumplings into the river to feed the fish, thus keeping them from eating the corpse of the poet. Today, Taiwanese Americans often eat *zongzi* at this festival, a glutinous rice pudding or dumpling wrapped in bamboo leaves and stuffed with pork, beans, and other ingredients. The Mid-Autumn Festival, *zhongchiu jie*, is celebrated on the fifteenth day of the eighth lunar month, when the full moon represents family harmony. The abundance of the autumn harvest is often displayed as

an offering to the moon goddess. Participants bake sweet, round mooncakes filled with a paste made from lotus or melon seeds or various beans. Some U.S. cities have organized street fairs to celebrate the Mid-Autumn Festival.

Health Care Issues and Practices There are no health issues specific to the Taiwanese American population. A healthy diet is embedded in the culture, based as it is on the five-element philosophy and the yin-yang dichotomy. Categories such as wet and dry and hot and cool are incorporated into each meal. The balance of such opposites is thought to be vital to good health. Taiwanese Americans rely heavily on non-Western forms of medical therapy such as acupuncture.

Death and Burial Rituals In the Taiwanese community funerals are a time for demonstrating respect for ancestors and publicly displaying family status. While the intricate kinship roles and patterns have partly broken down in the United States, funerals are still solemn affairs. Some mourners wear red to ward off the negative influences of death or to celebrate the long life and descendants of the deceased.

FAMILY AND COMMUNITY LIFE

Confucianism places a premium on family values and family cohesion. Throughout Chinese history, clans and lineages played significant roles, and in the Taiwanese American community such bonds persist. Whereas the extended family of three generations under one roof was once the norm in Taiwanese society, especially in rural, agricultural areas, the emphasis in recent years in both Taiwan and the United States has been on the smaller nuclear family. Often Taiwanese Americans have left family members behind, and sometimes mothers and fathers remain in Taiwan while sons and, increasingly, daughters come to the United States to build a new life. Relationships are maintained via telephone, the Internet, and periodic visits. It is still common for members of an extended family to live together in some cases, such as when a young person lives with relatives while attending college.

Within the family Chinese kinship terms are observed. Grandparents are *zufumu* if they are the parents of the father and *waizufumu* if they are the mother's parents. An older brother is called *gege*, a younger one *didi*; *jiejie* is an older sister while *meimei* is a younger one. Nomenclature that distinguishes rank, or seniority, and side of the family extends to uncles, aunts, and others. Such strict labeling eventually breaks down among Taiwanese families living in the United States.

Roles within families commonly depend on economic and educational status. Among blue-collar workers, even within double-income households, the husband is usually the dominant partner and male-female roles are more traditional. In professional families responsibilities tend to be divided more equally, and the higher income affords both parents time with their children. In general, Taiwanese Americans experience fewer divorces than other American families, partly as a result of the extended kinship bonds and the overlapping social relationships in the community. Long-term separations, however, in which the husband is forced for economic reasons to leave his family in the United States while he shuttles back and forth to Taiwan, strain marriages.

The Taiwanese American community is cohesive. New arrivals can count on networking to help them establish themselves, start businesses, and find jobs. Community members look out for one another, forming familial bonds and joining groups in specialized organizations and clubs.

Gender Roles In Taiwan women have been largely ruled over by the male members of the *jia*, or extended family unit. Although divorce is rare, a wife's failure to produce a male child is a viable reason for separation. Family duties are chiefly perceived as within the woman's sphere. In the Taiwanese American community, the need to take care of children and domestic affairs has contributed to limiting women's achievement in the workforce. The educational disparity between women and men is decreasing, however, and women more often take jobs outside the home.

Despite increased equality, gender disparities remain. According to the 2010 American Community Survey, 81.6 percent of Taiwanese American males had attained a bachelor's degree or higher, as compared to 68.2 percent of females. In terms of employment, 53.5 percent of Taiwanese American females are in the American labor force, as opposed to 60.3 percent of the total Taiwanese American population. The significant inequality between average Caucasian and Asian salaries in the United States is even greater for Asian women than it is for Asian men: Asian women earn approximately 70 percent of the salaries of white men who have similar educational and occupational backgrounds.

Education Taiwanese Americans value education highly; parents encourage their sons and daughters to pursue college degrees. Many immigrants arrive in the United States with university and postgraduate degrees in hand. Competition for the few places in Taiwanese universities is stiff, so many more Taiwanese immigrate to the United States to study. The value of a college education is instilled in succeeding generations. Parents often choose a home based on its being in a good school district and are very involved in all aspects of their children's education. Preparation for college begins in kindergarten, when children learn the importance of doing well and getting good grades so that they can get into a good college later on. Many Taiwanese American children enroll in SAT preparation courses and practice writing college admissions essays early. The community favors such California universities as University California, Berkeley; UCLA; and Stanford.

Birth and Birthdays Both before and after giving birth, a mother is given especially nutritious foods. Whereas in mainland China and Taiwan, the birth of a boy is still the greatest wish of all parents, Taiwanese Americans rejoice at the birth of children of either sex. The child's one-month birthday is a time of special celebration. Birthdays are generally commemorated according to the Western calendar.

Courtship and Weddings Taiwanese Americans no longer observe the elaborate, lengthy courtships common in their home country, where, during a "greater engagement," or *dading*, the families exchange gifts and present a dowry. Still, weddings are joyous occasions and are considered an important rite of passage. The marriage ceremony may be civil or religious and is always followed by a banquet. The couple is generally presented with envelopes filled with money. If the parents of either live in Taiwan, there may be banquets in both countries. In earlier times, the bride was sent back to Taiwan for cooking classes.

Relations with Other Americans Confucian cultural tradition emphasizes accomplishment over race or ethnicity. Thus Taiwanese do well in the multicultural environment in the United States and have generally gotten along well with other ethnic minorities. Friction may arise, however, especially where Taiwanese have settled in large numbers, such as in Monterey Park and Flushing. Immigrants from groups that have not fared as well resent the overall success and slowness to assimilate of the Taiwanese. Coming from a rich culture with ancient traditions, Taiwanese Americans do not take it for granted that all aspects of life in the United States are better than in Taiwan, and they are not eager to cast off their heritage.

EMPLOYMENT AND ECONOMIC CONDITIONS

In general, Taiwanese arrive better prepared than the pre-1949 mainland Chinese immigrants: they tend to be better educated, have a profession, and know some English. Of the 215,441 Taiwanese American residents estimated in 2010 by the United States Census Bureau, for example, 64 percent of those reporting occupations were in professional, technical, executive, administrative, or managerial positions. Many others are blue-collar workers employed in restaurants and the garment industry. The full picture, however, includes 4.8 percent of the Taiwanese American population reporting no occupation. According to the 2011 American Community Survey, 5.7 percent of Taiwanese Americans (compared to 15.9 percent of the total U.S. population) lived below the poverty line.

Many Taiwanese entrepreneurs settle in the United States, encouraged by the Immigration Act of 1990. This act created preferences not only for those with key professional skills but also for those who

Taiwanese Americans in New York City protest against Chinese aggression towards Taiwan. ROBERT MILLER / AFP / GETTY IMAGES

could create employment opportunities in the United States by starting businesses or investing funds here. Taiwanese feel that it is important to start their own businesses, no matter how small, because doing so is a sign of success in Chinese society. As the U.S. economy slowed in the 1980s and early 1990s, however, Taiwanese American professionals were forced to take research or teaching positions in Taiwan's high-tech industries and universities, leaving their families in the United States. With the East Asia economic crunch of the late 1990s, and with improved economic conditions in the United States, the reverse migration has been somewhat rectified.

POLITICS AND GOVERNMENT

Since the United States officially established diplomatic relations with the People's Republic of China in 1979, Taiwan's position as an independent country has been precarious. Despite American insistence that the United States no longer officially supports an independent Taiwan, Congress passed the Taiwan Relations Act of 1979, authorizing continued social and economic ties with the island nation. Much of the political activity of Taiwanese Americans has been focused on influencing American public and political opinion regarding Taiwan. Various Taiwanese American political organizations monitor U.S.-Taiwanese relations. The World United Formosans for Independence organization, established in 1970 in Dallas, Texas, promotes a free and democratic Taiwan and publishes

the *Taiwan Tribune* to further this goal. The Formosan Association for Public Affairs in Washington, D.C., closely observes legislation affecting Taiwan and the Taiwanese people. Taiwanese sovereignty is also the aim of the lobbying group Taiwan International Relations, centered in Washington, D.C., while the Formosan Association for Human Rights, located in Kansas, focuses on human rights.

Taiwanese Americans maintain close relations with their former country, as many have family members there. The numerous groups that continue to monitor the political situation within Taiwan welcomed the increasing democratization of the 1990s. The end of martial law in 1987 and the reforms of Chiang Ching-kuo and Lee Teng-hui have encouraged Taiwanese Americans to expect a stronger position in the world for the people of Taiwan.

NOTABLE INDIVIDUALS

In *The Taiwanese Americans*, Ng noted that despite having a short history in this country and representing a relatively small percentage of the population, the immigrant group has made "a significant presence. [...] Most came after the immigration changes in 1965," Ng observed, "but they have already helped to alter the U.S. cultural landscape." Taiwanese Americans have worked to return U.S. attention to the Pacific Rim and, according to Ng, many Taiwanese Americans in business have become "cultural brokers in penetrating the markets of Asia." Taiwanese have brought capital and investment with them and are particularly prominent in academia. Others have become skilled workers in Silicon Valley businesses, valuable medical researchers, talented artists in film and music, and, in one case, an astronaut. The following is a list of individual Taiwanese Americans notable for their achievements.

Academia The first Asian in the country to lead a major university, Chang-lin Tien (1935–2002) was both a renowned educator and an administrator, serving as chancellor of the University of California, Berkeley, from 1990 to 1997. Born in Wuhan, China, Chang fled with his family to Shanghai in 1937 and to Taiwan in 1949. He graduated from National Taiwan University in 1955 then received an MA and PhD at Princeton in mechanical engineering. Conducting research at Berkeley in thermal radiation, he quickly made a name for himself, winning a Guggenheim Fellowship in 1965 and 1966 and an Alexander von Humboldt Foundation Fellowship in Germany in 1979.

Ray H. Liu (1942–), the author of books and more than fifty articles on mass spectrometry and clinical chemistry, is the graduate program director in forensic science at the University of Alabama at Birmingham and the editor of the *Forensic Science Review*. A professor of journalism at the University of Minnesota, Tsan-kuo Chang (1950–) wrote *The Press and China Policy: The Illusion of Sino-Soviet Relations, 1950–84*. Associate professor at the University of Texas at Arlington, Tsay-jiu Brian Shieh (1953–), researches compound semiconductor device modeling and vacuum microelectronics.

Business From 2001 to 2009 Taiwanese American Elaine Chao (1952–) served as the United States Secretary of Labor as the first Asian Pacific American woman on a presidential cabinet. Chao is a former director of the Peace Corps and the United Way of America and is married to Senator Mitch McConnell of Kentucky. Other successful Taiwanese Americans involved in business include John Chau Shih (1939–), president of S Y Technology in Van Nuys, California. Dean Shui-tien Hsieh (1948–) is a pharmaceutical company executive in Pennsylvania, and Helen Kuan Chang (1962–) is a public relations director for the San Jose Convention and Visitors Bureau. Architect Jennifer Jen-huey (1964–) works in San Francisco. Paul P. Hung (1933–) is an executive for Wyeth-Ayerst Labs, and Yeou-chuong Simon Yu (1958–) manages the engineering department for Monolith Technologies in Tucson, Arizona.

Film Film director and producer Ang Lee (1954–) immigrated to the United States in 1978 to study acting at the University of Illinois at Urbana-Champaign, but his lack of fluency in English prompted him to change his career goal to directing. In 1985 the New York University Film Festival selected Lee's *Fine Line* as the best movie of the year.

In 1992, after receiving funding from a Taiwanese production company, he made *Pushing Hands*, a film that became a box-office success in Taiwan and won the Taipei Golden Horse Film Festival Award. The movie was released in the United States in 1994. Lee's best-known films are *The Wedding Banquet* (1993) and *Eat Drink Man Woman* (1994). He also directed a movie version of Jane Austen's *Sense and Sensibility* (1995), which was nominated for seven Academy Awards, and the acclaimed 1997 movie *The Ice Storm*. His accolades continued with *Crouching Tiger, Hidden Dragon* (2000), the recipient of the Oscar for Best Foreign Language Film. In 2005 his film *Brokeback Mountain* won him another Academy Award for Best Director. His 2012 film *Life of Pi* garnered eleven nominations from the Academy.

Taiwanese American Doug Chiang (1962–) is a visual effects arts director at Industrial Light and Magic, the special effects company founded by George Lucas. Chiang was the visual effects arts director of *Death Becomes Her*, which won an Academy Award for Visual Effects in 1992. He has also won both an Academy Award and a British Academy Award for his work at Industrial Light and Magic. Chiang led the design team that provided the special effects for *Star Wars I: The Phantom Menace*, released in 1999.

Journalism Attorney Phoebe Eng (1961–) is the founder of *A. Magazine*, a periodical devoted to Asian American issues. With a readership of about 100,000, the magazine also reports on the media and the manner in which it covers Asian Americans and Asian American concerns. In 1999 Eng published *Warrior Lessons: An Asian American Woman's Journey into Power*, an examination of what it means to be an Asian woman in the United States. In 2005 Eng cofounded the Opportunity Agenda, a communications and national policy group that works with social justice groups to open avenues for success for all.

Music Renowned Taiwanese American violinist Cho-liang Lin (1960–) immigrated to the United States in 1975 to study at the Juilliard School. In 1991 he joined the faculty there, later becoming professor of violin at Rice University in Houston, Texas. Beginning in 2001 Lin served as music director of La Jolla's Music Society, developing their SummerFest chamber music festival. He is also the artistic director of the Hong Kong International Chamber Music Festival.

Science and Medicine Nobel Prize winner Yuan-tse Lee (1936–) is the son of a well-known painter in Taiwan. Lee opted for science over art, attending Berkeley in 1962 and working at Harvard University designing a mass spectrometer that could identify the paths of different ions as they separated. His work in the deflection and identification of the ions in chemical reactions won Lee the Nobel Prize in Chemistry in 1986. In 1994 he renounced his American citizenship to serve as president of the Academia Sinica in Taiwan. Paul Chu (1941–) has conducted researches in superconductivity that have earned him worldwide fame. Chu has been at the University of Houston since 1979. David Ho (1952–) is a medical researcher whose work on the use of AZT in AIDS treatment won him a "Man of the Year" citation on the cover of *Time* magazine in 1995. Edward Lu (1963–), a NASA astronaut, has participated in two Space Shuttle missions. He left NASA in 2007. William Wei-lien Chang (1933–), a well-known pathologist formerly of West Virginia University, wrote numerous research articles on cell population kinetics and colon cancer. Kong-cheng Ho (1940–), associate professor of neurology at the Medical College of Wisconsin, authored numerous publications on Alzheimer's disease and the development of the brain.

MEDIA

PRINT

Several nationally published daily newspapers are aimed at a general Chinese American audience. In addition, some newspapers are linked to Taiwan in both direct and indirect ways. The *World Journal*, for example, is affiliated with the media magnate Tih-wu Wang and his *United Daily News* of Taipei.

International Daily News

Established in 1981, the paper features news of the Taiwanese American community.

> 870 Monterey Pass Road
> Monterey Park, California 91754
> Phone: (323) 265-1317
> Fax: (323) 262-1425
> Email: idnchina@gmail.com
> URL: www.chinesetoday.com

Sampan

The only bilingual newspaper in New England serving the Asian community, *Sampan* is published twice monthly.

> Ling Mei Wong, Editor
> 87 Tyler Street
> 5th Floor
> Boston, Massachusetts 02111
> Phone: (617) 426-9492
> Fax: (617) 482-2316
> Email: editor@sampan.org
> URL: www.sampan.org

Sing Tao Daily

Published since 1938, this newspaper is one of the most widely read Chinese-language papers in the world. The New York office reports on both world and local news applicable to the entire Asian community.

> 108 Lafayette Street
> New York, New York 10013
> Phone: (212) 699-3800
> Fax: (212) 699-3828

> Email: info@nysingtao.com
> URL: us.nysingtao.com

Taiwan Today

This weekly Internet newsletter includes notes on events and happenings in Taiwan.

> Edwin Hsiao, Editor in Chief
> Friends of Free China
> 1629 K Street
> Washington, D.C. 20006
> Email: ttonline@mofa.gov.tw
> URL: www.taiwantoday.tw

Taiwan Tribune

This Chinese-language publication offers news and events of interest to the Taiwanese community around the world.

> P.O. Box 1527
> Long Island, New York 11101
> Phone: (609) 750-0731
> Email: taiwantribune@yahoo.com
> URL: www.taiwantribune.com

World Journal

This newspaper, publishing since 1976, offers Chinese-language news for the North American community. It is published in New York, Los Angeles, San Francisco, Chicago, Dallas, Vancouver, and Toronto.

> 14107 20th Avenue
> Whitestone, New York 11357
> Phone: (718) 746-8889
> Fax: (718) 746-6509
> Email: webmaster@worldjournal.com
> URL: http://ny.worldjournal.com

RADIO

KAZN-AM (1300)

Broadcasts programs in several Asian languages, including Chinese.

> 747 East Green Street
> Pasadena, California 91101
> Phone: (626) 568-1300
> URL: www.am1300.com

KUSF-FM (90.3)

Chinese news programming every morning.

> 2130 Fulton Street
> San Francisco, California 94117
> Phone: (415) 386-KUSF
> Email: kusf@usfca.edu
> URL: www.kusf.org

WKCR-FM (89.9)

Broadcasts a Chinese variety show each Saturday morning.

> Eric Ingram, Program Director
> Columbia University
> 2920 Broadway

New York, New York 10027
Phone: (212) 854-9920
Email: board@wkcr.org
URL: www.studentaffairs.columbia.edu/wkcr/

TELEVISION

KCNS-TV (38)

Programming in Cantonese and Mandarin.

Luis Mendoza, General Manager
1750 Montgomery Street
Suite 149
San Francisco, California 94111
Phone: (415) 945-7149
URL: www.kcns-tv.com

KSCI-TV (18)

Some Chinese programming.

1990 South Bundy Drive
Suite 850
Los Angeles, California 90025
Phone: (310) 478-1818
Fax: (310) 479-8118
Email: info@la18.tv
URL: www.la18.tv

KTSF-TV (26)

Chinese news programming and a Friday night movie
in Chinese.

100 Valley Drive
Brisbane, California 94005
Phone: (515) 468-2626
Fax: (415) 467-7559
URL: www.ktsf.com

ORGANIZATIONS AND ASSOCIATIONS

Many Taiwanese American organizations have been
founded to promote Taiwanese-U.S. relations, a
free Taiwan, or both. Others have formed around
business and professional themes and concerns.

Formosan Association for Human Rights (FAHR)

A national organization that monitors and promotes
human rights in Taiwan, with sixteen chapters and a
monthly newsletter.

Linda Lin, President
2403 Millikin Drive, Arlington
Texas 76012
Phone: (817) 261-3929
URL: www.fahrusa.org

Formosan Association for Public Affairs (FAPA)

Attempts to affect U.S. policy vis-à-vis Taiwan.

Mark L. Kao, President
552 7th Street SE
Washington, D.C. 20003
Phone: (202) 547-368
Fax: (202) 543-7891
Email: home@fapa.org
URL: www.fapa.org

North America Taiwanese Professors' Association (NATPA)

Professors and senior researchers of Taiwanese origin or
descent join to encourage educational exchange and
cultural understanding among the Taiwanese and
other peoples worldwide. The association promotes
scientific and professional knowledge, seeks to
further the welfare of Taiwanese communities in
North America and Taiwan, and sponsors research
and lectures on topics related to Taiwan.

Shyu-Tu Lee, President
P.O. Box 873704
Vancouver, Washington 98687-3704
URL: www.natpa.org

Taiwanese Association of America (TAA)

Promotes friendship and welfare among Taiwanese
Americans and those concerned with Taiwanese
human rights.

Shi Tadao, Chairman
Email: taausa@gmail.com
URL: www.taa-usa.org

Taiwan Benevolent Association of America (TBAA)

Promotes the culture of Taiwanese Americans, offering
them a group of like-minded peers. Several states,
including California, have TBAA chapters.

URL: www.tbaa.us

Taiwanese United Fund (TUF)

This organization encourages cultural exchange
and understanding between Taiwanese
Americans and other cultural communities in
the United States.

3001 Walnut Grove Ave
Suite 7
Rosemead, California 91770
Phone: (626) 569-0692
Fax: (626) 569-0637
Email: info@tufusa.org
URL: www.tufusa.org

MUSEUMS AND RESEARCH CENTERS

Center for Taiwan Studies (CTS)

As part of the University of California, Santa Barbara's
Department of East Asian Languages and Cultural
Studies, the CTS researches and promotes Taiwan-
related academic activities. Its aim is to study Taiwan
and Taiwanese culture as separate from China.

Kuo-Ch'ing Tu, Professor
University of California, Santa Barbara
HSSB Building
Room 2257
Santa Barbara, California 93106
Phone: (805) 893-8835
Email: kctu@eastasian.ucsb.edu
URL: www.eastasian.ucsb.edu/projects/
taiwancenter

SOURCES FOR ADDITIONAL STUDY

Chee, Maria W. L. *Taiwanese American Transnational Families: Women and Kin Work*. New York: Routledge, 2005.

Chen, Carolyn. *Getting Saved in America: Taiwanese Immigration and Religious Experience*. Princeton: Princeton University Press, 2008.

Copper, John F. *Taiwan: Nation-State or Province?* 2nd ed. Boulder: Westview Press, 1996.

Davison, Gary Marvin, and Barbara E. Reed. *Culture and Customs of Taiwan*. Westport, CT: Greenwood Press, 1998.

Harrell, Stevan, and Huang Chün-chieh, eds. *Cultural Change in Postwar Taiwan*. Boulder, CO: Westview Press, 1994.

Hsiang-shui Chen. *Chinatown No More: Taiwan Immigrants in Contemporary New York*. Ithaca, NY: Cornell University Press, 1992.

Ng, Franklin. *The Taiwanese Americans*. Westport, CT: Greenwood Press, 1998.

THAI AMERICANS

Megan Ratner

OVERVIEW

Thai Americans are immigrants or descendants of people from Thailand, a nation in Southeast Asia on the Indochine Peninsula. Formally known as Prathet Thai ("Sacred Territory of the Thai") or Muang Thai ("Land of the Free"), Thailand is bordered by Myanmar (Burma) on the north and west, Laos on the north and east, and Cambodia and Malaysia on the south. It possesses a 2,000-mile (3,216 kilometer) coastline on the Gulf of Thailand, which is part of the South China Sea. The country covers an area of 198,115 square miles (513,120 square kilometers), giving it a footprint a little bigger than the state of California.

Thailand ranks twentieth in world population figures, with an estimated 67 million people, according to *CIA World Factbook* data for 2012. Its population is predominantly Buddhist, at 94 percent, followed by just over 4 percent who identify as Muslim. Three-quarters of the population are ethnic Thai, followed by 14 percent Chinese and smaller numbers of Malay, Hmong, and hill tribes. Thailand has a fairly robust economy that has posted impressive growth rates since the 1980s. It exports rice, rubber, computer equipment, transportation and construction products, and some perishable goods, such as seafood.

Thai immigration to the United States was nearly nonexistent before 1960, when U.S. armed forces began arriving in Thailand during the Vietnam War. By the 1970s, some 5,000 Thais had immigrated to the United States, at a ratio of three women to every man. The largest concentration of Thai immigrants can be found in Los Angeles and New York City. The first wave of immigrants consisted of professionals, especially medical doctors and nurses, business entrepreneurs, and wives of men in the U.S. Air Force who had either been stationed in Thailand or had spent their vacations there while on active duty in Southeast Asia. Another influx of Thai immigration to the United States occurred during the 1980s, with more than 64,000 new arrivals.

According to 2011 American Community Survey figures published by the U.S. Census Bureau, there are an estimated 271,924 Thai Americans—a figure comparable to the population of Newark, New Jersey. The highest concentration of Thai Americans is in California, which counts more than 67,700 residents of Thai ancestry. Smaller but sizable numbers live in Texas, Florida, and New York state, with roughly 16,000, 15,000, and 11,000 in each, respectively. Most U.S. metropolitan areas, including cities across the midwest, feature pockets of Thai American settlement.

HISTORY OF THE PEOPLE

Early History Once known as the Kingdom of Siam, Thailand has been a regional power for centuries and bears a proud historical distinction as the only nation in Southeast Asia to have avoided colonization by a European power. Its population of 67 million is relatively homogenous, with roughly 75 percent of Thai ancestry. This Southeast Asian ethnic group is ethnolinguistically related to the people of Laos, the Shan in Myanmar, and a distinct ethnic group known as Dai, or Tai, that lives in China's southern provinces.

Thai origins may have been in Yunnan, China, the seat of an ancient kingdom. The Thais' southward migration in the early centuries CE led to the establishment of several nation states now known as Thailand, Laos, and Myanmar (Burma). By the sixth century CE an important network of agricultural communities had spread as far south as Pattani province, close to Thailand's modern border with Malaysia, and to the northeastern area of present-day Thailand. The Thai nation became officially known as "Syam" in 1851 under the reign of King Mongkut. Eventually this name became synonymous with the Thai kingdom and was the name by which the country was known for many years, in an Anglicized form as the Kingdom of Siam.

In the thirteenth and fourteenth centuries, several Thai principalities united and sought to break from their Khmer (early Cambodian) rulers. Sukhothai, which the Thai consider the first independent Siamese state, declared its independence in 1238 (or 1279, according to some records). The new kingdom expanded into Khmer territory and onto the Malay Peninsula. Sri Indradit, the Thai leader in the independence movement, became king of the Sukhothai Dynasty. He was succeeded by his son, Ram Khamhaeng, one of the most revered figures in Thai history. Ram Khamhaeng organized a writing system that became the basis for modern Thai and declared his devotion to local spirits as well as Theravada Buddhism. Modern Thais consider this period of their history as the golden age of Siamese religion, politics, and culture. It was also one of great expansion: under Ram Khamhaeng, the monarchy extended to Nakhon Si Thammarat in the south—a province on the eastern coast of the Malay Peninsula—to Vientiane and Luang Prabang in Laos, and to Pegu in southern Burma.

Ayutthaya was established as the capital city after Ram Khamhaeng's death in 1317. The Thai kings of Ayutthaya became quite powerful in the fourteenth and fifteenth centuries, adopting Khmer court customs and language and gaining more absolutist authority. During this period, Europeans—the Dutch, Portuguese, French, English, and Spanish—began to pay visits to Siam, establishing diplomatic links and Christian missions within the kingdom. Early accounts note that the city and port of Ayutthaya astonished its European guests, who remarked that London was nothing more than a village in comparison. On the whole, the Thai kingdom distrusted foreigners but maintained a cordial relationship with the then-expanding colonial powers. During the reign of King Narai, two Thai diplomatic groups were sent on a friendship mission to King Louis XIV of France in the 1680s.

In 1767 Ayutthaya suffered a devastating invasion from the Burmese, with whom the Thais had endured hostile relations for at least two hundred years. After several years of savage battle, the capital fell and the Burmese set about destroying everything the Thais held sacred, including temples, religious sculpture, and manuscripts. But the Burmese could not maintain a solid base of control, and they were ousted by Phraya Taksin, a first-generation Chinese Thai general who declared himself king in late 1767 and ruled from a new capital, Thonburi, which was across the river from Bangkok.

Following the death of Phraya Taksin in 1782, General Chao Phraya Chakri was crowned and given the title Rama I. Chakri moved the capital across the river to Bangkok. In 1809, Rama II, Chakri's son, assumed the throne and reigned until 1824. Rama III, also known as Phraya Nang Klao, ruled from 1824 through 1851; like his father, he worked hard to restore the Thai culture that had been almost completely destroyed in the Burmese invasion. Not until the reign of Rama IV, or King Mongkut, which began in 1851, did the Thai strengthen relations with Europeans. Rama IV worked with the British to establish trade treaties and modernize the government while managing to avoid British and French colonization. During the reign of Rama V (King Chulalongkorn), who ruled from 1868 to 1910, Siam gave up some territory to French Laos and British Burma. The short rule of Rama VI (1910–1925) saw the introduction of compulsory education and other educational reforms.

Modern Era In the late 1920s and early 1930s, a group of Thai intellectuals and military personnel—many of whom had been educated in Europe—embraced democratic ideology and were able to effect a successful—and bloodless—coup against the absolute monarchy in Siam. This occurred during the reign of Rama VII, between 1925 and 1935. In its place, the Thai developed a constitutional monarchy based on the British model, with a combined military-civilian group in charge of governing the country, with great reverence for the king and his dynasty. The country's name was officially changed to Thailand in 1939 during prime minister Plaek Phibunsongkhram's government. Phibunsongkhram had been a key military figure in the 1932 coup and seized increasing executive powers for himself.

Japan occupied Thailand during World War II, and Phibunsongkhram declared war on the United States and Great Britain. The Thai ambassador in Washington, however, refused to make the declaration. Seri Thai ("Free Thai") underground groups worked with the Allied powers both outside and within Thailand to vanquish the Japanese, and the end of World War II terminated Phibunsongkhram's regime. After a short stint of democratic civilian control, he regained control in 1948, only to have much of his power taken away by General Sarit Thanarat, another military dictator. By 1958, Thanarat had abolished the constitution, dissolved parliament, and outlawed all political parties. He maintained power until his death in 1963.

Army officers ruled the country from 1964 to 1973, during which time the United States was given permission to establish army bases on Thai soil to support their troops fighting in Vietnam. The generals who ran the country during the 1970s closely aligned Thailand with the United States during the war. Civilian participation in government was allowed intermittently. In 1983 the constitution was amended to allow for a more democratically elected National Assembly, and the monarchy exerted a moderating influence on the military and on civilian politicians, but the economy remained moribund and social strictures continued. This monarch was King Bhumibol Adulyadej, known as Rama IX. Born in 1927 in the United States while his father was a student at Harvard University, Adulyadej ascended to the throne in 1946 and had one son, Crown Prince Vajiralongkorn, in 1952.

The success of a pro-military coalition in Thailand's March 1992 elections touched off a series of disturbances in which fifty citizens died. The military violently suppressed a pro-democracy movement on the streets of Bangkok in May 1992, but following the intervention of the king, another round of elections was held in September of that year, and Chuan Leekpai, the leader of the Democrat Party, was elected. His government fell in 1995, and the chaos that resulted—along with the nation's large foreign debt—led to the collapse of the Thai economy in 1997. Slowly, with help from International Monetary Fund (IMF) loans, the nation's economy has recovered.

In 2001 a wealthy telecommunications entrepreneur, Thaksin Shinawatra, was elected Thailand's new prime minister. His five-year tenure was marked by several notable economic gains, including a significant reduction in the number of rural Thais living in poverty, but Shinawatra's regime was also tarnished by widespread corruption and other abuses of office. He was forced out in a 2006 military coup. A new constitution went into effect in 2007, followed by elections that same year.

In January 2008 widespread political protests occurred in Bangkok over a new coalition government formed by members of the People's Power Party (PPP) allied with the disgraced Shinawatra. Supporters of an opposition party, the People's Alliance for Democracy (PAD), organized widespread demonstrations in Bangkok. In spring 2009 the unrest prompted Prime Minister Abhisit Vejjajiva to declare a state of emergency in the capital, which eventually led to the dispersal of the protest camp by Thai army units in May 2010. Shinawatra's sister, Yingluck Shinawatra, led the newly created Pheu Thai Party to electoral victory in 2011 and became the first woman to serve as prime minister of Thailand. Although the country is technically a democracy, strict censorship laws prevent any public discussion of political corruption. These conditions exacerbate internal unrest.

SETTLEMENT IN THE UNITED STATES

There was little or no immigration from Thailand to the United Stated prior to the Vietnam War. However, both the war, which ended in 1975, and the passage of the U.S. Immigration and Nationality Act of 1965 vastly increased the number of Thais (and emigrants from other Southeast Asian countries) seeking a permanent place in America. The immigration-reform law, which abolished the previous "quota" system that favored immigrants of European origins, was signed by President Lyndon B. Johnson on October 3, 1965, and went into effect three years later.

The first Thai immigrants to the United States originally came to the Los Angeles area in the 1950s to gain educational or professional skills, enrolling at the University of Southern California (USC) and the University of California Los Angeles (UCLA). Many settled in a rundown section of Hollywood Boulevard between Normandie and Western avenues in apartment buildings that had been built during the 1920s and 1930s to house newcomers to the movie industry. The Thai student-immigrants were drawn there because of the low monthly rents and substandard housing stock. More young Thai men, mostly enrolled in medicine and science-degree programs, arrived in the 1960s and made the area their home, and some decided to stay in the United States instead of returning home, as their original intent had been. Thai-owned businesses sprang up, along with religious and community organizations. In 1999 this section of Hollywood Boulevard was officially designated Thai Town in a motion passed by the Los Angeles City Council, making it the first "official" Thai Town in the United States.

The next significant immigration of Thai Americans was composed mainly of spouses of U.S. military personnel in the 1960s and 1970s. Many of the first Thai women to gain "fiancé" visas were those from the villages around Udon Thani, the site of a U.S. military air base. A 1976 report published by the U.S. Department of Education noted that in 1968, 304 Thais came to the United States as spouses of returning U.S. military personnel; by 1971 that number had nearly quintupled to 1,481; and the peak year for Thai-born military wives was 1974, when 2,141 settled in the United States. Many of these women, while assimilating with seemingly little effort into their new American lives, nevertheless maintained strong ties to their families and homeland.

About 44,000 Thais immigrated to the United States in the 1970s. By the following decade, that number had risen to more than 64,000. Student or temporary visitor visas were a frequent avenue of entry into the United States. In the first years after the 1965 U.S. immigration-reform law, the Thais who came were mostly professionals, including almost the entire graduating class of a medical school in Chiang Mai, who in 1972 chartered their own plane to the United States. Thais who came to America in the 1980s fled worsening economic circumstances in Thailand. Some fell victim to unlawful labor practices in their search for a better life in the United States, namely in a few notable cases of garment-manufacturing sweatshops in California and the New York/ New Jersey area, where Asian small-business owners employed dozens of illegal immigrants in near slave-labor conditions.

According to the U.S. Census Bureau, the number of Thais in the United States more than doubled between 2000 and 2009, from 150,093 to 304,160. California registered a 44 percent rise in the number of Thai Americans in the first decade of the twenty-first century, from 46,868 in 2000 to 67,707 in 2010. Florida also experienced a significant spike (77 percent) in newcomers, from 8,618 to 15,333. As in California, New York state's population of Thai Americans rose by 44 percent, from 8,158 to 11,763. The number of Thai Americans in Texas grew by 66 percent in the same time frame, from 9,918 to 16,472. Most surprising was the triple-digit growth of Thai Americans in noncoastal and Eastern seaboard states like Montana and Maine, which saw growth rates of 83 percent and 114 percent, respectively, though the 2000 populations were admittedly small to begin with; in Wyoming, for example, there were 114 Thai Americans in 2000 and 259 in 2010 (a 127 percent increase).

After Los Angeles, the second-most-populous Thai-American community is centered in New York City's borough of Queens. The western Queens communities of Elmhurst, Jackson Heights, and

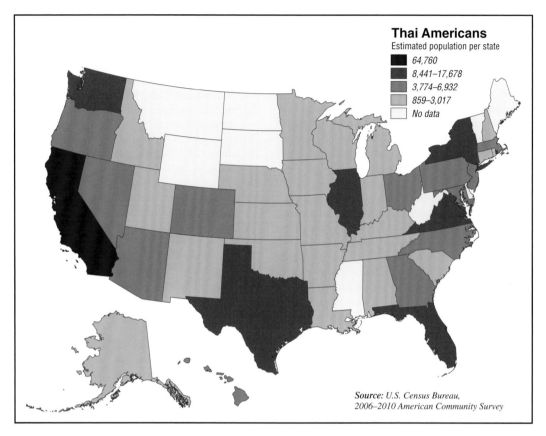

Thai Americans
Estimated population per state

- *64,760*
- *8,441–17,678*
- *3,774–6,932*
- *859–3,017*
- *No data*

Source: U.S. Census Bureau,
2006–2010 American Community Survey

Woodside are home to the largest concentration of Thai Americans in New York City. The San Francisco Bay Area also harbors a tight-knit Thai American population.

In California, New York, Texas, and Florida, first-, second-, and third-generation Thai Americans own an array of small businesses, including restaurants, gas stations, hair and nail salons, grocery stores, and even independent video stores that cater to a demand for Asian-origin programming. In general, Thai communities are tightly knit and mimic the social networks of their native land.

LANGUAGE

A member of the Tai language family, Thai is one of the oldest languages in East and Southeast Asia. Some anthropologists have hypothesized that it may even predate standard Chinese. Thai and Chinese share certain similarities because they are monosyllabic tonal languages; that is, because there are only 420 phonetically different words in Thai, a single syllable can have multiple meanings. Meanings are determined by five different tones (in Thai): a high or low tone; a level tone; and a falling or rising tone. For example, depending on the inflection and vowel length, the syllable *mai* can mean "widow," "silk," "burn," "wood," "new," "not?" or "not." In addition to the tonal similarities with Chinese, Thai has also borrowed from Pali and Sanskrit, most notably in the phonetic alphabet

conceived by King Ram Khamhaeng in 1283 and still in use today. The signs of the alphabet take their pattern from Sanskrit and early Khmer; there are also supplemental signs for tones, which are like vowels and can stand beside or above the consonant to which they belong. This alphabet bears some similarities to the alphabets of neighboring Laos and Cambodia.

Greetings and Popular Expressions Common Thai words and expressions include the following: *sawatdi*—"good morning," "good afternoon," or "good evening," as well as "good-bye" (by the host); *la kon*—"good-bye" (by the guest); *khopkhun*—"thank you"; *kho hai chok di*—"good luck"; *farang*—"foreigner"; *choen khrap* (if the speaker is male) or *choen kha* (if the speaker is female)—"please, you are welcome," "it's all right," "go ahead," or "you first" (depending on the circumstances).

In the 2004 U.S. Census Bureau report *We the People: Asians in the United States*, Thai Americans responded to questions about languages spoken in their household. Among those surveyed, 19.2 percent reported that only English is spoken at home; 33.9 percent said a language other than English is spoken in their home but said they speak English "very well." A little more than 46 percent reported that Thai or another language is the primary one used in their home, while self-reporting that they speak English less than "very well."

RELIGION

Nearly 95 percent of all Thais identify themselves as Theravada Buddhists. Theravada Buddhism originated in India and stresses three principal aspects of existence: *dukkha* (suffering, anxiety, "dis-ease"), *anicca* (impermanence, transiency of all things), and *anatta* (non-substantiality of reality; no permanence of the soul/self). These principles, which were articulated by Siddhartha Gautama in the sixth century BCE, contrast with certain Hindu beliefs in an eternal, blissful Self.

Gautama was given the title Buddha, or "enlightened one." He advocated the "eight-fold path," which requires high ethical standards and the ability to conquer desire. The concept of reincarnation is central to Buddhism. By feeding monks, making regular donations to temples, and worshipping regularly at the *wat* (temple), Thais try to improve their situation—acquire enough *bun* (merit)—to lessen the number of rebirths, or subsequent reincarnations, a person must undergo before reaching Nirvana, a state described as peace of mind, or freedom from all earthly suffering and attachment. In addition, the accumulation of *bun* helps determine the quality of the individual's station in future lives. *Tham bun*, or merit making, is an important social and religious activity for Thais. Because Buddhist teachings emphasize philanthropic donations as part of achieving merit, Thais tend to be supportive of a wide range of charities and practice generalized reciprocity.

Ordination into the Buddhist order of monks often serves to mark entry into the adult world. Ordination is restricted to men, although women can become nuns by shaving their heads, wearing white robes, and obtaining permission to reside in the nun's quarters on grounds within the temple. Many Thai men enter the monkhood at some point in their lives, often just prior to their marriage. Many only stay for a short period, sometimes as little as a few days, but in general they remain for at least one *phansa*, the three-month Buddhist Rains Retreat, which coincides with the rainy season. Most ordinations occur in July, just before the Rains Retreat.

During one of the first liminal stages of the ordination ritual, the candidate is called a *nak*, which means dragon, referring to a Buddhist myth about a dragon who tried to pass himself off as a human being and became a monk. In the ceremony, the *nak*'s head and eyebrows are shaved to symbolize his rejection of vanity. For three to four hours, a professional master of ceremonies sings of the mother's pain in giving birth to the child and emphasizes the many filial obligations of the young man, as well as his important obligations to the Buddhist order. The ceremony concludes with all relatives and friends gathered in a circle holding a *sai mongkhon* (white thread) and passing three lighted candles in a clockwise direction.

At a later stage in the ritual process, the *nak*, dressed in white (to symbolize purity), is carried on the shoulders of his friends under tall umbrellas in a colorful procession. He bows before his father, who hands him the saffron robes he will wear as a monk and leads him to the abbot, where four or more monks are seated on a raised platform before the main Buddha image. The *nak* asks permission for ordination after prostrating himself three times to the abbot. The abbot reads a scripture and drapes a yellow sash on the *nak*'s body to symbolize acceptance for ordination. He is taken out of view and dressed in the saffron robes by the two monks who will oversee his instruction. He then requests the ten basic vows of a novice monk and repeats each as it is recited to him.

The *nak*'s father presents alms bowls and other gifts to the abbot. Facing the Buddha, the candidate answers questions to show that he has met the conditions for entry into the monkhood. The ceremony concludes with all the monks chanting and the new monk pouring water from a silver container into a bowl to symbolize the transference of all merit he has acquired from being a monk to his parents. They in turn perform the same ritual to transfer some of their new merit to other relatives. The ritual's emphasis is on his identity as a Buddhist and his newfound adult maturity. At the same time, the rite reinforces the link between generations and the importance of family and community.

Thai Americans have accommodated themselves to the environment in the United States by adapting their religious practices when necessary. One of the most far-reaching of these changes was the switch from lunar calendar days to the conventional Saturday or Sunday services that are offered in the United States.

San Jose State University scholar of Theravada Buddhism Todd L. Perreira undertook an extensive survey of the membership of one temple in the San Francisco Bay area (Wat Buddhanusorn), polling members about their ethnicity and religious practices. He published the results of the study in a 2004 paper, "*Sasana Sakon* and the New Asian American: Intermarriage and Identity at a Thai Buddhist Temple in Silicon Valley." Perreira discovered that Thai American wives worship and participate in community activities with their non-Thai husbands to an unusually high degree. Just under a third of the couples who belonged to the *wat* were interracial unions—that is, Thai women married to non-Asian men. Perreira reflected that Wat Buddhanusorn, founded in the 1980s, was representative of the 150 Theravada Buddhist temples in the United States that serve Thai Americans. The practice of exogamy, or marrying outside of one's social group, is markedly higher for Asian-born women, who marry non-Asians but often retain their religious and other cultural ties to their homeland.

CULTURE AND ASSIMILATION

Thai Americans have adapted well to American society. Although they maintain their culture and many of their ethnic traditions, they accept the norms as practiced in U.S. society. This flexibility and adaptability has had a profound effect on first-generation American-born Thais, who tend to be quite assimilated, or "Americanized." According to members of the Thai-American community, the young people's acceptance of American ways has made these changes more acceptable to their parents, facilitating relations between "established" Americans and newcomers.

Perhaps the greatest contribution from the small Thai American community has been its cuisine. Thai restaurants remain a popular choice in most cities across the United States, and items from Thai cuisine have even made their way to grocery-store shelves.

Although Thai Americans retain many traditional beliefs, they often try to adjust their beliefs in order to live in the United States comfortably. Others have often perceived Thais as too adaptable and lacking in innovation. A common expression, *mai pen rai*, meaning "never mind" or "it doesn't matter," has been seen by some as an indication of Thai Americans' unwillingness to expand or develop ideas. Thai Americans are often mistaken for Chinese or Indochinese, which has led to misunderstandings and offended Thais, as Thai culture is bound up with Buddhism and has its own traditions, different from Chinese culture. In addition, Americans often assume Thais are refugees rather than immigrants by choice. This assumption is tied to the prevalence of so many other South Asians who came to the United States in the years after the Vietnam War, when U.S. immigration policies gave special preference to refugees from Laos, Cambodia, and the former South Vietnam. Thai Americans are anxious that their presence be seen as a benefit, not a burden, to American society.

Traditions and Customs Thais do not shake hands when they meet. Instead, they keep their elbows at their sides and press their palms together at about chest height in a prayer-like gesture called *wai*. The head is bent in this greeting; the lower the head, the more respect one shows. Children are supposed to *wai* adults, and they receive an acknowledgment in the form of *wai* or a smile in return. In Thai culture the feet are considered the lowest part of the body, both spiritually and physically. When visiting any religious edifice, feet must be pointed away from any Buddha images, which are always kept in high places and shown great respect. Thais consider pointing at something with one's feet to be the epitome of bad manners. The head is regarded as the highest part of the body; therefore Thais do not touch each other's hair, nor do they pat each other on the head. These customs remain common among Thai Americans.

Spirit Houses In Thailand, many houses and buildings have an accompanying spirit house, or a place for the property guardian spirit (*Phra phum*) to reside. Some Thais believe that the lack of a spirit house causes spirits to live with the family, which invites trouble. Spirit houses, which are usually about the same size as a birdhouse, are mounted on a pedestal and resemble Thai temples. In Thailand, large buildings such as hotels may have a spirit house as large as an average family dwelling. The spirit house is given the best location on the property and is shaded by the main house. Its position is planned at the time of the building's construction; then it is ceremonially erected. Corresponding improvements, including additions, are also made to the spirit house whenever modifications are made to the main house. Thai Americans continue to follow this custom in their new homeland.

Cuisine Perhaps the greatest contribution from the small Thai American community has been its cuisine. Thai restaurants remain a popular choice in most cities across the United States, and items from Thai cuisine have even made their way to grocery-store shelves. Thai cooking is generally light in calories, pungent, and flavorful, and some dishes can be quite spicy. The mainstay of Thai cooking, as in the rest of Southeast Asia, is rice. In fact, the Thai word *kao* means both "rice" and "food." Thai food is eaten with a spoon and fork.

Presentation of food for the Thai is a work of art, especially if the meal marks a special occasion. Thais are renowned for their ability to carve fruit: melons, mandarins, and pomelos (a large citrus fruit), to name just a few, are carved in the shapes of intricate flowers, classic designs, or birds. Staples of Thai cuisine include coriander roots, peppercorns, and garlic (which are often ground together), lemongrass, *nam pla* (fish sauce), and *kapi* (shrimp paste). The meal generally includes soup, one or two *kaengs* (dishes that include thin, clear, souplike gravy; although Thais describe these sauces as "curry," it is not what most Westerners know as curry), and as many *khruang khiang* (side dishes) as possible. Among these, there might be a *phat* (stir-fried) dish, something with *phrik* (hot chili peppers), or a *thot* (deep-fried) dish. Thai cooks typically use very few recipes, preferring to taste and adjust seasonings as they cook.

Traditional Dress Traditional clothing for Thai women consists of a *phasin*, or wraparound skirt (sarong), which is worn with a fitted, long-sleeved jacket. Men wear a loose-fitting cotton shirt and trousers. Among the most beautiful costumes are those worn by dancers of classical Thai ballet. Female dancers wear a tight-fitting under-jacket and a *phanung* (skirt), which is made of silk, silver, or gold brocade. The *phanung* is pleated in front, and a belt holds it in place. A pailletted and jeweled velvet cape fastens to the front of the belt and drapes down behind nearly to the hem of the *phanung*. A wide jeweled collar, armlets, necklace, and bracelets make up the rest of the costume, which is capped with a *chada*, the temple-style headdress. Dancers are sewn into their costumes before a performance. The jewels and metal thread can make the costume weigh nearly forty pounds. Men's costumes feature tight-fitting silver-thread brocade jackets with epaulets and an ornately embroidered collar. Embroidered panels hang from the belt, and the calf-length pants are made of silk. A male dancer's jeweled headdress has a tassel on the right, while the woman's is on the left. Dancers wear no shoes. For everyday life, Thais wear sandals or Western-style footwear. Shoes are always removed when entering a house. For the past one hundred years, Western clothing has become the standard form of clothing in Thailand's urban areas. Thai Americans wear typical American clothes for everyday occasions.

Holidays Thais are well known for enjoying festivities and holidays, even those not part of their culture; for example, Bangkok residents have been known to take part in the Christmas and even Bastille Day celebrations of the resident foreign communities. Thai holidays include New Year's Day (January 1); Chinese New Year; Magha Puja, which occurs on the full moon of the third lunar month (February) and commemorates the day when 1,250 disciples heard the Buddha's first sermon; Chakri Day (April 6), which marks the enthronement of King Rama I; Songkran (mid-April), the Thai New Year, an occasion when caged birds and fish are set free and water is thrown by everyone on everyone else; and Coronation Day (May 5). Visakha Puja, which occurs on the full moon of the sixth lunar month (May), is the holiest of Buddhist days, a celebration of Lord Buddha's birth, enlightenment, and death. Thai Americans celebrate these as well as a Buddhist Lenten period in July, and the Kathina, or robe-gifting event, in October. The Kathina is a time for Theravada Buddhists to honor their monks with special gifts. In the United States these celebrations are much shorter than some of the two- or three-day events in Thailand, and they are generally arranged around the weekend to accommodate work schedules. Thai Americans also celebrate Queen Sirikit's birthday on August 12 and King Rama X's birthday on December 5; these serve as a type of Mother's Day and Father's Day for Thai families, as they honor the royal family in Thailand by showing devotion to their own parents.

Death and Burial Rituals Many Thais consider *ngan sop* (the cremation ceremony) one of the most important of all communal religious rituals. It is a family occasion, and the presence of Buddhist monks is necessary. One *baht* coin is placed in the mouth of the corpse (to enable the dead person to buy his or her way into the next world), and the hands are arranged into a *wai* and tied with *sai mongkhon* (white thread). A banknote, two flowers, and two candles are placed between the hands. *Sai mongkhon* is used to tie the ankles as well, and the mouth and eyes are sealed with wax. The corpse is placed in a coffin with the feet facing west, the direction of the setting sun and of death.

THAI PROVERBS

Khwamlap mai mi nai lok.

> There are no secrets in the world.

Phuan kin ha ngai, phuan tai ha yak.

> Friends for a meal are easy to find, friends for life are difficult to find.

Ma kat ya kat top.

> If dogs bite, don't bite back.

Dressed for mourning in black or white, the relatives gather around the body to hear the sutras of the monks who sit in a row on raised padded seats or on a platform. On the day the body is cremated (which for persons of high rank can be as long as a year after the funeral ceremony), mourners carry the coffin feet first to the burial site. Mourners scatter rice on the ground to appease the spirits who are said to be drawn to the funeral activities. As tokens of respect for the deceased, the mourners throw candles and incense bouquets on the funeral pyre, which consists of piles of wood under an ornate paste pagoda. The most exalted guest then officiates at the cremation by lighting the pyre. Only the next of kin attend the actual cremation that follows, which is usually held a few yards from the ritual funeral pyre. The occasion is sometimes followed by a meal for guests who may have traveled from far away to attend the ceremony. On that evening and the two following, monks come to the house to chant blessings for the departed soul and for the protection of the living. According to Thai tradition, the departed family member is advancing along the cycle of death and rebirth toward the state of perfect peace; thus, sadness has no place at this rite.

Thai Americans often request the presence of a monk at a family member's deathbed. The monks pray for the sick and the dying and provide an important symbolic link to traditional Thai culture at this difficult time. Monks prepare the body for burial and chant at the pre-cremation funeral ceremony, which is held at a standard America mortuary-service provider. The funeral and mourning rituals may last from one to three days. Thai Americans honor their departed ancestors in the annual Songkran (Thai New Year ceremony) in mid-April.

FAMILY AND COMMUNITY LIFE

Traditional Thai families are closely knit, often incorporating servants and employees. Togetherness is a hallmark of the extended family structure: people never sleep alone, even in houses with ample room, unless they ask to do so. Virtually no one is left to live alone in an apartment or house. The Thai family is highly structured, and each member has his or her specific place based on age, gender, and rank within the family. They can expect help and security as long as they remain within the confines of this order. Relationships are strictly defined and named with terms so precise that they reveal the relation (parental, sibling, uncle, aunt, cousin), the relative age (younger, older), and side of the family (maternal or paternal). These terms are used more often in conversation than the person's given name. The biggest change that settlement in the United States has brought has been the diminishing of these extended families. They remain prevalent in Thailand, but the lifestyle and mobility of American society has made the extended Thai family hard to maintain. The conventional nuclear family, smaller in size and offering more privacy, seems to be preferable.

In 2011 the U.S. Census Bureau's American Community Survey reported that an estimated 35.4 percent of Thai Americans had never been married, 50.6 percent listed themselves as married, and 14 percent were separated, widowed, or divorced. Household type is another tool census-takers use to profile a community. In 2011, 48.2 percent of Thai American households were married-couple domiciles, and 11.1 percent were headed by a female head of household with no spouse present. Some 35.9 percent of Thai American households classified themselves as nonfamily households.

Gender Roles About 60 percent of Thai Americans are women, and a little more than half of them (54 percent) are married to non-Asian spouses. Their children generally retain strong ties to their mother's culture and traditions. Thai American women often bring an unusually high degree of cultural and religious practices into their households in comparison to other marriages between Asians and non-Asians.

Education Education has traditionally been of paramount importance to Thais. Educational accomplishment is considered a status-enhancing achievement. Until the late nineteenth century, the responsibility for educating the young lay entirely with the monks in the temple. Compulsory education in Thailand is through the sixth grade, and the literacy rate is over 90 percent. There are thirty-nine universities and colleges and thirty-six Teacher Training Colleges in Thailand to meet the needs of thousands of secondary school students who want higher educational attainment. Since the beginning of the twenty-first century, overseas study and degrees have been actively sought and highly prized.

Thai American students complete bachelor's degree programs at a rate nearly comparable to their counterparts in larger Asian American population subgroups. A 2011 survey published by the National Commission on Asian American and Pacific Islander Research in Education (CARE) and The Asian American and Pacific Islander Scholarship Fund (APIASF) showed that 40.9 percent of Thai Americans listed their educational attainment as a bachelor's degree, roughly the same as Asian Indians and Chinese students, but less than Japanese and Korean undergraduate degree rates. Of Thai Americans surveyed, 24 percent had completed an advanced degree.

Courtship and Weddings Unlike other Asian countries, Thailand has been far more permissive toward marriages of personal choice, though parents generally have some say in the matter. Thai Americans typically choose their own marriage partners. Marriages in Thailand tend to take place between families of equal social and economic status. There are no ethnic or religious restrictions, and intermarriage in Thailand is quite common, especially between Thai and Chinese, and Thai and Westerners.

Wedding ceremonies can be ornate affairs, or there may be no ceremony at all. If a couple lives together for a while and has a child together, they are recognized as "de facto married." Most Thais do have a ceremony, however—especially the wealthier members of the community, who consider this essential. Prior to the wedding, the two families agree on the expenses of the ceremony and the "bride price." The couple begins their wedding day with a religious ritual in the early morning and by receiving blessings from monks. During the ceremony, the bride and groom kneel side by side. An astrologer or a monk chooses a favorable time for the couple's heads to be linked with joined loops of *sai mongkhon* (white thread) by a senior elder. He pours sacred water over their hands, which they allow to drip into bowls of flowers. Guests bless the couple by pouring sacred water in the same way. The second part of the ceremony is essentially a secular practice. Thais do not make any vows to one another. Rather, the two linked but independent circles of thread serve to symbolically emphasize that the man and woman have each retained their individual identities while, at the same time, joining their destinies.

One tradition, practiced primarily in the countryside, is to have "sympathetic magic" performed by an older, successfully married couple. This duo lies in the marriage bed before the newlyweds, where they say many auspicious things about the bed and its superiority as a place for conception. They place symbols of fertility on the bed, such as a tomcat, bags of rice, sesame seeds, coins, a stone pestle, or a bowl of rainwater. The newlyweds are supposed to keep these objects (except the tomcat) in their bed for three days.

Even in cases in which the marriage has been sealed by a ceremony, divorce is a simple matter: if both parties consent, they sign a mutual statement to this effect at the district office. If only one party wants the divorce, he or she must show proof of the other's desertion or lack of support for one year. The divorce rate among Thais, both officially and unofficially, is

relatively low compared to the American divorce rate, and the remarriage rate is high. Though American legal practices differ in the event of divorce, the spirit of the law is still adhered to among Thai Americans, whose households tend to remain close-knit units.

Birth In order to keep evil spirits away, pregnant women are not given any gifts before a baby is born. These evil spirits are thought to be the spirits of women who died childless and unmarried. For a minimum of three days to a month after birth, the baby is still considered a spirit child, and it is customary to refer to the newborn as "frog," "dog," "toad," or other animal terms that are seen as helpful in warding off the attention of evil spirits. Parents often ask a monk or an elder to select an appropriate name for their child, usually of two or more syllables, which is used for legal and official purposes. Nearly all Thais have a one-syllable nickname. Like the formal name, a nickname is intended to keep the evil spirits away. These customs are prevalent among Thai Americans even several generations removed from immigration. One marked difference is the custom of bestowing a standard English-language name for children officially yet still referring to them by their pet name.

Health Care Issues and Practices Many Thai Americans travel back to Thailand for health care, including for serious medical conditions. This number is especially concentrated among naturalized U.S. citizens, who may travel back and forth without constraint. Thailand's medical practices focus on a patient's state of mind in addition to physical issues. Stress, diet, and family concerns are also judged as factors that affect treatment results. Furthermore, Thailand has an especially well-trained health-care workforce, with many specialists having earned their credentials at U.S. medical schools. Although this type of treatment is available in the Unites States as well, many Thai Americans trust the Thai health system and prefer to travel abroad to their homeland for health issues, finances permitting.

In the Los Angeles area, home to the largest population of Thai-descent Americans, health care professionals from the University of California-Los Angeles Medical Center founded the Thai Health and Information Services (THAIS). The group works to help newcomers and non-English-speaking Thais in Los Angeles County navigate health-care provider networks and social-service programs.

EMPLOYMENT AND ECONOMIC CONDITIONS

In Thailand, men tend to aspire to military or civil service jobs. Rural women have been traditionally engaged in running businesses, while educated women are involved in all types of professions. In the United States, most Thais own small businesses or work as skilled laborers. Many women have opted for nursing careers. There are no Thai-only labor unions, nor do Thais particularly dominate one profession.

According to the 2004 U.S. Census Bureau publication *We the People: Asians in the United States*, Thai Americans' labor-force participation is healthy. Census results show a 70.2 percent rate of employment for Thai American men ages sixteen and older.

A Thai American restaurateur and her two daughters own several Thai restaurants in the Sacramento, CA area. MICHAEL A. JONES / ZUMAPRESS / NEWSCOM

Thai American women were particularly active in the labor force, with 61.1 percent holding jobs outside the home. Aside from Filipino-American women, this was the highest percentage of women in the U.S. workforce among Asian population groups.

The same U.S. Census data tallied workforce participation by occupation. A significant number, 36.1 percent, of Thai Americans listed themselves as belonging to "management, professional, and related categories"; 32.5 percent reported they worked in one of the service professions, and another 19.6 percent held sales and office jobs. Their median earnings, by gender, were $41,128 for Thai American men and $31,700 for Thai American women. Thai Americans' median family income was $48,640 in 2004, with only 9.1 percent of Thai Americans classified as living below the poverty line. In comparison, the median household income for all U.S. households was $50,233 in 2006.

POLITICS AND GOVERNMENT

In 2006 voters in the California city of La Palma (Orange County) elected Gorpat Henry Charoen, who came to the United States from Thailand in 1979, to its city council. An engineer and information-technology specialist by training, Charoen was the first Thai American ever to be elected to public office in the United States. A year later, he was elected mayor of La Palma.

Thai Americans tend not to be active in community politics in this country; rather, they are more concerned with issues in Thailand. This reflects the general insulation of the community, where there are specific delineations between northern and southern Thais and where intercommunity outreach with other groups has been almost nonexistent. Thai Americans are quite active in Thai politics and they keep an active watch on economic, political, and social movements there.

In early 2006 some Thai Americans began staging weekly protests outside the Thai consulate in Los Angeles to voice their criticism of the mounting corruption in Thailand's Prime Minister Thaksin Shinawatra's regime. After Shinawatra was removed from office by a military coup later that year, his sister, Yingluck Shinawatra, became head of the Pheu Thai Party and, after the 2011 elections, Thailand's first female prime minister. Along with King Bhumibol Adulyadej, she welcomed U.S. President Barack Obama just days after his 2012 reelection. Obama was not the first sitting U.S. president to visit Thailand—Lyndon B. Johnson did so in 1966, as U.S. military involvement in Southeast Asia was about to escalate. Obama's 2012 visit commemorated 180 years of cooperation between the two nations.

NOTABLE INDIVIDUALS

Academia College professor Ira Sukrungruang was born in 1976 in the United States to Thai-immigrant parents. His 2010 memoir *Talk Thai: The Adventures of Buddhist Boy* recounts his experiences growing up in a fairly typical Thai household in Chicago and his struggles with assimilation.

Activism Joe W. Gordon is a naturalized U.S. citizen who was born Lerpong Wichaicommart in Thailand in the mid-1950s. In 2011, while visiting Thailand for the first time in more than thirty years, Gordon was arrested on charges of defaming Thailand's King Bhumibol Adulyadej on a website that Gordon had run from his U.S. address. The case served to highlight Thailand's strict censorship laws and restrictions on freedom of speech, especially a tight ban on any discussions of the royal family or succession matters. Gordon was released from prison in 2012 after he was granted a royal pardon.

Fashion Fashion designer Thakoon Panichgul was born in 1974 in Thailand's Chiang Rai Province and came to the United States as a child. He grew up in Nebraska and graduated from Boston University before moving to New York City to pursue a career in fashion. His eponymous label was launched in 2004 and gained an enormous boost when future first lady Michelle Obama wore his designs during 2008 campaign stops, including a significant photo-opportunity moment at that year's Democratic National Convention.

Music Singer and film star Tata Young is one of the most successful artists in Thai popular culture. Born Amita Marie Young in Bangkok in 1980 to a Thai mother and American father, she started her career as a teen singer of novelty tracks in the mid-1990s and branched out to film roles. Because she records in both Thai and English, Young has a strong fan base inside Thailand, across other parts of Asia, and among the Thai American community.

Performance The outdated term "Siamese twin" was originally used to describe a pair of conjoined twins from Thailand named Chang and Eng. Born in 1811 of mixed Thai-Chinese ancestry, Chang and Eng came to the United States as a sideshow curiosity and adopted the surname "Bunker." They married a pair of American sisters and had a total of twenty-one children before they died within three hours of one another in 1874.

Politics In 2012 voters in Illinois elected L. Tammy Duckworth as the first Thai American to U.S. Congress. Born Ladda Duckworth in Bangkok in 1968, she is the daughter of an ethnic Chinese woman and a U.S. Marine who met during the Vietnam War era. Duckworth followed her father into military service and was a helicopter pilot in the Iraq War when, in 2004, she was gravely injured by a rocket-propelled grenade. She lost both legs and became an advocate for disabled veterans. Duckworth removed a Republican incumbent from his seat in the U.S. House of Representatives in the 2012 election and arrived on Capitol Hill in 2013 to serve the Eighth Congressional District of Illinois.

Sports Major League Baseball player Johnny Damon (born 1973) is the son of a Thai woman and American father who was serving overseas. Damon was born at Fort Riley, Kansas, and grew up in the Orlando, Florida, area. He emerged as a superior high school athlete and made his major-league debut with the Kansas City Royals in 1995. Damon played for several other MLB franchises over his long career and is considered one of the best hitters and base-stealers of his generation.

Kultida (Tida) Punsawad, mother of professional golfer Tiger Woods, is one of the Thai women who came to the United States after becoming romantically involved with U.S. military personnel during the Vietnam War. Punsawad met U.S. Army officer Earl Woods in 1966, immigrated to the United States in 1968, and married him in 1969. Their son, nicknamed Tiger, was born in 1975, and within a few years the pint-size golf prodigy was demonstrating his talents on national television.

Stage and Screen Actress Brenda Song appeared in the Disney Channel series *The Suite Life of Zack & Cody*. She was born in California in 1988 to a mother of Thai ancestry; Song's father is Hmong. In 2010 the popular Disney star had a small but notable role in *The Social Network*, the fictionalized story about the founding of Facebook at Harvard University.

MEDIA

NAT TV

Offers satellite-based programming in Thai for North American audiences.

Bunyati Noppakun
10840 Vanowen Street
North Hollywood, California 91605
Phone: (818) 980-7999
Fax: (818) 985-8009
Email: info@nattv.com
URL: www.nattv.com

Siam Media

Founded in 1981, *Siam Media* is the oldest weekly Thai-language newspaper published in the United States; an English-language edition is also published.

Tang Sripipat
9266 Valley Boulevard
Rosemead, California 91770
Phone: (626) 307-9119
Fax: (626) 307-9040
Email: siammedia@gmail.com
URL: www.siammedia.org

Asian-Pacific News

Online news site for the Thai-Lao community.

Email: apacnews@hotmail.com
URL: http://asianpacificnews.com

ORGANIZATIONS AND ASSOCIATIONS

Association of Thai Professionals in America and Canada (ATPAC)

Promotes the advancement of scientific knowledge, technology, and education in Thailand.

Nisai Wanakule, President
14 Doric Avenue
Parsippany, New Jersey 07054
Phone: (973) 299-7992
Fax: (973) 299-1117
Email: mail@atpac.org
URL: www.atpac.org

Thai Community Development Center

Founded in 1994 in Los Angeles, the Thai Community Development Center promotes development and social-networking opportunities for families and businesses in Los Angeles's Thai Town.

Chanchanit (Chancee) Martorell, Executive Director
6376 Yucca Street
Suite B
Los Angeles, California 90028
Phone: (323) 468-2555
Fax: (323) 461-4488
URL: www.thaicdc.org

Thai Society of Southern California

Established in 1962 by Thai scholars and friends, the Thai Society of Southern California promotes the unity of Thais in California and fosters cultural exchange.

Nikun Khoongumjorn, President
P.O. Box 16034
Irvine, California 92623
Phone: (562) 285-7889
Email: contact@thaisocal.org
URL: www.thaisocal.org

MUSEUMS AND RESEARCH CENTERS

Center for Southeast Asian Studies, Northern Illinois University

The university's library has a dedicated collection of Southeast Asian materials numbering over 300,000 volumes, specializing in Thai studies.

Judy Ledgerwood, Director
520 College View Court
NIU
DeKalb, Illinois 60115
Phone: (815) 753-1771
Email: cseas@niu.edu
URL: www.cseas.niu.edu

Cornell University Southeast Asia Program

The center concentrates its activities on the social and political conditions in Southeast Asian countries, including the history and culture of Thailand. It studies cultural stability and change, especially the consequences of Western influences.

Tamara Loos, Director
180 Uris Hall
Ithaca, New York 14853-7601
Phone: (607) 255-2378
Fax: (607) 254-5000
URL: http://seap.einaudi.cornell.edu/

University of California-Berkeley Center for Southeast Asia Studies

This library contains a special Thai collection in addition to its substantial holdings on the social sciences and humanities of Southeast Asia. The entire collection comprises some 400,000 monographs, dissertations, microfilm, pamphlets, manuscripts, videotapes, sound recordings, and maps.

Jeffrey Hadler, Director
2223 Fulton Street
Suite 617
Berkeley, California 94720-2318
Phone: (510) 642-3609

Fax: (510) 643-7062
Email: cseas@berkeley.edu
URL: http://cseas.berkeley.edu

University of California-Los Angeles Center for Southeast Asian Studies

Founded in 1999, the Center for Southeast Asian Studies (CSEAS) promotes academic ties between scholars and students of Southeast Asian languages, nations, and cultures with counterparts in Asian nations.

Michael L. Ross, Director
11274 Bunche Hall
Box 951487
Los Angeles, California 90095-1487
Phone: (310) 206-9163
Fax: (310) 206-3555
Email: cseas@international.ucla.edu
URL: www.international.ucla.edu/cseas/

Yale University Southeast Asia Studies Collection

This collection of materials centers on the social sciences and humanities of Southeast Asia. Holdings include some 200,000 volumes.

Richard Richie, Curator
Sterling Memorial Library
P.O. Box 208240
New Haven, Connecticut 06520-8240
Phone: (203) 432-1859
Email: rich.richie@yale.edu
URL: www.library.yale.edu/southeastasia/southeas.htm

SOURCES FOR ADDITIONAL STUDY

Bao, Jiemin. "Thai American Middle-Classness: Forging Alliances with Whites and Cultivating Patronage from Thailand's Elite." *Journal of Asian American Studies* 12, no. 2 (2009): 163–90.

Chen, Edith Wen-Chu, and Grace J. Yoo, eds. *Encyclopedia of Asian American Issues Today*. Santa Barbara, CA: ABC-CLIO, 2010.

Cooper, Robert, and Nanthapa Cooper. *Culture Shock*. Portland, OR: Graphic Arts Center, 1990.

Hidalgo, Danielle Antoinette, and Carl L. Bankston III. "The Demilitarization of Thai American Marriage Migration, 1980–2000." *Journal of International Migration and Integration* 12, no. 1 (2011): 85–99.

Mannur, Anita. *Culinary Fictions: Food in South Asian Diasporic Culture*. Philadelphia: Temple University Press, 2010.

Padoongpatt, Tanachai Mark. "Too Hot to Handle: Food, Empire, and Race in Thai Los Angeles." *Radical History Review* 110 (2011): 83–108.

Perreira, Todd L. "*Sasana Sakon* and the New Asian American: Intermarriage and Identity at a Thai Buddhist Temple in Silicon Valley," in *Asian American Religions: The Making and Remaking of Borders and Boundaries*, edited by Tony Carnes and Fenggang Yang. New York: NYU Press, 2004.

Sukrungruang, Ira. *Talk Thai: The Adventures of Buddhist Boy*. Columbia: University of Missouri Press, 2010.

TIBETAN AMERICANS

Olivia Miller

OVERVIEW

Tibetan Americans are immigrants or descendants of immigrants from Tibet, a region northeast of the Himalayas in Asia. The Tibetans and the Chinese refer to different areas when defining Tibet. Chinese Tibet is officially known as the Tibet Autonomous Region (TAR) of the People's Republic of China and is located on the Qinghai-Tibet Plateau in southwest China. It is a landlocked region that is bordered on the west by India; on the south by Myanmar (Burma), India, Bhutan, and Nepal; on the east by the Chinese provinces of Sichuan and Yunnan; and in the north by the Xinjiang Uyghur Autonomous Region and the Chinese provinces of Sichuan and Yunnan. However, the Tibetans refer to a much larger area, "Ethnic Tibet" or "Greater Tibet," which includes the entire Tibetan Plateau and the northeastern and eastern provinces of Kham and Amdo. Tibet is the highest region in the world, with an average altitude of 14,000 feet above sea level. It has some of the world's largest mountains, including Mount Everest, the tallest mountain on Earth. Tibet has been called the "Roof of the World" and the "Land of Snows." TAR is approximately 1.2 million square kilometers (463,000 square miles), making up about 13 percent of China's total area. It is slightly smaller than Montana and Texas combined. Ethnic Tibet covers a quarter of China's total area and is approximately 2.3 million square kilometers (888,000 square miles), almost twice the area of TAR and a little bit larger than Mexico.

According to the Tibetan Youth Congress, the total population of Tibet is approximately six million, with almost half of them living in TAR. According to the Tibetan Autonomous Region's Bureau of Statistics, however, Tibet's population in 2010 was just more than three million. The disparity between these figures is a reflection of the intense conflict that exists between China and Tibet, as both sides seek data that supports their arguments about the nature of Tibetan autonomy and ethnicity. Tibet has the lowest population density of any Chinese province, mainly due to much harsh or uninhabitable terrain—there is an average of two people per square kilometer (five per square mile). About 85 percent live in the southern Yarlung Tsangpo River valley and the eastern valleys and forestland. The vast majority of Tibetans, more than 90 percent, practice Tibetan Buddhism, whose spiritual and political leader is the Dalai Lama. There are small Muslim, Christian, and Bönpos (followers of the Bön religion) communities. The majority of the population consists of Tibetan and Han Chinese. Ethnic Tibetan subgroups include the Topa from the far west, the Khampa from the east, and the Golok from the northeast. Tibet's government-in-exile (TGIE) claims that Tibet is becoming more populated with Chinese than with Tibetans. The 2000 Chinese Census says 5.9 percent of the population is Han Chinese, but this does not account for influxes of Chinese settlers, Chinese military, and Chinese government officials stationed in TAR. According to the Migration Policy Institute, the vice president of the Commission for Planning and Development in TAR stated that of the 200,000 residents of the city of Lhasa, only half were Tibetans; the remainder came from thirty-one other nonindigenous ethnic-minority groups (2002). Tibet's economy is mainly based on agriculture and animal husbandry, although since about the 1980s light industry, manufacturing, the military, mining, and tourism have also been important to the economy. TAR is the poorest part of China, and those in agricultural areas are extremely poor. In many areas there is no electricity, running water, schools, or health care. The barter system is still in use in many of these communities. According to the Chinese government, the 2002 per capita net income of urban Tibet residents was 6,448 yuan ($777.86 U.S.), with Tibetan farmers earning just 1,331 yuan ($160 U.S.) annually. At a 2010 meeting in Beijing, the Chinese government stated that it was working toward improving the rural Tibetan income to meet Chinese national standards by 2020 and implementing a free education system for rural children.

The earliest official Tibetan immigration to the United States took place in the late 1950s. Only a very small number of Tibetans came to the United States until the U.S. Immigration Act of 1990 granted "1,000 immigrant visas to 'displaced' Tibetans living in India and Nepal," according to Section 34 of the Act. They settled primarily in urban areas of New York, Minnesota, California, Wisconsin, and Massachusetts and found employment in a variety of occupations, including working in business, administration, teaching, nursing, and other health care occupations, with many finding "unskilled" work as nannies, construction workers, housekeepers, and store clerks. The immigrant population grew again starting in 1995, primarily due to the Family Reunification Program as well as professionals immigrating and visitors or students who chose to stay. Because the United States officially recognizes Tibet as part of China, Tibetan immigrants are legally considered "overseas Chinese." Many Tibetan immigrants take umbrage with this, and for the 2010 Census, many in the Tibetan community encouraged community members to list themselves as "other" rather than Chinese.

According to a February 2012 article in the *New York Times*, there are an estimated 14,000 people of Tibetan ancestry in the United States—about half the enrollment of Harvard University—with at least seven thousand in New York. The first group of one thousand Tibetans settled in six pilot cluster sites: San Francisco; Minneapolis–St. Paul, Minnesota; New York City and Ithaca, New York; Madison, Wisconsin; and Amherst, Massachusetts, as directed by the U.S. Immigration and Naturalization Service resettlement project. This group of immigrants then migrated to other areas of the northeast, the Great Lakes region, and the Intermountain West, as well as establishing small communities in Austin, Texas, and Charlottesville, Virginia. Colorado and Minnesota both have a high concentration of Tibetan immigrants; Minnesota's Tibetan population was estimated at three thousand in 2009. There are more than thirty Tibetan community associations in the United States.

HISTORY OF THE PEOPLE

Early History According to traditional lore, Tibetans trace their ancestry to the copulation of an ape (a manifestation of wisdom) and an ogress (a form of the goddess Tara). The Tibetan people are descendants of their offspring. Monkey gods are part of the religious folklore of India and other Buddhist countries. Chinese scholars claim that Tibetans descended from the Quiang, nomadic shepherds of western China who first appeared around 1000 BCE. Over the course of its history, Tibet ruled parts of China, India, Nepal, central Asia, and the Middle East. The Tibetan nation gained world prominence in the sixth and seventh centuries as a silk and spice trading center. The Mongolians under Genghis Khan conquered Tibet during the Middle Ages but bestowed political power on the head of the *Lamanists* Buddhist organization. In the seventeenth century, China gained sovereignty over Tibet and ruled until the British invaded in 1904. At the Anglo-Chinese convention in 1906, the Chinese again were recognized as the sovereign power in Tibet. By 1907, the governments of Britain and Russia agreed not to interfere in Tibetan affairs. The Tibetans rebelled against China in 1912 and expelled all Chinese officials. In 1913 the Dalai Lama, who had fled two years before, returned to Tibet. Tibet was made a British protectorate, and for the next several decades the Dalai Lama was allowed to reign.

Modern Era The People's Republic of China invaded Tibet in 1949 and, after defeating the small Tibetan army, established control of the province. In 1959 the Tibetans once again rebelled against the Chinese. According to a TGIE estimate first published in 1990, the People's Liberation Army of China (PLA) crushed the uprising, killing more than 87,000 Tibetans. (However, many Western scholars question this figure, pointing to the TGIE's initial statement that between five hundred and ten thousand people were killed in the uprising.) The Dalai Lama, members of his government, and roughly 80,000 Tibetans escaped from Tibet. They sought political asylum in India, Nepal, and Bhutan and announced the formation of a Tibetan government-in-exile. The government of India welcomed the Tibetan refugees but did not grant recognition to the Dalai Lama's TGIE. Since 1959, more than fifty-four refugee settlements have been established in India, Nepal, and Bhutan. Between 1959 and 1961, the PLA destroyed more than six thousand Tibetan monasteries, followed by years of breaking up monastic estates and establishing secular education. During China's Cultural Revolution in the 1960s and 1970s, there was organized vandalism against cultural sites, and many Buddhist monks and nuns were killed, tortured, or imprisoned.

The number of Tibetans who have died as a result of the Chinese invasion and China's half-century occupation of Tibet is disputed. The TGIE estimates that 1.2 million Tibetans died during the occupation between 1950 and 1979, but many scholars have contradicted this figure. More credible estimates, such as those of the demographer Yao Han, place the number of Tibetans who died or left Tibet during the first two decades of the Chinese occupation around 152,000, with many of these people migrating to India. The United Nations passed three resolutions on Tibet—in 1959, 1961, and 1965—expressing concern over human rights violations. There have been no UN resolutions since 1965; however, many countries have issued statements in support of Tibet and critical of Chinese human rights violations there. In 2012, the United Nations Human Rights Council issued a statement urging China "… to re-assess policies that undermine Tibetan and Uighur linguistic, religious and cultural traditions creating grievances and fostering unrest."

By the late 1990s more than 120,000 Tibetans were living in exile; by 2009 the number topped 128,000. The TGIE has been organized along democratic principles to preserve Tibetan culture and education and to seek the restoration of Tibet's freedom. Tibetan people throughout the world consider the TGIE, based in Dharamsala, India, to be the sole legitimate government of Tibet.

The Chinese government actively encourages Chinese immigration to Tibet, and Tibetans say they have become a minority within their own country. In 1999, various pro-Tibet organizations protested the World Bank's funding of China's Western Poverty Reduction Project (WPRP), which involved the transfer of about 61,775 non-Tibetan settlers into Tibet. According to the Tibetan Youth Congress, there are an estimated 300,000 to 500,000 Chinese troops in Tibet. China also uses Tibet for chemical warfare exercises and dumping nuclear waste from other countries. The International Campaign for Tibet confirmed the existence of a Chinese nuclear station in Tibet—the "Ninth Academy," near Lake Kokonor in Amdo province.

In March 2008 the largest protest against Chinese occupation since 1959 was begun in Lhasa, the capital city of TAR. It was initiated by monks from Sera and Drepung and then spread across Tibet, involving Tibetans from all walks of life. Chinese police broke up the protest with tear gas and gunfire, but it resumed for several more days and then turned into a riot. Tibetan anger was further fueled by reports that imprisoned monks and nuns were being mistreated or killed as a reaction to the street demonstrations. In retaliation, the shops of ethnic Chinese immigrants were ransacked and burned. The official Chinese media reports said eighteen people were killed by rioters. The Chinese mobilized as many as five thousand troops across the country where riots had spread. It has been estimated that the military killed between eighty and 140 Tibetans and arrested more than 2,300, provoking some in the international community to question Chinese adherence to human rights policies. Some international leaders protested by boycotting that year's Olympic Opening Ceremonies in Beijing. In March 2009, the fiftieth anniversary of the 1959 uprising, the Chinese government put Tibet under a de facto state of martial law to stop any possible repeat of protests and riots.

Between 2009 and late 2012, there were close to eighty self-immolations (suicide by setting oneself on fire), by Tibetans protesting Chinese rule and occupation. Five were Tibetans-in-exile in India and Nepal. In late 2012, U.S. Ambassador to the People's Republic of China Gary Locke urged China to meet with Tibetan representatives to "… address and re-examine some of the policies that have led to some of the restrictions and the violence and the self-immolations." United Nations High Commissioner for Human Rights Navi Pillay also urged Chinese authorities to "promptly address the longstanding grievances that have led to an alarming escalation in desperate forms of protest, including self-immolations, in Tibetan areas." In 2012, the Tibetan Youth Congress organized a hunger strike in front of UN headquarters in New York City to try to convince the United Nations to send a fact-finding delegation to Tibet and pressure China to stop (undeclared) martial law, allow the international media into Tibet, release all political prisoners, and stop patriotic Chinese re-education. Tibetans continue to leave their country in order to escape Chinese persecution. Many of these exiles seek assistance from the United Nations High Commission for Refugees (UNHCR), foreign donor agencies, and the governments of India, Nepal, Bhutan, and elsewhere, including the United States and Canada.

SETTLEMENT IN THE UNITED STATES

Very few Tibetans immigrated to the United States before 1992. Those who did were typically Tibetan monks or visiting students or professors who decided to stay. Most notably, Thubten Jigme Norbu, brother of the fourteenth Dalai Lama, came in 1952; from 1965 to 1987 he was a professor of Tibetan history at Indiana University. In 1985, there were approximately five hundred Tibetans in North America. More than thirty were employed by the Great Northern Paper Company in Maine.

Somewhat motivated by the Cold War and anti-communism, the United States supported an independent Tibet in the 1950s and 1960s. However, by 1972, when President Nixon visited China, support was waning. In 1978 the United States recognized Tibet as part of China, although there was often support for the Dalai Lama and the TGIE. For instance, in 1987 Congress passed an amendment criticizing China for subjecting Tibetans to famine, imprisonment, and political instability. Support for Tibet changed from supporting independence to a human rights issue. A 1988 congressional bill sponsored Tibetan refugee students to study in American universities; some of these students chose to remain and settled in the United States. Section 134 of the U.S. Immigration Act of 1990 granted one thousand visas to Tibetan refugees from India and Nepal, accounting for the beginning of the first significant wave of Tibetan immigrants to the United States. By 1995 these immigrants were allowed to bring their family members to the United States through the Family Reunification Program. Other Tibetans came to the United States as temporary visitors or students.

Tibetans fall under the legal definition of *refugee* as defined by the United Nations and adopted into United States law. However, due primarily to the adversarial political relationship between the United States and China, most Tibetans have not been legally considered refugees, but instead have been designated as "displaced persons." The U.S. government's reasoning for this is that Tibetans do not arrive directly from Tibet, but rather with documentation from India, Nepal, or other countries and, therefore, are not refugees. Although Tibetans do not qualify as refugees, the Immigration and Naturalization Service does identify them as asylum seekers, and they are officially recognized as "overseas Chinese."

After the Immigration Act of 1990, the first group of Tibetans arrived in 1992. The Tibetan United States Resettlement Project (TUSRP) was established to support their resettlement into the United States. They were settled into six pilot cluster sites: San Francisco; Minneapolis; New York City and Ithaca, New York;

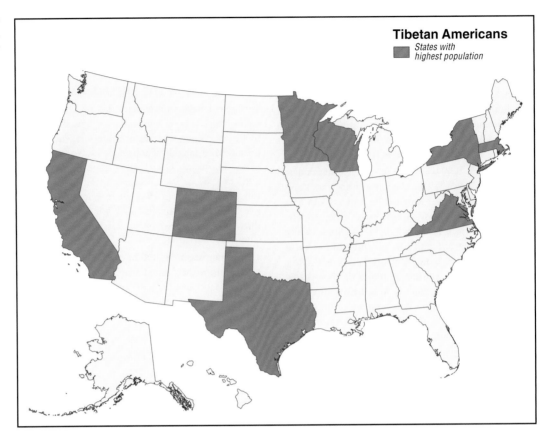

Tibetan Americans
*States with
highest population*

Madison, Wisconsin; and Amherst, Massachusetts. "Clustering" was a way to resettle members of the same ethnic group in close geographic proximity in order to help preserve ethnic identity, culture, and social cohesion and to make it easier to provide services to the group as a whole. Cluster site communities offered sponsorships and employment. After the initial pilot cluster sites, twenty-one new cluster sites in eighteen states were established, primarily in the northeast, Great Lakes region, and Intermountain West. Thanks primarily to the Family Reunification Program, more Tibetan immigrants arrived, so that by 2002 there were nearly 8,700 Tibetan immigrants in the United States, and by 2010 more than ten thousand. According to the Conservancy for Tibetan Art and Culture, the majority of Tibetans live in or near cities of 500,000 or more. In 2010, the largest group of Tibetan immigrants outside of India or Nepal was in New York City, with the highest concentration in the borough of Queens. Nearby Jersey City, New Jersey, also has a large Tibetan population.

Some initial cluster communities decreased in number of immigrants, while others, such as Minneapolis, gained immigrants. In Minneapolis, for example, the Tibetan population grew from 160 in 1992 to two thousand in 2008. These geographic moves were generally due to economic reasons and employment opportunities. The majority of the initial immigrants did not have the educational background to be professionals and, thus, worked in "unskilled"

nonprofessional jobs. Those with professional skills generally became nurses, teachers, and accountants. Tibetan immigrants who are already established in the United States sometimes sponsor other Tibetans to come to the United States to pursue higher education. Upon completing their education, these students have often decided to stay. This has presented some conflict in the Tibetan community at large. In India, the Dalai Lama has stated that it's good for Tibetans to go abroad for higher education, but once the educational pursuit is finished, they should return to India to serve their community and their government-in-exile. Conversely, some Tibetans feel that Tibetan Americans should send their children to be educated in India, such as to the Tibetan Children's Village, so they can get a suitable Tibetan education.

In the late 1990s and early 2000s, there was a movement of Tibetan Americans to Canada, where they could get refugee status that allowed them more protections and gave them full access to social services, unlike what their "displaced persons" status afforded them in the United States. However, a law in 2004 between the United States and Canada—the Canada-U.S. Safe Third-Country Agreement—stated that refugees had to claim refugee status in the country in which they first arrived. This greatly slowed down migration to Canada, as many Tibetans had to pass through the United States to get to Canada and thus had to remain in the United States.

In September 2005, President George W. Bush proposed a new program to resettle five thousand Tibetan refugees from Nepal to the United States after the 2001 assassination of Nepal's King Birendra and the rise of the Maoists. The resettlement was to take place in 2007; however, Nepal has refused to grant exit visas due to the country's political instability and opposition from China. United States officials have repeated their interest in taking these refugees, but China claimed that the program would interfere with internal affairs and violate Nepal's One China Policy that says that Tibet is part of China. China does not believe these Tibetan immigrants in Nepal are refugees and feels they should be punished in Nepal or sent home to TAR. This standoff continued into 2013 without a resolution in sight.

As is common in many immigrant communities, the older Tibetan immigrants tend to be more associated with the religious community and its values and activities, while the younger generation, who have been exposed to secular education and are more assimilated, rely more on secular values and institutions. Still, Tibetan immigrants across the generations have a strong sense of ethnic and cultural identity and have strong involvement in and support from many Tibetan community organizations and the larger worldwide Tibetan population.

LANGUAGE

Since the Chinese invasion and conquest of Tibet, Chinese has been the official language of commerce and government. It is also the primary language taught in Tibetan schools. But native Tibetans continue to speak their native language, which bears little resemblance to the languages of neighboring China and India. Tibeto-Burman, a language of the Sino-Tibetan family, is based on a form of Sanskrit that originated in India during the seventh century. Sino-Tibetan languages are a family of languages spoken from northeast India eastward to Taiwan and from China southward to the Malay Peninsula. Sino-Tibetan is generally divided into two large subfamilies: the Sinitic, comprising Mandarin, Cantonese, and the other languages of China; and the Tibeto-Burman, the best-known of which are Tibetan and Burmese. The Tibeto-Burman languages are spoken in Tibet, Nepal, Burma, western China, and the Assam State in India. Sino-Tibetan languages are distinguished from Western language families by two main traits: isolating monosyllabic characters and the use of tones. Tibetan is most closely related to Burmese and to other spoken dialects of Himalayan peoples, but the written script was adapted from Indian writing.

While many of the Tibetan Resettlement Programs established English as a Second Language (ESL) classes, in turn many Tibetan American communities established weekend Tibetan language classes to make sure that children raised in the United

TIBETAN PROVERBS

Tibetans liberally sprinkle proverbs into daily conversation as a substitute for slang phrases. Some examples include the following:

- Whatever happiness is in the world, it has arisen from a wish for the welfare of others; whatever misery is in the world, it has arisen from a wish for our own welfare.

- Look not on the height of the mountain, but look at the size of the mountain.

- Those who do not love comfort can do one hundred deeds; those who cannot love hardship cannot do one deed.

- If one does not cross the doorstep's sill, one cannot arrive anyplace.

- A braggart has no courage.

- Muddy water has no depth.

- Having eaten together, you should agree in counsel.

- The life of all living beings is like the bubbles of water.

- The stripes of wild beasts are on the outside, the stripes of man are on the inside.

- When the blind escorts the blind, both fall into the river.

- If one desires misery, let him buy an aged horse.

- If one is not happy inside, one's work cannot be done outside.

- If the mouth and stomach are considered first, then promise and debts follow later.

- If one is without soup on earth, of what use is a ladle in heaven?

- After calling a dog, one should not beat him.

- A hoe digs, a broom sweeps.

- When a man becomes old, he thinks of his homeland.

States remained literate in their home language. Retaining Tibetan language and literacy is perhaps seen as particularly important because, with Chinese being the official language in Tibet, preserving the Tibetan language is considered critical to the survival of ethnic and national identity. According to the 2000 U.S. Census, 5,110 Tibetan Americans spoke Tibetan at home.

In 2012, a two-day conference was held in California to discuss Tibetan language education for Tibetan immigrants in the United States. Workshops included discussion of successes in Tibetan language education in the previous two decades, improving teaching methods and curriculum, challenges of specific communities, using Uchen or Urney Tibetan script, and maintaining older students' interest in weekend classes. Tibetan teachers from around North America attended, as well as non-Tibetan language and bilingual education experts.

Both maintaining Tibetan fluency and learning the language of the immigrant's new home are considered important to Tibetan immigrants in the United States and worldwide. For instance, in Tibetan boarding schools in India, both Tibetan and the language of the "host country" are taught.

Common Expressions and Greetings *Tashidelek* means "hello" in Tibetan. An old Tibetan custom sometimes used today, though rarely among Tibetan Americans, is to greet a person by sticking the tongue out and pointing down the face. This was traditionally done as a sign of respect for someone of higher social standing, and it was sometimes repeated at the end of every sentence in a conversation. *Khe-rahng kah-bah phe-geh?* means "Where are you going?" and is used as a common greeting. *Po rhang-tsen* ("Tibetan freedom") is another common greeting.

There are different expressions for goodbye depending on who is leaving. *Kah-leh phe* is said to a person who is leaving or is said by two people who are leaving at the same time. *Kah-leh shu* is said to the person remaining behind.

Many Tibetan expressions and greetings relate to Buddhism. Buddha is always referred to, even in passing, as the "victoriously consummate one" because he won perfection after a long and continuous struggle with worldly desires.

RELIGION

Buddhism encompasses the cultural values and social structure of the Tibetan people. However, Buddhism was preceded by Bön, Tibet's earliest religion, which was founded by Shenrab Miwo of Shangshung in western Tibet. Bön was a religion that involved the violent worship of local mountain and lake spirits. Magic and ritual, including animal sacrifice, were strongly emphasized. With the advent of Buddhism in Tibet in the seventh century, the Bön religion diminished in influence, although it is still practiced in some areas of Tibet.

Before the Chinese takeover, Buddhist monasteries, temples, and hermitages were found in every village and town throughout Tibet. Nearly every Tibetan home had an altar. In 1959 there were more than 6,259 monasteries, with about 592,558 resident monks and nuns. These religious centers housed tens of thousands of statues and religious artifacts made of gold, silver, and other metals studded with jewels. In addition to housing texts on Buddhism, these centers were storehouses of works on literature, medicine, astrology, art, and politics of the Tibetan people.

From 1949 to 1979, China discouraged the practice of any religion in Tibet. Many religious artifacts were confiscated, taken to China, and destroyed; the majority of monasteries and nunneries in Tibet were also destroyed or closed; and many Buddhist monks and nuns were killed, tortured, or imprisoned. Buddhist monks and nuns are active in politics in Tibet, such as their critical role in the 2008 protests against the Chinese occupation.

Religion continues to be an important part of life for Tibetan Americans. However, religious institutions are not as central to Tibetan Americans as they are in Tibet or other main places of exile, such as India, Nepal, and Bhutan. In those countries Dharma centers are the main centers for spiritual and cultural community connection. There are about five hundred Dharma centers in the United States. They also serve Western practitioners of Tibetan Buddhism, and Tibetan Americans sometimes feel these Dharma centers are more oriented toward Westerners and their practice and community. For that reason, Tibetan Americans might visit the Dharma center just for holidays and special occasions—for instance, on *Losar* (the Tibetan New Year). Tibetan American cultural centers, which initially began in each cluster site, have become central places for celebrations and gatherings. Younger generations who have been more influenced by secular education and assimilation relate less to religious institutional settings like Dharma centers but are often still actively involved in cultural centers and politics.

CULTURE AND ASSIMILATION

The Tibetan Community Assistance Project (TCAP) was established in 1993 to set up an association wherever more than fifteen Tibetans settled. TCAP first assisted in finding jobs, housing, and crisis assistance. They developed into organizations to help Tibetans maintain their culture and to educate others about the plight of Tibet. TCAP organizes many events, including holiday parties and other celebrations, such as the Dalai Lama's birthday, and commemorations of historical days of protest; performances by local or traveling artists; talks by religious figures; and religious gatherings. They also organize protests or vigils when, for instance, Chinese delegates or government officials are visiting. They provide programs for children to learn or maintain the Tibetan language and to expose them to the music, dance, literature, and other cultural aspects of Tibet. They also run adult classes and programs.

Tibetan immigrants have very strong values about the importance of family. They often send money to support their families in Tibet or other places of exile. Additionally, they are strongly encouraged to pay annual dues, called *rangzen*—Tibetan freedom—to support the TGIE and are encouraged to participate in TGIE elections. Some Tibetan Americans feel they are living in the United States only until their country is liberated. Many believe, however, it is possible to maintain their Tibetan identity and still firmly embrace the opportunities in the United States.

Tibetans' strong connection to the family, as well as to the government-in-exile, sometimes prevents them from easily incorporating mainstream American culture or values. The traditional Tibetan emphasis on the value of community and family can come into opposition with American ideals about the importance of the individual. This opposition can create friction and conflict within the family, as well as stress for the younger generation trying to live in both worlds. Furthermore, it can be challenging for immigrants to adapt to the Western conveniences in the United States if they are used to living in an agrarian-based society with few (or no) modern conveniences.

As is common with many immigrant groups, assimilation is easier for the younger generations who are raised in the United States. Generational differences are present when families try to deal with, for instance, public schools. Parents may have difficulty understanding the requirements or values that dictate their children's secular educational environments, while children are more interested in assimilating. Additionally, although Americans may view Tibetan Americans as one homogenous group, in reality they come from different regions of Tibet with differing traditions and even regional differences in how language is spoken, such as accents or slang used. These regional differences in traditions, culture, and language can create conflict within communities.

Tibetans may assimilate into mainstream culture less readily than some other groups because they often come to the United States without strong educational or professional backgrounds and thus often have "unskilled" low-paying jobs. With the pressure of obtaining American "success," economic responsibility to their family here, and the cultural edict of sending financial support to family abroad and the government-in-exile, Tibetan immigrants frequently need to work long hours at tiring jobs to make ends meet. Finding the time and energy to embrace and learn the customs and culture of their new home, as well as, sometimes, to maintain their Tibetan cultural connections, can be challenging with the demands of their work life. However, Tibetan Americans do often receive help from the many established Tibetan assistance centers with jobs, housing, education, clothing, financial and legal assistance, and immigration and citizenship training, as well with cultural and educational opportunities.

Because Tibetan Americans come from diverse socioeconomic classes, they generally do not abide by the traditional Tibetan notion that wealth is a prerequisite for leadership. Additionally, leaders from the younger generation are sometimes critical of traditional Tibetan religious or political values and ideologies, which would not be acceptable behavior in Tibet.

In the contemporary United States, Tibetans Americans are sometimes presumed to be or are mistaken for Chinese. They suffer the pain of being misidentified as the Chinese, whom they feel are their oppressors, as well as being subject to anti-Chinese or anti-Asian discrimination. However, newspaper articles from locations where there are Tibetan communities tend to present Tibetan immigrants positively. For instance, the *Boston Globe*, the *Minneapolis Star Tribune* and the *Idaho Statesman* have described Tibetan immigrants as being a rich source of ancient culture. This may be partially a result of successful campaigns to increase Americans' awareness of, and concern for, the political struggles of Tibet

Traditions and Customs Tibetan cultural centers provide an important way for Tibetan Americans to maintain their traditions and customs, especially in multigenerational families who are concerned about their second- and third-generation children being exposed to enough Tibetan customs and traditions to maintain a strong sense of ethnic identity. The repression of their culture by the Chinese in their home country may also fuel the desire of some Tibetan American immigrants to maintain their traditions and customs, or be the "voice" of Tibetans, because it is difficult—and sometimes impossible—to maintain Tibetan traditions where the Chinese rule and free speech is prohibited. In addition to participation in cultural center events, Tibetan Americans maintain their customs and traditions in daily life, such as daily prayers, eating Tibetan food, wearing Tibetan clothing, and abiding by traditional Tibetan Buddhist ideals such as compassion and nonviolence. Some younger-generation Tibetans feel it's more important to be politically involved about Tibetan issues than it is to be involved in cultural events.

Tibetans do not use surnames, preferring single or double first names. For men, a middle name is given by the *lama*, a Buddhist holy man. Though some Tibetan Americans maintain their cultural tradition of having only one name, this is beginning to change, as many Tibetan Americans have adopted family names for purposes of documentation.

Tibetans throw pinches of *tsampa*, roasted barley flour, into the air to celebrate marriages, birthdays, New Year's Day, and other important events. The tradition dates from the seventh century, when it was a formality at the enthronement of kings. Throwing *tsampa* in the air is an expression of good wishes for one's own and others' happiness and for the overcoming of all obstacles.

Many Tibetan values are established through their Buddhist beliefs. *Vajras* (prayer wheels that are spun clockwise), bells, and beads are important in Tibetan Buddhism. The vajra symbolizes the enlightenment of

Buddhahood and is a symbolic rather than functional ritual object. Paired with the vajra, a bell represents wisdom, and as wisdom and method are perfectly unified, so the vajra and bell are never parted or employed separately. Vajras may have nine, five, or three spokes. The upper sets of spokes of a five-spoked vajra symbolize the five wisdoms of Buddhism. A bell's base must be round, above which is a vase topped by the face of the goddess Prajnaparamita. Above these are representations of a lotus, a moon disc, and finally a vajra. The hollow of the bell symbolizes wisdom recognizing emptiness, and the bell's clapper represents the sound of emptiness. The eight lotus petals are the four mothers and four goddesses, and the vase represents the vase containing the nectar of accomplishment.

Beads are mainly used to count mantras (prayers). Beads made of bodhi seed or wood are used to count mantras recited for four main purposes: to appease, to increase, to overcome, and to tame by forceful means. The string common to all beads should consist of nine threads, which symbolize Buddha Vajradhara and the eight *bodhisattvas* (enlightened beings). The large bead at the end stands for the wisdom that recognizes emptiness, and the cylindrical bead surmounting it represents emptiness itself; both symbolize having vanquished all opponents.

Cuisine Tibetan foods are practical, reflecting the nomadic and often severe lifestyle of Tibetans. Cuisine tends toward oils, dough, spices, and meats that are usually boiled then stir-fried. Mustard seed is grown in Tibet and is a common ingredient. The most common meat in Tibet is yak, and yak milk is used for yogurt and butter. In the United States, beef is usually substituted for yak, but there are a few yak ranches in Colorado and Wyoming, and it is served in some New York Tibetan restaurants. Butter is common to many dishes and even beverages. *Tsampa*, a staple of the Tibetan diet, is made by mixing highland barley flour with tea or butter. Though *tsampa* is difficult to find the United States, it can be procured and is an important element of Tibetan American cuisine.

A typical Tibetan dinner begins with spicy cold appetizers, followed by a main course of several hot dishes accompanied by noodles or dumplings. *Momo* are steamed dumplings made with onion, cumin, garlic, minced lamb or beef, and soya sauce and shaped like half-moons. Special small wooden dowels are used to roll out the dough, or store-bought dough is used. *Momos* are not eaten on the first day of the holiday of Losar because they look like purses for holding money, and on Losar one is supposed to focus on purification and family, not work or money. Other common dishes include *then thuk*, a noodle soup made with fresh spinach, onion, garlic, ginger, and meat; *shamday*, a Tibetan curry made with bean thread noodles, ginger, onion, turmeric, lamb or beef, potatoes, and a handful of seaweed; and *sha-balé*, a deep-fried dough surrounding beef or lamb to form meat pockets seasoned

with onion, ginger, garlic, cumin, and soya sauce. A favorite beverage is *po cha*, made of strong tea, rich butter, milk, and salt. *Chang*, a homemade Tibetan-style wine, is a popular drink. During Losar, homemade beer is often brewed using rice and barley, and *khapse* (deep-fried dough twists) and *dresil* (sweet rice cooked with sugar, nuts, raisins, and butter) are eaten as well as used as part of an offering.

Tibetan restaurants are now found in many U.S. cities. Some Tibetan American restaurants also serve certain Indian and Chinese dishes reflective of the tastes of immigrants who lived under Chinese occupation or emigrated from India. Rice, which is not grown in Tibet, is rarely served either in Tibetan restaurants or in Tibetan American homes.

Traditional Dress Tibetan Americans wear traditional dress, available in local stores and online, as well as common Western clothing. Both women and men adorn themselves with bright colors and jewelry, although women continue to wear more traditional dress than men. Traditional dress is more commonly worn for special occasions, holidays, family gatherings, and events, as well as, sometimes, at political actions. Western clothing has also become more common in Tibet, especially in larger cities with large Chinese populations.

Traditional Tibetan clothing is made from the wool of yaks or sheep. Fabric is woven in relatively narrow widths and long lengths, cut, and assembled side-to-side for garments, blankets, and other textiles. The decoration of textiles is achieved by *plangi* (tie-dying). Typical patterns, often used in various combinations, include circles inscribed with crosses, multi-color stripes, and Buddhist motifs. The use of strong colors is common. Garb worn in royal or urban circles in Tibet and Bhutan may be similar in form to the garments of nomadic citizens. However, royal costumes are made of silk and decorated with exquisitely fine, painstaking, woven designs.

Most Tibetan men and women wear the *nambu*, a wool sash about eight inches wide, usually white for poor people and colorful for the wealthy. Many Tibetans also wear yak-hide boots. These knee-high boots are slit in the back and tied at the top with a colorful garter. The upper portions of the boots are made of leather, felt, or cloth and are often red in color. Men also wear pouches on the right side of their belts to hold a small knife and a pair of chopsticks.

The headdress is the chief adornment for Tibetan women. Because symbols of family wealth are often worn in the hair, married women wear more ornaments than unmarried women. Traditional headdresses have a wooden framework covered with coral, pearls, amber, and turquoise. Tibetan women wear jewelry, including bangles and bracelets, as well as earrings that are so large that the holes in their earlobes may stretch to an eighth of an inch in diameter. Married women wear colorfully striped aprons. Tibetan women commonly

At the Tibetan Cultural Center in Bloomington, IN, Mongolian dancers perform. 2007 CRAIG LOVELL / EAGLE VISIONS PHOTOGRAPHY / ALAMY

braid their hair. Unmarried women sometimes wear special garments to indicate the wealth of their family so suitors can estimate the dowry they might receive.

Jewelry is of great value and is sometimes used as part of a dowry. Turquoise, coral, and silver are commonly used. Both men and women wear earrings. Religious jewelry is also worn, such as a prayer necklace with 108 beads (the number of books in Tibetan Buddhist scripture) and a *gau*, a pendant that holds a picture of the Dalai Lama or the owner's protector god.

Costumes for rituals usually include a mask, called *ba*. Masks serve various functions for the Tibetan people. Some are hung in temples or used in ritual ceremonies, and others are used in theatrical performances. The faces on the masks range from deities to men and animals, with the expressions carved to display a certain characteristic, such as honesty, harshness, greed, or humor. According to tradition, masks of Buddha may appear in either benevolent or wrathful manifestations. The *Rdo-rjegro-lod*, the wrathful guardian deity, and the *Bhairava Vajra*, the fearful guardian deity, are commonly seen in mask designs.

Dances and Songs Folkdances and songs are an integral part of Tibetan culture and play an important role in maintaining Tibetan culture in the United States. Most celebrations and events include traditional dances and music. Tibetan dance celebrates an enchanted world of wizards, demons, singing maidens, dancing yaks, with acrobatic dances, thunderous horns, and lilting melodies. The great Lama Dances are celebrated twice a year in honor of Guru Rinpoche, who brought Buddhism to Tibet in the eighth century. Their original purpose was to destroy the obstacles to the development of Buddhism. The dancers are costumed in elaborate robes and ornate masks. During the Shotun Festival, which takes places in the sixth month of the Tibetan calendar, the people dress in festival costumes and jewelry and congregate around their local monastery for special festivities. For these colorful ceremonies, all of the dancers wear elaborate silk brocade costumes with unique deity masks. Other Tibetan dances include the *Via bo Shana*, the black hat dance, which is performed by three people; *Ronshu Chinen*, a dance performed by the people of northeastern Tibet; and *Agi Ulu* (the dance of the maiden *Ulu*), a harvest dance from southwestern Tibet.

Tibetan dance and music classes and performances are common in the United States, especially for Tibetan youth. Learning and performing these dances is seen as an essential part of maintaining Tibetan culture. For instance, the Tibetan American Foundation of Minnesota calls its dance performances the "… cultural highlight of our festivals and celebrations, especially during His Holiness the Dalai Lama's regular visits to the Twin Cities." An annual cultural dance

Tibetan composer Nawang Khechog reads prayers across the street from the United Nations as part of a one week hunger strike to draw attention to human rights violations by China. Nawang Khechog lives in Colorado. DON EMMERT / AFP / NEWSCOM

competition is held for North American Tibetans. Performances in the United States by Chinese-backed Tibetan dance troupes are sometimes met with protests, as Tibetan American exiles feel these tours are used to promote China's occupation of Tibet and showcase the Chinese interpretation of Tibetan culture rather than authentic traditional Tibetan dance.

Tibetan music and song are primarily based in Tibetan Buddhist religion. The chant of Tibetan monks is recognized around the world as the music of Tibet. The Tibetans cultivated multiphonic singing, in which a singer intones three simultaneous notes, creating a complete chord. Chanting is accompanied by musical instruments unique to the area, such as the *dranyem*, a traditional stringed instrument. The most unusual Tibetan ritual instruments are long, copper *rag-dung* trumpets. These horns are used to play a drone for chanting. Tibetan copper curved horns are played at Buddhist celebrations. Tibetan wind bells are handcrafted, solid brass wind bells used to keep devils away from the home. *Tingsha* are miniature cymbals that are used to encourage "hungry ghosts" to accept offerings. Tibetans believe that by relieving the ghosts' hunger and making an offering, their suffering is diminished. This is important because,

according to Buddhist beliefs, enlightenment can be achieved only when all suffering is eliminated. Singing bowls are traditionally struck to produce a complex and beautiful sound designed to aid meditation. Craftsmen recite mantras as they make the bowls and, according to Tibetan legend, the mantras are absorbed into the metal and released when the bowl is played.

Holidays Tibetan Americans generally observe all the major holidays observed in Tibet, celebrating the festivals at Tibetan Buddhist centers, at home, or at local Tibetan associations or community centers. In addition to important holidays such as Losar, the Tibetan New Year, they also commemorate important dates such as the anniversary of the Lhasa uprising on March 10 and the Dalai Lama's birthday on July 6. Often, dance, theater, and music groups perform at holiday celebrations.

The Tibetan calendar is a lunar calendar and contains twelve or thirteen months, depending on the moon's cycles. The year in the Tibetan calendar is not the same as the Gregorian calendar—the year 2013 was the Tibetan year 2140, for instance.

Celebrations of Losar, the Tibetan New Year, begin on the first day of the first lunar month. In Tibet it is generally celebrated for three days, but Tibetan Americans often do the main celebration on one day in deference to their work schedules. Khapse, deep-fried dough twists that are sweet or salty, are given to visitors and left as offerings in temples or special home altars. On home altars there are also sweets/candy, dried fruit, candles made from butter, and green barley shoots that represent both new life and the staple grain of Tibet. Houses are decorated with "eight auspicious signs," such as conch shells, representing the Buddha's enlightenment, and eternal knots for love and harmony.

On the eve of Losar, people eat a soup called *guthuk* to help with a safe passage into the new year and to cleanse oneself and one's home of all the obstacles and negativities of the past year. Literally translated, *gu* means "nine," seen as a lucky number, and *thuk* is "pasta in soup." There must be at least nine ingredients in the soup, such as vegetables, grains, and dried cheese, and at least nine dumplings containing pieces of paper that have written on them various human characteristics. The trait you find in your dumpling is said to represent your natural character.

Houses are cleaned for Losar, and a pile of dust is put in the corner with tiny effigies made out of dough on top of the dust. After the traditional meal, the dust is brought outside and thrown on a fire in order to get rid of the house's demons. Traditional Tibetan dress is worn for Losar.

Tashi dalek, loosely translated as "may you have good fortune, good health, and success," is the traditional New Year's greeting. At Losar celebrations, when two people meet, one makes one of the seven Buddhist offerings, such as of flowers or food, then takes a pinch from the tip of a mound of *tsampa* and throws it into the air, yelling, "*Tashi delek!*" The person receiving the offering answers, "Tashi delek. May you achieve unchanging happiness, and may it ever increase."

Monlam is a fifteen-day prayer festival celebrating the Buddha's victory in a competition of displays of miracles. The Butter Festival occurs on the fifteenth day, commemorating when the fifth Dalai Lama dreamed of paradise and carved a model out of butter to show his followers. Butter carvings are commonly made by monks to commemorate this.

Saka Dawa, on the full moon of the fourth lunar month, is one of the most sacred days. It is the day the Buddha was born, was enlightened, and died.

The Dalai Lama's birthday, July 6, is celebrated with huge events across the Tibetan American communities, including educational and political events as well as large cultural celebrations, potlucks, dances, and parties.

Other celebrations include *Chocko Duchen*, commemorating the Buddha's first sermon; *Zamling Chisong*, World Purification Day; *Gadem Ngamchoe*, "Festival of Lamps," commemorating the death of *Tsongkapa*, the founder of the Yellow Hat school of Buddhism; and the "Scapegoat Festival," which includes ritualistic dances, theater, and processions. A dough figure representing evil in the world (the scapegoat) is made and ripped into pieces.

Health Issues Tibetan medicine has been practiced for more than 2,500 years and is still used today. Called *Soba Rig-pa*, it is a science of healing based on the use of herbs and precious metals. Tibetan medicine is used to treat chronic diseases such as rheumatism, arthritis, ulcers, chronic digestive problems, asthma, hepatitis, eczema, liver problems, sinus problems, anxiety, and problems connected with the nervous system. It is often seen as part of the alternative and complementary medical system.

A 2009 pilot survey from the University of Wisconsin–Madison studied the health and stress levels of Tibetan immigrants ages twenty-two to sixty-six in Dane County, Wisconsin. Results showed that 59 percent feel more stressed in the United States than they felt in their earlier place of residence. The most common stresses included concern about the Tibetan cause and the general political, economic, and cultural freedom of Tibetans; worrying about their relatives in other countries; and their experience with "structural discrimination and interpersonal prejudice in the United States."

Tibetan Americans who are in low-paying jobs experience the same challenges of other Americans in low-paying jobs with poor health insurance or no health insurance. Their low salaries may make it

cost-prohibitive to purchase health care for themselves and their families, which may in turn adversely affect their health.

Tibetan immigrants across the generations have a strong sense of ethnic and cultural identity and have strong involvement in and support from many Tibetan community organizations and the larger worldwide Tibetan population.

FAMILY AND COMMUNITY LIFE

Nomadic Tibetan family life was structured around tending yaks in the mountains of Tibet. Young children assumed duties essential to the family's survival. The Chinese conquest of Tibet brought dramatic changes to nomadic family life. Nomadic families were restricted to only one child per household, stripped of individual ownership of herds, and reorganized into a communal structure. In the Tibetan refugee community in India, the concept of family takes on a greater significance as a way of preserving Tibetan culture. Most families include several children and often extended relatives. Tibetan Americans maintain strong family bonds, and Tibetans work hard and prioritize spending time together.

Most Tibetans in the first wave of immigrants in the 1990s came as individuals. Called "anchor relatives," this group was typically made up of fathers who left their spouse and children at home in Tibet or India. They would establish themselves economically and socially in the United States before sending for the rest of the family, usually two to five years later. The separation was emotionally difficult for both the anchor relative and the family left behind. Some surveys show that anchor relatives turned to alcohol or gambling or had extramarital affairs. Additionally, when families were reunited, there was often stress due to the long separation. Cultural differences often sprouted within families whose members were used to living in different countries within disparate cultures.

Tibetan Americans remain connected to events in Tibet and are more strongly connected to these events because of family members who still live in Tibet or in exile in India and elsewhere. Once they reach the United States, Tibetan immigrants often financially support their families back home in Tibet, India, Nepal, or Bhutan. They may sacrifice their own welfare in order to support their family overseas or so they can save money toward paying for their families to join them in the United States.

Gender Roles Historically, both men and women in Tibet owned land and conducted business with equal status. Women kept their maiden name after marriage, and there were no specific prohibitions against women's rights under the government law. However, there were gender gaps. For instance, men typically held positions of political power and leadership, while the cooking and childrearing were seen as mainly the domain of women. Inequality between genders is seen in the essential spiritual arena, where nuns (*anis*) are regarded as inferior to monks. In some Tibetan monasteries, women are not allowed to enter the chapel out of fear that spirits may be offended.

Traditional Tibetan society practiced polyandry, whereby a woman could legally be married to two or three men, usually brothers, simultaneously. The practice, which developed as a way to prevent land divisions, began to decline in the mid-twentieth century but it is still maintained by some.

Thousands of women protested China's occupation of Tibet in 1959 by organizing the Tibetan Women's Association (TWA). The organization was brutally suppressed by Chinese soldiers. In 1984, Tibetan women in exile in India and Nepal revived the organization, whose main objective is to raise public awareness of the abuses faced by Tibetan women in Chinese-occupied Tibet. Through extensive publicity and interaction in national and international affairs, TWA alerts the international community to the gender-specific human rights abuses committed against Tibetan women in the form of forced birth-control policies such as sterilizations and abortions, and restrictions on religious, political, social, and cultural freedoms. In 1987, the TWA launched the Tibetan Nuns Project to assist newly exiled nuns with shelter, food, and clothing. Eleven Tibetan nuns visited the United States in April 1999 for a ten-month tour to call attention to the Chinese takeover of Tibet. The Tibetan-native nuns came from the refugee community in Nepal, where they were educated in the exile settlements before taking to the road to benefit Tibet through their contact with Americans. In 2007,

Tibetan Tenzin Choezom demonstrates at the Chinese Consulate in Houston, TX. AP IMAGES / DAVID J. PHILLIP

gender sensitization workshops were organized by the Regional Tibetan Women's Association in communities in India, including one for high school students.

Although they are not legally obligated to abide by the TGIE, Tibetan American women have benefited within their own communities from the edicts on gender equality by the government-in-exile. Generally, there is movement toward equal opportunity for men and women to become community leaders and to get a good education. However, Tibetan American women are still seen as the primary homemakers and childrearers and are subject to the same challenges as other American women in terms of discrimination.

Education Boys and girls have been treated equally in terms of educational policy since the Chinese occupation of Tibet began in the 1950s. Between 1988 and 1997, the United States Information Agency provided scholarships for Tibetan students and professionals to study in the United States. More than 140 students participated in the program, and almost all returned to India and Nepal upon completion of their studies in order to assist Tibetan refugee communities there.

An important motivation for Tibetan immigration to the United States is to attain a good education for children. According to a 2002 North American Tibetan Community Needs Assessment Project survey, 89 percent of Tibetan youth in the United States considered finishing high school very important, and 69 percent planned on attending college. Tibetan organizations vocally support these efforts. Since 1988, the Tibet Fund financially supports twenty-five Tibetan students per year, and the U.S. Department of State helps provide funding for fifteen Tibetan students per year from India, Nepal, and Bhutan to pursue higher education in the United States, either for a one-year certificate or training program or a two-year master's degree program. Additionally, the Tibet Fund supports basic education, vocational training, food, clothing, shelter, and medical care at three schools for newly arrived children and at other schools throughout the exile community. This work is supported, in part, through the U.S. State Department's annual Humanitarian Assistance grant.

Like other impoverished American children, Tibetan American children of low economic status often must attend poor public schools. The educational aspirations of Tibetan Americans have, however, motivated some immigrants to work extra jobs in order to be able to afford to send their children to private schools that will provide a better education for their children. As children become more assimilated into American mainstream culture, Tibetan community centers stress maintaining language and culture through after-school activities and programs.

Courtship and Weddings In Tibet, a wedding is a social event between two communities. The maternal uncle of the bride is the most honored figure at the wedding and presides over the event. In the early morning, the groom's wedding party comes to invite the bride for the wedding ceremony. The bride's head is covered with a red veil, and her feet do not touch the ground when she leaves her village. Upon arrival at the groom's village, the leader of the bridal party sprinkles sacred water at its entrance. When the bridal party reaches the groom's house, the bride and her chaperone (the maid of honor), who are dressed exactly alike, sit side-by-side to wait for the groom. The groom must select the true bride, to whom he will have sent certain items as a symbol of their relationship during courtship, usually rings, bracelets, or necklaces. The groom is expected to identify their symbolism and lift off the veil without making a mistake. The wedding guests and participants form a huge circle and dance the *Guozhan* wedding dance.

Following a tradition known as Tibetan "Sacred Horse" worship, many Tibetans bring a *longda*, also known as a "fortune horse" or "paper horse" to weddings or festivals. After the ceremony, guests throw the *longda*—a piece of paper about two inches wide and four inches long featuring a woodblock-printed horse—into the air, letting the wind blow it high and far, like horses running swiftly and serenely. The *longda* is said to bring humans' wishes to the gods.

Tibetan weddings that take place in the United States preserve many of the customs of Tibetan culture and also integrate some American customs. A Tibetan wedding in Madison, Wisconsin, for instance, was an arranged marriage between a Tibetan American and a Tibetan emigrant living in India. After a possible arrangement between the families, the groom was sent on a trip to India to meet his potential bride. He was not told at the time that this was what the trip was for, but the families had agreed that if the children liked each other, a marriage would be arranged. After two years of e-mails and phone calls, they decided to marry. At the wedding in Madison, a poster of the Dalai Lama hung over the makeshift altar. Guests were served sweet Tibetan tea and *de sil*, sweet rice cooked with coconut and raisins, to bring good luck to the couple. The bride wore the traditional rainbow-colored Tibetan aprons. The brother of the bride announced the wedding procession, but the parents of the bride were not there because they could not get visas. The couple bowed in front of the altar and the brother made introductions and then announced the scarf ceremony, which included guests draping *khata*, traditional Tibetan scarves, around the necks of the newly married couple and then leaving gifts on a table. People joined in Tibetan folkdances and songs. The couple also partook in the American customs of a champagne toast and cutting the wedding cake and feeding it to each other. Family and friends brought traditional Tibetan foods such as *tingmo* (braided white buns), *kalachana* (a spicy black bean dish), hand-shaped *kapse* (dough confection), and hand-made *momo* (meat dumplings).

Pema Dorjee discusses language with his students at the Tibet Fund in Manhattan. NICOLE BENGIVENO / THE NEW YORK TIMES / REDUX

As more Tibetan Americans assimilate, more are marrying outside of the Tibetan culture; thus more courtship and wedding rituals include mainstream American traditions.

Relations with Other Americans Because many Tibetans were exiled in India before immigrating to the United States, it follows that they would have connections in the Indian immigrant community. For instance, in Jackson Heights in Queens, New York, there is a neighborhood called "Little India" populated with stores, restaurants, and businesses owned by and oriented toward the Indian population. Many Tibetans live, work, and even own businesses in this neighborhood. Many speak Hindi with shop and restaurant owners and feel comfortable in this environment because of their time in India. Some Tibetan entrepreneurs have opened businesses in this neighborhood, such as the Yak Restaurant, which serves Tibetan food.

In areas where Tibetans make up only a very small part of the population, such as in New Mexico, Tibetans are sometimes mistaken for Latinos, Native Americans, or Chinese.

The strongest ties between Tibetan Americans with non-Tibetans revolve around Tibetan politics. There are many support groups founded by non-Tibetans, such as Students for a Free Tibet, International Tibet Independence Movement, the U.S.-Tibet Committee, and Friends of Tibet. Hollywood stars, most notably Richard Gere, also provide education about and support for Tibetan issues. Concerts to support Tibet, such as the rock-music Tibet Freedom Concerts, have featured such musicians as the Red Hot Chili Peppers and the Smashing Pumpkins.

EMPLOYMENT AND ECONOMIC CONDITIONS
Lack of fluency in English, lack of transferable skills, and lack of familiarity with the culture have created challenges in the workforce for Tibetan immigrants.

Some immigrants with advanced degrees are unable to find professional jobs because their degrees, from Nepal or India, are not recognized in the United States. According to a 1995 study by the scholar Julia Hess published in *Immigrant Ambassadors: Citizens and Belonging in the Tibetan Diaspora*, 920 Tibetan immigrants found that 4 percent did not have job skills, 23 percent had nontransferable skills, 21 percent had entry-level skills, 19 percent had technical skills, 16 percent were students, and 17 percent were professionals.

Typical jobs for Tibetan Americans have included data entry, construction work, store clerks, or other retail and service jobs. Women often find work as nannies, housekeepers, or secretaries. Businesses that have consistently hired Tibetan immigrants in New Mexico, for instance, include the Hyatt Hotel; Bandelier, a papermaking company; Wild Oats, a national health food chain; and Ten Thousand Waves, a local Japanese spa. Tibetan Americans in the professional world are generally teachers, accountants, businesspeople, nurses, or other health care workers. American perception of the "mystique" of Tibet's culture and its political situation has helped Tibetans get jobs, especially in more liberal settings such as natural foods stores. Even during the recession, there was low unemployment in the Tibetan American community. Some Tibetans have opened Tibetan restaurants or stores to serve the community. Many Tibetan immigrants settle in New York City because they can get undocumented jobs while they go through the asylum application process.

As younger generations become more assimilated in American schools and go on to higher education, their prospects for finding better-paying professional jobs increase.

POLITICS AND GOVERNMENT

Tibetan Americans feel strongly that maintaining their ethnic identity includes helping Americans understand the plight of Tibetans in Tibet and elsewhere. They have strong nationalistic ties to the government in exile in India—especially those who resided in India before immigrating to the United States—as well as a commitment to their home in the United States. Older-generation Tibetan Americans, or those not raised in the United States, tend to emphasize maintaining cultural and religious traditions while being politically active, while younger generations tend to be less connected to religious and cultural activities and more connected to political activities. Younger-generation Tibetans also feel more freedom to criticize traditional Tibetan customs as part of their political activities, perhaps because they have been raised with a juxtaposition of Western ideology and Tibetan values. For instance, younger-generation Tibetan Americans who embrace the idea of separation of church and state may feel comfortable criticizing some of the Dalai Lama's political policies and ideas even though they have great respect for him as a spiritual leader.

Tibetan associations are highly organized in the United States and lead protests, candlelight vigils, hunger strikes, boycotts, lobbying efforts, and more in support of Tibetan independence and human rights on national, international, and local levels. Local associations, for instance, organize protests, boycotts, and letter-writing campaigns when Chinese leaders are in their town, as well as join with national organizations to politically pressure businesses, the U.S. government, and the United Nations to take a stand for Tibetan independence and human rights.

Since the 1990s, many, if not most, in the Tibetan American community have been heavily involved in diverse and effective political actions promoting Tibetan independence and human rights. Their political campaign has been very successful. Holiday Inn Worldwide was faced with an international boycott of its hotel chain from 1993 to 1997, when the company announced it would not renew its management contract in Tibet—a contract that had been beneficial to the Chinese government. Holiday Inn's decision was part of the growing movement to return control of Tibet's economic affairs to Tibetans. A coalition of more than fifty organizations worldwide participated in the boycott, which attracted major grassroots support and celebrity interest and was highlighted at a Tibetan Freedom Concert in New York City in 1997. In 2009, the Tibetan Youth Congress of New York and New Jersey organized a march to commemorate the fiftieth anniversary of the 1959 uprising against the Chinese occupation of Tibet. Starting at Borough Hall in Brooklyn, approximately three thousand local Tibetans and their supporters walked over the Brooklyn Bridge to the United Nations, to the Chinese Consulate, and to Union Square. There were also educational panel discussions that people could attend after the rally.

Innumerable political protests, vigils, fasts, and more have taken place in response to the plight of Tibetans, both in Tibet and in exile. From 2009 to 2012, more than ninety-five people in Tibet, India, and Nepal—primarily young monks and nuns—set themselves on fire in protest against the Chinese government; nearly twenty-five of these self-immolations took place in November 2012. These protesters have been honored in Buddhist temples with fasts, demonstrations, and prayer vigils. Tibetan Americans have also participated in such events as the 2012 online Town Hall Meeting with U.S. Ambassador Gary Locke, who said, "We implore the Chinese to really meet with the representatives of the Tibetan people to address and re-examine some of the policies that have led to some of the restrictions and the violence and the self-immolations."

Tibetan Americans also participate in the political activities of the Tibetan government-in-exile, including voting in elections. Tibetan exile government officials sometimes tour the United States and are sponsored by local Tibetan community organizations to speak in their towns. For instance, when Prime Minister of the TGIE Lobsang Sangay toured the United States in 2011, the

Tibetan American Foundation of Minnesota sponsored his stop in the Twin Cities. The Dalai Lama also makes local stops when he tours the United States in addition to meeting with high government officials such as President Bill Clinton in 1993 and President George W. Bush in 2007. In 2011, the San Francisco Regional Tibetan Youth Congress organized a debate between four of the candidates of the Tibetan Parliament in Exile from North America in order to discuss politics, democracy, the Central Tibetan Administration, and the North American Tibetan community.

Older and first-generation Tibetan Americans often vote in Tibetan government-in-exile elections but not necessarily in American elections, despite citizenship. Younger Tibetans have become more involved in American politics and elections, believing they can have more influence not only over U.S. government decisions about the situation in Tibet, but also in how differing political parties and candidates will impact their lives in America. In the 2012 presidential election, the International Campaign for Tibet sent a questionnaire to both candidates, President Barack Obama and Governor Mitt Romney, asking about their stand on Tibet.

NOTABLE INDIVIDUALS

Literature Rinjing Dorje (1949–) of Seattle, Washington, is a folklorist, storyteller, and author of books on Tibetan humor and culinary arts, including *Tales of Uncle Tompa*, *Food in Tibetan Life*, and *The Renegade Monk of Tibet*. Dorje was raised in Nepal by a Tibetan father and Nepalese mother. He left Nepal in order to pursue his desire to become a writer.

Music Nawang Khechog (1956–) is a world music composer and musician who played with top musicians including Paul Simon, Kitaro, and Philip Glass. He often mixed traditional Tibetan windpipe instruments with Australian aboriginal and indigenous North American instruments. The Grammy nominee produced more than twenty albums. He worked with the Peacejam Foundation, an international education program organized by twelve Nobel Peace Laureates; trained youth in compassion through "Awakening Kindness" workshops; and worked with Deepak Chokra and others to create a video game called "The Journey to Wild Divine." He was born in Tibet, immigrated first to India, then Australia, and then the United States, where he lived in the Colorado mountains.

Tenzin Kunsel (1995–) is a Tibetan musician who began performing when she was five years old. She immigrated to the United States (New York) at the age of eight in 2003. She has performed at various fundraising events and venues in the United States and Europe, including for the Dalai Lama.

Yungchen Lhamo (1963–) is a popular Tibetan American musician whose name means "goddess of song." A New York City resident, she lived temporarily in Australia, where she won the Australian Recording Industry Award for best Folk/Traditional World Music

release. Her albums include *Tibetan Prayer*, *Tibet, Tibet*, *Coming Home*, and *Ama*. Her music is a mix of Buddhist chants and Western instruments.

Kesang Marstrand (1981–) is a folk musician born of a Tibetan father and Danish mother. In 2008 she released her debut album, *Bodega Rose*, which included the hit single *Tibet Will Be Free*. Her second album, *Hello Night* (2009), contains original children's lullabies.

Religion Thubten Jigme Norbu (1922–2008) was the eldest brother of the fourteenth Dalai Lama. He escaped Tibet in 1951 for the United States under the sponsorship of a CIA-front organization. He renounced his monastic vows when he came to the United States, and he began teaching at the University of Indiana in Bloomington in 1965. While there, he set up the Tibetan Cultural Center and built a *stupa*, a Buddhist pagoda, to memorialize "the million Tibetans" who died since 1959. He led walks for Tibetan independence across the United States in the 1990s. He disagreed with the Dalai Lama's stance for limited autonomy from the Chinese.

Chögyam Trungpa (1939–1987) was a Buddhist meditation master and teacher. A descendent of a line of important teachers of Tibetan Buddhism that is known for its emphasis on meditation, Trungpa was born in Tibet and fled to India during the 1959 revolt. In 1963, he received a sponsorship to study comparative religion at Oxford University in England, and in 1967 he was invited to Scotland to take over a meditation center. He moved to the United States in 1970 and traveled around the country teaching and giving seminars on Buddhism. He founded Vajradhatu (headquartered in Boulder, Colorado), the umbrella organization for the meditation centers throughout the world that were under his direction. He also founded 150 Shambhala meditation centers around the world. His style of teaching was seen as unconventional and sometimes controversial, as were some of his lifestyle choices, such as drinking, smoking, drug use, and having many sexual encounters.

Tarthang Tulku (1934–) is the founder and Head Lama of the Tibetan Nyingma Meditation Center in California, the founder of the Tibetan Aid Project, and the founder of Dharma Publishing, one of the first presses to print sacred Tibetan texts. He was born in Tibet, escaped to India, and then immigrated to the United States in 1969. He founded the Guna Center in 2009 to share Tibetan Buddhism through historical footage, web media, photo exhibitions, promotional material, and documentaries.

Ngawang Wangyal (1901–1983) was a Buddhist priest and scholar born in Tibet. After escaping to India in the early 1950s, he moved to the United States in 1955. In 1958 he established a Buddhist monastery in New Jersey and contributed to the spread of Tibetan Buddhism in the United States. He helped found the American Institute of Buddhist Studies in 1972. He also translated Tibetan and Sanskrit stories.

MEDIA

NEWSPAPERS AND PERIODICALS

Journal of the International Association of Tibetan Studies (JIATS)

The official publication of the International Association of Tibetan Studies, this is an online, scholarly, peer-reviewed journal.

> David Germano, Editor in Chief
> P.O. Box 400126
> University of Virginia, Charlottesville
> Virginia 22904-4126
> Email: thl@collab.itc.virginia.edu
> URL: www.thlib.org/collections/texts/jiats

Tibet Press Watch

Published bimonthly by International Campaign for Tibet, *Tibet Press Watch* promotes human rights and democratic freedoms for the people of Tibet.

> 1825 Jefferson Place NW
> Washington, D.C. 20006
> Phone: (202) 785-1515
> Fax: (202) 785-4343
> Email: info@savetibet.org
> URL: www.savetibet.org/media-center/
> tibet-press-watch

RADIO/BROADCAST STATIONS

Radio Free Asia

Provides accurate and timely news and information to Asian countries whose governments prohibit access to a free press.

> John A. Estrella, Vice President, Communications and Government Relations
> 2025 M Street NW
> Suite 300
> Washington, D.C. 20036
> Phone: (202) 530-4900
> Email: estrellaj@rfa.org; tibetnews@rfa.org
> URL: www.rfa.org/english

Tibet Online TV

Tibetonline.tv includes videos, audio shows, music, news, documentaries, and photos.

> Secretary, Dept. of Information and International Relations
> URL: tibetonline.tv

Central Tibetan Administration

> Gangchen kyisong
> Dharamsala, Himachal Pradesh 176216 India

Voice of America Tibet

A United States Act of Congress created Voice of America (VOA) Tibet in 1990 to establish Tibetan language programming for the people of Tibet. It broadcasts two one-hour television programs each week via satellite, plus forty-two hours of shortwave radio directly into Tibet. It is also available streamed and archived on the VOA Tibetan-language and English-language websites via RSS feeds, and broadcast on podcasts, mobile apps, and YouTube.

Tibetan Service Chief:

> Phone: (202) 382-5569

VOA Tibetan:

> VOA Tibetan EAP Room 2046
> 330 Independence Avenue SW
> Washington, D.C. 20237
> Phone: (202) 382-5595
> Email: contact-tibetan@voanews.com
> URL: www.voatibetanenglish.com

ORGANIZATIONS AND ASSOCIATIONS

The United States has a strong base of regional, state, and local organizations that support the Tibetan freedom movement, many of which are named "Friends of Tibet." Select national and international organizations are listed below.

Conservancy for Tibetan Art and Culture (CTAC)

This association supports activities dedicated to the preservation and promotion of Tibetan culture through teachings, exhibitions, symposia, and cultural research. Collaborating with Tibet Fund, Tibet House, and other experts and scholars, CTAC aims to increase awareness of Tibet's living cultural heritage among the Tibetan communities and the general public.

> Lodi Gyari, Board Chairperson
> Phone: (202) 828-6288
> Fax: (703) 538-4671
> Email: info@tibetanculture.org
> URL: tibetanculture.org

Tibetan Youth Congress (TYC)

TYC is a worldwide organization of young Tibetans working to restore complete independence for the whole of Tibet and for the preservation and promotion of religion and Tibet's unique culture and traditions. They organize political activities and host social, educational, and cultural activities and festivals. There are thirteen chapters in North America.

> McLeod Ganj
> Central Tibetan Administration
> Dharamsala, Himachal Pradesh 176216 India
> Phone: 91-1892-22155-4
> Email: tyc@tibetanyouthcongress.org
> URL: tibetanyouthcongress.org

The Tibet Fund

The Tibet Fund's mission is to preserve the distinct cultural and national identity of the Tibetan people. Since 1981, under the patronage of His Holiness the Dalai Lama, The Tibet Fund has been the primary funding organization for health care, education, refugee rehabilitation, religious and cultural preservation, elder care, and community and economic development programs serving more than 140,000 Tibetan refugees living in India, Nepal, and Bhutan.

Rinchen Dharlo, President
241 East 32ⁿᵈ Street
New York, New York 10016
Phone: (212) 213-5011
Fax: (212) 213-1219
Email: info@tibetfund.org
URL: www.tibetfund.org

Tibet Justice Center (formerly International Committee of Lawyers for Tibet)

The Tibet Justice Center is devoted solely to legal advocacy for Tibet, with projects related to asylum and immigration, the legal status of Tibet, and environmental self-determination and human rights.

Robert D. Sloane, President
440 Grand Avenue
Suite 425
Oakland, California 94610
Phone: (510) 486-0588
Email: tjc@tibetjustice.org
URL: www.tibetjustice.org

U.S. Tibet Committee

Independent human rights organization of Tibetan and American volunteers promotes public awareness of the current political situation in Tibet through lectures, conferences, demonstrations, and letter writing campaigns.

241 East 32ⁿᵈ Street
New York, New York 10016
Phone: (212) 481-3569
Email: ustc@igc.org
URL: www.ustibetcommittee.org

MUSEUMS AND RESEARCH CENTERS

Jacques Marchais Museum of Tibetan Art

This museum resembles a small Tibetan mountain temple tucked away from the world. Terraced sculpture gardens, a lily and fish pond, and a distant view of the lower Hudson Bay are the setting for Tibetan, Nepalese, Tibeto-Chinese, and Mongolian artifacts from the seventeenth to the nineteenth centuries or earlier. The museum also hosts public programs to further the understanding of the art and culture of Tibet.

Meg Ventrudo, Executive Director
338 Lighthouse Avenue
Staten Island, New York 10306
Phone: (718) 987-3500
Fax: (718) 351-0402
Email: mventrudo@tibetanmuseum.org
URL: www.tibetanmuseum.org

Los Angeles County Museum of Art (LACMA)

LACMA houses of the most comprehensive collections of Himalayan art, including seventy-five Tibetan and Nepalese *thangkas* and Tibetan paintings that once belonged to Giuseppe Tucci, one of the few scholars to enter Tibet in the middle of the twentieth century.

5905 Wilshire Boulevard
Los Angeles, California 90036
Phone: (323) 857-6000

Email: publicinfo@lacma.org
URL: www.lacma.org

The Metropolitan Museum of Art

The Met has a collection of Tibetan Buddhist art, Tibetan rugs, ritual utensils, arms and armor, and native costumes.

1000 Fifth Avenue
New York, New York 10028
Phone: (212) 535-7710
Email: education@metmuseum.org
URL: www.metmuseum.org

Museum of Fine Arts, Boston

The museum houses a permanent collection of Tibetan art from the fifteenth to the early twentieth century, including paintings, rugs, and metalwork.

465 Huntington Avenue
Boston, Massachusetts 02115
Phone: (617) 267-9300
Email: info@mfa.org
URL: www.mfa.org

Virginia Museum of Fine Arts

The Tibetan and Nepalese galleries showcase paintings and other cultural treasures of Tibet.

Alex Nyerges, Director
2800 Grove Avenue
Richmond, Virginia 23221-2466
Phone: (804) 340-1400
Email: visitorservices@vmfa.museum
URL: www.vmfa.state.va.us

SOURCES FOR ADDITIONAL STUDY

Goldstein, Melvyn C. *A History of Modern Tibet, 1913-1951.* Berkeley: University of California Press, 1989.

Goldstein, Melvyn C., and Cynthia M. Beall. "China's Birth Control Policy in the Tibet Autonomous Region." *Asian Survey* 31, no. 3 (1991): 285–303.

Hess, Julia Meredith. *Immigrant Ambassadors: Citizenship and Belonging in the Tibetan Diaspora.* Stanford: Stanford University Press, 2009.

Lee, Jonathan H. X., and Kathleen M. Nadeau, eds. "Tibetan Americans." In *Encyclopedia of Asian American Folklore and Folklife.* Santa Barbara: ABC-CLIO, 2010.

Moskin, Julia. "Tibetans' (Forbidden) Special Treat," *New York Times*, February 12, 2012.

Mullen, Eve. *The American Occupation of Tibetan Buddhism: Tibetans and Their American Hosts in New York City.* New York, Münster: Waxmann Verlag, 2001.

Pommaret-Imaeda, Francoise. *Tibet: An Enduring Civilization.* London: Thames and Hudson, 2003.

Ptak, Thomas Walter. *Tibetan Migration, Cultural Identity, and Place in Portland and New York City, A Thesis.* Eugene: University of Oregon, 2010.

Wangdi, Yosay. "'Displaced People' Adjusting to New Cultural Vocabulary, Tibetan Immigrants in North America." In *Emerging Voices: Experiences of Underrepresented Asian Americans.* New Brunswick: Rutgers University Press, 2008.

TLINGIT

Diane E. Benson ('L xeis')

OVERVIEW

The Tlingit (pronounced "Thlingit") people are an indigenous group from Southeast Alaska, an archipelago with a narrow strip of continental shoreline backed by the high coastal mountains that separate Alaska from British Columbia, Canada. Tlingit communities extended from south of Ketchikan (the southernmost city in present-day Alaska) northward across islands and the mainland as far as the Copper River area. Tlingit people also occupied some inland areas on the Canadian side of the border in British Columbia and the Yukon Territory. The mainland Tlingit of Alaska inhabited the Coast Mountains from 50 to 100 miles inland. The northernmost portion of Tlingit country is dominated by glaciers and ice fields with the majesty of the Fairweather and Saint Elias mountains overlooking the northern shores of the Gulf of Alaska. Fjords, mountains that dive into the sea, islands, and ancient trees make up most of this wet country that is part of one of the largest temperate rain forests in the world. The name *Tlingit* essentially means human beings. The word was originally used simply to distinguish a human being from an animal, since the Tlingit people believed that there was little difference between humans and animals. Over time the word came to be the tribal nation's name.

The Tlingit population at time of contact with Europeans is estimated to have been 10,000. Prior to the arrival of outsiders, Tlingit culture was heavily influenced by shamanism, a belief system in which spiritualists commune with the spirit world on behalf of the community. For sustenance the Tlingit hunted almost all of the subarctic land and sea mammals in the region, including Dall sheep, deer, bears, harbor seals, and sea lions. From late spring until early autumn, many Tlingit families relocated to "fish camps" where they fished and prepared salmon, halibut, and herring. Both fishing and hunting were spiritual endeavors for the Tlingit people and were practiced with ceremony and intention. Pre-contact Tlingit economy was marked by extensive trade, both internally and with neighboring tribes such as the Tsimshian, Haida, Eyak, and Athabaskan. Occasionally the Tlingit pushed out competing traders in order to maintain a monopoly of trade with some interior tribes. The Tlingit offered trade partners seaweed, fish oil, and blankets, among other things. Trade brought the community such items as walrus ivory, furs, copper, and slaves—which were the most valuable commodities. With the arrival of European and Russian settlers, Tlingit trade expanded to involve these groups, and by the nineteenth century, tobacco and manufactured goods, such as guns and ammunition, were indispensable to Tlingit culture.

Unlike American Indian groups in the continental United States, the Tlingit people do not have designated reservations. Today, many Tlingit people continue to occupy the territory of their ancestors; important centers of Tlingit culture can be found in the small coastal cities of Angoon, Hoonah, Kake, Klawock, Klukwan, Saxman, and Yakutat Sitka in Alaska and in Atlin, Carcross, and Teslin in the Canadian Yukon interior. Along with village tribal councils, Alaskan Natives are organized by regional corporations established by the Alaska Native Claims Settlement Act (ANCSA), which was passed by Congress and signed into law by President Richard Nixon in 1971. The Sealaska Corporation manages Tlingit and Haida communities. The Tlingit, Haida, and Tsimshian tribes are often discussed in conjunction with one another as a result of their geographical origins on the Northern Pacific coast and because of cultural similarities, such as their social structure and their reliance on waterways for food. Significant differences also exist among these groups, however, including their languages, which are not mutually intelligible. Contemporary Tlingit people are integrated into the broader Alaskan society and contribute significantly to the state's commercial economy.

In 2013 the Central Council of Tlingit and Haida tribes of Alaska claimed a combined worldwide enrollment of more than 28,000 members, and the 2010 U.S. Census reported that 26,080 individuals identified as Tlingit or Haida, singly or in combination with another ethnic identity. Out of that number, 9,777 identified solely as Tlingit. Most of the Tlingit population live in the urban communities of southeastern Alaska, though a significant number have made their homes all across the continent. Euro-Americans dominate the Southeast Alaska population, with the Tlingit people being the largest minority group in the region. According to the U.S. Census Bureau's American

Community Survey estimates for 2006 to 2010, the states with significant numbers of Tlingit-Haida were Alaska, California, Oregon, and Washington.

HISTORY OF THE PEOPLE

Early History Archaeological evidence suggests that Tlingit people first occupied present-day Southeast Alaska at least 11,000 years ago. Little is known about the origin of the Tlingit people, as archeological records cannot prove their movements. Yet Tlingit legends speak of migrations into the area from several possible directions, either from the north by crossing the Bering Strait land bridge, from the sea as Polynesian boaters, from more southern parts of the North American continent, or from the interior of the continent via numerous river channels. Oral traditions hold that the Tlingit came from the sources of several major rivers in the area. By contrast, the Haida people, with whom the Tlingit have had frequent interaction, have only been on the Alaska coast for about two hundred years but have resided since ancient times on the archipelago of Haida Gwaii, located roughly 60 miles off the British Columbia coast. The Tsimshian, another tribe with which the Tlingit historically interacted, also migrated to coastal Alaska relatively recently, having originated in the Skeena River basin of interior British Columbia.

Before the arrival of European explorers, groups of Tlingit people often traveled by canoe through treacherous waters for hundreds of miles to engage in war, attend ceremonies, trade, or marry. Through trade with other tribes as far south as the Olympic Peninsula—particularly the Tsimshian, Haida, Athabaskan, and

Eyak peoples—and even northern California, the Tlingit people gained fur, shells and tusks, canoes, and slaves; moreover the development of complex woven designs seen in Chilkat blankets (produced by Tlingit and other Northwest Coast peoples) is often attributed to Tsimshian influence.

In the mid-1700s the Spaniards and the British, attracted by the fur trade, penetrated the Northwest from the south, via the Juan de Fuca Islands in the Nootka Sound area. The Russians, also in search of furs, invaded the Aleutian Islands and moved southeast, travelling throughout the southwestern coast of Alaska toward Tlingit country. While the Tlingit traders may have heard stories of these strangers coming, they took little heed. Records show that Europeans arrived in Tlingit country for the first time in 1741, when Russian explorer Aleksey Chirikov sent a boatload of men ashore to obtain drinking water near the modern-day site of Sitka, where the expedition likely encountered Tlingit locals. When the group did not return for several days, Chirikov sent another boat of men to shore; they also did not return. Thereafter, contact with Tlingit people was limited until well into the 1800s.

After subduing the Aleut people, a group indigenous to the Aleutian Islands, and moving southward, Russian invaders began their occupation of Tlingit country. The Tlingit, having monopolized trade routes in every direction from Southeast Alaska, engaged in somewhat friendly and quite profitable trading with the newcomers until the Russians became more aggressive in their attempts to colonize the area and control trade routes. In 1802 Kiksadi Tlingit chief Katlian of the Sitka area successfully led his warriors against the Russians, who had set up a fort in Sitka. Eventually the Russians recaptured Sitka and maintained a base they called New Archangel, but they had little contact with the Sitka clans. For years the Tlingit resisted occupation and the use of their trade routes by outsiders. In 1854 a Chilkat Tlingit war party traveled hundreds of miles into the interior and destroyed a Hudson's Bay Company post at Fort Selkirk in the Yukon Valley.

Eventually, diseases and other hardships took their toll on the Tlingit people, making them more vulnerable. It is estimated that between 1836 and 1840, half of the Tlingit people in and near Sitka died of smallpox, influenza, and tuberculosis. At about this time white Americans arrived in Tlingit country hunting for gold and sought to occupy and control the land and its people. The weakening of the Tlingit allowed for American occupation, and Americans became firmly established in the land with the 1867 Alaska Purchase, a treaty with the Russian Empire. The treaty resulted from Russian fears of losing the Alaska territory through future conflict with Canadian British settlers. Knowing that the United States would be in a better position to defend the region, the Russian minister to the United States signed over the land to Secretary of State William Seward for $7.2

million. The document referred to the indigenous people of Alaska as "uncivilized tribes." and made them subject to the same regulations and policies as U.S. American Indians. As a result the Tlingit people were compelled to abide by the 1884 First Organic Act, which allowed Alaska Natives to remain in possession of already established land and settlements but denied them the ability to obtain titles for this land. The 1885 Major Crimes Act further eroded Alaskan Native sovereignty by classifying seven major crimes under federal jurisdiction if those crimes were perpetrated by a Native American against another Native American. The act stripped tribes of their right to deal with criminal matters according to traditional customs. Such acts are representative of numerous statutes imposed by the U.S. federal government that threatened Tlingit people politically, territorially, culturally, and socially.

The Tlingit fought American development of canneries, mines, and logging, exploitive commercial interests that conflicted with the Tlingit subsistence lifestyle and values of resourcefulness and stewardship. Disputes between the Americans and the decreasing number of Tlingit people proved futile for the Tlingit, because Americans displayed impressive military strength, technology, and an unwavering desire for settlement and expansion. After a disagreement involving the death of two Tlingit, the American military destroyed the Tlingit villages of Kake (in the 1860s) and Angoon (in 1882), further establishing American power and occupancy.

Modern Era In response to their subjugation to U.S. sovereignty, the Tlingit people founded the Alaska Native Brotherhood (ANB) in Sitka in 1912. The ANB's goals were to gain equality for the Native people of Southeast Alaska and to obtain for them the same citizenship and education rights as non-Natives. In 1915 the efforts of the ANB and the newly organized Alaska Native Sisterhood (ANS) prompted the territorial legislature to adopt a position similar to the 1887 Dawes Act, a federal legislative measure that allowed states to divide tribal land into allotments and provided for Natives to become U.S. citizens— if the Natives became "civilized" by rejecting certain tribal customs and relationships. Because of the latter clause, few Native people became citizens at this time; most had to wait until the U.S. Congress adopted the Citizenship Act of 1924. Through the ANB Tlingit people also actively pursued the right to vote. Unlike many Alaska Native people at the time who wanted to continue living as they had for many generations, Tlingit leaders sought increased political power. In 1924 William Paul, a Tlingit, won election to the Territorial House of Representatives, marking the beginning of a trend toward Native political influence.

The issues of Native citizenship, voting rights, fishing and fishing trap disputes, and the activities of ANB contributed to the rising tensions between the Tlingit and the newcomers. In the 1930s, 1940s, and 1950s, it was not uncommon to see signs that read "No Indians Allowed" on the doors of business establishments. Throughout the twentieth century, Alaska Natives made significant strides towards equality under United States laws and in reasserting tribal sovereignty, however. The ANB did much to fight prejudices and elevate the social status of the Tlingit and Haida people as American citizens, including sending ANS president Elizabeth Peratrovich to testify before the state senate. In the 1940s the state passed significant antidiscrimination laws, largely as a result of ANB efforts.

The 1971 ANCSA legislation abolished all Native land claims, instead giving Alaska Native regional and village corporations the titles to Native land along with monetary compensation. The act radically altered the relationship between the U.S. government and Alaska Native tribes and changed the way those tribes self-govern. In the last decades of the twentieth century, Tlingit activists focused efforts on the repatriation of cultural artifacts previously removed and held in museums.

The most pressing issues for the Tlingit continue to center on matters of tribal sovereignty, including hunting and fishing rights. Their ability to subsist off the land and sea is constantly endangered by logging, pulp mills, overharvesting of the waters by commercial fisheries, government regulations, and the area's increasing population. Legislation such as the Alaska

Tlingit mother and child. JOEL BENNETT / PETER ARNOLD / GETTY IMAGES

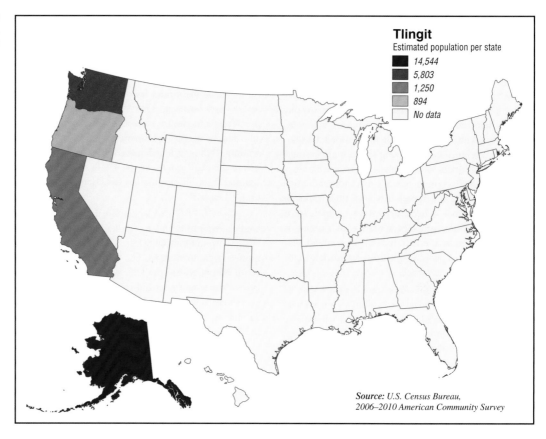

Tlingit
Estimated population per state

- 14,544
- 5,803
- 1,250
- 894
- No data

*Source: U.S. Census Bureau,
2006–2010 American Community Survey*

National Interest Lands Conservation Act of 1980 has made some concessions to Native concerns, but the Tlingit and others continue to fight for access to natural resources and their right to employ traditional methods. In the twenty-first century, Tlingit people have also turned their attention towards rebuilding their culture and identity through artistic and academic work. A traditional Tlingit canoe has been on display at the Smithsonian since 2008, and an annual multidisciplinary academic clan conference, "Sharing our Knowledge," most recently held in May 2012, has promoted educational outreach. Through such advocacy the Tlingit have found a way to both present and negotiate their own tribal identity and to educate non-Natives about their cultural values and practices.

SETTLEMENT IN THE UNITED STATES

Since contact with Europeans, centers of Tlingit society have largely remained on original Tlingit lands. The 1906 Native Allotment Act resulted in some Tlingit lands being placed in the hands of individual Tlingit. The law provided for conveyance of 160 acres to adult Natives as long as no tract of ground contained mineral deposits. Only a few allotments were issued in Southeast Alaska. The Native Townsite Act of 1926 also provided only for the conveyance of "restricted" title lands, meaning that such property could not be sold or leased without the approval of the U.S. secretary of the interior. Lands regained in this way by

villages or individuals failed to sufficiently meet the needs of a hunting and fishing people, however.

In 1929, seventeen years after its founding, the ANB began campaigning on land issues, and as a result Congress passed a law in 1935 allowing Tlingit and Haida peoples to sue the United States for the loss of their lands. By this time large sections of Tlingit country had become the Tongass National Forest. Glacier Bay had become a national monument, and, further south in Tlingit country, Annette Island was set aside as a reservation for Tsimshian Indians from Canada. In 1959—the same year that Alaska was admitted to the union as a state—the U.S. Court of Claims decided in favor of the Tlingit and Haida's suit for payment of land that was taken from them. The Tlingit-Haida land claims award specified 16 million acres without stipulating a definite monetary value; the actual monetary settlement took years to conclude.

In 1971 ANCSA mandated the settlement of all claims against the United States and the state of Alaska that were based on aboriginal right, title, use, or occupancy of land or water areas in Alaska. The law did not grant land to Tlingit individuals; rather, lands claimed by Southeast Natives under this act were placed under the control of the ANCSA-established regional corporation Sealaska and village corporations. Some village corporations had the option to provide individuals with land in some cases, but most villages designated the land for future development.

Throughout the twentieth and twenty-first centuries, Tlingit settlements became more geographically consolidated: rather than making use of winter villages and summer fishing camps, more Tlingit people remained in permanent towns. During the same time period, higher numbers of Tlingit people migrated from traditional villages to Alaskan cities such as Juneau, Anchorage, and Ketchikan, as well as to the continental United States. Large Tlingit communities can be found primarily on the Northwest Coast in such cities as Seattle and San Francisco in the 2010s. According to the American Community Survey estimates, in 2010 large numbers of Tlingit and Haida were residing in Alaska (14,544), Washington (5,803), California (1,250), and Oregon (894).

LANGUAGE

Classified as an isolate of the Na-Dené language family, which is dominated by Athapaskan languages, including those of interior groups, Tlingit can be separated into five mutually intelligible dialects, of which only three have survived into the twenty-first century. The Tlingit language is a tonal language that includes twenty-four sounds not found in English. The sounds of Tlingit are difficult and varied and include not only the more familiar rolling and drawn-out vowel sounds and deeper guttural (or "back-in-the-mouth") sounds but also pinched and air-driven sounds with consonants that are "voiceless" (except for the "n" sound, as in "naa"). Many of the sounds that have no English equivalents are pronunciations of consonants. Almost all Alaska Native languages have gutturals. Tlingit is unique in that it is not only guttural but also has glottalized stops and a series of linguistically related sounds called glottalized fricatives, which are breathy-voiced sounds that can change depending on the preceding letters.

Unlike the English alphabet of twenty-six letters, the Tlingit language has at least thirty-two consonants and eight vowels. The written alphabet was created with not only the familiar lettering of English but also with periods, underlined letters, and apostrophes to distinguish particular sounds. For example; the word *yéil* means "raven," and *yéil'* (with the apostrophe) means "elderberry." Tlingit grammar does not express concern with time, whereas English conveys some sense of time (past, present, and future tenses) with almost any verb usage. Tlingit verbs may provide the information about an action's frequency, however, or indicate the stopping or starting point of an action. The grammatical and phonological features of the language make it a difficult one to learn if it has not been absorbed since birth.

The earliest attempt to communicate in written Tlingit occurred in the nineteenth century. Bishop Innocent (Veniaminov) of the Russian Orthodox Church created the first alphabet for the Tlingit language and developed a Tlingit literacy program. The church supported bilingual education in its schools, but the Americans discouraged it and ultimately sought to suppress the use of the language completely. It was not until the 1960s that a Tlingit language literacy movement was resumed through the efforts of such linguists as Constantine Naish and Gillian Story, who created the popular alphabet that forms the basis of modern Tlingit orthography.

Unfortunately, efforts to suppress the language in the past created a situation in which there are not many young speakers, and the language may not survive. In 2000 the United Nations Education, Scientific and Cultural Organization (UNESCO) estimated that only three hundred fluent Tlingit speakers remained, and it listed the language as critically endangered. As the remaining fluent speakers age, several cultural and heritage centers have dedicated themselves to restoring and reviving Tlingit by teaching new speakers. The Sealaska Heritage Institute produces school curriculum and other educational tools, including a Tlingit dictionary, phrasebook, flashcards, and audio CDs; the institute also hosted immersion retreats in the mid-2000s at which participants agreed to speak only Tlingit for five days. *Alaskool.org* provides educational materials online for Tlingit educators. The Sitka school district provides middle school classes to help young people learn their native language, and the University of Alaska Southeast offers a minor in Tlingit language in order to afford students "an appreciation of the unique nature of the language."

Greetings and Popular Expressions Tlingit people do not use such greetings as hello, good-bye, good afternoon, or good evening. Some common expressions are: *Yoo xat duwasaakw … —*"My name is …"; *gunalchéesh*—"thank you"; *Yak'éi ixwsiteení—*"It's good to see you"; *Wáa sá iyatee?*—"How are you feeling?"; *Wa.éku.aa?*—"Where are you going?"; and *Haa kaa gaa kuwatee*—"It's good weather for us."

RELIGION

Tlingit people believe that all forms of life—plants, trees, birds, fish, animals, and human beings—are of equal value and that all should be accorded the same amount of respect. Traditionally, spirituality was present in every aspect of the Tlingit culture. Living closely with their surroundings, the Tlingit developed a belief system that derived significance from an animate natural environment. Shamanism, an ancient spiritual and healing tradition, was also a key element in Tlingit religion and culture. At least one shaman, or *ixt'*, was present in each Tlingit clan. The Tlingit believed that an ailing physical condition was a manifestation of a spiritual problem, invasion, or disturbance. In such cases a shaman was called in to combat a spirit or spirits called *yéiks* or the negative forces of a witch or "medicine man." Today, it is believed that Tlingit shamanism is all but extinct; anyone addressing such spiritual forces does so quietly, and most people are silent on the subject.

Institutionalized religion or places of worship were not a part of precontact Tlingit life. Dating from the first introduction of Christianity in the 1830s by Russian priests and later proselytizing by Americans, the Russian Orthodox and Presbyterian faiths have had the longest and most profound impact on Tlingit society and are well established in the Tlingit communities. Missionaries aimed to abolish traditional practices, shamanism in particular, while they worked to instill Christianity and other markers of Western culture. Other religions have become popular in Southeast Alaska, and a few Tlingit people are members of the Jehovah's Witnesses, the Baha'i Faith, and the fundamentalist Baptist churches. Today, many Tlingit people practice organized religion in conjunction with some traditional beliefs. Among those Tlingit who remain on ancestral lands and live in longstanding Tlingit communities, interest in practicing and preserving traditional religious practices and philosophy has seen a resurgence.

CULTURE AND ASSIMILATION

Throughout the nineteenth century, many Tlingit communities were affected by the influx of various industries. Fish canneries were established in Sitka and Klawock, gold mining began at Windham Bay, and a Presbyterian mission station was constructed at the location of present-day Haines. New settlements like Juneau (1880) and Ketchikan (1888) dramatically changed Tlingit lands and economic systems. A mixed cash-subsistence economy developed, altering traditional trade and material acquisition systems. Missionary schools that were determined to acculturate the Tlingit and other Alaska Natives instructed them in English language and American ways and denied the indigenous students access to their traditional language, foods, dances, songs, and healing methods. Although change was overwhelming and Americanization pervasive, Tlingit clan structures remained intact, and traditions survived in the original communities. At the turn of the twentieth century, it was not uncommon for Southeast Alaskan factories to retain clan leaders to prevent disputes between their employees and the Native communities.

Tlingit people believe that all life is of equal value; plants, trees, birds, fish, animals, and human beings are all equally respected.

By the same time the destruction and death brought on by disease, combined with the arrival of Western religions and medicines, had caused many Tlingit to abandon their faith in shamanism and traditional healing by the turn of the century. Smallpox and other epidemics of the early nineteenth century recurred well into the twentieth century. A number of communities, including Dry Bay and Lituya Bay, were overcome in 1918 and thereafter by bouts of influenza. Culturally fundamental traditional gatherings called potlatches became almost nonexistent in Tlingit country during the tuberculosis epidemics of the 1900s. These epidemics caused hundreds of Tlingit and other Southeast Alaskan people to be institutionalized; many of those who fell victim to these diseases were subsequently buried in mass graves. Tlingit people turned to the churches for relief, and in the process many were given new names to replace their Tlingit names, which had formed an important basis of identity and status in Tlingit society. Demoralization and hopelessness ensued and worsened with the government-sponsored internment of Aleut people, who were moved to Tlingit country during World War II because of Japanese incursions in the Aleutians. Some Tlingit families adopted Aleut children who had been orphaned as a result of widespread disease and intolerable living conditions.

When they were established, the Alaska Native Brotherhood and Sisterhood accepted acculturation as a goal for their members, believing that the abandonment of cultural traditions was in the peoples' best interests. Their organizational structure, however, reflected the traditional form of government that managed tribal and clan operations. Social and clan interactions and relationships continue to exist to this day despite all outside influences and despite the marked adaptations of Tlingit people to American society. The relatively recent revival of dances, songs, potlatches, language, and stories has strengthened continuing clan interactions and identities.

Traditions and Customs Tlingit peoples demand that respect be shown toward other individuals and clans. When a person feels insulted by another, payment must be made or a process performed to remove the damage publicly by the person or clan who was responsible for the insult. If this does not happen, bad feelings persist, negatively affecting relationships between clans. In the old ways if a Tlingit person was seriously harmed or murdered by another Tlingit person, the "eye for an eye" philosophy would determine punishment: someone from the opposing clan would have to sustain injury or die. That philosophy has been adapted to exist within formal legal boundaries. Criminal cases are tried strictly by American law, but the family of the perpetrator may also be subject to social sanctions according to traditional law. Payment by the perpetrator's clan to the harmed clan for the wrongdoing may also occur.

Many newcomers to Tlingit country, including some missionaries, erroneously reported that the Tlingit people worshiped totems, idolized animals or birds as gods, and held heathen rituals. As a result some religious leaders instructed their Native congregations to burn or destroy various elements of their art and culture, and a good deal of Tlingit heirlooms were destroyed in this way. These misconceptions undermined the complexity and power of Tlingit culture and society.

Cuisine The traditional diet of the Tlingit people relied heavily on the sea. Fish, seal, seaweed, clams, cockles, gum boots (chitons—a shell fish), and herring and salmon eggs, as well as berries and venison, still make up the primary foods of most traditional Tlingit people. Fish, such as halibut, cod, herring, and salmon, are prepared in many forms—most commonly smoked, dried, baked, roasted, or boiled. Sockeye, silver, humpy, and dog salmon are the fish best utilized for smoking and drying. The drying process takes about a week and involves several stages of cleaning, deboning, cutting strips, and hanging them usually near an open fire until firm. These strips serve as a food source throughout the year, as they are easily stored and carried.

Because southeastern Alaska is abundant with ocean life and wildlife, the Tlingit people could easily find and preserve foods in the warmer seasons, saving colder months for art, crafts, trade, and ceremonial gatherings. Today, although food sources have been impacted by population and industry, traditional foods are still gathered and prepared in traditional ways as well as in new and creative ways influenced by the various ethnic groups who have immigrated into the area, especially Filipino Americans (rice has become a staple of almost any Tlingit meal). Pilot bread, brought in by various seafaring merchants, is also common because it stores well and softens the consumption of oil delicacies such as eulachon (a type of fish) and seal oils. Fry bread is also an element of many meals and special occasions. Other influences on diet and food preparation besides standard American cuisine include Norwegian, Russian, and Chinese foods.

Other foods of the Tlingit include such pungent dishes as *xákwláee* (whipped berries often mixed with fish or seal oil), seal liver, dried seaweed, fermented fish eggs, abalone, grouse, crab, deer jerky, sea greens, *suktéitl'* (goose tongue, a plant food), rosehips, rhubarb, roots, *yaana.eit* (wild celery), and *s'ikshaldéen* (Hudson Bay tea).

In the modern era Tlingit cuisine has been impacted by Alaska's unique subsistence laws, which have helped Alaska Natives, particularly those in rural areas, to maintain priority access to fish, plants, and wildlife that were part of a traditional diet; the laws have also assisted in perpetuating the spiritually significant practices of fishing, hunting, and gathering. Specifically, the state amended 1971's ANCSA laws to prioritize subsistence users of resources over consumptive users. A 1989 federal court also gave Native Alaskan traditional practices precedence over fish and game regulations. Yet, in the twenty-first century, many non-native Alaskans and tourists seeking recreation opportunities and corporations with commercial interests continue to oppose subsistence and to argue about the finer points of such provisions.

Traditional Dress Traditionally, Tlingit men and women wore loincloths and skirts made of cedar bark. Because of the rainy weather in southeastern Alaska, they also wore raincoats made from natural elements such as spruce root or cedar bark. Today, Tlingit people dress much as other contemporary Americans do, although they often display their clan or family emblem on clothing or jewelry, as has been the custom for centuries. Robes, tunics, and other ceremonial regalia continue to be produced and worn, especially on ritual occasions such as memorial potlatches.

The most distinctive form of ceremonial dress prior to Americanization, and still the most admired, is the Chilkat robe. Although it is called the Chilkat robe after the Chilkat tribe of Tlingit who specialized in weaving, its origins are Tsimshian. The robe is made from mountain goat wool and cedar bark strips and generally exhibits an emblem of the clan. This garment takes a weaver one to five years to make. The technique not only involves horizontal weaving similar to that found in other cultures but also a symmetrical and circular (curvilinear) design. This complex art form came dangerously close to extinction in the twentieth century, but through the perseverance of individuals in and outside the tribe, there are now several weavers, older and younger, in the Tlingit and other Northwest nations today. This is also true of the recently revived art of the Raven's Tail robe, another complexly woven garment of black and white worn over the shoulders in the same cape fashion as the Chilkat robe. Raven's Tail weaving. Which employs geometric and herring bone patterns, is a skill that was not used for nearly two centuries, but with the resurgence of cultural interest, it is now being practiced throughout the Northwest coastal region. Chilkat and Raven's Tail weaving is also used to make leggings, medicine bags, dance purses, dance aprons, tunics, and shirts.

Chilkat robes are never worn as daily dress, but they are worn with pride at potlatches, celebrations, and sometimes for burial, if the deceased was of a particular social stature. The robes are a sign of wealth, and traditionally, if one owned such an item, he was generally a clan leader of great prestige. Giving away a Chilkat robe meant greater glory because only the wealthiest could afford to be so generous. Many Chilkat robes can be seen at Sealaska Heritage Foundation's Celebration, a biennial gathering in Juneau established in 1982 and featuring dance, art, cooking contests, and lectures to honor Tlingit, Haida, and Tsimshian culture.

Modern regalia for special occasions consists primarily of the button blanket, or dancing robe, which, although it is time-consuming and expensive to make, is much more available to the people than the Chilkat or Raven's Tail robe. Russian influence played a great part in the evolution of the button blanket, since trade provided the Tlingit people with the (usually) red, black, or blue felt from which the blanket is made. These robes are often intricately decorated with clan emblems through appliqué variations, mother of pearl (shell) button outlines, or solid beading of the design.

People wear the robes at gatherings in order to display their lineage and family crest, in much the same way as the Chilkat robe is worn.

Robes of any type are almost always worn with an appropriate headdress. Headdresses can be as simple as a headband or as intricate and rich as a carved cedar potlatch hat, which displays a crest and is decorated with color, inlaid with abalone shell, and finished with ermine. Russian influence inspired the sailor-style hat that many women wear for dancing, made of the same felt as the button blanket and completed with beaded tassels. Ornamentation traditionally included hair dressing, ear and nose piercing, labrets (piercings of the lower lip), bracelets, face painting, and tattooing. Most of these facets of adornment are practiced today, excluding the labret.

The formal dress of the Tlingit people not only displays power, wealth, and lineage; it is also an integral part of the social practices of the Tlingit. Ancestors and the opposite moiety (Raven or Wolf) are honored in the making and handling of a garment. Importance is also placed on the maker of the garment and the relationship of his or her clan to the clan of the wearer.

Traditional Arts and Crafts In addition to the ornate robes and headdresses made for ceremonial occasions, the Tlingit people are renowned for their elaborate totem poles and carved wooden canoes. Totem poles are tall wooden posts carved with bone or metal tools. Taken together, the images on a totem pole tell a story that falls into one of four main categories: family crest histories, clan histories, folk legends, or memorials. Today, many craftspeople carry on this tradition, and visitors can see both early and modern totem poles at the Sitka National Historical Park and the Totem Heritage Center in Ketchikan. Pole raisings are important events for many Tlingit people and are often accompanied by a potlatch.

As well as serving as an important means of transportation and hunting, canoes were also a source of artistic expression for coastal Tlingit tribes. Varying in size and shape based on their intended function, these boats were dugouts made from trees and could be up to 40 feet long with a carrying capacity of more than fifty people. Typically using red cedar or Sitka spruce, canoe makers employed adzes to hollow the log. They then softened it with boiling water and hot stones and shaped it to form bowed sides and a prow and stern. Canoes were usually painted and decorated using natural materials such as minerals or spruce gum. Craftsmen continue to make canoes by traditional methods, despite the time it takes. Traditional canoe making has become a symbol of the regeneration of Alaska Native culture in modern times. In 2008 the Smithsonian Institution commissioned a traditional Tlingit canoe that was paddled up the Potomac River before being displayed permanently in the Smithsonian Ocean Hall.

Once an integral part of Tlingit spirituality, shamans displayed their relationship with the spirit world through masks. Shaman masks traditionally represented the supernatural powers that shamans contacted while concealing the human form beneath. While the practice of shamanism has all but disappeared from contemporary Tlingit culture, these masks maintain an important role in Tlingit art. Also made from wood, shamans' masks covered either the entire face or, more frequently, only the top portion; they were intricately carved and painted. Some carvings represented animals in order to demonstrate the link between human and beast, but often the designs included humanistic features or distorted and asymmetrical semihuman features. Shamans' masks were only used during ceremonies and festivities. Contemporary artists continue this craft, elaborating and adapting their works of art to incorporate modern influences.

Dances and Songs Music is a highly valued part of Tlingit culture, so much so that songs and dances are treated as property of a clan or house and can only be performed with permission; doing so without permission was once considered a punishable offense. Today, music remains an integral aspect of Tlingit gatherings, and there are songs for nearly every occasion. Entrance songs typically mark the beginning of many celebrations. During an entrance song a singer and drummer lead viewers to gaze at dancers who display the crests of their clans. Additional types of songs include potlatch songs, mourning songs, *gunalcheesh* (thank you) songs, shaman songs, and others. Many songs do not contain discernable words, making them easy for younger generations to learn, while other songs are written in older dialects and have become untranslatable. Songs are often accompanied by drums, carved rattles, and dancing.

Similar to Tlingit songs, Tlingit dances are also specific to an occasion and carry a message. In traditional dances, performers wear regalia such as Chilkat blankets, masks, and headdresses; they are typically accompanied by a drum and move in such a way as to best display their exquisite regalia, often by spinning in circles. Dancers perform both individually and in groups, depending on the ceremony or occasion. Dancing continues to be a key aspect of Tlingit culture as an important way to carry on tradition. Modern Tlingit people of all ages maintain a connection to their culture through dancing with tribal troupes. Traditional songs and dances have been preserved in large part through the efforts of committed elders. Charlie Joseph Sr., also known as Kaal.átk', was a Tlingit elder who lived a precontact subsistence lifestyle well into the twentieth century and maintained a thorough knowledge of Tlingit traditions. Joseph has been recognized for his documentations of Tlingit songs and legends, which continue to be of use to contemporary cultural groups.

A widespread interest in Tlingit dancing, singing, and stories has generated the revival and development of a large number of traditional performance groups. The renowned Geisan Dancers of Haines have performed internationally, as have Kake's Keex' Kwaan Dancers and Sealaska Heritage Foundation's NaaKahidi Theatre. Other major dance groups include the Noow Tlein Dancers of Sitka, the acclaimed children's group Gájaa Héen Dancers of Sitka, and the Mt. Fairweather Dancers (led for many years by the late T'akdeintaan matriarch, Katherine Mills). Less famous but notable performance groups include the Tlingit and Haida Dancers of Anchorage, the Angoon Eagles, the Angoon Ravens, the Marks Trail Dancers, the Mt. Juneau Tlingit Dancers, the Mt. St. Elias Dancers, the Seetka Kwaan Dancers, the Killerwhale Clan, the Klukwan Chilkat Dancers, and the Klawock Heinya Dancers.

Holidays Potlatches are an integral part of both Tlingit history and modern-day life. A potlatch is a giant feast that marks a time for showing respect, paying debts, and displaying wealth. Tlingit people give grandly at potlatches to raise their stature. Traditionally, respect and honor for ancestry, name, house crest, family, and wealth determined how elaborate a potlatch was. Potlatches are given for various reasons and may be planned for years in advance. The most common potlatches given today are funeral potlatches, the 40-Day Party, memorial potlatches, adoption potlatches, naming potlatches, totem-pole-raising potlatches, and house- or lodge-building potlatches.

Sometimes, less elaborate potlatches are held to give names to youngsters or to those who have earned a new or second name. A naming potlatch may be held in conjunction with a memorial potlatch, as may an adoption potlatch. Adoption ceremonies are held for one or more individuals who have proven themselves by their long-term commitment to a Tlingit family or community and who have become members of the clan. The new members receive gifts and names and are obligated from that day forward to uphold the ways of that clan. Ceremony is always part of a potlatch: participants wear traditional dress, make painstaking preparations, give formal speeches in Tlingit and English, and observe proper Tlingit etiquette.

Health Care Issues and Practices Existing traditional health care practices consist primarily of physical healing through diet and local medicines, although this custom is rather limited. A few people today still use teas brewed from the devil's club; Hudson Bay tea leaves; and the roots, leaves, and flowers of various plants that cleanse the body, boost the immune system, and even heal wounds and illnesses. Overall, the Tlingit people use modern medical treatment through the existing, federally established health care systems.

Some Tlingit believe that people have a relationship with spirits, can communicate with animals and birds, and can learn from all life forms. Those who vocalize these experiences or abilities, however, feel vulnerable about being labelled mentally ill. Still considered radical by most modernized Tlingit and mental health specialists, this aspect of Tlingit culture is only now beginning to be discussed.

Health problems among the Tlingit are similar to those of other Alaska Native peoples. Extensive and continuous Indian Health Service data demonstrate their susceptibility to such illnesses as influenza, arthritis, hepatitis, cancer, and diabetes. Alcoholism is a more common disease, and although the suicide rate is not as high among the Tlingit as it is in more northern Native populations, it too has caused havoc and despair for some Tlingit communities. Providing social and emotional support for individuals, as well as for the family structure, has become a necessity for health care professionals and concerned tribal citizens. Since the Alaska Natives Commission's 1994 report was released stressing the link between health and culture, more and more communities are discussing the psychology of various forms of cultural and social oppression and how to recover spiritually, mentally, and physically.

Death and Burial Rituals Traditional Tlingit belief held that when the deceased were cremated, they sat near a warm hearth in a house in the spirit world, whereas those who were buried were fated to sit by the drafty door of the house, forever chilled by cold winds. Cremation was therefore the most common Tlingit death rite until the influence of Christianity made burial more acceptable in the late 1800s; burial has become the more widespread procedure. Regardless of whether the corpse is to be cremated or buried, a person's death requires a three-stage potlatch process to properly attend to the deceased person's transfer to the spirit world or future life. The first potlatch includes the mourning for and burial of the deceased and lasts between one and four days. George Emmons reported in his book *The Tlingit Indians* (1991) that this process traditionally took four to eight days. During this time the body is prepared for cremation or burial. Attendees sing songs of grief, and sometimes the family fasts. Feasts are prepared for guests of the opposite moiety. Afterward, the person is buried. During the second stage, a party is held for the deceased person's clan. The third stage, or memorial potlatch, usually takes place about a year later. The memorial potlatch is a ritual process of letting go emotionally of the deceased. It marks the final mourning and the release of the deceased to his or her future life; it includes speeches and payments of debts. The potlatch concludes with a celebration of life through happy stories and song. Although Canadian bans on potlatches existed in the mid-nineteenth century, contemporary Tlingit people uphold memorial potlatches as an important assertion of cultural continuity and as a symbol of an individual's passage into the afterlife.

THE REVERENCE OF THE CREST

Within Tlingit culture people belong to one of two lineages, Raven and Wolf, that are then divided into distinct matrilineal clans. Clans and clan houses have identifying crests, which represent the clan's "totem"; a totem can be any animal, celestial body, landmark, ancestor, or mystical being associated with that clan. A clan would be equally proud to have a snail or a killer whale on its crest, as there are no recognized superior species. When any "crested" living being dies, homage is expected, and appropriate respects are paid. Today, some indigenous communities of Southeast Alaska are still very sensitive to this tradition. Crests adorn paintings, totem poles, ceremonial garments, battle gear, dishes, and other objects and can be used in names of people, places, canoes, and heirlooms.

Each crest has stories and songs associated with it that belong to the clan. Ownership recognition of these sacred possessions among the Tlingit is a profound aspect of respect. Tlingit people do not tolerate misuse or misappropriation of their crests, names, songs, designs, stories, or other properties. Using a killer whale song, story, or crest design without acknowledging the owning clan or without its permission, for example, can be considered stealing. Almost a century ago two clans began a dispute over who owned a particular crest, a conflict discussed in detail in Frederica de Laguna's 1972 book *Under Mt. St. Elias: The History and Culture of the Yakutat Tlingit*. The issue developed into a social, political, and legal battle that lasted for decades and in many ways remains unresolved. Crest ownership sometimes conflicts with American notions of public domain. This contradiction, along with a growing interest by the general public in Tlingit art and culture, has raised concerns among the clans about how to protect their birthrights from distortion and acquisition.

FAMILY AND COMMUNITY LIFE

Ancient Tlingit people established a complex social structure based on matrilineal affiliation. At the highest level of this structure, Tlingit were divided into two descent groups, or moieties, either Raven or Wolf. Many Tlingit trace their lineage back to historical founding ancestors in one of these moieties. Each moiety is composed of dozens of clans, which are subdivided into house groups. For the most part Tlingit clans and house lineages lived in geographical dwelling areas called *kwáan*. A group of people who lived together in a *kwáan* shared residences, intermarried, and for the most part lived in peace. Some anthropological accounts estimate that fifteen to twenty *kwáan* existed at the time of European contact. Some house lineages and clans expanded beyond one *kwáan*. Among Tlingit communities are the *Sheet'ka-kwan* (People Dwelling on the Oceanside of Shee) of the Sitka area; the *Taku-kwan* of the Taku River area; and the *Heenya-kwan* of the Klawock area. Most of the urban communities of Southeast Alaska occupy the sites of many of the traditional *kwaan* communities.

Clan identities and relationships remain largely intact and are still acknowledged through naming and in social life. Biological relationships are one part of the family and clan structure; the other is the reincarnate relationship, which is based on the belief that descendants may be spiritually linked to clan ancestors, as expressed through traditional names that are passed on ceremonially. This aspect of Tlingit lineage is understood by the elders but not always acknowledged by younger members, although clan conferences are being held to educate people about this complex social system.

Prior to contact with Europeans, smaller Tlingit clans coexisted in a house or lodge, and larger clans lived in small settlements. Houses are the smallest unit of Tlingit society; they exercise rights, such as possessing property or access to fishing and hunting spots, and have their own chiefs. Like moieties and clans, houses are matrilineal and differentiated by their crests; the Snail House, the Brown Bear Den House, and the Owl House are some examples. Houses are still one of the ways Tlingit people identify themselves and their relationship to others.

Gender Roles Prior to contact with Europeans, labor in Tlingit society was complementary but not neatly divided between the genders. Men and women shared in the pursuit and production of food. Generally, men were responsible for hunting and fishing, and women were in charge of processing game and fish into food and other materials. Both genders also worked to gather berries and some shellfish. Because the Tlingit were a matrilineal society, women were awarded special duties: they often served as household bookkeepers, overseeing stores of goods and, later, money, and were generally in charge of the family home. This position gave Tlingit women a great deal of influence. While men governed more public aspects of Tlingit society, women were often looked to for private council, and they exercised considerable power both publicly and behind the scenes. Matters of rank and prestige outweighed issues of gender, however.

Education Tlingit children were traditionally raised with a great deal of family and community support. Uncles and aunts played a major role in a child's progress into adulthood. Matrilineal uncles and aunts often taught children how to survive physically and how to participate in society, and anyone from the clan could conceivably reprimand or guide the child. The role of the aunts and uncles has diminished, but in smaller, predominantly Tlingit communities, some children are still raised this way. Most Tlingit children are raised in typical American nuclear family households, however, and are instructed in American schools as are other American children.

Tlingit people place a strong emphasis on education, which elders point to as a main source of cultural preservation. Many Tlingit earn higher education degrees: 12 percent of the Tlingit population reported achieving a bachelor's degree or higher in the 2010 U.S. Census, which is above the average for American Indian and Alaska Native population. Traditional education usually occurs in dance groups, traditional survival camps, art camps, and Native education projects through the public education system.

Courtship and Weddings A defining feature of Tlingit marriage is the matching of opposites: an individual must marry someone of the opposite moiety. Generally speaking, courtship did not exist in traditional Tlingit society. Marriages were most often arranged by clan elders in consultation with the family. Matches aimed to pair individuals who held comparable ranking, and in the cases of high-ranking families, such matches were made for political advantage. Marriage ceremonies were not typically accompanied by pomp but instead involved the exchange of gifts and the bride's transfer to her husband's clan. More prominent families occasionally hosted a potlatch as a reception.

In Tlingit society today, a great deal of interethnic marriage occurs, changing some of the dynamics of family and clan relationships. Many Tlingit people marry Euro-Americans, and a few marry into other races or other tribes. Some of the interracial families choose to move away from the Tlingit communities and from Tlingit life. Others live in the communities but do not participate in traditional Tlingit activities. A few of the non-Tlingit partners are adopted by a clan of the opposite moiety of their Tlingit spouse and thereby further their children's participation in Tlingit society.

EMPLOYMENT AND ECONOMIC CONDITIONS

The Tlingit economy at time of contact was a subsistence economy supported by intensive trade. The cash economy and the American systems of ownership altered the lifestyle of Tlingit people dramatically; however, many Tlingit have adapted successfully. Job seekers find occupations primarily in logging and forestry, fishing and the marine industry, tourism, and other business enterprises or government services. Because of the emphasis on education, a significant number of Tlingit people work in professional positions as lawyers, health care specialists, and educators. The Sealaska Corporation and village corporations created under ANCSA also provide some employment in blue-collar work, office work, and corporate management. Not all positions within the corporations are held by Tlingit and Haida, as some jobs are filled by non-Natives. The corporations provide dividends—the only direct ANCSA compensation families receive for land they have lost, but these dividends are generally modest. Some of the village corporations have produced some lump sum dividends through timber sales and one-time sale of NOL's (net operating losses) to other corporations for tax purposes, but these windfalls are infrequent.

Since the ANCSA bill passed in 1971, differences in wealth distribution among the Tlingit have arisen that did not previously exist. Some of the Tlingit people are economically disadvantaged and can no longer rely on subsistence for survival. Welfare reliance has become an all-too-common reality for many families, while those in political and corporate positions may become more financially independent. As a result, shareholder dissension in the various Native corporations has increased periodically and has sometimes become very public. The issue has been explored extensively by contemporary scholars, including Kirk Dombrowski, a professor of anthropology at the John Jay College of Criminal Justice. In his 2001 book *Against Culture: Development, Politics, and Religion in Indian Alaska*, Dombrowski considered the relationship between "local, village-based inequalities" and the "larger process of resource extraction" that characterizes the Alaskan coastal region and plays out in the lives of Alaska Native communities.

In 2004 the University of Alaska Anchorage Institute of Social and Economic Research reported that, despite gaining more than 8,000 jobs between 1990 and 2000, Alaska Natives still suffered from high unemployment rates. Moreover, the group found that the income of Alaska Natives was only 50 to 60 percent of non-Native Alaskans' income, and Native families were three times as likely to be below the poverty line. Many of these conditions remained in the second decade of the twenty-first century. Tribal organizations such as the Central Council of Tlingit and Haida Indian Tribes of Alaska have stepped in to offer a variety of assistance programs for tribal members, including GED tutoring, job placement assistance, job training, Head Start, caregiver support for the elderly, and many others. Such programs offer Tlingit tribal members opportunities to be more competitive in the Alaska job market.

POLITICS AND GOVERNMENT

Tlingit people have been and continue to be very active in community and clan politics and in tribal, city, and state governments. Many Tlingit tribal members won seats in the territorial legislature in the 1920s and beyond, setting in motion Tlingit involvement in all aspects of politics and government. Tlingit activist and Alaska Native Sisterhood leader Elizabeth Peratrovich testified before the territorial legislature on February 8, 1945, making a plea for justice and equality regardless of race that prompted the signing of an antidiscrimination bill. Her efforts as a civil rights leader set a precedent for active Tlingit political involvement. Many Tlingit men fought in the World Wars, Korea, and Vietnam. Tlingit participation in the U.S. armed forces is common and generally supported by the families and their communities. Military honor guards often play a part in Tlingit ceremonies.

The Indian Child Welfare Act of 1978 provided the first real means for traditional Tlingit law to be practiced and recognized by the American government.

Since the act was passed, several tribal courts have been created and tribal judges placed. Today, Sitka is home to a very active tribal court, with Tlingit judges presiding over civil suits. Unlike tribal courts of the continental United States, however, Tlingit country tribal courts are not yet active in determining criminal cases, but tribal councils are considering such jurisdiction. Tribal councils and tribal courts are a much more integral part of the communities than they were twenty years ago, and many issues today are addressed and resolved by Tlingit communities at this level. In the 2010s the push for sovereignty in Tlingit country manifested in debates about jurisdiction over child support cases.

Since their formation ANCSA-created corporations have wielded a great deal of political power. Tlingit and Haida corporate officials are often courted by legislators and businessmen because of their influence on tribal members. The corporations are a strong lobby group in Alaska's capital because they not only control lands and assets but represent more than 17,000 Tlingit and Haida shareholders. Throughout the late twentieth century and into the twenty-first, Tlingit people have fought for rights to subsistence harvesting and fishing practices, for Alaskan Native equality with non-natives, and for sovereignty. A small faction called for the "decolonization" of the Tlingit tribe, and although this appeal was disregarded, it represented the larger questions faced by American Indians and Native Alaskans in the early decades of the twenty-first century regarding their tenuous position as both tribal members and U.S. citizens. Tlingit candidates for office tend to run on the Democratic ticket, including state house legislators Albert Kookesh (1997) and Bill Thomas (2005). Tlingit individuals also tend to support the Democratic Party. The 2012 Alaska state legislature was the first one in nearly twenty years that had no Tlingit representatives. Groups such as the nonprofit organization Alaska Native Vote work to register indigenous voters regardless party affiliation in hopes of increasing Native voting turnout at the polls.

NOTABLE INDIVIDUALS

Academia Elaine Abraham (1929–), bilingual educator, was the first Tlingit to enter the nursing profession. In the early years of her career, she cared for people on the Navajo reservation during a diphtheria epidemic, and in Alaska she nursed patients with tuberculosis and diphtheria during a time when many indigenous tribes feared modern medicine. Thereafter she served in major hospital supervisory positions and initiated such health programs as the original Southeast Health Aid Program and the Alaska Board of Health (now called the Alaska Native Health Board). An outstanding educator, she became assistant dean of students at Sheldon Jackson College and was appointed vice president of the college in 1972. In Fairbanks she cofounded the Alaska Native Language Center, and she established the Native Student

Services office while teaching the Tlingit language at Anchorage Community College. Her work in student services and indigenous understanding continues as Director of Alaska Native Studies for the University of Alaska in Anchorage. The recipient of many accolades, Abraham was inducted into the Alaska Women's Hall of Fame in 2011.

Lance Twitchell, who also goes by the Tlingit name X̱'unei, is a writer and professor whose work emphasizes the importance of Alaska Native language preservation and cultivation. Born in Skagway, Alaska, Twitchell graduated from the University of Minnesota with a degree in English and American Indian Studies and earned an MFA in creative writing from the University of Alaska Fairbanks. In addition to his numerous works of fiction, Twitchell is perhaps best known for his biweekly column in the *Juneau Empire* on Alaska Native languages and his contributions to the online news source the *Huffington Post*. He began teaching Tlingit language courses for the Skagway Traditional Council, where he was also a tribal administrator. He continued to teach Native languages in conjunction with anthropological and social sciences throughout his career and was a professor of Alaska Native languages at the University of Alaska Southeast. Twitchell has also been recognized for his multimedia art, which incorporates written media, Native design, and music.

Rosita Worl (1938–), anthropologist and president of the Sealaska Heritage Institute, grew up in Southeast Alaska and belongs to the Tlingit Eagle moiety and the Thunderbird clan. As a child Worl was removed from her family and taken to the Haines boarding house, where she learned to speak English and interact with non-Natives. As a young teenager she returned to her family home. After she completed high school, she attended Alaska Methodist University and later Harvard University, where she received a master's degree and a PhD in anthropology. Her academic research in the social sciences has focused on Alaska's arctic region and has included studies of the cultural ramifications of offshore oil drilling, as well as on indigenous whaling and seal-hunting practices. Worl teaches anthropology at the University of Alaska Southeast. As the president of the Sealaska Heritage Institute and a board member of the Sealaska Corporation, the Alaska Federation of Natives, and numerous other groups, Worl has spent her professional career working to uphold and protect Tlingit culture and Alaska Native cultural interests. She was inducted into the Alaska Women's Hall of Fame in 2012 in recognition of her academic and professional contributions to Tlingit, Haida, and Tsimshian cultural preservation.

Activism Elizabeth Peratrovich (1911–1958), civil rights activist, is recognized by Alaskans for her contributions to the equal rights struggle. In 1988 the State of Alaska set aside February 17 as Elizabeth Peratrovich Day; she is the only person in Alaska to have been honored in this way for political and social efforts. She is also celebrated annually by the Alaska Native Sisterhood (which she served as grand camp president) and the Alaska Native Brotherhood. She was inducted into the Alaska Women's Hall of Fame in 1989. Roy Peratrovich (1910–1989), Elizabeth's husband, is also honored by the Alaska Native Brotherhood and other Alaskans for his dedication to bettering the education system and for actively promoting school and social integration. His efforts frequently involved satirical letters to the newspapers that stimulated controversy and debate.

Government William L. Paul (1885–1977), attorney, became the first Alaska Native and first Tlingit in Alaska's territorial House of Representatives. He contributed to equal rights, racial understanding, and settlement of land issues. Frank J. Peratrovich (1895–1984) received a University of Alaska honorary doctorate for public service for his work as the Mayor of Klawock and as a territorial legislator in the Alaska house and senate. He was the first Alaska Native not only to serve in the senate but also to become senate president (1948).

Andrew P. Hope (1896–1968) was an active politician and contributed to the advancement of Tlingit people and social change. He was instrumental in the development of the Alaska Native Brotherhood and was one of Alaska's few Native legislators. Other Tlingit legislators include Frank See (1915–1998), mayor and businessman from Hoonah; Frank Johnson (1894–1982), teacher and lobbyist; and Frank Price (1886–1946).

Literature Nora Marks Dauenhauer (1927–), poet, scholar, and linguist, has dedicated her work to the survival of the Tlingit language, stressing the importance of story in culture. Besides authoring such poetry collections as *The Droning Shaman* (1988), she has edited a number of works with her husband, Richard Dauenhauer, including the bilingual editions of Tlingit oral literature, *Haa Shuka, Our Ancestors: Tlingit Oral Narratives* (1987); *Haa Tuwunaagu Yis, for Healing Our Spirit: Tlingit Oratory* (1990); and *Anóoshi Lingít Aaní Ká: Russians in Tlingit America: The Battles of Sitka 1802 and 1804*, which won the American Book Award. Together they have developed Tlingit language instruction materials, including *Beginning Tlingit* (1976) and the *Tlingit Spelling Book (1984)*, and instructional audio tapes. Nora Dauenhauer has written numerous papers on the subjects of Tlingit language oratory, and culture and has coauthored many other articles.

Performance Orators and storytellers in Tlingit history and within the society today are numerous. Ssome of the most noteworthy include Amy Marvin/Kooteen (1912–); Chookan Sháa, who also serves as song leader and as a lead drummer for the Mt. Fairweather Dancers; Robert Zuboff/Shaadaax' (1893–1974), traditional storyteller and humorist;

Johnny Jackson/Gooch Éesh (1893–1985), storyteller, singer, and orator; and Jessie Dalton/Naa Tlaa (1903–1997), an influential bilingual orator. Another well-respected orator was Austin Hammond/Daanawáak (1910–1993), a traditions bearer and activist. Hammond dedicated a song to the Tlingit people just before he died for use in traditional gatherings and ceremony as the Tlingit national anthem.

Gary Waid (1948–), has bridged the Western stage and traditional performance for nearly two decades, performing nationally and internationally in such productions as *Coyote Builds North America* (at Juneau's Perseverance Theatre, as a solo actor) and *Fires on the Water* (at Juneau's NaaKahidi Theatre, as a leading storyteller). He has also performed in educational films such as *Shadow Walkers* (2006; sponsored by the Alaska State Department of Education and Sealaska Heritage Foundation). Besides performing regularly in Alaska and on tour, Waid appeared in New York in *Summer Faced Woman* (1986) and *Lilac and Flag* (1994), a Perseverance Theatre Production coproduced with the Talking Band. He also performs Shakespeare and standard Western repertoire.

David Kadashan/Kaatyé (1893–1976) was an avid musician in both Tlingit and contemporary Western music during the big band era and became a traditional orator and song leader of standing. Archie James Cavanaugh is a jazz musician and recording artist, best known for his album *Black and White Raven* (1980), with some selections recorded with the late great Kaw and Creek Native American jazz saxophonist, Jim Pepper.

Visual Arts Nathan Jackson (1938–) is a master carver who has exhibited his works—totem poles, masks, bentwood boxes, and house fronts—in New York, London, Chicago, Salt Lake City, and Seattle. Jackson's more than fifty totem poles are on permanent display throughout the world and in a variety of public locations. His eagle frontlet is the first aspect of Native culture to greet airline passengers deplaning in Ketchikan. Two of his 40-foot totem poles decorate the entrance to the Centennial Building in Juneau, and other areas display his restoration and reproduction work. While best known for his totem poles, Jackson has created works in numerous types of media.

Jennie Thlunaut/Shax´saani Kéek' (1890–1986) of the Kaagwaantaan clan, award-winning master Chilkat weaver, taught the ancient weaving style to others and thereby kept the art alive. Jennie has woven more than fifty robes and tunics and has received many honors and awards. In 1983 Alaska's Governor Bill Sheffield named a day in her honor, but she chose to share the distinction by renaming her day Yanwaa Sháa Day in recognition of her fellow clanswoman, a language expert. Emma Marks/Seigeigéi (1913–2006), Lukaax.ádi, is acclaimed for her award-winning beadwork. The beaded ceremonial robes, aprons, and dance shirts of Esther Littlefield of Sitka (1906–1997) are on display in lodges and museums; and a younger artist, Ernestine Hanlon of Hoonah creates, sells, and displays her intricate cedar and spruce basket weavings throughout Southeast Alaska.

Sue Folletti/Shaxʹsaani Kéekʹ (1953–) was named after Jenni Thlunaut and is also Kaagwaantaan. A silver carver, she creates clan and story bracelets of silver and gold, traditionally designed earrings, and pendants that are sold and displayed in numerous art shows and were featured at the Smithsonian Institute during the Crossroads of the Continents traveling exhibit. Other exceptional Tlingit art craftsmen include Ed Kasko, master carver and silversmith from Klukwan; Louis Minard, master silversmith from Sitka; and developing artists such as Norm Jackson, a silversmith and mask maker from Kake, and Odin Lonning (1953–), carver, silversmith, and drum maker.

MEDIA

PRINT

Juneau Empire

A daily newspaper serving the greater Juneau region; regularly publishes columns by Tlingit writers such as Bertrand Adams Sr./Kadashan and Lance Twitchell, who often write about Alaska Native issues and concerns. The publication also runs a "Tlingit Word of the Week" feature.

John R. Moses, Managing Editor
3100 Channel Drive
Juneau, Alaska 99801
Phone: (907) 586-3740
Fax: (907) 586-9097
URL: juneauempire.com

ORGANIZATIONS AND ASSOCIATIONS

Alaska Native Brotherhood (ANB)/Alaska Native Sisterhood (ANS)

ANB (founded in 1912) and ANS (founded in 1915) promote community, education, and justice through a governing grand camp and subordinate camps (local ANB and ANS groups). Native education and equal rights are some of the many issues addressed by the membership, as are Tlingit and Haida well-being and social standing. The following contact information is for Camp No. 2.

Andrew Ebona, President
320 West Willoughby Avenue #100
Juneau, Alaska 99801
Phone: (907) 586-2049
Fax: (907) 586-3301

Central Council of the Tlingit and Haida Indian Tribes of Alaska (CCTHITA)

Founded in 1965, the council provides trust services through the Bureau of Indian Affairs (BIA) to Tlingit and Haida people and Tlingit and Haida villages in land allotment cases, operates health and tribal employment programs, and issues educational grants and scholarships.

Edward K. Thomas, President
320 West Willoughby Avenue
Suite 300
Juneau, Alaska 99801-9983
Phone: (907) 586-1432
Fax: (907) 586-8970
Email: webmaster@ccthita.org
URL: www.ccthita.org

CCTHITA Tlingit & Haida Washington Chapter

Based in Seattle, the Washington chapter of the CCTHITA is a local council serving Alaska Natives of the Tlingit and Haida tribes living in the greater Seattle area, who number in the thousands. The chapter helps to provide programs and services for tribal members who cannot access such services out of Alaska, doing so by hosting numerous cultural fund-raising events.

Jania Garcia, President
P.O. Box 14011
Seattle, Washington 98114
Phone: (206) 782-4329
Email: tlingit.haida.wa@gmail.com
URL: www.thwachapter.org

San Francisco Tlingit & Haida Community Council

A chapter of the Central Council of Tlingit and Haida Tribes of Alaska, the San Francisco council offers California-based Tlingit and Haida peoples a way to connect with other Alaska Natives in order to build community and share resources for tribal members living in a new location. The group also hosts powwows and other celebrations, holds regular meetings, and offers scholarships to tribal members.

Kathryn Paddock, President
Phone: (415) 887-9315
Email: Info@sfthcc.org
URL: http://sfthcc.org

Sealaska Corporation

Established in 1971 by the Alaska Native Claims Settlement Act, which settled indigenous land claims in Alaska, the Sealaska Corporation is the Alaska Native corporation regionally responsible for the Tlingit and Haida tribes. In this capacity the Sealaska group holds titles and deeds to the homeland of these tribes and manages business enterprises on behalf of more than 17,000 primarily Tlingit, Haida, and Tsimshian shareholders.

Albert Kookesh, Board Chair
1 Sealaska Place
Suite 400
Juneau, Alaska 99801
Phone: (907) 586-1512
Fax: (907) 586-2304
Email: corpsec@sealaska.com
URL: www.sealaska.com/page/home

MUSEUMS AND RESEARCH CENTERS

Alaska State Museum

The museum houses a varied collection of Southeast Alaska Indian art, with elaborate displays of traditional Tlingit regalia, carvings, artifacts, and totem designs.

Scott Carrlee, Curator of Museum Services
395 Whittier Street
Juneau, Alaska 99811-1718
Phone: (907) 465-2901
Fax: (907) 465-2976
Email: scott.carrlee@Alaska.gov
URL: www.museums.state.ak.us

Sheldon Jackson Museum

This museum houses Tlingit regalia, a canoe, a large spruce
root basket collection, and other traditional items and
artifacts, including house posts, hooks, woodworking
tools, bentwood boxes, and armor. It also contains a
large variety of Aleut and Eskimo art. The museum's
gift shop sells baskets and other Tlingit art.

Lisa Bykonen, Museum Protection and Visitor Services
Supervisor
104 College Drive
Sitka, Alaska 99835
Phone: (907) 747-8981
Fax: (907) 747-3004
Email: lisa.bykonen@alaska.gov
URL: www.museums.state.ak.us/sheldon_jackson/
sjhome.html

Sheldon Museum and Cultural Center

The museum's displays share the history of Haines, the
gold rush era, and Tlingit art. The cultural center
provides books and flyers on different aspects of
Tlingit art and history, as well as live demonstrations
in traditional crafts.

Jerrie Clarke, Director
11 Main Street
P.O. Box 269
Haines, Alaska 99827
Phone: (907) 766-2366
Fax: (907) 766-2368
Email: director@sheldonmuseum.net
URL: www.sheldonmuseum.org

Southeast Alaska Indian Cultural Center (SAICC)

Located in the Sitka National Historical Park, the SAICC
displays a model panorama of the Tlingit battles
against the Russians in 1802 and 1804, elaborate
carved house posts, and artifacts. The center shows
historic films and has a large totem park outside the
structure. Classes are conducted in Tlingit carving,
silversmithing, and beadwork, and artists remain
in-house while completing their own projects.

106 Metlakatla
Sitka, Alaska 99835
Phone: (907) 747-8061

Fax: (907) 747-5938
URL: www.nps.gov/sitk/parkmgmt/southeast-alaska-
indian-cultural-center.htm

Totem Heritage Center

The center promotes Tlingit and Haida carving and
traditional art forms and designs by offering
firsthand instruction. It provides brochures and
other information on artists in the area as well as
instructional literature.

601 Deermount Street
Ketchikan, Alaska 99901
Phone: (907) 225-5900
Fax: (907) 225-5901
Email: museum@city.ketchikan.ak.us
URL: http://www.city.ketchikan.ak.us/departments/
museums/totem.html

SOURCES FOR ADDITIONAL STUDY

Case, David S., and David A. Voluck. *Alaska Natives and American Laws*. Fairbanks: University of Alaska Press, 2012.

Dauenhauer, Nora Marks, and Richard Dauenhauer. *Haa Ḵusteeyí, Our Culture: Tlingit Life Stories*. Seattle: University of Washington Press; and Juneau, AK: Sealaska Heritage Foundation, 1994.

Dombrowski, Kirk. *Against Culture: Development, Politics, and Religion in Indian Alaska*. Lincoln: University of Nebraska Press, 2001.

Emmons, George Thornton. *The Tlingit Indians*. Seattle: University of Washington Press, 1991.

Goldschmidt, Walter R., and Theodore Haas. *Haa Aaní, Our Land: Tlingit and Haida Land Rights and Use*. Edited with an introduction by Thomas F. Thornton. Seattle: University of Washington Press; and Juneau, AK: Sealaska Heritage Foundation, 1998. Originally published 1946.

Kan, Sergei. "Shamanism and Christianity: Modern-Day Tlingit Elders Look at the Past." *Ethnohistory* 38, no. 4 (1991): 363–87.

———. *Symbolic Immortality: The Tlingit Potlach of the Nineteenth Century*. Washington, D.C.: Smithsonian Institution Press, 1989.

Jonaitis, Aldona. *Art of the Northern Tlingit*. Seattle: University of Washington Press, 1986.

Thornton, Thomas F. "Alaska Native Subsistence: A Matter of Cultural Survival." *Cultural Survival Quarterly* 22 (1998): 29–34.

———. *Being and Place among the Tlingit*. Seattle: University of Washington Press, 2008.

TONGAN AMERICANS

Amy Cooper

OVERVIEW

Tongan Americans are immigrants or descendants of immigrants from the Kingdom of Tonga, an archipelago of more than 150 tropical islands located in the South Pacific Ocean. Tonga's cluster of islands forms a roughly north-south line that lies between Fiji (on the west) and the Cook Islands and French Polynesia (on the east). The national capital, Nuku'alofa, is located on the island of Tongatapu. The Tongan islands, situated on the geologic formation called the Tongan Trench, are vulnerable to volcanoes and earthquakes. Only 36 of the islands in the archipelago are inhabited. The islands experience a cool season between May and December and a warm season between December and May. The total land area is approximately 290 square miles (750 square kilometers), slightly smaller than the area of Kansas City, Missouri.

In 2012 the *CIA World Factbook* estimated the population of the Kingdom of Tonga as 106,146 people, over 90 percent of whom were of Polynesian descent. About 300 Europeans also live on the islands. Christianity is the primary religion, with more than 30,000 people belonging to the Free Wesleyan Church. In Tonga the monarch is the head of the church, which is related to the Methodist Church in the United States. Other Christian religions with significant membership in Tonga include the Roman Catholic and Mormon churches. The Tongan economy relies heavily on tourism and on remittances from Tongan communities abroad, though it also exports fish and other agricultural products, primarily to New Zealand.

Waves of Tongan immigrants first arrived in the United States in the 1950s and 1960s. Many were converts to Mormonism who moved to Utah as a result of intensive missionary activity of the Church of Jesus Christ of Latter-day Saints. Tongans also immigrated to Hawaii after World War II. More came during the 1970s, and there was another boom in the 1980s. In addition to Utah, Tongans lived in large West Coast cities like Los Angeles and San Francisco. Tongans began moving to North Texas during the 1970s and 1980s.

The U.S. Census Bureau's American Community Survey estimated that there were almost 51,000 Americans of Tongan descent in 2012. The majority of Tongan Americans lived in California (20,000),

Utah (11,000), and Hawaii (8,000), with large communities also in the states of Texas, Nevada, Arizona, and Washington.

HISTORY OF THE PEOPLE

Early History Tongans are descended from the Lapita peoples who settled on the main island group of Tongatapu about 3,000 years ago. Beginning in the 10th century, they were ruled by a line of sacred, hereditary kings and queens called the Tu'i Tonga. Tongans were skilled canoe builders and navigators and for many centuries had political and cultural influence over neighboring islands. In 1600 power was transferred to the Tu'i Kanokupolu, from whom the current rulers are descended.

The Dutch were the first Europeans to visit the islands. Jacob Le Maire arrived in 1616, and Abel Janszoon Tasman followed in 1643. In contrast to his predecessors' short stints in the islands, Captain James Cook visited the Tongans several times between 1773 and 1777. He named the Tongan islands the Friendly Islands because of the warmth shown him by the native inhabitants. The European explorers found a socially stratified society of 15,000 to 20,000 indigenous inhabitants, with several chiefdoms ruled by hereditary leaders who often competed with each other; the authority of the Tu'i Tonga, the supreme chief, was in decline. The first missionaries arrived in 1797 and encountered a period of great unrest in which various chiefdoms were fighting for dominance. In 1826 the Methodist Mission successfully introduced Christianity to Tonga, and Marists introduced Roman Catholicism in 1842. King George Tupou I, the first king of modern Tonga, who had earlier converted to Methodism, established a constitution in 1875. He ruled until 1893. During his reign, Tonga was unified and became an independent nation. Germany, Great Britain, and the United States recognized Tonga's independence in 1876, 1879, and 1888, respectively.

Modern Era George I was succeeded by his great-grandson, George II. Under George II's reign, Tonga renounced its independence in return for protection from German invasion. In 1900 it became a British protectorate, agreeing to conduct all foreign affairs through a British consul and giving Britain veto power over its foreign policy and finances. Queen

Salote Tupou III ruled from George II's death in 1918 until her death in 1965 and was succeeded by her son, who became Taufa'ahau Tupou IV. It was during his reign that Tonga became a fully independent nation, regaining control from Britain on June 4, 1970.

The last decades of the twentieth century in Tonga were marked by unrest, financial instability, and attempts at political reform. In late 2006 Taufa'ahau Tupou IV died and was succeeded by King George Tupou V. Riots destroyed much of the downtown of the capital Nuku'alofa amid demands for implementation of political reforms. During his short reign (2006–2012), significant pro-democracy constitutional change was instituted, giving commoners increased political representation and establishing a fully elected parliament. Although the constitutional changes were significant, they did not affect land-tenure issues, an enshrined and hierarchical system of land control. The Tongan constitution gives the power to the nobility to lease land allotments to commoners, which, while having deep cultural significance, caused insecurity as the Tongan population grew. When King George Tupou V died in March 2012, he was succeeded by his younger brother, Prince 'Ulukalala Lavaka Ata, who had served as prime minister from 2000 to 2006. He took the title King George Tupou VI.

SETTLEMENT IN THE UNITED STATES

The United States Census categorizes Tongans as Pacific Islanders, the smallest ethnic group represented in the country. Pacific Islanders (who include Fijians, Samoans, and numerous other groups) have only been enumerated distinctly from Asians and Native Hawaiians in the U.S. Census since 1980. Tongan Americans and other Pacific Islanders are often confused with Samoans and Hawaiians. Tongans first came to Laie, Hawaii, in 1916 (Hawaii was a U.S. territory at the time). The number of immigrants increased dramatically at the end of World War II, when Mormon labor missionaries from Tonga migrated to Hawaii to build the church's Laie Hawaii Temple, Church College of Hawaii, and Polynesian Cultural Center. The first record of a Tongan immigrating to the mainland United States was in 1956. According to Immigration and Naturalization Service (INS) records for the 1950s, 14 Tongans were admitted in 1958, 4 were admitted in 1960, and a record 119 arrived in 1966. During the 1970s, Tongan migration ranged from 133 admissions in 1976 to 809 in 1979.

In 1980 the U.S. Census counted 6,200 Tongan Americans. Over the next decade, the Tongan American population grew, and by 1990 Tongan Americans numbered approximately 17,600. From 2001 through 2010, an annual average of 300 Tongans obtained legal permanent residence in the United States; most were immediate relatives of Tongans already living there. During those same years, more than 3,000 Tongans were admitted annually as temporary workers.

In the mainland United States, Tongans have settled primarily on the West Coast. Nearly 22 percent live in Utah, according to the American Community Survey's estimates for 2006–2010. Tongans initially moved to Utah because of their Mormon faith, encouragement from the Mormon church, and educational opportunities. The Mormon church helped Tongans immigrate to the United States by providing student and work visas, employment, and the opportunity for Tongans of marriageable age to meet spouses. Subsequently, relatives of all faiths went to Utah to join family members already there and to enjoy the low cost of living.

In 2011 California passed a bill requiring the state to collect data on a greater number of ethnic groups, including Tongan residents. Tongans were estimated to number between 20,000 and 23,000, though some estimate an additional 10,000 undocumented Tongans in California. Before 2011, California had collected data on eleven Asian and Pacific Islander ethnicities: Chinese, Japanese, Filipino, Korean, Vietnamese, Asian Indian, Hawaiian, Guamanian, Samoan, Laotian, and Cambodian. After 2012 the state also counted Bangladeshi, Hmong, Indonesian, Malaysian, Pakistani, Sri Lankan, Taiwanese, Thai, Fijian, and Tongan, which together made up 13.4 percent of California's population in 2010. The largest concentration of Tongans in Southern California was in the Los Angeles area. Officials in San Mateo County in Northern California estimated that there were 13,000 Tongan Americans in their county. According to the American Community Survey estimates for 2006–2010, the states besides California and Utah with large numbers of Tongan Americans included Hawaii, Arizona, Nevada, Texas, and Washington.

LANGUAGE

Tongan is the national language of Tonga, but both Tongan and English are official languages. Schools primarily teach in Tongan, and English as a second language is emphasized at all levels of schooling. Some high schools use English-only instruction, and increasingly in the twenty-first century, English has been associated with higher education and employment opportunities. In 2012 the U.S. Census Bureau estimated that 84 percent of Tongans in the United States spoke English very well and 38 percent spoke only English.

There are three primary social classes in Tonga: the king, a nobility made up of thirty-three families, and commoners. The Tongan language has different speech levels for addressing the three different social classes: *lea fakatu'i* (language of the king), *lea fakahou'eiki* (language of the chiefs), and *lea tu'a* (language of the commoners). When addressing or referring to the king, God, or Jesus, the "king's language" is used. The language of the chiefs is used to talk to and about nobility. Among commoners, and when anyone talks about a commoner, commoner's language is used. An example of this stratified language is the

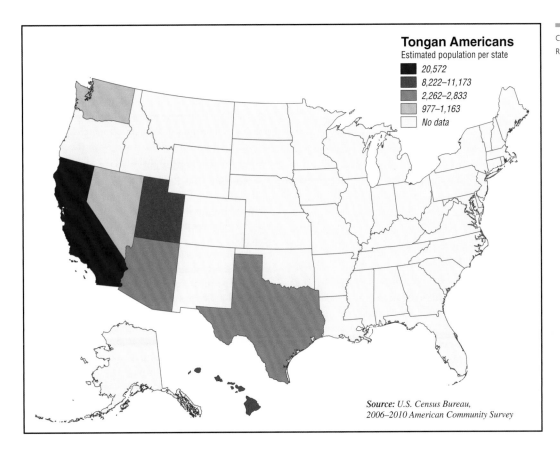

Tongan Americans
Estimated population per state

■ 20,572
■ 8,222–11,173
▨ 2,262–2,833
▨ 977–1,163
☐ No data

*Source: U.S. Census Bureau,
2006–2010 American Community Survey*

three verbs at different speech levels, all meaning "to go": *haʻele* (king), *meʻa* (chief), and *ʻalu* (commoner).

Linguistically, Tongan is related to Samoan and other Polynesian languages. Tongan vowels are pronounced as follows: *a* as in the English word "can"; *e* as in "bet"; *i* as in "in"; *o* as in "not"; and *u* as in "put." There are eleven consonants; *f, h, kl, m, n,* and *v* are pronounced as in English. However, the consonant *ng* (considered a single letter) is pronounced as in "singer" (not "linger"); the *p* is midway between the English "p" and "b;" the *s* has a slight "sh" sound; and the *t* is between the English "t" and "d." Accent stress is usually on the last syllable. An apostrophe called a glottal stop (') represents a space and a slight pause. Tongan is written in a standardized, Roman, orthography.

Greetings and Popular Expressions Common Tongan greetings and phrases include the following: *Mālō ʻe lelei*—Hello; *Mālō e tau maʻu e pongipongi ni*—Good morning; *Faka molemole*—Please; *Mālō*—Thank you; *Fēfē hake?*—How are you?; and *Nofo ā*—Goodbye.

RELIGION

Christian missionary activity has taken place in Tonga since 1797 and has had a great impact on the Tongan culture. Most Tongan Americans are Christian, primarily Methodist. In Tonga, according to the country's 2006 census, 37.3 percent of Tongans belonged to the

Free Wesleyan Church, 16.8 percent were Mormon, 15.6 percent belonged to the Free Church of Tonga, 11.3 percent of Tongans were Roman Catholic, and 14 percent belonged to other Christian denominations. In 2012 in California, where the majority of Tongan Americans lived, there were more than fifty Christian congregations of different denominations with Tongan ministries, clustered around Los Angeles and in the San Francisco Bay Area.

While denominations vary, Tongan traditions of dance and drumming may be interwoven with religious services and outreach. For instance, in 2001 the First United Methodist Church in Sanger, California, formed a hula dance and drum team that performed throughout the community. Tongan Americans value a religious service in their native language, and their ministers and congregations usually wear a *taʻovala*, the traditional woven mat wrapped around the waist. In 2012 the Pacific Islander National Caucus of United Methodists announced an expanded Pacific Islander ministry, saying, "There are now some 70 United Methodist congregations composed primarily of Pacific Islanders in the United States—a total of roughly 1.1 million people." The report also stated that the "system of mutuality that undergirds the Pacific Island culture and life plays an important role in ensuring that everyone participates in the world of building the ministry." In 2013 the United Methodists of the California-Nevada Annual

FISH IN COCONUT CREAM

Ingredients

For the fish:

2 cups red snapper fillets, skinned and pin bones removed, and cut into chunks

1 lemon, juice only

1 teaspoon salt

7 tablespoons coconut cream

For the salad:

2 tomatoes, chopped

½ cucumber, peeled and diced

1 shallot, finely sliced

½ fresh red chile, finely chopped

Preparation

Place fish chunks in a bowl. Pour over ⅘ of the lemon juice and salt. Leave to stand for 1 to 30 minutes depending on how raw you like your fish. The lemon juice and salt will 'cook' the fish. When the fish is 'cooked' to your liking, drain off the lemon juice and discard. Add the coconut cream and the remaining lemon juice to taste. Toss the salad ingredients together. To serve; mix the salad ingredients with the fish and season with salt and pepper.

Serves 2

Conference listed Tongan congregations in Palo Alto, Sacramento, Sunnyville–San Jose, San Carlos, San Bruno, and Reno, Nevada. The majority of United Methodist Tongan pastors in the United States were graduates of a private Methodist high school in Tonga.

In Tonga, where the king is the head of the church, religious observances affect the calendar. Government and shops close down for Good Friday. Tongans in the United States take that day off when possible. Tongans in both countries attend services leading up to the sunrise Easter service. Government in Tonga also takes a vacation that extends from the week before Christmas until the first week in January. Tongan Americans know that this is the best time to visit family in the South Pacific.

In 2011 there were thirty all-Tongan Mormon wards (congregations) in Utah, which made up three stakes (groups of congregations), two in Salt Lake County and one in adjacent Utah County.

CULTURE AND ASSIMILATION

Key to the preservation of the Tongan culture is the concept of *tauhi vaha'a*, a Tongan vow to maintain ties between family and community, helping to preserve the culture from outside influences. Among Tongan Americans, the older generation tried to pass on *anga fakatonga* (the Tongan way) of love and generosity toward family and community, but there was anxiety that among second-generation Tongan Americans the Tongan way was being transformed and deteriorating. Tongan culture is maintained and passed on at evening gatherings called *po-lotu*, where religion, family, and community are discussed, with the singing of hymns and other traditional songs.

Cuisine Tongan foods include various meats—pork, chicken, beef, lamb, and seafood—cooked wrapped in taro leaves with coconut milk. Meals will also include various starches such as yams, taro (a starchy tuber), sweet potatoes, and tapioca, and fresh tropical fruits. Traditional Tongan food may be cooked in an outdoor, dugout pit Tongans call an *umu* ("oo-moo"). The pit is lined with stones that are heated by a wood fire. Wrapped food is placed on the stones and then covered by blankets and then dirt. A whole pig may be roasted in the umu, or it may be spit roasted. Corned beef is popular and is also cooked with taro leaves (a dish called *lu pulu*). A feast may also be called an "umu," as in, "I'm throwing an umu in honor of my father who recently passed away." Guests may help to build the pit before the cooking gets started.

The drink made from the root of the kava plant is an important social and ceremonial beverage, often consumed by men in the evening at church and at social gatherings. Women are not allowed to drink it. It has a relaxing effect but is not alcoholic and is fully legal in the United States.

Traditional Dress A key element of Tongan and Tongan American identity is the *ta'ovala* ("tah oh vah-la"), a woven-leaf mat worn around the waist. Women sometimes wear a smaller version called a *kiekie* ("key-ah key-ah"). There are ta'ovala for everyday wear and fancier varieties for special occasions. In the United States, ta'ovala are worn at church, for funerals, and for other cultural celebrations.

Holidays Because Tongan Americans are Christian, they celebrate the Christian holidays of Christmas and Easter. They also celebrate the traditional New Year's Day (called *Ta'u Fo'ou*), during which children go caroling, singing hymns for friends and neighbors. Tongan Americans celebrate Sunday School Day, or Children's Day (called *FakaMē*), which is something like a first communion celebration. FakaMē is celebrated on the first Sunday in May and gives the children in the church an opportunity to dress in new clothes specially made for the occasion. The families attend church and then host a feast for the children. Another important holiday is Tonga Emancipation Day, celebrated on June 4 in commemoration of Tongan independence from Britain, which was gained in 1970.

In Tonga, on the island of Tongatapu, a weeklong celebration of the king's birthday occurs around July 4.

Named for the red flowering national tree, the Heilala Festival features sports and music competitions, feasts, military parades, a parade with decorated floats, and the annual crowning of Miss Heilala. Although Heilala is not celebrated in the United States, Tongan Americans, who visit their homeland often, may choose to go during this summer vacation time.

Tongan Methodist churches, in both Tonga and the United States, hold an annual fund-raising festival called the *Misinale*, or *Katoanga Misinale* (named for the English word "missionary"), where pledges are made to support the activities of the church. There may be dancing and singing while each family is called upon to make a donation.

Dances and Songs Tongans have a strong heritage of poetry, which is set to dance and music. The *lakalaka* is a formal, traditional line dance performed by both men and women that commemorates people, historical events, and places. New dances and songs are composed and choreographed for special occasions by Tongan poets. A more informal type of music is called *hiva kakala* (love songs). Young women perform solo dances (*tau'olunga*) to these songs at fund-raisers. The paddle dance (*me'etu'upaki*) features dancers who carry paddle-shaped boards painted or carved with abstract representations of the human body. Other popular dances include the *kailao*, which is a war dance, and the *ma'ulu'ulu*, which is an action dance similar to the lakalaka but performed while seated. Tongans also have a highly developed form of harmonization for singing hymns.

Traditional Arts and Crafts The most widely known Tongan crafts are bark cloth painting, called *tapa* or *ngatu*, and woven mats used as floor and wall coverings, bedding, and garments. The bark for the tapa is from the native Tongan mulberry tree and is soaked, beaten, and painted with dyes made from sap. Many pieces of bark may be glued together to make large mats to be worked on by a group of women. The woven mats are made from several different varieties of dried leaves, most commonly pandanus leaves. The art of tapa and mat making has continued in the United States, though the traditional materials are harder to obtain and sometimes substitutions are made.

Health Care Issues and Practices According to studies cited in a 2010 *California Journal of Health Promotion* article, Tongan Americans have high rates of chronic diseases, including diabetes, cardiovascular disease, and cancer. They are also more likely than the average American to be uninsured. In 2011 the American Community Survey reported that more than a quarter of Tongan Americans had no health insurance (while the U.S. average was 15 percent) and 22.4 percent of Tongan Americans with children under five years old were living below the poverty level (while the U.S. average was 18.8 percent). The issues of health, poverty, education, and immigration are

PIECES OF CLOTH, PIECES OF CULTURE

In 2004 the Oakland Craft and Cultural Arts Gallery in California held the exhibit *Pieces of Cloth, Pieces of Culture: Tapa from Tonga and the Pacific Islands*. On display were several dozen pieces of tapa and cultural objects from the anthropology collection of the California Academy of Sciences in San Francisco. In addition, a new, full-sized tapa was made for the exhibit by artist Siu Tuita and twelve other Tongan American women artists in collaboration with the Center for Art and Public Life at the California College of the Arts (CCA). Measuring 24 by 26 feet, it was said to be the first full-sized tapa created in the mainland United States. The project also involved a video documentary titled *Pieces of Cloth, Pieces of Culture: Tapa Making and Community Collaboration*, which may be purchased on DVD from the Center for Art and Public Life.

especially interrelated because family and community reliance is so important to the Tongan community. In 2011 an estimated 18.5 percent of Tongan Americans over the age of twenty-five had not graduated from high school (while the U.S. average was 14.4), and only 3.2 percent had graduate or professional degrees (as opposed to 10.5 percent for the overall U.S. population). Health professionals have seen a need to develop practices and materials specific to the Tongan American community. For instance, in 2010 the Tongan Community Service Center in Los Angeles developed Tongan-language educational materials on breast and cervical cancer.

FAMILY AND COMMUNITY LIFE

Both Tongan island communities and Tongan American communities are generally organized around large family units called *kainga*. The kainga encompass all blood relatives and can include people other than blood relations. Tongans see themselves as members of several overlapping groups of descent, and each person has a rank within the family structure. In this complex system, Tongans trace descent through both the mother's and father's lineage, called unilineal descent, and have social obligations to both groups.

Tongan households are large and include many generations and relations. Aunts, uncles, cousins, and other family members may all, at some time or another, live under the same roof, for the household can shift, depending on the needs of work, marriage, or education. Tongans have very specific obligations to each family member, depending on rank. They also rely on the status that their ties to the chiefs provide and hold strongly to the protocol of social obligations. Many Tongans are also tied to large social groups, including church groups (probably the most important), sports groups, and community associations.

Although many Tongan Americans feel that residence in the United States relieves them from the social obligations to village chiefs and others of high rank, when Tongan chiefs and their families visit the United States, they are typically welcomed with gifts and special treatment.

Family Celebrations Tongan Americans mark many different family celebrations in similar ways. Birthdays, weddings, funerals, graduations, and chiefly installment ceremonies are celebrated within families by feasts and the exchange of gifts, usually painted tapa cloth and woven pandanus mats. Women provide the *koloa*, or ceremonial wealth, which is normally redistributed at the next event. Men provide the food for the feast. In the United States it can be difficult to obtain tapa cloth and mats, so as a replacement Tongan American women create quilts as koloa. This has enabled Tongan Americans to participate in traditional exchanges more easily.

Courtship and Weddings In Tonga communities, a wedding may last up to three days. On the first day, tapa cloth may be presented to in-laws. The church ceremony usually happens on a Saturday, followed by a feast and more exchanges of tapa and other gifts. The bride and groom are each wrapped in special ta'ovala. The next day, as part of what is called the First Sunday celebration, newlyweds attend their first Sunday church service as a couple.

Although many Tongan Americans feel that residence in the United States relieves them from the social obligations to village chiefs and others of high rank, when Tongan chiefs and their families visit the United States, they are typically welcomed with gifts and special treatment.

Funerals In Tongan, a funeral is called a *putu*. The Tongan tradition is to hold religious services each night for the deceased until the burial. Families set the length of mourning times when a member dies. Tongan Americans carry on the tradition of the extended family preparing food and gathering for up to five days after the funeral. For Tongan funerals, a dark brown ta'ovala is worn. The size of the ta'ovala indicates the mourner's relationship to the deceased. A larger ta'ovala signifies a closer relationship. When a relative or close friend dies, adults and children wear black clothing and a ta'ovala.

Gender Roles Tongan culture is strongly gendered in particular and unique ways. Traditionally, Tongan women are associated with indoor, home-based work, but also with chiefly and dignified qualities. Men are associated with activity, outside work, and childish qualities. Tongan women symbolically rank lower than their husbands but higher than their brothers. A brother and all of his children are especially obligated to support his sister and her children. Tongan women and men spend much of their time in same-sex groups. In Tonga there is also a recognized "third gender" called *fakaleiti*, meaning "like a lady," in which biological males take on many qualities and roles associated with women in Tongan society. Fakaleiti are not necessarily gay men as understood in the United States, although, because Tongan Americans travel back and forth between the United States and Tonga, there is mutual influence.

Education Tonga boasts a literacy rate of nearly 100 percent. Although there was universal public education and almost universal literacy in Tonga, Tongan families did not emphasize higher education once they were in the United States. According to the American Community Survey's estimates in 2011, 18.5 percent of Tongan Americans age twenty-five or older had less than a high school diploma. Although more women than men (83 percent versus 79 percent) had at least a high school diploma, more men than women (15 percent versus 13 percent) had bachelor's and graduate degrees.

EMPLOYMENT AND ECONOMIC CONDITIONS

Tonga's economy is still agriculturally based, but there is a growing pattern of middle-class Tongans who have been educated abroad and who have started small businesses. Tonga also has an important tourist trade. Up to 46 percent of the "tourists" to Tonga are Tongans who have emigrated and are returning to visit. Tongans living abroad in the United States, New Zealand or Australia, often send money to family members still living on the islands.

Kainga participate in resource-sharing characteristic of the traditional redistributive economy in Tonga. This economy is based on three core values: *'ofa* (love), *faka'apa'apa* (respect), and *kavenga* (responsibility). Family groups rely on traditional economic cooperation to raise money for important occasions such as weddings, funerals, graduation, and home building. Tongan American family groups regularly participate in this tradition, though they are often not geographically near their families. Thus, the social structure necessitates that a Tongan American living in Utah or California fulfill an economic obligation to a relative still living in Tonga. The same Tongan American may receive goods from Tonga for an event in the future. In the United States, first-generation Tongan Americans could generally make more money than in Tonga, but by U.S. standards, they still are in relatively low-paying and low-status jobs. Tongan Americans may be more respected in the homeland—to which they have sent remittances and where they spend money when they visit—than they are in the United States, where they often live in crowded urban areas and hold low-paying service jobs. In Los Angeles in 2000, for instance, 28.5 percent of Tongans lived below the federal poverty line. In 2010 Tongan American unemployment was over 11 percent, higher than the national average.

POLITICS AND GOVERNMENT

The Kingdom of Tonga is a constitutional monarchy, and Tongans worldwide are both interested in the democratization of Tonga and loyal to the traditional king and class of chiefs. In the United States, the only Tongan elected to statewide office as of 2010 was Filia (Phil) Uipi, who served as a Republican in the Utah State Legislature from 1990 to 1994. Tongans in the United States tend to be more active in the Republican Party and to vote conservatively on social issues.

NOTABLE INDIVIDUALS

Journalism Sione Ake Mokofisi (1951–) is a Tongan American writer and photographer born Nukunuku, Tongatapu, Tonga. He was editor in chief of *Polynesia Magazine*, the online magazine published by the Literature and Arts Heritage Guild of Polynesia. Mokofisi has served as the editor of *Ke Alaka'i* (on the Brigham Young University–Hawaii campus), *Alaska Sports*, and *Rugby* magazines. He worked as a reporter at Hawaii's *Northshore News*, *Anchorage Daily News*, *Alaskan Journal of Commerce*, *Alaskan Oil & Natural Resources News*, and *Tongan International*, a Tongan newspaper based in New Zealand. He was also a founder of the Literature and Arts Heritage Guild.

Performing Arts Siu Tuita, artistic director of the Otufelenite Tongan Dance Ensemble, was born in Tonga and moved to Oakland, California, in the 1980s. A highly regarded musician, dancer, composer, and artist, Tuita teaches Tongan dance, song, and other cultural traditions, such as tapa making, to Tongans and non-Tongans in the San Francisco Bay Area.

The Jets, a pop music act popular in the 1980s, were a group of eight siblings from Minneapolis. Their parents, Maikeli and Vaké Wolfgramm, had emigrated from Tonga in 1965. Their big hits in the 1980s included "Crush On You" and "You Got It All." In the 1990s and into the twenty-first century the band recorded gospel music and music for the Mormon church, of which they are members.

Manisela "Monty" Fifita Sitake (1952–) was one of three founders of the Literature and Arts Heritage Guild of Polynesia in Salt Lake City, Utah. He was born in Nuku'alofa, Tonga, and graduated from Brigham Young University in Provo, Utah, with a degree in English literature in 1984. He, Filoi Manuma'a Mataele, and Sione Ake Mokofisi started the guild in 1998 to help Polynesians with artistic talents and skills. Sitake has served as the guild president since its inception. Sitake is also an author who writes

Indianapolis Colts defensive lineman Fili Moala #95, originally from Tonga, looks on from the sideline during a preseason game against the Pittsburgh Steelers in Pittsburgh, Pennsylvania 2012. GEORGE GOJKOVICH / GETTY IMAGES

in both Tongan and English. He prefers to write in his native tongue to preserve the Tongan language, and to encourage the importance of Polynesian literature. Sitake also plays guitar, ukulele, harmonica, and trumpet, and has recorded a compact disc mixing Tongan and western music.

Filoi Manuma'a Mataele (1968–) is vice president of the Literature and Arts Heritage Guild of Polynesia in Salt Lake City, Utah. He was born in Nuku'alofa, Tonga. He is also involved in small business and management.

Politics Filia (Phil) Uipi (1949–) was the first Polynesian to become a member of the Utah House of Representatives and the first Tongan to become a legislator outside of Tonga. He was born in Fotuha'a, Tonga. Upon graduating from the University of Utah Law School, Uipi was admitted to the state bar in 1986. A Republican, he was elected to two terms in the state legislature, representing District 36 from 1990 to 1994. He chaired the House Judiciary Committee during his second term. His voice was among those rallying for the establishment of the state Office of Polynesian Affairs (OPA). After leaving elected office, he served as the first chairman of the OPA's Polynesian Advisory Council.

Sports Vai Sikahema (1962–) was an NFL player (for the St. Louis Cardinals, the Philadelphia Eagles, and the Green Bay Packers) and sports anchor. He was born and grew up in Tonga, moving to the United States during high school. He attended Brigham Young University. Sikahema retired from the NFL in 1994 and became a sports anchor for NBC.

Etuini Haloti Ngata (1984–) began playing for the Baltimore Ravens of the NFL in 2006. He was born in California and played college football for the University of Oregon Ducks. Ngata has been chosen to play in the Pro Bowl four times.

MEDIA

Taimi 'o Tonga

Founded in 1989, *Taimi 'o Tonga* is a weekly newspaper distributed in Tonga, New Zealand, Australia, and the United States. Its associated website is *Taimi Online*.

Kalafi Moala, Publisher
Taimi Media Network
Vaiola Motu'a
Nuku'alofa
Kingdom of Tonga
Email: times@kalianet.to
URL: www.taimionline.com

ORGANIZATIONS AND ASSOCIATIONS

National Tongan American Society

Founded in 1994, this group advocates for and empowers Tongan Americans in Utah and across the United States.

3007 South West Temple
Salt Lake City, Utah 84115
Phone: (801) 467-8712
URL: www.ntasutah.org

Pacific Islanders' Cultural Association (PICA)

Supports Pacific Islanders in Northern California. Includes information on all Pacific Islands, links, the Northern California Outrigger Canoe Association, and Pacific Island News sources.

1016 Lincoln Boulevard #5
San Francisco, California 94129-1721
Phone: (415) 281-0221
Email: webmaster@pica-org.org
URL: www.pica-org.org

Tongan Community Service Center

An organization founded in 1988 that provides social services—including job training, youth leadership programs, health programs, and immigration assistance—to the Tongan community in Southern California.

13030 Inglewood Avenue #104
Hawthorne, California 90250
Phone: (310) 679-9899
Fax: (310) 679-9299
Email: office@tonganla.org

Tongan Interfaith Collaborative

A project of the Peninsula Conflict Resolution Center that began in 2004 as a response to significant delinquency and violence among Tongan youth.

Marco Durazo
1660 South Amphlett Boulevard
Suite 219
San Mateo, California 94402
Phone: (650) 513-0330
Fax: (650) 513-0335
URL: www.pcrcweb.org/pcrc-services/violence-prevention/pacific-islander-community-projects/

MUSEUMS AND RESEARCH CENTERS

Polynesian Cultural Center (PCC)

This organization, founded in 1963, seeks to preserve Polynesian cultures and provides information and education about arts, crafts, and lore. It sponsors several recognition awards and funds the Institute for Polynesian Studies at the Brigham Young University–Hawaii campus.

55-370 Kamehameha Hwy
Laie, Hawaii 96762
Phone: (800) 367-7060
URL: www.polynesia.com

SOURCES FOR ADDITIONAL STUDY

Addo, Ping-Ann. *Creating a Nation with Cloth: Women, Wealth, and Tradition in the Tongan Diaspora*. New York: Berghahn Books, 2013.

Ferdon, Edwin N. *Early Tonga: As the Explorers Saw It, 1616–1810*. Tucson: University of Arizona Press, 1987.

Lee, Helen Morton. *Tongans Overseas: Between Two Shores*. Honolulu: University of Hawai'i Press, 2003.

Longman, Jere. "An Island for Tongans in a Texas High School." *New York Times*, Oct. 8, 2008.

MacPherson, Cluny; Bradd Shore; and Robert Franco, eds. *New Neighbours: Islanders in Adaptation*. Santa Cruz: Center for South Pacific Studies, University of California, 1978.

Māhina, 'Okusitino. *Reed Book of Tongan Proverbs =: Ko E Tohi 'a E Reed Ki He Lea Tonga Heliaki*. Auckland, New Zealand: Reed, 2004.

Moala, Kalafi. *Tonga: In Search of the Friendly Islands*. Hawaii: Pasifika Foundation, 2009.

Otsuka, Yuko. "Making a Case for Tongan as an Endangered Language." *Contemporary Pacific* 19, no. 2 (2007): 446+.

Small, Cathy. *Voyages: From Tongan Villages to American Suburbs*. Ithaca, NY: Cornell University Press, 1997. Print.

TRINIDADIAN AND TOBAGONIAN AMERICANS

N. Samuel Murrell

OVERVIEW

Trinidadian and Tobagonian Americans are immigrants or descendants of people from the Republic of Trinidad and Tobago. Located off the northeastern coast of Venezuela, the republic comprises the two most southerly islands in the West Indies. Tobago, which lies twenty miles northeast of Trinidad, measures only 117 square miles (303 square kilometers). The island of Trinidad makes up 94 percent of the republic's land mass and is home to 96 percent of the population. It has a land mass of 1,865 square miles (5,128 square kilometers) and is about the size of Delaware. The land is primarily plains, with some hills and low mountains. The country celebrated fifty years of independence and freedom from British colonial rule in 2012.

According to the *CIA World Factbook* estimate for 2012, Trinidad and Tobago had approximately 1.23 million residents, most of whom lived on Trinidad. While the population of Tobago is predominantly of African descent, Trinidad supports several ethnic groups, including East Indians (40.3 percent); Africans (39.6 percent); and Europeans, Chinese, and Lebanese (1 percent). The remaining 18 percent includes individuals of mixed heritage. Roman Catholics (26 percent), Hindus (22.5 percent), Protestant Christians (25.8 percent), Anglicans (10.9 percent), and Muslims (5.8 percent) are the dominant religious groups on the islands. Unlike most English-speaking Caribbean countries, whose economies are based on tourism, Trinidad and Tobago's economy is primarily industrial. The republic's capital, Port of Spain, is an important commercial center, producing beer, rum, plastics, lumber, and textiles. Chief exports of Trinidad and Tobago include oil, sugar, citrus fruit, asphalt, and coffee.

The first immigrants from Trinidad and Tobago began to arrive in the United States in the early 1600s, initially as volunteer indentured workers until the first ship of slaves arrived in the British colonies in North America in 1629. By the 1640s most of the colonies had passed laws depriving Trinidadians of their rights and classifying them as property. These immigrants worked primarily in agriculture in the Southern colonies. The next significant waves of immigration happened during

the 1900s and consisted of two main groups of people: the educated elite and rural poor classes. Immigrants from the rural poor classes came in search of jobs. They tended to work in the industrial sector in the Northeast. Some of the elite immigrated to the United States around the time of the Black Power movement in the 1970s; they were losing their grip on political power in the republic with the rise of nationalism and independence, and in 1972 Britain passed a law restricting immigration from the Commonwealth islands to the British Isles. The number of Trinidadian and Tobagonian immigrants to the United States rose again in the late 1980s after oil prices fell, hurting the islands' petroleum industry and sending the republic into a deep recession. Immigration remained relatively high until 2000, when the Republic of Trinidad and Tobago experienced strong economic growth, encouraging people to stay in their home country. Trinidadian and Tobagonian Americans are now the second-largest group of English-speaking West Indian immigrants in the United States.

An American Community Survey conducted by the U.S. Census Bureau in 2011 estimated the number of people of Trinidadian descent living in the United States at 195,840 (less than 0.1 percent of the total U.S. population). Areas with a significant number of Trinidad Americans include Lakeview, New York; Naranja, Florida; Mount Rainier, Maryland; and Orange, New Jersey.

HISTORY OF THE PEOPLE

Early History The history of Trinidad and Tobago is one of invasion, conquest, and colonization. On July 31, 1498, Christopher Columbus first encountered the islands, which were inhabited by about 40,000 native people (Arawaks and Caribs), whom he called Indians. Columbus named the larger island Trinidad, in honor of the Holy Trinity, and called the smaller island Concepcion. Shortly after the founding of the first city, San Jose de Oruna (Saint Joseph), in 1592, the islands' native population began dying out, largely because of exposure to European diseases and poor treatment, and by 1783 the native population had been reduced to fewer than 1,490 people. By 1800 they were virtually extinct.

Trinidad remained an underdeveloped outpost for almost two hundred years until the King of Spain issued the Cedular of Population in 1783 and began enticing planters to migrate to Trinidad with their slaves. In 1791 thousands of French colonists, fleeing the revolution in the French colony of Saint-Domingue (in Hispaniola), settled in Trinidad, bringing enslaved Africans with them. While Trinidad was largely ignored during the early years of colonization in the Americas, Tobago fell to a number of European explorers. The island passed through the hands of Great Britain, France, Holland, and other invading European countries at least twenty-two times during its history until it was finally ceded to Britain in 1814.

In January 1889 Trinidad and Tobago united as one nation under British rule. Africans had been brought to Tobago as slaves in the early 1600s and began to be imported into Trinidad in great numbers in the early 1700s. After the British government abolished slavery in 1834, East Indian and Chinese laborers were brought to Trinidad as indentured servants. Between 1842 and 1917 more than 170,000 East Indians, Chinese, and Portuguese (from Madeira) were enticed into working on the islands' vast plantations. Lured by the fertile soil and unexplored natural resources, many former American slaves migrated to the island as well. Consequently, by 1900 more than 70,000 blacks had settled in Trinidad and Tobago.

Modern Era Trinidad and Tobago was governed by British royalists and dominated by Scottish, French, and Spanish colonists until its independence in 1962. Prior to independence, nonwhites had little or no voice in government affairs. After World War I, however, they began protesting through strikes and demonstrations organized by such civil rights leaders as Arthur Cipriani, Uriah Buzz Butler, and others involved with the powerful Oil Field Workers Trade Union and the Manual and Metal Workers Union.

In 1947 the British government plotted the formation of a West Indian Federation, which came to fruition in 1958 and included the British colonies of Trinidad and Tobago, Barbados, Jamaica, and the Leeward and Windward Islands. Port of Spain was chosen as the federation's capital. The federation was designed to foster political and cultural solidarity and to break down economic barriers among the islands. It collapsed in 1961, however, when Jamaica seceded from the union, becoming an independent nation. Trinidad and Tobago attained independence on August 31, 1962, and became a republic within the Commonwealth in 1976. In 1965 Trinidad and Tobago joined the Organization of American States (OAS) and the Caribbean Free Trade Association (CARIFTA), which was renamed the Caribbean Community (Caricom) in 1974. Trinidad and Tobago enjoyed substantial prosperity from the 1960s to the early 1980s due to the success of the oil industry, but prices plummeted in the late 1980s, sending the country into a serious recession.

In 1990 the radical Muslim organization Jamaat-al-Muslimeen staged an attempted coup in the capital, Port of Spain. They blew up police headquarters, demanded the prime minister's resignation, and called for new elections. Armed members of the group occupied the lower House of Parliament, where they held several hostages, including the prime minister, politicians, and building staff. Still other members of the group seized control of a state-run television station. The government declared a state of emergency. The six-day standoff between the insurgents and the country's defense forces lasted until the Muslimeen were promised amnesty in exchange for releasing the hostages.

Trinidad's economy underwent radical changes in the 1990s. Sleepy villages grew into towns, and towns developed into bustling cities. Products from the United States that had been impossible to buy gradually made their way onto shelves in Trinidad and Tobago. By 2009 there were malls in many places across the country, some selling upscale European and American brands at European and American prices. Young people were carrying cell phones. Young men were wearing the baggy pants that had been popular in the United States five years earlier, and young women were showing cleavage. The skyline in Port of Spain was filling with skyscrapers in accordance with Prime Minister Patrick Manning's plans to elevate Trinidad to the status of a first-world nation by 2020.

If Trinidad were to succeed, it would be the first Caribbean country to do so. Thanks to the country's petroleum and natural gas industries, the economy prospered between 2000 and 2009, and the republic increased its humanitarian aid to neighboring countries. Because of its proximity to Venezuela, a country with vast oil reserves and whose president, Hugo Chávez, challenged U.S. power in the region, Trinidad became an area of interest to the United States. As of 2012 the FBI had established a base of operations there. Groups of Muslim extremists had also become more visible in Trinidad, leading to concerns that al-Qaida would attempt to gain a foothold there.

In general, religious orthodoxy was on the rise, existing side-by-side with the rampant consumerism popular with the dominant culture. The gap between the wealthy and the poor had widened, resulting in increased crime, including a dramatic rise in the number of murders. The prime minister called a "limited" state of emergency on August 22, 2011, in response to a wave of violent crime in which eleven people were killed in one weekend. Reports stated that the violence was a backlash against the government's earlier attempts to shut down drug trafficking on the islands.

SETTLEMENT IN THE UNITED STATES

Trinidadian and Tobagonian immigration to the United States, which dates back to the seventeenth century, was spasmodic and is best studied in relation to the major waves of Caribbean immigration. The first documented account of black immigration to the British colonies in North America from the Caribbean dates back to 1619, when a small group of voluntary indentured workers arrived in Jamestown, Virginia, on a Dutch frigate. The immigrants worked as free people until 1629, when a Portuguese vessel arrived with the first shipload of blacks captured off the west coast of Africa. In the 1640s Virginia and other states began instituting laws that took away the freedom of blacks and redefined them as chattel, or personal property. Trinidad, like many other islands in the British West Indies, served as a clearinghouse for slaves en route to North America. The region also acted as a "seasoning camp" where newly arrived blacks were "broken in" psychologically and physically to a life of slavery, as well as a place where they acquired biological resistance to deadly European diseases.

Since the turn of the twentieth century, there have been three distinct waves of Caribbean immigrants into the United States. The first wave was modest and lasted from about 1900 to the 1920s. Between 1899 and 1924 the number of documented, English-speaking Caribbean immigrants entering the United States increased annually from 412 in 1899 to 12,245 in 1924, although the actual number of Caribbean residents in the United States was probably twice as high. Immigration fell substantially after 1924, when the U.S. government established national quotas on African and Caribbean countries. By 1930 there were only 177,981 documented foreign blacks in the United States—less than 2 percent of the aggregate black population. Approximately 72,200 of the foreign blacks were first-generation emigrants from the English-speaking Caribbean.

Most Trinidadians and Tobagonians who entered the United States during that period were industrial workers, civil servants, laborers, and former soldiers disillusioned by the high unemployment rate in Trinidad and Tobago after World War I. The number of new arrivals dropped significantly during the Great Depression (1932–1937), as more blacks returned to the Caribbean than came to the United States. Only a small number of professionals and graduate students migrated to the United States in the years just prior to World War II, some with the intention of staying for a short time on a student or worker's visa and others planning to remain permanently.

The second and weakest immigration wave from the Caribbean to the United States was rather sporadic and occurred between the late 1930s and the passage of new immigration policies in the 1960s. As late as the 1950s, the number of Trinidadians and Tobagonians arriving in the United States was low in comparison to other foreign countries. This was partially due to the passage of the 1952 McCarran-Walter Act, which removed explicit race barriers to immigration but tightened the provisions for admission and deportation, making it easy for immigration officials to continue to prevent the entry of nonwhite

people. Prospective immigrants were screened using a strict and subjective loyalty test. U.S. immigration policy during the Cold War had a stated preference for "political" as opposed to "economic" refugees. Political refugees were those from eastern European countries in the Soviet bloc, whereas economic refugees tended to be from poor, developing countries in the southern hemisphere, including those from Trinidad and Tobago. After the republic achieved independence in 1962, only one hundred Trinidadian and Tobagonian immigrants were permitted to enter the United States annually.

Still, a small group, mainly from Trinidad's middle class, immigrated between the waning of the Depression and the changing of U.S. immigration laws. This group consisted mainly of white-collar workers, students, and people joining their families already living in the United States. With the opening of a U.S. naval base on Trinidad in 1940, Trinidadian and Tobagonian military personnel were stationed in the U.S. Virgin Islands and Florida, and some served under U.S. and British command in Europe. After World War II some of these soldiers migrated to America in search of jobs and improved economic opportunity. Because of laws restricting immigration, only 2,598 documented Trinidadian and Tobagonian immigrants entered the United States between 1960 and 1965.

The third and largest wave of Caribbean immigration occurred from 1965 to 2000. It was greatly influenced by the American civil rights movement, which exposed the racism inherent in U.S. immigration policy. The 1965 Hart-Cellar Immigration Reform Act, which established uniform limits of no more than 20,000 persons per country annually for the eastern hemisphere and no per country limits in the western hemisphere (up to a total of 120,000), enabled Trinidadian and Tobagonian immigrants to seek legal immigration and naturalization status in larger numbers. A clause in the Act of 1965, which gave preference to immigrants whose relatives were already U.S. citizens and therefore capable of sponsoring newcomers, also encouraged many Trinidadian and Tobagonian residents to migrate to the United States.

Census data concerning racial and ethnic groups in the United States is controversial. The census bureau's definitions of race are complex and constantly changing, making it hard to follow population trends over time. Another problem is the bureau's data collection methods, which assume that populations are evenly distributed throughout a census tract, even when reliable data from other sources show that they are not. Historically, people of Caribbean or West Indies descent have been lumped together, making it difficult to find information about Trinidadians and Tobagonians that is not mixed with information about Jamaicans, Bahamians, and others from the region.

That said, from 1966 to 1970, 23,367 Trinidadian and Tobagonian immigrants, primarily from the educated elite and rural poor classes, legally migrated to the United States. From 1971 to 1975 the figure climbed to 33,278. It dropped to 28,498 from 1976 to 1980, and only half that amount between 1981 and 1984, when the administration of President Ronald Reagan began placing greater restrictions on immigration to the United States. Fewer than 2,300 Trinidadian and Tobagonian immigrants arrived in 1984, and that number scarcely increased the following four years during Reagan's second term of office. In the 1980s more than half of Trinidadian and Tobagonian immigrants in the United States were living in New York City. A small number of European-Trinidadians migrated during the latter half of the twentieth century, primarily because, with the rise of nationalism on the islands, they were losing their grip on political power in the republic, and Britain had also restricted immigration from the Commonwealth islands to the British Isles. A larger number immigrated in the late 1980s through 2000 when oil prices fell, sending the republic into a deep recession. The number of people from Trinidad and Tobago coming to the United States dropped significantly between 2000 and 2010.

Of the approximately 195,000 Trinidadian Americans living in the United States in 2011, 34.2 percent had been born in the United States. Fifty-five percent of the foreign-born population had become naturalized citizens. The highest concentrations of Trinidadian Americans lived in Florida (29,186), New York (89,476), New Jersey (11,737), and Maryland (9, 471). Family connections, employment opportunities, racial tolerance, access to higher education, and weather conditions are some of the reasons for the heavy concentration of Trinidadian immigrants on the Eastern seaboard.

LANGUAGE

The official language of Trinidad and Tobago, a former British colony, is English, although Hindi is also spoken widely in Indian communities, both in the republic and in the United States. French, Spanish, and English patois are also common, as well as Hindustani, a dialect of Hindi. Trinidadians and Tobagonians speak English with a wide variety of accents and innovations due to the impact of Spanish, French, Indian, and African languages. The styles of English therefore range from standard British English, usually spoken in formal conversations, to the more common Trinidad English, a mixture of Spanish, French, British, and African. No sharp break exists between Trinidad English and standard English. Almost all Trinidadian and Tobagonian Americans speak English at home.

Greetings and Popular Expressions Trinidadian and Tobagonian greetings include "Wah happenen day?" (casual); "How is the daughter doing?" (casual); "Take care daughter" (good-bye to a young woman friend). Some devout Hindus and Muslims greet with the name *Krishna* or *Allah*, respectively. Common

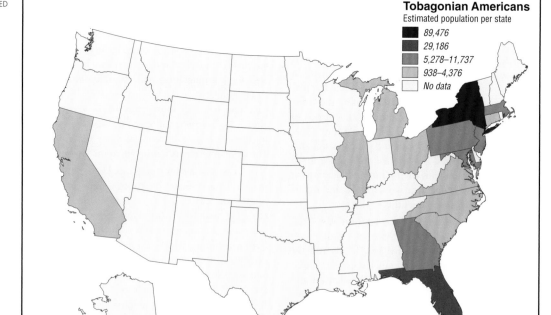

Trinidadian and Tobagonian Americans
Estimated population per state

- 89,476
- 29,186
- 5,278–11,737
- 938–4,376
- No data

Source: U.S. Census Bureau,
2006–2010 American Community Survey

Trinidadian and Tobagonian expressions include "Let's lime" (let's hang out); "Never see, come see" (someone who is unaccustomed to things); "Same khaki pants" (things never change); and "He/she doh eat nice" (to say a person is arrogant or formidable).

RELIGION

Because of British, Spanish, and French influences, most Trinidadian and Tobagonian citizens are associated, in some way, with Christianity. People of East Indian descent on the islands practice Hinduism and Islam. And a small number of people (9 percent) follow the African-centered religions of Shango, Spiritual Baptist, Obeah, Rastafari, or Rada. Shango and Spiritual Baptist, also known as "Shouters," are the two most common Afro-centric religious traditions, although Rastafari is growing in popularity.

Trinidadian Shango, which is part of the legacy of African traditional culture and religion, incorporates a mixture of Catholic rituals and elements of African spiritual beliefs and focuses on animal sacrifices, drums, and supernatural manifestations. Spiritual Baptists place great emphasis on participatory worship, and Obeah followers, sometimes called "shadow catchers," believe that they have supernatural powers, can control the spirits of the living and the dead, and can harness a shadow and force it to do specific protective tasks. Rastafarianism is a part secular, part religious movement that started with the poor and laborer classes in Jamaica in the 1930s and spread to other countries. Rastafarians ideology is anticolonialist and supports the economic and political independence of black people everywhere. The Rada religion arrived with tribal members from West Africa around 1850. Similar to Shango, Rada practitioners in Trinidad incorporate aspects of Roman Catholicism into their faith, as well as aspects of Hinduism and Haitian Voodoo.

Because of the negative stigma attached to these folk religions by other religious groups and by the general Trinidadian and Tobagonian public, it is difficult to tell how many immigrants are Spiritual Baptist, Shango, or Obeah followers in the United States. In order to be inconspicuous, many followers of such religions meet in private.

Trinidadians and Tobagonians generally practice two forms of baptism: infant baptism and adult baptism. Among the more traditional Christian denominations (Catholic, Anglican, Lutheran, Presbyterian, and Methodist), infants are baptized by sprinkling water on their heads. When they reach the age of accountability, a confirmation ceremony is performed. In other Protestant Christian and Afro-centric Christian traditions, the infants are blessed at a dedication ceremony and baptized after their faith in Christ is professed voluntarily. The subjects are dipped into a river, the sea, or a baptismal fount near the sanctuary by a minister or an elder of the church. Shangoes and Spiritual

Baptists often dip blindfolded individuals three times into the river or sea. Some of these baptismal practices operate underground in the United States.

CULTURE AND ASSIMILATION

Trinidadian and Tobagonian immigrants generally select one of two options: they either make a quick livelihood in the United States before returning home, or they join American society permanently, usually immersing themselves in black culture. Many of the early Trinidadians and Tobagonians age thirty-five and older did return to their native land. Later immigrants often chose the second option and increasingly became part of the distinctly Caribbean communities in New York City and Florida.

Trinidadian and Tobagonian immigrants have had to adjust in a number of ways while assimilating into American society. Some have given up their Trinidad and Tobago citizenship and strong ties to Caribbean nationalism for American citizenship and values. They have had to adjust to new cultural traditions and social roles in the United States, as well as American stereotypes of their ethnic groups. Trinidadian and Tobagonian immigrants of the first and second waves arrived in the United States at the height of Jim Crow segregation and, consequently, suffered tremendous racial prejudice. Even though they came from a country where racial categories and stereotypes were not unknown, they resented having to fight the social, political, and economic issues in American society. Many immigrants have also had to

Girls perform at the 41st West Indian American Day Parade and Carnival in Brooklyn, New York City. MICHEL SETBOUN/ GLOW IMAGES

PELAU

Ingredients

3 tablespoons vegetable oil

¾ cup sugar (white or brown)

1 2.5–3 pound chicken, cut up

1 onion, chopped

1 clove garlic, minced

1½ cup pigeon peas, soaked overnight

2 cups rice

3 cups water

1 cup coconut milk

2 cups hubbard squash, cubed

2 carrots, chopped

¼ cup chopped parsley

1 teaspoon dried thyme

1 bunch green onions, chopped including the green parts

¼ cup ketchup

3 tablespoons butter

Preparation

Heat the oil in a heavy pot or skillet. With the heat on high, add the sugar and let it caramelize until it is almost burned, stirring constantly. Add the chicken and stir until all the pieces are covered with the sugar. Reduce the heat to medium, add the onion and garlic and cook, stirring constantly for 1 minute.

Drain the pigeon peas and add them to the pot along with the rice, water, and coconut milk. Reduce the heat and simmer, covered, for 30 minutes.

Add the remaining ingredients, stir until well mixed, cover and continue simmering until the vegetables are tender, about 20–30 minutes.

Serves 4

adjust to a major change in weather, particularly in the North, which, for older generations, has been especially difficult. Traditionally "safe" Caribbean neighborhoods in New York City, for example, have become battle zones for gangs and drug dealers, and some immigrants have become victims of crimes. Moreover, Trinidadian and Tobagonian immigrants living in non-Caribbean communities often feel isolated; they carry the dual burden of speaking with a foreign accent and being visibly identifiable as a minority in a European-based society.

The experiences of Trinidadian and Tobagonian immigrants in the United States continue to be mixed. Historically their home country has a higher poverty rate than that of African Americans, but according to

a 2011 study done by the republic's Central Statistical Office, the poverty level in that country was 21.8 percent, almost identical to the poverty level among African Americans. Trinidadian and Tobagonian immigrants often settle in blighted urban areas of the United States where educational resources are scarce. As a population, they have not attainted the social or economic status of the average U.S. citizen. But coming from an English-speaking country gives them an advantage over non-English speaking immigrants from the Caribbean.

There are differences of opinion among sociologists about what happens to second-generation immigrants from the Caribbean. Some believe that people of Caribbean descent born in the United States who see themselves as African American and who assimilate into the U.S. culture are less likely to succeed economically or socially, while others argue that assimilation helps them do well.

It has been suggested that, because Trinidadians and Tobagonians come from a culture where blacks are the majority, this group has more social and cultural capital and higher self-esteem. Their accents set them apart from their peers, and whites often differentiate these groups and treat the foreign-born immigrants better. These advantages appear to erode over time, leaving American-born Trinidadian and Tobagonians in a similarly disadvantaged position as other African Americans.

Traditions and Customs Trinidad and Tobago is a multifaceted country with a profusion of customs and traditions that come together to form the "Trinibago" culture. Two of the most dominant cultures in Trinidad and Tobago are mixed-black (often called Creole) and East Indian. The first is a mixture of African, English, Spanish, and French cultures. Spanish influence is evident in the islands' music, festivals (especially the Parang festival), and dance. Even though France never occupied Trinidad, French planters on the island left their unmistakable mark in terms of language, religion, and class consciousness. The republic's East Indian culture is celebrated through *Divali* (Festival of Lights), *Hosay* (Muslim New Year festival), East Indian music, and various philosophical beliefs and practices foreign to Western cultures. For example, everyone is expected to take off their shoes at the door before stepping inside an Indian Muslim house, and new homes are often blessed in a special ceremony. There are rites for conception, birth, puberty, marriage, death, and the planting and harvesting of crops.

Cuisine Trinidadians and Tobagonians have retained many of their cooking traditions in the United States, although eating habits have changed somewhat to better suit America's fast pace. Breakfast varies from a full meal to a very light one and may include fresh coconut water and coconut jelly. Because Trinidad and Tobago is a highly Westernized nation, oatmeal, cornflakes, cocoa, coffee, and rolls are also common breakfast foods. Lunches and dinners generally consist of meat, rice, green vegetables, and fruits. Most native dishes contain meat or fish, although many of the favorites in Trinidad and Tobago (manicou, tatoo, venison, armadillo, lappe, quenk, duck, shark, flying fish, shrimp, kingfish, chip-chip, and cascadou) are not readily available in the United States. Such vegetables as pumpkin, cabbage, onion, and *melongene* (eggplant) are also well liked. One popular Trinidadian and Tobagonian dish is *pelau*, or rice mixed with pork or chicken and various local vegetables. *Calaloo* (a green, leafy vegetable that is served cooked) is sometimes combined with taro, dasheen, or tania leaves, okra, pumpkin, and crab to make a dish called calaloo and crab. Other popular dishes are dumpling and pig-tail or cow-heel soup, *souse* (well-cooked pickled pigs feet), and chicken stew. Coconut ice cream and fruits are popular Trinidadian and Tobagonian desserts. Many meals, especially during special occasions, are served with *mauby* (a drink made from the bark of a tree), Guinness stout, and Carib and Stag beers.

East Indian dishes of Trinidad and Tobago include *dhalpurie* (roti—unleavened bread—with split pea filling and, often, curried chicken or goat), *paratha roti* or *buss-up-shut* (shredded roti), and *doubles* (two pieces of flat fried bread, called *barra*, sandwiching curried chickpeas). *Doubles* are a popular street food. Two special dishes of Tobago are curry crab and dumplings and *accra*, which is seasoned saltfish pounded and shaped into small cakes and fried. Some foods are eaten seasonally, in keeping with harvest time and religious traditions. Trinidadians and Tobagonians in the United States often substitute American foods for their native dishes and prepare traditional foods only when dining with family or for special occasions.

Traditional Dress In their homeland Trinidadians and Tobagonians wear a variety of clothing suited for the tropics. In the United States, however, only Trinidadians and Tobagonians of East Indian descent have retained their unique cultural dress. Blacks from the republic have no special clothing, except carnival dress, which they share with other ethnic groups. Carnival takes place on the Monday and Tuesday leading up to Ash Wednesday. It is a sort of "last hurrah" before the start of Lent, which traditionally marks forty days of self-sacrifice for Catholics. The tradition in Trinidad and Tobago began with West African slaves. The exuberant festival combines days of calypso and soca music, dancing, parades, and costumes and is celebrated by everyone on the islands, regardless of religious affiliation. The costumes can be elaborate and costly. Some are massive, requiring the support of cars and trucks, while others might consist of simply loincloths and beads. Carnival costuming in Trinidad and Tobago and in New York City (where a Carnival takes place every year) is an extremely expensive cultural and commercial affair, providing

department stores, fabric stores, and hardware stores with hundreds of millions of dollars in revenue every year. Designers Peter Minshall, Peter Samuel, and Edmond Hart are well known in the United States for their costume talents.

Dances and Songs In New York City and Miami it is common to hear *parang* (a type of folk music brought to Trinidad and Tobago by Spanish-speaking immigrants from Venezuela) and *chawta* (East Indian drumming and vocals) in predominantly Caribbean neighborhoods. But the most popular Trinidadian and Tobagonian music in the United States is calypso and *soca* (a less socially conscious and faster-paced, party-oriented local music). Calypso is played on steelpan, a style of metal drums that originated in Trinidad and Tobago. The steelpan was created in the 1930s, but its roots extend to the African hand drums brought to the islands by slaves in the 1700s. Music was made by hitting the instrument with an open hand, a fist, or a stick. Over the years, the instrument has evolved from being made from a hodgepodge of everyday metal objects and kitchen utensils to state-of-the-art percussion instruments that are played by musicians around the world.

Calypso originated in Trinidad among African slaves in the 1800s. Although it has its roots in African oral traditions, it was sung in French dialect until 1883, when calypsonians began singing in English. Calypsonians play an important role in Caribbean society, functioning as poets, philosophers, and social commentators within social, political, and religious circles. Mighty Sparrow (Slinger Francisco), the "Calypso King of the World," won the Carnival crown in 1956 for his song "Jean and Dinah." Sparrow's 1962 calypso "Model Nation" captures the feelings of Trinidadians and Tobagonians toward their newly achieved status of independence: "The whole population of our little nation / Is not a lot; / But, oh what a mixture of races and culture / That's what we got; / Still no major indifference / Of race, color, religion, or finance; / It's amazing to you, I'm sure, / We didn't get our independence before."

During the 1980s calypso also became a forum for discussing women's rights. Although less popular than Mighty Sparrow, such female calypsonians as Singing Francine, Lady Jane, Twiggy, and Denise Plummer established their voices in Trinidadian and Tobagonian society. Their message is twofold: women should not tolerate abuse, and men should treat women as equals, especially in domestic partnerships.

Steel bands are popular in the United States among Trinidadian and Tobagonian Americans. Bands such as the Trinidad and Tobago Social Club of Boston, Sistas Wit Style (from Los Angeles), and 3Ni Productions (from Philadelphia) were popular at annual Carnival celebrations in the United States.

TRINIDAD AND TOBAGO PROVERBS

According to Lisa Winer in the introduction to her *Dictionary of the English/Creole of Trinidad and Tobago*, the country has been influenced by a wider variety of ethnic groups, languages, and cultures than any of the other islands in the Caribbean. As a result, proverbs used there come from many sources,

British-inspired proverbs include:

■ In for a penny, in for a pound.

■ A penny wise and a pound foolish.

■ Make hay while the sun shines.

Afro-Caribbean sayings commonly used by Trinidadians and Tobagonians include the following:

■ Do not cut you nose to patch you bottom.

■ If you see you neighbor house catch fire wet yours.

■ No money no love.

■ A man who cannot rule his house is *tootoolbay*.

■ What you head consent you bottom pay for.

■ Don't dance with two left feet.

Two common East Indian proverbs are:

■ Corn "nuh" grow where rain "nuh" fall.

■ Don't trust you neighbor unless you neighbor trusts you.

In Trinidad some popular expressions are "Monkey know what tree to climb" (people who are up to no good know who to interfere with); "You can't play sailor and 'fraid powder" (you have to face the consequences of your actions); and "All skin teeth eh laugh" (do not be deceived by friendly appearances). Tobagonians use some expressions that are different from those used in Trinidad, including, "Ah nuh fuh want ah tongue, mek cow cyar talk" (some things might just be beyond your power); "Belly full man does tell hungry gut man keep heart" (well-to-do people offer words of consolation but never any tangible assistance); and "Do not let the candle cost more than the funeral" (in an effort to solve one problem, be wary of creating further problems).

Trinidad and Tobago is known for its lively rhythmic dances set to the tunes of calypso and steel band music. Immigrants from the republic perform a variety of dances, including ballet, folk dancing, limbo, wining (dancing that involves moving the hips in a seductive fashion), hula hoop, *gayelle* (stick dancing), and *mocojumby* (a costumed dancer on stilts). Jump-up, a celebrative, emotionally charged, and physically exhausting dance, has a free-for-all style and is usually performed during Carnival.

Holidays Special holidays celebrated by Trinidadians and Tobagonians include Emancipation Day (August 1), Independence Day (August 31), Republic Day (September 24), and Boxing Day (December 26). Other popular festivals in Trinidad and Tobago are *Phagwa* (honoring the Hindu god Lord Krishna), *Divali* (a Hindu celebration with millions of lights honoring Mother Laskami), and *Hosay* (the Muslim New Year festival). However, Carnival is perhaps the best known of Trinidadian and Tobagonian annual celebrations; it takes place from Friday through Tuesday before Ash Wednesday of the Lenten season. Carnival Friday through Sunday are public holidays, but Carnival Monday and Tuesday are not official holidays.

Carnival was introduced to Trinidad by the French as an urban festival celebrated by the upper class until emancipation. It then became a festival for all classes, allowing people to break from their normal routine and, through calypso, indirectly criticize and ridicule the government. The Grand Steel Drum tournament known as Panorama is held on the Saturday of Carnival. On the first night of Carnival there is a "pan around the neck" competition (in reference to the way the steel pans are carried when the band is in motion). A junior carnival for school-age children takes place on Saturday, and the panorama finals are held Saturday night. On Sunday night, able calypsonians vie for the title of "calypso monarch" at the *Dimanche Gras*, and the "King and Queen of Carnival" are named. Monday and Tuesday see lots of "carnivalling," or dancing and masquerading with fantastic costumes. On the final day of Carnival, celebrants drink and dance to the point of exhaustion.

Trinidadian and Tobagonian Americans show off their Afro-Caribbean heritage at Carnival celebrations in the United States. First celebrated in the United States in New York City in the 1920s as a privately sponsored indoor family affair during the pre-Lenten season, it evolved into New York City's Labor Day Carnival (called West Indian Day Carnival). The celebration, modeled after Trinidad and Tobago's Carnival, is one of the largest scheduled street events in New York, rivaling the Saint Patrick's Day and Macy's Thanksgiving Day parades. It was first organized by Jesse Wattle on the streets of Harlem in 1969 and was moved to the Eastern Parkway in Brooklyn a few years later by Rufus Gorin. The festival features

A Trinidadian American performs at the annual West Indian parade in Crown Heights, Brooklyn, NY. CLARENCE HOLMES PHOTOGRAPHY / ALAMY

four nights of concerts, a steel band contest, and children's pageants on the grounds of the Brooklyn Museum. The Labor Day Carnival climaxes with a lengthy procession on the Eastern Parkway. Its overall purpose is to promote unity among Caribbeans and Americans.

Health Issues and Practices There are no documented medical problems unique to Trinidadians and Tobagonians in the United States or in Trinidad and Tobago. During the 1970s alcohol and drug abuse in Trinidad and Tobago was relatively low, but it increased steadily over the next three decades. A World Health Organization study from 2004 reported that alcoholism was much higher among men (14 percent) than women (1.1 percent). The report also stated that alcohol use was high among Indo-Trinidadians and low among Afro-Trinidadians. According to the study, 47 percent of hospitalizations for men were connected in some way to alcohol consumption or abuse. Since the 1980s the country has experienced significant increased use of illegal drugs, particularly marijuana and cocaine. The government initiated a National Anti-Drug Plan beginning in 2008 to address the issue.

The average life expectancy in Trinidad and Tobago is seventy-three years for women and sixty-eight years for men. Major causes of death among adults include heart disease, cerebra-vascular disease, malignant neoplasm, and diabetes mellitus. The infant mortality rate is relatively low; seventeen of every one thousand babies die in their first year. In the United States, life expectancy among Trinidadians and Tobagonians has decreased somewhat due to socioeconomic, health, and crime conditions. Most native Trinidadians and Tobagonians use either free or low-cost medical care provided by the government of Trinidad and Tobago, and compared to other developing countries, they enjoy relatively good health. A majority of families living in the United States have health insurance coverage through their jobs. According to an American Community Survey taken in 2011, 59.6 percent of Trinidadian and Tobagonian Americans had private health insurance. Another 27.5 percent were covered by public insurance programs, and 18.6 percent had no coverage.

Death and Burial Because of the multifaceted nature of its religious culture, Trinidad and Tobago have many different funeral practices. Among Hindus, a dying person is administered water from a tulsi leaf (India's most sacred plant). East Indians in Trinidad and Tobago began cremating their dead after 1930, and the practice was carried over to the United States. The Hindu funeral is an elaborate ceremony, and on the tenth day of mourning for an immediate family member, males may shave their heads, leaving only a lock of hair in the center.

Christians bury their dead after conducting a formal funeral church service. On the night before the funeral, there is a wake for the dead, during which friends and family come to offer condolences, sing dirges, and drink rum. In the Catholic faith, a priest recites the last rites to a dying member of the church and offers Mass for a soul that may have departed to purgatory before making peace with God. Afro-centric religions (Obeah, Shango, and Spiritual Baptist) also bury their dead after performing special rites. They have a Nine Night service to ensure that the shadow of the deceased does not return on the ninth evening after death to visit family members. This practice is occasionally performed after Christian, Muslim, and Hindu deaths as well.

Despite Trinidad and Tobago's culturally diverse people, the family, regardless of ethnic background, fulfills certain basic roles. In the United States, it is the family's responsibility to maintain traditions and enforce strong family values in the community.

FAMILY AND COMMUNITY LIFE

Gender Roles Traditionally Trinidadian and Tobagonian men were the sole providers of income for their families while women were held accountable for raising children and managing the home. Since the mid-1970s, however, family planning and other measures have helped Trinidadian and Tobagonian women to enjoy the same educational, professional, and property rights as men. Many of these women entered traditionally male-dominated fields such as medicine, law, and journalism. In the United States, where two-income families are often the rule rather than the exception, Trinidadian and Tobagonian women often work as managers, office clerks, service industry workers, nurses, and domestics. The median earnings for male and female full-time workers in the United States in 2012 were almost on a par, with men earning an average of $42,347 and women earning $39,782.

Education There is a high literacy rate among Trinidadian and Tobagonian immigrants in the United States, resulting from the high premium they place on education. In fact, they are often critical of the American education system, which contrasts sharply with the strong British educational system of their homeland. Some Trinidadian and Tobagonian immigrants try to shield their children from racism and miseducation by sending them to private schools

either taught or founded by Caribbean people. St. Mark's Academy, founded in Crown Heights, New York, in 1977 by a Guyanese man, has educated hundreds of Caribbean students, many of whom are now leaders in their communities. A 2008 study conducted by Philip Kasinitz and his colleagues at City University of New York (CUNY) showed that black immigrant students were achieving greater success in college than their African American and Puerto Rican peers.

In 2012 more than 88 percent of Trinidadian and Tobagonian Americans had a high school diploma or higher. Another 26.3 percent had college degrees, and 9.4 percent of those also had graduate or professional degrees. Females had a higher rate of postgraduate education. Data from the Current Population Survey in 2010 and the 2000 U.S. Census indicated that the schooling and wages of children of African immigrants from places like Trinidad and Tobago consistently exceed those of third-generation and later African Americans.

Trinidadian and Tobagonian immigrants who are in the United States legally are often active in civic and political affairs. Many take a keen interest in their children's education by joining school PTOs and PTAs and attending school board meetings.

Courtship and Weddings In Trinidad and Tobago, marriages can be performed in a religious or a civil ceremony. Most Trinidadian and Tobagonian weddings, like most Afro-Caribbean weddings in general, follow Christian traditions. There is an engagement period that lasts from a few months to several years. Traditionally the bride's parents were responsible for supplying the bride's dress and the cost of the reception, and the groom and his parents provided the ring and the new home. In the United States this practice varies. In some cases the parties are already living together, and the wedding ceremony legalizes the relationship in the eyes of the law and the community.

In ancient Indian tradition, Hindu authorities prescribed eight different forms of marriages, or *ashrams*, but only two of these were ever practiced among Trinidadian and Tobagonian East Indians. The more traditional of these, which is no longer practiced, was called *aqua* (matchmaker) and dictated that parents choose their children's partners. Such marriages took place at a young age, usually during puberty, because it was believed that postponing the wedding of a daughter for too long would bring bad luck. The ritual itself involved performing a *saptapadi* (a seven-step ritual) around a fire. In most traditional Hindu weddings, the groom is not allowed to see his bride until late in the ceremony, after she exchanges her yellow sari for a red one.

In modern times Hindu marriages involve bargaining between the two sets of parents. Often there is a short preliminary ceremony, or *chheka*, during which the family priest and the father of the bride travel to the house of the prospective groom to deliver a dowry.

By accepting the token sum, the groom is obligated to marry the young woman. These events last three days, from Friday night to Sunday. The bride's hands are painted with henna. The groom wears a beaded and embroidered four-piece Indian suit, and the bride changes her outfit throughout the three days, wearing up to three different dresses. The main ceremony takes place at the bride's home, and friends and relatives assist in setting up the *mantro* (nuptial tent). The wedding is followed by a large reception, with music, jokes, singing, chanting, beating drums, and the throwing of flowers in the air. Often there is another ceremony and a vegetarian feast at the groom's home. No alcohol is served.

For those on the islands who have no strong religious affiliation, weddings are festive occasions. Typically the groom wears tails and a top hat, and the bride wears a pale satin dress of any color, though white is very popular. After the ceremony, the wedding party parades through the streets, singing and dancing their way to the reception on foot. The music at the reception is often provided by a steel band. Guests are served crab dumplings and Indian food such as roti. The traditional black wedding cake is wrapped in mosquito net and carried in to the reception on the head of a guest.

EMPLOYMENT AND ECONOMIC CONDITIONS

Economically Trinidadian and Tobagonian immigrants have had mixed experiences in the United States. Individuals who are not living in the United States legally, as well as those who are waiting for legal status, tend to be exploited by employers and landlords. Legal immigrants from Trinidad and Tobago are often well educated and work in a variety of occupations.

The American Community Survey for 2011 reports that 71.7 percent of Trinidadian and Tobagonian Americans over the age of sixteen were employed, and 8.1 percent were unemployed. The employment rate for women was roughly equal to that of men. Of those employed, 75 percent worked for a private company, 19.5 percent worked for a government agency, and 5.4 percent were self-employed. Management, business, science, and the arts were the most popular type of occupations, with 34 percent of Trinidadian and Tobagonian Americans working in those areas. There were 23.6 percent working in the service industry and another 25.6 percent in sales or office work. Women were recorded as having a 10 percent higher rate of management positions than their male counterparts. The median household income was $51,013.

POLITICS AND GOVERNMENT

Caribbean people have been active in American politics since the early 1800s. After slavery was abolished in the British West Indies in 1834, a number of Trinidadians, Jamaicans, and Barbadians supported the African repatriation movement and worked for the abolition of slavery in collaboration with their black counterparts in the United States. This political activity led to what became known as the Pan-African Movement, supported by W.E.B. DuBois, Marcus Garvey, and others. The Trinidad-born attorney H. Sylvester Williams, who had ties to the United States, was one of the leaders of the first Pan-African Congress, which met in London in 1900.

During the 1920s Caribbean immigrants were drawn to socialist and black nationalist groups in the United States; the majority of the members in Jamaican-born Marcus Garvey's Universal Negro Improvement Association were from the West Indies. Caribbean American political activity reached a new level in the mid-1930s when Trinidadian and Tobagonian immigrants began playing an important role in the Democratic Party in New York. Mervyn Dymally (1926–2012), a Trinidadian immigrant, founded the Caribbean Action Lobby to mobilize ethnic ties into a political interest group focusing on international and local relations. The first black to serve as lieutenant governor in California and the first foreign-born person elected to the U.S. Congress, Dymally was a leading proponent for aid to the English-speaking Caribbean.

Trinidadian George Padmore (1903–1959), the great Pan-Africanist who was highly decorated in Ghana, founded the International African Service Bureau in London in 1937. In the 1930s and 1940s Padmore, C.L.R. James, and Eric Williams joined DuBois and others in criticizing foreign interference in Africa and discrimination against blacks in the United States. In the 1960s Trinidadian Stokely Carmichael, or Kwame Toure (1941–1998), a black nationalist and civil rights organizer, served as a major force behind the Student Nonviolent Coordinating Committee (SNCC). In the late 1960s the black power movement in the United States attracted the Caribbean's urban poor, and many organizations were formed throughout Trinidad and Tobago using its slogan. Among these were the Black Panthers, the African Unity Brothers, the African Cultural Association, and the National Freedom Organization.

The government of Trinidad and Tobago does not allow Trinidadians and Tobagonians to hold dual citizenship. Therefore, naturalized U.S. citizens do not vote in the republic's elections. Nonetheless, whether they are U.S. citizens or temporary residents, most Trinidadian and Tobagonian Americans maintain constant communication with their home country. They read the *Trinidad Guardian*, the *Punch*, the *Bomb*, the *Express*, and other national papers and watch news programs broadcast over satellite. Temporary residents also vote in Trinidad and Tobago's general elections and remit funds regularly to family and relatives in the republic.

THE AMERICAN MILITARY IN TRINIDAD AND TOBAGO

Trinidad's rich deposit of oil and its strategic location have attracted many foreign powers over the years, most notably the United States. In 1940 President Franklin Delano Roosevelt leased three strategic military bases in British-Caribbean territories (one of which was Trinidad and Tobago) from Winston Churchill's British government. The Americans built a sizable air strip in Port of Spain and a superb naval installation at Trinidad's well-placed deep-water harbor at Chaguaramas Bay.

These actions resulted in increased employment and major development projects (through the U.S. Navy and Public Works Department), including the building of roads and bridges for wartime operations and the recruitment of many Trinidadians and Tobagonians by the U.S. Navy during World War II. Furthermore, American interest in the republic eased the immigration process to the United States. Many Trinidadian and Tobagonian immigrants who have become naturalized U.S. citizens continue to serve in the U.S. military, though in smaller numbers than during World War II. Because few of these individuals identify themselves as Trinidadian and Tobagonian immigrants, it is difficult to accurately access their number in the U.S. armed forces.

Historically the U.S. government has maintained good diplomatic relations with Trinidad and Tobago, which in recent years has received federal loans to recover from its economic recession. In spite of strained relations between the U.S. government and the late Prime Minister Eric Williams over the closing of the U.S. naval base in Chaguaramas in the 1970s, the oil boom in Trinidad (between the 1960s and the early 1980s) kept Trinidadians and Tobagonians a favorite of the United States among people of the Caribbean Basin.

NOTABLE INDIVIDUALS

Trinidadians and Tobagonians have enriched American culture in many ways. The following individuals are some of the most notable.

Academia Eric Williams (1911–1981), the late prime minister of Trinidad and Tobago and vice chancellor of the University of the West Indies, taught at Howard University and gave lectures at several other distinguished American colleges and universities. His books *Capitalism and Slavery* and *Columbus to Castro* have been reprinted dozens of times since they were first published in the 1940s and continue to attract interest in the United States.

Trinidadian Hindu American Anantanand Rambachan received his undergraduate degree from the University of the West Indies in Trinidad and his Ph.D. from the University of Leeds in the United Kingdom. Rambachan is a professor and the first non-Christian chair of religion, philosophy, and Asian

studies at St. Olaf, a Lutheran college in Minnesota. He is a member of the Theological Education Steering Committee of the American Academy of Religion; the Advisory Council of the Centre for the Study of Religion and Society, University of Victoria, British Columbia, Canada; an adviser to Harvard University's Pluralism Project; and a member of the Consultation on Population and Ethics, a nongovernmental organization affiliated with the United Nations.

Fashion Anya Ayoung-Chee (1981–) holds dual American and Trinidadian citizenship. She was born in New York to Trinidadian parents of Chinese descent and moved to Trinidad at the age of two. After high school she studied graphic art and design in the United States and England. Ayoung-Chee won the title of Miss Trinidad and Tobago Universe in 2008. She was the winner of the television reality show *Project Runway* in 2011, and the prize enabled her to start her own line of clothing, Pilar. She is also involved in philanthropic work through TallMan, her family's foundation.

Journalism Lakshmi Singh, the daughter of an Indo-Trinidadian father and Puerto Rican mother, joined National Public Radio as a newscaster in 2000, covering midday broadcasts.

Born in California and raised in St. Thomas, Virgin Islands, Gabrielle Reece (1970–) is the daughter of a Trinidadian planter. The professional American volleyball player, model, and actress has also appeared as a sports commentator for ESPN, NBC, and MTV and as a spokesperson for Nike.

Literature C.L.R. James (1901–1989) edited the *International African Opinion* and wrote dozens of articles and books on Marxism, revolution, and Afro-Caribbean and American history and politics. He spent the first thirty years of his life in Trinidad and lived in England from 1932 to 1938, pursuing his literary career and making a name for himself as an advocate for West Indian independence. He lived in the United States for fifteen years, writing and speaking about socialism and race politics, and again later in his life, teaching college. One of James's most renowned works is *Black Jacobins* (1938), which documents the black struggle in the Haitian Revolution. The C.L.R. James Institute in New York, named in his honor, was founded in 1983 as an affiliate of Cambridge University's Centre for African Studies.

Earl Lovelace (1935–) is a novelist who spent his early years in Tobago and later Trinidad. He attended Howard University in Washington, D.C., received his master's degree from Johns Hopkins University, and was a visiting writer at the University of Iowa's prestigious writing program. He has taught creative writing at universities in the United States, the West Indies, and England. Lovelace received a Guggenheim fellowship in 1980 and a grant from the National Endowment for the Humanities in 1986. He has written six novels and won several awards for fiction, including the Commonwealth Writers' Prize for his novel *Salt* (1996).

John Stewart is a popular Trinidadian American writer who did his undergraduate and graduate study in the United States at California State University, Stanford University, and the University of California-Los Angeles. His short stories have appeared in, among other places, *The Faber Book of Contemporary Caribbean Short Stories* (1990) and *Best West Indian Short Stories* (London: Nelson, 1981). He is the recipient of a Royal Society of Literature Award for *Last Cool Days* (1996). He was a professor and director of African American and African Studies at the University of California-Davis. Among his best-known works are *A Bend in the River* (1979), shortlisted for the Booker Prize and No. 83 on the Modern Library's list of the top 100 novels written in the English language of the twentieth century; and *A House for Mr. Biswas* (1961), his first novel to receive international acclaim.

Lynn Joseph (1963–), a Trinidadian-born author who migrated to the United States during her college years, writes children books for Trinidadians and Tobagonians in the United States and the Caribbean. Perhaps her best-known book is the young-adult fiction book *The Color of My Words* (2000).

Music Heather Headley (1974–) is the daughter of a pastor who grew up singing in church choirs. Her family moved from Trinidad to the United States in the early 1990s. After graduating from Northwestern University, she was cast in the role of Nala in the original cast of *Lion King* on Broadway. She won a Tong Award for Best Actress in a Musical for her portrayal of Aida in Elton John and Tim Rice's stage production of that classic. Her 2009 R&B-gospel album *Audience of One* won a Grammy.

Nickie Minaj (born Onika Tanya Maraj, 1982) is a Trinidad-born rapper, singer-songwriter, and television personality who moved to Queens, New York, at the age of five. There she studied to be an actress before breaking into the music scene. Her first studio album, *Pink Friday* (2010), hit number one on the U.S. Billboard 200 and was certified platinum. Minaj has received music awards from BET, MTV, and others, and the *New York Times* claimed that she may be the most important female rapper of all time. In 2013 she became an *American Idol* judge.

Politics Stokely Carmichael (1941–1998) emigrated from Trinidad and Tobago to the United States at the age of eleven. He received his undergraduate degree from Howard University. In the 1960s Carmichael changed his name to Kwame Ture and began his career as an activist by leading the Student Nonviolent Coordinating Committee (SNCC.) He later became a leader in the Black Panther Party, eventually earning the title "Honorary Prime Minister" of that group. Carmichael is perhaps most famous for popularizing the term "Black Power." The Black Panthers expelled him in 1967. His two books, *Black Power Politics of Liberation in America* (1967) and *Stokely Speaks: Black Power Back to Pan-Africanism* (1971), are highly regarded.

Republican politician Jennifer Carroll (1959–) was born in Trinidad and moved to the United States at the age of eight. She served for seven years in the Florida state legislature and was elected lieutenant governor of Florida in 2011.

Maurice Gumbs was one of the founders of The Harriet Tubman Democratic Club, a political advocacy group dedicated to educating and empowering the constituents of the Bronx. Gumbs ran for several New York State offices in the 1980s and 1990s. He was born in Trinidad and as of 2012 lived in Brooklyn, New York.

Mervyn Dymally (1926–2012) left Trinidad at the age of eighteen and moved to the United States. He was elected to the California state house in 1962, becoming the first foreign-born black to hold office in that body. He became California's first black state senator in 1966 and its first black lieutenant governor in 1974. Starting in 1980 he served six terms in the U.S. House of Representatives, where he was leader of the Congressional Black Caucus. He returned to state politics in 2002, serving another three terms in the state house.

Sports Kareem Abdul-Jabbar (born Ferdinand Lewis Alcindor Jr. in 1947) is a first-generation Trinidadian American who was one of the greatest centers in basketball history. He was named Most Valuable Player by the National Basketball Association six times and is the NBA's all-time leading scorer.

Hasley Crawford (1950–) is a Trinidadian and Tobagonian sprinter who lived and trained in the United States. In 1976 he became his country's first Olympic champion and the first Olympic 100 meter champion from a Caribbean country. A stadium was renamed in his honor in Port of Spain in 2001.

Boxer Leslie Stewart (1961–) was born in Trinidad. He was reigning World Boxing Association Light Heavyweight Champion for several months in 1987 and officially retired in 2000. He lives in Miami.

Ato Boldon (1973–) was born in Trinidad and moved to the United States at age fourteen. At eighteen he competed in the 1992 Summer Olympics in Barcelona as a sprinter for the Trinidad and Tobago team. Bolton won his first Olympic medal in 1996. Unable to compete in the 1999 Commonwealth Games due to a temporary injury, he worked as a sports commentator and analyst for the BBC for two years. In 2002, after winning a total of four Olympic medals, he had a serious hip injury from an auto collision with a drunk driver, effectively ending his running career. He has since been a broadcaster for CBS, NBC, and ESPN. In 2006–2007 he served in the Trinidad and Tobago Parliament as an Opposition Senator. He lives in Los Angeles.

Stage and Screen Geoffrey Holder (1930–), an outstanding American producer, director, and choreographer, was born in Port of Spain and has lived in the United States for more than fifty years. In 1975 he won a Tony Award for directing and designing costumes for *The Wiz*.

Nia Long (1970–) is an American actress of Afro-Trinidadian descent. She appeared in the television series *The Fresh Prince of Bel-Air* and *Third Watch* along with films *Boyz n the Hood* (1991), *Deep Cover* (1992), *The Best Man* (1999), and others.

MEDIA

There are many periodicals, papers, radio stations, and television networks in the United States that cater to the Caribbean population.

PRINT

Everybody's Caribbean Magazine

A New York magazine founded in 1977 by a Grenadian who lived in Trinidad and New York, it reflects the demographic interest and views of the American Caribbean community.

1630 Nostrand Avenue
Brooklyn, New York 11226
Phone: (718) 941-1879
Fax: (718) 941-1886
Email: info@everbodysmag.com
URL: www.everybodysmag.com

Caribbean Life

Self-described as the voice of the New York Caribbean community.

One Metrotech Center
Suite 1001
Brooklyn, New York 11201
Phone: (718) 260-2500
Email: CaribbeanLife@CNGLocal.com
URL: www.caribbeanlifenews

New York Carib News

Weekly newspaper tabloid founded in 1981, covering Caribbean politics in New York.

35 West 35th Street
Suite 705
New York, New York 10001
Phone: (212) 944-1991
Fax: (212) 944-2089
Email: info@nycaribnews.com
URL: www.nycaribnews.com

RADIO

KISS-FM and WBLS 107.5 FM

Two of New York City's top radio stations, KISS FM and WBLS, merged in 2012. The reorganized station continues to air "Caribbean Fever," a show hosted by Dahved Levy on Saturdays from noon to 4:00 p.m. and Sundays from 8:00 p.m. to midnight, featuring a mix of talk and Caribbean music.

Dahved Levy, Show Host
Phone: (212) 447-1000
Fax: (212) 447-5211
Email: info@wbls.com
URL: www.wbls.com

WLIB 1190 AM

A New York City religious radio station (with the tagline "Your Praise and Inspirations Station") that plays a Caribbean gospel show on Saturdays from 2:00 p.m. to 6:00 p.m. In addition to music and gospel celebrity profiles, the show also features news from Caribbean communities in New York and abroad. Owned and operated by WBLS.

Ricardo Bryan, Show Host
Phone: (212) 447-1000
Fax: (212) 447-5211
Email: info@wbls.com
URL: www.wbls.com

TELEVISION

Caribbean International Network (CIN)

A New York-area television station launched in 1992 that offers twenty-seven hours of Caribbean programming a week. Channel 73 reaches all five boroughs of New York, plus Connecticut and New Jersey, and has an estimated 18.9 million viewers.

Stephen Hill, CEO
Phone: (347) 448-4345
Fax: (876) 754-8449
Email: mail@cintvjamaica.com
URL: www.cintvjamaica.com

TEMPO TV

Featuring Caribbean music videos, dramas, news, and documentaries, TEMPO reaches more than three million viewers in the Caribbean. In the United States it is broadcast on New York Cablevision Channel 1105, as well as streaming at www.gottempo.com.

Frederick Morton, Jr., Founder and CEO
Tempo Networks, LLC
58 Park Place, Third Floor
Newark, New Jersey 07102
Phone: (973) 508.1000
Fax: (973) 508.1002
URL: www.gottempo.com

ORGANIZATIONS AND ASSOCIATIONS

African Caribbean Political Action Committee (ACPAC)

Political action committee dedicated to social, political, and economic inclusion for residents in the African Caribbean diaspora. ACPAC also supports United States policies that strengthen bilateral relations and create economic opportunities for Caribbean and African nations.

Phone: (267) 223-5015
Email: info@africancaribbeanpac.org

California Caribbean Chamber of Commerce

The Chamber of Commerce is dedicated to improving and creating business opportunities for Caribbean

Americans and to making the community a desirable place to live.

Lloyd Eastwick
4452 Ocean View Blvd. #201
Montrose, California 91020
Phone: (818) 249-7706
Fax: (818) 249-3920
URL: www.calcaribchamber.com

Caribbean American Political Action Committee (C-PAC)

C-PAC was founded in November 2005 with the goal of advancing the political agenda of Caribbean Americans currently residing in and around the Washington, D.C., metropolitan area (including Maryland and northern Virginia). C-PAC's overarching mission is to be the unified political voice of the area's vibrant and growing Caribbean community.

Thomas Layne
1701 Pennsylvania Ave. NW
Suite 300
Washington, D.C. 20006
Phone: (202) 349-1498

Citizens and Friends of Trinidad and Tobago

The mission of this corporation is to ensure access to medical care and to improve the lives of children in need who are part of the Trinidadian and Tobagonian community of Southern California and in the Caribbean.

420 South Grand Avenue
Los Angeles, California 90071
Phone: (310) 762-2253
Email: citizensfriends@cftt.us
URL: www.cftt.us

Trinidad and Tobago Folk Arts Institute

The mission of this organization is to inform the rest of the world about Trinidad and Tobago's rich cultural heritage. The Institute hosts forums on the republic's history and politics in conjunction with Medgar Evers College of the City University of New York, Brooklyn. Sponsors musical performances and organizes tributes to outstanding steel bands.

Les Slater, Director
3522 Farragut Road
Brooklyn, New York 11210
Phone: 718-252-6161
Email: slatertalentmart@yahoo.com

There are a number of important Trinidadian and Tobagonian organizations in the United States: Trinidad Alliance; Caribbean Action Lobby (founded by Mervyn Dymally); West Indian American Day Carnival Association (founded by Rufus Gorin in New York); West Indian Cricket Club (with branches in Ohio, New York, Washington, D.C., Florida, and other states); Brooklyn Council for the Arts; and Trinidad and Tobago-New York Steel Band Club. There is also the Caribbean American Chamber of Commerce and the Caribbean American Media Studies Inc., dedicated to the study and dissemination of information about recent West Indian immigrants.

MUSEUMS AND RESEARCH CENTERS

Caribbean Culture Center of the African Diaspora Institute (CCCADI)

CCCADI brings together people of African descent living in the Americas to promote common cultures and to introduce others to the religious, cultural, artistic, and philosophical contributions made by members of the African diaspora. The center offers a variety of educational, professional and artistic programs designed to appeal to audiences of all ages.

Laura B. Moreno, Assistant Director
1825 Park Ave.
Suite 602
New York, New York 10035
Phone: (212) 307-7420
Email: info@cccadi.org
URL: www.cccadi.org

W.E.B. Du Bois Institute for African and African American Research

A research center at Harvard University dedicated to the study of the history, culture, and social institutions of Africans and African Americans. The Institute sponsors readings, art exhibits, and publications covering topics relevant to the African diaspora. Its archive contains research on issues affecting Trinidadian and Tobagonian Americans.

Amy Gosdanian, Executive Assistant
104 Mount Auburn Street, 3R
Cambridge, Massachusetts 02138
Phone: (617) 495.8508
Fax: (617) 495.8511
Email: gosdan@fas.harvard.edu
URL: www.dubois.fas.harvard.edu

Institute of African American Affairs

This institute is part of New York University and is devoted to research, documentation, and celebration of African and African diaspora arts and culture in the Atlantic as well as other parts of the world.

Manthia Diawara, Director
New York University
14A Washington Mews, 4th Floor
New York, New York 10003
Phone: (212) 998-2130
URL: www.africanastudies.as.nyu.edu

SOURCES FOR ADDITIONAL STUDY

Allsop, Richard. *Dictionary of Caribbean English Usage.* Oxford: Oxford University Press, 1996.

Epstein, James. *Scandal of Colonial Rule: Power and Subversion in the British Atlantic During the Age of Revolution.* Cambridge: Cambridge University Press, 2012.

Foner, Nancy. *New Immigrants in New York.* New York: Columbia University Press, 1987.

Kasinitz, Philip. *Caribbean New York.* New York: Cornell University Press, 1992.

Lum, Kenneth Anthony. *Praising His Name in the Dance: Spirit Possession in the Spiritual Baptist Faith and Orisha Work in Trinidad, West Indies.* Singapore: Harwood, 2000.

Palmer, Colin A. *Eric Williams and the Making of the Modern Caribbean* Chapel Hill: University of North Carolina Press, 2008.

Read, Jen'nan Ghazal, and Michael O. Emerson. "Racial Context, Black Immigration and the U.S. Black/White Health Disparity." Social Forces 84, no. 1 (2005): 181–99.

Sakamoto, Aurthur, Hyeyoung Woo & ChangHwan Kim. "Does an Immigrant Background Ameliorate Racial Disadvantage? The Socioeconomic Attainments of Second-Generation African Americans." Sociological Forum 25, no. 1 (2010): 123–46.

Sander, Reinhardt W. *The Trinidad Awakening: West Indian Literature of the 1930s.* Westport, CT: Greenwood, 1988.

Williams, A. R. "The Wild Mix of Trinidad and Tobago," *National Geographic*, 185, no. 3, (1984): 66–88.

TUNISIAN AMERICANS

Grace Waitman

OVERVIEW

Tunisian Americans are immigrants or descendants of immigrants from Tunisia, a small nation in northern Africa bordered to the north and east by the Mediterranean Sea. Algeria lies to the west, and Libya to the southeast. A long, narrow country with more than 700 miles of coastline, Tunisia has a diverse climate, with abundant rainfall in the north and an arid climate in the south. It occupies 163,610 square kilometers, a region slightly smaller than the state of Wisconsin.

The 2013 *CIA World Factbook* listed the population of Tunisia as 10,835,873, a number marginally smaller than the population of Ohio. People of Arab ethnicity comprise 98 percent of the population, and Europeans and people of various other ethnicities make up the remaining 2 percent. Approximately 98 percent of the people living in Tunisia practice Islam. Tunisia has a growing market-oriented economy founded on diverse sources of revenue, with only 3.8 percent of the population living below the poverty line. A revolution in 2010 and 2011, at the beginning of the widespread upheaval of the Arab Spring, had severe ramifications on the economy, and the nation has faced significant challenges in recovering from the turmoil.

Small numbers of Tunisian immigrants first arrived in the United States in the late 1950s, not long after the Republic of Tunisia achieved independence from France, and in 1969, after a devastating flood in Tunisia. Between 1981 and 1992 approximately seven hundred Tunisian students came to the United States as part of the Technology Transfer Program. About 40 percent remained in the country. Immigration diversity legislation passed by Congress in 1995 brought more Tunisians to the United States, as did the 2010 to 2011 uprising in Tunisia that led to the overthrow of the government. A 2000 U.S. Census Brief indicated that the number of Tunisians living in the country increased from 2,376 in 1980 to 4,735in 2000. According to the Department of Homeland Security's 2011 Yearbook of Immigration statistics, between 2002 and 2011 an average of 450 Tunisians obtained legal resident status in the United States per year.

An accurate estimate of the number of Tunisian Americans residing in the United States remains difficult to determine, because information about Americans of Tunisian heritage is not provided by the U.S. Census Bureau. The Tunisian Community Center (TCC; an electronic network representing Tunisian Americans since 1999), however, estimated that as of 2010 approximately 13,500 Tunisian Americans resided in the United States. The TCC reported that the majority lived in Washington, New York, Florida, California, Minnesota, and Texas.

HISTORY OF THE PEOPLE

Early History Archeological evidence suggests that present-day Tunisia was populated by small farming communities as long ago as 4000 BCE and for several millennia thereafter by the nomadic Berber tribes of North Africa. The Phoenicians settled the area sometime in the tenth century BCE and ruled in northern Africa until the eighth century BCE. Because invading Greek and Roman armies destroyed most of the records, accurate historical information is difficult to obtain; however, historians believe that the Phoenicians built the city of Carthage, located in what is now a suburb of Tunis, sometime in the ninth century BCE. Over the course of several centuries, the settlement developed into a central hub in the Mediterranean region and was widely known as a strong naval power. By around 146 BCE, however, Carthage had been devastated by the three Punic Wars that Rome had waged against the city. Ultimately, the land passed to the Roman Empire.

Rome controlled the North African territory until the fifth century CE. The eastern half of the Roman Empire, which had come to be known as the Byzantine Empire, survived as a Greek-speaking continuation of Roman rule after the Western Roman Empire crumbled; the Byzantines ruled North Africa until the Arab conquest of 648 to 669 transferred power to a succession of Berber and Arab dynasties. Tunisia came under Arab domination during the next several centuries, despite challenges from the Berbers. At this time the region was the site of multiple waves of immigration, and Tunisia underwent a massive transformation. One larger group of immigrants consisted of Spanish Jews and Muslims, who arrived in the late 1400s. By 1574 the region had been assimilated into the Ottoman Empire, and Tunisia remained an Ottoman territory for the next three hundred years.

In the late 1500s three rulers of Berber descent established political entities or large spheres of influence along the Mediterranean coast. They were known by Europeans as the Barbary States, and each was governed by a *pasha*, or *bey*. Although they lived independently of Ottoman rule, they conspired with the Ottomans to resist European exploration and settlement in the Mediterranean and North Africa. Operating from ports in present-day Algeria, Tunisia, and Libya, Barbary pirates, as they were called, conducted raids on European ships travelling throughout the Mediterranean, capturing Christian slaves for trade in the Muslim Middle East and North Africa. Over the course of three hundred years, these pirates took more than one million slaves. Eventually, although the European powers were often fighting among themselves on the continent, they collaborated to subdue the pirates. Over time, the state in present-day Algiers grew to be the largest, and Tunis shrank, both in area—because of Ottoman administrative decisions—and population, as a result of a series of plagues and epidemics that ravaged the area in the eighteenth and early nineteenth centuries.

France colonized Algeria in 1830, and in 1881 the French invaded Tunis, establishing a protectorate that lasted until 1956. The Treaty of Bardo, signed by the bey, set the terms of French rule; it essentially secured French protection for the bey's land holdings and dynasty but imposed restrictions on his capacity to intervene in internal governance and affairs, making him a figurehead. The French encouraged European settlement of the coast, and by the turn of the century, nearly 150,000 French colonists lived in Tunisia, along with approximately 100,000 Italians and a significant number of British.

Modern Era Chafing under with French rule, Tunisian insurgents began forming revolutionary organizations early in the twentieth century and clamored for independence. The Young Tunisian Party, formed in 1907, was the first of these groups to gain considerable backing, but they were mistrusted by poor Tunisians, and many of their leaders were quickly expelled by the French. Nevertheless, they succeeded in kindling a revolutionary spirit in Tunis, and in 1920 the Constitutional Liberty Party, known as Destour, was formed. A larger and better organized group of intellectuals, Destour was able to carry the movement further. They, too, had trouble earning the trust of the masses, however. In 1934 a radical faction of Destour established Neo Destour and, under the leadership of Habib Bourguiba, a Tunisian who had been educated in Paris in law and political science, was finally able to win widespread support from the population at large. He was imprisoned several times for his activities. French losses to Germany in World War II weakened their control over Tunisia. The Nazis released Bourguiba from prison, but he was loath to negotiate with them and risk exchanging one form of colonial tyranny for another.

In the decade following World War II, Bourguiba, who had become known as a gradualist, continued seeking independence from French rule. While he was in prison again, from 1952 to 1954, however, Tunisian rebels resorted to violence, persisting until French leader Pierre Mendes-France initiated a plan for partial withdrawal from Tunisia. Mendes-France agreed to restore the conditions that had been in place in 1881 at the signing of the Treaty of Bardo.

With this step, Bourguiba was released from prison, and Tunisia established a Neo-Destour government. Bourguiba finally secured complete independence for the country in March 1956, becoming its prime minister; in July 1957 Tunisia became a republic and Bourguiba its president. Tunisia adopted a constitution in June 1959 based in part on the French model of government that organized power around a strong presidential figure. Within this government, the military could not interfere in politics. Under Bourguiba's leadership, Tunisia experienced rapid increases in its literacy rate, relatively consistent economic growth, and low unemployment and poverty. His improvements also included a free educational system and the discontinuation of polygamy.

Bourguiba remained the head of the government for more than thirty years, until 1987, when rumors of his dementia led to a bloodless overthrow by Zine el-Abidine Ben Ali. As president Ben Ali purported to continue many of the effective reforms that Bourguiba had established. His presidency was marked by suspiciously unanimous elections, however, with his party winning more than 90 percent of the vote in 1999 and 2004. In addition the party secured all directly elected positions in 1994, 1999, and 2004. Under his leadership reports were common of infringements on previously established freedoms and of abusive conditions for detained individuals. Tunisians were also beginning to experience extreme economic inequality, despite the fact that the economy overall was thriving at the end of the twentieth century. Public opinion shifted completely away from Ben Ali when he introduced modifications to the constitution that allowed him to seek a fifth term in office (at which time he was again elected in a suspicious landslide).

In late December 2010 a Tunisian produce seller name Mohamed Bouazizi set himself on fire in front of the governor's office to protest the harassment, humiliation, and loss of livelihood he had suffered at the hands of the government. His death ushered in a revolution as protestors demanded Ben Ali's resignation. Ben Ali eventually complied, voluntarily stepping down on January 14, 2011. The Tunisian Revolution was the first of a series of uprisings in the Arab world known as the Arab Spring, in which widespread civil protests throughout the region and overthrew governments in Egypt, Yemen, and Libya as well as Tunisia. In October 2011, in the first election after the revolution, the Ennahda (Renaissance) Party gained a plurality in the Tunisian parliament.

A moderate Islamic party, Ennahda promised to create a secular state. In the aftermath of the revolution, significant numbers of people fled Tunisia, most of them attempting to immigrate to Italy. According to a report from *Al Monitor*, which covers the Middle East, more than 40,000 Tunisians left the country in 2011. Political unrest has persisted; on September 14, 2012, twenty Islamists attacked the U.S. Embassy in Tunis, killing two people, and on February 6, 2013, Chokri Belaid, a lawyer and radical secularist, was murdered outside his home. Fundamentalist Sunni Muslims, commonly called Salafists, are believed to have been responsible for both acts of violence.

SETTLEMENT IN THE UNITED STATES

In 1797 the United States and the Ottoman emperor signed a Treaty of Peace and Friendship in Tunis. Despite U.S. aggression in the Barbary Wars (1801–1805 and 1815) that ultimately ended piracy in the Mediterranean, relations between Tunisia and the American government remained strong. It was not until the mid-1950s, however, that Tunisians began even modest immigration to the United States. Because the U.S. Census Bureau has compiled a minimal amount of data on Tunisian immigrants, it is only possible to surmise why Tunisians may have come to the United States at this time. Tunisian independence from the French Protectorate in 1956 may

have allowed for an increase in emigration. Another possible explanation is the arrival of U.S. Peace Corps volunteers in the early 1960s, bringing Western influences with them.

More Tunisian immigrants arrived in the United States in 1969 after thirty-eight days of rain caused widespread flooding in Tunisia, killing 540 people, destroying 70,000 homes, and making 300,000 people into refugees—almost 7 percent of the total population of Tunisia at the time. In the 1970s the United States Agency for International Development (USAID) began to fund major projects in Tunisia, designating $45 million to help the country establish itself as a modernized nation built on a knowledge economy. As part of the project, which ran from 1981 to 1992, the Technology Transfer Program provided funds for approximately 700 Tunisians to study in the United States. The Academy for Education Development released a report in 1991 estimating that 40 percent of these students remained in the United States and that most of the other 60 percent returned to Tunisia and took jobs in the country's technology sector. Most Tunisians who remained pursued careers in business and maintained close ties to the business community in Tunisia. They also encouraged Tunisian students to pursue degrees in the United States and set up scholarship funds to help pay for their education here.

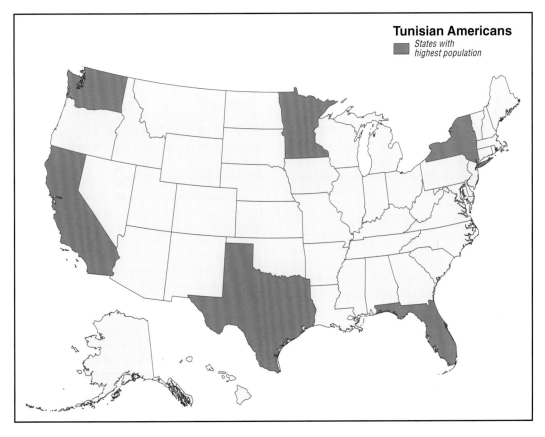

Tunisian Americans
States with highest population

In 1995, under the Clinton administration, Congress created the Diversity Immigrant Visa program, which instituted a lottery for immigrants desiring permanent resident visas. Participation was restricted to countries from which fewer than 50,000 documented immigrants had arrived in the United States during the previous five years. In part because of this legislation and the growing network between the Tunisian American and Tunisian business communities, there were well over 4,000 Tunisians living in the United States in the late 1990s. In 1999 the TCC was formed with express purpose of creating an online presence that united the various local Tunisian American communities throughout the United States and strengthened ties between the immigrant community and Tunisia. It is not possible to determine what role the vibrant online community that has grown out of this venture has played in recent Tunisian immigration to the United States.

Tunisian Americans' combination of smooth assimilation into American society and sustained ties to the home country may be a result of Tunisia's historical amalgamation of many lasting outside influences, including those of the Phoenicians, Carthaginians, Greeks, Romans, Ottomans, Berbers, French, Spanish, and Italians.

According to the 2000 Census (published in 2003), around 80 percent of Tunisian Americans lived in six U.S. states: Washington (20 percent), New York (15 percent), Florida (12 percent), California (12 percent), Minnesota (12 percent), and Texas (12 percent).

LANGUAGE

The official language of Tunisia is standard Arabic, although many people who engage in commercial activities also speak French, English, Italian, or German. Other languages spoken include Tunisian Arabic—a Maghrebi (the Maghreb being the region of North Africa west of Egypt) dialect related to Maltese and influenced by Berber, French, Turkish, Italian, and Spanish—and Shelha, a Berber language. Because of Tunisia's long-standing history as a French protectorate, a minority speak French. The ability to speak French is often as a mark of status. In more recent years schools have taught children both French and English.

Many Tunisian Americans speak standard Arabic, Tunisian Arabic, and English. Many of the younger immigrants who have arrived since 2010 already spoke some English.

Greetings and Popular Expressions The following phrases are examples of greetings or popular expressions in Tunisian Arabic: *aaslemma*—"hello"; *bislemma*—"goodbye"; *sbalakher*—"good morning"; *sahhelkher*—"good night"; and *aaeshik*—"thank you."

RELIGION

Tunisia has a long tradition of religious tolerance. About 98 percent of the population practice Sunni Islam, and the government recognizes the major holidays and festivals on the Muslim calendar as national holidays. The government has protected the rights of the Jewish and Christian minorities to practice their faith and celebrate their holidays. While all Tunisian youth study Islam in public school, they may if they wish, take additional courses in Christian and Jewish history. Most Tunisian Americans continue to practice their Islamic faith, engaging in the customary ritual of praying five times daily and adhering to the ways in which their families have traditionally celebrated religious rituals. Local chapters of the TCC, which offer Tunisian Americans opportunities to maintain religious and other cultural practices, frequently hold festivals in honor of the major Islamic religious holidays.

CULTURE AND ASSIMILATION

In 2011, in the immediate aftermath of the revolution, Tunisian American Young Professionals was established to stimulate Tunisian American investment in the new government. At the time the group worked directly with Habib Bourguiba Jr., the son of the president, to organize relief efforts. The group has created the Thomas Jefferson Scholarship, which pays for first- and second-year Tunisian undergraduates to study at an American university for a year. The group also provides venture capital for fledgling Tunisian businesses, primarily located in Tunisia.

Tunisian Americans' combination of smooth assimilation into American society and sustained ties to the home country may be a result of Tunisia's historical amalgamation of many lasting outside influences, including those of the Phoenicians, Carthaginians, Greeks, Romans, Ottomans, Berbers, French, Spanish, and Italians. In addition, living across the sea from some of Europe's great empires and maritime powers, the Tunisians have a considerable legacy of interacting with different cultures and conducting international business.

Traditions and Customs Tunisia possesses a rich and decorated history of participation in and support of the arts, which are a critical element of the country's traditions and customs. A recent Tunisian artistic tradition is collaborative painting, which was begun in 1988 by journalist Hechmi Ghachem as a way to help artists circumvent the oppression of the Ben Ali regime. Ghacem encouraged artists who had been unable to release their own work to collaborate on a canvas. Typically, one of these collaborative paintings features the shared efforts of five artists working on a canvas approximately 6 feet by 5 feet, and the finished products tend to be colorful and abstract. Over time a set of unwritten rules evolved. For example, once a work is begun, no new members are permitted to join the group, and artists in the group are free to paint over the work of the other artists. Before the project gets underway, one person is designated to solve disputes. In 2008 Ted Black, a former Broadway producer who had recently taken up painting, met Ghacem on a visit to Tunisia and brought the idea back to Manhattan and Connecticut, where collaborative painting has become quite popular. Black has since toured the northeastern United States and Europe, giving lectures and hosting collaborative sessions at such venues as Yale University, the American Islamic Congress Center in Boston, and the Sorbonne in Paris.

Cuisine One of the most popular appetizers in Tunisia is *harissa*, which consists of dried chili peppers, garlic, cumin, and olive oil. Another popular dish, especially among vegetarians, is *salata mechouia*, a dip made from grilled peppers, olive oil, onion, and garlic, usually served with bread. Nonvegetarians sometimes eat *salata mechouia* with shredded tuna served on top. Another favorite, *salata tounisa* is created from cucumber, tomato, onion, olive oil, and lemon. This dish is also often garnished with tuna. Other meal starters include *tajine*, a baked casserole made from egg, meat, and spices; and *brik*, which contains egg, olive oil, parsley, and tuna and is served in triangle-shaped portions.

One of the most popular entrees in Tunisia is couscous, a staple food throughout North Africa made from grains enhanced with spices and other ingredients. Tunisians are also fond of grilled fish, including *loup* (European sea bass), *dourade* (similar to snapper), and *rouget* (red mullet). Many Tunisian diners offer *ojja*, a stew that includes various meats, tomatoes, harissa, onion, olive oil, garlic, peppers, and egg. This extremely spicy dish, when served with spicy sausage, is called *ojja merguez*. Finally, for dessert Tunisians eat fruit and *makroudh*, a honey-based pastry with a date filling.

Couscous and grilled fish are very popular among Tunisian Americans, who serve these dishes at home and at festivals, events, and other celebrations sponsored by their organizations. Tunisian Americans sometimes share their native culture with the community through food festivals. In Johnson City, Tennessee, for example, the Tunisian American Chamber of Commerce sponsors Taste of Tunisia, a well-attended, upscale culinary experience.

Dances and Songs Classical Tunisian music is a blend of Greek, Ottoman, and, most notably, Andalusian influences. In the thirteenth century, Muslims fleeing religious persecution in Andalusia, a large area covering most of southern Spain, came to present-day Morocco, Tunisia, and Algeria. Among the many aspects of Muslim culture that these refugees brought with them was *malouf*, a complexly arranged form of classical music played by orchestras consisting of sitars, flutes, violins, and drums. The form became part of the Tunisian national identity in 1956,

TUNISIA'S CINEMATIC TRADITION

Tunisia has a rich cinematic tradition that dates from the early days of the French protectorate, when the brothers Auguste and Louis Lumiere, French pioneers of the motion picture camera, filmed street scenes in Tunis in 1896. European and North African filmmakers have been making movies there since the 1920s, and throughout the latter half of the twentieth century, Tunisia's coastal landscape and traditional architecture has attracted numerous celebrated directors, including George Lucas, who shot much of *Raiders of the Lost Ark* (1981) there, and Roman Polanski, who filmed *Pirates* (1986) in Tunisia. Three of the *Star Wars* movies were partly filmed in Tunisia. Some of the most successful Tunisian films, such as *As-Soufraa* (1975; The Ambassadors) and *Rih Essedd* (1986; Man of Ashes), have focused on social issues including racism, prostitution, and sexual tourism.

when Tunisia gained independence from France and Bourguiba promoted the music as part of his effort to forge a new national consciousness. While Tunisians remain proud of malouf, they tend to listen to it only at weddings and perhaps at government events that invoke Tunisian culture.

Modern Tunisian music follows common genres with its own unique twist. A vibrant underground heavy metal scene has evolved in Tunisia since the first decade of the twenty-first century. Many credit the group Neshez—founded in 1994 by guitarist Heikal Guiza and drummer Skander Bouassida—with starting the movement. The duo plays a wide range of fast-paced, percussion-driven songs that include aspects of numerous musical genres, including jazz, reggae, soul, grunge, and even malouf. According to their website, the band's name means "discord or nonsense." They have released more than one hundred titles. Most of the young Tunisian metal bands play cover songs and sing in English.

Rap music has also grown quite popular in Tunisia, and in the years leading up to the revolution, rap stars acquired considerable social clout as a result of bold lyrics that objected to the machinations of the Ben Ali regime. All of these artists risked arrest, and several endured punishment. For example, less than two weeks before Ben Ali fled the country, Hamada Ben Amor, who raps under the name El General, was forcibly removed from his home by government officials and detained for eight days, probably for a song titled "Mr. President Your People Are Dying." Tunisia's biggest rap star is Balti, who is acknowledged as one of founders of the hip-hop tradition in the country. A respected social critic, he provided a calming voice in the aftermath of the revolution, advocating for a peaceful reconstruction of Tunisian society. In an interview with CNN on March 2, 2011, he said,

TUNISIAN PROVERBS

- Because he has so many trades, he is unemployed.

- Don't trust the horses if they run away, or the whores if they repent.

- He ate one fig, and he thought the autumn had come.

- He who is covered with other people's clothes is naked.

- He who spends a night with a chicken will cackle in the morning.

- He who wants to be famous will have many a sleepless night.

"The stone which brought down the government we can use to rebuild the country."

Tunisian Americans have a reputation for following events in their country closely and are aware of the burgeoning music scene and such figures as Balti and El General. Most also know and take some measure of pride in the malouf tradition. They may play a classical piece if they are inclined to invoke Tunisian culture at a wedding or other large family gathering. In general, however, musical tastes among Tunisian Americans tend to be similar to mainstream American musical tastes.

Holidays Tunisians celebrate the Muslim holidays, most notably Eid al-Fitr (usually in late August), which marks the end of Ramadan, the traditional month of fasting; and Eid al-Adha (late October or early November), which honors Abraham's agreement to sacrifice his son to God. Tunisian Sufis (who make up about 1 percent of the country's Muslim population) celebrate Mawlid—the Prophet Muhammad's birthday—in early August. In addition, many Tunisians make pilgrimages to Mecca and Medina in Saudi Arabia. Nonreligious national holidays include Independence Day, or National Day (March 20), which commemorates the end of the French Protectorate in 1956; and Republic Day (July 25), which honors the founding of the republican government in 1957. Tunisian Americans celebrate Muslim holidays in traditional fashion and may observe Tunisian secular holidays by taking the day off of work.

FAMILY AND COMMUNITY LIFE

Families in Tunisia tend to be large by Western standards, with many having more than five children. Wealthier families and families in which both spouses have college degrees, however, are likely to have fewer children. In the traditional Tunisian family, the oldest man is considered the head of the family. The rest of the males, in order of age, are ranked below him. The wife is next, followed by the remaining females. To outside observers, traditional Tunisian family dynamics may appear harsh. Family members are known to quarrel, and when a family member encounters difficulty outside the home, he or she may expect only a modicum of help. While this dynamic exists in families in many different cultures, it is perhaps more noticeable in Tunisia, and Tunisian families may at times appear to be divided against each other.

In recent decades, especially among the wealthy and educated classes, traditional family mores changed as more women went to college and pursued careers. In the years leading up to the revolution, Tunisian society became increasingly secularized and democratic, and the pace of social change increased after the Arab Spring. Many families that clung to traditional values during this time endured bitter intergenerational feuds as young Tunisian men and women demanded greater degrees of self-expression, especially when courting and choosing a career. In wealthy families an increasing number of children, especially females, sought college education in Europe. Tunisian American families tend to resemble American families, and they have avoided the tensions that accompany radical social change.

Gender Roles Tunisians traditionally followed conventional gender roles, with men serving as breadwinners and woman maintaining responsibility for domestic chores. Some of the reforms enacted during Bourguiba's presidency gave women more opportunities to acquire advanced education and to work in professional jobs outside the home. Most working Tunisian women must still manage a majority of the domestic responsibilities. While some Tunisian men have accepted women as equals in the workplace and the home, many have been resistant to women's expanded roles and their rise in social status.

Tunisian American women experience somewhat greater acceptance and freedom than do their counterparts in Tunisia, but, similarly, they often assume the majority of the domestic responsibilities even if they hold a job.

Education In Tunisia elementary school attendance is obligatory, but children usually follow different pathways beginning as early as middle school, with some steered towards a vocational future and others encouraged to pursue intellectual interests. Most children do not hold jobs, but male teenagers may be commissioned as apprentices.

Both men and women are encouraged to pursue higher education. Enrollment has grown briskly since the mid-1990s, when the Tunisian government committed to improving the country's higher education system by adding more universities and improving existing facilities. Between 1995 and 2005 university enrollment more than tripled from about 100,000 students to more than 350,000. By 2005 spending on education accounted for nearly 7.4 percent of the gross domestic product, with 2 percent going to higher education. Most students focus on either business or technology.

Tunisian Americans are encouraged to pursue business and technology and are known to perform well in school. Tunisian Americans in the workforce also value education and have set up scholarship funds and exchange programs to enable Tunisians to study at American universities.

Courtship and Weddings Many Tunisian marriages are arranged, and if they are not explicitly arranged, young couples are expected to seek the counsel of their parents and follow their advice. Families help select a spouse based on set of rational considerations, including wealth, family reputation, and, with regard to the prospective bride, modesty. Prenuptial contracts are mandatory, and divorce rates are high—almost 50 percent in the major metropolitan areas. In one typical wedding ritual, the bride enters the groom's house while he stays outside, and he joins her privately in an inner chamber. The couple then remain secluded for the consummation of the marriage. Prior to Bourguiba's presidency, polygamy was common. With the introduction of his reforms, however, women can no longer be forced into marriage, they must be of a certain age to be married, and polygamy is not permitted.

As in other conservative Muslim societies, unmarried couples are not permitted to display affection publically and are expected to refrain from sex. Since the revolution, however, temporary, or *urfi*, marriages have helped young Tunisian lovers circumvent such restrictions. In an urfi marriage the couple proclaims "We got married" before two witnesses, and their union is considered to be sanctified by Allah. These marriages, which have been common among impoverished Tunisians for a long time, have become a trend on Tunisian college campuses and among young professionals. Urfi marriages are not recognized by the government, but a popular movement is working to legalize them.

Tunisian Americans may adopt the courtship and dating rituals practiced in U.S. culture, but they are likely to adhere to their parent's wishes when selecting a spouse. Like Tunisians, Tunisian Americans often see marriage as an institution intended to produce children and raise them in accordance with the principals of Islam.

Tunisian swimmer Oussama Mellouli swam for, and continues to train with, the USC Trojans in California. FRANCOIS XAVIER MARIT / AFP / GETTY IMAGES

EMPLOYMENT AND ECONOMIC CONDITIONS

The small size of the Tunisian American community and their relatively recent arrival make it difficult to determine what types of jobs these immigrants most commonly hold. Many Tunisian Americans are well educated, and because they have a strong level of English proficiency, they hold professorships in universities around the United States. A large percentage of Tunisian Americans have pursued careers in business.

POLITICS AND GOVERNMENT

Although they have had a minimal impact on American politics, Tunisian Americans are heavily invested in the security and stability of Tunisia. They maintain close ties with relatives and friends there, primarily through social media. This keeps them abreast of Tunisian politics and has also given them a voice in the country's attempts to restructure its government and economy since the overthrow of President Ben 'Ali. Both individually and through participation in their organizations, Tunisian Americans have advocated for the need to maintain strong ties between their home country and the United States. Tunisian Americans have shown solidarity with other Americans by denouncing terrorist activities, such as the attack on the U.S. embassy in Libya in September 2012.

NOTABLE INDIVIDUALS

Education Ali Khemili, who was born and raised in Tunisia, conceptualized and launched the Tunisian Community Center, the website that serves as a virtual network through which Tunisian Americans can connect for many different purposes. He manages a Tunisia-focused nonprofit organization in Albany, New York, named Nidaa Tounes (the Call of Tunisia).

Fashion Sulaika Zarrouk was raised in Manhattan by her Tunisian-born painter father and her United Nations-associated mother. An eco-conscious designer, she has created various handbag lines, including her Felix Ray line for Target, and she has been featured in *Elle* magazine.

Science and Medicine Nelly Alia-Klein, a scientist with the U.S. Department of Energy, was named Woman of the Year in Medicine by the *Village Beacon Record* in 2011. She attended Columbia University and is a professor at the Icahn School of Medicine at Mount Sinai in Manhattan.

Mohamed Laoucet Ayari, a space researcher, is a professor at the University of Colorado Boulder, where he received a PhD in 1988.

Sports The swimmer Oussama Mellouli (1984–) won three Olympic medals in 2008 and 2012. Previously, he swam for the University of Southern California.

ORGANIZATIONS AND ASSOCIATIONS

American Tunisian Association

This nonprofit, first established in 1966 and reorganized in 1989, aims to raise awareness and understanding of Tunisia in the United States. It caters especially to members in the Washington, D.C., area.

6225 32nd Place NW
Washington, D.C. 20015
Phone: (202) 966-3238
URL: http://americantunisianassociation.com

Tunisian American Young Professionals

Organized after Tunisian uprisings of 2010 and 2011, the organization strives to connect Tunisian American professionals, to create opportunities for them, and to raise awareness about the challenges faced by Tunisians and Tunisian Americans.

Email: info@tayp.org
URL: www.tayp.org

Tunisian Community Center (TCC)

This landmark association, founded in 1999, serves as a virtual network through which Tunisian Americans can connect, find information, and organize. It sponsors Tunisian American Day annually in several cities and runs various other programs, including the Tunisian Student Federation, which helps establish Tunisian student clubs at American universities. It also publishes the *Community Gazette Newsletter*, an online monthly that circulates information about Tunisia to interested parties and members of the TCC virtual network.

Phone: (339) 224-4822
Fax: (518) 383-9453
URL: www.tunisiancommunity.org

Tunisian Student Association in North America (TUSANA)

This organization serves students of Tunisian origin or descent at the University of Houston, as well as other interested parties. The group advocates for awareness and understanding of Tunisia and its characteristics.

University of Houston
4800 Calhoun Boulevard
Campus Activities Box 284
Houston, Texas 77204-3031
Email: uh.tusana@yahoo.com
URL: www.uh.edu/tusana

MUSEUMS AND RESEARCH CENTERS

University of Georgia-Tunisia Educational Partnership

This e-learning project, sponsored by the University of Georgia, is designed to augment educational opportunities for Tunisian students by facilitating connections between university personnel and educational professionals in Tunisia.

Takoi Hamrita, Director
University of Georgia
597 D. W. Brooks Drive

Athens, Georgia 30602
Phone: (706) 542-1973
Fax: (706) 542-8806
Email: thamrita@uga.edu
URL: http://tunisia.uga.edu/about.php

SOURCES FOR ADDITIONAL STUDY

Abadi, Jacob. *Tunisia since the Arab Conquest: The Saga of a Westernized Muslim State*. Ithaca, NY: Ithaca Press, 2013.

Anderson, Lisa. *The State and Social Transformation in Tunisia and Libya, 1830–1980*. Princeton, NJ: Princeton University Press, 1987.

Hejaiej, Monia. *Behind Closed Doors: Women's Oral Narratives in Tunis*. Rutgers, NJ: Rutgers University Press, 1996.

King, Stephen J. *Liberalization against Democracy: The Local Polices of Economic Reform in Tunisia*. Bloomington: Indiana University Press, 2003.

Murphy, Emma C. *Economic and Political Change in Tunisia: From Bourguiba to Ben Ali*. New York: Palgrave Macmillan, 1999.

Zussman, Mira. *Development and Disenchantment in Rural Tunisia: The Bourguiba Years*. New York: Westview Press, 1992.

TURKISH AMERICANS

Donald Altschiller

OVERVIEW

Turkish Americans are immigrants or descendants of immigrants from the Republic of Turkey, a country that straddles the border between Europe and Asia. On its western, European side, Turkey adjoins Greece and Bulgaria; on the eastern, Asian side, it shares borders with Armenia, Georgia, Azerbaijan, Iran, Iraq, and Syria. The Black Sea lies to the north and the Mediterranean to the west and southwest. Its location on two continents has been a crucial factor in the country's variegated history and culture. Modern Turkey embraces bustling cosmopolitan centers, pastoral farming communities, barren wastelands, placid Aegean islands, and steep mountain ranges. The country's area of almost 300,000 square miles (777,000 square kilometers) includes about 10,000 square miles (26,000 square kilometers) of European Turkey, known as Thrace, and approximately 290,000 square miles (750,000 square kilometers) of Asian Turkey, known as Anatolia or Asia Minor. The whole of Turkey is slightly smaller than the combined area of Texas and Louisiana.

In July 2012 Turkey's population was estimated at 79.7 million people by the *CIA Factbook*, with an annual growth rate of 1.2 percent. Almost 99.8 percent of the population is Muslim, mostly Sunni. Turkey is a secular state, however, and Jews and Christians may freely practice their religious faiths. Kurds, who are also mainly Muslims, are the largest ethnic minority in Turkey, making up 18 percent of the population. Other minorities include Greeks, Armenians, and Roma. In 2005 Turkey and seven other European countries signed onto the Decade of Roma Inclusion initiative (committing to work toward social and socioeconomic equality of the Roma population). Subsequently, Turkey officially counted 500,000 Roma among its residents, though others estimate the number at closer to 2.5 million. After an economic crisis in 2001, Turkey's economy has shown unusual strength and growth, weathering the global economic downturn in 2008. While Turkey has an increasingly diverse economy, 25 percent of the population still works in agriculture.

Although they have disagreed on the number, historians estimate that 25,000 to 50,000 Muslim Turks came to the United States between 1890 and 1924,

most of them male peasants from both the European and Asian areas of Turkey: from Thrace because the edges of the Ottoman Empire were breaking down, and from Anatolia because U.S. missionaries were active among the Armenians there. Most of these immigrated to Detroit, Boston, and smaller towns in Massachusetts, such as Lowell and Salem, where they worked in factories and lived in neighborhoods close to other immigrants from the Ottoman Empire, including Armenians, Jews, and Greeks. Turkish Sephardic Jews founded congregations in Seattle and New York. According to Talat Sai Halman in the *Harvard Encyclopedia of American Ethnic Groups* (1980), the majority of this first wave of immigrants, up to 86 percent, returned to Turkey after it gained independence in 1923. From the 1980s through the beginning of the twenty-first century, about 4,000 Turkish immigrants arrived each year. This last wave was much more diverse, containing more women, both religious and secular people, and both working class and professionals.

The 2010 U.S. Census tallied 177,841 Turkish Americans; however, according to a 2004 article by Ilhan Kaya in the *Journal of Muslim Minority Affairs* ("Turkish-American Immigration History and Identity Formations"), former Turkish ambassador to the United States Mehmet Ezen estimated that 350,000 to 500,000 people of Turkish descent lived in the United States at that time. Although there are Turkish Americans in every state, the highest concentrations are in the large urban areas of New York, California, New Jersey, Florida, Virginia, and Texas.

HISTORY OF THE PEOPLE

Early History The Turks, who have inhabited the Anatolian Peninsula since the eleventh century, are relative newcomers to a land that has seen many successive civilizations. Beginning around 2000 BCE, pre-Hittites, Hittites, Phrygians, Lydians, Persians, Greeks, and Romans lived in or ruled the region. After the collapse of Roman Empire in the West in about 450 CE, Anatolia became the heartland of the Byzantine Empire (a Greek continuation of Roman rule in the eastern Mediterranean), with its capital in Byzantium (renamed Constantinople, for Constantine the Great, in the fourth century) and its state religion Christianity.

Turkish American writer Elif Batuman at the Melbourne Writers Festival in Australia. BEOWULF SHEEHAN / ZUMAPRESS / NEWSCOM

Originally nomadic peoples from the steppes of Central Asia, Turkish tribes began moving west toward Europe around the first century CE. In the middle of the fifth century, the first group, the Huns, reached Western Europe. Others established kingdoms in Turkestan and Persia before the tenth century, by which time they had converted to Islam from Zoroastrianism or other polytheistic tribal religions. Later that century a new Turkish dynasty, the Seljuqs, came to power in Turkestan and then in Persia. From there they began to make incursions into Anatolia in the early eleventh century. In 1071 the Seljuqs crushed the Byzantine army at Manzikert in eastern Anatolia, capturing the emperor himself. This important battle marked the effective end of Byzantine power in eastern Anatolia, and the beginning of Turkish dominance.

The main branch of the Seljuqs continued to rule in Persia and Mesopotamia (present-day Iran and Iraq), while another branch, known as the Seljuqs of Rum (Rome), quickly penetrated the entire Anatolian Peninsula. Of the original population, who were Christian Greek and Armenian speakers, some fled to Constantinople or the West and a few remained Christian under the generally tolerant rule of the Muslim Turkish tribes. Over the centuries, however, most converted to Islam and began to speak Turkish, melding with the dominant Turks, whom they had originally outnumbered.

During the 1100s the Seljuqs struggled with Byzantines and later with the Christian Crusaders from Europe for control of western Anatolia, especially along the Aegean coast, from which these assailants had been fighting to drive the Turkish tribes for more than two hundred years. The strongly centralized Seljuq state reached the peak of its power in the early thirteenth century; shortly thereafter, local internal revolts, combined with the Mongol invasions from the east, began to erode its authority. By the early fourteenth century, Seljuq rule had collapsed completely.

Of ten local emirates, or kingdoms, that arose in Turkish Anatolia in the ensuing power vacuum, one quickly came to preeminence: that of Osman, who ruled in northwestern Anatolia and founded the Osmanli, or Ottoman, dynasty. Osman's son, Orhan, expanded his father's dominions in Anatolia and in the 1350s undertook the first Ottoman conquests in Europe, wrestling several towns in eastern Thrace from the Byzantines and crushing the Bulgars and Serbs in battle. His successors, Murad and Bayezid, continued the string of Asian and European conquests. By the early 1400s the territory of the once-mighty Byzantine Empire had been reduced to a small island of land around Constantinople surrounded by Ottoman territory.

As Ottoman power had increased, so had the pomp of those who wielded it. Murad, for example, had taken the title of sultan (meaning "authority" or "power") rather than the less majestic bey or emir, which were military ranks. Ottoman capitals also became increasingly grand. Muhammad (or Mehmed) II undertook a massive building program in Constantinople, constructing houses, baths, bazaars, inns, fountains, gardens, a huge mosque, and an imperial palace. He also encouraged the original inhabitants who had fled to return—Jews, Greeks, and Armenians, many of whom were craftsmen, scholars, or artists—and made trade agreements with Venetian and Florentine merchants. Now commonly referred to as Istanbul, the city became a hub of culture and commerce.

Sultan Muhammad II's eldest son and successor, Bayezid II, ruled from 1481 to 1512, during the height of the Roman Catholic Inquisition and the expulsion of Jews from Spain and Portugal. Although Jews had lived in Anatolia continuously since at least the fourth century BCE, Bayezid II's welcome to the Jews expelled by Spain's King Ferdinand brought thousands into a safe haven in the Ottoman Empire. In "History of the Turkish Jews" (on the *Sephardi Center* website), Naim Güleryüz, curator of the Jewish Museum of Turkey, wrote that in 1477 there were 1,647 Jewish households in Istanbul—11 percent of the city's total population—while by 1527 there were 8,070 Jewish households.

The Ottoman Empire reached its peak under Muhammad's great-grandson, Suleiman, who took power in 1520. By the time of his death in 1566, the empire had reached its apogee, with the Ottomans controlling areas of northern Africa, southern Europe, and western Asia. Over the next century the Ottomans ultimately maintained hegemony over the lands Suleiman had conquered but were vulnerable to local rebellions and unable to keep pace with European political, scientific, and social developments. By the end of the seventeenth century, the empire had stagnated, and over the course of the following two centuries, it lost large tracts of land to the Russians, Austrians, and Persians, among other foreign adversaries. By the late nineteenth century, after a decisive defeat to the Russian Empire in the Russo-Turkic War of 1877 to 1878, the Ottoman Empire was on the brink of dissolution.

Modern Era In 1908 a nationalist group known as the Young Turks revolted and took control of the empire. They joined World War I on the side of Germany and the Central Powers in 1914. Within the empire the war proved particularly tragic for the Armenian people who, influenced culturally and politically by both the Ottomans and the Russians, had formed diaspora communities in the Russian, Persian, and Ottoman empires. The Young Turks

initiated a policy of mass deportation and extermination of the Armenian people living within the Ottoman Empire. Historians estimate that as many as 1.5 million Armenians were killed in what is known as the first genocide of the twentieth century.

After World War I Mustafa Kemal, a military hero who became known as Atatürk (Father of the Turks), organized the Turkish army, drove the Greeks from Turkey, and founded the Republic of Turkey in 1923, marking the end of the Ottoman Empire. After assuming the office of president (which he held from 1923 until his death in 1938), Atatürk began a series of revolutionary reforms that transformed Turkey into a modern nation. In a symbolic break with the Ottoman past, he moved the capital from Istanbul to Ankara and replaced religious law with civil, criminal, and commercial laws based on those of Switzerland. Atatürk also encouraged Turks to imitate European dress and customs. Among other language reforms, he changed the Islamic call to prayer from Arabic to Turkish. According to Naim Turfan in the *Oxford Encyclopedia of the Islamic World*, Atatürk believed that Islam was the most rational and natural religion and

Hundreds of people, including many Turkish Americans and members of the Occupy Wall Street movement, protest in Zuccotti Park, New York City, in solidarity with demonstrators in Istanbul who were trying to stop a popular park from being demolished to make way for a shopping center. June, 2013. SPENCER PLATT / GETTY IMAGES

that a secular Turkish government would be the best vehicle for the advancement of the voluntary adherence of individual Muslim believers.

Turkey remained neutral for the better part of World War II, officially joining the Allies in 1945 in what was largely recognized as a diplomatic manoeuver. Emerging from a one-party system under Atatürk's Republican People's Party, by the mid-1940s Turkey's government evolved into a parliamentary democracy which, despite interference from the military in the early 1970s, maintained its independence from the powerful army throughout the 1980s.

The country began to experience political turmoil in the early 1990s as various Islamist parties gained strength and threatened Turkey's avowed commitment to secular government. In 1996 one of these, the Welfare Party, became the largest party and created a coalition government under Prime Minister Necmettin Erbakan. By the end of the decade, the military demanded that Erbakan resign and dissolve his party, and he agreed. While this peaceful coup said much about Turkey's political stability, in the early part of the twenty-first century some fifty quarrelsome political parties were registered in Turkey, and the nation continued to struggle to maintain its secularity. Abdullah Gül, who had been associated with Islamist parties, was elected President in 2007. Prime Minister Recep Tayyip Erdoğan, in power since 2003, was reelected for the third time in 2011 and has been considered the most influential Turkish leader of the twenty-first century. Turkey formally applied to be part of the European Union in 2005; as of 2012, the application was still pending.

SETTLEMENT IN THE UNITED STATES

Precise statistics on Turkish American immigration prior to 1890 are difficult to obtain. According to the U.S. Immigration and Naturalization Service Statistical Yearbook for 2001, the number of immigrants from the Ottoman Empire was minuscule from 1820 through 1860, averaging less than twenty people per year. Between 1895 and 1924, these immigration records stated, between 18,000 and 22,000 Turks arrived in the United States. One of the difficulties in arriving at an accurate count is that between 1820 and 1920, some 300,000 immigrants entering the United States had passports from the Ottoman Empire, the majority of them Armenian, Greek, and other ethnic minorities. Although most of the individuals from this wave (80 to 86 percent) returned to Turkey following the establishment of the republic in 1923, they were among the first large groups of Muslim immigrants to the United States and their contributions were just beginning to be unearthed in 2000.

The early Turkish immigrants were almost entirely male. In the culture of Anatolian Turkey, men did not feel comfortable bringing their wives and families until they were able to plant secure economic roots in the United States. According to Frank Ahmed, author of *Turks in America* (1986), the *Salem Evening News* wrote extensively about the sizable Turkish community on the North Shore of Boston, including those in the towns of Peabody, Salem, and Lynn. Many Turkish immigrants worked in Massachusetts, in the leather factories of Lynn and Salem and the wire factories of Worcester. Others obtained work in factories in New York, Detroit, and Chicago. Forced to work long hours with low pay in unsanitary and unsafe conditions, some Turkish workers were involved in strikes against management, who generally viewed the Turks as "good workers," according to Ahmed.

Before 1920 as many as 2,000 Turks arrived in Peabody, worked in the growing leather tanning industry, and then left after 1923. In 1918 in Cleveland, Ohio, where almost one thousand Turkish laborers lived, some founded an Islamic association and purchased burial plots, yet by 1950 all but a dozen or so had moved back to Turkey or elsewhere. In 1910 a large Turkish community lived in Detroit, where the Ford motor plant offered well-paid factory work and where earlier Armenian and Greek immigrants from the Ottoman Empire had paved the way. In 1919 one of the first U.S. mosques was built there. Historian John Grabowski noted in *Prospects and Challenges* (2005) that the settlement patterns of Turks from the Balkans and Turks from Anatolia differed somewhat. The Anatolians predominated in Massachusetts and Detroit, while in the Ohio and the Pennsylvania industrial belt, Balkan Turks were more common.

Early Turkish immigrants often settled into rooming houses. Frequently, a Turk would rent the house and sublease rooms to his fellow countrymen. Although the accommodations were spare, the newly arriving immigrants managed, to a degree, to replicate village life at home. They ate Turkish food (pilaf, lamb, and vegetable dishes) and slept on mattresses without a bedstead.

Despite being hardworking and industrious, many Turks did not escape the prejudice frequently directed at newcomers. Occasionally, they were called "Ali Hassans" or "Abdul Hamids," and some newspapers ridiculed the "terrible Turks" and Islam. Among the Turks, however, there was much tolerance for Turkish minorities, especially Turkish Jews, who were fully accepted and respected by their recently arriving compatriots.

Because of the precarious situation in Turkey and their concern for their families, most Turks stayed for a decade or less and had returned to their Anatolian villages before the Great Depression. A small number of Turks stayed in the United States, learned English, and married American women. As a result, the diminished Turkish American community became more close-knit. Social life revolved around coffee houses and benevolent societies. In Peabody coffee houses on Walnut Street became a congregating place for the

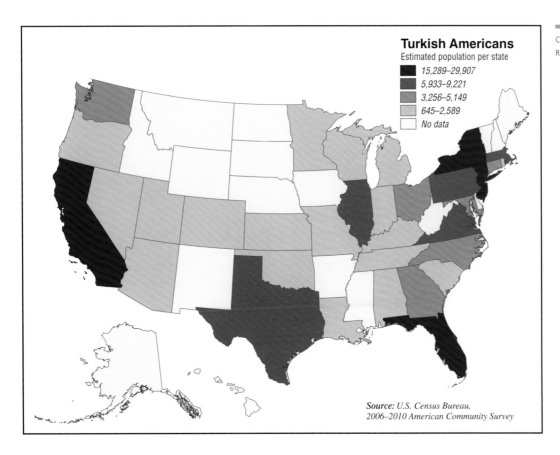

Turkish Americans
Estimated population per state

- 15,289–29,907
- 5,933–9,221
- 3,256–5,149
- 645–2,589
- No data

*Source: U.S. Census Bureau,
2006–2010 American Community Survey*

Turks living in the area. It was here that community members exchanged news about their villages while sipping Turkish coffee and eating sweet pastries.

Unlike the earlier wave of immigrants, the post–World War II generation was highly educated and included almost four thousand engineers and physicians. These numbers would undoubtedly have been higher, but strict U.S. immigration regulations, enforced from the mid-1920s until 1965, established an annual quota of 100 Turkish immigrants. Again, many of these professionals returned to Turkey after living in the United States for a brief period.

The third wave of Turkish immigration began in the 1980s and continued into the twenty-first century. It has been much more diverse in terms of education and occupations and has included men, women, and families. The number of Turkish immigrants has risen to more than two thousand per year. Many opened small businesses in the United States and created Turkish American organizations, thus developing Turkish enclaves, particularly in New York City. Others came for educational purposes.

All three waves have brought Turks to large urban centers. The immigrants often follow relatives or people from the same hometown to the same U.S. location, which is called *hemşerilik* in Turkish. The greatest number have settled in New York City, Boston, Chicago, Detroit, Los Angeles, San Francisco, and

Rochester. Other concentrations of Turkish Americans may be found along the East Coast in Connecticut, New Jersey, Maryland, Virginia, and Florida. The U.S. Census Bureau's American Community Survey reported that in 2010, Turkish Americans were living in thirty-six states, among them Arizona (2,477), Georgia (4,126), Pennsylvania (6,319), Texas (9,221), and Washington (5,149).

LANGUAGE

Like Mongolian, Korean, and Japanese, Turkish belongs to the Altaic language family. More than 100 million people living in Turkey and Central Asia speak Turkic languages. During the Ottoman era Turkish was written in Arabic script, from right to left. Ottoman Turkish borrowed heavily from other languages, and its varying forms of Arabic script made it difficult to use. Atatürk eliminated Arabic script, substituting the Latin alphabet with some letter modifications to distinguish certain Turkish sounds. Many Arabic and Persian loan words were removed, while words from European languages were phoneticized. The alphabet consists of twenty-nine letters—twenty-one consonants and eight vowels—six of which do not occur in English. Turkish does not use gendered words and makes no distinction between he, she, and it. Historians believe that the language reforms were generally a positive development. Literacy is now more commonplace, and the language gap between economic classes has been reduced. The Turks are very expressive and often use body language to communicate.

There are several Turkish American organizations and community centers in the United States that teach the Turkish language to the children of Turkish Americans. Despite this effort, relatively few second- and third-generation Turkish Americans speak Turkish, a trend that will greatly affect the future of this community.

Greetings and Popular Expressions Common expressions among Turks and Turkish Americans include: *merhaba* (MEHR-hah-bah)—"hello"; *günaydın* (gew-nahy-DUHN)—"good morning"; *iyi akşamlar* (EE ahk-shahm-LAHR)—"good evening"; *Nasılsınız?* (NAHS-suhl-suh-nuhz)—"How are you?"; *İyiyim* (ee-YEE-yihm)—"I am fine"; *teşekkür ederim* (tesh-ek-KEWR eh-dehr-eem)—"thank you"; *Saatler olsun*! (sa-at-LER OL-sun)—"May it last for hours!" (said after a bath, shave, or haircut); *Geçmiş olsun*! (GESH-meesh OL-sun)—"May it be in the past!" (said in cases of illness).

RELIGION

Most Turkish Americans practice Sunni Islam, but in a particularly Turkish way, influenced by Sufism and Turkish nationalism. When Atatürk led independent Turkey into secular statehood in 1923, religious law was replaced with civil law, leaving religious preference and practice up to the individual. Turkish Islam is marked by moderation, compatibility with modernity, diversity, and democracy. Turks who immigrated to the United States between 1940 and 1980 were largely secular and did not form their own religious organizations, often worshiping in Arab, Pakistani, or other South Asian mosques.

The larger wave of immigration after 1980 brought more diversity and also a desire to establish Turkish religious organizations. In 1980 Turkish Americans founded the United American Muslim Association (UAMA) in Brooklyn, New York, to teach Islam and to build or rent mosques for prayer. By 2012 the UAMA listed more than twenty associated mosques in New York, Connecticut, California, Ohio, Massachusetts, and Illinois. Its headquarters, Fatih Camii, remain in Brooklyn, and its website is in Turkish with an English translation option.

Turkish mosques are distinctive in several ways: they display the Turkish flag, their prayers and sermons are often in Turkish, and they are often named for mosques in Turkey, which are in turn named for Ottoman Sultans such as Fatih, Suleymaniye, Selimiye, or Osman Gazi. Ilhan Kaya's 2003 dissertation for Florida State University, "Shifting Turkish American Identity Formations in the United States," found that Turkish American mosques have retained some practices of mosques in Turkey, such

as using rose perfume and curtaining off the women's prayer space. Kaya also reported a substantial Suleymancilar movement (followers of the Sufi master Suleyman Hilmi Tunahan) in the United States. The Suleymanci religious communities raise money for mosques and religious education. Another important Turkish American religious movement follows Fethullah Gülen, a Sunni Muslim who came to the United States in 1999 and as of 2012 lived in the Poconos in Pennsylvania. Gülen's followers, though religiously conservative in the Turkish context, are committed to interfaith dialogue and service to the common good.

CULTURE AND ASSIMILATION

Turkish culture is a unique blend of European, Asian, North African, and Middle Eastern influences. Turkish cuisine, customs, applied arts, and fine arts reflect a rich diversity as well as robust adaptability.

At the beginning of the twenty-first century, more than half of Turkish people in the United States were first-generation Americans: the U.S. Census Bureau's American Community Survey estimated in 2010 that of the nearly 180,000 Turkish Americans, 98,000 were born in Turkey. In his 2009 study "Identity across Generations" (*Middle East Journal* 63, no. 4), a look at first- and second-generation Turkish Americans, Ilhan Kaya found that most lived in urban neighborhoods near other Turks, and though acclimating to American culture, first-generation immigrants still felt out of the mainstream—for instance, only using English when they had to and relying on community networks for jobs and housing.

Harassment and fear of harassment after the September 11, 2001, Al Qaeda attacks on the World Trade Center and Pentagon pushed Muslim Turkish American communities to separate themselves from Arab Muslims and identify more closely with Western culture; some Turkish Americans changed their names, some women stopped wearing the *hijab* (head scarf), and some male students shaved their beards in an effort to blend in more. At the same time the aftermath of September 11 included a breaking of the isolation of Turkish American communities as they wanted others to get to know them. Turkish American mosques and organizations coordinated interfaith dialogues and conferences to teach others about their faith and culture. After the devastation of Hurricane Sandy in November 2012, the *Wall Street Journal* reported on an initiative called "Young Peace Builders" that paired Brooklyn Jewish and Turkish American teenagers in helping at a soup kitchen, among other activities, in an effort to foster understanding between the two communities and to benefit the larger society.

Cuisine Turkish food is widely regarded as one of the world's major cuisines. It is noted for its careful preparation and rich ingredients. A typical Turkish meal begins with soup or *meze* (hors d'oeuvres), followed in succession by the main course (usually red meat, chicken, or fish), vegetables cooked in olive oil, dessert, and fresh fruit. Turkish coffee, served in small cups, completes the feast.

Favorite soups include wedding soup, which combines chicken and beef broth, eggs, lemon, and vegetables; lentil soup, which uses beef broth, flour, butter, and paprika; and *tarhana* soup, which is made with a dried preparation of flour, yogurt, tomato, and red pepper flakes. Although soup is usually served at the beginning of a meal, tripe soup—featuring a sauce of vinegar and garlic—is served after a complete dinner and is usually accompanied by alcoholic drinks.

Among the best-known Turkish appetizers are *borek*, a pastry roll filled with cheese or ground meat; and *dolma*, made from stuffed grape leaves, green pepper or eggplant. The meze tray features salads and purees and may also include eggplant, caviar, lamb or veal, fried vegetables with yogurt sauce, and a wide variety of seafood.

Seafood prepared as a main course may be grilled, fried, or stewed. *Kofte* (meatballs) are another specialty, served grilled, fried, or stewed with vegetables. A sauce of buttermilk, made of yogurt and water, accompanies meat dishes. Fresh vegetables, cooked in olive oil and served either hot or cold, are essential to Turkish cuisine. Eggplant, peppers, green beans, and peas are the primary vegetables. Rice pilaf, which sometimes contains currants and pine nuts, is served as a side dish. *Rakl*, a drink similar to anisette, is often consumed as an alternative to wine.

The final touch to a meal is a tray of fresh fruits, often a combination of peaches, apples, pears, raisins, figs, oranges, or melons. Typical Turkish desserts include *baklava*, a flaky pastry dipped in syrup; *bulbul yuvasi*, thin pastry leaves with walnut filling and lemon peel syrup; *sekerpare*, sweet cookies; and *lokma*, Turkish fritters. Puddings are also popular, including *muhallebi*, or milk pudding, and *sutlac*, rice pudding.

Döner kebab, meat (usually beef, lamb, or veal) cooked on a vertical spit then sliced thinly and served on flatbread, is more widely known in the United States in its Greek version, the gyro. Popular around the world, döner kebab houses proliferate in the large urban areas were Turks have settled, including Boston, New York, Seattle, Chicago, San Diego, and Los Angeles.

At the beginning or end of a meal, diners often say "*afiyet olsun*," which means "may what you eat bring you well-being." "*Elinize saglik*," or "bless your hands," expresses praise to the chef.

Traditional Dress Along with his many other reforms, Atatürk succeeded in making Western-style dress, at least among men, widespread in Turkey. Consequently, Turkish Americans dress no differently than most other Americans. Atatürk also outlawed the traditional *fez*, a brimless, cone-shaped red hat, and made brimmed felt hats mandatory, because they prevented men from touching their foreheads to the ground in prayer. Traditional dress for women requires that they be covered from head to foot. Most Turkish garments are made from wool. The *kepenek*, a heavy, hooded mantle shaped from a single piece of felt, sheltered herders from the rain and cold and served as a blanket or a tent. Turkish Americans only wear traditional costume for parades or other heritage festivals.

Music The distinctive styles of Turkish music, influenced by Arabic, Byzantine, Persian, and Roma motifs, falls into two broad categories: traditional (classic) music and folk music. In the days of the Ottoman Empire, the sultan supported traditional music, or court music, which incorporates a wide array of musical instruments, most commonly Turkish varieties of lutes, woodwinds, flutes, violins, and zithers. Turkish village (folk) music comprises dance tunes, folk songs, and lullabies unique to each regions. The most commonly used folk music instruments include the *davul* (bass drum), *shawm* (a traditional woodwind, predecessor of the oboe), *saz* or *baglama sazi* (long-necked lute), *kemence* (Black Sea fiddle), *darbukka* (vase drum), *gayda* (reed or back pipe), and *kaval* (flute).

Turkish popular music in the twentieth and early twenty-first centuries included *fasil*, a Roma-influenced nightclub version of traditional classic music, and *arabesk*, which combines Turkish folk songs, Arabic music, and other styles. Turkish Sephardic Jews, Sufis, and Janissaries contributed to the musical richness and diversity. Sufi music is mostly associated with followers of both the Mevlevi (whirling dervishes) and Bektashi orders of Sufism. Janissary music is a military music that also influenced some European composers.

Turkish musicians popular in the United States include Esref Inceoglu, who sings traditional and contemporary music.

Holidays Turkey observes both civil and religious holidays. Whereas dates for civil holidays are determined by the Western (Gregorian) calendar, religious holidays are set by the Muslim lunar calendar, resulting in observances occurring on different days each year. Government offices are closed for all holidays and frequently for a day or two before or after as well.

Many Turkish Americans celebrate New Year's Day on January 1 and both National Sovereignty and Children's Day on April 23. This holiday commemorates the founding of the Grand National Assembly in 1923. At the same time, Atatürk proclaimed it a day to honor children, making it a unique international holiday. Atatürk's birthday is honored on May 19 (officially known as Atatürk Memorial and Youth and Sports Day), and his death is memorialized on November 10. In Turkey this day is marked by a national moment of

GENDER EQUALITY FOR TURKISH WOMEN

Women in Turkey achieved the right to vote in 1930, one of the many reforms enacted during the presidency of Atatürk. His attitude toward women was considered feminist for his time. While it is not uncommon for Turkish American women to have professional occupations, traditional deference to men is still strong among Turkish American women in the early twenty-first century. In an article for the *Huffington Post* ("All Women Need to Lean in, Including Women of Turkey," March 29, 2013), Senay Ataselim-Yilmaz, chief operating officer of Turkish Philanthropy Funds, wrote about Turkey's contradictory attitudes about gender equality, as well as about her own experience as a Turkish American woman. Even though she had been a feminist from an early age, she said, "I recognized that I am still affected by the culture I was raised in. All of us do. I hold myself back out of respect. I listen more than I speak. I give up my seat at the table when a senior man shows up." She urged Turkish women to bring about cultural and institutional change by taking on leadership roles: "Women of Turkey should acknowledge the cultural barriers that restrict her behavior and should not let that restrain her standing in the society."

silence throughout the nation at precisely 9:05 a.m., the time of Atatürk's death. Victory Day (August 30) celebrates the Ottoman victory over the Greeks in 1922, and Turkish Independence Day (October 29) recognizes the proclamation of the republic by Atatürk in 1923. A unique American tradition, begun on April 24, 1984, is Turkish American Day, during which Turkish Americans march down New York's Fifth Avenue. In May 2005 Patterson, New Jersey, also began holding an annual Turkish Day and Festival, when thousands of Turkish Americans hold a parade and attend concerts of traditional and popular Turkish music.

FAMILY AND COMMUNITY LIFE

In Turkey family life centers on the male head of the household, as he is the one who traditionally provides for his family. Children are expected to obey their parents, even after reaching adulthood, and must also show respect for all persons older than themselves, including older siblings. Parental authority in Turkey is so great that parents often arrange for the marriages of their children. The extended family is of extreme importance in Turkey; family members often work in the same business, and in the United States, the Turkish American family remains close-knit.

Gender Roles Among Turkish Americans men participate in community affairs and women are expected to manage the household. Very few Turkish women immigrated to the United States before World War II, and even into the twenty-first century, many were first-generation Americans. These women were deeply interested in and affected by debates in Turkey

around such issues as whether women should wear headscarves at work and school. Turkish American women differ on this issue: some wear the headscarf and others do not. An area of gender separation that has been more generally retained in the United States is the gathering of men at Turkish coffee houses to drink coffee and tea and watch sports. Although no signs prohibit women, Turkish women would never enter.

Education Turkish American parents have made great efforts to nurture their children's Turkish, American, and Muslim identities. In a 2012 study of the children of first-generation, college-educated Turkish American parents, Zeynap Isik-Ercan found that children enjoyed many social as well as academic benefits from mentoring relationships with other Turkish Americans in Sunday schools where they studied Turkish language and history. At least two Turkish communities have started private elementary schools, open to anyone, at which Turkish and Muslim culture are taught and shared: Amity School in Brooklyn and Pioneer Academy of Science in Clifton, New Jersey. The Fatih Mosque in Brooklyn provides summer camps and religious and cultural education for children.

According to the American Community Survey's 2010 estimates, 51 percent of Turkish Americans over the age of twenty-five had at least a bachelor's degree (59 percent of males and 48 percent of females), and 26 percent had a graduate degree.

EMPLOYMENT AND ECONOMIC CONDITIONS

Early Turkish immigrants to the United States were predominantly from Turkey's rural community. They settled in large, industrial cities and found employment as unskilled laborers. The majority came to earn money so that they could improve their economic situation and that of their families in Turkey. After the 1950s people of a skilled and highly educated class immigrated to the United States, the majority of whom were medical doctors, engineers, and scientists. Since 1980 the Turkish immigrants have included unskilled and semiskilled workers as well as students and professionals. In 2012 Turkish Americans were visible in virtually every field, according to the American Community Survey. Although the majority were professionals and enjoyed a middle-class lifestyle, the community also included blue-collar restaurant workers, gas station attendants, hair stylists, construction workers, and grocery clerks.

POLITICS AND GOVERNMENT

The many political factions in Turkey are reflected in the Turkish American community. All Turkish Americans, however, are united in their concern for Turkey and take great pride in their ethnic heritage. Many Turks living in the United States refuse to abandon their Turkish citizenship.

Before the 1970s Turkish Americans were not often involved in American politics. The Turkish invasion of Cyprus in 1974, however, in which the U.S. government supported Greece, mobilized many in the community. The small Turkish American population was not able to counter the influence of the much larger and more powerful Greek American organizations, however.

Turkish Americans proudly point to Turkey's membership in NATO and its military and political support of the U.S. government during the 1991 Persian Gulf War. After September 11, 2001, Turkish Americans became more politically visible and active. As the United States entered the war in Iraq, Turkey became much more important in American foreign affairs, and Turkish Americans paid very close attention to the development of the political relationship between the two countries.

In 2002 Tarkan Öcal became the first Turkish American to run for public office, contending for a seat in the Florida State Senate. Jak Karako ran for a seat in the New York State Senate in 2005. In 2006 Osman Bengür ran in Maryland for U.S. Congress, and Rıfat Sivişoğlu ran for county office in DuPage, Illinois, in 2008. All Democrats, none of these candidates won their elections. Few ran in the following election cycles, but Turkish Americans began contributing more heavily to political campaigns.

In 2007 Adam Schiff, a Democrat in the U.S. House of Representatives, introduced the Armenian Genocide resolution recognizing the Turkish massacre of Armenians in 1915. This created a political sore point for Turkish Americans, who characterize the events as ethnic clashes between the Armenian and Turkish communities. As of 2013 the bill had not passed, but it evoked very strong reactions and prompted a greater tendency in Turkish Americans to vote Republican. In 2013 Turkish Americans circulated a petition to President Obama calling on him to also recognize the 1992 Khojaly Massacre during the Nagorno-Karabakh War (1988–94), in which Armenian and Russian forces occupied the Azerbaijani town of Khojaly and killed at least 613 civilians, including 106 women, 63 children, and 70 elders.

In 2009, as the Turkish American community pursued further grassroots political involvement, the Turkish Coalition of America began leading Congressional delegations to Turkey, and by 2013 the group had led sixteen delegations, with more than 155 members participating. In April 2012 several Turkish American umbrella groups—the Federation of Turkish American Associations, the Turkish Coalition of America, the Assembly of Turkish American Associations, and the Washington-based Turkish American Community Centers—began the Thirty-second Annual Turkish-American National Convention with a seminar titled "Grassroots Day," which urged Turks to participate actively in U.S. politics.

NOTABLE INDIVIDUALS

Arts Tunç Yalman (1925–2006) was an Istanbul-born actor, translator, and writer and the artistic director of the Milwaukee Repertory Theater.

Business Muhtar A. Kent (1952–) has been the CEO of Coca-Cola Company since 2008. Born in New York, where his father was the Turkish consul-general, Kent found his first position at Coca-Cola through a newspaper ad in 1978.

Literature Journalist and essayist Elif Batuman (1977–) was born in New York City. She taught at Stanford University, publishing her work in the *New Yorker* and *Harper's Magazine*. Her book *The Possessed: Adventures with Russian Books and the People Who Read Them* was published in 2010.

An area of gender separation that has been more generally retained in the United States is the gathering of men at Turkish coffee houses to drink coffee and tea and watch sports. Although no signs prohibit women, Turkish women would never enter.

Alev Lytle Croutier (1945–) is the most-often-read Turkish American woman novelist. She was born in İzmir, Turkey, and came to the United States in 1983 to attend Oberlin College in Ohio. She made documentary films in Turkey, Japan, Europe, and the United States and wrote screenplays, including that of *Tell Me a Riddle* (1980), based on Tillie Olsen's 1956 novella. She is the author of the nonfiction best-sellers *Harem: The World Behind the Veil* (1989) and *Taking the Waters: Spirit, Art, and Sensuality* (1992) as well as the novels *The Palace of Tears* (2000), *Seven Houses* (2002), and *Leyla: The Black Tulip* (2003), a novel for young readers.

Selma Ekrem (1902–1986) was the granddaughter of a prominent exiled Ottoman playwright and grew up among other exiles. She came to the United States at the age of twenty-one in 1923 and lived in Connecticut and Massachusetts until her death in 1986. Her book *Unveiled: The Autobiography of a Turkish Girl* (circa 1930; republished in 2005) is the earliest Turkish American work that records a first-generation immigrant's recollection of her past life in Ottoman Turkey.

Poet, translator, and cultural historian Talat Sait Halman (1931–) is one of the best-known Turkish American writers. Born in Istanbul, he received an MA from Columbia University in political science, international relations, and international law. In 1971 he returned to Turkey to serve as minister of culture. Halman published two poetry collections in English, *Shadows of Love* (1979) and *A Last Lullaby* (1990), and several books of Turkish-language poetry. He has also translated major Turkish literary works into English and has written and lectured extensively in the United States about Turkish cultural history.

Medicine Mehmet Cengiz Oz (1960–), born in Cleveland, Ohio, is a popular television health advice personality known as "Dr. Oz." Oz is vice-chairman of surgery and director of the Cardiovascular Institute at Columbia University and the founder of the Complementary Medicine Program at New York Presbyterian Hospital.

Music Founder and chief executive officer of Atlantic Records, Ahmet Ertegun (1924–) is an influential force in the music business. The son of a Turkish ambassador to the United States, he attended St. John's College in Annapolis, Maryland. The young Ahmet always loved jazz, especially the music of black performers. He and his brother Nesuhi promoted jazz concerts in Washington, D.C., at locales ranging from the Jewish Community Center to the National Press Club and the Turkish embassy. Duke Ellington and Lester Young attended some of these informal jazz sessions. Ertegun invested $10,000 with a record collector friend and started Atlantic Records. Four decades later it had become a conglomerate worth $600 million. Ertegun has been dubbed the "Greatest Rock 'n' Roll Mogul in the World."

Arif Mardin (1932–) is one of the major popular music producers and arrangers in United States. His clients include Aretha Franklin, the Bee Gees, Carly Simon, Roberta Flack, and Bette Midler. Born into a prominent Istanbul family, he received a scholarship to Boston's Berklee College of Music, where he obtained a BA in music in 1958. After briefly meeting Ahmet Ertegun at the Newport Jazz Festival, he joined Atlantic Records and is currently its vice president.

Born in Istanbul, musician and singer Ahu Gural moved in 2010 to New York, where she performs pop, jazz, arias from the famous operas, and classical Turkish music.

Science and Mathematics Feza Gürsoy (1921–1993) was the J. Willard Gibbs Professor Emeritus of Physics at Yale University. He contributed major studies on the group structure of elementary particles and the symmetries of interactions. Gürsoy helped bridge the gap between physicists and mathematicians at Yale. He won the prestigious Oppenheimer Prize (1977) and the Wigner Medal (1986).

MEDIA

Turk of America

Founded 2002, the first Turkish American nationwide business magazine aims to report news about the Turkish community in the United States. It is published in print and online.

One Bridge Plaza North
Suite 275
Fort Lee, New Jersey 07024
Phone: (201) 250 4376
URL: www.turkofamerica.com

ORGANIZATIONS AND ASSOCIATIONS

American Turkish Friendship Association (ATFA)

This organization is dedicated to addressing the social, cultural, and educational needs of Turkish Americans.

A. Tarik Ilhan, Executive Director
3949 University Drive
Fairfax, Virginia 22030
Phone: (703) 267-5751
Fax: (703) 267-5785
Email: info@atfa.us
URL: www.atfa.us

American Turkish Society (ATS)

Founded in 1949, the ATS has a membership of 400 American and Turkish diplomats, banks, corporations, businessmen, and educators. It promotes economic and commercial relations as well as cultural understanding between the people of the United States and Turkey.

Selen Ucak, Executive Director
3 Dag Hammarskjold Plaza
New York, New York 10017
Phone: (212) 583-7614
Fax: (212) 583-7615
Email: info@americanturkishsociety.org
URL: www.americanturkishsociety.org

Assembly of Turkish American Associations (ATAA)

The ATAA, founded in 1979, has approximately 10,500 members. It coordinates the activities of regional associations whose purpose is to present an objective view of Turkey and Turkish Americans and to enhance understanding between these two groups.

1526 18th Street NW
Washington, D.C. 20036
Phone: (202) 483-9090
Fax: (202) 483-9092
Email: assembly@ataa.org
URL: www.ataa.org

Turkish Coalition of America

An organization founded in 2007 that fosters understanding between the United States and Turkey and works to build the next generation of Turkish American leaders through scholarships and internships.

G. Lincoln McCurdy, Executive Director
1510 H Street NW
Suite 900
Washington, D.C. 20005
Phone: (202) 370-1399
Fax: (202) 370-1398
URL: www.tc-america.org

Turkish Women's League of America (TWLA)

Founded in 1958, the TWLA unites Americans of Turkish origin to promote equality and justice for women. The organization encourages cultural and recreational activities to foster relations between the people of Turkey, the United States, and other countries, including the new Turkish republics of the former Soviet Union.

Sermin Özçilingir, President
821 United Nations Plaza, Second Floor
New York, New York 10017
Phone: (212) 682-8525
Fax: (212) 215-5310
Email: atkbnewyork@gmail.com
URL: http://atkb.org/

SOURCES FOR ADDITIONAL STUDY

Acehan, Işıl. *Outposts of an Empire: Early Turkish Migration to Peabody, Massachusetts.* Ankara: Department of History, Bilkent University, 2005.

Ahmed, Frank. *Turks in America: The Ottoman Turk's Immigrant Experience.* Greenwich, CT: Columbia International, 1986.

Akcapar, Sebnem Koser. "Turkish Associations in the United States: Towards Building a Transnational Identity." *Turkish Studies* 10, no. 2 (2009): 165–93.

Balgamis, A. D., and Kemal H. Karpat. *Turkish Migration to the United States: From Ottoman Times to the Present.* Madison: Center for Turkish Studies, University of Wisconsin, 2008.

Grabowski, John J. *Prospects and Challenges: The Study of Early Turkish Immigration to the United States.* Piscataway, NJ: Transaction Periodicals Consortium, Rutgers University, 2005.

Hostler, Charles Warren. *The Turks of Central Asia.* Westport, CT: Praeger, 1993.

Kaya, Ilhan. "Religion as a Site of Boundary Construction: Islam and the Integration of Turkish Americans in the United States." *Alternatives: Turkish Journal of International Relations* 6, nos. ½ (Spring/Summer 2007): 139–55.

———. "Turkish-American Immigration History and Identity Formations." *Journal of Muslim Minority Affairs* 24, no. 2 (October 2004): 295–308.

Senyurekli, A. R., and C. Menjivar. "Turkish Immigrants' Hopes and Fears around Return Migration." *International Migration* 50, no. 1 (2012): 3–19.

Spencer, William. *The Land and People of Turkey.* New York: J. P. Lippincott, 1990.

UGANDAN AMERICANS

Olivia Miller

OVERVIEW

Ugandan Americans are immigrants or descendants of people from the Republic of Uganda, a landlocked country on the equator in East Africa. Uganda is bordered by Sudan to the north; Kenya to the east; Lake Victoria, Tanzania, and Rwanda to the south; and Congo (formerly Zaire) to the west. The country has great natural beauty, with an incredible variety of mammal species and birds. The country's tropical forests, tea plantations, rolling savannahs, and arid plains are home to half of Africa's bird species. Uganda is fairly flat but high, with an average altitude of 3,280 feet above sea level. Its topography varies from the lush and fertile shores of Lake Victoria in the southeast to semi-desert in the northeast. The capital city, Kampala, is on the shores of Lake Victoria. The White Nile, flowing out of the lake, winds through much of the country. Uganda's land area is 91,459 square miles (236,880 square kilometers), about the size of Oregon.

According to the *CIA World Factbook*, Uganda's estimated 2012 population of 34 million is made up of a complex and diverse range of peoples, including the Baganda, Banyakole, Basoga, Bakiga, Iteso, Langi, and Acholi ethnic groups, among others, as well as Europeans, Asians, and Arabs. The Baganda make up the largest portion of the population, about 16.9 percent. The majority—84 percent—of the population is Christian, evenly divided between Catholic and Protestant; 12 percent is Muslim; and 4 percent follows indigenous belief systems. Uganda's gross domestic product ranks just outside the top 40 percent of the countries ranked, falling 94th of 229. With its considerable natural resources, the country's economy relies heavily on farming. As of 2010 coffee was Uganda's number one export, and fish was second. In 2006, billions of barrels of oil reserves were discovered in western Uganda, and plans were subsequently established to build refineries and develop infrastructure to get the oil onto the international market.

Although there has been speculation that Arab traders may have brought the first Ugandans to the United States as slaves between 1619 and 1865, what is confidently known about Ugandan immigration to the United States is limited to the latter half of the twentieth century. Ugandans began immigrating to the United States in the late 1950s and early 1960s, both to seek education and better lives for themselves and to escape the brutal regime of Idi Amin. They tended to settle on the East Coast at first but later spread to urban areas throughout the country. Because the education they received in Uganda often did not serve them well in the United States, they frequently took menial jobs in factories and the transportation industry. While men were often the first to venture to the United States, in recent years, women and children have come as well.

According to the U.S. Census Bureau's American Community Survey estimates for 2009–2011, there were approximately 12,000 people of Ugandan ancestry residing in the United States, and the states with the largest population of Ugandan Americans were Massachusetts (2,181), California (1,711), Maryland (1,131), Minnesota (643), and Texas (435).

HISTORY OF THE PEOPLE

Early History The ancestors of today's Bantu-speaking people, who include the Baganda and other groups, were likely the earliest occupants (in about the fourth century CE) of the low-lying plateau north of Lake Victoria. The population gradually moved southwest and developed a way of life based on farming and herding. Kingdoms emerged, and they remained strong from the fourteenth century until the nineteenth century. Uganda's inland location kept it isolated from Arab and European trading until the nineteenth century. When Arab traders reached the interior of Uganda in the 1830s, they found several kingdoms with well-developed political institutions dating back several centuries. Buganda (the kingdom of the Baganda people) dominated the region, and Bunyoro was its greatest rival.

The first traders came in search of slaves and ivory. In the 1860s British explorers arrived, seeking the source of the Nile River. Protestant missionaries arrived in 1877, followed by Catholic missionaries in 1879. Baganda converts to Christianity and Islam clashed with the Buganda ruler, King Mwanga, and eventually overthrew him. The kingdom then separated along Catholic and Protestant lines. This weakening of Buganda coincided with growing European interest in the area. Imperial powers from Europe soon attempted to conquer Buganda and its neighbors. The Treaty of Berlin in 1890 defined the various European countries' spheres of influence in Africa, and subsequently Uganda, Kenya, and the islands of Zanzibar and Pemba became British protectorates. Colonial agents established the Uganda Protectorate in 1894.

Colonial administrators introduced coffee and cotton as cash crops and adopted a policy of indirect rule, giving the traditional kingdoms autonomy but favoring the recruitment of Baganda tribespeople for civil service. Few Europeans settled permanently in Uganda, but Pakistanis, Indians, and Goans arrived in large numbers. Agricultural production increased dramatically during World War I and again during the 1920s and 1930s. In the 1930s and 1940s, native Ugandans began to agitate for economic and political self-determination. In the mid-1950s schoolteacher Milton Obote, a member of the Langi people, created a loose coalition that led Uganda to independence in 1962.

Modern Era Ethnic and regional rivalries beset newly formed political parties with the arrival of independence in October 1962. Assisted by his army chief of staff Idi Amin, Prime Minister Obote crushed the opposition and became president, abolishing the Bagandan monarchy. Obote rewrote the constitution to consolidate virtually all powers in the presidency and then began to nationalize, without compensation, $500 million worth of foreign assets. In 1971 Idi Amin led a military coup that ousted Obote. Under the government of Amin, Uganda endured eight years of mass murder and destruction. Amin's main targets were the Acholi and Langi tribespeople, the professional classes, which included intellectuals and entrepreneurs, and the country's 70,000-strong Asian community. In 1972 all Asians were given ninety days to leave the country with nothing but the clothes that they wore. The economy disintegrated because the Asian population had been the backbone of trade, industry, and health care, and the education system suffered lasting damage. Government-sanctioned brutality became commonplace. Amin went to war with Tanzania in 1978, then fled Uganda the following year when the Tanzanian military pushed into the heart of Uganda.

In 1980 Milton Obote returned from exile to resume control. Human rights abuses continued. Between half a million and a million people perished during the reigns of Amin and his successors from 1971 to 1986, and armless, legless, and facially disfigured torture victims survive in the population today. Rebels drove Obote from office in 1985, however. Yoweri Kaguta Museveni, leader of the National Resistance Army, set up a new government in January 1986. Museveni stated his goal of bringing peace and security to Uganda. He won strong support from citizens, and about 300,000 Ugandan refugees returned from across the Sudanese border.

In the 1990s Uganda worked to recover from two decades of instability and civil war. A new constitution was ratified on July 12, 1995. Museveni won democratic, nonpartisan elections in 1994, in 1996, and again in 2001. International leaders saw the 1996 elections as Uganda's final step towards rehabilitation. By the end of the twentieth century, Uganda had set up new economic development projects and export initiatives and renewed its commitment to education and social services.

However, the Lord's Resistance Army (LRA), a militant movement in northern Uganda, southern Sudan, and the Democratic Republic of Congo, threatened the peace. Wanting to establish a society based on the Ten Commandments, the group stepped up its activity in the early 2000s, murdering, raping, and kidnapping tens of thousands of innocent people and abducting many children for use as soldiers and as sex and labor slaves. While peace talks with the rebel group have continued on and off since the 1990s, as of 2013 peace had not been reached.

Since the 1980s, Uganda and other Sub-Saharan African nations have faced a devastating public health crisis with the HIV/AIDS epidemic. Uganda was at the forefront of implementing prevention and treatment programs, and has made major strides in lowering infection rates. In 1991, 15 percent of the population in Uganda was HIV positive, but by 2009 that number had dropped to 6.5 percent.

Ugandan politics drew international attention on October 14, 2009, when David Bahati submitted the Anti-Homosexuality Bill, which included provisions for the death penalty and life imprisonment. A vote on the bill, which is widely acknowledged to have been inspired by U.S. fundamentalist Christians, was postponed for two years due to protests from human rights activists throughout the world. Bahati resubmitted the bill in 2012, and as of 2013 the controversy remained unresolved.

SETTLEMENT IN THE UNITED STATES

In 1975, according to immigration records, 859 Ugandan immigrants arrived in the United States, most fleeing Idi Amin's terror. (Of note is the fact that a number of the African Asians expelled from Uganda by Idi Amin in 1972 immigrated to the United States but were counted in a separate category from Ugandans.) In 1976 and 1977, 359 and 241 Ugandans arrived in the United States, respectively. Immigration fell to less than 150 each year in the late 1980s and early 1990s, during the time of political stability in Uganda. Between 1946 and 1990, the number of Ugandan refugees granted permanent residence status in the United States was generally less than 50 per year. The Diversity Visa (DV) Program, a lottery established in 1990 under the terms of the Immigration and Nationality Act, makes available 50,000 permanent resident visas annually to people from countries with low rates of immigration to the

A former refugee from Uganda poses in Ithaca, New York, in 2006. He helps African orphans through music therapy. CARA ANNA / AP IMAGES

United States. In 1993, 87 Ugandans won the lottery; in 1994, 79; in 1996, only 10; and in 1998, 215. In 2012, 419 Ugandans won the lottery.

Ugandan immigrants often join family members already in the United States. While the first immigrants settled in East Coast cities, significant communities have developed in metropolitan areas such as Atlanta; Sacramento, California; Dallas; Denver; and St. Petersburg, Florida, immigrants with professional employment are geographically scattered. Some newly arrived Ugandans receive assistance from Catholic Social Services and other humanitarian relief agencies. According to the American Community Survey estimates for 2011, there were more than 12,000 Ugandan Americans living in the United States, and the states with the highest populations of Ugandan Americans were Massachusetts, California, Maryland, Minnesota, and Texas.

LANGUAGE

Uganda adopted English as its official language after it became independent in 1962. In their home country, Ugandans study English in grade school, and it is the language used by courts and most news media. Although English is the language of business, government, and education, most Ugandans speak an African language as well. While the vast majority of Uganda's forty-seven languages are still in use, the country's three major language groups are Bantu, Central Sudanic, and Nilotic. Following independence, Bantu-language speakers comprised roughly two-thirds of the population. Bantu speakers live in the southern portion of Uganda, the Nilotic languages are spoken in the northern region of the country, and the Central Sudanic languages are concentrated in a small area in the upper northwest. Luganda, a Bantu language spoken by over

16 million Baganda people in southern Uganda, is the most widely spoken language in the country. In 2005 the government named Swahili the country's second official language. While many people in Uganda speak Swahili, the language is a sensitive topic among many Ugandans because it was the official language of the country under Amin's rule and is thus associated with the brutal acts of the military and police.

In the United States, Ugandans usually speak English outside the home, both in personal and professional circles. Inside the home, many Ugandan Americans speak their native tongues. While many Ugandan American children grow up hearing the native languages at home and are able to speak and understand them, most cannot read or write them, and the level of proficiency drops with each generation.

Greetings and Popular Expressions In Luganda a person greets someone by saying "*Oli otya?*" (How are you?), and the response may be "*Bulungi*" (I am fine) or "*Gyendi*" (I am okay). Shaking hands is common. In parting one might say, "*Siiba bulungi*" (Have a nice day), or "*Tunaalabagana*" (See you later). "*Weebale*" means "Thank you," and "*Kale*" means "You're welcome."

RELIGION

According to the *CIA World Factbook*, the majority of Uganda's population is Christian, with 42 percent identifying as Catholic and 42 percent identifying as Protestant (including 35.9 percent Anglican, 4.6 percent Pentecostal, and 1.5 percent Seventh-day Adventist). The remaining 16 percent of Ugandans follow either Islam (12 percent), local indigenous religions (3 percent), or no religion at all (1 percent). These percentages are also true of the Ugandan American population. Similar to Ugandans, Ugandan Americans largely stay loyal to their denominations.

Local indigenous religions may include belief in a creator as well as in ancestral and other spirits. Worshippers convey respect for the dead, who are thought to help the living, through prayer and sacrifices—and some practitioners serve as mediators with those who have died. In the Bunyoro region, some people believe the spirits to be the early mythical rulers, the Chwezi.

Ugandan Americans find that factors such as tight work or study schedules often limit their ability to practice their faith in the United States, and often they become less devout. Even though Uganda Americans tend to maintain their religious affiliation, they become more open to alternative ways of practicing their religion. Most Ugandan Americans of the Christian faith attend Sunday service regularly. Those who practice Islam find a mosque where they worship every Friday and attend events. The ones with no access to a mosque generally stay faithful by practicing their faith privately. When they reach the United

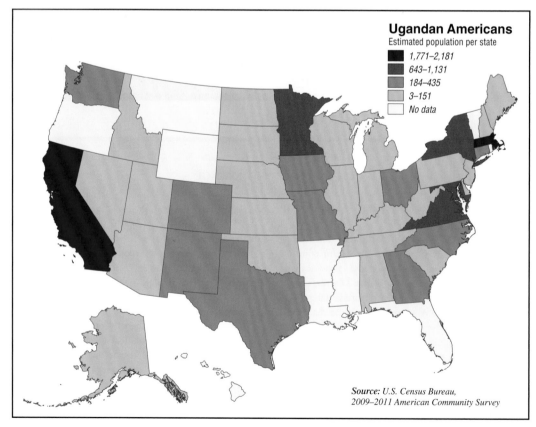

Ugandan Americans
Estimated population per state
- 1,771–2,181
- 643–1,131
- 184–435
- 3–151
- No data

Source: U.S. Census Bureau, 2009–2011 American Community Survey

States, the small percentage of Ugandans who practice indigenous religions often abandon public practice of them in favor of religions that have a greater presence in the new country.

CULTURE AND ASSIMILATION

Given the ethnic diversity of Uganda's population, Ugandan culture is a mixture of various traditions and practices. However, some common characteristics apply to the population at large. Because Ugandans tend to require less personal space than Americans, standing close and touching hands, arms and shoulders during conversation is common among members of the same sex. When men and women talk, however, the only appropriate touch is an initial handshake. In addition, most Ugandans prefer indirect over direct eye contact, and women and children are expected to cast their gazes down or away when talking with men or their elders. In conversation, Ugandans often illuminate ideas with stories and proverbs, and humor plays an important role in most exchanges, even when Ugandans are discussing ostensibly serious matters. Long periods of silence can be considered rude.

With regard to attending social events, Ugandans are not overly concerned with punctuality; arriving within an hour or two of an event's beginning is considered acceptable. Although promptness, even for social events, is highly valued in the United States, it is hard for Ugandan immigrants to view lateness for social gatherings differently than they did in Uganda.

Two traditions that Ugandan Americans consider important and are determined to maintain are respect for elders by the young and putting the community ahead of the individual. Nevertheless, television and peer pressure, among other factors, can undermine efforts to preserve these ideals. Many Ugandan Americans have succeeded in carrying over these values to the younger generations, but success varies depending on the level of assimilation.

Cuisine Ugandan main dishes usually center on beef, goat, mutton, or fresh fish and the starch that comes from *ugali*, or maize meal, which is cooked into a thick porridge until it sets hard and then served in flat bricks. Ugandans eat *chapati*, a bread that resembles a pita and is used to dip in curries and sauces; originally from India, its presence in Uganda is a legacy of the Asian community that was exiled from Uganda in the 1970s. A staple food is *matoke*, a dish of green cooking bananas, steamed and then mashed. Other food crops include millet bread, cassava, sweet potatoes, white potatoes, yams, beans, peas, groundnuts (peanuts), cabbage, onions, pumpkins, and tomatoes.

Fruits such as oranges, papaws (papayas), and pineapple are often served as between-meal snacks. Groundnuts are an important part of the diet. They are roasted, pounded to a pulp, and then made into a sauce that may accompany meat, matoke, or vegetables. Groundnut stew consists of meat strips cooked with onions and tomatoes, to which peanut butter and milk are added to create a sauce. The dish is served over rice. Ugandans also enjoy bananas and plantains prepared in a number of different ways, including boiling, baking, and roasting.

Drinks include *mwenge bigere*, a fermented banana beer, and *waragi*, a sugarcane-based alcoholic beverage. A popular Ugandan-American dessert is peanut orange cake, made from a typical cake batter with orange peel, vinegar, and peanut butter added.

Ugandan Americans have been successful in preserving the cooking of traditional dishes. How often these dishes are prepared depends on the availability of the foods. In states that have big Ugandan American populations, such as California and Massachusetts, families eat traditional food every day because the ingredients are readily available. Areas with large Latino and Asian American populations tend to have ethnic foods in abundance, which means the ingredients for traditional Ugandan dishes are available and Uganda Americans can cook traditional dishes at home and at social events. There are even restaurants that serve Ugandan food. In areas where families have to drive miles to get these foods, traditional Ugandan cuisine is cooked only on special occasions or once a week. For Ugandan Americans with full-time jobs, the time it takes to prepare a Ugandan meal can make it difficult to cook traditional dishes. Some families cook one big meal once a week and they keep everything refrigerated and serve it in smaller portions throughout the week. While first-generation Ugandan immigrants enjoy these traditional dishes, those of the second and third generation are less enthusiastic because they have been exposed to a variety of other foods at school and other places. They will eat traditional Ugandan food but expect an American side dish to accompany the meal.

The Ugandan American restaurant Karibu serves a variety of traditional Ugandan fare. Located in Waltham, Massachusetts—home to a large community of Ugandan Americans—the eatery's slogan is "A Taste of Africa." Although it boasts traditional cuisine from all over Africa, Karibu is best recognized for its Ugandan offerings, which include cassava, matoke (green bananas), Irish potatoes (white potatoes), ugali, and *mbuzi* (goat stew).

Traditional Dress Ugandans Americans wear American-style clothing, in both public and private realms, though they might don traditional garb for special occasions, like religious ceremonies or meetings or celebrations with other Ugandans. Typical clothing among women consists of *busuti* or *gomasi*, which are colorful saris, though the style varies from one tribe to another. For men, the *kanzu*, an ankle-length robe, used to be regarded as the national dress. It was replaced by the safari suit, then by Western-style shirts and pants.

GROUNDNUT STEW

Ingredients

3 fresh chile peppers, seeds removed, minced

1 pound carrots

1 pinch mixed dried herbs

1 1-inch piece fresh ginger

6 tablespoons natural peanut butter

2 onions, chopped

1 pound tomatoes, chopped

1 pound stewing beef, cut into chunks

salt

black pepper

Preparation

Mix chiles with the peanut butter, ginger, herbs, vegetables and tomatoes.

Place meat in a saucepan with a tight fitting lid and add the vegetable mixture and some seasoning. The meat and vegetables will add moisture to the dish as it cooks. Cover and cook very gently for about 1½ hours or until the meat is tender.

Serves 4

Dances and Songs Music and dance play a large role in Ugandan culture. Each tribe has specific dances, such as the Imbalu dances of the Bagisu people on the slopes of Mount Elgon in eastern Uganda and the Runyege dances native to the area around Masindi in western Uganda. Traditional story-songs tell tales of magic birds and animals, with songs and narrative interwoven. W. Moses Serwadda, a musician, folklorist, and faculty member at Makarere University in Uganda, compiled a book, *Songs and Stories from Uganda* (1974), of traditional work and game story songs and lullabies. The songs appear in the original Luganda language, with phonetic pronunciation, English translation, and an explanation of the story or purpose of each.

Each tribe has its own musical history. Songs are passed down from generation to generation. *Ndigindi* (lyre), *entongoli* (harp), *amadinda* (xylophone), and *lukeme* (thumb piano) are common musical instruments in Uganda.

Many Ugandan Americans, especially first-generation immigrants, enjoy watching and participating in traditional Ugandan music and dances. It gives them a sense of pride. At important occasions, viewers can expect to see people jumping up and performing numerous traditional dances. Second- and third-generation Ugandan Americans learn to

perform these dances at functions as well. However, with so many influences in the United States, like video games, sports, and work pressures, many parents do not have enough time to instill these traditions in their children.

Holidays Ugandan Americans celebrate many Christian holidays, including Christmas, Easter, and Good Friday. Those who are Muslim honor Islamic holidays such as Hari Raya Puasa (the sighting of the new moon, which signifies the first day of the Muslim calendar and the end of Ramadan, the fasting month). In addition, the entire country of Uganda observes Women's Day in early March as well as several holidays associated with independence and events during the civil wars: NRM (National Resistance Movement) Anniversary Day is January 26; Martyrs' Day is June 3; Heroes' Day is June 9; and Independence Day is October 9.

Health Issues Because Uganda has a poor health care system, Ugandans who have immigrated to the United States typically receive much better health care than those in their native country. Health insurance coverage by an employer is a valued benefit of life in America.

The AIDS epidemic devastated the population of Uganda. In the 1980s the country had the highest reported incidence of the disease, with more than 15 cases per 100,000 people. By mid-1990, 17,400 AIDS cases had been diagnosed in the country, and the number was doubling every six months. At the peak of the epidemic in Uganda, in 1991, 15 percent of the adult population—and 30 percent of pregnant women—was HIV-positive. Grassroots and government prevention programs led to a decline in the virus, however. In 2009, 6.5 percent of the adult population, or 1.2 million people, were living with HIV or AIDs. Ugandan life expectancy, which was thirty-seven years in 1998, had increased to fifty-three years by 2012.

FAMILY AND COMMUNITY LIFE

Uganda has a wide variety of cultures, traditions, and lifestyles, but in most parts of the country the family consists of an extended group that includes aunts, uncles, cousins, and neighbors. Ugandans may refer to members of their extended families as brothers and sisters, even if this designation is not accurate in the genetic sense of these terms. The entire community participates in child-rearing, and families are, for the most part, free of the larger cultural influences that intrude on raising children, such as the negative effects of the mass media and the pressure to maintain a high material standard of living. The largest cultural group, the Baganda people, have historically emphasized blood ties through the clan system. Clan members all have at least one male ancestor in common, and there are believed to be somewhere between forty-five and fifty-five original clans. Clan councils once regulated many aspects of Baganda life, including marriage and land use. The Baganda have traditionally sent their children to live with people of higher social standing in the group to create ties and provide avenues for social mobility.

The structure of the Ugandan American family, on the other hand, closely resembles that of a traditional American family: Ugandan Americans tend to establish single-family homes, although they may have difficulty adapting to the American methods of child-rearing in the confines of a nuclear family and relatively isolated neighborhoods. In Uganda children are likely to regard their parents as the sole authority figures in their lives and to see the rest of their community as a collective of people working in concert with their parents to instill a unified set of values. In the United States, a number of factors disrupt this cohesion. For example, whereas in Uganda neighbors would likely be available to watch children during the day, Ugandan American parents often need to send their children to day-care and thus are more likely to feel they have less control over the influences to which their young children are exposed.

Gender Roles Ugandan women have traditionally been subordinate to men, despite the substantial economic and social responsibilities of women in Ugandan society. Their fathers, brothers, and husbands hold authority over them, and as late as the 1980s, women in some rural areas had to kneel when speaking to men. This was the case even though women not only had significant domestic responsibilities but also contributed to the economy through agricultural work. Polygamous marriage practices also disadvantaged women. Even so, women's rights groups began organizing even before Uganda became independent. In 1960 the Uganda Council of Women called for marriage, divorce, and inheritance laws to be put in writing and publicized.

The violence during Idi Amin's rule created hardships for women, as public services, schools, hospitals, and markets often became inaccessible. They had to take care of their families in extreme conditions. These difficulties, however, may have forced women to become more independent. Ugandan women's activism has continued. In 1987 Museveni appointed Joyce Mpanga minister for women and development, and she pledged that the government would improve women's wages, job opportunities, and status. The Uganda Association of Women Lawyers set up a legal aid clinic in early 1988 to defend women's property and custody rights. In the early 1990s women became increasingly involved in Ugandan government. In 1997 Ugandan women held 18 percent of the seats in the Parliament of Uganda, and by 2012 that number had grown to 35 percent. In 1994 Specioza Kazibwe became the first female vice president of an African nation. She held that office until 2003. In 2011 Rebecca Kadaga was elected Speaker of the Parliament.

UGANDAN PROVERBS

The following are some examples of proverbs in Lugandan:

Akwagala, akubuulirira.

He who loves you, warns you.

Akunoonya ameewola takunoonya masasula.

One who seeks you out for a loan doesn't look for you when payment is due.

Kyawa okubuulirirwa akyawa okumanya.

One who hates advice hates knowledge.

Akukyaye bw'awerekera akubanja, teweebaka.

If you see your enemy with your creditor, you will have a sleepless night.

Akakuli mu linnyo tikaganya lulimi kutereera.

The little morsel between your teeth gives your tongue no rest.

Agayirira ebitono agwa kiserebetu.

Carelessness in small things leads little by little to ruin.

Abaagalana tebafunda.

Those who love each other need only a small place.

In the United States there is a greater degree of equality among Ugandan American men and women in the home and in the workplace. This is mostly due to the nature of work available to men and women in the United States. Whereas in Uganda, the protocols of rural life may divide work along gender lines, in the United States, Ugandan American men and women have access to many of the same jobs and can earn similar wages for their labor. Some Ugandan American men have difficulty adapting to these evolving gender roles, which can lead to problems in their relationships. This tension can be exacerbated by the fact that Ugandan women who immigrate to the United States often find work before their partners do. The situation generally improves as Uganda American women and men become more familiar with mainstream American culture.

Education While not compulsory, education in Uganda is highly regarded. Education is divided into four levels: seven years of primary; three to four years of lower secondary; two years of upper secondary; and then postsecondary, consisting of university, teachers' colleges, or commercial training. While there has traditionally been a fee for primary and lower secondary schooling, thereafter, education

NON-AGGRESSION PERCEIVED AS PASSIVITY

The West has traditionally viewed Ugandans as passive people, but this observation is a generality that sheds little insight on Ugandan people, and there is a historical and cultural basis for what Westerners perceive as passivity among Ugandans. Their non-aggressive behavior, which Westerners have at times interpreted as willing servitude, results from centuries of tribal structure that discouraged individual self-promotion. The culture of the Baganda was authoritarian, and obedience to the king was crucial. As David Lamb writes in *The Africans* (1987), among Ugandans "one's well-being depended on an allegiance to a man or a group of tribal barons, and that attachment did not include the right to question. The tradition of giving all power to a village chief, the era of colonialism, and the repressiveness of men like Obote and Amin had taught them obedience, even servitude. They had learned the art of survival."

is free. In early 1997 the Ugandan government launched the Universal Primary Education Program as a step toward free primary education for all citizens. Under this program, the government would pay for four children per family to attend primary school at any public school.

Despite the Ugandan emphasis on education, the country's average literacy rate in 2002 was 67 percent: 77 percent for men and 58 percent for women. In addition, fewer women than men received higher education, and only 3 percent of people attending technical institutions were female. Many Ugandans immigrate to the United States for educational opportunities.

EMPLOYMENT AND ECONOMIC CONDITIONS

Ugandan Americans have pursued a variety of occupations. Numerous Ugandan Americans are professionals and intellectuals who fled during Amin's reign of terror. While many such professionals (such as physicians, journalists, and teachers) have been able to continue their careers in the United States, a significant number have had to accept work for which they are overqualified. Many work as nurses and nurse's aides or seek other employment in the health care professions. No matter what jobs they find, Ugandan Americans are likely to subsist on tight budgets so that they can send money back to Uganda. Many send thousands of dollars per year and network with people in Uganda to develop social programs such as AIDS education workshops. They also raise money for weddings in Uganda and also to ship the bodies of the deceased home for local funerals. This practice of sending remittances, which Ugandans call *kyeyo*, is

common among nearly all Ugandans living abroad. The Bank of Uganda reported that in 2010, Ugandans living outside the country sent more than $750 million to Uganda.

POLITICS AND GOVERNMENT

Most Ugandan Americans are politically conservative, though since the turn of the twenty-first century there has been a slight shift to the left that has coincided with a rise in social status among some segments of the Ugandan American population. In the United States, Ugandan Americans have played only a marginal role in local, state, and national politics, primarily because adapting to American life and honoring obligations to extended family still residing in Uganda leaves little time for engagement in American politics.

Ugandan Americans do, however, tend to remain interested in the local political issues of Uganda. They avidly follow the news and information coming out of Uganda and continue to follow the trends there. Ugandan Americans have joined other Africans in organizations such as the National Summit on Africa to influence U.S. policy on Uganda. A major piece of Africa-related legislation, the African Growth and Opportunity Act, passed in 2000, encourages the import of goods from sub-Saharan Africa by allowing them to come into the United States duty-free and in unrestricted quantity. Many Ugandan Americans provide assistance in educating their siblings and relatives in Uganda because they believe that educated citizens can improve the country. Ugandans in the diaspora have successfully lobbied for the right to hold dual citizenship. The 2008 Uganda Citizenship and Immigration Control Bill was signed by the president of Uganda in 2009 and permits Ugandan citizens eighteen years and older who acquire the citizenship of another country to keep their Ugandan citizenship. As of 2013 Ugandan Americans and others in the Ugandan diaspora were lobbying for the right to cast absentee ballots in Ugandan elections.

NOTABLE INDIVIDUALS

Fashion Kiara Kabukuru (1975–), fashion model, immigrated to the United States as a refugee in 1981. She was discovered by a modeling scout in Los Angeles and went on to appear in ads for Cover Girl, Chanel, and Calvin Klein as well as on the cover of *Vogue*.

Journalism Larry Kaggwa, professor of journalism at Howard University in Washington, D.C., is a native Ugandan and a veteran journalist and educator. Since receiving an MA in journalism from UCLA (1969) and a PhD in journalism from Southern Illinois University (1972), he has written for various U.S. newspapers, including the *Asbury Park Press*, the *Washington Post*, the *Oakland Tribune*, the *Los Angeles Times*, and the *Hartford Courant*. He has presented scholarly papers in forums across the country and is dedicated to developing daily newspapers at historically black universities. Kaggwa is adviser to the student chapter of the Society of Professional Journalists.

Music James Makubuya, an ethnomusicologist and musician, was born was born in Gayaza, Uganda, and earned a PhD at UCLA in 1995. He became a professor of music at Indiana's Wabash College in 2000. Makubuya plays a variety of traditional Ugandan instruments, including the *endongo* (an eight-stringed bowl lyre) and other stringed instruments, the *amadinda* (a type of xylophone), and the *engoma* (a type of drum). He has recorded a number of albums, and the film *Mississippi Masala* (1991) is one of several that has featured his music.

Musician, singer, dancer, choreographer, storyteller, playwright, and actress Namu Lwanga, a native Ugandan living in the United States, has a degree in ethnomusicology and has mastered and performs a wide variety of Ugandan traditional instruments. She wrote, acted in, and produced plays in Uganda before coming to the United States. A recipient of the 1996 Parents' Choice Award for her *Web of Tales* video, Lwanga produces videos, albums, and performances that focus on Ugandan traditional movements. She won the Kenyan International Music Festival with an ensemble composition based on Uganda's war-torn past.

Born and raised in Uganda, musician Samite Mulondo fled to Kenya as a political refugee in 1982, then immigrated to the United States in 1987. Singing and playing the *kalimba* (thumb piano), marimba, *litungu* (a type of lyre), and various flutes, he has produced nine CDs and the score for the 2009 PBS film *Taking Root: The Vision of Wangari Maathai*. As founder of Musicians for World Harmony, he travels the world, using music to promote peace, understanding, and harmony. He is the subject of the documentary *Song of the Refugee*, distributed by PBS in 1998.

Sports Betty Okino (1975–), gymnast, was born in Uganda and immigrated to the United States with her family when she was a child. She competed in the 1992 Olympics. After retiring from gymnastics, she made several appearances in small roles on television shows such as *Everybody Hates Chris* and *Sabrina, the Teenage Witch*.

Kato Serwanga (1976–), born in Uganda, played football in the NFL for the New England Patriots (1998–2000), the Washington Redskins (2001), and the New York Giants (2002–2003). His twin brother, Wasswa Serwanga, was also an NFL player; he played for the San Francisco 49ers (1999) and the Minnesota Vikings (2000–2001).

Mathias Kiwanuka (1983–), a Ugandan American born in Indianapolis, is a linebacker for the New York Giants football team. He is a grandson of Benedicto Kiwanuka (1922–1972), the first prime minister of Uganda.

Stage and Screen Ntare Mwine (1967–) is an actor, playwright, and photographer born in New Hampshire to parents from Uganda. He received accolades for his one-man show *Biro* (2003), about a HIV-positive Ugandan rebel, which he performed in New York, London, and throughout Africa. Mwine has also acted in various televisions shows, including *ER*, *CSI*, and *Heroes*.

MEDIA

PRINT

Daily Monitor

A privately owned daily newspaper in Uganda that reports on local, national, and international news, as well as sports and entertainment. It is considered a reliable source of information for Ugandans living abroad.

Plot 29/35 8th Street
P.O. Box 12141
Kampala, Uganda
Email: editorial@ug.nationalmedia.com
URL: www.monitor.co.ug

New Vision

A state-owned multimedia venture that includes newspaper, magazine, and Internet publishing and is read by many Ugandans living abroad.

Barbara Kaija, Editor in Chief
Plot 19/21, First Street
Industrial Area
Kampala, Uganda
Email: editorial@newvision.co.ug
URL: www.newvision.co.ug

RADIO

Radio Uganda USA

Founded in 2009, this Internet radio station allows Ugandan Americans to stay abreast of Ugandan political, economic, and social issues. The site runs programs in both English and Luganda and be accessed anywhere over the Internet.

24 Crescent Street
Suite 105
Waltham, Massachusetts 02453
Phone: (781) 472-4986
URL: www.radiougandausa.com

ORGANIZATIONS AND ASSOCIATIONS

Pacific Northwest Uganda American Association

This organization serves the Ugandan American community in the Pacific Northwest, providing economic opportunities and sponsoring cultural events.

Stephen Kato Katende, Chairman
P.O. Box 80425
Seattle, Washington 98108
Email: infor@pnuaaonline.org
URL: www.pnuaaonline.org

Ugandan North American Association

The Ugandan North America Association is the largest formal association of Ugandans in the diaspora. Its objectives are to "promote the social, cultural and economic development of the Ugandan community in North America and beyond." In addition to providing programs and services year-round for Ugandans in North America, the organization encourages fellowship among Ugandans living on this continent; fosters social, cultural, and business contacts; has local chapters in major cities; and sponsors an annual convention.

Ssennoga Francis, President
1337 Massachusetts Avenue
Suite 153
Arlington, Massachusetts 02476
Phone: (855) 873-8622
Email: info@unaa.org
URL: www.unaa.org

MUSEUMS AND RESEARCH CENTERS

Museum for African Art

Founded in 1984, this museum is dedicated to the arts and cultures of Africa and the African diaspora. In addition to organizing exhibitions related to historical and contemporary African art, the museum also issues publications and sponsors events. Past events have included the lecture series "Conversations with a Continent," which dedicated a session to Uganda.

1280 Fifth Avenue
Suite 20A
New York, New York 10029

Phone: (212) 444-9795
Fax: (212) 444-9796
Email: administration@africanart.org
URL: www.africanart.org

SOURCES FOR ADDITIONAL STUDY

Arthur, John A., Joseph Takougang, Thomas Owusu, and Janet Awokoya, eds. *Africans in Global Migration.* Plymouth, UK: Lexington Books, 2012.

Baingana, Doreen. *Tropical Fish: Stories out of Entebbe.* Amherst: University of Massachusetts Press, 2005.

Burge, Kathleen. "'Little Kampala': With Students Pioneering the Way, 1,500 Ugandans Now Call Waltham Home." *Boston Globe*, August 20, 2009.

Conrad, N. L. "The Effect of Character and Values on Ugandan Adaptation to America." *Journal of Cultural Diversity* 16, no. 3 (2009): 99–108.

Edel, May M. *The Chiga of Uganda.* New Brunswick, NJ: Transaction Publishers, 1996.

Lamb, David. *The Africans.* New York: Vintage Books, 1987.

Martelle, Scott. "Ntare Mwine's Journey of Discovery: The Los Angeles-based actor Reconnects with His Ugandan Roots as He Embodies a Continent's Plight in His Solo 'Biro.'" *Los Angeles Times*, October 19, 2005.

Muwanguzi, Samuel, and George W. Musambira. "Communication Experiences of Ugandan Immigrants during Acculturation to the United States." *Journal of Intercultural Communication* 30 (2012).

Otiso, Kefa M. *Culture and Customs of Uganda.* Westport, CT: Greenwood Press, 2006.

UKRAINIAN AMERICANS

Marianne P. Fedunkiw

OVERVIEW

Ukrainian Americans are immigrants or descendants of people from Ukraine, an eastern European country along the northern coast of the Black Sea. Ukraine is bordered by the Sea of Azov, Moldova, and Romania to the south; Hungary, Slovakia, and Poland to the west; Belarus to the north; and Russia to the north and northeast. After Russia, Ukraine is the second-largest country in Europe in terms of area and is mainly composed of geographically diverse plains and plateaus. Ukraine's total land area is 233,089 square miles (603,700 square kilometers), roughly 90 percent of the size of Texas.

According to a 2012 report by the Ukrainian State Statistics Service, Ukraine has a population of 45,559,235. An overwhelming majority of the population (83 percent) belongs to one of the Orthodox churches: Ukrainian Orthodox–Kyiv Patriarchate (50.4 percent), Ukrainian Orthodox–Moscow Patriarchate (26.1 percent), or Ukrainian Autocephalous Orthodox (7.2 percent). Approximately 10 percent of the population participates in the Catholic Church, while a small percentage identifies as Protestant, Muslim, or Jewish. Ukraine's economy continues to struggle, ranking last among the economies of other European countries and in the bottom 20 percent of the Index of Economic Freedom. However, Ukraine's fertile soil has created a solid agricultural market, and the country has some of the richest mineral deposits on the globe. It also ranks as the sixth-largest arms trader in the world.

Although individual Ukrainians had come to the United States in the eighteenth and early nineteenth centuries, the first major wave of Ukrainian immigrants arrived in the late nineteenth century during the period of American industrialization. This group, numbering more than 350,000, began to arrive in 1877. Many were strikebreakers in the Pennsylvania mines. The second substantial wave of immigration, which consisted of approximately 40,000 Ukrainians, occurred between 1920 and 1939. During this period, Ukraine was divided into several countries, including Russia, Poland, Czechoslovakia, and Romania. Many of the immigrants fled religious and political oppression. Following the passage of the 1948 Displaced Persons Act, the United States opened its doors to thousands of Ukrainian refugees. The fourth and largest wave of Ukrainians emigrated in the early 1990s following the collapse of the Soviet Union. The wave continued into the twenty-first century as close to 7,000 Ukrainians immigrated to the United States each year. While most early Ukrainian immigrants were men, it became common after the fall of the Soviet Union for entire families to immigrate to the United States.

According to 2010 U.S. Census figures, 976,314 people of Ukrainian descent lived in the United States. States with the largest number of Ukrainian Americans included New York, Pennsylvania, California, New Jersey, Ohio, and Illinois.

HISTORY OF THE PEOPLE

Early History The earliest evidence of human settlement in Ukraine dates back 150,000 years. Early settlers of the territory included the Cimmerians (the first nomadic horsemen to appear in Ukraine, about 1500 to 1000 BCE), the Scythians (who appeared in the early seventh century BCE), and colonists from the Greek Empire (who appeared in the fourth century BCE). The direct ancestors of modern-day Ukrainians were the Slavs, who arrived in the early seventh century CE and built what would become the medieval state of Kyivan Rus'. However, the area remained relatively underdeveloped until the arrival of the Varangians (or Vikings or Normans) in the mid-ninth century.

Following the reign of Varangian Prince Oleh, Prince Ihor ruled Kyivan Rus'. After Ihor was killed, his wife Olha took over leadership as their son Sviatoslav was still too young to rule. Her influence was especially apparent years later when her grandson Volodymyr became prince. Olha had converted from paganism to Christianity in 955 and is credited, along with Volodymyr, with bringing Christianity to a pagan land in 988.

The reign of Jaroslav the Wise (1036–1054) is often seen as the pinnacle of the history of Kyivan Rus'. Among Jaroslav's contributions were more than four hundred churches in Kyiv alone and the establishment of *Ruska pravda* (Rus' justice), the basic legal code of the country. Jaroslav's reign was followed by a period of relative decline, beginning with feuds among his sons and grandsons. He had divided his kingdom among his sons with the idea that the eldest would hold a position of seniority and maintain unity. However, as each principality became almost autonomous, Kyiv declined as the political and economic center of Ukraine. In 1240 the state fell to the Mongols under Ogodei Khan and Batu, the grandson of Genghis Khan.

From the latter half of the thirteenth century until the sixteenth century, Ukraine was ruled first by Lithuania (Grand Prince Algirdas began to occupy Kyiv in 1362) and then Poland under Casimir the Great (1310–1370). The Ukrainians, or Ruthenians (as they called themselves during this period), preferred to be ruled by the Lithuanians, who treated them as equals. In 1385 an alliance between Lithuania and Poland was struck to consolidate power against the growing power of Muscovy. Thus, the fourteenth and fifteenth centuries were years of struggle to keep Ukrainians free from Poland, Hungary, and Lithuania, and from the boyars, or noblemen. At the heart of many of these battles was religion—Catholics in Poland and Lithuania effectively shut out Orthodox Ukrainians from power.

The late sixteenth and early seventeenth centuries were periods of recolonization in Ukraine, particularly in the provinces of Kyiv and Bratslav. In 1569 the regions of Kyiv, Volhynia, and Bratslav (Podillia) were annexed to the Kingdom of Poland. A new society of Cossacks grew out of the plains of the Dnipro River. Unlike the serfs of the sixteenth century, these were free men who organized to fend off marauding Tatars. The Cossacks ruled for decades, freeing Ukraine from Polish rule and helping to defend the country from Turks, Tatars, and other invaders. One of the most notable of the Cossack hetmans (leaders) was Bohdan Khmelnytsky, who ruled from 1648 to 1657. During this time he led an uprising and mass peasant revolt against the Poles, which led to a new ruling state with Khmelnytsky as leader. The new states formed a tumultuous relationship with Russia in order to fight Poland. There was also a treaty signed with Muscovy in 1654 to help protect against invaders. However, after Khmelnytsky died in 1657, Ukraine's position weakened, and the nation was eventually betrayed by its ally, Russia, which entered into an agreement with Poland to divide Ukraine.

Ukraine tried several times to loosen the grip of Russia and Poland. In 1708–1709 hetman Ivan Mazepa led the Cossacks to fight alongside Sweden's King Charles XII in the Swedish king's war with Russia's Peter I. But the Swedes and Cossacks lost, and Peter destroyed the hetman's capital. By the late seventeenth century, only one-third of the hetmanate that Khmelnytsky controlled in his heyday as leader remained.

In the late eighteenth century, Russia annexed much of eastern Ukraine, taking the provinces of Kyiv, Volhynia, and Podillia away from Poland and wresting Crimea from the Turks. This transfer meant that Orthodox Christianity, which had been persecuted under Polish rule, could be practiced. In addition, by 1831, Russian replaced Polish as the official language of Ukraine. Meanwhile, Austria gained possession of much of western Ukraine, including the province of Ruthenia and what had been Galicia. However, the fight for a free Ukraine continued. One of its major figures was the poet, patriot, and painter Taras Shevchenko (1814–1861), who, though born a serf, established Ukrainian as a language of literature. His works tell of the glories and sufferings of the nation during a time when Ukrainian was banned from schools, books, and the performing arts.

Modern Era During World War I, Ukraine became caught between Austria and Russia, though by 1915–1916, little of Ukraine was left under Russian control. When the Bolsheviks overthrew the Russian czar, and in 1917 the provisional Russian government, Ukraine was poised for freedom. On January 22, 1918, Ukraine declared itself independent of Russia and used the help of German and Austrian troops to drive out the Russians. But the tenuous alliance with Germany and Austria quickly broke down, and Ukraine's freedom was short lived. By April 1918 Ukraine had instituted a new government that was acceptable to the Germans. Meanwhile, Galicia, which had freed itself of Austrian rule and declared independence in 1918, soon fell to Poland. Four years of war followed, and in 1922 the new Union of Soviet Socialist Republics reconquered Ukraine, making it one of the original republics. Aside from being lost and rewon during World War II, Ukraine remained part of the Soviet Union until the Soviet Union was dissolved in 1991.

The collapse of the Soviet Union caused a great deal of political, social, and economic turmoil. Largely dependent on Soviet imports and exports, Ukraine lost close to 60 percent of its GDP between 1991 and 1999. The Ukrainian government struggled to stabilize the economy, and in 1993, under the leadership of president Leonid Kravchuk, the economy suffered drastic inflation. With the economy faltering, crime and corruption were widespread. Ukrainians protested Kravchuk's regime and backed Leonid Kuchma in the 1994 elections; however Kuchma's presidency (1994–2005) was marked by increased censorship and political corruption. Many Ukrainians left the country, taking advantage of the U.S. green card lottery, which since 1990 has allowed thousands of Ukrainians to establish new lives in the United States.

By the end of the 1990s, the Ukrainian economy stabilized with the help of the introduction of a new currency, the hryvnia, as well as structural and economic reforms that allowed exports to grow by 10 percent per year and the economy to grow annually at approximately 7 percent. In 2004 prime minister Viktor Yanukovych won the presidential election, but the Ukrainian Supreme Court later declared the results null and void after discovering that Yanukovych had rigged the contest. Yanukovych's opponent, Victor Yushchenko, led the public outcry, known as the Orange Revolution, and eventually became president, with Yulia Tymoshenko as prime minister. In 2006 Yanukovych returned as prime minister with the Alliance of National Unity Party, but after Yushchenko dissolved parliament in 2007, Tymoshenko was reelected prime minister. In 2010 Yanukovych beat out Tymoshenko to become president once again.

SETTLEMENT IN THE UNITED STATES

Most Ukrainian immigrants came from western Ukraine, particularly the Lemko and Transcarpathian regions. In search of prosperity, they read advertisements that promised earnings ten to twenty times greater than they could hope for in Ukraine. Leaving their families, they traveled to the ports of Bremen, Hamburg, Rotterdam, and Antwerp, and were packed into steerage on ships for the long journey to the United States. Prior to the opening of Ellis Island in 1892, Ukrainian immigrants arrived at immigration ports such as Castle Garden in New York City, Washington Avenue Immigration Station in Philadelphia, Port of Boston, and Baltimore, where they sought work in construction and mining. After 1892 Ukrainians, like other immigrants, arrived at the immigration checkpoint at Ellis Island, where they waited in fear as many were sent back to Europe. Those who made it through found work in the coal mines of northeastern Pennsylvania and in the factories, steel mills, and foundries of Chicago; Detroit; Cleveland and Akron, Ohio; and Rochester, Buffalo, and Syracuse, New York.

Before World War I, 98 percent of Ukrainians settled in the northeastern states, and 70 percent lived in Pennsylvania alone. Men who had left wives and children in Ukraine worked to save money and bring their families to the United States. Ukrainians settled in urban villages near other Slavs, Poles, Jews, Hungarians, and Slovaks, seeking a sense of community to replace the one they had in the Old Country. Their lives centered on the neighborhood church, saloon, general store, and boarding houses.

Few of the early Ukrainian Americans farmed. By the time the first wave crossed the ocean, most of the free land in the United States had been distributed. These new immigrants had no money to buy land. Later, isolated groups such as the Stundists (Baptist Evangelicals) began to farm, mainly in Vermont, Massachusetts, and Pennsylvania. Small groups of Ukrainian Americans followed Orthodox priest Ahapii Honcharenko (1832–1916)—often considered the first nationality-conscious Ukrainian—to Alaska in the 1860s and Dr. Nicholas Sudzilovsky-Russel to Hawaii in 1895. Sudzilovsky-Russel was elected to the Hawaiian senate in 1901 and greatly aided the more than 375 Ukrainians whom dishonest agents had lured to Hawaii and forced to work as slaves on plantations until they repaid the cost of their four-month sea voyage. Eventually these workers were released from their contracts, and most returned to North America.

The second wave of Ukrainian immigration, which covers the period between the two world wars, was considerably smaller than the first, numbering only about 15,000. During this wave, the number of Ukrainians in Pennsylvania dropped, while the Ukrainian American populations of New Jersey and New York grew (especially in New York City). Sizable communities also sprang up in Ohio and Illinois. Unlike first-wave immigrants, these Ukrainians were aware of and vocal about their nationalism, so much so that they began engaging in political infighting. Until that time, Ukrainian Americans were polarized along religious lines; now socialists and conservatives fought from either end of the political spectrum. In addition, second-wave immigrants more readily assimilated to American clothing and language than the first immigrants.

The third major wave, which occurred after the end of World War II, consisted of refugees. These mostly well-educated Ukrainians (including 2,000 university students, 1,200 teachers and scholars, 400 engineers, 350 lawyers, and 300 physicians) had fled their homes during the war and had little interest in returning while the Soviet government was in place. They saw both the United States and Canada as temporary homes, although most would never return to live in Ukraine. The majority of these immigrants had spent time in the postwar refugee camps in Austria and Germany. Eight of these displaced person camps housed two-thirds of the Ukrainian refugees; the rest were privately accommodated. Between 1947 and 1951 these refugees were resettled, with the majority (80,000) going to the United States, 30,000 going to Canada, 20,000 to Australia, 20,000 to Great Britain, 13,000 to Brazil and Argentina, 10,000 to Belgium, and 10,000 to France.

The refugees concentrated in large cities, particularly Buffalo, Chicago, Cleveland, Detroit, Minneapolis, New York, Philadelphia, Rochester, and Syracuse. They gravitated to neighborhoods where Ukrainian Americans already lived and had set up churches and a community infrastructure. Third-wave immigrants were often better educated than previous immigrants and enjoyed the benefits of established social assistance systems, schools, and immigrant aid societies. However, despite their education, many Ukrainian American professionals had to work in menial jobs until they grasped the language and had enough money to establish a practice as doctors, lawyers, or engineers. Some found the adjustment difficult and never returned to their professions, instead taking jobs administering Ukrainian institutions and organizations, many of which were brought from Ukraine by immigrants.

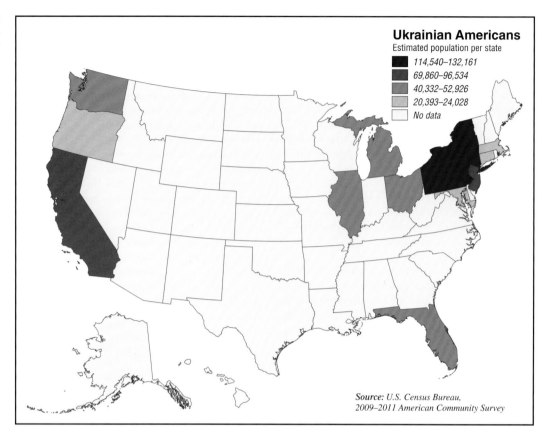

Source: U.S. Census Bureau,
2009–2011 American Community Survey

The Ukrainian American population steadily increased throughout the late twentieth and early twenty-first centuries. According to the 1990 U.S. Census, 740,803 Americans (0.3 percent) reported their ancestry as Ukrainian. Of those who said they were Ukrainian Americans, just over two-thirds listed it as their primary ancestry. The census also gave as ethnicity choices Carpatho-Rusyn, Central European, Russian, and Slavic, as when many of the first Ukrainians arrived in the United States, they were identified with labels other than Ukrainian, including some of these choices. The 2010 Census reported that there were 976,314 Americans of Ukrainian descent, the majority of whom were living in the northeast. The largest population lived in New York (148,700), followed by Pennsylvania (122,291). Although Ukrainians are least likely overall to live in the west, California was the third-ranked state with a population of 83,125. Other sizable communities exist in New Jersey, Washington, and Illinois.

LANGUAGE

Ukrainian belongs to the Slavic group of Indo-European languages and is the second-most widely spoken language of the twelve surviving members of this group. Historically, the literary language of Old Church Slavonic was common to all of Ukraine, in addition to the dialects of the regions. The three main dialect groups—northern, southeastern, and southwestern—are fairly similar to each other. The alphabet is made up of thirty-three Cyrillic characters, the last of which does not stand alone but follows various consonants to soften the sound. Each letter has a particular sound, so reading is relatively simple and the words are pronounced phonetically.

Ukrainian was the primary language of almost all first-generation Ukrainian Americans. Because of the political situation at home, many also spoke Polish, Russian, or German. In 1980 less than 17 percent listed their primary language as Ukrainian. The Ukrainian language is taught at several universities and colleges, including Stanford University, University of Chicago, University of Illinois–Urbana-Champaign, Harvard University, University of Michigan, University of Pennsylvania, and Kent State University. Ukrainian language collections are found in many public libraries including in Brooklyn, Cleveland, Denver, Detroit, Minneapolis, and New York.

Ukrainians have established large and vibrant communities in the United States. Like other immigrant groups, Ukrainians established their communities around their church. Many church services are still performed in Ukrainian, but English is quickly becoming the exclusive language. The 2011 American Community Survey indicates that 65 percent of Ukrainian Americans speak English only, with approximately 16 percent reporting that they speak English less than very well. The survey also indicates that close to 34 percent of Ukrainian Americans speak a language other than English. According to the demographer Oleh Wolowyna of the Center for Demographic and Socio-economic Research of Ukrainians in the United States, 14 percent of households speak Ukrainian and 15 percent speak Russian.

Greetings and Popular Expressions Common Ukrainian greetings based upon the time of day include *Dobredeyn*—"good day"; *Dobrey ranok*—"good morning"; and *Dobra nich*—"good night." Other often used expressions include *Diakoyu*—"thank you"; *proshu* (used both for "please" and "you are welcome"), and *dopobachynya* (literally, "until we see each other again," although more commonly translated as "goodbye"). For festive occasions the phrase *mnohaya lita* is used, which means "many happy years." A corresponding song titled "Mnohaya lita" is the standard birthday song and is used for toasts on any happy occasion such as an anniversary or wedding.

There are standard specific greetings and replies for Christmas and Easter. During the Christmas season, a visitor enters the home saying, *Christos rodyvsia*—"Christ is born"—and the host's reply is *Slavim yoho*—"Let us praise him." At Easter the greeting changes to *Christos voskrys*—"Christ has risen"—and the reply changes to *Voistenu voskrys*—He is risen indeed.

RELIGION

Most Ukrainian Americans belong to one of two faiths, Catholic (Eastern or Byzantine Rite) or Eastern Orthodox. Catholic Ukrainians are almost twice as numerous as Orthodox Ukrainians. The first Ukrainian Catholic church in the United States, St. Michael the Archangel, was built in Shenandoah, Pennsylvania, in 1885 under the direction of reverend Ivan Volansky, an immigrant priest who had arrived the year before. In the late nineteenth century, there was a struggle within the Ukrainian Catholic Church, and in 1890 Volansky was called back to Lviv by his superiors, who had buckled under pressure from Vatican authorities. The Vatican claimed he was an Eastern Rite Catholic and that the Latin Rite American Catholic bishops opposed the organization of separate Ukrainian Catholic parishes. This controversy led some Ukrainians to switch to the Russian Orthodox faith. In 1913 the Vatican finally acceded to the demands of Ukrainian Catholics in the United States and established an exarchate to organize all Ukrainian Catholic parishes, which numbered more than two hundred at the time, a separate administrative unit that reported only to the Pope.

Ex-Catholic Ukrainians set up the Ukrainian Orthodox Church in the United States in 1928. Thousands of Catholic Ukrainians converted to the Russian Orthodox Church after the consecrated priest of a Minneapolis parish, Alexis Toth, who was a widower, was not accepted by the Roman Catholic archbishop because he had been married. Toth broke away to join the Orthodoxy; his 365 parishioners followed him, and tens of thousands of immigrants from Galicia, Lemkivshchyna, and Transcarpathia filled out the ranks.

Ultimately, there were many battles among the dominant religious groups of Ukraine, which included Byzantine Rite Catholic Rusyns, as they called themselves; Ukrainian Catholics; and Orthodox Russians. Today both the Ukrainian Catholic Church (Byzantine Rite) and Orthodoxy remain strong in the United States.

Ukrainian Protestants include the Stundists sect, a Baptist denomination that settled in the United States in 1890. This group settled in several states including North Dakota, where they established a settlement called Kiev, named after the city in which they had lived in Ukraine. In 1905 Ukrainian Protestants founded the Ukrainian Evangelical Alliance of North America, and in 1922 the Union of Ukrainian Evangelical Baptist Churches was established to consolidate the Ukrainian Protestant parishes.

After 1989, when both Ukraine and the United States relaxed immigration restrictions, Ukrainian immigrants brought with them aspects of their religious community. American missionaries also travelled to Ukraine to establish Orthodox, Protestant, and Roman Catholic churches. Churches in both countries adopted and rejected aspects of each church depending on local preference. For example, Ukrainian American churches incorporated traditions that were familiar to the diasporic community, performing ceremonies in Russian and Ukrainian. Church leaders synthesized practices by allowing English and broadening definitions of appropriate clothing. At the same time, church services remained in predominantly Ukrainian- or Russian-speaking neighborhoods, maintaining a delicate balance that retained tradition and incorporated American practices to attract younger members.

Because the United States modeled itself as a melting pot for newly arrived immigrants, Ukrainian Americans assimilated more thoroughly and more quickly than their neighbors to the north, the Ukrainian Canadians.

CULTURE AND ASSIMILATION

Because the United States modeled itself as a melting pot for newly arrived immigrants, Ukrainian Americans assimilated more thoroughly and more quickly than their neighbors to the north, the Ukrainian Canadians. This was in part because the first immigrants moved to heavily populated urban centers where they tended to disappear into the sea of other immigrants and American citizens. As the decades passed, the number of new Ukrainian immigrants dropped as assimilation continued. By 1980 fewer than 17 percent of people of Ukrainian descent said Ukrainian was their primary language.

Nevertheless, through church, cultural, political, and business organizations, many Ukrainian Americans and their children and grandchildren continue to celebrate their heritage. Traditionally, Ukrainian Americans have not moved far from their original settlement sites in the northeastern states of Pennsylvania, New York, and New Jersey. Some of the strongest Ukrainian American institutions were established early in the history of immigration. The most forward-thinking have changed with the times and deemphasized nationalist concerns in favor of drawing members with cultural, business, and social activities. Credit unions, youth organizations, and professional and business clubs are strong in the communities they serve.

One of the most common misconceptions about Ukrainian Americans was that they were simply Russians, Poles, Hungarians, or Austrians. Many Americans grouped them into these categories because depending on when they arrived, Ukraine was occupied by Russia (or the Soviet Union), Poland, or the Austro-Hungarian Empire. In addition, even in their early settlement patterns, new Ukrainian immigrants tended to settle near other immigrants, particularly others from Eastern and Central Europe such as Polish, Russian, and Jewish immigrants. Because of the similarities in language, Ukrainians, Poles, and Russians could communicate easily even before they learned English, which gave them the sense of the community they had left behind when they crossed the ocean to the United States.

Because many first-wave Ukrainian immigrants were strikebreakers in the Pennsylvania mines, there was tension between them and the established English, Irish, and Welsh miners. Ukrainians also stood out for speaking a foreign language, eating different food, and wearing different clothes—at least upon arrival. They also tended to group together, further isolating themselves from the Americans. However, first-generation children helped quicken assimilation of Ukrainian Americans by playing in the streets with non-Ukrainian children and picking up the language and customs.

Nevertheless, discrimination was a significant part of Ukrainian American life. Those Americans who reviled these immigrants called Ukrainians Huns (because they came from the Hungarian part of the Austrian Empire) or bohunks (a derivative of "Bohemians"). Ukrainian immigrants were disparaged for being illiterate, dirty with mine dust, and willing to do work no one else would. In *Ukrainians in North America: An Illustrated History*, Orest Subtelny notes that this so-called "scum of Europe" was thought to be contaminating once civilized towns in Pennsylvania by forcing out those who had given stability to the area: the English, Irish, Welsh, and Scottish. In 1897 the state of Pennsylvania passed a discriminatory measure that required nonnaturalized American miners and workers to pay an additional tax.

Ukrainian Americans have always had a great interest in events in the Old Country. For decades Ukrainian organizations based in the United States have been formed to make political pleas on behalf of those in the occupied homeland and to send material and financial aid. These organizations led marches on the White House protesting the Polish occupation of eastern Galicia in 1922 and a 1933 march by Detroit Ukrainian Americans to protest the Soviet man-made famine that year.

The most striking political development for Ukrainians was the declaration of Ukraine's independence in 1991 after the breakup of the Soviet Union. Today the country continues to cope with democracy and a new form of government, as well as the transition to economic and social independence. Much of the infrastructure of business and government has been redesigned entirely, and Ukrainian Americans are eagerly monitoring the progress of change. Another concern is the continuing effects of the Chernobyl nuclear disaster in eastern Ukraine in the 1980s. Ukrainian Americans have raised considerable support, both financial and material, to aid victims, particularly orphans, of the disaster.

Traditions and Customs Before Ukraine adopted Christianity in 988, inhabitants of the region believed in pagan gods who ruled over the sun, stars, and moon. Modern folk beliefs are still connected to the sun, stars, and moon, as well as dreams, the seasons, and agriculture. In fact, many of the pagan customs blended over time with Christian beliefs, particularly those related to the family (e.g., birth, marriage, and funeral customs), the community, and seasonal agricultural rites.

Songs and folk tales play a significant role in these ancient customs. There are specific songs for harvest festivals, New Year's celebrations, Christmas, and Easter. These songs celebrate both pagan beliefs and Christian traditions and have always been important to Ukrainian Americans. The earliest immigrants, who had little money, often spent their rare free hours gathered together playing and singing. This tradition has continued not only in established choirs and ensembles but also as part of Ukrainian youth groups, camps, and Saturday language classes. These language classes are also a place where children of immigrants have been taught about their country's history, geography, and culture.

Examples of ancient customs still practiced today include the spring rites and songs (*vesnianky*) and the traditions associated with the Kupalo (harvest) festival. During the festival, young maidens make wreaths of wildflowers and set them afloat in a stream; their fortune is determined by the young men who retrieve the wreaths while facing the spirits of the night. Often these rituals are practiced by Ukrainian American youths at summer camps, youth organizations, and cultural festivals.

Cuisine Ukrainian cooking is a robust mix of meat, vegetable, and grain dishes. It is similar to, and has been influenced by, the cuisines of Poland, Russia, Turkey, Hungary, Romania, and Moldova. Although Ukrainian Americans enjoy access to a wider variety of food than Ukrainians, many traditional Ukrainian foods survive in the United States. Breads dominate the pantries of Ukrainian American households— Ukraine is, after all, known as the "breadbasket of Europe." Special breads such as *paska*, which is made for Easter, are featured during the holidays and at weddings; they are often decorated with braids or birds made of dough. Bread is also featured as a ceremonial ingredient at special occasions, whether to solicit a divine blessing for the start of a farm task, to welcome guests to a celebration, or to symbolically part with the dead at a *tryzna*, or wake.

The dishes most readily associated with Ukrainians are *borscht* (a soup of red beets), *holubtsi* (cabbage rolls), *pyrohy* and *varenyky* (dough dumplings filled with potatoes and cheese, sauerkraut, or fruit such as cherries), and *kielbassa* (smoked sausage). Potatoes are the most often used vegetable in traditional Ukrainian cooking, although garlic, onions, cabbage, cucumbers, tomatoes, and beets are also staples. In addition, mushrooms are a common ingredient used to spice up a meal and are often included in stuffing.

The best showcase for traditional Ukrainian cuisine is the meatless Christmas Eve meal, which traditionalists prepare on January 6 under the Julian calendar. This meal features twelve courses, symbolic of the twelve apostles present at the Last Supper. The meal begins with *kutya* (cooked wheat, ground poppy seed, and honey) and continues with pickled herring or pickled mushrooms, *borscht*, one or more preparations of fish, *holubtsi* with buckwheat or rice, *varenyky* with sauerkraut or potatoes, beans with prunes, sauerkraut with peas, baked beets, and mushroom sauce. The feast ends with a dessert of pastries—*makivnyk* (poppy seed cake), *khrusty* (cookies made of fried bands of dough, sprinkled with icing sugar), *pampushky* (doughnuts), *medivnyk* (honey cake), or *compote* (stewed dried fruit). The tradition, although slightly modified, continues in the United States. Ukrainian restaurants in New York and New Jersey offer the traditional meal between December 24 and January 6. Restaurants like Veselka in New York's East Village offer a unique fusion of American and Ukrainian foods. Veselka's menu offers vegetarian items and adaptations of traditional items like *varenyky* made with goat cheese and sweet potatoes.

Traditional Dress Modern Ukrainians dress in clothes that are basically indistinguishable from those of other Europeans. The traditional costumes of Ukraine vary from region to region. In Kubijovyc and Struk's *Encyclopedia of Ukraine*, Ukrainian folk dress is

A PLACE AT THE TABLE

Ukrainian festive dinners have a religious context. At Christmas a special place is set at the table to welcome the spirits of dead relatives. At Easter the food that makes up the ceremonial meal is taken to church in a basket decorated with the finest embroidered linens to be blessed. Older generations attempted to retain religious customs and symbolism after immigrating to the United States, but their children married people from other ethnic groups and abandoned or modified certain customs. For example, some families celebrate Christmas twice, on December 25 and January 7. In order to meet the demands of the double holiday, some families temper their celebrations. In spite of the dilution of urban communities due to increases in the cost of living, which forced younger generations to move to the suburbs, many Ukrainian Americans, in particular Orthodox Ukrainians, continue to observe traditions such as setting an extra place at the table.

divided into five different regional forms: the Middle Dnipro region, Polisia, Podillia, central Galicia and Volhynia, and Subcarpathia and the Carpathian Mountain region. The first region around the Dnipro River is characterized by women wearing a *plakhta* (a wraparound skirt), a *kersetka* (a blouse with wide sleeves and a bodice), and an *ochipok* (a headdress). Men wear cut shirts. These clothes date back to the time of the ruling hetmanate.

In Polisia the clothes date back even further to the princely era. The well-known Ukrainian embroidered blouse and the colorful red woven skirt are worn by the women. Men dress in a shirt worn outside their trousers and a grey woolen cap (*maherka*) or a tall felt hat (*iolomok*). In the third region, Podillia, women wear multicolored, embroidered blouses and the men's mantle. In central Galicia and Volhynia, linen is a popular fabric, and women wear corsets and head wraps that resemble turbans. The men don caftans, felt overcoats, or jackets. One of the most recognizable and colorful Ukrainian costumes comes from the Carpathian Mountain region, or Lemkivshchyna. There women's skirts are decorated with folds and pleats, while men wear tunics and *leibyks*—the Lemko felt vests.

The greatest native folk dress showcase for Ukrainian Americans is at dance festivals. The swirling ribbons of color and flashes of billowing satin pants tucked into red boots mix with linen shirts, laced leather slippers, and felt hats as dancers representing different regions of Ukraine share the stage.

Dances and Songs Ukrainian music has a rich history. Some of the oldest Ukrainian traditions survive today through Christmas carols, originally sung in pagan times to celebrate the first long day of the season, and Easter songs, or *hayivky* (songs of spring).

UKRAINIAN AMERICAN PROVERBS

Proverbs are a rich part of Ukrainian culture and are handed down from generation to generation.

- A smart man seeks all from himself; a fool looks for everything in others.

- Fear God—and you will not fear any person.

- He who thinks rarely always has time to talk.

- Snow falls upon a pursuit that is put off.

- A wise man does not always say what he knows, but a fool does not always know what he says.

- Life is the road to death.

- It is difficult to learn to thank God if we cannot thank people.

- The rich man is not he who has great riches but he who squanders little money.

- A good heart does not know pridefulness.

- Brotherhood is greater than riches.

- A black dog or a white dog is still a dog.

There are also songs to herald the arrival of summer and the harvest. During the era of Cossack rule, other forms of music arose. The lyrico-epic *dumas* told of the struggles of the Cossacks. Music flourished in the seventeenth and eighteenth centuries when there were organized singing guilds. Notable Ukrainian composers include Semen Artemovsky, author of the opera *Zaporozhian beyond the Danube* (1863), and Mykola Lysenko, who collected thousands of folk songs and composed original songs and operas. In the United States the first Ukrainian American choir was organized in 1887 in Shenandoah, Pennsylvania. Traditional instruments include the *bandura*, or *kobza*, whose strings are plucked to make music; the *sopilka*, a free-reed wind instrument; the stringed percussion dulcimer, or *tsymbaly*, which is played by hitting the strings with small hammers; and the violin.

Ukrainian folk dances differ in style and costume depending on the region and the occasion being celebrated. While dancers from central Ukraine wear bright pants, embroidered shirts, and swirling skirts and aprons, Hutsul dancers from the Carpathian mountain region wear felt hats and linen trousers tucked into leather slippers. They also brandish long wooden axes over which the men leap or on which the women balance. Dance themes deal with relations between men and women, and particular occupations such as reaper, cobbler, cooper, or smith.

Among the most popular dances are the *hopak* and *kozachok*. The *hopak* was first danced by the Cossacks of the Zaporizhian Sich in the sixteenth century and then spread to the rest of Ukraine. Today it is associated with the Kyiv region and incorporates both male and female dances. It is a fast-tempo, improvised dance with complex acrobatic movements; the men leap over one another and high into the air while the women spin and step around them. The *kozachok* also originated during the Cossack period in the sixteenth century. It is a folk dance with male and female roles that often begins with a slow, melodic introduction before breaking into a quick tempo. During the seventeenth and eighteenth centuries, it was performed not only in Ukraine but also in the royal courts of Russia, France, Hungary, and Poland. Both the *hopak* and *kozachok* are standards of Ukrainian folk dance today.

The 1920s and 1930s were decades of growth in Ukrainian dance, theater, and music in the United States. A number of theaters and music halls were opened; the first was in New York City in 1924. In 1932 Ukrainian American singers and dancers performed in a concert commemorating the bicentennial of George Washington's birth, and the New York Association of Friends of Ukrainian Music was created in 1934. Another highlight of the period was a performance by more than 300 Ukrainian American dancers from Vasyl Avramenko's dance school at the Metropolitan Opera House in New York City in 1931.

Holidays Ukrainian Americans all celebrate the same holidays but at different times depending on which calendar they use. The major holidays are religious. According to the Julian calendar, which is often used by Orthodox worshippers, Christmas is celebrated on January 7, with the ritual dinner held the night before, and Easter falls on a different Sunday each year. For those who adhere to a more modern model, Christmas and Easter are celebrated on December 25 and on the appropriate Sunday on the Gregorian calendar.

One occasion Ukrainians do not traditionally celebrate is birthdays. More important are name days, which celebrate certain saints. For example, people named Stephen or Stepany celebrate St. Stephen's Day on January 9, according to the Julian calendar. The other major holiday is on January 22, which commemorates the establishment of a free Ukraine on that date in 1918.

Health Care Issues and Practices There are no known afflictions specific to ethnic Ukrainians, although immigrants who experienced the Chernobyl reactor meltdown of the late 1980s are wary of the radiation exposure they received. To some degree, folk medicine retains its place in the Ukrainian American community in both attitude and practice. Traditionally, the mentally challenged were considered

"God's people," and physical diseases were driven out by squeezing, sucking, shouting, or beating. Diseases could also be charmed away by using magic incantations and prayers or treated by using medicinal plants, baths, bleeding (e.g., leeches or cupping), or massages. However, these methods tended to fall out of favor as Ukrainians were assimilated into the American mode of health care.

Ukrainians have readily joined the American medical establishment and are well represented in the medical fields, including dentistry and chiropractic. As health care professionals immigrated to the United States, regional associations of Ukrainian American physicians quickly sprang up in major northeastern cities where Ukrainian Americans concentrated.

FAMILY AND COMMUNITY LIFE

During the early waves of immigration, men came to the United States, settled, and then brought over their wives and children. Those who were single often sought to start a family after finding a job and a place to live. They tended to seek women who were of the same ethnic background, if only for ease of communication. With each generation there has been a greater tolerance and incidence of marriage outside Ukrainian culture. Divorce was, and still is, relatively rare among Ukrainian Americans; it made little economic sense to early immigrants and was forbidden by the Catholic faith to which the majority of immigrants subscribed.

Because of geography and time, finding a wife or husband was not always easy. Dating for early immigrants, who worked long hours and had relatively little free time, was a quick practice centered on Ukrainian social events. Couples sometimes attended church hall dances or concerts. Even today *zabavas* (dances) are prime meeting places for young people. Some men left a wife behind in Ukraine and married again in the United States. A newspaper story published in 1896 told of an immigrant from Galicia who left a wife there and married once in New Jersey and again in Michigan. After being arrested and then returning to his wife in Ukraine, he discovered his two children had grown to four.

Like many other European immigrants, first-generation Ukrainian Americans as they aged often moved in with one of their adult children, serving as babysitters for their grandchildren and freeing the parents to work. This practice helped to maintain Ukrainian culture and language in the United States, and many children went to school speaking only Ukrainian.

Both boys and girls were expected to help with household chores, especially in households where part of the income came from taking in boarders. However, the duties may have differed between the sexes. Considerable responsibility fell on the older siblings to take care of the younger children. Much was expected of the firstborn so that they could become successful and productive American citizens.

Gender Roles Most Ukrainian American women in the early twentieth century were employed as domestics, often far from the foundry towns in large coastal cities. Around the turn of the twentieth century, Passaic, New Jersey, had a high concentration of single Ukrainian American women. Ukrainian American women played a large role not only in raising their families but also in adding to the family income by working as domestics, taking in boarders, working in kitchens or factories, or contributing to the family business. Working as a domestic often meant thirteen-hour workdays, seven days a week, with just Sunday evenings free.

These women were also responsible for maintaining Ukrainian language and culture in the United States, specifically through festive occasions such as Christmas and Easter. Wives and mothers would spend hours baking and cooking multicourse celebratory dinners, participating in the religious life of their family and community, and serving on various women's nationalistic committees. Many women joined organizations whose purpose was to promote Ukrainian interests in the diaspora.

In addition to joining groups that accepted men, women formed their own associations such as the Ukrainian National Women's League of America, a national nonpartisan, nonsectarian organization founded in 1925 to unite women of Ukrainian birth and descent living in the United States and promote their common philanthropic, educational, civic, and artistic interests. Other notable organizations included the Ukrainian Women's Alliance and the United Ukrainian Women's Organizations of America. The first congress of Ukrainian Women in the United States was held in New York in 1932. Women's organizations managed to combine Ukrainian and American interests (for instance, celebrating the birthdays of female poet Lesia Ukrainka along with those of George Washington and Abraham Lincoln in February) and tended to be less insular than men's organizations.

Ukrainian American women have taken prominent roles in the household. Although the first two waves of immigrants maintained relatively traditional gender roles, the more egalitarian social structure of the United States created some tension between men and women. Life in the United States often created an unsettling feeling for women who attempted to balance their public and private lives. The goals of Western feminism, such as equality in the workplace, were foreign to many Ukrainian American women since they had worked side by side with Ukrainian American men for half a century. Nevertheless, Ukrainian American women quickly established themselves in the workforce and public sphere.

Education Education for the first Ukrainian American immigrants was a luxury few could afford. With each new wave, Ukrainians came to the United States better educated. Many of the artists and professionals who arrived between the world wars had been educated in Europe and pursued work in the United States as soon as they learned English. A growing number of Ukrainian Americans studied at American schools and encouraged their children, boys and girls, to do the same. Wherever possible, children were educated in parochial schools because religion played a large role in their lives. Those who went on to postsecondary education tended to concentrate in the professions of medicine, law, engineering, graduate studies, and the arts.

Soon after the third major wave of immigration, Ukrainian American students established a network based on their common ethnic background. For example, the Federation of Ukrainian Students Organization of America, based in New York City, held its first congress April 10–12, 1953. The congress included twenty-two regional and university associations of students across the United States. The federation went on to establish the Harvard Ukrainian Research Institute in 1973 but remained dormant between 1996 and 2006 until it was restored by students from Columbia, Rutgers, the University of Michigan, and Villanova. According to the 2011 American Community Survey, approximately 54 percent of Ukrainian Americans age twenty-five or over have a bachelor's degree or higher.

Courtship and Weddings Ukrainian marriage and courtship traditions vary across the country according to region. Weddings are major celebrations that begin with negotiations for the bride's hand in marriage. The groom's family appoints a *starosta* (negotiator), who serves as an intermediary between the families of the prospective bride and groom. Originally, this figure did much of the work, even haggling over the dowry of the bride. Today, if couples wish to include a *starosta*, they do so as a symbolic gesture toward a close relative or family friend, and the role often translates into master or mistress of ceremonies.

Before the wedding, a shower or *divych vechir* ("maidens' evening") is hosted by the close friends and relatives of the bride. These are often large gatherings of women held in community banquet halls, although today they may be smaller, more intimate affairs hosted in homes. The groom and bride attend and after a full meal sit beneath a wreath and open the gifts the guests have brought.

One wedding day custom that is often retained by Ukrainian Americans is a blessing at the home of the bride's parents, which precedes the church wedding ceremony. The bride, groom, and members of the immediate family join a priest to bless the impending union. Then everyone moves on to the church, where a ceremony, possibly including a full mass, takes place. During the ceremony certain customs are maintained, such as placing crowns or wreaths of myrrh on the heads of the couple or binding the bride's and groom's hands with a long embroidered linen called a *rushnychok*. The priest then may lead them in a circle around the altar three times. The bride also may say a prayer at the altar and give a gift of flowers to the Virgin Mary in hopes that she will bless the bride as a wife and mother.

Ukrainian wedding celebrations are large and alive with song, dance, and lots of food. It is not unusual to have more than 300 guests fill a church hall or banquet room. At the beginning of the reception, the bride and groom are greeted with bread and salt by their godparents. The bread represents the wish that they should never know hunger, and the salt, that they should never know bitterness. After the greeting, the newlyweds and their attendants sit at the head table and the dinner begins. Today wedding dinners reflect the tastes of the couple and their families and can include favorite Ukrainian and American dishes such as pierogi and roast beef. Although many couples have a wedding cake, they may also have a traditional *kolach*, a bread made with decorative flour and stalks of wheat, with braids of dough adorning the top. The name is derived from the word *kolo* ("circle"), which symbolizes eternity.

Dancing after dinner is an integral part of any Ukrainian wedding. At one point in the evening, the bride's veil is removed and replaced with a kerchief, symbolizing her change from maiden to married woman. As the guests watch, encircling the bride and groom, bridesmaids place the veil on the heads of unmarried women who dance with their boyfriends, their fiancés, or groomsmen. Some couples choose to incorporate throwing the bouquet and garter into the festivities.

Baptisms Within the first year of a baby's birth, the child is christened. Close family friends or relatives are chosen as godparents to participate in the religious ceremony. This festive occasion is often followed by a banquet hosted by the new parents. The link between godparent and child is maintained throughout the child's life. Often, for years after, the godparents are referred to as *chresna* (godmother) and *chresny* (godfather).

Funerals Ukrainian funerals are ritualistic and religious. The ceremony and burial are preceded by one or two *panakhydy*. These brief evening ceremonies are held in the funeral home, and friends and family of the deceased join for a memorial service. The ceremony is conducted by a priest and ends with the singing of the funeral song "Vichnaya Pam'yat" ("Eternal Memory").

Funerals may include a mass in a church. Family and friends accompany the casket to the grave site (few people are cremated) and then repair to a church, community hall, or family member's home for a *tryzna*, or funeral remembrance luncheon. One of the most significant features of a Ukrainian funeral is the memorial service, which is repeated forty days after the death and then again annually. There is also a festival, originally associated with the pagan cult of the dead, called Zeleni sviata, or Rosalia, which is dedicated to visiting and celebrating the dead. It is held on Pentecost, fifty days after Easter. Today people meet at the cemetery to have a special mass in honor of the dead.

EMPLOYMENT AND ECONOMIC CONDITIONS

Most of the early immigrants of the late nineteenth century worked in the steel mills, coal mines, and foundries of the northeastern states. Within the ethnic urban communities where they lived, other entrepreneurial Ukrainian Americans opened grocery or general stores, butcher shops, and taverns. Women contributed to the family income by taking in boarders and doing their laundry and cooking. Overall, it was characteristic of the first generation of settlers to remain in the job, or at least the industry, in which they began. Although their pay was not substantial, Ukrainian Americans as a group rarely took advantage of government assistance or unemployment benefits. They were also among the most law-abiding immigrants. In *Ukrainians in North America: An Illustrated History*, Orest Subtelny notes that between 1904 and 1908, only 0.02 percent of Ukrainian Americans were accused of breaking any law.

By the time of the second immigration wave, there was a shift in employment trends. Second-generation Ukrainian Americans had better higher education opportunities, and second-wave immigrants tended to be better educated than first-wave immigrants. The university graduation rate among Ukrainian Americans grew, with medicine, law, engineering, and teaching as the principal professions. This trend was also reflected in the growth of Ukrainian American professional and business clubs across the United States. According to the American Community Survey, close to 47 percent of employed Ukrainian Americans work in management, business, science, and arts occupations, and 27 percent are employed in educational services, health care, and social assistance.

POLITICS AND GOVERNMENT

From the earliest years of mass immigration, Ukrainian Americans were involved in local, state, and national politics. For example, Dr. Nicholas Sudzilovsky-Russel became presiding officer of the Hawaiian senate on February 10, 1901. In 1925 George Chylak began a five-year term as mayor of Olyphant, Pennsylvania. Mary Beck (Mariia Bek), born in 1908 in Ford City, Pennsylvania, was the first woman elected to the Detroit Common Council. She served as the council's president from 1952 to 1962 and was the acting mayor of Detroit from 1958 to 1962. In state politics, lawyer O. Malena took a seat in the Pennsylvania legislature in 1932, lawyer S. Jarema won a seat in the New York legislature in 1935, and judge John S. Gonas took a seat in the Indiana legislature in 1936. Gonas was also

a state senator from 1940 to 1948 and a Democratic candidate for vice president in 1960.

Ukrainian Americans also garnered the attention of government. On March 16, 1917, president Woodrow Wilson proclaimed April 21 a day "upon which the people of the United States may make such contributions as they feel disposed to aid the stricken Ruthenians (Ukrainians) in the belligerent countries," following discussion in Congress about the Ukrainian cause. President Dwight D. Eisenhower unveiled a statue of Taras Shevchenko, poet laureate of Ukraine, in Washington, D.C., to commemorate the 150th anniversary of the poet's birth.

Although some Ukrainians belonged to Communist organizations such as the Haidamaky (established in 1907 in New York), most tended to be conservative in their politics and therefore supported the Republican Party. But in 1910 the Ukrainian National Association of America (UNA) encouraged Ukrainian Americans to vote for the Socialist Party since neither Republicans nor Democrats were addressing the concerns of workers. Leftist factions included the Ukrainian Workers Association, which broke away from the UNA in 1918, and the Ukrainian Federation of Socialist Parties in America. The other choice for Ukrainian Americans in the 1920s was the conservative monarchist Sich movement.

Ukrainian Americans were also involved in supporting political change in Ukraine. Demonstrations were frequent in the 1920s and 1930s and included the participation of thousands of men, women, and children. Ukrainian Americans picketed the White House in 1922 over the Polish occupation of eastern Galicia. About 20,000 Ukrainian Americans marched in Philadelphia in 1930 to protest the Polish occupation of western Ukraine, and a 1933 march in Detroit was held to protest the Soviet-induced famine in Ukraine.

Voting trends for Ukrainian Americans are difficult to determine; however anecdotal evidence suggests that most Ukrainian Americans continued to lean to the right and are more likely to vote Republican. Many Ukrainian Americans are wary of the Democratic Party's proximity to communism. However, political analysts who researched the 2008 and 2012 elections found that Ukrainian Americans, like many other groups, did not strictly vote for one party or another. In addition, increased pressure on Ukraine from the Obama administration and the European Union to hold fair elections was met with favor by many Ukrainian American communities.

Ukrainian Americans tend to identify with their European counterparts. The Republican Party's appeal for rigid immigration reform was seen as an impediment to Ukrainian communities in New York, New Jersey, and the Midwest. In the 2012 presidential election, for example, analysts looked to groups that were typically not acknowledged in the national debate, such as Ukrainian Americans. Although observers assumed Ukrainian Americans would vote Republican, Democratic candidate Barack Obama won the battleground states with large populations of Ukrainian Americans, such as Pennsylvania and Ohio. Analysts surmised that Obama's appeal to Ukraine to stabilize its political process and continue its efforts toward democratization may have swayed many Ukrainian Americans to support the president.

Political groups such as the U.S.–Ukraine Foundation and the Ukrainian American Coordinating Council lobby the U.S. government not only to support the domestic interests of the Ukrainian American community but also to promote open cultural, educational, and social relations between the United States and Ukraine. The Ukrainian American Bar Association continues to serve as a watchdog group for human rights issues in Ukraine by monitoring its advancement and application of the rule of law. The Shevchenko Scientific Society, which was founded in Ukraine in 1873 and in the United States in 1947, includes Albert Einstein and Max Planck among its members and supports science and research activities. The Ukrainian Congress Committee of America, founded in 1940, coordinates legal and material support for Ukrainians in Europe while raising the profile of Ukraine in the United States. Finally, the Ukrainian National Association of America, originally established in 1894 as a fraternal benefit society to provide insurance to Ukrainian immigrants, supports the social education and welfare of Ukrainian immigrants while providing aid to the Old Country.

Military Early records reveal that Ukrainian Americans served in George Washington's army during the American Revolution. Mykola Bizun, Ivan Lator, Petro Polyn, and Stephen Zubley are just some of the Ukrainians named in Washington's register. Another group fought in the Union Army during the U.S. Civil War. Joseph Krynicky, Ivan Mara, and Andrey Ripka served as Union Army officers; the military dead included Ukrainian Americans Julius Koblansky, Petro Semen, and I. H. Yarosh.

Most significant for the Ukrainian Americans during the years of World War I was the concurrent bid for a free Ukraine. World War I was heralded as an opportunity to defeat Austria or Russia, both of which ruled parts of Ukraine. The Federation of Ukrainians in America was formed in 1915 to inform the American public about Ukrainian goals. In 1917—the same year that President Wilson declared April 21 as Ukrainian Day—dreams were realized and the Ukrainian People's Republic was established. However, Wilson supported the Russian empire, and the free Ukraine soon fell. In addition, many Ukrainians, particularly in Canada, were deemed to be Austrian citizens, and thousands were incarcerated as enemy aliens.

During World War II thousands of Ukrainian Americans served in the armed forces. Nicholas Minue

of Carteret, New Jersey, was posthumously awarded the Congressional Medal of Honor for his single-handed destruction of a German machine gun position. Nestor Chylak Jr., who went on to be an American League baseball umpire, received the Purple Heart and Silver Star and was almost blinded during the Battle of the Bulge. Lieutenant Colonel Theodore Kalakula was awarded the Silver Star and two oak leaf clusters for saving medical supplies during a Japanese air raid and for his attack against the Japanese after the company commander had been wounded. Kalakula was also the first Ukrainian American graduate of West Point.

Since World War II Ukrainian Americans have served in every U.S. war and conflict. As such, the Ukrainian American Veterans Association (UAV) was incorporated in 1987 as a national organization. While there is no official count of Ukrainian Americans in the military, the UAV estimates that there are approximately 90,000 living veterans as of 2013 and that over 200,000 Ukrainian Americans have served in the U.S. armed forces since World War II. In 2011 the UAV began fundraising efforts for a national monument honoring Ukrainian Americans who have served in the military.

NOTABLE INDIVIDUALS

Academia George Kistiakovsky (1900–1982), a research chemist, immigrated in 1925 to the United States, where he became a research fellow at Princeton University. In 1930 he joined the faculty of Harvard University. He was author of more than two hundred articles on chemical kinetic gas-phase reactions, molecular spectroscopy, and thermochemistry of organic compounds. He received many awards including the U.S. President's Medal of Merit in 1946, the Exceptional Service Award of the U.S. Air Force in 1957, and the National Medal of Sciences from the president in 1965. He also served as a consultant to the Manhattan Project, the initiative to develop the atomic bomb in the early 1940s, and was appointed head of the explosives division of the Los Alamos Laboratory. In 1959 he was named special assistant for science and technology by President Eisenhower. Kistiakovsky's daughter, Vera (born in 1928 in Princeton, New Jersey), was an accomplished academic in her own right. She completed her PhD in nuclear chemistry at the University of California–Berkeley in 1952 and became a professor of physics at the Massachusetts Institute of Technology in 1963.

Other Ukrainian American academics include George Vernadsky (1887–1973), a historian at Yale University from 1946 to 1956 and author of a five-volume history of Russian and a biography of hetman Bohdan Khmelnytsky. Stephen Timoshenko (1878–1972), a specialist in theoretical and applied mechanics, vibration, and elasticity, taught at the University of Michigan and Stanford University from 1927 to 1960. Lew Dobriansky (1918–2008) was an economist and author of *Decisions for a Better America* (1960).

Myron Kuropas (1932–) was a professor of educational foundations at Northern Illinois University and special assistant for ethnic affairs to president Gerald Ford in 1976–1977. Kuropas wrote several books on Ukrainians in North America including *To Preserve a Heritage: The Story of the Ukrainian Immigration in the United States* (1984).

Art Edward Kozak (1902–1992) was born in Hirne, Ukraine. Having studied at the Art Academy in Lviv, he immigrated to the United States, becoming a citizen in 1956. In addition to participating in exhibitions across the United States, Canada, and Europe, he illustrated a number of books and from 1951 to 1954 was a performer on WWJ-TV in Detroit. He established painting studios in Detroit and Warren, Michigan, in 1950. For his efforts in educational films, he was twice awarded first prize by the American Teachers' Association.

Fellow artist Jacques Hnizdovsky (1915–1985), born in Pylypcze, Ukraine, studied at the Academy of Fine Arts in Warsaw and Zagreb, Croatia, before settling in New York City in 1949. His career included a number of one-man shows in North America and Europe. He was best known for his wood cuts, and his work is featured in collections in the Boston Museum of Fine Arts, the Philadelphia Museum of Art, the White House, and the Museum of Modern Arts, Spain.

Another influential figure in the arts community was sculptor Alexander Archipenko (1887–1964), who settled in the United States in 1923. He opened an art school in New York in 1939 and served as sculptor in residence at a number of American universities. At the time of his death, he had just completed his 199th one-man exhibition.

Ukrainian American artists established their own association in 1952. More than one hundred painters, graphic artists, and sculptors were part of the original group, which included Kozak, Hnizdovsky, Michael Moroz, Michael Chereshnovsky and Nicholas Mukhyn. Yaroslava Surmach-Mills (1925–2008), another well-known artist, was born in New York City. She graduated from the Cooper Union Art School and worked as an art instructor, art editor for *Humpty Dumpty Magazine*, and illustrator for numerous children's books. Her work *Carol Singers* was chosen as a UNICEF Christmas card design in 1965.

Journalism There are many Ukrainian Americans who have contributed to a rich heritage of Ukrainian-language journalism in the United States. Ivan Volansky (1857–1926) published *Ameryka*, the first Ukrainian newspaper in the United States, in 1886. Hundreds of women and men played an important role in the rapid growth of the Ukrainian press in the United States. A partial list includes Cecilia Gardetska (1898–?), who worked on journals in Ukraine and the United States, including *Nashe Zhyttia* (*Our Life*) in Philadelphia, and served

as the head of the Department of Journalists for the Federation of Ukrainian Women's Organizations in the United States. Another important figure was Bohdan Krawciw (1904–1975), who edited more than fifteen journals and newspapers and was general editor of the second volume of *Ukraine: A Concise Encyclopedia*, published in 1971. Finally, Volodymyr Nestorovych (1893–?) was an editor of a number of Ukrainian-language newspapers in the United States, although he was an engineer and economist by occupation.

Literature Tania Kroitor Bishop, born Shevchuk, published *An Overture to Future Days* (1954), a volume of poetry written in English and Ukrainian, and translated several works from Ukrainian into English. A circle of young poets who called themselves the New York Group of Poets—among them Bohdan Boychuk (1927–), Patricia Kylyna (Patricia Nell Warren), Yuriy (George) Tarnawsky (1934–), and B. Pevny (1931–)—published its first volume of modern poetry in 1959. In addition to publishing plays and poetry, Boychuk became a U.S. citizen in 1955 and worked as an engineer.

Music Professor Alexander Koshetz (1875–1944) directed the first concert of Ukrainian church music to an American audience at Carnegie Hall in New York City in 1936. Hryhory Kytasty (1907–1984), musical director, composer, and *bandurist*, was the author of more than thirty melodies of Ukrainian songs for solo and choir with *bandura* (a traditional stringed instrument) or piano accompaniment. He directed the Bandurists Ensemble in numerous concerts throughout Europe, the United States, and Canada.

Other notables in music include Nicholas Malko, director of the Chicago Symphony Orchestra, from 1945 to 1957; Mykhailo Haivoronsky (1892–1949), composer and founder of the United Ukrainian Chorus in the United States in 1930; Paul Pecheniha-Ouglitzky (Uhlytsky) (1892–1948), double-bass player, composer, and conductor, who lived and worked in New York and was orchestrator for NBC Radio; Virko Baley (1938–), pianist, composer, champion of Ukrainian modern music and chamber music, and conductor of the Las Vegas Symphony Orchestra; and Neko Case (1970–), an American-born singer-songwriter who established an extensive fan base.

Science and Technology Aeronautical engineer Igor Sikorsky, born in Kyiv in 1889 (died 1972), immigrated to the United States and formed the Sikorsky Aero Engineering Company in 1923. This company built the S-29, the first twin-engine plane made in the United States. Sikorsky is also credited with designing the first helicopter (the VS-300, first flown in 1939) and the S-40 (the first large American four-engine clipper, built in 1931). Michael Yarymovich (1933–) served as chief scientist of the U.S. Air Force and assistant director to the Apollo Flight Systems in the 1960s. In 1975 he was appointed assistant administrator for

Ukrainian American actor
Mila Kunis in London,
2013. KEITH MAYHEW /
ALAMY

engineering at Rutgers University before going to war from 1942 to 1946. He was nearly blinded at the Battle of the Bulge and was awarded the Silver Star and Purple Heart. His officiating career in the major leagues spanned three decades, from 1954 to 1978, when he retired as an umpire in the American League.

Football is another sport in which Ukrainian Americans have excelled. Bronko (Bronislav) Nagurski (1908–1990) was a famous tackle for the Chicago Bears in the 1930s and 1940s. He helped lift the Bears from ninth to third place in the league and was an all-league player for three consecutive years. He was elected to the National Football Hall of Fame in 1951. He also made a career as a professional wrestler and won the world heavyweight title in 1937 and 1939. Charles Bednarik (1925–), center for the Philadelphia Eagles from 1949 until 1962, was elected to the National Football Hall of Fame in 1967.

Ukrainian American boxers include Steve Halaiko (1908–2001), a member of the 1928 U.S. Olympic team and Golden Gloves champion, and John Jadick (1908–1970), junior welterweight champion in the 1930s. Wrestler Mike Mazurki (1909–1990) (born Michael Mazurski) went on to a career in films in the 1940s. In the 1960s golfers Mike Souchak (1927–2008) and Steve Melnk (1947–) achieved success. Soccer star Zenon Snylyk (1933–2002) was a member of the 1964 U.S. Olympic and World Cup teams.

Stage and Screen Ukrainian Americans who found their way to Hollywood include director Edward Dmytryk (1908–1999), who directed a number of films including *Murder My Sweet*, *Crossfire*, and *The Caine Mutiny*. William Tytla (1904–1968) made his mark in Hollywood animation. Born in Yonkers, New York, he worked at Walt Disney Studios as an animator, creating the characters of Dumbo and the Seven Dwarfs, before moving to Paramount, Famous Studios, and Twentieth Century Fox, where he was director of a cartoon series that included Popeye, Little Audrey, and Little Lulu.

Academy Award-winner Jack Palance, born Walter Palahniuk (1919–2006), made his first film, *Panic in the Streets*, in 1950. He began his career as a professional boxer in the 1940s after he returned from a tour of duty in the U.S. Army Air Corps. He made his stage debut on Broadway in *Silver Tassel* in 1949 and appeared in stage productions of *Julius Caesar*, *The Tempest*, and *A Streetcar Named Desire*. Among his more than fifty films are *Shane*, *Batman*, and *City Slickers*, for which he won an Academy Award for Best Supporting Actor in 1991. He had his own television series, *Bronk*, in 1975 and appeared on various programs over more than four decades.

Other Ukrainian Americans involved in film are Nick Adams, born Adamschock (1931–1968); Anna Sten, born Stenski-Sujakevich (1908–1993), star of *The Brothers Karamazov* and *Nana*; and 1940s Hollywood leading man John Hodiak (1914–1955), who was married to actress Anne Baxter and starred in

Laboratory and Field Coordination of the Energy Research and Development Administration.

Sports Many Ukrainian Americans became successful in the National Hockey League (NHL). Terry Sawchuk (1929–1970) was elected to the Hockey Hall of Fame in 1971 with 103 career shutouts as a goalie, having played twenty-one seasons with Detroit and Toronto. Bill Mosienko (1921–1994), a right wing for the Chicago Black Hawks, was selected for the all-star team in 1947 and scored a record three goals in twenty-one seconds in one 1952 game. New York Ranger teammates Walter Tkaczuk (1947–) and Dave Balon (1938–2007) were two-thirds of the NHL's highest-scoring line during the 1969–1970 season. In 1971 Johnny Bucyk (1935–), Vic Stasiuk, and Bronko Horvath formed the famous "Uke" line in the all-star game. More recently, Ukrainian American hockey players have included Mike Bossy, (1957–) Dale Hawerchuk (1963–), and Mike Krushelnyski (1960–).

Nestor Chylak Jr. (1922–1982), a baseball umpire, was born in Peckville, Pennsylvania, and studied

Alfred Hitchcock's *Lifeboat* and *The Harvey Girls* with actress Judy Garland.

Mila Jovovich (1975–), born in Kyiv, appeared in numerous fantasy and science fiction films, including *The Fifth Element* (1997) and the *Resident Evil* series (2002–2012). Mila Kunis (1983–), an American-born actress of Ukrainian descent, became famous through her role in the hit television comedy *That '70s Show* (1998–2006). She appeared in numerous films, including *Forgetting Sarah Marshall* (2008), *Friends with Benefits* (2011), and *Black Swan* (2010), for which she received nominations for a Golden Globe Award for Best Supporting Actress and a Screen Actors Guild Award for Outstanding Performance by a Female Actor in a Supporting Role.

One of the most versatile individuals in Ukrainian dance and film was Vasyl Avramenko (1895–1981). Born in Stebliv, Ukraine, he founded the First School of Ukrainian National Dances in Kalisz, Poland, in 1921. After he immigrated to the United States, he directed performances at the Metropolitan Opera House, the 1893 World's Fair in Chicago, and the White House in 1935. He also took dance tours to Brazil, Argentina, Australia, and Israel throughout the 1950s, 1960s, and 1970s, and established his own dance studio in New York in 1952. In addition, he did work in film. In 1936 he organized a Ukrainian film company and produced two movies using the texts of the Ukrainian classic plays *Zaporozhets za Dunayem* (*The Cossack from beyond the Danube*) and *Natalka Poltavka* (Natalka from Poltava).

MEDIA

PRINT

America

Published by the Providence Association, an insurance company, this weekly tabloid is printed separately in Ukrainian and English. First published in 1912, this Catholic paper appears in print and online, and covers politics, sports, and news about Ukraine and the United States.

Leo Iwaskiw, Editor
817 North Franklin Street
Philadelphia, Pennsylvania 19123
Phone: (877) 857-2284
Email: info@provassn.com
URL: www.provassn.com/news.htm

New Star Ukrainian Catholic Newspaper

The organ of the St. Nicholas Diocese in Chicago, this bulletin of church news has a circulation of 3,500 and is published in both Ukrainian and English every three weeks.

John Lucas, Editor
2208 West Chicago Avenue
Chicago, Illinois 60622
Phone: (312) 772-1919
Email: churchatnewstar@cs.com
URL: www.esnucc.org/offices/new-star

Svoboda

This daily Ukrainian-language newspaper includes local and Ukrainian news stories and advertisements. The English-language newspaper *Ukrainian Weekly* is published out of the same location.

Petro Chasto, Editor
or
Roma Hadzewych
2200 Route 10
Parsippany, New Jersey 07054
Phone: (973) 292-9800
Fax: (973) 644-9510
Email: svoboda@svoboda-news.com
URL: www.svoboda-news.com

ORGANIZATIONS AND ASSOCIATIONS

Ukrainian Academy of Arts and Sciences in the United States

Founded in 1950, this academy was established to organize and sponsor scholars pursuing Ukrainian studies. The facilities include a museum and library with material on the history of Ukrainian immigration to the United States and books on Ukrainian history and literature. The academy also publishes a scholarly journal, *Annals of the Ukrainian Academy of Arts and Sciences*.

Albert Kipa, Professor Laureate
206 West 100th Street
New York, New York 10025-5018
Phone: (212) 222-1866
Fax: (212) 864-3977
Email: uvan@verizon.net
URL: www.uvan.us

Ukrainian American Youth Association

This organization operates summer camps and offers various cultural and recreational activities.

Andriy Bihun, President
136 Second Avenue
New York, New York 10003
Phone: (212) 477-3084
Email: ky-usa@cym.org
URL: www.cym.org/us/

Ukrainian Catholic Church

The first parish in the United States was established in 1885 in Shenandoah, Pennsylvania.

Metropolitan Stefan Soroka, Archbishop
Archdiocese of Philadelphia
827 North Franklin Street
Philadelphia, Pennsylvania 19123
Phone: (215) 627-0143
Email: ukrmet@catholic.org
URL: www.ukrarcheparchy.us

Ukrainian National Women's League of America

This nonpartisan, nonsectarian organization sponsors educational scholarships and cultural events.

Marianna Zajac, President
108 Second Avenue
New York, New York 10003

Phone: (212) 533-4646
Fax: (212) 254-2672
Email: unwla@unwla.org
URL: www.unwla.org

Ukrainian Orthodox Church in America

This church was founded in 1928 by Ukrainians who
emigrated from Russia, Bukovina, Galicia, and
Poland.

Metropolitan Anton, Eparchial Bishop
135 Davidson Avenue
Somerset, New Jersey 08873
Phone: (212) 927-2287
Email: consistory@uocofusa.org
URL: www.uocofusa.org

MUSEUMS AND RESEARCH CENTERS

Harvard Ukrainian Research Institute

Established January 22, 1968, with financial and
moral support from large numbers of Ukrainian
Americans, Ukrainian Studies at Harvard began
in 1957.

Michael S. Flier, Director
H34 Kirkland Street
Cambridge, Massachusetts 02138
Phone: (617) 495-4053
Fax: (617) 495-8097
Email: huri@fas.harvard.edu
URL: www.huri.harvard.edu

Shevchenko Scientific Society

Founded in 1947 in New York City to support research
and to assist immigrant Ukrainian scholars in
adjusting to life in the United States, this society was
named for the famous nineteenth-century Ukrainian
poet Taras Shevchenko. The society organizes
scientific sessions, lectures, and conferences, and
maintains archives and a library.

Leonid Rudnytzky, World Council President
63 Fourth Avenue
New York, New York 10003
Phone: (212) 254-5130
Fax: (212) 254-5239
Email: info@shevchenko.org
URL: www.shevchenko.org

Ukrainian Institute of America

Founded in 1948, this institute maintains a permanent
exhibition of Ukrainian folk arts; sponsors lectures,
concerts, and conferences; and houses a Ukrainian
historical gallery. It was established with funds
from Volodymyr Dzus, a wealthy Ukrainian
industrialist.

Daniel Swistel, President
2 East 79th Street
New York, New York 10021

Phone: (212) 288-8660
Email: mail@ukrainianinstitute.org
URL: www.ukrainianinstitute.org

Ukrainian Museum–Archives

Established in 1952, this museum emphasizes the
period of the Ukrainian Revolution and Ukrainian
immigration to the United States after World War
II. The archives include about 20,000 volumes in
addition to archival materials.

Andrew Fedynsky, Director
1202 Kenilworth Avenue
Cleveland, Ohio 44113
Phone: (216) 781-4329
Email: staff@umacleveland.org
URL: www.umacleveland.org

Ukrainian National Museum

This museum was established in 1958 through the
merger of the Ukrainian Archive–Museum in Chicago
and the Ukrainian National Museum and Library of
Ontario, Canada.

Taras Szmagala, Sr., Executive Director
2249 W. Superior St.
Chicago, Illinois 60612
Phone: (312) 421-8020
Email: info@ukrainiannationalmuseum.org
URL: www.ukrainiannationalmuseum.org

SOURCES FOR ADDITIONAL STUDY

Gregorovich, Andrew. *Ukrainian Fraternal Association
Centennial 1910–2010.* Scranton, OH: Ukrainian
Fraternal Association, 2010.

Kubijovyc, Volodymyr, and Danylo Husar Struk, eds.
Encyclopedia of Ukraine. Toronto: University of
Toronto Press, 1984–1993.

Kuropas, Myron B. *The Ukrainian Americans: Roots
and Aspirations 1884–1954.* Toronto: University of
Toronto Press, 1991.

Lushnycky, Alexander. *Ukrainians of Greater Philadelphia.*
Chicago: Arcadia, 2007.

———. *Ukrainians of the Delaware Valley.* Chicago:
Arcadia, 2009.

Pawliczko, Ann Lencyk, ed. *Ukraine and Ukrainians throughout the World: A Demographic and Sociological Guide to
the Homeland and Its Diaspora.* Toronto: University of
Toronto Press for the Shevchenko Scientific Society, 1994.

Satzewich, Vic. *The Ukrainian Diaspora.* New York:
Routledge, 2002.

Shtohryn, Dmytro M., ed. *Ukrainians in North America.*
Champaign, IL: Association for the Advancement of
Ukrainian Studies, 1975.

Subtelny, Orest. *Ukrainians in North America: An Illustrated
History.* Toronto: University of Toronto Press, 1991.

Wertsman Vladimir. *The Ukrainians in America
1608–1975.* New York: Oceana, 1976.

URUGUAYAN AMERICANS

Jane E. Spear

OVERVIEW

Uruguayan Americans are immigrants or descendants of people from Uruguay, a country on the Atlantic seaboard of South America. Bordered on the west by Argentina and on the north and northeast by Brazil, Uruguay is bounded on the southeast by the Atlantic Ocean, and to the south it fronts the Río de la Plata, a broad estuary that opens out into the South Atlantic. Three-fourths of the land is grassland, ideal for raising cattle and sheep. Uruguay's total land area is 68,037 square miles (176,215 square kilometers), slightly smaller than the state of Washington.

According to the *CIA World Factbook*, the population of the country was 3,316,328 in July 2012. In 2006 47.1 percent of Uruguayans were Roman Catholic, with another 11.1 percent non-Catholic Christians and 23.2 percent nondenominational; atheists or agnostics accounted for 17.2 percent, and 0.3 percent was Jewish. Uruguay's per capita GDP (gross domestic product) in 2008 of $12,200 placed it fourth among South American countries. Agriculture and agri-industry accounted for 12 percent of the total GDP and for about 70 percent of total exports.

The first significant immigration of Uruguayans to the United States occurred between 1963 and 1975, propelled by a declining economy in Uruguay. Largely a well-educated group, Uruguayan immigrants settled in urban areas, with the heaviest concentration in the New York-New Jersey metropolitan area, where many found employment in managerial and professional positions. Typically Uruguayans immigrating to the United States have been young and middle class. The Visa Waiver Program allowed Uruguayans to enter the United States without a visa from 1999 through early 2003, but the heavy influx and alleged security concerns led to the end of the exemptions later in 2003.

According to the 2010 Census there were 58,884 people of Uruguayan descent in the United States, just more than 1 percent of the total Hispanic American population. New York and California have the largest number of people of Uruguayan descent. Uruguayan Americans have a high degree of cultural assimilation.

HISTORY OF THE PEOPLE

Early History The Charrua Indians were the largest group of indigenous inhabitants in the land area that was to become Uruguay. In 1516, when the Spanish navigator Juan Díaz de Solís landed on Uruguayan shores, the Charruas immediately killed him and his crew. Uruguay did not possess the gold, uranium, and other precious metals abundantly present in other South American countries that were sought by the Spanish conquistadors as well as other Europeans. Because of that, very few Europeans had any interest in developing settlements there. In 1680 Portuguese soldiers arrived from Brazil and established the first city in Uruguay, Colonia del Sacramento. The Spanish colonists who founded Montevideo in 1726 did so more to prevent Portuguese expansion into Uruguay than for an interest in the land. During much of the early to mid-1700s the Portuguese and Spanish battled for control of the entire area. By 1777, the year following the United States's declaration of independence from England, the Spanish had established control over most of Uruguay. It then became a Spanish colony, a section of the Viceroyalty of La Plata. La Plata included Argentina, Paraguay, and portions of Brazil, Bolivia, and Chile. The natives battled with the Europeans during this period and were defeated. Those who escaped death in battle or by the hitherto unknown diseases the Europeans had brought with them retreated to the interior regions of the South American continent. This accounts for the predominance of whites in Uruguay even in modern times.

José Gervasio Artigas was a soldier who organized his own army to fight for freedom from Spanish colonial rule. In 1811 Artigas's near-defeat of the Spaniards when he laid siege to Montevideo was thwarted when Portuguese troops arrived from Brazil and attacked the Uruguayan forces. Neither Artigas nor his followers would submit to Portuguese or Spanish rule, so they fled inland to the Argentine province of Entre Rios, nearly emptying Uruguay of people. When the Spanish surrendered in 1814 and ended Spanish rule, Artigas captured Montevideo for Uruguay. Two years later, in 1816, the Portuguese again attacked, and this time the struggle lasted four years. At that time the Portuguese made Uruguay a part of Brazil, and Artigas went into exile.

By 1825, when a group of Uruguayan patriots known as "The Thirty-Three" staged a rebellion against Brazil, the renewed fight for Uruguayan independence emerged. Their armies gained control of the countryside within months with the support of

Argentina. After British intervention sparked because of a blockade that threatened British trade, Argentina and Brazil recognized Uruguay as an independent republic. The country adopted its first constitution in 1830. Fructuoso Rivera became the nation's first president. In 1835 Manuel Oribe followed as second president, but an attempt by Rivera to regain power in 1836 began a civil war. Rivera's commanders, known as the Colorados, generally more liberal, and Oribe's commanders, the Blancos, primarily conservative, fought for sixteen years until 1851, when the Colorados defeated the Blancos. The two groups eventually developed into Uruguay's two major political parties, and the struggles between the two forces continued for much of the rest of the nineteenth century, with power shifting back and forth between them. The Colorados had gained control in 1865 with Brazil's help. The Blancos subsequently received assistance from Paraguay. Brazil, Argentina, and Uruguay then joined forces against Paraguay in what was called the War of the Triple Alliance, defeating Paraguay in 1870. The Colorados became the dominant party, as immigrants flowed into Montevideo from all over South America and Europe.

Modern Era While some Colorado leaders were dictators, under the rule of the liberal Colorado José Batlle y Ordóñez, president from 1903 to 1907 and again from 1911 to 1915, Uruguay entered an era of social and governmental reform. Batlle held to democratic ideals and advocated social justice for all. During his leadership new laws established free education, minimum wages and workers' rights, free medical care for the poor, and marriage and divorce legislation. The government took benevolent control of public utilities and factories and established national banks and railroads.

With its stable domestic economy and social welfare programs, Uruguay prospered even during the Great Depression and World War II, when its products, especially meat and wool, were in demand by the Allies, with whom they joined forces. Uruguay had cut all diplomatic ties with Germany, Japan, and Italy in 1942 but did not declare war on them until 1945, near the end of the conflict, and no Uruguayan troops fought in World War II. When the United Nations was founded in 1945, Uruguay became a charter member.

Uruguayans approved a new constitution in 1951 that abolished the presidency and set up a nine-member National Council of Government. The intention of the new government was to allow the Colorados and the Blancos to share power. But by the next year Uruguay's economy began to collapse. Foreign trade was no longer prosperous because of a loss of agricultural exports. Inflation and the cost of social programs grew rapidly. The grave economic situation continued into the 1960s. Many Uruguayans left for other countries, principally Argentina, the United States, Australia, Spain, Brazil, and Venezuela. By 1967 the

inefficient National Council was abolished in favor of the re-establishment of the presidential government.

Economic downturn gave rise to political unrest. One group of urban guerrillas known as the Tupamaros kidnapped foreign ambassadors and other personnel and murdered a Uruguayan official. When President Juan María Bordaberry was elected in 1972, he declared war on the Tupamaros. He crushed the movement in a few months, but by 1973 Bordaberry was president in name only. The military took control of the government and suspended the constitution, replacing Bordaberry in 1976 with Aparicio Méndez. General Gregorio Álvarez succeeded him in 1981. At this time many of the country's artists, intellectuals, and politicians were persecuted for espousing beliefs different from those of the military regime and consequently went into exile abroad, mostly to Spain, Sweden, Mexico, the Netherlands, and Belgium. The late 1970s and early 1980s saw political unrest throughout Latin America. Uruguay maintained the world's highest ratio of political prisoners to general population; other Latin American governments also committed crimes against their people that encouraged some to flee to the United States.

Many Uruguayans who left the country for political reasons chose to return in 1984 when Julio María Sanguinetti, the leader of the Colorado Party, was elected president, signaling a return to civilian government. Sanguinetti faced all of the same problems that the nation had faced since the 1960s, only this time they were worse. Major economic problems, including inflation, foreign debt, and unemployment, were major issues. In 1989 Luis Alberto Lacalle won the presidency, and the Blanco party returned to dominance. His plans to privatize companies, taking them out of government control, and his call for smaller wage increases worried the workers, who organized strikes in opposition to such plans. In 1992 the voters rejected the plans to privatize, and in 1994 Sanguinetti was reelected to the presidency.

In 1991 Uruguay joined Argentina, Brazil, and Paraguay to form MERCOSUR, the southern common market. Until the mid-1990s China was the largest foreign investor in Uruguay; however, the MERCOSUR alliance began to change that. Uruguay also made agreements with Chile and Bolivia and continued to extend its economic rebuilding efforts to the other South American countries and elsewhere around the world.

The power of the two traditional political parties, the National (Blanco) and Colorado, began to decline in the 1990s, and by the end of the twentieth century, the Frente Amplio, a coalition of various left-of-center factions, had become the largest political force in the country. In 2004 the Frente Amplio candidate, Tabaré Vázquez, was elected president, and his party held a majority in Parliament. His administration won popular approval by fostering economic growth and by reexamining human rights abuses committed during the period of military dictatorship. Vázquez was succeeded by another Frente Amplio candidate, José Mujica, a former Tupamaro guerrilla, who was inaugurated for a five-year term on March 1, 2010. Mujica said that his model was Brazilian President Luiz Inácio Lula da Silva, a left-leaning former trade unionist known for a centrist approach.

SETTLEMENT IN THE UNITED STATES

Before the 1960s the economy of Uruguay provided its citizens with middle-class affluence, and emigration was limited. With a comfortable standard of living, adequate employment opportunities, a favorable social welfare and health insurance system, and democratic freedoms, few Uruguayans felt the need to leave. On the whole, even the poorest of Uruguayans enjoyed certain benefits that kept them satisfied enough to stay in their own country. For those who left the cultural and recreational opportunities of the cities, where 85 percent of all Uruguayans lived, the proposition of going to neighboring countries such as Argentina, with its familiar language and proximity to the home country, was more appealing than moving to the United States. Those who pursued business or educational opportunities in the United States and elsewhere often returned home.

Two factors changed the complacency of Uruguayans. First, there were economic and political problems in Uruguay after World War II, particularly money and employment crises during the 1960s and 1970s. Second, an oppressive military regime took control of the government. These factors motivated people to leave Uruguay, and those leaving in vast numbers were the ones that the country could least afford to lose—well-educated professionals and the young. This, too, marked the beginning of the social security crisis. As the aging population retired and young people left the country, the burden on the country's financial resources grew. Of Uruguay emigrants from 1963 to 1975, 17.7 percent of them were aged fourteen years or younger, 68 percent of them were between the ages of fifteen and thirty-nine, and only 14.3 percent were over forty years of age. The continued employment problems of the late 1980s represented yet another impetus for the youth of Uruguay to seek employment and make new lives elsewhere. Some of them went to the United States, but the largest population of Uruguayan emigrants continued to reside in Argentina. More than 40 percent of Uruguayan immigrants in the United States in 2000 were between the ages of twenty-five and forty-four. Older immigrants often enter under family reunification. It is common among young Uruguayan couples with small children to bring one of the children's grandmothers to the United States to care for the children and the home while the parents are employed outside the home.

The most significant wave of Uruguayan immigration to the United States occurred in the 1960s

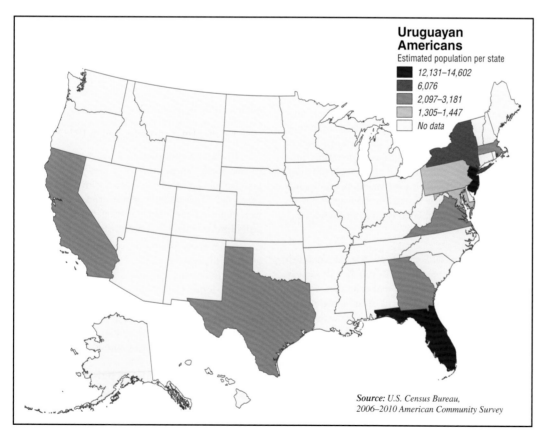

Uruguayan Americans
Estimated population per state

- 12,131–14,602
- 6,076
- 2,097–3,181
- 1,305–1,447
- No data

Source: U.S. Census Bureau, 2006–2010 American Community Survey

and 1970s. An estimated 180,000 people left Uruguay between 1963 and 1975, when the country's economy suffered a devastating slump. Between 1975 and 1985, during the period of oppressive military control, 150,000 Uruguayans left the country, according to statistics from the General Directorate of Statistics and Census of the Republic of Uruguay. As late as 1989 only 16,000 of those citizens had returned to their native country. When these two figures are added together, the emigration figure stands at approximately one-tenth of the population.

By the mid-1990s 10 percent of the U.S. population, an estimated 27 million people, was of Hispanic origin, though slightly fewer than 7,000 Uruguayans immigrated to the United States between 1990 and 2000. In 2000 Uruguayans accounted for 1.3 percent of the South American-born population in the United States. According to the 2010 United States Census, the number of Uruguayan immigrants was so small that it was included in the 882 who emigrated from South American countries other than Brazil, Colombia, Ecuador, and Peru. Many Uruguayan immigrants went to New York City, New Jersey, and Long Island. Two other significant centers of Uruguayan American population were Washington, D.C., and Florida.

Tighter security measures after the terrorist attacks on September 11, 2001, made United States officials aware of an increased number of Uruguayans who were working without a permit or overstaying their ninety-day limitation. This led to a revocation of Uruguayans from the Visa Waiver Program. According to Uruguay's Office of Welcome and Returns, in 2011 thirty Uruguayans per month were deported from the United States. In addition to these, other Uruguayans began voluntarily returning after the Uruguayan economy grew 8.5 percent in 2010 and unemployment reached the lowest level since 1986.

Uruguay's democratic history and multicultural tradition make it easier for immigrants from that country to adapt to life in the United States. According to a 2006 study conducted by the National Bureau of Economic Research, Uruguayan Americans show a high degree of economic and cultural assimilation. Yet many second- and third-generation immigrants maintain pride in their Uruguayan heritage and work at passing their cultural identity on to their children.

LANGUAGE

Spanish is the official language of Uruguay. As much as one-third of the population is of Italian descent in the coastal areas, and Italian is spoken in these regions by older people of Italian descent. A colloquial tongue known as *Rioplatense* consisting of Spanish with Italian influences is also used. English is taught in schools and is heard frequently, especially in the coastal areas, where tourism is concentrated.

When adjusting to life in the United States, Uruguayans find that Spanish is the language, next to English, most frequently spoken by other Uruguayans. Because of this, some Uruguayans do not find their

adjustment to life in the United States to be as difficult as it is for other immigrants. In 2000, 93.3 percent of Uruguayan immigrants spoke a language other than English in the home. For nearly 90 percent of them Spanish was the primary language. Forty-five percent were less than proficient in English.

RELIGION

The Spanish explorers brought the Roman Catholic religion with them to Uruguay. The faith did not play as important a role as it did with Uruguay's neighbors, even in the early colonial days. Uruguay's indigenous population resisted conversion, reducing the influence of the Catholic Church. After independence in 1828, the secular influence pervaded. Still, the Catholic population enjoyed its own parochial schools and its own political party and movements. The Union Civica del Uruguay (Civic Union of Uruguay), a Catholic political party, was founded in 1912, although it never won any significant percentage of the national vote. In 1962, influenced by progressive trends within the Catholic Church, the party changed its name to the Partido Democrata Cristiano (Christian Democratic Party, or PDC). The Third Conference of Latin American Bishops, held in Mexico in 1979, had a radical impact on Uruguay. The bishops called for a "preferential option for the poor," inspiring Uruguayan Catholics to provide temporary hospice for the radical Tupamaros when they were given amnesty in 1985.

Other faiths represented in Uruguay include Protestantism and Judaism. Protestant denominations grew in prominence throughout the twentieth century. By the late 1980s the Protestant population in Uruguay was estimated at 2 percent or slightly higher. From 1960 to 1985 the number of Protestants increased in Uruguay by 60 percent. The Jewish population of Uruguay settled primarily in Montevideo and accounted for approximately 2 percent of the population. Beginning in 1970 the Jewish population began to decrease, mostly due to emigration.

By the twenty-first century Uruguay was the most secular South American country. Less than half of the population was Catholic, compared with 73.6 percent in Brazil and 92 percent in Argentina, and many Catholics were nominal rather than practicing. More than 17 percent identified themselves as atheists or agnostics.

Uruguayan Americans compose such a small group within the Hispanic American population that information on their religious identification is minimal. For some, Catholicism continues to be central in their lives. A smaller number, some of whom are converts from the Roman Catholic Church, belong to a Protestant denomination, and an increasing number do not identify with any religious group.

CULTURE AND ASSIMILATION

Uruguayan Americans are as diverse as their native counterparts in Uruguay. For educated and sophisticated Uruguayan professionals, fitting into a cosmopolitan lifestyle in New York demanded little adjustment, except to climate. In their own country Uruguayans of several different classes lived a Westernized, cultured existence. The large Spanish-speaking population in the United States has reduced cultural adjustments because of language barriers.

Traditions and Customs Many of the customs of other Latin American nations are observed in Uruguay. When people greet each other, they usually shake hands. Public embraces and the use of first names are used only among close friends and family members. Meetings even among friends are formal, whether in public places or corporate settings. The eased sense of time among Latin Americans is apparent among Uruguayans—meetings often do not start on time, and no one is reprimanded or considered ill-mannered for being late. Even in informal social settings, polite custom requires that if invited to a Uruguayan's home, the visitor should send flowers or chocolates to the hostess ahead of time rather than at the time of the visit. Conversation in Uruguay in polite social settings does not include politics. The much-loved national pastime of football, known as soccer in the United States, is always a safe topic. Uruguayans in the United States also tend to follow Uruguayan football and their national teams.

Cuisine Uruguayans are mainly of European descent, and this is reflected in their cuisine, which is strongly influenced by Spanish and Italian cooking, with more subtle influences from German and French culinary traditions. Uruguayans love meat, especially beef, as evidenced by the large number of cattle they raise. In the 1990s it was estimated that cattle and sheep *estancias*, or farms, took up four-fifths of the country's land. *Asado*, a Uruguayan barbecue considered the national dish, includes different cuts of beef, ribs, sausages, sweet breads, chitterlings, and other organ meats cooked over a wood fire. Another traditional meal, *parrillada criolla*, is a barbecued mixture of *chorizo*, a Latin American sausage, *rinones*, or kidneys, and strips of beef. Also popular is *morcilla dulce*, a blood sausage mixed with orange peels and walnuts. *Milanesa* is deep-fried steak that has been breaded with Italian-seasoned crumbs. Because much of the population is of Italian heritage, pasta is usually served daily and is an integral element of a good meal. However, pasta is never served with beef dishes such as *asado* or *churrasco* (steak usually served with tomatoes and lettuce or with mashed potatoes). Uruguayans prefer freshly made pasta to the dry pasta popular in the United States. Another dish reflecting Italian roots is *faina*, made with chickpea flour and boiled with oil and salt, similar to polenta (boiled cornmeal) in texture.

Other favored dishes include *buseca*, which is soup made with calf's tripe, haricot or other white beans, peeled tomatoes, garlic, and Parmesan cheese. It combines Hispanic influences, from the Spanish soup *menudo*, made with tripe and hominy, with Italian elements, adding cheese and garlic to the soup. Potato *gramajo*, made with eggs and potatoes, and *pascualina*, a Uruguayan spinach pie made with Spanish olive oil and cheddar cheese, are two other dishes enjoyed by Uruguayans. *Chivito*, an original Uruguayan dish, consists of steak in a bun with bacon and eggs, usually accompanied by French fries, tomato, and lettuce. *Chivito* means "goat" in Spanish, but there is no goat in this dish. Uruguay has the reputation of being the dessert capital of Latin America. Favorite sweet treats include *masassurtidas*, the term given to many varieties of pastries; *pasta frola*, a pastry cake spread with quince preserves; and *chaja*, a sponge cake topped with whipped cream and crushed meringue cookies. *Dulce de leche*, Spanish for "candied milk," is a thickened caramel-like sauce made from sweetened milk that is used in a variety of Uruguayan desserts—as a filling for cookies and cakes or as an accompaniment for flan and ice cream.

Uruguayan *candombe* drummers play together in drum circle at Lummus Park, South Beach, Miami, FL. JEFF GREENBERG / PHOTOEDIT

Jugos, or juices, are popular beverages, with *naranja* (orange), *pina* (pineapple), and papaya being favorites. *Licuados* are juices mixed with milk or water. The most popular is *yerba mate*, or simply *mate*, a beverage of green tea. Sometimes a special ceremony surrounds the drinking of *mate*. A hollowed-out gourd or a china cup is almost filled with the green tea. A metal straw is inserted, and boiling water is then poured over the leaves. The mate is passed around to friends and family seated in a circle, with each person adding more hot water as it is passed. Between 1973 and 1985, the period of military control, people met one another in public squares for this tea ceremony. The ceremony provided a subterfuge, allowing citizens to congregate with less fear that the military police would arrest them on charges of illegal political conspiracy.

Dances and Songs Uruguayans appreciate many forms of music, whether it comes from the popular guitar, introduced by Spanish settlers, and the songs of the *gauchos*, or from a formal orchestra. In addition to the guitar, the accordion is played along with many of the traditional folk songs and dances. The most popular dance in Montevideo is the *candombe* performed by the African slave ancestral population. The drumbeats of the Afro-Uruguayans reach their loudest and most festive during the Uruguayan Mardi Gras; the dance has been an official part of that celebration since 1870.

The tango, the music form most associated with Uruguay, was created from the union of the *milonga*, music derived from traditional Spanish folk songs, with the rhythms of African slave music. Originally a duel-like dance that men danced with men, it later became a dance between men and prostitutes. The violent and erotic elements made it scandalous among the upper classes, and the dance won widespread acceptance in Uruguay only after it became popular in Paris and New York. The national dance is the pericon, a circle dance involving six or more couples. Small pockets of Uruguayan Americans incorporate traditional music into their community celebrations of the Uruguayan carnival each year in places such as Chicago; Elizabeth, New Jersey; and Springfield, Massachusetts.

Holidays In Uruguay the church and state are separate, and therefore holidays are secularized (non-religious). For instance, Christmas Day is celebrated as "Family Day" rather than as a religious holiday. Other holidays that Uruguayans celebrate include Kings' Day (January 5), commemorating the visit of the Three Kings, with presents sometimes exchanged; Semana de Turismo, or Tourism Week, which coincides with Easter; Desembarco de los Treinta y Tres (Landing of the Thirty-Three, April 19), commemorating the fight by thirty-three Uruguayan patriots for independence from Portuguese-Brazilian occupation in 1825; Labor Day (May 1); Artigas's Anniversary (June 19), celebrating the national hero José Gervasio Artigas, who began the struggle for independence in 1811;

and Todos Santos, or All Souls Day, on November 2. Mardi Gras, or *Carnaval*, is celebrated in Uruguay as in other Latin American countries, although not with as much vigor as it is in Rio de Janeiro. Uruguayans, including Uruguayan Americans, also celebrate their nation's Independence Day on August 25 with traditional music and food.

FAMILY AND COMMUNITY LIFE

Gender Roles As early as 1900 the patriarchal tradition was beginning to disappear in Uruguay. Following the decree making divorce legal in 1907 and allowing women to file on the grounds of cruelty, women became socially emancipated, a process furthered by changes in the divorce law in 1912 that required no cause to be specified in divorce cases. By 1919 women were allowed to keep their own bank accounts separate from their husbands, and they were already beginning to enter the workforce. Cheap, readily available domestic labor made it easier for middle-class women to work, and by 1985 more than 45 percent of them were employed outside the home. Because women were provided equal access to education at all levels from early in the twentieth century, they began entering the professions at increasing rates. They gained the vote in 1932, but their participation in actual governance remained low into the twenty-first century. In 2009, 11.5 percent of Uruguayan lawmakers were women, markedly lower than the 21.5 percent average for the Americas and the world average of 18.4 percent.

Machismo, the aggressively strong masculine character associated with patriarchy in Latin American countries, may have been less dominant in Uruguay than in neighboring nations, but males were still encouraged to display traditional "masculine" traits. Feminine traits were viewed as weaker, and a strong strain of paternalism that saw women as in need of protection remained part of the culture. Social gatherings tended to divide along gender lines. In many ways gender relationships in the United States were similar to those to which Uruguayan immigrants had been accustomed in their native country, thus easing adjustment to North American culture.

Education At the end of the twentieth century Uruguay had a literacy rate of nearly 95 percent for people over fifteen years of age. Education is mandatory by law for children between the ages of six to fifteen years, and public education is free to all Uruguayans through the university level. However, rural communities have only elementary-level schools, so children must go to the cities to attend high school or university. There is only one public university in Uruguay, the University of the Republic in Montevideo, which has approximately 35,000 students, but there is also a teacher training institute and a nationwide system of vocational, or trade, schools. There are also several important private universities, including the Catholic

University of Uruguay. Education is prized, and consequently many Uruguayan Americans pursue education and professional careers in the United States. Coeducation has long been the norm, and since the 1980s the number of females enrolled in higher education has often exceeded the number of males.

Among foreign-born Uruguayan Americans in 2000, 71.1 percent had graduated from high school, and 22.1 percent held a college degree. Since Uruguayans encourage their children to enter professions they see as prestigious (law, medicine, economics, and administration), it is hardly surprising that more than 10 percent of Uruguayan immigrants held a graduate or professional degree. The gap between the number of university graduates and the opportunities in the most respected fields contributes to Uruguay's high rate of emigration among young professionals.

EMPLOYMENT AND ECONOMIC CONDITIONS

The majority of Uruguayans have long held a middle-class lifestyle, with women as likely to be in the labor force as men. Many citizens who emigrated to the United States and elsewhere left because economic conditions did not allow them to continue to maintain their affluence and secure employment. Regarding those who left Uruguay from 1963 to 1975, the following statistics were available: 12.8 percent of the emigrants were professionals, technicians, managers, and administrators; 16 percent were office employees; 12.4 percent were salespeople; and 47.6 percent were drivers, skilled and unskilled workers, and day laborers. The divisions of labor and professions for those Uruguayan Americans living in the United States were not determined officially by the U.S. government census figures. According to 2000 census data, 30.1 percent of foreign-born Uruguayans in the United States were employed in management, professional, or related occupations with another 24.3 percent employed in sales and office work. The median family income was $52,362, with 25.4 percent making $50,000–$75,000, 28 percent making in excess of $75,000, and 14 percent living below the poverty level.

POLITICS AND GOVERNMENT

Uruguayans, whether living at home or abroad, tend to follow the politics of their native land. For the political exiles of the 1970s, democratic freedoms were crucial to their decision to leave. The return of those freedoms in the 1980s likewise were a major factor in their decision to return.

Uruguayans, under the direction of David P. Michaels and President Sanguinetti, formed the Uruguayan American Chamber of Commerce (UACC) in 1996 to further business and economic ties between the United States and Uruguay. The UACC has offices in Miami and in New York City.

An Uruguayan immigrant stocks snacks at a U.S. hotel while she works to obtain citizenship with the help of her employer. AP IMAGES / ALAN DIAZ

NOTABLE INDIVIDUALS

Art Bruno Fonseca (1958–1994), oldest son of Uruguayan sculptor Gonzalo Fonseca, was a painter and sculptor whose work is in collections at the Metropolitan Museum, the Museum of Modern Art, the Smithsonian, and many other public and private collections.

Caio Fonseca (1959–), younger brother of Bruno Fonseca, is a classically trained pianist whose paintings have been described as an interchange between painting and music. His work has been displayed in many museums, including the Whitney Museum of American Art in New York and the Smithsonian in Washington, D.C.

Literature Ida Vitale (1923–) is a major voice in Latin American literature. The author of more than thirty books, she is best known for her poetry. She was a leading figure in the Uruguayan art movement known as the Generation of 1945. *Garden of Silica* (2010), her first poetry anthology to appear in English, included work from 1960 to 2010. Living in exile since 1973, she became a resident of Austin, Texas, in 1989.

Isabel Fonseca (1963–) is the youngest of Uruguayan sculptor Gonzalo Fonseca's four children and the sister of the painters Caio Fonseca and Bruno Fonseca. The author of the nonfiction work *Bury Me Standing: The Gypsies and Their Journey* (1995), a book about the lives of Roma people, she published *Attachment*, her debut novel, in 2009. She is married to the writer Martin Amis.

Music Uruguayan-born Enrique Graf (1953–) is an internationally acclaimed pianist. He is also founder and artistic director of the International Piano Series in Charleston, South Carolina, and the Young Artist Series in the Piccolo Spoleto Festival. He is co-director of Music Fest Perugia, Italy.

Gabriel Eduardo "Gabe" Saporta (1979–), son of Jewish Uruguayan parents, was the lead singer and bassist of Midtown, a pop punk band from 1998 to 2004. In 2006 he formed the band Cobra Starship and signed to Pete Wentz's Decaydance record label. The band, featured on the soundtrack to the films *Snakes on a Plane* and *TNMT*, headlined its first tour in 2008. The band's fourth album was released in 2009.

Sports and Entertainment Pedro Piedrabuena (1971–), born in Montevideo, is an American professional three-cushion billiards player who has been United States national champion five times (2002, 2004, 2007, 2011, and 2012). He settled in San Diego, California.

MEDIA

Although there is an absence of specifically Uruguayan American media, Uruguayan immigrants have access to a wealth of Spanish-language media in the United States. They also have Internet access to *El Pais*, Uruguay's most popular daily newspaper. Social media such as Facebook and Orkut, Google's social networking site, are also popular among Uruguayans and Uruguayan Americans.

TELEVISION

Jonathan Del Arco (1966–), an actor best known for his roles as Hugh Borg on *Star Trek: The Next Generation*, as the transgender character Sophia Lopez on *Nip/Tuck*, and as Dr. Morales, the medical examiner on the critically acclaimed *The Closer*, immigrated to the United States with his family when he was ten.

Actress Natalia Cigliuti (1978–) first found success as Lindsey Warner in *Saved by the Bell: The New Class* (1993–1995). She also appeared as Anita Santos Warner on the popular soap opera *All My Children* from 2004 to 2006.

ORGANIZATIONS AND ASSOCIATIONS

Uruguayan American Chamber of Commerce

Founded in 1985 through a joint initiative with Dr. Julio Sanguinetti during his first term as president of Uruguay and David P. Michaels, a British-born economic and political strategist whose wife is Uruguayan, the organization acts as a catalyst and facilitator for trade and investment with Uruguay.

David P. Michaels
401 East 88th Street
Suite 12-A
New York, New York 10128
Phone: (212) 722-3306
Fax: (212) 996-2580
Email: gateway@uruguaychamber.com
URL: www.uruguaychamber.com

Uruguayan-American Foundation (UAF)

UAF is a nonprofit organization whose main mission is to seek tax-deductible contributions for nonprofit organizations, schools, and children at risk in Uruguay.

Lydia Aguirre, President
Phone: (301) 299-6493
Email: lydia.aguirre@uruguayanamericanfoundation.org
URL: http://uruguayanamericanfoundation.org

MUSEUMS AND RESEARCH CENTERS

The Blanton Museum of Art: Latin American Collection

The Blanton's collection of Latin American art features more than 2,100 modern and contemporary paintings, prints, drawings, and sculptures. Works by more than a dozen Uruguayan and Uruguayan American artists are included.

Simone J. Wicha, Director
University of Texas at Austin
200 E. Martin Luther King Jr. Boulevard
Austin, Texas 78701
Phone: (512) 471-7324
Fax: (512) 471-7023
Email: info@blantonmuseum.org
URL: http://collection.blantonmuseum.org/
IT_14?sid=13037464&x=615508

The David Rockefeller Center for Latin American Studies at Harvard University

The center works to increase knowledge of the cultures, economies, histories, environments, and contemporary affairs of Latin America. Activities directly related to Uruguay that are sponsored by the center include internships for graduate students, lectures on the country's politics and economy, and performances by Uruguayan artists.

Merilee S. Grindle, Director
1730 Cambridge Street
Cambridge, Massachusetts 02138
Phone: (617) 495-3366
Fax: (617) 496-2802
Email: merilee_grindle@harvard.edu
URL: www.drclas.harvard.edu

The Museum of Latin American Art (MOLAA)

Founded in 1996, MOLLA is the only museum in the United States exclusively dedicated to modern and contemporary Latin American art. Works by Uruguayan artists are in its collections.

Stuart A. Ashman, President and CEO
628 Alamitos Avenue
Long Beach, California 90802
Phone: (562) 437-1689
URL: www.molaa.org

The Stone Center for Latin American Studies at Tulane University

The Stone Center coordinates the research and teaching activities of over one hundred faculty members across several Tulane campuses. It also hosts conferences, symposia, film series, and other activities. Activities specific to Uruguay sponsored by the Stone Center include a conference in 2012 on democracy in Latin America.

Thomas F. Reese, Executive Director
100 Jones Hall
New Orleans, Louisiana 70118

Phone: (504) 865-5164

Email: rtsclas@tulane.edu

URL: http://stonecenter.tulane.edu/pages/detail/62/
Roger-Thayer-Stone-Center-for-Latin-American-Studies

SOURCES FOR ADDITIONAL STUDY

Finch, M. H. J., and Alicia Casas de Barran. *Uruguay*. Vol. 102 of *World Bibliographical Series*. Oxford: Clio Press, 1989.

Janer, Zilkia. *Latino Food Culture*. Westport, CT: Greenwood Press, 2008.

Solari, Aldo, and Rolando Franco. "The Family in Uruguay." In *The Family in Latin America*, edited by Man Singh Das and Clinton J. Jesser. Ghaziabad, India: Vikas, 1980 pp. 46–83.

Taglioretti, Graciela. *Women and Work in Uruguay*. Paris: United Nations Educational, Scientific, and Cultural Organization (UNESCO), 1983.

Taylor, Philip B., Jr. *Government and Politics of Uruguay*. Westport, CT: Greenwood Press, 1984.

Verdesio, Gustavo. "An Amnesic Nation: The Erasure of Indigenous Pasts by Uruguayan Expert Knowledges." In *Beyond Imagined Communities: Reading and Writing the Nation in Nineteenth-Century Latin America*, pp. 196–224 Washington, D.C.: Woodrow Wilson Center Press, 2003.

Weinstein, Martin. *Uruguay: Democracy at the Crossroads*. Boulder, CO: Westview Press, 1988.

VENEZUELAN AMERICANS

Drew Walker

OVERVIEW

Venezuelans Americans are immigrants or descendants of people from Venezuela, a country situated on the northern coast of South America. It is bounded by the Atlantic Ocean and Caribbean Sea to the north, Brazil to the south, Colombia to the west and southwest, and Guyana to the east. The land of Venezuela can be divided into three main regions: coastal mountains, plains, and forest. The coastal mountains are confined to a small part of the north of the country, whereas the plains and forest areas make up most of the landscape. The Orinoco River divides the country between north and south. Venezuela is the sixth-largest country in South America, covering an area of 352,143 square miles (912,050 square kilometers), a little more than twice the size of California. The contiguous United States is almost nine times as big as Venezuela.

According to preliminary results of the 2011 census by the *Institutor Nacional de Estadística* (National Institute of Statistics), Venezuela had a population of 28,946,101 inhabitants. The overwhelming majority of citizens, between 90 and 95 percent, are Roman Catholic. About 2 percent are Protestant. There are small Muslim and Jewish communities. The Muslim community of more than 100,000 is concentrated among people of Lebanese and Syrian descent living in Nueva Esparta State and around Caracas. The Jewish community of approximately 13,000 is mainly found in Caracas. Santería, a belief system that fuses ideas from African religions and Catholic doctrine and that involves worshipping deceased Venezuelan people of importance, is growing in popularity in Caracas and coastal areas. The majority of citizens are of mixed European and indigenous or black heritage. Venezuela is the fifth-largest member of OPEC for oil production. Oil revenues accounted for roughly 95 percent of export earnings, about 40 percent of federal budget revenues, and around 12 percent of the GDP. Venezuela had one of the highest inflation rates in the world (roughly 28 percent) in 2011.

There is no clear record of early settlement by Venezuelans in the United States, although there were migrations between South America and the United States, including by Europeans who first settled in Venezuela and then immigrated to the United States. Between 1910 and 1930 there were significant migrations from South America to the United States, but the number of immigrants specifically from Venezuela is unknown. Most of the South Americans in these migrations settled in urban areas in the northeastern United States as well as in Chicago, Los Angeles, and San Francisco. Economic and political crises in Venezuela since the 1980s have made middle-class lifestyles harder to attain, spurring immigration of Venezuelan professionals to the United States and elsewhere. Since 1999 President Hugo Chávez's social and economic policies prompted a surge of middle- and upper-class Venezuelans to move to the United States.

According to the U.S. Census Bureau, there were 215,023 Venezuelan Americans—a number comparable to the population of Irvine, California—living in the United States in 2010 (about 0.4 percent of the Hispanic or Latino population). The community is based primarily in southern Florida. Populations of Venezuelan Americans are more concentrated than most other South American immigrant groups, with the exception of the Guyanese and Ecuadorians. States with significant Venezuelan populations include Florida, New York, Texas, New Jersey, and California.

HISTORY OF THE PEOPLE

Early History Archaeologists estimate that the first people arrived in present-day Venezuela around 14,000 BCE. Venezuela was inhabited by a number of indigenous groups, including the Caracas, Arawak, and Cumangotos. By the time Christopher Columbus and the Spanish arrived in 1498, the area was populated with an estimated half a million indigenous inhabitants. At first assuming the land to be a large island, Columbus traveled east along the coast, where he encountered the wide mouth of the great Orinoco River. Knowing that no island could produce such a large river and outflow, Columbus realized that he was encountering a landmass much larger than he had assumed. When another explorer, Alonso de Ojeda, arrived a year later, he sailed westward along the coast. Ojeda observed houses built on stilts above the coastal water. These houses reminded Ojeda of the great Italian city of Venice, and he named the land "Venezuela," Spanish for "Little Venice." From 1500 to 1541 a series of Spanish settlements arose on the coast of Venezuela. Caracas, the capital, was founded in 1567. Over the following centuries, European and African populations in Venezuela continued to grow.

Modern Era As the Spanish empire grew in South America and the Caribbean, Venezuela moved from the control of one province to the next until 1717, when Venezuela was placed under the control of the viceroyalty of the Virreynato de la Nueva Granada in the Colombian city of Bogotá. Due to its difficult climate and the perceived lack of gold and other resources, Venezuela was largely ignored by the Spanish empire.

By the end of the eighteenth century, resistance to colonial rule in Venezuela grew. In 1806, a revolution began, headed by Francisco de Miranda. After trying to establish an alternative government in the capital city of Caracas, de Miranda was arrested and sent to Spain, where he died in prison a few years later. With the loss of Miranda, Simon Bolívar, a man who was to become the national hero of Venezuela, took control of the independence movement.

In 1819 Colombia (which had just become an independent nation), Ecuador, and Venezuela were united into one state named Gran Colombia. In 1821 Bolívar and his army defeated the Spanish in Venezuela and won independence. In 1829 Gran Colombia was split up into three separate countries, and Venezuela became an independent country.

Following Bolívar's death in 1830, a series of dictators ruled Venezuela. During this time, periods of civil war, and political and economic instability were frequent. In 1945 Rómulo Betancourt, the leader of the Acción Democrática (Democratic Action) party took over the government. In 1947 a new constitution was created, and well-known novelist Rómulo Gallegos became Venezuela's first democratically elected president. This new democratic regime was in power only six months when a coup toppled the government, and a military officer named Marcus Pérez Jiménez took control. Jiménez was overthrown in 1958, and Betancourt was elected president; he stepped down in 1963. Betancourt was followed by a series of democratically elected presidents.

For a time, Venezuela was one of the most stable and wealthy countries in the region. With some of the world's largest oil reserves, it benefited from the high oil prices of the 1970s and 1980s. However, when oil prices started to drop, political instability increased. Carlos Andrés Pérez became president in 1989 and introduced economic reforms that increased the gross domestic product but again concentrated wealth to a small elite, provoking violent opposition by the many poor and unemployed. Pérez was nearly overthrown by two coups, was impeached in 1993, and was subsequently imprisoned for misuse of government funds. Former President Rafael Caldera was elected to the office again in 1994. He promised to stabilize the economy and end corruption, but inflation, austerity measures, and record-low oil prices meant a drop in the standard of living for most Venezuelans, leading to further protests.

In 1998 Hugo Chávez Frías was elected president by a large majority. He claimed to represent the needs of the poor and promised radical social reform. A new constitution was created in 1999, dissolving the bicameral parliament, establishing a single National Assembly, and giving greater powers to the president. Chávez's agenda polarized the country, and again there were violent protests. In 2002 he was replaced by a military coup but returned to power after two days. Dissent continued with a nine-week strike and subsequent referendum that Chávez survived. He was elected to a new term in 2006. In 2011 Chávez announced he was diagnosed with cancer but was still running for reelection. He won another term in office in 2012.

The varied history of Venezuela has made for a country rich with ethnic and cultural diversity. Approximately two-thirds of the population is mestizo (of mixed European and Indian ancestry) or mulatto-mestizo (African, European, and Indian), approximately one-fifth of European descent, and approximately one-tenth mainly of African ancestry. Although there is a statistically small Native Indian population, there are thirty-eight distinct Indian peoples within Venezuela.

SETTLEMENT IN THE UNITED STATES

There is no definitive accounting of Venezuelan immigration to the United States before the twentieth century. Many Europeans immigrated to Venezuela between the eighteenth and early nineteenth centuries and later migrated to the United States. They brought children and grandchildren who were born in Venezuela and grew up in Venezuelan culture, with Spanish as their first language.

Between 1910 and 1930 ten times more South Americans than Central Americans immigrated to the United States, with estimates of more than 4,000 per year. Again, there are no definitive breakdowns, so it is not clear how many emigrated from Venezuela specifically. Many came hoping for better educational opportunities and then remained once their schooling ended. Frequently, they were joined by relatives.

Census data show a continuing rise in Venezuelan immigration to the United States since the 1970s. In 1970 there were 17,321 Venezuelan immigrants; in 1980, 38,120; in 1990, 50,823; and in 2000, 116,867. The overwhelming majority of Venezuelan Americans, 70.4 percent, identified as white; 19.1 percent identified as "other race," 6.7 percent identified as two or more races; and 2.1 percent identified as black/Negro. Less than 1 percent identified as Latin American Indian or Asian/Pacific Islander.

During the 1980s and 1990s political and economic crisis and instability in Venezuela stimulated

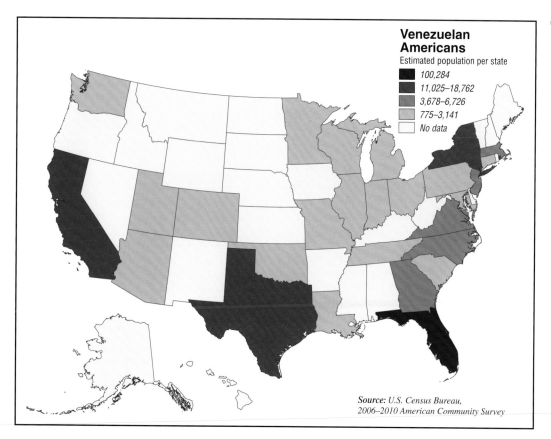

Venezuelan Americans

Estimated population per state

■ 100,284
■ 11,025–18,762
■ 3,678–6,726
□ 775–3,141
□ No data

*Source: U.S. Census Bureau,
2006–2010 American Community Survey*

immigration to the United States. According to the United Nations *Human Development Report 2000*, real wages in Venezuela decreased nearly 70 percent between the 1980s and 1990s, and the probability of being poor increased from 2.4 percent to 18.5 percent. Obtaining or maintaining a middle-class life-style became more challenging, and immigration to the United States grew more enticing, especially for professionals, manual laborers, entrepreneurs, and bureaucrats. With changing economic and social policies in Venezuela, immigration allowed many Venezuelans to protect personal property and capital investments. A 2002 survey found that more than half of Venezuelans under the age of twenty-four wanted to leave the country.

Immigration to the United States increased significantly after 1999 when Hugo Chávez came to power in Venezuela and enacted major changes in economic and social policies. The soaring crime rate was another impetus for many to leave (in 2010, there were 13,387 murders in Venezuela compared with 6,000 in 1999). Between 2000 and 2006 the Venezuelan American community in the United States grew by more than 94 percent. The 2010 U.S. Census reported 215,023 Venezuelan Americans, a 135 percent rise over the 2000 population; by 2011 there were 244,123. Some analysts likened Venezuelan immigration to the United States after the election of Chávez to Cuban immigration to the United States after

Fidel Castro took power. Cuban Americans who were against Castro immigrated to the United States and continued to be vocal and active about their opposition to Castro, also getting involved with U.S. politics generally, just as Venezuelan Americans who opposed their national leader, Chávez, came to the United States but continued their vocal opposition to Chávez and became involved in the U.S. political scene.

Although many Venezuelan Americans are found in California, Texas, and New Jersey, the majority settled in Florida (41 percent), generally in the greater Miami/Fort Lauderdale area near other South American communities. Weston, a suburb of Fort Lauderdale, is known as "Westonzuela" because of its high Venezuelan population. The Venezuelan population is concentrated on a state level, but within those states Venezuelans also settle outside of Latino communities in suburbs where they share class and educational backgrounds with non-Latinos. Consequently, they become strongly linked to mainstream American society.

South American immigrants tend to be more demographically similar to Cuban immigrants than other Latino groups. They are generally better educated and have higher incomes that correspond to lower poverty rates and unemployment. South American immigrants tend toward white-collar managerial and technical occupations and demonstrate a more equal male-to-female ratio of immigrants than many other Latin American immigrant groups in the United States. Venezuelan Americans in particular are generally younger and more educated than other Latin American groups. In 2000, 42.8 percent of Venezuelan immigrants had a bachelor's degree or higher, and 41.7 percent worked in professional or managerial occupations. The median age was thirty-two, and 52.7 percent were female and 47.3 percent were male. The majority, 68.8 percent, were not U.S. citizens. Recent Venezuelan immigrants, like many other immigrants from Latin America, often faced the challenges of undocumented status, ethnic concentration, and uncertainty about the impact of the political and economic stability of Venezuela.

LANGUAGE

Spanish is the official language of Venezuela, though there are more than twenty-five indigenous languages. English is required in private high schools and some public schools. Spanish and English are the predominant languages of the Venezuelan American community. Venezuelan American families stress education, and English proficiency is high, but strong family values also put an emphasis on teaching and preserving Spanish. Most children speak Spanish in the home and are bilingual. Some have adapted "Spanglish," Spanish combined with a liberal usage of English words.

People often stand closer together when speaking than one does in mainstream American culture. Using your hands when you speak is common, as well as using gestures to communicate without speaking. For instance, you can ask for the price of something or request payment by rubbing the thumb and index finger together while rotating the palm up. The diminutive form, constructed by adding -ito at the end of a word, is often used to show affection.

Common Venezuelan Expressions and Slang

Cheever *and* **Verbatim**

> Very well done, cool, excellent

Ester plead *(literally, "to be bald")* **and ester limpid** *("to be clean")*

> To be broke or out of money

Reecho

> Awesome or astonishing; also used when someone is angry

Pioneers las pilas *(literally, "to insert batteries")*

> To be aware or to watch out for

Dejar el pelero *(literally, "leave the hair")*

> To leave a mess

Pana

> Friend, buddy; also used to indicate someone is a good person

Soyao

> Kooky.

RELIGION

Venezuelans generally have a strong religious foundation and strong beliefs in religion and destiny. As in Venezuela, the vast majority of Venezuelan Americans are Roman Catholic; a very small number are Protestant, Muslim, or Jewish. Although religious by the strength of their beliefs, Venezuelan American Catholics' attendance at Mass and other official religious functions is infrequent when compared with other Hispanic or Latino groups.

Many Venezuelan traditions synthesize secular or cultural beliefs with religious beliefs, as well as official and unofficial doctrine. Hispanic, Indian, African, and indigenous customs often combine with Catholic beliefs. For instance, María Lionza, who is popular among Venezuelans of all social classes, blends Catholic belief, traditional Afro-Venezuelan folk culture, and native Indian myth. She is revered as a goddess of nature, love, peace, and harmony. Lionza is characterized by traits similar to the Virgin Mary and is often the center for many complex rituals about food, fortune, healing, and safety. She is referred to as "the Queen" or the "Spirit Queen" by her followers and is seen as a figure of inspiration.

People in secular positions are sometimes revered as "saints" because of their good works and the positive influence they have had on others. Dr. José Gregorio Hernández, for instance, was a medical doctor with an illustrious career before his death in 1918. He was seen as having an unusual ability to heal and was venerated for inspiring health and healing. Some claimed to have been granted miracles after praying to him. His image and story have made him so famous that in 1949, Venezuelan Catholic Church officials began the process leading to beatification. He was granted the title of "venerable" in 1985. Simon Bolívar, a military and political leader instrumental in achieving independence from Spain, is honored as a great man. Pictures of him often occupy a prominent place in the homes of Venezuelan Americans.

CULTURE AND ASSIMILATION

Large-scale Venezuelans immigration to the United States is a fairly recent phenomenon—it began to rise each decade from the 1970s and then saw a particularly significant rise after Chávez took power in 1999. As a consequence, there is less research specifically on the Venezuelan American community than some other Hispanic or Latino communities, such as those coming from Mexico, Cuba, or Puerto Rico. Venezuelan Americans do share some characteristics with other Hispanic or Latino immigrants, such as language or, in some cases, religion, culture, and family values. However, there are some less common characteristics, such as patterns of immigration, history, levels of education, work, and professional backgrounds.

The majority of Venezuelan immigrants were not politically persecuted, and thus their feelings for their home country are generally not as hostile as those of some other immigrant groups. Venezuelan Americans lack a long immigration history in the United States, which also accounts for a strong connection to their home country. Before the economic and political unrest of the early twenty-first century, Venezuela was often considered one of the most desired places to live in South America, boasting a high standard of living—albeit with frequent economic inequality—and vast cultural and geographic diversity. A Venezuelan expression indicates this pride: *Venezuela un pais para querer* ("Venezuela is a country to love"). Venezuelan Americans maintain their pride in their national heritage and culture. Political organizations, for instance, work on both American and Venezuelan issues. Venezuelan restaurants, such as El Arepazo in Doral, Florida, have become community centers where there are celebrations, protests, weekly dominoes sessions, and television screens showing Venezuelan soap operas and news footage about and from Venezuela.

It is not uncommon for Venezuelan American immigrants to have traveled to the United States prior to emigrating, giving them a familiarity with American culture. Some immigrants intended to be in the United States temporarily, but as the political and economic situation in Venezuela changed, they decided to stay. In this way, they are seen as similar to Cuban immigrants who moved to the United States at the beginning of the Castro regime.

The majority of Venezuelan Americans are from middle- or upper-class backgrounds, identify themselves as white, rarely immigrate due to political persecution, and often seek higher education. Most Venezuelan Americans descend from the Spanish (mainly), Italians, Portuguese, Germans, and French. They sometimes settle in suburban areas, not necessarily concentrated with other Venezuelan immigrants, but rather with others of similar class and educational backgrounds. For these reasons, their assimilation into mainstream culture can be less challenging than that of some other Hispanic or Latino groups, whose members are people of color or impoverished. Nonetheless, Venezuelan immigrants still do experience challenges when trying to assimilate, maintain their cultural heritage and values, and cope with a new environment. Differences in language, family and gender roles, and racial issues (that were not necessarily present in Venezuela) are challenges that Venezuelan Americans face. Undocumented immigrants face further challenges.

Traditions and Customs Depending on an individual's history, his or her family traditions may reflect those of several different ethnic groups. The majority of Venezuelans are of mixed heritage, although many Venezuelan Americans consider themselves white and identify more with white Western cultures. Their culture is heavily influenced by the Spaniards, and so cultural attributes found within the Venezuelan American community are also seen among Caribbean peoples

and Colombian Americans who were influenced by the Spaniards as well. It is often difficult to separate the religious elements of Venezuelan American culture from the more secular elements.

Honesty, generosity, optimism in the face of difficulties, and a good sense of humor are important parts of daily life. A common Venezuelan expression reflects these attitudes: *Al mal tiempo, buena cara* ("In bad weather, put on a good face"). People doing business with Venezuelans are advised that, unlike in other cultures where how strongly competent you are or the details of your specific business proposals may be of the most importance, in Venezuela it is more important whether people think you are trustworthy, worthy of respect, and have good relationships in order to make a profitable business partnership. In the business world it is said there are not relationships between companies but between people. Business meetings may often start, for instance, with what would might be considered extensive "small talk," such as personal questions about one's background and family, so that people will become better acquainted before a business transaction occurs. Similar to many other Latino cultures, schedules are often more "flexible"—being fifteen minutes to an hour late is not seen as problematic.

Venezuelans take great pride in their country and the heroes of the independence movement, such as liberator Simon Bolívar. However, Venezuelans have also long been influenced by American and European popular culture, especially in the more major urban areas such as Caracas. Due to these influences, a great deal of emphasis is placed on popular culture. Fashion is important. Baseball is a passion for many Venezuelan Americans, and they are often loyal supporters of hometown teams. Soccer is also a popular sport. Television programs, both in Spanish and English, are a great source of entertainment for Venezuelan Americans. *Telenovelas*, or soap operas, are particularly popular. Dominoes is a favorite pastime.

Cuisine Many types of traditional cuisine are found within the Venezuelan American community. Venezuelan cuisine has a good deal in common with that of other Latin American and Caribbean countries. Among the many foods enjoyed are arepas, which are small pancakes made from corn. Arepas are often stuffed with different fillings, including beef, shrimp, ham, sausage, eggs, salad, avocado, and octopus. Another specialty is the empanada, a crescent-shaped deep-fried turnover made of cornmeal that is stuffed with chicken, cheese, or beef. *Pepitos*, bread with grilled chicken or sliced meat that is served with onions, is a popular "fast-food" dish. *Cachitos*, bread rolls filled with ham, and *golfeados*, which look like cinnamon rolls but are made with brown sugar and cheese, are commonly found in Venezuelan American bakeries. *Guyanés* is a commonly used soft, salty, white cheese. Popular condiments include garlic, tomato,

GOLFEADOS

Ingredients

2 cups all-purpose flour

1 teaspoon or envelope granulated dry yeast

½ cup sugar

1 teaspoon salt

1 beaten egg

½ cup warm water and ⅓ cup water for syrup

3 tablespoons melted butter, plus a little more for coating pastry

1 tablespoon cold butter (to grease the baking sheet)

3 tablespoons sweet aniseed

2 cups grated papelón or brown sugar

2 cups crumbled queso blanco, soft and fresh

Preparation

In a bowl, combine the flour, instant yeast, sugar, salt, beaten egg, and ½ cup of warm water. Incorporate the 3 tablespoons of melted butter and knead the mixture until you have a soft dough that can be extended. Make a ball and let it rest on a lightly greased plate. Cover with a kitchen cloth and let rise until volume is doubled.

When dough is finished rising, knead again on a floured surface and use the rolling pin to extend it into a ½-inch-thick rectangle.

Coat the dough with more melted butter and spread it with 2 tablespoons of aniseed, 1½ cups of papelón, and 1½ cups of queso blanco.

Roll the dough into a cylinder shape and cut it into smaller rolls to form approximately ¾-inch golfeados. Place the golfeados on a greased baking sheet. Cover with a kitchen cloth and let rest for half an hour.

While the dough rests, preheat the oven to 350°F. In a small pot over medium-low heat, prepare the syrup with ½ cup of papelón, ⅓ cup of water, and a tablespoon of aniseed. Stir constantly. Once you have a syrup consistency, remove from the heat and set aside.

After resting for 30 minutes, bake the golfeados for 20 minutes or until light golden brown. Take them out and thoroughly coat them in the papelón syrup, sprinkle with remaining crumbled cheese, and bake for another 5 minutes.

bacon sauces, and *salsa blanca* (made from mayonnaise and parsley).

A Venezuelan dish often served during Christmas is *hallaca*, which consists of chopped beef, pork, or chicken with vegetables and olives. This mixture is folded into a corn dough, wrapped in banana leaves, and steamed. Also commonly served at Christmas is *ensalada de gallina*, a salad of diced potatoes, carrots, apples, onions, and peas mixed with shredded chicken in a mayonnaise-mustard-olive oil dressing. The most popular Christmas drink is *ponche crema*, a creamy alcoholic drink similar to eggnog, with rum as the base.

Another popular Venezuelan drink is *tizana*, which consists of chopped fruit and fruit juice; fruits used to make *tizana* include papaya, banana, watermelon, cantaloupe, orange, and pineapple. *Pampero*, an aged rum, is a popular alcoholic beverage.

Cafecito, a thick black coffee served in a very small cup, is often offered to visitors as a gesture of hospitality and friendship. Offering hot appetizers to visitors is also a popular tradition.

Dances and Songs The Venezuelan American community listens to many forms of traditional and popular music. Perhaps the most well-known Venezuelan music is the *joropo*, the traditional music of *los llanos*, or "the plains," which features the accordion, harp, *cuatro venezolano* (a small, guitarlike instrument), and maracas. The *joropo* musical form accompanies a song called "Alma Llanera," which has become the unofficial national anthem of Venezuela; an energetic dance performed by couples often is seen with this song.

Other traditional styles of music include salsa and merengue, also common in the Caribbean. *Gaita Zuliana*, from the region of Zulia State, is very popular during the Christmas season. Venezuelan Americans enjoy traditional Venezuelan music and a full range of popular music.

Folk dances are common in Venezuela and generally are reflective of a particular region and the interaction of European and indigenous heritages, rituals, and beliefs. Venezuelan Americans come from a variety of regions and may have different folk dance traditions. Additionally, although folk dance is taught and performed by some Venezuelan Americans, most prefer modern dances. Parties, concerts, and nightclubs featuring salsa or merengue often provide Venezuelan Americans with opportunities to dance. *Reggeaton*, which combines Latin rhythms and hip-hop, is popular with young people.

Venezuelan American dancer and choreographer Tina Ramirez founded the American dance company Ballet Hispanico in New York in 1970. The company describes itself as one that "reflects, explores, and expands the essence of the diaspora of Latino cultures." It has performed for more than 2 million people in the United States, Europe, and South America.

Holidays For many Venezuelan Americans, Carneval, celebrated forty days before Easter, is the main festival of the year. Many Venezuelan Americans visit Venezuela during Carneval to reunite with family and friends. In the United States, groups gather to celebrate with music, drinking, singing, and dancing. Venezuelan Americans also often simultaneously celebrate July 4, American Independence Day, and

July 5, Venezuelan Independence Day, with an outdoor fiesta. Christmas is an important holiday, with many family gatherings and traditional foods, including *hallaca*, *pan de jamón* (ham bread), *ensalada de gallina*, *pernil de cochino horneado* (baked pork leg), and desserts such as *dulce de lechoza*, papaya in a raw sugar cane syrup; *panettone*, a sweet bread loaf; and *turrón*, nougat with almonds. A *quinceanera* celebrates a girl's fifteenth birthday and marks her transition into womanhood. Mother's Day is also considered an important holiday.

Health Care Issues and Practices As a group, Venezuelan Americans do not suffer from health problems that differ significantly from those of other Americans. Some Venezuelan Americans prefer to visit practitioners of traditional medicine, such as herbalists. Traditional medical remedies are readily available in many areas with large Hispanic American populations. The Venezuelan American community of southern Florida opened a medical center to address the needs of low-income Venezuelans.

FAMILY AND COMMUNITY LIFE

Family ties are strong among Venezuelan Americans. There is a strong value of sharing collective responsibility and the importance of the family—the *familiarismo*. *Familiarismo* includes more than the immediate family. Grandparents, aunts, uncles, cousins, and sometimes even more distant relatives are all considered important parts of the family. Additionally, *padrinos* and *madrinas* are people very close to the family, either because they are godparents to children or old family friends. Children are taught at an early age to view the family as the key unit of society. Venezuelan Americans may be geographically distant from this extended family and may depend more on community members, neighbors, or even institutions than the family support system traditionally in place in Venezuela, especially as they become more assimilated into mainstream culture. The heavy reliance on family ties and connections is a great strength for Venezuelan Americans, who count on family members for support, especially in times of crisis, and with whom they gather for holidays and celebrations. Wealthy family members are expected to help less economically stable family members. The tight-knit family structure, however, can also limit the ability of individuals to assimilate into the greater society and economy of the United States.

Family roles are generally clearly defined and hierarchically organized by age, gender, and sometimes education. The eldest in a family has the most authority, and parental authority is an important value. Grandmothers are especially revered for passing on moral and religious instruction. Honesty and dignity are also important values within families and the community.

The connection between family and community dynamics is often strong, and the pull of the family often leads to concentrations of Venezuelan Americans in urban areas in which cultural, business, and political networks may form that otherwise might not exist.

Gender Roles Gender roles in the Venezuelan American community are complex and varied, They align with other Latino and Hispanic cultures that designate a binary gender system of machismo for males and *marianismo* for females. Machismo puts men in the public sphere—the workplace, politics, and bars, for example—whereas *marianismo* keeps women in the private sphere of the home. Men are viewed as the economic providers in the family, and women are expected to raise the children, take care of the home, and be responsible for the moral education of the family. Women are expected to submit to the will of male family members but are simultaneously considered greatly important and powerful because the family is so central in the culture. A popular expression is *"madre no hay mas que una, padre puede ser cualquiera"*; that is, "mother is only one, father could be anyone." Family decisions, such as which school children will attend or which car to purchase, are usually made jointly. The degree of conformity to these roles varies from urban to rural settings and among different social classes.

As is becoming more common in Venezuela, many Venezuelan American women are active in the workforce, and many families have two working parents. Grandparents or extended family may care for young children, or children may attend daycare. Women are engaged in a variety of professions, including business, social work, and teaching. Possessing a high degree of literacy, many Venezuelan American women and their female children have found greater opportunities than their mothers and grandmothers did in Venezuela. Venezuelan American women sometimes experience workplace discrimination because of their immigrant status, language difficulties, or differing cultural values.

Education Many Venezuelan immigrants already have high educational status; some come to the United States specifically for a higher education. As a group, middle-class Venezuelan Americans share a proportionately higher education level than many other Hispanic American groups. In 2000, 42.8 percent of Venezuelan immigrants boasted a bachelor's degree or higher. Venezuelans have not encountered great difficulty in achieving success in institutions of higher education.

The teaching and preservation of Spanish is often regarded as a family priority, and many Venezuelan Americans try to ensure their children's fluency in Spanish. Mothers traditionally oversee the educational pursuits of their children.

Courtship and Weddings Courtship in Venezuela is similar to that in Western countries and remains so when Venezuelans immigrate to the United States. Opportunities for courtship are abundant within the

Venezuelan Americans converged at the Washington Monument to express concern over Hugo Chavez's presidency. JERRY ARCIERI / CORBIS

Venezuelan American community. Single people meet and mix at school parties, weddings, festival celebrations, and nightclubs. Groups of young men and women often meet in clubs to dance and listen to music. In most instances, young people are allowed to choose whom they wish to date. Although dating outside of one's race or social class is often frowned upon by parents and other family members, marriages to "locals" are not uncommon. Some Venezuelan Americans first come to the United States to study and then marry a "local" and stay in the United States. These couples and families, including ones that are of mixed races, experience the privileges of being more connected to the mainstream culture, the discrimination that comes from being a "mixed" couple (one partner native Venezuelan and one born in the United States), and sometimes less connection or shunning by their Venezuelan families.

In traditional Venezuelan culture, men are expected to ask permission (*pedir la mano*) of their expected father-in-law before proposing. Most weddings include two marriage ceremonies: a civil ceremony for legal recognition and an optional religious ceremony. The ceremonies may be separated by one day or many, according to the couple's preference. After the civil ceremony there may be a first reception with a small number of very close family and friends. A reception after the religious ceremony is generally large, sometimes with 150 guests, dancing, and food; it is paid for by the family of the bride. It's considered good luck for the newly wedded couple to sneak out without saying good-bye to guests.

Religious ceremonies are an important part of the Venezuelan culture. The majority of Venezuelan American marriages are performed by the Roman Catholic Church. Following the wedding mass, a celebration is held. The wedding couple receives gifts, traditional dishes are served, and entertainment is provided. In some cases, the wedding celebration lasts for several days.

EMPLOYMENT AND ECONOMIC CONDITIONS

Many Venezuelans who immigrate to the United States are professionals, entrepreneurs, upper-level bureaucrats, or manual laborers. Many migrate in an effort to protect their personal property and capital investments. Some from the upper class change their standard of living after arrival; although they may have owned a number of shops and had a chauffeur in Venezuela, their lives are more modest, though still middle class, in the United States.

Venezuelan Americans are prominent in a variety of professions, particularly banking and the petroleum industry, as oil production is so prominent an economic force in Venezuela. In places such as Weston, Florida, where large communities of Venezuelans live, many have opened Venezuelan cafes and bakeries. Venezuelan Americans also work within the television, publishing, and radio industries, and some are not only becoming politically active, but are seeking jobs in politics.

According to the 2000 census, 41.7 percent of Venezuelan Americans worked in professional and managerial occupations, and 11.2 percent worked in service occupations.

POLITICS AND GOVERNMENT

Many Venezuelan Americans are politically active both in U.S. politics and in opposing the Chávez government. In this way, they have been likened to Cuban Americans. Organizations such as Independent Venezuelan-American Citizens in Florida encourage Venezuelan participation in local politics.

Venezuelan Americans maintain strong ties with Venezuela. Whether in business, family, or community life, Venezuelan Americans closely monitor events within Venezuela. Visits to the homeland are relatively frequent among first-generation immigrants, and visits by Venezuelans to relatives in the United States are also quite common.

Many Venezuelan Americans have established careers in local politics and government. A growing number of Venezuelan Americans are also pursuing government service on the federal level. The political allegiances of Venezuelan Americans extend across the entire spectrum of American politics.

NOTABLE INDIVIDUALS

Academia Leo Rafael Reif (1950–), an electrical engineer and academic administrator was named the president of the Massachusetts Institute of Technology (MIT) in 2012. He had previously served as MIT's provost, the head of MIT's Department of Electrical Engineering and Computer Science, and director of the MIT Microsystems Technology Laboratories. He was born in Venezuela to Eastern European Jewish parents who had immigrated there. He originally came to the United States for graduate school. Reif holds numerous patents. In 2012 he received the Tribeca Disruptive Innovation Award for his work in developing MITx, the university's initiative in developing free online college courses available to learners anywhere via an Internet connection.

Activism Thor Leonardo Halvorssen Mendoza, born in Caracas in 1976, is a Venezuelan American human rights advocate, film producer, and writer. He is a regular contributor to the *Huffington Post* and *Forbes* magazine. Mendoza founded the Oslo Freedom Forum, an annual gathering of human rights activists, and the Moving Picture Institute, a film production company and nonprofit organization. He is also the president of the Human Rights Foundation, devoted to protecting liberty in the Americas. In 2010 he bought the traditionally leftist Norwegian news magazine *Ny Tid*.

Architecture Monica Ponce de Leon (1965–), a Venezuelan-born architect and educator, was raised in Caracas and immigrated to Miami with her family after graduating from high school. She was a founding partner, along with Nader Tehrani, in the award-winning firm Office dA and also served as dean and Eliel Saarinen Collegiate Professor at the A. Alfred Taubman College of Architecture and Urban Planning at the University of Michigan. In 2002 she received an Academy Award in Architecture from the American Academy of Arts and Letters, and in 2008 she was named a United States Artist fellow. Her work with Office dA has received numerous awards, including the Cooper-Hewitt National Design Award (2007), thirteen Progressive Architecture Awards, and the Harleston Parker Medal (2002). In 2008 the firm's Macallen Building was named one of the top ten green projects by the American Institute of Architects Committee on the Environment. After Office dA disbanded in 2010, she established her own practice, MPdL Studio, with offices in New York, Boston, and Ann Arbor, Michigan.

Art Marisol Escobar (1930–) is a renowned Venezuelan American sculptor and painter. During the 1960s, Escobar gained international fame as a sculptor. Known for her strong political commitments and eccentric artistic style, she created works that sparked controversy, changing significantly in inspiration and style over the following decades. Escobar's works can be found both in private art collections and in art museums. In the 1990s, she continued to produce new work and became active in public education concerning the spread and treatment of AIDS. In 1997, she was given the Premio Gabriela Mistral award from the Organization of American States for her contribution to Inter-American culture.

Fashion Carolina Herrera (1939–) is an internationally known fashion designer and entrepreneur. She was born in Venezuela and became a naturalized American citizen in 2009. Her father was the governor

Venezuelan American Marisol Escobar is an award-winning sculptor. MIXPIX / ALAMY

of Caracas. Herrera was inducted into to the Fashion Hall of Fame in 1981, and she received the MODA Award for Top Hispanic Designer in 1987. In 2002 King Juan Carlos I of Spain presented her with Spain's Gold Medal for Merit in the Fine Arts. She has also won the International Center in New York's Award of Excellence (2002), Womenswear Designer of the Year award (2004), and the Geoffrey Beene Lifetime Achievement Award (2008).

Film, Television, and Theater Fred Armisen (1966–) is an American comedian, musician, and actor best known as a cast member of the television program *Saturday Night Live* and for his comic portrayal of foreign characters in films such as *Euro Trip* (2004), *Anchorman* (2004), and *Cop Out* (2010). He cocreated and costarred with Carrie Brownstein in the TV sketch comedy series *Portlandia* (2011–). His mother is Venezuelan, and his father is of German and Japanese descent.

Arthur Albert was born Arturo Albert in 1946 in Caracas. He is an American cinematographer and television director. His work as a cinematographer has included the films *Happy Gilmore* (1996) and *Saving Silverman* (2001). He has also directed episodes of *ER*, *The Wonder Years*, and *The Gates*.

Horacio Bocaranda (born in 1965) was a Venezuelan American television and film director and has also worked in radio. He is sometimes known as Steve Bocaranda or Steve Horacio Bocaranda. He won Orquidea's Gold *Director Destacado* (Director Prize), and his colleagues considered him one of the best Venezuelan film directors. His films include *The Celibacy* (2010) and *Immigrants* (2004). He has directed or acted in more than 1,300 commercials and has produced shows such as the Latin Billboard Music Awards.

Jesse Corti was born in Venezuela in 1955 and was raised in Paterson, New Jersey. He was the voice of the character Lefou in the 1991 Disney animated film *Beauty and the Beast* and played Courfeyrac in the original Broadway show *Les Misérables*. He has also appeared on television shows such as *24, Heroes, Desperate Housewives, The West Wing, Judging Amy*, and *Law & Order*. He received a Clio award for his Drug Free America commercial in 1990.

Wilmer Eduardo Valderrama is an actor of Venezuelan and Columbian descent. He was born in 1980 in Miami, moved to Venezuela when he was three years old, and then moved to Los Angeles when he was thirteen. He is known for the role of Fez in the sitcom *That '70s Show*, hosting the MTV series *Yo Momma*, and voicing the character of Manny in the children's show *Handy Manny*. In 2012 he played Detective Efrem Vega in the TV series *Awake*.

Government Peter Miguel Camejo (1939–2008) was an activist and politician. In the 1976 presidential election, he ran for president for the Socialist Workers Party. Ronald Reagan called him one of the "ten most dangerous men in California." In the 2004 U.S. presidential election, he was Ralph Nader's vice presidential running mate. He also served as the Green Party gubernatorial candidate three times in California; in 2006 he received 2.3 percent of the vote. Camejo also ran in the California recall election of 2003, finishing fourth in a field of 135 candidates (with 2.8 percent of the vote).

P. Michael McKinley, an American diplomat, was born in Venezuela and grew up in Brazil, Mexico, Spain, and the United States. In 2010 the U.S. Senate confirmed McKinley as U.S. ambassador to Bogotá, Colombia. He served as the U.S. ambassador to Peru from 2007 to 2010. He also published a book on the colonial history of Venezuela.

Alberto (Al) G. Santos, born in 1965, was the Democratic mayor of Kearny, New Jersey, in 2012. Santos formerly served as councilman for one year. Santos was elected mayor in 2000, and was subsequently reelected in 2001, 2003, 2005, and 2009. Santos was born in Caracas to Portuguese immigrant parents, and in 1970 he moved with his family to New Jersey.

Federico Moreno, born in 1952, immigrated to the United States with his family in 1963. He attended the University of Notre Dame and received a bachelor's degree in government. After teaching at Atlantic Community College and Stockton State College, Moreno attended law school and earned his law degree from the University of Miami. In 1986 Moreno became a judge in Dade County, Florida, and later served for three years as a judge in Florida's Circuit Court. In 1990 President George H. W. Bush appointed Moreno to the U.S. District Court for the Southern District of Florida.

Ana María Distefano is a prominent government official. Born in 1951, Distefano attended the University of Pittsburgh, where she received a bachelor's degree in 1983. After holding several positions in the private sector, she came to work for the U.S. Department of Commerce in its Minority Business Development Agency and later in the public information office in its Bureau of the Census. Distefano received awards and honors from the National Association of Hispanic Journalists, Hispanic Association of Media Arts and Science, National Association of Black Journalists, and Public Relations Society of America, among others.

Journalism Elizabeth Pérez is a Cuban-Venezuelan Emmy-winning television journalist and presenter working for CNN en Español, based in Atlanta, Georgia. She was born in Cuba and moved to Venezuela at an early age with her family. She immigrated to the United States in 2000. She worked as a CNN sports anchor and as an entertainment reporter for Telemundo.

Music Singer and lyricist Mariah Carey was born in New York City in 1970; her father was of Venezuelan descent. Her debut album, *Mariah Carey* (1990), soared to number one on the *Billboard* charts and remained there for more than five months. Seven million copies of the album were sold, and four singles from the album reached number one on the pop charts. In 2000 she left Columbia and signed a record-breaking $100 million recording contract with Virgin Records. In 2002 she signed a multimillion-dollar contract with Island Records. Her single "We Belong Together" (2005) was named "Song of the Decade" by *Billboard*. In 2009 she starred in the well-received film *Precious*. She has won five Grammy Awards, seventeen World Music Awards, eleven American Music Awards, and thirty-one Billboard Music Awards.

María Conchita Alonso (1957–), better known as María Conchita, is a Cuban American, raised in Venezuela, and a three-time Grammy Award–nominated singer/songwriter and actress. She moved from Cuba to Venezuela when she was five and later to the United States, where she became a citizen. In addition to her singing, she is well-known as an actress and has appeared in many films including *Moscow on the Hudson* (1984) with Robin Williams. She also appeared in Broadway plays, such as *Kiss of the Spider Woman* (1993), and played Lucía, the mother of Gabrielle Solis, on the hit show *Desperate Housewives.* She is an outspoken critic of both Castro and Chávez.

Musician and composer Ed Calle was born Eduardo J. Calle in Caracas and eventually moved to Miami. He was nominated for Latin Grammy Awards in 2005 for *Ed Calle Plays Santana* and in 2007 for *In the Zone.* He has also been an associate professor at Miami Dade College.

Performance Tina Ramirez, an American dancer and choreographer, was born in Venezuela in 1929. She moved to New York as a young child. Ramirez studied Spanish dance, classical ballet, and modern dance, and performed professionally in all, as well as on Broadway and on television specials. She was best known as the founder and artistic director of Ballet Hispanico, the leading Hispanic dance company in the United States. Ballet Hispanico was thought to give Hispanic culture to American dance in the manner that Alvin Ailey gave African American culture to American dance. Ballet Hispanico included a company, school, and educational programs and had performed for more than 3 million people on three continents, including at venues such as the Kennedy Center and Jacob's Pillow. In 2005 Ramirez won the National Medal of Arts, the nation's highest cultural honor. Among many other awards, she received the Honor Award from Dance/USA in 2009 and the Award of Merit from the Association of Performing Arts Presenters in 2007.

Iliana Veronica Lopez de Gamero is a Venezuelan American ballet dancer. Born in 1963, Lopez de Gamero danced with the San Francisco Ballet, Ballet Corps of the Cleveland Opera House, and as a soloist for the Berlin Opera House and Düsseldorf Opera House. She was a finalist at the IV International Ballet Competition in Moscow in 1981 and was principal dancer of the Miami City Ballet in 1987.

Science and Technology Manuel Blum was renowned for his contributions to theoretical computer science. He was born in Caracas in 1938 and moved to the United States in the 1950s to attend the Massachusetts Institute of Technology, where he later became a professor. Blum received the Turing Award in 1995 in recognition of his research on the complexity of computation. In 2001 he accepted a professorship at Carnegie Mellon University.

Scientist Francisco Dallmeier, born in Caracas in 1953, is recognized as a leading ornithologist and a prominent figure in the area of biodiversity research. He served as director of the La Salle University Museum of Natural History from 1973 to 1977, biologist and educational coordinator for INELMECA from 1977 to 1981, program manager for the Smithsonian Institute's Man and the Biosphere Biological Diversity Program from 1986 to 1988, was acting director of the program from 1988 to 1989, and then director

after 1989. In 2002 Dallmeier joined Secretary of State Colin Powell's delegation to Gabon to discuss the U.S. initiative on the conservation of Central Africa biodiversity and protected areas, and was appointed interim director of the Smithsonian Center for Latino Initiatives.

Sports Venezuelan Americans are great fans of baseball. Unlike other South American countries, baseball rather than soccer is the national sport. Baseball was first introduced to Venezuela as a result of the oil boom of the early twentieth century. The sport quickly spread from oil workers' camps to every city, town, and village across the country. Many Venezuelan Americans enjoy playing baseball and actively support major and minor league Venezuelan teams. Many current and former professional baseball players in the United States are Venezuelan Americans.

Luis Aparicio (1934–) was one of baseball's greatest shortstops. Aparicio held records for number of games played by a shortstop, double plays, and assists. He was Rookie of the Year in 1956 and played on All-Star teams from 1958 to 1964 and from 1970 to 1972. In 1984, Aparicio was inducted into the Baseball Hall of Fame.

Oswaldo José "Ozzie" Guillén Barrios (1964–) was a baseball player and manager. He managed the Chicago White Sox from 2004 to 2011 and the Miami Marlins in 2012. He played in Major League Baseball as a shortstop for the White Sox (1985–1997), Baltimore Orioles (1998), Atlanta Braves (1998–1999), and Tampa Bay Devil Rays (now known as the Tampa Bay Rays; 2000). He batted left-handed and threw right-handed. He was known for his speed, intensity, and defensive abilities, as well as his love for the game. In 2005, he became the first Latino manager in major league history to win a World Series.

Dave Concepción (1948–), another talented shortstop, played with the Cincinnati Reds from 1970 to 1988, was named captain of the Reds in 1973, played in three World Series, and was a member of All-Star teams in 1972 and from 1975 to 1982. His nineteen-season major league career ranks as the longest period of continual service time for the Cincinnati Reds. He was on nine League All-Star teams, won five Golden Glove awards, and was voted Most Valuable Player in 1982. In 2000, he was inducted into the Reds Hall of Fame.

Marcy Hinzmann (1982–) was an American figure skater of Venezuelan heritage. She competed in pairs skating. In 2005, she and partner Aaron Parchem won the bronze medal at the U.S. Figure Skating Championships and qualified for the Olympic team the following year, where they placed thirteenth. She ended her competitive career in 2006 and skates professionally on Royal Caribbean Cruise ships with her husband, Lee Harris.

MEDIA

PRINT

There were more than 800 Spanish-language newspapers in the United States in 2011, including a few specifically oriented toward the Venezuelan American population or with sections (print or digital) specifically oriented toward them. Small neighborhood newspapers specifically oriented toward Venezuelan Americans also exist, especially in South Florida. In 2010 and the beginning of 2011, many long-standing Hispanic newspapers saw slight decreases in print circulation. However, mirroring English-language general-circulation papers, they grew into other media forms and partnerships.

El Venezolano News

El Venezolano News communicates news about Venezuela to residents in the United States. The Venezolano News Editorial Group was established in Miami in 1992 with the weekly the *Venezuelan*. It expanded to other cities, including Orlando and Houston, as well as internationally to Venezuela, Panama, Colombia, and Costa Rica. It won a National Journalism Award in 2002. Its readers were mostly Venezuelans, followed by Colombians, Cubans, Argentines, and other nationalities, with ages ranging from twenty-five to sixty-five, generally men and women with university degrees and a "purchasing power" of $72,000 annually.

José Hernández, Grupo Editorial El Venezolano
8390 NW 53 Street
Suite 318
Doral, Florida 33166
Phone: (305) 717-3206
Fax: (305) 717-3250
Email: joseyelim@gmail.com
URL: www.elvenezolanonews.com/

Venezuela Al Dia

Venezuela Al Dia is a weekly print and online newspaper, with daily news from South Florida. It distributes 20,000 copies across Dade, Broward, and Palm Beach counties and produces editions in Orlando and Venezuela. Its mission is to provide timely and balanced information about Venezuela and its areas of influence: Latino América, the United States, and around the world.

Armando Chirinos, Editor
7791 NW 46 Street
Suite 101
Miami, Florida 33166
Phone: (305) 470-8250
Email: miami@venezuelaaldia.com
URL: http://venezuelaaldia.com/

Diario Las Americas

Diario Las Americas is a Florida-based Spanish newspaper "for Freedom, Culture, and hemispheric solidarity." It has a microsite specifically devoted to Venezuelan issues at www.diariolasamericas.com/micrositio/60/venezuela.

Alejandro J. Aguirre, Deputy Editor and Publisher
2900 NW 39 Street
Miami, Florida 33142

Phone: (305) 633-3341
Fax: (305) 635-7668
URL: www.diariolasamericas.com

RADIO

In 2009 there were 1,323 Spanish-language stations in the United States, including music, news, and other programming of interest to the Hispanic and Latino community and the Venezuelan American community. News talk remains a small part of that, with 96 stations using that format. The major radio companies were Univision Radio, Bustos Media, and Entravision. Spanish-language radio took a harder hit during the recession years of 2009 and 2010 than general market stations and had very small growth. It is also now possible to live stream numerous radio stations from Venezuela.

TELEVISION

In 2012 Radio Caracas Television, headquartered in Caracas, brought RCTV's Spanish-language programming, including ten popular soap operas—*telenovelas*—through the online video service Hulu. RCTV's shows, which also include documentaries and features, will be part of the Hulu Latino offering. RCTV also licensed more than 1,300 hours of programming to Netflix for its Latin American subscription service, which also launched in 2012.

ORGANIZATIONS AND ASSOCIATIONS

Independent Venezuelan American Citizens

Independent Venezuelan American Citizens is a nonprofit organization founded in Miami in 2004 to help legal residents within the Latin American community change their status to American citizens at no cost.

Ernesto Ackerman, President
Email: ceo@ivac.org
URL: www.ivac.org

The Venezuelan American Association of the United States, Inc. (VAAUS)

The Venezuelan American Association of the United States, Inc. (VAAUS), is a private, nonprofit business organization founded in 1936 to promote investment and commerce between the United States and Venezuela. VAAUS sponsors programs held in New York City.

641 Lexington Avenue
Suite 1430
New York, New York 10022
Phone: (212) 233-7776
Fax: (212) 233-7779
Email: info@andean-us.com
URL: www.venezuelanamerican.org

The Venezuelan American Chamber of Commerce of the United States

The Venezuelan American Chamber of Commerce of the United States is a self-financing nongovernmental organization established in 1991. Its objectives include promoting businesses, mentoring and supporting youth through the Young Entrepreneurs Chapter, and recognition as a principal binational trade association of commerce and industry between Venezuela and United States.

1600 Ponce de Leon Boulevard
10th Floor
#1033
Coral Gables, Florida 33134
Phone: (786) 350-1190
Fax: (786) 350-1191
URL: www.venezuelanchamber.org

MUSEUMS AND RESEARCH CENTERS

The Venezuelan American Endowment for the Arts (VAEA)

The mission of The Venezuelan American Endowment for the Arts (VAEA) is to promote through the visual and performing arts a deeper and richer understanding by Venezuelan citizens of U.S. culture and by U.S. citizens of Venezuelan culture. VAEA aims to do this by supporting activities such as exhibitions, performance, and the distribution and dissemination of works and information regarding visual and performing arts in both countries and by providing funding and other support to individuals and organizations.

30 West 61st Street
Suite 17C
New York, New York 10023
Email: contact@vaearts.org
URL: http://vaearts.org/

The Smithsonian Latino Center

The Smithsonian Latino Center ensures that Latino contributions to the arts, sciences, and humanities are highlighted, understood, and advanced through the development and support of public programs, research, museum collections, and educational opportunities at the Smithsonian Institution. The Smithsonian Latino Center lists almost one hundred Latino museums and museums with Latino collections across the United States.

600 Maryland Avenue
Suite 7042 MRC 512
Washington, D.C. 20024
Phone: (202) 633-1240
URL: http://latino.si.edu/

SOURCES FOR ADDITIONAL STUDY

Gonzalez, Angel, and Minaya Ezequiel. "Venezuelan Diaspora Booms under Chávez." *The Wall Street Journal*, October 17, 2011.

Meier, Matt S., with Conchita Franco Serri and Richard A. Garcia. *Notable Latino Americans: A Biographical Dictionary*. Westport, CT: Greenwood Press, 1997.

Rudolph, Donna Keyse, and G. A. Rudolph. *Historical Dictionary of Venezuela*. Lanham, MD: Scarecrow Press, 1996.

Semple, Kirk. "Rise of Chávez Sends Venezuelans to Florida." *The New York Times*, January 23, 2008.

Waters, Marcy C.; Reed Ueda; and Helen B. Marrow. *The New Americans: A Guide to Immigration Since 1965*. Cambridge, MA: Harvard University Press, 2007.

VIETNAMESE AMERICANS
Carl L. Bankston III

OVERVIEW

Vietnamese Americans are immigrants or descendants of people from the Socialist Republic of Vietnam, a long, narrow, "S"-shaped country that extends about 1,000 miles from southern China southward to the Gulf of Thailand. It is bordered on the west by Laos and Cambodia and on the east by the South China Sea. At the center of the "S," Vietnam is less than 30 miles wide. The northern and southern parts of the country are somewhat wider, with the north reaching a maximum width of 350 miles. Vietnam's land area is 127,243 square miles (329,556 square kilometers). In total land area this is about 6,000 square miles larger than New Mexico, the fifth-largest state of the United States.

According to the *CIA World Factbook*, Vietnam had a population of 91,519,289 in July 2012. The government does not encourage religion, and the *World Factbook* reported that in 1999 (the most recent year for which religious statistics were available), 80.5 percent of the people reported for the Vietnamese census that they had no religion. In reality, however, most Vietnamese practice the mutually compatible religions of Buddhism, Confucianism, and Taoism. Another 9.3 percent identified themselves as Buddhist, 6.7 percent Catholic, 1.5 percent as Hoa Hao (a Vietnamese religion largely based on Buddhism), 1.1 percent as Cao Ðai (a religion that combines elements of Catholicism, Buddhism, Confucianism, and other faiths), 0.5 percent as Protestant (these are mainly mountain tribesmen, among whom missionaries were more lately active), and 0.1 percent (including all the Cham) as Muslim. The ethnic Vietnamese, who made up an estimated 85.7 percent of the population in the 1999 census, are thought to be descendants of peoples who migrated into the Red River Delta of northern Vietnam from southern China. Minority groups include the Tay, Thai, Muong, Khmer, Mong, Nung, and others. There are also about three million members of mountain tribes; about two million ethnic Chinese, most of whom live in large cities; about 500,000 Khmer, or ethnic Cambodians; and about 50,000 Cham, descendants of a Malayo-Polynesian people who dominated the area that is now southern Vietnam before the arrival of the Vietnamese in the fifteenth century. Although Vietnam has been developing rapidly in recent decades, it remains a relatively low-income country with an estimated per capita Gross Domestic Product of $3,500 in 2012. Agriculture employed 48 percent of the workforce in 2012, followed by industry (40.7 percent) and the service sector (29.6 percent). The country produces many agricultural goods for export, as well as manufactured goods such as clothes and electronics.

Large-scale immigration from Vietnam to the United States began in 1975, when the Vietnamese arrived as refugees at the end of the Vietnam War. The U.S. government initially took charge of their resettlement by establishing camps and helping to find sponsors in various locations around the country, although the largest population ended up in California. Many were professionals—medical and white collar—with ties to the U.S. military. Vietnamese Americans have rapidly transformed themselves from refugees to a large and well-established American minority. They have achieved rapid upward mobility, and young Vietnamese Americans have often been distinguished by their success in U.S. schools.

According to the 2010 U.S. Census, 1,632,717 people described themselves as of Vietnamese ancestry (slightly more than the total population of Philadelphia, the fifth most populous city in the United States). This made them the fourth-largest Asian group in the United States, after Chinese, Asian Indians, and Filipinos. Vietnamese Americans had settled all over the nation, often in identifiable ethnic communities; California was home to more than one-third (37.3 percent, according to the 2010 Census) of the Vietnamese American population. Another 13.1 percent lived in Texas, 4.4 percent in Washington State, 3.8 percent in Florida, and 3.5 percent in Virginia. Smaller populations lived in Pennsylvania, Massachusetts, Georgia, and other states. The largest Vietnamese American settlement is in Orange County, California, home to about one out of every ten Vietnamese in the United States.

HISTORY OF THE PEOPLE

Early History The first known historical records of the Viets in the Red River Delta of what is now northern Vietnam were written by the Chinese in the second century BCE Vietnamese archaeologists have traced their civilization back even further, to the Phung-Nguyen culture that existed before 2000 BCE.

Whereas the village constituted the basis of rural Vietnamese folk culture, many of the nation's formal institutions were introduced from the great neighbor to the north, China, including Chinese forms of government, Chinese written characters, and Chinese-style Buddhism. Even the name of the country is derived from Chinese: *viet* is a variant pronunciation of the Chinese word *yueh*, which designates the "hundred" tribes that populated the southern region of China; and *nam*, which is the same as *nan* in Chinese, means "south."

As the Chinese empire of the Han dynasty extended its control over the area to the south, the Viets accepted Chinese administrative designations for their territory, and the local rulers were redefined as prefectural and district officers. Despite some early rebellions against Chinese rule (one in particular was instigated by the Trung sisters, who remain Vietnamese national heroes for their struggles against the Chinese in the first century CE), Vietnam was a part of the Chinese empire until a war for independence in the tenth century succeeded. The influence of Chinese culture remained strong among the elites, as did their distrust of their powerful neighbor; not much changed for villagers.

Until the fifteenth century the Vietnamese occupied only the northern part of what we now know as Vietnam. The southern portion comprised Champa, the empire of the Cham people; and part of the Khmer, or Cambodian, territory. By 1471, however, under the rulers of the Vietnamese Le dynasty (1428–1788; modeled after the Chinese "emperors"), Vietnam succeeded in conquering almost the whole of Champa. This victory not only brought the newly enlarged country into conflict with the Khmers but also gave it its present elongated shape, wide at the top and bottom and exceedingly narrow in the middle, where the mountains that run down its center approach the coast. This geographical feature, often described as two heads and a little body, divides the country into two regions. During the eighteenth century, although nominally still under the rule of the Le dynasty, Vietnam was split between the powerful Trinh family in the north and the Nguyen family, who controlled the south.

Modern Era Whereas Vietnam's early history was dominated by its struggles with neighboring China, modern Vietnam has been greatly influenced by France. Vietnam's early contacts with Europe were primarily forged through Catholic missionaries, particularly Jesuits, who arrived in 1615. Alexandre des Rhodes, a French Jesuit, along with some of his Portuguese colleagues, was instrumental in creating a new system of writing, which was later adopted throughout Vietnam. This form of writing became known as *quoc ngu*—national language—and uses the Latin alphabet to transcribe the Vietnamese spoken language phonetically. The system was adopted throughout Vietnam at the beginning of the twentieth century.

Through the work of missionaries, the French gained influence in Vietnam long before the arrival of French soldiers and administrators. In 1788 a peasant rebellion known as the *Tay-son* reunified the country under the rule of a rebel leader who had himself proclaimed emperor. The surviving heir of the southern Nguyen family, Nguyen Anh, sought the assistance of France. Because of the revolution gathering force in France, the claimant to the Vietnamese throne received only token French ships and volunteer troops that nonetheless helped him reestablish himself at Saigon in 1789.

Nguyen Anh's son, the Emperor Minh-mang, facilitated a revival of the Confucian religion to stabilize the country and to support his own position as an emperor. The spread of Catholicism presented a danger to the Confucian order in the eyes of Minh-mang, who consequently initiated a policy of persecution against Catholics in 1825.

By the nineteenth century the French were struggling to catch up to other European countries in the competition for colonies. The French Emperor Napoleon III took up the cause of the Catholics in Vietnam and used their persecution as a pretext for invading the country. His envoys seized Saigon and the three surrounding provinces in 1862. In the 1880s, following a war between France and China (which still claimed sovereignty over Vietnam), the French extended their control over the rest of Vietnam. They held the southern part, known as Cochinchina, as a colony, and the central and northern parts—respectively named Tonkin and Annam—as protectorates.

As in other parts of Southeast Asia, the system of colonial domination created in the late nineteenth century was maintained until the rise of an Asian imperial power, Japan. A variety of Vietnamese nationalist movements had developed in response to French rule. The anti-imperialist stance expressed in Lenin's analysis of colonialism attracted some Vietnamese, including the young man who joined the French Socialist Party in 1920 and later became known by the adopted name of Ho Chi Minh. Following the surrender of France to Japan's ally, Germany, in June 1941, Ho Chi Minh's forces were left as the only effective resistance to Japan in Vietnam.

When Japan surrendered in August 1945, the Communist-dominated nationalist organization called the Viet Minh staged the August Revolution and easily seized power. The last of the French-controlled Vietnamese emperors, Bao-dai, abdicated, and Ho Chi Minh declared the country's independence, proclaiming the creation of the Democratic Republic of Vietnam on September 2, 1945. While the Viet Minh retained control of Hanoi and the north, however, the British helped reestablish French colonial power in the south. After the British left in January 1946 and the Chinese left in the spring of that same year, the country was again divided into north and south.

France was not interested in seeing a truly independent power in Vietnam, and the Viet Minh had no desire to see their country continue under colonial rule. In late 1946 and early 1947, tensions between the two sides erupted into combat, and the first Vietnam War began. In February 1947, following the Battle of Hanoi, France reoccupied Hanoi, and the Viet Minh assumed the position of guerrillas, fighting in the mountains.

It was a long time before either side was able to gain a decisive victory. In the late 1940s France, realizing that it could not win the war militarily, added a political dimension to the conflict, accusing the Viet Minh of fighting for Communism and not for independence. France created a State of Vietnam in the south in 1946. The United States and other non-Communist countries quickly recognized the new Vietnamese state, while China, the Soviet Union, and other Communist countries recognized the government of the Democratic Republic of Vietnam. In the early 1950s the growing army of the Democratic Republic of Vietnam, under the command of General Vo Nguyen Giap, began a series of offensives against the French. They achieved a famous victory at Dien Bien Phu in May 1954. The French defeat at Dien Bien Phu led to an international conference on Vietnam in Geneva, which resulted in a ceasefire and a temporary division of the country into North Vietnam, governed by the Democratic Republic from Hanoi, and South Vietnam, under Ngo Dinh Diem as prime minister in Saigon. The Democratic Republic of Vietnam (North Vietnam), the State of Vietnam (South Vietnam), Cambodia, Laos, France, the Soviet Union, the People's Republic of China, and the United Kingdom signed the agreement known as the Geneva Accords. The United States acknowledged the agreement, but declined to sign it. Some South Vietnamese who sympathized with Ho Chi Minh's government moved north. About one million northerners, between 600,000 and 800,000 of whom were Catholics, fled south on U.S. and French aircraft and naval vessels.

Ngo Dinh Diem proved to be an energetic leader, putting down armed religious sects and criminal groups. He also demanded that France remove all its troops from Vietnam. In 1955 Diem organized and won elections in the south. Supported by the United States, Diem refused to take part in the elections for national reunification that had been promised by the Geneva Conference. His action led to terrorism and other forms of resistance to his regime in many parts of South Vietnam.

The U.S. government had begun to show an interest in Vietnam during World War II, when it gave supplies and other forms of assistance to Ho Chi Minh's anti-Japanese forces. After the war, however, containment of international Communism became its primary foreign policy objective, and the Americans increasingly dedicated themselves to preserving Diem's anti-Communist South Vietnamese government in order to keep the North Vietnamese from taking over the whole country. A Catholic, Diem relied heavily on Catholic support, and, in doing so, he alienated the Buddhist majority. This created opportunities for North Vietnamese-supported insurgents in South Vietnam, who organized themselves into the National Liberation Front. Their members became known as the Viet Cong.

In 1961 President Kennedy sent military advisors to South Vietnam to assist the beleaguered Diem government. Diem became increasingly unpopular in his own country, however, and in 1963 he was overthrown by a military coup, apparently with the knowledge and consent of the American government. The new leaders of South Vietnam proved less able to maintain control than Diem, and by 1965, with the South Vietnamese government on the verge of collapse, President Johnson sent in U.S. ground troops to stave off a takeover by the Communist north, beginning an escalation of American involvement in the war in Vietnam.

Until the end of 1967, American military and political leaders believed they were winning the war by decisively defeating North Vietnamese forces and putting down antigovernment rebels in the south. At the beginning of 1968, the Viet Cong and North Vietnamese troops launched the Tet offensive, which, though it ended in a U.S. military victory, was a public relations and propaganda disaster, increasing the American people's opposition to the war. It convinced U.S. leaders that victory, if possible at all, would not be quick or easy. In 1973 negotiations between the United States and North Vietnam, known as the Paris peace talks, resulted in the United States agreeing on a timetable for withdrawing its troops and turning the war over to the South Vietnamese army. The South Vietnamese government was no better prepared to defend itself than it had been in 1965, and in April 1975 the South Vietnamese capital of Saigon fell to an invasion of North Vietnamese and National Liberation Front troops.

For twenty years after the fall of Saigon, the United States and Vietnam had no formal relations. In the summer of 1995, under the administration of President William J. ("Bill") Clinton, the United States finally announced the full normalization of relations between the two countries. During the late 1990s and early 2000s, Vietnam began to move away from strict socialist policies and to encourage the growth of a market economy, although the country remained under the control of its Communist Party. In 2001 the United States and Vietnam signed a bilateral trade agreement. Former Vietnamese refugees to the United States who took American citizenship were now able to visit their former homeland.

SETTLEMENT IN THE UNITED STATES

On April 18, 1975, less than two weeks before the fall of Saigon, President Gerald Ford authorized the entry of 130,000 refugees from the three countries of Indochina (Cambodia, Laos, and Vietnam) into the United States, 125,000 of whom were from the now defunct nation of South Vietnam. This first large group of Vietnamese in the United States, now known as "the first wave," arrived in the mid- to late-1970s. They typically had close ties with the American military and tended to be the elite of South Vietnam. According to data collected by the U.S. Department of State in 1975, more than 30 percent of the heads of households in the first part of the wave had been trained in the medical professions or in technical or managerial occupations, 16.9 percent were in transportation occupations, and 11.7 percent were in clerical and sales occupations. Only 4.9 percent were fishermen or farmers—occupations of the majority of people in Vietnam. More than 70 percent of the first-wave refugees from this overwhelmingly rural nation came from urban areas.

During the months of April and May 1975, six camps opened in the United States to receive refugees and prepare them for resettlement. After they were interviewed, given medical examinations, and assigned to living quarters, they were sent to one of nine voluntary agencies, or VOLAGs. These VOLAGs, the largest of which was the United States Catholic Conference, assumed the task of finding sponsors, individuals or groups who would assume financial and personal responsibility for refugee families for up to two years.

Despite the fact that many first-wave arrivals were from privileged backgrounds, few were well prepared to take up a new life in America. The majority did not speak English, and all found themselves in the midst of a strange culture. The American refugee agencies attempted to scatter them around the country, so that this new Asian population would not be too visible in any one place and so that no one city or state would be burdened with caring for a large number of new arrivals. Nevertheless, although at least 1 percent of the Southeast Asian population in 1976 resided in each of twenty-nine states, California had already become home to the largest number of refugees, with 21.6 percent of all the Southeast Asians in the United States.

The large wave in 1975 was followed by smaller waves, with only 3,200 Vietnamese arriving in 1976 and 1,900 in 1977. These numbers increased dramatically in 1978 as a result of an enlarged resettlement program developed in response to the lobbying of concerned American citizens and organizations. Political and economic conditions in Vietnam were driving large numbers of Vietnamese from their country, often in small unseaworthy boats. News of their hostile reception in neighboring countries and their sufferings at the hands of pirates created pressure in the United States to expand the refugee program. In 1978, 11,100 Vietnamese entered the United States. Then in January 1979 Vietnam invaded neighboring Cambodia, and the following month war broke out between Vietnam and China. Consequently, the

number of Vietnamese admitted to the United States that year rose to 44,500. Many of the second wave were Chinese citizens of Vietnam. As the war continued, the number of fleeing Indochinese rose steadily. Some were Cambodians or Laotians, but Vietnam, with its larger population, was the homeland of the majority of refugees. In 1980, 167,000 Southeast Asians, 95,200 of whom were Vietnamese, arrived in the United States. They were followed in 1981 by 132,000 more Southeast Asians, 86,100 of whom were Vietnamese.

Unlike the first refugees, the second wave came overwhelmingly from rural backgrounds and usually had limited education. Indeed, they appear to have been the least educated and the least skilled of any legal immigrants to the United States in recent history. Their hardships were increased by the time of their arrival: 1980 was a year of high inflation rates, and from 1981 to 1983 the United States saw the most severe economic recession of the previous fifty years.

While first-wave refugees came directly to the United States, those in the second wave tended to come through refugee camps in Southeast Asia. Agencies under contract to the U.S. Department of State organized classes to teach English and familiarize refugees with American culture. VOLAGs were still charged with finding sponsors prior to resettlement.

By the early 1980s secondary migration (a term that refers to immigrants who move a second time after arriving in the United States) had somewhat concentrated the Vietnamese American population in states with warmer weather. According 1984 data from the Southeast Asian Resource Action Center (SEARAC), more than 40 percent of Vietnamese Americans were living in California, mostly in the large urban centers. Texas, the state with the next-largest number, had 7.2 percent of the Vietnamese American population. Vietnamese Americans established a presence throughout the United States, but California and Texas continued to be home to the largest numbers into the 2000s. Orange County, California, had an especially notable concentration, as it was home to Little Saigon, the largest Vietnamese community in the nation. In 2011 estimates from the U.S. Census Bureau's American Community Survey placed the Vietnamese American populations of the cities of Westminster, site of Little Saigon, and adjacent Garden Grove at nearly 88,000 people.

The number of Vietnamese and other Indochinese coming to the United States never again reached the high points of 1980 and 1981. The influx did continue, however, with roughly 24,000 Vietnamese reaching America every year through 1986. Many of those leaving Vietnam for the United States in the 1980s emigrated legally through the Orderly Departure Program (ODP). Established by the governments of the United States and Vietnam—despite the fact that there were no formal diplomatic

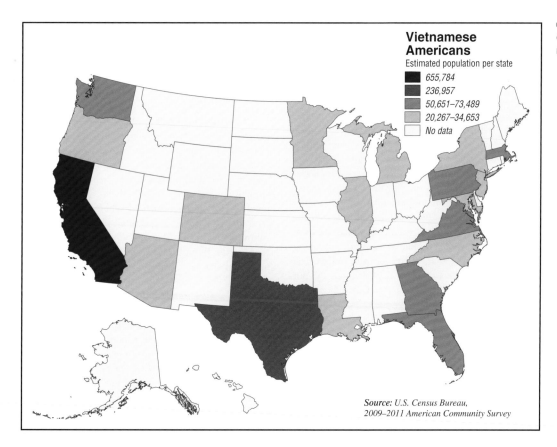

Vietnamese Americans

Estimated population per state

- 655,784
- 236,957
- 50,651–73,489
- 20,267–34,653
- No data

Source: U.S. Census Bureau, 2009–2011 American Community Survey

relations between the two countries—the program allowed those interviewed and approved by U.S. officials in Vietnam to leave the country. The United States was particularly interested in two groups: former South Vietnamese soldiers, who were in prisons and reeducation camps; and Amerasians, the roughly 8,000 children of American fathers and Vietnamese mothers who had been left behind at the end of the war. Although an estimated 50,000 Vietnamese were resettled in the United States through the ODP between late 1979 and 1987, refugees also continued to pour out of Vietnam by boat and land across war-torn Cambodia to Thailand.

After Vietnam and the United States established diplomatic relations in 1995, the numbers of refugees arriving on U.S. soil dropped sharply; that year there were 32,250; in 1996, 16,107 arrived; and in 1997, only 6,612 immigrated. In 2010 the United States admitted 873 Vietnamese refugees, according to data from the U.S. Department of Homeland Security. Because family reunification is a major basis for legal admission to the United States, however, Vietnamese began arriving in fairly large numbers as immigrants rather than as refugees. From 2002 through 2011 a yearly average of more than 30,000 people born in Vietnam entered the United States as legal permanent residents, according to the 2011 *Yearbook of Immigration Statistics* of the Department of Homeland Security.

Vietnamese Americans worked in a wide range of occupations by the 2000s, but Vietnamese beauty and nail salons were so common that they became almost a stereotypical business for Vietnamese Americans. The American Community Survey in 2010 estimated that hairdressers and cosmetologists made up more than 11 percent of all Vietnamese Americans in the labor force, a larger number than any other occupational concentration. The most common industries, along with beauty shops, included miscellaneous personal services, eating and drinking establishments, and electrical machinery, which together employed more than one-fifth of all Vietnamese workers in the United States.

While California is home to the highest numbers of Vietnamese Americans, other states with large populations include Texas, Florida, Washington, and Virginia. Americans of Vietnamese descent also reside in Georgia, Massachusetts, and Pennsylvania.

LANGUAGE

Vietnamese words are generally monosyllabic. Two or more one-syllable words may be joined together, however, usually connected by a hyphen, to form a compound word. Vietnamese is a tonal language; the meanings of words are determined by the pitch or tone at which the words are spoken. Several of these tones are also found in English, but English does not use the tones in the same way. In Vietnamese the sound *ma* pronounced with a falling tone and the sound *ma* pronounced with a low rising tone are actually two different words. The first means "but," and the second means "tomb." There are six of these tones in Vietnamese. In modern written Vietnamese, which uses the romanized system of writing introduced by European missionaries, the tones are indicated by diacritical marks, or marks written above and below the vowel in each syllable. A word without any mark is spoken with a midlevel tone. When the word has an acute accent over the vowel, it is spoken with a voice that starts high and then rises sharply. When the word has a grave accent over the vowel, it is pronounced with a voice that starts at a low level and then falls even lower. A tilde over the vowel indicates a high broken tone, in which the voice starts slightly above the middle of the normal speaking voice range, drops, and then rises abruptly. A diacritical mark that looks like a question mark without the dot at the bottom is placed over a vowel to indicate the low rising tone that sounds like the questioning tone in English. A dot written under a vowel means that the word should be pronounced with a voice that starts low, drops a little bit lower, and is then cut off abruptly. Most non-Vietnamese who study the language agree that the tones are the most difficult part of learning to speak it properly.

One of the most interesting features of Vietnamese is its use of status-related pronouns, a feature that it shares with many other Asian languages. While English has only one singular first-person pronoun, one singular second-person pronoun, and two singular third-person pronouns, Vietnamese has words that perform the function of pronouns but that depends on the relationship between the speaker and the person addressed. When a student addresses a teacher, for example, the word used for "you" is the respectful *thay*, which means "teacher." Many of the words used as pronouns express family relations, even when the Vietnamese are speaking with nonfamily members. Close friends are addressed as *anh* ("older brother") or *chi* ("older sister"). To address someone more politely, especially someone older than oneself, one uses the words *ong* (literally, "grandfather") or *ba* (literally, "grandmother"). In this way the fundamental Vietnamese values of respect for age, education, and social prestige and the central place of the extended family in Vietnamese life are embodied in the language itself.

The dialect of northern Vietnam, known as *tieng bac*, is slightly different from that of southern Vietnam, known as *tieng nam*. One of the most notable differences is that the Vietnamese letter *d* is pronounced like the consonant *y* in the southern dialect and somewhat like the *z* in the northern dialect. Although the southern dialect is more common among Vietnamese Americans, many who are from families that moved south in 1954 speak the northern dialect.

Although many Vietnamese Americans speak English well and use it outside the home, the vast majority retain their birth language. In 2010, according to census data, 82 percent of Vietnamese Americans reported that they spoke Vietnamese at home. Many young American-born Vietnamese Americans speak the ancestral language mainly with their parents and feel more comfortable speaking English in public or with their friends.

Greetings and Popular Expressions Some common Vietnamese greetings and expressions are: *chao ong* (jow ohm)—"hello" (to an older man or to show respect); *chao anh* (jow ahn)—"hello" (to a male friend); *chao ba* (jow ba)—"hello" (to an older woman); *chao co* (jow go)—hello (to a younger woman); *Di dao?* (dee dow)—"Where are you going?" (commonly used as a greeting); *Manh gioi khong?* (ohm mahn yoi kohm)—"Are you well?" (used in the sense of the English "How are you?"); *cam on* (gahm ung)—"thank you"; *khong co gi* (kohm gaw yi)—"you are welcome" (literally, the expression means "that is nothing!"); *Chuc mung nam moi* (chook meung nam meuey)—"Happy New Year." Because Vietnamese uses tones and also contains some sounds not found in English, the suggested pronunciations are only approximate.

RELIGION

Although Buddhism is the religion of the overwhelming majority of people in Vietnam, roughly 30 percent of Vietnamese Americans are Catholics, according to 2012 data from the Pew Forum on Religion and Public Life. The rituals and practices of Vietnamese Catholics are the same as those of Catholics everywhere, but some observers have claimed that the Vietnamese Catholic outlook is heavily influenced by Confucianism. Vietnamese Catholics belong to four types of parishes in the United States. The first is the usual Catholic parish, consisting of all Catholics in the territory assigned to a church. The second, the multicultural parish, includes special Vietnamese services and programs as part of a parish serving more than one ethnic group. The third, known in Catholic administration as a personal parish, is a specifically Vietnamese parish, in which a church is designated to serve Vietnamese members in order to provide rites and services in Vietnamese. Finally, a large residential concentration of Vietnamese may lead to the creation of a regular territorial parish, most or all of whose members are Vietnamese.

Vietnamese Catholics are widely recognized as among the most devout Catholics in the United States. Vocations to the priesthood and to other religious orders from Vietnamese Americans are among the most numerous of any American ethnic group. As a result it has become common for Vietnamese priests to serve parishioners of all ethnic backgrounds in churches across the nation.

Vietnamese Buddhists are almost always Mahayana Buddhists, the general school of Buddhism also found in China, Japan, Korea, and Tibet. One of the major types of Vietnamese Mahayana Buddhism is known as Pure Land Buddhism (in Vietnamese, *Tinh Độ Tông*, pronounced "tin doh tohng"), in which adherents recite prayers and chants to reach a state of enlightenment or to be reborn in the Pure Land. Vietnamese Buddhism is also heavily influenced by the tradition known in Vietnamese as *Tien*, which is more commonly known in the West by its Japanese name, *Zen*. This discipline emphasizes the achievement of enlightenment through meditation. Thich Nhat Hanh, a Vietnamese Zen master who was nominated for the Nobel Peace Prize by Martin Luther King Jr., is widely known in the United States, even outside the Vietnamese American community, for his stories, poems, and sermons. Vietnamese Buddhist temples have been established in many locations in the United States.

Vietnamese religions also include minority faiths. Two of the most notable are *Hoa Hao* ("hoh-uh how") and *Cao Đai*("gow dye"). The first is based on Buddhism but is recognized as a distinct religion. The second is a syncretistic religion, one that brings together elements of different belief systems. It includes influences from Buddhism, Confucianism, and Catholicism and recognizes individuals from both Asian and European history and traditions as saints. Both of these religions have followers among Vietnamese Americans.

CULTURE AND ASSIMILATION

Courtesy and respect are key traditional Vietnamese values to which most Vietnamese Americans still adhere. Children are expected to show respect for parents and younger people are expected to show respect for their elders. In Vietnamese the polite way to address someone is with the first name preceded by a title (a translated example might be Mr. Sam), although Vietnamese Americans have generally adopted the wider American custom of using last names for the sake of formality. Vietnamese Americans generally retain the traditional Vietnamese values of modesty and humility and consider boasting and showing off rude.

Maintaining Vietnamese traditions is a major concern in most Vietnamese American communities, and adult Vietnamese Americans often worry that their children may be losing distinctive cultural characteristics. Other Vietnamese Americans have made a conscious effort to assimilate completely into American society (for instance, by changing the last name Nguyen to Newman or Winn), but most retain their sense of ethnicity. Many Vietnamese Americans have adopted Western first names, however. Those who live in areas largely populated by Vietnamese typically remain more culturally distinctive than those who reside in suburban areas, surrounded by Americans of other ethnic backgrounds.

Cuisine Rice is the basis of most Vietnamese meals. In fact, the word *com* (gum), which means

VIETNAMESE AMERICAN MEMOIRS

Vietnamese Americans, struggling to adjust to life in a new country and a new language, are only beginning to establish a literature of their own. Most Vietnamese communities have their own newspapers, which frequently offer poems and stories in Vietnamese. The memoir has become an important literary form for Vietnamese American authors attempting to reach a wider English-speaking audience. Two important memoirs by Vietnamese American authors are *The Vietnamese Gulag* (1986) by Doan Van Toai and *When Heaven and Earth Changed Places* (1989) by Le Ly Hayslip. The latter work has also been made into a film by Oliver Stone (*Heaven & Earth*, 1993), and Hayslip has published a second memoir, *Child of War, Woman of Peace* (1993). Jade Ngoc Quang Huynh's *South Wind Changing: A Memoir* (1994), which tells of the author's youth and university education in Saigon, imprisonment in a reeducation camp, flight to America, and efforts to become a writer, met with great critical acclaim.

"cooked rice," is also used to denote "food" in general. In Vietnamese, "Have you eaten yet?" is expressed as "Have you eaten rice yet?" Rice is combined with a variety of side dishes, which are usually quite spicy. Popular dishes include *ca kho* ("ga khaw"; braised fish), *ca chien* ("ga cheeyen"; fried fish), *thit ga kho sa* ("tit ga khaw sa"; chicken braised with lemongrass), *thit bo xao* ("tit baw sow"; stir-fried beef), and *suon xao chua ngot* ("sow chewa ngawt"; sweet and sour spare ribs). Egg rolls, known as *cha gio* ("cha yaw"), are served with many Vietnamese meals and at almost all Vietnamese festive occasions. A rice noodle soup, *pho* ("fuh"), is one of the most popular breakfast and lunch foods. Vietnamese restaurants have become common in the United States, and their delicious foods are one of the most widely appreciated contributions of Vietnamese Americans to American life. Restaurants specializing in pho, in particular, have become common throughout the United States and cater to both non-Vietnamese and Vietnamese customers.

Traditional Dress Vietnamese men, even in Vietnam, long ago adopted Western dress. Many Vietnamese American women, however, still wear the traditional *ao dai* ("ow yai") on most special occasions. The ao dai consists of a long, mandarin-collared shirt that extends to the calves, slit at both sides to the waist. This is worn over loose black or white pants. Ao dais may come in many colors, and their flowing simplicity makes them among the most graceful forms of dress.

The conical Vietnamese hat known as the *non la* (literally, "leaf hat") may be seen often in areas where large numbers of Vietnamese Americans reside. Designed for protection from the hot sun of Southeast Asia, the non la is light and provides comfortable shade when the wearer is working outdoors.

Traditional Arts and Crafts Vietnam is known for its elaborate lacquerware items, including the bowls, chopsticks, and boxes featured in Vietnamese shops in California's Westminster-Garden Grove area, Houston's Vietnamese district, and many other locations. Traditional lacquer paintings frequently decorate Vietnamese American restaurants. Vietnamese silk painting, calligraphy, and woodblock prints are available in many locations in the United States, especially during the Tet celebration.

Dances and Songs Dancing is popular in Vietnam and among Vietnamese Americans. Most of the dances are the same as those in the West. The most notable traditional dance is the Dragon Dance, or Lion Dance, commonly performed during the lunar New Year festival and the Mid-Autumn festival in most Vietnamese American communities.

Historically, Vietnamese music included both court music and folk music, involving numerous stringed and percussion instruments and a wide range of styles. Both were heavily influenced by Chinese music. For the most part, though, contemporary people in Vietnam and Vietnamese Americans listen to pop or rock music sung in Vietnamese.

Many Vietnamese Americans have adopted American family patterns, but most of these still attempt to retain close ties with their extended families, so that even when adult children marry and leave the household, parents often encourage them to live nearby.

Holidays The most important Vietnamese holiday is Tet, which marks both the beginning of the lunar New Year and the beginning of spring. Tet usually falls in late January or early February. Traditional families may hold a ceremony the afternoon before Tet during which deceased ancestors are invited to come back and spend the festival days with the living. As in Western New Year's celebrations, fireworks may set off at midnight, heralding the coming year. Several young men dressed up as a dragon, the symbol of power and nobility, perform the dragon dance on the streets or other open spaces. The dragon dance also has become an important part of the cultural exhibitions in schools and other places. On the morning of Tet families awaken early and dress in their best clothes. People offer each other New Year's wishes and give the children lucky red envelopes containing money. Tet is considered a time for visiting and entertaining guests, and non-Vietnamese are heartily welcomed to most of the celebrations and ceremonies.

Many Vietnamese Americans, especially Buddhists, also celebrate the traditional holiday of *Trung Nguyen*, or Wandering Souls Day, which falls in the middle of the seventh lunar month (usually around August). On this holiday tables filled with food are offered to the wandering souls of ancestors. In some cases money and clothes made of special paper may be burned at this time.

Trung Thu, or the Mid-Autumn Festival, held on the fifteenth day of the eighth lunar month (usually around September) is one of the loveliest of Vietnamese holidays. Bakers in Vietnamese communities begin to prepare weeks before the festival by making moon cakes of sticky rice. People fashion lanterns of cellophane paper in many different shapes and place candles inside them. On the night of the festival, children form a procession and travel through the streets with their bright lanterns, dancing to the beat of drums and cymbals.

Health Care Issues and Practices Many older Vietnamese continue to suffer from the strains of war and exile. Younger Vietnamese, who sometimes find themselves straddling two cultures, express confusion over discrepancies between the expectations of their parents and those of the larger society. Nevertheless, Vietnamese Americans as a whole do not exhibit mental health problems that prevent them from functioning well in American society.

Vietnamese Americans generally have a high opinion of the American medical establishment. The profession of medical doctor is the most highly esteemed by Vietnamese Americans, and it is a source of great pride to Vietnamese American parents to have a child who is a doctor or a nurse.

Tuberculosis was a serious problem among Vietnamese refugees, but sufferers were kept in refugee camps overseas until it was determined that the disease was cured. As a result the incidence of tuberculosis among Vietnamese Americans now appears to be very low.

Many older Vietnamese Americans still follow traditional health practices. One of the most common of these is known as "coining": rubbing a coin, sometimes heated with oil, on the skin to draw out illnesses. For headaches or sore throats, a customary healing method involves skin pinching: pinching the head or throat with the fingers and thumb in order to move blood and remove the pain. In the practice known as cupping, small heated glasses are placed on the skin in order to create a vacuum, which is thought to pull the source of the illness out of the body.

Death and Burial Rituals Many Vietnamese Americans continue to follow traditional Vietnamese funeral customs, which can be divided into three parts. The first task involves washing and dressing the body of the departed. Funeral clothes are white, because white, not black, is the color associated with death among the Vietnamese. In Vietnam family members wash the body, but in the United States a funeral home generally performs the washing. The family of the departed also dresses in white as a sign of mourning. The body is placed in a coffin, and the mourning relatives pay their respects. Vietnamese Buddhists typically place a bowl of rice and an egg on top of the coffin. Christians usually place a card with the baptismal name of the departed on the coffin.

The second part of the funeral rite is a visitation, which, in the United States, usually takes place at a funeral home. Extended family members, neighbors, and friends pay their respects. They usually bring flowers, sometimes attaching envelopes with money to help the family with funeral expenses.

In the last stage of the funeral, the surviving head of the family or a family representative gives a short speech to thank visitors and invite them to the cemetery. The mourners usually follow the hearse to the burial.

Recreational Activities International football, known in the United States as soccer, is one of the most popular sports in Vietnam and among Vietnamese Americans. Vietnamese Americans also brought with them the Southeast Asian game of *sepak takraw*, or *cau may* in Vietnamese, which is similar to hacky sack. It is played with a rattan ball that players must keep in the air using their feet, knees, chest, and head without touching it with their hands. Many Vietnamese Americans enjoy badminton and volleyball. Chess and dominoes are among the most popular table games in Vietnamese American communities.

FAMILY AND COMMUNITY LIFE

The extended family is the heart of Vietnamese culture, and preservation of family life in their new home is one of the most important concerns of Vietnamese Americans. While American families are generally nuclear, consisting of parents and their children, the Vietnamese tend to think of the family as including maternal and paternal grandparents, uncles, aunts, and cousins. Many Vietnamese Americans have adopted American family patterns, but most of these still attempt to retain close ties with their extended families, so that even when adult children marry and leave the household, parents often encourage them to live nearby.

Older and newly arrived Vietnamese Americans often display indirectness and extreme politeness in dealing with others. Out of respect, they tend to avoid looking other people in the eyes, and they frequently try not to express open disagreement with others. U.S.-born Vietnamese youth often have the mannerisms and cultural traits of other American adolescents, which sometimes leads to intergenerational conflict and to complaints by older people that the younger people are "disrespectful."

Gender Roles Vietnamese culture is patriarchal, but relations between male and female Vietnamese Americans have become much more egalitarian, although most still regard men as the heads of families. Vietnamese families strongly encourage higher education for both young men and women. Still, almost all community leaders are men, and young Vietnamese

VIETNAMESE PROVERBS

Che de lam ko de.
> Criticism is easy, but making art is hard.

Noi de, lam kho.
> Talking is easy, doing is hard.

Xem ban biet nguoi.
> People are known by their friends.

Kong co lua sao co khoi.
> There is no smoke without fire.

Tre cao te dau.
> The higher you climb, the more it hurts to fall.

An qua nho ke trong cay.
> When you eat the fruit, remember those who took care of the tree.

American women often voice frustration at the expectation that they should be primarily wives and mothers, even if they work outside the home.

It is common for Vietnamese American women to work outside the home. According to the American Community Survey's estimates for 2010, 73 percent of Vietnamese American women between the ages of twenty-five and sixty-five were in the labor force, compared to 86 percent of Vietnamese American men in that age group.

Education Education is highly valued in Vietnamese culture, and the knowledge and level of study children attain is viewed as a reflection on the entire family. In a study of achievement among Southeast Asian refugees (*The Boat People and Achievement in America: A Study of Family Life and Cultural Values*, 1989), Nathan Caplan, John K. Whitmore, and Marcella H. Choy found that in both grades and scores on standardized tests, Vietnamese American children ranked higher than other American children, although they did show deficiencies in language and reading. Even Catholic Vietnamese Americans usually attend public schools.

The great respect accorded to learning leads a large proportion of young Vietnamese Americans, both male and female, to pursue higher education. In 2010 almost two-thirds of those between the ages of eighteen and twenty-four were in college, according to data from the American Community Survey, compared with 41 percent of white Americans and 38 percent of black Americans in the same age group. High school dropout rates among young Vietnamese Americans were the same as those of whites and lower than those of members of many other minority groups. Among white Americans and Vietnamese Americans aged sixteen to nineteen, 5.1 percent were neither enrolled in high school nor high school graduates, compared to 8 percent of black American and 15.1 percent of Hispanic youth.

Courtship and Weddings Dating is almost unknown in Vietnam, and couples who do date are almost always accompanied by chaperones. Some Vietnamese American parents still feel uncomfortable with the idea of their daughters going out alone with young men. Still, American-style dating has become fairly common among young Vietnamese Americans. Most marry within their ethnic group. Among those who marry non-Vietnamese, women are much more prevalent than men. In 2010, according the American Community Survey, an estimated 89 percent of married Vietnamese American men and 82 percent of married Vietnamese American women had Vietnamese spouses. Those who were married to members of other racial and ethnic groups most often had spouses classified as "white," including 5 percent of Vietnamese American men and 12 percent of Vietnamese American women.

Because Vietnamese Americans adhere to different religions and have been significantly influenced by mainstream American wedding practices, the nature of weddings among community members varies greatly. The traditional Vietnamese custom, still followed by some Vietnamese Americans, requires the bride and groom to remain apart from each other the day before the wedding in order to avoid bad luck. On the evening before the wedding, the bride's mother will comb the bride's hair with several symbolic combs. The wedding ceremony may be held at the bride's house or, among Catholics, at a church. Red is considered the traditional color of weddings, and some brides wear a red *ao dai*, but many others wear a Western-style white wedding gown. After the ceremony the bride and groom and their families typically hold a large banquet, during which they thank guests who have given them gifts, money, and blessings.

Relations with Other Americans Vietnamese Americans generally maintain good relations with members of other American groups. The women often intermarry with other groups; in 2011 one out of every eight married Vietnamese American women had a white spouse. Occasionally, however, tensions have arisen between Vietnamese Americans and others as a result of cultural misunderstandings, prejudice, or economic competition. In the early period of their settlement, Vietnamese American shrimpers and fishers along the Gulf Coast were involved in well-publicized conflicts with others in the industry, in part because the Vietnamese did not always follow unwritten rules about who could fish in which areas. Several violent episodes resulted, including, at the beginning of the 1980s, demonstrations and the burning of Vietnamese-owned boats by members of the Ku Klux

Klan on the Texas Gulf Coast. There have also been some tensions over the years between Vietnamese shop owners and their customers in predominantly African American neighborhoods. Vietnamese youth gangs in California and other areas have clashed with other ethnically and racially based youth gangs.

Philanthropy Many individual Vietnamese Americans who have achieved financial success in the United States have become active philanthropists. The Vietnamese American nuclear physicist Doan L. Phung, born in Hanoi, has supported projects for Vietnamese Americans and for people in Vietnam. In 2008 Phung announced that he was donating three million dollars as a challenge grant for the Vietnamese American NGO (nongovernmental organization) network, which consists of Vietnamese American organizations engaged in humanitarian and development work in Vietnam. Duy-Loan T. Le, an engineer and executive with Texas Instruments, works with her company's Vietnamese Initiative, aimed at promoting minority career advancement and has served on the boards of directors of other nonprofit organizations.

In addition to these individual philanthropists, many Vietnamese American organizations are devoted to promoting the welfare of their own and others' groups. The Vietnamese American Chamber of Commerce, in particular, is heavily involved in philanthropic activities.

Surnames Vietnamese people usually have three names: a family name, a middle name, and a given name. In contrast to the Western custom, the family name traditionally comes first, although Vietnamese Americans frequently put their family names last when interacting with non-Vietnamese. The Vietnamese custom is to address people by their given name, not their family name, even in formal circumstances. Thus, someone named Vuong Quang Anh (where Vuong is the surname) would be addressed as Ong Anh (Mr. Anh). Vietnamese Americans who use Western given names follow the Western tradition, however, addressing Joseph Vuong as Mr. Vuong. The Vietnamese surname Nguyen (pronounced, roughly, "ngwi-in") is by far the most common. Other common surnames include Le, Pham, Tran, Huynh, Hoang, Phan, Phu, Pho, Dang, and Bui. Children take the surname of their father, but women typically do not change their family name when they marry.

EMPLOYMENT AND ECONOMIC CONDITIONS

Vietnamese Americans may be found in almost all occupations, but hairdressing and cosmetology are particularly common employments, accounting for more than one out of every ten Vietnamese Americans in the labor force in 2010, according to census information. Work as a manicurist (which the census placed within the hairdresser and cosmetologist category) was an ethnic specialty among Vietnamese Americans. Other common occupations listed in the 2010 census, in order of frequency, were electrical equipment assembly, unclassified management and supervisory roles, computer systems analysis, computer science, cooking, computer software development, accounting and auditing, cashiering, retail sales, and restaurant work. In the southern states along the Gulf Coast, Vietnamese fishermen and shrimpers play an important role in the fishing industry.

Small business ownership is common among Vietnamese Americans. According to the 2007 Survey of Business Owners conducted by the U.S. Census Bureau, Vietnamese Americans owned 229,149 firms, with total receipts of 28.8 billion dollars. Two-thirds of Vietnamese-owned businesses in the United States were in repair, maintenance, personal services, laundry services, and retail sales sectors.

Vietnamese Americans in general have adapted well to the American economy. In 2010 the median income for Vietnamese American households was $67,000, compared to around $50,000 for the general American population. An estimated 15 percent of Vietnamese Americans lived below the poverty level, however, according to the American Community Survey's estimates for 2010. This was higher than the poverty rate for white non-Hispanics (10 percent) and Asians in general (12 percent) but lower than the poverty rates of both black Americans (27 percent) and Hispanics (27 percent).

POLITICS AND GOVERNMENT

During the 1980s and 1990s, Vietnamese Americans tended to be primarily interested in the political situation in Vietnam and were not yet heavily involved in American politics. By the twenty-first century, however, political involvement among Vietnamese Americans became much more prevalent. Many Vietnamese American neighborhoods established associations to promote civic participation, engaging in activities such as citizenship drives and voter registration drives. By 2010 only almost 83 percent of all Vietnamese Americans were U.S. citizens. An estimated 44 percent were naturalized citizens and 39 percent were citizens by birth. Vietnamese Americans belong to both major American political parties, but they are more likely to be Republicans than Democrats.

NOTABLE INDIVIDUALS

Academia Huynh Sanh Thong (1926–2008) was a scholar and translator of Vietnamese literature. Thong was the first editor of *The Vietnam Forum* and *Lac Viet*, two literature and literary anthology series on Vietnamese history, folklore, economics, and politics. Both of these collections are part of the Southeast Asian Refugee Project of the Yale Council on Southeast Asia Studies.

Nguyen Xuan Vinh (1930–) is professor emeritus of aerospace engineering at the University of Michigan. He has published widely in mathematics and astrodynamics. In 2006 he received the Dirk Brouwer Award for lifetime achievement from the American Astronautical Society.

Art and Entertainment Tila Tequila, the stage name of Tila Nguyen (1981–), is an actress and model. She was born to a Vietnamese refugee family in Singapore and grew up in Texas. Much of her early publicity came from posing for *Playboy* and other men's magazines. She has since had her own reality television show and has appeared in other entertainment ventures.

Film Dustin Nguyen, born Nguyen Xuan Tri (1963–) in Saigon, fled with his family to the United States in 1975. Nguyen graduated from high school in Missouri and attended Orange Coast College in California, where he became interested in acting. He moved to Hollywood to pursue this interest and became famous for the character he played on the television series *21 Jump Street* from 1986 to 1990. Since then he has appeared in a number of films, including *Little Fish* (2005), in which he starred opposite Cate Blanchett.

Government Joseph Cao (1967–), known in Vietnamese as Cao Quang Anh, has been the most prominent Vietnamese American elected official. Born in Saigon, he arrived in the United States in 1975. He spent six years in a Jesuit seminary, intending to become a Catholic priest, but shifted to a secular career. In 2000 he graduated from Loyola Law School in New Orleans, Louisiana. A Republican, Cao became the first Vietnamese American to serve in the U.S. Congress when Louisiana's second district elected him to the House of Representatives in 2009. A survey conducted in 2011 by the political magazine *National Journal* identified Cao as the most liberal Republican member of the House. His term ended that year after he lost a reelection bid to an African American Democrat in a majority African American and heavily Democratic district.

Tony Lam (1930–) immigrated to the United States from Vietnam in 1975. He opened a Vietnamese restaurant in Garden Grove, California, and became active in civic affairs. In 1992 Lam became the first Vietnamese American to serve as an elected official when he won a seat on the Westminster City Council. In 1999 he sparked controversy among Vietnamese Americans when he refused to join in protests against a local video game store that had displayed a poster of Vietnamese Communist leader Ho Chi Minh. After three terms in office, Lam decided not to stand for reelection in 2002.

Literature Andrew Lam (1964–) is a journalist and short story writer. The son of a South Vietnamese army officer, he fled Vietnam with his family in 1975,

the day before Saigon fell. He has published essays and news stories in a wide variety of publications. His most recent book of short stories is *Birds of Paradise Lost* (2013), about Vietnamese refugees and their lives in the San Francisco Bay Area.

Monique Truong (1968–) is a writer who fled Vietnam with her family in 1975, when she was six years old. Her best-known work is *The Book of Salt* (2003), a novel about a Vietnamese cook working for Gertrude Stein and Alice B. Toklas.

Sports Howard Bach (1979–) arrived in the United States at the age of two. He competed in badminton at the 2004 Summer Olympics. In 2005 he and his partner, Tony Gunawan, became the first Americans to win the gold medal at the World Badminton Championships.

MEDIA

RADIO AND TELEVISION

VNCR FM (106.3)

Vietnam California Radio is a Vietnamese-language radio station in Orange Country, California, in operation since 1993.

14861 Moran Street
Westminster, California 92683
Phone: (714) 891-8142
Fax: (714) 891-8190
Email: info@radiovncr.com
URL: www.radiovncr.com

KREH AM (900)

Radio Saigon Houston is a Vietnamese-language radio station that serves greater Houston.

URL: http://radiosaigonhouston.net

Saigon TV

The most popular Vietnamese-language television channel in the United States, with local affiliates in Los Angeles, San Francisco, and San Jose as well as nationwide satellite availability.

14775 Moran Street
Westminster, California 92683
Phone: (714) 230-8476
Fax: (714) 379-8083
URL: http://www.saigontv.us

PRINT

Nguoi Viet Daily News

The longest-running and largest-circulating U.S. daily newspaper in Vietnamese.

Dinh Quang Anh Thai, Editor
14771 Moran Street
Westminster, California 92683
Phone: (714) 892-9414
Fax: (714) 894-1381
URL: www.nguoi-viet.com

Thoi Luan

A Vietnamese community newspaper in Westminster, California.

9361 Bolsa Avenue
Westminster, California 92683
Phone: (714) 775-3547
URL: http://thoiluanonline.com

Vietnam Daily News

A daily community newspaper serving the greater San Francisco area.

Nguyen Can
2350 South Tenth Street
San Jose, California 95112
Phone: (408) 292-3422
Fax: (408) 292-5153
URL: www.vietnamdaily.com

ORGANIZATIONS AND ASSOCIATIONS

National Association for the Education and Advancement of Cambodian, Laotian, and Vietnamese Americans (NAFEA)

NAFEA seeks to support Indochinese Americans by providing them with equal educational opportunities; advancing their rights; acknowledging and publicizing their contributions in American schools, culture, and society; and encouraging appreciation of Indochinese cultures, peoples, education, and language. The organization facilitates the exchange of information and skills among Indochinese professionals and other professionals working with Indochinese Americans. It works to forward the legislative needs of Indochinese Americans in education, health, social services, and welfare.

Chahhany Sak-Humphry, President
University of Hawaii at Manoa
Spalding Hall 255
2540 Maile Way
Honolulu, Hawaii 96822
Phone: (808) 956-8070
Fax: (808) 956-5978
Email: sak@hawaii.edu
URL: www.nafeaonline.org

Viet Heritage Society

A nonprofit organization whose mission is to preserve and promote Vietnamese culture and history.

Nick Nghia Nguyen, Executive Director
696 East Santa Clara Street
Suite 200
San Jose, California 95112
Phone: (408) 821-9330
Fax: (408) 287-8505
URL: vietheritagesociety.org

Vietnamese American Chamber of Commerce

Seeks to advance commerce, education, philanthropy, and cultural exchange for Vietnamese Americans.

Tam Ngyen, President
16511 Brookhurst Street
Suite B
Fountain Valley, California 92708
Phone: (714) 775-6050
Fax: (888) 308-9730
Email: info@vacoc.com
URL: www.vacoc.com

Vietnamese American Young Leaders Association of New Orleans (VAYLA-NO)

A community-based organization dedicated to youth organizing and youth empowerment.

Minh Nguyen, Executive Director
4646 Michoud Boulevard
Suite 2
New Orleans, Louisiana 70129-1800
Phone: (504) 253-6000
Fax: (504) 754-7762
Email: contact@vayla-no.org
URL: www.vayla-no.org

MUSEUMS AND RESEARCH CENTERS

Southeast Asian Resource Action Center (SEARAC)

A national organization for advancing the interests of Cambodian, Laotian, and Vietnamese Americans. The organization's resource center is one of the best sources of information on these groups.

1626 16th Street NW
Washington, D.C. 20009
Phone: (202) 667-4690
Email: searac@searac.org
URL: http://www.searac.org/content/publications-and-materials

Viet Museum

A museum documenting the experience of Vietnamese Americans in leaving their ancestral country and resettling in the United States, located in the History Park in San Jose's Kelley Park.

1650 Senter Road
San Jose, California 95112
Phone: (408) 287-2290
Fax: (408) 287-2291
URL: www.vietmuseum.org

Vietnamese American Oral History Project

A project at the University of California, Irvine working to assemble, preserve, digitize, and disseminate the life stories of Vietnamese Americans in Southern California.

Thuy Vo Dang, Project Director
Department of Asian American Studies
3110 Humanities Gateway
Irvine, California 92697-6900
Phone: (714) 367-4475
Email: vaohp@uci.edu
URL: http://sites.uci.edu/vaohp

SOURCES FOR ADDITIONAL STUDY

Bankston, Carl L., III, and Danielle Antoinette Hidalgo. "The Waves of War: Immigrants, Refugees, and New Americans from Southeast Asia." In *Contemporary Asian America*, 2nd edition, edited by Min Zhou and James V. Gatewood. New York: New York University Press, 2007.

Caplan, Nathan; John K. Whitmore; and Marcella H. Choy. *The Boat People and Achievement in America: A Study of Family Life and Cultural Values.* Ann Arbor: University of Michigan Press, 1989.

Dao, Vy, and Carl L. Bankston III. "Vietnamese in the United States." In *Language Diversity in the United States*, edited by Kim Potowski. New York: Cambridge University Press Press, 2009.

Freeman, James M. *Hearts of Sorrow: Vietnamese-American Lives*. Stanford, CA: Stanford University Press, 1989.

Lieu, Nhi T. *The American Dream in Vietnamese*. Minneapolis: University of Minnesota Press, 2011.

Rutledge, Paul. *The Vietnamese Experience in America*. Bloomington: Indiana University Press, 1992.

Tenhula, John. *Voices from Southeast Asia: The Refugee Experience in the United States*. New York: Holmes & Meier, 1991.

Valverde, Kieu-Linh Caroline. *Transnationalizing Vietnam: Community, Culture, and Politics in the Diaspora*. Philadelphia: Temple University Press, 2012.

Zhou, Min, and Carl L. Bankston III. *Growing Up American: How Vietnamese Children Adapt to Life in the United States*. New York: Russell Sage Foundation,1998.

———. *Straddling Two Social Worlds: The Experience of Vietnamese Refugee Children in the United States*. New York: ERIC Clearinghouse in Urban Education, 2000.

VIRGIN ISLANDER AMERICANS

Lolly Ockerstrom

OVERVIEW

Virgin Islander Americans include immigrants from the British Virgin Islands and their descendants, and migrants from the U.S. Virgin Islands to other areas of the United States. Because U.S. citizenship was conferred on U.S. Virgin Islanders in 1927, people from the U.S. Virgin Islands who move to the United States are not considered immigrants. The Virgin Islands are located about 50 miles east of Puerto Rico, with the Atlantic Ocean lying to the north and east of the islands and the Caribbean Sea to the south and west. The islands are peaks of submerged mountains that rise from a submarine plateau. Their total land area is 193 square miles (500 square kilometers). The British Virgin Islands, which include four larger islands and more than thirty smaller islands, are collectively smaller than Washington, D.C., while the U.S. Virgin Islands, which comprise four larger islands and more than fifty smaller islands and cays, are approximately twice that size.

According to the *CIA World Factbook*, the population of the British Virgin Islands was 31,148 in July 2012, and the population of the U.S. Virgin Islands was 105,275. The majority of the population is black West Indian, with 82 percent of British Virgin Islanders and 76 percent of U.S. Virgin Islanders claiming this ethnicity. A substantial minority of U.S. Virgin Islanders are of European descent (more than 13 percent), while the largest minority group among British Virgin Islanders (11.2 percent) is of Indian or mixed ancestry. Virgin Islanders are largely Protestant (59 percent of U.S. Virgin Islanders and 84 percent of British Virgin Islanders). The U.S. Virgin Islands also has a substantial Roman Catholic population (34 percent), while the Catholic population in the British Virgin Islands is significantly smaller (10 percent). The economies of the British and U.S. Virgin Islands are among the most prosperous in the Caribbean. Tourism is the primary economic activity throughout the Virgin Islands, accounting for 45 percent of the national income in the British Virgin Islands and 80 percent in the U.S. Virgin Islands.

Immigration data for Virgin Islanders is severely limited. Historically, immigrants from the Virgin Islands have been grouped with other Caribbean immigrants and are significantly outnumbered by immigrants from Cuba, Puerto Rico, and other Caribbean nations. The Caribbean population in the United States remained small until after the American Civil War. By 1900 the foreign-born black population in the United States had increased fivefold since 1850. Most of the black immigrants who entered the United States between 1899 and 1924, the pinnacle of early black immigration, were from the Caribbean. Caribbean immigrants settled mostly in the Northeast, particularly in New York City. By 1930 almost a quarter of black Harlem was of Caribbean descent. Since the mid-twentieth century, when the tourism boom in the Virgin Islands began, immigration from the islands has been negligible. In 2009 about 3.5 million Caribbean immigrants resided in the United States, though less than 2.1 percent were from the Virgin Islands.

According to 2011 estimates by the U.S. Census Bureau's American Community Survey, 17,657 people claiming U.S. Virgin Islands ancestry resided in the mainland United States, with the largest numbers residing in the states of Florida (6,039) and New York (3,736). Information on people of British Virgin Islander ancestry residing in the United States is limited because they are grouped with immigrants from other Caribbean British territories—dubbed the British West Indies.

Most of the black immigrants who entered the United States between 1899 and 1924, the pinnacle of early black immigration, were from the Caribbean. Caribbean immigrants settled mostly in the Northeast, particularly in New York City. By 1930 almost a quarter of black Harlem was of Caribbean descent.

HISTORY OF THE PEOPLE

Early History Native peoples inhabited the Virgin Islands thousands of years before Christopher Columbus arrived on his second voyage to the New World in 1493. The Arawaks are thought to have arrived on the islands about 100–200 CE, while the Ciboneys came between 300 and 400 BCE. The Caribs arrived much later, about 100 to 150 years before Columbus. The Arawak and Carib Indians originated in Central America and traveled to the Virgin Islands through what is now Trinidad and the Lesser Antilles. It is not known where the Ciboneys originated. Various theories hold that they moved south from Florida, north from South America, or east from Central America. There was no firsthand study of these people, though twentieth-century archaeological studies have made it possible to reconstruct the social and cultural patterns of the first Virgin Islanders. Ancient petroglyphs, or rocks incised with figures hundreds of years ago, exist throughout the region and have provided the only written record of these earlier times.

The Arawaks, Caribs, and Ciboneys crafted articles from stone, shell, bone, and wood. They also worked with other natural materials from the local environment, including hemp, fiber, grass, cotton, and skins, to fashion such everyday items as bowls, mortars and pestles, flints, and celts. The Arawaks and Caribs produced pottery from yellow and red clay, although the Ciboneys do not appear to have worked in clay at all. Only the Caribs made mats from grasses. All three tribes were fish-eating cultures and hunters and gatherers who crafted dugout canoes from cedar and silk-cotton trees to use for transportation. The Arawaks were the most skilled in cultivating the soil to grow crops. Of the three groups, the Caribs were the most warlike. Their principal weapons were bows with poisoned arrows. The Arawaks preferred spears. Both the Carib and Arawak tribes also used javelins and clubs.

Around 1550 the native tribes were forced off the islands when Charles V of Spain declared them enemies. By the time the Dutch arrived in the mid-seventeenth century, very few natives remained. In 1648 the Dutch built the first permanent settlement on Tortola, the largest of the islands, although British planters took control of Tortola in 1666 and by 1672 had annexed the rest of the islands, including Anegada, Jost Van Dyke, and Virgin Gorda, making them part of the Leeward Islands colony. These colonizers established cotton and sugarcane plantations, and sugarcane eventually became the basis of the economy. By the end of the eighteenth century, sugar, molasses, and rum were the main exports.

While the Dutch and the British were vying for supremacy in the present-day British Virgin Islands, the Danish West India Company was working to establish a settlement on St. Thomas, today part of the U.S. Virgin Islands. By 1672 a small settlement was in place, though a few years later the Danes and the British were both claiming St. John. The British, not eager to alienate the Danes, yielded ground, and 1694 saw the successful establishment of a Danish settlement on the island. The Danes established trade and commerce, developing plantations for growing sugar, cotton, coffee, and

livestock, which demanded a continuous supply of cheap labor. This led to the use of indentured white servants and black slaves from Africa. In 1733 the Danes purchased St. Croix from the French, and the three islands became the Danish West Indies. A plantation economy flourished on St. John and St. Croix that comprised mainly sugar plantations. St. Thomas developed as a center of commerce, including the slave trade.

The plantation system that depended on slave labor lasted little more than a century in the British Virgin Islands. The last public auction of slaves was held in 1803, and five years later Great Britain abolished the slave trade. In 1834 the Proclamation of Emancipation declared the freedom of 5,133 slaves in the British Virgin Islands. By then more than 63 percent of the white population had left the islands. Many plantation holdings were given or sold to former slaves, and fishing and farming became mainstays of the economy.

The plantation system in the Danish islands survived slightly longer. Slavery was abolished the day after a rebellion on St. Croix on July 2, 1848. However, after emancipation occurred, labor riots became a problem. Planters abandoned their land, the economy suffered, and the population declined. By the end of the nineteenth century, natural disasters had intensified the bleak economic conditions.

Despite attempts by the Danish government to improve conditions on the Virgin Islands, agriculture and trade declined. At the outbreak of World War I, Denmark could no longer afford to maintain the islands, and it began discussions with the United States regarding the purchase of the islands as early as 1863. However, negotiations broke off when the U.S. Senate failed to ratify the purchase proposal. Talks resumed in 1914, and on March 31, 1917, the United States took possession of the islands in exchange for $25 million in gold.

Modern Era The United States wanted the islands chiefly to defend access to the Panama Canal and to prevent Germany from acquiring a strategic position in the Caribbean during World War I. U.S. naval officers governed the U.S. Virgin Islands from 1917 until 1931, when the United States appointed Paul D. Pearson the first civilian governor. Pearson set up ambitious programs to invigorate the islands' economy, and the Virgin Islands Company was established to encourage homestead farming, revive the sugarcane industry, and improve the port of St. Thomas. Although social services improved during the first years of U.S. ownership, the U.S. Virgin Islands remained impoverished as a result of continued failures in trade and agriculture since the nineteenth century. When Herbert Hoover became the first U.S. president to visit the islands in 1931, he characterized the U.S. Virgin Islands as the "effective poorhouse" of the United States.

During World War II the U.S. Virgin Islands took on strategic military importance as the United States routed convoys through the Caribbean. Military bases were constructed on the islands, warships were anchored in the Virgin Islands' harbors, and roads were built. Agricultural laborers left farming, first for jobs in construction and then for jobs in tourism. The Tourist Development Board was established in 1952, and sugar production was phased out in 1966. By 1954 more than 60,000 tourists had visited the U.S. Virgin Islands, spending an estimated $4 million. When Cuba was closed to Americans in 1959, the number of tourists arriving in the U.S. Virgin Islands rose to 200,000.

The British Virgin Islands remained part of the Leeward Islands colony until 1956, when they became a crown colony. In 1958 they chose not to join the West Indies Federation in order to preserve close economic ties with the U.S. Virgin Islands. A constitutional order in 1967 established a ministerial government, and H. Lavity Stoutt became the first chief minister. Since then constitutional changes have gradually increased the autonomy of the British Virgin Islands. The British Overseas Territory Act in 2002 made the islands a territory rather than a colony and granted British citizenship to the islanders. In 2007 a new constitution negotiated with the United Kingdom granted a greater degree of self-government to the islands.

In the late twentieth century, tourism became increasingly important in the Virgin Islands, transforming the islanders' way of life but not always in positive ways. The rapid rise in tourism during the 1960s placed strain on the existing infrastructure, which was unable to keep up with new demands. Traditional ways of life were severely disrupted. Inadequate planning for future needs resulted in damage to the environment, racial tensions, and rising crime rates. During the 1970s U.S. Virgin Islands governor Juan Luis and the U.S. Virgin Islands Chamber of Commerce identified crime as the islands' most severe problem. The crime rate began to fall in the late 1970s.

Between 1950 and 1970, the population of the U.S. Virgin Islands mushroomed from 26,665 to 63,200. In 1970 the number of visitors to the U.S. Virgin Islands rose to 1.5 million, and in 2005 there were 2.6 million visitors. In 1996 the U.S. Department of Interior transferred Water Island, located a quarter mile off the south shore of St. Thomas, to the U.S. Virgin Islands, and by the end of the twentieth century, the population of the territory had reached 102,000. The islands have become particularly popular for sailing and as a tax haven for the rich. Tax laws and subsidies favorable to industry have attracted new businesses. These include watch-assembly operations, textile manufacturing, and oil refining. Immigrants from other Caribbean islands have come to the Virgin Islands seeking employment, while others have come to retire.

SETTLEMENT IN THE UNITED STATES

Prior to the twentieth century, immigrants to the United States from the Virgin Islands were considered part of the larger group of Caribbean immigrants. During the eighteenth and nineteenth centuries, Caribbean immigrants formed a substantial part of free communities of African descent in the United States. For example, in 1860 one in five Bostonians of African descent had been born in the Caribbean. However, records fail to distinguish Virgin Islanders from other Caribbean groups except in the case of individuals such as Denmark Vesey, a free artisan in South Carolina who is credited with forming an insurrection plot in 1822, perhaps the most elaborate ever conceived by American slaves.

Early Caribbean immigrants defied stereotypes of blacks as uneducated slaves. Many were skilled craftsmen, teachers, journalists, lawyers, and doctors. Because immigration laws favored the highly skilled, 37.9 percent of immigrants of African descent who had occupations between 1899 and 1931 were skilled workers. Between 1927 and 1931 the number rose to 52.4 percent. The Caribbean population in the United States remained relatively small until after the Civil War. The number of black immigrants to the United States, most of them from the Caribbean, grew from 412 in 1899 to 12,243 in 1924, the high point of the early black migration. The number of foreign-born immigrants of African descent and their American-born children reached 55,000 in 1900 and 178,000 in 1930. These immigrants settled mostly in the Northeast. In fact, so many settled in New York City that by 1930 almost a quarter of black Harlem was of Caribbean origin. By the 1930s a third of New York's black professionals, including doctors, dentists, and lawyers, as well as a disproportionate number of businesspeople, came from the Caribbean.

In the 1940s migration trends reversed, and more Caribbean people returned home than entered the United States. Nevertheless, British and U.S. Virgin Islanders continue to feel strong ties with the United States, which remains the top destination for Virgin Islanders looking for opportunities outside their homeland. In 2011 the U.S. Census Bureau's American Community Survey reported that an estimated 17,657 people of U.S. Virgin Islands ancestry resided in the mainland United States. Florida and New York are the two states with the largest number of Virgin Islander Americans.

LANGUAGE

Most U.S. Virgin Islanders speak English, although the Census Bureau reported in 2010 that 28 percent of people living in the U.S. Virgin Islands spoke a language other than English in the home. Citizens of other Caribbean islands have immigrated to the U.S. Virgin Islands to work, bringing their languages with them. Immigrants from Puerto Rico and Santo Domingo speak Spanish, while immigrants from St. Lucia,

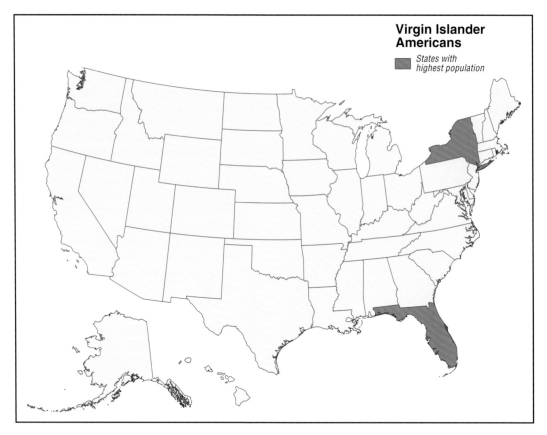

Virgin Islander Americans

States with highest population

Dominica, French Guyana, Haiti, and other places speak French Creole. In the British Virgin Islands there is a small Spanish-speaking community from the Dominican Republic.

Although English is the dominant language, Virgin Islanders attach unique cultural associations to many common English expressions. *Good morning*, *Good afternoon*, and *Good night* are considered warmer greetings than *hello* or *hi* and are commonly used among friends. Virgin Islanders are fond of the saying, "What a *kallaloo!*" The word *kallaloo* refers to a soup of seaweed and greens, but islanders use the word to refer to any kind of mess. Another frequently invoked word is *limin'*, which means lying back and enjoying the day.

RELIGION

The religious beliefs of Virgin Islanders reflect the history of the two territories and their cultural variety. Christianity is the dominant religion in the British Virgin Islands. Protestants account for about 86 percent of the population. Of that 86 percent, Methodists claim 33 percent, followed by Anglicans with 17 percent. Roman Catholics account for only 10 percent. The U.S. Virgin Islands, in contrast, have a substantially higher Catholic population, about 34 percent, a figure that has increased with the influx of immigrants from Puerto Rico and other predominantly Catholic countries. Most U.S. Virgin Islander Protestants are Baptists (42 percent),

with Episcopalians accounting for 17 percent. Small communities of Muslims, Hindus, and Jews can also be found on the islands. In addition, as is true throughout the Caribbean, some islanders practice the religious rituals of their African ancestors, including animism and ancestor worship. Belief in ghosts and *obeah*, or magic, is often found blended with mainstream religion.

CULTURE AND ASSIMILATION

Virgin Islanders claim allegiance to two distinct cultural identities, as they are simultaneously Virgin Islanders and citizens of either the United Kingdom or the United States. As such, Virgin Islanders have developed art forms, clothing, cuisine, and traditions unique to their region and its Caribbean and African history.

During the late 1960s issues of acculturation and assimilation for many black Virgin Islanders became a reversal of the usual immigrant experience. Large numbers of whites from the U.S. mainland migrated to the islands, threatening to overwhelm Virgin Islander culture. Marilyn Krigger, a professor at the College of the Virgin Islands on St. Thomas, maintained that black students at the school experienced a serious crisis of identity as a result of this migration. Chief among the students' observations was that faculty members were mostly white Americans from the mainland. As public school teachers, who were also from the mainland, were largely unaware of local history, customs, foods, and other aspects of island life, the distinctive history and culture of the Virgin Islands became endangered. Unlike ethnic groups that struggle to maintain a balance between their cultural past and their new homeland in the United States, U.S. Virgin Islanders had to struggle for cultural survival in their own land.

Separate black and white communities began to emerge as a result of economic disparities. There were great discrepancies between blacks' and whites' wages and status in business. Educational segregation developed as whites sent their children to expensive private schools out of the reach of most black Virgin Islander families. All-white residential areas appeared as well, and an atmosphere of distrust and hatred arose. For Virgin Islanders who came to the U.S. mainland, cultural identity remained a troublesome issue, and they struggled to balance their identity as U.S. citizens with memories of Virgin Islands life. Because most black Virgin Islanders are descendants of slaves, they tend to identify with black mainlanders.

Traditions and Customs Culturally Virgin Islanders belong to the larger group of Caribbean islanders. For centuries the Caribbean has been a crossroads for trade, commerce, and military maneuvers for people from all over the world. Many different cultures from Africa, Europe, Asia, and Australia have brought their own traditions to the Virgin Islands, enriching the already complex tapestry of Caribbean island traditions. Stories about jumbies, or spirits, who walk around in homes and on the streets, are a Caribbean tradition. Such stories are often used to warn children of the consequences of bad choices.

Cuisine Several different cultures have left an imprint on the Virgin Islands, producing a cuisine that represents a wide range of tastes and traditions. Seafood, chutneys, and curries are all typical of Virgin Islands fare. Baked plantains are common, as are chicken legs, *kallaloo* (a soup made with greens), johnnycakes (unleavened fried bread), and cassava bread. *Souse*, a stew served at all festivities, is made of a pig's head, tail, and feet and is flavored with lime juice. Fish is either fried or boiled and is eaten with *fungi*, a cornmeal dumpling. Conch is cooked in garlic sauce and served hot or cold in salads or as a main dish, as well as in chowder or as a fritter. The native tania root is cooked into a soup. Pâté turnovers, pastries filled with spiced beef or salt fish, are served at sidewalk stalls. Sugar cakes, made with fresh coconut, are very popular among natives and tourists alike.

More than 250 species of plants, exotic fruits, nuts, and vegetables are produced on the Virgin Islands, including coconuts, grapes, soursop, mammee apple, custard apple, sugar apple, cashew, and papaya. Cassava, arrowroot, and sweet potatoes are also native to the islands, as are several species of squash, beans, and cacao. When Columbus and the Spaniards arrived in 1493, explorers introduced new foods to the area, including sugarcane, which became one of the most important trade crops during the seventeenth and eighteenth centuries. Oregano and cumin arrived from Europe, while lemons, oranges, and bananas came from the Canary Islands. The British introduced fruit buns, ginger beer, and breadfruit, and the Dutch brought from Indonesia nutmeg, mace, cloves, and cinnamon. The French contributed methods of preserving fruits using rum, which became the drink of the Caribbean. Virgin Islands bay rum became one of the most important export products for islanders.

Other drinks of the Virgin Islands include *maubi*, made from the bark of the *maubi* tree using herbs and yeast. Cruzan rum, one of the U.S. Virgin Islands' biggest exports, has been distilled on the island of St. Croix since the seventeenth century. Other popular island drinks are the piña colada and soursop, made of soursop fruit plus milk, water, sugar, and spices.

As African slaves who worked the plantations received plots of their own on which to grow food, they began to incorporate food from the Virgin Islands into traditional African recipes. They cooked with plantains, yams, beans, and okra, as well as salt pork and salt fish. To add flavor, they used chili peppers such as the scotch bonnet. When slavery was abolished, indentured servants arrived to the islands from Asia, bringing with them curries from East India and stir-fried cuisine from China.

Music Caribbean calypso music, steel drums, and reggae are well known to music lovers throughout the world. The precursor of the calypso was known as the *kareso*, a term most likely derived from the Hausa word *kaiso* ("bravo"), which is used to signify approval for a singer. Quelbe, the official music of the Virgin Islands according to a 2001 law in the British Virgin Islands and a 2004 law in the U.S. Virgin Islands, is a fusion of African and European music. The scratch band sound of Quelbe began with slaves who, forbidden their native drum beating and dances by Danish law, used a number of homemade percussive instruments including bamboo flutes, steel triangles, and dried gourds to create their sound. As the music evolved, Virgin Islanders incorporated European sounds and added guitar, tambourine, and the "pipe" (an old tail pipe) to replace the bass drum and the ukulele. Quelbe songs comment on topics as varied as current events, cheating spouses, and rum smuggling. To preserve the tradition and heritage of Quelbe, schools throughout the islands have a youth steel band and chorus.

In the British Virgin Islands, scratch bands are known as *fungi*, named for a local cornmeal dish made with ingredients ranging from okra to onions to green peppers. As the dish fuses flavors to produce something new and tasty, the music combines African and European influences to create a new sound that is distinctive to the islands.

Dances and Songs The most famous folk dance of the Virgin Islands is the quadrille, a square dance of French origin changed to fit local musical rhythms

VIRGIN ISLANDER PROVERBS

Creole proverbs are often more colorful than their English equivalents.

Buddy, me a walkin' behin'.

> Meaning something similar to "Discretion is the better part of valor."

Yo' mout' is a one-room house.

> Speak up (or used ironically, You talk too much).

Bettah fo' sure dan for sorry.

> Haste makes waste.

Man got two wife; him sleep hungry.

> You can get too much of a good thing.

Yo' a run from de jumbie a' meet de coffin.

> Out of the frying pan, into the fire.

and tastes. The quadrille is performed by four couples in 6/8 or 2/4 meter. Dancers wear period costumes: women don dresses with layers of ruffles while men wear dark pants, white shirts, and cummerbunds. A scratch band provides the music, and dancers respond to the commands of a caller. Although the dance declined in popularity during the 1950s and 1960s, it regained favor during the 1970s, partly through the performances of the Milton Payne Quadrille Dance Company of Christiansted, St. Croix, which formed in 1969. One year later the Mungo Niles Cultural Dancers were founded with the goal of promoting the culture of the Virgin Islands. The group provided free weekly dance instruction throughout the Virgin Islands and went on tour to New York and Washington, D.C., during the 1980s. Other well-known dance groups include the St. Croix Heritage Dancers and the St. Croix Cultural Dancers.

Holidays The major holiday in the U.S. Virgin Islands is Carnival, which occurs during the last two weeks of April on St. Croix and in June on St. Thomas. In the Virgin Islands, the first week of Carnival is devoted to calypso song competitions and the second to community activities, including parades, marches, singing, and dancing. Streets are filled with stalls selling local foods, drinks, and produce. The festivities begin with the opening of the calypso tent, where song competitions take place. At the end of the first week, judges announce the new calypso king or queen, a much-sought-after honor. During the second week, attractions include the Children's Village, which offers a Ferris wheel, merry-go-round, and other rides, and J'ouvert, a 4:00 a.m. tramp through town ending

with fireworks at the harbor. A children's parade traditionally takes place on the Friday of the second week from 10:00 a.m. until 2:00 p.m, and an all-day adult parade is held the following day. Each parade is filled with dance troupes, floats, music, and exotic costumes that reflect the year's theme. The famed Mocko Jumbi dancers, wearing elaborate costumes with headdresses, perform traditional African dances on 17-foot stilts. They are thought to represent spirits hovering over the street dancers.

The British Virgin Islands celebrate Carnival in a similar fashion but at a different time. Carnival is held for two weeks in late July and early August to coincide with Emancipation Day, a celebration of the abolishment of slavery in the British Empire held on the first Monday in August. A cultural rather than religious holiday, Carnival boosts local pride and the local economy and is financed by a government grant. Although its popularity waned during the first half of the twentieth century, interest in Carnival was revived in 1952 by a radio personality known as Mango Jones, who later served as delegate to the U.S. Congress. American novelist Herman Wouk wrote of Carnival in his famed *Don't Stop the Carnival* (1965): "Africa was marching down the main street of this little harbor town today; Africa in undimmed black vitality, surging up out of centuries of island displacement, island slavery, island isolation, island ignorance; Africa, unquenchable in its burning love of life."

Other Virgin Islands holidays are related to hurricane season. The fourth Monday in July is Hurricane Supplication Day, which is marked by special church services where celebrants pray for safety from the storms that at times have ravaged the islands. The holiday is thought to have derived from fifth-century English rogation ceremonies held following a series of storms, although Rogation Day is also a Christian feast day preceding Ascension Day. The word *rogation*, from the Latin *rogare*, means to beg or supplicate. Islanders mark the end of hurricane season in October with Hurricane Thanksgiving Day, featuring church services in which participants express thanks for having been spared during the season.

Christmas and Easter are important holidays in the Virgin Islands, as Christianity is predominant among the islands' many religious traditions. Other holidays popular in the U.S. Virgin Islands include New Year's Day (January 1) and U.S. Independence Day (July 4). U.S. Virgin Islanders also celebrate many of the same nationally recognized holidays as other Americans, including Martin Luther King Jr. Day in January, Presidents' Day in February, Memorial Day in May, Labor Day in September, Columbus Day in October, and Veterans' Day in November. In addition residents celebrate Virgin Islands Thanksgiving in October and U.S. Thanksgiving in November.

Several holidays honor the history of the U.S. Virgin Islands. Islanders observe Emancipation Day on July 3 to mark the date the Virgin Islands slaves gained freedom from Danish colonists on St. John. The festivities, held at Coral Bay, St. John, include storytelling, games, and music, along with the sale of native foods and plants. Participants characterize the celebration as a cultural and spiritual gathering that emphasizes local culture and history rather than entertainment. March 31, Transfer Day, marks the day ownership of the U.S. Virgin Islands passed from Denmark to the United States, while June 16 is Organic Act Day, recognizing the islands' constitution. Liberty Day, which celebrates freedom of the press, is on November 1.

Holidays celebrated in the British Virgin Islands include the birthday of the islands' longest-serving minister Lavity Stoutt on March 5, Commonwealth Day on March 12, the British sovereign's birthday on the second Saturday in June, and Saint Ursula's Day on October 21. (Ursula is the patron saint of the British Virgin Islands.)

FAMILY AND COMMUNITY LIFE

Virgin Islander family structure tends to be traditional, with men serving as heads of the family and women managing child care. Although an increasing number of women engage in paid employment, they tend to work part time or in cottage industries so they can work at home and take care of small children. One in three households in the U.S. Virgin Islands is headed by a woman, and almost 20 percent of U.S. Virgin Islander children under eighteen are under the primary care of grandparents. Extended families and kin groups are of great importance in the British Virgin Islands, where several women may combine households or couples may rear the children of siblings, godchildren, or children from other relationships.

Gender Roles As in other parts of the world, gender roles in the Virgin Islands are changing as more women join the labor force. As Hilde Kahne and Janet Z. Giele report in *Women's Work and Women's Lives: The Continuing Struggle Worldwide* (1992), important socioeconomic transformations have taken place in Latin America and the Caribbean since the post–World War II period, resulting in the emergence of new roles for women. Women have benefited from lower fertility rates, smaller family sizes, increased educational opportunities, and greater participation in the labor force. However, despite some gains, women in the Virgin Islands have suffered from poverty and inequities in income, and Virgin Islanders have continued to view women's earnings from outside the home largely as supplemental. Many regard uncompensated work such as child care, cooking, and cleaning as women's work.

The rapid shift from rural to urban communities between 1940 and 1970 in the Virgin Islands and elsewhere in the Caribbean slowed somewhat in the 1970s. By then, however, major social and economic changes had occurred. Domestic service remains the most common occupation for Caribbean women, although street peddling—known as "higgling"—has become more prominent in the eastern Caribbean. Higglers travel among the islands to sell fresh produce or to market handcrafted items. Women with small children frequently become employed doing piecework at home, which allows them to remain with their children—though it also enables employers to exploit women. Nevertheless, whatever their employment, women in the Virgin Islands have increasingly contributed to the economies of their households.

Education The Virgin Islands rank among the world's most literate regions and have a 98 percent adult literacy rate—although this was not always the case. The 2010 U.S. Census reported that of U.S. Virgin Islanders over the age of twenty-five, 30.5 percent held a high school diploma and 11.8 percent held a bachelor's degree or higher. School attendance is compulsory between the ages of five and sixteen, and the government provides free public education for these students. The U.S. Department of Education also provides free lunches for all public school students. In conjunction with New York University, U.S. Virgin Island schools conduct a teacher training program. In the British Virgin Islands, education is compulsory for children aged five to seventeen, but about a third of students who enter primary school fail to complete their Caribbean Secondary Education Certificate.

The University of the Virgin Islands, founded in 1962 in St. Thomas as a junior college, became the University of the Virgin Islands in 1972. In 2012 it reported enrollment of 2,420. Of the students, 71 percent were women, prompting a discussion among islanders over why young Virgin Islands men were not seeking higher education. Jessica Dinisio reported in *Uvision* that many Virgin Islanders attributed the low enrollment among young men to cultural and societal pressures: young men were expected to enter the workforce and earn money. Others felt that the numbers represented a growing desire among young women to attain economic independence.

EMPLOYMENT AND ECONOMIC CONDITIONS

Although the U.S. Virgin Islands' economy is historically agricultural, the islands lack sufficient rain and high-quality soil to support large-scale agricultural production. Agriculture has not supported the economies of the Virgin Islands since the nineteenth century. On St. Croix and St. John, sorghum, fruit, and vegetables are produced, and leaves from the bay tree forest on St. John are used for making bay rum. Cattle raised on St. Croix are exported to Puerto Rico, but these operations occur on a small scale.

Tourism is the mainstay of the Virgin Island economies, with 30 percent of U.S. Virgin Islanders working in the tourist trade. The territory's largest single employer is Hess Oil Virgin Islands, the biggest

A painting by John Trumbull of American forefather Alexander Hamilton, who was from the Virgin Islands. NIDAY PICTURE LIBRARY / ALAMY

oil refinery in the world, located on St. Croix. Most manufacturing is performed on a small scale, and most products are exported to the continental United States, including petroleum products, alumina, chemicals, clocks and watch parts, meat, and ethanol. Fishing in island waters is for sporting rather than commercial endeavors. The average annual wages for Virgin Islanders in 2010 was $37,130. Virgin Islanders who come to the U.S. mainland frequently do so to further their education or seek employment in fields not found on the islands. However, those who come to the mainland often think of their move as temporary. Students in particular anticipate returning to the Virgin Islands once they have completed their education, even though many express concern that employment prospects in the islands are limited.

On the British Virgin Islands, small farms are involved in raising livestock and crops such as bananas, sugarcane, citrus fruits, coconuts, mangoes, and various root crops. However, most agricultural products are for local consumption. Fishing is a growing industry, but manufacturing is limited to rum, paint, and building materials such as sand and gravel. As in the U.S. Virgin Islands, financial services and tourism are the foundation of the British Virgin Islands economy, which is among the most prosperous in the world.

POLITICS AND GOVERNMENT

From 1917 to 1931 the U.S. Virgin Islands were under the authority of the U.S. Navy. In 1931 the U.S. Department of the Interior took administrative responsibility for the territory, and the president appointed a governor for the islands. A legislature of fifteen locally elected members from the three main islands has been in place since 1954. Members are elected for two-year terms. In 1970 Virgin Islanders won the right to vote for their governor, who is elected for a four-year term, and since 1972 islanders have elected one delegate to the U.S. Congress, who votes on House of Representatives committees and speaks in debate on the floor. However, the representative is not allowed to vote on bills, and U.S. Virgin Islanders cannot vote in U.S. presidential elections.

Several constitutional conventions have dealt with the voting and legislative rights of U.S. Virgin Islanders. The Organic Act of 1936, which established a constitutional government for the islands, granted universal suffrage. That same year, the first political party on the islands was organized. Since the purchase of the Virgin Islands by the United States, islanders have continued to agitate for more home rule. While expressing their opposition to any form of annexation as a state, the islanders have made it clear they are opposed to independence from the United States. Thus the Virgin Islands remain an unincorporated territory rather than an autonomous territory.

The political structure of the British Virgin Islands mirrors that of other overseas territories of the United Kingdom. The executive branch consists of the Queen, who is head of state, a governor general appointed by the Queen, a premier (known as the chief minister prior to a 2007 constitutional change), and a cabinet of ministers who advise the premier. One difference from the usual British system of governance is that the legislative branch is unicameral, consisting of the fifteen-member House of Assembly.

NOTABLE INDIVIDUALS

Art and Literature Virgin Islander artists generally identify with Caribbean arts, literature, and music. However, studies of Caribbean literature rarely focus on Virgin Islanders, instead offering critical readings of work by such writers as Derek Walcott of St. Lucia, V. S. Naipaul of Trinidad, and Jamaica Kincaid of Antigua. Anthologies of Caribbean writing often omit Virgin Islanders from their collections. Thus, although the Virgin Islands Humanities Council has published short, amateur collections of Virgin Island poetry, Virgin Islands writers have yet to drawn critical attention for their work.

Education Barbara Christian (1943–2000) was professor of African American studies at the University of California–Berkeley and author of *Black Women Novelists: The Development of a Tradition* (1980).

Government Virgin Islander Alexander Hamilton (1755–1804) was a political philosopher and the first U.S. secretary of the Treasury. Roy Emile Alfredo Innis (1934–), born on St. Croix, is a civil rights activist who has served as national chairman of the Congress of Racial Equality since 1968.

Music Composer Alton Augustus Adams Sr. (1889–1987), whose music was performed by John Philip Sousa, was the first African American bandmaster in the U.S. Navy. Theodore Walter "Sonny" Rollins (1930–) was an influential jazz musician whose skill on the tenor saxophone earned him the Miles Davis Award at the Montreal Jazz Festival in 2010 and Kennedy Center Honors on his eighty-first birthday in 2011.

Sports Tahesia Harrigan (1982–) is a professional sprinter who competed in the 2008 Summer Olympics in Beijing. Before turning professional, she was an all-American at the University of Alabama and the University of Minnesota. Joseph O'Neal Christopher (1935–) is credited as the first baseball player from the Virgin Islands to appear in a major league game. He first played with the Pittsburgh Pirates in 1959, later moving to the New York Mets (1962–1965) and Boston Red Sox (1966). Tim Duncan (1976–) plays for the San Antonio Spurs basketball team. A fourteen-time NBA all-star, he is the only player in NBA history to be selected to both all-NBA and all-defensive teams during each of his first thirteen seasons.

Stage and Screen Kelsey Grammer (1955–), a five-time Emmy winner born on St. Thomas, is best known for his role as psychiatrist Dr. Frasier Crane on the NBC sitcoms *Cheers*, *Wings*, and *Frasier*. Actress and hip-hop model Karrine Steffans (1978–) is an American author, most notably of the *Vixen* series of books, and has appeared in more than twenty music videos. Born on St. Thomas, she moved to the mainland United States at age ten.

MEDIA

ORGANIZATIONS AND ASSOCIATIONS

Virgin Islands Association, Inc.

VIA was organized to serve as a resource network for all Virgin Islanders abroad, to promote fellowship among members, and to foster a connection with the Virgin Islands. The group has coordinated hurricane relief efforts for the Virgin Islands and has raised money to purchase hospital equipment for the islands.

Clarence Beverhoudt, President
P.O. Box 75903
Washington, D.C. 20013
Email: dcmetrovia@gmail.com
URL: www.viadc.org

Virgin Islander American and runner Tahesia Harrigan competes in a race in Puerto Rico in 2010. LUIS ACOSTA / AFP / GETTY IMAGES

SOURCES FOR ADDITIONAL STUDY

Boyer, William W. *America's Virgin Islands: A History of Human Rights and Wrongs*. Durham, NC: Carolina Academic Press, 1983.

Dookhan, Isaac. *A History of the Virgin Islands of the U.S.* 2nd ed. Kingston, Jamaica: Canoe Press, 1994.

Eggleston, George T. *Virgin Islands*. Huntington, NY: Krieger, 1973.

James, Winston. "New Light on Afro-Caribbean Social Mobility in New York: A Critique of the Sowell Thesis." *New Critical Though: A Reader*. Ed. Folke Lindahl and Brian Meeks. Kingston, Jamaica: University of the West Indies Press, 2001.

Lewis, Gordon K. *The Virgin Islands: A Caribbean Lilliput*. Evanston, IL: Northwestern University Press, 1972.

Maurer, Bill. *Recharting the Caribbean: Land, Law, and Citizenship in the British Virgin Islands*. Ann Arbor: University of Michigan Press, 1997.

O'Neal, Eugenia. *From the Field to the Legislature: A History of Women in the Virgin Islands*. Westport, CT: Greenwood, 2001.

Pfeffer, Randall S. *Virgin Islands*. Oakland, CA: Lonely Planet, 2001.

Tyson, George F., and Arnold R. Highfield, eds. *The Kamina Folk: Slavery and Slave Life in the Danish West Indies*. St. Thomas: Virgin Islands Humanities Council, 1994.

WELSH AMERICANS

Evan Heimlich

OVERVIEW

Welsh Americans are immigrants or descendants of immigrants from Wales, a country on the west coast of Great Britain that is part of the United Kingdom. The Irish Channel and Atlantic Ocean surround Wales to the north, west, and south, while its eastern border is shared with England. Much of the terrain is mountainous. In the northwest is the rugged Snowdonia range, named for Mount Snowdon, which, at 3,560 feet (1,085 meters), is the highest point in Britain south of Scotland. Wales has a total area of 8,023 square miles (20,779 kilometers), making it slightly smaller than the state of New Jersey.

The 2011 United Kingdom census placed the population of Wales at just over 3 million. About 57 percent of Welsh are Christian, with the Church of Wales, a member of the Anglican Communion, the largest denomination, followed by Roman Catholicism. About a third of Welsh declare no religion. The country also has a small but significant population of Muslims in its capital city of Cardiff. From the dawn of the Industrial Revolution, Wales was a source of many of the United Kingdom's mineral and metallurgical needs, particularly coal from the coalfields of South Wales; today, these industries have declined as the economy has become more dependent on tourism, services, and public sector spending.

Significant Welsh immigration to America began in the eighteenth century, with particularly large numbers gravitating toward the mid-Atlantic states, Appalachia, and the South. Many early Welsh Americans were farmers who lived in rural religious communities, though later immigrants found work in coal mines, factories, and other urban industrial operations. Welsh Americans assimilated into American society with relative ease; only a few scattered areas of the country retain distinctly Welsh populations and culture. Some in the Welsh American community say that the group and its contributions to American culture are too hidden; this has contributed to a resurgence in Welsh American pride in recent decades and an increase in Americans identifying with their Welsh heritage.

According to the U.S. Census Bureau, in 2011 there were an estimated 1.8 million Americans (around 0.5 percent of the population) claiming Welsh ancestry. It is likely that more Americans have Welsh roots but no longer identify with them; a much larger percentage of Americans, about 4 percent, have a Welsh surname, according to a 2006 study by the government of Wales. California, Pennsylvania, Ohio, and Texas are the states with the largest numbers of Welsh Americans. Other significant communities of people of Welsh descent can be found in Florida, New York, and Washington. There is a significant population of Welsh American Mormons in the West as well, especially in Utah and Idaho.

HISTORY OF THE PEOPLE

Early History Wales, known in Welsh as Cymru, was named for its inhabitants. The Welsh trace their ancestry to two distinct groups of people—the Iberians who arrived from southwestern Europe in Neolithic times and the Celtic tribes who arrived in the late Bronze Age. Fierce fighters, they resisted the Anglo-Saxon invaders, who could not understand their language and called them *wealas* (strangers). They called themselves *Cymry* (fellow countrymen). Although populations and cultures overlap between Wales and England, Wales and its culture remained remarkably distinct.

The Roman Empire took Wales along with Britain in the first century CE. However, Wales remained a frontier area, little influenced by Roman culture. With the collapse of Roman power in the 400s, Germanic tribes from northern Europe began settling in southeastern Britain. Most numerous were the Angles and the Saxons, related peoples who became the English. The Celts resisted this long influx of alien settlers but were gradually pushed west. By about 800 CE they occupied only Britain's remotest reaches, where their descendants—the Highland Scots, the Cornish of the southwest coast, and the Welsh—live today. The Irish are also Celtic.

Over the following centuries, the Welsh, isolated from other Celts, developed a distinctive culture. However, their identity was shaped by the presence of their powerful English neighbors. Wales became a western refuge from the invasion and conquest by hostile tribes from Europe. This refuge was made inaccessible by its mountainous terrain and also lay farther west than most conquerors could effectively extend.

In the fifth century CE, early Welsh Christianity blossomed with the monasteries of St. David. In the late eighth century, Anglo-Saxon rulers of England—who were not yet Christians—built an earthen barrier named Offa's Dike (named after Offa, the Anglo-Saxon king of Mercia) to keep Welsh people from raiding eastward. This boundary still marks the separation between Wales and England.

In 1066 William the Conqueror (c. 1028–c. 1087) defeated the English and, with his French-born Norman nobles and knights, took power in England and determined to subdue the unruly Welsh. Over the next century, the Normans built a series of wooden forts throughout Wales from which Norman lords held control over surrounding lands. In the late 1100s they replaced the wooden strongholds with massive, turreted stone castles. From about 1140 to 1240, Welsh princes such as Rhys ap Gruffydd and Llewellyn the Great rose up against the Normans, capturing some castles and briefly regaining power. After Llewellyn's death in 1240, Welsh unity weakened. The English king Edward I conquered Wales in 1282, building another series of massive castles to reinforce his rule. Under Edward and his successors, Welsh revolts against the English continued. Most important was the rebellion of Owain Glyndwr in the 1400s. Despite his failure, Glyndwr strikes a heroic chord in Welsh memory as the last great leader to envision and fight for an independent Wales.

During the 1400s the Welsh increasingly became involved in English affairs, taking part in the War of the Roses. In 1485 a young Welsh nobleman named Henry Tudor won the Battle of Bosworth Field against King Richard III, thus securing his claim to the English throne. The Welsh rejoiced at having a Welshman as king of England. King Henry VII (reigned 1485–1509), as he was called, restored many of the rights that the Welsh had lost under English occupation. Under his son, Henry VIII (reigned 1509–1547), Wales and England became unified under one political system. Elizabeth I, daughter of Henry VIII, was the last Tudor monarch. By the time of her death in 1603, English language, law, and customs had become entrenched in Welsh life.

Today, nearly all Welsh Americans speak English exclusively, but several Welsh cultural organizations arrange Welsh courses and events in major American cities, and some Welsh Americans are very interested in exploring their heritage by learning their ancestral language.

Modern Era Since the end of the Tudor monarchy, the history of the Welsh people has been closely tied to that of their English neighbors. As England underwent rapid industrialization in the eighteenth and nineteenth centuries, the rich coalfields and slate quarries of Wales, along with its copper and ironworks, became vital components of English industrial might. The population grew quickly during this period, particularly in the south, around the capital of Cardiff and the coal-mining regions, where about two-thirds of Wales's population still lives. The Welsh economy suffered through several slumps in the twentieth century as extractive industries declined. By the late twentieth and early twenty-first centuries, the economy was more dependent on tourism, the service industry, and the public sector.

About four out of five Welsh people have adopted English as their sole language. Yet the Welsh have attempted to create their own national character. In the twentieth century Welsh nationalist sentiments were revived significantly, particularly amid concerns about the death of the Welsh language and the flooding of the Welsh Tryweryn Valley in 1965 to make a drinking-water reservoir for the English city of Liverpool. In the 1960s a brief period of militant action by Welsh nationalists destroyed English infrastructure and government offices. In 1979 the Welsh held their first referendum for a sovereign Welsh assembly, which was rejected by a large majority. In a second referendum in 1997, however, a slim majority voted in favor of the assembly. The National Assembly for Wales was established in 1999 and retains limited autonomy from the British Parliament. Its power was further expanded by Welsh voters in 2011.

SETTLEMENT IN THE UNITED STATES
Early Welsh immigrants generally came to the United States within waves of British migrants. Many were non-Anglican Christians seeking religious freedom. Others were prompted by opportunities for exploration, farming, and higher-paying industrial jobs in the United States. Some important early British settlers in North America—including Pilgrims and founders of the United States—were Welsh or Anglo-Welsh, not English.

There are common tales among the Welsh of ancestors who reached America centuries before Christopher Columbus, led by Madoc (or Madog) ap Owain Gwynedd. From the sixteenth century, there were many published reports by those who claimed to have found Welsh Indians in North America. No one ever proved the legends, but they nevertheless helped propel Welsh immigration. They also motivated important exploration. For example, in 1792 John Evans (1779–1847), a Welsh Methodist, searched for Welsh Indians around the northern reaches of the Missouri River. According to some versions of the legend, Madoc landed on the shores of Alabama; in 1953 the Daughters of the American Revolution in Mobile erected a plaque commemorating the event, but it was later removed. Although the various claims of the existence of Welsh-speaking Indians have not been proved, the existence of Americans descended from Welsh and Indian ancestors offers some possible corroboration.

However, even discounting the legendary Madoc, the Welsh came to the American continent early relative to other Europeans. Most of the early immigrants were farmers or missionaries. At first the Welsh settled in or near British colonies, among fellow Welsh Americans who shared their religious denomination. Baptists led the way. John Miles (c. 1621–1683), founder of the first Baptist church in Wales in 1649, suffered religious persecution both before and after he led Welsh Baptists to Massachusetts in 1662. At first the colony refused to tolerate them, but eventually it granted them land. They established there the town of Swansea and the First Baptist Church, which stands today as the oldest Welsh church in the United States.

Two decades after Baptists first arrived, Welsh members of the Society of Friends, or Quakers, founded the second and much larger Welsh settlement in America. Quakers were persecuted in Wales and England because they professed to value their "inner light" over Church and Bible. Among the Quaker leaders in England was William Penn (1644–1718), who claimed to have had a Welsh grandfather. In 1681 Penn obtained a vast tract of territory south of New York. Although his intention was to call it "New Wales," British authorities objected, and it was named Pennsylvania instead. The Quakers that Penn led there included many from Wales, and Pennsylvania became the heart of Welsh settlement.

In 1797 preacher Morgan John Rhys (1760–1804) founded a new homeland called Cambria for Welsh Americans in western Pennsylvania where they could live together and preserve their language and customs. Although Beulah, the township at the center of the settlement that he established, has not survived, Ebensburg, its second township, still exists. Meanwhile, a large population of Welsh immigrants settled in Philadelphia, which soon flourished and became one of the most important cities in the United States. Pennsylvania continues to have the largest population of Welsh Americans today.

After Britain's Religious Toleration Act of 1689 gave Quakers and other Protestant dissenters freedom of worship, Welsh emigration subsided until the late eighteenth century, when agricultural economics motivated a new wave of emigration. Welsh farmers had reaped poor harvests for years when they heard of the United States' expansion into the fertile Ohio Valley; meanwhile in Wales, acts of British Parliament limited people's access to farmland by enclosing common land and open moorlands. Concerned by the streams of emigrants leaving Wales, the British government passed measures to prevent skilled workmen from emigrating.

Beginning in the 1830s, large numbers of skilled Welsh industrial workers immigrated to the United States to work in its new factories, particularly after the American Civil War. These workers were mostly from southern Wales, Britain's main source of coal and iron. For each of the decades from 1881 to 1931, more than 10,000 Welsh immigrants were recorded by American authorities, up from just over 1,000 in the 1850s. The peak year for Welsh immigration to the United States was 1900, with more than 100,000 immigrants recorded in that year alone.

American regions from New York to Wisconsin and Minnesota to Oregon offered Welsh immigrants work in their traditional occupations and drew concentrations of descendants of Welsh shepherds and dairy farmers. After the Civil War, in Wisconsin, Iowa, Minnesota, Missouri, and Kansas, many Welsh American men entered trades, while young women found service work in private homes. Some Welsh American fruit growers became pioneers of orchard industries in the Pacific Northwest. Copper workers went to Baltimore; silver miners moved to Colorado; and, after 1849, prospectors for gold rushed to California. Slate quarrymen settled in New England and the Delaware Valley. Because so many Welsh immigrants were coal miners, they settled in the greatest concentrations in the coal regions of Pottsville, Wilkes-Barre, and Scranton. Steelworkers went to Pittsburgh, Cleveland, and Chicago.

Throughout the nineteenth century knowledgeable Welsh industrial workers immigrated to the United States to fill positions in ironworks not only as workers but also as industrial pioneers and leaders. After David Thomas (1794–1882) perfected techniques of burning anthracite coal to smelt iron ore, an American coal company brought him in 1839 from Wales to the great anthracite coalfields in Pennsylvania, where he developed the United States' anthracite iron industry. The new industry drew the Welsh by the thousands. At the beginning of the twentieth century, Scranton recorded nearly 5,000 natives of Wales, and more than 2,000 in Wilkes-Barre, who came to mine coal for Thomas's process. From the time of the Civil War to the end of World War I, Scranton claimed the largest concentration of Welsh people in the world outside Wales and England.

Another segment of Welsh American migration followed the tinplate-production industry. Glamorganshire, in southern Wales, dominated the world market as the main producer of tinplate until the United States, a principal market for Welsh tinplate, focused on producing it. To protect its own young tinplate industry, the United States passed the 1890 McKinley Tariff to raise prices of imported tinplate, throwing the Welsh industry into a depression and effectively drawing hundreds of workers from Wales to its new tinplate works. The Welsh American tinplate producers, centered in Philadelphia and Ohio, dominated the field for several generations. Many of the industrial workers who immigrated to the United States from Wales became executives and capitalists in their own right. In addition to their major roles in the development of American coal, iron, and steel industries, Welsh Americans in the mid-nineteenth century also built the American slate industry. Immigrants from North Wales prospected for and dug the United States' early slate quarries along the borders between Pennsylvania and Maryland, and between New York and Vermont.

Robert D. Thomas, a Congregational minister, authored what became for the Welsh of the post-Civil War period a convenient and detailed guidebook in their own language concerning the available land opportunities in the United States. After its publication in 1872, *Hanes Cymry America* (*History of the Welsh in America*) became popular in Wales and likely helped encourage further emigration.

In the mid- to late nineteenth century, a significant number of Welsh Mormon converts, primarily from southern Wales, immigrated to Salt Lake City, Utah, and surrounding regions. Mormonism founder Joseph Smith had converted Dan Jones (1810–1862), a Welsh immigrant, to the religion, then sent him on a mission to Wales in 1844. Jones in turn converted thousands, most of whom immigrated to the United States, settling in Utah and Idaho. Many worked in coalfields or as farmers. Welsh Americans contributed much to Mormon culture; for example, they founded the Mormon Tabernacle Choir in 1847.

Welsh immigration to the United States began to decline during the Great Depression. Precise numbers are difficult to identify because Welsh immigrants have been counted along with all other immigrants from the United Kingdom since the 1920s. That said, the number of Americans claiming Welsh ancestry has risen from about 1 million in the 1990 Census to about 1.8 million in 2011. This is most likely because more Americans are choosing to identify with their Welsh heritage. States with the highest number of Welsh Americans include California, Pennsylvania, Ohio, Texas, Florida, New York, and Washington.

Welsh Americans' part of the American story is evidenced by place names such as Bangor, Bryn Mawr, and Haverford, along with many counties and communities named for Welsh Americans in Ohio, Pennsylvania, and the South. Communities with significant proportions of Welsh Americans include the cities of Scranton; Philadelphia; Emporia, Kansas; and Malad City, Idaho; as well as Jackson County, Ohio, and the village of Cambria, Wisconsin.

LANGUAGE

Cymraeg, the Welsh language, is in the Indo-European language family. It descends from Celtic and relates closely to Breton, the language of Brittany; to Highland Scots Gaelic; and to Irish Gaelic. To outsiders, the language looks difficult and sounds strange, with lilting, musical tones in which one word seems to slur into the next. Indeed, the first letter of a word may change depending on the word before it. This is called *treiglo*, and it achieves a smoothness treasured by the Welsh ear. Welsh also contains elusive sounds such

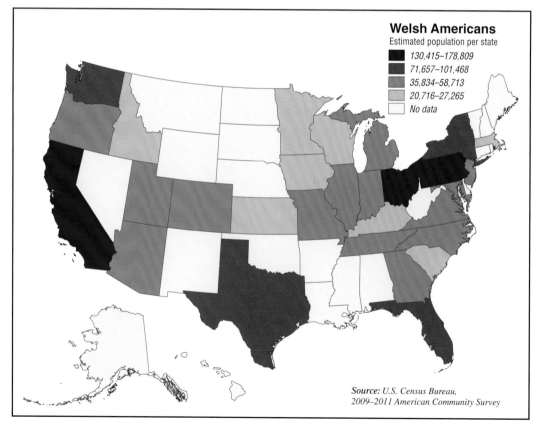

Welsh Americans
Estimated population per state

- 130,415–178,809
- 71,657–101,468
- 35,834–58,713
- 20,716–27,265
- No data

Source: U.S. Census Bureau, 2009–2011 American Community Survey

as "ll" (in the name Llewellyn or Lloyd, for example), which is pronounced almost like a combination of "f," "th," and "ch," though not quite. Welsh words nearly always accent their second-to-last syllable.

Welsh culture has struggled not only against the English church but also against the English language. When England industrialized Wales, extracting its abundant coal and iron ore, it divided the inhabitants into a rural group in which Welsh was spoken and an urban group in which English was the primary language. Late in the nineteenth century, battles over Welsh culture moved into the field of education as England prohibited Welsh public schools from teaching in Welsh. The Welsh maintained their culture, though, through their traditional Sunday schools and through nationalism.

According to the 2011 UK census, about one-fifth of Welsh residents aged three or over can speak the Welsh language today. However, it is rarely spoken among Welsh Americans. In the early days of Welsh immigration to the United States, Welsh churches used Sunday schools to perpetuate the Welsh language by teaching adults and children to read the Bible in Welsh. Because of the Sunday school movement, many early Welsh Americans became literate in their own language. This dedication waned over the generations, however, as Welsh churches merged with non-Welsh congregations and the population more fully acculturated. Today, nearly all Welsh Americans speak English exclusively, but several Welsh cultural organizations arrange Welsh courses and events in major U.S. cities, and some Welsh Americans are very interested in exploring their heritage by learning their ancestral language.

RELIGION

Welsh and Welsh American identities have centered on Christian religious traditions of strictness, evangelicalism, and reform. Mormonism and scattered versions of pre-Christian paganism also figure in Welsh American religion.

In seventeenth- and eighteenth-century Wales, religious nonconformity preserved Welsh identity by halting the expansion of the Anglican Church and the full absorption of Wales into English culture. As Welsh churches pitted their religious fundamentalism against the English establishment in the eighteenth century, their progressivism foreshadowed contributions of Welsh Americans to American Puritanism and progress. Around the year 1700, when English rule still dominated Welsh religion, the reform movement came from within the church and received its great stimulus from the pietistic evangelism introduced by John Wesley (1703–1791) and George Whitfield (1714–1770). Soon these men, and Welshmen of similar beliefs, were emphasizing the necessity of abundant preaching within the church and the need for experiencing a rebirth in religious conviction as a necessary part in the salvation of the individual.

WELSH PROVERBS

Adfyd a ddwg wybodaeth, a gwybodaeth ddoethineb.

Adversity brings knowledge, and knowledge wisdom.

Gwna dda dros ddrwg, uffern ni'th ddwg.

Repay evil with good, and hell will not claim you.

Mwyaf y brys, mwyaf y rhwystr.

More the hurry, more the obstacles.

Rhaid cropian cyn cerdded.

You must crawl before walking.

After this evangelical movement, which came to be known as Methodism, spread through Wales, Welsh Methodists split from Wesley and from English Methodists and followed Whitfield into Calvinism, calling themselves Calvinist Methodists. Welsh Methodists, furthermore, withdrew from the Anglican Church and precipitated a consolidation of Welsh culture.

Welsh Christian denominations shared many common traits, including strict adherence to marriage vows, observance of Sunday as a day for religious activities alone, and commitment to simple living. Nevertheless, divisive religious differences arose over church organization, baptism of infants, and Calvinist ideas such as predestination. Throughout the early period of Welsh immigration, Welsh Americans kept close to congregations that shared their religious beliefs and heritage, and a number of churches held services in Welsh. Today there are few American churches that are distinctly Welsh, but many churches throughout the country bear the name of St. David, the patron saint of Wales, often indicating their Welsh American roots.

In the United States, as in Wales, Welsh churches operated Sunday schools; children and adults attended separate classes in which teachers used Socratic methods of questioning. Welsh American churchgoers sang hymns and testified, respectively, on Tuesday and Thursday nights, and they regularly held *gymanvas*, preaching festivals.

Welsh Americans are still notably active in the Mormon Church. In 2004 the British Broadcasting Corporation reported on a journey of eighty Welsh American Mormons to their ancestral villages in Wales.

In pre-Christian Wales, the Druids (a special class of leaders) dominated a religion in which Celts worshipped a number of deities according to rites associated with nature. Although paganism is all but dead in Wales, a small but visible subculture of Welsh/Celtic nature-worship has gained popularity

WELSH MUSICALITY

The Welsh take pride in their language's musicality and expressiveness, and they cherish the traditional oratorical skills of poets and priests. In literature, the canonization of Welsh poet Dylan Thomas (1914–1953) is a matter of Welsh American pride. Thomas wrote English-language poems that drew from Welsh culture and preaching styles. The art of oral storytelling that flourished in medieval Wales left as its written legacy the *Mabinogion*. Preachers of sermons mastered versions of a chanting style called *hwyl*, and each preacher characteristically followed his own melody through a major key to a climax in a minor key. With their hwyl, Welsh preachers led congregations in fervent evangelical revivals.

in the United States since the 1960s, when two members of the Parent Kindred of the Old Religion in Wales brought Hereditary Welsh Paganism to the United States. Today, Welsh Pagans can be found in Georgia, Wisconsin, Minnesota, Michigan, California, and West Virginia. Welsh Pagans form circles with names such as The Cauldron, Annwfn, and Y Tylwyth Teg. Members often take symbolic Welsh names like Lord Myrddin Pendevig, Lady Gleannon or Gwyddion, Tiron, and Siani. Welsh Pagans in the United States also use the Welsh language in their rituals.

CULTURE AND ASSIMILATION

Welsh Americans forged their identity through churches, education, and dominance of particular industries, most notably coal mining and ironworks. The visibility of Welsh American communities waxed and waned with their churches. At first, as new territories opened in North America, Welsh missionary work expanded to fill the opportunities to convert new souls. In eighteenth-century Pennsylvania, Quaker, Baptist, and Presbyterian churches anchored communities in which Sunday schools helped shape Welsh American identities. These early Welsh Americans eventually became Americanized in their habits and English in their speech. During the nineteenth century, however, the clergy that led Welsh American congregations increasingly focused on Welsh identity. Their work, coupled with frequent exchanges of visitors from Wales and between Welsh American communities, drew together a Welsh American identity that better resisted acculturation.

By the turn of the twentieth century, Welsh Americans had almost fully acculturated. More Welsh immigrants and their descendants joined occupations outside their traditional industries. The contexts of their ethnic identities also changed as Eastern European and Italian immigrants entered the coal mines: to the newcomers, Welsh immigrants and Welsh Americans

seemed more similar than ever to Anglo, Yankee, or established "mainstream" Americans.

While their long history in the United States, large proportion of English speakers, and similarity to other British Americans have reduced the visibility of Welsh Americans as a distinct ethnic group, churches, organizations, and festivals continue to sustain Welsh American culture, and traditional Welsh American ethnic identity remains strong in a few communities around the country, including southeastern Ohio; upstate New York's Slate Valley; Scranton, Pennsylvania; and Chicago, where the iconic Wrigley Building is annually illuminated in the Welsh national colors for St. David's Day.

Dances and Songs The traditional Welsh *eisteddfod* is a festival celebrating Welsh writing and oratory that dates back to the twelfth century. Since the 1830s Welsh Americans have also competed in their own eisteddfods. Especially in Pennsylvania, Ohio, Iowa, and Utah, strong traditions of eisteddfod have inspired expert choirs in their performances of Bach, Handel, Mendelssohn, and other classical composers of sacred music. Today the United States usually sends the largest delegation of "Welshmen in Exile" to the annual National Eisteddfod of Wales, the world's largest. The "exiles" march in ranks by country to the singing of the Welsh nostalgic hymn *"Unwaith Eto Yng Nghymru Annwyl"* ("Once Again in Dear Wales").

Because few Welsh Americans today speak or write in Welsh, Welsh Americans have mostly replaced the eisteddfod with the *Gymanfa Ganu*, or Welsh singing festival. The Gymanfa Ganu started in Wales in 1859, and by the 1920s it had spread to the United States. In Wales each church denomination sponsors its own Gymanfa Ganu, but in the United States the festivals include all denominations. The Welsh North American Association, formerly known as the National Gymanfa Ganu Association of the United States and Canada, has organized such events for many years. It originated in 1929 with a gathering of 2,400 Welsh Americans at Niagara Falls and continues to meet at key Welsh American and Canadian cities each year on Labor Day. In recent years these have included Scranton, Cleveland, Pittsburgh, Chicago, and Toronto.

Cuisine Most Welsh Americans do not eat a distinctly "Welsh" cuisine, although traditional dishes are served at Welsh cultural festivals. These dishes typically feature basic ingredients of dairy products, seafood, lamb, or beef and simple vegetables such as potatoes, carrots, and leeks. The leek is a national symbol of Wales and its most popular vegetable, often featured in soups and stews. One favorite dish, Anglesey eggs, consists of leeks and mashed potatoes topped with hard-boiled eggs and a cheese sauce. In Welsh rabbit (often called rarebit by the English), eggs, cheese, milk, Worcestershire sauce, and beer are combined into a rich melted mixture that is poured over toast. There are very few Welsh restaurants in the United States; some Welsh dishes may be found in British pubs and restaurants, however, which is fitting as the two cuisines have heavily influenced each other. Wales also has a rich brewing history, and pale-malted Welsh beer is a distinct style, although it has yet to penetrate the American market as significantly as Irish or English beers.

Traditional Dress Like most Welsh in Wales, Welsh Americans do not maintain a distinct style of dress in day-to-day life. Traditional costumes, commonly worn at events such as eisteddfods, feature colorful stripes and checks, with a wide-brimmed hat for women that looks like a witch's hat with the top half of the cone removed.

Holidays By far the most important holiday specific to the Welsh and to Welsh Americans is St. David's Day, March 1. The patron saint of the Welsh, St. David (c. 500–589) was an archbishop and ascetic who founded monastic communities and churches throughout Wales. St. David's Day, which commemorates his death, represents an annual opportunity for rallying Welsh consciousness and celebrating culture worldwide. Several American communities hold festivals, and some Episcopal churches hold memorial services. The largest St. David's Day festival in the United States is in Los Angeles; other significant festivals and banquets are held in Philadelphia; Chicago; and Knoxville, Tennessee.

FAMILY AND COMMUNITY LIFE

Early Welsh Americans, many of them members of evangelical Christian sects, were known for living a modest, even austere lifestyle, with what many would now think of as strict traditional attitudes toward family, work, and church. Today, however, the attitudes and behaviors of Welsh Americas in general are similar to those of most other well-established European American ethnic groups.

EMPLOYMENT AND ECONOMIC CONDITIONS

The Welsh traditionally worked in farming or, during the Industrial Age, in the heavy industries of coal, iron, and steel. Because these industries had developed earlier in Wales, Welsh immigrants to the United States tended to know the work better than workers from elsewhere. Thus Welsh immigrants took leading roles in the United States' developing industries. Welsh American industrial bosses especially preferred to hire Welsh American workers and, more specifically, those from their own religious denomination. As a result Welsh Americans dominated coal mining, and many coal mines were manned mostly with a particular denomination of Welsh Americans. Welsh Americans also dominated the nineteenth-century tin-plate industry in Pennsylvania.

Today more Welsh Americans are employed in nonindustrial occupations, though some still work in the coal, iron, and steel industries in rural areas.

According to the American Community Survey's five-year estimates for 2006–2010, about half of Americans claiming Welsh ancestry worked in "management, business, science and art occupations," as opposed to about a third of Americans overall. Their median household income of about $62,000 was well higher than the American average of $51,000, and their poverty rate of 4.4 percent was lower than the American average of about 11 percent.

POLITICS AND GOVERNMENT

George Washington supposedly once said that "Good Welshman Make Good Americans." In the founding of the United States, cultural history positioned Welsh immigrants as American revolutionaries. The Welsh, who already tended to resent English control, were strongly inclined toward revolution in France, Britain, and America. The United States can trace the derivation of its trial-by-jury system through England to Wales. Although it is unclear exactly where Welsh culture contributed to the founding moments of the United States, Welsh Americans claim the Welshness of Jeffersonian principles, especially that certain rights are inalienable, that rights not assigned to governments are reserved for the people, and that church and state must remain separate. In February 1776 the Welsh philosopher Richard Price (1723–1791) published in London *Observations on the Nature of Civil Liberty*, appealing "to the natural rights of all men, those rights which no government should have the power to take away"; five months later, Welsh American Thomas Jefferson published similar ideas in the Declaration of Independence.

The Welsh influence on early American politics was pronounced. Five of the first six American presidents were of Welsh descent. Throughout the nineteenth century, nearly 75 percent of Welsh immigrants became citizens, a higher percentage than any other group. Welsh Americans found themselves on both sides of the Civil War, however; Abraham Lincoln and Jefferson Davis, for instance, could both claim Welsh heritage.

In accord with their religious views, Welsh Americans in the nineteenth and twentieth centuries were avid supporters of temperance, Prohibition, and Sabbath-enforcing Blue Laws. They also played a major role in fighting for women's suffrage. In addition, Welsh Americans have been labor leaders. In 1871 Welsh American coal miners led their union in a historic strike in which they protested a 30 percent wage decrease, ultimately to no avail.

Welsh Americans are hardly distinct as a political block today, owing to their widespread distribution throughout American regions and classes. Yet during the 2008 and 2012 presidential elections, the *Times of London* noted what it called a new trend of American candidates and their families, including Hillary Clinton and Ann Romney (wife of 2012 Republican

American jazz pianist Bill Evans (1929–1980) performs during a concert in New York City, 1959. BOB PARENT / GETTY IMAGES

given the middle name Lincoln, Wright changed it to Lloyd in the 1880s to honor his maternal relations after his father abandoned the family. Wright's building designs revolutionized American architecture, particularly residential architecture, with modern forms that blended into their natural environments. He named his home in Wisconsin "Taliesen," a Welsh word meaning poet or magician.

Business Some of the United States' greatest business figures have been Welsh Americans, including pioneering communications executive William Fargo (1818–1881), cofounder of Wells Fargo; banker and financier J. P. Morgan (1837–1913); and aviation and Hollywood magnate Howard Hughes (1905–1976). Whiskey maker Jack Daniel (1849–1911) and restaurateur Bob Evans (1918–2007) were also of Welsh descent.

Government Welsh Americans played a major role in the development of American democracy. Seventeen signers of the Declaration of Independence were of Welsh extraction. The greatest Welsh American colonial patriot was probably Thomas Jefferson (1743–1826), whose ancestors came from the foot of Mount Snowden in Wales to the colony of Virginia; Jefferson could even speak Welsh. Indeed, five of the first six American presidents were of Welsh descent: John Adams (1735–1826); Jefferson; James Madison (1751–1836); James Monroe (1758–1831); and John Quincy Adams (1767–1848). Other Welsh Americans include Gouverneur Morris (1752–1816), who wrote the final draft of the Constitution of the United States, and Supreme Court chief justice John Marshall (1755–1835), commonly considered the "father of American constitutional law."

Frontiersman Daniel Boone (1734–1820), who served in the Virginia General Assembly, and Meriwether Lewis (1774–1809), who led the Lewis and Clark Expedition and later became governor of the Missouri Territory, were of Welsh descent.

Other American presidents of at least partial Welsh descent include Abraham Lincoln (1809–1865)—though some dispute his Welshness; Calvin Coolidge (1872–1933); and Richard Nixon (1913–1994). Robert E. Lee (1807–1870), general of the Confederate Army, and Jefferson Davis (1808–1889), president of the Confederacy, were Welsh Americans. So were secretaries of state Daniel Webster (1782–1852), William Seward (1801–1872), and Charles Evan Hughes (1862–1948), who also served as governor of New York and chief justice of the Supreme Court.

Prominent American statespeople in recent years have included Hillary Rodham Clinton (1947–), First Lady, senator, and secretary of state, whose father was of Welsh-English descent. On the presidential campaign trail in 2012, Ann Romney (née Davies, 1949–), wife of Republican candidate Mitt Romney, served Welsh cakes in honor of her Wales-born father.

presidential candidate Mitt Romney), publicly citing their Welsh roots to appeal to voters.

NOTABLE INDIVIDUALS

Academia and Education Welsh Americans played a major role in the establishment of significant American academic institutions. Elihu Yale (1649–1721) helped launch Yale University; Welsh-born theologian Morgan Edwards (1722–1795) was a founder of Brown University; and Martha Carey Thomas (1857–1935) cofounded and served as president of Bryn Mawr College. Catharine E. Beecher (1800–1858), sister of Harriet Beecher Stowe, founded seminaries for women. Helen Parkhurst (1887–1973), originator of the Dalton Plan of individualized student contracts, established the Dalton School in New York.

Architecture One of the most influential American architects of the twentieth century, Frank Lloyd Wright (1867–1959), was born in rural Wisconsin into a then-prominent Welsh American family on his mother's side, the Lloyd Joneses. Originally

Literature Notable Welsh Americans in literature include abolitionist Harriet Beecher Stowe (1811–1896), author of *Uncle Tom's Cabin* (1852); novelist Jack London (1876–1916), author of *The Call of the Wild* (1903) and *White Fang* (1906); novelist Kate Wiggin (1856–1923), author of *Rebecca of Sunnybrook Farm* (1903); and humorist/poet Ogden Nash (1902–1971).

Medicine Medical scientist Alice Catherine Evans (1881–1975) was the first woman president of the Society of American Bacteriologists. Pioneer nutritionists Mary Swartz Rose (1874–1941) and Ruth Wheeler (1877–1948) were of Welsh descent, as was the women's health reformer Mary Nichols (1810–1884). Mary Whiton Calkins (1863–1930) was the first female president of the American Psychological Association and of the American Philosophical Association.

Music Welsh American musicians include popular vocalists Shirley Bassey (1937–), known for her James Bond themes; former teen idol Donny Osmond (1957–) and his sister, Marie (1959–); and jazz pianist Bill Evans (1929–1980), composer of "Waltz for Debby" and a brief member of the Miles Davis sextet. Pop singers Christina Aguilera (1980–) and Kelly Clarkson (1982–) are of Welsh descent, as is Tommy Lee (1962–) of the metal band Mötley Crüe.

Religion Welsh preacher Morgan John Rhys (1760–1804), who came to the United States in 1794, preached that slavery contradicted the principles of the Christian religion and the rights of man; he also stirred controversy with a sermon in which he said that no land should be taken from Native Americans without payment.

Stage and Screen Welsh Americans in Hollywood have included the pioneering movie producer D. W. Griffith (1875–1948), who is best known for the epic *The Birth of a Nation* (1915); actor and comedian Bob Hope (1903–2003); actress Bette Davis (1908–1989); actor-director Richard Burton (1925–1984); comic actor Leslie Nielsen (1926–2010); Wales-born Sir Anthony Hopkins (1937–), who became a U.S. citizen in 2000; and actress Susan Sarandon (1946–).

MEDIA

PRINT

Ninnau and Y Drych

Monthly magazine containing news and information for Americans and Canadians of Welsh ancestry.

Arturo Roberts, Publisher and Executive Editor
11 Post Terrace
Basking Ridge, New Jersey 07920
Phone: (908) 766-4151
Fax: (908) 221-0744
Email: ninnaupubl@cs.com
URL: www.ninnau.com

North American Journal of Welsh Studies

Published annually by the North American Society for the Study of Welsh History and Culture, this multidisciplinary journal features scholarship on Welsh and Welsh American topics.

Paul Ward, Editor
University of Huddersfield
Department of History, English, Languages, and Media
Huddersfield, HD1 3DH United Kingdom
Phone: +44 1484 472452
Email: paul.ward@hud.ac.uk
URL: www.welshstudiesjournal.org

ORGANIZATIONS AND ASSOCIATIONS

Welsh American Society of Northern California

Promotes Welsh culture in Northern California, including St. David's Day events and Welsh language classes. Also offers scholarships to students pursuing Welsh language or history studies.

Email: secretariat@wasnc.org
URL: www.wasnc.org

Welsh Heritage Week

An annual weeklong celebration of Welsh culture sponsored by the Welsh Harp and Heritage Society, with Welsh language classes, singing, folk music, and food. It is held in a different U.S. city each summer.

Welsh American actor Anthony Hopkins arrives at the World Premiere of 'The Muppets' at El Capitan Theatre in Los Angeles, 2011. HUBERT BOESL / DPA PICTURE ALLIANCE ARCHIVE / ALAMY

Beth Landmesser, Director
Email: hwyl@infionline.net
URL: www.welshheritageweek.org

Welsh North American Association (WNAA)

Founded in 1929 in Niagara Falls and formerly known as the Welsh National Gymanfa Ganu Association, the WNAA organizes a Gymanfa Ganu, or Welsh singing festival, every year in a different North American city. It also publishes hymnals and promotes Welsh culture generally.

Dr. Megan Williams, Executive Secretary
P.O. Box 1054
Trumansburg, New York 14886
Phone: (607) 279-7402
Email: IHQ@theWNAA.org
URL: www.thewnaa.org

The Welsh Society of Philadelphia

Founded in 1729, this is among the oldest of Welsh societies, which exist in several U.S. cities. Like other American Welsh societies, it seeks to keep alive Welsh culture and heritage, assist immigrants to the United States from Wales, and maintain scholarship and charitable programs.

Charles Lentz, President
P.O. Box 7287
Saint Davids, Pennsylvania 19087-7287
Email: membership@philadelphiawelsh.org
URL: www.philadelphiawelsh.org

MUSEUMS AND RESEARCH CENTERS

Cymdeithas Madog—The Welsh Studies Institute in North America

"Dedicated to helping North Americans learn, use, and enjoy the Welsh language," the Welsh Studies Institute acts as a clearinghouse for those interested in Welsh literature, music, and language resources. For nearly four decades, it has organized an annual *Cwrs Cymraeg* (Welsh language institute) in a U.S. city, with language courses, music and arts, and education about Welsh American heritage.

Rebecca Blaevoet, Secretary
1 Coed-Y-Moeth Road
Aberbargoed, CF81 9DR United Kingdom
Email: secretary@madog.org
URL: www.madog.org

Madog Center for Welsh Studies, University of Rio Grande

The Madog Center maintains a research center and library and organizes conferences and activities to preserve the Welsh language and culture.

Jeanne Jones Jindra, Director
University of Rio Grande
P.O. Box 500, Rio Grande
Ohio 45674
Phone: (740) 245-7186
Email: welsh@rio.edu
URL: www.rio.edu/madog

SOURCES FOR ADDITIONAL STUDY

Ashton, E. T. *The Welsh in the United States*. Hove, Sussex: Caldra House, 1984.

Dodd, A. H. *The Character of Early Welsh Emigration to the United States*. Cardiff: University of Wales Press, 1957.

Hartmann, George Edward. *Americans from Wales*. New York: Farrar, Straus and Giroux, 1978.

Holt, Constance Wall. *Welsh Women: An Annotated Bibliography of Women in Wales and Women of Welsh Descent in America*. Metuchen, NJ: Scarecrow, 1993.

Jones, Aled, and William D. Jones. *Welsh Reflections: Y Drych and America, 1851–2001*. Ceredigion, Wales: Gwasg Gomer, 2001.

Jones, William D. *Wales in America: Scranton and the Welsh, 1860-1920*. Chicago: University of Chicago Press, 2005.

Lewis, Ronald L. *Welsh Americans: A History of Assimilation in the Coalfields*. Chapel Hill: University of North Carolina Press, 2009.

Thomas, Erin Ann. *Coal in Our Veins: A Personal Journey*. Logan: Utah State University Press, 2012.

Thomas, R. D. Hanes. *Cymry America: A History of the Welsh in America*. Translated by Phillips G. Davies. Lanham, MD: University Press of America, 1983. First published 1872.

Van Vugt, William. *British Buckeyes: The English, Scots, and Welsh in Ohio, 1700-1900*. Kent, Ohio: Kent State University Press, 2006.

Welsh Assembly Government. *Keeping Up with the Joneses: The Story of Wales and the Welsh in the USA*. Welsh Assembly Government, 2004.

Williams, David. *Cymru Ac America: Wales and America*. Cardiff: University of Wales Press, 1975. First published 1946.

YEMENI AMERICANS

Drew Walker

OVERVIEW

Yemeni Americans are immigrants or descendants of people from Yemen, a country on the southern tip of the Arabian Peninsula. Yemen is bordered by two countries, Saudi Arabia to the north and Oman to the east, and by two bodies of water, the Gulf of Aden to the south and the Red Sea to the west. The northern border with Saudi Arabia is part of a vast desert and remains mostly uncharted. Yemen's total land area is 204,849 square miles (527,969 square kilometers), roughly a third larger than the state of California.

According to a census conducted by the Yemeni government in April 2011, Yemen had a population of about 25 million. The overwhelming majority of Yemeni citizens were Muslims, with nearly 54 percent belonging to a Sunni order of Islam and almost 45 percent belonging to a Shiite order. There were also small groups of Christians, Jews, and Hindus. Yemen is among the poorest countries on the Arabian Peninsula. Compared with other countries in the Arab world, Yemen's oil reserves are sparse, although it has vast reserves of natural gas.

Yemenis began to arrive in the United States in the late nineteenth and early twentieth centuries, settling mainly in the east and working in factories that employed the growing immigrant population in the United States. Until the 1990s nearly all Yemeni immigrants were adult males who had left Yemen to earn money to support their families. These men sent funds home monthly and typically returned to their native villages in Yemen every two years to reconnect with their wives and children. In the 1990s Yemeni women and children began immigrating to the United States in greater numbers, and increasingly Yemenis started coming to the United States for college or to find professional work.

The National Association of Yemeni Americans estimates that as of 2012 there were between 80,000 and 90,000 Yemeni Americans living in the United States (about 5 percent of the total Arab American population). Areas with a significant number of Yemeni Americans include Dearborn, Michigan; Buffalo, New York; the San Joaquin Valley of central California; New York City; and Washington, D.C.

HISTORY OF THE PEOPLE

Early History From approximately 1000 BCE to 100 BCE, most of the area today known as Yemen was controlled by a group of kingdoms that derived their status and wealth through the trade in spices and other products, primarily frankincense and myrrh. Both frankincense and myrrh were forms of gum taken from trees that covered much of Yemen's lands. These substances had medicinal properties and were highly valued in the ancient world for their ritual and healing powers. The peoples of the southern Arabian Peninsula were among the first to domesticate the camel, and by the eleventh century BCE they were using large numbers of these animals in caravans to transport their products from their center of production in the city of Qana (today Bir 'Ali) to the great markets of Gaza in Egypt. Also included in these caravans were gold and other fine goods that arrived in Yemen by sea from India.

The three largest and most enduring of the kingdoms that ruled the area were the Kingdom of Saba, which was located in the southwestern area of the Arabian Peninsula, the Kingdom of Ma'in, located in what is today northwest Yemen, and the Kingdom of Hadhramaut in today's southeastern Yemen. Other kingdoms that prospered in the southern portion of the Arabian Peninsula during the first millennium BCE included the Kingdom of Awsan and the Kingdom of Qataban. The Sabaean capital of Ma'rib, located approximately 70 miles from Yemen's present day capital city of Sana'a, was the most productive agricultural center in the region. In the eighth century BCE the Sabaeans completed a dam there that provided irrigation for the arable terrain surrounding Ma'rib, which allowed the Sabaeans to profit from agriculture as well as the spice trade. Regarded as one of the most impressive engineering accomplishments of the ancient world, the earthen dam stood for more than 1,000 years and fostered the growth of the surrounding 25,000-acre area into a center of early Yemeni culture.

In the second century BCE, the Himyar Kingdom, which developed along the coast of the Red Sea at the port of Aden in the southwestern corner of the Arabian Peninsula and grew rich through trade with powers in Africa, emerged as a rival to the Sabaeans, as well as the other powers in the region. In 25 BCE the Himyarites conquered the Sabaeans and began to expand eastward. Fighting continued in throughout the southern Arabian Peninsula for the next three centuries with the Sabaeans periodically regaining lost territory and maintaining control of the region. In 280 CE they finally succumbed to the Himyars, who then controlled the territory extending from the Red Sea in the west to the Arabian Desert in the north and the Persian Gulf in the east.

The Himyarites remained the dominant native power in Yemen from 300 to 520, but over the course of those two centuries various foreign influences grew in the area, weakening the Himyarites politically and economically. The spread of Christianity in the ancient Mediterranean world diminished the popularity of ritual fragrances, and the decreasing demand for the region's spices due to competition from the Byzantines eventually led to the demise of Himyarite wealth in the spice trade. By the fourth century both Christianity and Judaism had been introduced to the region, and the Ethiopian forces occupied the eastern portion of the kingdom.

In 570 the great dam at Ma'rib, which had been assiduously maintained up through the 400s, broke and was subsequently abandoned. By this time the Himyarites had established an alliance with Persia, which led to the expulsion of the occupying Ethiopian forces. Islam was introduced to southern Arabian Peninsula in the early to mid-seventh century. After centuries of exploitation by Christians and Jews in Yemen, the spread of Islam was quick and decisive. The Prophet Muhammad sent his son-in-law to be governor, leading to the establishment of the mosques in Janadiyah and Sana'a', still today the two most famous mosques in Yemen. From this point on Yemen was ruled by a series of Muslim holy men and governors known as caliphs and imams. Rulers from different Muslim groups controlled Yemen over the following centuries. Most prominent among these groups was an Iraqi Shi'ite sect introduced in the ninth century known as the Zaydi.

A turning point in the history of Yemen occurred around the early fifteenth century, when reputedly Sheik 'Ali ibn 'Umar' introduced a Yemeni specialty—coffee—to the greater Mediterranean world. It was at this point that Yemen became an area of conflict between the Ottoman Empire, the Egyptians, and various European countries over the trade in coffee. At first providing an economic boom that lasted for centuries in some areas of Yemen, coffee by the eighteenth century was being grown and sold elsewhere around the world. The result was yet another rapid decline in the position of Yemen in the world economy. By 1517 the Zaydi imams of Yemen could no longer resist the forces from outside and were absorbed for the first time into the Ottoman Empire, a period of domination that lasted until approximately 1630, at which time the Zaydi forces expelled the Turks from the highlands in southern and central Yemen. The Ottomans maintained control of small areas along the coast but gradually gave way to a combination of British and local interests there.

Modern Era The British first arrived in Aden in 1609 and over the course of two centuries developed the village into a major port with the help of the Sultanate of Lahej, a local group that had separated from Zaydi rule. Aden served as a key stopping point for the many ships in the British-owned East India Company that were traveling back and forth between England and India. In the early nineteenth century the British sent troops to Aden to protect their ships against attacks from pirates, and in 1839 the Sultan of Lahej ceded the port and the surrounding area to the British. Over the remainder of the century, the Ottomans gradually moved north while the British continued to spread their influence in the south. In 1904 the British and the Ottomans formally divided Yemen into northern and southern territories, but even so the entire region remained a patchwork of small kingdoms, some more powerful than others. The colonial powers exerted influence primarily in the larger cities.

The Ottomans withdrew from North Yemen in 1918, at the close of World War I, but the British remained in the South until 1967. With the Ottomans gone, Imam Yahya Mohammad emerged as the dominant ruler in the north and established the Mutawakkilite Kingdom of Yemen there. The Kingdom of Yemen joined the Arab League in 1945 and the United Nations in 1947. Both Yahya and his son Assad tried to expand the kingdom in the south, but the British would not relent and citizens within the kingdom were clamoring for democratic rule. In 1962 revolutionary forces backed by Arab nationalists from Egypt deposed the Yahya dynasty and established the Yemen Arab Republic (YAR) in north Yemen. Civil war and royalist insurrections continued for eight years but stopped abruptly in 1970 when Saudi Arabia formally recognized the sovereignty of the republic.

Throughout the first half of the twentieth century the British administered in southern Yemen in conjunction with local imams and sheikhs, establishing the West Aden Protectorate to oversee the major port at Aden and a looser confederacy called the East Aden Protectorate to administer the remainder of the southern peninsula. Tension in the area escalated in the late 1950s when Egyptian president Gamal Adbul Nasser attempted to draw North Yemen into the United Arab Republic and encouraged the people of the south to rise up against both colonial and local dynastic rulers. In the early 1960s the British backed Saudi efforts to dismantle the newly formed Yemen Arab Republic in the north, but their strategy backfired and fighting spilled into the south. Hostilities continued until 1967, when the British finally left the area after a temporary shutdown of the Suez Canal (which connects the Mediterranean Sea and the Red Sea) severely diminished their economic prospects there. On November 30, 1967, the National Liberation Front (NLF), a coalition of rebel forces, established the People's Republic of South Yemen.

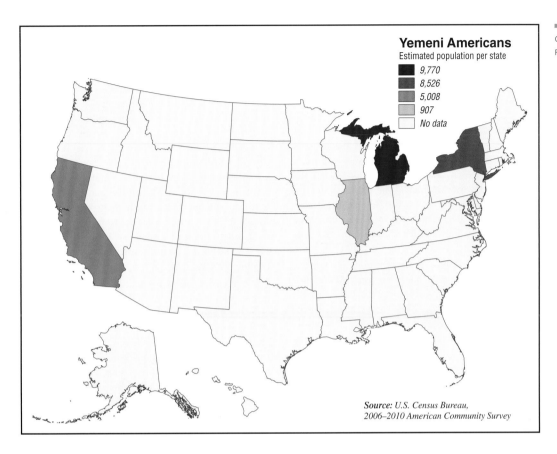

Yemeni Americans
Estimated population per state

- 9,770
- 8,526
- 5,008
- 907
- No data

*Source: U.S. Census Bureau,
2006–2010 American Community Survey*

By 1970 a Marxist faction within the coalition had gained control of the country and established a single-party state in the south called the People's Democratic Republic of Yemen.

During the 1970s the two Yemens engaged in a series of short border wars, which after much turmoil resulted in the drafting of a constitution establishing the unification of the north and south. It was not until May 1990 that the full merger finally took place, creating a unified country named the Republic of Yemen. The only republic on the Arabian Peninsula, Yemen began holding free elections in 1990, with universal suffrage for all citizens at least 18 years of age (in 1967 the PDRY had become the first country in the Arab world to grant women the right to vote). Nevertheless, corruption in government was widespread in Yemen, as the country was run almost exclusively by the General People's Congress party. In January 2011, in the midst revolutions throughout the Arab world, riots spread across Yemen, and President Ali Abdullah Saleh faced demands to step down. Saleh, who had been president since 1990, finally complied, and in February 2012 his vice president, Abd Rabbuh Mansur Al-Hadi, ran unopposed and was elected the new president.

SETTLEMENT IN THE UNITED STATES

There is no specific record of when the first Yemeni Americans arrived in the United States. It is most likely that they came shortly after the Suez Canal was opened in 1869, facilitating travel between the Red Sea and the Mediterranean. By 1890 there are records of a small number immigrating, and there are also records showing that some Yemenis obtained U.S. citizenship by fighting in the First World War. Many early Yemeni immigrants first settled within preexisting Lebanese and Palestinian communities in New York and other eastern cities. After orienting themselves to their new surroundings, many Yemenis set off for the Midwest, where the labor force was quickly growing. As they headed west out of New York, many Yemeni Americans found factory work in Buffalo, New York, and Dearborn, Michigan.

During the Great Depression of the 1930s, the flow of Yemeni immigration slowed dramatically, but it resumed again in greater numbers after the end of World War II in 1945. One route of immigration into the United States was through Vietnam, where many Yemenis had worked in warehouses and shops and on the docks as watchmen. Through a loophole in immigration laws, Yemeni immigrants who were not literate in their mother tongue (which was a requirement for all immigrants entering into the United States) could bypass regulations and thus be admitted. Yemeni immigration often took the form of chain migration, in which already established immigrants would secure visas for their relatives in Yemen. Yemeni men typically emigrated alone and sent money home to their families, traveling back to Yemen periodically to visit.

With the elimination of the quota system for immigration in 1965, Yemenis could more easily enter the United States and obtain work visas, leading to a great increase in the number of Yemeni immigrants. By the mid-1970s, more than 5,000 Yemeni Americans had found work as migrant farmers in California's San Joaquin Valley. The Yemeni American population in that region, however, began to dwindle in the 1990s as many of the original Yemeni settlers retired after saving money and moving back to Yemen. Many of their children left the valley to find work elsewhere in the United States. By 2010 there were only about 400 Yemeni Americans still residing in the valley. Some of those who stayed opened small businesses, such as restaurants and convenience stores.

During the 1990s Yemeni immigrants continued to settle in Buffalo and Dearborn, where they were able to find factory work. In 1991 the First Gulf War brought insecurity to Yemen, and many Yemeni immigrants in the United States were uncomfortable about having left their families behind. Airfares also increased, making return visits to Yemen more expensive. For many Yemeni men seeking work in the United States, it made more financial sense to bring their families with them.

According to Abdulhakem Alsadah, a licensed social worker in the Yemeni American community in Dearborn, Michigan, and the president of the National Association of Yemeni Americans (NAYA), in the late twentieth century there was an increase in the number of schools in Yemen, and consequently Yemeni immigrants in the twenty-first century have tended to be better educated than previous generations. In the past Yemeni immigrants were often illiterate and found work in assembly-line jobs. Many immigrants now arrive in the United States with high school and college degrees and expect a greater degree of social mobility than past generations, seeking careers as teachers, doctors, lawyers, pharmacists, and engineers.

LANGUAGE

The official language of Yemen is Arabic, and the vast majority of Yemeni Americans speak Arabic as well as English. Arabic dialects common among Yemenis and Yemeni Americans include the Sanaani or Northern Yemeni dialect (spoken by roughly 30 percent of the people in Yemen); the Ta'izzi-Adeni or Southern Yemeni dialect (about 27 percent); the Hadramidialect (about 1 percent); and the Mehri dialect (about 0.2 percent).

Second and third generation Yemeni Americans tend to speak Arabic with their parents and grandparents. In addition to learning Arabic in their homes, the children of Yemeni immigrants often study Arabic on weekends at a local mosque, where the language is frequently taught in religion classes. Younger generations are less likely to write in Arabic. If the first settlers in the family were literate in Arabic, then their children are more likely to read and write in the language.

RELIGION

Most Yemeni Americans are Muslim, and the majority of first generation immigrants adhere to the mandates of their faith. In the traditional practice of Islam, the observance of daily rituals is required, especially the practice of praying at five set times each day. The first prayer takes place at dawn. If there is a local mosque, men attend this prayer there, while women pray at home. The midday prayer takes place when the sun has reached its highest point in the sky. After this prayer, people eat their midday meals. The remaining set times for prayer are in the afternoon, at sunset, and in the evening when the sky has become completely dark.

Yemeni Americans tend to be among the most devout immigrants from the Arabic world, and they generally make every effort to follow these prayer rituals. In many work situations in the United States, however, the rituals cannot be followed. For example, many factory managers do not allow Yemeni workers to leave their posts during work shifts to pray. Likewise, Yemeni American students typically attend public schools, where they are often not given the opportunity to leave class to pray. Yemeni American Muslims are likely to observe their religion's prohibitions of alcohol and drug use and its emphasis on dressing modestly, whether in traditional or Western clothing.

Like most Muslims, Yemeni Americans observe Ramadan, the ninth month of the Islam calendar, by redirecting their hearts to God through self-control, sacrifice, and more vigilant observance of the rules of Islam, including the call to be kindhearted and charitable to the unfortunate. Ramadan is the most important holiday in Islam and lasts twenty-nine to thirty days. From dawn to dusk each day during this period, Muslims fast and abstain from other practices such as smoking and sex. During the fast, neither food nor water may be consumed. Many Yemeni American teenagers take pride in meeting the challenges of the fast. Though they are not obligated to do so, many younger children also try to fast. Each day at sundown during Ramadan, Muslims share a large meal at which family members celebrate having completed the day's fast and renew their vow to fast the following day. For Yemeni Americans, as with other Muslims, these meals can be festive. Extended families may get together, or neighbors may come over.

Ramadan ends with a holiday known as Eid al-Fitr, a three-day festival that marks the start of Shawwal, the tenth month in the Islam calendar. Yemeni Americans observe this holiday in the same way that most transplanted Muslims do, by coming together as a community for prayer and a large feast on the first day of the festival. In Muslim countries, schools and other institutions are closed for the duration of the festival. Although there is no general observance of Eid al-Fitr in the United States, most Yemeni Americans do not go to school or work on the first day of the festival.

Yemeni Americans also observe Eid al-Adha, or the Festival of Sacrifice, in the same way that most Muslims do. Eid al-Adha is a three-day festival held during the second week of Dhul Hijjah, the last month in the Islamic calendar. This holiday commemorates the Prophet Abraham's willingness to sacrifice everything for God, including the life of his son. On the last day of the festival, to celebrate God's sparing Abraham's son, Muslims slaughter a lamb or goat and distribute its meat among family, friends, and the needy. Eid al-Adha takes place after the Hajj, or traditional Muslim pilgrimage to the holy city of Mecca in Saudi Arabia.

Because of the cost of travel, the challenges of building a new life in the United States, and the obligation to visit family in Yemen, it is generally difficult for Yemeni Americans to make the pilgrimage to Mecca. However, in the early twenty-first century, increasing numbers of older Yemeni Americans have made the journey. In addition, younger and middle-aged Yemeni Americans who have professional jobs are likely to make the pilgrimage.

CULTURE AND ASSIMILATION

Yemeni immigrants have traditionally demonstrated a strong resistance to assimilation, tending to marry and live within the Yemeni community. In states such as Michigan, New York, and California, Yemeni cultural activities tend to take place at the mosque, where members of the community not only gather in prayer but also get together for social activities, such as traditional concerts or dances. Nevertheless, even as they try to maintain their cultural heritage, many Yemeni immigrants adopt some of the customs and attitudes of their new homes. This works in complex ways to modify the immigrants' identities in the host country and in Yemen. For example, older Yemeni immigrants who have been successful at work tend to seek the material goods that many other Americans seek, such as a nice house and an impressive car. Yemeni American teenagers listen to popular American music and participate in the athletic activities common to other American students, including track and field, baseball, football, and soccer.

Regardless of income level, Yemeni immigrants tend to maintain close ties to their homeland. Most try to make at least one visit back to their native village, often bringing with them items from their host culture. Those who acquire significant wealth commonly use their money to build an extended-family house in Yemen. The design of these structures is typically based on American architectural styles. Whether old or young, Yemeni immigrants acquire great status in their home villages and are often revered when

YEMENI PROVERBS

La budd min Sana'a wa lau taal al-safr.

(You must visit Sana'a, however long the journey takes.)

ratl hakya tafham wiqya.

(From a pound of talk one gets but an ounce of understanding.)

Ya gharib kun adib.

(A foreigner should be well behaved.)

Jaarak al-qarib wa la akhuk al-ba'id.

(Look to your neighbor who is near you rather than to your distant brother.)

Kun namla wa takul sukr.

(Work like an ant and you'll eat sugar.)

Man maat al-yaum salim min dhanb bukra.

(He who dies today is safe from tomorrow's sin.)

Yaddi fi fumuh wa yadduh fi 'aini.

(My fist is in his mouth, but his fist is in my eye, meaning "six of one, half a dozen of the other".)

La sadiq illa fi waqt al-dhiq.

(A friend in time of need is a friend indeed.)

Qird fi 'ain ummuh ghazaal.

(A monkey in its mother's eye is like a gazelle, meaning love is blind.)

Lau kan al-kalaam min fidha fa al-samt min dhahab.

(If speech is of silver, then silence is golden.)

Ma ghaab 'an al-nadhr ghaab 'an al-khaatir.

(Out of sight, out of mind.)

Idha sahibak 'asl la talhusuh kulluh.

(If you have honey, don't lick the pot clean.)

Tal'ab bi hanash wa taquluh dudah.

(You play with a snake and call it a worm.)

they return. Young adults returning to Yemen with an American education typically get the best jobs. Returning retirees are frequently among the richest people in their villages.

Traditions and Customs Yemeni culture, as reflected in its traditions and customs, is a rich mixture

LAMB SOUP

Ingredients

1 pound lean lamb cut into 1–2 cm pieces (keep some bones from the meat to add flavor if available).

1 onion, finely chopped

2 ripe tomatoes, chopped

1–2 tablespoons of tomato paste

1 teaspoon salt

1 teaspoon garam masala

½ teaspoon red pepper

¼ teaspoon black pepper

pinch of ground cinnamon

1½ cups orzo

1 cup fresh cilantro, chopped

1 teaspoon dried ground mint leaves

Preparation

In a saucepan fry the onion until soft then add the meat and continue to fry until brown. Add the spices, salt, tomatoes, tomato paste and plenty of water to cover (about 6½ cups). Cover and simmer for 1 hour. Add the orzo and cilantro. Add more water if necessary and stir. Continue to simmer until the pasta is cooked. Just before serving, add the dried mint.

Serve with lemon wedges, for squeezing into soup, and fresh bread.

of Islamic influences and more ancient traditions and practices. Most Yemeni Americans are aware of and take great pride in the long history of their people. They are also proud of the beauty of the landscape of Yemen and of their great achievements in architecture and construction, and images of sites in Yemen often decorate the walls of gathering places and homes in the United States. In addition to their traditional skill as builders, Yemeni Americans can point to a reputation for fine craftsmanship that has endured for thousands of years.

A Yemeni custom practiced by Yemeni Americans in various social situations is the chewing of *qat*. *Qat* is a seedless plant that grows up to 20 feet high and does best between 3,000 and 6,000 feet above sea level. Its leaves are harvested throughout the year in Yemen and neighboring countries. *Qat*, which is chewed like tobacco, is said to have a stimulant and euphoric effect. Although *qat* was banned in the United States in 1993, Yemeni Americans still use it, and for some in the community, celebrations are thought to be incomplete without it. Various adverse effects of long-term use, however, including depression and damage to teeth and liver, have deterred widespread use of *qat* among younger generations of Yemeni Americans.

Cuisine The national dish of Yemen, widely cooked in the United States, is *salta*, a heavily spiced chicken or lamb stew served with lentils, beans, chickpeas, fenugreek, and coriander, all on a bed of rice. Another dish is *shurba*, a more soup like stew made with lentils, fenugreek, or lamb. There are many kinds of bread, of which the most popular made at home is *khubz tawwa*. In addition, *lahuh*, a pancake-like bread made from sorghum, is eaten on special occasions. *Bint al sahn* is a sweet bread dipped in honey and clarified butter.

Yemeni Americans usually consider lunch the main meal of the day. While at home many Yemeni Americans eat the traditional way—without utensils and using bread to scoop up the food. Common midday meals include *ahseed*, a doughy mixture of flour and salt water that is dipped into a sour broth, and *holba*, which consists of ground fenugreek seeds that are soaked in water and then mixed with a rich soup. Yemeni Americans are also partial to lamb and fish, which they eat heavily spiced with a side dish of rice. The most popular sweet is *binta saheen*, a fluffy, layered bread dish with melted butter between each layer and honey spread across the top.

Clothing Yemeni people, regardless of where they live, are known for their love of beautiful fabrics. Yemen was once esteemed for its production of textiles and for the importation of high-quality, colorful textiles from around the world. In the twentieth century textile production in Yemen decreased substantially, though Yemeni merchants continued to import high-quality products from Kashmir. Traditionally only the wealthy could afford these fine fabrics, and garments made from them long served as markers of class and money. Less wealthy Yemenis bought textiles imported from Malaysia and Indonesia. Many Yemeni Americans continue to wear traditional clothing around the house and at special secular and religious gatherings. Yemeni Americans, however, typically earn wages that permit them to buy materials that resemble, and often surpass, what is reserved for the upper classes in Yemen.

For men of the highlands in Yemen, the most distinctive and important article worn was the *djambia*, a curved dagger. Different forms of these daggers were used to distinguish classes, and each class was forbidden to wear the wrong dagger. The traditional garment of men from the Tihama area of Yemen is an embroidered skirt, or *futah*, which is wrapped around the hips and fastened with a belt. In the highlands a shorter, calf-length skirt was worn with a jacket, belt, and dagger.

The traditional clothing of Yemeni women varied a great deal. Brightly colored cotton dresses with very wide long sleeves, including brass and silver adornment, were commonly worn in different areas. Some women wear an outfit, popularized in Yemen in the twentieth century, that consists of a pleated black skirt, veil, and head covering known as the *sharshaf*. Others wear the *abaya*, a loose black coat that covers head to foot. It comes in different fabrics and styles, which denote status. Some women use georgette, a less expensive crepe fabric, while wealthier women tend to wear coverings made from chiffon. Coverings may also be modestly embroidered.

Second and third generation Yemeni Americans tend to dress conservatively whether wearing traditional or Western style clothes. Women are more likely than men to wear traditional dress. Although it is not required, many Yemeni American women wear a veil and cover themselves from head to toe. Very few adorn themselves with jewelry. If they do wear Western clothes, Yemeni American women tend not to wear tight-fitting jeans or immodest tops. Tattoos are not common among Yemeni American men or women.

Dances and Songs The position of Yemen as a vital crossroads between the Indian Ocean and the Red Sea led to a great variety in musical expression. Like much of Yemeni culture, the music is often distinct from that of its neighboring Arab lands. Local accents, rhythms, modes of speech, and poetic forms figure strongly in the distinctive styles of Yemeni music and song. Traditional music from Yemen commonly consists of small-scale performances of an accompanied voice with a strongly poetic text. A range of instruments are used in the accompaniment, including the *'ud* (or oud), a plucked string instrument common throughout the Middle East and North Africa, and percussion instruments. In Yemen, as well as among Yemeni Americans, different poetic and musical forms are used depending on the context; both *razfah* (in which dancers have swords) and *balah* are performed at wedding celebrations.

Holidays In addition to traditional Muslim holidays such as Ramadan, Eid al-Fitr, and Eid al-Adha, Yemeni Americans sometimes observe major state holidays of Yemen. The most important is the Yemeni Day of National Unity (often referred to as Unity Day), which commemorates the unification of North and South Yemen on May 22, 1990. In Dearborn, Michigan, community leaders typically celebrate this holiday by renting a hall or some other large space and inviting local, state, or national politicians to address a large gathering of the Yemeni American community. For the Yemeni Americans who attend, the Yemeni Day of National Unity is a time to celebrate pride both in their native land and in the United States. In other areas of the country, Yemeni Americans often share a traditional meal with family and with friends who have migrated from the same village in Yemen.

On September 26, some Yemeni Americans celebrate Revolution Day. This holiday honors the liberation of North Yemen from the Yahya dynasty and the formation of the Yemen Arab Republic in 1962. Some Yemeni Americans also celebrate National Day, October 14, which marks the 1963 revolt in South Yemen against the British. The British were eventually expelled from Yemen on November 30, 1967, an official holiday in Yemen known as Independence Day. In Dearborn, festivities for Revolution Day and National Day are considerably more subdued than the observance of the Yemeni Day of National Unity and might consist of a meal with a few guests or a small local gathering with a speaker and some food. In other areas of the United States, these state holidays pass with little to no fanfare. Although Independence Day, on November 30, is important in Yemen, very few Yemeni Americans observe the holiday.

FAMILY AND COMMUNITY LIFE

Traditionally young Yemeni men have immigrated alone to the United States, leaving their wives and children in Yemen and sending money home from their jobs in the United States. The money was often used to purchase land in Yemen for a family homestead. In the United States these immigrants have typically lived in inner-city apartments or houses with several other men in the same situation. In the twenty-first century, whether as single men or in families, a great many Yemeni immigrants still live in communities with large Arab populations and frequent places where Yemenis congregate. In areas with large Arab populations, access to newspapers, magazines, books, and other media in Arabic help maintain a sense of community and common interest. Mosques are an important part of family and community life for many Yemeni Americans.

Education In the past, many first generation immigrants who attended school struggled with their studies because they had difficulty learning English. Those who persevered through elementary and high school tended to excel in college. Most first generation immigrants who arrived in the United States before 1990, however, did not complete their education and instead were employed as laborers in farm and factory work. These immigrants tended to encourage their children to study, and thus many second and third generation Yemeni Americans have found professional jobs.

Knowledge of the Quran and other sacred literature is highly respected in the community, as is higher education. Since the 1990s a growing number of Yemenis have come to the United States to pursue college and graduate degrees.

Courtship and Weddings Although there are only a small number of traditional Muslim weddings in the Yemeni American community, those that do take place are impressive social events. In such marriages, the match between a bride and bridegroom is still arranged by their respective parents. Typically, the family of a man who is considering marriage

A Yemen emigre cooks for customers at the Yemen Cafe in Hamtramck, Michigan, 2011. SCOTT OLSON / GETTY IMAGES

evaluates potential candidates for him to marry and help him determine the right one. The future groom and his father then pay a visit to the potential bride's family to discuss the matter, and the potential bride traditionally serves tea to the visitors. After the father of the man asks the father of the bride-to-be if he agrees to the union, it is the custom for the father of the woman to ask for time to discuss it with his wife, daughter, and other family members. If the father of the woman agrees the marriage, a ceremony of betrothal is held in which the groom and his father present an engagement ring to the father of the bride along with a gift of clothes for the bride and her mother. A bride price, which is paid by the father of the groom, is decided upon. Customarily, the greatest share of the bride price is spent purchasing jewelry and clothing for the bride.

The wedding traditionally lasts for at least three days. In the presence of a scholar of Islamic law called a *qadi*, papers of marriage are signed. As part of the ceremony it is the custom for the groom to ask his future father-in-law, "Will you give me your daughter in marriage?" The father of the bride answers, "Yes, I will give you my daughter to be your wife." The *qadi* then asks the father of the bride if his daughter agrees to the arranged marriage. After answering that she agrees, the bride's father clasps right hands with the groom. The *qadi* lays a white cloth over their hands and recites the first sura of the Quran, known as the *fatiha*. The celebration of the marriage is then inaugurated by the groom's father, who throws a handful of raisins onto the carpet. The

raisins are thought to be signs of a happy future for the newlyweds, and the guests try to pick up as many of them as possible.

The most important and public part of the wedding celebrations takes place on the Friday following the marriage ceremony. After going to midday prayers in a group, the men march through the street with the groom, who carries a golden sword. The women gather at the house of the bride, where decorative patterns are painted on her hands and feet with henna dye. When the sun sets and evening prayers have ended, the men take to the street for a procession called the *zaffa*. They slowly approach the house of the groom, all the while singing. The bride arrives accompanied by her father and other male relatives, and when she enters the house she officially becomes a member of her new husband's family.

Gender Roles For decades, gender roles in Yemeni American communities followed traditional patterns, with men working in factories or fields and women tending to domestic chores and raising children. Yemeni boys in the San Joaquin Valley often began working in the fields in their early teens and, in cities such as Dearborn and Buffalo, they typically began factory work in their late teens. Meanwhile, in addition to learning how to manage the home, Yemeni American girls were encouraged to study and were often asked to tutor younger siblings. Yemeni American girls tended to develop good study habits and to perform well in school. Through the 1990s and early 2000s they entered the professional work force, often in the fields of teaching or pharmaceutics, in increased numbers.

The role of women in the Yemeni American community is complex—in part because almost 70 percent of Yemeni Americans are men—and varies according to age, social class, and occupation. The practice of wearing a veil depends on what part of Yemen a woman comes from. A woman's educational level has a strong influence on how she relates to older women, who are often less educated. Traditionally, in addition to homemaking, women have taken part in farming activities and have assisted with small business ventures, such as convenience stores and restaurants. Second and third generation Yemeni women are more likely to have professional jobs and often find work as nurses and teachers.

Conflicts between economic necessity and tradition have commonly arisen for Yemeni American women. In more traditional Yemeni American families, difficulty speaking English, as well as customs restricting the roles of women in public, have led to a cloistered, isolated life for women. Such conflicts, however, are less common among second and third generation Yemeni American women and those women who arrived in the 1990s and 2000s, who have been encouraged to attend college and seek jobs.

EMPLOYMENT AND ECONOMIC CONDITIONS

Beginning in the second half of the twentieth century, many Yemeni Americans worked as factory workers in industries such as automobile manufacturing. Later, farm work became an occupation for many. In the twenty-first century Yemeni Americans held a wide variety of occupations, from small local merchants to university professors. After the economic crisis that began in the United States in 2007, many Yemeni Americans working in the auto industry were laid off.

Yemeni Americans have a reputation for being exceptionally hard workers. In the early 1900s Henry Ford wrote a letter to the British Counsel in South Yemen asking him to find 200 to 300 Yemeni men interested in working in his factory in the United States. In the note Ford said that Yemeni workers were the "most honest, decent, and hardworking" people he employed. The letter is on display at the Henry Ford Museum in Dearborn, Michigan. Yemeni workers in the San Joaquin Valley earned a similar reputation; in the 1970s many of the younger Yemeni workers there would get up at 4:30 in the morning to work in the fields before attending class at the local high school. The second and third generation Yemeni Americans who have remained in the valley tend to run successful small businesses. Many attribute their success to the discipline they acquired watching their fathers work in the fields.

POLITICS AND GOVERNMENT

Yemeni Americans vote in large numbers, but their participation in the American political system is otherwise limited, partially because of the expense of entering political life. Yemeni Americans have tended to vote for Democratic candidates at both the local and national level, although since 2000 Yemeni Americans have become more religious and more conservative.

In South Dearborn, Michigan, Arab Americans (mostly Yemeni) line up to vote for the next U.S. President at Salina Intermediate School in 2004. FARAH NOSH / GETTY IMAGES

One of the most influential Yemeni American political groups is the Yemeni American Political Action Committee, the political arm of its parent organization, the Yemeni American Public Affairs Council (YAPAC), based in Dearborn, Michigan. The group's website (www.yapac.org) states that its mission is to "educate, integrate, and advocate on behalf of the general public and specifically those of Yemeni American heritage" by "shaping public policy and opinion through engagement of decision makers in government, institution, media, and public at large."

NOTABLE INDIVIDUALS

Academia Nasser Zawia became a professor of pharmacology and toxicology at the University of Rhode Island, Kingston, in 1999 and previously taught at Meharry Medical College in Nashville, Tennessee. He has been on the editorial boards of several journals, including *Neurotoxicology* and *Journal of Environmental Protection Science*. Zawia's primary research focus has been on the adverse effects of environmental agents on the development of the brain. Zawia also worked as a staff fellow at the National Institute for Environmental Health Sciences (NIEHS/NIH). Known for his work on heavy metals and developmental gene expression, Zawia has written extensively in the field of toxicology and is widely published in both national and international journals.

Literature The poet Ali Mohammed Luqman was born in Aden, Yemen, in 1918. He began to write poetry while still in his teens. In 1936 he went to India, where he attended al-Ghira Muslim University. Afterward he attended the American University of Cairo, earning a bachelor's degree in journalism in 1947. Returning to Aden, Luqman became the editor of his father's newspaper, *Fatat al-Jezira*. In 1943 he published his first collection of poetry, titled *Overwhelmed Melody*. Luqman is noted for being the first poet to introduce Arabic poetic plays in the region of Aden. Because of political turmoil in Yemen, he eventually moved to the United States, where he died in December 1979.

Medicine and Science Rashid A. Abdu graduated from the George Washington University School of Medicine and Health Sciences in 1960 and later became a surgeon at St. Elizabeth Medical Center in Youngstown, Ohio. He made several trips to Yemen, where he conducted clinics to improve the quality of medical education and broaden the access to medical care. In 2005 Abdu published a memoir titled *Journey of a Yemeni Boy*, which chronicles his experiences in the United States and Yemen.

MEDIA

Online newspapers published for the Arab American community and of interest to Yemeni Americans include the following. More information and URLs can be found on the media website for Yemen at www.al-bab.com/yemen/media/med.htm.

Yemen Observer

English-language newspaper based in Yemen and published triweekly. Faris Sanabani established the paper in 1996 and has since expanded publication to include five other periodicals that appear in Arabic and English.

URL: www.yobserver.com

Yemen Times

Published weekly on Mondays (in English). Established in 1991, it has become highly influential. In 1995 the paper and its editor/publisher, Professor Abd al-Aziz al-Saqqaf, won the National Press Club's International Award for Freedom of the Press.

URL: www.yementimes.com

ORGANIZATIONS AND ASSOCIATIONS

American Association of Yemeni Scientists and Professionals

Founded in 2004, the association serves Yemenis across the globe by promoting higher education and creating a network where Yemeni students can find mentors, obtain academic support, and receive professional advice that helps them choose careers, prepare for their jobs, and succeed in the workplace. Has chapters in Providence (Rhode Island), Washington, D.C., San Francisco, New York, and Detroit.

P.O. Box 1566
Kingston, Rhode Island 02881
Phone: (401) 874-5909
Email: info@aaysp.org
URL: www.aaysp.org

National Association of Yemeni Americans

Founded in 2000 in Dearborn, Michigan, to improve the quality of life for Yemeni Americans. Provides a number of programs and services, including translation, assistance with work and school applications, voter registration, advice on starting small businesses, and substance abuse prevention.

Ahmed Alammari
2770 Salina Street
Dearborn, Michigan 48120
10415 Dix Avenue
Dearborn, Michigan 48120
Phone: (313) 842-8402
Fax: (313) 842-3135
URL: www.mynaya.org

Yemen American Cultural Center

Phone: (313) 841-3395
Fax: (313) 841-3395 or (313) 843-8973

Yemeni American Public Affairs Council

Sponsors lectures and conducts programs that help Yemeni Americans assimilate into mainstream American life and advances Yemeni American interests in local, state, and national politics.

10500 Dix Avenue #102
Dearborn, Michigan 48120
Phone: (313) 841-3395
Fax: (313) 841-3395 or (313) 843-8973
Email: info@yapac.org
URL: www.yapac.org

MUSEUMS AND RESEARCH CENTERS

Arab American National Museum

Documents the history of all Arab American immigrant communities.

Anan Ameri
13624 Michigan Avenue
Dearborn, Michigan 48126
Phone: (313) 624-0200
Email: ameri@accesscommunity.org
URL: www.arabamericanmuseum.org

American Institute for Yemeni Studies

Promotes scholarly research on Yemen and fosters ties between Yemeni and American academic communities. Maintains a lecture series in Sanaa, the capital of Yemen, and provides funding for fellowships.

Michael Carroll
Institute for the Study of Muslim Society and Civilizations
Boston University
232 Bay State Road, Room 426
Boston, Massachusetts 02215
Phone: (617) 358-4649

Fax: (617) 358-4650
Email: mcarroll@bu.edu
URL: www.aiys.org

SOURCES FOR ADDITIONAL STUDY

Abdu, Rashid A. *Journey of a Yemeni Boy*. Pittsburgh: Dorrance Publishing, 2005.

Abraham, Nabeel, Sally Howell, & Andrew Shryock, eds. *Arab Detroit 9/11: Life in the Terror Decade*. Detroit: Wayne State University Press, 2011.

Abraham, Nabeel & Andrew Shryock, eds. *Arab Detroit: From Margin to Mainstream*. Detroit: Great Lakes Books, 2000.

Colburn, Marta. *From the Queen of Sheba to the Republic of Yemen: K-12 Resource Guide and Classroom Ideas*. Ardmore, PA: American Institute of Yemeni Studies, 2006.

Friedlander, Jonathan, ed. *Sojourners and Settlers: The Yemeni Immigrant Experience*. Salt Lake City: University of Utah Press, 1988.

Haiek, Joseph R., ed. *Arab American Almanac*. 3rd edition. Glendale, CA: The News Circle Group Publishing Co., 1984.

Sarroub, Loukia K. *All American Yemeni Girls: Being Muslim in a Public School*. Philadelphia: University of Pennsylvania Press, 2005.

Staub, Shalom. *Yemenis in New York City: The Folklore of Ethnicity*. Philadelphia: Balch Institute Press, 1989.

"The Yemeni Immigrant Community in Detroit: Background, Emigration, and Community Life." In *Arabs in the New World*, ed. Sameer Y. Abraham and Nabeel Abraham. Detroit: Wayne State University Press, 1983.

YUPIK

Oscar Kawagley

OVERVIEW

The Yupik are an indigenous people who have traditionally lived in the southwest and south-central regions of Alaska as well as along the eastern edge of Siberia. The bulk of the population that resides in Alaska lives along the floodplain of the Yukon and the Kuskokwim Rivers. Their villages are located along the Bering Sea and Bristol Bay coasts as well as the delta of the two rivers. The name *Yupik* (plural *Yupiit*) derives from the word *yuk*, which means "person," and *pik*, which means "real." Hence, the Yupik refer to themselves as the real people. Additionally, when the word is divided with an apostrophe, as in *Yup'ik*, it refers specifically to the Yup'ik people of Central Alaska. Without an apostrophe, the term *Yupik* encompasses all the Yupik people in general, including those inhabiting eastern Siberia.

According to the Alaska Native Heritage Center, the Yup'ik population was approximately 16,500 people before first contact with European Americans in the early 1800s. Primarily a hunting people, the Yup'ik were highly mobile, following the migratory patterns of game, fish, and plants. Significant amounts of their travel were done by skin boats through the marshy waterways that make up the river deltas in the region. The Yup'ik economy was largely subsistence-based. In a region that could experience temperature extremes of negative 80 degrees Fahrenheit in the winter and 90 degrees Fahrenheit in the summer, daily life focused almost exclusively on survival.

The Yup'ik people, like other Alaska Natives, do not reside on reservations. For the most part, they occupy their traditional hunting and fishing lands along the western coast of Alaska and along the floodplains of the Yukon and Kuskokwim Rivers. The Yup'ik live in seventy or so villages, which typically have between 150 and 800 residents. Many others have settled in the larger cities of Bethel and Dillingham. While the Yup'ik people's lands are rich in flora and fauna, they do not contain a great deal of commercial resources. This enabled them to continue their traditional lifestyles relatively undisturbed for much longer than native peoples who occupied more commercially viable lands.

According to the U.S. Census Bureau, in 2010 there were nearly 29,000 Yup'ik living in the United States, which is approximately the number of participants in the annual Marine Corps Marathon in Washington, D.C. They are the most populous Native Alaskan tribe. While some Yup'ik have moved to the larger metropolitan areas of Alaska and a few have even ventured into the lower forty-eight states, the vast majority of Yupik people still occupy their traditional lands in Alaska, primarily in communities that border waterways. Small numbers of Yup'ik also reside in California, Oregon, and Washington.

HISTORY OF THE PEOPLE

Early History The earliest settlers in Alaska crossed the Bering land bridge and took up residence in modern-day Alaska approximately 12,000 years ago. Archeologists believe it was peoples associated with the Norton culture, which emerged 2,500 years ago, who first set up permanent residence in western Alaska. They were known to occupy permanent houses and maintained largely non-migratory lifestyles. Their subsistence was based on harvesting available flora and fauna, and they relied primarily on caribou, salmon, and sea mammals.

Approximately 1,000 years ago, the Norton peoples of western Alaska were displaced by the Thule peoples, who had superior tool-making abilities, which included the use of kayaks and umiaks (a boat similar to a kayak), ceramics, and superior housing structures. Archaeologists do not agree about whether this displacement was a process of peaceful dispersion or a violent invasion. However, it is known that interregional skirmishes were fairly common at that time. Once situated in Western Alaska, the Thule established an exclusively maritime-based economy in the region. In a research paper on the Yup'ik, Ahnie Litecky notes, "the Thule tradition formed the basis of Yup'ik culture on the eve of foreign contact" ("The Dwellers Between: Yup'ik Shamans and Cultural Change in Western Alaska," 2011).

According to Yupik creation mythology, the first Man was born from a pea pod, which had been created by a mythical Raven. The Raven then set about teaching Man how to survive in the harsh climate, creating other creatures on which Man could subsist. In the traditional Yupik belief system, Raven was seen as an essential provider of life and sustenance.

Modern Era While the Yupik's traditional homelands are rich in sustenance-providing resources, the land does not contain abundant commercial resources. For this reason, the Yupik did not have to contend with European American visitors until much later than some of their Native Alaskan counterparts. The first arrivals were Russian fur traders during the early 1800s who sought trade opportunities and generally promoted peaceful interactions. As trade in the region grew, the Yupik fell prey to a number of diseases, including smallpox, measles, tuberculosis, and influenza, which were brought in by Western encroachment. There were two particularly severe influenza outbreaks, in 1852–1853 and again in 1861. It is estimated that by 1858, nearly 60 percent of the Yupik population had died from communicable diseases. Mortality issues aside, the early visitors did not greatly attempt to alter the Yupik's daily lives, leaving them free to continue their seasonal pursuit of food and game.

Russian Orthodox missionaries arrived in around 1845 and set about converting the Yupik people. A Moravian mission was established in the town of Bethel in 1885. Jesuit missionaries founded a mission on Nelson Island in 1888. These visitors set about the task of "civilizing" the Yupik, encouraging them to abandon their traditional lifestyles. These efforts caused tension, both among the Yupik themselves and between the Yupik and the missionaries. As industries pushed more boldly into the Alaska region, the Yupik supplied fish and lumber to miners and steamship captains.

By 1916 it was reported that some Yupik along the Kuskokwim River had been convinced to live in log cabins, eat cultivated produce, and wear Western clothing. Many Yupik received education, health care, and Christian teaching from federal employees and missionaries living in the region. These efforts often came at the expense of the Yupik's native culture. By the second half of the twentieth century, improved access to health care and a reduction in infant mortality had enabled the Yupik population to rebound, exceeding their aboriginal numbers.

From the 1950s onward, federal efforts were periodically undertaken to lessen the cycle of poverty endemic to many Native Alaskan peoples, with mixed success. In 1971, with the passage of the Alaska Native Claims Settlement Act (ANCSA), the Yupik and other Alaskan tribes received monetary compensation for relinquishing their historic land claims. The ANCSA established twelve for-profit corporations to administer land and money on behalf of the tribes. While many feared that passage of the act would expedite the Americanization of Alaska's Native peoples, many have noted that, since its passage, the ANCSA has helped to fuel the search for a cultural identity for the Native people of Alaska.

SETTLEMENT IN THE UNITED STATES

The Yupik people have traditionally lived in the southwestern area of Alaska, on and around the floodplain of the Yukon and Kuskokwim Rivers, with nearly seventy villages along the Bering Sea and Bristol Bay coasts. The Yupik traditionally led seminomadic lives, moving from village to village in pursuit of plants and game.

Today, the majority of Yupik people still reside in southwest Alaska, though many have moved from their traditional small villages to the larger cities of Bethel and Dillingham. Small numbers of Yup'ik also reside in Washington, California, and Oregon.

Yupik villages typically have schools, medical clinics, government and community buildings, and airstrips. Most village homes have electricity, running water, and flush toilets. In the Yupik villages today, 90 percent of the economy is based on the public sector, whether from public aid or government jobs. Only 10 percent of the typical village economy is based on fishing, crafts, and private sector service. The Yupik economy has not experienced strong integration into the larger state economy. Most Yupik—by both tradition and necessity—engage in hunting and fishing to supplement their incomes.

LANGUAGE

The two main dialects of the Yupik language are Siberian Yupik (spoken on St. Lawrence Island) and Central Alaskan Yup'ik or Cup'ik (spoken in southwest Alaska). The Central Alaskan Yup'ik language is the strongest of any Alaska Native language today, with at least 10,000 speakers. Nevertheless, these dialects are becoming grammatically impoverished, and there has been much debate among the Yupik over whether their language should be taught at home or in school. As a result, English is becoming the dominant language. Some villages still prefer to speak primarily Yupik and regard English as a secondary language. Even these villages, however, are losing pieces of language. The younger generation communicates mainly in English. For the first time in the history of the Yupik people, a generation gap is steadily widening. The Yupik realize their world view is embedded in the language—that its webbing is ineluctably intertwined in the nuances, inflections, and subtleties of the words. Therefore many Yupik people wish the language to be revived, taught, and maintained by parents, village members, and the schools.

Greetings and Popular Expressions The following are examples of greetings and expressions in Central Yup'ik:

cama-i—hello (good to see you); *waqaa*—Hi! What's up?; *Cangacit?*—How are you?; *piura*—goodbye; *quyana*—thank you; *quyana tailuci*—you're welcome; and *Alussistuaqegcikici*—Merry Christmas.

These are examples of greetings and expressions in Siberian Yupik:

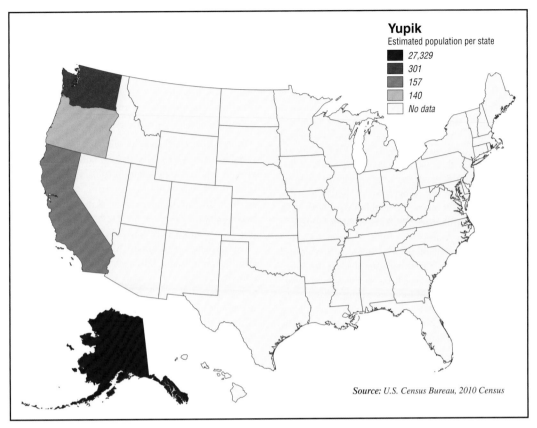

Yupik
Estimated population per state
- 27,329
- 301
- 157
- 140
- No data

Source: U.S. Census Bureau, 2010 Census

Natesiin?—How are you?; *esghaghlleqam-ken*—good-bye (I'll see you); *igamsiqanaghhalek*—thank you; *quyanaghhalek tagilusi*—welcome; and *Quyanaghhalek Kuusmemi*—Merry Christmas.

RELIGION

Today most Yupik are Christian. Traditionally, however, the Yupik believed in a *Ellam Yua* ("thlam yu-a"), a Spirit of the Universe. The most important figure, however, was the Raven, the creator of the world and human beings. The Raven had the powers of the spirits as well as the weaknesses of human beings. It provided many wonderful things for the Yupik, such as the sun, moon, and stars for light, and life for all the earth's inhabitants. But the Raven possessed human frailties such as greed, making mistakes, and hurting others and itself. It was the indomitable trickster, changing in form to a human or a plant.

The Yupik people traditionally believed that everything of the earth possessed a spirit—that is, consciousness. Such awareness meant that all things in nature, including animals and plants, were mindful of who they gave themselves to and how they were treated. A hunter who cared for and heeded taboos would be a successful provider, because the animals would give themselves to the hunter knowing that they would be well taken care of. Since the Yupik people believed that everything in nature has a spirit, some anthropologists described them as pantheistic.

This is not the case. Because animals and other things possessed spirits, they were honored and respected, but not worshipped. The purpose of this spirituality was to live in harmony with everything of the human, natural, and spiritual worlds.

Because the Yupik people had to kill living things in order to survive, they developed rituals and ceremonies to regain a sense of peace with the world and its creatures. This was their method of reciprocation to Mother Earth. Land is important to the Yupik people, for human beings and spirits occupy the same space. The land is described in action words: it is a process, ongoing and dynamic.

Shamans traditionally played a central part in Yupik life. They were often called upon to help fight or prevent illness. Some specialized in bone healing; others used herbs for curing diseases; and still others called upon spirits of animals, such as the bear and eagle, or spiritual beings for aid. The Yupik believed that animal spirits and spirit helpers lived on the moon. Powerful medicine people would experience out-of-body travel to the moon, the sea, the spiritual world, other villages, animal kingdoms, and other far-off places. They were citizens of two worlds—the earth and places where the spirits dwelled. They traveled readily and learned much from their experiences, which they conveyed to their village. Today the influence of the shamans has been replaced by Christian practices.

CULTURE AND ASSIMILATION

The Yupik people did not readily accept the missionaries' efforts to educate them according to Western principles. The resistance was led by shamans, village leaders, and elders. It was not superior knowledge, weapons, or methods of non-Natives that defeated the leaders, but the diseases that members of the dominant society brought with them. The Yupik people had no resistance to these new illnesses. The shamans, who treated ailments using spiritual methods, stood by helplessly while many of their people succumbed to these foreign diseases. Whole villages were wiped out, orphaning many children and young adults. It was during this time that the missionaries were able to establish their churches and orphanages, building schools to teach a different language and way of life. The cognitive and cultural imperialism of the dominant society forced the Yupik to conform to this system. Under the teachings of the missionary-teachers, the youngsters were faced with corporal punishment for using their mother tongue and practicing their traditional ways. Being told their language and ways were inferior mentally scarred many students. To this day, the Yupik people suffer many related psychosocial problems.

The goal of traditional Yupik education was to teach the youth to live in harmony in the human world, as well as the natural and spiritual worlds. It was their belief that everything in the universe (plants, animals, rivers, winds) had a spirit, which mandated respect. Everything possessing a spirit meant that everything had a consciousness or awareness and therefore must be accorded human respect. Such a way of life led the Yupik to possess only that which was absolutely necessary and taught them to enjoy to the utmost the little they had. The Yupik people have been bombarded by Western society's institutions for a little more than 100 years. These outside values and ways wreaked havoc upon their world view. Most Yupik are aware of who they are and where they came from, but the clash of Western and Yupik values and traditions has caused many Yupik people to suffer from a depression that is spiritual in nature.

Cuisine The Yupik region is rich with waterfowl, fish, and sea and land mammals. Salmon are a staple source of food and are caught in set nets. The nets are let out of a boat perpendicular to the river shoreline and allowed to drift downriver for approximately one-half mile. When the net is pulled in, fishers remove their catch. The fish are taken to the fish camp, where they are unloaded into holding boxes. The fish are beheaded and split by the women. The split fish are hung to dry. When the surface of the flesh begins to harden, they are moved to the smoke house, where they are smoked and preserved for winter use. Some of the fish are salted, frozen, or buried underground for later use. Today about half the Yupik people's food is supplied by subsistence activities; the other half is purchased from the commercial stores.

The tundra provides berries for making jams, jellies, and *akutaq*, a Yupik delicacy commonly called "Eskimo ice cream"—a concoction of vegetable shortening, berries, and sugar. Today there are many variations of this dessert. Yupik women have incorporated many new ingredients, such as raisins, strawberries, dried peaches, apples, and mashed potatoes, to create innovative and tasty mixtures.

Traditional Dress In the past, Yupik clothing was made from the pelts of such animals as Alaskan ground squirrels, muskrat, mink, land otter, wolf, beaver, red fox, caribou, wolverine, and moose, in addition to fish and waterfowl skins. Yupik women made parkas, pants, boots, and gloves from these skins. For special occasions, the women wore squirrel-skin parkas with many designs and tassels on them. A well-made parka showed that the owner had fine skills; if a woman with a beautiful parka was of marrying age, parents of young men assessed her as a possible wife for the son. Women sometimes tattooed their chins. Both men and women pierced their lips and noses and adorned them with stone or glass beads.

Holidays Traditionally, the Yupik observed five dominant ceremonies and several minor ceremonies throughout the year. The dominant ceremonies were *Nakaciuq* (Bladder Festival), *Elriq* (Festival of the Dead), *Kevgiq* or *Kivgiq* (Messenger Feast), *Petugtaq* (Asking Festival, in which people requested certain items), and *Kelek* (invitation). These were ceremonies of thanksgiving to the *Ellam Yua* (Spirit of the Universe) and Mother Earth. All Yupik rituals and ceremonies incorporated meditation on the integration of the human, natural, and spiritual worlds. Of the several original ceremonies, only the Messenger Feast is still observed. The celebration, which takes place in the spring, experienced a resurgence around 1990. None of the other traditional ceremonies are still practiced. One reason may be that few elders who remain remember the songs and dances. All traditional ceremonies required singing songs in a prescribed order, and making changes was taboo. Often ceremonies required very elaborate paraphernalia, such as masks, drums, clay lamps, food, and designated leaders with special costumes. Much time was spent in preparation for the performances. The rehearsals for traditional ceremonies were not to be observed by the villagers. The Yupik people today observe the Western holidays, into which they have begun to incorporate some of their traditional practices, including singing and dancing.

Health Care Issues and Practices Traditionally the Yupik were a healthy people in spite of occasional famines and diseases. Presently, the two biggest problems with the growing population are water and sewage. As a result of pollution, water from the rivers and lakes is no longer potable. Wells must be drilled and sewage lagoons built, but there are inherent problems with this approach. The land on which this must take place is marshy and presents difficulties for control. Federal and state agencies are constantly asked to grant more funding for these activities. However, the matter becomes more problematic each year. The solutions require expensive undertakings.

Suicide among young Yupik men is high. This is generally attributed to problems Native youth have with identity and finding a meaningful place in society. The Bethel and Dillingham region has a wide range of chronic health problems, including otitis media (ear infection), cancer, cardiovascular disease, diabetes, tooth and gum disease, obesity, and sexually transmitted diseases. The Yupik people are only now beginning to assume a role in stemming these maladies.

In many Yup'ik villages in Alaska, primary medical care is provided by community health aides. Such aides generally receive a rudimentary introduction to health practices, including diagnosis, medication, and emergency care from the Kuskokwim Community College in Bethel. As they advance, they receive more training. If health aides encounter a situation about which they know little, they call a physician in the Public Health Service Hospital in Bethel. Critical situations require the patient be transported to the hospital with one of the many local air services. If modern treatment and pharmaceuticals do not work, the practitioners may try traditional Yupik treatments. Often, the two treatments will work in concert to heal the patient.

FAMILY AND COMMUNITY LIFE

In the past, Yupik village life revolved around a structure known as a *qasgi*, which was where the men and boys over the age of five ate and slept. It was in the qasgi that the elder generation imparted instruction on hunting and how to read the signs of nature, which were necessary for the next generation to survive. In addition, the qasgi could be heated to high temperatures in order to perform sweat ceremonies. Extended families of nearly thirty persons made up the basic social unit of Yupik life.

Many Yupik family traditions are being lost due to the pressure to make money as well as to the appeal of mainstream American culture. As with the dominant society, divorce and one-parent families are on the rise among Yupik people. The number of single teenage mothers has increased. The nuclear family, which was once very important to Yupik people, is crumbling. Few Yupik youth know who the members of their extended family are, knowledge that was important for survival in the past.

Traditionally there was no dating among the Yupik people. Marriages were arranged by parents. Today many Yupik people date and fall in love. Only very traditional families arrange marriages. With new modes of transportation, such as three- and four-wheelers, snow machines, airplanes, and boats with powerful outboard motors, Yupik people can visit loved ones in distant villages.

In many Yupik villages in Alaska, primary medical care is provided by community health aides. Such aides generally receive a rudimentary introduction to health practices, including diagnosis, medication, and emergency care.

Gender Roles In times past, Yupik men and women had very distinct roles in the village. The men were providers, and the women were caregivers. Children were treasured by the parents, because they were insurance that the elders would be taken care of in later years. Fathers, grandfathers, and males of the extended family and community educated the boys. Mothers, grandmothers, and women of the extended family and community taught the girls. It was said that the community raised the children.

According to Yupik tradition, the father is the head of the family, but the mother's role as preparer of food is equally important. She tends to the plants and animals, giving proper care and observing taboos. In traditional Yupik culture, plant and animal foods are thought to have consciousness and an awareness of how the woman takes care of them. If pleased with the care, they give of themselves to the hunter again after reincarnation. Some of these beliefs are still observed by traditional families.

Education All Yup'ik village schools are publicly funded by the state of Alaska. Ancillary funds are received from the federal government, required by such laws as the Indian Education, Johnson-O'Malley, Title VII Bilingual, and the Migratory Education acts. A growing number of Yupik students have been dropping out of elementary and high schools because they do not see any value in the knowledge and skills taught there. The schools provide inferior schooling for Native youth. They often graduate without mastering either the Yupik language or English. They are usually very weak in mathematics and the sciences. Many do not pursue higher education, and most of those who do enroll in college ultimately drop out. Those few that do earn college degrees typically do not return to their villages, because their new knowledge and skills cannot fit into the community nor does a position exist.

Many Yup'ik students who have enrolled in the University of Alaska system have registered in education programs, giving them the opportunity to return to their home villages to teach. Nationwide, there have tended to be very few Native students enrolling in mathematics and science courses. That began to change, however, in 1995 when the

THE MOLLY HOOTCH CASE

In 1972 a sixteen-year-old Yupik girl named Molly Hootch was the lead plaintiff in a suit brought against the State of Alaska demanding that a school be built in her village of Emmonak so that she would not have to be sent away to a boarding school in order to continue her education. Native children of Alaska who came from small villages were often sent to Bureau of Indian Affairs schools in places as far away as Oregon and Oklahoma. When a settlement of the suit was reached, the State of Alaska was required to construct numerous schools in remote Alaskan villages, thus opening the door to a quality education for many native Alaskan children. These schools are often referred to as "Molly Hootch schools."

University of Alaska founded the Alaska Native Science and Engineering Program (ANSEP). The program, which begins with pre-college courses for high school students, is part of an effort to increase the number of students studying those subjects. It has been very successful, raising student retention rates to 70 percent—three times the national retention rate for Native students in science and engineering studies. Graduates of the program have gone on to find jobs in their chosen fields.

The Yupik elders, community members, parents, teachers' aides, teachers, and university professors have been pioneers in exploring mathematics and the sciences in Yupik thought. This effort attempts to use Yupik skills and ways of thinking as the basis for mathematics and sciences curricula. Yupik people have begun to realize they have knowledge that is not understood by the dominant society. Schooling has been based on the outside world with a concomitant feeling that what the Yupik know is of little importance. Today the Yupik are challenging this train of thought and have taken a keen interest in changing it. They are promoting education that focuses on their language, knowledge, and skills from elementary through high school. Making their community their laboratory will edify and strengthen the identity of the Yupik youth.

EMPLOYMENT AND ECONOMIC CONDITIONS

Well over 50 percent of Yupik villagers qualify for government assistance. Yupik unemployment is as high as 80 percent in some villages. Jobs are scarce, and the Alaska Native Commission claims that the few subsidized public service positions are generally occupied by transient or permanently settled non-Natives. The main industries in the Bethel and Dillingham regions are seasonal fisheries and government-funded jobs. These regions are not rich in natural resources. Some small pockets of gold,

platinum, and cinnabar exist. Profiting from such resources, however, conflicts with the Native concept of living in harmony with nature. Mining activities require that the surface of the environment be altered and make it unproductive for animal habitats, berries, and edible plants. Corporate leaders in the Yupik community are reluctant to invest in ventures that will alter the environment.

Because the Yupik women's role requires them to stay in the village, some have assumed leadership roles as village corporations' presidents. A growing number of Yupik women are taking on other jobs in the community. Many women have become bilingual teachers and counseling aides in the schools. Others work as community health aides and practitioners.

POLITICS AND GOVERNMENT

The Yupik people were governed by egalitarianism whereby each member of the village had the same rights and responsibilities. They had a traditional council composed of elders who held meetings to address problems and issues affecting the village. They chose a chief, a servant-leader who often was the best hunter-provider in the village. The chief and council would address a problem, striving for consensus to arrive at a solution. Sometimes there would be an issue that no one agreed upon. It would be tabled for the next meeting. If, at the succeeding meeting, there still was no agreement, the matter would be dropped. The chief was kept in power as long as he or she used common sense and did not become arrogant or try to make decisions on his or her own. The chief was strictly a servant of the people and was expected to uphold their will.

Several forms of governmental entities usually operate within the modern village, which is confusing to the local people as well as agents of other institutions. Villagers and agents wonder with which entity they are supposed to work. Each village has a traditional or Indian Reorganization Act (IRA) council, a municipal office funded by the state of Alaska, a health center funded by the federal government, and a village corporation. Each of these has a prescribed function within the village. The IRA or tribal council was established under the auspices of the federal government; the health center is under the Yukon-Kuskokwim Health Corporation funded by the federal Indian Health Service; and the village corporation, established under the Alaska Native Claims Settlement Act (ANCSA), has responsibilities for business ventures and village lands.

The Indian Self-Determination and Education Act (1975) has had the biggest impact on the Yupik villages. This law allows the Yupik villages to contract services operated by the federal government, including schools, social services, general assistance, child welfare, health services, and game management. Many of these services have been taken over by regional corporations or by organized clusters of villages. Funding for these activities is always a problem; the sources of funding are consistently looking for ways to cut programs.

The Yupik region belongs to the Alaskan Federation of Natives, Inc. (AFN), which is a statewide organization representing all Native regions. This organization functions year-round with one annual meeting of representatives from every region. The AFN tries to address all issues affecting the Alaskan Native people, presenting many resolutions to various government agencies and institutions. The Yupik people are always well represented. Being from a region where there are many elderly people who do not speak English, they have purchased communications technology that translates English to Yupik for the duration of the meeting. They are the only native group to use translators. This gives some indication of the importance of the AFN annual meeting to the Yupik people.

The majority of the Alaskan Native people belong to the Democratic Party, and the people of the Bethel and Dillingham regions vote heavily Democratic.

Military Service Since World War II, many Yupik men have joined the armed forces. Today many young Yupik men are members of the Army National Guard. Most villages have a guard unit. The headquarters of the 297th Infantry Battalion is in Bethel. It provides opportunities for income as well as training. A number of Yupik men have become officers.

NOTABLE INDIVIDUALS

Activism Caleb Pungowiyi (1942–2011) was a Siberian Yupik from Savoonga Village on St. Lawrence Island. He was the former president of the Inuit Circumpolar Conference and the Robert Aqqaluk Newlin Sr. Memorial Trust. Throughout his life, Pungowiyi worked to give a voice to his people in state, national, and world affairs. In addition, he served on the National Science Foundation Office of Polar Programs Advisory Committee, was the Marine Mammal Commission's Special Advisor on Native Affairs, and worked with the Steering Committee of the Alaska Native Science Foundation.

William Tyson (1916–1993) was born in Kanillik, a small Yupik village near Sheldon's Point located across Norton Sound from Nome. In 1977 Tyson was ordained a deacon in the Roman Catholic Church.

At the Alaskan Native Heritage Center in Anchorage, a Yupik dancer performs. DAVID SANGER PHOTOGRAPHY / ALAMY

He was an advocate for Natives statewide and fought for the Alaska Native Claims Act (which was passed into law in 1972) and tribal enrollment. He did not hesitate to voice his strong concerns about the survival of his people and the land on which they lived. He was a shareholder for Calista Regional Corporation. He and his wife, Marie, founded the Greatland Traditional Dancers in 1983 after learning that no such group existed for urban students in Anchorage. Reverend Tyson received many awards throughout his life. He was named Elder of the Year by the Alaska Federation of Natives and Parent of the Year by the Alaska Native Education Council, and the Johnson O'Malley Program named a scholarship after him.

Art Lucy Beaver (1899?–2012) was a renowned and revered Yup'ik skin sewer. She was viewed by many as an icon within the Yup'ik community, and the clothing she made—mukluks and parkas in particular—were highly sought after. She was particularly well known for the intricate fur designs and beadwork she sewed onto clothing. A photo of her, taken by Alaskan photographer Myron Rosenberg, has become a classic portrait of the Yup'ik people. The picture shows her with her great-grandson sleeping in her lap, while both of them wear heavy fur parkas.

Phillip Charette is an artist who specializes in contemporary art in the Yup'ik tradition. His works include Yup'ik masks, fine-art prints, mixed-media sculpture, healing jewelry, and Yup'ik drums. Although he grew up in the continental United States, he spent his summers with his Native American grandparents in Alaska. He creates Native American art that builds on the traditions and cosmology (world view) of the Yup'ik people. His works have been displayed throughout the United States and abroad, in galleries and museums, including the Smithsonian National Museum of the American Indian, the Santa Fe Indian Art Market, the Portland Art Museum, and many others. Charette earned a master's in education from Harvard University in 1994.

Emily Johnson, who grew up in Sterling, Alaska, is a choreographer, performer, and director of the performance company Catalyst. She has earned numerous awards, including a grant from the Native Arts and Cultures Foundation. Johnson's "performance installations," which she has brought to audiences throughout the United States, Canada, and Russia, combine storytelling, video, movement, and music. She was also a 2009 and 2010 MAP Fund Grant recipient, a 2009 McKnight Fellow, and a 2009 and 2011 MANCC Choreographer Fellow. She was the winner of the 2012 Outstanding Production ("new art, dance and performance") Bessie Award.

Politics Todd Palin (1964–), husband of former Alaska governor and 2008 vice-presidential nominee Sarah Palin, had a great-grandmother who was a full-blooded Yup'ik. Her Yup'ik name was Ahchitmook. Palin has worked for British Petroleum in the North Slope oil fields and is a four-time champion snowmobile racer. He was an advisor to his wife during her governorship. He appeared in the reality television show *Sarah Palin's Alaska*, which aired from 2010 to 2011.

Sports Falon Ring (1994–), from Anchorage Alaska, is a rising star in the world of kickboxing and mixed martial arts. At the age of sixteen, he claimed the International Kickboxing Federation's bantamweight championship belt. He has also won championships in jiu-jitsu and titles in two divisions at the Southwest Grapplefest.

MEDIA

RADIO AND TELEVISION

KYUK-AM (640) and KYUK-TV (Channel 4)

Native American–owned and operated public radio and television stations located in Bethel, Alaska. The stations have many tapes of Yupik songs, myths, legends, and stories as well as videotapes of the Yupik people.

Mike Martz, General Manager
P.O. Box 468
Bethel, Alaska 99559
Phone: (907) 543-3131
Fax: (907) 543-3130
URL: www.kyuk.org

PRINT

The Bristol Bay Times

Provides news coverage for southwest Alaska.

Carey Restino, News Editor
P.O. Box 241582
Anchorage, Alaska 99524
Phone: (907) 770-0820
Fax: (907) 770-0822
URL: www.thebristolbaytimes.com

The Delta Discovery

A native-owned weekly newspaper that covers the Yukon-Kuskokwim Delta.

P.O. Box 1028
401 Ridgecrest Drive
Bethel, Alaska 99559
Phone: (907) 543-4113
Email: realnews@deltadiscovery.com
URL: www.deltadiscovery.com

ORGANIZATIONS AND ASSOCIATIONS

Alaska Native Knowledge Network

Serves as a resource for compiling and exchanging information related to Alaska native knowledge systems and ways of knowing.

University of Alaska Fairbanks
P.O. Box 756730
Fairbanks, Alaska 99775

Phone: (907) 474-5897
Email: fyankn@ankn.uaf.edu
URL: www.ankn.uaf.edu

Calista Elders Council

Provides financial assistance to Calista Region
    Shareholders and descendants of Calista
    Shareholders enrolled in formal programs of study.

Carlos Soto, Education and Development Director
Phone: (907) 279-5516
Email: info@calistaheritage.org
URL: www.calistaheritage.org

Yup'ik Women's Coalition

Committed to ending violence against women and
    children in Yup'ik villages through strengthening
    traditional Yup'ik beliefs and teachings.

Lenora Hootch, Executive Director
General Delivery
Emmonak, Alaska 99581
Phone: (907) 949-1718
Fax: (907) 949-1434
Email: emmows@hughes.net
URL: www.yupikwomen.org

MUSEUMS AND RESEARCH CENTERS

Alaska Native Heritage Center

A renowned cultural center and museum where all
    people can expand their understanding of Alaska's
    indigenous people.

Steven Alvarez, Director of Education
8800 Heritage Center Drive
Anchorage, Alaska 99504
Phone: (907) 330-8000
Fax: (909) 330-6608
URL: www.alaskanative.net

Anchorage Museum at Rasmuson Center

Collects, preserves, interprets, and exhibits the art, history,
    anthropology, and science of Alaska.

James Pepper Henry, Museum Director
625 C Street
Anchorage, Alaska 99501
Phone: (907) 343-4326
Fax: (907) 929-9290
Email: museum@anchoragemuseum.org
URL: www.anchoragemuseum.org

Sheldon Jackson Museum

The museum's collection has been called a jewel in the
    crown of Alaska ethnographic collections.

Debbie Doland, Visitor Services Staff
104 College Drive
Sitka, Alaska 99835
Phone: (907) 747-8981
Fax: (907) 747-3004
URL: www.museums.state.ak.us/sheldon_jackson/
sjhome.html

University of Alaska Museum of the North

The museum's collections include some 1.4 million
    artifacts and specimens relating to the region's
    biological diversity and cultural traditions.

Jennifer Arseneau, Education and Public Programs
Manager
907 Yukon Drive
Fairbanks, Alaska 99775
Phone: (907) 474-7505
Email: museum@uaf.edu
URL: www.uaf.edu/museum

Yupiit Piciryarait Cultural Center and Museum

Consists of three galleries. One contains permanent
    exhibits of clothing, household, and hunting
    and gathering implements used by the people
    of the Yukon-Kuskokwim Delta in ancient and
    contemporary times. The other two galleries are used
    for short-term exhibitions.

Vivian Korthius
420 Chief Eddie Hoffman (State) Highway
Bethel, Alaska 99559
Phone: (907) 543-1819
Fax: (907) 543-1885
Email: vkorthius@avcp.org
URL: www.ypmuseum.org

SOURCES FOR ADDITIONAL STUDY

Andrew, Frank. *Paitarkiutenka / My Legacy to You.* Seattle:
    University of Washington Press, 2008.

Fienup-Riordan, Ann. *The Real People and the Children of
    Thunder: The Yup'ik Eskimo Encounter with Moravian
    Missionaries John and Edith Kilbuck.* Norman:
    University of Oklahoma Press, 1991.

———. *Wise Words of the Yup'ik People: We Talk to You
    Because We Love You.* Lincoln: University of Nebraska
    Press, 2005.

———. *Yuungnaqpiallerput / The Way We Genuinely Live:
    Masterworks of Yup'ik Science and Survival.* Seattle:
    University of Washington Press, 2007.

Fienup-Riordan, Ann, and Alice Rearden. *Ellavut, Our Yup'ik
    World & Weather: Continuity and Change on the Bering
    Sea Coast.* Seattle: University of Washington Press, 2012.

Henkelman, James W., and Kurt H. Vitt. *Harmonious to Dwell.*
    Bethel: The Moravian Seminary and Archives, 1985.

Litecky, Ahnie. "The Dwellers Between: Yup'ik Shamans
    and Cultural Change in Western Alaska." MA thesis,
    University of Montana, 2011. http://etd.lib.umt.edu/
    theses/available/etd-05102011-142458/unrestricted/
    Litecky_Ahnie_Thesis.pdf.

Meade, Marie, transl. *Agayuliyararput: Kegginaqut,
    Kangiit-llu = Our Way of Making Prayer: Yup'ik
    Masks and the Stories They Tell.* Seattle: University of
    Washington Press, 1996.

Napoleon, Harold. *Yuuyaraq: The Way of the Human
    Being.* Fairbanks: Center for Cross-Cultural Studies,
    University of Alaska, Fairbanks, 1990.

Oswalt, Wendell H. *Bashful No Longer: An Alaskan
    Ethnohistory, 1778–1988.* Norman: University of
    Oklahoma Press, 1990.

ZUNI

Kristin King-Ries

OVERVIEW

The Zuni are a Pueblo people that traditionally occupied northwestern New Mexico along the middle section of the Zuni River, a varied terrain that includes deserts, plains, forests, foothills, and mountains. By the thirteenth century, six Zuni villages were spread throughout a 25-square-mile area that bordered present-day Arizona and lay just south of what is now Gallup, New Mexico. The whole of Zuni territory, however, extended far beyond to include the Zuni Mountains to the north and east and a stretch of desert to the west and south. The tribe's name for itself is *A:shiwi* (pronounced AH-shee-wee) which means "the people." The word *Zuni* is derived from the name given to the A:shiwi by one of their neighbors, the Keres Tribe, and used by the Acoma Pueblo people. The Spanish learned the name from the Acoma and brought it into common use.

The population of the Zuni Tribe before contact with Europeans was estimated at 6,000 people, according to the Smithsonian Institute's *Handbook of North American Indians*. The tribe's prosperous economy during the pre-Columbian era was based on farming, mining, hunting, fishing, craft-making, and inter-tribal trade. In 1540 one of the first European visitors to Zuni territory, the Spanish explorer Francisco Vásquez de Coronado, described the village of Hawikuh as a walled village containing two hundred "very good homes," a quantity of turquoise, and abundant food.

The most geographically isolated of the Pueblo Indians, the Zuni people continue to live on the land of their ancestors in the Zuni River valley, but on a much smaller scale. When the federal government created the Zuni Indian Reservation in 1877, it reduced the tribe's territorial holdings to approximately one-tenth of their original size. In the first half of the 1900s, a series of U.S. government dam projects severely restricted the flow of the Zuni River, making farming less viable. By World War II the tribal economy had shifted away from agriculture and grew to include wage work, craft production and herding.

According to the Zuni Tribe's website, as of 2013 there were 12,000 enrolled members of the Zuni Tribe. The tribal government estimates that 90 percent of the tribal members live on the Zuni Reservation (which is also commonly referred to as Zuni Pueblo) in New Mexico.

HISTORY OF THE PEOPLE

Early History The Zuni are descendants of two earlier tribes, the Mogollon and the Anasazi. Anthropologists estimate the Mogollon arrived in the Zuni River valley between 700 and 800 CE and that the Anasazi arrived approximately three or four hundred years later, in around 1100 CE. Both groups built permanent structures, lived in villages, and engaged in trade with tribes from as far away as Mexico and the Great Plains.

The emergence of Zuni culture dates to the thirteenth century. Religion was central to daily life, as tribal members showed respect and gratitude to the Zuni deities and spirits with prayers, rituals, and offerings of food and tobacco. Extended family also played an important role in the culture. Families were matrilineal (tracing lineage through women), and they were grouped into clans of people who shared a common maternal ancestor. The head of each clan, usually an elder woman, distributed farmland to clan members based on need. Tribal government was run on the village level by a *pekwin* (a secular leader) and a council of priests.

Traditionally, the Zuni people traveled great distances to visit their sacred sites, some as far away as the Grand Canyon and parts of Arizona, but their villages were always in the Zuni River valley. As early as 1250, Zuni villages served as trade centers for tribes throughout the Southwest. The Zunis traded such items as salt, corn, turquoise, cloth, jewelry, and pottery in exchange for copper and parrot feathers from tribes in Mexico, buffalo hides from the Great Plains tribes, and coral and seashells from California tribes.

The first Europeans to encounter the Zuni were a party of Spanish explorers that arrived in Zuni territory in 1539 and found a well-organized civilization. After the Zuni executed their leader, the Spaniards returned to Mexico, spreading fantastical accounts about the Zuni towns, which they called the Seven Cities of Cibola. The following year, Francisco Vásquez de Coronado led a large force of conquistadors into Zuni territory looking for treasure, converts to Christianity, and new Spanish subjects. The Zuni had anticipated their arrival by evacuating the main village and assembling a force of several hundred warriors. Although advanced weaponry enabled the Spanish troops to prevail, the conquistadors soon abandoned the village when they did not find the fabled gold. A number of Spanish priests and soldiers stayed on, attempting to gain converts to Catholicism and enforce Spanish colonial authority. That group departed two years later. The Zuni's geographic isolation caused the Spanish to leave them alone for the next four decades, unlike the Rio Grande Pueblos, who were subject to demands for food and clothing for Spanish soldiers.

By the 1600s, however, the Zuni's remote location no longer exempted them from Spanish interference. Spain had set up a colonial government in New Mexico in 1598, and during the first decade of the century, colonial governors traveled to Zuni territory repeatedly in search of exploitable resources. An influx of foreigners spread deadly diseases among the Zuni. In the late 1620s Spanish soldiers forced the tribe to permit Franciscan priests to take up residence in Zuni territory, causing great resentment and anger among tribal members. By 1632, after Zuni builders completed work on two mission compounds they had been ordered to build, some Zunis killed two priests and destroyed the missions. The surviving priests fled, and the Zuni population retreated for two years to a fortress town on the high ground of Dowa Yallane (Corn Mountain). Following this episode, the Zunis enjoyed another period of respite from Spanish rule until 1680, when the tribe joined other Pueblo tribes in a battle to oust the Spanish colonial authorities. This became known as the Pueblo Revolt.

The Zuni tribe continued to resist the conversion efforts of the Catholic missionaries. There were few converts to Catholicism during the seventeenth, eighteenth, and early nineteenth centuries. Adherence to the traditional Zuni religion remained strong. Nevertheless, the Zuni were influenced by their invaders in other ways. One of the most devastating was exposure to foreign germs the Spaniards carried. Although population figures from that time are not entirely reliable, the number of Zunis declined precipitously (possibly by as much as 75 percent) after the first European contact as a result of multiple measles and smallpox epidemics during the sixteenth and seventeenth centuries. During this time, the Spanish also introduced horses to the area, which proved to be harmful for the Zuni, as their once-peaceful neighbors, the Navajos and Apaches, began raiding Zuni farms and villages to acquire horses for themselves.

Modern Era In the early 1800s Spanish influence on the Zunis declined but was replaced by American and Mexican interests in the present-day Arizona–New Mexico region. U.S. influence in Zuni territory began at the start of the 1800s, with the influx of Americans seeking to trade with tribal members and to trap animals for their fur. In 1821 the Spanish colonial government ceded their claims in southwestern North America to Mexico, and the Mexican government recognized all Native Americans in the region as full citizens, which allowed the Zuni

to practice their traditions without interference. In the 1840s, however, Zuni freedom was threatened by rising tension between the United States and Mexico and continued conflict with neighboring tribes. At the start of the Mexican-American War in 1846, the Zuni welcomed American troops in the area in exchange for promises of protection against the Navajo. In 1848, with the signing of the Treaty of Guadalupe Hidalgo to end the Mexican-American War, the U.S. government took possession of Zuni territory, and as a result the Zuni became even more dependent on the government for protection against the Navajo and other antagonistic tribes. Initially, the outlook was good for the Zuni, as the U.S. government, the Zuni, and the Navajo agreed to a treaty in 1850 that gave assurances of Zuni tribal sovereignty and guaranteed U.S. protection of Zuni lands from Navajo raids.

In the post–Civil War era, however, the federal government failed to abide by the terms of the 1848 and 1850 treaties. For example, in the late 1840s prospectors on their way to California for the gold rush drove their wagons through Zuni territory in ever-increasing numbers, violating Zuni territorial rights as defined by the treaties. In 1857 the government further violated those rights by authorizing the construction of a wagon road through Zuni territory in response to pressure from U.S. citizens to facilitate westward expansion. Furthermore, instead of being protected from raiding parties by U.S. troops, the Zuni were subjected to increased attacks by the Apache and Navajos during the 1860s.

In 1877 the U.S. government established the Zuni Reservation, reducing the tribal lands by 90 percent and undermining the authority of Zuni leaders by excluding many sacred sites from the reservation. The government also began sending ethnologists to study the Zuni and other Southwestern tribes. The ethnologists were responsible for attracting tourists to the territory through articles on Zuni culture published in the mainstream press and for removing (by stealing and in some cases purchasing) large quantities of Zuni artifacts and sacred objects to send to museums. The most accomplished of these ethnologists was Frank Hamilton Cushing, who lived among the Zunis in New Mexico from 1879 to 1884. Some tribal members and scholars believe that Balowahdiwa, a tribal leader, welcomed Cushing into his home in the hope that Cushing could one day help the Zuni get their land back from the U.S. government. Whether or not this was Balowahdiwa's motive, it is known that he angered some in the tribe by allowing Cushing to witness religious ceremonies that had been closed to outsiders. Through the connection with Cushing, Zuni leaders did gain access to U.S. authorities. In 1882 Cushing arranged for six prominent Zuni tribal members to visit Washington, D.C., where they had a chance to observe U.S. society and meet with President Chester Arthur. As a result, an 1883 executive order was issued to return certain outlying farms to the tribe.

Continued encroachments on Zuni lands throughout the 1870s and 1880s far outweighed these modest gains. Mormon missionaries had opened the first school in Zuni territory in 1876, and the Presbyterians opened their school on reservation lands the following year. In 1881 the southern line of the transcontinental railroad was completed, with the tracks located a mere 40 miles north of the Zuni territory. This brought new business to the area, such as glass making and lumber milling, but also brought more outsiders who were disrespectful of Zuni traditions.

In the early part of the twentieth century, President Woodrow Wilson signed an executive order that returned another 80,000 acres to the Zuni Reservation. More land was returned in 1935 and 1940, bringing the total acreage to roughly 400,000. However, a number of private enterprises, along with the U.S. Army Corps of Engineers projects—which included clear-cutting in the mountains above the Pueblo, dam-building (six in under ten years), and overgrazing—caused serious erosion and watershed damage on the reservation. The flow of the Zuni River was greatly diminished as a result of the dams, rendering farming on the reservation nearly impossible.

Zuni tribal members left the reservation in large numbers for the first time during World War II. More than two hundred Zuni men joined the U.S. Army to fight in Europe, where they were exposed to different cultures and ideas. Upon return, some of these veterans brought with them behaviors that clashed with traditional ways and upset the tribal elders. The veterans also brought G.I. benefits, which enabled them to pay for training and education and thereby helped the tribe adjust to the modern world. In the 1950s the tribe began the long process of seeking justice for all the losses they had suffered at the hands of the U.S. government. In 1987 the U.S. Supreme Court held that 14.8 million acres had been taken from the Zuni without payment, and in 1990 Congress passed the Zuni Land Conservation Act, allocating $25 million to the Zuni Tribe in exchange for settling the case. The money from the settlement that did not go to paying fees and expenses was placed in trust for the rehabilitation and maintenance of eroded lands and for the development of the tribe's human, natural, and cultural resources.

During the twenty-first century, tourism remains an important source of revenue for the Zuni. While well-paid full-time jobs are hard to come by on the Zuni Reservation, and unemployment remains high, many Zunis have found ways to stay in their ancestral home. Those who leave for college or other opportunities often return. Because the reservation has remained the site for the many religious ceremonies that still take place, living there continues to be a priority for many tribal members.

SETTLEMENT IN THE UNITED STATES

Unlike most of the Native American tribes in the United States, the Zuni Tribe has been able to remain in their ancestral homeland. However, the Spanish invasions in the seventeenth century caused a gradual consolidation of the population. The Zuni were living in six villages in 1540. Due to repeated Spanish invasions, by the 1700s the bulk of the population had moved to Halona (later renamed Zuni) for security reasons—it was easier to defend one village than to defend six. Demand for housing in Halona grew exponentially and led to higher population density.

Paradoxically, when the Zuni adopted the Spanish practice of raising livestock, they needed to expand their grazing lands. Burros enabled the Zuni to transport supplies and produce over longer distances, and they began to farm and graze their herds in camps as far as 25 miles away from Halona. Established in the early 1700s, these camps were used only in the summers. By the late 1700s places such as Nutria had become year-round settlements. As of 2012 an estimated 90 percent of enrolled Zuni Tribe members continue to live in Zuni Pueblo on the reservation in New Mexico. A small number live in the nearby town of Blackrock. The main reservation encompasses an estimated 418,304 acres of forests, rivers, streams and sagebrush prairie, and sandstone mesas. The Zuni Tribe owns additional lands outside the reservation boundaries in Catron County, New Mexico, and Apache County, Arizona.

LANGUAGE

Zuni language is what linguists refer to as an isolate. That is, Zuni is not derived from or similar to any other languages. For thousands of years, the language was spoken but not written. In the twentieth century people began to create a written version of Zuni.

The story of language change among the Zuni is more complex than that of many other tribes. Zuni territory was occupied by the Spanish colonizers, including a considerable number of missionaries who actively tried to bring Spanish culture and language to the people. Yet there is no evidence that the Spanish presence, although long-term, led to the use of Spanish as a first language. Even as some Zunis recognized the need to learn to speak Spanish (and later English), through the nineteenth century, the vast majority spoke only Zuni. Pressure for linguistic change came in the twentieth century, when more Zuni were sent to boarding schools, where typically it was school policy to suppress tribal language. After World War II, when many Zuni veterans returned to the reservation, the use of English began to increase. In the 1960s and thereafter, English became increasingly widespread on the reservation, due primarily to increased access to American popular culture via radio and television.

The Zunis have maintained the vitality of their language to a much greater extent than the vast majority of other native peoples. The pattern, however, is for young Zunis to have only a passive knowledge of

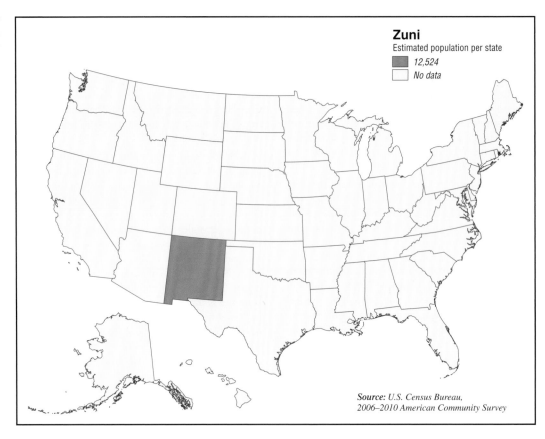

Zuni
Estimated population per state

▨ 12,524
☐ No data

*Source: U.S. Census Bureau,
2006–2010 American Community Survey*

the Zuni language, and when they do use "Zuni" it is really a slang form of Zuni. The elders do not understand it, and the young people do not understand traditional Zuni. In the mid-1990s there were still many elders throughout the community who spoke Zuni fluently and households that spoke it exclusively. Nevertheless, many Zunis feared they would lose the language, and the community has taken steps to preserve it by incorporating Zuni language classes into the public school curriculum on the reservation, offering cultural enrichment classes, and creating an oral history project to record traditional songs, stories, and dialog between elders. According to the U.S. Census Bureau's American Community Survey estimates for 2006–2010, among Zuni ages five and older, 23.6 percent reported speaking only English at home; the rest spoke another language at home (presumably Zuni). However, the vast majority—93.1 percent—reported being fluent in English.

RELIGION

According to the Zuni creation story, the tribe was called by emissaries of the sun god to come up and join the world. The people emerged from the fourth level of the underworld at a site that is now known as the Grand Canyon and were dazzled by the sun's brilliance. They were told to grow toward the light. From the entering place they embarked on a spiritual

journey in search of *Itiwana* (the "middle place"). Along their journey they were joined by a pair of witches who introduced them to corn and taught them to believe in an afterlife. The group divided into smaller groups, and one of these traveled up the Little Colorado River to the Zuni River valley, where they found Itiwana. However, the spot was already occupied and an epic battle ensued. With assistance from their twin war gods, the Zuni prevailed. According to their story, once the Zuni had defeated their enemies, they changed from a war-loving people to a peace-loving people. Over time the Zuni groups that had split off during the migration from the Grand Canyon found their way to Itiwana.

The Zunis have long been the subjects of anthropological studies and outside exploitation, such as the studies conducted by U.S. government-sponsored anthropologists in the 1870s. As a result the tribe has taken steps to ensure the privacy of knowledge about rituals and religious ceremonies. In 2002 the governor of Zuni Pueblo, Malcolm Bowekaty, testified before the U.S. Senate Committee on Indian Affairs, requesting that the government respect the tribe's privacy in these matters. For that reason, information on particular aspects of Zuni rituals is difficult to obtain.

In general terms, it is known that the Zuni religion is based on ancestor worship and involves a complex series of ceremonies with strong connections to the seasons and the landscape. Changes in season are observed by the performance of specific prayer dances. For example, dances calling for rain are performed during growing season. Dances to celebrate a bountiful harvest are performed in the fall. Ceremonial dances of this nature ensure harmony in the world and secure the tribe's survival, and therefore in the past everyone in the community was expected to participate.

In addition to rituals and ceremonies performed by the entire Zuni Tribe, there are six spiritual societies, each with its own rituals, ceremonies, and priesthood. Membership in these societies was restricted. Traditionally, Zuni tribal members also made regular offerings of sacred meal to their ancient ancestors and prayed to them three times a day. Structures called *kivas* were built to house certain religious ceremonies. Often these were located within the terraced blocks of the village rather than as stand-alone structures. A typical structure had flagstone floors, a fire pit with a ventilation system, an ash pit, a platform, an anchor for a loom, and a place for sacred objects representing Zuni gods.

Of all the tribes in New Mexico, the Zuni were the least influenced by missionaries. Spanish Catholics arrived in Zuni territory in 1629, but their early attempts to convert tribal members met with limited success. After a few decades of tolerating the mission in their midst, tribal members evicted the Catholics. From the 1700s until the 1950s, the Mission of Nuestra Señora de Guadalupe, one of the many Spanish missions established in present-day New Mexico for native peoples, was abandoned. When the Catholic Church paid to restore the building in 1960, it hired Zuni painters to fill the interior walls with murals depicting Zuni spirits and landscape. Masses were held until the end of the twentieth century, but now the church functions as a museum. Zuni religious leaders have a long tradition of visiting it for ceremonial purposes, and the old building plays a symbolic role in Zuni feasts and dances.

Over time, the Americans have had considerably more success in converting Zuni people to Christianity than the Spanish had. According to 2010 data from McKinley County, where the Zuni Reservation, is located, close to 40 percent of tribal members now practice Christianity. An estimated 55 percent of those are Catholics, 17 percent are Mormons, and the rest are Protestants of different denominations. While tribal members in the twenty-first century continue to observe traditional Zuni religious ceremonies and make pilgrimages to distant shrines, only a slim majority of Zuni people practice the traditional religion.

CULTURE AND ASSIMILATION

Zuni Tribe members in the twenty-first century have adopted aspects of mainstream U.S. culture. For example, they speak English, attend U.S. colleges, and use cell phones, computers, and other electronic gadgets. Even so, their traditional culture remains very strong. The tribe's ability to maintain its traditional culture and resist assimilation has made it one of the most intriguing cultures to American scholars, as the Zuni people are among the most heavily studied of all indigenous groups in the Western Hemisphere.

Cuisine Zuni cuisine includes foods such as chilies, onions, and herbs, which traditionally were grown in small gardens adjacent to the village. Corn was grown in larger fields. Salt was also an important part of the traditional Zuni diet. One of the sacred places for the Zuni is the Salt Lake, some miles from the reservation, where Zuni tribal members have traveled annually over thousands of years to collect salt. Men hunted deer and antelope meat and other smaller game. Boiling and cooking on hot stones were two traditional cooking methods. Later, when Europeans introduced wheat and adobe ovens, bread became a staple. Some traditional Zuni foods include baked beans, hominy (a form of porridge made from ground corn), cornbread, chili, and soups. The Zuni diet still includes corn, chilies, onions, and salt, but it has incorporated all types of foods from mainstream U.S. culture.

Traditional Dress Given the warm desert climate of the Zuni homeland, men and women in the past did not need much in the way of clothing. Men wore breechcloths, and women wore a style of dress called a *manta*, which covered one shoulder and left the other bare. Both men and women wore deerskin moccasins. Adults of both sexes wore their hair in buns, although some chose to wear their hair loose, with men's hair at shoulder-length and women's hair longer. The Zuni people were famous for their jewelry. Originally they used tin and copper to fashion bracelets and necklaces. Later Zuni jewelry makers switched to silver.

For religious ceremonies, people painted their skin. Men sometimes wore ceremonial masks or crowns of feathers. Women would paint their moccasins and wear leather leggings tied to their shins. Europeans' moral sensibilities influenced Pueblo fashion. Zuni people added other items to their ceremonial dress. Women began wearing shawls and long-sleeved dresses. Men started wearing shirts and leggings, and kilts replaced breechcloths. When Catholic missionaries arrived in the 1630s, they encouraged women to wear additional garments under their dresses.

Traditional clothing is seen as an important symbol of Zuni history. It is still worn for tribal ceremonies, and dance outfits are handed down from generation to generation. On the reservation, day-to-day wear includes contemporary American clothing such as jeans and T-shirts, but some Zuni have ancient designs embroidered on their clothing.

Traditional Arts and Crafts The Zuni tribe has a long tradition of painting. Zuni artists painted symbols of the sun and images of animals on stone slabs and carved small animal figurines, which are now called "fetishes," out of stone and shell. Later they began painting murals on the walls of kivas, where religious ceremonies were performed. The interior of the Catholic mission church at Zuni Pueblo has been painted with sacred images of Zuni spirits and of the landscape as it appears in each of the four seasons. Zuni pottery is typically decorated with black, white, red, and gray paint. In the era before the reservations were created, designs on pottery included squiggled lines, solid triangles with dots, and interlocking spirals, in addition to dragonflies, spotted frogs, and tadpoles. Owls, bears, and the Rain Bird were also used as motifs. Other traditional Zuni crafts include basket making and stone carving.

Dances and Songs The Zuni tribe distinguishes between religious dances, which are closed to the public, and social dancing, which anyone can enjoy. Social dances are held in a variety of public settings, such as high schools, powwows, fairs, and parades.

Holidays The Sha'lak'o Festival, perhaps the biggest Zuni holiday, takes place every December. Dancers dress in elaborate traditional clothing to celebrate the New Year. They bear six giant masked figures representing the *shalako*, the messengers of the gods, to bless the houses that have been built since the previous festival. Festivities begin with the ritual crossing of the small river that runs through the Pueblo, then the dancers continue through every street in the Pueblo. There is also an annual Rain Dance in June.

Of all the tribes in New Mexico, the Zuni were the least influenced by missionaries. Spanish Catholics arrived in Zuni territory in 1629, but their early attempts to convert tribal members met with limited success. After a few decades of tolerating the mission in their midst, tribal members evicted the Catholics.

Health Care Issues and Practices A study of health care among the Zuni published in *Social Science and Medicine* magazine in 1980 stated that up to 90 percent of non-emergency patients sought care from traditional healers before going to the Public Health Services clinic. According to the Zuni Hospital website, traditional medicine and beliefs have continued to be part of Zuni health practices into the twenty-first century. Significant health problems among Zuni tribal members include high rates of alcoholism, drug abuse, and diabetes linked to kidney disease. Native Americans are three times more likely than whites to suffer from kidney disease, and Zunis are even more at risk than members of other tribes. Due to the Zuni population's predisposition, medical researchers have conducted a number of studies on the reservation aimed at finding

solutions to the problem. One recent study was funded by the National Institutes of Health in 2011.

FAMILY AND COMMUNITY LIFE

The traditional Zuni family consisted of grandparents, parents, children, and other relatives living together in four to six rooms, which included living rooms, cooking rooms, and storage rooms. The floors in these rooms were paved with flagstones and had corner fireplaces with chimneys. Living rooms typically had low benches built into the walls that served as seating during the day and beds at night. Any religious ceremonies conducted in the home took place in a living room. Cooking rooms were often located on the rooftops and had grinding stones, clay pots, cooking stones, and places for drying and preserving food. Families also had storage rooms, and most families stored at least a one-year supply of food in case of drought.

Prior to contact with Europeans, most Zuni families lived side-by-side in the large terrace blocks in villages. By the late 1800s Zuni housing had shifted from five- or six-story connected terraces that opened onto central plazas to two- or three-story free-standing houses with less emphasis on central plazas. This resulted in families living in smaller groups. Regardless of the particulars of their living arrangements, elders in Zuni communities have always been regarded as leaders and teachers.

Gender Roles Traditional Zuni culture had three genders. There were women, men, and *lhamanas* (men-women), biological males who preferred to live, dress, and work as women. Some even took husbands. Zuni people honored lhamanas as valued members of their community, but U.S. authorities vehemently opposed the practice, and the tradition disappeared in the twentieth century.

In Zuni society women were in charge of the home, childrearing, and preparing, cooking and preserving food. Women made pottery; they were responsible for digging their own clay and shaping, firing, and painting the pots. Men were in charge of the public sphere, assuming the roles of priests, farmers, warriors, hunters, fishermen, and medicine men. They made tools, utensils, and jewelry. They also wove baskets and cloth. At a young age, boys began working alongside their fathers or uncles to learn the family occupation. They underwent two painful initiation ceremonies, the first between the ages of five and nine, when they were old enough to help in the fields, and the second in their early teens, when they were considered ready to take on a man's work. Girls were usually spared initiation and stayed home to help their mothers.

Education Initially the U.S. government allowed religious groups to open schools on reservations. Mormon missionaries opened a school in Zuni territory in 1876; they were followed by Presbyterian missionaries the next year. Attendance at both schools was low. Zuni tribal members resisted being "Americanized," and the white teachers on the Zuni Reservation complained that no matter what they taught the children during the day, they would go home in the afternoon and revert to their traditional customs and habits.

One unfortunate episode at the Presbyterian school had significant long-term consequences for Zuni education. In 1897 a teacher named Mary DeSette asked the U.S. cavalry to send troops to the Zuni reservation to arrest tribal members who had accused a fellow Zuni of being a witch. DeSette and her colleagues also asked the troops to enforce school attendance, and as a result they occupied the reservation for several months. The difficulties at the Presbyterian day school eventually led the BIA to establish the Zuni Agency Black Rock Boarding School in 1907, in order to remove children from their families and force them to assimilate. To aid in the process of assimilation, the school made classes in Christianity and attendance at Sunday services mandatory. The kindergarten-through-fifth-grade institution stayed in operation for at least two decades. Most of the education was vocational, teaching girls home economics of the dominant culture and boys skills like blacksmithing and carpentry, none of which was of use when they returned to the reservation. Eventually the school shifted its emphasis to teaching modern farming techniques.

Unlike many other American Indian boarding schools of the time, the Black Rock Boarding School did not send soldiers to enforce attendance. However, the school followed the military-style model used by all federal Indian boarding schools, including regular inspections, marching drills, and uniforms. Students were forbidden to speak Zuni. Boy students were allowed to visit home on the weekends, but girls were required to stay on campus for the entire nine months of the school year except during Shalako in December, when all the students went home for a week to celebrate the festival with their families.

From the 1930s to the 1950s, Zuni students could either attend the BIA day school near home or go to Albuquerque for boarding school. In 1956 the federal government turned over the Zuni schools to the state of New Mexico. By 1978 the Zuni Tribal Council had agreed that the state had failed to provide adequate schooling on the reservation and passed a resolution to create a Zuni-run school district with the use of BIA funds. One of the first changes made was the inclusion of a bilingual program.

The Zuni Public School District opened in 1980, and as of 2012 the Zuni operated two elementary schools, one middle school, and two high schools, all located on the reservation. In 2012 the district had a total of 1,425 students enrolled with an average class size of 13. The U.S. Census Bureau's American Community Survey estimates for 2006–2010 showed that 80.1 percent of Zunis over the age of twenty-four had a high school degree or higher (a rate slightly lower than that of the general U.S. population, which was 85.6 percent). The percentage of Zuni who had earned a bachelor's degree or higher was only 5.2 percent (whereas the rate for the general U.S. population was 28.2 percent).

Courtship and Weddings Traditionally, when a girl reached puberty she was considered eligible for marriage. Once she decided who she wanted to marry, she would seek family approval by consulting with her mother. If the family approved, the couple would spend their nights together for a number of weeks to see if the union would work. Typically the man would go to the bride's family's home at night and leave at dawn. Either party could call off the relationship during this stage. Those couples who decided to get officially married celebrated their wedding ceremony with an exchange of gifts between members of both families. Women from the bride's family exchanged clothes, food, and jewelry with women from the groom's family. The bride was expected to grind a large quantity of corn to give to her mother-in-law. In exchange, the mother-in-law gave the bride an outfit of clothes. If a man wanted to bypass these rituals, he could simply arrive at his prospective bride's home with many gifts and ask her father for permission to marry. The father would consult the daughter, and if she agreed, the marriage would take place. Marriages were considered personal and not subject to regulation by tribal authorities. Couples could get divorced by having the man move out of the matrilineal residence. The children typically stayed with the mother's family.

Today Zuni weddings more closely resemble modern U.S. weddings, with an official ceremony held in front of guests. Many Zunis get married at Zuni Pueblo, with the bride wearing traditional Zuni clothing. A 2007 article in *Smithsonian* magazine describes a modern Zuni wedding: the bride, attended by bridesmaids, wore white moccasins and deer-hide leggings on her calves; a white blouse with a black tunic; four large turquoise brooches pinned on her skirt; a shawl draped across her shoulders, and many silver-and-turquoise bracelets and rings. Like many American brides, she walked down the aisle to the song "Here Comes the Bride," and her father gave her away to the groom.

EMPLOYMENT AND ECONOMIC CONDITIONS

As of 2012 there were numerous tribal enterprises on the Zuni Reservation, including a museum, a forest-products business, and a cell phone company. The tribe operated the Zuni Public Library, a radio station, a medical clinic, and many other programs. There were several small businesses operating on the reservation, including four gas stations, a technology firm, a hair salon, a law office, restaurants, art galleries, a bed and breakfast, a hospital, and a bank. There was also a Department of Tourism.

Most Zunis living on the reservation are engaged in creating art or crafts. Of these, inlay silver jewelry is perhaps the most popular, followed by fetish carvings and pottery. Many of these artists and craftspeople work out of their homes. The Zuni Craftsmen's Cooperative Association and Pueblo of Zuni Arts and Crafts promote the sale of this work to local as well as national outlets. There are also websites dedicated to selling Zuni arts and crafts. Traditional Zuni art and crafts are protected under the 1990 Indian Arts and Crafts Act which forbids non-Indians from marketing their products as Indian made.

According to the U.S. Census Bureau's American Community Survey (ACS) estimates for 2006–2010, the median income among people of Zuni descent was $36,036 (while the median income for the U.S. population in general was $51,914). The ACS reported that poverty rate in Zuni Pueblo was at 31.8 percent during the period between 2007 and 2011. Evelyn Blanchard, an organizer for the New Mexico Center for Law and Poverty, said that racism is still a problem for Native Americans in New Mexico, and that this is evident in the job market.

POLITICS AND GOVERNMENT

Anthropologists have characterized traditional Zuni government as a theocracy because of the critical role played by priests. In Zuni society, there were two groups of priests, Rain priests and Bow priests. Rain priests were in charge of the sacred sphere and enacted the rituals for bringing rain to Zuni territory, and they alone prayed to the Creator, Awonawilona. The Bow priests prayed to the gods responsible for the tribe's military endeavors, enforced the decisions of the sacred priests, and appointed and monitored the *pekwins*, who were the secular leaders of village governments. The council of Bow priests left day-to-day management of the tribe to the pekwins, because if the priests became involved in mediating community conflicts, their hearts would be considered no longer pure and their prayers would lose power. Every village had its own council and its own pekwin.

One of the terms of the truce with Spain in 1692 was the establishment of a parallel civil government. Pekwins and their councils continued to have jurisdiction over spiritual matters and ethical conduct in Zuni villages, while the civil council governed all other aspects of village life. Initially, the Spanish governor selected the leaders of the civil council (a governor, lieutenant governor, and council) from the top Bow priests, but by the mid-1800s, Zuni elders were in charge making of those appointments. From roughly 1821 to 1848, the period of Mexican jurisdiction over Zuni territory, the tribe was left to govern themselves as they saw fit.

The U.S. government took over jurisdiction of present-day New Mexico and Arizona after defeating the Mexican army in the Mexican-American War but initially did nothing to change the structure of Zuni tribal governance. However, while the system of parallel councils remained largely unchanged until the end of the nineteenth century, other measures were taken that compromised the Zuni's capacity to govern themselves. For example, Christian missionaries had backing from U.S. troops to establish schools on the reservation, persecute tribal members for practicing their traditional religion, and force the men to cut their hair, all of which seriously undermined the authority of the Bow priests. U.S. troops occupied the reservation during the late 1890s, further eroding the tribe's political autonomy. In the early twentieth century the U.S. government took more overt and aggressive measures to control Zuni tribal governance. It opened an office of the Bureau of Indian Affairs (BIA) near Zuni Pueblo in 1902, in effect ending self-governance for the tribe. The BIA's power was far-ranging, from supervising federal programs and local activities to exercising ultimate veto power over the secular council.

In 1934 the Indian Reorganization Act (IRA) authorized the Zuni Tribe to hold elections and elect their own leaders once again. However, the system was very different from the traditional government and caused much division and debate. Under the IRA provisions, tribal members elected a governor, lieutenant governor, and six council members by a simple majority of male tribal members. Elected officials served one-year terms. Women were not permitted to vote until 1965. The tribe adopted its first constitution in 1970, and the U.S. government formally recognized the Zuni Tribal Council as the official tribal government.

As of the early twenty-first century, the Tribal Council consists of five council members, and all tribal members eighteen and older are eligible to vote. The most important issues in contemporary Zuni politics include land rights, reparations and monetary compensation, repatriation of tribal artifacts, respect for grave sites, cultural preservation, and grazing rights. The Zuni have had success in a number of areas with their dealings with the federal government. In the late 1980s the tribe won a lawsuit against the U.S. government that awarded $25 million in compensation for the illegal acquisition of their land between 1876 and 1939. In 1990, as a result of intense effort on the part of Zuni politicians, the Native American Graves Protection Repatriation Act was passed. Many sacred objects that had been stolen or bought by outsiders and shipped to museums, galleries, and private collections in distant places have since been returned to the tribe. The tribe reached a settlement in 2004 with the U.S. Department of Interior that resulted in a $20 million award to help pay for restoration of riparian (riverbank) lands and the purchase of additional water rights.

NOTABLE INDIVIDUALS

Activism Edmund Ladd Lewis (1926–1999) worked for the National Park Service (NPS) as the Pacific archeologist and spent twenty-six years restoring and preserving ancient Polynesian cultural sites in Hawaii. Ladd continued to advocate for his own tribe and helped repatriate the Zuni war gods, among other artifacts. He was an interpreter for the Zuni in landmark lawsuits against the U.S. government for broken treaties, and he played a key role in the success of the "repatriation" case for all American Indians. Ladd became an internationally renowned lecturer and writer as well as a consultant for universities and museums throughout the world, including the Smithsonian Institution. After thirty-four years with the NPS, he helped found the New Mexico Museum of Indian Art and Culture in Santa Fe, where he also served as curator until the year he died.

James Enote is a farmer, scientist, artist, writer, and advocate for his tribe. Enote has served as project leader of the Zuni Conservation Project, as head of the Zuni Department of Natural Resources, and as the executive director of the A:Shiwi A:wan Museum and Heritage Center, where he has been involved in repatriating Zuni artifacts and working on a cultural mapping project.

Margaret Lewis was born into the Cherokee tribe but married a Zuni man and lived most of her life in Zuni territory. Lewis was one of the few fluent English speakers on the reservation during the treaty era and assisted the tribe in many ways, including serving as its interim governor in 1917. Lewis is a controversial figure in part because for years she opened her home to many anthropologists who visited Zuni Pueblo to study and record the tribe's culture.

Art Alex Seotewa (1934–) was born into the Crane Clan and raised by his maternal grandfather, a high priest of the north and a tribal leader. Seotewa attended college in Albuquerque, New Mexico, on a scholarship until he was drafted into the U.S. Army. When he returned home to Zuni Pueblo after serving in the Korean War, he began his life as an artist. Eventually he was asked by the Catholic Church to paint murals in the newly restored Nuestra Señora de Guadalupe Church representing a synthesis of Zuni beliefs and Roman Catholicism. His murals, two panels that are 50 feet long and 15 feet high, took him more than two decades to paint and were completed in 1991. The works depict thirty masked *kachinas* (spirit beings) set against the Zuni landscape along with images of Jesus descending to the Pueblo on a cloud. The murals have attracted visitors from all over the world.

Eileen Yatsattie (1960–) followed in the footsteps of her grandmother and great-grandmother, both traditional Zuni potters. She started her career as an artist in 1973, while still quite young. Yatsattie is known for collecting her own clay, in the tradition of her Zuni ancestors, and making her own dyes using natural materials. She has studied with distinguished artists such as the late Hopi potter Daisy Nampeyo Hooee and the late Acoma potter Jennie Laate.

A Zuni man is shown with only a loin cloth and bow and arrow, c. 1909. SIMEON SCHWEMBERGER / BUYENLARGE / GETTY IMAGES

Politics Norman Cooeyate is a former governor of Zuni Pueblo (2006–2010). Born and raised on the reservation, Cooeyate earned his undergraduate degree in biology at the University of New Mexico and attended medical school there until he left to manage a National Institutes of Digestive, Diabetes & Kidney Disorders project in Zuni, New Mexico. He is a member of many boards, including the Native American Advisory Group.

MEDIA

RADIO

KSHI Radio 90.9 FM

The Zuni radio station went on air in 1977 and broadcasts announcements in both Zuni and English. Programming includes Pueblo news, current events, and a mix of contemporary rock and pop music.

Duane Chimoni, General Manager
Phone: (505) 782-4144

ORGANIZATIONS AND ASSOCIATIONS

All Indian Pueblo Council (AIPC)

The AIPC represents the twenty Pueblos of New Mexico, offers programs to revitalize and promote Pueblo culture and languages, and lobbies on behalf of the Pueblos on issues involving water, land, and cultural rights.

Melissa Felipe, Office Manager
2401 12th Street NW

Albuquerque, New Mexico 87104
Phone: (505) 881-1992
Fax: (505) 883-7682
Email: execdir.aipc@gmail.com
URL: www.aipcnm.org

Pueblo of Zuni

The official government of the Zuni Tribe deals with a broad range of issues affecting the health and well-being of tribal members, including tribal governance, economy, environment, employment, education, historic preservation, culture, tourism, and inter-governmental affairs.

P.O. Box 339
1203B State Hwy 53
Zuni, New Mexico 87327
Phone: (505) 782-7000
Fax: (505) 782-7202
URL: www.ashiwi.org

MUSEUMS AND RESEARCH CENTERS

A:shiwi A:wan Museum & Heritage Center

Founded in 1992, this tribally owned museum features exhibits from prehistoric Zuni history and art ranging from mural paintings depicting the creation story to work by contemporary artists. The archive includes old films, photographs, and recorded oral histories. The museum also supports cultural programs such as Zuni language and culture classes.

Jim Enote, Executive Director
02 East Ojo Caliente Road
P.O. Box 1009
Zuni, New Mexico 87327
Phone: (505) 782-4403
Fax: (505) 782-4503
Email: aamhc_museum@yahoo.com
URL: www.ashiwi-museum.org

Kennedy Museum of Art at Ohio University

The Kennedy Museum houses a noteworthy collection of Zuni arts and crafts, which includes jewelry and other silver work.

Beth Tragert, Administrative Associate
Lin Hall
Ohio University
Athens, Ohio 45701
Phone: (740) 593-1304
Email: kennedymuseum@ohio.edu
URL: www.ohio.edu/museum

SOURCES FOR ADDITIONAL STUDY

Blake, Kevin S., and Jeffrey S. Smith. "Pueblo Mission Churches as Symbols of Permanence and Identity." *Geographic Review* 90, no. 3 (2000): 359–80.

Bonvillian, Nancy. *The Zuni: Indians of North America.* Philadelphia: Chelsea House Publishers, 2006.

Cushing, Frank Hamilton. *Cushing at Zuni: The Correspondence and Journals of Frank Hamilton Cushing 1879–1884.* Edited by Jesse Green. Albuquerque: University of New Mexico Press, 1990.

Dodge, William. *Black Rock: Zuni Cultural Landscape and the Meaning of Place.* Biloxi: University Press of Mississippi, 2007.

Eckert, Suzanne L. "Zuni Demographic Structure, A.D. 1300–1680: A Case Study on Spanish Contact and Native Population Dynamics." *Kiva* 70, no. 3 (2005): 207–26.

Ostler, James. *Zuni: A Village of Silversmiths.* Zuni, NM: A:Shiwi Publishers, 1996.

Roscoe, William. *The Zuni Man-Woman.* Albuquerque: University of New Mexico Press, 1992.

Stevenson, Matilda Coxe. *The Zuni Indians: Their Mythology, Esoteric Fraternities and Ceremonies.* Washington, D.C.: Government Printing Office, 1904.

Wyaco, Virgil. *A Zuni Life: A Pueblo Indian in Two Worlds.* Albuquerque, NM: Side Canyon Press, 2004.

The Zuni People. *Zunis: Self-Portrayals.* Translated by Alvian Quam. Albuquerque: University of New Mexico Press, 1972.

ANNOTATED BIBLIOGRAPHY

Acuña, Rodolfo, and Guadalupe Compean. *Voices of the U.S. Latino Experience*. Westport, CT: Greenwood Press, 2008. The history of Latinos in the United States derived from letters, memoirs, speeches, articles, essays, interviews, treaties, government reports, testimony, and more.

Aguirre, Adalberto. *Racial and Ethnic Diversity in America: A Reference Handbook*. Santa Barbara, CA: ABC-CLIO, 2003. Examines, through current and historical census data, the populations and social forces that contribute to the racial and ethnic diversity of the United States.

Alba, Richard D., and Victor Nee. *Remaking the American Mainstream: Assimilation and Contemporary Immigration*. Cambridge, MA: Harvard University Press, 2003. Demonstrates the importance of assimilation in American society by looking at language, socioeconomic attachments, residential patterns, and intermarriage.

Alba, Richard D., and Mary C. Waters. *Next Generation: Immigrant Youth in a Comparative Perspective*. New York: New York University, 2011. An examination of second-generation immigrant youth in the United States and Western Europe.

American Ethnic Writers. Rev. ed. Pasadena, CA: Salem Press, 2009. Compiles and describes the works of African American, Asian American, Jewish American, Hispanic/Latino, and Native American writers.

Anderson, Wanni W., and Robert G. Lee, eds. *Displacements and Diasporas: Asians in the Americas*. New Brunswick, NJ: Rutgers University Press, 2005. An interdisciplinary look at the experiences of Asians in North and South America and how they have been shaped by the social and political dynamics of the countries in which they have settled as well as by their countries of origin.

Angell, Carole S. *Celebrations around the World: A Multicultural Handbook*. Golden, CO: Fulcrum, 1996. A month-by-month look at festivals from around the world.

Anglim, Christopher. *Encyclopedia of Religion and the Law in America*. 2nd ed. Amenia, NY: Grey House, 2009. Covers topics from prayer in schools to holiday displays on public property; includes a description of major cases.

Atwood, Craig D., et al. *Handbook of Denominations in the United States*. 13th ed. Nashville: Abingdon Press, 2010. This frequently updated handbook serves as a guide to the many denominations that make up the American religious experience.

Axtell, Roger E. *Gestures: The Do's and Taboos of Body Language around the World*. Rev. ed. New York: Wiley, 1998. Lists, illustrates, and explains the meaning of gestures from eighty-two countries around the world.

Banks, James A., ed. *Encyclopedia of Diversity in Education*. Thousand Oaks, CA: SAGE, 2012. A guide to research and statistics, case studies, best practices, and policies.

———, ed. *Handbook of Research on Multicultural Education*. 2nd ed. San Francisco: Jossey-Bass, 2004. A guide to advances in the research of multicultural education.

———. *Teaching Strategies for Ethnic Studies*. 8th ed. Boston: Pearson/Allyn & Bacon, 2009. Examines the current and emerging theory, research, and scholarship in the fields of ethnic studies and multicultural education.

Barkan, Elliott Robert, ed. *Immigrants in American History: Arrival, Adaptation, and Integration*. Santa Barbara, CA: ABC-CLIO, 2013. Covers the arrival, adaptation, and integration of immigrants into American culture from the 1500s to 2010.

Barkley, Elizabeth F. *Crossroads: The Multicultural Roots of America's Popular Music*. 2nd ed. Upper Saddle River, NJ: Pearson Prentice Hall, 2007. A comparative exploration of the music of Native Americans, European Americans, African Americans, Latino Americans, and Asian Americans.

Bayor, Ronald H., ed. *The Columbia Documentary History of Race and Ethnicity in America*. New York: Columbia University Press, 2004. Seeks to shed light on the many ways in which immigration, racial histories, and ethnic histories have shaped contemporary American society.

———, ed. *Multicultural America: An Encyclopedia of the Newest Americans*. Santa Barbara. CA: Greenwood, 2011. Profiles fifty of the largest immigrant groups in the United States.

Benson, Sonia, ed. *The Hispanic American Almanac: A Reference Work on Hispanics in the United States*. 3rd ed. Detroit: Gale, 2003. Examines the history and culture of Hispanic Americans with coverage of events, biographies, and demographic information.

Berlin, Ira. *The Making of African America: The Four Great Migrations*. New York: Viking, 2010. Interprets the history of African Americans by examining the forced migration of slavery, the relocation of slaves to interior southern states, the migrations to the north, and the more recent arrival of immigrants from African and Caribbean nations.

Berzok, Linda Murray, ed. *Storied Dishes: What Our Family Recipes Tell Us about Who We Are and Where We've Been*. Santa Barbara, CA: Praeger, 2011. An exploration of family history through recipes.

Bird, Stephanie Rose. *Light, Bright, and Damned Near White: Biracial and Triracial Culture in America*. Westport, CT: Praeger, 2009. Explores the challenges for, and psychological issues of, people with ethnically mixed ancestry.

Blank, Carla. *Rediscovering America: The Making of Multicultural America, 1900–2000*. New York: Three Rivers Press, 2003. A retelling of American history through the contributions of women, African Americans, Asian Americans, Hispanic Americans, and Native Americans, immigrants, artists, "renegades, rebels, and rogues."

Bona, Mary Jo, and Irma Maini, eds. *Multiethnic Literature and Canon Debates*. Albany: State University of New York Press, 2006. Critiques the debate over the inclusion of multiethnic literature in the American literary canon.

Boosahda, Elizabeth. *Arab-American Faces and Voices: The Origins of an Immigrant Community*. Austin: University of Texas Press, 2003. Looking at the long history of Arab Americans in the United States, this book includes personal interviews, photographs, and historical documents.

Bowler, Shaun, and Gary M. Segura. *The Future Is Ours: Minority Politics, Political Behavior, and the Multiracial Era of American Politics*. Thousand Oaks, CA: SAGE, 2012. A data-based examination of whether and how minority citizens differ from members of the white majority in political participation.

Brettell, Caroline. *Constructing Borders/Crossing Boundaries: Race, Ethnicity, and Immigration*. Lanham, MD: Lexington Books, 2008. Essays on a diverse range of immigrant populations from past to present that look at the boundaries and borders created by the social construction of race and ethnicity.

Bronner, Simon J., ed. *Encyclopedia of American Folklife*. Armonk, NY: M. E. Sharpe, 2006. Looks at the oral and written literary traditions, songs, and stories that make up a community's identity.

Brooks, Christopher Antonio, ed. *The African American Almanac*. 11th ed. Farmington Hills, MI: Gale Cengage Learning, 2011. A continually updated work from Gale's series of multicultural reference sources. Provides chronology, biography, events, and demography.

Buenker, John D., and Lorman A. Ratner, eds. *Multiculturalism in the United States: A Comparative Guide to Acculturation and Ethnicity*. Rev. ed. Westport, CT: Greenwood Press, 2005. Discusses how American culture has affected immigrants as well as how it has been shaped by them.

Cannato, Vincent J. *American Passage: The History of Ellis Island*. New York: Harper, 2009. Tells the story of Ellis Island from 1892 to 1924 using a variety of primary sources.

Carlisle, Rodney P., general ed. *Multicultural America*. 7 vols. New York: Facts On File, 2011. Presents the social history, customs, and traditions of ethnic groups throughout American history.

Carter, Susan B., ed. *Historical Statistics of the United States: Earliest Times to the Present*. 5 vols. New York: Cambridge University Press, 2006. Provides a historical perspective on statistics about the U.S. population, economy, government, and international relations.

Cesari, Jocelyne, ed. *Encyclopedia of Islam in the United States*. Westport, CT: Greenwood Press, 2007. Based on primary documents, this encyclopedia provides historical context for the current state of the practice of Islam in the United States.

Chi, Sang, and Emily Moberg Robinson, eds. *Voices of the Asian American and Pacific Islander Experience*. Santa Barbara, CA: Greenwood, 2012. Explores the experiences, views, and politics of recent Asian immigrants, emphasizing the diversity of experiences and viewpoints of individuals within the different nationalities and generations. Based on primary documents.

Ciment, James, and John Radzilowski, eds. *American Immigration: An Encyclopedia of Political, Social, and Cultural Change*. 2nd ed. 4 vols. Armonk, NY: M. E. Sharpe, 2013. American immigration from historic and contemporary perspectives. Primary documents include laws and treaties, referenda, Supreme Court cases, historical articles, and letters from 1787 to 2013.

Cohen, Selma Jeanne, ed. *International Encyclopedia of Dance*. 6 vols. New York: Oxford University Press, 2004. The definitive reference book for dance, documenting all types and styles of dance from around the world and throughout history.

Condra, Jill, ed. *The Greenwood Encyclopedia of Clothing through World History*. 3 vols. Westport, CT: Greenwood Press, 2008. Examines the history of clothing from all corners of the globe from pre-history to modern times.

Coontz, Stephanie, ed. *American Families: A Multicultural Reader*. 2nd ed. New York: Routledge, 2008. Brings together articles that look at the ethnic and racial diversity within families.

Cullum, Linda, ed. *Contemporary American Ethnic Poets: Lives, Works, Sources*. Westport, CT: Greenwood Press, 2004. Presents the lives and works of seventy-five poets.

Cordry, Harold V. *The Multicultural Dictionary of Proverbs: Over 20,000 Adages from More than 120 Languages, Nationalities and Ethnic Groups*. Jefferson, NC: McFarland, 1997. Presents 1,300 headings arranged by nationality, with a focus on European cultures.

Daniels, Roger. *Coming to America: A History of Immigration and Ethnicity in American Life*. 2nd ed. New York: Perennial, 2002. An overview of immigration to the United States from the colonial era to the beginning of the twenty-first century.

Danilov, Victor J. *Ethnic Museums and Heritage Sites in the United States*. Jefferson, NC: McFarland, 2009. A directory of all ethnic heritage sites in the United States.

Danky, James P., and Wayne A. Wiegand, eds. *Print Culture in a Diverse America*. Urbana: University of Illinois Press, 1998. Examines the multicultural world of reading and readers in the United States.

Davis, Rocío G., ed. *The Transnationalism of American Culture: Literature, Film, and Music*. New York: Routledge, 2012. A study of the border-crossing aspects of literature, film, and music.

Dinnerstein, Leonard, and David M. Reimers. *Ethnic Americans: A History of Immigration*. 5th ed. New York: Columbia University Press, 2009. Chapters examine the history of immigration to the United States chronologically, from the fifteenth century to 2008.

Dinnerstein, Leonard, Roger L. Nichols, and David M. Reimers. *Natives and Strangers: A History of Ethnic Americans*. 5th ed. New York: Oxford University Press, 2010. Examines the history of American ethnic groups and their impact on the character and social fabric of the United States.

Dodge, Abigail Johnson. *Around the World Cookbook*. New York: DK Publishing, 2008. A children's cookbook with fifty step-by-step recipes for preparing ethnic cuisine.

Ellicott, Karen, ed. *Countries of the World and Their Leaders Yearbook 2014*. 2 vols. Detroit: Gale, 2014. U.S. Department of State reports looking at all social, political, legal, economic, and environmental aspects for selected countries of the world.

Fleegler, Robert L. *Ellis Island Nation: Immigration Policy and American Identity in the Twentieth Century*. Philadelphia: University of Pennsylvania Press, 2013. Uses World War II films, records of Senate subcommittee hearings, and anti-Communist propaganda to view the evolution in the debate over immigration in the United States.

Franco, Dean J. *Ethnic American Literature: Comparing Chicano, Jewish, and African American Writing*. Charlottesville: University of Virginia Press, 2006. Provides a comparative approach to American ethnic literature.

Frazier, John W., Eugene L. Tettey-Fio, and Norah F. Henry, eds. *Race, Ethnicity, and Place in a Changing America*. 2nd ed. Albany: State University of New York Press, 2011. Looks at how race and ethnicity affects all aspects of everyday life.

Fredrickson, George M. *Diverse Nations: Explorations in the History of Racial and Ethnic Pluralism*. Boulder, CO: Paradigm Publishers, 2008. A comparative exploration of slavery and race relations in the United States, Europe, South Africa, and Brazil.

Gillota, David. *Ethnic Humor in Multiethnic America*. New Brunswick, NJ: Rutgers University Press, 2013. Investigates the role of humor in the national conversation on race and ethnicity and the response of contemporary comedians to multiculturalism.

Gilton, Donna L. *Multicultural and Ethnic Children's Literature in the United States*. Lanham, MD: Scarecrow Press, 2007. The history of and contemporary trends in U.S. multicultural children's literature.

Glenn, Evelyn Nakano. *Unequal Freedom: How Race and Gender Shaped American Citizenship and Labor*. Cambridge, MA: Harvard University Press, 2002. A comparative look at the history of inequality and specifically how labor and citizenship have been defined, enforced, and challenged in the United States.

González, Alberto, et al., eds. *Our Voices: Essays in Culture, Ethnicity, and Communication*. 5th ed. New York: Oxford University Press, 2012. Short first-person accounts that examine the varieties of intercultural communication covering discourses of gender, race, and ethnicity.

Grant-Thomas, Andrew, and Gary Orfield, eds. *Twenty-First Century Color Lines: Multiracial Change in Contemporary America*. Philadelphia: Temple University Press, 2009. The result of work initiated by the Harvard Civil Rights Project, this book provides an overview of contemporary racial and ethnic conditions in the United States.

Graves, Joseph L., Jr. *The Race Myth: Why We Pretend Race Exists in America*. New York: Dutton, 2004. Writing from a scientific perspective, Graves posits that racial distinctions are in fact social inventions, not biological truths.

Greene, Victor R. *American Immigrant Leaders, 1800–1910: Marginality and Identity*. Baltimore: Johns Hopkins University Press, 1987. The history of immigration through the lives of those who led.

Handlin, Oscar. *The Uprooted: The Epic Story of the Great Migrations That Made the American People*. 2nd ed. Philadelphia: University of Pennsylvania Press, 2002. Looks specifically at European migration to the United States during the late nineteenth and early twentieth centuries.

Hoerder, Dirk, ed. *The Immigrant Labor Press in North America, 1840s–1970s: An Annotated Bibliography*. New York: Greenwood Press, 1987. A look at the European immigrant press in the United States.

Jackson, Kenneth T., ed. *The Encyclopedia of New York City*. New Haven, CT: Yale University Press; New York: New York Historical Society, 2010. Entries on every aspect of the life and culture of the population of New York City.

Johansen, Bruce E. *Native Americans Today: A Biographical Dictionary*. Santa Barbara, CA: Greenwood Press, 2010. Biographical profiles of Native Americans from the twentieth and twenty-first centuries.

Johnson, Michael. *Encyclopedia of Native Tribes of North America*. Richmond Hill, Ontario: Firefly Books, 2007. An illustrated encyclopedia that provides information on North America's Native American populations.

Koppelman, Kent L., ed. *Perspectives on Human Differences: Selected Readings on Diversity in America*. Boston: Allyn & Bacon, 2011. An anthology of essays and short stories that explores issues of human diversity from multiple perspectives.

Kukathas, Uma, ed. *Race and Ethnicity*. Farmington Hills, MI: Greenhaven Press, 2008. Reflections on racial and ethnic identity in the United States as represented through institutional classification and the media.

Kurian, George Thomas, and Barbara A. Chernow, eds. *Datapedia of the United States: American History in Numbers*. 4th ed. Lanham, MD: Bernan Press, 2007. Based on historical statistics of the United States and the annual Statistical Abstract of the United States, Datapedia provides statistics in twenty-three areas for the years 1790–2003 with demographic projections to 2050. Updated regularly.

Lee, Erika, and Judy Young. *Angel Island: Immigrant Gateway to America*. New York: Oxford University Press, 2010. A comprehensive history of the Angel Island Immigration Station in the San Francisco Bay.

Lippy, Charles H., and Peter W. Williams, eds. *Encyclopedia of Religion in America*. Washington, DC: CQ Press, 2010. Explores origins, development, influence, and interrelations of faiths practiced in North America.

Mason, Patrick L., ed. *Encyclopedia of Race and Racism*. 2nd ed. 4 vols. Detroit: Macmillan Reference USA, 2013. A survey of the anthropological, sociological, historical, economic, and scientific theories of race and racism in the modern era.

McDonald, Jason. *American Ethnic History: Themes and Perspectives*. New Brunswick, NJ: Rutgers University Press, 2007. Looks at the reasons different ethnic groups have come to the United States, their treatment and adaptations, and the aspects that together build a sense of ethnic identity.

Min, Pyong Gap, ed. *Encyclopedia of Racism in the United States*. 3 vols. Westport, CT: Greenwood Press, 2005. Seeks to provide an understanding of U.S. minority groups and their experiences with the dominant culture.

Morgan, George G. *How to Do Everything: Genealogy*. 3rd ed. New York: McGraw-Hill, 2012. A guide to genealogical research in the twenty-first century.

Morrison, Joan, and Charlotte Fox Zabusky. *American Mosaic: The Immigrant Experience in the Words of Those Who Lived It*. Pittsburgh, PA: University of Pittsburgh Press, 1993. First-person accounts of the experiences of immigrants from Europe, Asia, the Middle East, South America, and South Africa.

Nelson, Emmanuel S., ed. *The Greenwood Encyclopedia of Multiethnic American Literature*. 5 vols. Westport, CT: Greenwood Press, 2005. Entries on authors and literature from multiethnic America.

Nettl, Bruno, et al., eds. *Garland Encyclopedia of World Music*. 10 vols. with CDs. New York: Garland, 1998–2002. A comprehensive look at music around the world by region and country. Also available online through Alexander Street Press.

Neusner, Jacob, ed. *World Religions in America: An Introduction*. 4th ed. Louisville, KY: Westminster John Knox Press, 2009. Each chapter examines the religious beliefs and practices of a separate American immigrant group.

Nimer, Mohamed. *The North American Muslim Resource Guide: Muslim Community Life in the United States and Canada.* New York: Routledge, 2002. Presents the history and contemporary status of Muslim communities in the United States. Also provides a directory of organizations, schools, centers, publications, and more.

Norton, Donna E. *Multicultural Children's Literature: Through the Eyes of Many Children.* 2nd ed. Upper Saddle River, NJ: Pearson/Merrill Prentice Hall, 2005. Highlights outstanding multicultural literature for children and young adults.

Ochoa, George, and Carter Smith. *Atlas of Hispanic-American History.* Rev. ed. New York: Facts on File, 2009. Using text, maps, and illustrations, this volume looks at the history of Hispanic American cultures.

Olson, James Stuart, and Heather Olson Beal. *The Ethnic Dimension in American History.* 4th ed. Malden, MA: Wiley-Blackwell, 2010. A survey of the role that ethnicity has played in shaping the history of the United States.

Overmyer-Velázquez, Mark. *Latino America: A State-by-State Encyclopedia.* 2 vols. Westport, CT: Greenwood Press, 2008. A chronological account of the presence and contributions of Latinos in each state and the District of Columbia from the beginning of recorded American history to the present.

Parrillo, Vincent N. *Strangers to These Shores: Race and Ethnic Relations in the United States.* 10th ed. Boston: Allyn & Bacon, 2011. A frequently updated text on racial and ethnic relations in the United States that looks at the experiences of more than fifty racial, ethnic, and religious groups.

Pinder, Sherrow O., ed. *American Multicultural Studies: Diversity of Race, Ethnicity, Gender, and Sexuality.* Thousand Oaks, CA: SAGE, 2013. Provides an interdisciplinary view of multicultural studies in the United States that addresses current and continuing issues of race, gender, ethnicity, sexuality, cultural diversity, and education.

Queen, Edward L., et al., eds. *Encyclopedia of American Religious History.* 3rd ed. 3 vols. New York: Facts On File, 2009. Covers the social and cultural histories of religious practices in the United States.

Ramsey, Paul J., ed. *The Bilingual School in the United States: A Documentary History.* Charlotte, NC: Information Age Pub., 2012. A history of bilingual education in the United States from the nineteenth century forward.

Rappoport, Leon. *Punchlines: The Case for Racial, Ethnic, and Gender Humor.* Westport, CT: Praeger, 2005. Looks at ethnic, racial, and gender humor as an instrument of prejudice and as a defense against it.

Recinos, Harold J., ed. *Wading through Many Voices: Toward a Theology of Public Conversation.* Lanham, MD: Rowman & Littlefield, 2011. Examines Christian theology as expressed by different immigrant and minority groups in the United States as well as its impact and implications for public discourse.

Reimers, David M. *Other Immigrants: The Global Origins of the American People.* New York: New York University Press, 2005. Chronicles the history of black, Hispanic, and Asian immigrants to the American continent from the fifteenth century through World War II.

Rhodes, Leara. *The Ethnic Press: Shaping the American Dream.* New York: Peter Lang, 2010. Documents the history of immigrants in America through an examination of their newspapers and their impact on American culture.

Rose, Christine, and Kay Germain Ingalls. *The Complete Idiot's Guide to Genealogy.* 3rd ed. New York: Alpha, 2012. The how-tos of exploring personal heritage through genealogical practice.

Rudnick, Lois Palken, Judith E. Smith, and Rachel Lee Rubin, eds. *American Identities: An Introductory Textbook.* Malden, MA: Blackwell, 2006. A collection of critical essays and primary documents taken from American history, literature, memoir, and popular culture that focuses on American identities of ethnicity and gender from World War II to the present.

Rumbaut, Rubén G., and Alejandro Portes, eds. *Ethnicities: Children of Immigrants in America.* Berkeley: University of California Press, 2001. Draws on the Children of Immigrants Longitudinal Study to look at second-generation immigrant youth from families of Mexican, Cuban, Nicaraguan, Filipino, Vietnamese, Haitian, Jamaican, and West Indian origin.

Sadie, Stanley. *The New Grove Dictionary of Music and Musicians.* 29 vols. New York: Grove, 2001. A 29-volume encyclopedic look at music from all time periods and all countries covering folk music and folk instruments as well as the classical tradition. Updated by Oxford Music Online.

Shay, Anthony. *Choreographing Identities: Folk Dance, Ethnicity and Festival in the United States and Canada.* Jefferson, NC: McFarland, 2006. A look at the importance of dance in the representation of cultural identity.

Sherrow, Victoria. *Encyclopedia of Hair: A Cultural History*. Westport, CT: Greenwood Press, 2006. Everything about hair across cultures and throughout time.

Shinagawa, Larry Hijime, and Michael Jang. *Atlas of American Diversity*. Walnut Creek, CA: AltaMira Press, 1998. A visual exploration through maps and charts of the social, economic, and geographic state of an ethnically diverse United States.

Shorris, Earl. *Latinos: A Biography of the People*. New York: W. W. Norton, 1992. Looks at Latino history from the time of the Spanish conquest of North and South America.

Snodgrass, Mary Ellen. *World Clothing and Fashion: An Encyclopedia of History, Culture, and Social Influence*. Armonk, NY: M. E. Sharpe, 2013. Approaches fashion from a global, multicultural, social, and economic perspective, covering prehistory to the present time.

Spickard, Paul R., ed. *Race and Immigration in the United States: New Histories*. New York: Routledge, 2012. Each essay looks at a particular aspect of immigrant experience, drawing attention to the ways the experiences differ depending on country of origin.

Statistical Abstract of the United States. Washington, DC: U.S. Gov. Print. Off., 1878–2012. The *Statistical Abstract* was compiled and published annually by the U.S. Census Bureau through 2012; beginning in 2013 it was instead published digitally by ProQuest. Provides an annual update of statistics about the characteristics and conditions of most aspects of life in the United States. For the historical perspective see *Historical Statistics of the United States: Earliest Times to the Present*, edited by Susan B. Carter.

Stave, Bruce M. Salerno, John F. Sutherland, and Aldo Salerno. *From the Old Country: An Oral History of European Migration to America*. New York: Maxwell Macmillan International, 1994. A compilation of oral histories describing the experience of migration and all aspects of the transition to life in a new country.

Strobel, Christoph. *Daily Life of the New Americans: Immigration since 1965*. Santa Barbara, CA: Greenwood, 2010. A history of twentieth- and twenty-first-century American immigrants through first-person and biographical narratives.

Stuhr, Rebecca. *Autobiographies by Americans of Color 1980–1994: An Annotated Bibliography*. Troy, NY: Whitston, 1997.

Stuhr, Rebecca, and Deborah Stuhr Iwabuchi. *Autobiographies by Americans of Color, 1995–2000: An Annotated Bibliography*. Albany, NY: Whitston, 2003. These two works together provide a comprehensive bibliography with extensive annotations for autobiographical works and oral histories.

Takaki, Ronald T. *A Different Mirror: A History of Multicultural America*. Boston: Little, Brown, 1993.

———. *Double Victory: A Multicultural History of America in World War II*. Boston: Little, Brown, 2000.

———. *Strangers from a Different Shore: A History of Asian Americans*. Boston: Little, Brown, 1989. Ronald Takaki was a pioneer in the field of ethnic studies. His books were among the very first to carefully and comprehensively explore the history and contemporary experiences of immigrants who crossed the Pacific to North America.

Thernstrom, Abigail M., and Stephan Thernstrom, eds. *Beyond the Color Line: New Perspectives on Race and Ethnicity in America*. Stanford, CA: Hoover Institution Press, Stanford University, 2002. Examines social, political, and economic changes that have taken place within ethnic America and the persistence of attitudes that create conditions of inequality.

Thernstrom, Stephan, ed. *Harvard Encyclopedia of American Ethnic Groups*. Cambridge, MA: Belknap Press of Harvard University, 1980. Although this work has never been updated, it continues to serve as a foundational text on the history and makeup of the population of the United States.

Thompson, William N. *Native American Issues: A Reference Handbook*. 2nd ed. Santa Barbara, CA: ABC-CLIO, 2005. An assessment of the problems faced by Native Americans, both historically and in the twenty-first century.

Ueda, Reed, ed. *A Companion to American Immigration*. Malden, MA: Blackwell, 2006. Scholarly essays on a range of topics, including law, health, politics, prejudice and racism, housing, education, labor, internationalism, and transnationalism.

Upton, Dell, ed. *America's Architectural Roots: Ethnic Groups That Built America*. New York: Preservation Press, 1986. An illustrated overview of the ethnic derivations of American architecture.

U.S. Census Bureau. *2000 Census of Population and Housing: Population and Housing Unit Counts* and *Summary Social, Economic, and Housing Characteristics*. Washington, DC: U.S. Dept. of Commerce, Economics, and Statistics Administration, U.S. Census Bureau, 2003. Two separate publications from the United States decennial census providing demographic and economic statistics on all populations within the United States.

Verbrugge, Allen, ed. *Muslims in America*. Detroit: Greenhaven Press, 2005. Looks at different aspects of life for Muslims in the United States, including gender, family, college life, politics, and the repercussions of 9/11, with narratives of personal experiences.

Vigdor, Jacob L. *From Immigrants to Americans: The Rise and Fall of Fitting In*. Lanham, MD: Rowman & Littlefield, 2009. A view of the challenges of belonging in the United States, with chapters on economics, linguistics, citizenship, neighborhoods, and family.

Walch, Timothy, ed. *Immigrant America: European Ethnicity in the United States*. New York: Garland, 1994. Examines the experiences of European immigrants to specific regions of the United States.

Waldman, Carl. *Encyclopedia of Native American Tribes*. 3rd ed. New York: Facts On File, 2006. Covers more than 200 American Indian tribes of North America.

Walkowitz, Rebecca L., ed. *Immigrant Fictions: Contemporary Literature in an Age of Globalization*. Madison: University of Wisconsin Press, 2006. A look at contemporary literature by immigrant authors from China, Eastern Europe, and other countries. Includes interviews.

Webb, Lois Sinaiko, and Lindsay Grace Roten. *The Multicultural Cookbook for Students*. Rev. ed. Santa Barbara, CA: Greenwood Press, 2009. Recipes are arranged by region and country and are preceded by an account of the geography, history, and culinary traditions of their country of origin.

Weil, François. *Family Trees: A History of Genealogy in America*. Cambridge, MA: Harvard University Press, 2013. A history of the practice of genealogy from its early methodology to the use of the database Ancestry.com and DNA testing; from a preoccupation with social status to an acceptance and celebration of diverse ethnic heritage.

Welsch, Janice R., and J. Q. Adams. *Multicultural Films: A Reference Guide*. Westport, CT: Greenwood Press, 2005. Provides brief synopses and critiques of motion pictures that explore race and ethnicity.

Wertsman, Vladimir. *What's Cooking in Multicultural America: An Annotated Bibliographic Guide to Over Four Hundred Ethnic Cuisines*. Lanham, MD: Scarecrow Press, 1996. An annotated bibliography to cookbooks, covering the cuisines of more than four hundred ethnic groups from all continents.

Wills, Chuck. *Destination America*. New York: DK Pub., 2005. Through personal accounts, letters, diaries, photographs, statistics, maps, and charts, examines the reasons immigrants leave home to travel to the United States and the conditions of their lives once they arrive.

York, Sherry. *Ethnic Book Awards: A Directory of Multicultural Literature for Young Readers*. Worthington, OH: Linworth, 2005. Provides an alphabetical listing of titles winning various book awards, including the Coretta Scott King, Carter G. Woodson, and Tomás Rivera Mexican American Children's book awards.

PERIODICALS

African American Review (1992–). Terre Haute: Dept. of English, Indiana State University. Print and online. Continues *Black American Literature Forum* (1976–1991). History and criticism of African American literature.

Amerasia Journal (1971–). Los Angeles: University of California, Los Angeles; and Yale Asian American Students Association. Print and Online. An interdisciplinary journal studying all aspects of Asian American society, jointly published by the UCLA Asian American Studies Center and the Yale Asian American Students Association.

Callaloo (1976–). Baltimore, MD: Johns Hopkins University Press. Print and Online. An African diaspora literary journal founded at Southern University in Baton Rouge, Louisiana, and now sponsored by Texas A&M University and published by Johns Hopkins University Press.

Ethnic NewsWatch (1998–). ProQuest Information and Learning. Online. Newspaper articles from the ethnic American presses. Dates of coverage depend on arrangements with each particular newspaper. Searchable via keywords and broad ethnic group.

Ethnic Studies Review: The Journal of the National Association for Ethnic Studies (1996–). Tempe, AZ: National Association for Ethnic Studies. Print and Online. A multidisciplinary international journal devoted to the study of ethnicity, ethnic groups and their cultures, and intergroup relations. Preceded by *Explorations in Ethnic Studies*.

Hispanic American Historical Review (HAHR) (1918–). Durham, NC: Duke University Press. Print and Online. Covers Latin American history and culture.

International Migration Review: IMR (1966–). New York: Center for Migration Studies. Print and Online. A quarterly interdisciplinary, peer-reviewed journal created to encourage and facilitate the study of all aspects of international migration.

Journal of American Ethnic History (1981–). Champaign: University of Illinois Press. Print and Online. Addresses various aspects of American immigration and ethnic history, including history of emigration, ethnic and racial groups, Native Americans, immigration policies, and the processes of acculturation.

Journal of Intercultural Studies (1980–). Melbourne: River Seine Publications. Print and Online. Covers cultural studies, sociology, gender studies, political science, cultural geography, urban studies, race, and ethnic studies.

MELUS: Society for the Study of the Multi-Ethnic Literature of the United States (1974–). Storrs: University of Connecticut, Dept. of English. Provides interviews and reviews that explore and bring light to the multiethnic character of American literature.

Multicultural Education (1993–). San Francisco: Caddo Gap Press. An independent quarterly magazine featuring research on promising pedagogical practices in art, music, and literature.

Rebecca Stuhr

SUBJECT INDEX

Volume numbers are denoted in **bold** (e.g., Armstrong, Louis, **1**:54). Main entry page ranges are represented as ***bold/italic*** (e.g., Acadians, **1**:*1–15*). Page numbers in italics refer to photographs and illustrations.

B

Babylonian Empire, **2**:557

Baca, Jimmy Santiago, **1**:121, **3**:214

Bacalhau (codfish casserole), **1**:348

Bacall, Lauren, **2**:576

Bacalodo (food), **3**:531

Baccarin, Morena, **1**:353

Bach, Howard, **4**:510

Bacharach, Burt, **2**:575

Bachelet Jeria, Michelle, **1**:480

Bachelis, Faren, **4**:48

Bachi, Pietro, **4**:160

Bacho, Peter, **2**:133

Baci, **3**:56–57

BACI (Burmese American Community Institute), **1**:378, 380

Back to Africa movement, **1**:37, **2**:533

Back to the Future (film), **3**:123

Backslider (Peterson), **3**:241

Bad Spirit (mythology), **3**:379

BADA (Burmese American Democratic Alliance), **1**:379, 380

Baderinwa, Folosade (Sade) Olayinka, **3**:340

Badminton, Indonesian Americans, **2**:409

Badr, M. Safwan, **4**:340

Baez, Alberto Vinicio, **3**:215

Baeza, Braulio, **3**:455

Baganda people, **4**:449–452, 454, 456
    See also Ugandan Americans

Bagdasarian, Ross, **1**:162

Bagels, Belarusan origin, **1**:269

Baglama sazi (lute), **4**:443

Bagpipes, **1**:365, **4**:106

Bagration, Teymuraz, **2**:203

Bah, Hamjat Jallomy, **4**:171

Baha'ism
    Iranian Americans, **2**:435, 436, 439
    Jamaicans and Jamaican Americans, **2**:527

Bahamas, overview, **1**:211–213

The Bahamas Weekly (news source), **1**:219

Bahamian American Association, Inc. (BAAI), **1**:220

Bahamian American Cultural Society, **1**:220

Bahamian Americans, **1**:*211–220*
    cultural aspects, **1**:211, 214–217, *215,* 218–220
    economic and political aspects, **1**:211, 213–214, 218
    family and community life, **1**:*217,* 217–218
    history and settlement, **1**:211–214, *213*

Bahamian Standard English, **1**:214–215

Bahasa Malaysia language, **3**:157

Bahasan Indonesia language, **2**:403–404

Bahati, David, **4**:450

Baho vigorrón (food), **3**:321

Bahr, Stephen, **3**:236, 239

Báiki: The North American Sámi Journal, **2**:148

Bailey, E. G., **3**:99

Bajan dialect, **1**:241–242

Bajraktarević, Tea, **4**:146

Bak, Sunny, **2**:409

Bakardade (sculpture), **1**:257

Baker, Bill John, **1**:455

Baker, Ella, **1**:55

Baker, Eugene M., **1**:303

Baker, Herman, **2**:43

Baker, James, **1**:339

Baker, Josephine, **2**:159

Baker, Sidney, **1**:183

Baker Book House, **2**:43

Bakersfield Daily Californian (newspaper), **1**:263

Baklava
    Chaldean Americans, **1**:446
    Macedonian Americans, **3**:146
    Syrian Americans, **4**:336
    Turkish Americans, **4**:443

Balaban, Barney, **2**:573

Balabanov, Hristo, **1**:359

Balaguer, Joaquin, **2**:16

Balah (dance), **4**:539

Balanchine, George, **2**:*204,* 205, **4**:42

Balanchivadze, George. *See* Balanchine, George

Balboa, Vasco Núñez de, **2**:275

Balch Institute for Ethnic Studies, **2**:521, **3**:77, **4**:162, 220, 328

Baldacci, John, **1**:137

Baldvinsdottir, Helga Steinvor, **2**:398

Baldwin, Alec, **2**:472

Baley, Virko, **4**:471

Bali
    dance, **2**:406, *407*
    Hinduism, **2**:401, 404

Balkan Wars, **1**:359, 360, **4**:135

Ball games
    Basque Americans, **1**:261
    Choctaws, **1**:513
    Creeks, **1**:559
    Grenadian Americans, **2**:259
    Vietnamese Americans, **4**:507

Ballet
    Cambodian Americans, **1**:387
    Estonian Americans, **2**:104, *104*
    Georgian Americans, **2**:*204,* 205
    Japanese Americans, **2**:554

Ballet Hispanico, **4**:490, 495

Baloch people, **2**:433

Balon, Dave, **4**:472

Balowahdiwa (Zuni leader), **4**:556

Balti (Tunisian artist), **4**:431–432

Baltic Appeal to the United Nations (BATUN), **3**:74

Baltic Women's Council, **2**:103

Baltic World Council, **2**:103

Baltimore, Maryland
    Belarusan Americans, **1**:265
    Jewish Americans, **2**:559

Balzary, Michael. *See* Flea (musician)

Balzekas Museum of Lithuanian Culture, **3**:127

Bamba, Ahamadou, **4**:124

Banac, Ivo, **1**:586

Banaha (song), **1**:537

Bananas
    Ecuadorians, **2**:52
    Garifunas, **2**:186
    Guatemala, **2**:186
    Hondurans and Honduran Americans, **2**:186, 345, 346, 347–348

Banateo, Dado, **2**:131

Bandak, Lily, **2**:588

Bandak Arab African Foundation, **2**:589

Bean dishes
Asian Indian Americans, **1**:169
Basque Americans, **1**:257
Belizean Americans, **1**:294
Chilean Americans, **1**:484
Creeks, **1**:559
Nicaraguan Americans, **3**:320–321
Bearden, Romare, **1**:57
Beastie Boys, **2**:574
Beatrix (queen of the Netherlands), **2**:36
Beatty, Warren, **4**:98
Beatty, Willard, **3**:263
Beauregard, Pierre Gustave Toutant, **1**:575
Beausoleil, Joseph Broussard dit, **1**:13
BeauSoleil (musical group), **1**:13
Beautiful Hills of Brooklyn (Cassedy), **3**:123
The Beautiful Things that Heaven Bears (Mengestu), **2**:116
Beauty industry, Vietnamese Americans, **4**:503, 508
Beauty pageants
Dominican Americans, **2**:25
Druze, **2**:31
Filipino Americans, **2**:127, 133
Beaver, Fred, **1**:563, **4**:119
Beaver, Lucy, **4**:552
Beaver medicine bundles, **1**:307
Beaver Wars, **2**:478
Beck, Mary, **4**:469
Beck, Richard, **2**:398
Becker, Marion Rombauer, **2**:218
Beckford, George, **2**:534
Bedawiyet language, **2**:88
Bednarik, Charles, **4**:218, 472
Bedouins, **2**:579, 580, 582, 583, 584–585
Bedoya, Alejandro, **1**:529
Bedwardism, **2**:527
Beecher, Catharine E., **4**:530
Beechey, F. W., **2**:422
Beer
Australian Americans, **1**:184
Austrian Americans, **1**:195
Belgian Americans, **1**:279
Czech Americans, **1**:627

German Americans, **2**:212, 217, 218
Irish Americans, **2**:466
Wales, **4**:529
Before the Mayflower (Bennett), **1**:31, 36
Before the Rain (film), **3**:152
Beg, Teodor, **1**:587
Begay, Fred, **3**:274
Begay, Harrison, **3**:273
Beggs, Joseph, **1**:588
Begich, Mark, **1**:585, 587
Begich, Nick, **1**:587
Behar, Ruth, **1**:602
Beiguan (music style), **4**:349
Beilin, Israel, **4**:42
Bektashi Order, **1**:65
Bekwerban marriage, **2**:114
Belafonte, Harry, **2**:529, 535
Belanger, J. William, **2**:178
Belarus, overview, **1**:265–267
Belarus Digest (online newsletter), **1**:273
Belarus Today (newspaper), **1**:273
Belarus TV, **1**:273
Belarusan-American Association (BAZA), **1**:269, 271, 272, 273
Belarusan American Community Center, **1**:273
Belarusan Americans, **1**:*265–287*
cultural aspects, **1**:268–270, *271, 272,* 272–274, *273*
economic and political aspects, **1**:271
family and community life, **1**:271
history and settlement, **1**:265–268, *267*
Belarusan Autocephalous Orthodox Church (BAOC), **1**:268
Belarusan language, **1**:268
Belarusian Telegraph Agency, **1**:273
Belarusian Youth Movement of America, **1**:271, 272, 273
Belejcak, Thomas. *See* Bell, Thomas
Belfast Peace Agreement, **4**:90
Belgian-American Association, **1**:286
Belgian American Chamber of Commerce, **1**:286
Belgian American Educational Foundation, **1**:284, 286

Belgian American Heritage Society of West Virginia, **1**:287
Belgian Americans, **1**:*275–287*
cultural aspects, **1**:278–281, *283,* 284–287
economic and political aspects, **1**:276–277, 283–284
family and community life, **1**:*281,* 281–283
history and settlement, **1**:275–277, *277*
Belgian endive, **1**:280
Belgian Ethnic Island (Wisconsin), **1**:277, 282
Belgian lace, **1**:280
Belgian Laces (bulletin), **1**:286
Belgian Researchers (organization), **1**:287
Belgian waffles, **1**:280
Belgium
Congo region colonization, **1**:532
overview, **1**:275–276, 284
Belgrano-Deutsch language, **1**:144
Belini, Esther G., **3**:273–274
Belisle, Eugene-Louis, **2**:179
Belize
Garifunas and Garifuna Americans, **2**:185, 186, 187, 189, 190
history, **1**:289–290
Belize Cultural Foundation, **1**:296, 297, 299
Belize Culture and Heritage Association (BCHA), **1**:299
Belize in America, **1**:299
Belize Kriol English, **1**:292
Belize Settlement Day. *See* Garifuna Settlement Day
Belizean Americans, **1**:*289–299*
cultural aspects, **1**:289, 292–295, *297,* 297–299, *298*
economic and political aspects, **1**:290, 291, 296–297
family and community life, **1**:295–296
history and settlement, **1**:289–292, *291*
Belizean Melody Music Show (radio program), **2**:194
Belizean National Day, **1**:295

C

on Romani Americans, **4**:12

Tibetan Americans, **4**:383

Vietnam relations, **4**:501

Clinton, Hillary Rodham, **4**:*139*

Albanian American relations, **1**:64

French/French-Canadian ancestry, **2**:162, 180–181

on Romani Americans, **4**:7, 12

Welsh ancestry, **4**:529, 530

Clipa (magazine), **4**:27

Clitoridectomy

Kenyan Americans, **3**:7

Liberian Americans, **3**:97

Nigerian Americans, **3**:335

Sierra Leonean Americans, **4**:173

Close the Gap campaign (Australia), **1**:181

Clothing. *See* Dress

CMAS (Center for Mexican American Studies), **3**:216

CNC (Cuban American National Council), **1**:604

CNFS (Chicagoland Nepali Friendship Society), **3**:287

CNHS (Cherokee National Historical Society), **1**:464

Coalition for Korean American Voters, **3**:35

Coalition of Progressive Liberians in the Americas (COPLA), **3**:99

Coalition of Women from Asia and the Middle East, **2**:440

Cobb, Tyrus, **4**:145

Cobell v. Salazar (class-action lawsuit), **1**:315

Coccia, Elda, **2**:515

Coccia, Joseph, **2**:515

Cochran, George, **1**:461

Coconut Grove graveyard, **1**:218

Coconuts

Garifuna cuisine, **2**:189

Guamanian cuisine, **2**:267–268

Hawaiian cuisine, **2**:322

Cocorioko Newspaper, **4**:165, 168, 177

Cod Wars, **2**:388

Code Noir (black code), **1**:568

Code of Handsome Lake, **3**:377

Code Talkers, Navajo, **3**:272

Codrescu, Andrei, **4**:26

Cody, Buffalo Bill, **2**:198

Coe, Peter, **1**:586

Coelho, Peter "Tony," **3**:504

Coffee, Robin, **1**:462

Coffee drinking

Chaldean Americans, **1**:444

Croatian Americans, **1**:582

Cypriot Americans, **1**:612

Ecuadorian Americans, **2**:53

Eritrean Americans, **2**:91

Finnish Americans, **2**:143

Garifunas and Garifuna Americans, **2**:191

Jordanians and Jordanian Americans, **2**:584

Turkish Americans, **4**:440–441

Coffee production, Yemen, **4**:534

Cohen, William Howard. *See* Cosell, Howard

Cohn, Harry, **2**:573

Cohn, Jack, **2**:573

Coining (healing practice), **1**:389, **4**:506

Colbert, Claudette, **2**:163–164

Colchi people, **2**:197

See also Georgian Americans

Cold War

Guam, **2**:264

Iceland, **2**:388

Japan, **2**:538

Lithuania, **3**:113

Soviet Union, **4**:33

Cole, Johnnetta B., **1**:52, **4**:131

Cole, Thomas, **2**:84

College of Menominee Nation, **3**:183, 185, 191

Colleton, John, **1**:240

Collier, John, **3**:263

Collins, Billy, **2**:471

Collor de Mello, Fernando, **1**:344, 352

Colombia, overview, **1**:519–521, **2**:48

Colombia Unites Us, **1**:528

Colombian American Association (CAA), **1**:530

Colombian American Coalition of Florida, **1**:530

Colombian American Cultural Society, **1**:530

Colombian American Service Association (CASA), **1**:530

Colombian Americans, **1**:*519–530*

cultural aspects, **1**:523–525, *526*, 528–530, *529*

economic and political aspects, **1**:519, 522, 524, *524*, 527–528

family and community life, **1**:526–527

history and settlement, **1**:519–523, *521*

Colón, Jesús, **3**:537

Colón, Miriam, **3**:536

Colon, Mirtha, **2**:190, 193

Colon, Teofilo, Jr., **2**:*189*

Colonialism effects

Africa, **1**:32, 42

Aleuts, **1**:75–76, 77, 81, 83

Algeria, **1**:87

Apache, **1**:114, 116, 118

Argentina, **1**:141–142

Australia, **1**:179–180

Bahamas, **1**:211–212

Bangladesh, **1**:222

Barbados, **1**:238–240, 245, 246

Belize, **1**:289–290

Bolivia, **1**:319–320

Brazil, **1**:344

Burma, **1**:373–374, 375

Cambodia, **1**:382

Canada, **1**:395–396, 397

Cape Verde, **1**:407–410

Catawba Indian Nation, **1**:434

Cherokees, **1**:454, 456

Chile, **1**:479

Colombia, **1**:520

Congo region, **1**:532, 534

Costa Rica, **1**:543

Cuba, **1**:591–592

Cyprus, **1**:608, 609

Ecuador, **2**:48

Egypt, **2**:62

Eritrea, **2**:87

Ethiopia, **2**:108

Garifunas and Garifuna Americans, **2**:188

Ghana, **2**:226

Greece, **2**:239

G

H

Jobs, Steve, **1**:136, **4**:340

Jochumsson, Matthias, **2**:393

Jodo Shinshu sect, **2**:542

Joest, Ricardo Manduro, **2**:347

John Canoe dance, **2**:190, 530

John Chryostom, St., **4**:19

The John Dau Foundation, **4**:303

John J. Burns Library, Boston College, **2**:475

John Paul II (pope), **1**:596, 601

Johns Hopkins University Center for Canadian Studies, **1**:405

Johnson, Alvin, **2**:10

Johnson, Dwane "The Rock," **3**:409, **4**:71

Johnson, Earvin, **1**:56

Johnson, Elias, **2**:489

Johnson, Emily, **4**:552

Johnson, Jack, **2**:235

Johnson, James Patrick, **4**:71

Johnson, James Weldon, **1**:55, 219, *219*

Johnson, John H., **1**:57

Johnson, Kenneth, **1**:563

Johnson, Lyndon B.
  Blackfoot programs, **1**:313
  civil rights support, **1**:49
  Dominican Republic, **2**:16
  on Romanian Americans, **4**:25
  Taiwanese Americans, **4**:345
  Thai Americans, **4**:366
  Vietnam relations, **4**:501

Johnson, Melvin, **2**:148

Johnson, Michael G., **3**:301

Johnson, Omotunde, **4**:176

Johnson, Philip, **3**:272

Johnson, Robert L., **1**:40

Johnson, Sargent, **1**:56

Johnson, Shoshana, **3**:455, *455*

Johnson, Sonia, **3**:240

Johnson, Viena Pasanen, **2**:147

Johnson-Reed Act of 1924. *See* Immigration Act of 1924

Johnson Sirleaf, Ellen, **3**:93

Joint Baltic American National Committee, **2**:103, **3**:119

Joint Region Edge (online publication), **2**:272

Jojola, Ted, **3**:519

Jolson, Al, **3**:*124*

Jonáă, Charles, **1**:628, 629

Jonas, Susanne, **2**:288

Jones, Dan, **4**:526

Jones, George Heber, **3**:26

Jones, Grace, **2**:535

Jones, Jim, **1**:162, **2**:297

Jones, Mango, **4**:518

Jones, Marion, **1**:298, *298*

Jones, Mary Harris "Mother," **2**:470

Jones, Norah, **1**:176

Jones-Jackson, Patricia, **4**:171

Jonestown Massacre, **2**:297

Jong, Erica, **2**:574

Jonkunnu. *See* John Canoe dance

Jordache Enterprises, Inc., **2**:501–502

Jordan
  Arab Americans, **1**:125, 126
  Druze, **2**:27
  embassy, **2**:589
  history, **2**:579–581
  Israel, **2**:494, 579, 580, 581
  United States, **2**:588
  See also Jordanian Americans

Jordan, June, **2**:534

Jordan, Michael, **1**:56

Jordan National Committee for Women (JNCW), **2**:587

Jordan Times (newspaper), **2**:589

Jordanian Americans, **2**:*579–589*
  cultural aspects, **2**:582–586, 588–589, *589*
  economic and political aspects, **2**:587–588
  family and community life, **2**:586–587
  history and settlement, **2**:579–582, *582*

Jordanian Bedouins, **2**:579, 580, 583

Joropo (music style), **4**:490

Joseph, Carole M. Berotte, **2**:314

Joseph, Lawrence, **1**:137

Joseph, Lynn, **4**:423

Joseph Fielding Smith Institute for Church History, Brigham Young University, **3**:233

Joseph Smith: Rough Stone Rolling (Bushman), **3**:241

Josephy, Alvin M., Jr., **3**:304

Joshi, Sushma, **3**:285–286

Jour des Aleux (Ancestors' Day), **2**:311

Jourgenson, Al, **1**:603

Le Journal de Lowell (newspaper), **2**:181

Le Journal Francais des États-Unis, **2**:164

Journal of Baltic Studies, **2**:105

Journal of British Studies, **2**:85

Journal of Cherokee Studies, **1**:463

Journal of Croatian Studies, **1**:588

Journal of Palestine Studies, **3**:446–447

Journal of Scotch-Irish Studies, **4**:99

Journal of the International Association of Tibetan Studies, **4**:384

Journalism contributions
  Afghan Americans, **1**:28
  African Americans, **1**:53–54
  Albanian Americans, **1**:70
  Arab Americans, **1**:137
  Argentinean Americans, **1**:148–149
  Asian Indian Americans, **1**:176
  Australian Americans, **1**:186
  Austrian Americans, **1**:198
  Barbadian Americans, **1**:246
  Basque Americans, **1**:262
  Belarusan Americans, **1**:272
  Bolivian Americans, **1**:328
  Brazilian Americans, **1**:353
  Bulgarian Americans, **1**:359, 369
  Burmese Americans, **1**:379
  Cambodian Americans, **1**:391
  Canadian Americans, **1**:402
  Choctaws, **1**:517
  Congolese Americans, **1**:539–540
  Croatian Americans, **1**:587
  Czech Americans, **1**:629
  Danish Americans, **2**:11
  Dominican Americans, **2**:24
  Dutch Americans, **2**:43
  Ecuadorian Americans, **2**:59
  Egyptian Americans, **2**:70
  English Americans, **2**:84
  Estonian Americans, **2**:104

K

N

Sicangu Sun Times (newspaper), **4**:205

Sicilian Americans, **4**:*151–163*

> cultural aspects, **4**:154–158, 160–163

> economic and political aspects, **4**:159–160

> family and community life, **4**:158–159

> history and settlement, **4**:151–153, *153*

Sicilian language, **4**:154

Sicilian Vespers Revolt, **4**:152

Sickle cell disease

> African Americans, **1**:41

> Garifuna and Garifuna Americans, **2**:351

> Moroccan Americans, **3**:253

> Nigerian Americans, **3**:335

> Saudi Arabians, **4**:80

Sidama people, **2**:107

Sidamon-Eristoff, Constantine, **2**:203

Siddiq, Jawid, **1**:28

Siddiqi, Dina, **1**:232–233

Siddique, Palbasha, **1**:233

Siddiqui, Asif Azam, **1**:232

Sidhwa, Bapsi, **3**:435

Sidibe, Gabourey, **4**:131

Sierra Leone Truth and Reconciliation Commission (SLTRC), **4**:167

Sierra Leonean Americans, **4**:*165–178*

> cultural aspects, **4**:168–173, 176–178

> economic and political aspects, **4**:175–176

> family and community life, **4**:173–175

> history and settlement, **4**:165–168, *169*

Sigerist, Henry E., **4**:326

Signani (liquor), **1**:326

Signs Following (faith), **4**:*93*

Sigurðardottir, Jóhanna, **2**:389

Sigurðsson, Jón, **2**:388

Sihamoni, Norodom. *See* Norodom Sihamoni

Sihanouk, Norodom. *See* Norodom Sihanok

Siirtolaisuusinstituutti/Institute of Migration, **2**:150–151

Sikahema, Vai, **4**:409

Sikander, Shahzia, **3**:434, *435*

Sikh American Chamber of Commerce (SACC), **4**:191

Sikh American Legal Defense and Education Fund (SALDEF), **4**:191

Sikh Americans, **4**:*179–192*

> Asian Indian Americans, **1**:165, 166, 168, 169

> cultural aspects, **4**:182–188, 189–191

> economic and political aspects, **4**:189

> family and community life, **4**:188–189

> history and settlement, **4**:179–182, *181*

Sikh Coalition, **4**:191

Sikh Foundation, **4**:191

Sikh History Museum and Library, **4**:191

Sikh Independence Day Parade, **4**:*187*

Sikh Research Institute, **4**:191

Sikhchic (magazine), **4**:190

Sikorsky, Igor, **4**:42, 471

Siksika language, **1**:305–306

Siku (musical instrument), **1**:323

Silberman, Jerome. *See* Wilder, Gene

Silent Night (song), **1**:194

Silicon and Synapse, **2**:69

Silk, George, **3**:297

Silko, Leslie Marmon, **3**:520

Sills, Beverly, **2**:575

Silva, Clarence Richard, **3**:505

Silva, Horace. *See* Silver, Horace

Silva, Justiano, **3**:505

Silva, Monica da, **1**:353

Silva Greaves, Abilio de, **3**:504

Silveira, Maria, **3**:505

Silver, Horace, **1**:416–417

Silver Bluff Baptist Church, **1**:37

Silver mining, **3**:412

Silvercraft Cooperative Guild, **2**:371

Silverheels, Jay, **2**:489

Silverman, Belle. *See* Sills, Beverly

Silverman, Carol, **4**:3, 5–6, 8, 11

Silverman, Sarah, **2**:576

Silvetti Adorno, Juan Fernando, **1**:149

Simenon, Georges, **1**:285

Simic, Charles, **4**:146

Simitian, Joe, **1**:160

Simmons, Al, **3**:489

Simmons, Gene, **2**:384

Simms (Simoncic), Eddie, **4**:230

Simon, Paul, **4**:263

Simon, Paul (1941–), **2**:384, 575

Simon Paneak Memorial Museum, **2**:430

Simonovich, Milletta, **4**:142

Simons, Menno, **1**:97, **3**:171, 172

Simply Ming (television show), **3**:501

Simply Scottish Radio (radio program), **4**:111

Simpson, James H., **3**:262

Simpson, Jerry, **1**:400

Simpson, Mona, **1**:137

Simpson-Miller, Portia, **2**:525

Sinatra, Frank, **2**:519, **4**:161

Sinclair, Madge, **2**:535

Sing, Lillian, **1**:503

Sing Alleluia (album), **3**:177

Sing and Rejoice (hymnbook), **3**:176

Sing Tao Daily (newspaper), **1**:504, **4**:354

Singel, Mark, **1**:429

Singh, Lakshmi, **4**:422

Singh, Manmohan, **4**:182

Singh, Ranjit, **4**:180

Singing bowls (Tibet), **4**:378

Singstad, Ole, **3**:355

Sinh (skirt), **3**:57

Sinhala/Tamil New Year, **4**:289–290

Sinnolai, Satu Khampoui, **3**:56

Sino-Japanese Wars (1894-1895 and 1937-1945), **2**:538, **4**:344

Sioux, **4**:*193–207*

> cultural aspects, **2**:370, **4**:196–201, 203–207

> economic and political aspects, **4**:202–203

> family and community life, **4**:201–202

> history and settlement, **4**:193–196, *197*

Sioux Indian Museum at the Journay Museum, **4**:207

Touceda, Julian Albert, **2**:354

Touma, Habib Hassan, **4**:80

Toure, Kwame. *See* Carmichael, Stokely

Tourism

    Apache region, **1**:120

    Australia, **1**:184

    Barbados, **1**:245

    Guam, **2**:264, 265, 271

    Hawaiians, **2**:327

    Jamaica, **2**:534

    Menominee region, **3**:185, 191

    Navajo region, **3**:270

    Oneida region, **3**:383

    Paiute region, **3**:421

    Pueblo region, **3**:518

    Virgin Islands, **4**:515, 519–520

Tourtière (French-Canadian dish), **2**:158

Tousey, Sheila, **3**:193

Toussaint, Pierre, **2**:307

Tovil (dances), **4**:289

Toyota v. United States (1925), **2**:124

TPS (Temporary Protected Status), **4**:50

Tracey, Patrick, **2**:467

Trachten (garments), **1**:195, **4**:323

Tracy, Alexandre de Prouville, **2**:168

Tracy, Spencer, **2**:472

Traditional arts and crafts. *See* Arts and crafts traditions

Traditional medicine

    Aleuts, **1**:80–81

    Amish, **1**:104

    Apache, **1**:118

    Bahamian Americans, **1**:217

    Belgian Americans, **1**:279

    Belizean Americans, **1**:295

    Catawba Indian Nation, **1**:437

    Cherokees, **1**:459

    Costa Rican Americans, **1**:546

    Guatemalan Americans, **2**:284

    Haitian Americans, **2**:311

    Hawaiians, **2**:323

    Hmong Americans, **2**:337–338

    Honduran Americans, **2**:351

    Hopis, **2**:364

    Irish Americans, **2**:467

Iroquois Confederacy, **2**:484–485

Mexican Americans, **3**:205

Mongolian Americans, **3**:227

Navajos, **3**:265, 266–267

Nepalese Americans, **3**:283

Nicaraguan Americans, **3**:322

Ojibwe, **3**:364, 367

Oneidas, **3**:381

Pacific Islander Americans, **3**:407

Paiutes, **3**:419

Pakistani Americans, **3**:432

Tibetan Americans, **4**:379

Zuni, **4**:560

Traditions and customs

    Acadians, **1**:7–8

    African Americans, **1**:38

    Albanian Americans, **1**:66

    Amish, **1**:100–102

    Arab Americans, **1**:130

    Asian Indian Americans, **1**:169

    Australian Americans, **1**:183–184

    Austrian Americans, **1**:194–195

    Bahamian Americans, **1**:216

    Bangladeshi Americans, **1**:228

    Barbadian Americans, **1**:243

    Basque Americans, **1**:256–257

    Belarusan Americans, **1**:269

    Belgian Americans, **1**:279

    Belizean Americans, **1**:293–294

    Blackfoot, **1**:308–309

    Bolivian Americans, **1**:322–323

    Brazilian Americans, **1**:347–348

    Bulgarian Americans, **1**:364, 367

    Cambodian Americans, **1**:386

    Cape Verdean Americans, **1**:412

    Carpatho-Rusyn Americans, **1**:425–426

    Catawba Indian Nation, **1**:436

    Chaldean Americans, **1**:444–445

    Cherokees, **1**:456, 457

    Cheyenne, **1**:471

    Chilean Americans, **1**:484, 486

    Choctaws, **1**:512–513, 514

    Colombian Americans, **1**:523

    Congolese Americans, **1**:536

    Costa Rican Americans, **1**:546–547

Creeks, **1**:559

Creoles, **1**:571

Croatian Americans, **1**:582

Cypriot Americans, **1**:611–612

Czech Americans, **1**:623

Danish Americans, **2**:6

Druze Americans, **2**:30–31

Egyptian Americans, **2**:65

English Americans, **2**:80

Eritrean Americans, **2**:90

Filipino Americans, **2**:125

Finnish Americans, **2**:143–144

French Americans, **2**:158

French-Canadian Americans, **2**:174

Garifunas and Garifuna Americans, **2**:189

Georgian Americans, **2**:200

German Americans, **2**:212–213

Ghanaian Americans, **2**:229–230

Greek Americans, **2**:243

Grenadian Americans, **2**:258

Guamanian Americans, **2**:267

Guyanese Americans, **2**:297–298

Hawaiians, **2**:320–321

Hmong Americans, **2**:336

Hopis, **2**:*362*, 362–363

Icelandians and Icelandic Americans, **2**:392

Indonesian Americans, **2**:404–405, *405*

Indos, **2**:416–417

Inupiat, **2**:424–425

Iraqi Americans, **2**:449–450

Iroquois Confederacy, **2**:482, *486*

Israeli Americans, **2**:496–497

Jamaican Americans, **2**:529

Japanese Americans, **2**:545, *545*

Jewish Americans, **2**:564–565

Jordanian Americans, **2**:583

Kenyan Americans, **3**:4

Klamaths, **3**:16–17

Korean Americans, **3**:29, 32

Kurdish Americans, **3**:46–47

Laotian Americans, **3**:57

Latvian Americans, **3**:70–71

Lebanese Americans, **3**:84

X

Y